fundamentals of corporate finance

3e

McGraw·Hill Australia

A Division of The McGraw·Hill Companies

National Library of Australia Cataloguing-in-Publication Data

Fundamentals of corporate finance.

3rd ed.
Includes index.
For tertiary students.
ISBN 0 07 471308 6.

1. Corporations - Finance - Textbooks. I. Ross, Stephen A.

658.15

Published in Australia by
McGraw-Hill Australia Pty Limited
Level 2, 82–84 Waterloo Road
Macquarie Park, NSW 2113, Australia
Editorial Director: Michael Tully
Senior Sponsoring Editor: Ailsa Brackley du Bois
Developmental Editor: Valerie Reed
Publishing Services Manager: Jo Munnelly
Production Editors: Narelle Segecic/Leanne Peters/Katrina O'Brien
Marketing Manager: Susan Talty
Director of E-Learning: Cameron Craig
Permissions Editor: Colette Hoeben
Freelance Editor: Catherine Page
Cover and Internal Design: Ramsay Macfarlane
Proofreader: Tim Learner
Typesetter: Sun Photoset
Indexer: Marjorie Flood
Printed by: Kyodo Printing Co. (Singapore) Pte Ltd

fundamentals of
corporate finance

3e

ROSS · THOMPSON · CHRISTENSEN
WESTERFIELD · JORDAN

**McGraw-Hill
Irwin**

Boston   Burr Ridge, IL   Dubuque, IA   Madison, WI   New York
San Francisco   St. Louis   Bangkok   Bogotá   Caracas   Kuala Lumpur
Lisbon   London   Madrid   Mexico City   Milan   Montreal   New Delhi
Santiago   Seoul   Singapore   Sydney   Taipei   Toronto

how to use this book

In addition to illustrating pertinent concepts and presenting up-to-date coverage, *Fundamentals of Corporate Finance 3e* strives to present the material in a way that makes it coherent and easy to understand. To meet the varied needs of its intended audience, *Fundamentals of Corporate Finance 3e* is rich in valuable learning tools.

Writing style

The writing style in *Fundamentals of Corporate Finance 3e* is informal and readers consistently find the relaxed style both approachable and likeable. Throughout, we try to convey our considerable enthusiasm for the subject.

Learning objectives

We set learning objectives at the start of each chapter to keep readers focused on the main issues.   (See Chapter 6, page 186)

Study tips

At the beginning of each chapter, we give you invaluable and practical study tips. These provide you with tools to help you to arrive at the best decision or outcome. (See Chapter 7, page 216)

Introduction

At the start of each chapter, we discuss the key aspects of the chapter, and tell you not only what we will be covering, but why it is important and how this information is used in the business world.   (See Chapter 4, page 107)

Extensive examples

Every chapter contains a variety of detailed, worked examples. Based on our classroom testing, these examples are among the most useful learning aids because they provide both detail and explanation.

Examples are found in the main body of the text.

Numbered examples are also included throughout.

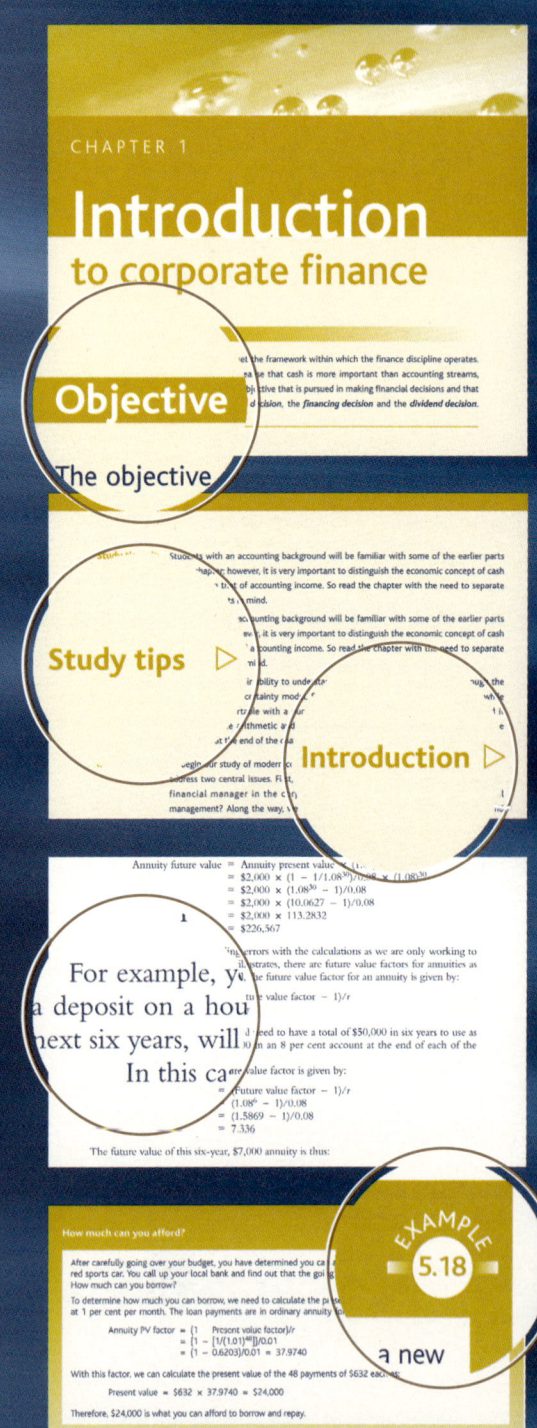

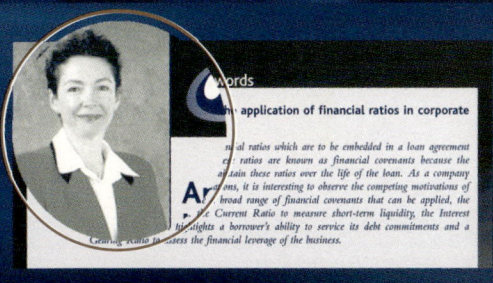

Boxed essays, In their own words

A unique series of brief essays, written by distinguished scholars and practitioners, are included on key topics in the text. As well as classics such as Fischer Black on dividends, we have new contributions from international experts and Australians prominent in finance. Tom Smith, Professor of Finance at the Australian National University, writes on the three ideas of finance, while Australian company director Annabelle Chaplain draws on her experience as a career banker to write on loan agreements. In all cases, the essays are enlightening, informative and entertaining. (See Chapter 3, page 89)

Using Excel

In new sections to some chapters, we give you step by step information on how to utilise the many functions of Excel to perform the required calculations.

(See Chapter 6, page 207; Chapter 7, page 240)

Real world data

To help you become familiar with the presentation and format of financial information, we have included screen dumps from financial reporting agencies like Bloomberg, to illustrate movements in the money market, bonds and share trading on the Stock Exchange. (See Chapter 1, page 21)

Key terms

Within each chapter, key terms are highlighted in gold boldface type the first time they appear. Key terms are defined in the text, and there is a running glossary in the margin of the text for quick reminders. (See Chapter 9, page 283)

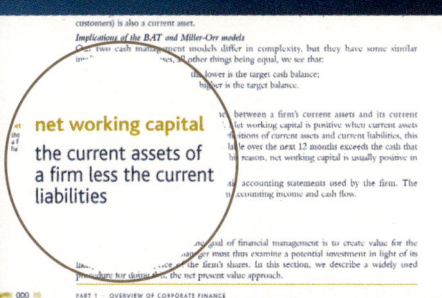

For added reference, there is a comprehensive list of key terms at the end of each chapter (see Chapter 9, page 307), and a glossary at the end of the book.

Concept building

Chapter sections are intentionally kept short to promote a step by step, building block approach to learning.

Each section is followed by a series of short concept questions that highlight the key ideas just presented. Students use these questions to make sure they can identify and understand the most important concepts as they read. (See Chapter 5, page 150).

how to use this book

Highlighted concepts

Throughout the text, important ideas are pulled out and presented in a highlighted box—signalling to students that this material is particularly relevant and critical for their understanding. (See Chapter 4, page 123)

Key elements and summary

At the end of each chapter, a concise but thorough summary is provided, highlighting the key principles discussed and explained in the chapter. (See Chapter 12, page 419)

Self-test questions

Comprehensive self-test questions appear at the end of each chapter, followed by detailed solutions and comments on the solutions. These frequently combine topics covered in the chapter to illustrate how they fit together.

End-of-chapter problems

We have found that students learn better when they have plenty of opportunity for practice. We therefore provide extensive end-of-chapter questions and problems. For the most part, there are at least 15, and as many as 57, problems for each chapter. This greatly exceeds what is typical in an introductory textbook. The questions and problems range in difficulty from relatively easy practice problems to thought-provoking 'challenge' problems designed to intrigue enthusiastic students. The problems are annotated so that students and instructors can readily identify particular types.

Suggested readings

A short, annotated list of books and articles to which the interested reader may refer for additional information follows each chapter. Included are both classic works that have stood the test of time, and contemporary publications.

On the web

We have referenced web sites that relate to various chapter topics. These sites can be explored to undertake additional research and to help deepen understanding.

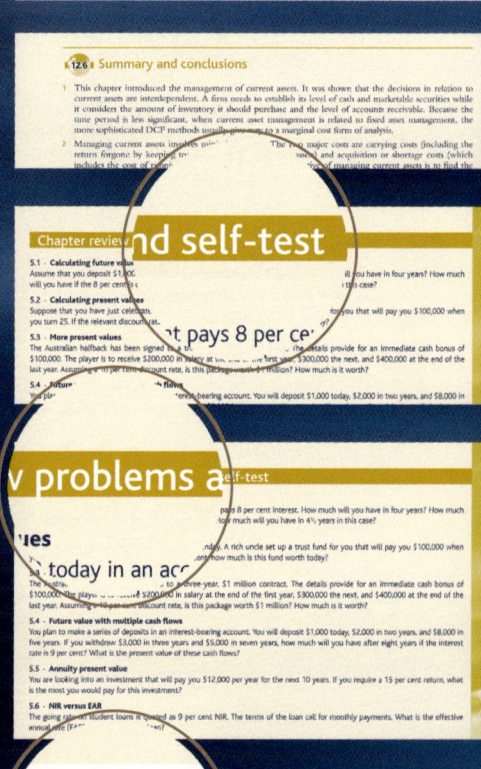

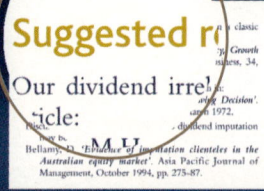

Welcome to McGraw-Hill's

It's all about flexibility. Today. You want to be able to teach your course, your way. McGraw-Hill offers you extensive choices in content selection and delivery backed by uncompromising service.

Your course: Connect your students with leading texts and study guides, websites, online readings, online cases, online course materials and revision programs. To assist you in teaching your course, McGraw-Hill provides you with cutting edge resources, including online testing and revision, instructor's manuals and guides, test banks, visual resources and PowerPoint slide shows. Your McGraw-Hill Academic Sales Consultant is trained to help match your course with our content, today.

Your way: Your McGraw-Hill Academic Sales Consultant, our instructional designer, and our E-learning team are trained to help you customise our content for your existing or new course. We carefully examine and match your course to our content and then discuss what, how, and when you would like it to be delivered — online or in print. It is that easy.

Your guarantee: Our programs are backed by our unique service guarantee. If you are a loyal McGraw-Hill customer, we will convert your course to our content each time your course changes — we use only qualified instructional designers or we consult with your own academic staff. Ask about our Course Conversion Program today!

your course

Text

Text supplements for academics:
Instructors CD-ROM, PowerPoint Presentations, Solutions, Instructor's Manuals, videos

Text supplements for students:
Study Guides and Case Booklets

Text website:
Online Learning Centre

Cases & News Online:
PowerWeb and Online Newsletters

Revision online:
MaxMark, GradeSummit

your way

Online testing & revision:
WebMCQ

Online course delivery:
WebCT, Blackboard, PageOut

Custom Publishing & Cases

www.mcgraw-hill.com.au/contenttoday

e-student

Introduction

The new *Online Learning Centre* with *PowerWeb* that accompanies this text is an integrated online product to assist you in getting the most from your course.

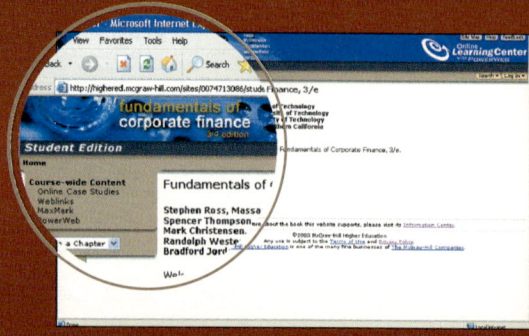

As a leading publisher of electronic material, McGraw-Hill has been producing a variety of online tools to assist in course-work for many years. This is the first time that they have been integrated into the one area for easy student access.

The Premium content areas, which are accessed by registering the code at the front of this text, provide you with excellent online resources. As soon as you register, you will have seamless access to *PowerWeb* articles, the *MaxMark* revision program and subject-specific news feeds. Each component of the *Online Learning Centre* is described below and can be found in both the student edition and the instructor edition. The *Information Centre* provides you with additional text information.

MaxMark

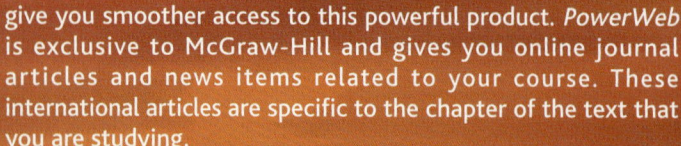

Unique to McGraw-Hill, *MaxMark* is a self-paced learning tool that consists of approximately 30 interactive, multiple-choice questions for every chapter of the book, with extensive feedback. *MaxMark* is designed to help you maximise your marks by allowing you to set time limits, randomise questions and switch the extensive feedback on or off. *MaxMark* is a *Premium* content item and access is by registration of the code at the front of this text. If you need to purchase another *Premium* content code, you can do so at your campus bookstore or on the book's web site.

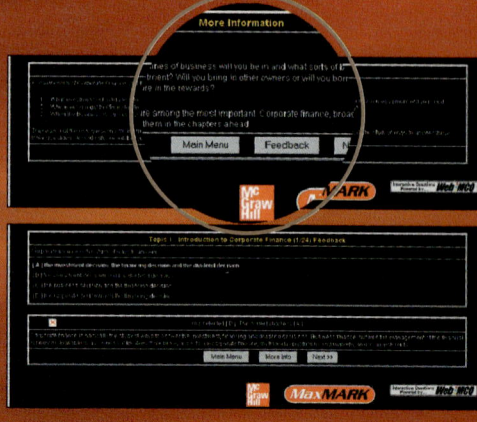

PowerWeb

PowerWeb has been built into your *Online Learning Centre* to give you smoother access to this powerful product. *PowerWeb* is exclusive to McGraw-Hill and gives you online journal articles and news items related to your course. These international articles are specific to the chapter of the text that you are studying.

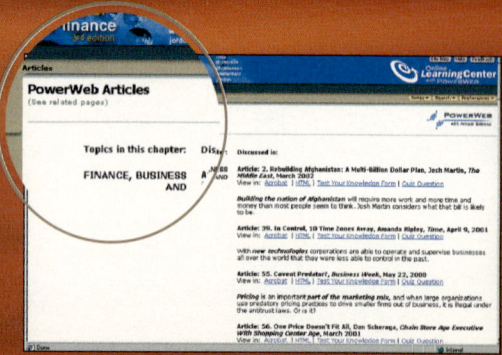

The selected *PowerWeb* articles are available in full and have been selected by a team of international academics to give you exposure to current events and ideas in international finance. The articles are up to date and updated annually.

Quizzes can be taken after reading each article. *PowerWeb* articles are selected to help you develop a level of knowledge that your peers and future employers are bound to respect.

PowerWeb is a *Premium* content item and access is by registration of the code at the front of this text. If you need to purchase another *Premium* content code, you can do so at your campus bookstore or on the book's web site.

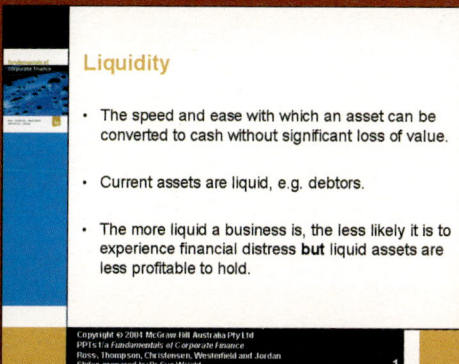

PowerPoint slides

These slides summarise learning objectives and key points contained in each chapter. They can be downloaded as a valuable revision aid.

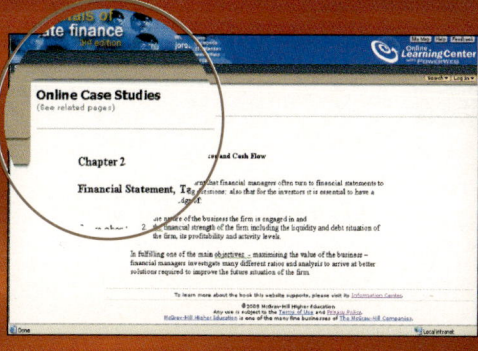

Online case studies

Case studies are provided for most chapters. They are an ideal learning resource, and will help you to quickly relate the theory to real world events. The case studies cover topical items in the financial news that are relevant to the topics in each chapter. Questions are included to give you the hands-on experience of working through the scenarios for yourself.

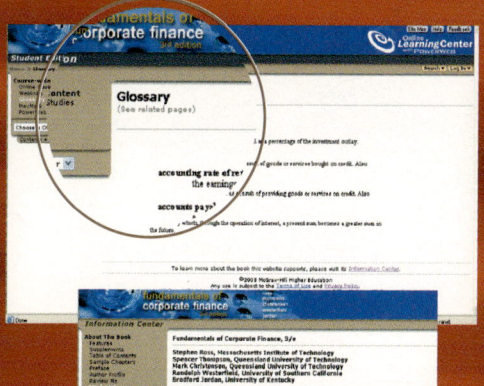

Glossary

Unsure of a finance term? The online glossary contains a quick reference to key terms and definitions.

Wish list

What do you want to see online or in future editions of this text? Email us your with your feedback.

e-instructor

Instructor's Resource and Solutions Manual

Prepared by the authors, the instructor's resource manual takes lecturers step by step through the chapters, providing detailed outlines. Areas of finance in which students experience most of their difficulties are identified and lecturing tips and student guidance hints are given to help. Other study suggestions and teaching aids are also presented.

Comprehensive rationales and solutions to end of chapter questions and problems are included.

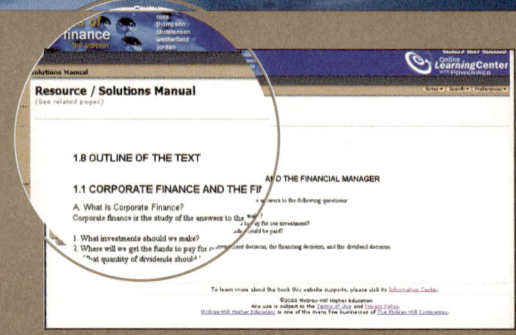

PowerPoint Slides

PowerPoint slides summarise the key points of each chapter. They can be downloaded and adapted to individual lecturers' requirements. The PowerPoints have been prepared by Dr Sue Wright of Macquarie University.

Test bank

The bank contains 40 comprehensive multiple-choice and true/false questions for each chapter. It is formatted for delivery in WebMCQ format if required. The test bank has been expanded and revised by Dr Madhu Veeraraghavan of the University of Auckland.

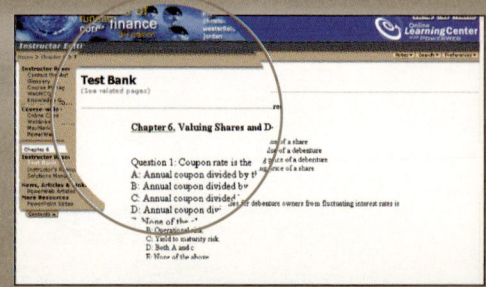

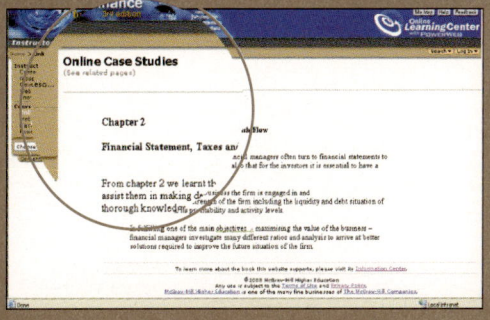

Online case studies

Case studies are provided for most chapters. They are an ideal learning resource, and will help link theoretical aspects of the text to real world events. The case studies cover topical items in the financial news relevant to each chapter. The case studies can be used for student assignments, as questions and solutions are included. Prepared by Dr Samanthala Hettihewa of the University of Western Sydney.

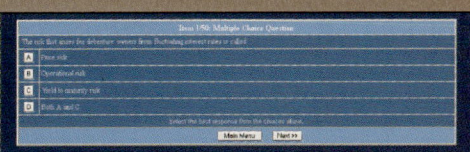

WebMCQ

You can set up your own online assignments and exams using our powerful and flexible online quizzing tool. Sophisticated tracking and reporting capabilities allow you to highlight topics where students are weak and target these areas in tutorials.

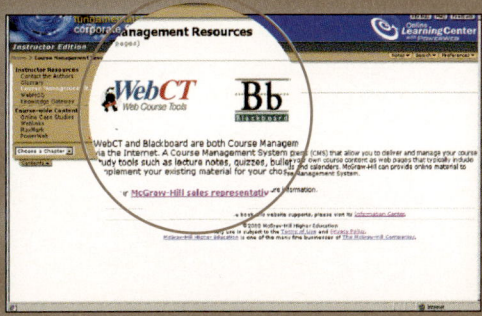

WebCT/Blackboard

If you are using WebCT or Blackboard to deliver your course, a fully functional WebCT and Blackboard cartridge is available. This contains all of the resources from the *Online Learning Centre*, with additional options to integrate PowerWeb, MaxMark and other online products.

Contact the authors

The authors welcome your feedback and comments on the text. Email links are provided for instructors.

contents in brief

contents

PART 1 ▸ Overview of corporate finance

CHAPTER 1 | Introduction to corporate finance

CHAPTER 2 | Financial statements, taxes and cash flow

PART 2 ▸ Financial statements and long-term financial planning

CHAPTER 3 | Working with financial statements

PART 3 ▶ Valuation of future cash flows

PART 6 ▶ Current investment decisions

PART 9 ▸ **Special topics in corporate finance**

in their own words

about the US originating authors

Stephen A. Ross

Stephen Ross is presently the Franco Modigliani Professor of Finance and Economics at the Sloan School of Management, Massachusetts Institute of Technology. One of the most widely published authors in finance and economics, Professor Ross is recognised for his work in developing the *Arbitrage Pricing Theory* and his substantial contributions to the discipline through his research in signalling, agency theory, option pricing, and the theory of the term structure of interest rates among other topics. A past president of the American Finance Association, he currently serves as an associate editor of several academic and practitioner journals. He is a trustee of CalTech, a director of the College Retirement Equity Fund (CREF), and Freddie Mac. He is also the co-chairman of Roll and Ross Asset Management Corporation.

Randolf W. Westerfield

Randolf W. Westerfield is Dean of the University of Southern California School of Business Administration and holder of the Robert R. Dockson Dean's Chair of Business Administration.

He came to USC from The Wharton School, University of Pennsylvania, where he was the chairman of the finance department and a member of the finance faculty for 20 years. He was the senior research associate at the Rodney L. White Center for Financial Research at Wharton. His areas of expertise include corporate financial policy, investment management and analysis, mergers and acquisitions, and stock market price behaviour.

Professor Westerfield serves as a member of the Board of Directors of Health Management Associates (NYSE: HMA), William Lyon Homes Inc (NYSE: WLS), the Lord Foundation, and the AACSB International. He has been consultant to a number of corporations, including AT&T, Mobil Oil, and the Pacific Enterprises, as well as to the United Nations, the U.S. Department of Justice and Labor, and the State of California.

Bradford D. Jordan

Bradford D. Jordan is Professor of Finance and the National City Bank Professor at the University of Kentucky, Carol Martin Gatton College of Business and Economics. He has a long-standing interest in both applied and theoretical issues in corporate finance and has extensive experience teaching all levels of corporate finance and financial management policy. Professor Jordan has published numerous articles on issues such as cost of capital, capital structure, and the behaviour of security prices. He is a past president of the Southern Finance Association, and he is co-author (with Charles J. Corrado) of *Fundamentals of Investments: Valuation and Management*, a leading investments text published by McGraw-Hill/Irwin.

Spencer Thompson

Spencer Thompson was formerly Professor of Finance, Head of the School of Finance and Head of the Department of Accounting and Law at the Queensland University of Technology. He has extensive teaching experience, having taught finance at degree, masters and doctorate levels for more than 20 years. Prior to his teaching he worked in industry as Managing Director of a group of service companies, controlling the day-to-day finance activities for a diverse set of business organisations. In addition he has maintained contact with senior professional bodies. He has served on several educational committees and has been Australian and State President in these organisations. He obtained his undergraduate degree from the University of Queensland with first class honours, the Thomas Brown Prize and the University Medal. His doctoral research looked at the changing characteristics of corporate risk.

Mark Christensen

Mark Christensen has a long-standing interest in both applied and theoretical issues in corporate finance. He has had extensive experience teaching all levels of corporate finance at the Queensland University of Technology and for numerous national and international institutes and professional bodies. He has a practical and interactive approach to learning and he helps understanding by developing concepts in a logical and easy to follow manner—this approach flows through to the text. Mark regularly consults in both the private and government sectors in the areas of discounted cash flow analysis, financial management, WACC and beta estimation. His applied research interests also extend to corporate valuation and risk management. He has a keen interest in finance education and regularly speaks to the broader community to further public understanding of corporate finance.

acknowledgements

We would like to join McGraw-Hill in thanking all those whose suggestions and input have refined and improved *Fundamentals of Corporate Finance*. In particular, the following people contributed opinions and feedback on the third edition and reviewed the manuscript:

Hamish Anderson	*Massey University*
Dawn Cable	*Macquarie University*
Mahendra Chandra	*Edith Cowan University*
Mark Coleman	*University of Adelaide*
Ben Jacobsen	*James Cook University*
Jennifer Kofoed	*Central Queensland University*
Mara Koplin	*University of Wollongong*
Fred McDougall	*University of Adelaide*
Ian McEwin	*Australian Defence Force Academy*
Michael Ntalianis	*Victoria University of Technology*
Stanley Paulo	*Lincoln University*
Toan Pham	*University of New South Wales*
Michael Poe	*University of Technology Sydney*
Tony Stanger	*Flinders University of South Australia*
Trevor Tonkin	*Swinburne University of Technology*
Madhu Veeraraghavan	*University of Auckland*
Mark Wilson	*University of Canberra*

Special thanks are due to our technical reviewers:

Ben Jacobsen	*James Cook University*
Trevor Tonkin	*Swinburne University of Technology*

We would like to acknowledge our fellow academics and colleagues whose input to previous editions have helped to develop this text. They are listed below with their affiliations at the time of review:

Cheryl Cliffe	*University of Auckland*
Mara Koplin	*University of Wollongong*
Helen Lange	*University of New South Wales*
Lyndon Lyons	*Griffith University – Nathan*
Brian Millanta	*Macquarie University*
Brian Phelan	*Curtin University of Technology*
Madhu Veeraraghavan	*Griffith University – Gold Coast*
Sue Wright	*Macquarie University*
Rex Zeeman	*University of Southern Queensland*
David Zhiwei Lin	*Monash University*

We owe a big vote of thanks to our respective wives, Irene and Sue, and to our families for their forebearance and understanding during the period we devoted to preparing this new edition.

Thanks are also due to the staff at McGraw-Hill, including Ailsa Brackley du Bois for her early initiative in commissioning and getting this new edition started, Valerie Reed and freelancer Catherine Page.

Instructor's Resource Authors

MaxMark and Test Bank

Thoroughly revised by Madhu Veeraraghavan

Dr Madhu Veeraraghavan is a Senior Lecturer of Finance at the Department of Accounting and Finance, The University of Auckland Business School, New Zealand. He holds a PhD in finance from Griffith University, Australia. His research interests are in the area of empirical and theoretical asset pricing, evaluating portfolio performance and behavioural finance.

PowerPoints

Prepared by Sue Wright

Dr Sue Wright is a Senior Lecturer in the Department of Accounting and Finance at Macquarie University. She has taught in the areas of Corporate Finance, Introductory Accounting, Finance and Financial Statement Analysis at both undergraduate and postgraduate levels for 18 years. Her current research interests are in capital market reactions to financial statement reporting, in particular intangible assets, and accounting and finance education. She has published articles in academic journals on a wide range of finance topics, and is a co-author on past and current accounting and finance textbooks.

Online case studies

Researched and written by Samanthala Hettihewa

Dr Samanthala Hettihewa is a Senior Lecturer in the School of Economics and Finance, University of Western Sydney. She has published articles in several domestic and international refereed journals, including the *Journal of Business Ethics*, *Research in International Business and Finance*, *Journal of Small Business Economics*, *Indian Journal of Applied Economics*, *JASSA (the journal of the Securities Institute of Australia)* and *Teaching Review*. She has also published two university textbooks, two instructors' manuals, and contributed to books.

preface

In the challenging business environment that will face graduates today, it is imperative that they have the capacity to be adaptive and to expand their knowledge. The finance understanding that they obtain must be applicable to all types of commercial activity in both the private and public sectors. The education must facilitate any change in career. The basic principles taught must have wide application in all sectors. Today's dynamic commercial environment makes it very important that graduates have the capacity to expand their knowledge. The challenge facing finance academics is to keep materials up to date, and distinguish the permanent changes from transitional fads. It is with this in mind that we approached the new edition of our textbook, *Fundamentals of Corporate Finance*. We provide a framework for understanding that allows readers to embrace the innovations borne of changing environments and financial markets.

The underlying philosophy

Our experience of existing finance texts is that they present corporate finance as a collection of unrelated topics which are unified by virtue of being bound together between the covers of one book. In many cases, this perception is only natural because the subject is treated in a way that is both topic-oriented and procedural. How often have finance academics heard students complain that they could solve a specific problem if they knew which formula to apply? To overcome this problem, our overriding concern in the text is to develop the basic logic of financial decision making.

Distinctive features

The institutional framework
The text outlines the current Australian corporate finance environment, with discussion of the fundamental changes that have taken place in financial markets, instruments, corporations law and taxation law.

An emphasis on intuition
The chapters are always careful to separate and explain the principles at work on an intuitive level before launching into specifics. The underlying ideas are discussed first in very general terms and then by way of examples that illustrate in more concrete terms how a financial manager might proceed in a given situation. Icons in the margins, 'The basic idea' and 'A closer look' assist students to orient themselves.

A unified valuation approach
The importance of the time value of money in finance is quickly identified. This leads to the acceptance of net present value (NPV) as the basic concept underlying corporate finance. The basic notion, that NPV represents the excess of market value over cost, often is lost in an overly mechanical approach to NPV that emphasises computation at the expense of understanding. In contrast, every topic covered in *Fundamentals of Corporate Finance 3e* is firmly rooted in valuation, and care is taken throughout to explain how particular decisions are made to maximise value.

A managerial focus
The approach of the text is to develop and explain financial management as a set of ideas and principles that work together rather than as simple formulae and procedures. We instil an understanding of finance by emphasising the financial and economic environment that underlies financial management. Readers not only learn the basics of corporate finance but how to apply these concepts in the decision-making process. *Fundamentals of Corporate Finance 3e* emphasises the role of the financial manager as decision-maker, and stresses the need for managerial input and judgment.

Keep it simple
Contemporary finance theory can be divided into three fundamental areas of study: the time value of money, diversification and derivative instruments. The time value of money drives most calculations and all valuation concepts. Diversification is

fundamental to risk protection and thus has given rise to the capital asset pricing model as the focus of finance theory. The study of derivates such as options allows us to expand the analysis of risk control, through the study of hedging, and to expand the understanding of asset values. These are simple concepts but many finance texts have made them very difficult to comprehend. Our text aims to aid teaching and learning by stripping the difficult presentations to an understandable level. More complicated issues such as Descartes' Rule of Signs, or Interest Rate Parity have been explained in simple terms without weakening the quality of the presentation.

E-commerce

We make extensive reference to web sites related to the various chapter topics. By exploring these sites, students are able to deepen their understanding of the relevant topics, as well as launch further research projects.

In addition, new sections in selected chapters explain how the many functions of Excel can be used to perform the financial calculations covered in the chapter.

For added realism, screen dumps from information providers like Bloomberg have been used to show movements in the money market or trading patterns in shares.

Intended audience

This text is designed explicitly for a first course in business or corporate finance. The typical student will not have previously taken a course in finance, and no previous knowledge of finance is assumed. Since this course is frequently part of a common business core, the text is intended for majors and non-majors alike. In terms of background or prerequisites, the book is nearly self-contained. Some familiarity with basic accounting principles is assumed, but even these are reviewed very early on. The only other tool the student needs is basic algebra. As a result, students with diverse backgrounds will find the text very accessible.

This is just a sampling. We have taken a very close look at what is likely to be relevant in the 21st century, and we have taken a fresh, modern approach to many traditional subjects. In doing so, we eliminated topics of dubious relevance, downplayed purely theoretical issues, and minimised the use of extensive and elaborate computations to illustrate points that are either intuitively obvious or of limited practical use.

Unlike virtually any other introductory text, *Fundamentals of Corporate Finance 3e* provides extensive real-world practical advice and guidance. We try to go beyond just presenting dry, standard textbook material to show how to actually *use* the tools discussed in the text. When necessary, the approximate, pragmatic nature of some types of financial analysis is made explicit, possible pitfalls are described, and limitations are outlined.

Mark Christensen
Spencer Thompson

flexible delivery

We have found that the phrase 'so much to do, so little time' accurately describes an introductory finance course. For this reason, we designed *Fundamentals of Corporate Finance 3e* to be as flexible and modular as possible. There are a total of nine parts, and, in broad terms, the instructor is free to decide the particular sequence, giving great control over the topics covered, the sequence in which they are covered and the depth of coverage.

Within each part, the first chapter generally contains an overview and survey. Thus, when time is limited, subsequent chapters can be omitted. Finally, the sections placed early in each chapter are generally the most important, and later sections can often be omitted without loss of continuity.

After **Part One**, either **Part Two**, on financial statements analysis, long-range planning and corporate growth, or **Part Three**, on time value and share and debt valuation, follows naturally.

Part Two can be omitted entirely if desired.

After Part Three, most instructors will probably want to move directly into **Part Four**, which covers net present value, discounted cash flow valuation and capital budgeting.

Part Five contains two chapters on risk and return. The first one, on market history, is designed to give students a feel for typical rates of return on risky assets. The second one discusses the expected return/risk trade-off, and develops the security market line in a highly intuitive way that bypasses much of the usual portfolio theory and statistics.

Part Six looks at current investment decisions and such important issues as cash and liquidity management and credit management.

Parts Seven and Eight look at the financing decision. Part Seven introduces the institutional framework of financing looking at the essential features of debt and equity instruments, with one of the most detailed and current descriptions of the Australian capital markets.

Cost of capital, dividend policy and capital structure policy are covered in three consecutive chapters in Part Eight. The chapter on dividends can be covered independently if desired; however, its positioning fits in neatly with the explanation of the influence of Australian taxation law. The chapter on capital structure can be omitted without creating any loss of continuity.

Lastly, **Part Nine** covers four important topics: options and option-like securities, mergers, international finance and leasing. These chapters contain somewhat greater depth of coverage than the basic text chapters and may be covered partially in courses where time is limited or completely in courses that give special emphasis to these topics.

text highlights of this edition

The basic principles of finance theory have remained reasonably constant for many years; however the market is continually changing. Graduates must be prepared to change employment from industry to industry or between private and public enterprises.

Therefore the authors' objectives for the revision were:

▶ to update and refine the text to ensure its continued relevance to graduating students

▶ to ensure that the revised edition relates closely to the needs of lecturers and students by avoiding the concentration on elaborate technical exceptions and keeping the language as simple as possible

▶ to, as far as possible, expose users to current market developments and jargon

▶ to identify clearly the universal application of finance theories so that finance graduates begin to develop an element of versatility

Chapter	Features of interest	New to this edition
Chapter 1 Introduction to corporate finance	▶ The investment, financing and dividend decisions ▶ The objective of the firm ▶ Two-period model	▶ section 1.1 looks at the executive structure of business using a real world example ▶ provides an excellent description of the agency problem ▶ additional problems
Chapter 2 Financial statements, taxes and cash flow	▶ Book versus market value ▶ Approved accounting standards ▶ Non-cash items ▶ Time and costs ▶ Taxation	▶ accounting terminology updated throughout the chapter ▶ taxation updated: section 2.3
Chapter 3 Working with financial statements	▶ Sources and uses of cash ▶ Ratio analysis ▶ Problems with financial statement analysis	▶ ratios currently used in practice are explained in section 3.3 ▶ introduces the 'Global Industry Classification Standard' used from 1 July 2002 by the ASX, in section 3.4
Chapter 4 Long-term financial planning and corporate growth	▶ The planning process ▶ Forecasting financial statements ▶ Sustainable growth	▶ accounting terminology is updated throughout the chapter ▶ section 4.4 looks at growth and external finance, financial policy and the determinants of growth
Chapter 5 First principles of valuation: the time value of money	▶ Compounding, discounting, rule of 72 ▶ Multiple cash flows ▶ Annuities and perpetuities ▶ Comparing interest rates	▶ interest rates and values revised to reflect current markets ▶ An extensive coverage is provided of financial mathematics. Current methods used in practice to package interest arrangements are used throughout the examples to show effective interest rates ▶ the use of Excel to make time value calculations is explained in a boxed section

text highlights of this edition

Chapter	Features of interest	New to this edition
Chapter 6 Valuing shares and bonds	▶ Bond valuation, semi-annual coupons, interest rate risk, bond reporting ▶ Ordinary share valuation model ▶ Constant growth, zero growth, changing growth rates across time ▶ Share market reporting	▶ explains the difference between bonds, debentures and unsecured notes ▶ section 6.2 uses recent data to describe share market reporting ▶ a boxed section shows how to use Excel to value bonds
Chapter 7 Net present value and other investment criteria	▶ Net present value ▶ Payback, discounted payback, accounting rate of return ▶ Internal rate of return and its problems ▶ Present value index ▶ Calculating using Excel	▶ explanations expanded in the examples ▶ a boxed section shows how to use Excel to calculate NPV and IRR ▶ additional problems
Chapter 8 Making capital investment decisions	▶ Relevant and project cash flows ▶ Depreciation, capital gains, inflation ▶ Incremental analysis ▶ Setting the bid price, valuing options ▶ Investments with different lives	▶ enhanced explanations, for example see table 8.3 and accompanying notes ▶ additional problems
Chapter 9 Project analysis and evaluation	▶ Sources of value ▶ Scenario analysis, sensitivity analysis, simulation analysis ▶ Break-even ▶ Operating leverage	▶ section 9.2 looks at estimation error and at introducing an upper and lower bound analysis
Chapter 10 Some lessons from capital market history	▶ Percentage returns, inflation and returns, Fisher effect ▶ Historical record and risk premium ▶ Variability of returns ▶ Normal distributions ▶ Capital market efficiency	▶ the historical behaviour in the Australian market is described using recent data: see for example Figures 10.4-10.9 and Tables 10.1-10.4 ▶ the Bloomberg database is introduced: see Figure 10.1 for an example ▶ calculations have been updated based on current information ▶ the market reaction around September 11, 2001 is looked at in Figure 10.12
Chapter 11 Return, risk and the security market line	▶ Individual and portfolio expected return, variance ▶ Announcements, surprises ▶ Risk, diversification, beta ▶ CAPM security market and capital market lines ▶ Portfolio attributes ▶ SML and cost of capital ▶ CAPM problems	▶ CAPM theory is reinforced by adding section 11.9 on portfolio characteristics. This section revisits mathematically the earlier portfolio attributes identified within the explanation of capital market theory ▶ A new section 11.11 is included, looking at problems with the CAPM. The section introduces some contemporary CAPM research without confusing students with technical detail. The broad area covered relates to the difficulties in estimating beta.

Chapter	Features of interest	New to this edition
Chapter 12 Current investment decisions	▶ Investments involved ▶ The operating and cash cycles ▶ The inventory model ▶ The cash budget	▶ maintains the descriptions used in previous editions and includes additional questions
Chapter 13 Cash and liquidity management	▶ Reasons for holding cash ▶ Target cash balance ▶ BAT model ▶ Miller and Orr model ▶ Miller and Orr and bank overdraft ▶ Regulation of financial intermediaries	▶ introduces new statistics to look at the importance of cash to Australian firms in the introduction ▶ a new section on direct transfers, section 13.3 ▶ section 13.5 on regulation of financial intermediaries has been updated
Chapter 14 Credit management	▶ Credit and receivables ▶ Terms of sale ▶ Analysing credit policy ▶ Optimal credit policy	▶ rewritten for clearer explanations ▶ additional end-of-chapter problems
Chapter 15 Australian financial markets: short-term financing	▶ Financial system ▶ Financial markets and securities ▶ Financial intermediaries ▶ Short-term financial sources	▶ examples updated: see Telstra ▶ financial market information updated, section 15.2 ▶ listed market information updated ▶ financial intermediaries information updated: section 15.3 ▶ recent stock exchange statistics provided
Chapter 16 Long-term financing	▶ Corporate long-term debt ▶ Callable debentures and debenture refunding ▶ Preference shares ▶ Ordinary shares	▶ Village Roadshow preference shares used in section 16.5 ▶ updated figures on the size of the capital market in section 16.7
Chapter 17 Issuing securities to the public	▶ Public issues ▶ Underpricing ▶ Value of the firm ▶ Cost of issuing ▶ Rights issues ▶ Issuing debt	▶ updated legal and ASX requirements ▶ revised examples, see Table 17.1 ▶ revised equity capital raising: Table 17.13 ▶ updated statistics on underpricing in world markets: see Ritter's 'In their own words' essay

text highlights of this edition

Chapter	Features of interest	New to this edition
Chapter 18 Cost of capital	▸ Cost of equity ▸ Using the dividend growth model ▸ Using the SML ▸ Cost of debt ▸ Cost of preference shares ▸ Weighted average cost of capital	▸ current risk premium statistics: see section 18.2 ▸ examples updated, see Example 18.3 ▸ updated tax rates throughout
Chapter 19 Dividends and dividend policy	▸ Cash dividends ▸ Does dividend policy matter? ▸ Dividend imputation ▸ Real world factors ▸ Employee share ownership plans	▸ statistics updated: see introduction ▸ updated capital gains tax and dividend imputation, section 19.3 ▸ special dividends Telstra example in section 19.6 ▸ Australian equity raising 2001, Figure 19.4
Chapter 20 Financial leverage and capital structure policy	▸ The capital structure question ▸ The cost of equity ▸ Capital structure and taxes ▸ Capital structure and bankruptcy ▸ Capital structure and imputation	▸ recent statistics: see Table 20.7 for 2002 debt to equity ratios
Chapter 21 Options, corporate securities and futures	▸ Share options ▸ Valuing options ▸ Black-Scholes OPM ▸ Futures trading	▸ Australian options market February 2003, Table 21.1 ▸ Option turnover 1988-2001, Table 21.2 ▸ revised option trading section ▸ new section 21.7 on futures ▸ short-term interest futures: Table 21.4 ▸ term structure of interest rates: see Figure 21.6 ▸ additional problems
Chapter 22 Mergers, acquisitions and takeovers	▸ Legal forms of acquisitions ▸ Gains from acquisitions	▸ example of the ACCC acting against market power, section 22.4 ▸ AMP and inefficient management consequences in section 22.4
Chapter 23 International corporate finance	▸ Terminology ▸ Foreign exchange rates ▸ Purchasing power parity ▸ International Fisher effect ▸ Exchange rate risk	▸ revised schedule of international currency symbols: Table 23.1 ▸ revised exchange rates in Table 23.2 and examples throughout the chapter
Chapter 24 Leasing	▸ Types of leases ▸ Taxation and leases ▸ Evaluation of leasing ▸ Setting lease premiums	▸ a new section on selecting the interest rate to use in lease evaluation after Table 24.4

PART ONE

Overview

of corporate finance

CHAPTER 1

Introduction
to corporate finance

Objective

The objective of this chapter is to begin to set the framework within which the finance discipline operates. At the end of the chapter students should realise that cash is more important than accounting streams, there should be a good understanding of the objective that is pursued in making financial decisions and that the three major decisions are the *investment decision*, the *financing decision* and the *dividend decision*.

Study tips ▷ Students with an accounting background will be familiar with some of the earlier parts of the chapter; however, it is very important to distinguish the economic concept of cash income from that of accounting income. So read the chapter with the need to separate the two concepts in mind.

Students vary in the way they understand the principles being introduced through the two-period perfect certainty model. Some prefer a diagrammatic presentation while others are comfortable with a numerical presentation. Understanding is reinforced if students do the arithmetic and label the values on the diagrams (for example, see Problem 13 at the end of this chapter).

Introduction ▷ To begin our study of modern corporate finance and financial management, we need to address two central issues. First, what is corporate finance and what is the role of the financial manager in the corporation? Second, what is the goal of financial management? Along the way, we will look at the corporate form of organisations and discuss some conflicts that can arise within the corporation. We will also take a brief look at financial markets in Australia. Finally, a simplistic model is introduced to begin the analysis of investment, financing and dividend decisions made by firms.

 **1.1** ■ Corporate finance and the financial manager

In this section, we discuss where the financial manager fits in the corporation. We start by looking at what corporate finance is and what the financial manager does.

What is corporate finance?

Imagine that you were to start your own business. No matter what type you started, you would have to answer the following three questions in some form or another:

1 What investments should you take on? That is, what lines of business will you be in and what sorts of buildings, machinery and equipment will you need?
2 Where will you get the financing to pay for your investment? Will you bring in other owners or will you borrow the money?
3 When the business is successful, how will you share in the rewards?

These are not the only questions by any means, but they are among the most important. Corporate finance, broadly speaking, is the study of ways to answer these three questions. Accordingly, we will be looking at each of them in the chapters ahead.

The financial manager

A striking feature of large corporations is that the owners (the shareholders or equityholders) are usually not directly involved in making business decisions, particularly on a day-to-day basis. Instead, the corporation employs managers to represent the owners' interests and make decisions on their behalf. In a large corporation, the financial manager would be in charge of answering the three questions we raised above.

The financial management function is usually associated with a top officer of the firm, such as a General Manager-Finance or some other Executive Financial Officer. Figure 1.1 is a simplified organisation chart that highlights the finance activity in a large firm. As shown, the General Manager-Finance coordinates the activities of the Corporate Treasurer and the Accountant. With the downsizing and cost-cutting exercises that most firms have introduced in the last decade there has been a tendency to centralise or concentrate the financial functions of organisations. The Accounting office handles cost and financial accounting, tax payments and management information systems. The Corporate Treasurer's office is responsible for managing the firm's cash, its financial planning and its capital expenditures. These treasury activities are all related to the three general questions raised above, and the chapters ahead deal primarily with these issues. Our study thus bears mostly on activities usually associated with the treasurer's office. In some organisations the Corporate Treasurer is called the financial manager and our study is an analysis of financial management. The market tends to believe the skill of the management team is important to firm value. When Coles Myer appointed John Fletcher as Chief Executive Officer (CEO) in August 2000 the value of the company rose by $1.2 billion in expectation of better company performance. Subsequently this belief was shown to be incorrect and the share price fell from a high of around $9 to less than $6 in 2003.

 1.2 ■ The Statement of Financial Position and corporate financial decisions

In this section, we take a closer look at the key areas and questions in financial management. We will be grouping and labelling the types of financial management decisions to study them separately. Our discussion focuses on the Statement of Financial Position[1] model of the firm.

FIGURE 1.1

A simplified organisation chart

The exact titles and organisation differ from company to company.

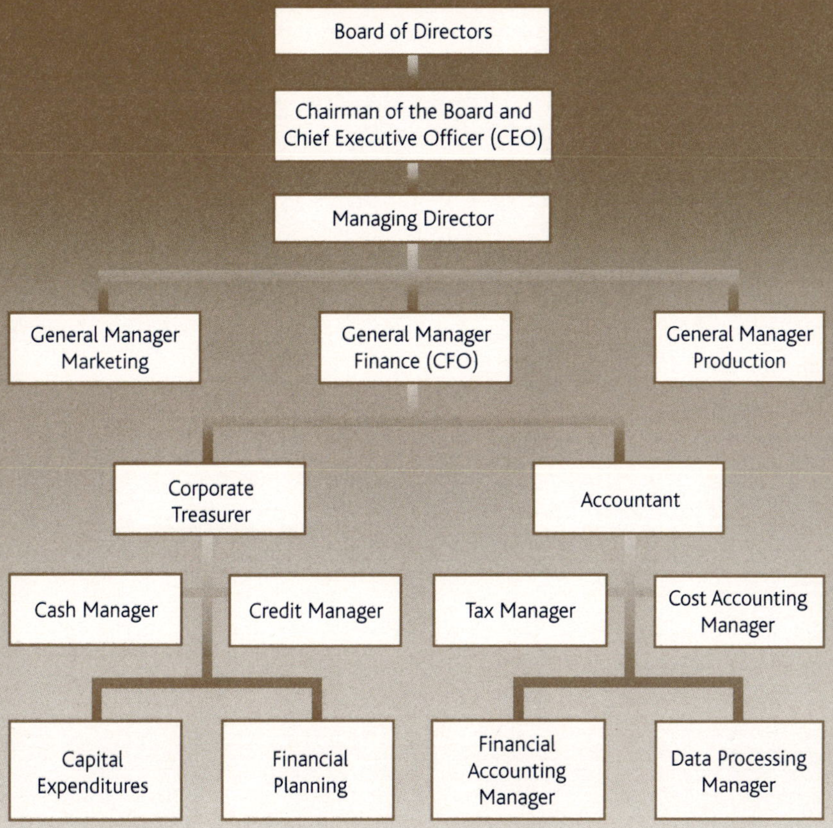

```
                    ┌─────────────────────┐
                    │  Board of Directors │
                    └─────────────────────┘
                              │
                ┌─────────────────────────────┐
                │  Chairman of the Board and  │
                │ Chief Executive Officer (CEO)│
                └─────────────────────────────┘
                              │
                    ┌─────────────────────┐
                    │  Managing Director  │
                    └─────────────────────┘
                              │
        ┌─────────────────────┼─────────────────────┐
┌───────────────┐   ┌───────────────┐     ┌───────────────┐
│ General Manager│   │ General Manager│     │ General Manager│
│   Marketing   │   │ Finance (CFO) │     │  Production   │
└───────────────┘   └───────────────┘     └───────────────┘
                              │
               ┌──────────────┴──────────────┐
        ┌───────────────┐            ┌───────────────┐
        │   Corporate   │            │  Accountant   │
        │   Treasurer   │            │               │
        └───────────────┘            └───────────────┘
```

Cash Manager	Credit Manager	Tax Manager	Cost Accounting Manager

Capital Expenditures	Financial Planning	Financial Accounting Manager	Data Processing Manager

The Statement of Financial Position

The Statement of Financial Position is a snapshot of the firm. It is a convenient means of organising and summarising what a firm owns (its *assets*), what a firm owes (its *liabilities*), and the difference between the two (the firm's *equity*) at a given point in time. Figure 1.2 (overleaf) illustrates how the Statement of Financial Position is constructed. As shown, the left-hand side lists the assets of the firm, and the right-hand side lists the liabilities and equity.

Assets: The left-hand side

Assets are classified as either *current* or *non-current*. A non-current asset is one that has a relatively long life. Non-current assets can either be *tangible*, such as a truck or a computer, or *intangible*, such as a trademark or patent. A current asset has a life of less than one year. This means that the asset will convert to cash within 12 months. For example, inventory would normally be purchased and sold within a year and is thus classified as a current asset. Obviously, cash itself is a current asset. Accounts receivable (money owed to the firm by its customers) is also a current asset.

Liabilities and owners' equity: The right-hand side

The firm's liabilities are the first thing listed on the right-hand side of the Statement of Financial Position. These are classified as either *current* or *non-current*. Current liabilities, like current assets, have a life of less than one year (meaning they must be paid within the year) and are listed before non-current liabilities. Accounts payable (money the firm owes to its suppliers) is one example of a current liability.

A debt that is not due in the coming year is classified as a non-current liability. A loan that the firm will pay off in five years is one such long-term debt. Firms borrow long term from a variety of sources. We will tend to use the terms *debt* and *debtholders* to refer to the amount owed and to whom it is owed, respectively.

Finally, by definition, the difference between the total value of the assets (current and non-current) and the total value of the liabilities (current and non-current) is the *shareholders' equity*, also called owners' equity. This feature of the Statement of Financial Position is intended to reflect the fact that, if the firm were to sell all of its assets and use the money to pay off its debts, then whatever residual value remains belongs to the shareholders. So, the Statement of Financial Position 'balances' because the value of the left-hand side always equals the value of the right-hand side.

Net working capital

net working capital
current assets less current liabilities

As indicated in Figure 1.2, the difference between a firm's current assets and its current liabilities is called **net working capital**. Net working capital is positive when current assets exceed current liabilities. Based on the definitions of current assets and current liabilities, this means that the cash that will become available over the next 12 months exceeds the cash that must be paid over that same period. For this reason, net working capital is usually positive in a healthy firm.

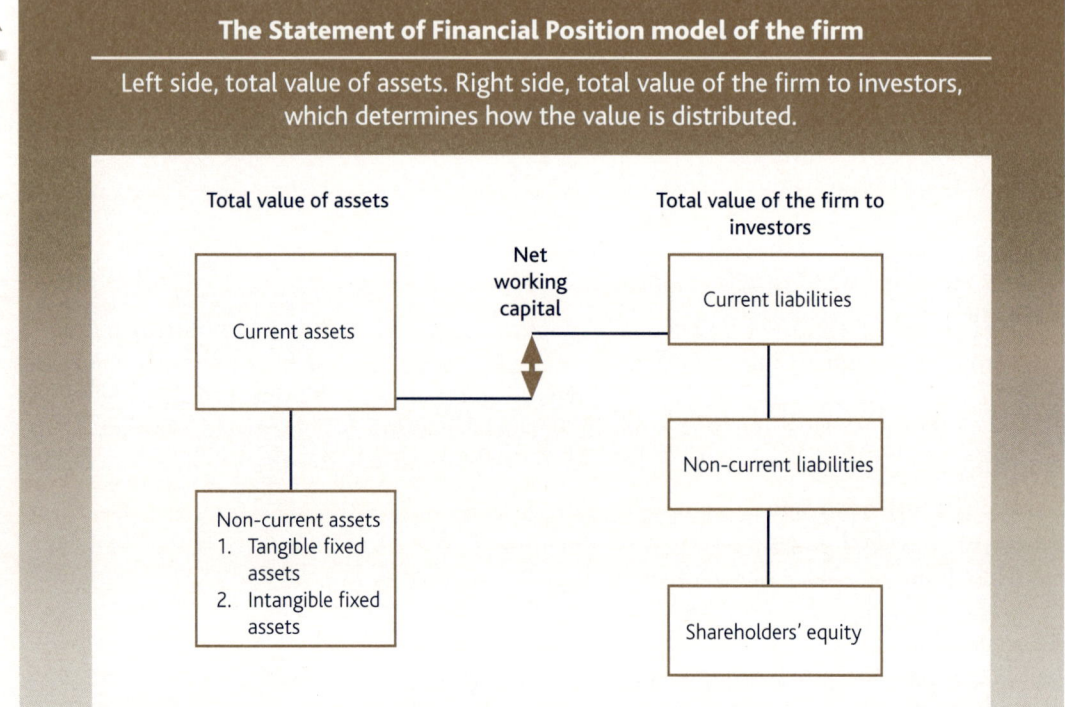

FIGURE 1.2

The Statement of Financial Position model of the firm

Left side, total value of assets. Right side, total value of the firm to investors, which determines how the value is distributed.

Total value of assets

Total value of the firm to investors

Current assets

Net working capital

Current liabilities

Non-current assets
1. Tangible fixed assets
2. Intangible fixed assets

Non-current liabilities

Shareholders' equity

Building the Statement of Financial Position

A firm has current assets of $1000, non-current assets of $5000, current liabilities or short-term debt of $700, and non-current liabilities or long-term debt of $2000. What does the Statement of Financial Position look like? What is shareholders' equity? What is net working capital?

In this case, total assets are $1000 + $5000 = $6000 and total liabilities are $700 + $2000 = $2700, so shareholders' equity is the difference: $6000 − $2700 = $3300. The Statement of Financial Position would thus look like:

Assets		Liabilities and equity	
Current assets	$1000	Current liabilities	$ 700
Non-current assets	5000	Non-current liabilities	2000
		Shareholders' equity	3300
		Total liabilities and	
Total assets	$6000	shareholders' equity	$6000

Net working capital is the difference between current assets and current liabilities, or $1000 − $700 = $300.

Corporate financial decisions

The three main questions in corporate finance are suggested by the organisation of the Statement of Financial Position. These questions, in the order we will study them, are:

1. What assets should we buy? This is the *investment decision*.
2. What is the best way to raise cash to fund assets, and what is the best mixture of debt and equity? This is the *finance decision*.
3. Should the firm be successful, what dividends should be paid? This is the *dividend decision*.

The job of the financial manager is to answer these questions.

Investment decision

In the investment decision concerning non-current assets or **capital budgeting**, the financial manager tries to identify investment opportunities that are worth more to the firm than they cost to acquire. Loosely speaking, this means that the value of the cash flow generated by an asset exceeds the cost of that asset.

capital budgeting
the process of planning and managing a firm's investment in non-current assets

Financial managers must be concerned not only with how much cash they expect to receive, but also with when they expect to receive it and how likely they are to receive it. Evaluating the size, timing and risk of future cash flows is the essence of capital budgeting. As we will discuss, this evaluation is complicated by a number of factors.

Cash flow size

Cash flows are often not easily observed, particularly from outside the firm, because much of the information we receive is in the form of accounting statements. However, accounting income is not cash flow, and it is important not to confuse the two.

For accounting purposes, a sale may be recorded at the time of the sale, but the cash inflow obviously does not occur until payment is actually made, assuming that it *is* actually made. Similarly, a cost may be recorded as such when the obligation to pay has occurred, not when the bill is actually paid. These are just two examples of the difference; we will examine this subject in more detail in the next chapter. For now, we just note that standard accounting practice often ignores both the timing and the risk associated with cash flows. As a result, accounting income or earnings can be very different from cash flow.

EXAMPLE 1.2 **Cash flow versus accounting profit**

Gemstone Pty Ltd refines and trades gold. At the beginning of the year, it spent $9 million in cash to acquire, process and refine one tonne of gold. At the end of the year, it sold the gold for $10 million, but it has not yet collected the cash from the sale. What would accounting for Gemstone's year look like? What really happened in terms of cash flow?

The standard accounting view is that the sale is recorded when it is made, not necessarily when collection takes place. Thus, the year looks like:

Gemstone Pty Ltd
Statement of Financial Performance for the year ended 30 June

Sales	$ 10,000,000
– Costs	9,000,000
Profit	$ 1,000,000

In the accounting view, Gemstone had a profit of $1 million for the year. The corporate financial manager, who is worried about the size of the firm's cash flow, would see things a little differently. In terms of how much cash came in and how much cash went out, we have:

Gemstone Pty Ltd
Corporate Finance View—Cash Flow for the year ended 30 June

Cash inflow	$ 0
– Cash outflow	9,000,000
Net cash flow	– $ 9,000,000

As Example 1.2 illustrates, the corporate finance perspective is concerned with whether or not cash flows are actually created in a particular period.

Cash flow timing
In addition to wondering if cash flows are actually created, the timing of cash flows is important. For most of us, a dollar now is more valuable than a dollar to be received, say, three years from now. There is, therefore, a trade-off between the size of an investment's cash flow and when that cash flow is received.

Cash flow timing

Gemstone Pty Ltd is evaluating two new products, code-named, with great originality, Product A and Product B. Both products cost $10,000 to launch and have a lifespan of four years. The cash flows from the two are anticipated to be:

Year	Product A	Products B
1	$ 0	$ 4,000
2	0	4,000
3	0	4,000
4	20,000	4,000
Total	$ 20,000	$16,000

Which of these two proposals is better? Product A has greater total cash flow. Product B returns cash to the firm more quickly. Without more information, it is not possible for us to say objectively which of these is more valuable. We need to know, among other things, the trade-off between cash now and cash later.

Cash flow risk

The nature of the world is such that the future is mostly unknown. What is almost certain is that whatever happens will be a surprise. As a result, dealing with economic uncertainty and reacting to surprises are fundamental to the financial manager's job. In particular, assessing the risk associated with promised future cash flows is critical, because the size and the timing of those flows are usually not known with certainty today.

Comparing risky cash flows

Gemstone Pty Ltd is debating an overseas expansion. It is considering Japan and Europe as possible locations. Europe is thought to be relatively safe, but Japan is considered risky. In either case, the venture would last only one year.

Gemstone's financial analysts have summarised their conclusions about the two sites by coming up with three scenarios: pessimistic; most likely; and optimistic. The cash flows under the three scenarios are:

	Pessimistic	Most likely	Optimistic
Europe	$ 75,000	$ 100,000	$ 125,000
Japan	5,000	150,000	200,000

Based only on the most likely cash flow projections, Japan is the better location. When we consider all the possibilities, however, it is not clear which location is better. Japan has greater potential for loss or gain. Once again, we do not have enough information. What we need to know is the trade-off between the size of the potential cash flows and the risk of the cash flows.

As the examples in this section illustrate, the need to evaluate projected future cash flows is an unavoidable part of financial management. As a result, much of this book is devoted to techniques aimed at analysing cash flow timing and risk.

Capital structure

capital structure
the mix of debt and
equity maintained
by a firm

A firm's **capital (or financial) structure** refers to the specific mixture of debt and equity the firm uses to finance its operations. The financial manager has two concerns in this area. First, how much should the firm borrow; that is, what mixture is best? The mixture chosen will affect both the risk and value of the firm. Second, what are the least expensive sources of funds for the firm?

If we picture the assets of the firm as a pie, then the firm's capital structure determines how that pie is sliced. In other words, what percentage of the firm's cash flow goes to debtholders and what percentage goes to shareholders. Firms have a great deal of flexibility in choosing a financial structure. Whether one structure is better than any other for a particular firm is the heart of the capital structure issue.

In addition to deciding on the financing mix, the financial manager has to decide exactly how and where to raise the money. The expenses associated with raising long-term financing can be considerable, so different possibilities must be carefully evaluated. Also, corporations borrow money from a variety of lenders in a number of different, and sometimes exotic, ways. Choosing among lenders and among loan types is another of the jobs handled by the financial manager.

Working capital management

Managing the firm's working capital is a day-to-day activity that ensures the firm has sufficient resources to continue its operations and avoid costly interruptions. This involves a number of activities all related to the firm's receipt and disbursement of cash.

Some of the questions about working capital that must be answered are:

1 How much cash and inventory should we keep on hand?
2 Should we sell on credit? If so, what terms will we offer, and to whom will we extend them?
3 How will we obtain any needed short-term financing? Will we purchase on credit or will we borrow short term and pay cash? If we borrow short term, how and where should we do it?

These are just a few of the issues that arise in managing a firm's working capital.

Dividend decision

The financial manager needs to decide what dividends the firm will pay, if any. Should the firm not pay a dividend then, all else being equal, the firm will reinvest the funds in profitable investment projects and the firm will grow. The growth of the firm via the profitable investment projects will be reflected in an increased share price. The shareholders do not receive a dividend but the value of their investment in the firm has increased.

The three areas of corporate financial management we have described—investment decision, financing decision and dividend decision—are very broad categories. Each includes a rich variety of topics, and we have indicated only a few of the questions that arise in the different areas. The chapters ahead contain greater detail.

Concept questions

1.2a *What is the capital budgeting decision?*
1.2b *Into what category of financial management does cash management fall?*
1.2c *What is the specific mixture of debt and equity that a firm chooses to use called?*

1.3 ■ The corporate form of business organisation

Large firms in Australia, such as BHP Billiton and Commonwealth Bank of Australia, are almost all organised as companies or corporations. We examine the three different legal forms of business organisation—sole proprietorship, partnership, and corporation—to see why this is so. Each of the three forms has distinct advantages and disadvantages in terms of the life of the business, the ability of the business to raise cash, and taxes. A key observation is that, as a firm grows, the advantages of the corporate form may come to outweigh the disadvantages.

Sole proprietorship

A **sole proprietorship** is a business owned by one person. This is the simplest type of business to start and is the least regulated form of organisation. Depending on where you live, you can start up a proprietorship by doing little more than registering a business name and opening your doors. For this reason, many businesses that later become large corporations start out as small proprietorships, and there are more proprietorships than any other type of business.

sole proprietorship
a business owned by a single individual

As the owner of a sole proprietorship, you keep all the profits. That is the good news. The bad news is that the owner has *unlimited liability* for business debts. This means that creditors can look beyond business assets to the proprietor's personal assets for payment. Similarly, there is no distinction between personal and business income, so all business income is taxed as personal income.

The life of a sole proprietorship is limited to the owner's lifespan and, importantly, the amount of equity that can be raised is limited to the proprietor's personal wealth. This limitation often means that the business has difficulty in exploiting new opportunities because of insufficient capital. Ownership of a sole proprietorship cannot easily be transferred, since this requires the sale of the entire business to a new owner.

Partnership

A **partnership** is similar to a proprietorship, except that there are two or more owners (partners). In a partnership, all the partners share in gains or losses, and all have unlimited liability for partnership debts, not just some particular share. The way partnership gains (and losses) are divided is described in the *partnership agreement*. This agreement can be an informal oral agreement, such as 'let's start a lawnmowing business...', or a lengthy, formal written document.

partnership
a business formed by two or more owners

The advantages and disadvantages of a partnership are basically the same as those for a proprietorship. Partnerships based on a relatively informal agreement are easy and inexpensive to form. Partners have unlimited liability for partnership debts, and the partnership terminates when a partner sells out or dies. All income is taxed as personal income to the partners, and the amount of equity that can be raised is limited to the partners' combined wealth. Ownership by a partner is not easily transferred because a new partnership must be formed.

Based on our discussion, the primary disadvantages of sole proprietorship and partnership as forms of business organisation are:

1 unlimited liability for business debts on the part of the owners;
2 limited life of the business; and
3 difficulty of transferring ownership.

These three disadvantages add up to a single, central problem: the ability of such businesses to grow can be seriously limited by an inability to raise cash for investment.

Company

The **company** is the most important form (in terms of size) of business organisation in Australia. A company is a legal 'person' separate and distinct from its owners, and it has many of the rights, duties and privileges of an actual person. Companies can borrow money and own property, can sue and be sued, and can enter into contracts. A company can even be a partner in a partnership, and a company can own shares in another company.

Not surprisingly, starting a company is somewhat more complicated than starting the other forms of business organisation, but not greatly so for a small business. Forming a company involves preparing a *constitution*.

The constitution contains rules describing how the company regulates its own existence. For example, it describes how directors are elected. These regulations may be a very simple statement of a few rules and procedures, or they may be quite extensive for a large company. The regulations may be amended or extended from time to time by the shareholders.

In a large company, the shareholders and the management are usually separate groups. The shareholders elect the board of directors, who then select the managers. Management is charged with running the company's affairs in the shareholders' interest. In principle, shareholders control the company because they elect the directors.

As a result of the separation of ownership and management, the corporate form has several advantages. Ownership (represented by shares) can be readily transferred, and the life of the company is therefore not limited. The company borrows money in its own name. As a result, the shareholders in a company have limited liability for corporate debts. The most they can lose is what they have invested plus any uncalled amount.

The relative ease of transferring ownership, the limited liability for business debts, and the unlimited life of the business are the reasons why the company form is superior when it comes to raising cash. If a company needs new equity, for example, it can sell new shares and attract new investors. The number of owners can be huge; larger companies have many thousands of shareholders. For example, the 2002 Annual Report of ANZ showed it had 199,556 shareholders. In such cases, ownership can change continuously without affecting the continuity of the business.

The company form does have some disadvantages. There are expenses involved with 'setting up' the company. As the company is a legal person it is required to lodge taxation returns and certain annual statutory returns have to be filed with the Australian Securities and Investments Commission (ASIC). Because of the size of some companies, the control tends to move away from the owners and rest with the managers of the firm. Consider the case of One.Tel, where working directors paid themselves millions of dollars in bonuses; many believe this contributed to the company's failure in 2001.

As the discussion in this section illustrates, the need for outside investors and creditors means that the company form will generally be the best option for large businesses. We focus on companies in the chapters ahead because of the importance of the corporate form in Australia and in other economies. Also, a few important financial management issues, such as dividend policy, are unique to companies. However, businesses of all types and sizes need financial management, so the majority of the subjects we discuss affect every form of business.

Concept questions

1.3a *What are the three forms of business organisation?*
1.3b *What are the primary advantages and disadvantages of a sole proprietorship or partnership?*
1.3c *Why is the corporate form superior when it comes to raising cash?*

 1.4 | ## The goal of financial management

Assuming that we restrict ourselves to for-profit businesses, the goal of financial management is to make money or add value for the owners. This goal is a little vague, of course, so we examine some different ways of formulating it in order to come up with a more precise definition. Such a definition is important because it leads to an objective basis for making and evaluating financial decisions.

Possible goals

If we were to consider possible financial goals, we might come up with some ideas like the following:

- survival
- avoid financial distress and bankruptcy
- beat the competition
- maximise sales or market share
- minimise costs
- maximise profits
- maintain steady earnings growth.

These are only a few of the goals we could list. Furthermore, each of these possibilities presents problems as a goal for the financial manager.

For example, it is easy to increase market share or unit sales; all we have to do is lower our prices or relax our credit terms. Similarly, we can always cut costs simply by doing away with things like research and development or maintenance. We can avoid bankruptcy by never borrowing any money or never taking any risks, and so on. It is not clear that any of these actions are in the shareholders' best interests.

Profit maximisation would probably be the most commonly cited goal, but even this is not a very precise objective. Do we mean profits this year? If so, then actions such as deferring maintenance, letting inventories run down, and other short-run cost-cutting measures will tend to increase profits now, but these activities are not necessarily desirable.

The goal of maximising profits may refer to some sort of 'long-run' or 'average' profits, but it is still unclear exactly what this means. First, do we mean something like accounting net profit or earnings per share? As we will see in more detail in the next chapter, these accounting numbers may have little to do with what is good or bad for the firm. Second, what do we mean by the long run? As a famous economist once remarked, in the long run, we are all dead! More to the point, this goal does not tell us what the appropriate trade-off is between current and future profits.

The goals we have listed above are all different, but they do tend to fall into two classes. The first of these relates to profitability. The goals involving sales, market share and cost control all relate, at least potentially, to different ways of earning or increasing profits. The second group, involving bankruptcy avoidance, stability and safety, all relate in some way to controlling risk. Unfortunately, these two types of goal are somewhat contradictory. The pursuit of profit normally involves some element of risk, so it is not really possible to maximise both safety and profit. What we need, therefore, is a goal that encompasses both these factors.

A decision rule

The financial manager in a corporation makes decisions for the shareholders of the firm. Given this, instead of listing possible goals for the financial manager, we really need to answer a more fundamental question: From the shareholders' point of view, what is a good financial management decision?

If we assume that shareholders buy shares because they seek to gain financially, then the answer is obvious: Good decisions increase the value of the shares, and poor decisions decrease the value.

Given our observations, it follows that the financial manager acts in the shareholders' best interests by making decisions that increase the value of the shares. The appropriate goal for the financial manager can thus be stated quite easily: The goal of financial management is to maximise the current value per share of the existing shares.

> The goal of financial management is to maximise the current value per share of the existing shares.

The goal of maximising the value of the shares avoids the problems associated with the different goals we listed above. There is no ambiguity in the criterion, and there is no short-run versus long-run issue. We explicitly mean that our goal is to maximise the *current* share value.

Since the goal of financial management is to maximise the value of the shares, we need to learn how to identify those investments, financing and dividend arrangements that favourably impact on the value of the firm. This is precisely what we will be studying. In fact, we could have defined corporate finance as the study of the relationship between business decisions and the value of the shares in the business.

A more general goal

Given our goal as stated above (maximise the value of the shares), an obvious question comes up: What is the appropriate goal when the firm has no traded shares? Companies are certainly not the only type of business, and the shares in many companies rarely change hands, so it can be difficult to say what the value per share is at any given time.

As long as we are dealing with for-profit businesses, only a slight modification is needed. The total value of the shares in a company is simply equal to the market value of the owners' equity. Therefore, a more general way of stating our goal is: Maximise the market value of the owners' equity.

With this in mind, it does not matter whether the business is a proprietorship, a partnership or a company. For each of these, good financial decisions increase the market value of the owner's equity and poor financial decisions decrease it. In fact, although we choose to focus on companies in the chapters ahead, the principles we develop apply to all forms of business. Many of them even apply to the not-for-profit sector.

Finally, our goal does not imply that the financial manager should take illegal or unethical actions in the hope of increasing the value of the equity in the firm. What we mean is that the financial manager best serves the owners of the business by identifying goods and services that add value to the firm because they are desired and valued in the free marketplace.

The financial manager undertakes the three decisions—the investment, financing and dividend decisions—in trying to meet the firm's objective of maximising the value of equity. Table 1.1 displays the interrelationship of the three decisions and the firm's objective. The financial manager is concerned with the efficient sourcing of funds and ensures the effective use of them. The manager cannot be efficient and effective without trying to meet the firm's objective.

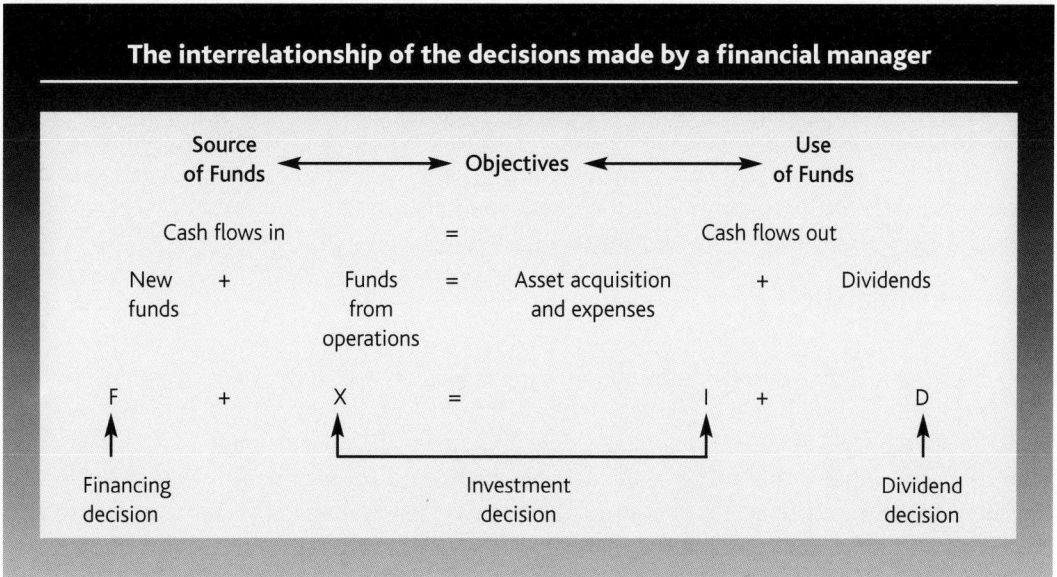

The interrelationship of the decisions made by a financial manager

TABLE 1.1

The source of funds can be simply broken into new funds raised (the financing decision) and funds from running the operations of the business (part of the investment decision). The use of funds similarly can be broken into asset and non-asset expenditure (the other part of the investment decision) and payments to the firm's owners (the dividend decision). Because the equation reduces to three interrelated decisions (financing, investment and dividend) the financial manager cannot make or change one decision without affecting at least one other type of decision. For example, if the financial manager decides to increase the dividends (the cash returns to owners) then the financing must be increased or the expenditure on investments reduced or some combination of both.

Concept questions

1.4a *What is the goal of financial management?*
1.4b *What are some shortcomings of the goal of profit maximisation?*
1.4c *Can you give a definition of corporate finance?*
1.4d *Show how the three decisions a financial manager makes are interrelated.*

1.5 ▪ The agency problem and control of the corporation

We have seen that the financial manager acts in the best interest of the shareholders by taking actions that increase the value of the shares. However, we have also seen that in large companies ownership can be spread over a huge number of shareholders. This dispersion of ownership arguably means that management effectively controls the firm. In this case, will management necessarily act in the best interests of the shareholders? Put another way, might not management pursue its own goals at the shareholders' expense? We briefly consider some of the arguments below.

Agency relationships

The relationship between shareholders and management is called an *agency relationship*. Such a relationship exists whenever someone (the principal) hires another (the agent) to represent their interests. For example, you might hire someone (an agent) to sell a car that you own while you are away at university. In all such relationships, there is a possibility of conflict of interest between the principal and the agent. Such a conflict is called an **agency problem**.

agency problem
the possibility of conflicts of interest between the shareholders and management of a firm

Suppose that you do hire someone to sell your car and that you agree to pay them a flat fee when the car sells. The agent's incentive in this case is to make the sale, not necessarily to get you the best price. If you paid a commission of, say, 10 per cent of the sale price instead of a flat fee, then this problem might not exist. This example illustrates that the way an agent is compensated is one factor affecting agency problems.

Management goals

To see how management and shareholder interests might differ, imagine that the firm has a new investment under consideration. The new investment will have a favourable impact on the share value, but it is also a relatively risky venture. The owners of the firm will wish to take the investment (because the share value will rise), but management may not because there is the possibility that things will turn out badly and management jobs will be lost. If management does not take the investment, then the shareholders may have lost a valuable opportunity. This is one example of an *agency cost*.

More generally, agency costs refer to the costs of the conflict of interests between shareholders and management. These costs can be indirect or direct. An indirect agency cost is a lost opportunity such as the one we have just described.

Direct agency costs come in two forms. The first type is a corporate expenditure that benefits management but costs the shareholders. Perhaps the purchase of a luxurious and unneeded corporate jet would fall under this heading. The second type of direct agency cost is an expense that arises from the need to monitor management actions. Paying outside auditors to assess the accuracy of financial statement information could be one example.

It is sometimes argued that, left to themselves, managers would tend to maximise the amount of resources over which they have control or, more generally, corporate power or wealth. This goal could lead to an overemphasis on corporate size or growth. For example, cases where management is accused of overpaying to buy up another company just to increase the size of the business or to demonstrate corporate power are not uncommon. Obviously, if overpayment does take place, such a purchase does not benefit the shareholders.

Our discussion indicates that management may tend to overemphasise organisational survival to protect job security. Also, management may dislike outside interference, so independence and corporate self-sufficiency may be important goals.

Do managers act in the shareholders' interests?

Whether managers will, in fact, act in the best interest of shareholders depends on two factors. First, how closely are management goals aligned with shareholder goals? This question relates to the way managers are compensated. Second, can management be replaced if it does not pursue shareholder goals? This issue relates to control of the firm. As we will discuss, there are a number of reasons to think that, even in the largest of firms, management has a significant incentive to act in the interest of shareholders.

Managerial compensation

Management will frequently have a significant economic incentive to increase share value for two reasons. First, managerial compensation, particularly at the top, is usually tied to financial performance in general and often to the share value in particular. For example, managers are frequently given the option to buy shares at a bargain price. The more the share is worth, the more valuable this option is. The second incentive managers have relates to job prospects. Better performers within the firm will tend to get promoted. More generally, those managers who are successful in pursuing shareholder goals will be in greater demand in the labour market and thus command higher salaries.

Late in 2002 and during 2003 stories of corporate 'generosity' surfaced frequently. Some of the payments that were made to executives were:

- $33 million payout from the Commonwealth Bank to Chris Cuffe;
- approximately $30 million by BHP Billiton to Brian Gilbertson;
- nearly $13 million from Coles-Myer to Dennis Eck;
- about $3 million from Coles-Myer and AMP to Stan Wallis (though Wallis, bowing to public pressure, decided he would not accept the $1.6 million from AMP); and
- an undisclosed amount, thought to be around $20 million, to Paul Batchelor, the former chief of AMP.

Andrew Mohl, the chief executive of AMP who was appointed in 2002, was reported as saying while he could understand shareholders' anger regarding the huge payouts they were necessary to meet contract requirements or avoid the long-winded process for discharging employees. He argued that it could take between 18 and 24 months to terminate an employee when the issue was performance. Three warnings and counselling had to be given prior to any termination steps.

In 2003 the ASX talked about making it a listing requirement that all executive reward packages be fully disclosed in the annual reports. In addition increasing pressure was being put on the government to legislate to control executive rewards.

These issues highlight the agency problem. Shareholders' control of their agent executives is dependent on the flow of information to them. The amount of information supplied is governed by the company's need to keep important competitive information secret and the objective of keeping shareholders informed.

Control of the firm

Control of the firm ultimately rests with shareholders. They elect the board of directors, who, in turn, hire and fire management. The mechanism by which unhappy shareholders can act to replace existing management is called a *proxy fight*. A proxy is the authority to vote on behalf of another shareholder. A proxy fight develops when a group solicits proxies in order to replace the existing board, and thereby replace existing management.

Another way that management can be replaced is by takeover. Those firms that are poorly managed are more attractive as acquisitions than well-managed firms because a greater profit potential exists. Thus, avoiding a takeover by another firm gives management another incentive to act in the shareholders' interest.

The available theory and evidence are consistent with the view that shareholders control the firm and that shareholder wealth maximisation is the relevant goal of the corporation. Even so, there will undoubtedly be times where management goals are pursued at the expense of the shareholders, at least temporarily. With the large number of recent corporate failures and many of the excesses of management that have been disclosed, much more emphasis has been placed upon sound corporate governance. More disclosure is now required in relation to directors' and senior officers' remunerations; directors' responsibilities and liabilities have been reinforced and tightened under law; and more responsibility has been placed on the audit process. Best corporate practice demands the establishment of an internal audit committee to scrutinise any transaction where there may be a conflict of management and shareholder interest.

Stakeholders

Our discussion thus far implies that management and shareholders are the only parties with an interest in the firm's decisions. This is an oversimplification, of course. Employees, customers, suppliers, and even the government all have a financial interest in the firm.

stakeholder
someone other than a shareholder or debtholder who potentially has a claim on a firm

Taken together, these various groups are called **stakeholders** in the firm. In general, a stakeholder is someone other than a shareholder or debtholder who potentially has a claim on the cash flows of the firm. Such groups will also attempt to exert control over the firm, perhaps to the detriment of the owners.

Concept questions

1.5a *What is an agency relationship?*
1.5b *What are agency problems and how do they come about? What are agency costs?*
1.5c *What incentives do managers in large corporations have to maximise share value?*

Clifford W. Smith Jr.

In their own words

Clifford W. Smith Jr* on market incentives for ethical behaviour

Ethics is a topic that has been receiving increased interest in the business community. Much of this discussion has been led by philosophers and has focused on moral principles. Rather than review these issues, I want to discuss a complementary (but often ignored) set of issues from an economist's viewpoint. Markets impose potentially substantial costs on individuals and institutions that engage in unethical behaviour. These market forces thus provide important incentives that foster ethical behaviour in the business community.

At its core, economics is the study of making choices. I thus want to examine ethical behaviour simply as one choice facing an individual. Economic analysis suggests that in considering an action, you identify its expected costs and benefits. If the estimated benefits exceed the estimated costs, you take the action; if not, you don't. To focus this discussion, let's consider the following specific choice: Suppose you have a contract to deliver a product of a specified quality. Would you cheat by reducing quality to lower costs in an attempt to increase profits? Economics implies that the higher the expected costs of cheating, the more likely ethical actions will be chosen. This simple principle has several implications.

First, the higher the probability of detection, the less likely an individual is to cheat. This implication helps us understand numerous institutional arrangements for monitoring in the marketplace. For example, a company agrees to have its financial statements audited by an external public accounting firm. This periodic professional monitoring increases the probability of detection, thereby reducing any incentive to misstate the firm's financial condition.

Secondly, the higher the sanctions imposed if cheating is detected, the less likely an individual is to cheat. Hence, a business transaction that is expected to be repeated between the same parties faces a lower probability of cheating because the lost profits from the foregone stream of future sales provide powerful incentives for contract compliance. However, if continued corporate existence is more uncertain, so are the expected costs of foregone future sales. Therefore firms in financial difficulty are more likely to cheat than financially healthy firms. Firms thus have incentives to adopt financial policies that help credibly bond against cheating. For example, if product quality is difficult to assess prior to purchase, customers doubt a firm's claims about product quality. Where quality is more uncertain, customers are only willing to pay lower prices. Such firms thus have particularly strong incentives to adopt financial policies that imply a lower probability of insolvency.

Thirdly, the expected costs are higher if information about cheating is rapidly and widely distributed to potential future customers. Thus information services like Consumer Reports, *which monitor and report on product quality, help deter cheating. By lowering the costs for potential customers to monitor quality, such services raise the expected costs of cheating.*

Finally, the costs imposed on a firm that is caught cheating depend on the market's assessment of the ethical breach. Some actions viewed as clear transgressions by some might be viewed as justifiable behaviour by others. Ethical standards also vary across markets. For example, a payment that if disclosed in the United States would be labelled a bribe might be viewed as a standard business practice in a third-world market. The costs imposed will be higher the greater the consensus that the behaviour was unethical.

Establishing and maintaining a reputation for ethical behaviour is a valuable corporate asset in the business community. This analysis suggests that a firm concerned about the ethical conduct of its employees should pay careful attention to potential conflicts among the firm's management, employees, customers, creditors, and shareholders. Consider Sears, the department store giant that was found to be charging customers for auto repairs of questionable necessity. In an effort to make the company more service oriented (in the way that competitors like Nordstrom are), Sears had initiated an across-the-board policy of commission sales. But what works in clothing and housewares does not always work the same way in the auto repair shop. A customer for a man's suit might know as much as the salesperson about the product. But many auto repair customers know little about the inner workings of their cars and thus are more likely to rely on employee recommendations in deciding on purchases. Sears's compensation policy resulted in recommendations of unnecessary repairs to customers. Sears would not have had to deal with its repair shop problems and the consequent erosion of its reputation had it anticipated that its commission sales policy would encourage auto shop employees to cheat its customers.

* **Clifford W. Smith Jr.** is the Epstein Professor of Finance at the University of Rochester's Simon School of Business Administration. He is an advisory editor of the *Journal of Financial Economics*. His research focuses on corporate financial policy and the structure of financial institutions.

1.6 Financial markets and the corporation

We have seen that the primary advantages of the corporate form of organisation are that ownership can be transferred more quickly and easily than with other forms and that money can be raised more readily. Both of these advantages are significantly enhanced by the existence of financial markets, and financial markets play an extremely important role in corporate finance.

The interplay between the corporation and the financial markets is illustrated in Figure 1.3. The arrows in Figure 1.3 trace the passage of cash from the financial markets to the firm and from the firm back to the financial markets.

FIGURE
1.3

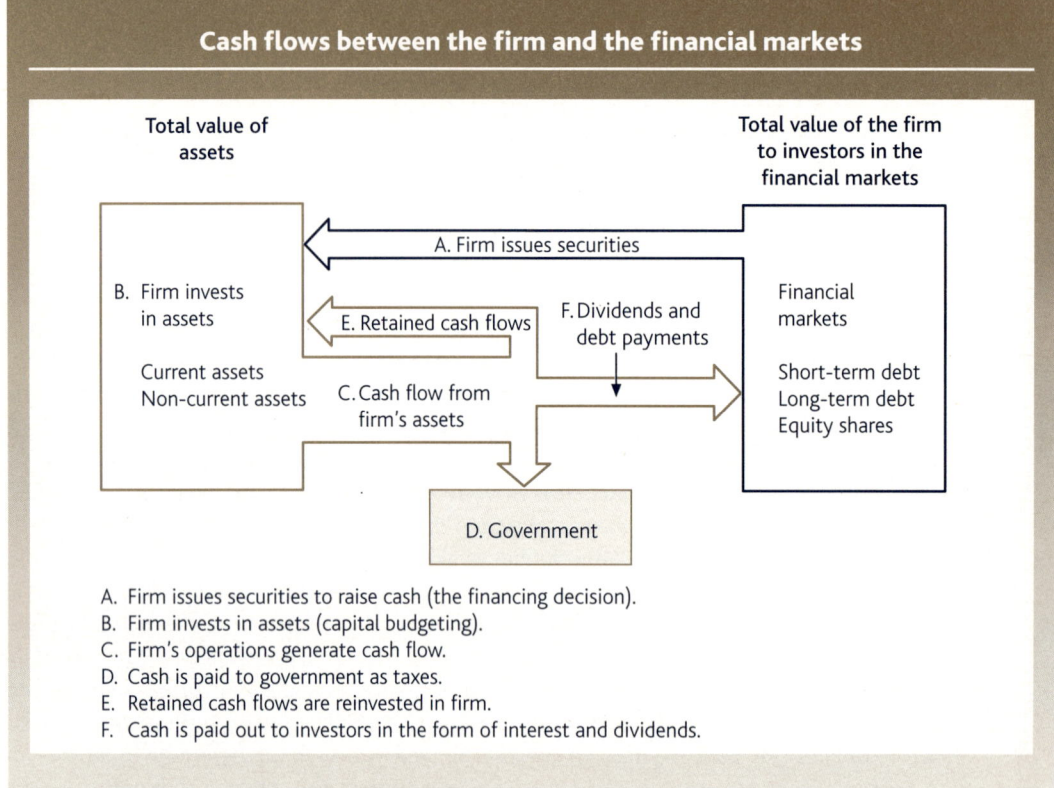

Cash flows between the firm and the financial markets

Total value of assets

Total value of the firm to investors in the financial markets

A. Firm issues securities

B. Firm invests in assets

Current assets
Non-current assets

E. Retained cash flows

F. Dividends and debt payments

C. Cash flow from firm's assets

Financial markets

Short-term debt
Long-term debt
Equity shares

D. Government

A.   Firm issues securities to raise cash (the financing decision).
B.   Firm invests in assets (capital budgeting).
C.   Firm's operations generate cash flow.
D.   Cash is paid to government as taxes.
E.   Retained cash flows are reinvested in firm.
F.   Cash is paid out to investors in the form of interest and dividends.

Suppose we start with the firm selling shares and borrowing money to raise cash. Cash flows to the firm from the financial market (A). The firm invests the cash in current and non-current assets (B). These assets generate some cash (C), some of which goes to pay corporate taxes (D). After taxes are paid, some of this cash flow is reinvested in the firm (E). The rest goes back to the financial markets as cash paid to debtholders and shareholders (F).

The financial market, like any market, is just a way of bringing buyers and sellers together. In financial markets, it is debt and equity securities that are bought and sold. Financial markets differ in detail, however. The most important differences concern the types of securities that are traded, how trading is conducted, and who the buyers and sellers are. Some of these differences are discussed below.

Money versus capital markets

money markets
financial markets where short-term debt securities are bought and sold

Financial markets can be classified as either **money markets** or **capital markets**. Short-term debt securities of many varieties are bought and sold in money markets. These short-term debt securities are often called money market 'instruments' and are essentially IOUs. For example, *commercial paper* or *bills* represent short-term borrowing by large companies and are money market instruments. Capital markets are the markets for long-term debt and shares.

capital markets
financial markets where long-term debt and equity securities are bought and sold

The money market is a *dealer market*. Generally speaking, dealers buy and sell something for themselves, at their own risk. A car dealer, for example, buys and sells cars. In contrast, brokers and agents match buyers and sellers, but do not actually own the commodity. A real estate agent or broker, for example, does not normally buy and sell houses.

The largest money market dealers are the banks and merchant banks whose shareholders are primarily large banks. These banks, along with other market participants, are connected electronically via telephone and computer, so the money market has no actual physical location. The data that they access electronically is provided by a number of suppliers. One such supplier is now the mayor of New York—Mike Bloomberg. The following is one of many money market screens that are provided by Bloomberg.

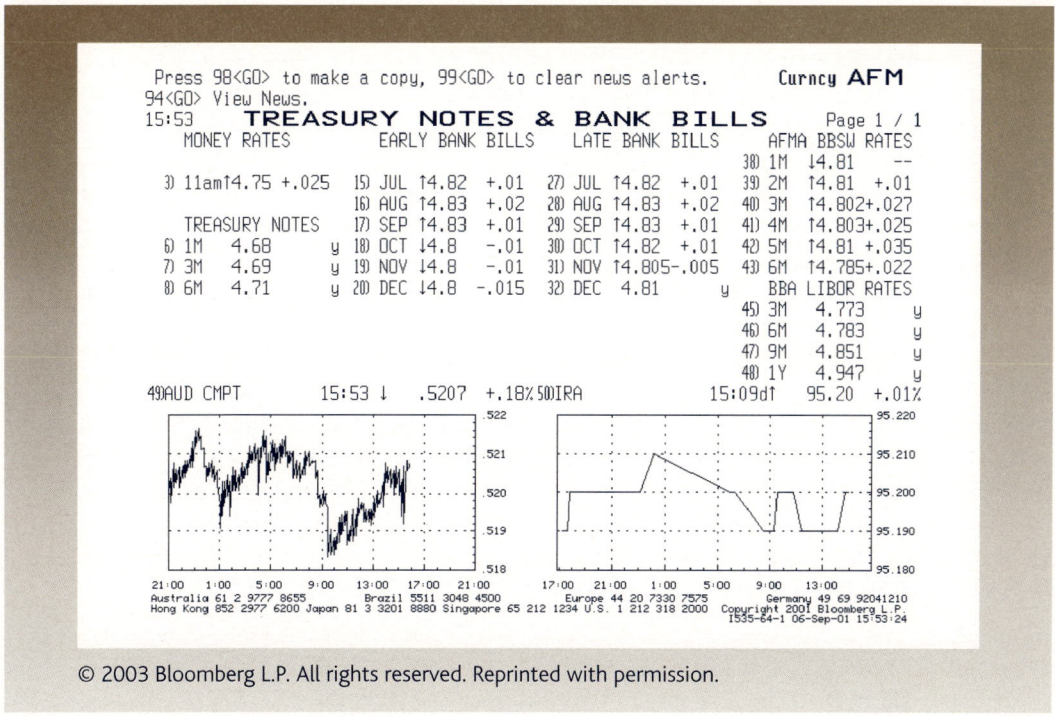

Primary versus secondary markets

Financial markets function as both primary and secondary markets for debt and equity securities. The term *primary market* refers to the original sale of securities by governments and companies. The *secondary markets* are where these securities are bought and sold after the original sale. Equities are, of course, issued solely by companies. Debt securities are issued by both governments and companies. In the discussion below, we focus on corporate securities only.

Primary markets

In a primary market transaction, the company is the seller, and the transaction raises money for the company. Companies engage in two types of primary market transaction: public offerings and private placements. A public offering, as the name suggests, involves selling securities to the general public, while a private placement is a negotiated sale involving a specific buyer. These topics are covered in some detail in Part Seven, so we only introduce the bare essentials here.

Most publicly offered debt and equity securities are 'underwritten'. *Underwriters* are firms that specialise in marketing securities. When a public offering is underwritten, an underwriter or *syndicate* contracts to purchase from the firm those securities that remain unsold to the public. The underwriters profit by charging a fee for this service.

By law, public offerings of debt and equity must be accompanied with a prospectus which must be lodged with ASIC. The prospectus basically sets out information that investors and their advisers would require to help make an informed decision about the securities.

The accounting, legal and underwriting costs of public offerings can be considerable. Partly to avoid the various regulatory requirements and the expense of public offerings, debt and equity are often sold privately to large financial institutions such as life insurance companies or superannuation funds. Such private placements do not have to be registered with ASIC and do not require the involvement of underwriters.

Secondary markets

A secondary market transaction involves one owner or debtholder selling to another. It is therefore the secondary markets that provide the means for transferring ownership of corporate securities.

The equity shares of most of the large firms in Australia trade in an organised market. This market is the Australian Stock Exchange (ASX). Those who can trade on the share market are brokers who are members of the ASX.

Until October 1987, all stock exchange transactions were conducted using the open outcry system on the trading floor. In October 1987, a computer-based trading system known as SEATS (Stock Exchange Automated Trading System) was introduced. In October 1990 the trading floors were closed, and all shares are now traded on SEATS. SEATS trading terminals are located in brokers' offices and allow the operators to enter bids and offers for automatic execution. The bids and offers are executed in order of priority at time of entry for a given price. The market for any shares can be monitored through the trading terminals.

Bloomberg also provides information about the Australian share market. The following is an example for Coles Myer. It can be seen that at 12.26 pm on 16 May 2002 the highest bid price was $6.71 and the lowest ask price was $6.72.

```
CML AU A$ ↑  6.72  +.04  N 16s N 6.71/6.72 N  3596x4460
At 12:26 Vol 2,904,634 Op 6.71 N Hi 6.77 N Lo 6.68 N ValTrd 19489540
      BEST BID/OFFER        COLES MYER LTD              A$
```

BID

Size	Price		Size	Price
860	2 6.56	16	3596	4 6.71
18351	18 6.55	17	43426	11 6.70
5000	1 6.54	18	17365	5 6.69
13160	4 6.53	19	25109	20 6.68
8900	5 6.52	20	25085	13 6.67
11070	7 6.51	21	16030	10 6.66
77315	61 6.50	22	12539	13 6.65
11644	8 6.49	23	2000	2 6.64
9200	7 6.48	24	7100	2 6.63
16520	10 6.47	25	650	2 6.62
11400	8 6.46	26	4860	4 6.61
47230	34 6.45	27	51144	37 6.60
14573	6 6.44	28	1300	2 6.59
2171	3 6.43	29	5800	5 6.58
8750	8 6.42	30	14435	3 6.57

ASK

	Price	Size		Price	Size
1	6.72 2	4460	16	6.88 3	6000
2	6.73 4	11667	17	6.89 1	1000
3	6.74 2	55437	18	6.90 8	17883
4	6.75 8	34116	19	6.91 2	3000
5	6.76 2	16000	20	6.92 1	600
6	6.77 4	4497	21	6.93 1	4000
7	6.78 7	39408	22	6.94 1	3600
8	6.79 3	2549	23	6.95 10	13000
9	6.80 21	59549	24	6.96 1	800
10	6.81 4	5226	25	6.97 1	3000
11	6.82 3	13500	26	6.98 7	16520
12	6.83 4	3159	27	6.99 10	23578
13	6.84 5	45188	28	7.00 39	36006
14	6.85 8	8300	29	7.02 1	500
15	6.86 1	500	30	7.04 1	1000

```
MAG  8:28 How Murdoch dropped $8 billion one day and picked it up overnight
AFR  5:10 Uphill task for Coles in Asia
BN   5/15 Woolworths Introduces a Stock-Option Plan for 150 Executives
Australia 61 2 9777 8600      Brazil 5511 3048 4500      Europe 44 20 7330 7500      Germany 49 69 920410
Hong Kong 852 2977 6000 Japan 81 3 3201 8900 Singapore 65 212 1000 U.S. 1 212 318 2000   Copyright 2002 Bloomberg L.P.
                                                                                     G974-327-2 16-May-02 12:28:12
```

Listing

Shares that trade on an organised exchange are said to be *listed* on that exchange. In order to be listed, firms must meet certain minimum criteria concerning, for example, asset size and number of shareholders. As these companies are of greater public interest, the ASX requires additional reports to those required under the *Corporations Act* 2001.

Concept questions

1.6a *How are money and capital markets different?*
1.6b *What is a dealer market?*
1.6c *What are the common elements of open outcry trading and SEATS trading?*

1.7 ■ The two-period perfect certainty model

We stated in Section 1.4 of this chapter that corporate finance was concerned with the investment, financing and dividend decisions. We will analyse these decisions using a model called the two-period perfect certainty model. To enable us to do this, we will view the world as being comprised of three major elements—individuals, firms and capital markets. The theory of business finance is concerned with how individuals and firms allocate resources through time.

We shall develop a model that explains the behaviour of firms and individuals under three assumptions. You will see that two of the three assumptions are unrealistic. Do not worry about the realism of the assumptions because in later chapters when we look at the issues in more detail you will see that the conclusions are still valid.[2]

These assumptions are, first, *perfect certainty*. All of the firm's future cash flow opportunities are known exactly. As the future is known there is no risk, so therefore the market rate of interest for all participants is a rate that reflects no risk. This rate we will call the *market rate*.

The second assumption is that of *perfect capital markets*. All investors and firms have equal and costless access to all information about present cash flows. There are no transaction costs. This is a world without taxes. The last assumption is that of *rational investors*. All investors are utility or wealth maximisers who prefer more wealth to less.

Two-period model

The certainty model is restricted to a single interval of time of unspecified length, so that there is only now (period 1) and the future (period 2).

Individuals will allocate their resources (make decisions about consumption) through time according to two criteria. These criteria are, first, their tastes and preferences with respect to current or future consumption; and second, the investment opportunities that they have available to them.

The complete consumption tastes and preferences of individuals in a two-period world may be represented as in Figure 1.4 (overleaf). A few points are worth noting. Each curve represents combinations of period 1 and period 2 consumption to which the individual is indifferent. This means that the individual has no particular preference with respect to the position on a particular curve. These utility curves are convex to the origin, representing a declining marginal rate of substitution.

FIGURE
1.4

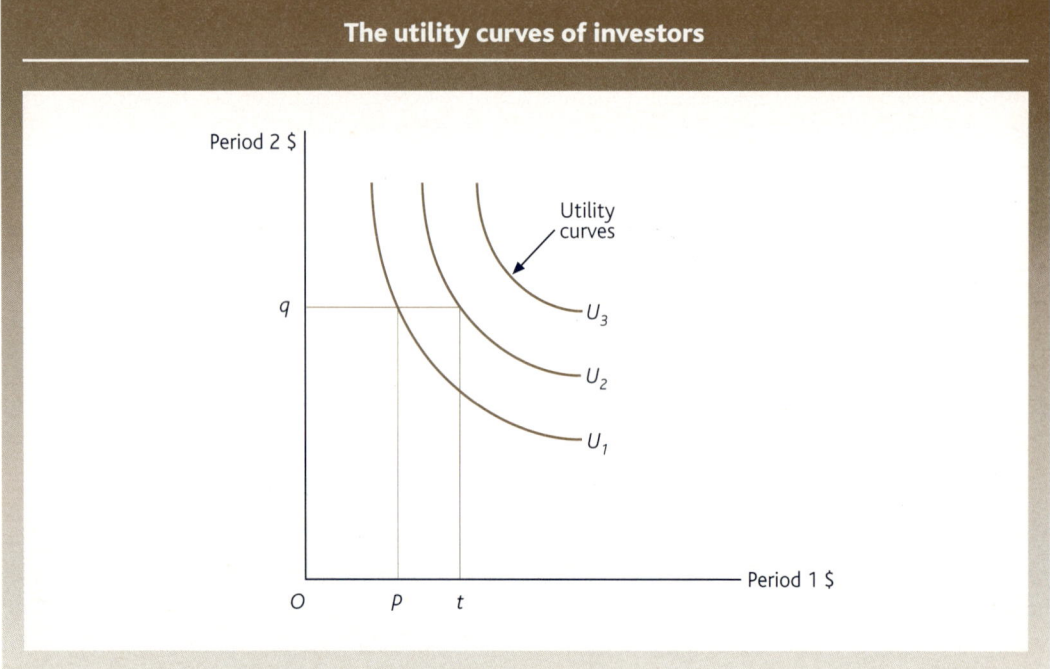

The utility curves of investors

Each succeeding curve represents increasing utility to the individual, therefore the curves cannot meet. If we assume individuals prefer more consumption to less consumption, progressing from a lower curve to a higher curve makes individuals more 'well off'. Thus the (t,q) combination in Figure 1.4 is more desirable than the (p,q) combination. The individual is better off to the extent of (p,t) of period 1 consumption. U_2 is better than U_1.

Representation of opportunities

It is useful to identify two types of investment opportunity facing individuals in our two-period world. These are firms and capital markets. This means that an individual can invest in a firm by buying shares or, alternatively, invest the money in the capital market (for example, a bank).

We will consider investment in a firm first of all. Consider Figure 1.5. A firm has an initial endowment (the capital that a firm starts off with) of (O,a_1) in period 1. The combinations of period 1 and period 2 dollars which the firm may produce from this endowment are shown by the *production possibility frontier* in Figure 1.5. The slope of the production possibility frontier represents attainable combinations of period 1 and period 2 dollars given the endowment. The *production possibility frontier* shows the ability of the firm in converting period 1 dollars into period 2 dollars.

The production frontier is concave to the origin. This implies a declining marginal rate of transformation of period 1 dollars into period 2 dollars (or diminishing marginal returns). Thus, an investment of (a_1,a_2) dollars in period 1 produces a return of (O,x_2) dollars in

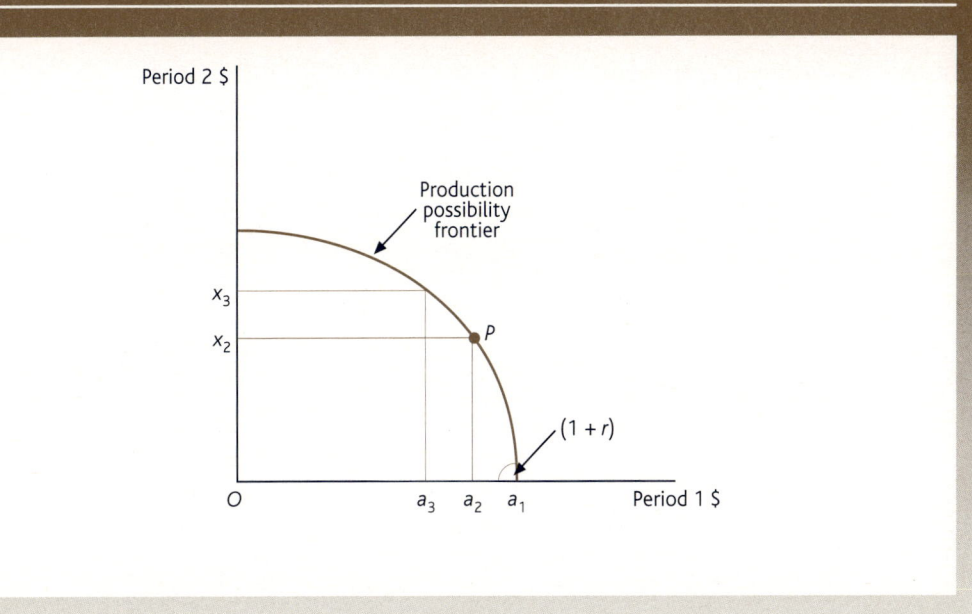

period 2; while an equal investment of (a_2,a_3) dollars in period 1 produces only (x_2,x_3) dollars in period 2. The diminishing returns are demonstrated by (x_2,x_3) being less than (O,x_2).

The curve assumes small investments. The slope of the curve at any point represents the rate at which period 1 dollars are transformed into period 2 dollars (r). Suppose the firm decides to invest (a_1,a_2) dollars in period 1 (that is, follow its production frontier from a_1 up to P). It has an initial endowment of (O,a_1) and consequently funds not invested, of (O,a_2) dollars, are currently available for distribution to owners in period 1 as a dividend. The investment of (a_1,a_2) dollars in period 1 produces a return or dividend in period 2 of (O,x_2) dollars. Thus by production at P, the firm pays dividends to its owners of (O,a_2) dollars in period 1 and (O,x_2) dollars in period 2.

The shape of the production frontier is determined by the technical efficiency of the firm (its ability to convert period 1 dollars into period 2 dollars) and the shape is independent of the initial endowment.

The firm and one owner

Consider Figure 1.6 (overleaf). The owner would require the firm to move along its production curve to Q, the point of tangency between the production frontier and the owner's utility curve U_2. It is at this point that the owner's utility is maximised as this is the utility curve furthest from the origin that can be reached given the firm's technical efficiency and its resources. It is assumed that firms are created by individuals so as to maximise their utility. Q is unique. It is the only point of production at which the owner's utility is maximised.

FIGURE
1.6

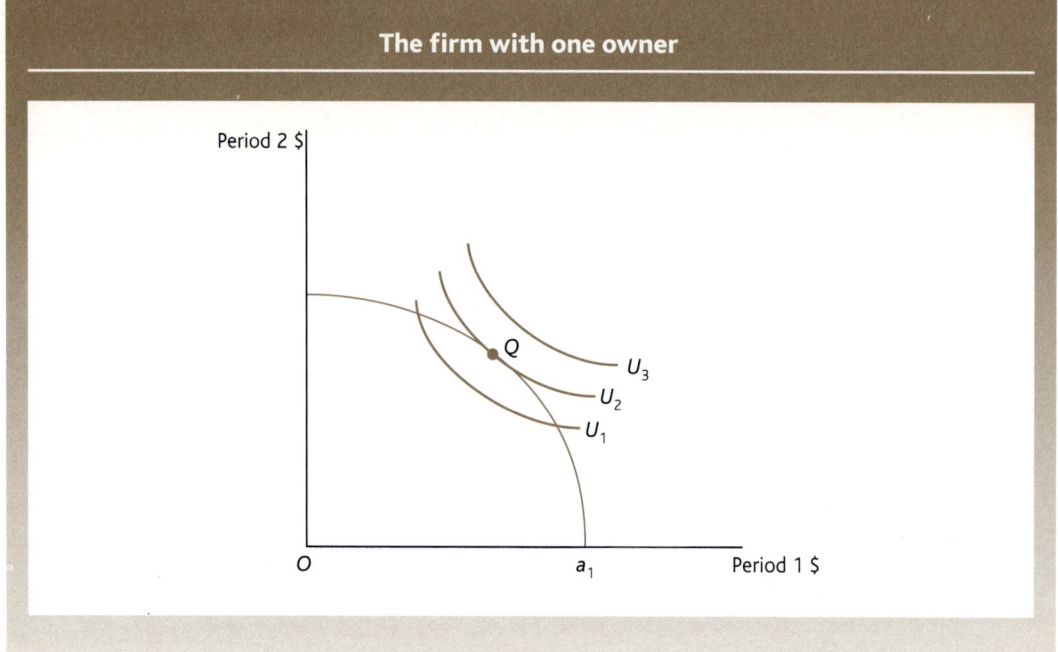

The firm with one owner

The firm with multiple owners

Now consider Figure 1.7. The firm now has many owners and not all owners have the same set of utility curves. Some prefer more consumption now and less later (U_c), while other owners prefer less consumption now and more later (U_a). In the case of one owner, the firm had a unique production point. However, where there is more than one owner, the firm faces a dilemma—which owner do they please?

FIGURE
1.7

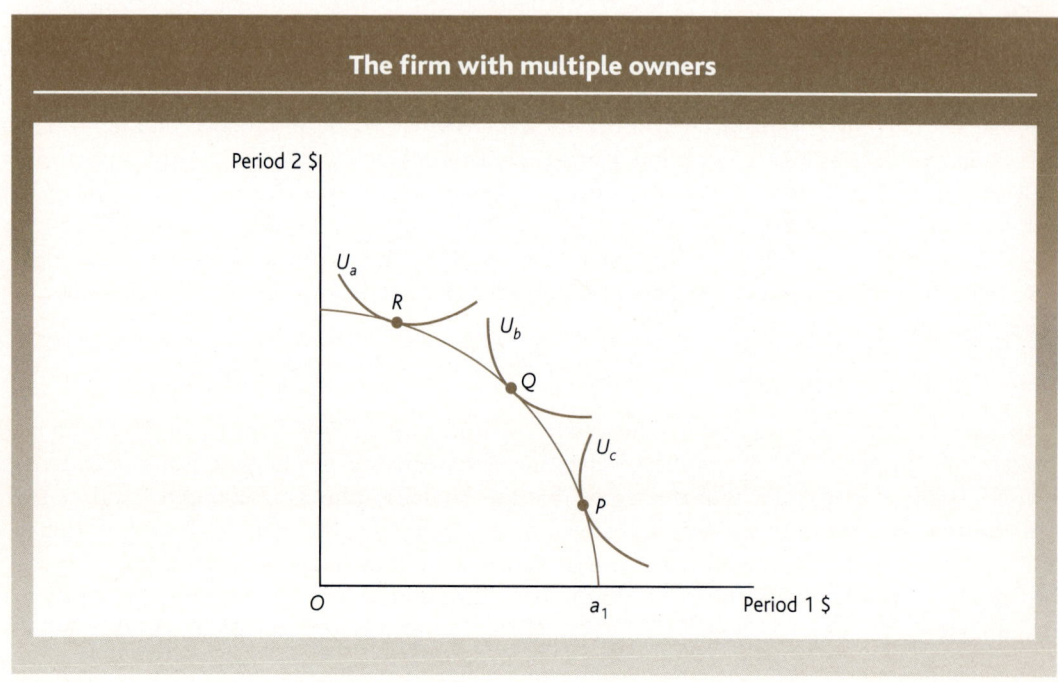

The firm with multiple owners

The point of tangency between the production frontier and each set of individual utility curves for the various owners will differ. Thus, there is no one unique point of production which maximises the happiness of all owners. Owner A wants the firm to produce at R, owner B at Q and owner C at P. What does the firm do? No unique freely chosen solution exists that will maximise the individual utility functions of the individual owners. However, by introducing a capital market we are able to find such a solution.

Perfect capital markets

A perfect capital market (PCM) implies that borrowing and lending rates must be the same and this, coupled with the certainty assumption, guarantees that there is only one rate of interest prevailing in the market and this is equal to the riskless rate (i).

If you look at Figure 1.8 you will see that an individual has an endowment of (O,a_1) in period 1 dollars. With the market rate of interest (i), the individual can trade period 1 consumption for period 2 consumption or vice versa by lending or borrowing in the market. Suppose the individual invests (a_1,c_1) in period 1 so that the period 1 consumption is (O,c_1), the individual will have a period 2 consumption of (O,c_2). If the individual were to invest an additional amount of (c_1,d_1) dollars, (O,d_1) dollars is available for consumption in period 1 and in period 2, (O,d_2).

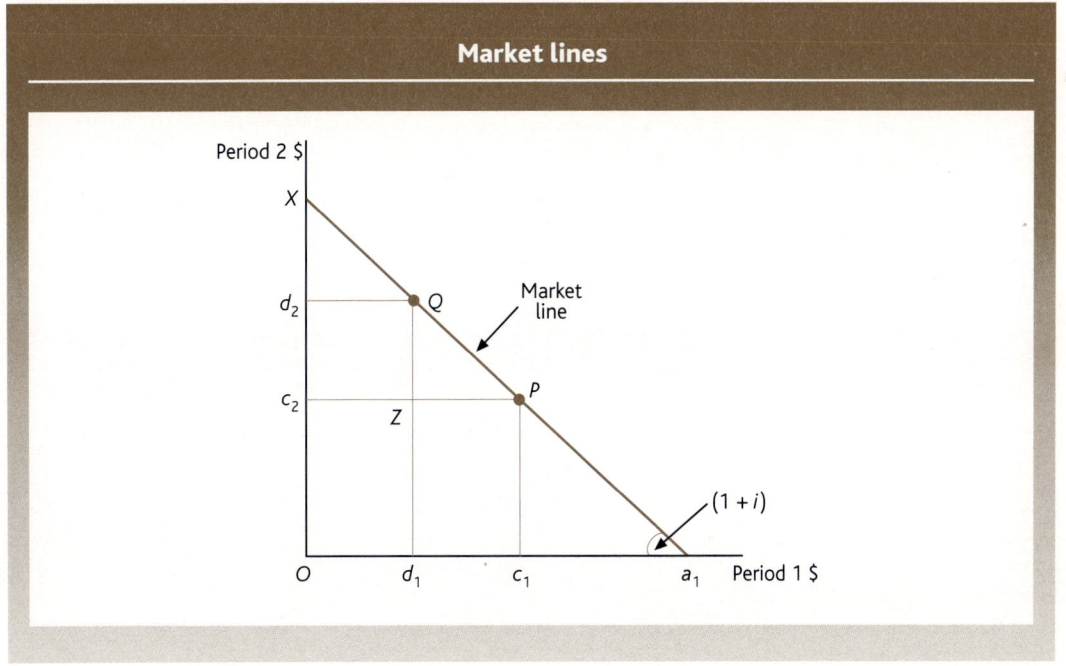

Market lines

FIGURE 1.8

From trigonometry:

Slope of (a_1,X) = tan of the angle (Oa_1X)

$$= \frac{(O,X) \text{ period 2 dollars}}{(O,a_1) \text{ period 1 dollars}}$$

$$= (1 + i)$$

Therefore, the slope tells us how much period 2 consumption we get from investing in period 1.

By investing (a_1, c_1) at rate i, the period 2 return is (O, c_2). Therefore $(a_1, c_1) \times (1 + i)$ equals (c_1, P). (c_1, P) equals (O, c_2). Also (c_1, d_1) equals (Z, P) and $(Z, P) \times (1 + i)$ equals (Z, Q) and (Z, Q) equals (c_2, d_2).

EXAMPLE 1.5 — Investing in the market

You have $100 today and the market rate of interest is 10 per cent. The present value of your wealth is $100. If you were to invest $40 of period 1 dollars, the period 2 return would be $40 × 1.1 = $44. Therefore:

Period 1 consumption is $60
Period 2 consumption is $44
Present value is $60 + ($44 ÷ 1.1) = $100

Students should be aware that moving from period 1 to period 2 is a process of finding the accumulated value for one period, and moving from period 2 to period 1 is discounting for one period. This is explained in great detail in Chapter 5. The present value will always be that value as represented from point O to where the market line touches the period 1 axis.

This means that with a perfect capital market, by borrowing and lending at the market rate of interest i, an individual can move up and down the market line (a_1, X) taking any desired combination of period 1 and period 2 consumption for the given initial endowment.

Firms, one owner and capital markets

In Figure 1.9, a firm has an initial endowment of (O, a_1) in period 1 and a production frontier of (a_1, Q, X). The firm should invest the amount (a_1, d_1) and pay a current dividend of (O, d_1). Its investment will produce a period 2 dividend of (O, d_2).

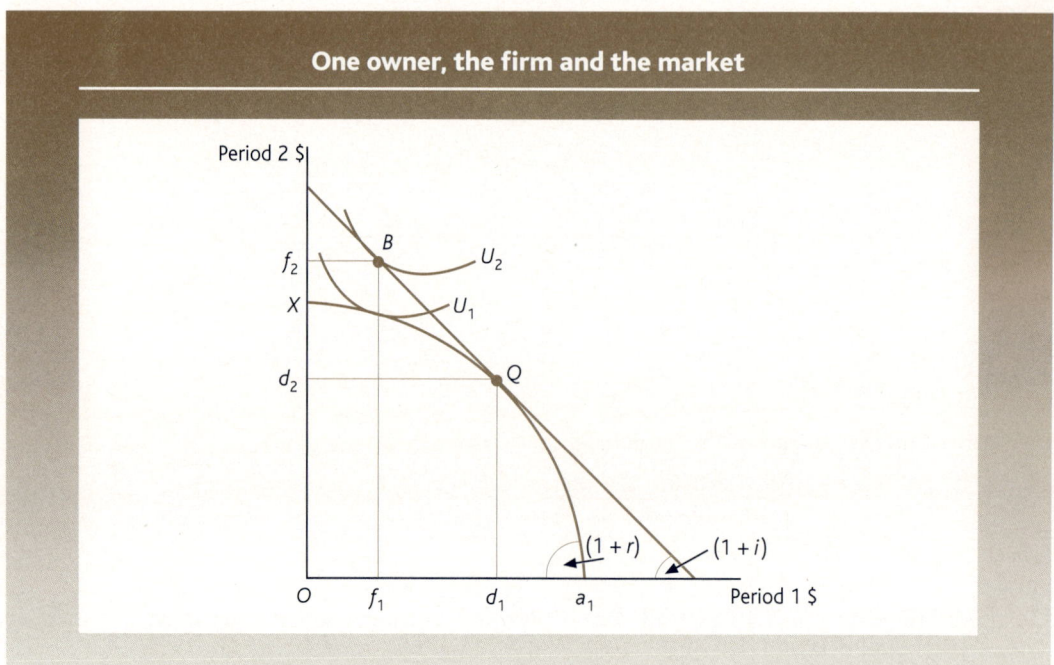

FIGURE 1.9 — One owner, the firm and the market

The reason that the firm should invest funds until it reaches point Q on its production frontier is that, by doing so, it places the owner on the highest possible utility curve given the resources (O,a_1). Although the firm pays a dividend of (O,d_1) (more than what the owner wants in period 1 consumption—the owner actually wants (O,f_1)), the owner can invest the excess amount (d_1,f_1) in the market and so move from Q up the market line to its point of tangency B with one of the owner's utility curves. The owner invests (d_1,f_1) at the market rate i, which means a period 2 return of $(d_1,f_1) \times (1 + i)$ or (d_2,f_2) in addition to the firm's period 2 dividend of (O,d_2).

The owner can attain this pattern because of the existence of a perfect capital market, even though the dividend pattern of the firm is (O,d_1) and (O,d_2). In other words, the utility of an individual would be less without a perfect capital market. Q is the unique solution that maximises the owner's utility.

Note that $(1 + i)$ is the market rate of interest. $(1 + r)$ is the internal rate of return for the firm (or the rate at which the firm can transform period 1 dollars into period 2 dollars). Below Q on the production frontier $(1 + r) > (1 + i)$; at Q, $(1 + r) = (1 + i)$; and above Q, $(1 + r) < (1 + i)$. This means that up to point Q, the return by the firm's investing is greater than investing in the market, at Q they are equal, and above Q the return is greatest where investment is in the market.

Case of many owners

With a perfect capital market as in Figure 1.10, all owners can attain their desired investment/consumption preference, maximising their utility for a given amount of resources (O,a_1). Their utility is higher than they could have attained had the market not existed.

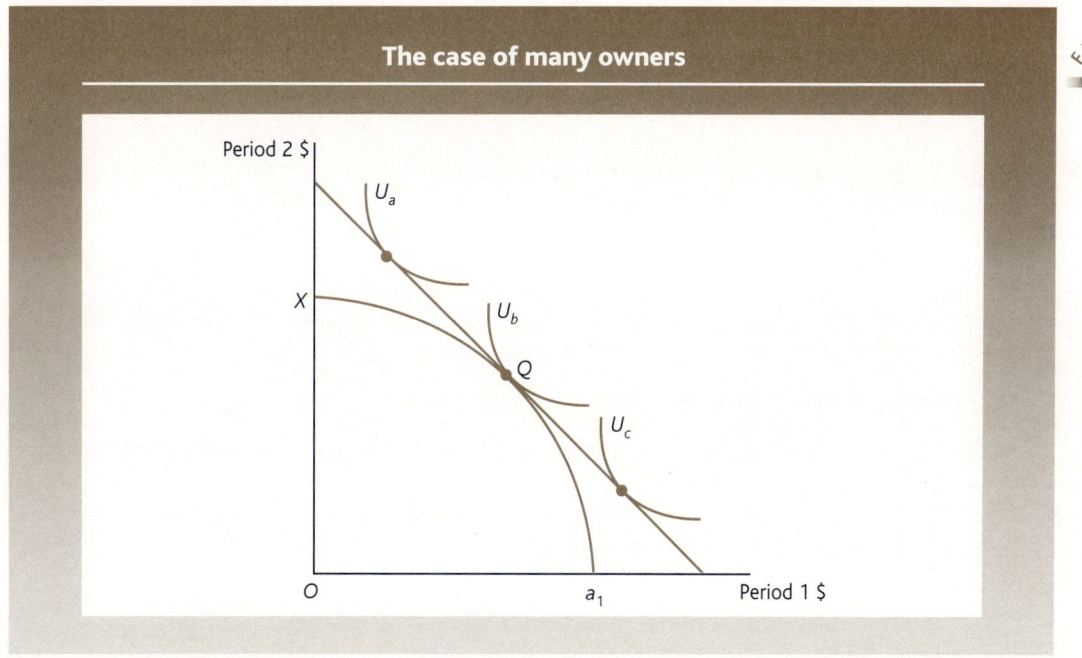

The case of many owners

FIGURE 1.10

Fisher's separation theorem

In a perfect capital market, it is possible to separate the firm's investment decisions from the owners' consumption decisions. It is not necessary to impose a dictatorial solution upon the owners. By producing at Q, all owners can attain their desired investment/consumption pattern and it is at a maximum.

Market value rule

Consider Figure 1.11. The firm has an initial endowment of (O, a_1) but the value of the firm is (O, V_1).

$$
\begin{aligned}
\text{Value of the firm} &= (O, V_1) \\
&= (O, d_1) + (d_1, V_1) \\
&= (O, d_1) + (O, d_2) \div (1 + i) \\
&= \text{period 1 dividend} + \text{PV of period 2 dividend} \\
&= \text{present value of future dividends}
\end{aligned}
$$

Thus, maximising the value of the firm is consistent with maximising shareholder wealth and shareholder utility.

Market value of the firm

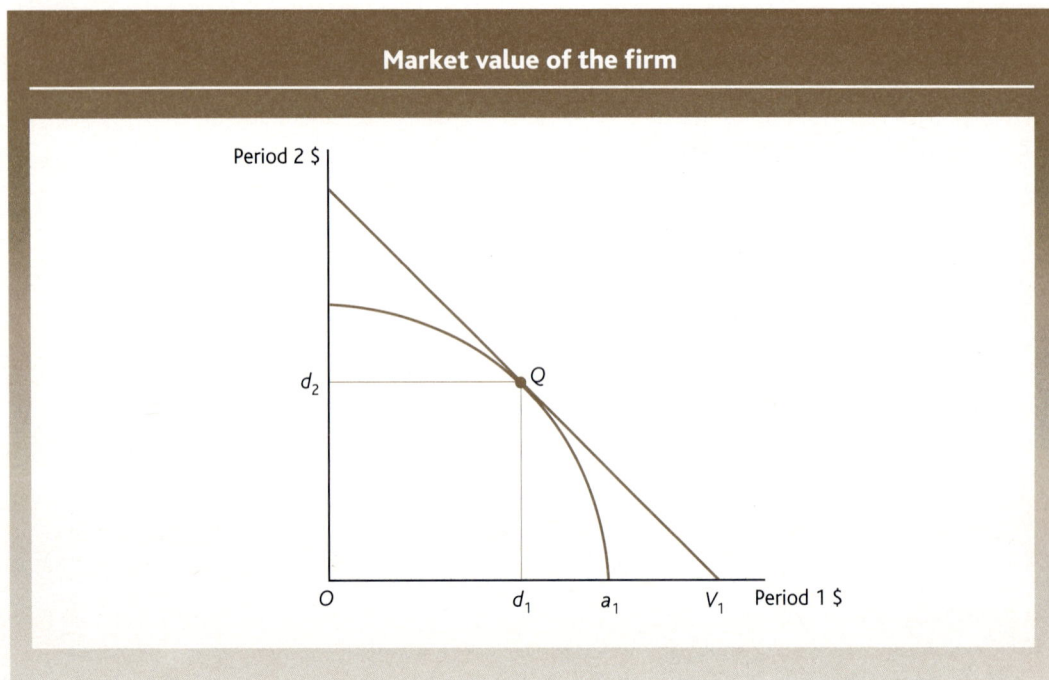

Firm decisions with imperfect capital markets

Consider Figure 1.12, where $i_L < i < i_B$; that is, when the lending or investing interest rate is less than the borrowing interest rate.

Imperfections in the capital market have led to a situation in which the borrowing and lending rates differ. For borrowers the optimal point of production is Y_B and for lenders the optimal point is Y_L.

> When borrowing and lending rates differ (that is, when there are imperfections in the market), there is no longer a unique production decision that would be made by any current owner regardless of the owner's tastes (Arrow's Impossibility Theorem).

Note that market imperfections should not exist in a competitive market.

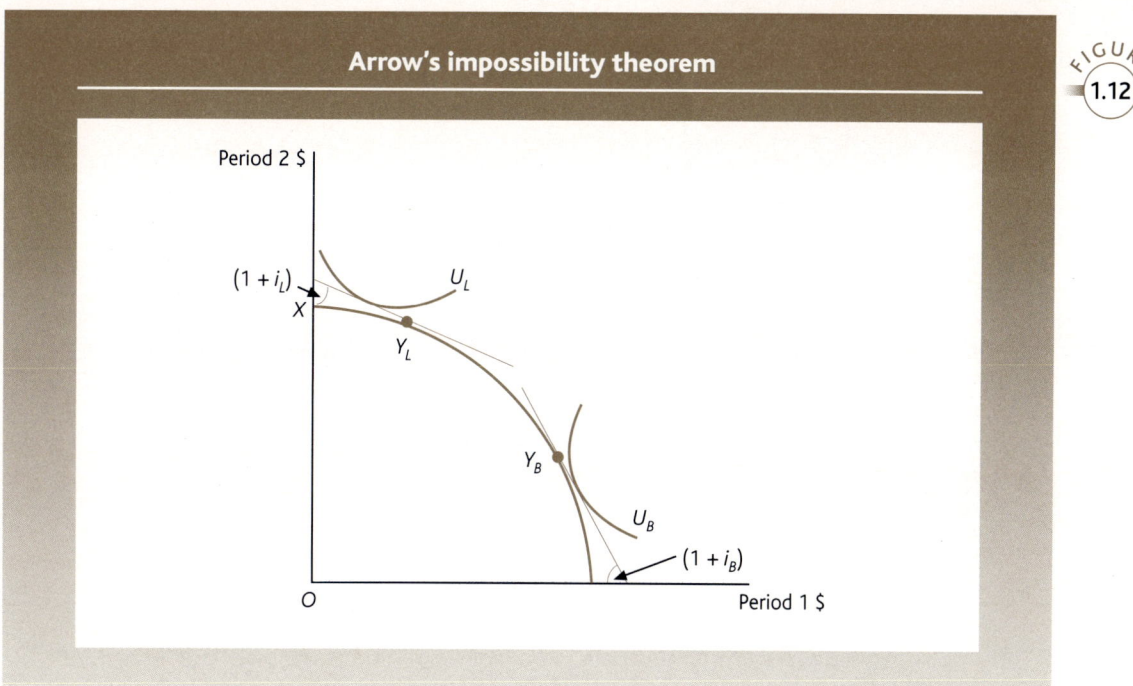

Arrow's impossibility theorem

FIGURE 1.12

The investment decision

Refer to Figure 1.13. Q is the optimal point of production for the firm because it is at this point that the wealth and utility of all owners is maximised. A question arises: *What decision rule exists that allows the firm to identify point Q?* There exist two rules, being the *net present value rule (NPV)* and the *internal rate of return rule (IRR)*. These are discussed in detail in Part Four.

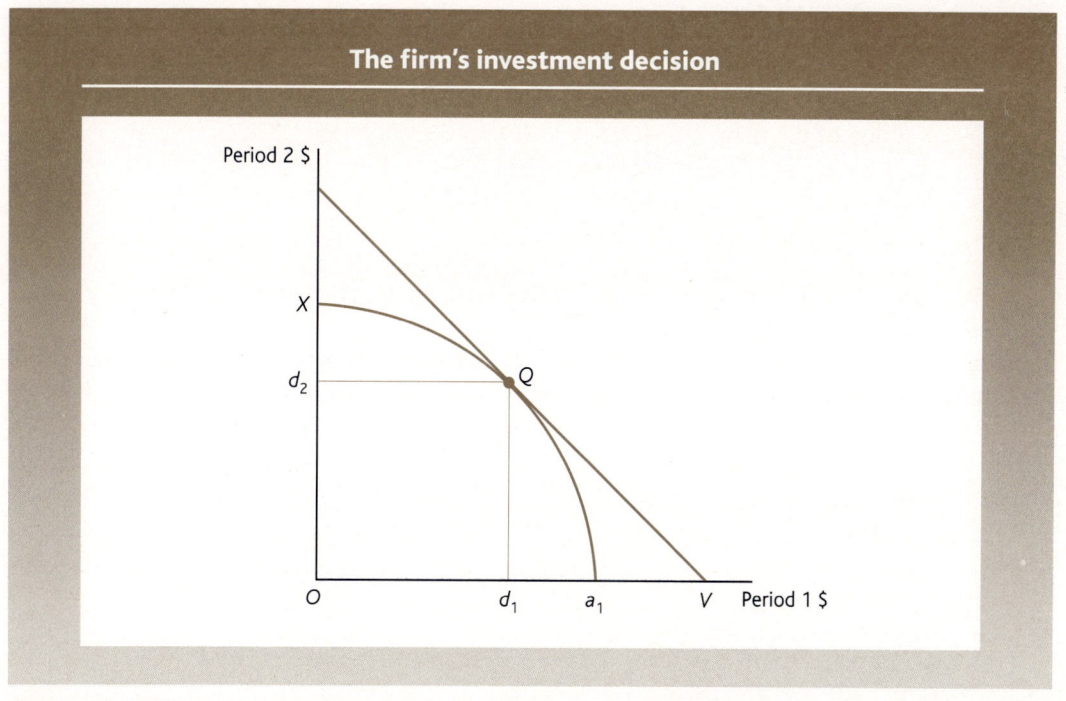

The firm's investment decision

FIGURE 1.13

Net present value (NPV) rule

In a two-period world, the NPV rule is as follows:

$$NPV = \left(\frac{X_2}{1 + i} - I_1 \right)$$

That is, the NPV is the period 2 cash flow return from undertaking a project (X_2), discounted by the market rate of interest $(1 + i)$, after deducting the period 1 outlay cost of the project (I_1).

Example:

Outlay	$10,000 (period 1)
Rate of return	15%
Return	$11,500 (period 2)
Market return	10%

$$
\begin{aligned}
NPV &= (\$11,500/1.1) - \$10,000 \\
&= \$10,455 - \$10,000 \\
&= \$455
\end{aligned}
$$

Should the project be accepted? The period 1 cost of the project is $10,000 and the period 1 return from the project is $10,455 (that is, in today's dollars, wealth has increased by $455 because the project is undertaken). The decision rule to follow is:

if NPV is	+ve	accept project
if NPV is	−ve	reject project
if NPV is	0	indifferent

Refer to Figure 1.13 again. Assume that the firm has an initial endowment of $15,000 and has the opportunity to invest in one project requiring an outlay of $10,000 and returning $11,500 in period 2. The period 1 investment (a_1,d_1) would be $10,000 and the period 1 dividend (O,d_1) would be $5000. The period 2 return or dividend (O,d_2) is $11,500.

$$
\begin{aligned}
\text{Value of the firm} &= (O,d_1) + (O,d_2) \div (1 + i) \\
&= \$5000 + \$11,500 \div 1.1 \\
&= \$5000 + \$10,455 \\
&= \$15,455 \\
&= (O,d_1) + (d_1,a_1) + (a_1,v_1) \\
&= \$5000 + \$10,000 + \$455
\end{aligned}
$$

The firm increased in value in period 1 dollars from $15,000 (O,a_1), the initial endowment, to $15,455 (O,V), the value of the firm. The marginal increase (a_1,V_1) is $455, the NPV (that is, positive NPV projects increase firm value by the amount of the NPV). It follows that if negative NPV projects were undertaken, firm value would decrease by the amount of the negative NPV project. *Question*: When would a firm undertake a negative NPV project? *Answer*: It would not unless regulation forced it to.

Internal rate of return (IRR) rule

The second decision rule is IRR. The IRR is found by solving for r in the following equation:

$$\frac{X_2}{1 + r} - I_1 = 0$$

$$\frac{11,500}{1 + r} - 10,000 = 0$$

$$r = 15\%$$

The accept/reject decision rule for IRR is:

if $r > i$	accept	i.e. the NPV is +ve
if $r < i$	reject	i.e. the NPV is −ve
if $r = i$	indifferent	i.e. the NPV is 0

The rationale is that if the firm were to invest funds in the project, the return is 15 per cent compared with the market return of 10 per cent. What should the firm do? Invest funds. Referring yet again to Figure 1.13, it can be seen that below Q on the production frontier, the slope of the frontier (r) is greater than the slope of the market line (i). That segment from a_1 to Q represents projects with a return greater than the market return (or a positive NPV). At Q, the slope of the frontier is equal to the slope of the market line and at this point $r = i$ and projects would have a zero NPV. From Q to X, the slope of the frontier is less than the slope of the market line $r < i$ and projects would have a negative NPV.

If used correctly, the NPV and IRR rules give the same *accept/reject* decisions for a project. In Part Four, we will examine the mechanics of these rules in detail. We will identify problems in the use of IRR when a choice has to be made between projects and when cash flows do not follow a normal pattern.

Financing decision

Under conditions of certainty and perfect capital markets, there is only one interest rate prevailing in the market and this is the riskless rate (i). Because there is no risk, there is no real distinction between the equity securities that a firm might issue and its debt securities. Consequently, questions of capital structure (combinations of debt and equity) do not exist. Questions of the amount of funds required by the firm are pertinent.

In Figure 1.14 (overleaf), the firm has an initial endowment of (O,a_1) and, given this endowment, can produce at point R and maximise firm value. *Should the firm borrow more funds?* From R to Q, the slope of the frontier is greater than the slope of the market line ($r > i$), representing positive NPV projects. The projects can only be undertaken if the firm borrows more funds.

The firm borrows (O,b_1) in period 1 dollars and invests these funds to move up the frontier to the optimal point Q. The increase in the period 2 return from the investment is (P,R). Of this return, some must be repaid as a cost of borrowing (P,B). The increase in the period 2 return for the firm's equityholders is (B,R) and firm value increases by (V_1,V), the NPV of the further investments undertaken from borrowed funds.

FIGURE 1.14

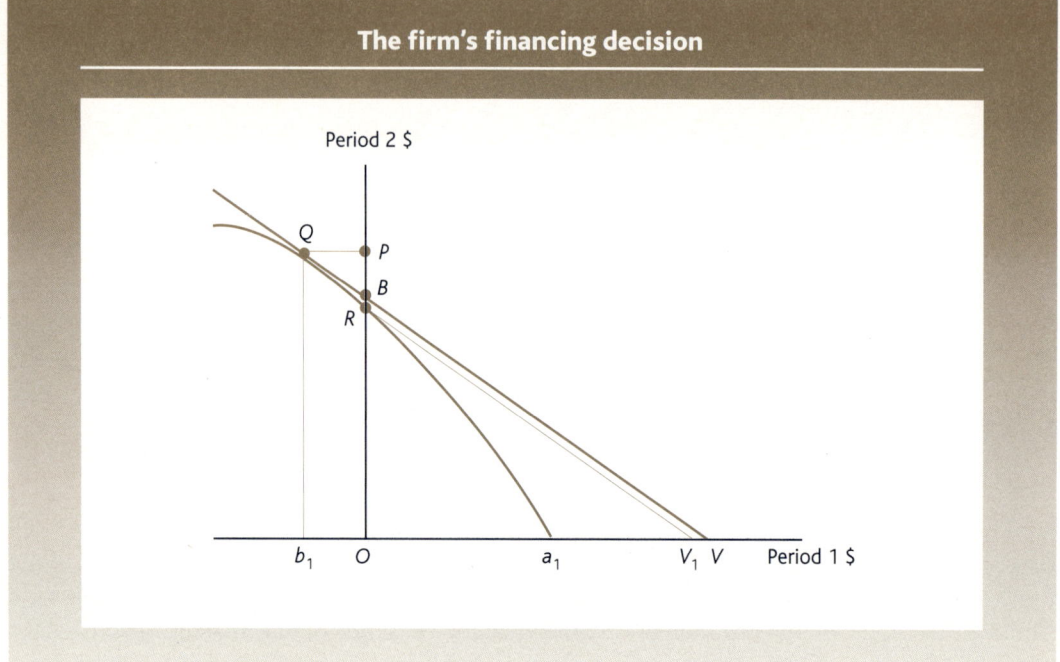

The firm's financing decision

Assume a market rate of interest of 10 per cent. The initial endowment (O,a_1) is $5,000 and a period 2 return from this (O,R) is $10,000. The NPV (a_1,v_1) at this stage is $4091 [$10,000 $\div$ 1.1 − $5000]. Further opportunities exist which require funding (O,b_1) of $10,000 and would return in period 2 dollars (P,R) $12,000.

If $10,000 is borrowed at 10 per cent, the repayments for monies borrowed must be (P,B) $11,000, leaving a net period 2 return to equityholders of $1,000 (B,R). The NPV of the further investment is $909 (V_1,V), which is the same as the period 2 increase in return to equityholders discounted ($1,000 $\div$ 1.1).

Total funds invested were $15,000 (a_1,b_1) giving a total period 2 return of $22,000 (O,P) of which equityholders received $11,000 (O,B) and therefore firm value is $10,000 (O,V); being the endowment of $5,000 (O,a_1), the NPV without borrowing (a_1,V_1) of $4,091, and the NPV from the further investments of $909 (V_1,V).

Question: What changed firm value: the financing decision (how much funds) or the investment decision (what was done with the funds)? *Answer*: The investment decision. Referring to the previous example, if the firm had borrowed $20,000 instead of $10,000, then $10,000 would have been invested in projects returning $12,000 and the other $10,000 invested in the market returning $11,000, giving a total return of $23,000 in period 2. $22,000 ($20,000 × 1.1) would have to be repaid, leaving $1,000 for equityholders as before. *The financing decision does not affect firm value, but the investment decision does.*

Dividend decision

Similarly, the dividend decision does not affect firm value. Refer to Figure 1.15 *(this example is totally independent of Figure 1.14)* and assume an initial endowment of $10,000 (O,a_1) returning $15,000 (O,R) in period 2. The firm borrows $5,000 (O,b_1) at 10 per cent and invests up to Q, returning $6,000 (P,R) in period 2. The firm will have to repay $5,500

(P,B) in period 2 and the return to equityholders will be $15,500 (O,B) in period 2 dollars, or firm value is $14,091 (O,V). Firm value is made up of the initial endowment of $10,000, the NPV before borrowing of $3,636 [$15,000 ÷ 1.1 − $10,000] and the NPV of the further investments of $455 [$6000 ÷ 1.10 − $5000].

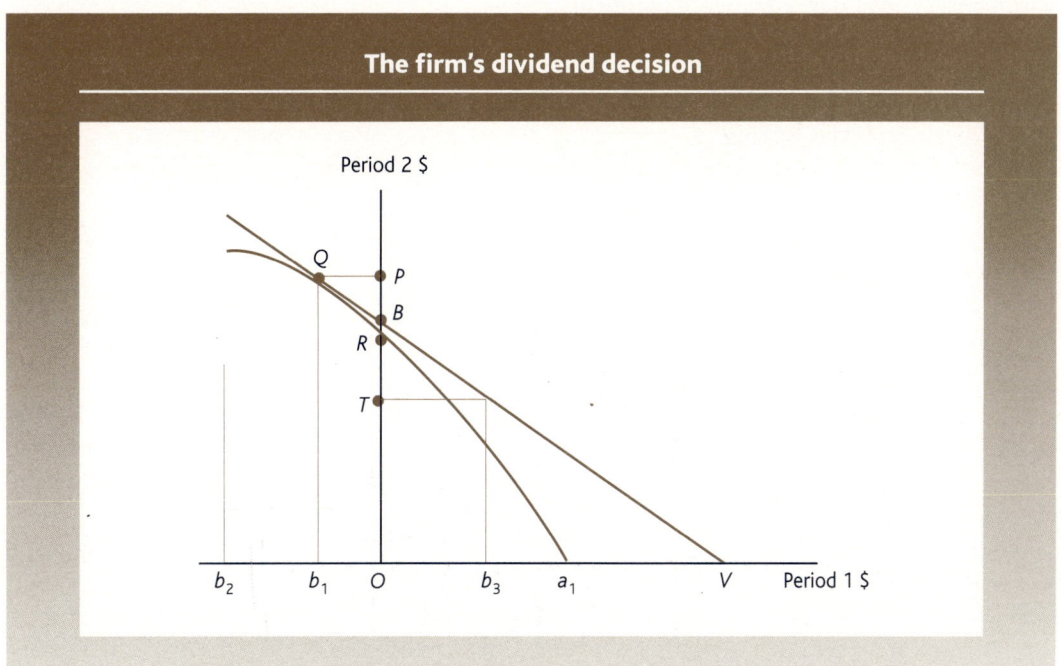

The firm's dividend decision

FIGURE 1.15

In this example, insufficient funds exist for a period 1 dividend. To pay a period 1 dividend of (say) $5,000, the firm could borrow the $5,000 ($b_1,b_2$) and pay the dividend ($O,b_3$) (note: b_1,b_2 = O,b_3). Repayments for the borrowing of the dividend would be $5,500 ($B,T$) and the period 2 dividend to equityholders would reduce from $15,500 (O,B) to $10,000 (O,T). Are the equityholders any better off? No. The present value of the dividend stream is $5,000 for period 1 and $10,000 ÷ 1.1 = $9,091, the present value of the period 2 dividend. Present value of the dividend stream is $14,091, the same as before.

Of the three decisions facing the financial manager of the firm, *it is only the investment decision that affects firm value* when the assumptions of perfect certainty and perfect capital markets hold. When we drop the assumption of certainty and introduce the problems of uncertainty we will see that it is still the *investment decision* that drives value and *not* how the investments are *financed* or how the distributions (*dividends*) are made to the owners.

Concept questions

1.7a *What are the three decisions made by the financial manager of a firm?*
1.7b *If a firm maximises its value, what happens to shareholder utility?*
1.7c *In a two-period perfect certainty world, what decision affects firm value?*

1.8 ▪ Outline of the text

A CLOSER LOOK

Now that we have completed a quick tour through the concerns of corporate finance, we can take a closer look at the organisation of this book. The text is organised into the following nine parts:

Part One: Overview of Corporate Finance
Part Two: Financial Statements and Long-Term Financial Planning
Part Three: Valuation of Future Cash Flows
Part Four: Capital Budgeting
Part Five: Risk and Return
Part Six: Current Investment Decisions
Part Seven: Long-Term Financing
Part Eight: Cost of Capital and Long-Term Financial Policy
Part Nine: Topics in Corporate Finance

Part One of the text contains some introductory material (this chapter) and goes on to explain the relationship between accounting profit and cash flow. Part Two explores financial statements and how they are used in finance in greater depth.

Parts Three and Four contain our core discussion on valuation. In Part Three, we develop the basic procedures for valuing future cash flows, with particular emphasis on shares and bonds (or debentures). Part Four draws on this material and deals with capital budgeting and the effect of long-term investment decisions on the firm.

In Part Five, we develop some tools for evaluating risk. We then discuss how to evaluate the risks associated with long-term investments by the firm. The emphasis in this section is on coming up with a benchmark for making investment decisions.

The important area of managing assets to be used in the next trading cycle of a business is covered in Part Six. It deals with current investment decisions.

Parts Seven and Eight deal with the related issues of long-term financing, dividend policy and capital structure. We discuss corporate securities in some detail and describe the procedures used to raise capital and sell securities to the public. We also introduce and describe the important concept of the cost of capital. We go on to examine dividends and dividend policy and the important considerations in determining a capital structure.

The final part, Part Nine, contains several important special topics. There is a chapter on the subject of options and option-like securities such as company options and convertible notes, a chapter on mergers and acquisitions, a chapter on international aspects of corporate finance, and a final chapter on leasing.

1.9 ■ Summary and conclusions

This chapter has introduced you to some of the basic ideas in corporate finance. In it, we saw that:

1 Corporate finance has three main areas of concern:
   • What investments should you take on? That is, what lines of business will you be in and what sorts of buildings, machinery, and equipment will you need? This is the investment decision.
   • Where will you get the financing to pay for your investment? Will you bring in other owners or will you borrow the money? This is the financing decision.
   • When the business is successful, how will you share in the rewards? This is the dividend decision.

2 The goal of financial management in a for-profit business is to make decisions that increase the value of the shares or, more generally, increase the market value of the equity.

3 If you keep in mind the important relationships in Table 1.1, you will always remember that the three decisions of financial management (investment, financing and dividend decisions) are interrelated and should be solved together.

4 The corporate form of organisation is superior to other forms when it comes to raising money, transferring ownership interest and perpetual succession.

5 There is the possibility of conflicts between shareholders and management in a large corporation. We called these conflicts 'agency problems' and discussed how they might be controlled and reduced.

6 The advantages of the corporate form are enhanced by the existence of financial markets. Financial markets function as both primary and secondary markets for corporate securities.

7 By using a simple model, the three decisions of the financial manager were examined. It was concluded that the investment decision alone affects firm value.

Of the topics discussed thus far, the most important is the goal of financial management: maximising the value of the equity. Throughout the text, we will be analysing financial decisions, but we always ask the same question: How does the decision under consideration affect the value of the equity?

Key terms

Agency problem *16*
Arrow's impossibility theorem *30*
Capital budgeting *7*
Capital markets *20*

Capital structure *10*
Company *12*
Fisher's separation theorem *29*
Money markets *20*

Net working capital *6*
Partnership *11*
Sole proprietorship *11*
Stakeholder *18*

Endnotes

1 Historically the Statement of Financial Position was known as the balance sheet. Balance sheet is still the international term.

2 A Nobel prize-winning economist once stated: 'the assumptions are not the point of enquiry. The fruitfulness of a model is its predictive power or its ability to explain'. This simply means that if a model with seemingly unrealistic assumptions is used but the model does explain real world phenomena, then the model is useful.

On the web

There are many sites which can help with the study of Corporate Finance. Throughout this book, we have listed sites relevant to specific chapters. For this chapter, you might find more information on general aspects of corporate finance at the sites listed:

http://www.asx.com.au (This is the Australian Stock Exchange site. Links from here provide a very good overview of the corporate finance sector.)

http://www.personalinvestor.com.au (This site provides overall information on investment.)

http://www.afr.com.au (The *Australian Financial Review*—this newspaper is an excellent daily resource.)

http://www.bloomberg.com (This is a financial news service site—a link provides Australian financial information, and currency conversion tables are also available.)

http://www.abc.net.au (The Australian Broadcasting Corporation maintains up-to-date financial information.)

Maximise Your Marks!
There are 30 interactive questions on introductory corporate finance waiting online for you at www.mhhe.com/au/ross3e. The questions are written with additional feedback for incorrect answers, and text excerpts with page references for follow-up study.

International Articles!
To read more on introductory corporate finance and to see current international articles, just go to www.mhhe.com/au/ross3e and click on *PowerWeb Articles* for this chapter.

Questions and problems

1 · Firm goals

Suppose you were the financial manager of a not-for-profit business (a not-for-profit charity, perhaps). What kinds of goals do you think would be appropriate?

2 · Firm goals

Evaluate the following statement: 'Managers should not focus on the current share value because doing so will lead to an overemphasis on short-term profits at the expense of long-term profits.'

3 · Firm goals

Can our goal of maximising the value of the shares conflict with other goals, such as avoiding unethical or illegal behaviour? In particular, do you think subjects like customer and employee safety, the environment, and the general good of society fit in this framework, or are they essentially ignored? Try to think of some specific scenarios to illustrate your answer.

4 · Firm goals

Would our goal of maximising the value of the shares be different if we were thinking about financial management in a foreign country? Why or why not?

5 · Two-period perfect certainty model

Explain and illustrate what is meant by the **separation theorem**. Discuss its significance for corporate financial management.

6 · Two-period perfect certainty model

'Thus when borrowing and lending rates differ, there is no longer a unique production decision that would be made by any current shareholder regardless of his tastes.' Discuss.

7 · Two-period perfect certainty model

A firm has assets of $10,000. The assets are held in either cash or an immediately liquid form. The firm is entirely owned by equityholders, who possess 1,000 shares in total.

The firm has several capital budgeting proposals. For simplicity, we assume perfect certainty and that time ends one period from the present. The proposals are:

Proposal	Outlay	Next period's return
1	$2000	$2400
2	$2000	$2100
3	$2000	$2150
4	$2000	$2180
5	$2000	$2250
6	$2000	$2150

Assume a perfect capital market. The return earned in the market over the period will be 10 per cent.

a   Which proposals should the firm undertake to maximise the value of the firm?

b   If the firm follows your advice from (a), how much money will it invest in period 1, and what will the **total** period 1 and period 2 dividends be?

c   What will the period 1 and period 2 dividends be on a **per share** basis?

d   What is the maximum that an owner of 200 shares can consume in one period's time, if he wishes to consume $100 immediately?

e   What is the maximum that an owner of 200 shares can consume now if only $500 is required in one period's time?

f   What is the maximum that an owner of 200 shares can consume in one period's time, if she wishes to consume $1000 immediately?

8 · Two-period perfect certainty model

Assume the two-period perfect certainty model for a firm.

a   Briefly explain the firm's investment policy and its investment decision rule.

b   Briefly explain the firm's optimal debt/equity (capital structure) ratio.

c   Explain and illustrate the firm's dividend decision.

9 · Two-period perfect certainty model

You are a financial analyst with Cute Looks Cosmetics Company (CLC Co.). The company has six independent investment opportunities available to it at the present time, and the following details are supplied by a junior analyst:

Project	Outlay	Present value of expected cash flows
1	$500,000	$610,000
2	150,000	142,500
3	350,000	420,000
4	450,000	531,000
5	200,000	240,000
6	400,000	420,000

Projects are not divisible (that is, you cannot undertake *part* of a project; they must be accepted in their entirety, or not at all). Because of its unwillingness to borrow additional funds, senior management of CLC Co. has decided that **capital expenditure in the current period must be limited to $1,000,000.** The market rate of interest for firms in the CLC Co. risk class is 10 per cent.

a   Given its budget constraint, which combination of the above investments should the firm undertake? Why?
b   Comment on the desirability of management's budget policy.

10 · Two-period perfect certainty model

Assume a two-period world, perfect certainty and perfect capital markets. A firm has an initial endowment of $500,000 and has the following investment opportunities available to it:

Proposal	Outlay	Period 2 Return	IRR
1	$100,000	$145,000	45%
2	350,000	420,000	20%
3	200,000	270,000	35%
4	250,000	287,500	15%
5	400,000	440,000	10%

The projects are not divisible (that is, you cannot invest in a fraction of a project: you must invest in 100 per cent of each proposal or none of it). Assume that the market rate of interest is 17 per cent.

a   If management does not want to (or cannot) raise any additional funds:
   i   Which projects will they undertake?
   ii   How much of the initial endowment will they spend?
   iii   What **period 1** dividend will be paid to shareholders?
   iv   What will the **period 2** dividend be?
   v   What is the value of this firm under the current capital rationing policy?
b   If management only allows **one** new project to be accepted, which project would you recommend? (Think carefully about this.)
c   If the capital rationing restrictions were removed:
   i   Which projects would the firm undertake?
   ii   What is the total amount of funds required for your selection?
   iii   Is it necessary to borrow any funds? If so, how much would the firm need to borrow?
   iv   What is the **period 1** dividend? **Period 2**?
   v   What is the value of the firm?
   vi   Has the firm's value increased over the value under budget restraint ((a)(v) above)? What does this tell you about budget policies?
d   i   What could the firm do if it wanted to pay a dividend in **period 1** of $100,000?
   ii   What will be the **period 2** dividend paid?
   iii   What is the value of the firm if it pays the **period 1** dividend? What does this tell you about the effect of dividend payments on firm value?

11 · Two-period perfect certainty model

Assume a perfect certainty two-period world. A firm has the following investment opportunities available:

Project	Outlay	Period 2 cash
1	$121,800	$152,250
2	98,760	125,425
3	110,000	118,250
4	105,700	121,555

The market rate of interest is 10 per cent.

a   Calculate the internal rate of return for each project.
b   Assuming that management are only willing to accept one project, which project should management select? Briefly explain the reasoning behind your answer.
c   Assume the firm has an initial endowment of $300,000 and **all desirable projects are undertaken**. What period 1 and period 2 dividends will be paid?

12 · Two-period perfect certainty model

Assume a perfect certainty two-period world. A firm has the following investment opportunities available:

Project	Outlay	IRR%
1	$110,000	22
2	60,000	30
3	76,000	9
4	90,000	17
5	93,000	6

The market rate of interest is 10 per cent.

a   If the firm had an initial endowment of $500,000 and undertook all desirable projects, what would be the value of the firm?
b   Britney is a shareholder of the firm and she owns 10 per cent. What dividend would she receive in period 1 and period 2 if the firm undertakes all desirable investments?
c   Assume the dividends are the only income Britney receives and the firm plans to pay $23,000 in period 1 and $34,000 in period 2. If she requires $50,000 in period 1, how much will she have available to spend in period 2?

13 · Two-period perfect certainty model

Assume a perfect certainty two-period world. A firm has the following investment opportunities available:

Project	Outlay	Period 2 cash
1	$100,000	$122,000
2	50,000	65,000
3	86,000	93,740
4	92,000	107,640
5	95,000	100,700

The firm has been established with shareholder contributions of $200,000 and no other funds have been raised. The market rate of interest is 10 per cent and the firm undertakes all desirable investments. Draw and label a diagram that illustrates the investment, financing and dividend decisions of the firm using the above data (it is not necessary to draw it to scale). In addition to drawing the diagram, calculate the following values and use the labels indicated:

Value	Label
Initial endowment	oa
Borrowings	ob_1
Repayment for borrowings	PB
Net present value	aA
Firm value	OA
Period 2 dividend	OB

14 · Rates of return, wealth creation through borrowing

The market rate of interest is 8 per cent.

a What is the net present value of an investment that requires an outlay of $500 and returns $527 in one year's time?

b What is the rate of return on an investment that requires an outlay of $660 and returns $759 in one year's time?

c Which of the following investments would you make if you had savings of $20,000?

	Outlay Period 1	Cash flows Period 2
A	$2,000	$2,460
B	5,000	5,900
C	7,000	7,460
D	3,000	3,340
E	10,000	10,800
F	6,000	6,680

d After making your chosen investments in part (c), assume you wish to buy a new car for $10,000. You can borrow the money you need at the market rate of interest and repay it in one period. How much will you have available for spending in period 2 if you buy the car?

e Return to part (c) and assume you only have $13,000 in savings. What should you do to maximise your returns?

f In period 1 dollars, what would be your value if you maximised your return as in part (e)? What is the increase in your wealth?

g In period 1 dollars, what would be your value if you refused to borrow? What is the increase in your wealth if you borrow? Is it poor financial policy to borrow? Based on your answers to (f) and (g), how would you formulate an investment decision model?

15 · Simple present value

Assume a two-period perfect certainty world. Wendy will receive the following dividends:

Industry	Period 1	Period 2
Retailing	$ 6,000	$ 8,500
Manufacturing	7,000	8,050
Mining	5,000	5,750
Building	11,000	12,650
Service	6,000	8,900

Wendy will require $19,000 in period 1 and $19,760 in period 2 for her consumption needs. In addition she wishes to purchase a new car in period 1 which will cost $38,000. The market rate of return is 8 per cent.

a How could Wendy rearrange the income so that she can do all she wants?

b How much of a shortage or surplus will Wendy have in period 2$?

c How much shortage or surplus will she have in period 1$?

16 · Internal rate of return and production frontier

Assume a two-period perfect certainty world. A property developer is looking at the following seven proposals:

Proposal	Nature	Period 1 outlay	Period 2 cash flow
A	Land development	$ 305,555	$ 351,388
B	Housing	472,890	524,908
C	Commercial arcade	1,792,600	2,043,564
D	Movie theatre	875,000	1,023,750
E	Big Chook	490,000	588,000
F	Faster Fish	530,050	630,760
G	Crazy Cheap	615,000	744,150

a Plot a production frontier for the property developer. Show each of the proposals as a point on the frontier.

b Rank the proposals where the highest rank is the proposal that would plot closest to the period 1 axis. Which proposals would you advise the developer to accept?

17 · Selecting investments

Consider Problem 16 with the additional information that the market rate of interest is 10 per cent.

a   Which proposals would you advise the property developer to accept?
b   What would be the effect on the wealth of the property developer if he followed your advice?

18 · Effect of rationing

Refer to Problem 16. If the property developer has a rule that he will only accept proposals that return one and a half times the market rate, what will be the effect on his wealth if he follows the rule? Do you think the rule is a good one? Why? Would your answer change if the property developer was operating in a risk environment and the future is not known with certainty?

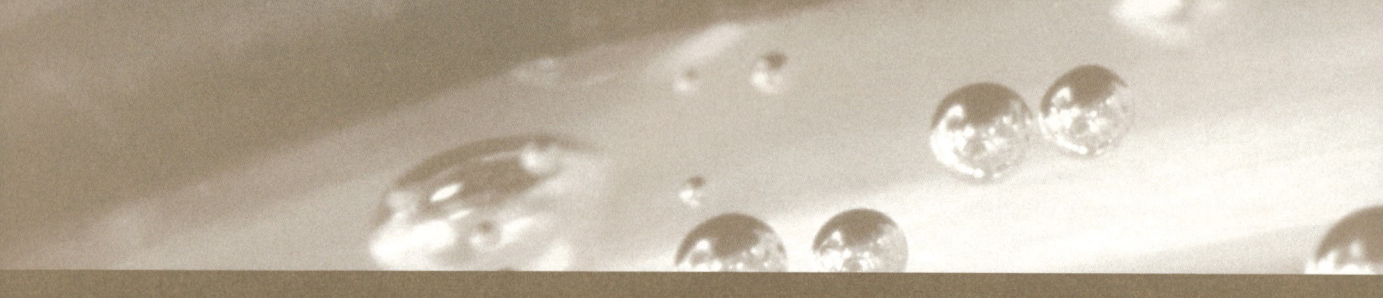

CHAPTER 2

Financial
statements, taxes and cash flow

Objective

Our emphasis in this chapter is not on preparing financial statements. Instead, we recognise that financial statements are frequently a key source of information for financial decisions, so our goal is to briefly examine such statements and point out some of their more relevant features. We pay special attention to some of the practical details of cash flow.

Study tips ▷ As you read, pay particular attention to two important differences:

1 the difference between accounting value and market value; and

2 the difference between accounting profit and cash flow.

These distinctions will be important throughout the book.

Students who have studied accounting may read the chapter lightly but they should pay particular attention to debt versus equity (in section 2.1), Examples 2.1 and 2.2, non-cash items (in section 2.2), time and costs (in section 2.2) and taxes (section 2.3).

Introduction ▷ Corporate finance managers often turn to financial statements to assist them in making decisions. Financial statements are a record of what has happened in the business. Finance managers need to understand this before decisions about the future of the business can be made. The financial decisions are made to maximise the value of the business. Value and cash flow are closely related. It is most important to understand where the cash flow comes from and where it goes to. This chapter will explain the link between financial statements and cash flow.

2.1 The Statement of Financial Position

Statement of Financial Position

financial statement showing a firm's accounting value on a particular date

As we discussed briefly in Chapter 1, the **Statement of Financial Position** is an accountant's snapshot of a firm's value as at a particular date. Here we take a closer look at what is listed on the Statement of Financial Position and some of the things to keep in mind when looking at one.

Statements of Financial Position are prepared in either a narrative form or a T account form. The narrative form lists assets and deducts liabilities to arrive at net assets. The net assets then equate to the shareholders' equity. The T account form (the method we use for illustrative purposes) lists the firm's assets on the left-hand side and the liabilities and shareholders' equity are shown on the right-hand side. The Statement of Financial Position always 'balances' because the value of the left-hand side equals the value of the right-hand side. That is, the value of the firm's assets is equal to the sum of its liabilities and shareholders' equity:[1]

$$\text{Assets} \ = \ \text{Liabilities} \ + \ \text{Shareholders' equity} \tag{2.1}$$

This is the Statement of Financial Position identity or equation, and it always holds because shareholders' equity is defined as the difference between assets and liabilities.

Table 2.1 shows a simplified Statement of Financial Position for the fictitious Pigeon Ltd. The assets in the Statement of Financial Position are listed in order of the length of time it takes for them to convert to cash in the normal course of business. Similarly, the liabilities are listed in the order in which they would normally be paid.

TABLE 2.1

Pigeon Company Ltd

Pigeon Ltd
Statement of Financial Position as at 30 June 200X+1 ($ in millions)

	200X+1	200X		200X+1	200X
Assets			**Liabilities and equity**		
Current assets			*Current liabilities*		
Cash	$ 220	$ 104	Creditors	$ 266	$ 232
Debtors	688	455	Notes payable	123	196
Inventory	555	553		389	428
Total	$1,463	$1,112			
Non-current assets			*Non-current liabilities*		
Net plant and equipment	1,709	1,644	Long-term loans	454	408
			Total liabilities	$ 843	$ 836
			Shareholders' equity		
			Capital	640	600
			Retained earnings	1,689	1,320
			Total equity	$2,329	$1,920
			Total liabilities		
Total assets	$3,172	$2,756	**and equity**	$3,172	$2,756

The structure of the assets for a particular firm reflects the line of business that the firm is in and the managerial decisions that have to be made. Some of the managerial decisions relate to how much cash and inventory to hold, what should be the credit policy, what non-current assets should be acquired, and so on.

The liabilities side of the Statement of Financial Position primarily reflects managerial decisions about capital structure and the use of debt. For example, in 200X+1, total long-term debt for Pigeon was $454 and total equity was $640 + $1,689 = $2,329, so total long-term financing was $454 + $2,329 = $2,783. Of this amount, $454 ÷ $2,783 = 16.31% was long-term debt. This percentage reflects capital structure decisions made in the past by the management of Pigeon Ltd.

There are three particularly important things to keep in mind when examining a Statement of Financial Position: liquidity, debt versus equity, and market value versus book value.

Liquidity

Liquidity refers to the speed and ease with which an asset can be converted to cash. Gold is a relatively liquid asset; a unique manufacturing company is not. Liquidity really has two dimensions: ease of conversion versus loss of value. Any asset can be converted to cash quickly if we cut the price enough. A highly liquid asset is therefore one that can be sold quickly without significant loss of value. A non-liquid asset is one that cannot be quickly converted to cash without a substantial price reduction.

Assets are normally listed on the Statement of Financial Position in order of decreasing liquidity, meaning that the most liquid assets are listed first. Current assets are relatively liquid and include cash and those assets that we expect to convert to cash over the next 12 months. Debtors, for example, represent amounts not yet collected from customers on sales already made. Naturally, we hope these will convert to cash in the near future. Inventory is probably the least liquid of the current assets, at least for some businesses.

Non-current assets are, for the most part, relatively non-liquid. These consist of tangible things such as buildings and equipment that do not convert to cash at all in normal business activity. Intangible assets, such as a trademark, patent or goodwill, have no physical existence but can be very valuable. Like tangible fixed assets, they will not ordinarily convert to cash and are generally considered non-liquid.

Liquidity is valuable. The more liquid a business is, the less likely it is to experience financial distress (that is, difficulty in paying debts or buying needed assets). Unfortunately, liquid assets are generally less profitable to hold. For example, cash holdings are the most liquid of all investments, but they sometimes earn the least return of all. There is therefore a trade-off between the advantages of liquidity and foregone potential profits.

Debt versus equity

To the extent that a firm borrows money, it usually gives first claim to the firm's cash flow to creditors. Equityholders are entitled only to the residual value, the portion left after creditors are paid. The value of this residual portion is the shareholders' equity in the firm and is just the asset value less the value of the firm's liabilities:

$$\text{Shareholders' equity} = \text{Assets} - \text{Liabilities} \qquad (2.2)$$

This is true in an accounting sense because shareholders' equity is defined as this residual portion. More importantly, it is true in an economic sense: If the firm sells its assets and pays its debts, what is left belongs to the shareholders.

The use of debt in a firm's capital structure is called financial leverage.[2] The more debt a firm has (as a percentage of assets), the greater is its degree of financial leverage. As we discuss further in later chapters, debt acts like a lever in the sense that using it can greatly magnify both gains and losses. So financial leverage increases the potential reward to shareholders, but it also increases the potential for financial distress and business failure. The following simple example illustrates the levered effect for equityholders.

Imagine an investment that requires an outlay of $100 and returns $20 per annum. If you use your own money (equity) the return is 20% ($20/$100). An alternative to this is to use only $50 of your own money and borrow $50 (debt) at say 15 per cent. The interest repayment of the money borrowed is $7.50 ($50 × 15%). In this case the investment returns $20 of which $7.50 is for interest, leaving you $12.50. The $12.50 is the return for your $50 investment, so you magnified your return to 25% ($12.50/$50). As you use only $50 per investment, you have the financial ability to undertake two investments.

Market value versus book value

The values shown on the Statement of Financial Position for the firm's assets are book values and generally are not what the assets are actually worth. Under **Generally Accepted Accounting Principles (GAAP)**, audited financial statements in Australia show assets at historical cost. In other words, assets are 'carried on the books' at what the firm paid for them, no matter how long ago they were purchased or how much they are worth today. The directors of a company have the right to revalue the non-current assets of the business if they want. The valuation considers the nature of the assets and is performed regularly, determining a fair value for the assets. The fair value for the assets would be the market value if there were an observable market value for the assets.

For current assets, market value and book value might be somewhat similar, since current assets are bought and converted to cash over a relatively short span of time. In other circumstances, they might differ quite a bit. Moreover, for non-current assets, it would be purely a coincidence if the actual market value of an asset (what the asset could be sold for) were equal to its book value. For example, a pastoralist might own enormous tracts of land purchased a century or more ago, for hundreds or thousands of times less than what it is worth today. The Statement of Financial Position would nonetheless show the historical cost.

The Statement of Financial Position is potentially useful to many different parties. A supplier might look at the size of creditors to evaluate the capability of the firm to pay its bills. A potential lender would examine the liquidity and degree of financial leverage. Managers within the firm can track things like the amount of cash and the amount of inventory that the firm keeps on hand. Uses such as these are discussed in more detail in Chapter 3.

Managers and investors will frequently be interested in knowing the value of the firm. This information is not on the Statement of Financial Position. The fact that Statement of Financial Position assets are listed at cost means that there is no necessary connection between the total assets shown and the value of the firm. Indeed, many of the most valuable assets that a firm might have—good management, a good reputation, talented employees—do not appear on the Statement of Financial Position at all.

Similarly, the shareholders' equity figure on the Statement of Financial Position and the true value of the equity need not be related. For financial managers, then, the accounting value of the equity is not an especially important concern; it is the market value that matters. Henceforth, whenever we speak of the value of an asset or the value of the firm, we will normally mean its market value. So, for example, when we say that the goal of the financial manager is to increase the value of the equity, we mean the market value of the equity.

EXAMPLE
2.1

Market versus book values

The Holdingon Company Pty Ltd has non-current assets with a book value of $700 and an appraised market value of about $1,000. Net working capital is $400 on the books, but approximately $600 would be realised if all the current accounts were liquidated. Holdingon has $500 in long-term debt, both book value and market value. What is the book value of the equity? What is the market value?

We can construct two simplified Statements of Financial Position, one in accounting (book value) terms and one in economic (market value) terms:

Holdingon Company Pty Ltd
Statements of Financial Position
Market Values versus Book Values

Assets			Liabilities		
	Book	Market		Book	Market
Net working capital	$ 400	$ 600	Long-term debt	$ 500	$ 500
Non-current assets	700	1,000	Equity	600	1,100
	1,100	1,600		1,100	1,600

In this example, shareholders' equity is actually worth almost twice as much as what is shown on the books. The distinction between book and market values is important precisely because book value can be so different from true economic value.

Concept questions

2.1a *What is the Statement of Financial Position identity?*
2.1b *What is liquidity? Why is it important?*
2.1c *What do we mean by financial leverage?*
2.1d *Explain the difference between accounting value and market value. Which is more important to the financial manager? Why?*

 # 2.2 ■ The Statement of Financial Performance

The **Statement of Financial Performance** measures performance over some period of time, usually a year. The profit equation is:

$$\textbf{Revenues} - \textbf{Expenses} = \textbf{Profit} \tag{2.3}$$

If you think of the Statement of Financial Position as a snapshot, then you can think of the Statement of Financial Performance as a video recording covering the period between a before and an after picture. Table 2.2 (overleaf) gives a simplified Statement of Financial Performance for Pigeon Ltd.

Statement of Financial Performance

financial statement summarising a firm's performance over a period of time

TABLE
2.2

Pigeon Ltd

Pigeon Ltd
Statement of Financial Performance for the year ended 30 June 200X+1
($ in millions)

Revenue	$ 1,509
Cost of goods sold	699
Depreciation	65
Earnings before interest and tax	745
Interest	70
	675
Tax 30%	203
Net profit after tax	$ 472
Dividends	$103
Retained earnings	$369

The first thing reported on a Statement of Financial Performance would usually be revenue and expenses from the firm's principal operations. Subsequent parts include, among other things, financing expenses such as interest paid. Taxes paid are reported separately. The last item is profit (the so-called bottom line). Profit is often expressed on a per-share basis and called earnings per share (EPS).

As indicated, Pigeon paid cash dividends of $103. The difference between net profit and cash dividends, $369, is retained earnings for the year. This amount is added to the cumulative retained earnings account on the Statement of Financial Position. If you look back at the two Statements of Financial Position for Pigeon Ltd, you will see that retained earnings did go up by this amount, $1,320 + $369 = $1,689.

EXAMPLE
2.2   **Calculating earnings and dividends per share**

Suppose that Pigeon Ltd had 400 million shares outstanding at the end of 200X+1. Based on the Statement of Financial Performance above, what was EPS? What were dividends per share?

From the Statement of Financial Performance, Pigeon Ltd had a net profit of $472 million for the year. Since 400 million shares were outstanding, EPS was $472 ÷ 400 = $1.18 per share. Similarly, dividends per share were $103 ÷ 400 = $0.2575 per share.

When looking at a Statement of Financial Performance account, the financial manager needs to keep three things in mind: approved accounting standards; cash versus non-cash items; and time and costs.

Approved accounting standards and the Statement of Financial Performance

A Statement of Financial Performance prepared using approved accounting standards will show revenue when it accrues. This is not necessarily when the cash comes in. The general rule is to recognise revenue when the earnings process is virtually complete and the value of an exchange of goods or services is known or can be reliably determined. In practice, this principle usually means that revenue is recognised at the time of sale, which need not be the same as the time of the collection of cash.

Costs shown on the Statement of Financial Performance are based on the matching principle. The basic idea here is first to determine revenues as described above and then match those revenues with the costs associated with producing them. So, if we manufacture and then sell a product on credit, the revenue is realised at the time of sale. The production and other costs associated with the sale of that product would likewise be recognised at that time. Once again, the actual cash outflows may have occurred at some very different time.

As a result of the way revenues and costs are realised, the figures shown on the Statement of Financial Performance may not be at all representative of the actual cash inflows and outflows that occurred during a period.

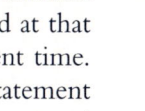

THE BASIC IDEA

Non-cash items

A primary reason that accounting profit differs from cash flow is that a Statement of Financial Performance contains **non-cash items**. The most important of these is depreciation. Suppose a firm purchases an asset for $5,000 and pays in cash. Obviously, the firm has a $5,000 cash outflow at the time of purchase. However, instead of deducting the $5,000 as an expense, an accountant might depreciate the asset over a five-year period.

non-cash items
expenses charged against revenues that do not directly affect cash flow, such as depreciation

If the depreciation is straight-line and the asset is written down to zero over that period, then $5,000 \div 5 = $1,000 would be deducted each year as an expense. The important thing to recognise is that this $1,000 deduction is not cash—it is an accounting number. The actual cash outflow occurred when the asset was purchased.

The depreciation deduction is simply another application of the matching principle in accounting. The revenues associated with an asset would generally occur over some length of time. So the accountant seeks to match the expense of purchasing the asset with the benefits produced from owning it.

As we will see, for the financial manager, the actual timing of cash inflows and outflows is critical in coming up with a reasonable estimate of market value, so we need to learn how to separate the cash flows from the non-cash accounting entries.

Time and costs

It is often useful to think of the future as having two distinct parts: the short run and the long run. These are not precise time periods. The distinction has to do with whether costs are fixed or variable. In the long run, all business costs are variable. Given sufficient time, assets can be sold, debts can be paid, and so on.

If our time horizon is relatively short, however, some costs are effectively fixed—they must be paid no matter what (rates, for example). Other costs, such as wages for labour and payments to suppliers are still variable. As a result, even in the short run, the firm can vary its output level by varying expenditures in these areas.

The distinction between fixed and variable costs is important, at times, to the financial manager, but the way costs are reported on the Statement of Financial Performance is not a good guide as to which costs are which. This is because, in practice, accountants tend to classify costs as either product costs or period costs.

Product costs include such things as raw materials, direct labour expense, and manufacturing overhead. These are reported on the Statement of Financial Performance as costs of goods sold, but they include both fixed and variable costs. Similarly, period costs are incurred during a particular time period and are reported as selling, general and administrative expenses. Once again, some of these period costs may be fixed and others may be variable. The general manager's salary, for example, is a period cost and is probably fixed, at least in the short run.

Concept questions

2.2a *What is the Statement of Financial Performance equation?*
2.2b *What are the three things to keep in mind when looking at a Statement of Financial Performance?*
2.2c *Why is accounting profit not the same as cash flow? Give two reasons.*

 ## Taxes

Taxes can be one of the largest cash outflows that a firm experiences. The size of the tax bill is determined by the *Income Tax Assessment Act* 1997 (Tax Act), an often amended and changed set of laws. In this section, we examine corporate and personal tax rates and how taxes are calculated.

If the various rules of taxation seem bizarre or convoluted to you, keep in mind that the Tax Act is the result of political, not economic, forces. As a result, there is no reason why it has to make economic sense.

Corporate and personal tax rates

There have been several changes in tax rates over the years of the current Act, however there has been little change in the method of levying tax; for example, consider the corporate and personal tax rates in effect for 2002 as shown in Table 2.3. For individuals the marginal tax rate increased as the level of taxable income increased. Companies on the other hand had a flat rate of tax which was 30 per cent. Companies did not enjoy a tax-free threshold as is the case with individuals.

Personal and corporate taxes	
Personal rates for the year ended 30 June 2003	
Taxable income	**Tax rate**
$0–6,000	Nil
6,000–20,000	Nil + 17% of excess over 6,000
20,001–50,000	2,380 + 30% of excess over 20,000
50,001–60,000	11,380 + 42% of excess over 50,000
60,001 +	15,580 + 47% of excess over 60,000
Company rates	
Private and public companies (other than life assurance companies)	30%

TABLE 2.3

An important feature of the current tax law is evident when corporate tax rates are compared to personal tax rates: the corporate tax rate is below the top personal rate; however, this has not always been the situation.

Average versus marginal tax rates

In making financial decisions, it is frequently important to distinguish between average and marginal tax rates. Your **average tax rate** is your tax bill divided by your taxable income, in other words, the percentage of your income that goes to pay taxes. Your **marginal tax rate** is the extra tax you would pay if you earned one more dollar. The percentage tax rates shown in Table 2.3 are all marginal rates. Put another way, the tax rates in Table 2.3 apply to the part of income in the indicated range only, not all income.

average tax rate
total taxes paid divided by total taxable income

marginal tax rate
amount of tax payable on the next dollar earned

The difference between average and marginal tax rates can best be illustrated with a simple example. Suppose that your individual taxable income is $28,500. What is the tax liability? From Table 2.3, we can figure out the tax liability as:

Tax on $0–$6,000		=	Nil
Tax on $6,000–$20,000	17% ($20,000 − $6,000)	=	2,380
Tax on Balance ($28,500 − $20,000)	30% ($28,500 − $20,000)	=	2,550
		=	$4,930

Your total tax is thus $4,930.

In our example, what is the average tax rate? You had a taxable income of $28,500 and a tax liability of $4,930, so the average tax rate is $4,930 ÷ $28,500 = 17.30%. What is the marginal tax rate? If you made one more dollar, the tax on that dollar would be 30 cents, so your marginal rate is 30 per cent.

EXAMPLE 2.3

Deep in the heart of taxes

Flat Ltd has a taxable income of $85,000. What is its tax bill? What is its average tax rate? Its marginal tax rate?

From Table 2.3 above, the tax rate applied to all the taxable income for companies is 30 per cent. So Flat must pay 0.30 × $85,000 = $25,500. The average tax rate is thus $25,500 ÷ $85,000 = 30%. The marginal rate is 30 per cent, which equals Flat's average tax rate.

With a flat rate tax, there is only one tax rate, and this rate is the same for all income levels. With such a tax, the marginal tax rate is always the same as the average tax rate.

So we have the situation in Australia that companies are taxed at a flat rate but individuals are subjected to a progressive tax rate scale. As Table 2.4 (overleaf) shows, this can provide some strange relationships. While the average and marginal tax rates of individuals increase as the level of taxable income increases, the company rate remains at a flat 30 per cent. Up to a taxable income of $74,244, company tax is more than individual tax. At this level of taxable income both companies and individuals would pay the same tax. For taxable income levels higher than $74,244 individual tax is greater than company tax. Notice that the percentage of taxable income paid in taxes does not increase for companies as taxable income increases. In the case of individual taxpayers, the higher the taxable income the larger the percentage of taxable income is paid in taxes.

TABLE
2.4

Comparison of individual and company tax[3] at various income levels					
	Individual			Company	
Taxable income $	Amount $	Average rate %	Marginal rate %	Amount $	Average and marginal rate %
30,000	5,380	17.93	30	9,000	30
40,000	8,380	20.95	30	12,000	30
60,000	15,580	25.97	47	18,000	30
74,244	22,275	30.00	47	22,275	30
80,000	24,980	31.23	47	24,000	30
100,000	34,380	34.38	47	30,000	30

It will normally be the marginal tax rate that is relevant for decision making. The reason is that any new cash flows will be taxed at that marginal rate. Since financial decisions usually involve new cash flows or changes in existing ones, this rate will tell us the marginal effect on our tax liability.

Concept questions

2.3a *What is the difference between a marginal and an average tax rate?*

2.3b *Do the wealthiest corporations (and individuals) receive a tax break in terms of a lower tax rate on some of their income? Explain.*

 ## 2.4 Cash flow

At this point, we are ready to discuss one of the most important pieces of financial information that can be gleaned from financial statements: cash flow. There is no standard financial statement for presenting this information in the way that we wish. We will therefore discuss how to calculate cash flow for Pigeon Ltd and point out how the result differs from standard financial statement calculations.

From the Statement of Financial Position, we know that the value of a firm's assets is equal to the value of its liabilities plus the value of its equity. Similarly, the cash flow from assets must equal the sum of the cash flow to debtholders (or creditors) plus the cash flow to shareholders (or owners):

Cash flow from assets = Cash flow to debtholders + Cash flow to shareholders (2.4)

This is the cash flow identity. It says that the cash flow from the firm's assets is equal to the cash flow paid to suppliers of capital to the firm. We discuss the various things that make up these cash flows next.

Cash flow from assets

Cash flow from assets involves three components: operating cash flow; capital spending; and additions to net working capital. **Operating cash flow** refers to the cash flow that results from the firm's day-to-day activities of producing and selling. Expenses associated with the firm's financing of its assets are not included since they are not operating expenses.

As we discussed in Chapter 1, some portion of the firm's cash flow is reinvested in the firm. Capital spending refers to the net spending on non-current assets (purchases of non-current assets less sales of non-current assets). Finally, additions to net working capital is the amount spent on net working capital. It is measured as the change in net working capital over the period being examined and represents the net increase in current assets over current liabilities. The three components of cash flow are examined in more detail below.

cash flow from assets

the total of cash flow to debtholders and cash flow to shareholders, consisting of the following: operating cash flow, capital spending, and additions to net working capital

operating cash flow

cash generated from a firm's normal business activities

Operating cash flow

To calculate operating cash flow, we want to calculate revenues minus costs, but we do not want to include depreciation since it is not a cash outflow, and we do not want to include interest because it is a financing expense. We do want to include taxes, because taxes are, unfortunately, paid in cash.

If we look at the Statement of Financial Performance, Pigeon Ltd had earnings before interest and taxes (EBIT) of $745. This is almost what we want since it does not include interest paid. We need to make two adjustments. First, recall that depreciation is a non-cash expense. To get cash flow, we first add back the $65 in depreciation since it was not a cash deduction. The other adjustment is to subtract the $203 in taxes since these were paid in cash. The result is operating cash flow:

Pigeon Ltd
200X+1 Operating Cash Flow

Earnings before interest and taxes	$ 745
+ Depreciation	65
– Taxes	203
Operating cash flow	$ 607

Pigeon Ltd thus had a 200X+1 operating cash flow of $607.

There is an unpleasant possibility for confusion when we speak of operating cash flow. In accounting practice, operating cash flow is often defined as net profit plus depreciation. For Pigeon Ltd, this would amount to (from Table 2.2) $472 + $65 = $537.

The accounting definition of operating cash flow differs from ours in one important way: interest is deducted when net income is computed. Notice that the difference between the $607 operating cash flow we calculated and this $537 is $70, the amount of interest paid for the year.

This accounting definition of cash flow thus considers interest paid to be an operating expense. Our definition treats it properly as a financing expense. If there were no interest expense, the two definitions would be the same.

EXAMPLE 2.4

Operating cash flow versus profit

During the year, Maxi Ltd had sales and costs of $600 and $300, respectively. Depreciation was $150 and interest paid was $30. Taxes were calculated at a straight 30 per cent. Dividends were $30. All figures are in millions of dollars. What was operating cash flow for Maxi? Why is this different from profit?

The easiest thing to do here is to go ahead and create a Statement of Financial Performance. We can then pick up the numbers we need. Maxi's Statement of Financial Performance is given in the table below.

Maxi Ltd
Statement of Financial Performance for the year ended 30 June 200X+1
($ in millions)

Net sales	$ 600
Cost of goods sold	300
Depreciation	150
Earnings before interest and tax	150
Interest paid	30
Taxable income	$ 120
Taxes	36
Net profit	$ 84

Retained earnings	$ 54	
Dividends	$ 30	

Net profit for Maxi is thus $84. We now have all the numbers we need; so referring back to the Pigeon Ltd example, we have:

Maxi Ltd
200X+1 Operating Cash Flow

Earnings before interest and taxes	$ 150
+ Depreciation	150
− Taxes	36
Operating Cash Flow	$ 264

As Example 2.4 illustrates, operating cash flow is not the same as profit, because depreciation and interest are subtracted when profit is calculated. If you recall our earlier discussion, we do not subtract these in computing operating cash flow because depreciation is not a cash expense and interest paid is a financing expense, not an operating expense.

To finish our calculation of cash flow from assets for Pigeon Ltd, we need to consider how much of the $607 operating cash flow was reinvested in the firm. We consider spending on non-current assets first.

Capital spending

Net capital spending is just money spent on non-current assets less money received from the sale of these assets. At the end of 200X, net non-current assets were $1,644. During the year, we wrote off (depreciated) $65 worth of non-current assets on the Statement of Financial Performance. So, if we did not purchase any new non-current assets, we would have had $1,644 − $65 = $1,579 at year's end. The 200X+1 Statement of Financial Position shows $1,709 in net non-current assets, so we must have spent a total of $1,709 − $1,579 = $130 on non-current assets during the year:

Ending non-current assets	$1,709
− Beginning non-current assets	1,644
+ Depreciation	65
Net investment in non-current assets	$ 130

This $130 is our net capital spending for 200X+1.

Calculating net capital spending

EXAMPLE 2.5

Going back to Maxi (Example 2.4), suppose that beginning net non-current assets were $500 and ending net non-current assets were $750. What was the net capital spending for the year?

From the Statement of Financial Performance for Maxi, depreciation for the year was $150. Net non-current assets rose by $250. We thus spent a total of $150 to cover the depreciation and an additional $250 as well, for a total of $400.

Could net capital spending be negative? The answer is yes. This would happen if the firm sold off more assets than it purchased. The 'net' here refers to purchases of non-current assets net of any sales.

Additions to net working capital

In addition to investing in non-current assets, a firm will also invest in current assets. For example, going back to the Statement of Financial Position in Table 2.1, we see that, at the end of 200X+1, Pigeon had current assets of $1,463. At the end of 200X, current assets were $1,112, so during the year Pigeon invested $1,463 − $1,112 = $351 in current assets.

As the firm changes its investment in current assets, its current liabilities will usually change as well. To determine the additions to net working capital, the easiest approach is to take the difference between the beginning and ending net working capital (NWC) figures. Net working capital at the end of 200X+1 was $1,463 − $389 = $1,074. Similarly, at the end of 200X, net working capital was $1,112 − $428 = $684. So, given these figures, we have:

Ending NWC	$ 1,074
− Beginning NWC	684
Addition to NWC	$ 390

Net working capital thus increased by $390. Put another way, Pigeon Ltd had a net investment of $390 in NWC for the year.

Cash flow from assets

Given the figures we have come up with, we are ready to calculate cash flow from assets. The total cash flow from assets is given by operating cash flow less the amounts invested in non-current assets and net working capital. So, for Pigeon, we have:

Pigeon Ltd
200X+1 Cash Flow from Assets

Operating cash flow	$ 607
− Net capital spending	130
− Additions to NWC	390
Cash flow from assets	$ 87

From the cash flow identity above, this $87 cash flow from assets equals the sum of the firm's cash flow to debtholders and cash flow to shareholders. We consider these next.

EXAMPLE 2.6 · Change in NWC and cash flow from assets

Suppose that Maxi started the year with $2,130 in current assets and $1,620 in current liabilities. The corresponding ending figures were $2,260 and $1,710. What was the addition to NWC during the year? What was cash flow from assets? How does this compare to profit?

Net working capital started out as $2,130 − $1,620 = $510 and ended up at $2,260 − $1,710 = $550. The addition to NWC was thus $550 − $510 = $40. Putting together all the information for Maxi we have:

Maxi Ltd
200X+1 Cash Flow from Assets

Operating cash flow	$ 264
− Net capital spending	400
− Additions to NWC	40
Cash flow from assets	−$ 176

Maxi had a cash flow from assets of negative $176. Profit was positive at $84. Is the fact that cash flow from assets is negative a cause for alarm? Not necessarily. The cash flow here is negative primarily because of a large investment in non-current assets. If these are good investments, then the resulting negative cash flow is not a worry.

Based on Example 2.6, it would not be at all unusual for a growing corporation to have a negative cash flow. As we see next, the negative cash flow means that the firm raised more money by borrowing and selling shares than it paid out to creditors and shareholders that year.

Cash flow to debtholders and shareholders

cash flow to debtholders
a firm's interest payments to lenders less net new borrowings

cash flow to shareholders
dividends paid out by a firm less net new equity raised

The cash flows to debtholders and shareholders represent the net payments to creditors and owners during the year. They are calculated in a similar way. **Cash flow to debtholders** is interest paid less net new borrowing; **cash flow to shareholders** is dividends less net new equity raised.

Cash flow to debtholders

Looking at the Statement of Financial Performance in Table 2.2, Pigeon paid $70 in interest to debtholders. From the Statements of Financial Position in Table 2.1, long-term debt rose by $454 − $408 = $46. So, Pigeon Ltd paid out $70 in interest, but it borrowed an additional $46. Net cash flow to debtholders is thus:

Pigeon Ltd
200X+1 Cash Flow to Debtholders

Interest paid	$ 70
− Net new borrowing	46
Cash flow to debtholders	$ 24

Cash flow to shareholders

From the Statement of Financial Performance, dividends paid to shareholders amount to $103. To get net new equity raised, we need to look at the issued capital and reserves. Table 2.1 tells us how much equity the company has sold. During the year, this account rose by $40, so $40 in net new equity was raised. Given this, we have:

Pigeon Ltd
200X+1 Cash Flow to Shareholders

Dividends paid	$ 103
− Net new equity	40
Cash flow to shareholders	$ 63

The cash flow to shareholders for 200X+1 was thus $63.

The last thing that we need to do is to check that the cash flow identity holds, to be sure that we did not make any mistakes. From above, cash flow from assets is $87. Cash flow to debtholders and to shareholders is $24 + $63 = $87, so everything balances.

Cash flow to debtholders and shareholders

We saw that Maxi had cash flow from assets of −$176 (Example 2.6). The fact that this is negative means that Maxi raised more money in the form of new debt and equity than it paid out for the year. For example, suppose we know that Maxi did not sell any new equity for the year. What was cash flow to shareholders? To debtholders?

Since it did not raise any new equity, Maxi's cash flow to shareholders is equal to the cash dividend paid:

Maxi Ltd
200X+1 Cash Flow to Shareholders

Dividends paid	$ 30
− Net new equity	0
Cash flow to shareholders	$ 30

Now, from the cash flow identity the total cash paid to debtholders and shareholders was −$176. Cash flow to shareholders is $30, so cash flow to debtholders must be equal to −$176 − $30 = −$206:

Cash flow to debtholders + Cash flow to shareholders	= −$176
Cash flow to debtholders + $30	= −$176
Cash flow to debtholders	= −$206

From the Statement of Financial Performance account (Example 2.4), interest paid is $30. We can determine net new borrowing as follows:

Maxi Ltd
200X+1 Cash Flow to Debtholders

Interest paid	$ 30
− Net new borrowing	236
Cash flow to debtholders	−$ 206

As indicated, since cash flow to debtholders is −$206 and interest paid is $30, Maxi must have borrowed $236 during the year to help finance the non-current asset expansion.

Concept questions

2.4a *What is the cash flow identity? Explain what it means.*
2.4b *What are the components of operating cash flow?*
2.4c *Why is interest paid not a component of operating cash flow?*

 2.5 ■ Summary and conclusions

This chapter has introduced you to some of the basics of financial statements, taxes and cash flow. In it we saw that:

1 The book values on an accounting Statement of Financial Position can be very different from market values. The goal of financial management is to maximise the market value of the equity, not its book value.

2 Net profit as it is computed on the Statement of Financial Performance is not cash flow. A primary reason is that depreciation, a non-cash expense, is deducted when net profit is computed.

3 Marginal and average tax rates can be different, and it is the marginal tax rate that is relevant for most financial decisions.

4 There is a cash flow identity much like the Statement of Financial Position identity. It says that cash flow from assets equals cash flow to debtholders and shareholders.

The calculation of cash flow from financial statements is not difficult. Care must be taken in handling non-cash expenses, such as depreciation, and in not confusing operating costs with financing costs. Most of all, it is important not to confuse book values with market values, and accounting income with cash flow.

Key terms

Average tax rate *53*
Cash flow from assets *55*
Cash flow to debtholders *58*
Cash flow to shareholders *58*

Generally Accepted Accounting
    Principles (GAAP) *48*
Marginal tax rate *53*
Non-cash items *51*

Operating cash flow *55*
Statement of Financial
    Performance *49*
Statement of Financial Position *46*

Suggested readings

There are many excellent textbooks on accounting and financial statements. Two that we have found helpful are:
Carnegie, G., Jones, B., Norris, G., Wigg, R. and
    Williams, B. *Accounting: Financial and Organisational
    Decision Making*, McGraw-Hill, Sydney, 1998.

Deegan, C. *Australian Financial Accounting,* 3rd edn,
    McGraw-Hill, Sydney, 2002.

Endnotes

1 The terms *owners' equity, shareholders' equity* and just plain *equity* are used interchangeably to refer to the equity in a corporation. The term *net worth* is also used. Variations exist in addition to these.

2 Another term often used to denote the existence of debt is 'gearing'. A geared firm is one where some of the financing is provided by debt.

3 In 1985, a system was introduced in Australia whereby shareholders may be allowed a credit for the tax paid by the company. This system of tax credits is discussed in later chapters.

On the web

There are numerous web sites that help provide an understanding of accounting and financial statements. A starting point is the McGraw-Hill Finance Supersite: go to http://www.mcgraw-hill.com.au/mhhe/fin/supersite.htm then click on the links to Accounting and to Finance.

Another idea is to review the financial information available on corporate web sites like:

http://www.bhpbilliton.com (BHP Billiton—the annual report is available, including financial tables and information)

http://www.telstra.com (Telstra—the latest annual report is available, with full financial information)

http://www.commbank.com.au (the Commonwealth Bank)

http://www.national.com.au (National Australia Bank)

http://www.ato.gov.au (Australian Tax Office)

Maximise Your Marks!

There are 30 interactive questions on financial statements, taxes and cash flow waiting online for you at www.mhhe.com/au/ross3e. The questions are written with additional feedback for incorrect answers, and text excerpts with page references for follow-up study.

International Articles!

To read more on financial statements, taxes and cash flow and to see current international articles, just go to www.mhhe.com/au/ross3e and click on *PowerWeb Articles* for this chapter.

Chapter review problem and self-test

2.1 · Cash flow for Royalist Ltd

This problem will give you some practice working with financial statements and figuring out cash flow. Based on the following information for Royalist Ltd, prepare a Statement of Financial Performance account for 200X+1 and Statements of Financial Position for 200X and 200X+1. Next, following our Pigeon Ltd examples in the chapter, calculate cash flow for Royalist, cash flow to debtholders, and cash flow to equityholders for 200X+1. Use a 30% tax rate throughout. You can check your answers below.

	200X	200X+1
Sales	$3,790	$3,990
Cost of goods sold	2,043	2,137
Depreciation	975	1,018
Interest	225	267
Dividends	200	225
Current assets	2,140	2,346
Non-current assets	6,770	7,087
Current liabilities	994	1,126
Non-current liabilities	2,869	2,956

Answer to self-test problem

2.1 · In preparing the Statements of Financial Position, remember that shareholders' equity is the residual. With this in mind, Royalist's Statements of Financial Position are as follows:

Royalist Ltd
Statements of Financial Position as at 30 June 200X and 200X+1

	200X	200X+1		200X	200X+1
Current assets	$ 2,140	$ 2,346	Current liabilities	$ 994	$ 1,126
Non-current assets	6,770	7,087	Non-current liabilities	2,869	2,956
			Equity	5,047	5,351
Total assets	$ 8,910	$ 9,433		$8,910	$9,433

The Statement of Financial Performance is straightforward:

Royalist Ltd
200X+1 Statement of Financial Performance

Sales	$3,990
Costs	2,137
Depreciation	1,018
Earnings before interest and taxes	$ 835
Interest paid	267
Taxable income	$ 568
Taxes (30%)	170
Net profit	$ 398

Retained earnings	$ 173
Dividends	$ 225

Notice that retained earnings are just net profit less cash dividends. We can now pick up the figures we need to get operating cash flow:

Royalist Ltd
200X+1 Operating Cash Flow

Earnings before interest and taxes	$ 835
+ Depreciation	1,018
− Current taxes	170
Operating cash flow	$1,683

Next, we get the capital spending for the year by looking at the change in non-current assets, remembering to account for the depreciation:

Ending non-current assets	$ 7,087
− Beginning non-current assets	6,770
+ Depreciation	1,018
Net investment in non-current assets	$ 1,335

After calculating beginning and ending NWC, we take the difference to get the addition to NWC:

Ending NWC	$ 1,220
− Beginning NWC	1,146
Addition to NWC	$ 74

We now combine operating cash flow, net capital spending, and the addition to net working capital to get the total cash flow from assets:

Royalist Ltd
200X+1 Cash Flow from Assets

Operating cash flow	$1,683
− Net capital spending	1,335
− Additions to NWC	74
Cash flow from assets	$ 274

To get cash flow to debtholders, notice that non-current borrowing increased by $87 during the year and that interest paid was $267; so:

Royalist Ltd
200X+1 Cash Flow to Debtholders

Interest paid	$ 267
− Net new borrowing	87
Cash flow to debtholders	$ 180

Finally, dividends paid were $225. To get net new equity, we have to do some extra calculating. Total equity was up by $5,351 − $5,047 = $304. Of this increase, $173 was from additions to retained earnings, so $131 in new equity was raised during the year. Cash flow to shareholders was thus:

Royalist Ltd
200X+1 Cash Flow to Shareholders

Dividends paid	$ 225
− Net new equity	131
Cash flow to shareholders	$ 94

As a check, notice that cash flow from assets ($274) does equal cash flow to debtholders plus cash flow to shareholders ($180 + $94 = $274).

Questions and problems

1 · Preparing a Statement of Financial Performance

Prepare a Statement of Financial Performance from the following information: sales, $500,000; cost of goods sold, $200,000; administrative expenses, $100,000; interest paid, $50,000. The tax rate is 30 per cent.

2 · Statement of Financial Performance

The Colin Company Pty Ltd had sales of $2,500, cost of goods sold of $900, depreciation of $650, and interest paid of $550. If the tax rate is 30 per cent and all taxes are paid currently, what is net profit?

3 · Calculating OCF

Based on the information in problem 2, what is Colin's operating cash flow?

4 · OCF versus net profit

What is the difference between net profit and operating cash flow? Could operating cash flow be positive if net profit is negative?

5 · OCF versus net profit

The Wildlife Corporation Ltd reported the following income data:

	200X $000	200X+1 $000
Net Sales	$1,000	$ 800
Cost of goods sold	560	320
Operating expenses	75	56
Depreciation	300	200

The tax rate is 30 per cent.

a   Prepare a Statement of Financial Performance for both years.

b   Determine operating cash flow for both years.

c   Comment on the difference between accounting profit and cash flow for Wildlife.

6 · OCF and net profit

During 200X+1, the Smooth Tyre Company Ltd has gross sales of $1 million. Its cost of goods sold and selling expenses are $300,000 and $200,000, respectively. Smooth also has notes payable of $1 million. The interest rate is 10 per cent. Depreciation was $100,000. The tax rate is 30 per cent.

a   What are Smooth's earnings before interest and taxes?

b   What is its net profit?

c   What is its cash flow from operations?

7 · Liquidity

What is liquidity? Explain why we say that liquidity has two dimensions.

8 · Preparing a Statement of Financial Position

Prepare a Statement of Financial Position for Wolff Ltd as at 30 June based on the following information: cash, $4,000; patents, $82,000; creditors, $6,000; debtors, $8,000; machinery and other tangible non-current assets, $40,000; non-current debt, $70,000; accumulated retained earnings, $38,000. (*Hint*: Remember that Assets = Liabilities + Equity.)

9 · Statement of Financial Position calculations

Following are the non-current liabilities and shareholders' equity of the Control Systems Company's Statement of Financial Position as at 30 June 200X. During 200X+1, Control issues $10 million of new ordinary shares, but no additional debt. Control generates $5 million of net profit and pays out $3 million in dividends. Complete the account balances shown for 30 June 200X+1.

	30 June 200X	30 June 200X+1
Non-current liabilities	$50,000,000	
Share capital	100,000,000	
Retained earnings	20,000,000	
	170,000,000	

10 · Tax rates

Your sole source of income is from a family partnership. The partnership generated income of $155,000 in 200X+1. Your share of the partnership profits is 30 per cent, however you have personal tax deductions of $1000. Based on Table 2.3 in the chapter, calculate your tax liability for the year. What is the average tax rate? The marginal tax rate?

11 · Tax rates

a In problem 10, what would the answers be if your share of the partnership income was 50% and your tax-deductible expenses were $3,265?

b If it is expected that the profit of the partnership will not change from its current level and that your expenses will remain constant at $3,265, is it advisable for you to convert your partnership to a company? It will only cost $1,000 and because it is you and your partner it could be done easily.

12 · Cash flow

Perfect Pty Ltd began the year with $70,000 in non-current assets. Depreciation for the year was $18,000. Ending non-current assets were $81,000. What was Perfect's net capital spending for the year?

13 · Calculating changes in NWC

Babe Co. Ltd's beginning current assets were $660. Ending current assets were $930. Current liabilities rose from $280 to $590. What was Babe's NWC at the beginning and the end of the year? How much did Babe invest in NWC for the year?

14 · Calculating depreciation

Mel Ltd invested $75,000 total in capital equipment for the year. Beginning non-current assets were $157,000 and ending non-current assets were $143,000. What was depreciation for the year?

15 · Market value versus book value

Comet Ltd has 5 million shares on issue, selling at $2.30 each. Its Statement of Financial Position shows net assets as $12.4 million. What is the difference between market and book value? Which is more relevant? Why?

16 · Computing cash flows

Consider the following financial statement information for Proact Ltd:

Proact Ltd
Partial Statements of Financial Position as at 30 June 200X and 200X+1

	200X	200X+1		200X	200X+1
Current assets	$176	$208	Current liabilities	$ 98	$116
Non-current assets	770	881	Non-current liabilities	569	576

Proact Ltd
Statement of Financial Performance for the period ended 30 June 200X+1

	200X+1
Sales	$ 1,995
Costs	647
Depreciation	228
Interest	116

a What is owners' equity for 200X and 200X+1?

b What is net working capital for 200X and 200X+1? What is the addition to NWC for 200X+1?

c What was net profit for 200X+1? What was operating cash flow? Assume a 30 per cent tax rate.

d In 200X+1, Proact purchased $500 in new non-current assets. How much in non-current assets did Proact sell? What was the cash flow from assets for the year?

e During the year 200X+1, Proact raised $50 in new non-current liabilities. How much must Proact have paid off during the year? What was the net cash flow to debtholders for the year?

Use the following information for Sunshine Ltd to work Problems 17 and 18:

	200X	200X+1
Sales	$ 1,145	$ 1,200
Depreciation	128	128
Cost of goods sold	450	537
Other expenses	110	98
Interest	85	96
Cash	640	735
Receivables	912	967
Notes payable	122	103
Non-current liabilities	2,349	2,666
Non-current assets	5,556	5,637
Accounts payable	664	659
Inventory	1,440	1,489
Dividend	100	110

17 · Statements

Draw up a Statement of Financial Performance and a Statement of Financial Position for Sunshine Ltd for 200X and 200X+1. The tax rate is 30 per cent.

18 · Computing cash flows

For 200X+1, calculate Sunshine's cash flow from assets, cash flow to debtholders, and cash flow to shareholders. The tax rate is 30 per cent.

19 · Computing cash flows

The following is an extract from the Statement of Financial Performance of Kylie Dance Recordings (KDR) for the year ended 200X.

Total Sales	$127m	
Cost of records sold	25m	($1.9m was prepaid in 200X–1)
Manufacturing costs	18m	
Administration costs	9m	(includes $0.5m bad debts written off)
Depreciation plant	2m	
Goodwill written off	3m	
Net profit	50m	

KDR knows that accounting net profit does not represent the true economic result of operations. Provide KDR with a better measure of the change in economic worth for the period.

20 · Cash receipts

Clutch has provided the following information:

	200X–1	200X
Receivables	$ 500,000	$ 440,000
Credit sales	560,000	680,000
Bad debts written off	4,000	5,000
Debtors' payments	625,000	

What were the cash receipts for Clutch from its accounts receivable in 200X?

21 · Depreciation

The following information has been supplied by the accountant of Hands.

	200X	200X–1
Plant and equipment	$ 77,000	$ 75,000
Plant scrapped	5,000	3,000
Additions	15,000	35,000

How much depreciation did Hands write off in 200X?

22 · Working on financial statements

Based on the following information for Trouble and Strife Limited, prepare a statement of financial performance for 200X and statements of financial position for 200X and 200X–1. Calculate cash flow from assets, cash flow to creditors and the cash flow to shareholders in 200X. *Use a 35 per cent tax rate throughout the problem*.

	200X	200X–1
Sales	$ 4,507	$ 4,203
Costs of goods sold	2,633	2,422
Depreciation	952	785
Interest	196	180
Dividends	250	225
Current assets	2,429	2,205
Net fixed assets	7,650	7,344
Current liabilities	1,255	1,003
Long-term debt	2,085	3,106

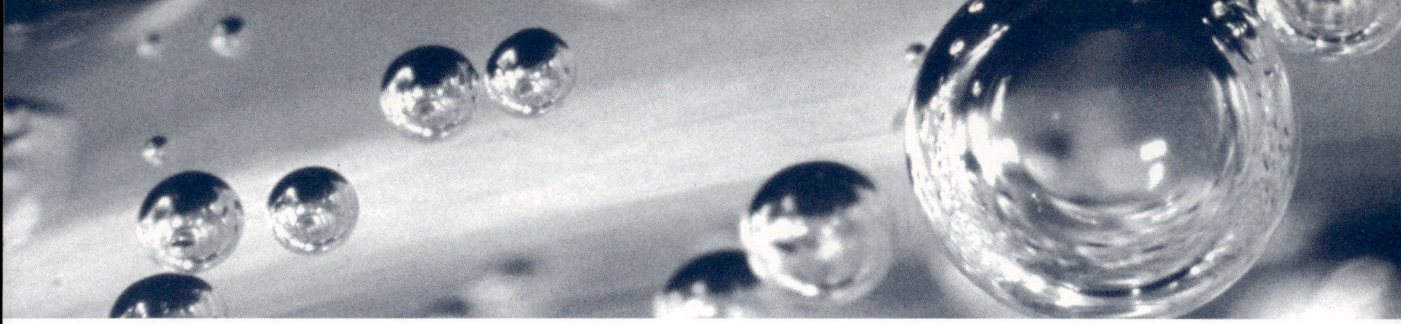

PART TWO

Financial
statements and long-term financial planning

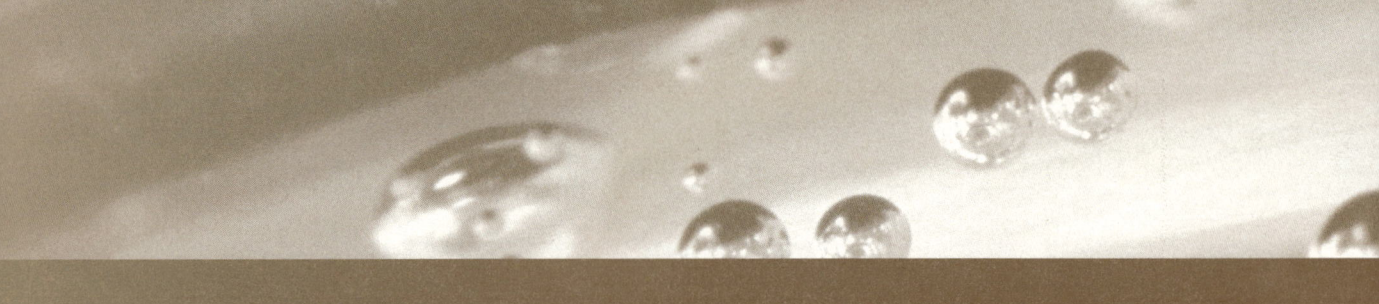

CHAPTER 3

Working
with financial
statements

Objective

Our goal here is to expand your understanding of the uses (and abuses) of financial statement information. In Chapter 2, we discussed some of the essential concepts of financial statements and cash flows. This chapter, and the next, continues where our earlier discussion left off.

In a perfect world, the financial manager has full market value information about all of the firm's assets. This will rarely (if ever) happen. So the reason that we rely on accounting figures for much of our financial information is that we almost always cannot obtain all (or even part) of the market information that we want. The only meaningful yardstick for evaluating business decisions is whether or not they create economic value (see Chapter 1). However, in many important situations, it will not be possible to make this judgment directly because we cannot see the market value effects.

Furthermore, as we shall see, there are many different ways of using financial statement information and many different types of user. This diversity reflects the fact that financial statement information plays an important part in many types of decision.

Study tips ▷ Financial statement information will crop up in various places in the remainder of the book. Part Two is not essential for understanding this material, but it will help give you an overall perspective of the role of financial statement information in corporate finance.

A good working knowledge of financial statements is desirable simply because such statements, and numbers derived from those statements, are the primary means of communicating financial information both within the firm and outside the firm. In short, much of the language of corporate finance stems from ideas we discuss in this chapter.

We recognise that accounting numbers are often just pale reflections of economic reality, but frequently they are the best available information. For privately held companies, not-for-profit businesses and smaller firms, for example, very little direct market value information exists at all. The accountant's reporting function is crucial in these circumstances.

Clearly, one important goal of the accountant is to report financial information to the user in a form that is useful for decision making. Ironically, the information frequently does not come to the user in such a form. In other words, financial statements do not come with a user's guide. This chapter and the next are first steps in filling this gap.

Introduction ▷ When making a financial decision a financial manager needs to have a clear understanding of where cash is coming from and how it is being used. If the benefit from using the cash is greater than the cost of the funds then firm value should increase. Cash flow statements illustrate the flow of funds in the past.

Cash flow is just one type of financial statement. In order to understand the business the financial statements are analysed in terms of liquidity, profitability, and so on. Ratios are easy to use to help analyse a business.

3.1 Cash flow and financial statements: A closer look

At the most fundamental level, firms do two different things: They generate cash and they spend it. Cash is generated by selling a product, an asset or a security. Selling a security involves either borrowing or selling an equity interest (i.e. shares) in the firm. Cash is spent by paying for materials and labour to produce a product and by purchasing assets. Payments to creditors, lenders and owners also require spending cash.

In Chapter 2, we saw that the cash activities of a firm could be summarised by a simple identity:

> Cash flow from assets = Cash flow to debtholders + Cash flow to equityholders

This cash flow identity summarises the total cash result of all the transactions that the firm engaged in during the year. In this section, we return to the subject of cash flows by taking a closer look at the cash events during the year that lead to these total figures.

Sources and uses of cash

sources of cash
a firm's activities that generate cash

uses of cash
the activities of a firm in which cash is spent. Also applications of cash

Those activities that bring in cash are called **sources of cash**. Those activities that involve spending cash are called **uses (or applications) of cash**. What we need to do is to trace the changes in the firm's Statement of Financial Position to see how the firm obtained its cash and how the firm spent its cash during some period.

To get started, consider the Statement of Financial Position for Common Ltd in Table 3.1. Notice that we have calculated the changes in each of the items on the Statement of Financial Position.

Looking over the Statement of Financial Position for Common, we see that quite a few things changed during the year. For example, Common increased its net non-current assets by $149 million and its inventory by $29 million. Where did the money come from? To answer this and related questions, we need to identify first those changes that used up cash (uses) and those that brought in cash (sources).

A little common sense is useful here. A firm uses cash by either buying assets or making payments. So, loosely speaking, an increase in an asset account means that the firm bought some net assets, a use of cash. If an asset account went down, then, on a net basis, the firm sold some assets. This would be a net source. Similarly, if a liability account goes down, then the firm has made a net payment, a use of cash.

Given this reasoning, there is a simple, albeit mechanical, definition that you may find useful. An increase in an asset account or a decrease in a liability or equity account is a use of cash. Likewise, a decrease in an asset account or an increase in a liability (or equity) account is a source of cash.

TABLE 3.1

Common Ltd			
Statement of Financial Position as at 30 June 200X+1 ($ in millions)			
	200X+1	200X	Change
Current assets			
Cash	$ 148	$ 84	+ $64
Receivables	188	165	+ 23

Common Ltd (*continued*)

TABLE 3.1

Statement of Financial Position as at 30 June 200X+1 (*continued*)

	200X+1	200X	Change
Inventory	422	393	+ 29
Total current assets	758	642	+ 116
Non-current assets			
Plant	2,880	2,731	+ 149
Total non-current assets	2,880	2,731	+ 149
Total assets	3,638	3,373	+ 265
Current liabilities			
Creditors	344	312	+ 32
Notes payable	224	231	− 7
Total current liabilities	568	543	+ 25
Non-current liabilities			
Borrowings	457	531	− 74
Total non-current liabilities	457	531	− 74
Total liabilities	1,025	1,074	− 49
Net assets	2,613	2,299	+ 314
Shareholders' funds			
Capital	550	500	+ 50
Retained Earnings	2,063	1,799	+ 264
Total shareholders' funds	2,613	2,299	+ 314

Looking back at Common, we see that *inventory rose by $29m*. This is a *net use* since Common effectively paid out $29m to increase inventories. Creditors rose by $32m. This is a source of cash since Common effectively has borrowed an additional $32m by the end of the year. *Notes payable*, on the other hand, *went down by $7m*, so Common effectively paid off $7m worth of current debt—a *use of cash*.

Based on our discussion, we can summarise the sources and uses from the Statement of Financial Position as follows:

($ in millions)

Source of cash:

Increase in creditors	$ 32
Increase in issued capital	50
Increase in retained earnings	264
Total sources	$ 346

	($ in millions)
Uses of cash:	
Increase in receivables	$ 23
Increase in inventory	29
Decrease in notes payable	7
Decrease in non-current debt	74
Net non-current asset acquisitions	149
Total uses	282
Net addition to cash	$ 64

The net addition to cash is the difference between sources and uses, and our $64m result here agrees with the $64m change shown on the Statement of Financial Position.

This simple statement tells us much of what happened during the year, but it does not tell the whole story. For example, the increase in retained earnings is profit (a source of funds) less dividends (a use of funds). It would be more enlightening to have these reported separately so we could see the breakdown. Also, we have only considered net non-current asset acquisitions. Total or gross spending would be more interesting to know.

To further trace the flow of cash through the firm during the year, we need a Statement of Financial Performance. For Common, the results for the year are shown in Table 3.2.

Notice here that the $264m addition to retained earnings we calculated from the Statement of Financial Position is just the difference between the profit of $385m and the dividend of $121m.

TABLE 3.2

Common Ltd

Statement of Financial Performance for the year ended 30 June 200X+1 ($ in millions)

Sales	$ 2,311
Cost of goods sold	1,344
Depreciation	276
Earnings before interest and tax	$ 691
Interest	141
Taxable income	550
Taxes (30%)	165
Profit	$ 385

Retained earnings	$264
Dividends	$121

statement of cash flows

a firm's financial statement that summarises its sources and uses of cash over a specified period

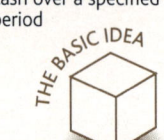
THE BASIC IDEA

The statement of cash flows

The presentation of cash flows in annual reports is determined by an *Accounting Standard*. We present the particular format in Table 3.3 for this statement. The basic idea is to group all the changes into one of three categories: operating activities, financing activities and investment activities.

Do not be surprised if you come across different arrangements. The types of information presented will be very similar; the exact order can differ. The key thing to remember in this

TABLE
3.3

Common Ltd

Statement of Cash Flows for the period ended 30 June 200X+1 ($ in millions)

Operating activities	
Cash from operations (including interest and working capital)	$ 799
Dividends paid	(121)
Income tax paid	(165)
Cash flow from operating activities	$513
Investing activities	
Acquisition of non-current assets	(425)
Cash flow from investing activities	(425)
Financing activities	
Proceeds from sale of shares	50
Decrease in borrowings	(74)
Cash flow from financing activities	(24)
Net cash flows—increase in cash	64
Reconciles to increase in cash	64
Cash from operations	
Sales	2,311
Cost of goods sold	(1,344)
	967
Increase in current liabilities	25
Increase in current assets	(52)
Interest	(141)
	799

case is that we started out with $84m in cash and ended up with $148m, for a net increase of $64m. We're just trying to see what events led to this change.

Going back to Chapter 2, there is a slight conceptual problem here. Interest paid should really go under financing activities but, unfortunately, that's not the way the accounting standard treats interest. The reason is that interest is deducted as an expense when profit is computed. Also, as shown, notice that our net purchase of non-current assets was $149m. Since we wrote off $276m worth (the depreciation), we must have actually spent a total of $149m + $276m = $425m on non-current assets.

Once we have this statement, it might seem appropriate to express the change in cash on a per-share basis, same as we did for net income. Ironically, despite the interest that we might have in some measure of cash flow per share, standard accounting practice expressly prohibits reporting this information. The reason is that accountants feel that cash flow (or some component of cash flow) is not an alternative to accounting income, so only earnings per share are to be reported.

Now that we have the various cash pieces in place, we can get a good idea of what happened during the year. Common's major cash outlays were non-current asset acquisitions and cash dividends. They paid for these activities with cash generated from operations.

Common also retired some non–current debt and increased current assets. Finally, current liabilities were virtually unchanged, and a relatively small amount of new equity was sold. Altogether, this short sketch captures Common's major sources and uses of cash for the year.

Concept questions

3.1a *What is a source of cash? Give three examples.*

3.1b *What is a use or application of cash? Give three examples.*

3.2 Financial statements of publicly listed firms

The contents and presentation of financial statements is determined by accounting standards. Those interested in the setting of and compliance with accounting standards include accountants, the government, regulators and other users of financial statements. The financial statements should be prepared so that users can make sound resource allocation decisions. This is not always the case, as evidenced by the number of corporate collapses, the largest of late being Enron.

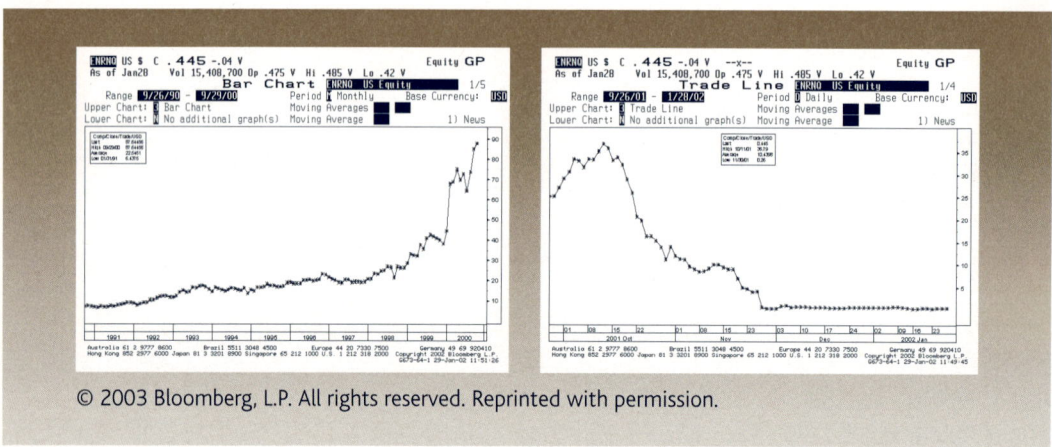

The chart on the left is Enron during the rise of the company, when the share price reached US$90. The chart on the right shows Enron trading at 44.5 cents per share.

The presentation of financial statements

The next thing we might want to do with the financial statements is to compare them to those of other similar companies. We would immediately have a problem, however. It is almost impossible to compare directly the financial statements for two companies because of differences in size.

For example, Woolworths and the local Foodland shop are obviously serious rivals in the grocery market, but Woolworths is much larger (in terms of assets), so it is difficult to compare them directly. For that matter, it is difficult to compare financial statements from different points in time for the same company if the company's size has changed.

To start making comparisons, one obvious thing we might try to do is to somehow standardise the financial statements. A useful and very common way of doing this is to work with percentages instead of total dollars. We can do this by way of ratios.

Ratio analysis

A way of avoiding the problem of comparing companies of different sizes is to calculate and compare **financial ratios**. Such ratios allow us to compare and investigate the relationships between different pieces of financial information. Using ratios eliminates the size problem since the size effectively divides out. We are then left with percentages, multiples or time periods.

There is a problem in discussing financial ratios. Since a ratio is simply one number divided by another, and since there is a substantial quantity of accounting numbers out there, there is a huge number of possible ratios we could examine. Everybody has their favourite. We will restrict ourselves to a representative sampling.

In this section, we only want to introduce you to some commonly used financial ratios. We do not choose the ones we think are best in some sense. Some of the definitions may strike you as illogical or not as useful as others. If they do, don't be concerned. As a financial analyst, you can always decide how to compute your own ratios. The ratio calculations used in this section are those commonly used by research analysts.

What you do need to worry about is the fact that different people and different sources frequently do not compute these ratios in exactly the same way, and this leads to much confusion. The specific definitions we use here may or may not be the same as ones you have seen or will see elsewhere. If you are ever using ratios as a tool for analysis, you should be careful to document how you calculate each one.

We will defer much of our discussion of how ratios are used, and some problems that come up with using them, to the next section. For now, for each of the ratios we discuss, several questions come to mind:

1 How is it computed?
2 What is it intended to measure, and why might we be interested?
3 What is the unit of measurement?
4 What might a high or low value be telling us? How might such values be misleading?
5 How could this measure be improved?

Financial ratios are traditionally grouped together into the following categories:

1 Liquidity ratios
2 Capital structure or financial leverage ratios
3 Asset management or turnover ratios
4 Profitability ratios
5 Market value ratios

financial ratios
relationships determined from a firm's financial information and used for comparison purposes

---

Ratio Analysis

FIGURE 3.1

In order to indicate some of the problems involved in calculating ratios, we have provided abridged information which might appear in the annual report of Highrise Company Ltd. Summary information relating to the notes provided to the accounts is also set out. The note information will assist in calculating some of the ratios. It is not complete and only provides enough information for the purposes of this chapter. Accordingly the notes are not numbered in sequence; however, the numbers are typical of those that might be found in an annual report.

(continued)

FIGURE 3.1

Ratio Analysis (*continued*)

Highrise Company Ltd
Statement of Financial Performance

	Note	$000
Operating profit before income tax	2,3,4	33,121
Income tax		11,687
Operating profit after tax		21,434
Retained profits beginning		19,274
Available for appropriation		40,708
Dividends paid		16,701
Retained profits end		24,007

Notes to the Statement of Financial Position and Statement of Financial Performance

Note	Item	$000
2	Sales Revenue	$381,079
	Cost of Goods Sold	192,250
3	Amortisation	2,602
	Depreciation	11,274
	Interest	2,238
	Finance Lease Charges	41
4	Significant Items	− 446
8	Gross Trade Debtors	39,407
10	Beginning Inventory	56,438
17	Trade Creditors	16,306
	Bank Overdraft	1,603
	Secured Bank Loans (short term)	524
	Lease Liability (short term)	206
	Unsecured Bank Loans (short term)	5,210
19	Secured Bank Loans (long term)	2,895
	Unsecured Bank Loans (long term)	19,972
	Other Loans (long term)	8,934
	Lease Liability (long term)	75
21	Number of Shares	139,654,000
Other	Market Price	$2.23
	Dividends per Share	12c
	Total Intangibles	$32,916

Highrise Company Ltd
Statement of Financial Position

	Note	$000
Current assets		
Cash		5,641
Receivables	8	41,112
Investments		5,230
Inventories	10	60,078
Other		4,251
Total current assets		116,312

Ratio Analysis (*continued*)

	Note	$000
Non-current assets		
Receivables		408
Investments		2,078
Property, plant and equipment		66,266
Intangibles		28,273
Other		6,310
Total non-current assets		103,335
Total assets		219,647
Current liabilities		
Creditors and borrowings	17	31,329
Provisions		28,518
Total current liabilities		59,847
Non-current liabilities		
Creditors and borrowings	19	31,876
Provisions		2,360
Total non-current liabilities		34,236
Total liabilities		94,083
Net assets		125,564
Shareholders' equity		
Share capital	21	69,827
Reserves		31,730
Retained profits		24,007
Total shareholders' equity		125,564

Liquidity ratios

As the name suggests, liquidity ratios as a group are intended to provide information about a firm's short-term solvency. The primary concern is the firm's ability to pay its bills over the short run without undue stress. Consequently, these ratios focus on current assets and current liabilities.

For obvious reasons, liquidity ratios are particularly interesting to short-term creditors. Since financial managers are constantly working with banks and other short-term lenders, an understanding of these ratios is essential.

One advantage of looking at current assets and liabilities is that their book values and market values are likely to be similar. Often (but not always), these assets and liabilities just do not live long enough for the two to get seriously out of step. On the other hand, like any type of near-cash, current assets and liabilities can and do change fairly rapidly, so today's amounts may not be a reliable guide to the future.

Current ratio

One of the best known and most widely used ratios is the *current ratio*. As you might guess, the current ratio is defined as:

$$\text{Current ratio} = \frac{\text{Current assets}}{\text{Current liabilities}} \qquad (3.1)$$

For Highrise, the current ratio is:

$$\text{Current ratio} = \$116{,}312 \div \$59{,}847$$
$$= 1.94$$

Because current assets and liabilities are, in principle, converted to cash over the following 12 months, the current ratio is a measure of short-term liquidity. The unit of measurement is either dollars or times. So, we could say that Highrise has $1.94 in current assets for every $1 in current liabilities, or we could say that Highrise has its current liabilities covered 1.94 times over.

To a creditor, particularly a short-term creditor such as a supplier, the higher the current ratio the better. To the firm, a high current ratio indicates liquidity, but it may also indicate an inefficient use of cash and other short-term assets. Barring some extraordinary circumstances, we would expect to see a current ratio of at least 1, because a current ratio of less than 1 would mean that net working capital (current assets less current liabilities) is negative. This would be unusual in a healthy firm, at least for most types of business.

The current ratio, like any ratio, is affected by various types of transactions. For example, suppose the firm borrows long term to raise money. The short-run effect would be an increase in cash from the issue proceeds and an increase in long-term debt. Current liabilities would not be affected, so the current ratio would rise.

Finally, note that an apparently low current ratio may not be a bad sign for a company with a large reserve of untapped borrowing power.

EXAMPLE 3.1 ■ Current events

Suppose a firm were to pay off some of its suppliers and short-term creditors. What would happen to the current ratio? Suppose a firm buys some inventory. What happens in this case? What happens if a firm sells some merchandise?

The first case is a trick question. What happens is that the current ratio moves away from 1. If it is greater than 1 (the usual case), it will get bigger, but if it is less than one, it will get smaller. To illustrate this, suppose the firm has $4 in current assets and $2 in current liabilities for a current ratio of 2. If we use $1 in cash to reduce current liabilities, then the new current ratio is ($4 − $1) / ($2 − $1) = 3. If we reverse this to $2 in current assets and $4 in current liabilities, the current ratio would fall to 1/3 from 1/2.

The second case is not quite as tricky. Nothing happens to the current ratio because cash goes down while inventory goes up—total current assets are unaffected.

In the third case, the current ratio would usually rise because inventory is normally shown at cost and the sale would normally be at something greater than cost (the difference is the markup). The increase in either cash or receivables is therefore greater than the decrease in inventory. This increases current assets, and the current ratio rises.

The quick (or acid-test) ratio

Inventory is often the least liquid current asset. It is also the one for which the book values are least reliable as measures of market value, since the quality of the inventory may not be considered. Some of it may be damaged, obsolete or lost.

More to the point, relatively large inventories are often a sign of short-term trouble. The firm may have overestimated sales and overbought or overproduced as a result. In this case, the firm may have a substantial portion of its liquidity tied up in slow-moving inventory.

One type of account often found in current liabilities is a bank overdraft. A bank overdraft is theoretically at call, meaning that the bank can call on the firm to repay the debt at any time. Banks fortunately do not do this unless the firm is experiencing liquidity problems and therefore once a bank overdraft facility is established, a firm effectively uses it as a source of long-term financing.

To further evaluate liquidity, the *quick* or *acid-test ratio* is computed just like the current ratio, except inventory is omitted from current assets and the bank overdraft (if any) is omitted from current liabilities:

$$\text{Quick ratio} = \frac{\text{Current assets} - \text{Inventory}}{\text{Current liabilities} - \text{Bank overdraft}} \qquad (3.2)$$

Notice that using cash to buy inventory does not affect the current ratio, but it reduces the quick ratio. Again, the idea is that inventory is relatively illiquid compared to cash.

For Highrise, this ratio was:

$$\text{Quick ratio} = \frac{\$116,312 - \$60,078}{\$59,847 - \$1,603}$$
$$= 0.97$$

The quick ratio here tells a somewhat different story from the current ratio, because inventory accounts for more than half of Highrise's current assets. To exaggerate the point, if this inventory consisted of, say, unsold nuclear power plants, then this is a cause for concern.

One of the early corporate failures in Australia was Mainline Corporation Limited. It is interesting to observe the current and quick ratios for the period before it crashed in 1975.

	1969	1970	1971	1972	1973
Current ratio	0.64	0.85	1.32	1.27	1.15
Quick ratio	0.26	0.45	0.31	0.48	0.16

There was a relatively small decline in the current ratio in 1973 but a large drop in the quick ratio in the same year. The quick ratio indicated the liquidity problem that the firm was facing.

Capital structure measures

This group of ratios is intended to address the firm's long-run ability to meet its obligations or, more generally, its financial leverage. These are sometimes called *financial leverage ratios* or just *leverage ratios*. We consider three commonly used measures and some variations.

Net debt/equity ratio

The *net debt/equity ratio* takes into account all interest-bearing debt of all maturities to all ordinary equity. It can be defined in several ways, one being:

$$\text{Net debt/equity} = \frac{\text{Interest-bearing debt} - \text{Cash}}{\text{Ordinary shareholders' equity} - \text{Intangibles}} \quad (3.3)$$

$$= \frac{\$39,419^* - \$5,641}{\$125,564}$$

$$= 0.27$$

In this case, an analyst might say that Highrise uses 27 cents of interest bearing debt for each dollar of ordinary shareholders funds. Whether this is high or low or whether it even makes any difference depends on whether or not capital structure matters, a subject we discuss in Part Eight.

Various debt structure ratios are used to assess the gearing or leverage of a company.

Net interest cover

Another common measure of long-term solvency is the *net interest cover ratio*. You will find that in some cases lenders call interest by another name. An example of this is when you undertake a finance lease. The interest in a finance lease is called a finance lease charge, but it is just another name for interest.

$$\text{Net interest cover} = \frac{\text{EBIT}}{\text{Net interest, including finance lease charges}} \quad (3.4)$$

$$= \frac{\$33,121 + \$446 + \$2,238 + \$41}{\$2,238 + \$41}$$

$$= 15.7 \text{ times}$$

EBIT is earnings before interest, finance lease charges, taxes and significant items. It is an indication of the ability of the company to service the debt obligation. For Highrise, the interest bill is covered 15.7 times over; that is, the earnings of the company are 15.7 times larger than the interest commitment that the company has to meet.

Debt to gross cash flow

A problem with the net interest cover ratio is that it is based on EBIT, which is not really a measure of cash available to pay interest. The reason is that depreciation and amortisation, non-cash expenses, have been deducted. A variation of net interest cover is the *debt to gross cash flow ratio* which gives an indication of how many years it would take the company to pay any outstanding interest-bearing debt.

$$\text{Debt to gross cash flow} = \frac{\text{Interest-bearing debt}}{\text{Net Profit after Tax} + \text{Depreciation} + \text{Amortisation}} \quad (3.5)$$

$$= \frac{\$39,416^*}{\$21,880^{**} + \$11,274 + \$2,602}$$

$$= 1.1 \text{ years}$$

*Interest-bearing debt = Bank overdraft + Secured bank loans + Lease liability + Unsecured bank loans + Other loans
  = \$1,603 + (\$524 + \$2,895) + (\$206 + \$72) + (\$5,210 + \$19,972) + \$8,934
  = \$39,416

**Net profit after tax = Profit after tax adjusted for significant items
  = \$21,434 + \$446
  = \$21,880

If the company decided to repay its debt, it could do so in 1.1 years.

Asset management or turnover measures

We next turn our attention to the efficiency with which Highrise uses its assets. The measures in this section are sometimes called *asset utilisation ratios*. The specific ratios we discuss can all be interpreted as measures of turnover. What they are intended to describe is how efficiently or intensively a firm uses its assets to generate sales. We first look at two important current assets, inventory and receivables.

Inventory turnover and days' sales in inventory

During the year, Highrise had a cost of goods sold of $192,250. Inventory at the end of the year was $60,078. With these numbers, *inventory turnover* can be calculated as:

$$\text{Inventory turnover} = \frac{\text{Cost of goods sold}}{\text{Inventory}} \qquad (3.6)$$

$$= \frac{\$192,250}{\$60,078}$$

$$= 3.2 \text{ times}$$

In a sense, we sold off or turned over the entire inventory 3.2 times.[1] As long as we are not running out of stock and thereby foregoing sales, the higher this ratio is, the more efficiently we are managing inventory.

If we turned our inventory over 3.2 times during the year, then we can immediately figure out how long it took us to turn it over on average. The result is the average *days' sales in inventory*:

$$\text{Days' sales in inventory} = \frac{365 \text{ days}}{\text{Inventory turnover}} \qquad (3.7)$$

$$= \frac{365}{3.2}$$

$$= 114 \text{ days}$$

This tells us that, roughly speaking, inventory sits 114 days on average before it is sold. Alternatively, assuming we used the most recent inventory and cost figures, it will take about 114 days to work off our current inventory.

So, for example, we frequently hear things like 'Majestic Motors has a 60 days' supply of cars. Thirty days is considered normal'. This means that, at current daily sales, it would take 60 days to deplete the available inventory. We could also say that we have 60 days of sales in inventory.

It might make more sense to use the average inventory in calculating turnover. Inventory turnover would then be $192,250/[($60,078 + $56,438)/2] = 3.3 times.[2] It really depends on the purpose of the calculation. If we are interested in how long it will take us to sell our current inventory, then using the ending figure (as we did initially) is probably better.

In many of the ratios we discuss below, average figures could just as well be used. Again, it really depends on whether we are worried about the past, in which case averages are appropriate, or the future, in which case ending figures might be better. Also, using ending figures is very common in reporting industry averages; so, for comparison purposes, ending figures should be used in this case. In any event, using ending figures is definitely less work, so we will continue to use them.

Receivables turnover and days in receivables

Our inventory measures give some indication of how fast we can sell product. We now look at how fast we collect on those sales. The *receivables turnover* is defined in the same way as inventory turnover:

$$\text{Receivables turnover} = \frac{\text{Sales}}{\text{Accounts receivable (trade debtors)}} \qquad (3.8)$$
$$= \frac{\$381,079}{\$39,407}$$
$$= 9.7 \text{ times}$$

Loosely speaking, we collected our outstanding credit accounts and reloaned the money 9.7 times during the year.[3]

This ratio makes more sense if we convert it to days, so the *days' sales in receivables* is:

$$\text{Days' sales in receivables} = \frac{365 \text{ days}}{\text{Receivables turnover}} \qquad (3.9)$$
$$= \frac{365}{9.7}$$
$$= 38 \text{ days}$$

Therefore, on average, we collect on our credit sales in 38 days. For this reason, this ratio is very frequently called the *average collection period (ACP)*.

Also, note that if we are using the most recent figures, we could also say that we have 38 days' worth of sales that are currently uncollected. We will learn more about this subject when we study credit policy in a later chapter.

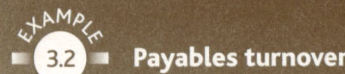

EXAMPLE
3.2 ■ **Payables turnover**

Here is a variation on the receivables collection period. How long, on average, does it take for Highrise Corporation to pay its bills? To answer, we need to calculate the accounts payable turnover rate using cost of goods sold. We will assume that Highrise purchases everything on credit.

The cost of goods sold is $192,250, and accounts payable (trade creditors) is $16,306. The turnover is therefore $192,250/$16,306 = 11.8 times. So payables turned over about every 365/11.8 = 31 days. On average, then, Highrise takes 31 days to pay. As a potential creditor, we might take note of this fact.

Asset turnover ratios

Moving away from specific accounts like inventory or receivables, we can consider several 'big picture' ratios. For example, *fixed asset turnover* is:

$$\text{Fixed asset turnover} = \frac{\text{Sales}}{\text{Net non-current assets}} \qquad (3.10)$$
$$= \frac{\$381,079}{\$103,335}$$
$$= 3.7 \text{ times}$$

With this ratio, it probably makes more sense to say that, for every dollar in non-current assets, we generated $3.70 in sales.

Our final asset management ratio, the *total asset turnover*, comes up quite a bit. We will see it later in this chapter and in the next chapter. As the name suggests, the total asset turnover is:

$$\text{Total asset turnover} = \frac{\text{Sales}}{\text{Total assets}} \qquad (3.11)$$
$$= \frac{\$381,079}{\$219,647}$$
$$= 1.74 \text{ times}$$

In other words, for every dollar in assets, we generate $1.74 in sales.

EXAMPLE 3.3

More turnover

Suppose you find that a particular company generates $0.40 in sales for every dollar in total assets. How often does this company turn over its total assets?

The total asset turnover here is 0.40 times per year. It takes $1/0.40 = 2.5$ years to turn them over completely.

Profitability measures

The four measures we discuss in this section are probably the best known and most widely used of all the financial ratios. In one form or another, they are intended to measure how efficiently the firm uses its assets and how efficiently the firm manages its operations. The focus in this group is on the bottom line, net profit.

Profit margin

Companies pay a great deal of attention to their *profit margin*:

$$\text{Profit margin} = \frac{\text{Net profit}}{\text{Sales}} \times 100\% \qquad (3.12)$$
$$= \frac{\$21,434}{\$381,079} \times 100\%$$
$$= 5.6\%$$

This tells us that Highrise, in an accounting sense, generates 5.6 cents in profit for every dollar in sales.

All other things being equal, a relatively high profit margin is obviously desirable. This situation corresponds to low expense ratios relative to sales. However, we hasten to add that other things are often not equal.

For example, lowering our sales price will normally increase unit volume, but profit margins will normally shrink. Total profit (or more importantly, operating cash flow) may go up or down; so the fact that margins are smaller is not necessarily bad. After all, isn't it possible that, as the saying goes, 'Our prices are so low that we lose money on everything we sell, but we make it up in volume!'?[4]

Return on assets

Return on assets (ROA) is a measure of profit per dollar of assets. It can be defined in several ways, but the most common is:

$$\text{Return on assets} = \frac{\text{Net Profit}}{\text{Total assets}} \times 100\% \qquad (3.13)$$

$$= \frac{\$21{,}434}{\$219{,}647} \times 100\%$$

$$= 9.8\%$$

Return on investment

Return on investment is similar to the return on assets except that in the top line of the equation we use EBIT. EBIT is the earnings of the firm that is shared between the equityholders, debtholders and the government in the form of taxation. It is the return to the firm as a whole. It is calculated as earnings before finance lease charges, interest, tax and significant items.

$$\text{Return on investment} = \frac{\text{EBIT}}{\text{Total assets}} \times 100\% \qquad (3.14)$$

$$= \frac{\$33{,}121 + \$446 + \$2{,}238 + \$41}{\$219{,}647} \times 100\%$$

$$= 16.3\%$$

Return on equity

Return on equity (ROE) is a measure of how the shareholders fared during the year. Since benefiting shareholders is our goal, ROE is, in an accounting sense, the true bottom-line measure of performance. ROE is usually measured as:

$$\text{Return on equity} = \frac{\text{Net profit}}{\text{Total equity}} \times 100\% \qquad (3.15)$$

$$= \frac{\$21{,}434}{\$125{,}564} \times 100\%$$

$$= 17.1\%$$

For every dollar in equity, therefore, Highrise generated 17 cents in profit, but, again, this is only correct in accounting terms.

Because ROA and ROE are such commonly cited numbers, we stress that it is important to remember that they are accounting rates of return. For this reason, these measures should properly be called return on **book** assets and return on **book** equity. In fact, ROE is sometimes called return on net worth. Whatever it's called, it would be inappropriate to compare the result to, for example, an interest rate observed in the financial markets. We will have more to say about accounting rates of return in later chapters.

The fact that ROE exceeds ROA reflects Highrise's use of financial leverage. We will examine the relationship between these two measures in more detail below.

Market value measures

Our final group of measures is based, in part, on information that is not necessarily contained in financial statements—the market price of the shares. Obviously, these measures can only be calculated directly for publicly traded companies.

Highrise has 139,654,000 shares issued to shareholders and the shares sell for $2.23 per share at the end of the year. Recalling that Highrise's net profit was $21,434,000, its earnings per share (EPS) is:

$$EPS = \$21,434/139,654 = \$0.1535$$

Price/earning ratio

The first of our market value measures, the *price/earning (P/E) ratio* (or multiple), is defined as:

$$P/E \text{ ratio} = \frac{\text{Price per share}}{\text{Earnings per share}} \tag{3.16}$$

$$= \$2.23/0.1535 = 14.5 \text{ times}$$

This means that Highrise shares sell for 14.5 times earnings, or we might say that at the current rate of earnings, it will take Highrise 14.5 years to earn the equivalent of what an investor would pay for the shares today.

Since the P/E ratio measures how much investors are willing to pay per dollar of current earnings, higher P/Es are often taken to mean that the firm has significant prospects for future growth. Of course, if a firm had no or almost no earnings, its P/E would probably be quite large; so, as always, care is needed in interpreting this ratio.

Market-to-book ratio

A second commonly quoted measure is the *market-to-book ratio*:

$$\text{Market-to-book ratio} = \frac{\text{Market value per share}}{\text{Book value per share}} \tag{3.17}$$

$$= \frac{\$2.23}{(\$125,564/139,654)}$$

$$= \frac{\$2.23}{\$0.90}$$

$$= 2.48 \text{ times}$$

Notice that book value per share is total equity divided by the number of shares outstanding.

Since book value per share is an accounting number, it reflects historical costs. In a loose sense, the market-to-book ratio therefore compares the market value of the firm's investments to their cost. A value less than 1 could mean that the firm has not been successful overall in creating value for its shareholders.

This completes our definitions of some common ratios. We could tell you about more of them, but these are enough for now. We'll leave it here and go on to discuss some ways of using these ratios instead of just how to calculate them. Table 3.4 summarises the ratios that we discussed.

TABLE 3.4

Common Financial Ratios

I. Short-term solvency or liquidity ratios

Current ratio $= \dfrac{\text{Current assets}}{\text{Current liabilities}}$

Quick ratio $= \dfrac{\text{Current assets} - \text{Inventory}}{\text{Current liabilities} - \text{Bank overdraft}}$

II. Long-term solvency or financial leverage ratios

Net debt/equity ratio $= \dfrac{\text{Total financial debt} - \text{Cash}}{\text{Total equity}}$

Debt/equity ratio $=$ Total debt/Total equity

Equity Multiplier $=$ Total assets/Total equity

Net interest cover $= \dfrac{\text{EBIT}}{\text{Interest} + \text{finance charges}}$

III. Asset utilisation or turnover ratios

Inventory turnover $= \dfrac{\text{Costs of goods sold}}{\text{Inventory}}$

Days' sales in inventory $= \dfrac{365 \text{ days}}{\text{Inventory turnover}}$

Receivables turnover $= \dfrac{\text{Sales}}{\text{Accounts receivable}}$

Days' sales in receivables $= \dfrac{365 \text{ days}}{\text{Receivables turnover}}$

Fixed asset turnover $= \dfrac{\text{Sales}}{\text{Non-current assets}}$

Total assets turnover $= \dfrac{\text{Sales}}{\text{Total assets}}$

IV. Profitability ratios

Debt to gross cash flow $= \dfrac{\text{Financial debt}}{\text{Net profit after tax} + \text{Depreciation} + \text{Amortisation}}$

Profit margin $= \dfrac{\text{Net profit}}{\text{Sales}}$

Return on assets (ROA) $= \dfrac{\text{Net profit}}{\text{Total assets}}$

Return on equity (ROE) $= \dfrac{\text{Net profit}}{\text{Total equity}}$

ROE $= \dfrac{\text{Net profit}}{\text{Sales}} \times \dfrac{\text{Sales}}{\text{Assets}} \times \dfrac{\text{Assets}}{\text{Equity}}$

ROI $= \dfrac{\text{EBIT}}{\text{Total assets}}$

TABLE
3.4

Common Financial Ratios (*continued*)

V. Market value ratios

$$\text{Price/earning ratio} = \frac{\text{Price per share}}{\text{Earnings per share}}$$

$$\text{Market-to-book ratio} = \frac{\text{Market value per share}}{\text{Book value per share}}$$

Concept questions

3.2a *What are the five groups of ratios? Give two or three examples of each kind.*

3.2b *Turnover ratios all have one of two figures as numerators. What are they? What do these ratios measure? How do you interpret the results?*

3.2c *Profitability ratios all have the same figure in the numerator. What is it? What do these ratios measure? How do you interpret the results?*

Annabelle Chaplain

❝❞ In their own words

Annabelle Chaplain* on the application of financial ratios in corporate lending negotiations

In the corporate market, the financial ratios which are to be embedded in a loan agreement are crucial to negotiations. These ratios are known as financial covenants because the borrower is legally bound to maintain these ratios over the life of the loan. As a company director overseeing these negotiations, it is interesting to observe the competing motivations of each party. While there are a broad range of financial covenants that can be applied, the more common ones are: the Current Ratio to measure short-term liquidity, the Interest Cover Ratio which highlights a borrower's ability to service its debt commitments and a Gearing Ratio to assess the financial leverage of the business.

The financial ratios selected as covenants governing a loan agreement must be very clearly defined. Terms such as Interest Cover and Gearing are often calculated very differently and can produce very different outcomes. For example, a number of lenders use EBIT (earnings before interest and tax) divided by interest expense to measure Interest Cover while others argue that EBITDA (earnings before interest and tax, depreciation and amortisation) divided by interest expense measures a company's position more accurately because it removes the impact of non-cash items like depreciation from the analysis. An EBITDA/Interest expense set at 2 times is an easier test to meet than EBIT/Interest expense also set at 2 times, as EBIT will always be less than EBITDA (unless D + A = 0). (continued)

The lender typically uses financial ratios as an early warning signal of a company's financial health, a trigger to vary pricing during the course of the loan (usually upward) and when certain ratio levels are breached, to enforce specific obligations on the borrower under the loan agreement. In this case, the lender wants to ensure that the ratios are properly constructed to provide adequate comfort that the loan will be repaid. The borrower's perspective is naturally quite different. The borrower is concerned to ensure that these ratios do not restrict flexibility, expansion plans or, indeed, trigger a default situation. For example, if a company's revenues and profits are affected by the building cycle, then it must ensure that there is sufficient buffer for those years when cash flow is expected to be tighter. For an infrastructure business with significant capital expenditure in the early years and revenues that are slow to ramp up, there are sometimes different levels of ratios set, with different consequences, varying over the course of the loan. Certain trigger points may be relaxed or even waived in the early years until the time when both parties—lender and borrower—agree that the business should perform at a sustained level.

Ultimately, the right level for any business is determined by looking at projected cash flows and testing a number of downside sensitivities. The more potentially volatile the cash flows, the higher the financial covenant breach levels should be, and if they are breached in the projections, debt should be 'sized' to ensure there are no breaches. It is also important to understand that while there are generally accepted levels in the marketplace for interest cover, liquidity and gearing, there is no one right answer. The debt rating firm Standard & Poor's produces comparisons on companies that they rate; but the ratios are always a matter for negotiation between individual lenders and borrowers. Companies that are very similar can have quite different financial covenants applied to their loan arrangements. There are many reasons for this. Variances can depend on the industry, the lender's appetite for a certain type of risk and, not to be underestimated, the borrower's powers of negotiation.

* Annabelle Chaplain is a director of several companies, both public and private sector. Prior to this, she spent over 20 years in banking and has experience in corporate banking, project finance, public sector financing and treasury.

3.3 ‖ The Du Pont identity

As we mentioned in discussing ROA and ROE, the difference between these two profitability measures is a reflection of the use of debt financing or financial leverage. We illustrate the relationship between these measures in this section by investigating a famous way of decomposing ROE into its component parts.

To begin, let us recall the definition of ROE:

$$\text{Return on equity} = \frac{\text{Net profit}}{\text{Total equity}}$$

If we were so inclined, we could multiply this ratio by Assets/Assets without changing anything:

$$\text{Return on equity} = \frac{\text{Net profit}}{\text{Total Equity}} = \frac{\text{Net profit}}{\text{Total Equity}} \times \frac{\text{Assets}}{\text{Assets}}$$
$$= \frac{\text{Net profit}}{\text{Assets}} \times \frac{\text{Assets}}{\text{Equity}}$$

Notice that we have expressed the return on equity as the product of two other ratios—return on assets and a ratio which we will call the equity multiplier:

$$\text{ROE} = \text{ROA} \times \text{Equity multiplier}$$
$$= \text{ROA} \times (1 + \text{debt/equity ratio})$$

Looking back at Highrise and using total liabilities/total shareholders' equity as the debt/equity ratio, the ratio is 0.75 ($94,083/$125,564) and ROA was 9.8 per cent. Our work here implies that Highrise's return on equity, as we previously calculated, is:

$$\text{ROE} = 9.8\% \times 1.75 = 17.1\%$$

We can further decompose ROE by multiplying the top and bottom by total sales:

$$\text{ROE} = \frac{\overline{\text{Sales}}}{\text{Sales}} \times \frac{\overline{\text{Net profit}}}{\text{Assets}} \times \frac{\overline{\text{Assets}}}{\text{Equity}}$$

If we rearrange things a bit, ROE is:

$$\text{ROE} = \frac{\overline{\text{Net profit}}}{\text{Sales}} \times \frac{\overline{\text{Sales}}}{\text{Assets}} \times \frac{\overline{\text{Assets}}}{\text{Equity}} \qquad (3.18)$$
$$= \text{Profit margin} \times \text{Total asset turnover} \times \text{Equity multiplier}$$

What we have now done is to partition the return on assets into its two component parts, profit margin and total asset turnover. This last expression is called the **Du Pont identity**, after the Du Pont Corporation, which popularised its use.

Du Pont identity
popular expression breaking ROE into three parts: operating efficiency, asset use efficiency, and financial leverage

We can check this relationship for Highrise by noting that the profit margin was 5.6 per cent and the total asset turnover was 1.73. ROE should thus be:

$$\text{ROE} = \text{Profit margin} \times \text{Total asset turnover} \times \text{Equity multiplier}$$
$$= 5.6245\% \times 1.73496 \times 1.74928$$
$$= 17.1\%.$$

This 17.1 per cent ROE is exactly what we had before.

The Du Pont identity tells us that ROE is affected by three things:

1 operating efficiency (as measured by profit margin)
2 asset use efficiency (as measured by total asset turnover)
3 financial leverage (as measured by the equity multiplier)

Weakness in either operating or asset use efficiency (or both) will show up in a diminished return on assets, which will translate into a lower ROE.

Considering the Du Pont identity, it appears that the ROE could be leveraged up by increasing the amount of debt in the firm. It turns out that this will only happen if the firm's ROA exceeds the interest rate on the debt. More importantly, the use of debt financing has a number of other effects, and, as we discuss at some length in Part Eight, the amount of leverage a firm uses is governed by its capital structure policy.

The decomposition of ROE we've discussed in this section is a convenient way of systematically approaching financial statement analysis. If ROE is unsatisfactory by some measure, then the Du Pont identity tells you where to start looking for the reasons.

Concept questions

3.3a *Return on assets (ROA) can be expressed as the product of two ratios. Which two?*

3.3b *Return on equity (ROE) can be expressed as the product of three ratios. Which three?*

3.4 Using financial statement information

Our last task in this chapter is to discuss in more detail some practical aspects of financial statement analysis. In particular, we will look at reasons for doing financial statement analysis, how to go about getting benchmark information, and some of the problems that come up in the process.

Why evaluate financial statements?

As we have discussed, the primary reason for looking at accounting information is that we do not have, and cannot reasonably expect to get, market value information. It is important to emphasise that whenever we have market information, we would use it instead of accounting data. Also, if there is a conflict between accounting and market data, market data should be given precedence.

Financial statement analysis is essentially an application of 'management by exception'. In many cases, such analysis will boil down to comparing ratios for one business with some kind of average or industry ratio. Those ratios that seem to differ the most from the averages are tagged for further study.

Internal uses

Financial information has a variety of uses within a firm. Among the most important of these is performance evaluation. For example, managers are frequently evaluated and compensated on the basis of accounting measures of performance such as profit margin and return on equity. Also, firms with multiple divisions frequently compare the performance of those divisions using financial statement information.

Another important internal use that we will explore in the next chapter is planning for the future. As we will see, historical financial statement information is very useful for generating projections about the future and for checking the realism of assumptions made in those projections.

External uses

Financial statements are useful to parties outside the firm, including short-term and long-term lenders and potential investors. For example, we would find such information quite useful in deciding whether or not to grant credit to a new customer.

We would also find such information useful in evaluating our main competitors. We might be thinking of launching a new product. A prime concern would be whether the competition would jump in shortly thereafter. In this case, we would be interested in our competitors' financial strength to see if they can afford the necessary development.

Finally, we might be thinking of acquiring another firm. Financial statement information would be essential in identifying potential targets and deciding what to offer.

Choosing a benchmark

Given that we want to evaluate a division or a firm based on its financial statements, a basic problem immediately comes up. How do we choose a benchmark or a standard of comparison? We describe some ways of getting started in this section.

Time-trend analysis

One standard we could use is history. Suppose we found that the current ratio for a particular firm is 2.4 based on the most recent financial statement information. Looking back over the last 10 years, we might find that this ratio has declined fairly steadily over that period.

Based on this, we might wonder if the liquidity position of the firm has deteriorated. It could be, of course, that the firm has made changes that allow it to use its current assets more efficiently, that the nature of the firm's business has changed, or that business practices have changed. If we investigate, these are all possible explanations. This is an example of what we mean by management by exception—a deteriorating time trend may not be bad, but it does merit investigation.

Peer group analysis

The second means of establishing a benchmark is to identify firms that are similar in the sense that they compete in the same markets, have similar assets and operate in similar ways. In other words, we need to identify a *peer group*. There are obvious problems with doing this, since no two companies are identical. Ultimately, the choice of which companies to use as a basis for comparison is subjective.

One common way of identifying potential peers is based on the **Global Industry Classification Standard (GICS)** used by the Australian Stock Exchange. From 1 July 2002 the ASX industry classification became redundant. The Australian market has traditionally been associated with 24 industry sectors unique to Australia. GICS consists of 10 economic sectors aggregated from 23 industry groups, 59 industries, and 122 sub-industries; it currently covers over 12,000 companies globally. Firms with the same industry code are frequently assumed to be similar.

Some companies are hard to place because they are unique or because they have diverse operations. A company is classified within an Industry Classification on the basis of its sales revenue. Some companies are extremely diversified but they will be classified into one of a number of Industry Classifications. The basis of classification is the area from which most revenue is generated.

With these caveats about the Industry Classifications in mind, we can now take a look at a specific industry. Suppose that we are a small manufacturer of building materials. Table 3.5 (overleaf) contains some condensed common-size financial statements for this industry, which we might use to evaluate how our company is performing. For ease we have used 200X+1 for the most current year and 200X for the previous year.

There is a large amount of information here, most of which is self-explanatory. In Table 3.5, we have current information reported for the average of many different companies. For example, in the profit and loss summary, operating expenses on average in 200X+1 comprise 89.2 per cent of each sales dollar. We could calculate various ratios from this data. The net interest cover ratio (EBIT/Interest) would be 11.8/3.8, being an average of 3.1 times.

Global Industry Classification Standard (GICS)
a code used globally to classify a firm by its type of business operations

TABLE 3.5

Profile of an average building materials company

Statement of Financial Performance summary

	200X+1 %	200X %
Aggregate sales ($m)	**16,901.1**	**16,444,3**
Percentage analysis		
Sales	100.0	100.0
less Operating expenses	89.2	87.7
	10.8	12.3
add Other income	3.1	3.2
	13.9	15.5
less Depreciation	3.5	3.1
Trading profit	10.4	12.4
add Investment income	1.4	1.9
EBIT	11.8	14.3
less Interest	3.8	3.7
Pre-tax profits	8.0	10.6
less Tax	3.0	4.1
Net profit	5.0	6.5
less Minority interests	0.4	0.3
Net profit to shareholders	4.6	6.2
less Preference dividends	0.1	0.1
Earned for ordinary shares	4.5	6.1
less Dividends	3.9	4.5
Retained from normal operations	0.6	1.6

Statement of Financial Position summary (assets)

	200X+1 %	200X %
Assets		
Current assets		
Cash & liquids	3.8	4.3
Trade debtors	10.7	12.1
Stocks	11.4	11.7
Other current assets	3.5	3.3
	29.4	31.4
Investments		
Listed & unlisted	5.5	7.0
Deferred assets	8.4	7.9
Fixed assets		
Net plant & property	49.8	47.1
Intangibles	6.9	6.6
	100.0	100.0
Aggregate total assets		
$m	18,991.7	18,665.8

Profile of an average building materials company (*continued*)		TABLE 3.5

Statement of Financial Position summary (liabilities)		
	200X+1 %	200X %
Liabilities		
Shareholders' funds		
Ordinary shareholders' funds	44.1	40.1
Preference capital	1.3	1.5
Convertible notes	1.5	1.5
	46.9	43.1
Minority interests	4.3	3.7
Current liabilities		
Bank overdraft	0.8	0.7
Trade debtors	7.6	8.0
Tax provisions	2.4	3.2
Debt due one year	6.1	5.8
Other current liabilities	5.9	6.6
	22.8	24.3
Deferred liabilities		
Long-term debt	19.5	23.0
Other deferred liabilities	6.5	5.9
	26.0	28.9
	100.0	100.0
Aggregate total liabilities		
$m	18,991.7	18,665.8

Problems with financial statement analysis

We close out our chapter on financial statements by discussing some additional problems that can arise in using financial statements. In one way or another, the basic problem with financial statement analysis is that there is no underlying theory to help us identify which quantities to look at and to guide us in establishing benchmarks.

As we discuss in other chapters, there are many cases where financial theory and economic logic provide guidance in making judgments about value and risk. Very little such help exists with financial statements. This is why we can't say which ratios matter the most and what a high or low value might be.

One particularly severe problem is that many firms are conglomerates, owning more or less unrelated lines of business. The consolidated financial statements don't really fit any neat industry category. More generally, the kind of peer group analysis that we have been describing is going to work best when the firms are strictly in the same line of business, the industry is competitive, and there is only one way of operating.

Several other general problems frequently crop up. First, different firms use different accounting procedures for inventory, for example. This makes it difficult to compare statements. Second, different firms end their fiscal years at different times. For firms in seasonal businesses (such as a retailer with a large Christmas season), this can lead to difficulties in comparing Statements of Financial Position because of fluctuations in accounts during the year. Finally, for any particular firm, unusual or transient events, such as a one-time profit from an asset sale, may affect financial performance. In comparing firms, such events can give misleading signals.

Concept questions

3.4a *What are some uses for financial statement analysis?*
3.4b *What are industry classifications and how might they be useful?*
3.4c *Why do we say that financial statement analysis is 'management by exception'?*
3.4d *What are some of the problems that can come up with financial statement analysis?*

3.5 ■ Summary and conclusions

This chapter has discussed aspects of financial statements analysis:

1 *Sources and uses of cash.* We discussed how to identify the ways that businesses obtain and use cash, and we described how to trace the flow of cash through the business over the course of the year. We looked briefly at the statement of cash flows.

2 *Ratio analysis.* Evaluating ratios of accounting numbers is another way of comparing financial statement information. We therefore defined and discussed a number of the most commonly reported and used financial ratios. We also developed the famous Du Pont identity as a way of analysing financial performance.

3 *Using financial statements.* We described how to establish benchmarks for comparison purposes and discussed some of the types of information that are available. We then examined some of the potential problems that can arise.

After you have studied this chapter, we hope that you have some perspective on the uses and abuses of financial statements. You should also find that your vocabulary of business and financial terms has grown substantially.

Key terms

Du Pont identity *90*
Financial ratios *77, 88*
Global Industry Classification Standard (GICS) *93*

Sources of cash *72*
Statement of cash flows *74*
Uses of cash *72*

Suggested reading

There are many excellent textbooks on financial statement analysis. One that we have found helpful is:

Foster, G. *Financial Statement Analysis*, Prentice-Hall, New Jersey, 1986.

Endnotes

1 Notice that we used cost of goods sold in the top of this ratio (numerator). For some purposes, it might be more useful to use sales instead of costs. For example, if we wanted to know the amount of sales generated per dollar of inventory, then we would replace the cost of goods sold with sales.

2 Notice that we calculated the average as (beginning value + ending value)/2.

3 Here we have implicitly assumed that all sales are credit sales. If they are not, then we would simply use total credit sales in these calculations, not total sales.

4 No, it's not.

Maximise Your Marks!
There are 30 interactive questions on financial statements waiting online for you at www.mhhe.com/au/ross3e. The questions are written with additional feedback for incorrect answers, and text excerpts with page references for follow-up study.

International Articles!
To read more on financial statements and to see current international articles, just go to www.mhhe.com/au/ross3e and click on *PowerWeb Articles* for this chapter.

3.1 · Sources and uses of cash

Consider the following Statement of Financial Position and Statement of Financial Performance for Bigbrover Ltd. Prepare a statement of cash flows for the year ended 30 June 200X+1.

Bigbrover Ltd

Statement of Financial Position as at 30 June 200X+1, 200X ($ in millions)

	200X+1	200X
Assets		
Cash	$ 106	$ 120
Accounts receivable	192	224
Inventory	368	424
Net plant & equipment	5,354	5,228
Total assets	6,020	5,996
Liabilities & shareholders' equity		
Accounts payable	$ 144	$ 124
Notes payable	1,039	1,412
Long-term debt	2,077	1,804
	3,260	3,340
Capital	300	300
Retained earnings	2,460	2,356
Total	6,020	5,996

Bigbrover Ltd

Statement of Financial Performance for the period ended 30 June 200X+1

Sales	$ 3,756
Cost of goods sold	2,453
Depreciation	490
EBIT	813
Interest	613
Taxable income	200
Taxes (30%)	60
Net profit	140
Dividends	36
Retained earnings	104

3.2 · Financial ratios

Based on the Statement of Financial Position and Statement of Financial Performance in the previous problem, calculate the following ratios for 200X+1:

Current ratio
Quick ratio
Inventory turnover
Receivables turnover
Days in inventory
Days in receivables
Debt/Equity ratio
Net interest cover

3.3 · ROE and the Du Pont identity

Calculate the 200X+1 ROE for Bigbrover Ltd and then break down your answer into its component parts using the Du Pont identity.

Answers to self-test problems

3.1 · We've filled in the answers below. Remember, increases in assets and decreases in liabilities indicate that we spent some cash. Decreases in assets and increases in liabilities are ways of getting cash.

Bigbrover Ltd
Statement of Financial Position as at 30 June 200X+1, 200X ($ in millions)

	200X+1	200X	Change
Assets			
Cash	$106	$120	−14
Accounts receivable	192	224	−32
Inventory	368	424	−56
Net plant & equipment	5,354	5,228	126
Total assets	6,020	5,996	24
Liabilities & shareholders' equity			
Accounts payable	$144	$124	20
Notes payable	1,039	1,412	−373
Long-term debt	2,077	1,804	273
	3,260	3,340	−80
Capital	300	300	0
Retained earnings	2,460	2,356	104
Total	6,020	5,996	24

Cash from operations

Sales	$ 3,756
Cost of goods sold	(2,453)
	$ 1,303
Decrease in current liabilities	(353)
Decrease in current assets	88
Interest	(613)
	425

Operating activities

Cash from operations	425
Dividends paid	(36)
Income tax paid	(60)
	329

Investment activities

Acquisition of non-current assets	(616)

Financing activities

Increase in borrowings	273
Net cash flows	(14)
Reconciles to decrease in cash	(14)

Bigbrover used its cash primarily to purchase non-current assets and to pay off short-term debt. The major sources of cash to do this were additional long-term borrowing and, to a larger extent, cash from operations.

3.2 · We've calculated the ratios below based on the ending figures. If you don't remember a definition, refer back to Table 3.7.

Current ratio	$666/$1,183	= 0.56
Quick ratio	$298/$1,183	= 0.25
Inventory turnover	$2,453/$368	= 6.7 times
Receivables turnover	$3,756/$192	= 19.6 times
Days in inventory	365/6.7	= 54.5 days
Days in receivables	365/19.6	= 18.6 days
Debt/Equity ratio	$3,260/$2,760	= 1.18
Net interest cover	$813/$613	= 1.33 times

3.3 · The return on equity is the ratio of net profit to total equity. For Bigbrover, this is $140/$2,760 = 5.07%, which is not outstanding.

Given the Du Pont identity, ROE can be written as:

$$
\begin{aligned}
\text{ROE} &= \text{Profit margin} \times \text{Total asset turnover} \times \text{Equity multiplier} \\
&= \$140/\$3,756 \times \$3,756/\$6,020 \times \$6,020/\$2,760 \\
&= 3.73\% \times 0.624 \times 2.18 \\
&= 5.07\%
\end{aligned}
$$

Notice that return on assets, ROA, is 3.73% × 0.624 = 2.33%.

Questions and problems

1 · Changes in the current ratio

What effect would the following actions have on a firm's current ratio? Assume that net working capital is positive.

a   Inventory is purchased.
b   A supplier is paid.
c   A bank loan is repaid.
d   A long-term debt matures and is paid.
e   A customer pays off an account.
f   Inventory is sold.

2 · Liquidity and ratios

In recent years, Optax Ltd has greatly increased its current ratio. At the same time, the quick ratio has fallen. What has happened? Has the liquidity of the company improved?

3 · Calculating the equity multiplier

A firm has a debt/equity ratio of 0.40. What is its equity multiplier?

4 · ROA and ROE

If a company reports a 5 per cent profit margin, an asset turnover of 2 and a debt/equity ratio of 0.50, what is its ROA? Its ROE?

5 · Calculating the quick ratio

The Annul Company has a current ratio of 3. Its current inventory is $12,000. If current liabilities are $40,000 (including a bank overdraft of $2,000), what is the quick ratio?

6 · Cash flow and asset expenditure

For the year just completed, Council Ltd shows an increase in non-current assets of $220. The depreciation for the year was $75. How much did Council spend on non-current assets? Is this a source or use of cash?

7 · Common-size statements

The Quick Cure Company reports the following Statement of Financial Position information. Prepare a common-size Statement of Financial Position for 200X+1 (just like Table 3.5).

Quick Cure Corporation
Statements of Financial Position as at 31 December 200X and 200X+1 ($ in millions)

	200X	200X+1
Assets		
Current assets		
Cash	$1,482	$1,553
Accounts receivable	3,446	4,229
Inventory	8,402	8,430
Total	13,330	14,212
Non-current assets		
Net plant and equipment	53,408	56,354
Total assets	$66,738	$70,566
Liabilities & owners' equity		
Current liabilities		
Accounts payable	$8,885	$9,003
Notes payable	7,633	8,355
	$16,518	$17,358
Long-term debt	6,764	4,356
Owners' equity		
Capital	9,000	9,000
Retained earnings	34,456	39,852
Total	43,456	48,852
Total liabilities & equity	$66,738	$70,566

8 · Source and uses of cash
Based on the Statements of Financial Position in the previous question, what was the largest use of cash? The largest source of cash?

9 · Calculating ratios
Based on the Statements of Financial Position in question 7, calculate the following ratios for both years.
a   Current ratio
b   Quick ratio
c   Net debt/equity ratio, debt/equity ratio, and equity multiplier

10 · Calculating the average collection period
McGinn's Bakery has receivables of $24,388. Credit sales for the year just ended were $124,890. What is the receivables turnover? The days' sales in receivables? The average collection period?

11 · Calculating inventory turnover
The Sawnee Group has inventory totalling $9,950. Cost of goods sold last year was $74,882. What is the inventory turnover for the year? The days' sales in inventory?

12 · Calculating collection and payables periods
Consider the following information for Nogolf Ltd:

Credit sales	$5,885
Cost of goods sold	4,021
Accounts receivable	880
Accounts payable	642

How long does it take Nogolf to collect on its sales? How long does Nogolf take to pay its suppliers?

13 · Calculating COGS
Unclaimed Ltd has about 73 days' sales in inventory. What is its inventory turnover? If inventories are currently $5,000, what is the cost of goods sold?

14 · Calculating ROA
Sophia Ltd's net profit for the most recent year was $3,299 on sales of $80,320. Total assets were $120,655. What was ROA for Sophia?

15 · More sources and uses
Based only on the following information for Crayfish Pty Ltd, did cash go up or down? By how much? Classify each event as a source or a use of cash.

Decrease in inventory	$100
Decrease in accounts payable	200
Decrease in notes payable	300
Increase in accounts receivable	500

16 · Calculating net interest cover
The Yabby Group's net profit for the most recent year was $1,400. The tax rate was 30 per cent. Total interest paid was $4,000. Finance lease charges were $800. What was the net interest cover?

17 · ROE and the equity multiplier
The Charvil Company has a debt/equity ratio of 1. The return on assets is 10 per cent and total equity is $5 million. What is net profit? What is ROE? What is the equity multiplier?

Some recent financial statement information for Outback Enterprises is listed below. Use this information for Problems 18–22.

Outback Enterprises
Statement of Financial Performance and abbreviated Statement of Financial Position

Sales	$ 1,400
Cost of goods sold	700
Depreciation	200
Earnings before interest and taxes	$ 500
Interest paid	150
Taxable income	$ 350
Taxes	137
Net profit	$ 213
Retained earnings	$ 62
Dividends	$ 151

Assets	200X	200X+1	Liabilities and owners' equity	200X	200X+1
Current assets			Current liabilities		
Cash	$ 200	$ 503	Accounts payable	$ 500	$ 530
Accounts receivable	650	688	Notes payable	543	460
Inventory	1,045	700	Other	214	183
Non-current assets			Long-term debt	1,097	1,184
Net plant and equipment	$1,490	$1,689			
Total assets	$ 3,385	$ 3,580	Owners' equity		
			Capital	590	720
			Retained earnings	441	503
			Total liabilities and equity	$ 3,385	$ 3,580

18 · Ratios
Compute the following ratios for Outback Enterprises:

Short-term solvency ratios
- Current ratio _____
- Quick ratio _____

Asset management ratios
- Total asset turnover _____
- Inventory turnover _____
- Receivables turnover _____

Long-term solvency ratios
- Debt/equity ratio _____
- Equity multiplier _____
- Net interest cover _____

Profitability ratios
- Profit margin _____
- Return on assets _____
- Return on equity _____

19 · Du Pont identity
Construct the Du Pont identity for Outback Enterprises.

20 · Preparing a statement of cash flows
Prepare a statement of cash flows for Outback.

21 · Calculating the internal measure

For how many days could Outback continue to operate if its operations were suspended?

22 · Calculating P/E

Outback has 600 shares outstanding. The price per share is $4.00. What is the P/E ratio? The market-to-book ratio?

23 · Ratios and net profit

A firm has sales of $10 million, assets of $5 million, and a debt/equity ratio of 1.00. If its return on equity is 20 per cent, what is its net profit?

24 · Ratio and ROE

Roadfix Ltd has a net profit of $14,000. There are currently about 10 days' sales in receivables. Total assets are $100,000, total receivables are $4,000, and the debt/equity ratio is 0.40. What is Roadfix's profit margin? Its total asset turnover? Its ROE?

25 · Profit margin

In response to complaints about high prices, a grocery chain runs the following advertising campaign: 'If you pay your child 25 cents to go to buy $10 worth of groceries, then your child makes twice as much on the trip as we do.' You've collected the following information from the grocery chain's financial statements:

Sales	$114 million
Net profit	1.42 million
Total assets	8 million
Total debt	3 million

Evaluate the claim. What is the basis for the statement? Is this claim misleading? Why or why not?

26 · Sources and use of cash

Consider the following Statements of Financial Position for I E T Russ Limited.

	200X–1 ($millions)	200X ($millions)
Assets		
Current assets		
Cash	$210	$215
Accounts receivable	355	310
Inventory	507	328
Total	$1,072	$853
Fixed assets		
Net plant and equipment	$6,085	$6,527
Total assets	$7,157	$7,380
Liabilities and equity		
Liabilities		
Current liabilities		
Accounts payable	$207	$298
Notes payable	1,715	1,427
Total	$1,922	$1,725
Long-term liabilities	$1,987	$2,308
Total assets	$7,157	$7,380
Owners' equity		
Ordinary shares	$1,000	$1,000
Retained earnings	2,248	2,347
Total	$3,248	$3,347
Total liabilities and equity	$7,157	$7,380

What were the sources and uses of cash? Did the company become more liquid during the year? What happened to cash?

27 · Common size statements

I E T Russ would like to have a common sized statement of financial performance. In addition it would like an interpretation of the standardised net profit and to know how much of sales goes into the cost of goods sold. The most recent details that IET can supply are presented below:

Total sales		$4,053m
Cost of records sold		2,780m
Depreciation plant		550m
Earnings before interest and taxes		$723m
Interest paid		502m
Taxable income		$221m
Tax (30%)		66m
Net profit		$155m
Dividends	$55m	
Retained earnings	$100m	

28 · Financial ratios

Using the information supplied in Problems 26 and 27, calculate the following ratios for I E T Russ Limited:

Current ratio
Quick ratio
Inventory turnover
Receivables turnover
Days' sales in inventories
Days' sales in receivables
Total debt ratio
Long-term debt ratio
Times interest covered ratio

CHAPTER 4

Long-term

financial planning and corporate growth

Objective

The aim in this chapter is to explain long-range planning as a means of systematically thinking about the future and anticipating problems before they arrive. Financial planning establishes guidelines for change and growth in a firm. It normally focuses on the 'big picture'. This means that it is concerned with the major elements of a firm's financial and investment policies without examining the individual components of those policies in detail.

Our primary goal in this chapter is to discuss financial planning and to illustrate how the various investment and financing decisions that a firm makes are interrelated. In the chapters ahead, we will examine in much more detail how these decisions are made.

Study tip ▷ Remember that the three major decisions of the firm, the dividend decision, the investment decision and the financing decision, are interrelated. Over any period of time

Cash inflows for the firm = Cash outflows of the firm

Therefore,

New funds raised + Cash from operations = Investments + Dividends.

Where

New funds raised results from a financing decision;
Cash from operations results from a prior investment decision;
Investments is the current investment decision; and
Dividends is the current dividend decision.

If we are to change one of the components in the equation we must balance it by changing another. Now as we progress through the various processes for developing long-term financial plans we must keep in mind the need to balance any changes in our decisions with compensating changes in other parts of the equation.

Introduction ▷

A lack of effective long-range planning is a commonly cited reason for financial distress and failure. There are no magic mirrors, of course, so the best we can hope for is a logical and organised procedure for exploring the unknown. As one member of General Motor's board was heard to say, 'Planning is a process that at best helps the firm avoid stumbling into the future backwards.' In May 2002 Stan Wallis, the chairman of the Australian company Coles Myer, was reported as supporting the CEO John Fletcher's five-year strategy to return the company to strong consistent profits, setting the first year (2001–2002) goal as $400 million. While the numbers were important, it was just as important to know Coles Myer had a five-year strategy.

We first describe what is usually meant by financial planning. For the most part, we talk about long-term planning. Short-term financial planning is discussed in later chapters. We examine what the firm can accomplish by developing a long-term financial plan. To do this, we develop a simple, but very useful, long-range planning technique: the **percentage of sales approach**. We describe how to apply this approach in some simple cases, and we discuss some extensions.

percentage of sales approach

financial planning method in which accounts are varied depending on a firm's predicted sales level

To develop an explicit financial plan, management must establish certain elements of the firm's financial policy. These basic policy elements of financial planning are:

1   *The firm's needed investment in new assets.* This will arise from the investment opportunities that the firm chooses to undertake, and it is the result of the firm's investment decision.

2   *The degree of financial leverage the firm chooses to employ.* This will determine the amount of borrowing the firm will use to finance its investments in real assets. This is the firm's financing decision.

3   *The amount of cash the firm thinks it is necessary and appropriate to pay shareholders.* This is the firm's dividend decision.

4   *The amount of liquidity and working capital the firm needs on an ongoing basis.* This is dependent on the firm's net working capital policy.

As we will see, the decisions that a firm makes in these four areas will directly affect its future profitability, need for external financing and opportunities for growth. The types and amounts of assets that the firm plans on purchasing must be considered along with the firm's ability to raise the necessary capital to fund those investments.

Financial planning forces the corporation to think about goals. A goal frequently espoused by corporations is growth, and almost all firms use growth as a major component of their long-run financial planning. OPSM's stated growth goal has been simple but typical: to expand operations to be the leading optical retailer in Australia and New Zealand.

There are direct connections between the growth that a company can achieve and its financial policy. We show how financial planning models can be used to better understand how growth is achieved and how such models can be used to establish the limits on possible growth.

4.1 What is financial planning?

Financial planning formulates the way financial goals are to be achieved. A financial plan is thus a statement of what is to be done in the future. Most decisions have long lead times, which means they take a long time to implement. In an uncertain world, this requires that decisions be made far in advance of their implementation. If a firm wants to build a factory in 2006, for example, it might have to begin lining up contractors and financing in 2004, or even earlier.

Growth as a financial management goal

Because the subject of growth will be discussed in various places in this chapter, we need to start out with an important warning: growth, by itself, is not an appropriate goal for the financial manager. As we discussed in Chapter 1, the appropriate goal is increasing the market value of the owners' equity. Of course, if a firm is successful in doing this, then growth will usually result.

Growth may thus be a desirable consequence of good decision making, but it is not an end unto itself. We discuss growth simply because growth rates are so commonly used in the planning process. As we will see, growth is a convenient means of summarising various aspects of a firm's financial and investment policies. Also, if we think of growth as growth in the market value of the equity in the firm, then goals of growth and increasing the market value of the equity in the firm are not all that different.

Dimensions of financial planning

It is often useful for planning purposes to think of the future as having a short run and a long run. The short run, in practice, is usually the coming 12 months. We focus our attention on financial planning over the long run, which is usually taken to be the coming two to five years. This is called the **planning horizon**, and it is the first dimension of the planning process that must be established.

In drawing up a financial plan, all of the individual projects and investments that the firm will undertake are combined to determine the total needed investment. In effect, the smaller investment proposals of each operational unit are added up and treated as one big project. This process is called **aggregation**. This is the second dimension of the planning process.

Once the planning horizon and level of aggregation are established, a financial plan would need inputs in the form of alternative sets of assumptions about important variables. For example, suppose a company has two separate divisions: one for consumer products and one for gas turbine engines. The financial planning process might require each division to prepare three alternative business plans for the next three years:

1 *A worst case*. This plan would require making the worst possible assumptions about the company's products and the state of the economy. This kind of disaster planning would emphasise a division's ability to withstand significant economic adversity, and it would require details concerning cost cutting, and even divestiture and liquidation.

2 *A normal case*. This plan would require making most likely assumptions about the company and the economy.

3 *A best case*. Each division would be required to work out a case based on the most optimistic assumptions. It could involve new products and expansion and then would detail the financing needed to fund the expansion.

In this example, business activities are aggregated along divisional lines and the planning horizon is three years.

planning horizon
the long-range period that the financial planning process focuses on, usually the next two to five years

aggregation
process by which smaller investment proposals of each of a firm's operational units are added up and treated as one big project

What can planning accomplish?

Because the company is likely to spend a lot of time examining the different scenarios that will become the basis for the company's financial plan, it seems reasonable to ask what the planning process will accomplish.

Interactions

As we discuss in greater detail below, the financial plan must make explicit the linkages between investment proposals for the different operating activities of the firm and the financing choices available to the firm. In other words, if the firm is planning on expanding and undertaking new investments and projects, where will the financing be obtained to pay for this activity?

Options

The financial plan provides the opportunity for the firm to develop, analyse, and compare many different scenarios in a consistent way. Various investment and financing options can be explored, and their impact on the firm's shareholders can be evaluated. Questions concerning the firm's future lines of business and questions of what financing arrangements are optimal are addressed. Options such as marketing new products or closing plants might be evaluated.

Avoiding surprises

Financial planning should identify what may happen to the firm if different events take place. In particular, it should address what actions the firm will take if things go seriously wrong or, more generally, if assumptions made today about the future are seriously in error. Thus, one of the purposes of financial planning is to avoid surprises and develop contingency plans.

Feasibility and internal consistency

Beyond a general goal of creating value, a firm will normally have many specific goals. Such goals might be couched in terms of market share, return on equity, financial leverage, and so on. At times, the links between different goals and different aspects of a firm's business are difficult to see. Not only does a financial plan make explicit these links, but it also imposes a unified structure for reconciling differing goals and objectives. In other words, financial planning is a way of checking that the goals and plans made with regard to specific areas of a firm's operations are feasible and internally consistent. Conflicting goals will often exist. To generate a coherent plan, goals and objectives will therefore have to be modified, and priorities will have to be established.

For example, one goal a firm might have is 12 per cent growth in unit sales per year. Another goal might be to reduce the firm's total debt/equity ratio from 40 per cent to 20 per cent. Are these two goals compatible? Can they be accomplished simultaneously? Maybe yes, maybe no. As we discuss below, financial planning is a way of finding out just what is possible and, by implication, what is not possible.

The fact that planning forces management to think about goals and to establish priorities is probably the most important result of the process. The future is inherently unknown. What we can do is establish the direction that we want to travel and take some educated guesses at what we will find along the way. If we do a good job, then we won't be caught off guard when the future rolls around.

Concept questions

4.1a *What are the two dimensions of the financial planning process?*
4.1b *Why should firms draw up financial plans?*

4.2 Financial planning models: A first look

Just as companies differ in size and products, the financial planning process will differ from firm to firm. In this section, we discuss some common elements in financial plans and develop a basic model to illustrate these elements.

A financial planning model: The ingredients

Most financial planning models require the user to specify some assumptions about the future. Based on those assumptions, the model generates predicted values for a large number of other variables. Models can vary quite a bit in terms of their complexity, but almost all would have the elements that we discuss below.

Sales forecast

Almost all financial plans require an externally supplied sales forecast. In our models below, for example, the sales forecast will be the 'driver', meaning that the user of the planning model will supply this value and all other values will be based on it. This arrangement would be common for many types of business; planning will focus on projected future sales and the assets and financing needed to support those sales.

Frequently, the sales forecast will be given as growth rate in sales rather than as an explicit sales figure. These two approaches are essentially the same, since we can calculate projected sales once we know the growth rate. Perfect sales forecasts are not possible, of course, because sales depend on the uncertain future state of the economy. To help a firm come up with such projections, some businesses specialise in macroeconomics and industry projections.

As we discuss above, we will frequently be interested in evaluating alternative scenarios, so it isn't necessarily crucial that the sales forecast be accurate. In such cases, our goal is to examine the interplay between investment and financing needs at different possible sales levels, not to pinpoint what we expect to happen.

Pro-forma statements

A financial plan will have a forecasted Statement of Financial Position, a Statement of Financial Performance and a Statement of Cash Flows. These are called pro-forma statements, or pro-formas for short. The phrase pro forma literally means 'as a matter of form'. In our case, this means that the financial statements are the form we use to summarise the different events that are projected for the future. At a minimum, a financial planning model will generate these statements based on projections of key items such as sales.

In the planning models we describe below, the pro-formas are the output from the financial planning model. The user will supply a sales figure, and the model will generate the resulting Statement of Financial Performance and Statement of Financial Position.

Asset requirements

The plan will describe projected capital spending. At a minimum, the projected Statement of Financial Position will contain changes in total non-current assets and net working capital. These changes are effectively the firm's total capital budget. Proposed capital spending in different areas must thus be reconciled with the overall increases contained in the long-range plan.

Financial requirements

The plan will include a section on the financing arrangements that are necessary. This part of the plan should discuss dividend policy and debt policy. Sometimes firms will expect to raise cash by selling new shares or by borrowing. In this case, the plan will have to consider what kinds of securities have to be sold and what methods of issuance are most appropriate. These are subjects we consider in Parts Seven and Eight when we discuss long-term financing, capital structure and dividend policy.

The 'plug'

After the firm has a sales forecast and an estimate of the required spending on assets, some amount of new financing will often be necessary because projected total assets will exceed projected total liabilities and equity. In other words, the Statement of Financial Position will no longer balance.

Since new financing may be necessary to cover all of the projected capital spending, a financial 'plug' variable must be designated. The plug is the designated source or sources of external financing needed to deal with any shortfall (or surplus) in financing and thereby to bring the Statement of Financial Position into balance.

For example, a firm with a great number of investment opportunities and limited cash flow may have to raise new equity. Other firms with few growth opportunities and ample cash flow will have a surplus and thus might pay a large dividend. In the first case, external equity is the plug variable. In the second, the dividend is used.

Economic assumptions

The plan will have to state explicitly the economic environment in which the firm expects to reside over the life of the plan. Among the more important economic assumptions that will have to be made are the level of interest rates and the firm's tax rate.

A simple financial planning model

We can begin our discussion of long-term planning models with a relatively simple example. Vision Ltd's financial statements from the most recent year are as follows:

Vision Ltd
Financial Statements

Financial Performance			Financial Position		
Sales	$ 1,000	Assets	$ 500	Debt	$ 250
Costs	800			Equity	250
	$ 200		$ 500		$ 500

Unless otherwise stated, the financial planners at Vision assume that all variables are tied directly to sales and that current relationships are optimal. This means that all items will grow at exactly the same rate as sales. This is obviously oversimplified; we use this assumption only to make a point.

Suppose that sales increase by 20 per cent, rising from $1,000 to $1,200. Planners would then also forecast a 20 per cent increase in costs, from $800 to $800 $\times$ 1.2 = $960. The pro-forma Financial Performance Statement would be:

Pro-Forma Financial Performance Statement

Sales	$1,200
Costs	960
Profit	$ 240

The assumption that all variables will grow by 20 per cent will enable us to easily construct the pro-forma Financial Position as well:

Pro-Forma Financial Position

Assets	$600 (+100)	Debt	$300 (+50)
		Equity	$300 (+50)
	$600		$600

Notice that we have simply increased every item by 20 per cent. The numbers in parentheses are the dollar changes for the different items.

Now we have to reconcile these two pro-formas. How, for example, can profit be equal to $240 and equity increase by only $50? The answer is that Vision must have paid out the difference of $240 − $50 = $190, possibly as a cash dividend. In this case, dividends are the plug variable.

Suppose Vision does not pay out the $190. With this assumption, Vision's equity will grow to $250 (the starting amount) + $240 (profit) = $490, and debt must be repaid to keep total assets equal to $600.

With $600 in total assets and $490 in equity, debt will have to be $600 − $490 = $110. Since we started with $250 in debt, Vision will have to retire $250 − $110 = $140 in debt. The resulting pro-forma financial position would look like this:

Pro-Forma Financial Position

Assets	$600 (+100)	Debt	$110 (−140)
		Equity	$490 (+240)
	$600 (+100)		$600 (+100)

In this case, debt is the plug variable used to balance out projected total assets and liabilities.

This example shows the interaction between sales growth and financial policy. As sales increase, so do total assets. This occurs because the firm must invest in net working capital and non current assets to support higher sales levels. Since assets are growing, total liabilities and equity, the right-hand side of the Financial Position Statement, will grow as well.

The thing to notice from our simple example is that the way the liabilities and owners' equity change depends on the firm's financing policy and its dividend policy. The growth in assets requires that the firm decide on how to finance that growth. This is strictly a managerial decision. Also, in our example the firm needed no outside funds. This won't usually be the case, so we explore a more detailed situation in the next section.

Concept questions

4.2a *What are the basic components of a financial plan?*
4.2b *Why is it necessary to designate a plug in a financial planning model?*

 ## The percentage of sales approach

In the previous section, we described a simple planning model in which every item increased at the same rate as sales. This may be a reasonable assumption for some elements. For others, such as long-term borrowing, it probably is not, because the amount of long-term borrowing is something set by management, and it does not necessarily relate directly to the level of sales.

In this section, we describe an extended version of our simple model above. The basic idea is to separate the components of the Statement of Financial Performance and Statement of Financial Position into two groups, those that do vary directly with sales and those that do not. Given a sales forecast, we will then be able to calculate how much financing the firm will need to support the predicted sales level.

An illustration of the percentage of sales approach

The financial planning model we describe next is based on the percentage of sales approach. Our goal here is to develop a quick and practical way of generating pro-forma statements. We defer discussion of some 'bells and whistles' to a later section.

The Financial Performance Statement

We start out with the most recent Statement of Financial Performance for Future Ltd as shown in Table 4.1. Notice that we have still simplified things by including costs, depreciation, and interest in a single cost figure. We separate these out in a later section.

TABLE 4.1

Future Ltd	
Financial Performance Statement	
Sales	$1,000
Costs	800
Taxable income	200
Taxes (30%)	60
Net profit	140
Retained earnings	$ 112
Dividends	$ 28

Future has projected a 25 per cent increase in sales for the coming year, so we are anticipating sales of $1,000 × 1.25 = $1,250. To generate a pro-forma Financial Performance Statement, we assume that total costs will continue to run at $800/$1,000 = 80% of sales. With this assumption, Future's pro-forma Financial Performance Statement is as shown in Table 4.2. The effect here of assuming that costs are a constant percentage of sales is to assume that the profit margin is constant. To check this, notice that the profit margin was $140/$1,000 = 14%. In our pro-forma, the profit margin is $175/$1,250 = 14%; so it is unchanged.

TABLE 4.2

Future Ltd	
Pro-Forma Financial Performance Statement	
Sales (projected)	$1,250
Costs (80% of sales)	1,000
Taxable income	$ 250
Taxes (30%)	75
Net profit	$ 175

Next, we need to project the dividend payment. This amount is up to Future's management. We will assume that Future has a policy of paying out a constant fraction of net profit in the form of a cash dividend. From the most recent year, the **dividend payout ratio** was:

$$\text{Dividend payout ratio} = \text{Cash dividends/Net profit} \qquad (4.1)$$
$$= \$28/\$140 = 20\%$$

We can also calculate the ratio of retained earnings to net profit as:

$$\text{Retained earnings/Net profit} = \$112/\$140 = 80\%$$

This ratio is called the **retention ratio** and it is equal to 1 minus the dividend payout ratio, because everything not paid out is retained. Assuming that the payout and retention ratios are constant, the projected dividends and addition to retained earnings will be:

$$\text{Projected addition to retained earnings} = \$175 \times 80\% = \$140$$
$$\text{Projected dividends paid to shareholders} = \$175 \times 20\% = \underline{\quad 35}$$
$$\underline{\underline{\$175}}$$

The Financial Position Statement

To generate a pro-forma financial position statement, we start with the most recent statement:

TABLE 4.3

Future Ltd

Statement of Financial Position

Assets	($)	(%)	Liabilities & owners' equity	($)	(%)
Current assets			Current liabilities		
Cash	160	16%	Accounts payable	300	30%
Accounts receivable	440	44	Notes payable	100	n/a
Inventory	600	60			
Total	$1,200	120%	Total	$ 400	n/a
Non-current assets					
Net plant & equipment	$1,800	180%	Long-term debt	$ 800	n/a
			Shareholders' equity		
			Issued capital	$800	n/a
			Retained earnings	$1,000	n/a
			Total	$1,800	n/a
Total assets	$3,000	300%	Total liabilities & equity	$3,000	n/a

On our financial position statement, we assume that some of the items vary directly with sales while others do not. For those items that do vary with sales, we express each as a percentage of sales for the year just completed. When an item does not vary directly with sales, we write 'n/a' for 'not applicable'.

For example, on the asset side, inventory is equal to 60 per cent of sales ($600/$1,000) for the year just ended. We assume that this percentage applies to the coming year, so for each

dividend payout ratio

amount of cash paid out to shareholders divided by net profit

retention ratio

retained earnings divided by net profit. Also called the ploughback ratio

$1 increase in sales, inventory will rise by $0.60. More generally, the ratio of total assets to sales for the year just ended is $3,000/$1,000 = 3, or 300%.

This ratio of total assets to sales is sometimes called the **capital intensity ratio**. It tells us the assets needed to generate $1 in sales; so the higher the ratio is, the more capital intensive is the firm. Notice also that this ratio is just the reciprocal of the total asset turnover ratio we defined in the last chapter.

For Future, assuming this ratio is constant, it takes $3 in total assets to generate $1 in sales (apparently Future is in a relatively capital intensive business). Therefore, if sales are to increase by $100, then Future will have to increase total assets by three times this amount, or $300.

On the liability side of the Statement of Financial Position, we show accounts payable varying with sales. The reason is that we expect to place more orders with our suppliers as sales volume increases, so payables will change 'spontaneously' with sales. Notes payable, on the other hand, represent short-term debt such as bank borrowing. These will not vary unless we take specific actions to change the amount, so we mark them as 'n/a'.

Similarly, we use 'n/a' for long-term debt because it won't automatically change with sales. The same is true for issued capital. The last item on the right-hand side, retained earnings, will vary with sales, but it won't be a simple percentage of sales. Instead, we will explicitly calculate the change in retained earnings based on our projected net profit and dividends.

We can now construct a partial pro-forma Statement of Financial Position for Future. We do this by using the percentages we calculated above wherever possible to calculate the projected amounts. For example, non current assets are 180 per cent of sales; so, with a new sales level of $1,250, the non current asset amount will be 1.80 × $1,250 = $2,250, an increase of $2,250 − $1,800 = $450 in plant and equipment. Importantly, for those items that don't vary directly with sales, we initially assume no change and simply write in the original amounts. The result is the following:

TABLE 4.4

Future Ltd

Partial Pro-Forma Statement of Financial Position

Assets	Present year	Change from previous year	Liabilities & owners' equity	Present year	Change from previous year
Current assets			Current liabilities		
Cash	$ 200	$ 40	Accounts payable	$ 375	$ 75
Accounts receivable	550	110	Notes payable	100	0
Inventory	750	150			
Total	$1500	$ 300	Total	$ 475	$ 75
Non-current assets					
Net plant & equipment	$2250	$ 450	Long-term debt	800	0
			Shareholders' equity		
			Issued capital	800	0
			Retained earnings	$1140	140
			Total	$1940	$ 140
Total assets	$3750	$ 750	Total liabilities & owners' equity	$3215	$ 215
			External financing needed	$ 535	$ 535

Notice that the change in retained earnings is equal to the $140 addition to retained earnings that we calculated above.

Inspecting our pro-forma financial position statement, we notice that assets are projected to increase by $750. However, without additional financing, liabilities and equity will only increase by $215, leaving a shortfall of $750 − $215 = $535. We label this amount external financing needed (EFN).

A particular scenario

Our financial planning model now reminds us of one of those good news/bad news jokes. The good news is that we're projecting a 25 per cent increase in sales. The bad news is that this isn't going to happen unless we can somehow raise $535 in new financing.

This is a good example of how the planning process can point out problems and potential conflicts. If, for example, Future had a goal of not borrowing any additional funds and not selling any new equity, then a 25 per cent increase in sales would probably not be feasible.

If we take the need for $535 in new financing as given, Future has three possible sources: short-term borrowing, long-term borrowing and new equity. The choice of a combination among these three is up to management; we will illustrate only one of the many possibilities.

Suppose that Future decides to borrow the needed funds. In this case, they might choose to borrow some short-term and some long-term. For example, current assets increased by $300 while current liabilities rose by only $75. Future could borrow $300 − $75 = $225 in short-term notes payable and leave total net working capital unchanged. With $535 needed, the Remaining $535 − $225 = $310 would have to come from long-term debt. Table 4.5 shows the completed pro-forma Statement of Financial Position for Future.

TABLE 4.5

Future Ltd

Pro-Forma Statement of Financial Position

	Present year	Change from previous year		Present year	Change from previous year
Assets			**Liabilities & owners' equity**		
Current assets			Current liabilities		
Cash	$ 200	$ 40	Accounts payable	$ 375	$ 75
Accounts receivable	550	110	Notes payable	325	225
Inventory	750	150			
Total	$1,500	$ 300	Total	$700	$ 300
Non-current assets					
Net plant & equipment	$2,250	$ 450	Long-term debt	$ 1110	$ 310
			Shareholders' equity		
			Issued capital	800	0
			Retained earnings	1,140	140
			Total	$1,940	$ 140
Total assets	$3,750	$ 750	Total liabilities & equity	$3,750	$ 750

We have used a combination of short- and long-term debt as the plug here, but we emphasise that this is just one possible strategy; it is not necessarily the best one by any means. There are many other scenarios that we could (and should) investigate.

Now that we have finished our financial position statement, we have all of the projected sources and uses of cash. We could finish off our pro-formas by drawing up the projected statement of cash flows along the lines discussed in Chapter 3. We will leave this and instead investigate an important alternative scenario.

An alternative scenario

The assumption that assets are a fixed percentage of sales is convenient, but it may not be suitable in many cases. For example, we effectively assumed that Future was using its non current assets at 100 per cent of capacity because any increase in sales led to an increase in non-current assets. For most businesses, there would be some slack or excess capacity, and production could be increased by, perhaps, running an extra shift.

If we assume that Future is only operating at 70 per cent of capacity, then the need for external funds will be quite different. When we say '70 per cent of capacity', we mean that the current sales level is 70 per cent of the full capacity sales level:

$$\text{Current sales} = \$1{,}000 \qquad = 0.70 \times \text{Full capacity sales}$$
$$\text{Full capacity sales} = \$1{,}000/0.70 = \$1{,}429$$

This tells us that sales could increase by almost 43 per cent—from $1,000 to $1,429—before any new non-current assets were needed.

In our previous scenario, we assumed that it would be necessary to add $450 in non-current assets. In the current scenario, no spending on non-current assets is needed, because sales are projected to rise to $1,250, which is substantially less than the $1,429 full capacity level.

As a result, our original estimate of $535 in external funds needed is too high. We estimated that $450 in net new non-current assets would be needed. Instead, no spending on new net non-current assets is necessary. Thus, if we are currently operating at 70 per cent capacity, then we only need $535 − $450 = $85 in external funds. The excess capacity thus makes a considerable difference in our projections.

EXAMPLE
4.1

EFN and capacity usage

Suppose that Future were operating at 90 per cent capacity. What would sales be at full capacity? What is the capital intensity ratio at full capacity? What is EFN in this case?

Full capacity sales would be $1,000/0.90 = $1,111. From Table 4.3, non-current assets are $1,800. At full capacity, the ratio of non-current assets to sales is thus:

$$\text{Non current assets/Full capacity sales} = \$1{,}800/\$1{,}111$$
$$= 1.62$$

This tells us that we need $1.62 in non-current assets for every $1 in sales once we reach full capacity. At the projected sales level of $1,250, then, we need $1,250 × 1.62 = $2,025 in non-current assets. Compared to the $2,250 we originally projected, this is $225 less, so EFN is $535 − $225 = $310.

Current assets would still be $1,500, so total assets would be $1,500 + $2,025 = $3,525. The capital intensity ratio would thus be $3,525/$1,250 = 2.82, less than our original value of 3 because of the excess capacity.

These alternative scenarios illustrate that it is inappropriate to blindly manipulate financial statement information in the planning process. The results depend critically on the assumptions made about the relationships between sales and asset needs. We return to this point below.

Concept questions

4.3a *What is the basic idea behind the percentage of sales approach?*

4.3b *Unless it is modified, what does the percentage of sales approach assume about non-current asset capacity usage?*

4.4 External financing and growth

External financing needed and growth are obviously related. All other things being the same, the higher the rate of growth in sales or assets, the greater will be the need for external financing. In the previous section, we took a growth rate as given, and then we determined the amount of external financing needed to support that growth. In this section, we turn things around a bit. We will take the firm's financial policy as given and then examine the relationship between that financial policy and the firm's ability to finance new investments and thereby grow.

Once again, we emphasise that we are focusing on growth not because growth is an appropriate goal; instead, for our purposes, growth is simply a convenient means of examining the interactions between investment and financing decisions. In effect, we assume that the use of growth as a basis for planning is just a reflection of the very high level of aggregation used in the planning process.

EFN and growth

The first thing we need to do is establish the relationship between EFN and growth. To do this, we introduce the following simplified Financial Performance and Financial Position Statements for the Control Company:

TABLE 4.6

Control Company Financial Performance and Financial Position Statements

Statement of Financial Performance

Sales	$ 500
Costs	400
Taxable income	$ 100
Taxes (30%)	30
Net profit	$ 70

Retained earnings	$25	
Dividends	45	

Statement of Financial Position

Assets	($)	(% of sales)	Liabilities & equity	($)	(% of sales)
Current assets	$ 400	80%	Total debt	$450	n/a
Non-current assets	600	120	Owners' equity	550	n/a
Total assets	$1,000	200%		$1,000	n/a

Notice that we have simplified the financial position statement by combining current and non-current liabilities into a single total debt figure. Effectively, we are assuming that none of the current liabilities varies spontaneously with sales. This assumption isn't as restrictive as it sounds. If any current liabilities (such as accounts payable) vary with sales, we can assume that they have been netted out in current assets. Also, we continue to combine depreciation, interest, and costs on the Statement of Financial Performance.

The following symbols will be useful:

$$
\begin{aligned}
S &= \text{Previous year's sales} &&= \$500 \\
A &= \text{Total assets} &&= \$1,000 \\
D &= \text{Total debt} &&= \$450 \\
E &= \text{Total equity} &&= \$550
\end{aligned}
$$

In addition, based on our earlier discussions of financial ratios, we can calculate the following:

$$
\begin{aligned}
p &= \text{profit margin} &&= \$70/\$500 &&= 14\% \\
R &= \text{retention ratio} &&= \$25/\$70 &&= 36\% \\
\text{ROA} &= \text{return on assets} &&= \$70/\$1,000 &&= 7\% \\
\text{ROE} &= \text{return on equity} &&= \$70/\$550 &&= 12.7\% \\
D/E &= \text{debt/equity ratio} &&= \$450/\$550 &&= 0.82
\end{aligned}
$$

Suppose the Control Company is forecasting next year's sales level at $600, a $100 increase. The capital intensity ratio is $1,000/$500 = 2, so assets will need to rise by 2 × $100 = $200 (assuming full capacity usage). Notice that the percentage increase in sales is $100/$500 = 20%. The percentage increase in assets is also 20 per cent: $200/$1,000 = 20%. As this illustrates, assuming a constant capital intensity ratio, the increase in total assets will simply be $A \times g$, where g is growth rate in sales:

$$
\begin{aligned}
\text{Increase in total assets} &= A \times g \\
&= \$1,000 \times 20\% \\
&= \$200
\end{aligned}
$$

In other words, the growth rate in sales can also be interpreted as the rate of increase in the firm's total assets.

Some of the financing necessary to cover the increase in total assets comes from internally generated funds and shows up in the form of the addition to retained earnings. This amount is equal to net profit multiplied by the retention ratio, R. Projected net profit is equal to the profit margin, p, multiplied by projected sales, $S \times (1 + g)$. The projected addition to retained earnings for Control can thus be written as:

$$
\begin{aligned}
\text{Addition to retained earnings} &= p(S)R \times (1 + g) \\
&= 0.14(\$500)(36\%) \times 1.20 \\
&= \$25.2 \times 1.20 \\
&= \$30
\end{aligned}
$$

Notice that this is equal to last year's addition to retained earnings, $25, multiplied by $(1 + g)$.

Putting this information together, we need $A \times g = \$200$ in new financing. We will generate $p(S)R \times (1 + g) = \$30$ internally, so the difference is what we need to raise. In other words, we find that EFN can be written as:

$$\text{EFN} = \text{Increase in total assets} - \text{Addition to retained earnings} \quad (4.2)$$
$$= A(g) - p(S)R \times (1 + g)$$

For Control, this works out to be:

$$\text{EFN} = \$1,000(0.20) - 0.14(\$500)36\% \times 1.20$$
$$= \$200 - \$30$$
$$= \$170$$

We can check that this is correct by filling in a pro-forma balance sheet as follows:

Control Company
Statement of Financial Position

Assets	($)	Liabilities & equity	($)
Current assets	$ 480	Long-term debt	$ 450
Non-current assets	720	Owners' equity	580
Total assets	$ 1,200	Total liabilities & equity	$ 1,030
		External funds needed	$ 170

As we calculated, Control needs to raise $170.

Looking at our equation for EFN, we see that EFN depends directly on g. Rearranging things to highlight this relationship, we get:

$$\text{EFN} = -p(S)R + [A - p(S)R] \times g \quad (4.3)$$

Plugging in the numbers for Control, the relationship between EFN and g is:

$$\text{EFN} = -0.14(\$500)(36\%) + [\$1,000 - 0.14(\$500)(36\%)] \times g$$
$$= -\$25 + \$975 \times g$$

Notice that this is the equation of a straight line with a vertical intercept of −$25 and a slope of $975.

The relationship between growth and EFN is illustrated in Figure 4.1. The y-axis intercept of our line, −$25, is equal to last year's addition to retained earnings. This makes sense because, if the growth in sales is zero, then retained earnings will be $25, just as it was last year. Furthermore, with no growth, no net investment in assets is needed, so we run a surplus equal to the addition to retained earnings, which is why we have a negative sign.

The slope of the line in Figure 4.1 tells us that for every 0.01 (1% in sales growth, we need an additional $975 × 0.01 = $9.75 in external financing to support that growth.

Looking at Figure 4.1, there is one growth rate of obvious interest. What growth rate can we achieve with no external financing at all? This growth rate corresponds to the point where our line crosses the horizontal axis, that is, the point where EFN is zero. We can easily calculate this rate by setting EFN equal to zero:

$$\text{EFN} = 0 = -\$25 + \$975 \times g$$

For Control, this growth rate works out to be:

$$g = \$25/\$975 = 2.56\%$$

Control can therefore grow at a 2.56 per cent rate before any external financing at all is required.

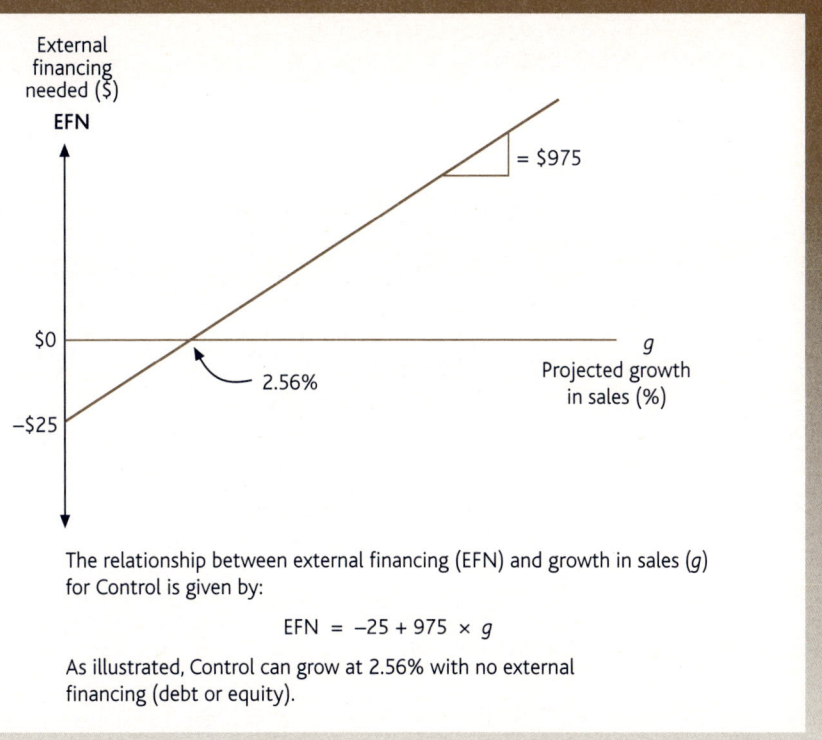

FIGURE
4.1

External financing needed and growth in sales for Control Company

The relationship between external financing (EFN) and growth in sales (g) for Control is given by:

$$EFN = -25 + 975 \times g$$

As illustrated, Control can grow at 2.56% with no external financing (debt or equity).

Financial policy and growth

If Control grows at 2.56 per cent or so every year, its equity would steadily increase due to additions to retained earnings. Its total debt would not increase because no external financing would be used. As a result, the total debt/equity ratio would decline.

Suppose that Control, for whatever reason, does not wish to sell any new equity. As we discuss in later chapters, one possible reason for this is simply that new equity sales can be very expensive. Alternatively, the current owners may not wish to bring in new owners or contribute additional equity.

In addition, we will assume that Control wishes to maintain its current debt/equity ratio. To be more specific, Control regards its current debt policy as optimal. We discuss why a particular mixture of debt and equity might be better than any other in later chapters. For now, we say that Control has a fixed **debt capacity** relative to total equity. If the total debt/equity ratio declines, then Control has excess debt capacity and can comfortably borrow additional funds.

debt capacity
the ability to borrow to increase firm value

Assuming that Control does borrow up to its debt capacity, what growth rate can be achieved? The answer is given by the following simple expression:

$$g^* = (ROE \times R)/(1 - ROE \times R) \qquad (4.4)$$

This growth rate is called the firm's **sustainable growth rate** (SGR).

sustainable growth rate
the growth rate a firm can maintain given its debt capacity, ROE, and retention ratio

For example, for the Control Company, we already know that the ROE is 12.7 per cent and the retention ratio, R, is 36 per cent. The sustainable growth rate is thus:

$$
\begin{aligned}
g^* &= (\text{ROE} \times R)/(1 - \text{ROE} \times R) \\
&= 0.127(0.36)/[1 - 0.127(0.36)] \\
&= 0.046/0.954 \\
&= 0.0482 \\
&= 4.82\%
\end{aligned}
$$

This tells us that Control can increase its sales and assets at a rate of 4.82 per cent per year without selling any additional equity and without changing its debt ratio or payout ratio. If a growth rate in excess of this is desired or predicted, then something will have to give.

To better see that the SGR is 4.82 per cent (and to check our answer), we can fill out the pro-forma financial statements assuming that Control's sales increase at exactly the SGR. What we seek to do is to verify that if Control's sales do grow at 4.82 per cent, all needed financing can be obtained without the need to sell new equity, and, at the same time, the total debt/equity ratio can be maintained at its current level of 0.82.

To get started, sales will increase from $500 to $500 × (1 + 0.0482) = $524. Assuming, as before, that costs are proportional to sales, the profit and loss account would be:

Control Company
Pro-Forma Statement of Financial Performance

Sales	$ 524
Costs (80% of sales)	419
Taxable income	$ 105
Taxes (30%)	32
Net profit	$ 73

Control Company
Pro-Forma Statement of Financial Position

Assets	($)	(% of sales)	Liabilities & equity	($)	(% of sales)
Current assets	$ 419	80%	Long-term debt	$ 450	n/a
Non-current assets	629	120%	Owners' equity	576	n/a
Total assets	1,048	200%	Total liabilities & equity	1,026	n/a
			External funds needed	$ 22	

Given that the retention ratio, R, stays at 36%, the addition to retained earnings will be $73 × 36% = $26, and the dividend paid will be $73 − $26 = $47.

We fill out the pro-forma Statement of Financial Position just as we did above. Note that, in this case, owner's equity will rise from $550 to $576 because the addition to retained earnings is $26.

As illustrated, EFN is $22. If Control borrows this amount, then total debt will rise to $450 + $22 = $472. The debt/equity ratio will therefore be $472/$576 = 0.82 as desired, thereby verifying our earlier calculations. At any other growth rate, something would have to change.

Determinants of growth

In the last chapter, we saw that the return on equity could be decomposed into its various components using the Du Pont identity. Since ROE appears prominently in the determination of the SGR, the factors that are important in determining ROE are also important determinants of growth. To see this, recall that from the Du Pont identity, ROE can be written as:

$$\text{ROE} = \text{Profit margin} \times \text{Total asset turnover} \times \text{Equity multiplier}$$

Using our current symbols for these ratios, ROE is:[1]

$$\text{ROE} = p(S/A)(1 + D/E)$$

If we substitute this into our expression for g^*, the sustainable growth rate (SGR), just above, then we see that the SGR can be written in greater detail as:

$$g^* = \frac{p(S/A)(1 + D/E) \times R}{1 - p(S/A)(1 + D/E) \times R} \qquad (4.5)$$

Writing the SGR out in this way makes it look a little complicated, but it does highlight the various factors that are important in determining the ability of a firm to grow.

If we examine our expression for the SGR, we see that growth depends on the following four factors:

1 **Profit margin**. An increase in profit margin, p, will increase the firm's ability to generate funds internally and thereby increase its sustainable growth.
2 **Dividend policy**. A decrease in the percentage of net profit paid out as dividends will increase the retention ratio, R. This increases internally generated equity and thus increases sustainable growth.
3 **Financial policy**. An increase in the debt/equity ratio, D/E, increases the firm's financial leverage. Since this makes additional debt financing available, it increases the sustainable growth rate.
4 **Total asset turnover**. An increase in the firm's total asset turnover, S/A, increases the sales generated for each dollar in assets. This decreases the firm's need for new assets as sales grow and thereby increases the sustainable growth rate. Notice that increasing total asset turnover is the same thing as decreasing capital intensity.

The sustainable growth rate is a very useful planning number. What it illustrates is the explicit relationship between the firm's four major areas of concern: its operating efficiency as measured by p, its asset use efficiency as measured by S/A, its dividend policy as measured by R, and its financial policy as measured by D/E.

Given values for all four of these, there is only one growth rate that can be achieved. This is an important point, so it bears restating:

> If a firm does not wish to sell new equity, and its profit margin, dividend policy, financial policy and total asset turnover (or capital intensity) are all fixed, then there is only one possible growth rate.

As we described early in this chapter, one of the primary benefits of financial planning is that it ensures internal consistency among the firm's various goals. The sustainable growth rate captures this element nicely. Also, we now see how a financial planning model can be used to test the feasibility of a planned growth rate. If sales are to grow at a rate higher than the sustainable growth rate, the firm must increase profit margins, increase total asset turnover, increase financial leverage, increase earnings retention, or sell new shares.

EXAMPLE
4.2 ■ **Sustainable growth**

Horizons Ltd has a total debt/equity ratio of 0.5, a profit margin of 3 per cent, a dividend payout of 40 per cent, and a capital intensity ratio of 1. What is its sustainable growth rate? If Horizons desires a 10 per cent SGR and plans to achieve this goal by improving profit margins, what would you think?

The sustainable growth rate is:

$$g^* = \frac{0.03(1)(1 + 0.5)(1 - 0.40)}{[1 - 0.03(1)(1 + 0.5)(1 - 0.40)]}$$

$$= 2.77\%$$

To achieve a 10 per cent growth rate, the profit margin will have to rise. To see this, assume that g^* is equal to 10 per cent and then solve for p:

$$0.10 = \frac{p(1)(1.5)(0.6)}{[1 - p(1.5)(0.6)]} = \frac{0.9p}{(1 - 0.9p)}$$

$$p = 1/9.9 = 10.1\%$$

For the plan to succeed, the necessary increase in profit margin is substantial, from roughly 3 per cent to about 10 per cent. This may not be feasible.

Concept questions

4.4a *What are the determinants of growth?*
4.4b *How is a firm's sustainable growth related to its accounting return on equity (ROE)?*

In their own words

Robert C. Higgins

Robert C. Higgins* on sustainable growth

Most financial officers know intuitively that it takes money to make money. Rapid sales growth requires increased assets in the form of accounts receivable, inventory, and fixed plant, which, in turn, require money to pay for assets. They also know that if their company does not have the money when needed, it can literally 'grow broke'. The sustainable growth equation states these intuitive truths explicitly.

Sustainable growth is often used by bankers and other external analysts to assess a company's creditworthiness. They are aided in this exercise by several sophisticated computer software packages that provide detailed analyses of the company's past financial performance, including its annual sustainable growth rate.

Bankers use this information in several ways. Quick comparison of a company's actual growth rate to its sustainable rate tells the banker what issues will be at the top of management's financial agenda. If actual growth consistently exceeds sustainable growth, management's problem will be where to get the cash to finance growth. The banker thus can anticipate interest in loan products. Conversely, if sustainable growth consistently exceeds actual, the banker had best be prepared to talk about investment products, because management's problem will be what to do with all the cash that keeps piling up in the till.

Bankers also find the sustainable growth equation useful for explaining to financially inexperienced small business owners and overly optimistic entrepreneurs that, for the long-run viability of their business, it is necessary to keep growth and profitability in proper balance.

Finally, comparison of actual to sustainable growth rates helps a banker understand why a loan applicant needs money and for how long the need might continue. In one instance, a loan applicant requested $100,000 to pay off several insistent suppliers and promised to repay in a few months when he collected some accounts receivable that were coming due. A sustainable growth analysis revealed that the firm had been growing at four to six times its sustainable growth rate and that this pattern was likely to continue in the foreseeable future. This alerted the banker to the fact that impatient suppliers were only a symptom of the much more fundamental disease of overly rapid growth, and that a $100,000 loan would likely prove to be only the downpayment on a much larger, multiyear commitment.

* Robert C. Higgins is Professor of Finance at the University of Washington. He pioneered the use of sustainable growth as a tool for financial analysis.

4.5 ▪ Some caveats of financial planning models

Financial planning models do not always ask the right questions. A primary reason is that they tend to rely on accounting relationships and not financial relationships. In particular, the three basic elements of firm value tend to get left out, namely, cash flow size, risk and timing.

Because of this, financial planning models sometimes do not produce output that gives the user many meaningful clues about what strategies will lead to increases in value. Instead, they divert the user's attention to questions concerning the association of, say, the debt/equity ratio and firm growth.

The financial model we used for the Control Company was simple; in fact, too simple. Our model, like many in use today, is really an accounting statement generator at heart. Such models are useful for pointing out inconsistencies and reminding us of financial needs, but they offer very little guidance concerning what to do about these problems.

In closing our discussion, we should add that financial planning is an iterative process. Plans are created, examined and modified over and over. The final plan will be a negotiated result between all the different parties to the process.

As such, the final plan will implicitly contain different goals in different areas and also satisfy many constraints. For this reason, such a plan need not be a dispassionate assessment of what we think the future will bring; it may instead be a means of reconciling the planned activities of different groups and a way of setting common goals for the future.

Concept questions

4.5a *What are some important elements that are often missing in financial planning models?*
4.5b *Why do we say that planning is an iterative process?*

■ 4.6 ■ **Summary and conclusions**

Financial planning forces the firm to think about the future. We have examined a number of features of the planning process. We described what financial planning can accomplish and the components of a financial model. We went on to develop the relationship between growth and financing needs, and discussed how a financial planning model is useful in exploring that relationship.

Corporate financial planning should not become a purely mechanical activity. If it does, it will probably focus on the wrong things. In particular, plans are all too often formulated in terms of a growth target with no explicit link to value creation, and they are frequently overly concerned with accounting statements. Nevertheless, the alternative to financial planning is 'stumbling into the future'.

Key terms

Aggregation *108*   Dividend payout ratio *114*   Retention ratio or ploughback ratio *114*
Capital intensity ratio *115*   Percentage of sales approach *107*   Sustainable growth rate *121*
Debt capacity *121*   Planning horizon *108*

Suggested readings

Approaches to building a financial planning model are contained in:

Carleton, W.T., Downes, D.H. and Dick, C.L., Jr. 'Financial Policy Models: Theory and Practice', *Journal of Financial and Quantitative Analysis*, Vol. 8, 1973, pp. 691–709.

Myers, S.C. and Pogue, G.A. 'A Programming Approach to Corporate Financial Management', *Journal of Finance*, Vol. 29, May 1974, pp. 579–99.

Warren, J.M. and Shelton, J.R. 'A Simultaneous-Equation Approach to Financial Planning', *Journal of Finance*, Vol. 26, December 1971, pp. 1123–42.

Sustainable growth is discussed in:

Higgins, R.C. 'Sustainable Growth Under Inflation', *Financial Management*, 10, Autumn 1981.

For a critical discussion of sustainable growth, see:

Rappaport, A. *Creating Shareholder Value: The New Standard for Business Performance*, The Free Press, New York, 1986.

Endnote

1 Remember that the equity multiplier is the same as 1 plus the debt/equity ratio.

Maximise Your Marks!
There are 30 interactive questions on long-term financial planning and corporate growth waiting online for you at www.mhhe.com/au/ross3e. The questions are written with additional feedback for incorrect answers, and text excerpts with page references for follow-up study.

International Articles!
To read more on long-term financial planning and corporate growth and to see current international articles, just go to www.mhhe.com/au/ross3e and click on *PowerWeb Articles* for this chapter.

Chapter review problems and self-test

4.1 · Calculating EFN

Based on the following information for the Assist Company, what is EFN if sales are predicted to grow by 20 per cent?

Assist Company
Financial Statements

Financial Performance Statement		Financial Position Statement			
Sales	$ 2,750	Current assets	$ 600	Long-term debt	$ 200
Cost of sales	2,400	Non-current assets	800	Equity	1,200
Tax (30%)	105				
Net profit	$ 245	Total	$ 1,400	Total	$ 1,400
Dividends	56				

4.2 · EFN and capacity use

Based on the information in Problem 4.1, what is EFN, assuming 75 per cent capacity usage for net non-current assets? Assuming 90 per cent capacity?

4.3 · Sustainable growth

Based on the information in Problem 4.1, what growth rate can Assist maintain if no external financing is used? What is the sustainable growth rate?

Answers to self-test problems

4.1 · EFN can be calculated easily as:

$$EFN = -p(S)R + [A - p(S)R] \times g \text{ (This is equation 4.3. Alternatively equation 4.2 could be used.)}$$

Where $p = \$245/\$2750 = 0.08909 = 8.909\%$

$R = 1 - \$56/\$245 = 0.77$

$= -0.08909 \times \$2,750 \times 0.77 + (\$1,400 - 0.08909(\$2750)(0.77) \times g$

$= -\$188.6 + (\$1,400 - \$188.6) \times 0.2$

$= -\$188.6 + \$1211.4 (0.2)$

$= -\$188.6 + \$242.28$

$= \$53.68$

We can check this by preparing the pro-forma statements using the percentage of sales approach. Note that sales are forecast to be $\$2,750 \times 1.2 = \$3,300$.

Assist Company
Financial Statements
Financial Performance Statement

Sales	$3,300	forecast
Cost of sales	2,880	87.27% of sales
Tax (30%)	126	
Net profit	$ 294	
Dividends	67.62	23% of net profit

Financial Position Statement

Current assets	$ 720	21.81% of sales	Long-term debt	$ 200.00
Non-current assets	960	29.09% of sales	Equity	1,426.38
Total	$1,680	50.90% of sales	Total	$1,626.38

4.2 · Full capacity sales are equal to current sales divided by the capacity utilisation. At 75 per cent of capacity:

$\$2,750 = 0.75 \times$ full capacity sales

$\$3,667 =$ full capacity sales

With a sales level of $3,300, no new non-current assets will be needed, so our earlier estimate is too high. We estimated an increase in non-current assets of $960 - $800 = $160. The new EFN would thus be $53.62 - $160 = $106.38, a surplus. No external financing is needed in this case.

At 90 per cent capacity, full capacity sales are $3,056. The ratio of non-current assets to full capacity sales is thus $800/$3,056 = 0.262. At a sales level of $3,300, we will thus need $3,300 × 0.262 = $864 in non-current assets, an increase of $64. This is $160 - $64 = $96 less than we originally predicted, so the EFN is now $53.62 - $96 = -$42.38, a small surplus. No additional financing is needed.

4.3 · **Assist** retains $R = (1 - 0.23) = 0.77$ of net profit. Return on equity for **Assist** is $245/$1,200 = 20.42%, so we can calculate the sustainable growth rate as $(ROE \times R)/(1 - ROE \times R) = (0.2042 \times 0.77)/(1 - 0.2042 \times 0.77) = 0.1572/0.8428 = 0.1865 = 18.65\%$.

From Problem 4.1, we saw that EFN can be written:

$$EFN = -\$188.6 + \$1,211.4 \times g$$

If we set this equal to zero and solve for g, we get:

$g = \$188.6/\$1,211.4$

$= 15.57\%$

Questions and problems

1 · Pro-forma statements

Consider the following simplified financial statements for the Ceedee Corporation:

Financial Performance Statement (200X)		Financial Position Statement (200X)			
Sales	$1,000	Assets	$ 500	Debt	$ 250
Costs	900			Equity	250
Net profit	$ 100	Total	$ 500	Total	$ 500

Ceedee has predicted a sales increase of 20 per cent. It has also predicted that every item on the Statement of Financial Position will increase by 20 per cent as well. Create the pro-forma statements and reconcile them. What is the plug variable here?

2 · Pro-forma statements and EFN

In the previous question, assume that Ceedee pays out half of net profit in the form of a cash dividend. Costs and assets vary with sales, but debt and equity do not. Prepare the pro-forma statements and determine the external financing needed.

3 · Calculating EFN

The most recent financial statements for Makemyday Ltd are shown below.

Financial Performance Statement		Financial Position Statement			
Sales	$ 500	Assets	$1,300	Debt	$ 800
Costs	200			Equity	500
Net profit	$ 300	Total	$1,300	Total	$1,300

Assets and costs are proportional to sales. Debt is not. No dividends are paid. Next year's sales are projected to be $550. What are external funds needed (EFN)?

4 · EFN

The most recent financial statements for Hag Pty Ltd are shown below.

Financial Performance Statement		Financial Position Statement			
Sales	$ 800	Assets	$2,400	Debt	$1,500
Costs	200			Equity	900
EBIT	600				
Taxes	200				
Net profit	$ 400	Total	$2,400	Total	$2,400

Assets and costs are proportional to sales. Debt is not. A dividend of $320 was paid, and Hag wishes to maintain a constant payout. Next year's sales are projected to be $920. What is EFN (external funds needed)?

5 · EFN

The most recent financial statements for Machoes Ltd are shown below.

Financial Performance Statement	
Sales	$ 500
Costs	440
Taxes	18
Net profit	$ 42

Financial Position Statement			
Current assets	$ 400	Current liabilities	$ 200
Non-current assets	800	Long-term debt	200
		Equity	800
Total	$1,200	Total	$1,200

Assets, costs, and current liabilities are proportional to sales. Long-term debt is not. Machoes maintains a constant 70 per cent dividend payout. Next year's sales are projected to be $640. What are external funds needed (EFN)?

6 · Calculating sustainable growth

The most recent financial statements for Tryhard Ltd are shown below.

Financial Performance Statement

Sales	$ 262
Costs	142
Taxes	36
Net profit	$ 84

Financial Position Statement

Current assets	$ 100	Debt	$830
Non-current assets	1,230	Equity	500
Total	$1,330	Total	$1,330

Assets and costs are proportional to sales. Debt is not. Tryhard maintains a constant 20 per cent dividend payout. No external financing is possible.

a   What is the sustainable growth rate?

b   Using the same information as in (a) but a tax rate of 25 per cent, provide the sustainable growth rate.

7 · Growth as a firm goal

Explain why growth by itself is not an appropriate goal for financial management. In particular, describe a scenario under which the goals of growth and maximisation of owners' wealth could be in conflict.

8 · Calculating new sales

The most recent financial statements for Drought Ltd are shown below.

Financial Performance Statement

Sales	$490
Costs	400
Taxes	27
Net profit	$ 63

Financial Position Statement

Current assets	$ 532	Long-term debt	$1,300
Non-current assets	1,998	Equity	1,230
Total	$2,530	Total	$2,530

Assets and costs are proportional to sales. Drought maintains a constant 30 per cent dividend payout and a constant debt-to-equity ratio. What is the maximum increase in sales that can be sustained assuming no new equity is issued?

9 · Calculating retained earnings from pro-forma financial performance statement

Consider the following financial performance statement for the AFLNRL Corporation:

AFLNRL Ltd

Financial Performance Statement

Sales	$4,000
Costs	3,000
Taxable income	$1,000
Taxes (30%)	300
Net profit	$ 700
Dividends	$126

A 10 per cent growth rate is projected. Prepare a pro-forma financial performance statement assuming that costs vary with sales and the dividend payout ratio is constant. What is the projected addition to retained earnings?

10 · Applying percentage of sales

The Financial Position Statement for AFLNRL Ltd is shown below. Based on this information and the Financial Performance Statement in the previous problem, supply the missing information using the percentage of sales approach. Assume that accounts payable vary with sales while notes payable do not. Put 'n/a' where needed.

AFLNRL Ltd

Financial Position Statement

Assets	($)	(%)	Liabilities and owners' equity	($)	(%)
Current assets			Current liabilities		
Cash	$ 500	___	Accounts payable	$2,000	___
Accounts receivable	1,000	___	Notes payable	1,000	___
Inventory	1,000	___	Total	$3,000	___
Total	$2,500	___	Long-term debt	$1,000	___
Non-current assets			Shareholders' equity		
Net plant and equipment	$3,000	___	Capital	500	___
			Retained earnings	1,000	___
			Total	$1,500	___
Total assets	$5,500		Total liabilities & equity	$5,500	

11 · EFN and sales

From the previous two questions, prepare a partial pro-forma Financial Position Statement, showing EFN, assuming a 10 per cent increase in sales.

12 · Calculating ROE

From the previous question, assuming that long-term debt is the plug, prepare the completed pro-forma Financial Position Statement. What is the projected ROE?

13 · Determinants of growth

Assuming a firm does not wish to sell new equity, what are the four determinants of growth? Explain how an increase in each of these affects the firm's growth rate. If these four elements are taken as fixed and no new equity will be issued, then what must be true?

14 · Using accounting statements

Evaluate the following statement: 'There is no finance in financial planning models.'

15 · EFN

Barcaldinel Ltd has $5,000 in total assets. The retention ratio is 0.50, the debt/equity ratio is 1, and the profit margin is 5 per cent. Sales for the year just ended were $2,000. If sales are to rise by 10 per cent, what is EFN?

16 · EFN and sales

In the previous question, what is the general relationship between growth in sales and EFN? Illustrate your answer graphically. What growth rate can be supported with no external financing? What would happen if growth were zero? How do you interpret this?

17 · Calculating SGR

In the previous question, what is the sustainable growth rate?

18 · SGR

If a firm has a 20 per cent ROE and a 40 per cent payout ratio, what is its sustainable growth rate?

19 · Percentage of sales issues

What are the advantages and disadvantages of the percentage of sales approach? In particular, is the assumption that many of the firm's costs and assets are directly proportional to sales a reasonable assumption? Does your answer depend on the time horizon being considered?

20 · SGR

Based on the following information, calculate the sustainable growth rate:

Profit margin	= 4%
Capital intensity ratio	= 2
Debt/equity ratio	= 0.5
Net profit	= $1,000
Dividends	= $300

What is the ROE here?

21 · SGR

Assuming the following ratios are constant, what is the sustainable growth rate?

Total assets/sales	= 1.0
Net profit/sales	= 0.05
Debt/equity	= 0.5
Dividends/net profit	= 0.6

22 · SGR

Assuming the following ratios are constant, what is the sustainable growth rate?

Sales/total assets	= 0.6
Net profit/sales	= 0.1
Debt/total assets	= 0.5
Retained earnings/net profit	= 0.8

23 · Growth and profit margin

A firm wishes to maintain a growth rate of 5 per cent per year, a debt-to-equity ratio of 0.5, and a dividend payout of 60 per cent. The ratio of total assets to sales is constant at 2. What profit margin must it achieve?

24 · Growth and D/E

A firm wishes to maintain a growth rate of 10 per cent per year and a dividend payout of 20 per cent. The ratio of total assets to sales is constant at 2, and profit margin is 10 per cent. What must the debt/equity ratio be?

25 · Growth and assets

A firm wishes to maintain a growth rate of 4 per cent per year, a debt-to-equity ratio of 0.5, and a dividend payout of 80 per cent. If the profit margin is 8 per cent and next year's sales are projected at $1,500, what is the total asset projection?

26 · SGR

Based on the following information, calculate the sustainable growth rate:

Profit margin	= 4%
Total asset turnover	= 2
Total debt ratio	= 0.5
Payout ratio	= 60%

27 · SGR and outside financing

You have collected the following information about Lostitl Pty Ltd:

Sales	= $4,000
Net profit	= $200
Dividends	= $50
Total debt	= $5,000
Total equity	= $10,000

What is the sustainable growth rate for Lostitl? If they do grow at this rate, how much borrowing will take place in the coming year? What rate could be supported with no outside financing at all?

28 · Constraints on growth

A firm wishes to maintain a growth rate of 8 per cent per year and a debt-to-equity ratio of .25. Profit margin is 4 per cent, and the ratio of total assets to sales is constant at 2. Is the growth rate possible? To answer, determine what the dividend payout must be. How do you interpret the result?

29 · Sustainable growth, ROA, and ROE

This is a challenge question. We saw that it is possible to determine the growth rate for a company that issues no new financing at all (debt or equity). Show that this growth rate is simply:

$$g = \frac{\text{ROA} \times R}{1 - \text{ROA} \times R}$$

This is a firm's internally financed growth rate, that is, the rate at which a firm can grow if it relies only on internal financing. (**Hint**: What is the sustainable growth rate for an all-equity company?)

30 · An alternative form for SGR

This is a challenge problem. Show that the SGR is given by

$$g^* = \frac{p(R)(1 + D/E)}{A/S - p(R)(1 + D/E)}$$

Then show that this is equivalent to the definition given in the chapter. (**Hint**: If the addition to retained earnings is $p(R)S$, then, to maintain a constant debt/equity ratio, the firm will have to borrow $p(R)S \times (D/E)$. For sustainable growth, this amount must exactly equal the firm's EFN.)

The following information is to be used for Problems 31, 32 and 33.

Mark Spence operates a mining firm and he has a tax rate of 34 per cent. His accountant Irene Sue has provided the following financial statements:

Financial Position	($000)
M S equity	$ 800
Current liabilities	500
Long-term liabilities	1,800
Total	$3,100
Represented by	
Current assets	$ 900
Fixed assets	2,200
Total	$3,100

Financial Performance	($000)
Sales	$4,250
Costs	3,875
Taxable income	$375
Tax at 34%	127.5
Net profit	$247.5
Owners salary	$82.6
Addition to retained earnings	164.9

31 · Calculating EFN

Assume the firm is operating at full capacity and that Mark Spence will draw a salary as a constant percentage of profit. Sales are predicted to grow at 10 per cent. Use the percentage of sales approach and calculate the EFN.

32 · EFN and capacity use

What is the EFN if capacity is 60 per cent for fixed assets? What if the capacity is 95 per cent?

33 · Sustainable growth

What growth can Mark Spence maintain if no external financing is used? What is the sustainable growth rate?

PART THREE

Valuation

of future cash flows

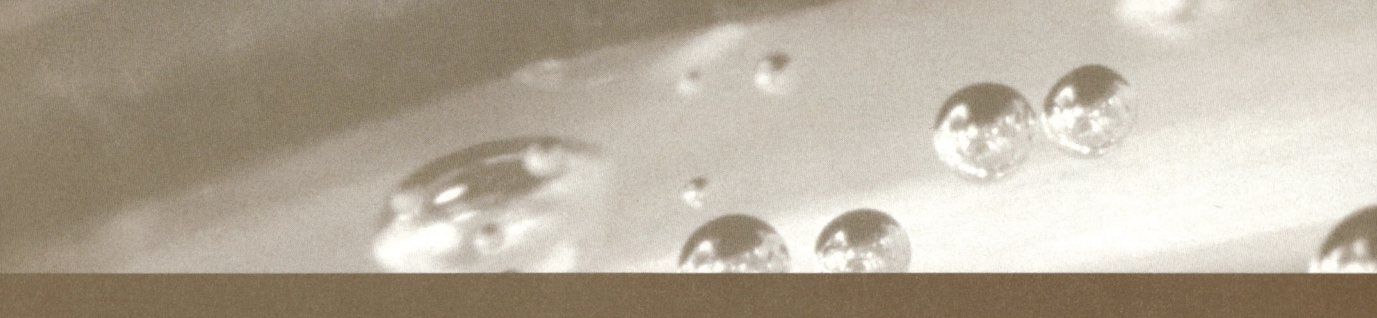

CHAPTER 5

First principles
of valuation: the time value of money

Objective

The objective of this chapter is to provide the financial base for business finance. Understanding the numbers associated with commercial contracts is very important in the competitive business environment of today. On a personal level, at some time in our lives we all incur debt or desire to make investments, and it is important to know the exact cost or the precise benefits involved. On completion of the chapter you should understand compounding and discounting in order to appreciate the value of future cash flows no matter how they are packaged. Our aim is to evaluate explicitly the trade-off between dollars today and dollars at some time in the future.

In this chapter, we look at the basic mechanics of common financial calculations. When you finish this chapter, you should have some very practical skills. For example, you will know how to calculate your own car payments or loan payments. You will also be able to determine how long it will take to pay off a loan. We will show you how to compare interest rates to determine which are the highest and which are the lowest, and we will also show you how interest rates can be quoted in different, and at times deceptive, ways.

A thorough understanding of the material in this chapter is critical to understanding material in subsequent chapters, so you should study it with particular care. We will present a large number of examples in this chapter. In many problems, your answer may differ from ours to some minor extent. This can happen because of rounding and is not a cause for concern.

Study tip ▷ Problems involving financial mathematics tend to be confusing for students and the best remedy is plenty of practice. It is important to understand the principles rather than rote learn answers to specific questions. Once the facts are changed marginally the problem may change significantly so that the answer committed to memory is of little use. Many of the issues raised in financial problems hinge upon the timing of the cash flows, so a very useful approach for students is to quickly plot a fund time line showing when cash flows occur. For example, consider plotting a periodic payment of $100 for three years starting in two years time, then stopping for three years and recommencing for a further two years. *What a mess! But it is simple if we use a fund time line such as:*

Year 0	1	2	3	4	5	6	7	8	9
Cash flows		100	100	100				100	100

Once the cash flow timeframe is correctly identified, the required calculations fall into place.

Introduction ▷ One of the basic problems faced by the financial manager is how to determine the value today of cash flows that are expected in the future. For example, when I retire I expect a superannuation payout of about $7 million. With this money it would be nice to buy a new home, go on a world trip, drive a Porsche and live my life out comfortably. Unfortunately, $7 million in about 30 years time equates to about $200,000 today. The exact value today depends on the time value of money, the subject of this chapter.

In the most general sense, the phrase 'time value of money' refers to the fact that a dollar in hand today is worth more than a dollar promised at some time in the future. On a practical level, one reason for this is that you could earn interest while you waited; so a dollar today would grow to more than a dollar later. The trade-off between money now and money later thus depends on, among other things, the rate you can earn by investing.

future value

the amount an investment is worth after one or more periods. Also compound value

The first thing we will study is **future value**. Future value refers to the amount of money an investment will grow to over some length of time at some given interest rate. Put another way, future value is the cash value of an investment at some time in the future. We start out by considering the simplest case, a single period investment.

Investing for a single period

Suppose you were to invest $100 in a savings account that pays 10 per cent interest per year. How much will you have in one year? You would have $110. This $110 is equal to your original principal of $100 plus $10 in interest that you earn. We say that $110 is the future value (FV) of $100 invested for one year at 10 per cent, and we simply mean that $100 today is worth $110 in one year, given that 10 per cent is the interest rate.

In general, if you invest for one period at an interest rate of r, your investment will grow to $(1 + r)$ per dollar invested. In our example, r is 10 per cent, so your investment grows to $(1 + 0.10) = 1.1$ dollars per dollar invested. You invested $100 in this case, so you ended up with $100 \times (1.10) = 110.

You might wonder if the single period in this example has to be a year. The answer is no. For example, if the interest rate were 2 per cent per quarter, your $100 would grow to $100 \times (1 + 0.02) = 102 by the end of the quarter. You might also wonder if 2 per cent every quarter is the same as 8 per cent per year. The answer is again no, but we'll explain why a little later.

Investing for more than one period

compounding

the process of accumulating interest in an investment over time to earn more interest

interest on interest

interest earned on the reinvestment of previous interest payments

compound interest

interest calculated each period on the principal amount and on any interest earned on the investment up to that point

simple interest

the method of calculating interest in which, during the entire term of the loan, interest is computed on the original sum borrowed

Going back to our $100 investment, what will you have after two years, assuming that the interest rate does not change? If you leave the entire $110 in the bank, you will earn $110 \times 0.10 = 11 in interest during the second year, so you will have a total of $110 + $11 = 121. This $121 is the future value of $100 in two years at 10 per cent. Another way of looking at it is that one year from now you are effectively investing $110 at 10 per cent for a year. This is a single-period problem, so you'll end up with $1.10 for every dollar invested, or $110 \times 1.1 = 121 in total.

This $121 has four parts. The first part is the $100 original principal. The second part is the $10 in interest you earned in the first year, along with another $10 (the third part) you earn in the second year, for a total of $120. The last $1 you end up with (the fourth part) is interest you earn in the second year on the interest paid in the first year: $10 \times 0.10 = 1.

This process of leaving your money and any accumulated interest in an investment for more than one period, thereby reinvesting the interest, is called **compounding**. Compounding the interest means earning **interest on interest**, so we call the result **compound interest**. With **simple interest**, the interest is not reinvested, so interest is earned each period only on the original principal.

EXAMPLE 5.1

Interest on interest

Suppose you locate a two-year investment that pays 14 per cent per year. If you invest $325, how much will you have at the end of the two years? How much of this is simple interest? How much is compound interest?

At the end of the first year, you will have $325 × (1 + 0.14) = $370.50. If you reinvest this entire amount and thereby compound the interest, you will have $370.50 × 1.14 = $422.37 at the end of the second year. The total interest you earn is thus $422.37 − $325 = $97.37. Your $325 original principal earns $325 × 0.14 = $45.50 in interest each year, for a two-year total of $91 in simple interest. The remaining $97.37 − $91 = $6.37 results from compounding. You can check this by noting that the interest earned in the first year is $45.50. The interest on interest earned in the second year thus amounts to $45.50 × 0.14 = $6.37, as we calculated.

We now take a closer look at how we calculated the $121 future value. We multiplied $110 by 1.1 to get $121. The $110, however, was $100 also multiplied by 1.1. In other words:

A CLOSER LOOK

$$
\begin{aligned}
\$121 &= \$110 \times 1.1 \\
&= (\$100 \times 1.1) \times 1.1 \\
&= \$100 \times (1.1 \times 1.1) \\
&= \$100 \times 1.1^2 \\
&= \$100 \times 1.21
\end{aligned}
$$

At the risk of belabouring the obvious, let us ask: How much would our $100 grow to after three years? Once again, in two years, we will be investing $121 for one period at 10 per cent. We will end up with $1.10 for every dollar we invest, or $121 × 1.1 = $133.10 in total. This $133.10 is thus:

$$
\begin{aligned}
\$133.10 &= \$121 \times 1.1 \\
&= (\$110 \times 1.1) \times 1.1 \\
&= (\$100 \times 1.1) \times 1.1 \times 1.1 \\
&= \$100 \times (1.1 \times 1.1 \times 1.1) \\
&= \$100 \times 1.1^3 \\
&= \$100 \times 1.331
\end{aligned}
$$

You're probably noticing a pattern to these calculations, so we can now go ahead and state the general result. As our examples suggest, the future value of $1 invested for t periods at a rate of r per period is:

$$\text{Future value} = \$1 \times (1 + r)^t$$

The expression $(1 + r)^t$ is sometimes called the future value interest factor (or just future value factor) for $1 invested at r per cent for t periods and can be abbreviated as FVIF (r,t).

In our example, what would your $100 be worth after five years? We can first compute the relevant future value factor as:

$$(1 + r)^t = (1 + 0.10)^5 = 1.1^5 = 1.61051$$

Your $100 will thus grow to:

$$\$100 \times 1.1^5 = \$161.05$$

The growth of your $100 each year is illustrated in Table 5.1. As shown, the interest earned in each year is equal to the beginning amount multiplied by the interest rate of 10 per cent.

In Table 5.1, notice that the total interest you earn is $61.05. Over the five-year span of this investment, the simple interest is $100 × 0.10 = $10 per year, so you accumulate $50 this way. The other $11.05 is from compounding.

TABLE
5.1

Future value of $100 at 10 per cent			
Year	Beginning amount	Interest earned	Ending amount
1	$100.00	$10.00	$110.00
2	110.00	11.00	121.00
3	121.00	12.10	133.10
4	133.10	13.31	146.41
5	146.41	14.64	161.05
	Total interest	$61.05	

FIGURE
5.1

Future value, simple interest, and compound interest

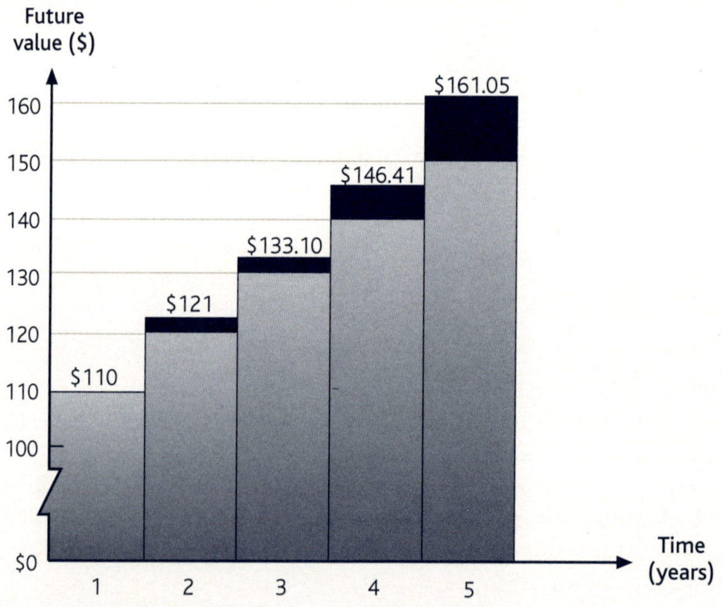

Growth of $100 original amount at 10% per year. Dark shaded area represents the portion of the total that results from compounding of interest.

Figure 5.1 (opposite) illustrates the growth of the compound interest in Table 5.1. Notice how the simple interest is constant each year, but the compound interest you earn gets bigger every year. The size of the compound interest keeps increasing because more and more interest builds up and there is thus more to compound.

Future values depend critically on the assumed interest rate, particularly for long-term investments. Figure 5.2 illustrates this relationship by plotting the growth of $1 for different rates and lengths of time. Notice that the future value of $1 after 10 years is about $6.20 at a 20 per cent rate, but it is only about $2.60 at 10 per cent. In this case, doubling the interest rate more than doubles the future value.

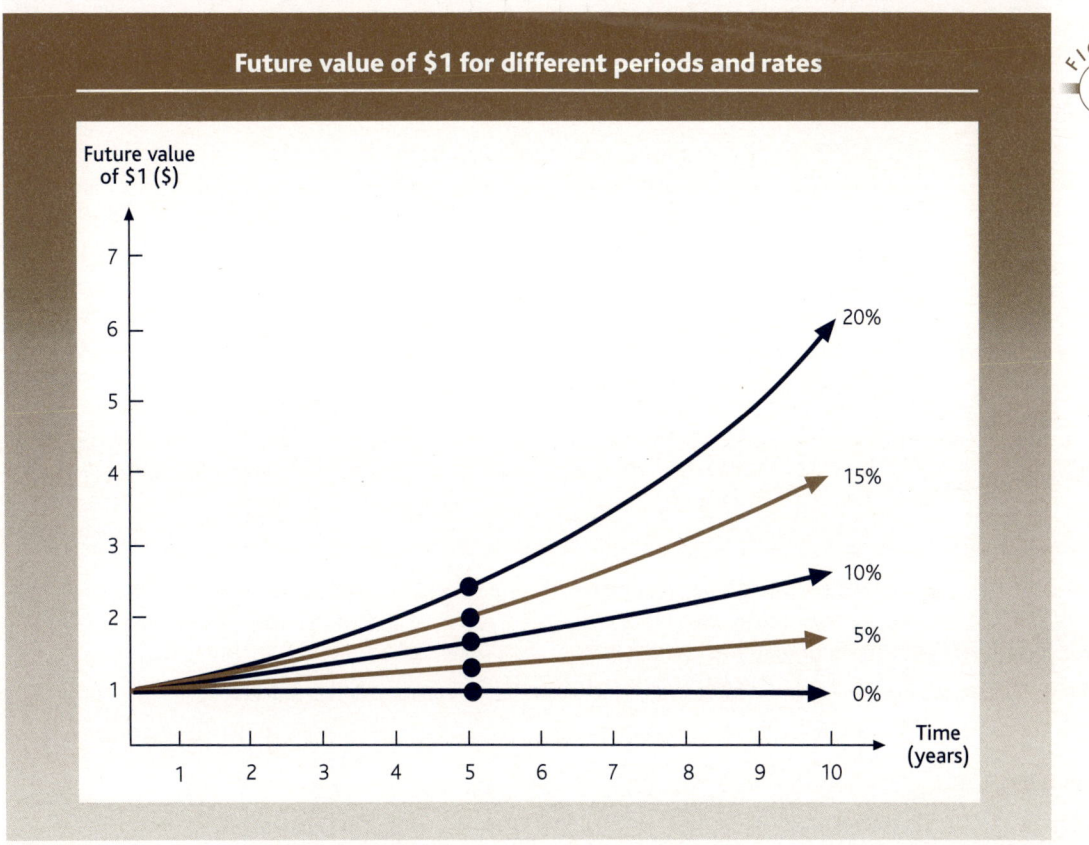

Future value of $1 for different periods and rates

FIGURE 5.2

To solve future value problems, we need to come up with the relevant future value factors. There are several different ways of doing this. In our example, we could have multiplied 1.1 by itself 5 times. This will work just fine, but it would get to be very tedious for, say, a 30-year investment.

Fortunately, there are several easier ways to get future value factors. Most calculators have a key labelled 'y^x'. You can usually just enter 1.1, press the y^x key, enter 5, and press the = key to get the answer. This is an easy way to calculate future value factors and it is quick and accurate.

Alternatively, you can use a table that contains future value factors for some common interest rates and time periods. Table 5.2 (overleaf) contains some of these factors. Table A.1 in the appendix at the end of the book contains a much larger set. To use the table, find the column that corresponds to 10 per cent. Then look down the rows until you come to five periods. You should find the factor that we calculated, 1.61051.

TABLE
5.2

Future value interest factors				
	Interest rate			
Number of periods	5%	10%	15%	20%
1	1.0500	1.1000	1.1500	1.2000
2	1.1025	1.2100	1.3225	1.4400
3	1.1576	1.3310	1.5209	1.7280
4	1.2155	1.4641	1.7490	2.0736
5	1.2763	1.6105	2.0114	2.4883

Tables such as 5.2 are not as common as they once were because they predate inexpensive calculators and are only available for a relatively small number of rates. Interest rates are often quoted to three or four decimal points, so the number of tables needed to deal with these accurately would be quite large. As a result, the 'real world' has moved away from using them. We will emphasise the use of a calculator in this chapter.

These tables still serve a useful purpose. To make sure that you are doing the calculations correctly, pick a factor from the table and then calculate it yourself to see that you get the same answer. There are plenty of numbers to choose from.

EXAMPLE 5.2 ■ Compound interest

You have located an investment that pays 12 per cent. That rate sounds good to you, so you invest $400. How much will you have in three years? How much will you have in seven years? At the end of seven years, how much interest have you earned? How much of that interest results from compounding?

Based on our discussion, we can calculate the future value factor for 12 per cent and three years as:

$$(1 + r)^t = 1.12^3 = 1.4049$$

Your $400 thus grows to:

$$\$400 \times 1.4049 = \$561.97$$

After seven years, you would have:

$$\$400 \times 1.12^7 = \$400 \times 2.2107 = \$884.27$$

Thus, you will more than double your money over seven years.

Since you invested $400, the interest in the $884.27 future value is $884.27 − $400 = $484.27. At 12 per cent, your $400 investment earns $400 × 0.12 = $48 in simple interest every year. Over seven years, the simple interest thus totals 7 × $48 = $336. The other $484.27 − $336 = $148.27 is from compounding.

The effect of compounding is not great over short time periods, but it really starts to add up as the time horizon grows. To take an extreme case, suppose one of your more frugal ancestors had invested $5 for you at a 6 per cent interest 200 years ago, how much would you have today? The future value factor is a substantial $(1.06)^{200} = 115,125.90$ (you won't

EXAMPLE 5.3

How much for that island?

To further illustrate the effect of compounding for long horizons, consider the case of Peter Minuit and the Indians. In 1626, Minuit bought all of Manhattan Island for about $24 in goods and trinkets. This sounds cheap, but the Indians may have had the better end of the deal. To see why, suppose that the Indians had sold the goods and invested the $24 at 10 per cent. How much would it be worth today?

Roughly 375 years have passed since the transaction. At 10 per cent, $24 will grow by quite a bit over that time. How much?

$$(1 + r)^t = 1.1^{375} = 3,328,564,170,000,000$$

This is 3,328 trillion. The future value is therefore $79,885,540,000,000,000 or almost $80 thousand trillion. Bill Gates of Microsoft fame is expected to be the first person to accumulate one trillion dollars. The Indians would have $80 thousand more if they could have earned compound interest at a rate of 10 per cent.

Well, $80 thousand trillion is a lot of money. How much? If you had it, you could buy Australia and most of the world. This example is something of an exaggeration, of course. In 1626, it would not have been easy to locate an investment that would pay 10 per cent every year without fail for the next 375 years.

---

find this one in a table), so you would have $5 × 115,125.91 = $575,629.52 today. Notice that the simple interest is just $5 × 0.06 = $0.30 per year. After 200 years, this amounts to $60. The rest is from reinvesting. Such is the power of compound interest!

A note on compound growth

If you are considering depositing money in an interest-bearing account, then the interest rate on that account is just the rate at which your money grows, assuming you don't remove any of it. If that rate is 5 per cent, then each year you simply have 5 per cent more money than you had the year before. In this case, the interest rate is just an example of a compound growth rate.

The way we calculated future values is actually quite general and lets you answer some other types of questions related to growth. For example, your company currently has 10,000 employees. You have estimated that the number of employees grows by 3 per cent per year. How many employees will there be in five years? Here, we start with 10,000 people instead of dollars, and we do not think of the growth rate as an interest rate, but the calculation is exactly the same:

$$10,000 \times (1.03)^5 = 10,000 \times 1.1593 = 11,593 \text{ employees}$$

There will be about 1,593 net new employees over the coming five years.

Concept questions

5.1a *What do we mean by the future value of an investment?*

5.1b *What does it mean to compound interest? How does compound interest differ from simple interest?*

5.1c *In general, what is the future value of $1 invested at r per period for t periods?*

Maars Ltd currently pays a cash dividend of $0.50 per share. You believe that the dividend will be increased by 4 per cent each year indefinitely. How big will the dividend be in eight years?

Here we have a cash dividend growing because it is being increased by management, but, once again, the calculation is the same:

$$\text{Future value} = \$0.50 \times (1.04)^8 = \$0.50 \times (1.3686) = \$0.68$$

The dividend will grow by $0.18 over that period. Dividend growth is a subject we will return to in a later chapter.

⟨⟨⟩⟩ In their own words

Tom Smith* on the three ideas of finance

A lot of students find finance a very confusing field at first. I think they become confused because they feel overwhelmed with the volume and diversity of topics. I have found that the field is much simpler than it seems. In fact, the field of finance can be viewed as being made up of three simple ideas:

1 *the time value of money;*
2 *diversification; and*
3 *arbitrage.*

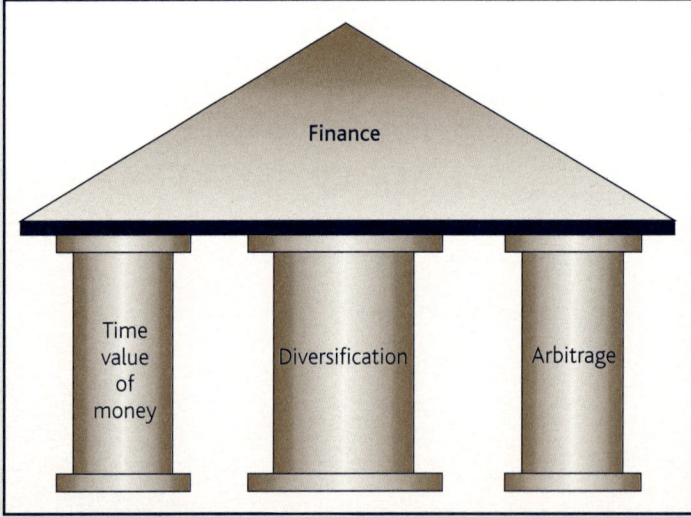

The time value of money
Finance is rooted in the idea of the time value of money. The idea is simple—a dollar today is worth more than a dollar tomorrow. This idea is the basis of all valuation. To value any asset:

Tom Smith

1 *Write down the asset's cash flows;*
2 *Calculate the present value of the asset's cash flows; and*
3 *Sum the present values.*

The value of the asset is the sum of the present values.

This approach can be used to determine the value of any asset, including mortgages, stocks, bonds, in fact all financing alternatives facing the firm; and investment proposals.

Diversification

The idea here is straightforward. If investors want to make as much money as they can with least risk, they should diversify. Why? Because diversification reduces risk. With a large portfolio holding, some assets will do very well, some will do very badly and most will perform up to expectations. Those that do very well will cancel out those that do very badly and fluctuations for the portfolio as a whole will be smooth and show little variation.

If everyone is diversified, this tells us something about how assets are priced—it gives us the required return for risk. It is this required return that is used as the discount rate in calculating present values under the time value of money idea.

Arbitrage

The simple idea here is that if there are two ways to get the same cash flow, they must have the same price. This idea is also known as valuation by arbitrage. The arbitrage idea is at the heart of the valuation of futures and options.

It is a very powerful idea and often lies at the centre of strategic decisions regarding value creation. You will only add value if others (e.g. competitors, investors) cannot replicate what you are doing at lower cost.

All three ideas come together and are used in the valuation of assets.

As you proceed through the topics in this text you may find it helpful to consider which of the three ideas the topic is based on.

* **Tom Smith** is Professor of Finance at the Australian National University.

5.2 ∎ Present value and discounting

When we discuss future value, we are thinking of questions like 'What will my $2,000 investment grow to if it earns a 6.5 per cent return every year for the next six years?' The answer to this question is what we called the future value of $2,000 invested at 6.5 per cent for six years (check that the answer is about $2,918).

There is another type of question that comes up even more often in financial management and is obviously related to future value. Suppose you need to have $10,000 in 10 years, and you can earn 6.5 per cent on your money. How much do you have to invest today to reach your goal? You can verify that the answer is $5,327.26. How do we know this? Read on.

The single period case

We have seen that the future value of $1 invested for one year at 10 per cent is $1.10. We now ask a slightly different question: How much do we have to invest today at 10 per cent to get $1 in one year? In other words, we know the future value here is $1, but what is the **present value (PV)**? The answer is not too hard to figure out. Whatever we invest today will be 1.1 times bigger at the end of the year. Since we need $1 at the end of the year:

present value

an amount that corresponds to today's value of a promised future sum

$$\text{Present value} \times 1.1 = \$1$$

or:

$$\text{Present value} = \$1/1.1 = \$0.91$$

or equivalently:

$$\text{Present value} = \$1 \times (1.1)^{-1} = \$0.91$$

In this case, the present value is the answer to the following question: 'What amount, invested today, will grow to $1 in one year if the interest rate is 10 per cent?' Present value is thus just the reverse of future value. Instead of compounding the money forward into the future, we discount it back to the present.

EXAMPLE 5.5 ■ Single period PV

Suppose you need $400 to buy textbooks next year. You can earn 7 per cent on your money. How much do you have to invest today?

We need to know the PV of $400 in one year at 7 per cent. Proceeding as above:

$$\text{Present value} \times 1.07 = \$400$$

We can now solve for the present value:

$$\text{Present value} = \$400 \times (1.07)^{-1} = \$373.83$$

or

$$\text{Present value} = \$400/(1.07) = \$373.83$$

Thus, $373.83 is the present value. Again, this just means that investing this amount for one year at 7 per cent will result in your having a future value of $400.

From our examples, the present value of $1 to be received in one period is generally given as:

$$PV = \$1 \times (1 + r)^{-1}$$

or

$$PV = \$1 \times [1/(1 + r)^1]$$

We next examine how to get the present value of an amount to be paid in two or more periods into the future.

Present values for multiple periods

Suppose you needed to have $1,000 in two years. If you can earn 7 per cent, how much do you have to invest to make sure that you have the $1,000 when you need it? In other words, what is the present value of $1,000 in two years if the relevant rate is 7 per cent?

Based on your knowledge of future values, we know that the amount invested must grow to $1,000 over the two years. In other words, it must be the case that:

$$\begin{aligned} \$1,000 &= PV \times 1.07 \times 1.07 \\ &= PV \times 1.07^2 \\ &= PV \times 1.1449 \end{aligned}$$

Given this, we can solve for the present value as:

$$\text{Present value} = \$1,000/1.1449 = \$873.44$$

or

$$\begin{aligned} \text{Present value} &= \$1,000 \times (1.07)^{-2} \\ &= \$1,000 \times 0.87344 = \$873.44 \end{aligned}$$

Therefore, $873.44 is the amount you must invest in order to achieve your goal.

Saving up

EXAMPLE 5.6

You would like to buy a new car (a good one). You have about $50,000 or so, but the car costs $68,500. If you can earn 9 per cent, how much do you have to invest today to buy the car in two years? Do you have enough? Assume the price will stay the same.

What we need to know is the present value of $68,500 to be paid in two years, assuming a 9 per cent rate. Based on our discussion, this is:

$$PV = \$68,500 \times 1.09^{-2} = \$68,500 \times 0.84168 = \$57,655.08$$

You're still about $7,655 short, even if you're willing to wait two years.

As you have probably recognised by now, calculating present values is quite similar to calculating future values, and the general result looks much the same. The present value of $1 to be received t periods in the future at a **discount rate** of r is:

$$PV = \$1 \times [1/(1 + r)^t] = \$1/(1 + r)^t = \$1 \times (1 + r)^{-t}$$

The quantity in brackets, $1/(1 + r)^t$ or $(1 + r)^{-t}$, goes by several different names. Since it's used to discount a future cash flow, it is often called a discount factor. With this name, it is not surprising that the rate used in the calculation is often called the discount rate. We will tend to call it this in talking about present values. The quantity in brackets is also called the present value interest factor for $1 at r per cent for t periods and is sometimes abbreviated as PVIF(r,t). Finally, calculating the present value of a future cash flow to determine its worth today is commonly called discounted cash flow (DCF) valuation.

To illustrate, suppose you needed $1,000 in three years. You can earn 15 per cent on your money. How much do you have to invest today? To find out, we have to determine the present value of $1,000 in three years at 15 per cent. We do this by **discounting** $1,000 back three periods at 15 per cent. With these numbers, the discount factor is:

discount rate

the interest rate that reduces a given future value to an equivalent present value

discounting

the process by which, through the operation of interest, a future sum is converted to its equivalent present value

$$1/(1 + 0.15)^3 = 1/1.5209 = 0.6575$$

or

$$(1 + 0.15)^{-3} = 0.6575$$

The amount you must invest is thus:

$$\$1,000 \times \text{PVIF}(15\%, 3 \text{ periods})$$
$$\$1,000 \times 0.6575 = \$657.50$$

We say that \$657.50 is the present or discounted value of \$1,000 to be received in three years at 15 per cent.

There are tables for present value factors just as there are tables for future value factors, and you use them in the same way (if you use them at all). Table 5.3 contains a small set. A much larger set can be found in Table A.2 in the Appendix.

In Table 5.3, the discount factor we just calculated (0.6575) can be found by looking down the column labelled 15% until you come to the third row.

TABLE 5.3

	Present value interest factors			
		Interest rate		
Number of periods	5%	10%	15%	20%
1	0.9524	0.9091	0.8696	0.8333
2	0.9070	0.8264	0.7561	0.6944
3	0.8638	0.7513	0.6575	0.5787
4	0.8227	0.6830	0.5718	0.4823
5	0.7835	0.6209	0.4972	0.4019

EXAMPLE 5.7 ■ Deceptive advertising?

Firms in the United States used to advertise things like 'Come try our product. If you do, we'll give you \$100 just for coming by!' If you read the fine print, what you find out is that they will give you a savings certificate that will pay you \$100 in 25 years or so. If the going interest rate on such certificates is 10 per cent per year, how much are they really giving you?

What you are actually getting is the present value of \$100 to be paid in 25 years. If the discount rate is 10 per cent per year, then the discount factor is:

$$1/1.1^{25} = 1/10.8347 = 0.0923$$

This tells you that a dollar in 25 years is worth a little more than nine cents today, assuming a 10 per cent discount rate. Given this, the promotion is actually paying you about $0.0923 \times \$100 = \$9.23$. Maybe this is enough to draw customers, but it is not \$100 in today's terms.

As the length of time until payment grows, present values decline. As Example 5.7 illustrates, present values tend to become small as the time horizon grows. If you look out far enough, they will always get close to zero. Also, for a given length of time, the higher the discount rate is, the lower is the present value. Put another way, present values and discount rates are inversely related. Increasing the discount rate decreases the PV and vice versa.

Several well-known Australian retailers are offering **interest free** purchase terms for periods up to two years. One may ask: How can they do that? Assume that a product has a retail price of $1,000, but the business is quite happy to receive $857.30 in cash for an immediate sale. This amount covers all costs and includes a level of profit. The choice for the firm is $857.30 now or $1,000 in two years time. We can show that at 8 per cent compound interest $857.30 will grow to $1,000 in two years, as:

$$\$857.30 \times (1.08) \times (1.08) = \$1,000$$

So the firm earns 8 per cent and the additional profits through the additional sales because of its generous credit terms.

What about the risk of some buyers defaulting in payment? A well-managed firm would collect statistics on defaults and use them to calculate the risk of some losses. A simple way to allow for this risk is to increase the interest rate. Consider the case where a firm buys a piece of furniture for resale at $1,365. The firm marks up its stock at 20 per cent to cover all overheads and its profit. In addition the firm can borrow funds at 7 per cent. Because of defaults it feels it would have to increase the interest rate to 10.5 per cent if it was to sell on interest free delayed payment conditions. What should be the super, discount price at which the furniture is offered to the public for two year interest free terms?

Cost to the retailer	$1,365
Mark-up for profit and overheads (20%)	273
Selling price required today	$1,638

Contract payment in two years $1,638 $\times$ $(1.105)^2$ = $2,000

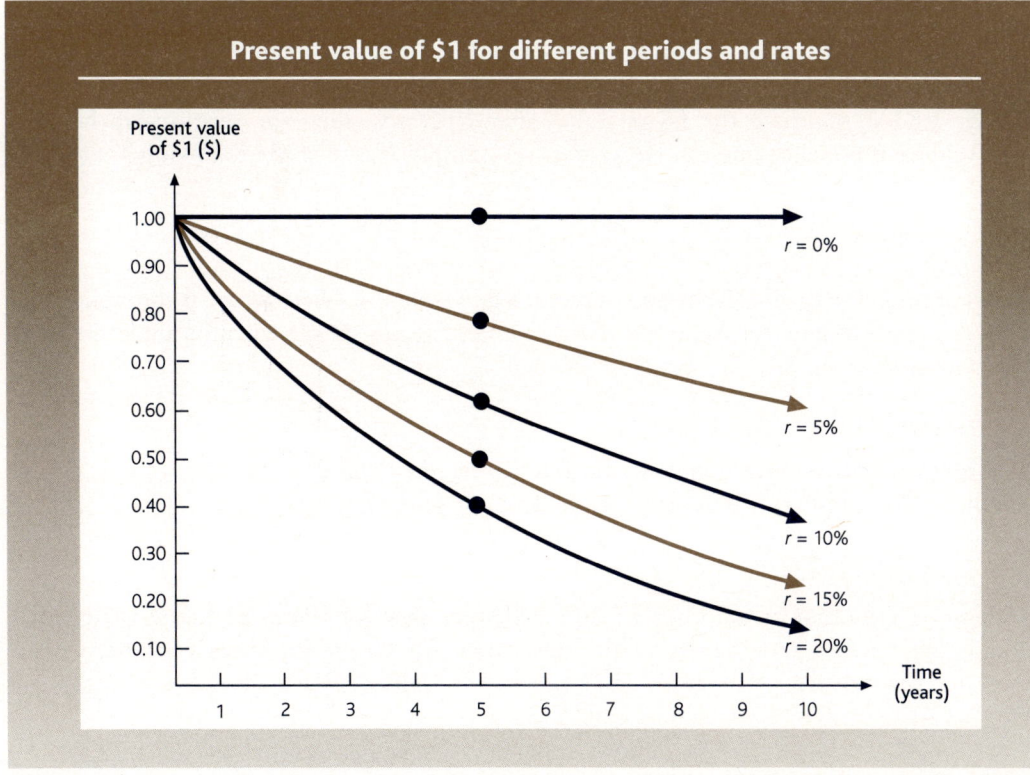

Present value of $1 for different periods and rates

FIGURE 5.3

So the super, discount, 'wholesale' price the firm would offer is a generous $2,000.

The relationship between time, discount rates, and present values is illustrated in Figure 5.3 (previous page). Notice that by the time we get to 10 years, the present values are all substantially smaller than the future amounts with any discount rate greater than zero.

Concept questions

5.2a *What do we mean by the present value of an investment?*

5.2b *The process of discounting a future amount back to the present is the opposite of doing what?*

5.2c *What do we mean by the discounted cash flow or DCF approach?*

 ## 5.3 More on present and future values

If you look back at the expressions that we came up with for present and future values, you will see that there is a very simple relationship between the two. We explore this relationship and some related issues in this section.

Present versus future value

What we called the present value factor is just the reciprocal of (that is 1 divided by) the future value factor:

$$\text{Future value factor} \;=\; (1 + r)^t$$
$$\text{Present value factor} \;=\; 1/(1 + r)^t \text{ or } (1 + r)^{-t}$$

In fact, the easy way to calculate a present value factor on many calculators is first to calculate the future value factor and then press the '$1/x$' key to flip it over.

If we let FV_t stand for the future value after t periods, then the relationship between future value and present value can be written very simply as one of the following:

$$PV \times (1 + r)^t \;=\; FV_t$$
$$PV \;=\; FV_t /(1 + r)^t \;=\; FV_t \times (1 + r)^{-t} \;=\; [FV_t \times [1/(1 + r)^t]$$

This last result we will call the basic present value equation. We will use it throughout the text. There are a number of variations that come up, but this simple equation underlies many of the most important ideas in corporate finance.

Determining the discount rate

It will turn out that we will frequently need to determine what discount rate is implicit in an investment. We can do this by looking at the basic present value equation:

$$PV \;=\; FV_t /(1 + r)^t$$

There are only four parts to this equation: the present value (PV), the future value (FV_t), the discount rate (r), and the life of the investment (t). Given any three of these, we can always find the fourth.

PART 3 · VALUATION OF FUTURE CASH FLOWS

Evaluating investments

 EXAMPLE 5.8

To give you an idea of how we will be using present and future values, consider the following simple investment. Your company proposes to buy an asset for $335. This investment is very safe. You will sell off the asset in three years for $400. You know that you could invest the $335 elsewhere at 10 per cent with very little risk. What do you think of the proposed investment?

This is not a good investment. Why not? Because you can invest the $335 elsewhere at 10 per cent. If you do, after three years it will grow to:

$$\$335 \times (1 + r)^t = \$335 \times 1.1^3$$
$$= \$335 \times 1.331$$
$$= \$445.89$$

Since the proposed investment only pays out $400, it is not as good as other alternatives that we have. Another way of saying the same thing is to notice that the present value of $400 in three years at 10 per cent is:

$$\$400 \times [1/(1 + r)^t] = \$400/1.1^3 = \$400/1.331 = \$300.53$$

This tells us that we only have to invest about $300 to get $400 in three years, not $335. We will return to this type of analysis later on.

Finding *r* for a single period investment

 EXAMPLE 5.9

You are considering a one-year investment. If you invest $1,250 you will get back $1,350. What rate is this investment paying?

First of all, in this single period case, the answer is fairly obvious. You are getting a total of $100 in addition to your $1,250. The rate of return on this investment is thus $100/$1,250 = 8 per cent.

More formally, from the basic present value equation, the present value (the amount you must invest today) is $1,250. The future value (what the present value grows to) is $1,350. The time involved is one period, so we have:

$$\$1,250 = \$1,350/(1 + r)^1$$
$$(1 + r) = \$1,350/\$1,250 = 1.08$$
$$r = 8\%$$

In this simple case, of course, there was no need to go through this calculation, but, as we describe below, it gets a little harder when there is more than one period.

For example, we might be offered an investment that costs us $100 and will double our money in eight years. To compare this to other investments, we would like to know what discount rate is implicit in these numbers. This discount rate is called the rate of return or sometimes just return for the investment. In this case, we have a present value of $100, a future value of $200 (double our money), and an 8-year life. To calculate the return, we can write the basic present value equation as:

$$PV = FV_t /(1 + r)^t$$
$$\$100 = \$200/(1 + r)^8$$

(continued)

EXAMPLE 5.9 ■ Finding *r* for a single period investment (*continued*)

It could also be written as:

$$(1 + r)^8 = \$200/\$100 = 2$$

We now need to solve for *r*. There are three ways we could do it:

1   Use a financial calculator.
2   Solve the equation for 1 + *r* by taking the eighth root of both sides. Since this is the same thing as raising both sides to the power of 1/8 or 0.125, this is actually easy to do with the 'y^x' key on a calculator. Just enter 2, then press y^x, enter 0.125, and press the = key. The eighth root is about 1.09, which implies that *r* is roughly 9 per cent.
3   Use a future value table. The future value factor after eight years is equal to 2. If you look across the row corresponding to eight periods in Table A.1, the closest factor is 1.9926, in the 9 per cent column, again implying that the return here is 9 per cent.

Actually, in this particular example, there is a useful 'rule of thumb' means of solving for *r*—the Rule of 72. For reasonable rates of return, the time it takes to double your money is given approximately by 72/*r*%. In our example, this is 72/*r*% = 8 years, implying that *r* is 9 per cent as we calculated. This rule is fairly accurate for discount rates in the 5 to 20 per cent range.

EXAMPLE 5.10 ■ Double your fun

You have been offered an investment that promises to double your money every 10 years. What is the approximate rate of return on the investment?

From the Rule of 72, the rate of return is approximately 72/*r* % = 10, so the rate is approximately 72/10 = 7.2%. Check that the exact answer is 7.177 per cent.

EXAMPLE 5.11 ■ Saving for uni

You estimate that you will need about $80,000 to send your child to university in eight years. You have about $35,000 now. If you can earn 20 per cent, will you make it? At what rate will you just reach your goal?

If you can earn 20 per cent, the future value of your $35,000 in eight years will be:

$$FV = \$35,000 \times (1.20)^8 = \$35,000 \times 4.2998 = \$150,493.59$$

So you will make it easily. The minimum rate you would need to earn is the unknown *r* in the following:

$$FV = \$35,000 \times (1 + r)^8 = \$80,000$$
$$(1 + r)^8 = \$80,000/\$35,000 = 2.2857$$

EXAMPLE 5.11

Saving for uni (*continued*)

Therefore, the future value factor is 2.2857. Looking at the row in Table A.1 that corresponds to eight periods, our future value factor is roughly halfway between the ones shown for 10 per cent (2.1436) and 12 per cent (2.4760), so you will just reach your goal if you earn approximately 11 per cent. To get the exact answer, we could use a financial calculator or we can solve for r:

$$(1 + r)^8 = \$80,000/\$35,000 = 2.2857$$
$$(1 + r) = 2.2857^{1/8} = 2.2857^{0.125} = 1.1089$$
$$r = 10.89\%$$

EXAMPLE 5.12

Only 18,262.5 days to retirement

You would like to retire in 50 years as a millionaire. If you have $10,000 today, what rate of return do you need to earn to achieve your goal?

The future value is $1,000,000. The present value is $10,000, and there are 50 years until payment. We need to calculate the unknown discount rate in the following:

$$\$10,000 = \$1,000,000/(1 + r)^{50}$$
$$(1 + r)^{50} = 100$$

The future value factor is thus 100. From Table A.1 the factor for 50 periods at 9 per cent is 74.358 and for 10 per cent it is 117.39. Therefore the answer lies between 9 and 10 per cent. You can verify that the implicit rate is close to 9.65 per cent.

Finding the number of periods

Suppose we were interested in purchasing an asset that costs $50,000. We currently have $25,000. If we can earn 12 per cent on this $25,000, how long until we have the $50,000? The answer involves solving for the last variable in the basic present value equation, the number of periods. You already know how to get an approximate answer to this particular problem. Notice that we need to double our money. From the Rule of 72, this will take $72/12 = 6$ years at 12 per cent.

To come up with the exact answer, we can again manipulate the basic present value equation. The present value is $25,000, and the future value is $50,000. With a 12 per cent discount rate, the basic equation takes the following form:

$$\$25,000 = \$50,000/(1.12)^t$$
$$\$50,000/\$25,000 = (1.12)^t = 2$$

We thus have a future value factor of 2 for a 12 per cent rate. We now need to solve for t. If you look down the column in Table A.2 that corresponds to 12 per cent, you will see that a future value factor of 1.9738 occurs at six periods. It will thus take about six years as we calculated. To get the exact answer, we have to explicitly solve for t (or use a financial calculator). If you do this, the answer is 6.1163 years, so our approximation was quite close in this case.[1]

EXAMPLE 5.13 **Waiting for Gayetime**

You've been saving up to buy the Gayetime Company. The total cost will be $10 million. You currently have about $2.3 million. If you can earn 5 per cent on your money, how long will you have to wait? At 16%, how long must you wait?

At 5 per cent, you'll have to wait a long time. From the basic present value equation:

$$\$2.3 = 10/(1.05)^t$$
$$1.05^t = 4.3478$$
$$\text{Log } 1.05 \times t = \text{Log } 4.3478$$
$$t = \text{Log } 4.3478/\text{Log } 1.05$$
$$t = 30.122 \text{ years}$$

At 16 per cent, things are a little better. Check for yourself that it will take about 10 years.

Concept questions

5.3a *What is the basic present value equation?*

5.3b *What is the Rule of 72?*

5.3c *In general, what is the present value of $1 to be received in t periods, assuming a discount rate of r per period?*

 ## 5.4 Present and future values of multiple cash flows

Thus far, we have restricted our attention to either the future value of a lump-sum present amount or the present value of some single future cash flow. In this section, we extend these basic results to handle any number of cash flows. We start with future value.

Future value with multiple cash flows

Suppose you deposit $100 today in an account paying 8 per cent. In one year, you will deposit another $100. How much will you have in two years? This particular problem is relatively easy. At the end of the first year, you will have $108 plus the second $100 you deposit for a total of $208. You leave this $208 on deposit at 8 per cent for another year. At the end of this second year, it is worth:

$$\$208 \times 1.08 = \$224.64$$

 FIGURE 5.4

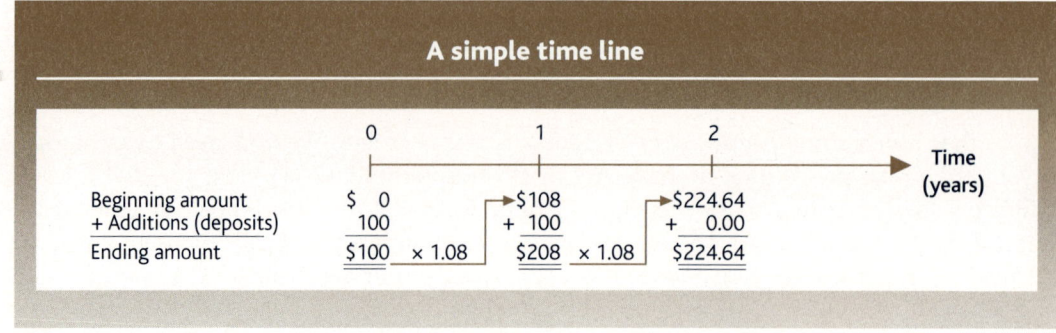

A simple time line

Figure 5.4 (opposite) is a time line that illustrates the process of calculating the future value of these two $100 deposits. Figures such as this one are very useful for solving complicated problems. Whenever you are having trouble with a present or future value problem, drawing a time line will usually help you to see what is happening.

Based on Example 5.14, there are two ways to calculate future values for multiple cash flows:

1 compound the accumulated balance forward one year at a time; or
2 calculate the future value of each cash flow first and then add them up.

These give the same answer, so you can do it either way.

To illustrate the two different ways of calculating future values, consider the future value of $2,000 invested at the end of each of the next five years. The current balance is zero, and the rate is 10 per cent. We first draw a time line as in Figure 5.5 (overleaf).

FIGURE 5.5

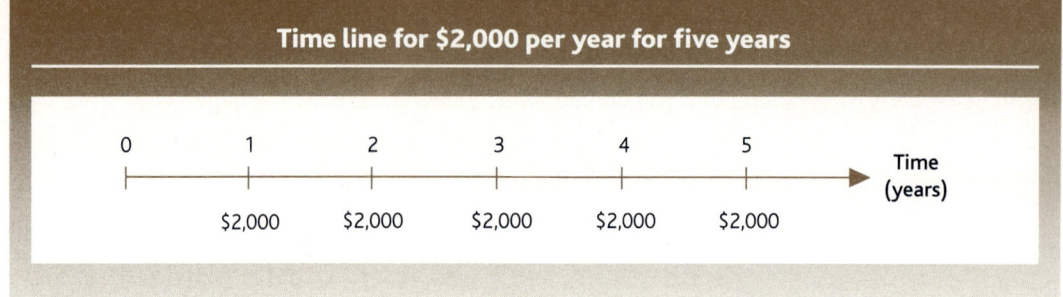

Time line for $2,000 per year for five years

On the time line, notice that nothing happens until the end of the first year when we make the first $2,000 investment. This first $2,000 earns interest for the next four (not five) years. Also notice that the last $2,000 is invested at the end of the fifth year, so it earns no interest at all.

Figure 5.6 illustrates the calculations involved if we compound the investment one period at a time. As illustrated, the future value is $12,210.20.

FIGURE 5.6

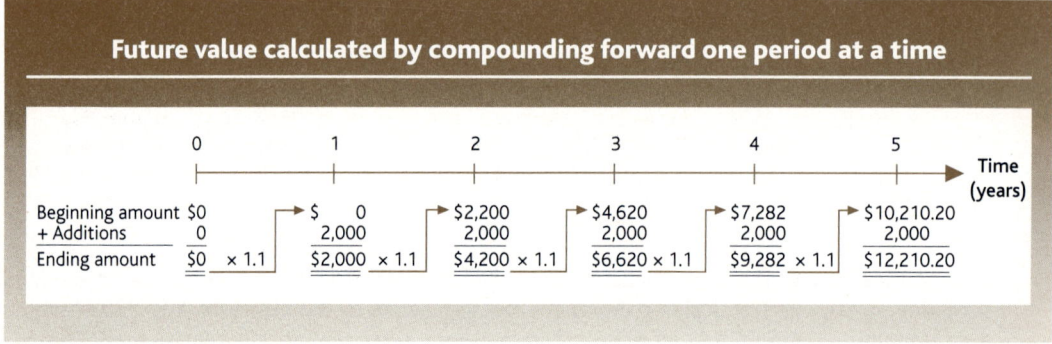

Future value calculated by compounding forward one period at a time

Figure 5.7 goes through the same calculations, but the second technique is used. Naturally, the answer is the same.

FIGURE 5.7

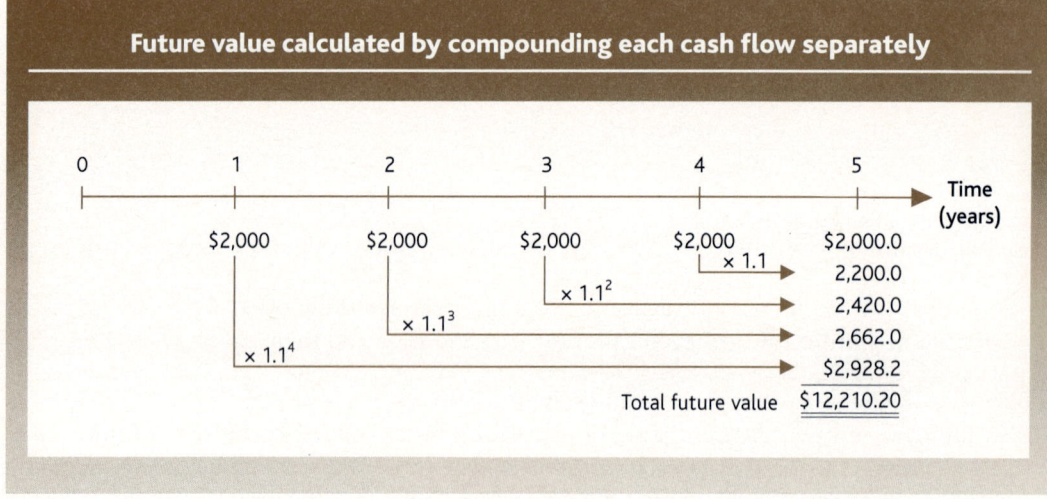

Future value calculated by compounding each cash flow separately

Saving up once again

If you deposit $100 in one year, $200 in two years, and $300 in three years, how much will you have in three years? How much of this is interest? How much will you have in five years if you do not add additional amounts? Assume a 7 per cent interest rate throughout.

We will calculate the future value of each amount in three years. Notice that the $100 earns interest for two years, and the $200 earns interest for one year. The final $300 earns no interest. The future values are thus:

$$
\begin{aligned}
\$100 \times 1.07^2 &= \$114.49 \\
\$200 \times 1.07 &= 214.00 \\
+ \$300 &= \underline{300.00} \\
\text{Total future value} &= \underline{\underline{\$628.49}}
\end{aligned}
$$

The future value is thus $628.49. The total interest is:

$$\$628.49 - (\$100 + \$200 + \$300) = \$28.49$$

How much will you have in five years? We know that you will have $628.49 in three years. If you leave that in for two more years, it will grow to:

$$\$628.49 \times (1.07)^2 = \$628.49 \times 1.1449 = \$719.56$$

Notice that we could have calculated the future value of each amount separately. Once again, be careful about the lengths of time. As we previously calculated, the first $100 earns interest for only four years, the second deposit earns three years interest, and the last earns two years interest:

$$
\begin{aligned}
\$100 \times (1.07)^4 &= \$100 \times 1.3108 &= \$131.08 \\
+ \$200 \times (1.07)^3 &= \$200 \times 1.2250 &= 245.01 \\
+ \$300 \times (1.07)^2 &= \$300 \times 1.1449 &= \underline{343.47} \\
\text{Total future value} & & = \underline{\underline{\$719.56}}
\end{aligned}
$$

Present value with multiple cash flows

It will turn out that very often we will need to determine the present value of a series of future cash flows. As with future values, there are two ways we can do it. We can either discount back one period at a time, or we can just calculate the present values individually and add them up.

Suppose that you needed $1,000 in one year and $2,000 more in two years. If you can earn 9 per cent on your money, how much do you have to invest today to cover these amounts exactly in the future? In other words, what is the present value of the two cash flows at 9 per cent?

The present value of $2,000 in two years at 9 per cent is:

$$\$2,000/1.09^2 = \$1,683.36$$

The present value of $1,000 in one year is:

$$\$1,000/1.09 = \$917.43$$

Therefore, the total present value is:

$$\$1,683.36 + \$917.43 = \$2,600.79$$

To see why $2,600.79 is the right answer, we can check to see that after the $2,000 is paid out in two years, there is no money left. If we invest $2,600.79 for one year at 9 per cent, we will have:

$$\$2,600.79 \times 1.09 = \$2,834.86$$

We take out $1,000, leaving $1,834.86. This amount earns 9 per cent for another year, leaving us with:

$$\$1,834.86 \times 1.09 = \$2,000$$

This is just as we planned. As this example illustrates, the present value of a series of future cash flows is simply the amount that you would need today in order to exactly duplicate those future cash flows (for a given discount rate).

An alternative way of calculating present values for multiple future cash flows is to discount back to the present one period at a time. To illustrate, suppose we had an investment that was going to pay $1,000 at the end of every year for the next five years. To find the present value, we could discount each $1,000 back to the present separately and then add them up. Figure 5.8 illustrates this approach for a 6 per cent discount rate. As Figure 5.8 shows, the answer is $4,212.37.

FIGURE 5.8

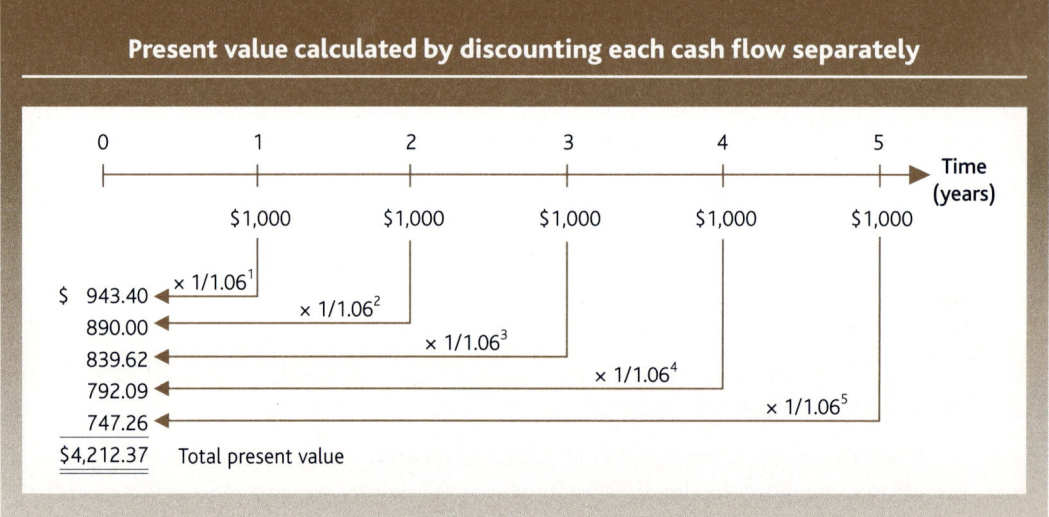

Present value calculated by discounting each cash flow separately

FIGURE 5.9

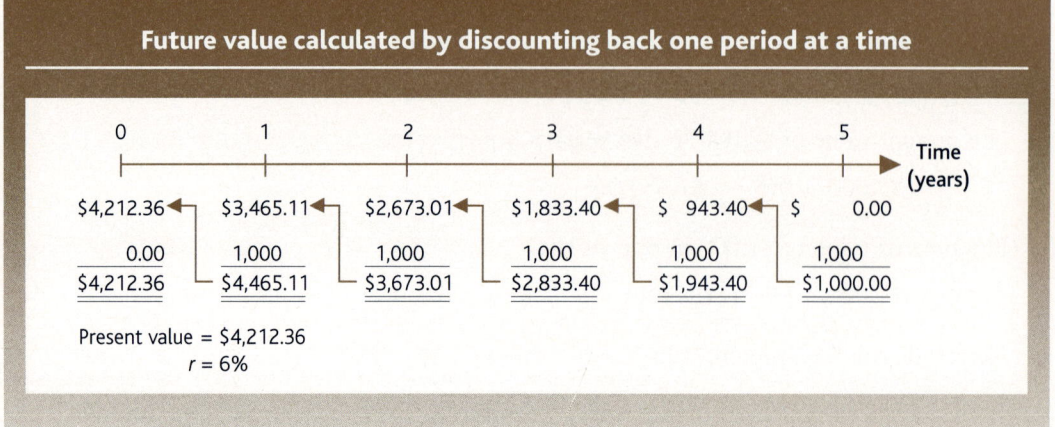

Future value calculated by discounting back one period at a time

Alternatively, we could discount the last cash flow back one period and add it to the next-to-the-last cash flow:

$$\$1,000/1.06 + \$1,000 = \$943.40 + \$1,000 = \$1,943.40$$

We could then discount this amount back one period and add it to the year three cash flow:

$$\$1,943.40/1.06 + \$1,000 = \$1,833.39 + \$1,000 = \$2,833.39$$

This process could be repeated as necessary. Figure 5.9 (opposite) illustrates this approach and the remaining calculations. The answer is the same as that obtained in Figure 5.8 when a small rounding error is ignored.

How much is it worth? EXAMPLE 5.16

You are offered an investment that will pay you $200 in one year, $400 the next, $600 the next, and $800 at end of the last year. You can earn 12 per cent on very similar investments. What is the most you should pay for this one?

We need to calculate the present value of these cash flows at 12 per cent. Taking them one at a time gives:

$$
\begin{aligned}
\$200 \times 1/1.12^1 &= \$200/1.1200 = & \$178.57 \\
\$400 \times 1/1.12^2 &= \$400/1.2544 = & 318.88 \\
\$600 \times 1/1.12^3 &= \$600/1.4049 = & 427.07 \\
\$800 \times 1/1.12^4 &= \$800/1.5735 = & \underline{508.41} \\
\text{Total present value} & & = \underline{\$1,432.93}
\end{aligned}
$$

If you can earn 12 per cent on your money, then you can duplicate this investment's cash flows by investing $1,432.93 elsewhere, so this is the most you should be willing to pay.

How much is it worth? Part 2 EXAMPLE 5.17

You are offered an investment that will make three $5,000 payments. The first payment will occur four years from today. The second will occur in five years, the third will follow in six years. If you can earn 11 per cent, what is the most this investment is worth today? What is the future value of the cash flows?

We will answer the questions in reverse order to illustrate a point. The future value of the cash flows in six years is:

$$\$5,000 \times (1.11)^2 + \$5,000 \times (1.11) + \$5,000 = \$6,160.50 + \$5,550 + \$5,000$$
$$= \$16,710.50$$

The present value must be:

$$\$16,710.50/(1.11)^6 = \$8,934.12$$

Let's check this. Taking them one at a time, the PV of the cash flows is:

$$
\begin{aligned}
\$5,000 \times (1/1.11^6) &= \$5,000/1.8704 &= \$2,673.20 \\
\$5,000 \times (1/1.11^5) &= \$5,000/1.6851 &= \$2,967.26 \\
\$5,000 \times (1/1.11^4) &= \$5,000/1.5181 &= \underline{\$3,293.65} \\
\text{Total present value} & & = \underline{\$8,934.12}
\end{aligned}
$$

This is as we previously calculated. The point we want to make is that we can calculate present and future values in any order and convert between them using the method that seems most convenient. The answers will always be the same as long as we stick with the same discount rate and are careful to keep track of the right number of periods.

 **5.5** ## Valuing equal cash flows: annuities and perpetuities

annuity

a series of cash flows of equal amount, equally spaced in time

We will frequently encounter situations where we have multiple cash flows that are all the same amount. For example, the most common type of loan repayment calls for the borrower to repay the loan by making a series of equal payments for some length of time. Almost all consumer loans (such as car loans) and home mortgages feature equal payments, usually made each month.

ordinary annuity

an annuity in which the time period from the date of valuation to the date of the first cash flow is equal to the time period between each subsequent cash flow. All cash flows occur at the end of the period

More generally, a series of constant or equal cash flows that occurs at the end of each period for some fixed number of periods is called an **ordinary annuity**, or, more correctly, the cash flows are said to be in ordinary annuity form. Annuities appear very frequently in financial arrangements, and there are some useful shortcuts for determining their values. We consider these next.

Present value for annuity cash flows

Suppose we were examining an asset that promised to pay $500 at the end of each of the next three years. The cash flows from this asset are in the form of a three-year, $500 annuity. If we wanted to earn 10 per cent on our money, how much would we offer for this annuity?

From the previous section, we can discount each of these $500 payments back to the present at 10 per cent to determine the total present value:

$$
\begin{aligned}
\text{Present value} &= \$500/1.1^1 + \$500/1.1^2 + \$500/1.1^3 \\
&= \$500/1.10 + \$500/1.21 + \$500/1.1331 \\
&= \$454.55 + \$413.22 + \$375.66 \\
&= \$1{,}243.43
\end{aligned}
$$

This approach works just fine. However, we will often encounter situations where the number of cash flows is quite large. For example, a typical home mortgage calls for monthly payments over 30 years, for a total of 360 payments. If we were trying to determine the present value of those payments, it would be useful to have a shortcut.

Since the cash flows on an annuity are all the same, we can come up with a very useful variation on the basic present value equation. It turns out that the present value of an annuity of C dollars per period for t periods when the rate of return or interest rate is r is given by:

$$
\begin{aligned}
\text{Annuity present value} &= C \times (1 - \text{Present value factor})/r \\
&= C \times \{1 - [1/(1 + r)^t]\}/r
\end{aligned}
$$

Another way of representing this formula is:

$$
\begin{aligned}
\text{Annuity present value} &= C \times (1 - \text{Present value factor})/r \\
&= C \times [1 - (1 + r)^{-t}]/r
\end{aligned}
$$

This discounting term is sometimes called the present value interest factor for annuities and abbreviated PVIFA (t,r).

The expression for the annuity present value may look a little complicated, but it is not difficult to use. Notice for the first formula that the term in curly braces, $\{1/(1 + r)^t\}$, is the same present value factor we have been calculating. In our example just above, the interest rate is 10 per cent and there are three years involved. The usual present value factor is thus:

$$\text{Present value factor} = 1/1.1^3 = 1/1.331 = 0.75131$$

To calculate the annuity present value factor, we just plug this in:

$$
\begin{aligned}
\text{Annuity present value factor} &= (1 - \text{Present value factor})/r \\
&= (1 - 0.75131)/0.10 \\
&= 0.248685/0.10 = 2.48685
\end{aligned}
$$

Just as we calculated before, the present value of our $500 annuity is then:[2]

$$\text{Annuity present value} = \$500 \times 2.48685 = \$1,243.43$$

Annuity tables

Just as there are tables for ordinary present value factors, there are tables for annuity factors as well. Table 5.4 (overleaf) contains a few such factors; Table A.3 in the Appendix contains a larger set. To find the annuity present value factor we just calculated, look for the row corresponding to three periods and then find the column for 10 per cent. The number you see at that intersection should be 2.4869, as we calculated. Once again, try calculating a few of these factors yourself and compare your answers to the ones in the table to make sure you know how to do it. If you are using a financial calculator, just enter $1 as the payment and calculate the present value; the result should be the annuity present value factor.

How much can you afford?

EXAMPLE 5.18

After carefully going over your budget, you have determined you can afford to pay $632 per month towards a new red sports car. You call up your local bank and find out that the going rate is 1 per cent per month for 48 months. How much can you borrow?

To determine how much you can borrow, we need to calculate the present value of $632 per month for 48 months at 1 per cent per month. The loan payments are in ordinary annuity form, so the annuity present value factor is:

$$
\begin{aligned}
\text{Annuity PV factor} &= (1 - \text{Present value factor})/r \\
&= \{1 - [1/(1.01)^{48}]\}/0.01 \\
&= (1 - 0.6203)/0.01 = 37.9740
\end{aligned}
$$

With this factor, we can calculate the present value of the 48 payments of $632 each as:

$$\text{Present value} = \$632 \times 37.9740 = \$24,000$$

Therefore, $24,000 is what you can afford to borrow and repay.

Finding the payment

Suppose you wished to start up a new business that specialises in the latest of health food trends, frozen bat milk. To produce and market your product you need to borrow $100,000. Because it strikes you as unlikely that this particular fad will be long-lived, you propose

TABLE 5.4

Annuity present value interest factors

Number of periods	Interest rate			
	5%	10%	15%	20%
1	0.9524	0.9091	0.8696	0.8333
2	1.8594	1.7355	1.6257	1.5278
3	2.7232	2.4869	2.2832	2.1065
4	3.5460	3.1699	2.8550	2.5887
5	4.3295	3.7908	3.3522	2.9906

to pay off the loan quickly by making five equal annual payments. If the interest rate is 18 per cent, what will the payment be?

In this case, we know the present value is $100,000. The interest rate is 18 per cent, and there are five years. The payments here are all equal, so we need to find the relevant annuity factor and solve for the unknown cash flow:

$$\text{Annuity present value} = \$100,000 = C \times (1 - \text{Present value factor})/r$$
$$\$100,000 = C \times (1 - 1/1.18^5)/0.18$$
$$= C \times (1 - 0.4371)/0.18$$
$$= C \times (3.1272)$$
$$C = \$31,977$$

Therefore, you'll make five payments of just under $32,000 each.

EXAMPLE 5.19

Finding the number of payments

You ran a little short during your semester break, so you put $1,000 on your credit card. You can only afford to make the minimum payment of $20 per month. The interest rate on the credit card is 1.5 per cent per month. How long will you need to pay off the $1,000?

What we have here is an annuity of $20 per month at 1.5 per cent per month for some unknown length of time. The present value is $1,000 (the amount you owe today). We need to do a little algebra:

$$\$1,000 = \$20 \times (1 - \text{Present value factor})/0.015$$
$$(\$1,000/20) \times 0.015 = 1 - \text{Present value factor}$$
$$0.75 = 1 - \text{Present value factor}$$
$$\text{Present value factor} = 0.25 = 1/(1 + r)^t$$
$$(1.015)^t = 1/0.25 = 4$$

At this point, the problem boils down to asking the question: 'How long does it take for your money to quadruple at 1.5% per month?' Based on the previous sections, the answer is about 93 months:

$$t = \text{Log } 4/\text{Log } 1.015 = 93.11.$$
$$\text{Proof } (1.015)^{93} = 3.99 \approx 4$$

It will take you about 93/12 = 7.75 years at this rate.

Finding the rate

The last question we might want to ask concerns the interest rate implicit in an annuity. For example, an insurance company offers to pay you $1,000 per year for 10 years if you will pay $6,710 up front. What rate is implicit in this 10-year annuity?

In this case, we know the present value ($6,710), we know the cash flows ($1,000 per year), and we know the life of the investment (10 years). What we do not know is the discount rate:

$$\$6{,}710 = \$1{,}000 \times (1 - \text{present value factor})/r$$
$$\$6{,}710/\$1{,}000 = 6.71 = (1 - \{1/(1 + r)^{10}\})/r$$

So, the annuity factor for 10 periods is equal to 6.71, and we need to solve this equation for the unknown value of r. Unfortunately, this is mathematically impossible to do directly. The only way to do it is to use a table or trial and error.[3]

If you look across the row corresponding to 10 periods in Table A.3, you will see a factor of 6.7101 for 8 per cent, so we see right away that the insurance company is offering just about 8 per cent. Alternatively, we could just start trying different values until we get very close to the answer. Using this trial and error approach can be a little tedious, but, fortunately, machines are good at repetitious calculations.

To illustrate how to find the answer by trial and error, suppose a relative of yours wants to borrow $3,000. She offers to repay you $1,000 every year for four years. What interest rate are you being offered?

The cash flows here have the form of a four-year $1,000 annuity. The present value is $3,000. We need to find the discount rate, r. Our goal in doing so is primarily to give you a feel for the relationship between annuity values and discount rates.

We need to start somewhere, so 10 per cent is probably as good a place as any to begin. At 10 per cent, the annuity factor is:

$$\text{Annuity present value factor} \doteq (1 - 1/1.10^4)/0.10 = 3.1699$$

The present value of the cash flows at 10 per cent is thus:

$$\text{Present value} = \$1{,}000 \times 3.1699 = \$3{,}169.90$$

You can see that we are already near the correct figure.

Is 10 per cent too high or too low? Recall that present values and discount rates move in opposite directions: Increasing the discount rate lowers the PV and vice versa. Our present value here is too high, so the discount rate is too low. If we try 12 per cent:

$$\text{Present value} = \$1{,}000 \times (1 - 1/1.12^4)/0.12 = \$3{,}037.35$$

Now we are almost there. We are still a little low on the discount rate (because the PV is a little high), so we will try 13 per cent:

$$\text{Present value} = \$1{,}000 \times (1 - 1/1.13^4)/0.13 = \$2{,}974.47$$

This is less than $3,000, so we now know that the answer is between 12 per cent and 13 per cent, and it looks to be about 12.5 per cent. For practice, work at it for a while longer and see if you find that the answer is about 12.59 per cent.

Future value for annuities

On occasion, it is also handy to know a shortcut for calculating the future value of an annuity. For example, suppose you plan to contribute $2,000 every year into a retirement account paying 8 per cent. If you retire in 30 years, how much will you have?

One way to answer this particular problem is to calculate the present value of a $2,000, 30-year annuity at 8 per cent to convert it to a lump sum, and then calculate the future value of that lump sum:

$$\text{Annuity present value} = \$2,000 \times (1 - 1/1.08^{30})/0.08$$
$$= \$2,000 \times 11.2578$$
$$= \$22,515.60$$

The future value of this amount in 30 years is:

$$\text{Future value} = \$22,515.60 \times 1.08^{30} = \$22,515.60 \times 10.0627 = \$226,567$$

We could have done this calculation in one step:

$$\text{Annuity future value} = \text{Annuity present value} \times (1.08)^{30}$$
$$= \$2,000 \times (1 - 1/1.08^{30})/0.08 \times (1.08)^{30}$$
$$= \$2,000 \times (1.08^{30} - 1)/0.08$$
$$= \$2,000 \times (10.0627 - 1)/0.08$$
$$= \$2,000 \times 113.2832$$
$$= \$226,567$$

Note that there are small rounding errors with the calculations as we are only working to four decimal places. As this example illustrates, there are future value factors for annuities as well as present value factors. In general, the future value factor for an annuity is given by:

$$\text{Annuity FV factor} = (\text{Future value factor} - 1)/r$$
$$\text{FVIFA} = [(1 + r)^t - 1]/r$$

For example, you think that you will need to have a total of $50,000 in six years to use as a deposit on a house. If you put $7,000 in an 8 per cent account at the end of each of the next six years, will you make it?

In this case, the annuity future value factor is given by:

$$\text{Annuity FV factor} = (\text{Future value factor} - 1)/r$$
$$= (1.08^6 - 1)/0.08$$
$$= (1.5869 - 1)/0.08$$
$$= 7.336$$

The future value of this six-year, $7,000 annuity is thus:

$$\text{Annuity future value} = \$7,000 \times 7.336$$
$$= \$51,352$$

Thus you will make it with $1,352 to spare.

In our example, notice that the first deposit occurs in one year and the last in six years. As we discussed earlier, the first deposit earns five years interest; the last deposit earns none.

Perpetuities

We have seen that a series of equal cash flows can be valued by treating those cash flows as an annuity. An important special case of an annuity arises when the equal stream of cash flows continues forever. Such an asset is called a **perpetuity** since the cash flows are perpetual.

Since a perpetuity has an infinite number of cash flows, we obviously cannot compute its value by discounting each one. Fortunately, valuing a perpetuity turns out to be the easiest possible case. Consider a perpetuity that costs $1,000 and offers a 12 per cent rate of return. The cash flow each year must be $1,000 $\times$ 0.12 = $120 in this case. More generally, the present value of a perpetuity (PV = $1,000) multiplied by the rate (r = 12%) must equal the cash flow (C = $120):

perpetuity
an annuity in which the cash flows continue forever

$$\text{Perpetuity present value} \times \text{Rate} = \text{Cash flow}$$
$$PV \times r = C$$

Therefore, given a cash flow and a rate of return, we can compute the present value very easily:

$$\text{PV for a perpetuity} = C/r = C \times (1/r)$$

For example, an investment offers a perpetual cash flow of $500 every year. The return you require on such an investment is 8 per cent. What is the value of this investment? The value of this perpetuity is:

$$\text{Perpetuity PV} = C \times (1/r) = \$500/0.08 = \$6,250$$

Another way of seeing why a perpetuity's value is so easy to determine is to take look at the expression for an annuity present value factor:

$$\text{Annuity present value factor} = (1 - \text{Present value factor})/r$$
$$= (1/r) \times (1 - \text{Present value factor})$$

As we have seen, when the number of periods involved gets very large, the present value factor gets very small. As a result, the annuity factor gets closer and closer to $1/r$. At 10 per cent, for example, the annuity present value factor for 100 years is:

$$\text{Annuity present value factor} = (1/0.10) \times (1 - 1/1.10^{100})$$
$$= (1/0.10) \times (1 - 0.000073)$$
$$= (1/0.10)$$

Preference shares

EXAMPLE
5.20

Preference shares are an important example of a perpetuity. When a corporation sells preference shares, the buyer is promised a fixed cash dividend every period forever. This dividend must be paid before any dividend can be paid to regular shareholders, hence the term preference.

Suppose Preferred Ltd wants to sell preference shares at $10 per share. A very similar issue of preference shares already on issue has a price of $4 per share and offers a dividend of $0.40 every year. What dividend will Preferred have to offer if the preference shares are going to sell? *(continued)*

EXAMPLE 5.20 **Preference shares (continued)**

The issue that is already out has a present value of $4 and a cash flow of $0.40 every year forever. Since this is a perpetuity:

$$\text{Present value} = \$4 = \$0.4 \times (1/r)$$
$$r = 10\%$$

To be competitive, the new Preferred Ltd issue will also have to offer 10 per cent so, if the present value is to be $10, the dividend must be such that:

$$\text{Present value} = \$10 = C \times (1/0.1)$$
$$C = \$1$$

Concept questions

5.5a *In general, what is the present value of an annuity of C dollars per period at a discount rate of r per period? The future value?*

5.5b *In general, what is the present value of a perpetuity? The future value?*

 # Comparing rates: the effect of compounding periods

The last issue we need to discuss has to do with the way interest rates are quoted. This subject causes a fair amount of confusion because rates are quoted in many different ways. Sometimes the way a rate is quoted is the result of tradition, and sometimes it is the result of legislation. Unfortunately, at times, rates are quoted in deliberately deceptive ways to mislead borrowers and investors. We will discuss these topics in this section.

Effective annual rates and compounding

If a rate was quoted as 10 per cent compounded semi-annually, then what this means is that the investment actually pays 5 per cent every six months. A natural question then arises: Is 5 per cent every six months the same thing as 10 per cent per year? It is easy to see that it is not. If you invest $1 at 10 per cent per year, you will have $1.10 at the end of the year. If you invest at 5 per cent every six months, then you'll have the future value of $1 at 5 per cent for two periods, or:

$$\$1 \times (1.05)^2 = \$1.1025$$

This is 0.0025 more. The reason is very simple. What has occurred is that your account is credited with $1 × 0.05 = 5 cents in interest after 6 months. In the following six months, you earned 5 per cent on that, which is an extra 5 × 0.05 = 0.25 cents.

As our example illustrates, 10 per cent compounded semi-annually is actually equivalent to 10.25 per cent per year. Put another way, we would be indifferent between 10 per cent compounded semi-annually and 10.25 per cent compounded annually. Anytime we have compounding during the year, we need to be concerned about what the rate really is.

In our example, the 10 per cent is called a **stated or nominal interest rate** (NIR). Other names are used as well. The 10.25 per cent, which is actually the rate that you will earn, is called the **effective annual interest rate** (EAR). To compare different investments or interest rates with different compounding frequencies, we will always need to convert to effective rates. Some general procedures for doing this are discussed next.

stated or nominal interest rate

a quoted interest rate where interest is charged more frequently than the basis on which the interest is quoted. The interest rate actually used to calculate the interest charge is taken as a proportion of the quoted nominal rate and compounded up to the full period of the nominal rate

Calculating and comparing effective annual rates

To see why it is important to work only with effective rates, suppose that you have shopped around and come up with the following three rates:

effective annual interest rate (EAR)

the actual rate of interest to be earned or paid

Bank A: 15%, compounded daily
Bank B: 15.5%, compounded quarterly
Bank C: 16%, compounded annually

Which of these is the best if you are thinking of opening an interest bearing account? Which of these is best if they represent loan rates?

To begin, Bank C is offering 16 per cent per year. Since there is no compounding during the year, this is the effective rate. Bank B is actually paying $0.155/4 = 0.03875$ or 3.875 per cent per quarter. At this rate, an investment of $1 for four quarters would grow to:

$$\$1 \times (1.03875)^4 = \$1.1642$$

The EAR, therefore, is 16.42 per cent. For a saver, this is much better than the 16 per cent rate Bank C is offering; for a borrower, it's worse.

Bank A is compounding every day. This may seem a little extreme, but it is very common to calculate interest daily. In this case, the interest rate is actually:

$$0.15/365 = 0.000411$$

This is 0.0411 per cent per day. At this rate, an investment of $1 for 365 periods would grow to:

$$\$1 \times (1.000411)^{365} = \$1.1618$$

The EAR is 16.18 per cent. This is not as good as Bank B's 16.42 per cent for a saver.

This example illustrates two things. First, the highest nominal rate is not necessarily the best. Second, the compounding during the year can lead to a significant difference between the nominal rate and the effective rate. Remember that the effective rate is what you get or what you pay.

If you look at our examples, we computed the EARs in three steps. We first divided the quoted rate by the number of times that the interest is compounded. We then added 1 to the result and raised it to the power of the number of times the interest is compounded. Finally, we subtracted the 1. If we let m be the number of times the interest is compounded, these steps can be summarised simply as:

$$EAR = [1 + (\text{Nominal rate})/m]^m - 1$$

For example, suppose you were offered 12 per cent compounded monthly. In this case, the interest is compounded 12 times a year; so m is 12. You can calculate the effective rate as:

$$
\begin{aligned}
EAR &= [1 + (\text{Nominal rate})/m]^m - 1 \\
&= [1 + 0.12/12]^{12} - 1 \\
&= 1.01^{12} - 1 \\
&= 1.126825 - 1 \\
&= 12.6825\%
\end{aligned}
$$

EXAMPLE 5.21 ▪ **What's the EAR?**

A bank is offering 12 per cent compounded quarterly. If you put $100 in an account, how much will you have at the end of one year? What's the EAR? How much will you have at the end of two years?

The bank is effectively offering 12%/4 = 3% every quarter. If you invest $100 for four periods at 3 per cent per period, the future value is:

$$
\begin{aligned}
\text{Future value} &= \$100 \times (1.03)^4 \\
&= \$100 \times (1.1255) \\
&= \$112.55
\end{aligned}
$$

The EAR is 12.55 per cent ($100 × (1 + 0.1255) = $112.55).

We can determine what you have at the end of two years in two different ways. One way is to recognise that two years is the same as eight quarters. At 3 per cent per quarter, after eight quarters, you would have:

$$\$100 \times (1.03)^8 = \$100 \times 1.2668 = \$126.68$$

Alternatively, the interest rate is effectively 12.55 per cent per year; so after two years you would have:

$$\$100 \times (1.1255)^2 = \$100 \times 1.2668 = \$126.68$$

Thus, the two calculations produce the same answer. This illustrates an important point. Whenever we do a present or future value calculation for a lump sum, the rate we use must be an actual or effective rate. In this case, the actual rate is 3 per cent per quarter. The effective annual rate is 12.55 per cent. It doesn't matter which one we use once we know the EAR.

EXAMPLE 5.22 ▪ **Quoting a rate**

Now that you know how to convert a nominal rate to an EAR, consider going the other way. As a lender, you know that you want to actually earn 18 per cent on a particular loan. You want to quote a rate that features monthly compounding. What rate do you quote?

In this case, we know the EAR is 18 per cent, and we know that this is the result of monthly compounding. Let n stand for the nominal rate. We thus have:

$$
\begin{aligned}
\text{EAR} &= [1 + (\text{Nominal rate})/m]^m - 1 \\
0.18 &= [1 + n/12]^{12} - 1 \\
1.18 &= [1 + n/12]^{12}
\end{aligned}
$$

We need to solve this equation for the quoted rate. This calculation is the same as the ones we did to find an unknown interest rate in Section 5.3:

$$
\begin{aligned}
1.18^{(1/12)} &= [1 + n/12] \\
1.18^{0.08333} &= 1 + n/12 \\
1.0139 &= 1 + n/12 \\
n &= 0.0139 \times 12 \\
&= 16.68\%
\end{aligned}
$$

Therefore, the rate you would quote is 16.68 per cent, compounded monthly.

EARs and NIRs

Sometimes it's not altogether clear whether a rate is an effective annual rate or not. A case in point concerns what is called the nominal interest rate or NIR on a loan.

Given that an NIR is calculated and displayed, an obvious question arises: Is an NIR an effective annual rate? Put another way, if a bank quotes a car loan at 12 per cent NIR, is the consumer actually paying 12 per cent interest? Surprisingly, the answer is no. There is some confusion over this point, which we discuss next.

The confusion over NIRs arises because lenders compute the NIR in a particular way. The NIR is simply equal to the interest rate per period multiplied by the number of periods in a year. For example, if a bank is charging 1.2 per cent per month on car loans, then the NIR that is reported is $1.2\% \times 12 = 14.4\%$. So, an NIR is in fact the nominal rate we have been discussing. For example, an NIR of 12 per cent on a loan calling for monthly payments is really 1 per cent per month. The EAR on such a loan is thus:

$$\begin{aligned} EAR &= [1 + NIR/12]^{12} - 1 \\ &= 1.01^{12} - 1 = 12.68\% \end{aligned}$$

What rate are you paying?

Depending on the issuer, a typical credit card agreement quotes an interest rate of 18 per cent NIR. Monthly payments are required. What is the actual interest rate you pay on such a credit card?

Based on our discussion, an NIR of 18 per cent with monthly payments is really $0.18/12 = 0.015$ or 1.5 per cent per month. The EAR is thus:

$$\begin{aligned} EAR &= [1 + 0.18/12]^{12} - 1 \\ &= 1.015^{12} - 1 \\ &= 1.1956 - 1 \\ &= 19.56\% \end{aligned}$$

This is the rate you actually pay.

The difference between an NIR and an EAR probably won't be all that great but it makes a monetary difference.

Taking it to the limit: a note on continuous compounding

If you made a deposit in a savings account, how often could your money be compounded during the year? If you think about it, there isn't really any upper limit. We've seen that daily compounding, for example, isn't a problem. There is no reason to stop here, however. We could compound every hour or minute or second. How high would the EAR get in this case? Table 5.5 (overleaf) illustrates the EARs that would result as 10 per cent is compounded at shorter and shorter intervals. Notice that the EARs do keep getting larger, but the differences get very small.

TABLE
5.5

Compounding frequency and effective annual rates		
Compounding period	Number of times compounded	Effective rate
Year	1	10.00000%
Quarter	4	10.38129%
Month	12	10.47131%
Week	52	10.50648%
Day	365	10.51558%
Hour	8,760	10.51703%
Minute	525,600	10.51709%

As the numbers in Table 5.5 seem to suggest, there is an upper limit to the EAR. If we let n stand for the nominal rate, then, as the number of times the interest is compounded gets extremely large, the EAR approaches:

$$\text{EAR} = e^n - 1$$

where e is Euler's (rhymes with 'toiler's') constant, 2.71828 (look for a key labelled 'e^x' on your calculator). For example, with our 10 per cent rate, the highest possible EAR is:

$$
\begin{aligned}
\text{EAR} &= e^n - 1 \\
&= 2.71828 e^{0.10} - 1 \\
&= 1.1051709 - 1 \\
&= 10.51709\%
\end{aligned}
$$

In this case, we say that the money is continuously or instantaneously compounded. What is happening is that interest is credited the instant it is earned, so the amount of interest grows continuously.

Concept questions

5.6a *If an interest rate is given as 12 per cent, compounded daily, what do we call this rate?*

5.6b *What is an NIR? What is an EAR? Are they the same thing?*

5.6c *In general, what is the relationship between a stated interest rate and an effective interest rate? Which is more relevant for financial decisions?*

5.6d *What does continuous compounding mean?*

 ## 5.7 Loan types and loan amortisation

Whenever a lender extends a loan, some provision will be made for repayment of the principal (the original loan amount). A loan might be repaid in equal instalments, for example, or it might be repaid in a single lump sum. Because the way that the principal and interest are paid is up to the parties involved, there is actually an unlimited number of possibilities.

There are a few forms of repayment that come up quite often, and more complicated forms can usually be built up from these. The three basic types are: pure discount loans, interest-only loans, and amortised loans. As we will see, working with these loans is a very straightforward application of the present value principles that we have already developed.

Pure discount loans

The pure discount loan is the simplest form. With such a loan, the borrower receives money today and repays a single lump sum at some time in the future. A one-year, 10 per cent pure discount loan, for example, would require the borrower to repay $1.1 in one year for every dollar borrowed today.

Because a pure discount loan is so simple, we already know how to value one. Suppose that a borrower was able to repay $25,000 in five years. If we, acting as the lender, wanted a 12 per cent interest rate on the loan, how much would we be willing to lend? Put another way, what value would we assign today to that $25,000 to be repaid in five years? Based on our work in this chapter, we know that the answer is just the present value of $25,000 at 12 per cent for five years:

$$
\begin{aligned}
\text{Present value} &= \$25,000/1.12^5 \\
&= \$25,000/1.7623 \\
&= \$14,186
\end{aligned}
$$

Pure discount loans are common where the loan term is short, say a year or less. Examples of this are bank bills or commercial paper with a term of less than one year. These types of securities are discussed in later chapters.

Interest-only loans

A second type of loan repayment plan calls for the borrower to pay interest each period and to repay the entire principal (the original loan amount) at some point in the future. Such loans are called interest-only loans. Notice that if there is just one period, a pure discount loan and an interest-only loan are the same thing.

For example, with a three-year, 10 per cent interest-only loan of $1,000, the borrower would pay $1,000 × 0.10 = $100 in interest at the end of the first and second years. At the end of the third year, the borrower would return the $1,000 along with another $100 in interest for that year. Similarly, a 50-year interest-only loan would call for the borrower to pay interest every year for the next 50 years and then repay the principal. In the extreme case, the borrower pays the interest every period forever and never repays any principal. As we discussed in the chapter, the result is a perpetuity.

Most corporate debentures (debt) have the general form of an interest-only loan. Because we will be considering debentures in some detail in the next chapter, we will defer a further discussion of them for now.

Amortised loans

With a pure discount or interest-only loan, the principal is repaid all at once. An alternative is an amortised loan where the lender may require the borrower to repay parts of the loan amount over time. The process of paying off a loan by making regular principal reductions is called amortising the loan.

A simple way of amortising a loan is to have the borrower pay the interest each period plus some fixed amount. This approach is not common.

For example, suppose a business takes out a $5,000, five-year loan at 9 per cent. The loan agreement calls for the borrower to pay the interest on the loan balance each year and to reduce the loan balance each year by $1,000. Since the loan amount declines by $1,000 each year, it is fully paid in five years.

In the case we are considering, notice that the total payment each year will decline. The reason is that the loan balance goes down, resulting in a lower interest charge each year, while the $1,000 principal reduction is constant. For example, the interest in the first year will be $5,000 × 0.09 = $450. The total payment will be $1,000 + $450 = $1,450. In the second year, the loan balance is $4,000, so the interest is $4,000 × 0.09 = $360, and the total payment is $1,360. We can calculate the total payment in each of the remaining years by preparing a simple amortisation schedule as follows:

TABLE 5.6

	Amortisation schedule				
Year	Beginning Balance	Total payment	Interest paid	Principal paid	Ending balance
1	5,000	1,450	450	1,000	4,000
2	4,000	1,360	360	1,000	3,000
3	3,000	1,270	270	1,000	2,000
4	2,000	1,180	180	1,000	1,000
5	1,000	1,090	90	1,000	0
Totals		6,350	1,350	5,000	

Notice that, in each year, the interest paid is just given by the beginning balance multiplied by the interest rate. Also notice that the beginning balance is given by the ending balance from the previous year.

The most common way of amortising a loan is for the borrower to make a single, fixed payment every period. Almost all consumer loans (such as car loans) and mortgages work this way. For example, suppose our five-year, 9 per cent, $5,000 loan was amortised this way. How would the amortisation schedule look?

We first need to determine the payment. From our discussion in the chapter, we know that the loan's cash flows are in the form of an ordinary annuity in this case, so we can solve for the payment as follows:

$$\$5,000 = C \times (1 - 1/1.09^5)/0.09$$
$$= C \times (1 - 0.6499)/0.09$$
$$= C \times 3.8897$$

This gives us:

$$C = \$5,000/3.8897$$
$$= \$1,285.46$$

The borrower will therefore make five equal payments of $1,285.46. Will this pay off the loan? We will check by filling in an amortisation schedule.

In our previous example, we knew the principal reduction each year. We then calculated the interest owed to get the total payment. In this example, we know the total payment. We will thus calculate the interest and then subtract it from the total payment to calculate the principal portion in each payment.

In the first year, the interest is $450 as we calculated before. Since the total payment is $1,285.46, the principal paid in the first year must be:

$$\text{Principal paid} = \$1,285.46 - \$450 = \$835.46$$

The ending loan balance is thus:

$$\text{Ending balance} = \$5,000 - \$835.46 = \$4,164.54$$

The interest in the second year is $4,164.54 × 0.09 = $374.81, and the loan balance declines by $1,285.46 − $374.81 = $910.65. We can summarise all of the relevant calculations in the following schedule.

Amortisation of a loan for $5,000 at 9 per cent per year				
Year	Beginning balance	Total payment	Interest paid	Principal paid	Ending balance
1	5,000.00	1,285.46	450.00	835.46	4,164.54
2	4,164.54	1,285.46	374.81	910.65	3,253.88
3	3,253.88	1,285.46	292.85	992.61	2,261.27
4	2,261.27	1,285.46	203.51	1,081.95	1,179.32
5	1,179.32	1,285.46	106.14	1,179.32	0.00
Totals		6,427.30	1,427.30	5,000.00	

TABLE 5.7

Since the loan balance declines to zero, the five equal payments do pay off the loan. Notice that the interest paid declines each period. This isn't surprising since the loan balance is going down. Given that the total payment is fixed, the principal paid must be rising each period.

If you compare the two loan amortisations in this section, you will see that the total interest is greater for the equal total payment case, $1,427.30 versus $1,350. The reason for this is that the loan is repaid more slowly early on, so the interest is somewhat higher. This doesn't mean that one loan is better than the other; it simply means that one is effectively paid off faster than the other. For example, the principal reduction in the first year is $835.46 in the equal total payment case compared to $1,000 in the first case.

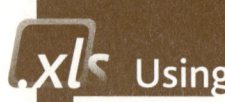

Using Excel

All of the calculations that have been performed in this chapter can be done in Excel. We will now show you various examples of the calculations. First you need to be in the program Excel. On the toolbar you should notice a function f_x. Click on this and you will see that you have a number of choices of functions. The ones that we will use are the financial functions. The Excel menu is reproduced below.

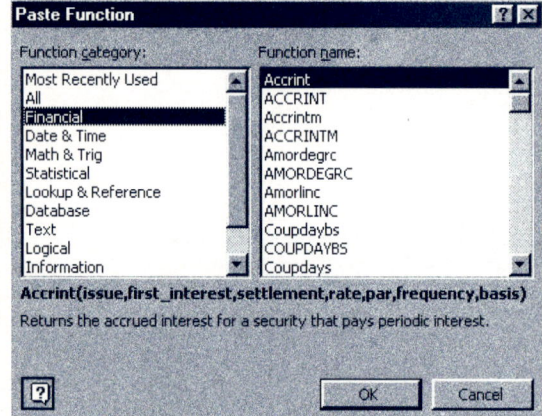

First, let us calculate the future value, FV. Assume that an investment pays 12 per cent and you have $400 to invest. What will be the value of the investment in three years time? Go to the financial functions and find FV. When you click onto this you should notice that there are up to five inputs required. The inputs are:

Rate = the rate of interest per period

Nper =   the total number of periods

Pmt = the payment per period—for an annuity

PV = the present value lump sum

Type = normally left blank

For the problem at hand the rate is 0.12 for 12 per cent, the Nper is 3 for three years, the Pmt is left blank (since it is not an annuity) and the PV is −400. The calculated answer will be $561.97. Notice that the PV is put in as a negative. For Excel and financial calculators to do the calculations, some cash flows need to be negative and others need to be positive. This may sound a bit strange, but think of an investment where you invest $100 and get back $110 in one periods time. What rate of return have you earned? The answer is 10 per cent. Now try this in Excel.

The function that will be used here is Rate within the financial functions. Click on rate and the inputs are Nper, Pmt, PV, FV and Type. The number of periods is 1, there is no payment as it is not an annuity, the present value is 100

and the future value is 110. If you put both the present value and future value in as positive figures then Excel cannot calculate an answer. If both the figures are positive it is like receiving (positive) $100 today and $110 in one years time. What rate of return have you earned? This does not make sense. You received $100 and then $110. To make sense of the problem, think that you outlay (negative cash flow) $100 and get back (positive cash flow) $110. Now Excel will calculate a rate of return of 10%.

Next we will try the PV function, but this time the problem will be an annuity. I can afford say $320 per month for car loan repayments. The finance company charges 8% per annum. How much can I afford to borrow if I am willing to enter a five-year loan? Now the problem requires me to enter particular data. Rate will be 0.08/12 because you are asked for the rate per period and the repayments are monthly therefore a period is a month. The Nper is 60 and the Pmt is −320. Remember to make the Pmt negative because this is a negative cash flow, a payment to the finance company. $15,781.90 is the amount that I can afford to borrow.

You plan to borrow $100,000 to buy a home. The bank is lending funds at 7 per cent and you are going to make monthly repayments. What will be the monthly repayment if you borrow the funds for 20 years? In this problem you need to solve for Pmt. When you click onto the Pmt function, you need to input Rate which will be 0.07/12, Nper which is 20 × 12 = 240 and PV which is $100,000. It is not necessary to enter either FV or type. FV is not necessary as you will be paying the loan off over 20 years so that in 20 years time you will owe nothing. Excel's default for FV is $0, which is what you want anyway. The calculated answer is $775.30. If you put the $100,000 in as a positive as you would be receiving this, Excel calculates $775.30 as a negative as you will be paying this amount every month.

Another Excel calculation is Nper. Mary currently has $500,000 invested in a fund earning 10 per cent per annum. She wishes to retire with $1,000,000. How many more years does she have to wait until the fund accumulates to $1,000,000? The answer is about 7.3 years.

Excel will also convert a nominal interest rate (NIR) into an effective interest rate (EAR) and vice versa. To calculate the effective rate, just click onto Effect within the financial functions (if you cannot see this function, make sure you have ticked the two Analysis ToolPak boxes under Tools, Add-ins). You need to input both the nominal rate and the number of compounding periods. To calculate a nominal rate, click onto Nominal. You need to input the effective rate and the number of compounding periods.

5.8 ■ Summary and conclusions

This chapter has introduced you to the basic principles of present value and discounted cash flow valuation. In it, we explain a number of things about the time value of money, including:

1   For a given rate of return, the value at some point in the future of an investment made today can be determined by calculating the future value of that investment.

2   The current worth of a future cash flow or series of cash flows can be determined for a given rate of return by calculating the present value of the cash flow(s) involved.

3   The relationship between present value (PV) and future value (FV) for a given rate r and time t is given by the basic present value equation:

$$PV = FV_t /(1 + r)^t$$

As we have shown, it is possible to find any one of the four components (PV, FV_t, r, t) given the other three.

4   A series of constant cash flows that arrive or are paid at the end of each period is called an ordinary annuity, and we describe some useful shortcuts for determining the present and future values of annuities.

5   Interest rates can be quoted in a variety of ways. For financial decisions, it is important that any rates are converted to effective rates before being compared. The relationship between a quoted rate, such as the nominal interest rate (NIR), and an effective annual rate (EAR) is given by:

$$EAR = (1 + Nominal\ rate/m)^m - 1$$

where m is the number of times during the year the money is compounded or, equivalently, the number of payments during the year.

The principles developed in this chapter will figure prominently in the chapters to come. The reason for this is that most investments, whether they involve real assets or financial assets, can be analysed using the discounted cash flow (DCF) approach. As a result, the DCF approach is broadly applicable and widely used in practice. For example, the next chapter shows how to value bonds and shares using an extension of the techniques presented in this chapter. Before going on, however, you might want to do some of the problems below.

Key terms

Annuity *160*
Compound interest *138*
Compounding *138*
Discount rate *147*
Discounting *147*

Effective annual interest rate (EAR) *167*
Future value (FV) *138*
Interest on interest *138*
Ordinary annuity *160*

Perpetuity *165*
Present value (PV) *146*
Simple interest *138*
Stated or nominal interest rate *167*

Suggested reading

One of the best places to learn more about the mathematics of present value is the owner's manual that comes with a financial calculator.

Endnotes

1 To solve for t, we have to take the logarithm of both sides of the equation:

$$1.12^t = 2$$
$$\log 1.12 \times t = \log 2$$

We can then solve for t explicitly:

$$t = \log 2/\log 1.12$$
$$= 6.1163$$

Almost all calculators can determine a logarithm; look for a key labelled 'log' or 'ln'. If both are present, use either one but you need to be consistent.

2 To solve this problem on a common type of financial calculator, you would need to do the following:

1. Enter the 'payment' of C = \$500 and press 'PMT'.
2. Enter the 'interest rate' of r = 10 % as 10 (not 0.10) and press 'i'.
3. Enter the number of periods as 3 and press 'n'.
4. Ask the calculator for the PV by pressing 'compute' and then 'PV'.

3 Financial calculators rely on trial and error to find the answer. That's why they sometimes appear to be 'thinking' before coming up with the answer. Actually, it is possible to solve directly for r if there are less than five periods, but it's usually not worth the trouble.

Maximise Your Marks!
There are 30 interactive questions on the time value of money waiting online for you at www.mhhe.com/au/ross3e. The questions are written with additional feedback for incorrect answers, and text excerpts with page references for follow-up study.

International Articles!
To read more on the time value of money and to see current international articles, just go to www.mhhe.com/au/ross3e and click on *PowerWeb Articles* for this chapter.

Chapter review problems and self-test

5.1 · Calculating future values
Assume that you deposit $1,000 today in an account that pays 8 per cent interest. How much will you have in four years? How much will you have if the 8 per cent is compounded quarterly? How much will you have in $4\frac{1}{2}$ years in this case?

5.2 · Calculating present values
Suppose that you have just celebrated your 19th birthday. A rich uncle set up a trust fund for you that will pay you $100,000 when you turn 25. If the relevant discount rate is 11 per cent, how much is this fund worth today?

5.3 · More present values
The Australian halfback has been signed to a three-year, $1 million contract. The details provide for an immediate cash bonus of $100,000. The player is to receive $200,000 in salary at the end of the first year, $300,000 the next, and $400,000 at the end of the last year. Assuming a 10 per cent discount rate, is this package worth $1 million? How much is it worth?

5.4 · Future value with multiple cash flows
You plan to make a series of deposits in an interest-bearing account. You will deposit $1,000 today, $2,000 in two years, and $8,000 in five years. If you withdraw $3,000 in three years and $5,000 in seven years, how much will you have after eight years if the interest rate is 9 per cent? What is the present value of these cash flows?

5.5 · Annuity present value
You are looking into an investment that will pay you $12,000 per year for the next 10 years. If you require a 15 per cent return, what is the most you would pay for this investment?

5.6 · NIR versus EAR
The going rate on student loans is quoted as 9 per cent NIR. The terms of the loan call for monthly payments. What is the effective annual rate (EAR) on such a student loan?

5.7 · It's the principal that matters
Suppose you borrow $10,000. You are going to repay the loan by making equal annual payments for five years. The interest rate on the loan is 14 per cent per year. Prepare an amortisation schedule for the loan. How much interest will you pay over the life of the loan?

5.8 · Just a little bit each month
You've recently finished your MBA at the Advancit School. Naturally, you must purchase a second-hand BMW immediately. The car costs about $21,000. The bank quotes an interest rate of 15 per cent NIR for a 72-month loan with a 10 per cent down-payment. You plan on trading the car in for a new one in two years. What will you monthly payment be? What is the effective interest rate on the loan? What will the loan balance be when you trade the car in?

Answers to self-test problems

5.1 · We need to calculate the future value of $1,000 at 8 per cent for four years. The future value factor is:

$$1.08^4 = 1.3605$$

The future value is thus $1,000 × 1.3605 = $1,360.50. If the 8 per cent is compounded quarterly, then the rate is actually 2 per cent per quarter. In four years, there are 16 quarters; so the future value factor is now:

$$1.02^{16} = 1.3728$$

The future value of your $1,000 is thus $1,372.80 in this case, which is a little more than before because of the extra compounding. Notice that we could have calculated the EAR first:

$$EAR = [1 + 0.08/4]^4 - 1 = 8.24322\%$$

The future value factor would then be:

$$1.0824322^4 = 1.3728$$

This is just as we calculated. To find the future value after 4.5 years, we could either use the actual quarterly rate with 18 quarters or the effective annual rate with 4.5 years. We will do both:

Future value $= \$1,000 \times (1.02)^{18} = \$1,000 \times 1.42825 = \$1,428.25$

or:

Future value $= \$1,000 \times (1.0824322)^{4.5} = \$1,000 \times 1.42825$
$= \$1,428.25$

5.2 · We need the present value of $100,000 to be paid in six years at 11 per cent. The discount factor is:

$1/1.11^6 = 1/1.8704 = 0.5346$

The present value is thus about $53,460.

5.3 · Obviously, the package is not worth $1 million because the payments are spread out over three years. The bonus is paid today, so it's worth $100,000. The present values for the three subsequent salary payments are:

$\$200,000/1.1 + 300,000/1.1^2 + 400,000/1.1^3$
$= \$200,000/1.1 + 300,000/1.21 + 400,000/1.3310$
$= \$181,819 + \$247,935 + \$300,526$
$= \$730,280$

The package is worth a total of $830,280 including the $100,000 bonus.

5.4 · We will calculate the future values for each of the cash flows separately and then add them up. Notice that we treat the withdrawals as negative cash flows:

$\$1,000 \times 1.09^8$ =	$\$1,000 \times 1.9926$ =	$\$1,992.60$
$\$2,000 \times 1.09^6$ =	$\$2,000 \times 1.6771$ =	$\$3,354.20$
$-\$3,000 \times 1.09^5$ =	$-\$3,000 \times 1.5386$ =	$-\$4,615.80$
$\$8,000 \times 1.09^3$ =	$\$8,000 \times 1.2950$ =	$\$10,360.00$
$-\$5,000 \times 1.09^1$ =	$-\$5,000 \times 1.0900$ =	$-\$5,450.00$
Total future value	=	$\$5,641.00$

This value includes a small rounding error as the answer is dependent on the number of decimal places used in the calculations.

To calculate the present value, we could discount each cash flow back to the present or we could discount back a single year at a time. However, since we already know that the future value in eight years is $5,641, the easy way to get the PV is just to discount this amount back eight years:

Present value $= \$5,641/1.09^8 = \$5,641/1.9926 = \$2,831$

We again ignore a small rounding error. For practice, you can verify that this is what you get if you discount each cash flow back separately.

5.5 · The most you would be willing to pay is the present value of $12,000 per year for 10 years at a 15 per cent discount rate. The cash flows here are in ordinary annuity form, so the relevant present value factor is:

Annuity present value factor $= (1 - (1/1.15^{10}))/0.15$
$= (1 - 0.2472)/0.15$
$= 5.0188$

The present value of the 10 cash flows is thus:

Present value $= \$12,000 \times 5.0188$
$= \$60,225$

This is the most you would pay.

5.6 · A rate of 9 per cent NIR with monthly payments is actually 9%/12 = 0.75% per month. The EAR is thus:

EAR $= [1 + 0.09/12]^{12} - 1 = 9.38\%$

5.7 · We first need to calculate the annual payment. With a present value of $10,000, an interest rate of 14 per cent, and a term of 5 years, the payment can be determined from:

$$\$10,000 = \text{Payment} \times (1 - 1/1.14^5)/0.14$$
$$= \text{Payment} \times 3.4331$$

Therefore, the payment is $10,000/3.4331 = \$2,912.84$ (actually, it's $2,912.8355; this will create some small rounding errors in the schedule below). We can now prepare the amortisation schedule as follows:

Year	Beginning balance	Total payment	Interest paid	Principal paid	Ending balance
1	10,000.00	2,912.84	1,400.00	1,512.84	8,487.16
2	8,487.16	2,912.84	1,188.20	1,724.64	6,762.52
3	6,762.52	2,912.84	946.75	1,966.09	4,796.44
4	4,796.44	2,912.84	671.50	2,241.34	2,555.10
5	2,555.10	2,912.84	357.74	2,555.10	0.00
Totals		14,564.20	4,564.20	10,000.00	

5.8 · The cash flows on the car loan are in annuity form, so we only need to find the payment. The interest rate is $15\%/12 = 1.25\%$ per month, and there are 72 months. The first thing we need is the annuity factor for 72 periods at 1.25 per cent per period:

$$\text{Annuity present value factor} = (1 - \text{Present value factor})/r$$
$$= (1 - \{1/1.0125^{72}\})/r$$
$$= (1 - \{1/2.4459\})/0.0125$$
$$= (1 - 0.4088)/0.0125$$
$$= 47.2925$$

The present value is the amount we finance. With a 10 per cent down payment, we will be borrowing 90 per cent of $21,000, or $18,900. So, to find the payment, we need to solve for C in the following:

$$\$18,900 = C \times \text{Annuity present value factor}$$
$$= C \times 47.2925$$

Rearranging things a bit, we have:

$$C = \$18,900 \times (1/47.2925)$$
$$= \$18,900 \times 0.02115$$
$$= \$399.64$$

Your payment is just under $400 per month.

The actual interest rate on this loan is 1.25 per cent per month. Based on our work in the chapter, we can calculate the effective annual rate as:

$$\text{EAR} = (1.0125)^{12} - 1 = 16.08\%$$

The effective rate is about one hundred basis points (1%) higher than the quoted rate.

To determine the loan balance in two years, we could amortise the loan out to see what the balance would be at that time. This would be fairly tedious to do by hand. We can instead simply calculate the present value of the remaining payments. After two years, we have made 24 payments, so there are $72 - 24 = 48$ payments left. What is the present value of 48 monthly payments of $399.64 at 1.25 per cent per month? The relevant annuity factor is:

$$\text{Annuity present value factor} = (1 - \text{Present value factor})/r$$
$$= (1 - \{1/1.0125^{48}\})/r$$
$$= (1 - \{1/1.8154\})/0.0125$$
$$= (1 - 0.5508)/0.0125$$
$$= 35.936$$

The present value is thus:

$$\text{Present value} = \$399.64 \times 35.936 = \$14,361.46$$

You will owe about $14,361 on the loan in two years.

Questions and problems

1 · Calculating present values

For each of the following, compute the present value:

Future value	Years	Interest rate	Present value
$15,530	10	12%	
10,665	13	6%	
12,324	23	4%	
15,180	4	32%	

2 · Calculating future values

For each of the following, compute the future value:

Present value	Years	Interest rate	Future value
$2,092	8	15%	
2,061	10	12%	
2,275	12	9%	
4,307	20	2%	

3 · Calculating interest rates

Assume that the cost of a university education will be $30,000 when your children enter uni in 15 years time. You presently have $10,000 to invest. What rate of interest must be earned on your investment to cover the cost of a university education 15 years from now?

4 · Present value with multiple cash flows

An investment has the following cash flows. If the discount rate is 8 per cent, what is the present value of these flows? What is the present value at 12 per cent? What is the present value if the interest rate is zero?

Year	Cash Flows
1	$200
2	400
3	800

5 · Calculating future values

What is the future value of $5,000 in 12 years, assuming a rate of 6 per cent compounded monthly?

6 · Calculating future values

A local bank is offering 6 per cent compounded monthly on savings accounts. If you deposit $1,500 today, how much will you have in two years? How much will you have in 2.5 years?

7 · Present value and multiple cash flows

You have just joined the investment banking firm of Super, Save and Growth. They have offered you two different salary arrangements. You can have $40,000 per year for the next two years; or $20,000 per year for the next two years, along with a $30,000 signing bonus today. If the interest rate is 8 per cent compounded quarterly, which do you prefer? For simplicity, assume the salaries are to be paid at the end of each year.

8 · Calculating EAR

Find the EAR in each of the cases below:

Stated rate (NIR)	Number of times compounded	Effective rate (EAR)
5%	semi-annually	
7%	quarterly	
20%	daily	
24%	infinite	

9 · Calculating NIR

Find the NIR or stated rate in each of the cases below:

Stated rate (NIR)	Number of times compounded	Effective rate (EAR)
	semi-annually	6%
	quarterly	8%
	daily	12%
	infinite	14%

10 · Calculating EAR

Generous Bank charges 8 per cent, compounded daily, on its personal loans. Meaner Bank charges 8.50 per cent, compounded semi-annually. As a potential borrower, which do you prefer?

11 · Present value with multiple cash flows

Investment A pays $100 per year for three years. Investment B pays $80 per year for four years. Which of these cash flow streams has the higher PV if the discount rate is 10 per cent? If the discount rate is 25 per cent?

12 · Calculating the number of periods

At 12 per cent interest, how long does it take for your money to double? To triple?

13 · Calculating present value

An investment will pay $55,000 in five years. If the appropriate discount rate is 4 per cent, continuously compounded, what is the PV?

14 · Calculating future value

The population of Ozland Settlement is growing at 2 per cent per year. The current population is 20 million. What will the population be in eight years? How long until the population exceeds half a billion?

15 · Calculating interest rates

You are offered an investment that requires you to invest $500 today in exchange for $1,259.09 in 12 years. What is the rate of return on this investment?

16 · Calculating interest rates

You are comparing two investments. Both require a $2,500 initial investment. Investment A returns $4,700 in eight years. Investment B pays $5,650 in 12 years. Which of these investments has the higher return?

17 · Calculating the number of periods

Solve for the unknown number of years in each of the following cases:

Present value	Future value	Interest rate	Time (years)
$100	$305	12%	
123	218	10%	
4,100	8,523	5%	
10,543	26,783	6%	
20,000	23,185	3%	

18 · EAR versus NIR

A typical rate for a credit card would be 1.25 per cent per month. Credit cards are legally required to report interest rates. If this was the NIR what rate should they report? What is the effective annual rate?

19 · Calculating present value

An investment offers $100 per year for 10 years. If the required return is 8 per cent, what is the value of the investment? What would the value be if the term were 30 years? 50 years? Forever?

20 · Calculating annuity cash flows

If you invest $50,000 today in exchange for a 12 per cent, 8-year annuity, what will the annual cash flow be?

21 · Calculating interest rates

Solve for the unknown interest rate in each of the following cases:

Present value	Future value	Interest rate	Time (years)
$1,100	$3,357		5
1,000	6,130		16
8,000	16,609		7
10,543	21,215		12

22 · Calculating annuity payments

You have determined that your company can afford a $15,000 annual payment for the next 10 years. A new computer system costs $100,000 in total. If you can borrow the money at 8 per cent, can you afford the new system?

23 · Present value and interest rates

What is the relationship between the value of an annuity and the level of the interest rate? What would happen to the value of an annuity if the interest rate were to suddenly increase? Illustrate your answer by calculating the present value of a 10-year annuity of $10 per year at 5, 10 and 15 per cent.

24 · Loan payments and EAR

If you borrow $12,000 at 14 per cent NIR for 60 months, what will your monthly payment be? What is the effective interest rate on this loan?

25 · EAR versus NIR

You have just concluded the purchase of a new warehouse. To finance the purchase, you've arranged for a 20-year mortgage for 80 per cent of the $400,000 purchase price. The monthly payment will be $3,000. What is the NIR on the loan? The effective annual rate?

26 · Calculating number of periods

One of your customers is having trouble paying her bills. You agree to a repayment schedule of $150 per month. You charge 1 per cent per month interest on late accounts. If the current account balance is $3,000, how long will it take until the debt is fully paid?

27 · Future value with multiple cash flows

If you deposit $2,000 at the end of each of the next eight years in an account paying 9 per cent interest, how much will you have in eight years? How much will you have in 10 years?

28 · Annuity values

This one is a little harder. In Problem 27, suppose you made the first deposit today. If you make 10 deposits in all, how much would you have in 10 years?

29 · Calculating EAR

A local loan shark offers 'four for eight on pay-day'. This means you get $4 today and you must repay $8 in 30 days when you get your next paycheque. What's the effective annual interest rate on this loan?

30 · Calculating number of periods

You think that the value of a piece of seaside real estate you just purchased will increase by 14 per cent per year. You paid $850,000 for the property and plan to sell when you can make a $200,000 profit. How long will you wait if the value does increase by 14 per cent per year?

31 · EAR versus NIR

If a loan has an NIR of 12 per cent, what is the effective annual rate (EAR) assuming the loan calls for semi-annual payments? If the loan calls for monthly payments?

32 · Calculating EAR

You are looking at an investment that has an effective annual rate of 10 per cent. What is the effective semi-annual return? The effective quarterly return? The effective monthly return?

33 · Calculating present value

It is estimated that a fund has a superannuation liability of $1 million to be paid in 24 years. To assess the value of the fund, financial analysts want to discount this liability back to the present. If the discount rate is 6 per cent, what is the present value of this liability?

34 · Calculating PV and break-even interest

Felicity Glamorous has to borrow funds at 10 per cent to purchase a necklace. She has a contract to sell the necklace for $70,000. Payment is to be received in two years time. The necklace cost $60,000 today and could be sold for this amount. Glamorous likes this arrangement as she does not have to give up the necklace for two years and by then fashions will possibly have changed. Does Glamorous have a good arrangement from a financial point of view? How much is it costing her to have the necklace for two years? What is the borrowing rate at which she would break even?

35 · Present value and multiple cash flows

You have won the Happyvalley lottery with the number 8888887. Lottery officials offer you the choice of the following alternative payouts:

> Alternative 1: $10,000 one year from now
> Alternative 2: $20,000 five years from now

Which should you choose if the discount rate is:

a   0 per cent?
b   10 per cent?
c   20 per cent?

36 · Present value and multiple cash flows

With an 8 per cent interest rate, calculate the present value of the following streams of payments:

a $1,160 per year forever with the first payment today
b $800 per year forever, with the first payment two years from today
c $2,420 per year forever, with the first payment three years from today

37 · Present value and multiple cash flows

What is the present value of cash flows of $2,000 per year, with the first cash flow received 5 years from today and the last one 24 years from today (a total of $40,000)? Use an 8 per cent interest rate.

38 · Present value of a perpetuity

Given an interest rate of 6 per cent per year, what is the value at date $t = 7$ of a perpetual stream of $60 payments coming at dates $t = 12, t = 13, t = 14$ and so on to infinity?

39 · Present value and after-tax cash flows

You have recently won the *Set For Life* jackpot in the lottery, with a payoff of $4,960,000. On reading the fine print, you discover that you have the following two options:

a   You could receive 31 payments of $160,000 per year with the first payment today. The income would be taxed at an average rate of 28 per cent. Assuming that the appropriate interest rate for you is 10 per cent, what is the present value of the after-tax cash flows? (Taxes are withheld when the cheques are mailed.)
b   You could receive $1,750,000 now. This would be taxed at an average rate of 28 per cent. With the after-tax amount of $1,260,000, you could take $446,000 now and buy a 30-year annuity with the remaining $814,000. The annuity would pay $101,055 at the end of each year, which would be taxed at an average rate of 28 per cent. Once again using a 10 per cent interest rate, what is the present value of the cash flows under this scenario?

Which option would you take?

40 · Present value and non-constant interest rates

What is the value of a 10-year annuity that pays $1,200 a year if the annuity's first cash flow starts at year 6 and the interest rate is 5 per cent for years 1 to 5 and 10 per cent thereafter?

41 · Calculating EAR with 'discount' interest

This question illustrates what is known as 'discount' interest. Imagine that you are discussing a loan with a somewhat unscrupulous lender. You want to borrow $100,000 for a year. The interest rate is 15 per cent. You and the lender agree that the interest on the $100,000 will be 0.15 × $100,000 = $15,000. So the lender deducts this amount from the loan and gives you $85,000. You repay the $100,000 in a year, thereby paying the $15,000 interest as agreed. In this case, we say that the discount is $15,000. What is wrong here?

42 · Calculating EAR with 'discount' interest

You are considering a one-year loan of $100,000. The interest rate is quoted on a discount basis (see the previous problem) as 9 per cent. What is the effective annual interest rate?

43 · Calculating EAR with points

You are looking at a one-year loan of $100,000. The interest rate is quoted as 8 per cent plus 200 basis points. 100 basis points on a loan is simply 1 per cent of the loan amount. The interest rate quotation in this example requires that the borrower pay 2 per cent to the lender upfront and repay the loan later with 8 per cent interest (another way of describing the upfront payment is as a loan application fee that will be deducted from the amount to be lent). What rate would you actually be paying here?

44 · Calculating EAR with points

The interest rate on a one-year loan is quoted as 4 per cent plus 500 basis points (see the previous problem). What is the effective annual rate (EAR)? Is your answer affected by the loan amount?

45 · Calculating EAR with 'add-on' interest

This problem illustrates a deceptive way of quoting interest rates called add-on interest. Imagine that you see an advertisement for Ripoff Retailing that reads something like this: '$1,000 Instant Credit! 12% Simple Interest! Forty Months to Pay! Low, Low Monthly Payments!' You're not exactly sure what all this means and somebody spilled ink over the NIR on the loan contract, so you ask for clarification. Roger Ripoff explains that if you borrow $1,000 for forty months at 12 per cent interest, in 3.3 years you will owe:

$$\$1,000 \times 1.12^{3.3} = \$1,000 \times 1.4535 = \$1,453.50$$

However, he is prepared to give you a saving and drop the amount to $1404.80 as an incentive to sign now.

Now Roger recognises that coming up with $1,404.80 all at once might be a strain; so, he lets you make 'low, low monthly payments' of $1,404.80/40 = $35.12 per month, even though this is extra bookkeeping work for him.

Is this a 12 per cent loan? Why or why not? What is the NIR on this loan? What is the effective annual rate (EAR)? Why do you think this is called 'add-on' interest?

46 · Calculating EAR

A local finance company quotes a 20 per cent interest rate on one-year loans. So, if you borrow $10,000, the interest for the year will be $2,000. Since you will pay a total of $12,000, the finance company requires you to pay $1,000 per month over the next 12 months. Is this a 20 per cent loan? What rate would legally have to be quoted? What is the effective annual rate?

47 · Calculating annuity payments

This is a classic 'retirement' problem. A timeline will help in solving it. Your friend is celebrating his 35th birthday today and wants to start saving for his anticipated retirement at age 65. He wants to be able to withdraw $10,000 from his savings account on each birthday for 10 years following his retirement; the first withdrawal will be on his 66th birthday. Your friend intends to invest his money in the local savings bank, which offers 8 per cent interest per year. He wants to make equal, annual payments on each birthday in a new savings account he will establish for his retirement fund.

a   If he starts making these deposits on his 36th birthday and continues to make deposits until he is 65 (the last deposit will be on his 65th birthday), what amount must he deposit annually to be able to make the desired withdrawals on retirement?

b   Suppose your friend has just inherited a large sum of money. Rather than making equal payments, he has decided to make one lump-sum payment on his 36th birthday to cover his retirement needs. What amount would he have to deposit?

48 · Present value with multiple cash flows

This is a challenge problem. In January 2003, Alfie 'Blocker' Lewis signed a contract to play for the Sydney Lions that guaranteed him a minimum of $9,955,000. The guaranteed payments were $875,000 in 2003, $650,000 in 2004, $800,000 in 2005, $1 million in 2006, $1 million in 2007, and $300,000 in 2008. In addition, the contract calls for $5,330,000 in deferred money payable at the rate of $240,000 per year from 2009 to 2025 and then $125,000 a year from 2026 to 2035. If the relevant rate of interest is 9 per cent and all payments are made on 1 July each year, what would the present value of these guaranteed payments be on 1 January 2003? If he were to receive an equal annual salary at the end of each of the 5 years from 2003 to 2008, what would his equivalent annual salary be? Ignore taxes throughout this problem.

49 · Future value and multiple cash flows

This is a challenge problem. A well-known insurance company offers a policy known as the 'estate creator six pay'. Typically, the policy is bought by a parent or grandparent for a child at the child's birth. The details of the policy are as follows: The purchaser (say, the parent) makes the following six payments to the insurance company:

1st birthday	$730	4th birthday	$855
2nd birthday	$730	5th birthday	$855
3rd birthday	$730	6th birthday	$855

After the child's 6th birthday, no more payments are made. When the child reaches age 65, he or she receives $143,723. If the relevant interest rate is 6 per cent for the first 6 years and 7 per cent for all subsequent years, is the policy worth buying?

50 · Calculating interest rates

This is a challenge problem. A financial planning service offers a university savings program. The plan calls for you to pay 6 annual payments of $1,000 each. The first payment occurs today, on your child's 12th birthday. Beginning on your child's 18th birthday, the plan will provide $3,000 per year for 4 years. What return is the investment offering?

51 · Present value of a perpetuity

This is a challenge problem. What is the value of an investment that pays $100 every other year forever, with the first cash flow occurring in one year? What would the value be if the first cash flow occurred in two years? The discount rate is 16 per cent per year.

52 · Ordinary annuity versus annuity due

This is a challenge problem. As we discussed in the chapter, an ordinary annuity has cash flows that occur at the end of each period and the first cash flow occurs in exactly one period. For an annuity due, things are slightly different. With this arrangement, we still have a fixed number of equal payments, but the first payment occurs today, not one period from now. The cash flows associated with a real estate lease, for example, are usually in the form of an annuity due because you have to pay the first month's rent up front.

a   Suppose you are comparing two annuities. Both offer 5 payments of $6,000. The interest rate in both cases is 6 per cent. One of these is an ordinary annuity and the other is an annuity due. What is the difference in their values?

b   What is the general relationship between the value of annuity due and the value of an ordinary annuity?

53 · Amortisation with equal payments

Prepare an amortisation schedule for a 3-year loan of $12,000. The interest rate is 9 per cent per year and the loan calls for equal annual payments. How much interest is paid in the third year? How much total interest is paid over the life of the loan?

54 · Amortisation with equal principal payments

Rework Problem 53 assuming that the loan agreement calls for a principal reduction of $4,000 every year instead of equal annual payments.

55 · Calculating a balloon payment

You have just arranged for a $1 million mortgage to finance the purchase of a large tract of land. The mortgage has a 12 per cent NIR, and it calls for monthly payments over the next 10 years. However, the loan has a 3-year balloon payment, meaning that the loan must be paid off then. How big will the balloon payment be?

56 · Rule of 72 and rate of return

An investment will double in ten years. What is the rate of return? Use the rule of 72 to check the calculated answer.

57 · Rule of 72 and the number of periods

An investment returns 9 per cent per year. If $15,000 is invested, how long before it doubles? Use the rule of 72 to check your answer.

CHAPTER 6

Valuing
shares and bonds

Objective

In this chapter, we will show how to value shares and bonds. The approach uses the basic procedures for valuing future cash flows that were introduced in the previous chapter. The principles involved apply to all assets whether they be shares, bonds, inventory, real estate, works of art and so on. Usually there are two elements in the future cash flows, namely the periodic flow of funds and the final return of capital. Items such as inventory and works of art will involve only the return of capital. Along the way, we introduce you to some of the terminology that commonly appears in these areas, and we also describe how the prices for these types of investments are reported in the financial press. On completion of the chapter you will have a full understanding of the principles of valuation which may be applied to estimating the worth of any item.

Note ▷ Throughout this and the next several chapters, we will generally assume that we know the appropriate discount rate. The question of what determines this discount rate and how we might go about measuring it is sufficiently important that we will devote several chapters to it later on in the text. For now, we focus on the relevant cash flows from financial assets and how to value them, given a suitable discount rate.

Remember that all valuation involves just three elements: the future cash flows, the interest rate and the present worth (identified as the present value). Think of the interest rate as the price of the future cash flows. If the price (interest rate) is high then we will obtain less of the present worth (value). Conversely if the price (interest rate) is low we will obtain more of the present worth (value). The object we are valuing involves a capital outlay on purchase, usually a cash flow while the object is held and a return of capital when the object is sold. It is as simple as this so let us see how these simple issues apply in valuing bonds and shares.

Introduction ▷ There are two important issues in relation to discount rates used in valuation. The first is how to identify the appropriate discount rate and the second is how to use it. Throughout this and the next several chapters, we will generally assume that we know the appropriate discount rate. The question of what determines this discount rate and how we might go about measuring it is so important that we will devote several chapters to it later on in the text. For now, we focus on the relevant cash flows from financial assets and how to value them given a suitable discount rate.

A postgraduate student was once heard to remark that, although several units of study in finance had been completed, it was still impossible to read and understand the financial pages in the daily press. If the graduate had access to the last section of this chapter this would have no longer been a problem. This section walks the student through the interesting and major items reported on the financial pages daily.

6.1 Bonds and bond valuation

When a company or government wishes to borrow money from the public on a long-term basis, it usually does so by issuing or selling debt securities called **bonds** or **notes**. These debt securities are both priced in the same way.

In this section, we describe the various features of bonds and some of the terminology associated with bonds. These subjects are discussed in greater detail in Parts Seven and Eight when we examine long-term financing and capital structure; we examine only the essentials in this chapter. We then discuss the cash flows associated with a bond and how bonds can be valued using our discounted cash flow procedure. We conclude this section with a discussion of how bond prices are quoted in the financial press.

bonds
long-term debt securities

notes
unsecured debt securities

Bond features and prices

A bond is normally an interest-only loan, meaning that the borrower will pay the interest every period, but none of the principal will be repaid until the end of the loan.[1] For example, suppose the state government wants to borrow $100 for 30 years. The interest rate on similar debt issued by similar state governments is 12 per cent. The government will thus pay $0.12 \times \$100 = \$12$ in interest every year for 30 years. At the end of 30 years, the government will repay the $100. As this example suggests, a bond is a fairly simple financing arrangement. There is, however, a rich jargon associated with bonds, so we will use this example to define some of the more important terms.

In our example, the $12 regular interest payments that the government promises to make are called **coupon payments**. Because the coupon payment is constant and usually paid every year or every half year, the type of bond we are describing is sometimes called a fixed interest security. The amount that will be repaid at the end of the loan is called the bond's **face value**, par value or redemption value. The market practice is to calculate prices on a face value of $100 rounded to three decimal places. A bond that sells for its par value is called a par value bond. Government bonds sometimes have much larger face or par values than corporate bonds. Finally, the annual coupon divided by the face value is called the **coupon rate** on the bond, which, in this case, is $12 \times \$100 = 12\%$; so the bond has a 12 per cent coupon rate.

The number of years until the face value is paid is called the bond's time to **maturity**. In our example, the bond had a maturity of 30 years when it was originally issued. Once the bond has been issued, the number of years to maturity declines as time goes by. Bond issues may have different maturities.

coupon payments
the stated interest payments made on a bond

face value
the principal amount of a bond that is repaid at the end of the term. Also par value

coupon rate
the annual coupon divided by the face value of a bond

maturity
specified date at which the principal amount of a bond is paid

Bond values and yields

As time passes, interest rates change in the marketplace. The cash flows from a bond, however, stay the same. As a result, the value of the bond will fluctuate. When interest rates rise, the present value of the bond's remaining cash flows declines, and the bond is worth less. When interest rates fall, the bond is worth more.

> This inverse relationship between interest rates and values is one of the fundamental concepts of finance theory. It is applicable to any cash flow that is being valued today.

To determine the value of a bond at a particular point in time, we need to know the number of periods remaining until maturity, the face value, the coupon payment, and the market interest rate for bonds with similar features. This interest rate required in the market on a bond is called the bond's **yield to maturity (YTM)**. This rate is sometimes called the bond's 'yield' for short. Given this information, we can calculate the present value of the cash flows as an estimate of the bond's current market value. Historically government debt issues were called bonds and company issues were called debentures or secured notes (or just notes). Today the tendency is to call them all bonds, so we will use this approach.

yield to maturity (YTM)

the market interest rate that equates a bond's present value of interest payments and principal repayment with its price

For example, suppose Borrow Ltd were to issue a bond with 10 years to maturity. The Borrow bond has an annual coupon payment of $8. Similar bonds have a yield to maturity of 8 per cent. Based on our discussion above, the Borrow bond will pay $8 per year for the next 10 years in coupon interest. In 10 years, Borrow will pay $100 to the owner of the bond. The cash flows from the bond are shown in Table 6.1. What would this bond sell for?

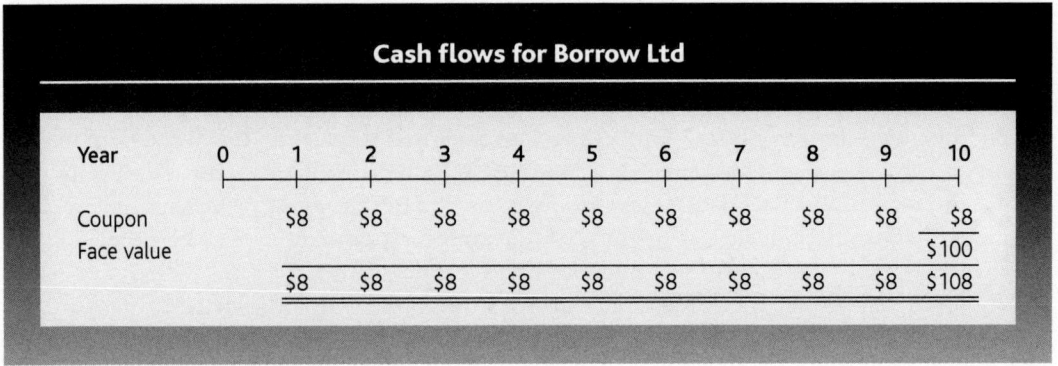

TABLE 6.1

Year	0	1	2	3	4	5	6	7	8	9	10
Coupon		$8	$8	$8	$8	$8	$8	$8	$8	$8	$8
Face value											$100
		$8	$8	$8	$8	$8	$8	$8	$8	$8	$108

Cash flows for Borrow Ltd

As illustrated in Table 6.1, the Borrow bond's cash flows have an annuity component (the coupon payments) and a lump sum (the face value paid at maturity). We thus estimate the market value of the bond by calculating the present value of these two components separately and adding the results together. First, at the going rate of 8 per cent, the present value of the $100 paid in 10 years is:

$$\text{Present value} = \$100/1.08^{10} = \$100/2.1589 = \$46.319$$

Second, the bond offers $8 per year for 10 years, so the present value of this annuity stream is:

$$
\begin{aligned}
\text{Annuity present value} &= \$8 \times (1 - 1/1.08^{10})/0.08 \\
&= \$8 \times (1 - 1/2.1589)/0.08 \\
&= \$8 \times 6.7101 \\
&= \$53.681
\end{aligned}
$$

We can now add the values for the two parts together to get the bond's value:

$$\text{Total bond value} = \$46.319 + 53.681 = \$100.00$$

This bond sells for exactly its face value. This is not a coincidence. The going interest rate in the market is 8 per cent. Considered as an interest-only loan, what interest rate does this bond have? With an $8 coupon payment, this bond pays exactly 8 per cent interest only when it sells for $100.

To illustrate what happens as interest rates change, suppose that a year has gone by. The Borrow bond now has nine years to maturity. If the interest rate in the market had risen to 10 per cent, what would the bond be worth? To find out, we repeat the present value calculations above with 9 years instead of 10, and a 10 per cent yield instead of an 8 per cent yield. First, the present value of the $100 paid in nine years at 10 per cent is:

$$\text{Present value} = \$100/1.10^9 = \$100/2.3579 = \$42.41$$

Second, the bond now offers \$8 per year for 9 years, so the present value of this annuity stream at 10 per cent is:

$$
\begin{aligned}
\text{Annuity present value} &= \$8 \times (1 - 1/1.10^9)/0.10 \\
&= \$8 \times (1 - 1/2.3579)/0.10 \\
&= \$8 \times 5.7590 \\
&= \$46.072
\end{aligned}
$$

We can now add the values for the two parts together to get the bond's value:

$$\text{Total bond value} = \$42.410 + \$46.072 = \$88.482$$

Therefore, the bond should sell for about \$88. We say that this bond, with its 8 per cent coupon, is priced to yield 10 per cent at \$88.482.

The Borrow Company bond now sells for less than its \$100 face value. Why? The market interest rate is 10 per cent. Considered as an interest-only loan of \$100, this bond only pays 8 per cent, its coupon rate. Since this bond pays less than the going rate, investors are only willing to lend something less than the \$100 promised repayment. Since the bond sells for less than face value, it is said to be a discount bond.

The only way to get the interest rate up to 10 per cent is for the price to be less than \$100 so that the purchaser, in effect, has a built-in gain. For the Borrow bond, the price of \$88.482 is \$11.518 less than the face value, so an investor who purchased and kept the bond would get \$8 per year and would have an \$11.518 gain at maturity as well. This gain compensates the lender for the below-market coupon rate.

Another way to see why the bond is discounted by \$11.518 is to note that the \$8 coupon is \$2 'too low' based on current market conditions. By this we mean that the bond would be worth \$100 only if it had a coupon of \$10 per year. In a sense, an investor who buys and keeps the bond gives up \$2 per year for nine years. At 10 per cent, this annuity stream is worth:

$$
\begin{aligned}
\text{Annuity present value} &= \$2 \times (1 - 1/1.10^9)/0.10 \\
&= \$2 \times 5.7590 \\
&= \$11.518
\end{aligned}
$$

This is just the amount of the discount.

What would the Borrow bond sell for if interest rates had dropped by 2 per cent instead of rising by 2 per cent? As you might guess, the bond will sell for more than \$100. Such a bond is said to sell at a premium and is called a premium bond.

This case is just the opposite of a discount bond. The Borrow bond now has a coupon rate of 8 per cent when the market rate is only 6 per cent. Investors are willing to pay a premium to get this extra coupon. In this case, the relevant discount rate is 6 per cent, and there are nine years remaining. The present value of the \$100 face amount is:

$$\text{Present value} = \$100/1.06^9 = \$100/1.6895 = \$59.189$$

The present value of the coupon stream is:

$$
\begin{aligned}
\text{Annuity present value} &= \$8 \times (1 - 1/1.06^9)/0.06 \\
&= \$8 \times (1 - 1/1.6895)/0.06 \\
&= \$8 \times 6.8017 \\
&= \$54.414
\end{aligned}
$$

PART 3 · VALUATION OF FUTURE CASH FLOWS

We can now add the values for the two parts together to get the bond's value:

$$\text{Total bond value} = \$59.189 + \$54.414 = \$113.603$$

Total bond value is therefore $13.603 in excess of par value. Once again, we can verify this amount by noting that the coupon payment is now $2 'too high'. The present value of $2 per year for nine years at 6 per cent is:

$$\begin{aligned}\text{Annuity present value} &= \$2 \times (1 - 1/1.06^9)/0.06 \\ &= \$2 \times 6.8017 \\ &= \$13.603 \end{aligned}$$

This is just as we calculated.

Based on our examples, we can now write the general expression for the value of a bond. If a bond has (1) a face value of F paid at maturity, (2) a coupon payment of C paid per period, (3) t periods to maturity, and (4) a yield of r per period, its value is:

$$\textbf{Bond value} = C \times (1 - 1/(1 + r)^t)/r + F/(1 + r)^t \qquad (6.1)$$
$$\text{Bond value} = \text{Present value of the coupon payments} + \text{Present value of the face amount}$$

Semi-annual coupons

EXAMPLE 6.1

In practice, bonds usually make coupon payments twice a year. So, if an ordinary bond has a coupon rate of 14 per cent, then the owner will get a total of $14 per year, but this $14 will come in two payments of $7 each. Suppose we were examining such a bond. The yield to maturity is quoted at 16 per cent.

Bond yields are quoted like nominal rates of interest; the quoted rate is equal to the actual rate per period multiplied by the number of periods. In this case, with a 16 per cent quoted yield and semi-annual payments, the true yield is 8 per cent per six months. The bond matures in seven years. What is the bond's price? What is the effective annual yield on this bond?

Based on our discussion, we know the bond will sell at a discount because it has a coupon rate of 7 per cent every six months when the market requires 8 per cent every six months. So, if our answer exceeds $100, we will know that we have made a mistake.

To get the exact price, we first calculate the present value of the bond's face value of $100 paid in seven years. This seven years has 14 periods of six months each. At 8 per cent per period, the value is:

$$\text{Present value} = \$100/1.08^{14} = \$100/2.9372 = \$34.046$$

The coupons can be viewed as a 14-period annuity of $7 per period. At an 8 per cent discount rate, the present value of such an annuity is:

$$\begin{aligned}\text{Annuity present value} &= \$7 \times (1 - 1/1.08^{14})/0.08 \\ &= \$7 \times (1 - 0.3405)/0.08 \\ &= \$7 \times 8.2442 \\ &= \$57.710 \end{aligned}$$

The total present value gives us what the bond should sell for:

$$\text{Total present value} = \$34.046 + \$57.710 = \$91.756$$

To calculate the effective yield on this bond, note that 8 per cent every six months is equivalent to:

$$\text{Effective annual rate} = (1 + 0.08)^2 - 1 = 16.64\%$$

The effective yield, therefore, is 16.64 per cent.

As we have illustrated in this section, bond prices and interest rates always move in opposite directions. When interest rates rise, a bond's value, like any other present value, will decline. Similarly, when interest rates fall, bond values rise. Even if we are considering a bond that is riskless in the sense that the borrower is certain to make all the payments, there is still risk in owning a bond. We discuss this next.

Interest rate risk

The risk that arises for bond owners from fluctuating interest rates is called interest rate risk. How much interest risk a bond has depends on how sensitive its price is to interest rate changes. This sensitivity directly depends on two things: the time to maturity and the coupon rate. As we shall see, you should keep the following in mind when looking at a bond:

1 All other things being equal, the longer the time to maturity, the greater the interest rate risk.
2 All other things being equal, the lower the coupon rate, the greater the interest rate risk.

We illustrate the first of these two points in Figure 6.1. As shown, we compute and plot prices under different interest rate scenarios for 10 per cent coupon bonds with maturities of 1 year and 30 years. Notice how the slope of the line connecting the prices is much steeper for the 30-year maturity than it is for the 1-year maturity. This tells us that a relatively small change in interest rates could lead to a substantial change in the bond's value. In comparison, the 1-year bond's price is relatively insensitive to interest rate changes.

FIGURE 6.1

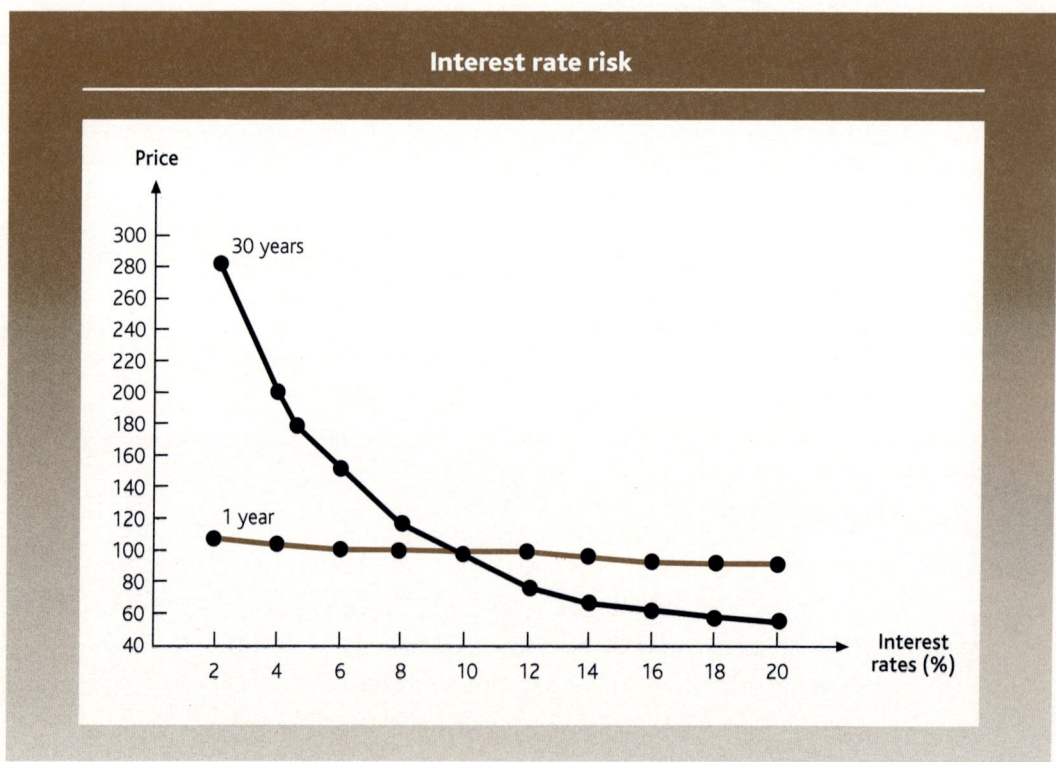

Intuitively, the reason that longer-term bonds have greater interest rate sensitivity is that a large portion of a bond's value comes from the $100 face amount. The present value of this amount isn't greatly affected by a small change in interest rates if it is to be received in one year. If it is to be received in 30 years, however, even a small change in the interest rate can have a significant effect once it is compounded for 30 years. The present value of the face amount will be much more volatile with a longer-term bond as a result.

The reason that bonds with lower coupons have greater interest rate risk is essentially the same. As we discussed above, the value of a bond depends on the present value of its coupon payments and the present value of the face amount. If two bonds with different coupon rates have the same maturity, then the value of the one with the lower coupon payment is proportionately more dependent on the face amount to be received at maturity. As a result, all other things being equal, its value will fluctuate more as interest rates change. Put another way, the bond with the higher coupon payment has a larger cash flow early in its life, so its value is less sensitive to changes in the discount rate.

Finding the yield to maturity: More trial and error

Frequently, we will know a bond's price, coupon rate, and maturity date, but not its yield to maturity. For example, suppose we were interested in a six-year, 8 per cent coupon bond. We are quoted a price of $95.514. What is the yield on this bond?

We've seen that the price of a bond can be written as the sum of its annuity and lump-sum components. With an $8 coupon for six years and a $100 face value, this price is:

$$\$95.514 = \$8 \times (1 - 1/(1 + r)^6)/r + \$100/(1 + r)^6$$

where r is the unknown discount rate or yield to maturity. We have one equation here and one unknown, but we cannot solve it for r explicitly. The only way to find the answer is to use trial and error.

This problem is essentially identical to the one we examined in the last chapter when we tried to find the unknown interest rate on an annuity. However, finding the rate (or yield) on a bond is even more complicated because of the $100 face amount.

We can speed up the trial-and-error process by using what we know about bond prices and yields. In this case, the bond has an $8 coupon and is selling at a discount. We thus know that the yield is greater than 8 per cent. If we compute the price at 10 per cent:

$$
\begin{aligned}
\text{Bond value} &= \$8 \times (1 - 1/1.10^6)/0.10 + \$100/1.10^6 \\
&= \$8 \times (4.3553) + \$100/1.7716 \\
&= \$34.842 + \$56.446 \\
&= \$91.288
\end{aligned}
$$

At 10 per cent, the value we calculate is lower than the actual price, so 10 per cent is too high. The true yield must be somewhere between 8 per cent and 10 per cent. At this point, it's a matter of 'guesstimating' to find the answer. You would probably want to try 9 per cent next. If you do, you will see that this is in fact the bond's yield to maturity.[2]

EXAMPLE
6.2 ■ **Bond yields**

You're looking at two bonds that are identical in every way except for their coupons and, of course, their prices. Both have 12 years to maturity. The first bond has a 10 per cent coupon rate and sells for $93.508. The second has a 12 per cent coupon rate. What do you think it would sell for?

Since the two bonds are very similar, they will be priced to yield about the same rate. We first need to calculate the yield on the 10 per cent coupon bond. Proceeding as before, the yield must be greater than 10 per cent since the bond is selling at a discount. The bond has a fairly long maturity of 12 years. We've seen that long-term bond prices are relatively sensitive to interest rate changes, so the yield is probably close to 10 per cent. A little trial and error reveals that the yield is actually 11 per cent:

$$
\begin{aligned}
\text{Bond value} &= \$10 \times (1 - 1/1.11^{12})/0.11 + \$100/1.11^{12} \\
&= \$10 \times 6.4924 + \$100/3.4985 \\
&= \$64.924 + \$28.584 \\
&= \$93.508
\end{aligned}
$$

With an 11 per cent yield, the second bond will sell at a premium because of its $12 coupon. Its value is:

$$
\begin{aligned}
\text{Bond value} &= \$12 \times (1 - 1/1.11^{12})/0.11 + \$100/1.11^{12} \\
&= \$12 \times 6.4924 + \$100/3.4985 \\
&= \$77.908 + \$28.584 \\
&= \$106.492
\end{aligned}
$$

Bond price reporting

If you were to look in the *Australian Financial Review* (or a similar financial newspaper), you would see information on various notes, bonds and debentures issued by large companies and semi-government and government bodies.

Each working day an estimated $7–$8 billion of securities is traded in Australian money and fixed interest markets. The profits of dealers is the difference, if any, between the price at which debt is bought from the issuer and the price at which debt is sold or placed in the market. The dealers are linked by an electronic dealing system. A typical system lists the issuer, the coupon, maturity date, quantity in millions, the yield to maturity bid by a buyer, the yield to maturity offered by a seller and the last traded yield.

One of the many financial reporting agencies is Bloomberg. Table 6.2 is one of the hundreds of thousands of Bloomberg reporting screens. This screen provides some basic information regarding an Australian Commonwealth Government Bond that has a coupon of $7\frac{1}{2}$ per cent and matures on 15 July 2005. Currently the bonds yield about 4.68 per cent. As the yield is less than the coupon, the bonds should trade at a premium. They do: they trade for a price of around $109.747. Notice that there are two yields quoted and two prices quoted. Think of these as being buy and sell quotes so that the other party to the transaction makes a profit (the difference between the two quotes). Normal dealing practice in the fixed interest market is to quote a yield calculated to two decimal places. The yield is then converted into a price, to three decimal places per $100 face value.

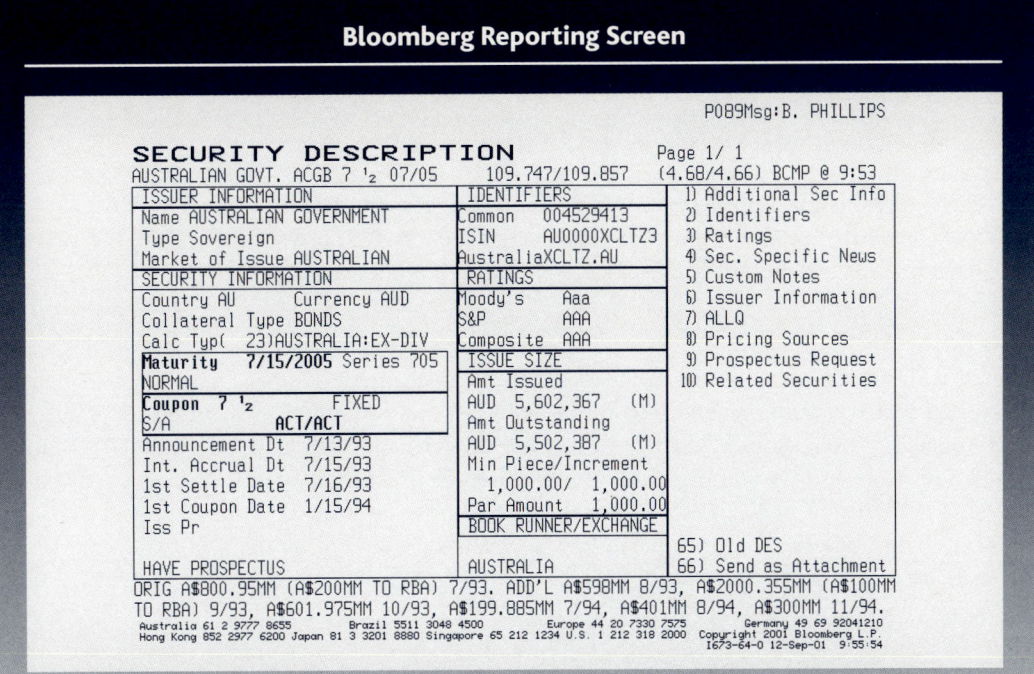

TABLE
6.2

Concept questions

6.1a *What are the cash flows associated with a bond?*

6.1b *What is the general expression for the value of a bond?*

6.1c *Is it true that the only risk associated with owning a bond is that the issuer will not make all the payments? Explain.*

6.1d *A bond has a coupon rate of 10%. It has 15 years to maturity and the current market value is less than the face value. If you are calculating the YTM by trial and error, should you start the calculations using 7%, 9%, 11% or 15%?*

6.2 ▪ Ordinary share valuation

A share is more difficult to value than a bond for at least three reasons. First, not even the promised cash flows are known in advance. Second, the life of the investment is essentially forever since a share has no maturity. Third, there is no easy way to observe the rate of return that the market requires. Nonetheless, as we will see, there are cases in which we can come up with the present value of the future cash flows for a share and thus determine its value.

Ordinary share cash flows

Imagine that you were to buy a share today. You plan to sell the share in one year. You somehow know that the share will be worth $7 at that time. You predict that the share will also pay a $0.10 per share dividend at the end of the year. If you require a 25 per cent return on your investment, what is the most you would pay for the share? In other words, what is the present value of the $0.10 dividend along with the $7 ending value at 25 per cent?

If you buy the share today and sell it at the end of the year, you will have a total of $7.10 in cash. At 25 per cent:

$$\text{Present value} = (\$7 + 0.1)/1.25 = \$5.68$$

Therefore, $5.68 is the value you would assign to the share today.

More generally, let P_0 be the current price of the share, and define P_1 to be the price in one period. If D_1 is the cash dividend paid at the end of the period, then:

$$P_0 = (D_1 + P_1)/(1 + r) \tag{6.2}$$

where r is the required return in the market on this investment.

Notice that we really haven't said much so far. If we wanted to determine the value of a share today (P_0), we would first have to come up with the value in one year (P_1). This is even harder to do, so we've only made the problem more complicated.

What is the price in one period, P_1? We don't know in general. Instead, suppose that we somehow knew the price in two periods, P_2. Given a predicted dividend in two periods, D_2, the share price in one period would be:

$$P_1 = (D_2 + P_2)/(1 + r)$$

If we were to substitute this expression for P_1 into our expression for P_0, we would have:

$$
\begin{aligned}
P_0 &= (D_1 + P_1)/(1 + r) \\
&= (D_1 + [D_2 + P_2]/[1 + r])/(1 + r) \\
&= D_1/(1 + r)^1 + D_2/(1 + r)^2 + P_2/(1 + r)^2
\end{aligned}
$$

Now we need to get a price in two periods. We don't know this either, so we can procrastinate again and write:

$$P_2 = (D_3 + P_3)/(1 + r)$$

If we substitute this back in for P_2, we would have:

$$
\begin{aligned}
P_0 &= D_1/(1 + r)^1 + D_2/(1 + r)^2 + P_2/(1 + r)^2 \\
&= D_1/(1 + r)^1 + D_2/(1 + r)^2 + ((D_3 + P_3)/(1 + r))(1 + r)^2 \\
&= D_1/(1 + r)^1 + D_2/(1 + r)^2 + D_3/(1 + r)^3 + P_3/(1 + r)^3
\end{aligned}
$$

You should start to notice that we can push the problem of coming up with the share price off into the future forever. Importantly, no matter what the share price is, the present value is essentially zero if we push it far enough away.[3] What we would be left with is the result that the current price of the share can be written as the present value of the dividends, beginning in one period and extending out forever:

$$P_0 = D_1/(1 + r)^1 + D_2/(1 + r)^2 + D_3/(1 + r)^3 + D_4/(1 + r)^4 + D_5/(1 + r)^5 + \ldots$$

One may wonder about the final dividend and ask the question 'should it be a final return of capital?' We may avoid the debate on this point by looking at it as a final liquidating dividend. That is where all the assets of the company are sold, all the liabilities are paid and the balance distributed to the shareholders as the liquidating dividend.

We have illustrated here that the price of the share today is equal to the present value of all of the future dividends. How many future dividends are there? In principle, there can be an infinite number. This means that we still cannot compute a value for the share, because we would have to forecast an infinite number of dividends and then discount them all. In the next section, we consider some special cases where we can get around this problem.

Growth Shares

You might be wondering about shares in companies that currently pay no dividends. Small, growing companies frequently plough back everything and thus pay no dividends. Are such shares worth nothing? It depends. When we say that the value of a share is equal to the present value of the future dividends, we don't rule out the possibility that some number of those dividends are zero. They just cannot all be zero.

Imagine a company that had a provision in its articles that prohibited the paying of dividends now or ever. The company never borrows any money, never pays out any money to shareholders in any form whatsoever, and never sells any assets. Such a company couldn't really exist because the shareholders could always vote to amend the constitution if they wanted to, which is highly probable. If it did exist, however, what would the shares be worth?

The shares would be worth absolutely nothing. Such a company is a financial 'black hole'. Money goes in, but nothing valuable ever comes out. Since nobody would ever get any return on this investment, the investment has no value. This example is a little absurd, but it illustrates that when we speak of companies that don't pay dividends, what we really mean is that they are not currently paying dividends.

Ordinary share valuation: Some special cases

There are a few very useful special circumstances where we can come up with a value for the shares. What we have to do is make some simplifying assumptions about the pattern of future dividends. The three cases we consider are: (1) the dividend has a zero growth rate, (2) the dividend grows at a constant rate, and (3) the dividend grows at a constant rate after some length of time. We consider each of these separately.

Zero growth
The case of zero growth is one we have already seen. A share in a company with a constant dividend is much like a preference share. From the previous chapter (Example 5.20), we know that the dividend on a preference share has zero growth and thus is constant through time. For a zero growth share, this implies that:

$$D_1 = D_2 = D_3 = D = \text{constant}$$

So, the value of the share is:

$$P_0 = D/(1 + r)^1 + D/(1 + r)^2 + D/(1 + r)^3 + D/(1 + r)^4 + D/(1 + r)^5 + \dots$$

Since the dividend is always the same, the share can be viewed as an ordinary perpetuity with a cash flow equal to D every period. The per-share value is thus given by:

$$P_0 = D/r \tag{6.3}$$

where r is the required return.

For example, suppose the One Rate Company has a policy of paying a $0.10 per share dividend every year. If this policy is to be continued indefinitely, what is the value of a share if the required return is 20 per cent? The shares in this case amount to an ordinary perpetuity, so a share is worth $0.10/0.20 = $0.50 per share.

Constant growth

Suppose we knew that the dividend for some company always grows at a steady rate. Call this growth rate g. If we let D_0 be the dividend just paid, then the next dividend, D_1, is:

$$D_1 = D_0 \times (1 + g)$$

The dividend in two periods is:

$$
\begin{aligned}
D_2 &= D_1 \times (1 + g) \\
&= [D_0 \times (1 + g)] \times (1 + g) \\
&= D_0 \times (1 + g)^2
\end{aligned}
$$

We could repeat this process to come up with the dividend at any point in the future. In general, from our discussion of compound growth in the previous chapter, we know that the dividend t periods in the future is given by:

$$D_t = D_0 \times (1 + g)^t$$

An asset with cash flows that grow at a constant rate forever is called a growing perpetuity. As we will see, there is a simple expression for determining the value of such an asset.

The assumption of steady dividend growth might strike you as peculiar. Why would the dividend grow at a constant rate? The reason is that, for many companies, steady growth in dividends is an explicit goal. This subject falls under the general heading of dividend policy, so we will defer further discussion of it to Chapter 19.

EXAMPLE 6.4 ■ **Dividend growth revisited**

The Constant Company has just paid a dividend of $0.30 per share. The dividend grows at a steady rate of 8 per cent per year. Based on this information, what will the dividend be in five years?

Here we have a $0.30 current amount that grows at 8 per cent per year for five years. The future amount is thus:

$$\$0.30 \times (1.08)^5 = \$0.30 \times 1.4693 = \$0.441$$

The dividend will therefore increase by $0.141 over the coming five years.

If the dividend grows at a steady rate, then we have replaced the problem of forecasting an infinite number of future dividends with the problem of coming up with a single growth rate, a considerable simplification. In this case, if we take D_0 to be the dividend just paid and g to be the constant growth rate, the value of a share can be written as:

$$
\begin{aligned}
P_0 &= D_1/(1 + r)^1 + D_2/(1 + r)^2 + D_3/(1 + r)^3 + \ldots \\
&= D_0(1 + g)^1/(1 + r)^1 + D_0(1 + g)^2/(1 + r)^2 + D_0(1 + g)^3/(1 + r)^3 + \ldots
\end{aligned}
$$

As long as the growth rate, g, is less than the discount rate, r, the present value of this series of cash flows can be written very simply as:

$$P_0 = D_0 \times (1 + g)/(r - g) = D_1/(r - g) \tag{6.4}$$

This elegant result goes by a lot of different names. We will call it the **constant dividend growth model**. By any name, it is very easy to use. To illustrate, suppose that D_0 is $0.23, r is 13 per cent, and g is 5 per cent. The price per share in this case is:

$$
\begin{aligned}
P_0 &= D_0 \times (1 + g)/(r - g) \\
&= \$0.23 \times (1.05)/(0.13 - 0.05) \\
&= \$0.2415/(0.08) \\
&= \$3.02
\end{aligned}
$$

constant dividend growth model
model that determines the current price of a share as its dividend next period divided by the discount rate less the dividend growth rate

We can actually use the dividend growth model to get the share price at any point in time, not just today. In general, the price of a share as of time t is:

$$
P_t = D_t \times (1 + g)/(r - g) = D_{t+1}/(r - g) \tag{6.5}
$$

In our example, suppose we were interested in the price of the share in five years, P_5. We first need the dividend at time 5, D_5. Since the dividend just paid is $0.23 and the growth rate is 5 per cent per year, D_5 is:

$$
D_5 = \$0.23 \times (1.05)^5 = \$0.23 \times 1.2763 = \$0.2935
$$

From the dividend growth model, the price of the share in five years is:

$$
P_5 = D_5 \times (1 + g)/(r - g) = \$0.2935 \times (1.05)/(0.13 - 0.05) = \$0.30817/0.08 = \$3.85
$$

Example 6.5 (overleaf) illustrates that the dividend growth model has the implicit assumption that the share price will grow at the same constant rate as the dividend. This really isn't too surprising. It tells us is that if the cash flows on an investment grow at a constant rate through time, so does the value of that investment.

You might wonder what would happen with the dividend growth model if the growth rate, g, were greater than the discount rate, r. It looks like we would get a negative share price, because $r - g$ would be less than zero. This is not what would happen.

Instead, if the constant growth rate exceeds the discount rate, then the share price is infinitely large. Why? If the growth rate is bigger than the discount rate, then the present value of the dividends keeps on getting bigger and bigger. Essentially, the same is true if the growth rate and the discount rate are equal. In both cases, the simplification that allows us to replace the infinite stream of dividends with the dividend growth model is 'illegal', so the answers we get from the dividend growth model are nonsense unless the growth rate is less than the discount rate.

Finally, the expression we came up with for the constant growth case will work for any growing perpetuity, not just dividends on ordinary shares. If C_1 is the next cash flow on a growing perpetuity, then the present value of the cash flows is given by:

$$
\text{Present value} = C_1/(r - g) = C_0(1 + g)/(r - g)
$$

Notice that this expression looks like the result for an ordinary perpetuity except that we have $r - g$ on the bottom instead of just r.

Non-constant growth

The last case we consider is non–constant growth. The main reason to consider this case is to allow for 'supernormal' growth rates over some finite length of time. As we discussed above, the growth rate cannot exceed the required return indefinitely, but it certainly could do so for some number of years. To avoid the problem of having to forecast and discount an

EXAMPLE
6.5

Retail Growth Company

The next dividend for the Retail Growth Company will be $0.40 per share. Investors require a 16 per cent return on companies such as Retail. Retail's dividend increases by 6 per cent every year. Based on the dividend growth model, what is the value of Retail's shares today? What is the value in four years?

The only tricky thing here is that the next dividend, D_1, is given as $0.40, so we won't multiply this by $(1 + g)$. With this in mind, the price per share is given by:

$$P_0 = D_1/(r - g)$$
$$= \$0.40/(0.16 - 0.06)$$
$$= \$0.40/(0.10)$$
$$= \$4.00$$

Since we already have the dividend in one year, the dividend in four years is equal to $D_1 \times (1 + g)^3 = \$0.40 \times (1.06)^3 = \$0.4764$. The price in four years is therefore:

$$P_4 = [D_4 \times (1 + g)]/(r - g)$$
$$= [\$0.4764 \times 1.06]/(0.16 - 0.06)$$
$$= \$0.505/(0.10)$$
$$= \$5.05$$

Notice in this example that P_4 is equal to $P_0 \times (1 + g)^4$:

$$P_4 = \$5.05 = \$4.00 \times (1.06)^4 = P_0 \times (1 + g)^4$$

To see why this is so, notice first that:

$$P_4 = D_5/(r - g)$$

However, D_5 is just equal to $D_1 \times (1 + g)^4$, so we can write P_4 as:

$$P_4 = D_1 \times (1 + g)^4/(r - g)$$
$$= [D_1/(r - g)] \times (1 + g)^4$$
$$= P_0 \times (1 + g)^4$$

infinite number of dividends, we will require that the dividends start growing at a constant rate sometime in the future.

To give a simple example of non-constant growth, consider the case of a company that is not currently paying dividends. You predict that in five years, the company will pay a dividend for the first time. The dividend will be $0.50 per share. You expect that this dividend will then grow at 10 per cent indefinitely. The required return on companies such as this one is 20 per cent. What is the price of a share today?

To see what the shares are worth today, we first find out what it will be worth once dividends are paid. We can then calculate the present value of that future price to get today's price. The first dividend will be paid in five years, and the dividend will grow steadily from then on. Using the dividend growth model, the price in four years will be:

$$P_4 = D_4 \times (1 + g)/(r - g)$$
$$= D_5/(r - g)$$
$$= \$0.50/(0.20 - 0.10)$$
$$= \$5.00$$

If a share will be worth \$5.00 in four years, then we can get the current value by discounting this back four years at 20 per cent:

$$P_0 = \$5.00/(1.20)^4 = \$5.00/2.0736 = \$2.41$$

A share is therefore worth \$2.41 today.

The problem of non-constant growth is only slightly more complicated if the dividends are not zero for the first several years. For example, suppose that you have come up with the following dividend forecasts for the next three years:

Year	Expected dividend
1	\$0.10
2	0.20
3	0.25

After the third year, the dividend will grow at a constant rate of 5 per cent per year. The required return is 10 per cent. What is the value of a share today?

As always, the value of a share is the present value of all the future dividends. To calculate this present value, we first have to compute the present value of the share price three years down the road, just as we did above. We then have to add the present value of the dividends that will be paid between now and then. So, the price in three years is:

$$P_3 = D_3 \times (1 + g)/(r - g)$$
$$= \$0.25 \times (1.05)/(0.10 - 0.05)$$
$$= \$5.25$$

We can now calculate the total value of a share as the present value of the first three dividends plus the present value of the price at time 3, P_3:

$$P_0 = D_1/(1 + r)^1 + D_2/(1 + r)^2 + D_3/(1 + r)^3 + P_3/(1 + r)^3$$
$$= \$0.10/1.10 + \$0.20/1.10^2 + \$0.25/1.10^3 + \$5.25/1.10^3$$
$$= \$0.091 + 0.165 + 0.188 + 3.944$$
$$= \$4.39$$

The value of a share today is thus \$4.39.

EXAMPLE

6.6

Supernormal growth

Fast Growth Ltd has been growing at a phenomenal rate of 30 per cent per year because of its rapid expansion and explosive sales. You believe that this growth rate will last for three more years and then drop to 10 per cent per year. If the growth rate then remains at 10 per cent indefinitely, what is the total value of the shares? Total dividends just paid were \$5 million for 10 million shares, and the required return is 20 per cent. *(continued)*

EXAMPLE 6.6 ■ **Supernormal growth (*continued*)**

Fast Growth is an example of supernormal growth. It is unlikely that a 30 per cent growth can be sustained for any extended length of time. To value the equity in this company, we first need to calculate the total dividends over the supernormal growth period:

$$D_1 = D_0 \times (1 + g)$$
$$= \$0.5 \times 1.3 = \$0.65$$
$$D_2 = D_1 \times (1 + g)$$
$$= \$0.65 \times 1.3 = \$0.845$$
$$D_3 = D_2 \times (1 + g)$$
$$= \$0.845 \times 1.3 = \$1.0985$$

The price at time 3 can be calculated as:

$$P_3 = D_3 \times (1 + g)/(r - g)$$

where g is the long-run growth rate. So we have:

$$P_3 = \$1.0985 \times (1.10)/(0.20 - 0.10) = \$12.0835$$

To determine the value today, we need the present value of this amount plus the present value of the total dividends:

$$P_0 = D_1/(1 + r)^1 + D_2/(1 + r)^2 + D_3/(1 + r)^3 + P_3/(1 + r)^3$$
$$= \$0.65/1.20 + \$0.845/1.20^2 + \$1.0985/1.20^3 + \$12.0835/1.20^3$$
$$= \$0.542 + 0.587 + 0.636 + 6.993$$
$$= \$8.76$$

The total value of the equity today is thus $87.6 million, being 10 million shares at $8.76 each. If there were, for example, 20 million shares, then the share price would be $87.6 million/20 million = $4.38.

Components of the required return

Thus far, we have taken the required return or discount rate, r, as given. We will have quite a bit to say on this subject in Chapters 10 and 11. For now, we want to examine the implications of the dividend growth model for this required return. Earlier, we calculated P_0 as:

$$P_0 = D_1/(r - g)$$

If we rearrange this to solve for r, we get:

$$(r - g) = D_1/P_0$$
$$r = D_1/P_0 + g \tag{6.6}$$

This tells us that the total return, r, has two components. The first of these, D_1/P_0, is called the **dividend yield**. Since this is calculated as the cash dividend divided by the current price, it is conceptually similar to the current yield on a bond.

dividend yield
a share's cash dividend divided by its current price

The second part of the total return is the growth rate, g. We know that the dividend growth rate is also the rate at which the share price grows (see Example 6.5). Thus, this growth rate can be interpreted as the **capital gains yield**, that is, the rate at which the value of the investment grows.[4]

capital gains yield
the dividend growth rate or the rate at which the value of an investment grows

To illustrate the components of the required return, suppose we observe a share selling for $2. The next dividend will be $0.1 per share. You think that the dividend will grow by 10 per cent more or less indefinitely. What return does this share offer you if this is correct?

The dividend growth model calculates total return as:

$$r = \text{Dividend yield} + \text{Capital gains yield}$$
$$r = D_1/P_0 + g$$

In this case, total return works out to be:

$$r = \$0.1/\$2 + 10\%$$
$$= 5\% + 10\%$$
$$= 15\%$$

This share, therefore, has a return of 15 per cent.

We can verify this answer by calculating the price in one year, P_1, using 15 per cent as the required return. Based on the dividend growth model, this price is:

$$P_1 = D_1 \times (1 + g)/(r - g)$$
$$= \$0.1 \times (1.10)/(0.15 - 0.10)$$
$$= \$0.11/0.05$$
$$= \$2.20$$

Notice that this $2.20 is $2 × (1.1), so the share price has grown by 10 per cent as it should. If you pay $2 for the share today, you will get a $0.1 dividend at the end of the year, and you will have a $2.20 − $2 = $0.2 gain. Your dividend yield is thus $0.1/$2 = 5%. Your capital gains yield is $0.2/$2 = 10%, so your total return would be 5% + 10% = 15%.

Share market reporting

If you look through the pages of the *Australian Financial Review* (or another financial newspaper), you will find information on a large number of shares. Table 6.3 reproduces a small section of the National Markets page for the Australian Stock Exchange (ASX) for 26 August 2002. In Table 6.3, locate the line for BHP.

Stock Market Reporting—Industrial Market

TABLE 6.3

ASX Code	Weekly Vol 000's	YTD Vol Mil	PCP Vol Mil	Mkt Cap Bil	Mkt/ Mkt NTA	EPS ¢ NTA	P/E Ratio	Div ¢ Shr	Div Cvr	Div Ytd %	Stock Name	Mrkt Call Code	Last Sale	Wk Mve +-	Buy	Sell	Nat Wk High	Nat Wk Low	Move Rel to Mkt	52 Wk High	52 Wk Low
BER	54.659	.940	.516	.008	.72	.8	4.10	13.4	3.25	1.26	5.91f	Berklee Ltd	2134	.55	+7	.50	.55	.55	.49	+12.99	.56	.26
BWI	103.200	2.894	1.053	.031	.81	1.1	4.55	19.3	9.24	.49	10.50	Beston Wine Ind unt	3211	.88	+4	.86	.88	.88	.85	+3.17	.96	.78
BYI	20.813	4.022	4.163	.022	.68	.6	2.56	15.6	-	-	-	Beyond Intl	2188	.40		.40	.46	.40	.40	-1.60	.85	.30
BYO	10.000	1.090	.924	.002	.12	.8	-4.54	-	-	-	-	Beyond Online	7354	.09		.09	.105	.09	.09	-1.60	.19	.08
BHP	71508.0	2314.76	1600.40	35.581	-	-	54.40	17.6	24.75	2.20	2.53f	BHP Billiton Ltd	2136	9.58	+65	9.55	9.59	9.66	8.95	+5.68	11.676	7.357
BSL	19653.8	319.714	-	2.220	-	-	-	-	-	-	-	BHP Steel Ltd	3099	2.80	+26	2.78	2.79	2.80	2.52	+8.64	3.04	2.47
BHL	49.575	.457	2.911	.835	1.41	3.0	27.84	15.3	9.92	2.81	2.33	Bidvest Plc cdi	6976	4.25		4.25	4.29	4.25	4.15	-1.60	5.00	2.70
BKV	28.700	8.821	3.205	.002	.07	1.2	-31.30	-	-	-	-	Big Kev's Ltd	7732	.087	+7	.087	.088	.087	.08	+7.15	.375	.075
BIG	-	1.547	11.725	.002	.07	.4	.75	3.3	-	-	-	Bigshop.Com.Au	7474	.025		.025	.035	.025	.025	-1.60	.085	.019
BBG	3007.58	87.563	76.960	1.757	.14	62.8	25.18	34.9	15.50	1.62	1.76f	Billabong Intl	2121	8.79	+63	8.75	8.80	8.85	8.10	+6.13	10.00	6.03
BNO	134.826	14.447	15.097	.025	.30	2.1	-4.86	-	-	-	-	Bionomics Ltd	7085	.63	+3	.63	.66	.64	.60	+3.40	1.01	.50

Source: *Australian Financial Review*, 26 August 2002

BHP is the ASX code for BHP Billiton Ltd, a company with a market capitalisation of $35.581 billion. Market capitalisation is simply the number of shares times the last sale price ($9.58). The unique call code assigned to the company is 2136. The last sale price for the share was $9.58 and there was a 65 cent positive price variation. The number of shares sold for the week, in multiples of 1000, was 71,508 (i.e., 71,508,000 shares changed hands). The buy and sell quotes are the closing buyer and seller quotes. The buy quote of 9.55 is the price that prospective buyers are bidding for the shares; the price that sellers are willing to accept in the market is 9.56. The dividend per share is $0.2475 and the dividend does appear to contain some franked amount (denoted by the small f).[5]

Times covered is 2.20. It is calculated by dividing the earnings of the company (54.40 cents) by its dividend (24.75 cents). The current dividend yield is 2.53 per cent. This is calculated by dividing the current dividend of 24.75 cents by the current market price of $9.58. With such a low dividend yield, the shareholders in BHP must be expecting a larger capital gain. The ratio of market price to current earnings per share is 17.6. A ratio of around 18 is average for the market.

While we are discussing the financial press, we may as well take you through other parts of the *Australian Financial Review*. We are jumping ahead here because we discuss options, futures, bank bills and currency exchanges in detail in later chapters. All we hope to achieve at this stage is an understanding of how to read the financial press. The other concepts covered will be explained in full later, so you may like to revisit this section after you have read Parts Seven, Eight and Nine.

In the Options part of the paper both call and put exchange traded options are listed. Options and futures are covered in Chapter 21. An option is basically a right to buy (call) or sell (put) an underlying asset (in this case a share) at a predetermined price (the strike or exercise price). Table 6.4 details Amcor call options.

TABLE 6.4

Call Options. Amcor Last Sale Price $8.75

Series	Ex Price	Fair Value	Last Sale	Vol '000s	Open Int	Implied Volatility Buyer	Implied Volatility Seller	Delta	Annual % Return
Amcor Ltd Last Sale Price $8.75									
Aug 02	.01	8.75	9.05	1557	1692	–	–	1.00	8.94
Aug 02	6.35	2.41	1.00	–	10	20.20	20.20	1.00	8.94
Aug 02	6.84	1.93	1.81	1	40	–	–	1.00	14.91
Aug 02	7.09	1.69	1.64	73	227	–	–	1.00	20.87
Aug 02	7.33	1.45	.89	85	462	–	–	1.00	20.87
Aug 02	7.82	.95	.88	200	1091	63.01	56.32	.94	14.91
Aug 02	8.06	.71	.86	13	232	48.37	40.79	.93	14.91
Aug 02	8.31	.47	.38	20	485	38.45	34.71	.87	20.87
Aug 02	8.55	.26	.21	41	2239	29.93	27.91	.74	35.78
Aug 02	8.80	.08	.10	266	1465	22.22	21.24	.43	45.32
Aug 02	9.04	.01	.04	89	723	21.91	21.37	.13	8.94
Aug 02	9.29	.00	.02	45	1478	20.77	20.44	–	.60
Nov 02	.01	8.72	8.31	1610	5662	–	–	–	–
Nov 02	7.57	1.22	1.31	6	8	–	–	.91	1.90

Call Options. Amcor Last Sale Price $8.75 (*continued*)

TABLE 6.4

Series	Ex Price	Fair Value	Last Sale	Vol '000s	Open Int	Implied Volatility Buyer	Implied Volatility Seller	Delta	Annual % Return
Amcor Ltd Last Sale Price $8.75									
Nov 02	7.82	1.01	1.06	8	42	–	–	.86	3.58
Nov 02	8.06	.83	.85	6	1131	12.47	9.77	.97	6.11
Nov 02	8.31	.64	.68	30	754	14.94	14.27	.83	8.64
Nov 02	8.55	.50	.48	30	572	16.89	16.47	.70	12.65
Nov 02	8.80	.35	.31	60	799	16.95	16.64	.57	14.76
Nov 02	9.04	.27	.27	44	887	18.64	18.39	.45	11.38
Nov 02	9.29	.20	.19	110	796	19.43	19.23	.35	8.22
Nov 02	9.53	.14	.21	–	30	20.01	19.84	.27	5.90
Nov 02	9.78	.09	.21	–	90	20.24	20.08	.20	3.96
Feb 03	7.50	1.72	–	3	3	–	–	.89	3.82
Feb 03	8.00	1.05	.91	–	16	13.42	12.68	.93	6.66
Feb 03	8.25	.88	.88	92	185	15.86	15.20	.83	8.41
Feb 03	8.50	.71	.78	86	131	16.19	15.87	.74	10.16
Feb 03	8.75	.59	.49	2	12	17.57	17.32	.64	12.89
Feb 03	9.00	.48	.48	7	92	18.36	18.14	.55	10.49
Feb 03	9.25	.39	.35	165	890	18.90	18.72	.47	8.41
Feb 03	9.50	.28	.30	113	113	18.29	18.14	.38	6.12
Apr 06	10.03	1.09	.25	–	162	7.61	7.48	.90	3.38

Source: *Australian Financial Review*, 26 August 2002

There are four series of options listed and these have maturity dates of August 2002, November 2002, February 2003 and April 2006 respectively. If the options are not exercised by these dates then they expire and are of no value. The February $8.50 exercise (Ex) price options are 'in the money'. This means that an Amcor share worth $8.75 can be purchased for $8.50. There are investors in the market willing to pay 78 cents for this right.

There are many tables in the Banking & Finance and National Markets sections of the paper. We will explain only two other tables to you. Table 6.5 lists interest rates.

Interest rates

TABLE 6.5

	Aug 16	Aug 23		Aug 16	Aug 23
Cash Rate: average 11am rate	4.75 pc	4.75 pc	**US Treasury Bonds:**		
Domestic Rates:			US 10 year Treasury Bond yields	4.18 pc	4.32 pc
90 day dealers bill rate	4.92 pc	5.02 pc	US 30 year Treasury Bond yields	4.98 pc	5.10 pc
180 day dealers bill rate	4.97 pc	5.07 pc	**US Federal Funds,** rate per annum	1.875 pc	1.688 pc
5 year Bond Yield	5.365 pc	5.535 pc	**US Bank Acceptances:**		
10 year Bond Yield	5.675 pc	5.835 pc	1 month bank buy	1.71 pc	1.76 pc
Bank Bill Swap Reference Rates: (Source: Bloomberg)			3 months bank buy	1.69 pc	1.73 pc
30 Days	4.902 pc	4.928 pc	6 months bank buy	1.60 pc	1.645 pc
60 Days	4.918 pc	4.962 pc	**German 10 yr Govt Bond Yld**	4.57 pc	4.687 pc
90 Days	4.942 pc	5.028 pc	**Japan, JGB No. 241 10yr yield**	1.280 pc	1.260 pc
180 Days	4.99 pc	5.078 pc			
Swap Rates: (Source: Commonwealth)					
Quarterly in arrears versus mean Bank Bill.					
1 year	5.05 pc	5.17 pc			
3 years	5.45 pc	5.595 pc			
5 years	5.70 pc	5.82 pc			

(continued)

TABLE 6.5

Interest rates (continued)

	Aug 16	Aug 23
Bank Bill Swap Reference Rate: Average Bid (Source: ANZ)		
30 Days	4.95 pc	4.98 pc
60 Days	4.97 pc	5.01 pc
90 Days	4.99 pc	5.08 pc
120 Days	5.01 pc	5.09 pc
180 Days	5.04 pc	5.13 pc
Calculated Cash Rate: (Source: ANZ)		
11 am cash Rate	4.75 pc	4.75 pc
AUD Forward Rate Agreements: (Source: Macquarie)		
1/4	4.96 pc	5.02 pc
3/6	4.97 pc	5.08 pc
6/9	5.09 pc	5.23 pc
Interest Rate Caps: (Source: Macquarie)		
Strike = prevailling swap rate: $ per million		
1 year	$2,600	$2,600
3 years	$15,500	$15,500
5 years	$28,000	$28,000
Commonwealth Bonds: (Source: Lewis Securities Ltd)		
3 year Indicator Rate—Index	5.16 pc	5.33 pc
10 year Indicator Rate—Index	5.60 pc	5.76 pc
London Inter Bank Offered Rates: $US		
3 months	1.758 pc	1.78 pc
6 months	1.739 pc	1.78 pc

UBS WARBURG INDICES (Source: UBS Warburg):	Aug 22	Aug 23	% rtn mth	% rtn year
Treasury 0 + yrs	4161.90	4154.28	+0.65	+4.16
Semi-Govt 0 + yrs	4261.95	4256.30	+0.75	+4.05
Credit 0 + yrs	3779.66	3776.23	+0.50	+3.53
Compsite 0 + yrs	3850.07	3844.80	+0.64	+3.92
Credit B 0 + yrs	1337.65	1336.45	+0.49	+3.54
Govt 0 + yrs	1271.56	1269.56	+0.70	+4.10
Bank 0 + yrs	4508.10	4508.62	+0.30	+2.95
Inflation 0 + yrs	2684.67	2678.82	+0.15	+5.13
Fixed Debt 0 + yrs	1215.74	1214.12	+0.63	+3.90
Float Rate 0 + yrs	1222.46	1222.44	+0.33	+2.84
Master Debt 0 + yrs	1217.58	1216.17	+0.55	+3.78

ABN AMRO BOND INDEX (Source: ABN AMRO Australia)	Aug 22	Aug 23	% chg	Mod Dur
Government	2014.113	2009.876	-0.210	4.579
Semi-Government	2032.191	2029.109	-0.152	4.354
Composite	2022.374	2018.648	-0.184	4.479
Composite 1–3 yr	1771.996	1770.627	-0.077	2.105
Composite 3–5 yr	1944.269	1941.318	-0.152	3.441
Composite 5–7 yr	2084.369	2080.420	-0.189	4.451
Composite 7+ yr	2239.243	2233.223	-0.269	6.589
B.I.G. Infl. Linked	2058.567	2056.058	-0.122	9.077
Liquids Infl. Linked	2086.011	2083.333	-0.128	9.489

Source: *Australian Financial Review*, 26 August 2002

On 23 August the 11 am rate was 4.75 per cent while the 30 day SWAP rate was 4.928 per cent. The 90-day bank bill rate was 5.08 per cent while in London it was 1.78 per cent. The 10-year bond yield in Australia was 5.835 per cent, while in the US the rate was 4.32 per cent.

In the retail market, as per Table 6.6, the Australian dollar was worth 53.68 US cents. If I wanted to convert US dollars back to Australian dollars, I would need 54.44 cents for one Australian dollar. Exchange rates are discussed in more detail in Chapter 23.

TABLE 6.6

Australian Dollar

Retail Market Exchange Rates

	buy/sell		buy/sell
US, dollar	0.5444/0.5368	**N Zealand**, dollar	1.1680/1.1433
$Aust equivalent	1.8369/1.8629	**Norway**, krone	4.1814/4.0638
UK, pound	0.3597/0.3512	**Pakistan**, rupee	On Ap/27.938
$Aust equivalent	2.7801/2.8474	**Papua NG**, kina	On Ap/1.8182
Europe, euro	0.5662/0.5492	**Philippines**, peso	On Ap/26.840
$Aust equivalent	1.7662/1.8208	**Saudi Arabia**, riyl	2.0712/1.9879
Brunei, dollar	0.9697/0.9207	**Singapore**, dollar	0.9653/0.9305
Canada, dollar	0.8548/0.8313	**Solomon Is.**, dollar	3.8232/3.5011
Denmark, kroner	4.1990/4.0769	**S Africa**, rand	5.9182/5.7418
Fiji, dollar	1.1980/1.1432	**Sri Lanka**, rupee	On Ap/50.01
Fr Pacific, franc	67.52/65.49	**Sweden**, krona	5.1899/5.0462
Hong Kong, dollar	4.2743/4.1612	**Switzerland**, franc	0.8293/0.8066
India, rupee	On Ap/24.870	**Thailand**, baht	23.67/21.68
Indonesia, rupiah	On Ap/On Ap	**Tonga**, pa'anga	1.2287/1.1405
Japan, yen	65.66/63.91	**Vanuatu**, vatu	76.60/72.73
Malaysia, ringgit	On Ap/On Ap	**W Samoa**, tala	1.8252/1.6675
Malta, pound	0.2367/0.2233	**Gold—1 oz**	562.00/579.00

* For up to A$25,000 equivalent
* Other currencies, on application
Source: Westpac Banking Corporation: August 23, 2002

Source: *Australian Financial Review*, 26 August 2002

Concept questions

6.2a *What are the relevant cash flows for valuing an ordinary share?*

6.2b *Does the value of a share depend on how long you expect to keep it?*

6.2c *What is the value of a share when the dividend grows at a constant rate?*

Using Excel

.xl

All the bond pricing calculations that have been performed in this chapter can be done in Excel. We will now show you various examples of the calculations. First you need to be in the program Excel. On the toolbar you should notice a function f_x. Click on this function and you will see that you have a number of choices of functions. The ones that we will use are the financial functions.

Let's calculate the present value, PV. Assume that a bond pays a 12 per cent coupon on a face value of $100 and that the term of the bond is three years. What will be the value of the bond if the yield is 10 per cent? In the financial functions, find PV. When you click onto this you should notice that there are up to five inputs required. The inputs are:

Rate = the rate of interest per period
Nper = the total number of periods
Pmt   = the payment per period—for an annuity
FV   = the future value lump sum
Type = normally left blank

For the problem at hand the rate is 0.10 for 10 per cent yield, the Nper is 3 for three years and the Pmt is 12 for the annual coupon. The future value is 100. The calculated answer will be −$104.97. Notice that the FV and Pmt need to be entered as negatives. Remember that for Excel and financial calculators to do the calculations, some cash flows need to be negative and others need to be positive. Think of an investment where you invest $104.97 and get back $12 each year for three years plus $100 in three years time.

Let's do the problem again, but this time assume that the coupon is paid semi-annually. Now the rate will be 0.05 for 5 per cent yield per half year and the Nper is now 6 for the six coupon payments. The Pmt will now be 6 for $6 per half-year and the FV will be the same. The calculated answer is now $105.07.

When we want to calculate the yield, the Excel function that we need to use is Rate. Let's assume that a four-year bond has an annual coupon of 8 per cent and again a face value of $100. It has a market price of $103.39. You need to calculate the yield.

The number of periods is 4 and the payment is 8. The future value is 100. Now Excel will calculate a rate of return or yield of 7%.

6.3 ▪ Summary and conclusions

This chapter has shown you how to extend the basic present value results of Chapter 5 in some important ways. In our discussion of debt and shares, we saw that:

1 Bonds are long-term debts. We examined the cash flows from a bond and found that the present value of the cash flows and, hence, the bond's value can be readily determined. We also introduced some of the terminology associated with bonds, and we discussed how bond prices are reported.

2 The cash flows from owning a share come in the form of future dividends. We saw that in certain special cases it is possible to calculate the present value of all the future dividends and thus come up with a value for a share. We discussed some of the terms that are associated with ordinary shares, and we also examined how share price information is reported.

This chapter completes Part Three of the book. By now, you should have a good grasp of what we mean by present value. You should also be familiar with how to calculate present values, loan payments, and so on. In Part Four, we cover capital budgeting decisions. As you will see, the techniques you learned in Chapters 5 and 6 form the basis for our approach to evaluating business investment decisions.

Key terms

Capital gains yield *203*
Coupon payments *188*
Coupon rate *188*
Current yield *202*

Dividend growth model *199*
Dividend yield *202*
Face value *188*

Maturity *188*
Par value *188*
Yield to maturity *189*

Suggested readings

The best place to look for additional information about valuing shares and bonds is in an investments textbook. Some good ones are:

Brealey, R., Myers, S., Partington, G. and Robinson, D. *Principles of Corporate Finance*, McGraw-Hill, Sydney, 2000.

Reilly, F. and Brown, K. *Investment Analysis and Portfolio Management*, Dryden Press, Orlando, Fl., 2000.

Endnotes

1 See Chapter 5 for details on basic loan types.

2 A financial calculator will find the yield to maturity for a bond. A common procedure would involve entering $8 (the coupon) as the payment (Pmt), 6 as the number of periods (*N* or *t*), $95.514 (the current market price) as the present value (PV), and $100 (the face value) as the future value (FV). If you solve for the interest rate (*i*), the answer should be 9 per cent.

3 The only assumption that we make about share price is that it is a finite number no matter how far we push it. It can be extremely large, just not infinitely so. Since no one has ever observed an infinite price, this assumption is plausible.

4 Here and elsewhere, we use the term capital gain a little loosely. For the record, a capital gain (or loss) is, strictly speaking, something defined by the Income Tax Assessment Act. For our purposes, it would be more accurate (but less common) to use the term price appreciation instead of capital gain.

5 Franking credits are discussed in detail in Chapter 19. They are taxation credits linked to the company dividend.

Maximise Your Marks!
There are 30 interactive questions on valuing shares and bonds waiting online for you at www.mhhe.com/au/ross3e. The questions are written with additional feedback for incorrect answers, and text excerpts with page references for follow-up study.

International Articles!
To read more on valuing shares and bonds and to see current international articles, just go to www.mhhe.com/au/ross3e and click on *PowerWeb Articles* for this chapter.

Chapter review problems and self-test

6.1 · Bond values

A bond has a 10 per cent coupon rate and a $100 face value. Interest is paid semi-annually, and the bond has 20 years to maturity. If investors require a 12 per cent yield, what is the bond's value? What is the effective annual yield on the bond?

6.2 · Bond yields

A Property Ltd bond carries an 8 per cent coupon, paid semi-annually. The face value is $100, and the bond matures in 6 years. If the bond currently sells for $91.137, what is its yield to maturity? What is the effective annual yield?

6.3 · Dividend growth and share valuation

Development Company has just paid a cash dividend of $0.20 per share. Investors require a 16 per cent return from investments such as this. If the dividend is expected to grow at a steady 8 per cent per year, what is the current value of a share? What will a share be worth in 5 years?

6.4 · More dividend growth and share valuation

In Problem 6.3, what would a share sell for today if the dividend is expected to grow at 20 per cent for the next 3 years and then settle down to 8 per cent per year?

Answers to self-test problems

6.1 · Since the bond has a 10 per cent coupon yield while investors require a 12 per cent return, we know that the bond must sell at a discount. Notice that, since the bond pays interest semi-annually, the coupons amount to $10/2 = $5 every six months. The required yield is 12%/2 = 6% every six months. Finally, the bond matures in 20 years, so there are a total of 40 six-month periods.

The bond's value is thus equal to the present value of $5 every six months for the next 40 six-month periods, plus the present value of the $100 face amount:

$$\text{Bond value} = \$5 \times [1 \times 1/(1.06)^{40}]/0.06 + \$100/(1.06)^{40}$$
$$= \$5 \times 15.04630 + \$100/10.2857$$
$$= \$75.232 + \$9.722$$
$$= \$84.954$$

Notice that we discounted the $100 back 40 periods at 6 per cent per period, rather than 20 years at 12 per cent. The reason is that the effective annual yield on the bond is $1.06^2 - 1 = 12.36\%$, not 12 per cent. We thus could have used 12.36 per cent per year for 20 years when we calculated the present value of the $100 face amount, and the answer would have been the same.

6.2 · The present value of the bond's cash flows is its current price, $91.137. The coupon is $4 every 6 months for 12 periods. The face value is $100, so the bond's yield is the unknown discount rate in the following:

$$\$91.137 = \$4 \times [1 \times 1/(1 + r)^{12}]/r + \$100/(1 + r)^{12}$$

The bond sells at a discount. Since the coupon rate is 8 per cent, the yield must be something in excess of that.

If we were to solve this by trial and error, we might try 12 per cent (or 6% per 6 months):

$$\text{Bond value} = \$4 \times [1 - 1/1.06^{12}]/0.06 + \$100/1.06^{12}$$
$$= \$4 \times 8.3838 + \$49.697$$
$$= \$33.535 + \$49.697$$
$$= \$83.232$$

This is less than the actual value, so our discount rate is too high. We now know that the yield is somewhere between 8 and 12 per cent. With further trial and error (or a little machine assistance), the yield works out to be 10 per cent, or 5 per cent every six months.

$$\text{Bond value} = \$4 \times [1 - 1/1.05^{12}]/0.05 + \$100/1.05^{12}$$
$$= \$4 \times 8.8633 + \$55.684$$
$$= \$35.453 + \$55.684$$
$$= \$91.137$$

By convention, the bond's yield to maturity would be quoted as $2 \times 5\% = 10\%$. The effective yield is thus $1.05^2 - 1 = 10.25\%$.

6.3 · The last dividend, D_0, was \$0.20. The dividend is expected to grow steadily at 8 per cent. The required return is 16 per cent. Based on the dividend growth model, the current price is:

$$P_0 = D_1/(r - g) = D_0 \times (1 + g)/(r - g)$$
$$= \$0.2 \times (1.08)/(0.16 - 0.08)$$
$$= \$0.216/(0.08)$$
$$= \$2.70$$

We could calculate the price in 5 years by calculating the dividend in 5 years and then using the growth model again. Alternatively, we could recognise that the share price will increase by 8 per cent per year and calculate the future price directly. We'll do both. First, the dividend in 5 years will be:

$$D_5 = D_0 \times (1 + g)^5$$
$$= \$0.2 \times 1.08^5$$
$$= \$0.2 \times 1.4693$$
$$= \$0.29387$$

The price in five years would therefore be:

$$P_5 = D_5 \times (1 + g)/(r - g)$$
$$= \$0.29387 \times (1.08)/0.08$$
$$= \$0.31738/0.08$$
$$= \$3.97$$

Once we understand the dividend model, however, it's easier to notice that:

$$P_5 = P_0 \times (1 + g)^5$$
$$= \$2.70 \times 1.08^5$$
$$= \$2.70 \times 1.4693$$
$$= \$3.97$$

Notice that both approaches yield the same price in 5 years.

6.4 · In this scenario, we have supernormal growth for the next three years. We need to calculate the dividends during the rapid growth period and the share price in 3 years. The dividends are:

$$D_1 = \$0.20 \times 1.20 = \$0.24$$
$$D_2 = \$0.24 \times 1.20 = \$0.288$$
$$D_3 = \$0.288 \times 1.20 = \$0.3456$$

After 3 years, the growth rate falls to 8 per cent indefinitely. The price at that time, P_3, is thus:

$$P_3 = D_3 \times (1 + g)/(r - g)$$
$$= \$0.3456 \times 1.08/(0.16 - 0.08)$$
$$= \$0.37325/0.08$$
$$= \$4.67$$

To complete the calculation of the share's present value, we have to determine the present value of the three dividends and the future price:

$$P_0 = D_1/(1 + r)^1 + D_2/(1 + r)^2 + D_3/(1 + r)^3 + P_3/(1 + r)^3$$
$$= \$0.24/1.16 + \$0.288/1.16^2 + \$0.3456/1.16^3 + \$4.67/1.16^3$$
$$= \$0.207 + \$0.214 + \$0.221 + \$2.99$$
$$= \$3.63$$

Questions and problems

1 · Bond Values

Debit Instruments has a bond issue outstanding that pays $6 annually. It has a face value of $100, and it will mature in eight years. Similar bonds are priced to yield 7 per cent. What would you expect this bond to sell for?

2 · Bond values with semi-annual coupons

In Problem 1, what would the bond be worth if it paid $3.50 every six months? Assume the rate is 3.5 per cent per six months. Why is this value different from the value in Problem 1?

3 · Semi-annual coupons

Ioyou bonds have a coupon rate of 7 per cent and mature in 15 years. Assuming semi-annual coupons, what is the value of this bond? Similar bonds yield 8 per cent.

4 · Calculating yields

In Problem 3, what would be the value of the bond if similar bonds yield 6 per cent?

5 · Bond values and yields

You have just purchased a newly issued $100 five-year bond at par. This bond (bond A) pays $3 in interest semi-annually ($6 per year). You are also negotiating the purchase of a $100 six-year bond that pays $5 semi-annually and has 5 years to maturity (bond B).

a   What is the rate required in the market (the yield) on these issued bonds?
b   What should you be willing to pay (at most) for bond B?
c   How will your answer to part (b) change if bond A pays $2 (instead of $3) in semi-annual interest but still sells for $100?

6 · Prices versus interest rates

What is the relationship between changes in interest rates and bond values? How is this relationship affected by the time to maturity? By the coupon rate?

7 · Bond values and yields

A particular bond is observed to have a coupon rate of 6 per cent and a yield to maturity that is also 6 per cent. What do you know about the value of the bond? What would you know if the yield to maturity were 4 per cent? 8 per cent?

8 · Interest rate risk

The Lendit Corporation has two bonds outstanding, both of which have a 10 per cent coupon rate (with annual coupons) and sell for their $100 par value. The first bond, bond A, has four years to maturity. The second bond, bond B, has eight years to maturity. If market interest rates were to rise by 2 per cent, which bond would have the larger price change? Calculate the new prices to illustrate your answer.

9 · Bond values and coupons

Your firm is contemplating selling some 10-year bonds to raise funds for a planned expansion. The firm currently has an issue outstanding with a $6 annual coupon, paid semi-annually. These bonds currently sell for $92.89, a discount relative to their $100 face value, and they have 10 years remaining to maturity. What coupon rate must the new issue have if it is to sell at par when it is issued?

10 · Note values

Bust Bank Ltd has suffered some financial reversals recently and is unable to meet its next several coupon payments. The notes in question will mature in 6 years and have a 16 per cent coupon rate. Coupons are paid annually. By arrangement with its creditors, Bust Bank will skip the next three coupons. The skipped coupons will be repaid at maturity without interest. Not surprisingly, investors view these notes as risky and require a 25 per cent return. What price would we expect to see on the notes?

11 · Bond yields

Issued bonds have a price of $84.87 and a coupon rate of 10 per cent paid annually. The bonds will mature in 12 years. What is the yield to maturity?

12 · Coupon rates

The Balancing Company has an outstanding debt issue that is currently selling for $90.06. The yield to maturity is 12 per cent, and the bonds mature in 8 years. Assuming that the face value is $100, what is the coupon rate?

13 · Share values and growth

Expand Ltd has experienced a steady growth of 8 per cent per year in its annual dividend. This growth is expected to continue indefinitely. The last dividend paid was $0.11 per share. Investors require a 12 per cent return on similar companies. What is the current price of Expand Ltd shares? What will the price be in 4 years?

14 · Share values and yield

In Problem 13, what is the dividend yield on Expand shares? What is the capital gains yield?

15 · Calculating required return

Future Fashions anticipates a dividend growth rate of 6 per cent forever. The market-required return is 20 per cent on similar securities. The next dividend is predicted to be $0.152 per share. What is the current price per share?

16 · Required returns

Jab Insurance Ltd shares currently sell for $5 per share. The last dividend was $0.20 per share. The dividend is expected to grow at 10 per cent. What is the required return on Jab shares? The dividend yield?

17 · Required returns

Suppose that a shareholder has just paid $5 per share for Windfall Company shares. The shares will pay a $0.20 per share dividend in the upcoming year, and this dividend is expected to grow at an annual rate of 10 per cent indefinitely. The shareholder felt that the price paid was an appropriate price, given an assessment of Windfall's risks. What is the annual required rate of return of this shareholder?

18 · Non-constant growth

Wealth-Girl Ltd has just paid a $0.40 dividend. The dividend is expected to grow at 12 per cent for the next four years. After that, the growth rate will be 5 per cent indefinitely. If the required return is 16 per cent, what is the current value of a share today?

19 · Non-constant growth

The Worthless Company does not currently pay dividends. You predict that dividend payments will begin in 4 years and that the first cash dividend will be $0.60. The dividend will grow at 8 per cent thereafter. If the required return is 25 per cent, what is the value of a share?

20 · Perpetuities

What is the value of an asset that pays $2 per year forever? Assume a 20 per cent required return. How would your answer change if the cash flow grows at a rate of 5 per cent per year forever? Assume that $2 was the most recent payment.

21 · Calculating growth

Shares in Mystery Ltd are selling for $6 per share. Mystery has paid a dividend of $0.40 per share, and the required return on similar shares is 12 per cent. Assuming that Mystery's dividend will grow at a constant rate in the future, what will that growth rate be?

22 · Calculating dividends

The Now Company's dividend growth rate is projected to be 6 per cent indefinitely. It has just paid a dividend. A share currently sells for $8.20 per share. Assuming that the market requires a 14 per cent return, what is the current dividend?

23 · Non-constant growth

Gromixs Ltd is experiencing a period of rapid growth. Earnings and dividends are expected to grow at a rate of 18 per cent during the next two years, 15 per cent in the third year, and then at a constant rate of 6 per cent thereafter. Gromixs' last dividend, which has just been paid, was $0.115. If the required return on the shares is 12 per cent, what is the price of a share today?

24 · Negative growth

Reversal Mining Company's ore reserves are being depleted, and its costs of recovering a declining quantity of ore are rising each year. As a result the company's earnings and dividends are declining at a rate of 10 per cent per year. If the dividend, which was just paid, was $0.05 and the required return is 14 per cent, what is the value of a share?

25 · Required returns

Onhold Ltd recently suspended its dividend payments. Management anticipates that a dividend of $0.25 per share will be restored in 5 years and that the dividend will be increased at a rate of 6 per cent per year thereafter. The shares currently sell for $1.20 per share. What is the required return in this case?

26 · Non-constant growth

Newsite Ltd is expanding rapidly. Its dividend growth rate for the coming year is projected at 25 per cent. This rate will decline by 5 percentage points per year until it reaches the industry average of 5 per cent. Once it reaches 5 per cent, it will stay there indefinitely. The most recent dividend was $0.85 per share, and the market requires a return of 16 per cent on investments such as this one. What is the price per share for Newsite?

27 · Required returns

This one's a little harder. In the previous question, suppose that the price per share was $12. If the dividend projections remain unchanged, what is the required return on Newsite shares?

28 · Negative growth

Cool Ltd's profitability has steadily declined because of increasing competition. The most recent dividend was $0.20 per share, but management anticipates that the dividend will decrease at a rate of 10 per cent per year indefinitely. If the required return is 20 per cent, what is a share worth?

29 · Negative growth

This is a challenge problem. Macrosoft Software is one of a myriad of companies selling word processor programs. Their newest and only program will cost $5 million to develop. First-year profits will be $1.2 million. However, as a result of competition, profits will fall by 4 per cent each year. All cash inflows occur at year end. If the market discount rate is 16 per cent, what is the value of the company?

30 · Capital gains versus dividends

This is a challenge problem. You have predicted the following dividends for the next three years on Noitall Production's shares:

Year	Projected dividend
1	$0.50
2	0.60
3	0.70

Beginning in the third year, you project that the dividend will grow at an 8 per cent rate indefinitely. The required return is 15 per cent.
a   Calculate the price today for the shares.
b   Calculate the price at years 1, 2 and 3.
c   Calculate the dividend yield and capital gains yield in each of the first four years. What do you observe?

31 · Bond value

Bandaid Bank Limited bonds have a 10 per cent coupon rate and $100 face value. Interest is paid semi-annually and they have 20 years to maturity. If investors require 12 per cent yield, what is the bond's value? What is the effective annual yield?

32 · Bond yield

Fixit Finance Limited carries an 8 per cent coupon, paid half-yearly. The par value is $100 and it matures in six years. If the bond currently sells for $91.137, what is its yield to maturity? What is the effective annual yield?

33 · Share value and dividend growth

The Bringapal Company has just paid a cash dividend of 20 cents per share. Investors require a 16 per cent return from investments such as this. If the dividend is expected to grow at a steady 8 per cent per year, what is the current value of the share? What will the share be worth in five years?

34 · Share value and dividend growth

Using the information from Problem 33, what would the share sell for today if the dividend was expected to grow at 20 per cent for the next three years and then settle down to 8 per cent indefinitely?

PART FOUR

Capital

budgeting

CHAPTER 7

Net present value and other investment criteria

Objective

This chapter looks at the methods used in practice to address the capital budgeting decisions faced by firms. Capital budgeting is probably the most important issue in corporate finance. Because these decisions involve cash flows that will occur for some considerable time into the future, many different procedures are used in practice. In addition any firm possesses a huge number of possible investments. Each of these possible investments is an option available to the firm. Some of these options are valuable and some are not. The essence of successful financial management, of course, is learning to identify which are which. With this in mind, our goal in this chapter is to introduce you to the techniques used to analyse potential business ventures to decide which are worth undertaking.

We present and compare a number of different procedures that are used in practice. Our primary goal is to acquaint you with the advantages and disadvantages of the various approaches. As we shall see, the most important concept in this area is net present value. We consider this approach first.

Study tip | Superior capital budgeting decisions will be made if the approach correctly identifies the cash flows, the timing of the cash flows, and the risk associated with the cash flows.

As we look at the various procedures used in practice, we should be evaluating whether the approach *takes into account all three* essential factors: if it does, it is an acceptable approach for making capital budgeting decisions.

Introduction ▷ In Chapter 1, we identified the three key areas of concern to the financial manager. The first of these was: 'What fixed assets should we buy?' We called this the capital budgeting decision. In this chapter, we begin to deal with this question.

The process of allocating or budgeting capital is usually more involved than simply deciding on whether or not to buy a particular fixed asset. We will frequently face broader issues, like whether or not we should launch a new product or enter a new market. Decisions such as these will determine the nature of a firm's operations and products for years to come, primarily because fixed asset investments are generally long-lived and not easily reversed once they are made.

The most fundamental decision that a business must make concerns its product line. What services will we offer or what will we sell? In what markets will we compete? What new products will we introduce? The answer to any of these questions will require that the firm commit its scarce and valuable capital to certain types of assets. As a result, all of these strategic issues fall under the general heading of capital budgeting. Capital budgeting could thus be given a more descriptive name: strategic asset allocation.

For the reasons we have discussed, the capital budgeting question is probably the most important issue in corporate finance. How a firm chooses to finance its operations (the capital structure question) and how a firm manages its short-term operating activities (the working capital question) are certainly issues of concern, but it is the fixed assets that define the business of the firm. Airlines, for example, are airlines because they operate aeroplanes, regardless of how they finance them.

We shall see that techniques that discount future cash flows are highly regarded as methods of capital investment appraisal. Conversely, techniques that do not discount future cash flows have a number of shortcomings and consequently leave a lot to be desired. Nevertheless it must be appreciated that the mere adoption of the preferred analytical tool is not in itself sufficient to guarantee superior performance. Other elements, such as marketing, product development, executive recruitment and training, staff relations, market position, the quality of the future cash flow estimates, the assessed risk of the investment, and so on, may have greater impact on the acceptability of the project and must be considered in the qualitative aspects of the investment. It follows that our emphasis is upon the quantitative aspects of the decision.

7.1 ■ Net present value

net present value (NPV)

the difference between an investment's market value and its cost

In Chapter 1, we argued that the goal of financial management is to create value for the shareholders. The financial manager must thus examine a potential investment in light of its likely effect on the price of the firm's shares. In this section, we describe a widely used procedure for doing this, the **net present value (NPV)** approach.

The basic idea

An investment is worth undertaking if it creates value for its owners. In the most general sense, we create value by identifying an investment that is worth more in the marketplace than it costs us to acquire. How can something be worth more than it costs? It's a case of the whole being worth more than the cost of the parts.

For example, suppose you buy a dilapidated house for $130,000 and spend another $45,000 on painters, plumbers, and so on to get it fixed up. Your total investment is $175,000. When the work is completed, you place the house back on the market and find that it's worth $225,000. The market value ($225,000) exceeds the cost ($175,000) by $50,000. What you have done here is to act as a manager and bring together some fixed assets (a house), some labour (plumbers, carpenters, and others), and some materials (carpeting, paint, and so on). The net result is that you have created $50,000 in value. Put another way, this $50,000 is the value added by management.

With our house example, it turned out after the fact that $50,000 in value was created. Things thus worked out very nicely. The real challenge, of course, was to somehow identify ahead of time whether or not investing the necessary $175,000 was a good idea in the first place. This is what capital budgeting is all about, namely, trying to determine whether a proposed investment or project will be worth more than it costs once it is in place.

For reasons that will be obvious in a moment, the difference between an investment's market value (in today's dollars) and its cost (also in today's dollars) is called the net present value of the investment, abbreviated as NPV. In other words, net present value is a measure of how much value is created or added today by undertaking an investment. Given our goal of creating value for the shareholders, the capital budgeting process can be viewed as a search for investments with positive net present values.

With our run-down house, you can probably imagine how we would go about making the capital budgeting decision. We would first look at what comparable, renovated properties were selling for in the market. We would then get estimates of the cost of buying a particular property and bringing it up to market. At this point, we have an estimated total cost and an estimated market value. If the difference is positive, then this investment is worth undertaking because it has a positive estimated net present value. There is risk, of course, because there is no guarantee that our estimates will turn out to be correct.

As our example illustrates, investment decisions are greatly simplified when there is a market for assets similar to the investment we are considering. Capital budgeting becomes much more difficult when we cannot observe the market price for at least roughly comparable investments. The reason is that we are then faced with the problem of estimating the value of an investment using only indirect market information. Unfortunately, this is precisely the situation that the financial manager usually encounters. We examine this issue next.

Estimating net present value

Imagine that we are thinking of starting a business to produce and sell a new product, say, organic fertiliser. We can estimate the start-up costs with reasonable accuracy because we know what we will need to buy to begin production. Would this be a good investment?

Based on our discussion, you know that the answer depends on whether or not the value of the new business exceeds the cost of starting it. In other words, does this investment have a positive NPV?

This problem is much more difficult than our 'fixed-up' house example, because entire fertiliser companies are not routinely bought and sold in the marketplace; so it is essentially impossible to observe the market value of a similar investment. As a result, we must somehow estimate this value by other means.

Based on our work in Chapters 5 and 6, you may be able to guess how we will go about estimating the value of our fertiliser business. We will first try to estimate the future cash flows that we expect the new business to produce. We will then apply our basic discounted cash flow procedure to estimate the present value of those cash flows. Once we have this estimate, we then estimate NPV as the difference between the present value of the future cash flows and the cost of the investment. As we mentioned in Chapter 5, this procedure is often called **discounted cash flow (DCF) valuation**.

discounted cash flow (DCF) valuation
the process of valuing an investment by discounting its future cash flows

To see how we might go about estimating NPV, suppose we believe that the cash revenues from our fertiliser business will be $20,000 per year, assuming that everything goes as expected. Cash costs (including taxes) will be $14,000 per year. We will wind down the business in eight years. The plant, property and equipment will be worth $2,000 as salvage at that time. The project costs $30,000 to launch. We use a 15 per cent discount rate on new projects such as this one. Is this a good investment? If there are 1,000 shares on issue, what will be the effect on the price per share from taking it?

From a purely mechanical perspective, we need to calculate the present value of the future cash flows at 15 per cent. The net cash inflow will be $20,000 cash profit less $14,000 in costs per year for eight years. These cash flows are illustrated in Table 7.1. As Table 7.1 suggests, we effectively have an eight-year annuity of $20,000 − $14,000 = $6,000 per year along with a single lump-sum inflow of $2,000 in eight years time. Calculating the present value of the future cash flows thus comes down to the same type of problem we considered in Chapter 5.

The present value is provided as follows:

$$\text{Present value} = \$6,000 \times (1 - 1/1.15^8)/0.15 + \$2,000/1.15^8$$
$$= \$6,000 \times 4.4873 + \$2,000/3.0590$$
$$= \$26,924 + \$654$$
$$= \$27,578$$

When we compare this to the $30,000 estimated cost, the NPV is:

$$\text{NPV} = -\$30,000 + \$27,578 = -\$2,422$$

Project cash flows ($000)									TABLE 7.1
Time (years)	0	1	2	3	4	5	6	7	8
Initial cost	−$30								
Inflows		$20	$20	$20	$20	$20	$20	$20	$20
Outflows		−14	−14	−14	−14	−14	−14	−14	−14
Net Inflow		6	6	6	6	6	6	6	6
Salvage									2
Net cash flow	−$30	$6	$6	$6	$6	$6	$6	$6	$8

Therefore, this is not a good investment. Based on our estimates, taking it would decrease the total value of the shares by $2,422. With 1,000 shares on issue, our best estimate of the impact of taking this project is a loss of value of $2,422/1,000 = $2.422 per share.

Our fertiliser example illustrates how NPV estimates can be used to determine whether or not an investment is desirable. From our example, notice that, if the NPV is negative, the effect on share value will be unfavourable. If the NPV were positive, the effect would be favourable. As a consequence, all we need to know about a particular proposal for the purpose of making an accept/reject decision is whether the NPV is positive or negative.

Given that the goal of financial management is to increase share value, our discussion in this section leads us to the net present value rule:

> An investment should be accepted if the net present value is positive and rejected if it is negative.

In the unlikely event that the net present value turned out to be exactly zero, we would be indifferent to taking the investment or not taking it.

Two comments about our example are in order. First and foremost, it is not the rather mechanical process of discounting the cash flows that is important. Once we have the cash flows and the appropriate discount rate, the required calculations are fairly straightforward. The task of coming up with the cash flows and the discount rate in the first place is much more challenging. We will have much more to say about this in the next several chapters. For the remainder of this chapter, we take it as given that we have estimates of the cash revenues and costs and, where needed, an appropriate discount rate.

The second thing to keep in mind about our example is that the –$2,422 NPV is an estimate. Like any estimate, it can be high or low. The only way to find out the true NPV would be to place the investment up for sale and see what we could get for it. We generally won't be doing this, so it is important that our estimates be reliable. Once again, we will have more to say about this later. For the rest of this chapter, we will assume the estimates are accurate.

EXAMPLE 7.1 ■ Using the NPV rule

Suppose we are asked to decide whether or not a new consumer product should be launched. Based on projected sales and costs, we expect that the cash flows over the five-year life of the project will be $2,000 in the first two years, $4,000 in the next two, and $5,000 in the last year. It will cost about $10,000 to begin production. We use a 10 per cent discount rate to evaluate new products. What should we do here?

Given the cash flows and discount rate, we can calculate the total value of the product by discounting the cash flows back to the present:

$$\text{Present value} = \$2{,}000/1.1 + \$2{,}000/1.1^2 + \$4{,}000/1.1^3 + \$4{,}000/1.1^4 + \$5{,}000/1.1^5$$
$$= \$1{,}818 + \$1{,}653 + \$3{,}005 + \$2{,}732 + \$3{,}105$$
$$= \$12{,}313$$

The present value of the expected cash flows is $12,313, but the cost of getting those cash flows is only $10,000, so the NPV is $12,313 − $10,000 = $2,313. This is positive; so, based on the net present value rule, we should take it.

As we have seen in this section, estimating NPV is one way of assessing the profitability of a proposed investment. It is certainly not the only way that profitability is assessed, and we now turn to some alternatives. As we will see, when compared to NPV, each of the ways of assessing profitability that we examine is flawed in some key way; so NPV is the preferred approach in principle, if not always in practice.

Concept questions

7.1a *What is the net present value rule?*

7.1b *If we say that an investment has an NPV of $1,000, what exactly do we mean?*

7.2 ■ The payback rule

It is very common in practice to talk of the payback on a proposed investment. Loosely, the payback is the length of time it takes to recover our initial investment or 'get our money back'. Because this idea is widely understood and used, we will examine it in some detail.

Defining the rule

We can illustrate how to calculate a payback with an example. Table 7.2 shows the cash flows from a proposed investment. How many years do we have to wait until the accumulated cash flows from this investment equal or exceed the cost of the investment? As Table 7.2 indicates, the initial investment is $50,000. After the first year, the firm has recovered $30,000, leaving $20,000 to be recovered. The cash flow in the second year is exactly $20,000, so this investment 'pays for itself' in exactly two years. Put another way, the **payback period** is two years. If we require a payback of, say, three years or less, then this investment is acceptable. This illustrates the payback period rule:

payback period
the amount of time required for an investment to generate cash flows to recover its initial cost

> Based on the payback rule, an investment is acceptable if its calculated payback is less than some prescribed number of years.

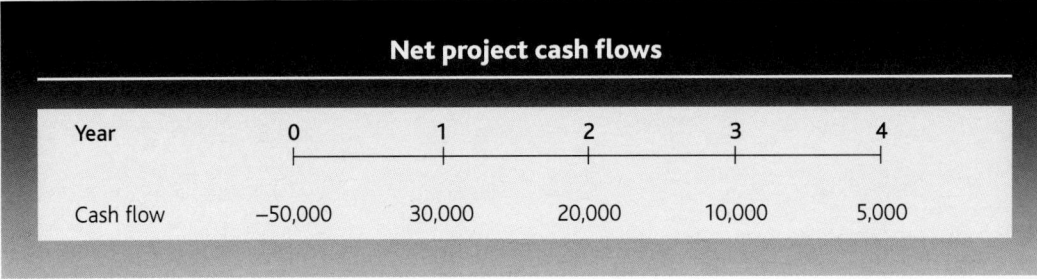

TABLE 7.2

Net project cash flows					
Year	0	1	2	3	4
Cash flow	−50,000	30,000	20,000	10,000	5,000

In our example, the payback works out to be exactly two years. This won't usually happen, of course. When the numbers don't work out exactly, it is customary to work with fractional years. For example, suppose the initial investment is $60,000, and the cash flows are $20,000 in the first year and $80,000 in the second. The cash flows over the first two years are $100,000, so the project obviously pays back sometime in the second year. After the first year, the project has paid back $20,000, leaving $40,000 to be recovered. To figure out the fractional year, note that this $40,000 is $40,000/$80,000 = $1/2$ of the second year's cash flow. Assuming that the $80,000 cash flow is paid uniformly throughout the year, the payback would thus be 1.5 years.

EXAMPLE 7.2 ■ **Calculating payback**

The projected cash flows from a proposed investment are:

Year	Cash flow
1	$100
2	200
3	500

This project costs $500. What is the payback period for this investment?

The initial cost is $500. After the first two years, the cash flows total $300. After the third year, the total cash flow is $800, so the project pays back sometime between the end of year 2 and the end of year 3. Since the accumulated cash flows for the first two years are $300, we need to recover $200 in the third year. The third year cash flow is $500, so we will have to wait $200/500 = 2/5 of the year to do this. The payback period is thus 2.4 years, or about two years and five months.

Now that we know how to calculate the payback period on an investment, using the payback period rule for making decisions is straightforward. A particular cut-off time is selected, say two years, and all investment projects that have payback periods of two years or less are accepted, and all of those that pay off in more than two years are rejected.

Table 7.3 illustrates cash flows for five different projects. The figures shown as the year 0 cash flows are the cost of the investment. We examine these to indicate some peculiarities that can, in principle, arise with payback periods.

TABLE 7.3

	Expected cash flows for projects A to E				
Year	A	B	C	D	E
0	−$100	−$200	−$200	−$200	−$50
1	30	40	40	100	100
2	40	20	20	100	−9,999
3	50	10	10	−200	
4	60		130	200	

The payback for the first project, A, is easily calculated. The sum of the cash flows for the first two years is $70, leaving us with $100 − $70 = $30 to go. Since the cash flow in the third year is $50, the payback occurs sometime in that year. When we compare the $30 we need to the $50 that will be coming in, we get $30/$50 = 0.60; so payback will occur 60 per cent of the way into the year. The payback period is thus 2.6 years.

Project B's payback is also easy to calculate: it never pays back because the cash flows never total up to the original investment. Project C has a payback of exactly 4 years because it supplies the $130 that B is missing in year 4. Project D is a little strange. Because of the negative cash flow in year 3, you can easily verify that it has two different payback periods, two years and four years. Which of these is correct? Both of them; the way the payback period is calculated doesn't guarantee a single answer. Finally, Project E is obviously unrealistic, but it does pay back in 6 months, thereby illustrating the point that a rapid payback does not guarantee a good investment.

Analysing the payback period rule

When compared to the NPV rule, the payback period rule has some rather severe shortcomings. First of all, the payback period is calculated by simply adding up the future cash flows. There is no discounting involved, so the time value of money is completely ignored. A payback rule also does not consider risk differences at all. The payback would be calculated the same way for both very risky and very safe projects.

Perhaps the biggest problem with the payback period rule is coming up with the right cut-off period, because we don't really have an objective basis for choosing a particular number. Put another way, there is no economic rationale for looking at payback in the first place, so we have no guide as to how to pick the cut-off. As a result, we end up using a number that is arbitrarily chosen.

Suppose we have somehow decided on an appropriate payback period, say two years or less. As we have seen, the payback period rule ignores the time value of money for the first two years. More seriously, cash flows after the second year are ignored entirely. To see this, consider the two investments, Long and Short, in Table 7.4. Both projects cost $250. Based on our discussion, the payback on Long is 2 + $50/$100 = 2.5 years, and the payback on Short is 1 + $150/$200 = 1.75 years. With a cut-off of two years, Short is acceptable and Long is not.

TABLE
7.4

Investment projected cash flows		
Year	Long	Short
1	$100	$100
2	100	200
3	100	0
4	100	0

Is the payback period rule giving us the right decisions? Maybe not. Suppose again that we require a 15 per cent return on this type of investment. We can calculate the NPV for these two investments as:

$$\text{NPV(Short)} = -\$250 + \$100/1.15 + \$200/1.15^2$$
$$= -\$250 + \$86.96 + \$151.23 = -\$11.81$$
$$\text{NPV(Long)} = -\$250 + \$100 \times (1 - 1/1.15^4)/0.15$$
$$= -\$250 + \$100 \times 2.8550 = \$35.50$$

Now we have a problem. The NPV of the shorter-term investment is actually negative, meaning that taking it diminishes the value of the shareholders' equity. The opposite is true for the longer-term investment—it increases share value.

Our example illustrates two primary shortcomings of the payback period rule. First, by ignoring time value, we may be led to take investments (like Short) that actually are worth less than they cost. Second, by ignoring cash flows beyond the cut-off, we may be led to reject profitable long-term investments (like Long). More generally, using a payback period rule will tend to bias us towards shorter-term investments.

TABLE
7.5

			Projects			
Year	A	B	C	D	E	F
0	–$900	–$900	–$900	–$900	–$900	–$900
1	300	300	100	600	600	300
2	300	300	200	200	200	300
3	300	300	600	100	100	300
4	–	300	–	–	100	–
Payback	3 yrs	3 yrs	3 yrs	3 yrs	3 yrs	3 yrs

Projects with different cash flows

Table 7.5 illustrates the shortcomings of the payback period rule. All of the projects have a payback of three years but clearly some are preferred to others. Project B is preferred to all other projects ignoring time value. E is preferred to D because it has the same pattern of cash flow in the first three years plus an additional $100 in year 4. D is preferred to C if time value is considered. D provides larger cash flows earlier in the life of the project. Obviously B is preferred to A because again it has the same pattern of cash flow plus an additional $300 in year four.

What about A and F? Both have the same payback period and cash flow pattern. Which one is preferred? If A was a relatively safe, low-risk project and F was an extremely high-risk project then A would be preferred to F but payback does not allow for this.

Redeeming qualities

Despite its shortcomings, the payback period rule is often used by large and sophisticated companies when making relatively small decisions. There are several reasons for this. The primary reason is that many decisions simply do not warrant detailed analysis because the cost of the analysis would exceed the possible loss from a mistake. As a practical matter, an investment that pays back rapidly and has benefits extending beyond the cut-off period probably has a positive NPV.

Small investment decisions are made by the hundreds every day in large organisations. Moreover, they are made at all levels. As a result, it would not be uncommon for a corporation to require, for example, a two-year payback on all investments of less than $10,000. Investments larger than this are subjected to greater scrutiny. The requirement of a two-year payback is not perfect for reasons we have seen, but it does exercise some control over expenditures and thus has the effect of limiting possible losses.

In addition to its simplicity, the payback rule has two other features to recommend it. First, because it is biased towards short-term projects, it is biased towards liquidity. In other words, a payback rule tends to favour investments that free up cash for other uses more quickly. This could be very important for a small business; it would be less so for a large corporation. Second, the cash flows that are expected to occur later in a project's life are probably more uncertain. Arguably, a payback period rule adjusts for the extra riskiness of later cash flows, but it does so in a rather draconian fashion—by ignoring them altogether. We should note here that some of the apparent simplicity of the payback rule is an illusion. The reason is that we still must come up with the cash flows first, and, as we discussed above, this is not at all easy to do. Thus, it would probably be more accurate to say that the concept of a payback period is both intuitive and easy to understand.

Summary of the payback period rule

To summarise, the payback period is a kind of 'break-even' measure. Because time value is ignored, you can think of the payback period as the length of time it takes to break even in an accounting sense, but not in an economic sense. The biggest drawback to the payback period rule is that it doesn't ask the right question. The relevant issue is the impact an investment will have on the value of our shares, not how long it takes to recover the initial investment.

Nevertheless, because it is so simple, companies often use it as a screen for dealing with the myriad of minor investment decisions they have to make. There is certainly nothing wrong with this practice. Like any simple rule of thumb, there will be some errors in using it, but it wouldn't have survived all this time if it weren't useful. Now that you understand the rule, you can be on the alert for those circumstances under which it might lead to problems. To help you remember, Table 7.6 lists the pros and cons of the payback period rule.

Advantages and disadvantages of the payback period rule

Advantages	Disadvantages
1 Easy to understand	1 Ignores the time value of money
2 Adjusts for uncertainty of later flows	2 Ignores cash flow beyond the cut-off date
3 Biased toward liquidity	3 Biased against long-term projects, such as research and development, and new projects

TABLE 7.6

Concept questions

7.2a *In words, what is the payback period? What is the payback period rule?*
7.2b *Why do we say that the payback period is, in a sense, an accounting break-even?*

7.3 ■ The discounted payback rule

We saw that one of the shortcomings of the payback period rule was that it ignored time value. There is a variation of the payback period, the **discounted payback period**, that fixes this problem. The discounted payback period is the length of time until the sum of the discounted cash flows is equal to the initial investment. The discounted payback rule would be:

> Based on the discounted payback rule, an investment is acceptable if its discounted payback is less than some prescribed number of years.

discounted payback period
the length of time required for an investment's discounted cash flows to equal its initial cost

To see how we might calculate the discounted payback period, suppose that we require a 12.5 per cent return on new investments. We have an investment that costs $300 and has cash flows of $100 per year for five years. To get the discounted payback, we have to discount each cash flow at 12.5 per cent and then start adding them. We do this in Table 7.7 (overleaf). In Table 7.7, we have both the discounted and the non-discounted cash flows. Looking at the accumulated cash flows, the regular payback is exactly three years (look for the $\Rightarrow$ in year 3). The discounted cash flows total $300 only after four years, however, so the discounted payback is four years as shown.[1]

TABLE
7.7

Ordinary and discounted payback

	Cash flow		Accumulated cash flow	
Year	Non-discounted	Discounted	Non-discounted	Discounted
1	$100	$89	$100	$89
2	100	79	200	168
3	100	70	⇒ 300	238
4	100	62	400	⇒ 300
5	100	55 (= NPV)	500	355

How do we interpret the discounted payback? Recall that the ordinary payback is the time it takes to break even in an accounting sense. Since it includes the time value of money, the discounted payback is the time it takes to break even in an economic or financial sense. Loosely speaking, in our example, we get our money back along with the interest we could have earned elsewhere in four years.

FIGURE
7.1

Future value of project cash flows

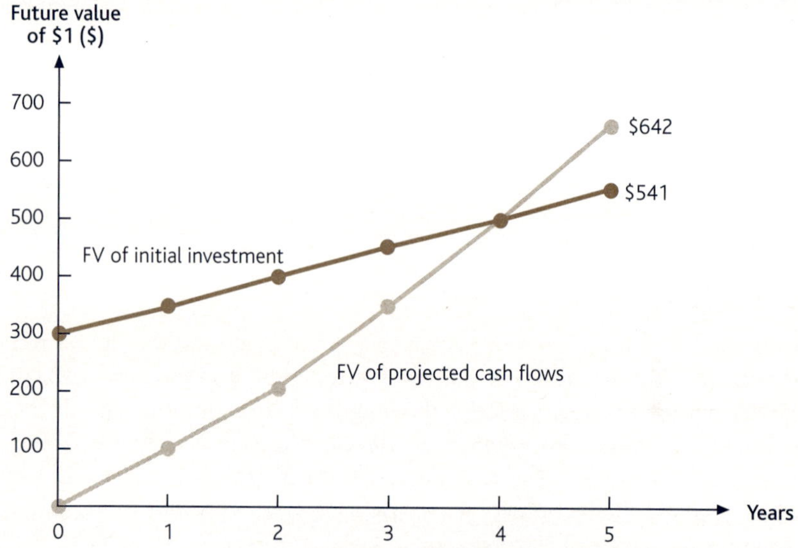

Future value
of $1 ($)

700

600

500 — FV of initial investment

400

300

200 — FV of projected cash flows

100

0   1   2   3   4   5   Years

$642

$541

Future value at 12.5%

Year	$100 Annuity (projected cash flows)	$300 Lump sum (projected investment)
0	$ 0	$300
1	100	338
2	213	380
3	339	427
4	481	481
5	642	541

Figure 7.1 (opposite) illustrates this idea by comparing the future value at 12.5 per cent of the $300 investment versus the future value of the $100 annual cash flows at 12.5 per cent. Notice that the two lines cross at exactly four years. This tells us that the value of the project's cash flows catches up and then passes the original investment in four years.

Table 7.7 and Figure 7.1 illustrate another interesting feature of the discounted payback period. If a project ever pays back on a discounted basis, then it must have a positive NPV.[2] This is true because, by definition, the NPV is zero when the sum of the discounted cash flows equals the initial investment. For example, the present value of all the cash flows in Table 7.7 is $355. The cost of the project was $300, so the NPV is obviously $55. This $55 is the present value of the cash flow that occurs after the discounted payback (see the last line in Table 7.7). In general, if we use a discounted payback rule, we won't accidentally take on any projects with a negative estimated NPV. The problem though is the rejection of positive NPV projects. If management had set a discounted payback period of three years in the above example, the project would have been rejected.

Based on our example, the discounted payback would seem to have much to recommend it. You may be surprised to find out that it is rarely used in practice. Why? Probably because it really isn't any simpler than NPV. To calculate a discounted payback, you have to discount cash flows, add them up, and compare them to the cost, just as you do with NPV. So, unlike an ordinary payback, the discounted payback is not especially simple to calculate.

A discounted payback period rule still has a couple of significant drawbacks. The biggest one is that the cut-off still has to be arbitrarily set and cash flows beyond that point are ignored.[3] As a result, a project with a positive NPV may not be acceptable because the cut-off is too short. Also, just because one project has a shorter discounted payback than another does not mean it has a larger NPV.

All things considered, the discounted payback is a compromise between a regular payback and NPV that lacks the simplicity of the first and the conceptual rigour of the second. Nonetheless, if we need to assess the time it will take to recover the investment required by a project, then the discounted payback is better than the ordinary payback because it considers time value. In other words, the discounted payback recognises that we could have invested the money elsewhere and earned a return on it. The ordinary payback does not take this into account.

Calculating the discounted payback

EXAMPLE 7.3

Consider an investment that costs $400 and pays $100 per year forever. We use a 20 per cent discount rate on this type of investment. What is the ordinary payback? What is the discounted payback? What is the NPV?

The NPV and ordinary payback are easy to calculate in this case because the investment is a perpetuity. The present value of the cash flows is $100/0.20 = $500, so the NPV is $500 − $400 = $100. The ordinary payback is obviously four years.

To get the discounted payback, we need to find the number of years such that a $100 annuity has a present value of $400 at 20 per cent. In other words, the present value annuity factor is $400/$100 = 4, and the interest rate is 20 per cent per period; so what's the number of periods? From Table A.3 the annuity factor for 8 years is 3.8372 and for 9 years it is 4.0310. Therefore the answer is a little less than nine years, so this is the discounted payback.

7.3a In words, what is the discounted payback period? Why do we say it is, in a sense, a financial or economic break-even measure?

7.3b What advantage(s) does the discounted payback have over the ordinary payback?

7.4 ▪ The accounting rate of return

accounting rate of return (ARR)

an investment's average net income divided by its average book value

Another attractive, but flawed, approach to making capital budgeting decisions is the **accounting rate of return (ARR)**. There are many different definitions of the ARR. However, in one form or another, the ARR is always defined as:

$$\frac{\text{Some measure of accounting profit}}{\text{Some measure of accounting value}}$$

The specific definition we will use is:

$$\frac{\text{Average net profit}}{\text{Average book value}}$$

To see how we might calculate this number, suppose we are deciding whether or not to open a store in a new shopping mall. The required investment in improvements is $500,000. The store would have a five-year life because everything reverts to the mall owners after that time. The required investment would be 100 per cent depreciated (straight-line) over five years, so the depreciation would be $500,000/5 = $100,000 per year. The tax rate is 25 per cent. Table 7.8 contains the projected revenues and expenses. Based on these figures, net profit in each year is also shown.

TABLE 7.8

Projected yearly revenue and costs for average accounting return					
	Year 1	Year 2	Year 3	Year 4	Year 5
Revenue	$433,333	$450,000	$266,667	$200,000	$133,333
Expenses	200,000	150,000	100,000	100,000	100,000
Earnings before depreciation	233,333	300,000	166,667	100,000	33,333
Depreciation	100,000	100,000	100,000	100,000	100,000
Earnings before taxes	133,333	200,000	66,667	0	−66,667
Taxes ($T_c = 0.25$)	33,333	50,000	16,667	0	−16,667
Net profit	$100,000	$150,000	$ 50,000	$ 0	$−50,000

$$\text{Average net profit} = \frac{(\$100,000 + \$150,000 + \$50,000 + 0 + -\$50,000)}{5}$$

$$= \$50,000$$

$$\text{Average investment} = \frac{(\$500,000 + 0)}{2}$$

$$= \$250,000$$

To calculate the average book value for this investment, we note that we started out with a book value of $500,000 (the initial cost) and ended up at $0. The average book value during the life of the investment is thus ($500,000 + 0)/2 = $250,000. As long as we use straight-line depreciation, the average investment will always be half of the initial investment.[4]

Looking at Table 7.8, net profit is $100,000 in the first year, $150,000 in the second year, $50,000 in the third year, $0 in year 4, and –$50,000 in year 5. The average net profit, then, is:

$$[\$100,000 + \$150,000 + \$50,000 + 0 + (-\$50,000)]/5 = \$50,000$$

The average accounting return is:

$$ARR = \text{Average net profit/Average book value} = (\$50,000/\$250,000) \times 100\% = 20\%$$

If the firm has a target ARR less than 20 per cent, then this investment is acceptable; otherwise not. The accounting rate of return rule is thus:

> Based on the average accounting return rule, a project is acceptable if its average accounting return exceeds a target average accounting return.

As we will see in the next section, this rule has a number of problems.

Analysing the accounting rate of return method

You recognise the chief drawback to the ARR immediately. Above all else, the ARR is not a rate of return in any meaningful economic sense. Instead, it is the ratio of two accounting numbers, and it is not comparable to the returns offered, for example, in financial markets.

One of the reasons that the ARR is not a true rate of return is that it ignores time value. When we average figures that occur at different times, we are treating the near future and the more distant future the same way. For example, there was no discounting involved when we computed the average net profit.

The second problem with the ARR is similar to the problem we had with the payback period rule concerning the lack of an objective cut-off period. Since a calculated ARR is really not comparable to a market return, the target ARR must somehow be specified. There is no generally agreed-upon way to do this. One way of doing it is to calculate the ARR for the firm as a whole and use this for a benchmark, but there are lots of other ways as well.

The third, and perhaps worst, flaw in the ARR is that it doesn't even look at the right things. Instead of cash flow and market value, it uses net profit and book value. These are both poor substitutes. As a result, an ARR doesn't tell us what the effect on share price will be from taking an investment, so it doesn't tell us what we really want to know.

Does the ARR have any redeeming features? About the only one is that it can almost always be computed. The reason is that accounting information will almost always be available, both for the project under consideration and for the firm as a whole through the accounting budget estimates. We hasten to add that once the accounting information is available, we can always convert it to cash flows, so even this is not a particularly important fact.

Concept questions

7.4a *What is an accounting rate of return (ARR)?*

7.4b *What are the weaknesses of the ARR rule?*

7.5 The internal rate of return

internal rate of return (IRR)

the discount rate that makes the NPV of an investment zero

We now come to the most important alternative to NPV, the **internal rate of return**, universally known as the **IRR**. As we will see, the IRR is closely related to NPV. With the IRR, we try to find a single rate of return that summarises the merits of a project. Furthermore, we want this rate to be an 'internal' rate in the sense that it only depends on the cash flows of a particular investment, not on rates offered elsewhere.

To illustrate the idea behind the IRR, consider a project that costs $100 today and pays $110 in one year. Suppose you were asked 'What is the return on this investment?' What would you say? It seems both natural and obvious to say that the return is 10 per cent because, for every dollar we put in, we get $1.10 back. In fact, as we will see in a moment, 10 per cent is the internal rate of return or IRR on this investment.

Is this project with its 10 per cent IRR a good investment? Once again, it would seem apparent that this is a good investment only if our required return is less than 10 per cent. This intuition is also correct and illustrates the IRR rule:

> Based on the IRR rule, an investment is acceptable if the IRR exceeds the required return. It should be rejected otherwise.

Imagine that we wanted to calculate the NPV for our simple investment. At a discount rate of r, the NPV is:

$$NPV = -\$100 + \$110/(1 + r)$$

Now, suppose we didn't know the discount rate. This presents a problem, but we could still ask how high the discount rate would have to be before this project was unacceptable. We know that we are indifferent to taking or not taking this investment when its NPV is just equal to zero. In other words, this investment is economically a break-even proposition when the NPV is zero because value is neither created nor destroyed. To find the break-even discount rate, we set NPV equal to zero and solve for r:

$$NPV = 0 = -\$100 + \$110/(1 + r)$$
$$\$100 = \$110/(1 + r)$$
$$1 + r = \$110/\$100 = 1.10$$
$$r = 10\%$$

This 10 per cent is what we have already called the return on this investment. What we have now illustrated is that the internal rate of return on an investment (or just 'return' for short) is the discount rate that makes the NPV equal to zero. This is an important observation, so it bears repeating:

> The IRR on an investment is the required return that results in a zero NPV when it is used as the discount rate.

TABLE 7.9

Project cash flows			
Year	0	1	2
	−$100	$60	$60

The fact that the IRR is simply the discount rate that makes the NPV equal to zero is important because it tells us how to calculate the returns on more complicated investments. As we have seen, finding the IRR turns out to be relatively easy for a single period investment. However, suppose you were now looking at an investment with the cash flows shown in Table 7.9 (opposite). As illustrated, this investment costs $100 and has a cash flow of $60 per year for two years, so it's only slightly more complicated than our single period example. However, if you were asked for the return on this investment, what would you say? There doesn't seem to be any obvious answer. However, based on what we now know, we can set the NPV equal to zero and solve for the discount rate:

$$\text{NPV} = 0 = -\$100 + \$60/(1 + \text{IRR}) + \$60/(1 + \text{IRR})^2$$

Unfortunately, the only way to find the IRR in general is by trial and error, either by hand or by calculator. This is precisely the same problem that came up in Chapter 5 when we found the unknown rate for an annuity and in Chapter 6 when we found the yield to maturity on a bond. In fact, we now see that in both of those cases we were finding an IRR.

In this particular case, the cash flows form a two-period, $60 annuity. To find the unknown rate, we can try various different rates until we get the answer. If we were to start with a 0 per cent rate, the NPV would obviously be $120 − $100 = $20. At a 10 per cent discount rate, we would have:

$$\text{NPV} = -\$100 + \$60/1.1 + \$60/(1.1)^2$$
$$= -\$100 + \$54.55 + \$49.58 = \$4.13$$

Now we're getting close. We can summarise these and some other possibilities as shown in Table 7.10. From our calculations, the NPV appears to be zero between 10 per cent and 15 per cent, so the IRR is somewhere in that range. With a little more effort, we can find that the IRR is about 13.1 per cent.[5] So, if our required return is less than 13.1 per cent, we would take this investment. If our required return exceeds 13.1 per cent, we would reject it.

TABLE 7.10

NPV at different discount rates	
Discount rates	NPV
0%	$20.00
5	11.56
10	4.13
15	−2.46
20	−8.33

By now, you have probably noticed that the IRR rule and the NPV rule appear to be quite similar. In fact, the IRR is sometimes simply called the discounted cash flow or DCF return. The easiest way to illustrate the relationship between NPV and IRR is to plot the numbers we calculated in Table 7.10. On the vertical or y-axis we put the different NPVs. We put discount rates on the horizontal or x-axis. If we had a very large number of points, the resulting picture would be a smooth curve called a **net present value profile**. Figure 7.2 (overleaf) illustrates the NPV profile for this project. Beginning with a 0 per cent discount rate, we have $20 plotted directly on the y-axis. As the discount rate increases, the NPV declines smoothly. Where will the curve cut through the x-axis? This will occur where the NPV is just equal to zero, so it will happen right at the IRR of 13.1 per cent.

net present value profile

a graphical representation of the relationship between an investment's NPVs and various discount rates

FIGURE
7.2

An NPV profile

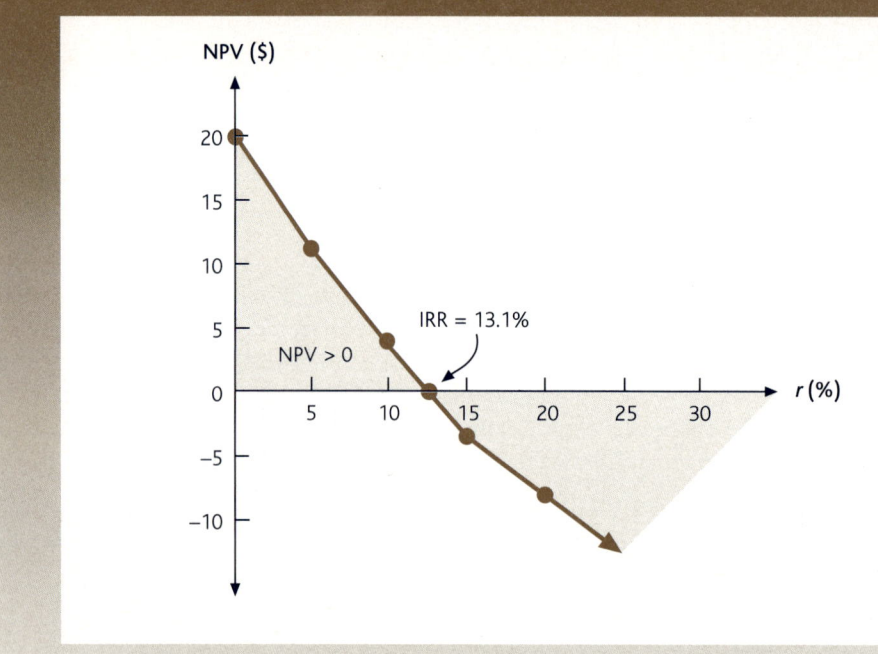

In our example, the NPV rule and the IRR rule lead to identical accept/reject decisions. We will accept an investment using the IRR rule if the required return is less than 13.1 per cent. As Figure 7.2 illustrates, however, the NPV is positive at any discount rate less than 13.1 per cent, so we would accept the investment using the NPV rule as well. The two rules are equivalent in this case.

Calculating the IRR

A project has a total up-front cost of $435.44. The cash flows are $100 in the first year, $200 in the second year, and $300 in the third year. What's the IRR? If we require an 18 per cent return, should we take this investment?

We will describe the NPV profile and find the IRR by calculating some NPVs at different discount rates. You should check our answers for practice. Beginning with 0 per cent, we have:

Discount rate	NPV
0%	$164.56
5	100.36
10	46.15
15	0.00
20	−39.61

The NPV is zero at 15 per cent, so 15 per cent is the IRR. If we require an 18 per cent return, then we should not take the investment. The reason is that the NPV is negative at 18 per cent (check that it is −$24.47). The IRR rule tells us the same thing in this case. We shouldn't take this investment because its 15 per cent return is below our required 18 per cent return.

At this point, you may be wondering whether the IRR and the NPV rules always lead to identical decisions. The answer is yes as long as two very important conditions are met.

1 The project's cash flows must be conventional, meaning that the first cash flow (the initial investment) is negative and all the rest are positive.
2 The project must be independent, meaning that the decision to accept or reject this project does not affect the decision to accept or reject any other.

The first of these conditions is typically met, but the second often is not. In any case, when one or both of these conditions are not met, problems can arise. We discuss some of these next.

Problems with the IRR

The problems with the IRR come about when the cash flows are not conventional or when we are trying to compare two or more investments to see which is best. In the first case, surprisingly, the simple question 'What's the return?' can become very difficult to answer. In the second case, the IRR can be a misleading guide.

Non-conventional cash flows

Suppose we have a strip-mining project that requires a $60 investment. Our cash flow in the first year will be $155. In the second year, the mine is depleted, but we have to spend $100 to restore the terrain. As Table 7.11 illustrates, both the first and third cash flows are negative.

Project cash flows

Year	0	1	2
	−$60	+$155	−$100

TABLE 7.11

To find the IRR on this project, we can calculate the NPV at various rates:

Discount rate	NPV
0%	−$5.00
10	−1.74
20	−0.28
30	0.06
40	−0.31

The NPV appears to be behaving in a very peculiar fashion here. First, as the discount rate increases from 0 per cent to 30 per cent, the NPV starts out negative and becomes positive. This seems backwards because the NPV is rising as the discount rate rises. It then starts getting smaller and becomes negative again. What's the IRR? To find out, we draw the NPV profile in Figure 7.3 (overleaf).

In Figure 7.3, notice that the NPV is zero when the discount rate is 25 per cent, so this is the IRR. Or is it? The NPV is also zero at $33^{1}/_{3}$ per cent. Which of these is correct? The answer is both or neither; more precisely, there is no unambiguously correct answer. This is the **multiple rates of return** problem. Many financial computer packages are not aware of this problem and just report the first IRR that is found. Others report only the smallest positive IRR, even though this answer is no better than any other.

multiple rates of return

one potential problem in using the IRR method if more than one discount rate makes the NPV of an investment zero

NPV profile

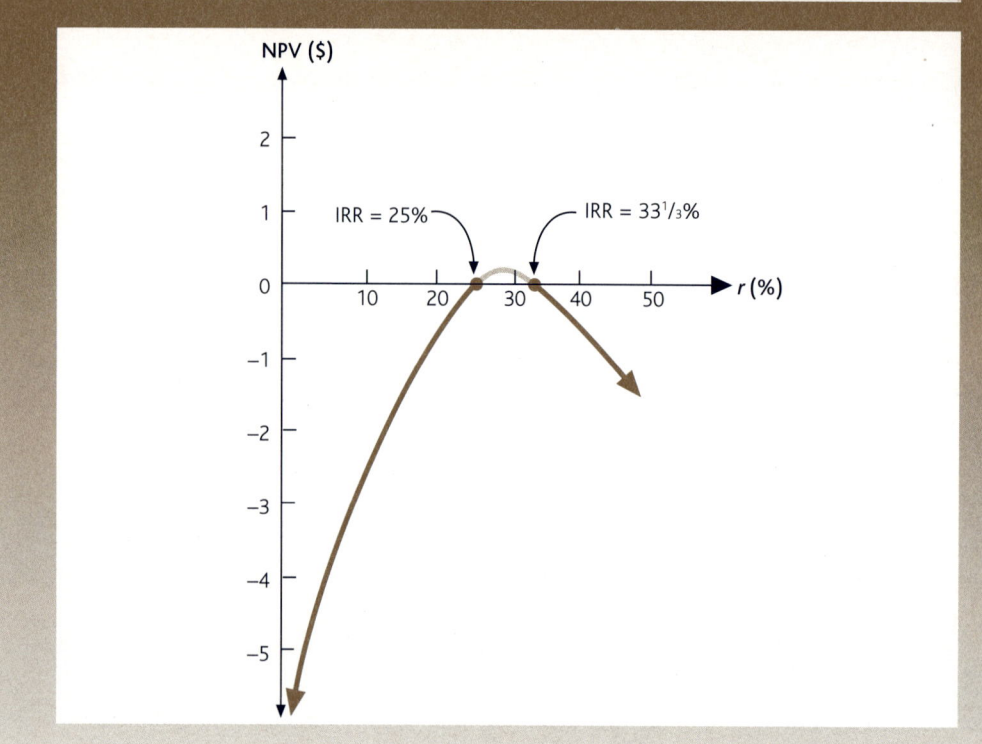

In our current example, the IRR rule breaks down completely. Suppose our required return were 10 per cent. Should we take this investment? Both IRRs are greater than 10 per cent, so, by the IRR rule, maybe we should. However, as Figure 7.3 shows, the NPV is negative at any discount rate less than 25 per cent, so this is not a good investment. When should we take it? Looking at Figure 7.3 one last time, the NPV is positive only if our required return is between 25 per cent and $33^1/3$ per cent.

The moral of the story is that when the cash flows aren't conventional, strange things can start to happen to the IRR. This is not anything to get upset about however, because the NPV rule, as always, works just fine. This illustrates that, oddly enough, the obvious question—What's the rate of return?—may not always have a good answer.

What is the IRR?

You are looking at an investment that requires you to invest $51 today. You'll get $100 in one year, but you must pay out $50 in two years. What is the IRR on this investment?

You are on the alert now to the non-conventional cash flow problem, so you probably wouldn't be surprised to see more than one IRR. However, if you start looking for an IRR by trial and error, it will take you a long time. The reason is that there is no IRR. The NPV is negative at every discount rate, so we shouldn't take this investment under any circumstances. For example, if the time value of money is zero and we simply add all the cash flows, the NPV is –$1. What's the return of this investment? There isn't any, as the investment will always be a loss.

'I think; therefore, I know how many IRRs there can be'

EXAMPLE
7.6

We have seen that it is possible to get more than one IRR. If you wanted to make sure that you had found all of the possible IRRs, how could you tell? The answer comes from the great mathematician, philosopher and financial analyst Descartes (of 'I think; therefore I am' fame). Descartes' Rule of Sign says that the maximum number of IRRs that there can be is equal to the number of times that the cash flows change sign from positive to negative and/or negative to positive. To be more precise, the number of IRRs that are bigger than −100 per cent is equal to the number of sign changes, or it differs from the number of sign changes by an even number. Thus, for example, if there are five sign changes, there are either five, three or one IRRs. If there are two sign changes, there are either two IRRs or no IRRs.

In our example with the 25 and 33¹/₃ per cent IRRs, could there be yet another IRR? The cash flows flip from negative to positive, then back to negative for a total of two sign changes. As a result, the maximum number of IRRs is two, and, from Descartes' rule, we don't need to look for any more. Note that the actual number of IRRs can be less than the maximum (see Example 7.5).

Mutually-exclusive investments

Even if there is a single IRR, another problem can arise concerning **mutually-exclusive investment decisions**. If two investments, X and Y, are mutually exclusive, then taking one of them means that we cannot take the other. For example, if we own one corner block, then we can build a petrol station or a block of flats, but not both. These are mutually-exclusive alternatives.

Thus far, we have asked whether or not a given investment is worth undertaking. There is a related question, however, that comes up very often: Given two or more mutually-exclusive investments, which one is the best? The answer is simple enough: The best one is the one with the largest NPV. Can we also say that the best one has the highest return? As we show, the answer is no.

To illustrate the problem with the IRR rule and mutually-exclusive investments, consider the cash flows from the following two mutually-exclusive investments:

mutually-exclusive investment decisions

one potential problem in using the IRR method if the acceptance of one project excludes that of another

Year	Investment A	Investment B
0	−$100	−$100
1	50	20
2	40	40
3	40	50
4	30	60
IRR	24%	21%

Since these investments are mutually exclusive, we can only take one of them. Simple intuition suggests that investment A is better because of its higher return. Unfortunately, simple intuition is not always correct.

To see why investment A is not necessarily the better of the two investments, we've calculated the NPV of these investments for different required returns:

Discount rate	Investment A	Investment B
0%	$60	$70
5%	43.13	47.88
10%	29.06	29.79
15%	17.18	14.82
20%	7.06	2.31
25%	−1.63	−8.22

The IRR for A (24%) is larger than the IRR for B (21%). However, if you compare the NPVs, you'll see that the investment with the highest NPV depends on our required return. B has greater total cash flow, but it pays back more slowly than A. As a result, it has a higher NPV at lower discount rates.

In our example, the NPV and IRR rankings conflict for some discount rates. If our required return is 10 per cent, for instance, then B has the higher NPV and is thus the better of the two even though A has the higher IRR. If our required return is 15 per cent, then there is no ranking conflict: A is better.

The conflict between the IRR and NPV for mutually-exclusive investments can be illustrated by plotting their NPV profiles as we have done in Figure 7.4. In Figure 7.4, notice that the NPV profiles cross at about 11.1 per cent. Notice also that at any discount rate less than 11.1 per cent, the NPV for B is higher. In this range, taking B benefits us more than taking A, even though A's IRR is higher. At any rate greater that 11.1 per cent, project A has the greater NPV.

FIGURE 7.4

NPV profiles for mutually-exclusive investments

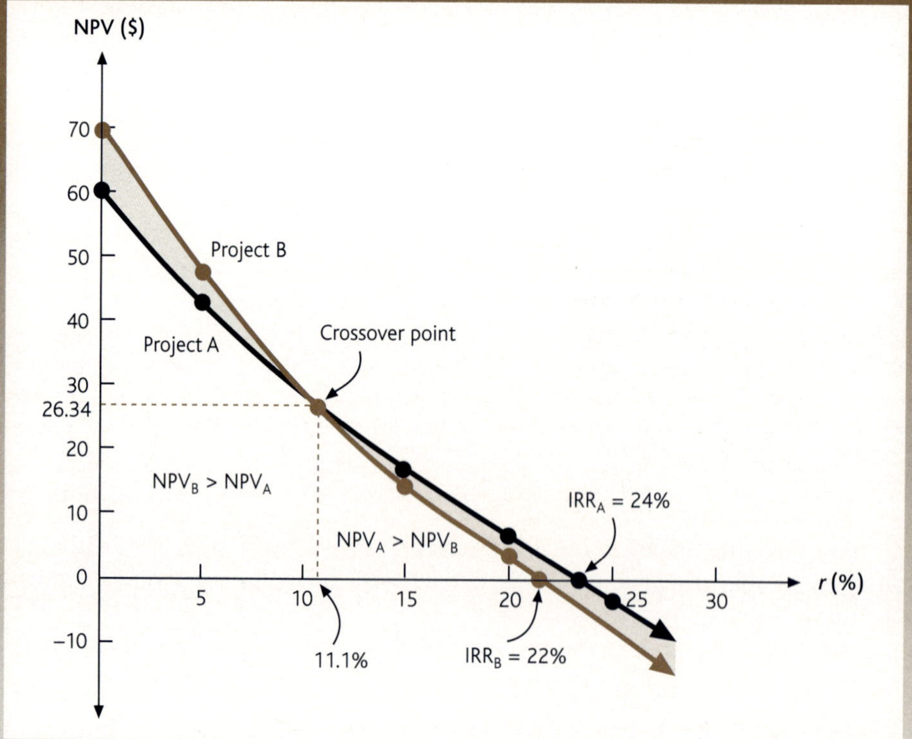

What this example illustrates is that whenever we have mutually-exclusive projects, we shouldn't rank them based on their returns. More generally, whenever we are comparing investments to determine which is best, IRRs can be misleading. Instead, we need to look at the relative NPVs to avoid the possibility of choosing incorrectly. Remember, we are ultimately interested in creating value for the shareholders, so the option with the higher NPV is preferred, regardless of the relative returns.

If this does not seem intuitive, think of it this way. Suppose you have two investments. One has a 10 per cent return and makes you $100 richer immediately. The other has a 20 per cent return and makes you $50 richer immediately. Which one do you like better? We would rather have $100 than $50, regardless of the returns, so we like the first one better.

EXAMPLE
7.7

Calculating the crossover rate

In Figure 7.4, the NPV profiles cross at about 11.1 per cent. How can we determine just what this crossover rate is? The crossover rate, by definition, is the discount rate that makes the NPVs of two projects equal. To illustrate, suppose we have the following two mutually-exclusive investments:

Year	Investment A	Investment B
0	−$400	−$500
1	250	320
2	280	340

What's the crossover rate?

To find the crossover, first consider moving out of investment A and into investment B. If you make the move, you will have to invest an extra $100 ($500 − $400). For this $100 investment, you will get an extra $70 ($320 − $250) in the first year and an extra $60 ($340 − $280) in the second year. Is this a good move? In other words, is it worth investing the extra $100?

Based on our discussion, the NPV of the switch, NPV(B − A) is:

$$NPV(B - A) = -\$100 + \$70/(1 + r) + \$60/(1 + r)^2$$

We can calculate the return on this investment by setting the NPV equal to zero and solving for the IRR:

$$NPV(B - A) = 0 = -\$100 + \$70/(1 + r) + \$60/(1 + r)^2$$

If you go through this calculation, you will find the IRR is exactly 20 per cent. What this tells us is that at a 20 per cent discount rate, we are indifferent between the two investments because the NPV of the difference in their cash flows is zero. As a consequence, the two investments have the same value, so this 20 per cent is the crossover rate. Check that the NPV at 20 per cent is $2.78 for both.

In general, you can find the crossover rate by taking the difference in the cash flows and calculating the IRR using the differences. It doesn't make any difference which one you subtract from which, so long as one of the investments has a positive NPV and the cash flows are conventional.[6] To see this, find the IRR for (A − B); you'll see it's the same number. Also, for practice, you might want to find the exact crossover in Figure 7.4. (A big hint: It's 11.0704%.)

Redeeming qualities of the IRR

Despite its flaws, the IRR is very popular in practice, more so than even the NPV. It probably survives because it fills a need that the NPV does not. In analysing investments, people in general, and financial analysts in particular, seem to prefer talking about rates of return rather than dollar values.

In a similar vein, the IRR also appears to provide a simple way of communicating information about a proposal. One manager might say to another: 'Remodelling the clerical wing has a 20 per cent return.' This may somehow be simpler than saying: 'At a 10 per cent discount rate, the net present value is $4,000.'

Finally, under certain circumstances, the IRR may have a practical advantage over NPV. We can't estimate the NPV unless we know the appropriate discount rate, but we can still estimate the IRR. Suppose we didn't know the required return on an investment, but we found, for example, that it had a 40 per cent return. We would probably be inclined to take it since it is very unlikely that the required return is that high.

Concept questions

7.5a *Under what circumstances will the IRR and NPV rules lead to the same accept/reject decisions? When might they conflict?*

7.5b *Is it generally true that an advantage of the IRR rule over the NPV rule is that we don't need to know the required return to use the IRR rule?*

7.6 The present value index

present value index (PVI)

the present value of an investment's future cash flows divided by its initial cost. Also benefit/cost ratio

benefit/cost ratio

the profitability index of an investment project. Also present value index

Another method used to evaluate projects is called the **present value index (PVI)** or **benefit/cost ratio**. This index is defined as the present value of the future cash flows divided by the initial investment. So, if a project costs $200 and the present value of its future cash flows is $220, the present value index value would be $220/$200 = 1.10. Notice that the NPV for this investment is $20, so it is a desirable investment.

More generally, if a project has a positive NPV, then the present value of the future cash flows must be bigger than the initial investment. The PVI would thus be bigger than 1.00 for a positive NPV investment and less than 1.00 for a negative NPV investment.

How do we interpret the PVI? In our example, the PVI was 1.10. This tells us that, per dollar invested, $1.10 in value or $0.10 in NPV results. The PVI thus measures the value created per dollar invested. For this reason, it is often proposed as a measure of performance for government or not-for-profit investments. Also, when capital is scarce, it may make sense to allocate it to those projects with the highest PVIs. We will return to this issue in a later chapter.

The PVI is obviously very similar to the NPV. However, consider an investment that costs $5 and has a $10 present value and an investment that costs $100 with a $150 present value. The first of these investments has an NPV of $5 and a PVI of 2. The second has an NPV of $50 and a PVI of 1.50. If these were mutually-exclusive investments, then the second one is preferred even though it has a lower PVI. This ranking problem is very similar to the IRR ranking problem we saw in the previous section. In summary, there seems to be little reason to rely on the PVI instead of the NPV.

An index similar to the PVI is the net present value index (NPVI). This index is defined as the net present value of the future cash flows divided by the initial investment. Returning to our earlier example, if a project costs $200 and the present value of its future cash flows is $220, the PVI would be 1.1 and the NPVI would be $20/$200 = 0.1. The NPVI differs from the PVI by a scale of one. The ranking problems associated with the PVI are also applicable to the NPVI.

Concept questions

7.6a *What does the present value index measure?*
7.6b *How would you state the PVI rule?*

7.7 ∎ The practice of capital budgeting

Given that NPV seems to be telling us directly what we want to know, you might be wondering why there are so many other procedures and why alternative procedures are commonly used. Recall that we are trying to make an investment decision and that we are frequently operating under considerable uncertainty about the future. We can only estimate the NPV of an investment in this case. The resulting estimate can be very 'soft', meaning that the true NPV might be quite different.

Because the true NPV is unknown, the astute financial manager seeks clues to assess whether the estimated NPV is reliable. For this reason, firms would typically use multiple criteria for evaluating a proposal. For example, suppose we have an investment with a positive estimated NPV. Based on our experience with other projects, this one appears to have a short payback and a very high ARR. In this case, the different indicators seem to agree that it's 'all systems go'. Put another way, the payback and the ARR are consistent with the conclusion that the NPV is positive.

On the other hand, suppose we had a positive estimated NPV, a long payback and a low ARR. This could still be a good investment, but it looks like we need to be much more careful in making the decision since we are getting conflicting signals. If the estimated NPV is based on projections in which we have little confidence, then further analysis is probably in order. We will consider how to go about this analysis in more detail in the next two chapters.

There have been a number of surveys conducted asking large firms what types of investment criteria they actually use. Table 7.12 presents the results of one such survey. Based on the results, the most important capital budgeting technique is some form of discounted cash flow (such as NPV or IRR). Some 75 per cent of the firms rank it as the most important.

In practice, the payback period is a popular tool; about 44 per cent of the responding firms use it. Other surveys are consistent with these results. The most common practice is to look at NPV or IRR along with non-discounted cash flow criteria such as payback and ARR. Given our discussion, this is sound practice.

Evaluation techniques	
Method	**% Respondents using**
ARR	33
Payback (non discounted)	44
IRR	72
NPV	75

TABLE 7.12

Source: Freeman and Hobbs (1991) Reproduced with the joint permission of CPA Australia and the Institute of Chartered Accountants in Australia.

Concept questions

7.7a *What are the most commonly used capital budgeting procedures?*

7.7b *Since NPV is conceptually the best procedure for capital budgeting, why do you think that multiple measures are used in practice?*

 Using Excel

Most of the calculations that have been performed in this chapter can be done in Excel. We will now show you various examples of the calculations. First you need to be in the program Excel. On the toolbar you should notice a function f_x. Click on this function and you will see that you have a number of choices of functions. The ones that we will use are the financial functions.

First, let's calculate the NPV. Assume that an investment has the following cash flows: an outlay of $100, then returns of $50 in year 1 and $70 in year 2. The required rate of return is 10%. The spreadsheet would look something like the following:

A	B	C
−100	50	70

To calculate the NPV, choose the NPV function. The formula will look like this:

= NPV(0.1, B1:C1) + A1

and the calculated NPV is $3.31.

Do not fall into the trap. Within the NPV function you need to indicate the discount rate and the range for discounting. Do not include in the range for discounting the year 0 figure. This is a very common error.

Now we need to calculate the IRR. The formula is:

= IRR (A1:C1, 0.1)

and the calculated IRR is 12.32.

Here you need to include the total range of figures that are used to calculate the IRR. The only concern is the guess figure for the IRR. If you do not guess, Excel assumes 10%. Why Excel asks you to guess is because of Descartes' Rule of Signs. Recall the problem:

Year	0	1	2
	−$60	+$155	−$100

If you use a guess of 10%, the calculated IRR is 25%. Now try a guess of 40%. The calculated IRR is now $33\frac{1}{3}$%. This was the second IRR. Excel recognises the dual answer problem and that is why the program asks you for a guess.

■ 7.8 ■ Summary and conclusions

This chapter has covered the different criteria used to evaluate proposed investments. The six criteria, in the order we discussed them, are:

1 Net present value (NPV)

2 Payback period

3 Discounted payback period

4 Accounting rate of return (ARR)

5 Internal rate of return (IRR)

6 Present value index (PVI)

We illustrated how to calculate each of these and discussed the interpretation of the results. We also described the advantages and disadvantages of each of them.

The most important concept in this chapter is net present value (NPV). We will return to this idea repeatedly in the chapters to come. We defined NPV as the difference between the market value of an asset or project and its cost. We saw that the financial manager acts in the best interest of the shareholders by identifying and undertaking positive NPV investments.

Finally, we noted that NPVs can't normally be observed in the market; instead, they must be estimated. Because there is always the possibility of a poor estimate, financial managers use multiple criteria for examining projects. These other criteria provide additional information about whether a project truly has a positive NPV.

Key terms

Accounting rate of return *228*
Benefit/cost ratio *238*
Discounted cash flow (DCF) *219*
Discounted payback period *225*
Internal rate of return *230*

Multiple rates of return *233*
Mutually-exclusive investment
  decisions *235*
Net present value *218*

Net present value profile *231*
Payback period *221*
Present value index *238*
Valuation *219*

Suggested readings

For a discussion of the capital budgeting techniques used by large firms, see:

Bierman, H. Jr and Smidt, S. *The Capital Budgeting Decision: Economic Analysis of Investment Projects*, 8th edn, Macmillan Company, New York, 1993.

Freeman, M. and Hobbs, G. 'Capital Budgeting: Theory versus practice', *The Australian Accountant*, September 1991, pp. 36–41.

Rachlin, R. and Sweeney, H.W.A. (eds) *Handbook of Budgeting*, 3rd edn, John Wiley and Sons, New York, 1993.

Schall, L. and Sundem, C. 'Capital Budgeting Methods and Risk: A Further Analysis', *Financial Management*, Vol. 9, Spring 1980, pp. 7–11.

Endnotes

1 In this case, the discounted payback is an even number of years. This will not ordinarily happen. Calculating a fractional year for the discounted payback period is more involved than it is for the ordinary payback, but it is not commonly done.

2 This argument assumes that cash flows other than the first are all positive. If they are not, then these statements are not necessarily correct. Also, there may be more than one discounted payback.

3 If the cut-off were forever, then the discounted payback rule would be the same as the NPV rule. It would also be the same as the profitability index rule considered in a later section.

4 We would of course calculate the average of the six book values directly. In thousands, we would have ($500 + $400 + $300 + $200 + $100 + 0)/6 = $250.

5 With a lot more effort (or a financial calculator), we can find that the IRR is (to 15 decimal places) 13.0662386291808 per cent, not that anybody would ever want this many decimal places.

6 Imagine analysing two investments, both with negative NPVs. If crossover is used solely, it is possible to select that investment with the smallest negative NPV. This simply meant that the change from the larger negative NPV to the smaller negative NPV project is the same as going from 'very bad' to 'bad'. Remember that negative NPV investments should be rejected.

Maximise Your Marks!
There are 30 interactive questions on NPV and other investment criteria waiting online for you at www.mhhe.com/au/ross3e. The questions are written with additional feedback for incorrect answers, and text excerpts with page references for follow-up study.

International Articles!
To read more on NPV and other investment criteria and to see current international articles, just go to www.mhhe.com/au/ross3e and click on *PowerWeb Articles* for this chapter.

Chapter review problems and self-test

7.1 · Investment criteria

This problem will give you some practice calculating NPVs and paybacks. A proposed overseas expansion has the following cash flows:

Year	Investment A
0	−$100
1	50
2	40
3	40
4	15

Calculate the payback, the discounted payback, and the NPV at a required return of 15 per cent.

7.2 · Mutually-exclusive investments

Consider the following two mutually-exclusive investments. Calculate the IRR for each, and the crossover rate. Under what circumstances will the IRR and NPV criteria rank the two projects differently?

Year	Investment A	Investment B
0	−$100	−$100
1	50	70
2	70	75
3	40	10

7.3 · Accounting rate of return

You are looking at a three-year project with a projected net profit of $1,000 in year 1, $2,000 in year 2, and $4,000 in year 3. The cost is $9,000, which will be depreciated straight-line to zero over the three-year life of the project. What is the accounting rate of return (ARR)?

Answers to self-test problems

7.1 · In the table below, we have listed the cash flows, cumulative cash flows, discounted cash flows (at 15%), and cumulative discounted cash flows.

	Cash flow		Accumulated cash flow	
Year	Non-discounted	Discounted	Non-discounted	Discounted
1	$50	$43.48	$50	$43.48
2	40	30.25	⇒ 90	73.73
3	40	26.30	⇒ 130	⇒ 100.03
4	15	⇒ 8.58	145	108.61

Recall that the initial investment is $100. When we compare this to accumulated non-discounted cash flows, we see that payback occurs between years 2 and 3. The cash flows for the first two years are $90 in total, so, going into the third year, we are short by $10. The total cash flow in year 3 is $40, so the payback is $2 + \$10/\$40 = 2^1/_4$ years.

Looking at the accumulated discounted cash flows, we see that the discounted payback occurs right at three years. The sum of the discounted cash flows is $108.61, so the NPV is $8.61. Notice that this is the present value of the cash flows that occur after the discounted payback.

7.2 · To calculate the IRR, we might try some guesses, as in the following table:

Discount rate	NPV A	NPV B
0%	$60	$55
10	33.36	33.13
20	13.43	16.20
30	−1.91	2.78
40	−14.01	−8.09

Several things are immediately apparent from our guesses. First, the IRR of A must be just a little less than 30 per cent (why?). With some more effort, we find that it's 28.61 per cent. For B, the IRR must be a little more than 30 per cent (again, why?); it works out to be 32.37 per cent. Also, notice that at 10 per cent, the NPVs are very close, indicating that the crossover is in that vicinity.

To find the crossover exactly, we can compute the IRR on the difference in the cash flows. If we take the cash flows for A minus the cash flows for B, the resulting cash flows are:

Year	A − B
0	$0
1	−20
2	−5
3	30

These cash flows look a little odd, but the sign only changes once, so we can find an IRR. With some trial and error, you'll see that the NPV is zero at a discount rate of 10.61 per cent, so this is the crossover rate.

The IRR for B is higher. As we've seen, A has the larger NPV for any discount rate less than 10.61 per cent, so the NPV and IRR rankings will conflict in that range. Remember, if there's a conflict, we will go with the higher NPV. Our decision rule is thus very simple: Take A if the required return is less than 10.61 per cent, take B if the required return is between 10.61 per cent and 32.37 per cent (the IRR of B), and take neither if the required return is more than 32.37 per cent.

7.3 · Here we need to calculate the ratio of average net profit to average book value to get the ARR. Average net profit is:

Average net profit = ($1,000 + $2,000 + $4,000)/3 = $2,333.33

Average book value is:

Average book value = $9,000/2 = $4,500

So the accounting rate of return is:

ARR = $2,333.33/$4,500 = 51.85%

This is an impressive return. Remember, however, that it isn't really a rate of return like an interest rate or an IRR, so the size doesn't tell us a lot. In particular, our money is probably not going to grow at 51.85 per cent per year, unfortunately.

Questions and problems

1 · Calculate payback

An investment offers $2,000 per year for 10 years. What is the payback if the investment costs $11,000? If it costs $13,000? If it costs $22,000?

2 · Calculate payback

Would your answers change in Problem 1 if you were told that the $2,000 cash flows occurred at year end rather than evenly throughout the year?

3 · Calculate payback

Old Fashion is considering the following cash flows for two investments:

Year	Investment A	Investment B
0	−$1000	−$1000
1	520	410
2	630	550
3	977	1900

What are the paybacks on the two investments? If Old Fashion requires a two-year payback to take an investment, which of these two is acceptable? Is it necessarily the best investment? Explain.

4 · Calculate NPV

In the previous question, which of the two investments is better if we require a 5 per cent return?

5 · Calculate IRR

Compute the internal rate of return on a project with cash flows of:

Year	Cash flow
0	−$2100
1	1008
2	1505.28

6 · Payback

Suppose an investment pays $1000 per year and costs $6000. How many years does it take to pay back? If the discount rate is 5 per cent, what is the discounted payback period? If the discount rate is 20 per cent? Is the payback period affected by the different discount rates?

7 · Payback intuition

If a project has conventional cash flows, is the discounted payback always less than the regular payback? Explain.

8 · Payback intuition

If a project has conventional cash flows and a discounted payback that is less than the project's life, what do you know about its NPV? Explain.

9 · Budgeting techniques and their relationships

If a project has conventional cash flows and a positive NPV, what do you know about its benefit/cost ratio? IRR? Which will be the shortest and which will be the longest when we compare the payback, the project's life and the discounted payback?

10 · IRR

Compute the internal rate of return on a project with the following cash flows:

Year	Cash flow
0	−$12,000
1	11,000
2	2420

Assume the project is undertaken and it is found that the total outlay at the beginning was only $10,847.23. What is the revised IRR?

11 · IRR versus NPV

Consider the following cash flows for two mutually-exclusive investments:

	Year 0	Year 1	Year 2
Project A	−$100	$80	$90
Project B	−100	70	102

For what range of discount rates is project A better? Illustrate your answer with an NPV profile.

12 · Problems with IRR

Compute the internal rates of return (via trial and error) for the following sequences of cash flows:

Year	Project A	Project B
0	−$100	−$100
1	100	0
2	200	100
3	−100	200

13 · IRR versus NPV

Confident Colin, the president of Cartell Ltd, is evaluating the following two mutually-exclusive investments:

	Year 0	Year 1	Year 2
Project A	−$4000	$2410	$2930
Project B	−2000	1310	1720

Determine the IRR for each. If Colin chooses the project with the higher IRR, under what circumstances will his choice be incorrect? At what discount rate would Colin be indifferent between the two projects?

14 · Problems with IRR

Compute the internal rate of return (via trial and error) for the following cash flows:

Year	Project A	Project B	Project C
0	−$2000	−$1502	−$400
1	2000	500	−300
2	8000	1000	−200
3	−8000	1000	−969

15 · Calculate ARR

Dated Ltd is evaluating a four-year project with a projected net income of $4,266 in year 1, $4,910 in year 2, $6,482 in year 3, and $7,132 in year 4. The $20,000 cost will be depreciated straight-line to zero over the four-year life of the project. What is the accounting rate of return (ARR)?

16 · NPV versus the discount rate

An investment has a total installed cost of $16,061. The cash flows over a four-year life of the investment are projected to be $4,377, $6,036, $6,702, and $3,015. If the discount rate is zero, what is the NPV? If the discount rate is infinity, what is the NPV? What is the IRR on the investment? Based on these three points, sketch the NPV profile.

17 · Payback calculations

Mystery Ltd is examining a three-year investment but it is not sure which evaluation technique to use. The following information has been collected for the investment:

Year	Cash flow
0	−$100
1	50
2	40
3	60

Help Mystery by completing the table assuming a 12 per cent required return and answering the questions that follow the table.

	Cash flows and accumulated cash flows			
	Cash flow		Accumulated cash flow	
Year	Non-discounted	Discounted	Non-discounted	Discounted
1				
2				
3				

a   What is the payback rounded up to the next whole year? What is the payback if we use fractional years? What are we assuming about the cash flows when we calculate the fractional year?

b   What is the discounted payback? Don't calculate the fractional year.

c   What is the NPV of this investment if the required return is 12 per cent?

d   What is the NPV of this investment if the required return is 14 per cent?

e   Do you think computing the three techniques of evaluation helped Mystery?

18 · Calculating NPV and IRR

Consider the following cash flows on two investments:

Year	Investment A	Investment B
0	−$100	−$100
1	44	69
2	56	51
3	65	32

a   The required return is 15 per cent. The investments are not mutually exclusive. Calculate the NPV and IRR on both. Are they desirable?

b   Now suppose you wanted to combine the two investments into a single Investment C. Calculate the combined cash flows. What is the NPV of C? How does this NPV relate to the NPVs for A and B considered separately? Based on your answer, is there an obvious shortcut that we could have used to calculate the NPV of C?

c   Based on the combined cash flows, calculate the IRR for C. How does your answer relate to the IRRs for A and B? Is there an obvious shortcut that we could have used?

19 · Project choice using several techniques

You have been asked by Dizzy Days Ltd to consider the following cash flows for two mutually-exclusive investments:

Year	Investment A	Investment B
0	−$100	−$100
1	40	60
2	60	60
3	90	60

a   Based on the payback periods, which of these might you prefer?

b   Sketch the NPV profiles for both investments. Over what range is Investment A preferred?

c   Find the IRR for the two investments and indicate them on the graph.

d   Find the exact crossover point and indicate it on the graph.

e   Suppose the required return is 8 per cent. Which of these investments do you prefer?

20 · Applications of various techniques

The Coastalwater Co. owns 140 acres of prime ocean-front property. It is considering several different development options. One option is a hotel and resort complex (option A). Also under consideration is a more expensive multihotel/amusement park development (option B). The cash flows (in millions of dollars) for the two options are projected to be:

Year	Option A	Option B
0	−$600	−$800
1	−40	−60
2	95	175
3	203	210
4	245	270
5	290	375
6	1,240	1,510

a   What is the payback of option A? Option B?

b   Assuming a required return of 20 per cent, what are the present value indices or benefit/cost ratios for the projects? How do you interpret these?

c   Do the present value index and NPV criteria always rank projects the same way? Why or why not? Which of these two projects is preferable, again assuming a 20 per cent discount rate?

21 · Intuition

Projects A and B have the same cost, and both have conventional cash flows. The total cash inflows from A (non-discounted) are $400. The total for B is $360. The IRR for A is 20 per cent; the IRR for B is 18 per cent. What can you deduce about the NPVs for projects A and B? What do you know about the crossover rate?

22 · Problems with IRR

Consider the following cash flows. What is the IRR? If our required return is 30 per cent, should we take this investment? What is the NPV at 28 per cent? What's going on here? Sketch the NPV profile. When should we take this investment? Interpret your answer.

Year	Cash flow
0	$21,065
1	−10,000
2	−10,000
3	−10,000

23 · Payback and IRR

A project has perpetual cash flows of $C per period, a cost of $I, and a required return of r. What is the relationship between its payback and its IRR? What implications does your answer have for long-lived projects with relatively constant cash flows?

24 · NPV and the profitability index

If we define the NPV index as the ratio of NPV to cost, what is the relationship between this index and the present value index?

25 · Payback and NPV

This is a challenge problem. An investment under consideration has a payback of six years and a cost of $11,000. If the required return is 8 per cent, what is the worst-case NPV? Explain.

26 · Multiple IRRs

This is a challenge problem that is also useful for testing computer software. Consider the following cash flows. How many IRRs can there be? How many are there? (*Hint*: search between 20 per cent and 70 per cent.) When should we take this project?

Year	Cash flow
0	−$252
1	1,431
2	−3,035
3	2,850
4	−1,000

27 · Cash flow evaluation

A proposed expansion will result in the following cash flows:

Year	Cash flow
0	−$200
1	50
2	60
3	70
4	200

Ignore taxes. Calculate the payback, the payback reciprocal, the discounted payback and the net present value if the required return is 10 per cent.

28 · Mutually exclusive investments

Consider the following two mutually exclusive investments:

Year	Investment Whimp	Investment Stud
0	−$75	−$75
1	20	60
2	40	50
3	70	15

Calculate the internal rate of return for each and the crossover rate. Under what circumstances will the internal rate of return and the net present value rank the projects differently?

29 · Accounting rate of return

There is a three-year project that is expected to have the following net income:

Year	Net income
0	$2,000
1	4,000
2	6,000

The cost is $12,000, which will depreciate straight line to zero over the three-year life of the project. What is the accounting rate of return?

CHAPTER 8

Making
capital investment decisions

Objective

The aim of this chapter is to show how best to present the numbers for a proposed investment or project. Then how, based on the numbers, to make an assessment as to whether or not the investment or project should be undertaken. On completion of the chapter we will see that it is not our intention to account for the investment or project, following accepted accounting principles, but to evaluate the project or investment using economic cash flows.

Study tip ▷

We are considering the value of the organisation with or without the project or investment. It is a marginal analysis of shifting from one position (without the project or investment) to another (with the project or investment). So when we look at cash flows we look at increases or decreases in cash flows, not the absolute level of the cash flows. For example if an investment increases our cash flow from $10 to $15 then the relevant cash flow in determining whether the investment is acceptable is $5, not $10 or $15. The information provided for a specific decision may be complex; however, the analysis is simple as it reduces to three distinct steps. The three steps are:

1 *calculating the tax effect of the decision;*
2 *calculating the cash flows relevant to the decision; and*
3 *discounting the cash to make the decision.*

If these steps are used in the tabular form demonstrated throughout the chapter, the analysis is systematic. When students get to certain points in the table they will know what to look for in the analysis so that errors and omissions are minimised.

Introduction ▷

In the discussion that follows, we focus on the process of setting up a discounted cash flow analysis. From the last chapter, we know that the projected future cash flows are the key element in such an evaluation. Accordingly, we emphasise working with financial and accounting information to come up with these figures.

In evaluating a proposed investment, we pay special attention to deciding what information is relevant to the decision at hand and what information is not. As we shall see, it is easy to overlook important pieces of the capital budgeting puzzle.

We will wait until the next chapter to describe in detail how to go about evaluating the results of our discounted cash flow analysis. Also, where needed, we will continue to assume that we are given the relevant required return or discount rate. We continue to defer discussion of this subject to Part Five.

■ 8.1 ■ Project cash flows: A first look

The effect of undertaking a project is to change the firm's overall cash flows today and in the future. To evaluate a proposed investment, we must consider these changes in the firm's cash flows and then decide whether or not they add value to the firm. The first (and most important) step, therefore, is to decide which cash flows are relevant and which are not.

Relevant cash flows

incremental cash flows

the difference between a firm's future cash flows with a project or without the project

What is a relevant cash flow for a project? The general principle is simple enough: a relevant cash flow for a project is a change in the firm's overall future cash flow that comes about as a direct consequence of the decision to accept that project. Because the relevant cash flows are defined in terms of changes or increments in the firm's existing cash flow, they are called the **incremental cash flows** associated with the project.

The concept of incremental cash flow is central to our analysis, so we will state a general definition and refer back to it as needed:

> The incremental cash flows for project evaluation consist of any and all changes in the firm's future cash flows that are a direct consequence of undertaking the project.

This definition of incremental cash flows has an obvious and important corollary: Any cash flow that exists regardless of whether or not a project is undertaken is not relevant.

The stand-alone principle

stand-alone principle

evaluation of a project based on the project's incremental cash flows

In practice, it would be very cumbersome to calculate the future total cash flows to the firm with and without a project, especially for a large firm. Fortunately, it is not really necessary to do so. Once we identify the effect of undertaking the proposed project on the firm's cash flows, we need only focus on the resulting project's incremental cash flows. This marginal form of analysis is called the **stand-alone principle**.

What the stand-alone principle says is that, once we have determined the incremental cash flows from undertaking a project, we can view that project as a kind of 'mini firm' with its own future revenues and costs, its own assets and, of course, its own cash flows. We will then be interested primarily in comparing the cash flows from this mini firm to the cost of acquiring it. An important consequence of this approach is that we will be evaluating the proposed project purely on its own merits, in isolation from any other activities or projects.

Concept questions

8.1a *What is the relevant incremental cash flow for project evaluation?*
8.1b *What is the stand-alone principle?*
8.1c *An investment of $10,000 cash provides $500 each period; increasing the investment to $12,000 will provide $720. What are the relevant cash flows to evaluate the additional investment?*

■ 8.2 ■ Incremental cash flows

We are concerned here only with those cash flows that are incremental to a project. Looking back at our general definition, it seems easy enough to decide whether a cash flow is incremental or not. Even so, there are a few situations when mistakes are easy to make. In this section, we describe some of these common pitfalls and how to avoid them.

Sunk costs

A **sunk cost**, by definition, is a cost we have already paid or have already incurred the liability to pay. Such a cost cannot be changed by the decision today to accept or reject a project. Put another way, the firm will have to pay this cost no matter what. Based on our general definition of cash flow, such a cost is clearly not relevant to the decision at hand. So, we will always be careful to exclude sunk costs from our analysis.

sunk cost
a cost that has already been incurred and cannot be removed and therefore should not be considered in an investment decision

A sunk cost being irrelevant seems obvious given our discussion. Nonetheless, it is easy to fall prey to the sunken cost fallacy. For example, suppose Ports Corporation hires a financial consultant to help evaluate whether a rail line to the port should be built. When the consultant presents the report, Ports' CEO objects to the analysis because the consultant did not include the large consulting fee as a cost to the rail project. The consultant claims it is not relevant to the analysis.

Who is correct? By now, we know that the consulting fee is a sunk cost, because the consulting fee must be paid whether or not the rail line is built (this is an attractive feature of the consulting business).

Opportunity costs

When we think of costs, we normally think of out-of-pocket costs, namely, those that require us to actually spend some amount of cash. An **opportunity cost** is slightly different; it requires us to give up a benefit. A common situation arises where a firm already owns some of the assets that a proposed project will be using. For example, we might be thinking of converting a rustic wool store that we bought years ago for $1,000,000 into 'upmarket' town houses.

opportunity cost
the most valuable alternative that is given up if a particular investment is undertaken

If we undertake this project, there will be no direct cash outflow associated with buying the wool store since we already own it. For purposes of evaluating the town house project, should we then treat the wool store as 'free'? The answer is no. The wool store is a valuable resource used by the project. If we didn't use it here, we could do something else with it. Like what? The obvious answer is that, at a minimum, we could sell it. Using the wool store for the town house complex thus has an opportunity cost: We give up the valuable opportunity to do something else with it.

There is another issue here. Once we agree that the use of the wool store has an opportunity cost, how much should the town house project be charged? Given that we paid $1,000,000, it might seem that we should charge this amount to the town house project. Is this correct? The answer is no, and the reason is based on our discussion concerning sunk costs.

The fact that we paid $1,000,000 some years ago is irrelevant. It's sunk. At a minimum, the opportunity cost that we charge the project is what it would sell for today (net of any selling costs) because this is the amount that we give up by using it instead of selling it.[1]

Side effects

Remember that the incremental cash flows for a project include all the changes in the firm's future cash flows. It would not be unusual for a project to have side or spill-over effects, both good and bad. For example, if the Fuel Efficient Company (FEC) introduces a new car, some of the sales might come at the expense of other FEC cars. This is called **erosion**, and the same general problem could occur for any multi-line producer or seller. In this case, the cash flows from the new line should be adjusted downward to reflect lost profits on other lines.

erosion
the cash flows of a new project that come at the expense of a firm's existing projects

In accounting for erosion, it is important to recognise that any sales lost as a result of our launching a new product might be lost anyway because of future competition. Erosion is only relevant when the sales would not otherwise be lost.

Financing costs

In analysing a proposed investment, we will not include interest paid or any other financing costs such as dividends or principal repaid, because we are interested in the cash flow generated by the assets from the project. As we mentioned in Chapter 2, interest paid, for example, is a component of cash flow to debtholders, not cash flow from assets. Another issue, which may not be obvious at this stage of your studies, is that the interest rate we use to discount the cash flows reflects in part the financing costs of the project. If we were to include the negative cash flow of financing and the interest cost for discounting, it would result in taking to account this cost twice.

More generally, our goal in project evaluation is to compare the cash flow from a project to the cost of acquiring that project in order to estimate NPV. The particular mixture of debt and equity that a firm actually chooses to use in financing a project is a managerial variable and primarily determines how project cash flow is divided between owners and debtholders. This is not to say that financing arrangements are unimportant. They are just something to be analysed separately. We will cover this in later chapters.

Other issues

There are some other things to watch out for. First, we are only interested in measuring cash flow. Moreover, we are interested in measuring it when it actually occurs, not when it accrues in an accounting sense. Second, we are always interested in after-tax cash flow, since taxes are definitely a cash outflow. In fact, whenever we write incremental cash flows, we mean after-tax incremental cash flows. Remember, however, that after-tax cash flow and accounting profit are entirely different things.

Concept questions

8.2a *What is a sunk cost? An opportunity cost?*
8.2b *Explain what erosion is and why it is relevant.*
8.2c *Explain why interest paid is not a relevant cash flow for project valuation.*

Project cash flows

The first thing we need when we begin evaluating a proposed investment is a method of analysis. To help ensure that all facets of the project are considered, a three-stepped method is proposed. This simple approach involves as the first step the calculation of the tax payment. As you will see in the following example and in a later section, not all items relevant to the investment have a tax effect. It is necessary, therefore, to consider the tax effect items first so that one of the cash flow items—the tax payment—can be calculated. The second step involves the calculation of the total cash flow. In this step all cash flow items are considered. Once we have the cash flows, we can undertake the third step, which is to estimate the value of the project using the techniques we described in the previous chapter.

Getting started: Projected cash flows

Projected cash flows are a convenient and easily understood means of summarising the relevant information for a project. To prepare these statements, we will need to have estimates of quantities such as unit sales, the selling price per unit or total sales, the variable costs per unit, and total fixed costs. We will also need to know the total investment required.

To illustrate, suppose we are considering the purchase of a new machine for $28,000 to help cope with a temporary excess demand for our product. The salvage value at the end of its three-year life is $5,000. The net annual cash benefits are $20,000, $14,000 and $12,000 in years 1, 2 and 3. For this type of machine the depreciation rate is 25 per cent reducing balance. The tax rate is 30 per cent and tax is paid in the year of income. You require a 15 per cent return for this type of investment.

Example of an investment analysis

TABLE 8.1

	Year 0	Year 1	Year 2	Year 3
Step 1				
Calculation of the tax effect				
Annual benefits		20,000	14,000	12,000
Depreciation		(7,000)	(5,250)	(3,937)
Loss on sale				(6,813)
Taxable income		13,000	8,750	1,250
Step 2				
Calculation of cash flows				
Tax paid		(3,900)	(2,625)	(375)
Annual benefits		20,000	14,000	12,000
Salvage				5,000
Outlay	(28,000)			
Cash flow	(28,000)	16,100	11,375	16,625
Step 3				
Discounting				
Discount factor	1	0.8696	0.7561	0.6575
Discounted cash flows	(28,000)	14,000	8,601	10,931
NPV	$5,532			

Once again, notice that we have not deducted any interest expense. This will always be so. As we described earlier, interest paid is a financing expense, not a component of operating cash flow.

Project taxable income

To develop the cash flows from a project, we need first to calculate the marginal change in the taxable income caused by undertaking the project. After calculating the change in taxable income, the change in the tax payment can be easily determined.

Obviously the annual cash benefits generated by the investment are subject to income tax. Depreciation is a tax deduction where the asset is used for income-producing purposes.

As we note elsewhere, accounting depreciation is a non-cash deduction. As a result, depreciation has cash flow consequences only because it influences the taxable income and therefore the tax payment. The way that depreciation is computed for tax purposes is thus the relevant method for capital investment decisions. Not surprisingly, the procedures are governed by tax law. We now discuss some specifics of the depreciation system enacted by the Income Tax Assessment Act.

Calculating depreciation is normally very mechanical. While several ifs and buts are involved, the basic idea is that every depreciating asset has an effective life. Once an asset's tax life is determined, the depreciation for each year is computed by multiplying the cost of the asset by a fixed percentage.[2] The expected salvage value (what we think the asset will be worth when we dispose of it) and the actual expected economic life (how long we expect the asset to be in service) are not explicitly considered in the calculation of depreciation. We will discuss depreciation further later in this chapter.

The depreciation in our 'purchase of a new machine' example is calculated as follows:

Machine outlay	$28,000
Depreciation year 1—25% of $28,000	7,000
Depreciated value at the end of year 1	21,000
Depreciation year 2—25% of $21,000	5,250
Depreciated value at the end of year 2	15,750
Depreciation year 3—25% of $15,750	3,937
Depreciated value at the end of year 3	11,813
Salvage value	5,000
Loss on disposal	6,813

Refer back to Table 8.1 and you will see that taxation deductions have been claimed for depreciation of $7,000, $5,250 and $3,937 in years 1, 2 and 3 respectively, and a loss on sale at the end of year 3 of $6,813.

Cash flows

The first cash flow item is the tax payment. As the tax rate is 30 per cent, the effect on the tax payment from undertaking the investment is $3,900 ($13,000 × 30%) for the first year's taxable income. Notice that we have put the tax payment of $3,900 in the cash flow column for year 1. If tax was to be paid the year after the year of income then the tax payment would appear in the column for year 2.

If the investment had a tax loss in any year, then less tax would have to be paid on other income earned in that year. As this is an incremental form of analysis, it is assumed that the business is earning other income. The effect that this investment would then have on tax in the tax loss year would be a positive tax figure.

The second cash flow item is the annual cash benefits. This amount is the net of any cash revenue less any cash costs.

We have already looked at the salvage of the machine in order to calculate the loss on disposal, as there were tax effects associated with the salvage, but we now need to consider the cash flow. We will receive $5,000 in cash when we salvage the machine, so this figure should be included as a positive cash flow in year 3. *One of the most common mistakes made by students in completing this type of problem is to forget to include the influence of the salvage as a tax effect and a cash flow effect.*

The last cash flow item to consider is the outlay in year 0; that is, today. The machine costs $28,000 so it is included as a negative figure in year 0.

Discounted cash flow

For each of the years we total the cash flows. The cash flows are then discounted at the appropriate rate. The discounted cash flow is the value of the future period's cash flow today. Paying $28,000 today has a value today of $28,000. Receiving $16,100 in one year's time has a value today of $14,000 if the rate of discount is 15 per cent.

Given that the discounted cash flow is all in today's dollars, we simply add up the figures and the investment has a positive NPV of $5,532.

$$NPV = -\$28,000 + \$16,100/1.15 + \$11,375/1.15^2 + \$16,625/1.15^3$$
$$= \$5,532$$

> Remember there are three steps in the analysis—to calculate the tax effect, to calculate the cash flow and then to do the discounting.

So, based on these projections, the project creates over $5,000 in value and should be accepted. Also the return on investment obviously exceeds 15 per cent (since the NPV is positive at 15%). After some trial and error, we find that the IRR works out to be about 26.6 per cent.

NPV	Discount rate
12,012	5%
8,528	10%
5,532	15%
2,937	20%
672	25%
(1,317)	30%

In addition, if required, we could go ahead and calculate the payback. Inspection of the cash flow shows that the payback on this project is just over two years (check that it's about 2.03 years).[3]

Concept questions

8.3a *What is the three-step approach used to calculate a discounted cash flow?*

8.3b *In the purchase of the machine project, why did we consider the depreciation of the machine when depreciation is only a book entry?*

8.4 ▮ More on project cash flows

In this section, we take a closer look at some aspects of project cash flows. In particular, we discuss interest in more detail. We then examine current tax laws regarding depreciation, gain or loss on disposal, and capital gains tax. Finally, we work through an example that illustrates more fully the idea of NPV being an incremental form of analysis.

A CLOSER LOOK

Interest

In this and the previous chapter we told you to ignore interest costs. Sure interest may be a tax deduction, and additionally, it definitely has a cash flow effect, but still interest is ignored. Recall in our earlier machine example that the project cash flows were:

Year 0	Year 1	Year 2	Year 3
–$28,000	$16,100	$11,375	$16,625

and that the NPV was $5,532.

What would happen if we didn't have the money to purchase the machine? We would go to the bank. Which bank? Well it doesn't matter as long as we will be charged interest of no more than 15%, the required rate of return on the project.

We go to the bank and borrow $33,532, being the NPV amount of $5,532 and the outlay cost of $28,000. We put $5,532 in our pocket today, purchase the machine and then let the cash flows generated by the machine repay the loan. Table 8.2 displays the repayment schedule for the loan.

TABLE
8.2

		Interest			
Year	Amount	15%	Total	Repayment	Balance
1	33,532	5,030	38,562	16,100	22,462
2	22,462	3,369	25,831	11,375	14,456
3	14,456	2,169	16,625	16,625	0

Repayment schedule

You can see from the table that the cash flows generated by the investment repay the loan. We know that since the project has a positive NPV, any interest costs can effectively be met by the cash flows from the investment. To include interest costs in the cash flows, we would effectively be double counting (once by including the interest cost and then discounting to also reflect an interest cost).

What about the case where the bank wants to charge us more than 15 per cent or more than the required rate of return for the investment? What this means is that our discount rate is not high enough. We have analysed the investment and we want a return of 15 per cent. We take the project to a financier and the financier wants a return of 20 per cent. This means that the financier thinks that the project is more risky than we do. Either the financier is wrong or we are wrong.

As an aside, what do you think is the most that we can afford to pay as an interest rate in the case where the cash flows from the investment are paying off the loan? The answer is the IRR of the project. The IRR of our machine example was 26.6 per cent. If we were to borrow money at this rate then the cash flows from the investment would pay off the loan.

Table 8.2 provides further insight into understanding the NPV. NPV is the increase in wealth today from undertaking the project. Recall that we borrowed the outlay plus the NPV from the bank. The NPV of $5,532 we put into our pocket and the project paid the loan. What was the increase in wealth today from undertaking the project? The answer is obvious: the NPV, the $5,532 we pocketed today.

Depreciation

As we stated earlier, assets may be depreciated. The rate of depreciation is reflective of the asset's effective life. Generally the effective life of a depreciating asset is how long it can be used for a taxable purpose, having regard to the wear and tear you reasonably expect from your expected circumstances of use and assuming reasonable levels of maintenance. For most depreciating assets, you have a choice to either work out the effective life yourself or use an effective life determined by the Commissioner. For example for a computer the asset's effective life is four years.

There are two methods of depreciation: the prime cost (equivalent of the straight-line depreciation method in accounting) and the diminishing value method. The rate for the diminishing value method is 150 per cent of the prime cost rate. For example, if the prime cost rate is 25 per cent (an effective life of four years), then this asset can be depreciated at 37.5 per cent diminishing value. Diminishing value is the taxation equivalent to the reducing balance method in accounting.

Our intention in this chapter is to keep the issue simple. Depreciation is a non-cash expense of running a business. Depreciation is the way that the cost of the asset is claimed over the economic life of the asset. The only cash flow effect is the effect on the taxable income from claiming depreciation as a deduction.

Suppose we buy a machine for $10,000 and the effective life is six and two-third years, then the prime cost rate is 15 per cent. We will assume that we sell the machine at year 5 for $2,000, this being the termination value (called the salvage value in accounting). The possible taxation depreciation amounts are shown in Table 8.3.

Depreciation rates		
Rates	15%	22.5%
Life years	Prime cost	Diminishing value
1	$ 1,500	$ 2,250
2	$ 1,500	$ 1,744
3	$ 1,500	$ 1,351
4	$ 1,500	$ 1,047
5	$ 1,500	$ 812
Total Depreciation	$ 7,500	$ 7,204
Adjustable value year 5	$ 2,500	$ 2,796
Termination value	$ 2,000	$ 2,000
Gain/(Loss)	($ 500)	($ 796)
Total depreciation + Loss	$ 8,000	$ 8,000
Present value @ 10%*	$ 5,996**	$ 6,216

TABLE 8.3

* While the total tax claim is the same under all methods, the present values will be different because the tax claims are spread differently across time. For example, the diminishing value methods have the higher tax claims in the earlier years of the asset.

** The present value of the tax saving using prime cost depreciation is:

$$\$1500 \times (1 - 1.1^{-5})/0.1 + \$500 \times 1.1^{-5}$$
$$= \$5986 + \$310$$
$$= \$5996$$

For diminishing value it is:

$$\$2250 \times 1.1^{-1} + \$1744 \times 1.1^{-2} + \$1351 \times 1.1^{-3} + \$1047 \times 1.1^{-4} + \$812 \times 1.1^{-5} + \$796 \times 1.1^{-5}$$
$$= \$6216$$

For prime cost, the amount to be depreciated is the cost of the asset, which in this case is $10,000. The rate of depreciation is 15 per cent so the depreciation claim in each year will be $1,500 ($10,000 × 15%). Over a five-year period the total amount of depreciation is $7,500 ($1,500 × 5 years) so the adjustable value (being the unclaimed amount and commonly called the book value in accounting) of the asset at year 5 must be $2,500

($10,000 − $7,500). If the machine is sold for $2,000 (this is called the termination value for taxation purposes), then there is a loss on disposal of $500, which is a tax deduction. The total of the tax deductions is $8,000, being $7,500 in depreciation and $500 for loss on sale.

With diminishing value the rate for depreciation is 22.5 per cent (15% × 1.5). In the first year the depreciation is $2,250 ($10,000 × 22.5%) and the book value at the end of the year will be $7,750. In year 2 the amount that will be depreciated is $7,750 at the rate of 22.5%. The amount of depreciation in year 2 is therefore $1,744 ($7,750 × 22.5%).

Both methods have the same total amount claimed as a tax deduction of $8,000; the issue must be the timing of the tax deduction. Under the diminishing value methods more depreciation is claimed in the early years and less in the later years. Now, when do you want a $100 tax deduction, today or in five years time? It is the same question as whether you would rather receive $100, today or in five years time. The obvious answer is today. When we discount the deductions at a rate of 10 per cent we see the diminishing value methods have the highest present value so these are the preferred depreciation methods.

Gain or loss on disposal

When an asset is sold at a price (termination value) different to the book value of the asset (adjustable value), you will have a gain or loss (balancing adjustment) on sale. The reason that taxes must be paid on a gain is that the difference in sale price and book value is excess depreciation and the Taxation Office wants to recoup this excess.

If we purchase an asset for $12,000 and claim depreciation of $6,000 over the life of the asset then the book value of the asset is $6,000. If we sell the asset for $7,000 then we have a gain of $1,000. This gain arises because the amount claimed for depreciation, $6,000, is greater than the amount that should have been claimed for depreciation, being $5,000 ($12,000 − $7,000).

If we had sold the asset for $5,000, the amount of depreciation claimed would still be $6,000 but the amount that should have been claimed is $7,000 ($12,000 − $5,000). The $1,000 loss on disposal or balancing deduction is a tax deduction to us.

Capital gains tax

A capital gain occurs if an asset is sold for more than it cost. If you purchase a rental property for $100,000, hold it for twelve months and then sell it for $120,000, then you have gained. For taxation purposes, the calculation of a capital gain is complicated and depends upon whether the seller is an individual or an entity such as a company or trust.

The following section explains how capital gains tax is levied on assets acquired after 21 September 1999. The elements that contribute to the identification of a capital gain are the cost base, acquisition costs, disposals costs, selling price, improvements and additions and the general exemption. Theses elements are defined as follows:

The *cost base* is the purchase price, or a deemed purchase price in some situations, plus the acquisition, disposal and improvement costs.

Acquisition costs are the expenses incidental to the purchase of the asset.

Disposal costs are the expenses incidental to the sale of the asset.

Selling price is the sale price or deemed sale price of an asset.

Improvements and additions are the capital enhancements to the asset that add value to its cost base.

A general exemption is an exemption from tax that is provided for individuals and superannuation funds on disposals made after 21 September 1999.

Consider the example of land purchased on 22 September 1999 by Charlie Prince for $100,000 and sold for $200,000 on 23 September 2002. Legal costs including stamp duty on purchase were $5,000, while commission and legal costs at sale were $4,000. Clearing costs for the land were $10,000 and it was cleared in June 2002. The capital gain would be calculated as:

Selling price		$200,000
Costs		
Purchase price	$100,000	
Acquisition cost	5,000	
Improvements	10,000	
Selling costs	4,000	
Total cost base	119,000	(119,000)
Capital gain		81,000
Less General exemption 50%		40,500
Taxed capital gain		$40,500

The taxed capital gain is aggregated with the taxpayer's other assessable income and taxed at normal marginal tax rates. The old method of calculating capital gains is being phased out. This method involved indexing costs using the consumer price index.

Assume the same facts as above but now Charlie Prince purchased the land on 22 September 1985. The calculation adopted could be that shown; however, for purchases prior to 21 September 1999 only, a second approach is available, using consumer price index adjustments. The consumer price index was 71.3 in September 1985 and 123.4 in September 1999. The old method would calculate the capital gain as:

Selling price		$200,000
Cost base		
Purchase price	$100,000	
Acquisition cost	5,000	
	$105,000	
Indexed $105,000 × 123.4/71.3	$181,725	
Improvements	10,000	
Selling costs	4,000	
Indexed cost base		195,725
Capital gain		$4,275

Superannuation funds receive a one-third capital gains tax general exemption. Companies are placed poorly in relation to capital gains, as they do not receive the benefit of the general exemption.

Inflation

When a project is being evaluated, anticipated inflation would be reflected in the estimates of the future cash flows and the interest rate used as the discount rate in the analysis. As a result there will be no distortion to the analysis by not identifying inflation specifically. Because depreciation deductions are based on historic costs rather than replacement costs, some analysts argue that offsetting historic depreciation deductions against future inflation adjusted cash flows is overstating the cash saving resulting from the depreciation deductions. These analysts would reduce the depreciation deduction for the inflation factor.

Chapter 10 contains a discussion of real and nominal interest rates. A nominal rate includes the effect of inflation where a real rate is uninflated. If inflated cash flows are estimated then a nominal rate is required to discount. If uninflated cash flows are estimated then a real discount rate is required. Take the following example. The nominal rate is 17.7% and inflation is 7%. The real rate (you need to read Chapter 10) is 10%.[4]

Assume an anticipated inflation rate of 7 per cent

Including the effect of depreciation

	Year 1	Year 2
Depreciation	20,000	20,000
Taxable income	20,000	20,000
Tax benefit 30%	$ 6,000	$ 6,000

$$PV @ 17.7\% = \$6,000 \times 1.177^{-1} + \$6,000 \times 1.177^{-2}$$
$$= \$9,429$$

Adjusting the depreciation for anticipated inflation

	Year 1		Year 2	
Depreciation	20,000/1.07 =	18,691	20,000/1.07^2 =	17,468
Taxable income		18,691		17,468
Tax benefit 30%		$ 5,607		$ 5,240

$$PV @ 10\% = \$5607 \times 1.1^{-1} + \$5240 \times 1.1^{-2}$$
$$= \$9,429$$

Is it necessary to incorporate the inflation factor into the tax saving provided by the depreciation. If real cash flows are being estimated then adjustments for inflation are required to be made to depreciation. If nominal cash flows are being estimated (these are the cash flows incorporating inflation) then no adjustment is required to be made to depreciation.

Incremental form of analysis

We will use an example to illustrate the point that NPV is an incremental form of analysis. Most readers would be familiar with economic concepts such as marginal cost and marginal revenue, so you will not be surprised to hear the description 'incremental' is often replaced by 'marginal'. A manufacturer has a small factory, which generates revenue of $1,000,000 per year. The factory and office cash costs (being rent, rates, office staff) amount to $120,000 per annum. Factory labour costs for each of the ten employees are $25,000 per person per annum. The additional associated labour costs, like superannuation and annual leave, are 42 per cent of labour costs. The current machinery cost $1,500,000 three years ago and it is being depreciated over its estimated life of five years. If the machinery was scrapped today, its salvage value would be $850,000 and in two years it would be nothing.

The owner is considering purchasing new machinery for $1,000,000 with a two-year life. The advantage will be the saving of four employees. The new machinery will be worthless in two years. If the discount rate is 12 per cent, should the manager purchase the new machinery? To keep it easy, let us assume that the tax calculated at 30 per cent is paid in the year of income.

One approach that we could use is to calculate the NPV of the present situation. Table 8.4 provides this analysis.

TABLE
8.4

NPV of present situation

Year	0	1	2
Calculation of tax effect			
Revenue		1,000,000	1,000,000
Labour		−250,000	−250,000
On-costs		−105,000	−105,000
Factory costs		−120,000	−120,000
Depreciation		−300,000	−300,000
Taxable income		**225,000**	**225,000**
Calculation of cash flows			
Tax		−67,500	−67,500
Revenue		1,000,000	1,000,000
Labour		−250,000	−250,000
On-costs		−105,000	−105,000
Factory costs		−120,000	−120,000
Cash flow		457,500	457,500
DCF at 12%		408,452	364,716
NPV	$ 773,198		

We can ignore the outlay for the current machinery of $1,500,000 in the analysis because this occurred three years ago to be a sunk cost in relation to this analysis. The present situation has an NPV of $773,198, which is very good. The next step in this type of analysis is to calculate the NPV of the new situation. This is displayed in Table 8.5.

TABLE
8.5

New situation

Year	0	1	2
Calculation of tax effect			
Revenue		1,000,000	1,000,000
Labour		−150,000	−150,000
On-costs		−63,000	−63,000
Factory costs		−120,000	−120,000
Depreciation		−500,000	−500,000
Gain on sale	250,000		
Taxable income	**250,000**	**167,000**	**167,000**
Calculation of cash flows			
Tax	−75,000	−50,100	−50,100
Revenue		1,000,000	1,000,000
Labour		−150,000	−150,000
On-costs		−63,000	−63,000
Factory costs		−120,000	−120,000
Salvage	850,000		
Outlay	−1,000,000		
Cash flow	−225,000	616,900	616,900
NPV	$ 817,592		

If new machinery is purchased, the number of employees falls to six. The labour costs and the on-costs fall. The factory costs will remain at $120,000 per year. Depreciation will now be $500,000 per year as the owner is depreciating it to zero over two years ($1,000,000/2).

The old machinery cost $1.5m five years ago. It was being depreciated at a rate of $300,000 per year so that after three years it had been depreciated by $900,000 ($300,000 × 3) and the book value of the old machinery is $600,000 ($1,500,000 − $900,000). The old machinery is sold for $850,000 so that the gain on sale is $250,000 ($850,000 − $600,000).

The NPV of the new situation is $817,592. Should the owner buy the new machinery? The old NPV is $773,198 and the new NPV is $817,592, so the owner will be better off by $44,394 from changing over.

This method of analysis is difficult. What we did was calculate the NPV of the present situation. We then needed to calculate the NPV of the new situation to see the change in the NPV. This required two separate NPV calculations to examine the change in NPV. A preferred method of analysis is to perform an NPV calculation on only those variables that change when shifting from one method of production (as in this case) to another.

Let us do the analysis again using a marginal form of analysis as in Table 8.6.

TABLE 8.6

Marginal analysis			
Year	0	1	2
Calculation of tax effect			
Labour savings		100,000	100,000
On-costs savings		42,000	42,000
Depreciation—old		300,000	300,000
Depreciation—new		−500,000	−500,000
Gain on sale	250,000		
Taxable income	250,000	−58,000	−58,000
Calculation of cash flows			
Tax	−75,000	17,400	17,400
Labour		100,000	100,000
On-costs		42,000	42,000
Salvage	850,000		
Outlay	−1,000,000		
Cash flow	−225,000	159,400	159,400
NPV	$ 44,394		

In this case the revenue is not included, as it does not change so the marginal effect is zero. It is only the changed labour costs, both wages and on-costs, that are included. With depreciation, we were claiming $300,000 in depreciation and we will now be claiming $500,000 in depreciation. The marginal effect of depreciation is an increase of $200,000.

The NPV of the marginal changes is a positive $44,394. This tells us that the manufacturer is better off by $44,394 if the manufacturer changes to the new machinery.

The advantage of using a marginal form of analysis is that there will only be one calculation and not two. By using a marginal form we are implicitly analysing one option: that is, to do nothing. By analysing changes, we are implicitly comparing a new situation to an old situation. The sign of the NPV tells us whether it is sensible to change or not.

Samuel Weaver

Samuel Weaver* on capital budgeting at Hershey Foods Corporation

The capital program at Hershey Foods Corporation and most Fortune 500/1000 companies involves a three-phase approach: planning/budgeting, evaluation, and post-completion reviews.

The first phase involves identification of likely projects at strategic planning time. These are selected to support the strategic objectives of the corporation. This identification is generally broad in scope with minimal financial evaluation attached. As the planning process focuses more closely on the short-term plans, major capital expenditures are scrutinised more rigorously. Project costs are more closely honed, and specific projects may be reconsidered.

Each project is then individually reviewed and authorised. Planning, developing, and refining cash flows underlie the capital program at Hershey Foods. Once the cash flows have been determined, the application of capital evaluation techniques such as net present value, internal rate of return, and payback period is routine. Presentation of the results is enhanced using sensitivity analysis, which plays a major role for management in assessing the critical assumptions and resulting impact.

The final phase relates to post-completion reviews in which the original forecasts of the project's performance are compared to actual results and/or revised expectations.

Capital expenditure analysis is only as good as the assumptions that underlie the project. The old cliché of 'GIGO' (Garbage In, Garbage Out) applies in this case. Incremental cash flows primarily result from incremental sales or margin improvements (cost savings). For the most part, a range of incremental cash flows can be identified from marketing research or engineering studies. However, for a number of projects, correctly discerning the implications and the relevant cash flows is analytically challenging. For example, when a new product is introduced and is expected to generate millions of dollars worth of sales; the appropriate analysis focuses only on the incremental sales after accounting for cannibalisation of existing products.

One of the problems that we face at Hershey Foods deals with the application of net present value (NPV) versus internal rate of return (IRR). NPV offers the correct investment indication when dealing with mutually-exclusive alternatives. However, decision-makers at all levels sometimes find it difficult to comprehend the result. Specifically, an NPV of, say, $535,000 needs to be interpreted. It is not enough to know that the NPV is positive or even more positive than an alternative. Decision-makers seek a level of 'comfort' of how profitable the investment is by relating it to other standards.

Although the IRR may provide a misleading indication of which project to select, the result is provided in a way that can be interpreted by all parties. The resulting IRR can be mentally compared to expected inflation, current borrowing rates, the cost of capital, an equity portfolio's return, and so on. An IRR of, say, 18 per cent is readily interpretable by management. Perhaps this ease of understanding is why surveys indicate that most Fortune 500 or Fortune 1000 companies use the IRR method as a primary evaluation technique.

In addition to the NPV versus IRR problem, there are a limited number of projects for which traditional and capital expenditure analysis is difficult to apply because the cash flows can't be determined. When new computer equipment is purchased, an office building is renovated, or a parking lot is repaved, it is essentially impossible to identify the cash flows, so the use of traditional evaluation techniques is limited. These types of 'capital expenditure' decisions are made using other techniques that hinge on management's judgment.

* Samuel Weaver, Ph.D., was Manager of Corporate Financial Analysis for the Hershey Foods Corporation. He is a certified management accountant, and he currently serves on the board of trustees of the Financial Management Association. His current position is Professor of Finance at Lehigh University.

Concept questions

8.4a *Why is it preferred to perform a marginal form of analysis when doing NPV calculations?*

8.4b *How is depreciation calculated for depreciating assets under current tax law? What effect does expected salvage value and estimated effective life have on the calculated depreciation deduction?*

 8.5 # Some special cases of discounted cash flow analysis

To finish the chapter, we look at three common cases involving discounted cash flow (DCF) analysis. In the first case we consider a firm involved in submitting competitive bids. The second case values options, the right to undertake an action. The final case arises in choosing between equipment with different economic lives.

There are many other special cases that we could consider, but these three are particularly important because problems similar to these are so common. Also, they illustrate some very diverse applications of cash flow analysis and DCF valuation.

Setting the bid price

Early on, we used discounted cash flow to evaluate the purchase of a new machine. A somewhat different (and very common) scenario arises when we must submit a competitive bid to win a job. Under such circumstances, the winner is whoever submits the lowest bid.

There is an old saying concerning this process: the lowest bidder is whoever makes the biggest mistake. This is called the winner's curse. In other words, if you win, there is a good chance that you underbid. In this section, we look at how to go about setting the bid price to avoid the winner's curse. The procedure we describe is useful whenever we have to set a price on a product or service.

To illustrate how to go about setting a bid price, imagine that we are in the business of buying truck platforms and then modifying them to customer specifications for resale. A local distributor has requested bids for five specially modified trucks each year for the next four years, for a total of 20 trucks in all.

We need to decide what price per truck to bid. The goal of our analysis is to determine the lowest price we can profitably charge. This maximises our chances of being awarded the contract while guarding against the winner's curse.

Suppose we can buy the truck platforms for $10,000 each. The facilities we need can be leased for $24,000 per year. The labour and material cost to do the modification works out to be about $4,000 per truck. Total cost per year will thus be $24,000 + 5 × ($10,000 + $4,000) = $94,000.

We will need to invest $60,000 in new equipment. This equipment will be depreciated prime cost to a zero salvage value over the four years. It will be worth about $5,000 at that time. The relevant tax rate is 30 per cent. What price per truck should we bid if we require a 20 per cent return on our investment?

We start out by using our standard method of analysis and we put in the figures that we know (see Table 8.7).

TABLE 8.7

Preparing the bid					
Year	Year 0	Year 1	Year 2	Year 3	Year 4
Calculation of tax effect					
Revenue					
Labour & materials × 5		(20,000)	(20,000)	(20,000)	(20,000)
Platforms × 5		(50,000)	(50,000)	(50,000)	(50,000)
Lease		(24,000)	(24,000)	(24,000)	(24,000)
Depreciation		(15,000)	(15,000)	(15,000)	(15,000)
Gain on sale					5,000
Taxable income					
Calculation of cash flows					
Tax					
Revenue					
Labour & materials		(20,000)	(20,000)	(20,000)	(20,000)
Platforms		(50,000)	(50,000)	(50,000)	(50,000)
Lease		(24,000)	(24,000)	(24,000)	(24,000)
Outlay	(60,000)				
Salvage					5,000
Cash Flow					
DCF	(60,000)				
NPV					

With this in mind, here is the key observation: the lowest possible price we can profitably charge will result in a zero NPV at 20 per cent. The reason is that at that price, we earn exactly 20 per cent on our investment.

Given this observation, we first need to determine what the cash flow must be for the NPV to be equal to zero. To do this, we calculate the present value of the $5,000 salvage cash flow, after tax from the last year, and subtract it from the $60,000 initial investment:

$$\$60,000 - \$5,000(1 - 0.30)/1.20^4$$
$$= \$60,000 - \$1,688 = \$58,312$$

Once we do this, the cash flow is now an unknown ordinary annuity amount.

	Year 0	Year 1	Year 2	Year 3	Year 4
Cash flow	–$58,312	Cash flow	Cash flow	Cash flow	Cash flow

The four-year annuity factor for 20 per cent is 2.58873, so we have:

$$\text{NPV} = 0 = -\$58{,}312 + \text{Cash flow} \times 2.58873$$

This implies that:

$$\text{Cash flow} = \$58{,}312/2.58873 = \$22{,}525$$

So the cash flow (excluding the outlay and the salvage value) needs to be $22,525 each year (see Table 8.8).

TABLE 8.8

Preparing the bid					
Year	Year 0	Year 1	Year 2	Year 3	Year 4
Calculation of tax effect					
Revenue					
Labour & materials		(20,000)	(20,000)	(20,000)	(20,000)
Platforms		(50,000)	(50,000)	(50,000)	(50,000)
Lease		(24,000)	(24,000)	(24,000)	(24,000)
Depreciation		(15,000)	(15,000)	(15,000)	(15,000)
Taxable income					
Calculation of cash flows					
Tax					
Revenue					
Labour & materials		(20,000)	(20,000)	(20,000)	(20,000)
Platforms		(50,000)	(50,000)	(50,000)	(50,000)
Lease		(24,000)	(24,000)	(24,000)	(24,000)
Cash flow		22,525	22,525	22,525	22,525

We are not quite done. The final problem is to find out what sales price results in this cash flow of $22,525. The easiest way to do this is to recall that cash flow can be written as profit plus depreciation, the bottom-up definition. The depreciation here is $60,000/4 = $15,000. Given this, we can determine what profit must be:

$$
\begin{aligned}
\text{Cash flow} &= \text{Profit} + \text{Depreciation} \\
\$22{,}525 &= \text{Profit} + \$15{,}000 \\
\text{Profit} &= \$7{,}525
\end{aligned}
$$

From here, we work our way backwards up the profit and loss account. If profit is $7,525, then our profit and loss account is as follows:

Sales	?
Costs	$94,000
Depreciation	$15,000
Taxes (30%)	?
Profit	$ 7,525

So we can solve for sales by noting that:

$$
\begin{aligned}
\text{Profit} &= (\text{Sales} - \text{Costs} - \text{Depreciation}) \times (1 - T_c) \\
\$7,525 &= (\text{Sales} - \$94,000 - \$15,000) \times (1 - 0.30) \\
\text{Sales} &= \$7,525/0.70 + \$94,000 + \$15,000 \\
&= \$119,750
\end{aligned}
$$

If we wanted to check these figures to make sure that we are correct then the NPV analysis would be like Table 8.9.

TABLE 8.9

Complete analysis					
	Year 0	Year 1	Year 2	Year 3	Year 4
Calculation of tax effect					
Revenue		119,750	119,750	119,750	119,750
Labour & materials		(20,000)	(20,000)	(20,000)	(20,000)
Platforms		(50,000)	(50,000)	(50,000)	(50,000)
Lease		(24,000)	(24,000)	(24,000)	(24,000)
Depreciation		(15,000)	(15,000)	(15,000)	(15,000)
Gain on sale					5,000
Taxable income		10,750	10,750	10,750	15,750
Calculation of cash flows					
Tax (30%)		(3,225)	(3,225)	(3,225)	(4,725)
Revenue		119,750	119,750	119,750	119,750
Labour & materials		(20,000)	(20,000)	(20,000)	(20,000)
Platforms		(50,000)	(50,000)	(50,000)	(50,000)
Lease		(24,000)	(24,000)	(24,000)	(24,000)
Outlay	(60,000)				
Salvage					5,000
Cash flow	(60,000)	22,525	22,525	22,525	26,025
NPV	Zero				

Sales per year must be $119,750. Since the contract calls for five trucks per year, the sales price has to be $119,750/5 = $23,950. If we round this up a bit, it looks like we need to bid about $24,000 per truck. At this price, were we to get the contract, our return would be just over 20 per cent.

Setting the option value

A buy option is an arrangement that gives the holder the right to buy an asset at a fixed price sometime in the future. We cover options in detail in later chapters but we give you some preliminary understanding here.

Let us consider the case of Hilda Iris Lee Shirley Alive (known as Hils to all), a pensioner. Hils could use could use some extra cash but she does not want to sell her major asset, her home. She feels that, if she were to sell her home, she would lose her pension because the home is worth $800,000 as a result of its beachfront position. She is prepared to give you an option at a fee for the purchase of her home in ten years for a set price. This offer suits you as you are not ready to settle and you have several other investments you wish to undertake. Because of your salary and security, lenders are prepared to provide funds to you at 10 per cent for property investments. You cannot enforce the option and put Hils on the street until the full ten years pass, and if Hils should die before the 10 years lapse, her home would be rented and held in trust until the date of your contract. Also, the challenge is to set the fixed amount for the house purchase in ten years and the fee that should be paid now to Hils for the option.

You feel the home will be worth $1.2 million in ten years so this is the fixed amount you would be prepared to accept in the option. The fixed amount of the option contract is called the exercise or strike price. You also agree the current value of the house is $800,000. The maximum value of the option—the fee you will pay—is equal to the current value of the house less the present value of the exercise price.

$$\text{Option value} = \$800,000 - \$1,200,000(1.1)^{-10}$$
$$= \$800,000 - \$462,652$$
$$= \$337,348$$

Suppose you are not confident about the current value of the house and you have derived the following:

Value	Probability	Expected value
$700,000	25% = 0.25	0.25 × $700,000 = $175,000
$750,000	40% = 0.4	0.4 × $750,000 = $300,000
$800,000	30% = 0.3	0.3 × $800,000 = $240,000
$850,000	5% = 0.05	0.05 × $850,000 = $ 42,500
	100% = 1	$757,500

So the current expected value is $757,500.

In addition you feel there is a 10 per cent probability that the house will be worth less than $1.2 million. If the home is worth less than the exercise price you will not take up the option as the house could be purchased cheaper on the open market. You also feel there is a 15 per cent chance the house will be worth more than $1.2 million. In this case you would take up the option and purchase for the exercise price. In summary we have:

Condition	Probability	Expected value
Less than $1.2 m	0.1	Nil
$1.2 m	0.75	0.75 × $1.2m = $ 900,000
More than $1.2 m	0.15	0.15 × $1.2m = $ 180,000
	1	$1,080,000

With this additional information the option value calculation is:

$$\text{Value of the option} = \text{Asset value} \times \text{Probability of the value} - \text{Present value}$$
$$\text{of the exercise price} \times \text{Probability the exercise price}$$
$$\text{will be paid}$$
$$= \$757,500 - \$1,080,000(1.1)^{-10}$$
$$= \$757,500 - \$416,387$$
$$= \$341,113$$

There are many other characteristics of options we could discuss but we will leave those until later.

Evaluating equipment with different lives

The final problem we consider involves choosing among different possible systems, equipment or procedures. Our goal is to choose the most cost-effective, the one that provides the highest NPV or, if it is an analysis of costs, the lowest cost. The approach we consider here is only necessary when two special circumstances exist. First, the possibilities under evaluation have different economic lives. Second, and just as important, we need whatever we buy more or less indefinitely. As a result, when it wears out, we will buy another one.

We can illustrate this problem with a simple example. Imagine that we are in the business of manufacturing stamped metal subassemblies. Whenever a stamping mechanism wears out, we have to replace it with a new one to stay in business. We are considering which of two stamping mechanisms to buy.

Machine A costs $100 to buy and $10 per year to operate. It wears out and must be replaced every two years. Machine B costs $140 to buy and $8 per year to operate. It lasts for three years and must then be replaced. Ignoring taxes, which one should we go with if we use a 10 per cent discount rate?

In comparing the two machines, we notice that the first is cheaper to buy, but it costs more to operate and it wears out more quickly. How can we evaluate these trade-offs? We can start by computing the present value of the costs for each:

$$\text{Machine A: PV} = (\$100) + (\$10)/1.1 + (\$10)/1.1^2$$
$$= (\$117.36)$$

$$\text{Machine B: PV} = (\$140) + (\$8)/1.1 + (\$8)/1.1^2 + (\$8)/1.1^3$$
$$= (\$159.89)$$

Notice that all the numbers here are costs, so they are all in brackets. If we stopped here, it might appear that A is the more attractive since the PV of the costs is less. However, all we have really discovered so far is that A effectively provides two years worth of stamping service for $117.36, while B effectively provides three years worth for $159.89. These are not directly comparable because of the difference in service periods.

We need to somehow work out a cost per year for these two alternatives. To do this, we ask the question: 'What amount, paid each year over the life of the machine, has the same PV of costs?' This amount is called the **annual equivalent cost (AEC)**.

Calculating the AEC involves finding an unknown payment amount. For example, for machine A, we need to find a two-year ordinary annuity with a PV of ($117.36) at 10 per cent. Going back to Chapter 5, the two-year annuity factor is:

$$\text{Annuity factor} = [1 - 1/1.10^2]/0.10 = 1.7355$$

For machine A, then, we have:

$$\text{PV of costs} = (\$117.36) = \text{AEC} \times 1.7355$$
$$\text{AEC} = (\$117.36)/1.7355$$
$$= (\$67.62)$$

For machine B, the life is three years, so we first need the three-year annuity factor:

$$\text{Annuity factor} = [1 - 1/1.10^3]/0.10 = 2.4869$$

annual equivalent cost (AEC)

the present value of a project's costs calculated on an annual basis

We calculate the AEC for B just as we did for A:

$$\text{PV of costs} = (\$159.89) = \text{AEC} \times 2.4869$$
$$\text{AEC} = (\$159.89)/2.4869$$
$$= (\$64.29)$$

Based on this analysis, we should purchase B because it effectively costs $64.29 per year versus $67.62 for A. In other words, all things considered, B is cheaper. In this case, the longer life and lower operating cost is more than enough to offset the higher initial purchase price.

EXAMPLE
8.1
Annual equivalent costs

This extended example illustrates what happens to the AEC when we consider taxes. You are evaluating two different pollution control options. A filtration system will cost $1.1 million to install and $60,000 annually pre-tax to operate. It will have to be completely replaced every five years. A precipitation system will cost $1.9 million to install, but only $10,000 per year to operate. The precipitation equipment has an effective operating life of eight years. Prime cost depreciation is used throughout, and neither system has any salvage value. Which method should we select if we use a 12 per cent discount rate? The tax rate is 30 per cent.

We need to consider the AECs for the two approaches because they have different service lives, and they will be replaced as they wear out. The relevant information can be summarised as:

	Filtration system Years 1 to 5	Precipitation system Years 1 to 8
Calculation of tax effects		
Annual cost	(60,000)	(10,000)
Depreciation	(220,000)	(237,500)
Taxable income	(280,000)	(247,500)
Calculation of cash flows		
Tax benefit	84,000	74,250
Annual cost	(60,000)	(10,000)
Cash flow	$24,000	$64,250
Economic life	5 years	8 years
Annuity factor	3.6048	4.9676
Present value of cash flow	86,515	319,168
Outlay	(1,100,000)	(1,900,000)
NPV	($1,013,485)	($1,580,832)

Notice that the annual cash flow is actually positive in both cases because of the large tax effect of depreciation. This can occur whenever the operating cost is small relative to the purchase price.

To decide which system to purchase, we compute the AECs for both using the appropriate annuity factors:

Filtration system: ($1,013,485) = AEC × 3.6048
AEC = ($281,149) per year

Precipitation system: ($1,580,832) = AEC × 4.9676
AEC = ($318,229) per year

The filtration system is the cheaper of the two, so we select it. In this case, the longer life and smaller operating cost of the precipitation system are not sufficient to offset its higher initial cost.

Unequal life projects with cash inflows

When we are comparing projects with cash inflows and cash outflows but unequal lives we use the *annual equivalent benefit* (AEB). The steps required to calculate the AEB are the same as those used for AEC. The NPVs are calculated and then these are converted to the AEBs using the relevant PVIFA.

Annual equivalent benefit

We are considering installing a vending machine. A smaller, less expensive, machine only supplies soft drinks and has to be replaced every four years. A larger machine supplies soft drinks, chocolates and salted chips and has to be replaced every eight years. Major maintenance programs have to be conducted in Year 2 for the smaller machine and Year 4 for the larger. Suppose the required rate of return on vending machines is 20 per cent and the estimated cash flows are:

Years	Details	Smaller machine	Larger machine
0	cost	−$2,400	−$6,500
1	cash flow	3,000	3,600
2	cash flow	−500	3,600
3	cash flow	3,000	3,600
4	cash flow	3,000	−1,500
5	cash flow		3,200
6	cash flow		3,200
7	cash flow		3,000
8	cash flow		3,000
	NPV	$2,936	$4,253
	PVIFA	2.5887*	3.8372**
	AEB	$1,134	$1,108

* Four years at 20 per cent.

** Eight years at 20 per cent.

The NPVs tell us to select the larger machine whereas the correct decision, using the AEB, is the smaller machine, as we are $26 ($1,134 − $1,108) better off each year.

Concept questions

8.5a *Under what circumstances do we have to worry about unequal economic lives? How do you interpret the AEC?*

8.5b *In setting a bid price, we used a zero NPV as our benchmark. Explain why this is appropriate.*

8.5c *What is the difference between AEC and AEB?*

International Articles!

To read more on capital investment decisions and to see current international articles, just go to www.mhhe.com/au/ross3e and click on *PowerWeb Articles* for this chapter.

■ 8.6 ■ Summary and conclusions

This chapter described how to go about putting together a discounted cash flow analysis. In it, we covered:

1 The identification of relevant project cash flows. We discussed project cash flows and described how to handle some issues that often come up, including sunk costs, opportunity costs, financing costs and erosion.

2 Preparing and using projected cash flows.

3 The role of depreciation in projects' cash flows. We also went over the calculation of depreciation expense under current tax law.

4 Some special cases in using discounted cash flow analysis. Here we looked at two special issues: how to go about setting a bid price, and the unequal lives problem.

The discounted cash flow analysis we have covered here is a standard tool in the business world. It is a very powerful tool, so care should be taken in its use. The most important thing is to get the cash flows identified in a way that makes economic sense. This chapter gives you a good start on learning to do this.

Key terms

Annual equivalent cost (AEC) *271*   Incremental cash flows *252*   Stand-alone principle *252*
Erosion *253*   Opportunity cost *253*   Sunk cost *253*

Suggested reading

For more on the capital budgeting decision, see:

Bierman, H. Jr and Smidt, S. *The Capital Budgeting Decision: Economic Analysis of Investment Projects*, 8th edn, Macmillan Company, New York, 1993.

Endnotes

1 Economists sometimes use the acronym 'TINSTAAFL', which is short for 'there is no such thing as a free lunch', to describe the fact that only very rarely is something truly free. If the asset in question is unique, then the opportunity cost might be higher because there might be other valuable projects we could undertake that would use it. However, if the asset in question is of a type that is routinely bought and sold (a used car maybe), then the opportunity cost is always the going market price.

2 From 1 July 2001, the uniform capital allowance system (UCA) applies to most depreciating assets. Under the UCA, deductions for the cost of a depreciating asset are based on the decline in value of the asset.

3 We are guilty of an inconsistency here. When we calculated the NPV and IRR, we assumed that the cash flows occurred at year end. When we calculated the payback, we assumed that the cash flows occurred uniformly through the year.

4 Nominal rate = Real rate + Inflation rate + Cross-product
     = 10% + 7% + 10% × 7%
     = 17.7%

Chapter review problems and self-test

8.1 · Capital budgeting for project X

Based on the following information for project X, should we undertake the venture? To answer, use the three-stepped approach. Calculate taxable income and then the change in the tax payment caused by undertaking the project. All cash flows will need to be identified and finally the total cash flow will be discounted at the appropriate rate of 20 per cent. Use a 30 per cent tax rate throughout and assume that tax is paid in the year income is earned. For help, look back at our earlier examples.

Project X is a new type of audiophile-grade stereo amplifier. We think we can sell 500 units per year at a price of $10,000 each. Variable costs per amplifier will be 70 per cent of revenue, and the product should have a 4-year life. We require a 20 per cent return on new products such as this one.

Fixed costs for the project will be $610,000 per year. Further, we will need to invest a total of $1,100,000 in manufacturing equipment. This equipment may be depreciated at 15 per cent diminishing value. In 4 years, the equipment will be worth half of what we paid for it.

8.2 · Spending money to save money?

We're contemplating a new, mechanised welding system to replace our current manual system. It will cost $600,000 to get the new system. The cost will be depreciated straight-line to zero over its 4-year expected life. The system will actually be worth $100,000 at the end of four years.

We think the new system will save us $180,000 per year pre-tax in labour costs. The tax rate is 30 per cent. What are the NPV and return on buying the new system? The required return is 15 per cent.

Answers to self-test problems

8.1

	Year 0	Year 1	Year 2	Year 3	Year 4
Step 1					
Calculation of the tax effect					
Sales		5,000,000	5,000,000	5,000,000	5,000,000
Variable costs		(3,500,000)	(3,500,000)	(3,500,000)	(3,500,000)
Fixed costs		(610,000)	(610,000)	(610,000)	(610,000)
Depreciation		(165,000)	(140,250)	(119,213)	(101,331)
Loss on sale					(24,207)
Taxable income		725,000	749,750	770,788	764,463
Step 2					
Calculation of cash flows					
Tax paid		(217,500)	(224,925)	(231,236)	(229,339)
Annual benefits		5,000,000	5,000,000	5,000,000	5,000,000
Variable costs		(3,500,000)	(3,500,000)	(3,500,000)	(3,500,000)
Fixed costs		(610,000)	(610,000)	(610,000)	(610,000)
Salvage					550,000
Outlay	(1,100,000)				
Cash flow	(1,100,000)	672,500	665,075	658,764	1,210,661
Step 3					
Discounting					
Discount factor	1	0.8333	0.6944	0.5787	0.4823
Discounted cash flows	(1,100,000)	560,417	461,858	381,229	583,845
NPV	$887,348				

To develop the cash flow, we need to calculate the depreciation for each of the 4 years. The relevant rate is 15 per cent and the amount of depreciation and book values for the first 4 years are:

Cost	$1,100,000
Depreciation year 1	165,000
Book value year 1	935,000
Depreciation year 2	140,250
Book value year 2	794,750
Depreciation year 3	119,213
Book value year 3	675,537
Depreciation year 4	101,331
Book value year 4	574,207

There is a small rounding error of $1 because we are working in whole dollars. The equipment is sold for $550,000, which is less than the book value of $574,207. The loss on disposal is $24,207. Finally, we have to invest $1,100,000 to get started.

When we combine all this information, the projected cash flows for project X are:

Year 0	Year 1	Year 2	Year 3	Year 4
(1,100,000)	672,500	665,075	658,764	1,210,661

With these cash flows, the NPV at 20% is:

$$NPV = -\$1,100,000 + \$672,500/1.2 + \$665,075/1.2^2 + \$658,764/1.2^3 + \$1,210,661/1.2^4$$
$$= \$887,348$$

So this project appears quite profitable.

8.2

	Year 0	Year 1	Year 2	Year 3	Year 4
Step 1					
Calculation of the tax effect					
Labour savings		180,000	180,000	180,000	180,000
Depreciation		(150,000)	(150,000)	(150,000)	(150,000)
Gain on sale					100,000
Taxable income		30,000	30,000	30,000	130,000
Step 2					
Calculation of cash flows					
Tax paid		(9,000)	(9,000)	(9,000)	(39,000)
Labour savings		180,000	180,000	180,000	180,000
Salvage					100,000
Outlay	(600,000)				
Cash flow	(600,000)	171,000	171,000	171,000	241,000
Step 3					
Discounting					
Discount factor	1	0.8696	0.7561	0.6575	0.5718
Discounted cash flows	(600,000)	148,702	129,293	112,433	137,804
NPV	($71,768)				

You can see that the NPV is –$71,768, and the return on the new welding system is less than 15 per cent. The project does not appear to be profitable.

Questions and problems

1 · Calculating net profit

a   If a proposed new investment is undertaken by the New Frontier Company, it is expected to produce projected sales in year 5 of $225,000. Variable costs are 60 per cent of sales, and fixed costs are $18,000. Depreciation for the year will be $27,000. Prepare a projected Statement of Financial Performance assuming a 30 per cent tax rate.

b   Assume the sales and costs other than depreciation are cash. What cash flow would be included in a capital investment analysis?

c   Why is the answer to (b) different to the answer in (a)?

2 · Calculating cash flows

Consider the following Statement of Financial Performance:

Sales	$144,600
Costs	84,780
Depreciation	15,000
Taxes (30%)	?
Net profit	?

Fill in the missing numbers and then calculate the yearly cash flow assuming that tax is paid in the year of income. What is the tax benefit provided by the depreciation tax deduction (i.e. the tax shield)?

3 · Calculating cash flows

Proposed new home delivery services have projected sales of $131,956, costs of $92,875, and vehicle depreciation of $35,310. The tax rate is 30 per cent. Calculate the cash flow assuming that tax is paid in the year of income.

4 · Calculating depreciation

Club Comfort Cabins Ltd has recently purchased a piece of gambling equipment for $168,000. It can be depreciated at 15 per cent prime cost. Calculate the annual depreciation deduction and end of year book values using both the prime cost method and the diminishing balance method. The equipment is sold at the end of its 5-year life for $45,000.

5 · Depreciation

The new computer system of Tours Ltd cost $80,000. Tours will outgrow it in three years. When Tours sells it, it will probably only get 20 per cent of the purchase price. The computer will be depreciated at 25 per cent prime cost. Calculate the depreciation and book values for the three years. What will be the after-tax proceeds from the sale? Assume a 30 per cent tax rate.

6 · NPV application

A new photocopier costs $14,000. This cost will be depreciated prime cost to zero over 5 years. The photocopier will actually be worthless in 5 years. The new photocopier would save us $5,000 per year before taxes and operating costs. If we require a 10 per cent return, what is the NPV of the purchase? Assume a tax rate of 30 per cent and that tax is paid in the year of income.

7 · NPV application

In the previous question, suppose that an old photocopier was purchased 3 years ago for $4,800 and that it is being depreciated prime cost to zero over 8 years. If the old photocopier were to be sold today, it is reasonable to expect a salvage value of $2,000. Further, suppose that the new photocopier will actually be worth $2,000 in 5 years. What is the new NPV? Assume that tax is paid in the year after the year of income.

8 · NPV and depreciation

A new security process monitor costs $140,000. This monitor will be depreciated at a diminishing value rate of $33\frac{1}{3}$ per cent. The monitor will be worthless in 5 years but it will save costs of $50,000 per year before taxes. The required rate of return is 10 per cent and the rate of tax is 30 per cent. What is the NPV of the purchase if the tax is paid in the year the income is earned?

9 · Identifying relevant costs

Rick Bundy and Ed Carlton are considering building a new bottling plant to meet expected future demand for their new line of tropical ales. They are considering putting it on a plot of land they have owned for three years. They are in the process of analysing the idea and comparing it to some others. Bundy says, 'Ed, when we do this analysis, we should put in an amount for the cost of the land equal to what we paid for it. After all, it did cost us a pretty penny.' Carlton retorts, 'No, I don't care how much it cost—we have already paid for it. It is what they call a sunk cost. The cost of the land shouldn't be considered.' What would you say to Bundy and Carlton?

10 · NPV applications

Fire Alert Ltd believes it can sell 10,000 home smoke detectors per year at $30 apiece. They cost $20 each to manufacture (variable cost). Fixed production costs will run $30,000 per year. The necessary equipment costs $150,000 to buy and will be depreciated prime cost to a zero salvage value over the 5-year life of the project. The actual value will be essentially zero in 5 years. The discount rate is 14 per cent, and the tax rate is 30 per cent. What do you think of the proposal?

11 · Cash flows and IRR

Car Parts are contemplating the purchase of a $900,000 computer-based customer order management system. The system will be depreciated prime cost to zero over its 5-year life. It will be worth $330,000 at that time. The firm would save $500,000 before taxes per year in order processing costs. The relevant tax rate is 30 per cent and tax is paid in the year of income. What is the DCF return on this investment? And the net present value if the interest rate is 32% or 40%?

12 · Calculating AEC

You are evaluating 2 different sound mixers. The Jazzmaster costs $45,000, has a 3-year life, and costs $5,000 per year to operate. The Discomaster costs $65,000, has a 5-year life, and costs $4,000 per year to operate. The relevant discount rate is 12 per cent. Ignoring depreciation and taxes, compute the AEC for both. Which do we prefer?

13 · AEC

In the previous question, assume that prime cost (reflecting their respective lives) is used for both. Furthermore, each has a salvage value of $10,000. The relevant tax rate is 30 per cent and tax is paid in the year of income. Compute the AEC for both. Which is preferred now?

14 · AEC

Adder Ltd is looking at producing electronic chips for financial calculators. The company is considering alternative production methods. The costs and lives associated with each are:

Year	Method 1	Method 2
0	$90,000	$80,000
1	2,000	8,000
2	2,000	8,000
3	2,000	8,000
4		8,000

Assuming that Adder will not replace the equipment when it wears out, which should it buy? If it is going to replace it, which should it buy ($r = 10\%$)? Ignore depreciation and taxes in answering.

15 · Calculating cash flows and AEC

In the previous question, suppose that all the costs are before taxes and the tax rate is 30 per cent. The equipment used in method 1 will be worth $12,000 in salvage in 3 years. Both will be depreciated prime cost to zero over their respective lives. Method 2 will generate a $16,000 salvage value. Tax is paid in the year of income. What are the AECs in this case? Which is the preferred method?

16 · Cash flows and NPV

Weed Eater Ltd has developed a high-risk new garden-use laser-guided weed search and destroy system. Projected unit sales are as follows:

Year	Unit sales
1	42,400
2	52,000
3	60,800
4	68,800
5	36,800

The new system will be priced to sell at $115 each. The variable cost per unit is $85, and total fixed costs are $55,000 per year. The equipment necessary to begin production will cost a total of $6,500,000. This equipment is mostly industrial machinery and thus can be depreciated at a rate of 9 per cent diminishing value. In 5 years, this equipment will actually be worth about 30 per cent of its cost. The relevant tax rate is 30 per cent, tax is paid in the year of income, and the required return is 20 per cent. Based on these preliminary estimates, what is the NPV of the project?

17 · NPV application

Smallshow Ltd is thinking about replacing an old computer with a new one. The old one cost $50,000; the new one will cost $35,000. The new machine will be depreciated prime cost to zero over its 5-year life. It will probably be worth about $5,000 after 5 years.

The old computer is being depreciated at a rate of $5,000 per year. It will be completely written off in 5 years. If Smallshow does not replace it now, it will have to replace it in 5 years. Smallshow can sell it now for $12,000. In five years, it will probably be worth nothing. The new machine will save $5,000 per year in cooling costs. The tax rate is 30 per cent, tax is paid in the year of income, and the discount rate is 10 per cent. Should Smallshow purchase the new computer?

18 · Calculating required savings

This is a challenge problem. A proposed cost-saving device has an installed cost of $59,400. It can be depreciated at a rate of $33^{1}/_{3}$ per cent prime cost. It will actually function for 5 years, at which time it will have no value. The tax rate is 30 per cent and tax is paid in the year of income.

a   What must the pre-tax cost savings be for us to favour the investment? We require a 10 per cent return. (**Hint**: This one is a variation on the problem of setting a bid price.)

b   Suppose the device will be worth $11,000 in salvage (before taxes). How does this change your answer?

19 · Cash flows and capital budgeting choices

This is a challenge problem. Seals Co. has recently completed a $400,000, 2-year marketing study. Based on the results, Seals has estimated that 10,000 of its new cold rooms could be sold annually over the next 8 years at a price of $9,615 each. Subcontractors would install the cold rooms at a cost per installation of $7,400. Fixed costs to be incurred would be $12 million per year.

Start-up costs include $40 million to build production facilities and $2.4 million in land. The $40 million facility will be depreciated prime cost to zero over the project's life. At the end of the project's life, the facilities (including the land) will be sold for an estimated $8.4 million. The value of the land is not expected to change.

Finally, start-up would also entail fully-deductible expenses of $1.4 million at year zero. Seals is an ongoing, profitable business and pays taxes at a 30 per cent rate in the year of income on all income and gains. Seals uses a 10 per cent discount rate on projects such as this one. Should Seals produce the cold rooms?

20 · Calculating a bid price

This is a challenge problem. Woolie Ltd, a large retailer, has requested a bid for a new point-of-sale credit checkout system. The system would be phased in at a rate of 20 stores per year for 3 years. We can purchase the relevant hardware for $25,000 per installation. The labour and material cost to put the system together and install it is about $10,000 per site. We will need to purchase $250,000 worth of specialised equipment. This will be depreciated prime cost to a zero salvage value over 5 years. We will sell it in 3 years, at which time it should be worth about half of what we paid for it. The relevant tax rate is 30 per cent. What price per system should we bid if we require a 16 per cent return on our investment?

21 · Options

A neighbour has offered you an option at $388,996 to purchase additional farmland in 15 years for $1,050,000. If the interest rate is 8 per cent, what does he consider to be the value of the farmland?

CHAPTER 9

Project
analysis and evaluation

Objective

Capital investment decisions focus upon the future so that, apart from the risk of the investment, which is captured in the discount rate, there is uncertainty in relation to the estimates of future cash flows. The previous chapter showed us how to identify and organise the relevant cash flows for capital investment decisions. The task of this chapter is to assess the reliability of the net present value of the proposed project or investment, which we have calculated following the method developed earlier.

We begin by discussing the need for an evaluation of cash flow and NPV estimates. We go on to develop some tools that are useful for doing so. We also examine some additional complications and concerns that can arise in project evaluation.

Introduction ▷ Now we have a look at how firms make their capital budget investment decisions in the real world. Firms are faced with an uncertain future and yet they have to predict what their future benefits will be if they make current investments. They have to estimate the outcomes before they commit funds to current proposals. Forecasts have to be made and allowance has to be made for possible errors in predictions. Firms have to consider whether there will be any restrictions in obtaining the capital for all investments. We now address these issues.

9.1 ▪ Evaluating NPV estimates

As we discussed in Chapter 7, an investment has a positive net present value if its market value exceeds its cost. Such an investment is desirable because it creates value for its owner. The primary problem in identifying such opportunities is that most of the time we cannot actually observe the relevant market value. Instead, we estimate it. Having done so, it is only natural to wonder whether or not our estimates are at least close to the true values. We consider this question next.

The basic problem

Suppose we are working on a preliminary discounted cash flow (DCF) analysis along the lines we described in the previous chapter. We carefully identify the relevant cash flows and avoid such things as sunk costs. We add back any depreciation; we account for possible erosion; and we pay attention to opportunity costs. Finally, we double-check our calculations and, when all is said and done, the bottom line is that the estimated NPV is positive.

Now what? Do we stop here and move on to the next proposal? Probably not. The fact that the estimated NPV is positive is definitely a good sign but, more than anything, this tells us that we need to take a closer look.

If you think about it, there are two circumstances under which a DCF analysis could lead us to conclude that a project has a positive NPV. The first possibility is that the project really does have a positive NPV. That is the good news. The bad news is the second possibility: a project may appear to have a positive NPV because our estimate is inaccurate.

Notice that we could also err in the opposite way. If we conclude that a project has a negative NPV when the true NPV is positive, then we lose a valuable opportunity.

Projected versus actual cash flows

There is a somewhat subtle point we need to make here. When we say something like: 'The projected cash flow in year 4 is $700', what exactly do we mean? Does this mean that we think the cash flow will actually be $700? Not really. It could happen, of course, but we would be surprised to see it turn out exactly that way. The reason is that the $700 projection is based only on what we know today. Almost anything could happen between now and then to change that cash flow.

Loosely speaking, we really mean that, if we took all the possible cash flows that could occur in four years and averaged them, the result would be $700. We may have the following expectations:

Chance of the cash flow occurring	Cash flow	Expected value
5%	$1,200	$ 60
8%	1,000	80
15%	900	135
20%	800	160
25%	600	150
14%	500	70
8%	400	32
5%	260	13
100%	**Expected cash flow**	**$700**

So, we don't really expect a projected cash flow to be exactly right in any one case. What we do expect is that, if we evaluate a large number of projects, our projections are right on the average.

Forecasting risk

The key inputs into a DCF analysis are projected future cash flows. If these projections are seriously in error, then we have a classic GIGO (garbage-in, garbage-out) system. In this case, no matter how carefully we arrange the numbers and manipulate them, the resulting answer can still be grossly misleading. This is the danger in using a relatively sophisticated technique like DCF. It is sometimes easy to get caught up in number crunching and forget the underlying 'nuts and bolts' economic reality.

The possibility that we make a bad decision because of errors in the projected cash flows is called **forecasting risk** (or estimation risk). Because of forecasting risk, there is the danger that we think a project has a positive NPV when it really does not. How is this possible? It happens if we are overly optimistic about the future and, as a result, our projected cash flows don't realistically reflect the possible future cash flows.

> **forecasting risk** the possibility that errors in projected cash flows lead to incorrect decisions

So far, we have not explicitly considered what to do about the possibility of errors in our forecasts, so one of our goals in this chapter is to develop some tools that are useful in identifying areas where potential errors exist and where they might be especially damaging. In one form or another, we will be trying to assess the economic 'reasonableness' of our estimates. We will also be wondering how much damage will be done by errors in those estimates.

Sources of value

The first line of defence against forecasting risk is simply to ask: 'What is it about this investment that leads to a positive NPV?' We should be able to point to something specific as the source of value. For example, if the proposal under consideration involved a new product, then we might ask questions such as: 'Are we certain that our new product is significantly better than that of the competition? Can we truly manufacture at lower cost, or distribute more effectively, or identify undeveloped market niches, or gain control of a market?'

These are just a few of the potential sources of value. There are many others. A key factor to keep in mind is the degree of competition in the market. It is a basic principle of economics that positive NPV investments will be rare in a highly competitive environment. Therefore, proposals that appear to show significant value in the face of stiff competition are particularly troublesome, and the likely reaction of the competition to any innovations must be closely examined.

The point to remember is that in an efficient market, positive NPV investments are probably not all that common, and the number of positive NPV projects is almost certainly limited for any given firm. If we can't articulate some sound economic basis for thinking ahead of time that we have found something special, then the conclusion that our project has a positive NPV should be viewed with some suspicion.

Concept questions

9.1a *What is forecasting risk? Why is it a concern for the financial manager?*

9.1b *What are some potential sources of value in a new project?*

9.2 Scenario and other 'what if' analysis

Our basic approach to evaluating cash flow and NPV estimates involves asking 'what if' questions. Accordingly, we discuss some organised ways of going about a 'what if' analysis. Our goal in doing so is to assess the degree of forecasting risk and to identify those components that are the most critical to the success or failure of an investment.

Getting started

We are investigating a new project. Naturally, the first thing we do is estimate NPV based on our projected cash flows. We will call this the base case. Now, however, we recognise the possibility of error in those cash flow projections. After completing the base case, we thus wish to investigate the impact of different assumptions about the future on our estimates.

One way to organise this investigation is to put an upper and lower bound on the various components of the project. For example, suppose we forecast sales at 100 units per year. We know this estimate may be high or low, but we are relatively certain that it is not off by more than 10 units in either direction. We would thus pick a lower bound of 90 and an upper bound of 110. We go on to assign such bounds to any other cash flow components that we are unsure about.

When we pick these upper and lower bounds, we are not ruling out the possibility that the actual values could be outside this range. What we are saying, again loosely speaking, is that it is unlikely that the true average (as opposed to our estimated average) of the possible values is outside this range.

An example is useful to illustrate the idea here. The project under consideration costs $200,000, has a five-year life, and no salvage value. Depreciation is straight-line to a zero salvage. The required return is 12 per cent, and the tax rate is 30 per cent. In addition, we have compiled the following information:

	Base case	Lower bound	Upper bound
Unit sales	6,000	5,500	6,500
Price per unit	$80	$75	$85
Variable cost per unit	$60	$58	$62
Fixed costs per year	$50,000	$45,000	$55,000

With this information, we can calculate the base case NPV by first calculating net profit:

Sales	$480,000
Variable costs	360,000
Fixed costs	50,000
Depreciation	40,000
EBIT	30,000
Taxes (30%)	9,000
Net profit	$ 21,000

Cash flow is thus $30,000 + $40,000 − $9,000 = $61,000 per year. At 12 per cent, the five-year annuity factor is 3.6048, so the base case NPV is:

$$\text{Base case NPV} = -\$200,000 + \$61,000 \times 3.6048$$
$$= \$19,893$$

Thus, the project looks good so far.

To calculate the IRR we have:

$$\$200,000 = \$61,000 \times \text{PVIFA}(5,x\%)$$
$$3.2786 = \text{PVIFA}(5,x\%)$$

From Table A.3 we see that the factor for 5 years at 16% is 3.2743, so the IRR is close to 16%.

Scenario analysis

The basic form of 'what if' analysis is called **scenario analysis**. What we do is investigate what happens to our NPV estimate when we start asking questions like: 'What if unit sales realistically should be projected at 5,500 units instead of 6,000?'

scenario analysis
the determination of what happens to NPV estimates when we ask 'what if' questions

Once we start looking at alternative scenarios, we might find that most of the plausible ones result in positive NPVs. In this case, we have some confidence in proceeding with the project. If a substantial percentage of the scenarios looks bad, then the degree of forecasting risk is high and further investigation is in order.

There are a number of possible scenarios we could consider. A good place to start is the worst-case scenario. This will tell us the minimum NPV of the project. If this were positive, we would be in good shape. While we are at it, we will go ahead and determine the other extreme, the best case. This puts an upper bound on our NPV.

To get the worst case, we assign the least favourable value to each item. This means low values for inflows and high values for outflows. We do the reverse for the best case. For our project, these values would be:

	Worst case	Best case
Unit sales	5,500	6,500
Price per unit	$ 75	$ 85
Variable cost per unit	$ 62	$ 58
Fixed costs per year	$ 55,000	$ 45,000
Sales	$412,500	$552,500
Variable costs	341,000	377,000
Fixed costs	55,000	45,000
Depreciation	40,000	40,000
EBIT	(23,500)	90,500
Taxes (30%)	7,050	(27,150)
Net profit	($16,450)	$ 63,350
Yearly cash flow	23,550	103,350
NPV	(115,107)	172,556
IRR	−15.4%	43.0%

With this information, we can calculate the net profit and cash flows under each scenario (check these for yourself):

Scenario	Net profit	Cash flow	NPV	IRR
Base case	$21,000	61,000	$19,893	16%
Worst case*	−16,450	23,550	−115,107	−15.4%
Best case	63,350	103,350	172,556	43%

* We assume a tax credit in our worst-case scenario.

What we learn is that under the worst scenario, the cash flow is still positive at $23,550. That's good news. The bad news is that the return is −15.4 per cent in this case, and the NPV is −$115,107. Since the project costs $200,000, we stand to lose a little more than half of the original investment under the worst possible scenario. The best case offers an attractive 43 per cent return.

As we have mentioned, there is an unlimited number of different scenarios that we could examine. At a minimum, we might want to investigate two intermediate cases by going halfway between the base amounts and the extreme amounts. This would give us five scenarios in all, including the base case.

Beyond this point, it is hard to know when to stop. As we generate more and more possibilities, we run the risk of 'paralysis of analysis'. The difficulty is that no matter how many scenarios we run, all we can learn are possibilities, some good and some bad. Beyond that, we don't get any guidance as to what to do. Scenario analysis is thus useful in telling us what can happen and in helping us gauge the potential for disaster, but it does not tell us whether or not to take the project.

Sensitivity analysis

THE BASIC IDEA

sensitivity analysis

investigation of what happens to NPV when only one variable is changed

Sensitivity analysis is a variation on scenario analysis that is useful in pinpointing the areas where forecasting risk is especially severe. The basic idea with a sensitivity analysis is to freeze all of the variables except one and then see how sensitive our estimate of NPV is to changes in that one variable. If our NPV estimate turns out to be very sensitive to relatively small changes in the projected value of some component of project cash flow, then the forecasting risk associated with that variable is high.

To illustrate how sensitivity analysis works, we go back to our base case for every item except unit sales. We can then calculate cash flow and NPV using the largest and smallest unit sales figures.

	Base case	Worst case	Best case
Unit sales	6,000	5,500	6,500
Price per unit	$ 80	$ 80	$ 80
Variable cost per unit	$ 60	$ 60	$ 60
Fixed costs per year	$ 50,000	$ 50,000	$ 50,000
Sales	$480,000	$440,000	$520,000
Variable costs	360,000	330,000	390,000
Fixed costs	50,000	50,000	50,000
Depreciation	40,000	40,000	40,000
EBIT	30,000	20,000	40,000
Taxes (30%)	(9,000)	(6,000)	(12,000)
Net profit	$ 21,000	$ 14,000	$ 28,000
Yearly cash flow	61,000	54,000	68,000
NPV	19,893	(5,341)	45,126
IRR	15.9%	10.9%	20.8%

By way of comparison, we now freeze everything except fixed costs and repeat the analysis:

	Base case	Worst case	Best case
Unit sales	6,000	6,000	6,000
Price per unit	$ 80	$ 80	$ 80
Variable cost per unit	$ 60	$ 60	$ 60
Fixed costs per year	$ 50,000	$ 55,000	$ 45,000
Sales	$480,000	$480,000	$480,000
Variable costs	360,000	360,000	360,000
Fixed costs	50,000	55,000	45,000
Depreciation	40,000	40,000	40,000
EBIT	30,000	25,000	35,000
Taxes (30%)	(9,000)	(7,500)	(10,500)
Net profit	$ 21,000	$ 17,500	$ 24,500
Yearly cash flow	61,000	57,500	64,500
NPV	19,893	7,276	32,510
IRR	15.9%	13.5%	18.4%

What we see here is that, given our ranges, the estimated NPV of this project is more sensitive to projected unit sales than it is to projected fixed costs.

The results of our sensitivity analysis for unit sales can be illustrated graphically as in Figure 9.1. Here we place NPV on the vertical axis and unit sales on the horizontal axis. When we plot the combinations of unit sales versus NPV, we see that all possible combinations fall on a straight line. The steeper the resulting line is, the greater the sensitivity of the estimated NPV to the projected value of the variable being investigated.

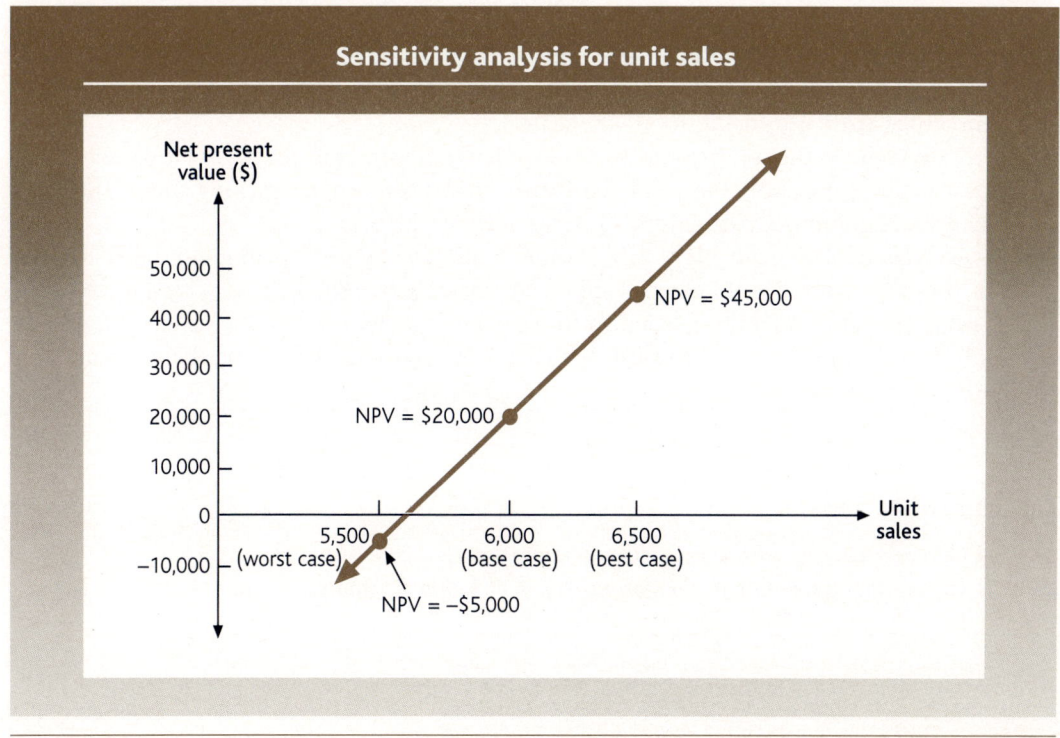

Sensitivity analysis for unit sales

FIGURE 9.1

As we have illustrated, sensitivity analysis is useful in pinpointing those variables that deserve the most attention. If we find that our estimated NPV is especially sensitive to a variable that is difficult to forecast (such as unit sales), then the degree of forecasting risk is high. We might decide that further market research would be a good idea in this case.

Because sensitivity analysis is a form of scenario analysis, it suffers from the same drawbacks. Scenario analysis is useful for pointing out where forecasting errors will do the most damage, but it does not tell us what to do about possible errors.

Simulation analysis

simulation analysis
a combination of scenario and sensitivity analyses

Scenario analysis and sensitivity analysis are widely used. With scenario analysis, we let all the different variables change, but we only let them take on a small number of values. With sensitivity analysis, we only let one variable change, but we let it take on a large number of values. If we combine the two approaches, the result is a crude form of **simulation analysis**.

If we want to let all the items vary at the same time, we have to consider a very large number of scenarios, and computer assistance is almost certainly needed. In the simplest case, we start with unit sales and assume that any value in our 5,500 to 6,500 range is equally likely. We start by randomly picking one value (or by instructing a computer to do so). We then randomly pick a price, a variable cost, and so on.

Once we have values for all the relevant components, we calculate an NPV. We repeat this sequence as much as we desire, probably several thousand times. The result is a large number of NPV estimates that we summarise by calculating the average value and some measure of how spread-out the different possibilities are. For example, it would be of some interest to know what percentage of the possible scenarios result in negative estimated NPVs.

Since simulation is an extended form of scenario analysis, it has the same problems. Once we have the results, there is no simple decision rule that tells us what to do. Also, we have described a relatively simple form of simulation. To really do it right, we would have to consider the interrelationships between the different cash flow components. Furthermore, we assumed that the possible values were equally likely to occur. It is probably more realistic to assume that values near the base case are more likely than extreme values, but coming up with the probabilities is difficult, to say the least.

For these reasons, the use of simulation is somewhat limited in practice. However, recent advances in computer software and hardware (and user sophistication) mean that it is becoming more common, particularly for large-scale projects.

We have recalculated the NPV 1,000 times with the help of a program called Crystal Ball. In the program we have allowed unit sales, price per unit, variable cost per unit and fixed costs to vary. Allowing the inputs to vary produced 1,000 NPVs. The NPV distribution is shown opposite. You can see that there is a less than 50 per cent chance that the NPV will be positive.

Concept questions

9.2a *What are scenario, sensitivity and simulation analyses?*
9.2b *What are the drawbacks to the various types of 'what if' analysis?*

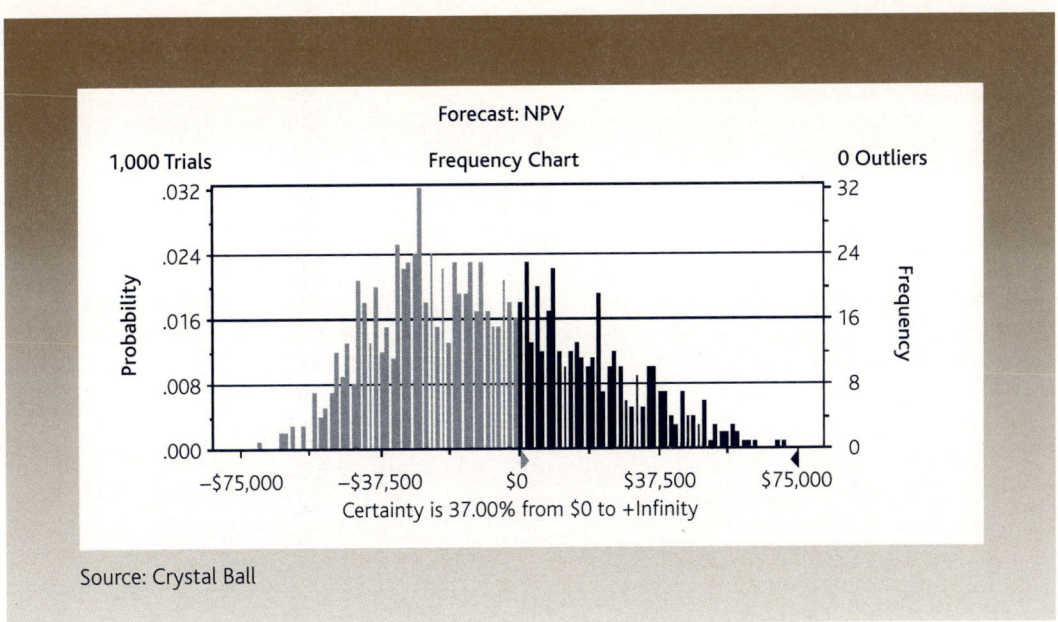

Source: Crystal Ball

Break-even analysis

It will frequently turn out that the crucial variable for a project will be sales volume. If we are thinking of a new product or entering a new market, for example, the hardest thing to forecast accurately is how much we can sell. For this reason, sales volume is frequently analysed more closely than other variables.

Break-even analysis is a popular and commonly used tool for analysing the relationship between sales volume and profitability. There are a variety of different break-even measures, and we have already seen several types. For example, we discussed how the payback period can be interpreted as the length of time until a project breaks even, ignoring time value.

All break-even measures have a similar goal. Loosely speaking, we will always be asking: 'How bad do sales have to get before we actually begin to lose money?' Implicitly, we will also be asking: 'Is it likely that things will get that bad?' To get started on this subject, we first discuss fixed and variable costs.

Fixed and variable costs

In discussing break-even, the difference between fixed and variable costs becomes very important. As a result, we need to be a little more explicit about the difference than we have been so far.

Variable costs

By definition, **variable costs** change as the quantity of output changes, and they are zero when production is zero. For example, direct labour costs and raw material costs are usually considered variable. This makes sense because if we shut down operations tomorrow there will be no future costs for labour or raw materials.

variable costs
costs that change when the quantity of output changes

We will assume that variable costs are a constant amount per unit of output. This simply means that total variable cost is equal to the cost per unit multiplied by the number of units. In other words, the relationship between total variable cost (VC), cost per unit of output (v), and total quantity of output (Q) can be written simply as:

$$\text{Variable cost} = \text{Total quantity of output} \times \text{Cost per unit of output}$$
$$\text{VC} = Q \times v$$

For example, suppose that v is $2 per unit and Q is 1,000 units, what will VC be?

$$\begin{aligned} \text{VC} &= Q \times v \\ &= 1{,}000 \times \$2 \\ &= \$2{,}000 \end{aligned}$$

Similarly, if Q is 5,000 units, then VC will be $5{,}000 \times \$2 = \$10{,}000$. Figure 9.2 illustrates the relationship between output level and variable costs in this case. In Figure 9.2, notice that increasing output by 1 unit results in variable costs rising by $2, so the slope of the line is given by $\$2/1 = \$2$.

FIGURE 9.2

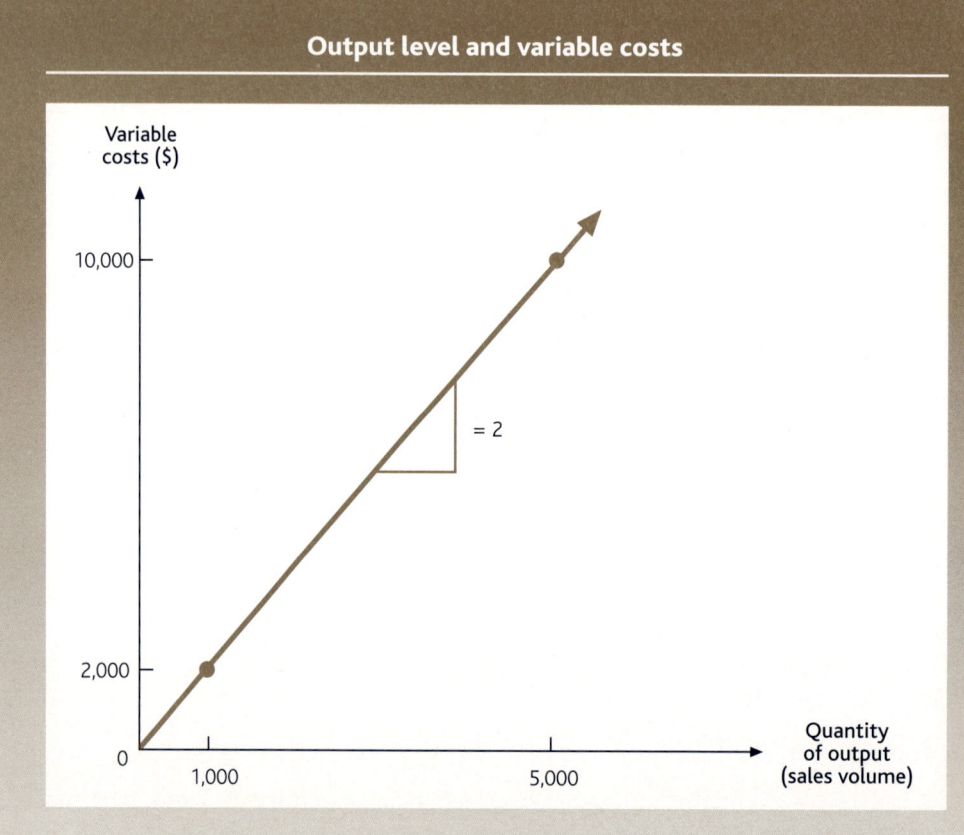

Output level and variable costs

EXAMPLE 9.1 ▪ Variable costs

Biro Ltd is a manufacturer of pens. It has received an order for 5,000 pens, and the company has to decide whether or not to accept the order. From recent experience, the company knows that each pen requires 5 cents in raw materials and 50 cents in direct labour costs. These variable costs are expected to continue in the future. What will Biro's total variable costs be if it accepts the order?

EXAMPLE
9.1

Variable costs (*continued*)

In this case, the cost per unit is 50 cents in labour plus 5 cents in material for a total of 55 cents per unit. At 5,000 units of output, we have:

$$VC = Q \times v$$
$$= 5,000 \times \$0.55$$
$$= \$2,750$$

Therefore, total variable costs will be $2,750.

Fixed costs

Fixed costs, by definition, do not change during a specified period. So, unlike variable costs, they do not depend on the amount of goods or services produced during a period (at least within some range of production). For example, the lease payment on a production facility and the managing director's salary are fixed costs, at least over some period.

Naturally, fixed costs are not fixed forever. They are only fixed during some particular time, say a quarter or a year. Beyond that time, leases can be terminated and executives 'retired'. More to the point, any fixed cost can be modified or eliminated given enough time; so, in the long run, all costs are variable.

Notice that during the time that a cost is fixed, that cost is effectively a sunk cost because we are going to have to pay it no matter what.

fixed costs
costs that do not change when the quantity of output changes during a particular time period

Total costs

Total costs (TC) for a given level of output are the sum of variable costs (VC) and fixed costs (FC):

$$TC = VC + FC$$
$$= v \times Q + FC$$

So, for example, if we have a variable cost of $3 per unit and fixed costs of $8,000 per year, our total cost is:

$$TC = \$3 \times Q + \$8,000$$

If we produce 6,000 units, our total production cost would be $3 × 6,000 + $8,000 = $26,000. At other production levels, we have:

Quantity produced	Total variable cost	Fixed cost	Total cost
0	$ 0	$8,000	$ 8,000
1,000	3,000	8,000	11,000
5,000	15,000	8,000	23,000
10,000	30,000	8,000	38,000

By plotting these points in Figure 9.3 (overleaf), we see that a straight line gives the relationship between quantity produced and total cost. In Figure 9.3 notice that total costs are equal to fixed costs when sales are zero. Beyond that point, every one-unit increase in production leads to a $3 increase in total costs, so the slope of the line is 3. In other words, the **marginal or incremental cost** of producing one more unit is $3.

marginal or incremental cost
the change in costs that occurs when there is a small change in output

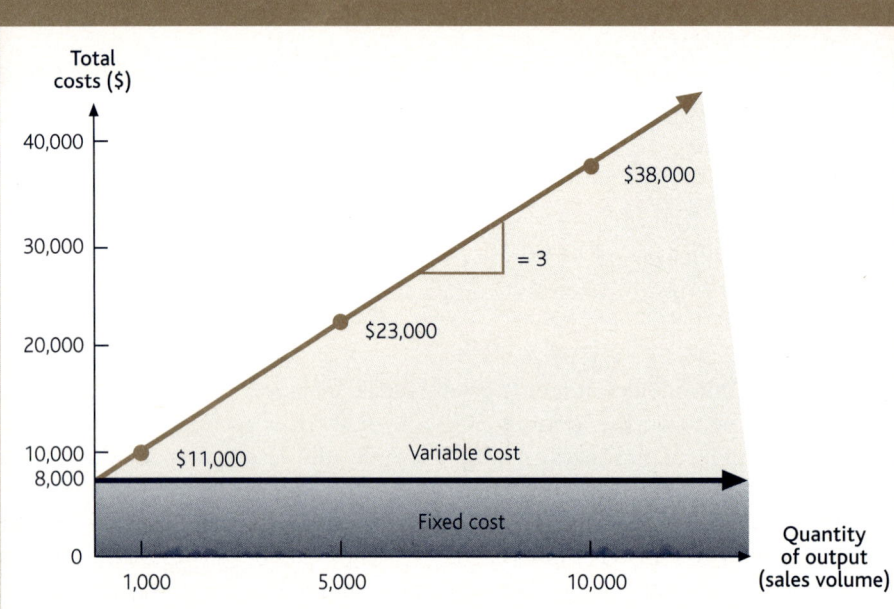

FIGURE 9.3

Output level and total costs

Total costs ($)

40,000

30,000

= 3

20,000 $23,000

$38,000

10,000
8,000 $11,000   Variable cost

Fixed cost

Quantity
of output
(sales volume)

0
          1,000   5,000   10,000

**marginal or
incremental
revenue**

the change in
revenue that
occurs when there
is a small change
in output

EXAMPLE 9.2 — Average cost versus marginal cost

Suppose Biro Ltd has a variable cost per pen of 55 cents. The lease payment on the production facility is $5,000 per month. If Biro produces 100,000 pens per year, what are the total costs of production? What is the average cost per pen?

The fixed costs are $5,000 per month or $60,000 per year. The variable cost is $0.55 per pen, so the total cost for the year assuming that we produce 100,000 pens is:

$$\text{Total cost} = v \times Q + FC$$
$$= \$0.55 \times 100,000 + \$60,000$$
$$= \$115,000$$

The average cost per pen is $115,000/100,000 = $1.15.

Now suppose that Biro has received a special, one-off order for 5,000 pens. Biro has sufficient capacity to manufacture the 5,000 pens on top of the 100,000 already produced, so no additional fixed costs will be incurred. Also, there will be no effect on existing orders. If Biro can get 75 cents per pen for this order, should the order be accepted?

What this boils down to is a very simple proposition. It costs 55 cents to make another pen. Anything we can get for this pen in excess of our 55 cents incremental cost contributes in a positive way toward covering our fixed costs. The 75 cent **marginal or incremental revenue** exceeds the 55 cent marginal cost, so Biro should take the order.

The fixed cost of $60,000 is not relevant to this decision because it is effectively sunk, at least for the current period. For the same reason, the fact that the average cost was $1.15 is irrelevant because this average reflects the fixed cost. As long as producing the extra 5,000 pens truly does not cost anything beyond the 55 cents per pen, then Biro should accept anything over that 55 cents.

Accounting break-even

The most widely used measure of break-even is **accounting break-even**. The accounting break-even point is simply the sales level that results in a zero project net profit.

accounting break-even

the sales level that results in zero project net profit

To determine a project's accounting break-even, we start off with some common sense. Suppose that we retail computer diskettes for $5 each. We can buy diskettes from a wholesale supplier for $3 each. We have accounting expenses of $600 in fixed costs and $300 in depreciation. How many diskettes do we have to sell to break even; that is, for net profit to be zero?

For every diskette we sell, we pick up $5 − $3 = $2 toward covering our other expenses. We have to cover a total of $600 + $300 = $900 in accounting expenses, so we obviously need to sell $900/$2 = 450 diskettes. We can check this by noting that, at a sales level of 450 units, our revenues are $5 × 450 = $2,250 and our variable costs are $3 × 450 = $1,350. The profit and loss account is thus:

Sales	$2,250
Variable costs	1,350
Fixed costs	600
Depreciation	300
EBIT	0
Taxes	0
Net profit	$ 0

Remember, since we are discussing a proposed new project, we do not consider any interest expense in calculating net profit or cash flow from the project. Also, notice that we include depreciation in calculating expenses here, even though depreciation is not a cash outflow. That is why we call it accounting break-even. Finally, notice that when net profit is zero, so are pre-tax profit and, of course, taxes. In accounting terms, our revenues are equal to our costs, so there is no profit to tax.

Figure 9.4 (overleaf) is another way to see what is happening. This figure looks like Figure 9.3 except that we add a line for revenues. As indicated, total revenues are zero when output is zero. Beyond that, each unit sold brings in another $5, so the slope of the revenue line is 5.

From our discussion above, we break even when revenues are equal to total costs. In Figure 9.4 the line for revenues and the line for total cost cross right where output is 450 units. As illustrated, at any level below 450, our accounting profit is negative and, at any level above 450, we have a positive net profit.

Accounting break-even: A closer look

In our numerical example, notice that the break-even level is equal to the sum of fixed costs and depreciation divided by price per unit less variable costs per unit. This is always true. To see why, we recall the following set of abbreviations for the different variables:

$$P = \text{Selling price per unit}$$
$$v = \text{Variable cost per unit}$$
$$Q = \text{Total units sold}$$
$$FC = \text{Fixed costs}$$
$$D = \text{Depreciation}$$
$$t = \text{Tax rate}$$

FIGURE
9.4

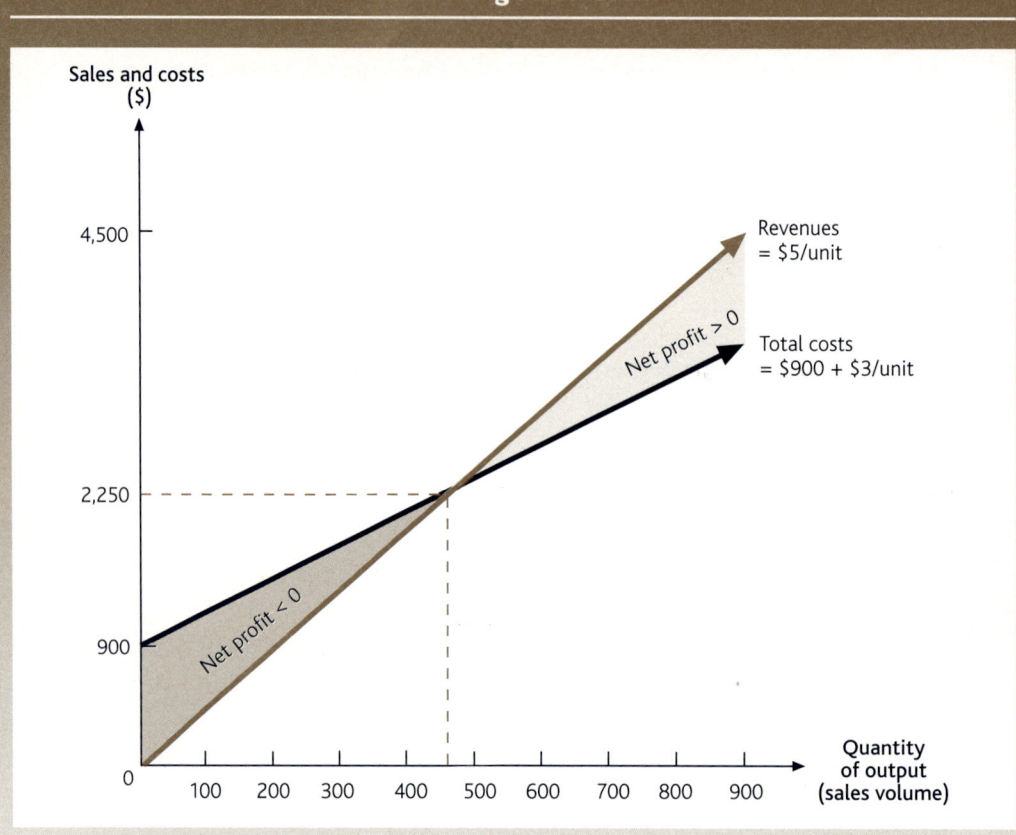

Accounting break-even

Project net profit is given by:

$$\text{Net profit} = (\text{Sales} - \text{Variable costs} - \text{Fixed costs} - \text{Depreciation}) \times (1 - t)$$
$$= (S - \text{VC} - \text{FC} - D) \times (1 - t)$$

From here, it is not difficult to calculate the break-even point. If we set net profit equal to zero, we get:

$$\text{Net profit} = 0 = (S - \text{VC} - \text{FC} - D) \times (1 - t)$$

Divide both sides by $(1 - t)$ to get:

$$S - \text{VC} - \text{FC} - D = 0$$

As we have seen, this says that, when net profit is zero, so is pre-tax profit. If we recall that $S = P \times Q$ and $\text{VC} = v \times Q$, then we can rearrange this to solve for the break-even level:

$$S - \text{VC} = \text{FC} + D$$
$$P \times Q - v \times Q = \text{FC} + D$$
$$(P - v) \times Q = \text{FC} + D$$
$$Q = (\text{FC} + D)/(P - v) \qquad (9.1)$$

This is the same result we described above.

Uses for the accounting break-even

Why would anyone be interested in knowing the accounting break-even point? To illustrate how it can be useful, suppose that we are a small speciality ice-cream manufacturer with a strictly local distribution. We are thinking about expanding into new markets. Based on the estimated cash flows, we find that the expansion has a positive NPV.

Going back to our discussion of forecasting risk, it is likely that what will make or break our expansion is sales volume. The reason is that, in this case at least, we probably have a fairly good idea of what we can charge for the ice cream. Further, we know relevant production and distribution costs with a fair degree of accuracy since we are already in the business. What we do not know with any real precision is how much ice cream we can sell.

Given the costs and selling price, however, we can immediately calculate the break-even point. Once we have done so, we might find that we need to get 30 per cent of the market just to break even. If we think that this is unlikely to occur because, for example, we only have 10 per cent of our current market, then we know that our forecast is questionable and there is a real possibility that the true NPV is negative. On the other hand, we might find that we already have firm commitments from buyers for about the break-even amount, so we are almost certain that we can sell more. In this case, the forecasting risk is much lower and we have greater confidence in our estimates.

There are several other reasons why knowing the accounting break-even can be useful. First, as we discuss in more detail below, accounting break-even and payback period are very similar measures. Like payback period, accounting break-even is relatively easy to calculate and explain.

Second, managers are often concerned with the contribution a project will make to the firm's total accounting earnings. A project that does not break even in an accounting sense actually reduces total earnings.

Third, a project that just breaks even on an accounting basis loses money in a financial or opportunity cost sense. This is true because we could have earned more by investing elsewhere. Such a project does not lose money in an out-of-pocket sense. As described below, we get back exactly what we put in. For non-economic reasons, such opportunity losses may be easier to live with than out-of-pocket losses.

Concept questions

9.3a *How are fixed costs similar to sunk costs?*
9.3b *What is net profit at the accounting break-even point? What about taxes?*
9.3c *Why might a financial manager be interested in the accounting break-even point?*

9.4 ▪ Operating cash flow, sales volume and break-even

Accounting break-even is one tool that is useful for project analysis. Ultimately, however, we are more interested in cash flow than accounting profit. So, for example, if sales volume is the critical variable, then we need to know more about the relationship between sales volume and cash flow than just the accounting break-even.

Our goal in this section is to illustrate the relationship between operating cash flow and sales volume. We also discuss some other break-even measures. To simplify matters somewhat, we will ignore the effect of taxes. We start off by looking at the relationship between accounting break-even and cash flow.

Accounting break-even and cash flow

Now that we know how to find the accounting break-even, it is natural to wonder what happens with cash flow. To illustrate, suppose that the Newland Sailboat Company is considering whether or not to launch its new Margo-class sailboat. The selling price will be $40,000 per boat. The variable costs will be about half that, or $20,000 per boat, and fixed costs will be $500,000 per year.

The base case

The total investment needed to undertake the project is $3,500,000. This amount will be depreciated straight-line to zero over the five-year life of the equipment and the salvage value is zero. Newland has a 20 per cent required return on new projects.

Based on market surveys and historical experience, Newland projects total sales for the five years at 425 boats, or about 85 boats per year. Ignoring taxes, should this project be launched?

To begin, the operating cash flow at 85 boats per year is:

$$\text{Operating cash flow} = 85 \times (\text{Sales} - \text{Variable cost}) - \text{Fixed cost}$$
$$= 85 \times (\$40,000 - \$20,000) - \$500,000$$
$$= \$1,200,000 \text{ per year}$$

At 20%, the five-year annuity factor is 2.9906, so the NPV is:

$$\text{NPV} = -\$3,500,000 + \$1,200,000 \times 2.9906$$
$$= -\$3,500,000 + \$3,588,720$$
$$= \$88,720$$

In the absence of additional information, the project should be launched.

Calculating the break-even level

To begin looking a little more closely at this project, you might ask a series of questions. For example, how many new boats does Newland need to sell for the project to break even on an accounting basis? If Newland does break even, what will be the annual cash flow from the project? What will be the return on the investment in this case?

Before fixed costs and depreciation are considered, Newland generates $40,000 − $20,000 = $20,000 per boat (this is revenue less variable cost). Depreciation is $3,500,000/5 = $700,000 per year. Fixed costs and depreciation together total $1.2 million, so Newland needs to sell $(FC + D)/(P − v) = \$1.2 \text{ million}/\$20,000 = 60$ boats per year to break even on an accounting basis. This is 25 boats less than projected sales; so, assuming that Newland is confident that its projection is accurate to within, say, 15 boats, it appears likely that the new investment will at least break even on an accounting basis.

To calculate Newland's cash flow in this case, we note that, if 60 boats are sold, net profit will be exactly zero. Recalling that operating cash flow for a project can be written as net profit plus depreciation (the bottom-up definition), the operating cash flow is obviously equal to the depreciation, or $700,000 in this case. The internal rate of return would be exactly zero (why?).

Payback and break-even

As our example illustrates, whenever a project breaks even on an accounting basis, the cash flow for that period will be equal to the depreciation. This result makes perfect accounting sense. For example, suppose we invest $100,000 in a five-year project. The depreciation is straight-line to a zero salvage, or $20,000 per year. If the project exactly breaks even every period, then the cash flow will be $20,000 per period.

The sum of the cash flows for the life of this project is 5 × $20,000 = $100,000, the original investment. What this shows is that a project's payback period is exactly equal to its life if the project breaks even every period. Similarly, a project that does better than break even has a payback that is shorter than the life of the project and has a positive rate of return.

The bad news is that a project that just breaks even on an accounting basis has a negative NPV and a zero return. For our sailboat project, the fact that we will almost surely break even on an accounting basis is partially comforting since our 'downside' risk (our potential loss) is limited, but we still don't know if the project is truly profitable. More work is needed.

Sales volume and operating cash flow

At this point, we can generalise our example and introduce some other break-even measures. From our discussion just above, we know that, ignoring taxes, a project's operating cash flow (OCF) can be written simply as EBIT plus depreciation:

$$OCF = [(P - v) \times Q - FC - D] + D \qquad (9.2)$$
$$= (P - v) \times Q - FC$$

For the Newland sailboat project, the general relationship (in thousands of dollars) between operating cash flow and sales volume is thus:

$$OCF = (P - v) \times Q - FC$$
$$= (\$40 - 20) \times Q - \$500$$
$$= -\$500 + \$20 \times Q$$

What this tells us is that the relationship between operating cash flow and sales volume is given by a straight line with a slope of $20 and a y-intercept of −$500. If we calculate some different values, we get:

Quantity sold	Operating cash flow
0	−$500
15	−200
30	100
50	500
75	1,000

These points are plotted in Figure 9.5 (overleaf). In Figure 9.5, we have indicated three different break-even points. We discuss these next.

Cash flow, accounting, and financial break-even points

We know from the discussion above that the relationship between operating cash flow and sales volume (ignoring taxes) is:

$$OCF = (P - v) \times Q - FC$$

If we rearrange this and solve it for Q, we get:

$$Q = (FC + OCF)/(P - v) \qquad (9.3)$$

This tells us what sales volume (Q) is necessary to achieve any given OCF, so this result is more general than the accounting break-even. We use it to find the various break-even points in Figure 9.5.

FIGURE 9.5

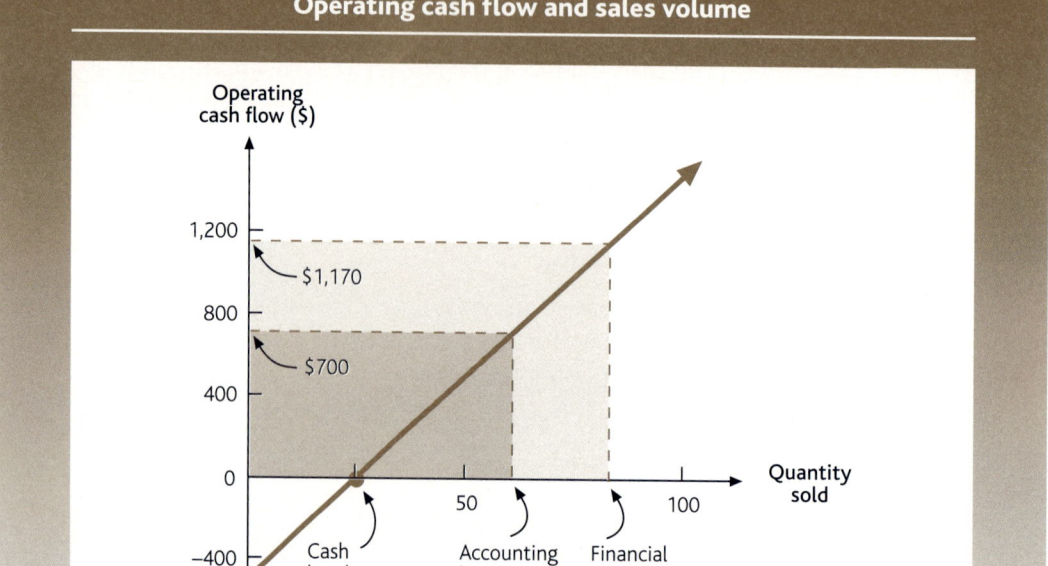

Operating cash flow and sales volume

Accounting break-even revisited

Looking at Figure 9.5, suppose operating cash flow was equal to depreciation (*D*). Recall that this corresponds to our break-even point on an accounting basis. To find the sales amount, we substitute the $700 depreciation amount for OCF in our general expression:

$$Q = (FC + OCF)/(P - v)$$
$$= (\$500 + \$700)/(\$20)$$
$$= 60$$

This is the same quantity we had before.

Cash break-even

We have seen that a project that breaks even on an accounting basis has a net profit of zero, but it still has a positive cash flow. At some sales level below the accounting break-even, the operating cash flow actually goes negative. This is a particularly unpleasant occurrence. If it happens, we actually have to supply additional cash to the project just to keep it afloat.

cash break-even
the sales level where operating cash flow is equal to zero

To calculate the **cash break-even** (the point where operating cash flow is equal to zero), we put in a zero for OCF:

$$Q = (FC + 0)/(P - v)$$
$$= \$500/\$20$$
$$= 25$$

Newland must therefore sell 25 boats to cover the $500 in fixed costs. As we show in Figure 9.5, this point occurs right where the operating cash flow line crosses the horizontal axis.

Notice that a project that just breaks even on a cash flow basis can cover its own fixed operating costs, but that is all. It never pays back anything, so the original investment is a complete loss (the IRR is −100%).

Financial break-even

The last case we consider is **financial break-even**, the sales level that results in a zero NPV. To the financial manager, this is the most interesting case. What we do is first determine what operating cash flow has to be for the NPV to be zero. We then use this amount to determine the sales volume.

financial break-even
the sales level that results in a zero NPV

To illustrate, recall that Newland requires a 20 per cent return on its $3,500 (in thousands) investment. How many sailboats does Newland have to sell to break even once we account for the 20 per cent per year opportunity cost?

The sailboat project has a five-year life. The project has a zero NPV when the present value of the operating cash flow equals the $3,500 investment. Since the cash flow is the same each year, we can solve for the unknown amount by viewing it as an ordinary annuity. The five-year annuity factor at 20 per cent is 2.9906, and the OCF can be determined as follows:

$$\$3,500 = OCF \times 2.9906$$
$$OCF = \$3,500/2.9906$$
$$= \$1,170$$

Newland thus needs an operating cash flow of $1,170 each year to break even. We can now plug this OCF into the equation for sales volume:

$$Q = (\$500 + \$1,170)/\$20$$
$$= 83.5$$

So Newland needs to sell about 84 boats per year. This is not good news.

As indicated in Figure 9.5, the financial break-even is substantially higher than the accounting break-even point. This will often be the case. Moreover, what we have discovered is that the sailboat project has a substantial degree of forecasting risk. We project sales of 85 boats per year, but it takes 84 just to earn our required return.

Overall, it seems unlikely that the Newland sailboat project would fail to break even on an accounting basis. However, there appears to be a very good chance that the true NPV is negative. This illustrates the danger in just looking at the accounting break-even.

What should Newland do? Is the new project all wet? The decision at this point is essentially a managerial issue—a judgment call. The crucial questions are:

1 How much confidence do we have in our projections?
2 How important is the project to the future of the company?
3 How badly will the company be hurt if sales do turn out low? What options are available to the company in this case?

We will consider questions such as these in a later section.

Concept questions

9.4a *If a project breaks even on an accounting basis, what is its operating cash flow?*
9.4b *If a project breaks even on a cash basis, what is its operating cash flow?*
9.4c *If a project breaks even on a financial basis, what do you know about its discounted payback?*

■ 9.5 ■ Operating leverage

We have discussed how to calculate and interpret various measures of break-even for a proposed project. What we have not explicitly discussed is what determines these points and how they might be changed. We now turn to this subject.

operating leverage

the degree to which a firm or project relies on fixed costs

degree of operating leverage

the percentage change in operating cash flow relative to the percentage change in quantity sold

The basic idea

Operating leverage is the degree to which a project or firm is committed to fixed production costs. A firm with low operating leverage will have low fixed costs compared to a firm with high operating leverage. Generally speaking, projects with a relatively heavy investment in plant and equipment will have a relatively high **degree of operating leverage**. Such projects are said to be capital intensive.

Whenever we are thinking about a new venture, there will normally be alternative ways of producing and delivering the product. For example, Newland Company can purchase the necessary equipment and build all the components for its sailboats in-house. Alternatively, some of the work could be farmed out to other firms. The first option involves a greater investment in plant and equipment, greater fixed costs and depreciation and, as a result, a higher degree of operating leverage.

Implications of operating leverage

Regardless of how it is measured, operating leverage has important implications for project evaluation. Fixed costs act like a lever in the sense that a small percentage change in operating revenue can be magnified into a large percentage change in operating cash flow and NPV. This explains why we call it operating 'leverage'.

The higher the degree of operating leverage, the greater the potential danger from forecasting risk. The reason is that relatively small errors in forecasting sales volume can get magnified or 'levered up' into large errors in cash flow projections.

From a managerial perspective, one way of coping with highly uncertain projects is to keep the degree of operating leverage as low as possible. This will generally have the effect of keeping the break-even point (however measured) at its minimum level. We will illustrate this point below, but first we need to discuss how to measure operating leverage.

Measuring operating leverage

One way of measuring operating leverage is to ask: 'If quantity sold rises by 5 per cent, what will be the percentage change in operating cash flow?' In other words, the degree of operating leverage (DOL) is defined such that:

$$\text{Percentage change in OCF} = \text{DOL} \times \text{Percentage change in } Q$$

Based on the relationship between OCF and Q, DOL can be written as[1]

$$\text{DOL} = 1 + \text{FC/OCF} \tag{9.4}$$

The ratio FC/OCF simply measures fixed costs as a percentage of total operating cash flow. Notice that zero fixed costs would result in a DOL of 1, implying that changes in quantity sold would show up one for one in operating cash flow. In other words, no magnification or leverage effect would exist.

To illustrate this measure of operating leverage, we go back to the Newland sailboat project. Fixed costs were $500 and $(P - v)$ was $20, so OCF was:

$$\text{OCF} = -\$500 + \$20 \times Q$$

Suppose Q is currently 50 boats. At this level of output, OCF is –$500 + $1,000 = $500.

If Q rises by 1 unit to 51, then the percentage change in Q is $(51 - 50)/50 = 0.02$, or 2%. OCF rises to $520, a change of $(P - v) = 20. The percentage change in OCF is $($520 - 500)/500 = 0.04$, or 4%. So a 2 per cent increase in the number of boats sold leads to a 4 per cent increase in operating cash flow. The degree of operating leverage must be exactly 2.00. We can check this by noting that:

$$\begin{aligned} DOL &= 1 + FC/OCF \\ &= 1 + \$500/\$500 \\ &= 2 \end{aligned}$$

This verifies our calculations above.

Our formulation of DOL depends on the current output level, Q. However, it can handle changes from the current level of any size, not just one unit. For example, suppose Q rises from 50 to 75, a 50 per cent increase. With DOL equal to 2, operating cash flow should increase by 100 per cent, or exactly double. Does it? The answer is yes, because, at a Q of 75, OCF is:

$$-\$500 + \$20 \times 75 = \$1,000$$

Notice that operating leverage declines as output (Q) rises. For example, at an output level of 75, we have:

$$\begin{aligned} DOL &= 1 + \$500/1,000 \\ &= 1.50 \end{aligned}$$

The reason that DOL declines is that fixed costs, considered as a percentage of operating cash flow, get smaller and smaller, so the leverage effect diminishes.

Operating leverage

EXAMPLE  9.3

The Purr Company currently sells gourmet cat food for $1.20 per can. The variable cost is 80 cents per can, and the packaging and marketing operation has fixed costs of $360,000 per year. Depreciation is $60,000 per year. What is the accounting break-even? Ignoring taxes, what will be the increase in operating cash flow if the quantity sold rises to 10 per cent above the break-even point?

The accounting break-even is $420,000/0.40 = 1,050,000 cans. As we know, the operating cash flow is equal to the $60,000 depreciation at this level of production, so the degree of operating leverage is:

$$\begin{aligned} DOL &= 1 + FC/OCF \\ &= 1 + \$360,000/\$60,000 \\ &= 7 \end{aligned}$$

Given this, a 10 per cent increase in the number of cans of cat food sold will increase operating cash flow by a substantial 70 per cent.

To check this answer, we note that if sales rise by 10 per cent, then the quantity sold will rise to $1,050,000 \times 1.1 = 1,155,000$. Ignoring taxes, the operating cash flow is $1,155,000 \times 0.40 - \$360,000 = \$102,000$. Compared to the $60,000 cash flow we had, this is exactly 70 per cent more: $102,000/$60,000 = 1.70.

Operating leverage and break-even

We illustrate why operating leverage is an important consideration by examining the Newland sailboat project under an alternative scenario. At a Q of 85 boats, the degree of operating leverage for the sailboat project under the original scenario is:

$$
\begin{aligned}
\text{DOL} &= 1 + \text{FC/OCF} \\
&= 1 + \$500/\$1,200 \\
&= 1.42
\end{aligned}
$$

Also, recall that the NPV at a sales level of 85 boats was $88,720, and that the accounting break-even was 60 boats.

An option available to Newland is to subcontract production of the boat hull assemblies. If they do, the necessary investment falls to $3,200,000, and the fixed operating costs fall to $180,000. However, variable costs will rise to $25,000 per boat since subcontracting is more expensive than doing it in-house. Ignoring taxes, evaluate this option.

For practice, see if you agree with the following:

$$
\begin{aligned}
\text{NPV at 20\% (85 units)} &= \$74,707 \\
\text{Accounting break-even} &= 55 \text{ boats} \\
\text{Degree of operating leverage} &= 1.16
\end{aligned}
$$

What has happened? This option results in slightly lower estimated net present value, and the accounting break-even point falls from 60 boats to 55 boats.

Given that this alternative has the lower NPV, is there any reason to consider it further? Maybe there is. The degree of operating leverage is substantially lower in the second case. If we are worried about the possibility of an overly optimistic projection, then we might prefer to subcontract.

There is another reason why we might consider the second arrangement. If sales turned out better than expected, we would always have the option of going ahead and starting to produce in-house at a later date. As a practical matter, it is much easier to increase operating leverage (by purchasing equipment) than to decrease it (by selling off equipment). As we discuss below, one of the drawbacks to discounted cash flow is that it is difficult to explicitly include options of this sort, even though they may be quite important.

Concept questions

9.5a *What is operating leverage?*
9.5b *How is operating leverage measured?*
9.5c *What are the implications of operating leverage for the financial manager?*

9.6 ▪ Additional considerations in capital budgeting

Our final task for this chapter is a brief discussion of two additional considerations in capital budgeting: managerial options and capital rationing. Both of these can be very important in practice but, as we will see, dealing explicitly with either of them is difficult.

Managerial options and capital budgeting

In our capital budgeting analysis thus far, we have more or less ignored the possibility of future managerial actions. Implicitly, we assumed that once a project is launched, its basic features cannot be changed. For this reason, we say that our analysis is static (as opposed to dynamic).

In reality, depending on what actually happens in the future, there will always be ways to modify a project. We will call these opportunities **managerial options**. There are a great number of these options. The way a product is priced, manufactured, advertised and produced can all be changed, and these are just a few of the possibilities. We discuss some of the most important ones in the next few sections.

Contingency planning

The various 'what if' procedures, particularly the break-even measures, in this chapter have another use. We can also view them as primitive ways of exploring the dynamics of a project and investigating managerial options. What we think about in this case are some of the possible futures that could come about and what actions we might take if they do.

For example, we might find that a project fails to break even when sales drop below 10,000 units. This is a fact that is interesting to know, but the more important thing is to then go on and ask: 'What actions are we going to take if this actually occurs?' This is called **contingency planning**, and it amounts to an investigation of some of the managerial options implicit in a project.

There is no limit to the number of possible futures or contingencies that we could investigate. However, there are some broad classes, and we consider these next.

The option to expand

One particularly important option that we have not explicitly addressed is the option to expand. If we truly find a positive NPV project, then there is an obvious consideration. Can we expand the project or repeat it to get an even larger NPV? Our static analysis implicitly assumes that the scale of the project is fixed.

For example, if the sales demand for a particular product were to greatly exceed expectations, we might investigate increasing production. If this is not feasible for some reason, then we could always increase cash flow by raising the price. Either way, the potential cash flow is higher than we have indicated because we have implicitly assumed that no expansion of price increase is possible. Overall, because we ignore the option to expand in our analysis, we underestimate NPV (all other things being equal).

The option to abandon

At the other extreme, the option to scale back or even abandon a project is also quite valuable. For example, if a project does not break even on a cash flow basis, then it can't even cover its own expenses. We would be better off if we just abandoned it. Our DCF analysis implicitly assumes that we would keep operating even in this case.

In reality, if sales demand were significantly below expectations, we might be able to sell off some capacity or put it to another use. Maybe the product or service could be redesigned or otherwise improved. Regardless of the specifics, we once again underestimate NPV if we assume that the project must last for some fixed number of years, no matter what happens in the future.

The option to wait

Implicitly, we have treated proposed investments as if they were 'go or no-go' decisions. Actually, there is a third possibility. The project can be postponed, perhaps in hope of more favourable conditions. We call this the option to wait.

For example, suppose an investment costs $120 and has a perpetual cash flow of $10 per year. If the discount rate is 10 per cent, then the NPV is $10/0.10 − $120 = −$20, so the project should not be undertaken now. However, this does not mean that we should forget about the project forever, because in the next period, the appropriate discount rate could be different. If it fell to, say, 5 per cent, then the NPV would be $10/0.05 − $120 = $80, and we would take it.

More generally, as long as there is some possible future scenario under which a project has a positive NPV, then the option to wait is valuable.

Options in capital budgeting: An example

Suppose we are examining a new project. To keep things relatively simple, we expect to sell 100 units per year at $1 net cash flow apiece into perpetuity. We thus expect the cash flow will be $100 per year.

In one year, we will know more about the project. In particular, we will have a better idea of whether it is successful or not. If it looks like a long-run success, the expected sales will be revised upwards to 150 units per year. If it does not, the expected sales will be revised downward to 50 units per year.

Success and failure are equally likely. Notice that, since there is an even chance of selling 50 or 150 units, the expected sales are still 100 units as we originally projected.

The cost is $550, and the discount rate is 20 per cent. The project can be dismantled and sold in one year for $400, if we decide to abandon it. Should we take it?

A standard DCF analysis is not difficult. The expected cash flow is $100 per year forever and the discount rate is 20 per cent. The PV of the cash flows is $100/0.20 = $500, so the NPV is $500 − $550 = −$50. We shouldn't take it.

This analysis is static, however. In one year, we can sell out for $400. How can we account for this? What we have to do is to decide what we are going to do one year from now. In this simple case, there are only two contingencies that we need to evaluate, an upward revision and a downward revision, so the extra work is not great.

In one year, if the expected cash flows are revised to $50, then the PV of the cash flows is revised downward to $50/0.20 = $250. We get $400 by abandoning the project, so that is what we will do (the NPV of keeping the project in one year is $250 − $400 = −$150).

If the demand is revised upward, then the PV of the future cash flows at year 1 is $150/0.20 = $750. This exceeds the $400 abandonment value, so we will keep the project.

We now have a project that costs $550 today. In one year, we expect a cash flow of $100 from the project. In addition, this project will either be worth $400 (if we abandon it because it is a failure) or $750 (if we keep it because it succeeds). These outcomes are equally likely, so we expect it to be worth ($400 + $750)/2, or $575.

Summing up, in one year, we expect to have $100 in cash plus a project worth $575, or $675 total. At a 20 per cent discount rate, this $675 is worth $562.50 today, so the NPV is $562.50 − $550 = $12.50. We should take it.

The NPV of our project has increased by $62.50. Where did this come from? Our original analysis implicitly assumed we would keep the project even if it was a failure. At year 1, however, we saw that we were $150 better off ($400 versus $250) if we abandoned. There was a 50 per cent chance of this happening, so the expected gain from abandoning is $75. The PV of this amount is the value of the option to abandon, $75/1.20 = $62.50.

Strategic options

Companies sometimes undertake new projects just to explore possibilities and evaluate potential future business strategies. This is a little like testing the water by sticking a toe in before diving. Such projects are difficult to analyse using conventional DCF because most of the benefits come in the form of **strategic options**; that is, options for future, related business moves. Projects that create such options may be very valuable, but that value is difficult to measure. Research and development, for example, is an important and valuable activity for many firms precisely because it creates options for new products and procedures.

strategic options
options for future, related business products or strategies

To give another example, a large manufacturer might decide to open a retail outlet as a pilot study. The primary goal is to gain some market insight. Because of the high start-up costs, this one operation won't break even. However, based on the sales experience from the pilot, we can then evaluate whether or not to open more outlets, to change the product mix, to enter new markets, and so on. The information gained and the resulting options for actions are all valuable, but coming up with a reliable dollar figure is probably not feasible.

We have seen that incorporating options into capital budgeting analysis is not easy. What can we do about them in practice? The answer is that we can only keep them in the back of our minds as we work with the projected cash flows. We will tend to underestimate NPV by ignoring options. The damage might be small for a highly structured, very specific proposal, but it might be great for an exploratory one.

Capital rationing

Capital rationing is said to exist when we have profitable (positive NPV) investments available but we can't get the needed funds to undertake them. For example, as division managers for a large corporation, we might identify $5 million in excellent projects, but find that, for whatever reason, we can spend only $2 million. Now what? Unfortunately, for reasons we will discuss, there may be no truly satisfactory answer.

capital rationing
the situation that exists if a firm has positive NPV projects but cannot find the necessary financing

Soft rationing

The situation we have just described is **soft rationing**. This occurs when, for example, different units in a business are allocated some fixed amount of money each year for capital spending. Such an allocation is primarily a means of controlling and keeping track of overall spending. The important thing about soft rationing is that the corporation as a whole isn't short of capital; more can be raised on ordinary terms if management so desires.

soft rationing
the situation that occurs when units in a business are allocated a certain amount of financing for capital budgeting

If we face soft rationing, the first thing to do is try to get a larger allocation. Failing that, then one common suggestion is to generate as large a net present value as possible within the existing budget.

Strictly speaking, this is the correct thing to do only if the soft rationing is a one-time event; that is, it won't exist next year. If the soft rationing is a chronic problem, then something is amiss. The reason goes all the way back to Chapter 1. Ongoing soft rationing means that we are constantly by-passing positive NPV investments. This contradicts the goal of the firm. If we are not trying to maximise value, then the question of which projects to take becomes ambiguous because we no longer have an objective goal in the first place.

Hard rationing

With **hard rationing**, a business cannot raise capital for a project under any circumstances. For large, healthy corporations, this situation probably does not occur very often, if at all. This is fortunate because with hard rationing our DCF analysis breaks down, and the best course of action is ambiguous.

hard rationing
the situation that occurs when a business cannot raise financing for a project under any circumstances

The reason that DCF analysis breaks down has to do with the required return. Suppose we say our required return is 20 per cent. Implicitly, we are saying that we will take a project with a return that exceeds this. However, if we face hard rationing, then we are not going to take a new project no matter what the return on that project is, so the whole concept of a required return is ambiguous. About the only interpretation we can make in this situation is that the required return is so large that no project has a positive NPV in the first place.

Hard rationing can occur when a company experiences financial distress, meaning that bankruptcy is a possibility. Also, a firm may not be able to raise capital without violating a pre-existing contractual agreement. Some of the issues relating to raising capital are discussed in Chapter 17.

Concept questions

9.6a *Why do we say that our standard discounted cash flow analysis is static?*

9.6b *What are managerial options in capital budgeting? Give some examples.*

9.6c *What is capital rationing? What types are there? What problems does it create for discounted cash flow analysis?*

9.7 ■ **Summary and conclusions**

In this chapter, we looked at some ways of evaluating the results of a discounted cash flow analysis. We also touched on some of the problems that can come up in practice. We saw that:

1. Net present value estimates depend on projected future cash flows. If there are errors in those projections, then our estimated NPVs can be misleading. We called this forecasting risk.

2. Scenario and sensitivity analyses are useful tools for identifying which variables are critical to a project and where forecasting problems can do the most damage.

3. Break-even analysis in its various forms is a particularly common type of scenario analysis that is useful for identifying critical levels of sales.

4. Operating leverage is a key determinant of break-even levels. It reflects the degree to which a project or a firm is committed to fixed costs. The degree of operating leverage tells us the sensitivity of operating cash flow to changes in sales volume.

5. Projects usually have future managerial options associated with them. These options may be very important, but standard discounted cash flow analysis tends to ignore them.

6. Capital rationing occurs when apparently profitable projects cannot be funded. Standard discounted cash flow analysis is troublesome in this case because NPV is not necessarily the appropriate criterion any more.

The most important thing to take away from this chapter is that estimated NPVs or returns should not be taken at face value. They depend critically on projected cash flows. If there is room for significant disagreement about those projected cash flows, the results from the analysis have to be taken with a grain of salt.

Despite the problems we have discussed, discounted cash flow is still the best way of attacking problems, because it forces us to ask the right questions. What we learnt in this chapter is that knowing the questions to ask does not guarantee that we will get all the answers.

Key terms

Accounting break-even *293*
Capital rationing *305*
Cash break-even *298*
Contingency planning *303*
Degree of operating leverage *300*
Financial break-even *299*
Fixed costs *291*

Forecasting risk *283*
Hard rationing *305*
Managerial options *303*
Marginal or incremental cost *291*
Marginal or incremental revenue *292*
Operating leverage *300*
Scenario analysis *285*

Sensitivity analysis *286*
Simulation analysis *288*
Soft rationing *305*
Strategic options *304*
Variable costs *289*

Suggested readings

For an interesting application of break-even analysis, see:
Reinhardt, U.E. 'Break-even Analysis for Lockheed's TriStar: An Application of Financial Theory', *Journal of Finance*, Vol. 28, September 1973, pp. 821–38.

The following articles are 'classics' on the subject of risk analysis in investment decisions:

Hertz, D.B. 'Risk Analysis in Capital Investment', *Harvard Business Review*, Vol. 42, January–February 1964, pp. 95–106.

——'Investment Policies that Pay Off', *Harvard Business Review*, Vol. 46, January–February 1968, pp. 96–108.

Endnote

1   To see this, note that, if Q goes up by 1 unit, OCF will go up by $(P - v)$. In this case, the percentage change in Q is $1/Q$, and the percentage change in OCF is $(P - v)/OCF$. Given this, we have:

$$\text{Percentage change in OCF} = \text{DOL} \times \text{Percentage change in } Q$$
$$(P - v)/OCF = \text{DOL} \times 1/Q$$
$$\text{DOL} = (P - v) \times Q/OCF$$

Also, based on our definition of OCF:

$$OCF + FC = (P - v) \times Q$$

Thus, DOL can be written as:

$$DOL = (OCF + FC)/OCF$$
$$= 1 + FC/OCF$$

On the web

Some of the issues in this chapter are given consideration at:

http://www.btonline.com.au (BT Funds Management)

http://www.ampbanking.com.au (AMP)

http://www.incomeinvest.com.au (a site providing advice and assistance for personal investors from Macquarie Equities)

Maximise Your Marks!

There are 30 interactive questions on project analysis and evaluation waiting online for you at www.mhhe.com/au/ross3e. The questions are written with additional feedback for incorrect answers, and text excerpts with page references for follow-up study.

International Articles!

To read more on project analysis and evaluation and to see current international articles, just go to www.mhhe.com/au/ross3e and click on *PowerWeb Articles* for this chapter.

Chapter review problems and self-test

Use the following base case information to work the self-test problems. You can check your answers just below.

A project under consideration costs $500,000, has a five-year life, and has no salvage value. Depreciation is straight-line to zero. The required return is 15 per cent, and the tax rate is 30 per cent. Sales are projected at 400 units per year. Price per unit is $3,000, variable cost per unit is $1,900, and fixed costs are $250,000 per year.

9.1 · Scenario analysis
Suppose you think that the unit sales price, variable cost, and fixed cost projections above are accurate to within 5 per cent. What are the upper and lower bounds for these projections? What is the base case NPV? What are the best- and worst-case scenario NPVs?

9.2 · Break-even analysis
Given the base case projections in the previous problem, what are the cash, accounting and financial break-even sales levels for this project? Ignore taxes in answering.

Answers to self-test problems

9.1 · We can summarise the relevant information as follows:

	Base case	Lower bound	Upper bound
Unit sales	400	380	420
Price per unit	$ 3,000	$ 2,850	$ 3,150
Variable costs per unit	$ 1,900	$ 1,805	$ 1,995
Fixed costs per year	$250,000	$237,500	$262,500

The depreciation is $100,000 per year, so we can calculate the cash flows under each scenario. Remember that we assign high costs and low prices and volume under the worst case and just the opposite for the best case.

Scenario	Unit sales	Price	Variable costs	Fixed costs
Base case	400	$3,000	$1,900	250,000
Worst case	380	2,850	1,995	262,500
Best case	420	3,150	1,805	237,500

	Base case	Worst case	Best case
Units	400	380	420
Sales	1,200,000	1,083,000	1,323,000
Variable costs	760,000	758,100	758,100
Fixed costs	250,000	262,500	237,500
Depreciation	100,000	100,000	100,000
EBIT	90,000	(37,600)	227,400
Tax (30%)	(27,000)	11,280	(68,220)
Net profit	63,000	(26,320)	159,180
Cash flow	163,000	73,680	259,180
NPV	46,409	(253,010)	368,823

At 15 per cent, the five-year annuity factor is 3.3522.

9.2 · In this case, we have $250,000 in cash fixed costs to cover. Each unit contributes $3,000 − $1,900 = $1,100 toward doing so. The cash break-even is thus $250,000/$1,100 = 227 units. We have another $100,000 in depreciation, so the accounting break-even is ($250,000 + $100,000)/$1,100 = 318 units.

To get the financial break-even, we need to find the OCF such that the project has a zero NPV. As we have seen, the five-year annuity factor is 3.3522 and the project costs $500,000, so the OCF must be such that:

$$\$500,000 = OCF \times 3.3522$$

So, to break even on a financial basis, the project's cash flow must be $500,000/3.3522, or $149,156 per year. If we add this to the $250,000 in cash fixed costs, we get a total of $399,156 that we have to cover. At $1,100 per unit, we need to sell $399,156/$1100 = 363 units.

Questions and problems

1 · Calculating cost and break-even

Zero Smoke Ltd manufactures petrol additives. The variable materials cost is $1.15 per litre and the variable labour cost is $2.60 per litre.

a What is the variable cost per litre?

b Zero Smoke incurs fixed costs of $320,000 during a year when total production is 280,000 litres. What are the total costs for the year?

c If the selling price is $5.30 per litre, does Zero Smoke break even on a cash basis? If depreciation is $130,000 per year, what is the accounting break-even point?

2 · Calculating break-even

In each of the following cases, calculate the accounting break-even and the cash break-even points. Ignore tax effects in calculating the cash break-even and explain any large discrepancies between the two points.

Unit price	Unit variable cost	Fixed costs	Depreciation
$2	$1	$100	$200
25	14	14,000	75,000
20,000	15,000	40,000,000	25,130,000

3 · Scenario analysis

Claw Hammers Manufacturers are evaluating a project that costs $70,000, has a 7-year life, and no salvage value. Assume that depreciation is straight-line to a zero salvage over the 7 years. Claw requires a return of 10 per cent on such projects. The tax rate is 30 per cent. Sales are projected at 15,000 units per year. Price per unit is $5.95, variable cost per unit is $2.63, and fixed costs are $25,000 per year.

a Calculate the accounting break-even point. What is the degree of operating leverage at the accounting break-even point?

b Calculate the base case cash flow and NPV. Suppose that you think that the sales projection is accurate only to within 25 per cent. Evaluate the sensitivity of NPV to changes in that projection.

c Suppose the projections given are all accurate to within 5 per cent except for sales volume, which is only accurate to within 15 per cent. Calculate the NPV under the best and worst cases.

4 · Calculating operating leverage

At an output level of 20,000 units, you calculate that the degree of operating leverage is 4. If output rises to 24,000 units, what will the percentage change in operating cash flow be? Will the new level of operating leverage be higher or lower? Explain.

5 · Leverage

In the previous question, suppose that fixed costs are $50,000. What is the operating cash flow at 12,000 units? The degree of operating leverage?

6 · Computing average cost

Dreamtime Ltd can manufacture fairies for $2.30 in variable raw materials cost and $24 in variable direct labour expense. Fairies sell for $36 each. Last year, production was 40,000 fairies. Fixed costs were $360,000. What were total production costs? What is the marginal cost per fairy? What is the average cost? If Dreamtime is considering a one-off order for an extra 1,000 fairies, what is the minimum acceptable total revenue from the order? Explain.

7 · Break-even intuition

A co-worker claims that looking at all this marginal this and incremental that is just a bunch of nonsense, and states: 'Listen, if our average revenue doesn't exceed our average cost, then we will have a negative cash flow, and we will go broke!' How do you respond?

8 · Degree of operating leverage and break-even intuition

If a project just breaks even on an accounting basis, show that the degree of operating leverage is:

$$DOL = 1 + (Fixed\ costs/Depreciation)$$

9 · Break-even intuition

If a project just breaks even on an accounting basis, what is its cash flow? Its payback? Its return? Explain. Suppose a project just breaks even on a financial basis. What is its discounted payback? What is its return? What is the return on a project that just breaks even on a cash basis?

10 · Break-even and fixed costs

A project is projected to break even on an accounting basis in its third year. Sales for the third year are projected at 12,000 units. Depreciation at that time will be $130,000. The price per unit less variable cost per unit is $15. What are the fixed costs?

11 · Break-even and variable costs

In the previous question, suppose fixed costs are $80,000 and the price per unit is $50. What is the variable cost per unit?

12 · Operating cash flow and leverage

A proposed project has fixed costs of $50,000 per year. The operating cash flow at 3,000 units is $125,000. What is the degree of operating leverage? If units sold rise from 3,000 to 4,000, what will the increase in operating cash flow be (ignore taxes)? What is the new degree of operating leverage?

13 · Forecasting risk

What is forecasting risk? In general, would the degree of forecasting risk be greatest for a new product or a cost-cutting proposal? Why?

14 · Options and NPV

What is the option to abandon? The option to expand? Explain why we tend to underestimate NPV when we ignore these options.

15 · Project analysis

You are considering a new product. It will cost $945,000 to launch, have a 3-year life, and no salvage value. Depreciation is straight-line to a zero salvage. The required return is 20 per cent, and the tax rate is 30 per cent. Sales are projected at 80 units per year. Price per unit will be $35,000, variable cost per unit is $21,900, and fixed costs are $500,000 per year.

a   Based on your experience, you think that the sales, variable cost, and fixed cost projections above are probably accurate to within 10 per cent. What are the upper and lower bounds for these projections? What is the base case NPV? What are the best- and worst-case scenarios?

b   Evaluate the sensitivity of your base case NPV to changes in fixed costs.

c   What is the cash break-even for this project?

d   What is the accounting break-even for this project? What is the degree of operating leverage at the accounting break-even point? How do you interpret this number?

16 · Break-even and taxes

If you were to include the effect of taxes in break-even analysis, what do you think would happen to the cash, accounting and financial break-even points?

This information relates to questions 17 to 21.

We are examining a new project. We expect to sell 500 units per year at $20 net cash flow each for the next 10 years. In other words, the annual operating cash flow is projected to be $20 × 500 = $10,000 per year. The relevant discount rate is 20%, and the initial investment is $55,000. Ignore taxation.

17 · Base case

What is the base case NPV?

18 · Abandonment value

After the first year, the project can be dismantled and sold for $40,000. If expected sales are revised based on the first years performance, when would it make sense to abandon the investment? In other words, at what level of expected sales would it make sense to abandon the project?

19 · Abandonment value

Explain how the $40,000 abandonment value can be viewed as the opportunity cost of keeping the project in one year.

20 · Abandonment

Suppose that you think it is likely that expected sales will be revised up to 750 if the first year is a success and revised down to 250 if the first year is not a success.

a   If success and failure are equally likely, what is the NPV of the project? Consider the possibility of abandonment in answering.

b   What is the value of the option to abandon?

21 · Abandonment

Suppose that the scale of the project can be doubled in one year in the sense that twice as many units can be produced and sold. Naturally, expansion would only be desirable if the project is a success. This implies that if the project is a success, projected sales after expansion will be 1,500. Again assuming that success and failure are equally likely, what is the NPV of the project? Note that abandonment is still an option if the project is a failure. What is the value of the option to expand here?

22 · Break-even intuition

This question concerns the effect of taxes on the accounting break-even measure.

a   Show that, when we consider taxes, the general relationship between operating cash flow (OCF) and sales volume (Q) can be written as:

$$Q = [FC + (OCF - t \times D)/(1 - t)]/(P - v)$$

b   Use the expression in part (a) to find the accounting break-even point for the Newland sailboat example in the chapter. Assume a 30 per cent tax rate.

c   In part (b), the accounting break-even should be the same. Why? Verify this algebraically.

23 · Operating leverage and taxes

This is a challenge question. Show that if we consider the effect of taxes, the degree of operating leverage can be written as:

$$DOL = 1 + [FC \times (1 - t) - D \times t]/OCF$$

Notice that this reduces to our previous result if $t = 0$. Can you interpret this in words?

PART FIVE

Risk

and return

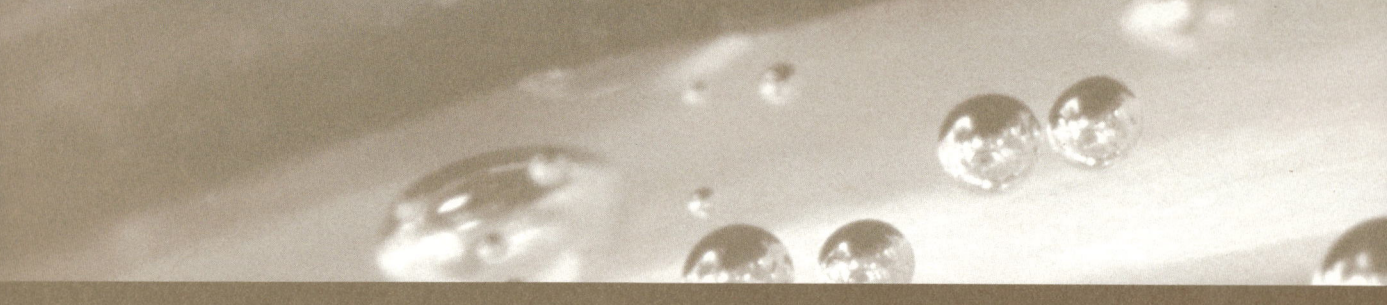

CHAPTER 10

Some lessons
from capital market history

Objective

Thus far, we haven't had much to say about what determines the required return on an investment. In one sense, the answer is very simple: The required return depends on the risk of the investment. The greater the risk is, the greater is the required return.

Having said this, we are left with a somewhat more difficult problem. How can we measure the amount of risk present in an investment? Put another way, what does it mean to say that one investment is riskier than another? Obviously, we need to define what we mean by risk if we are going to answer these questions. This is our task in this chapter and the next.

From the last several chapters, we know that one of the responsibilities of the financial manager is to assess the value of proposed real asset investments. In doing this, it is important that we first look at what financial investments have to offer. At a minimum, the return we require from a proposed non-financial investment must be greater than what we can get from buying financial assets of similar risk.

Our goal in this chapter is to provide a perspective on what capital market history can tell us about risk and return. The most important thing to get out of this chapter is a feel for the numbers. What is a high return? What is a low one? More generally, what returns should we expect from financial assets and what are the risks from such investments? This perspective is essential for understanding how to analyse and value risky investment projects.

Study tips ▷ Students of finance do not like the study of statistics. Similar to their real world contemporaries they would rather look at the management of funds, understanding shares, fixed interest securities and real estate than know how to calculate an average, a standard deviation, a variance or a covariance. In order to understand returns it is important that we understand these statistical concepts and part of that learning process is tedious calculation. Remember that throughout Chapters 10 and 11, as students of finance, we are focusing upon:

a the most likely outcome of a range of possible returns (that is, the average or expected return);

b how possible outcomes are spread around the most likely outcome (that is, the standard deviation or variance); and

c how the most likely outcome will change as other variables change (the covariance or correlation coefficient).

Introduction ▷ We start our discussion of risk and return by describing the historical experience of investors in financial markets. In 1931 in the United States, for example, the share market lost 43 per cent of its value. Just two years later, the share market gained 54 per cent. In more recent memory, the Australian market lost about 34 per cent of its value in the month of October 1987 alone.

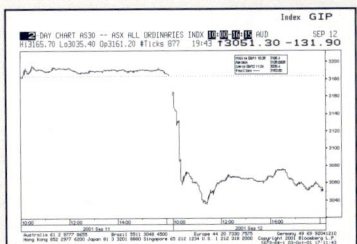

This chart displays the reaction of the Australian stock market to the news of September 11, 2001. The market index closed at around 3195 the night before the terrorist attack. The next morning the market had news of the attack and when it opened in Australia at 10 am, the news was quickly reflected in the market index. In minutes the market fell to around 3050, a drop of 145 points, or about 4.5 per cent. What lessons, if any, can financial managers learn from such shifts in the share market? We will explore several years of market history to find out.

Not everyone agrees on the value of studying history. On the one hand, there is philosopher George Santayana's famous comment, 'Those who do not remember the past are condemned to repeat it.' On the other hand, there is industrialist Henry Ford's equally famous comment, 'History is more or less bunk.' Nonetheless, based on recent events, perhaps everyone would agree with Mark Twain when he observed, 'October. This is one of the peculiarly dangerous months to speculate in shares in. The others are July, January, September, April, November, May, March, June, December, August, and February.'

There are two central lessons that emerge from our study of market history.

1 There is a reward for bearing risk.

2 The greater the potential reward, the greater the risk.

To understand these facts about market returns, we devote much of this chapter to reporting the statistics and numbers that make up the modern capital market history of Australia. In the next chapter, these facts provide the foundation for our study of how financial markets put a price on risk.

Returns

We wish to discuss historical returns on different types of financial assets. The first thing we need to do, then, is to discuss briefly how to calculate the return from investing.

Dollar returns

If you buy an asset of any sort, your gain (or loss) from that investment is called the return on your investment. This return will usually have two components. First, you may receive some cash directly while you own the investment. This is called the income component of your return. Second, the value of the asset you purchase will often change. In this case, you have a capital gain or capital loss on your investment.

To illustrate, suppose the Capital Project Company has several thousand shares on issue. You purchased some of these shares in the company at the beginning of the year. It is now year end, and you want to determine how well you have done on your investment.

First, over the year, a company may pay cash dividends to its shareholders. As a shareholder in Capital Project Company, you are a part owner of the company. If the company is profitable, it may choose to distribute some of its profits to shareholders (we discuss the details of dividend policy in later chapters). So, as the owner of some shares, you will receive some cash. This cash is the income component from owning the shares.

In addition to the dividend, the other part of your return is the capital gain or capital loss on the shares. This part arises from changes in the value of your investment. For example, consider the cash flows illustrated in Figure 10.1. The shares are selling for $3.70 each. If you buy 1,000 shares, you have a total outlay of $3,700. Suppose that, over the year, the shares paid a dividend of $0.185 per share. By the end of the year, then, you would have received income of:

$$\text{Dividend} = \$0.185 \times 1,000 = \$185$$

FIGURE 10.1

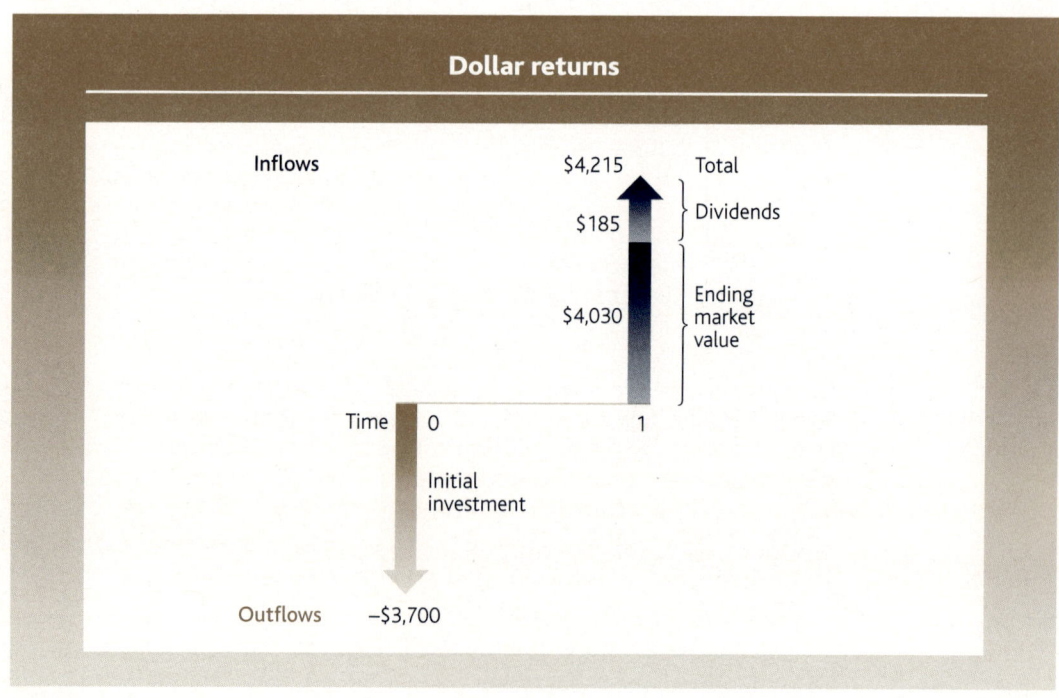

Dollar returns

Inflows

$4,215 Total

$185 } Dividends

$4,030 } Ending market value

Time 0 1

Initial investment

Outflows −$3,700

Also, the value of the shares rises to \$4.03 per share by the end of the year. Your 1,000 shares are worth \$4,030, so you have a capital gain of:

$$\text{Capital gain} = (\$4.03 - \$3.70) \times 1,000 = \$330$$

On the other hand, if the price had dropped to, say, \$3.48, you would have a capital loss of:

$$\text{Capital loss} = (\$3.48 - \$3.70) \times 1,000 = -\$220$$

A capital loss is the same thing as a negative capital gain.

The total dollar return on your investment is the sum of the dividend and the capital gain:

$$\textbf{Total dollar return} = \textbf{Dividend income} + \textbf{Capital gain (or loss)} \qquad \textbf{(10.1)}$$

In our first example, the total dollar return is thus given by:

$$\text{Total dollar return} = \$185 + \$330 = \$515$$

Notice that, if you sold the shares at the end of the year, the total amount of cash you would have would be your initial investment plus the total return. In the preceding example, then:

$$\begin{aligned}\textbf{Total cash if shares are sold} &= \textbf{Initial investment} + \textbf{Total return} \qquad \textbf{(10.2)}\\ &= \$3,700 + \$515\\ &= \$4,215\end{aligned}$$

Check that this is the same as the proceeds from the sale of the shares plus the dividends:

$$\begin{aligned}\text{Proceeds from share sale} + \text{Dividends} &= \$4.03 \times 1,000 + \$185\\ &= \$4,030 + \$185\\ &= \$4,215\end{aligned}$$

Suppose you hold on to your Capital Project shares and don't sell them at the end of the year. Should you still consider the capital gain as part of your return? Isn't this only a 'paper' gain and not really a cash flow if you don't sell them?

The answer to the first question is a strong yes, and the answer to the second is an equally strong no. The capital gain is every bit as much a part of your return as the dividend, and you should certainly count it as part of your return. That you actually decided to keep the shares and not sell (you don't 'realise' the gain) is irrelevant because you could have converted them to cash if you wanted to. Whether you choose to do so or not is up to you.

After all, if you insisted on converting your gain to cash, you could always sell the shares at year end and immediately reinvest by buying the shares back. There is no net difference between doing this and just not selling (assuming, of course, that there are no tax consequences from selling the shares and no brokerage). Again, the point is that whether you actually sell the shares or reinvest by not selling doesn't affect the return you earn.

Percentage returns

It is usually more convenient to summarise information about returns in percentage terms, rather than dollar terms, because that way your return doesn't depend on how much you actually invest. The question we want to answer is: How much do we get for each dollar we invest?

To answer this question, let P_t be the price of the share at the beginning of the year and let D_{t+1} be the dividend paid on the share during the year. Consider the cash flows in Figure 10.2. These are the same as those in Figure 10.1, except that we have now expressed everything on a per-share basis.

Percentage returns. Dollar return and per-share return

Inflows $4.215   Total

$0.185   } Dividends

$4.03   Ending market value

Time t $t+1$

Outflows   −$3.70

$$\text{Percentage return} = \frac{\text{Dividends paid at end of period} + \text{Change in market value over period}}{\text{Beginning market value}}$$

$$1 + \text{Percentage return} = \frac{\text{Dividends paid at end of period} + \text{Market value at end of period}}{\text{Beginning market value}}$$

In our example, the price at the beginning of the year was $3.70 per share and the dividend paid during the year on each share was $0.185. As we discussed in Chapter 6, expressing the dividend as a percentage of the beginning share price results in the dividend yield:

$$\begin{aligned} \text{Dividend yield} &= D_{t+1}/P_t \\ &= \$0.185/\$3.70 = 0.05 = 5\% \end{aligned}$$

This says that, for each dollar we invest, we get 5 cents in dividends.

The second component of our percentage return is the capital gains yield. Recall (from Chapter 6) that this is calculated as the change in the price during the year (the capital gain) divided by the beginning price:

$$\begin{aligned} \text{Capital gains yield} &= (P_{t+1} - P_t)/P_t \\ &= (\$4.03 - \$3.70)/\$3.70 \\ &= \$0.33/\$3.70 \\ &= 9\% \end{aligned}$$

So, per dollar invested, you get 9 cents in capital gains.

Putting it together, per dollar invested, we get 5 cents in dividends and 9 cents in capital gains; so we get a total of 14 cents. Our percentage return is 14 cents on the dollar, or 14 per cent.

To check this, notice that you invested $3,700 and ended up with $4,215. By what percentage did your $3,700 increase? As we saw, you picked up $4,215 − $3,700 = $515. This is a $515/$3,700 = 14% increase.

Calculating returns

EXAMPLE 10.1

Suppose you buy some shares for $2.50 per share. At the end of the year, the price is $3.50 per share. During the year, you got a $0.20 dividend per share. This is the situation illustrated in Figure 10.3. What is the dividend yield? The capital gains yield? The percentage return? If your total investment was $1,000, how much do you have at the end of the year?

Cash flow—An investment example

FIGURE 10.3

Your $0.20 dividend per share works out to a dividend yield of:

Dividend yield $= D_{t+1}/P_t$
$= \$0.20/\$2.50 = 0.08 = 8\%$

The per-share capital gain is $1.00, so the capital gains yield is:

Capital gains yield $= (P_{t+1} − P_t)/P_t$
$= (\$3.50 − \$2.50)/\$2.50$
$= \$1/\$2.50$
$= 40\%$

The total percentage return is thus 48 per cent.

If you had invested $1,000, you would have $1,480 at the end of the year, a 48 per cent increase. To check this, note that your $1,000 would have bought you $1,000/$2.50 = 400 shares. Your 400 shares would then have paid you a total of 400 × $0.20 = $80 in cash dividends. Your $1.00 per share gain would give you a total capital gain of $1.00 × 400 = $400. Add these together, and you get the $480.

Concept questions

10.1a *What are the two parts of total return?*

10.1b *Why are unrealised capital gains or losses included in the calculation of returns?*

10.1c *What is the difference between a dollar return and a percentage return? Why are percentage returns more convenient?*

10.2 Inflation and returns

So far, we haven't worried about inflation in calculating returns. Since this is an important consideration, we consider the impact of inflation next.

Real versus nominal returns

nominal return
return on an investment not adjusted for inflation

real return
return adjusted for the effects of inflation

The returns we calculated in the previous section are called **nominal returns** because they weren't adjusted for inflation. Returns that have been adjusted to reflect inflation are called **real returns**.

To see the effect of inflation on returns, suppose that prices are currently rising by 5 per cent per year. In other words, the inflation rate is 5 per cent. We are considering an investment that will be worth $115.50 in one year. It costs $100 today.

We start by calculating the percentage return. In this case, there is no income component, so the return is the capital gains yield of ($115.50 − $100)/$100 = 15.50%. Once again, we have ignored the effect of inflation, so this 15.50 per cent is the nominal return.

What is the impact of inflation here? To answer, suppose pizzas cost $5 each at the beginning of the year. With $100, we can buy 20 pizzas. Since the inflation rate is 5 per cent, pizzas will cost 5 per cent more, or $5.25, at the end of the year. If we take the investment, how many pizzas can we buy at the end of the year? Measured in pizzas instead of dollars, what is our return?

Our $115.50 from the investment will buy us $115.50/$5.25 = 22 pizzas. This is up from 20 pizzas, so our pizza return is (22 − 20)/20 = 10%. What this illustrates is that even though the nominal return on our investment is 15.5 per cent, our buying power has only gone up by 10 per cent because of inflation. Put another way, we are really only 10 per cent richer. In this case, we say that the real return is 10 per cent.

Alternatively, with 5 per cent inflation, each of the $115.50 nominal dollars we get is worth 5 per cent less in real terms, so the real dollar value of our investment in a year is:

$$\$115.50/1.05 = \$110$$

What we have done is to deflate the $115.50 by 5 per cent. Since we give up $100 in current buying power to get the equivalent of $110, our real return is again 10 per cent. Because we have removed the effect of future inflation here, this $110 is said to be measured in current dollars.

The difference between nominal and real returns is important and bears repeating.

Your nominal return on an investment is the percentage change in the number of dollars you have.

Your real return on an investment is the percentage change in how much you can buy with your dollars, in other words, the percentage change in your buying power.

The Fisher effect

Our discussion of real and nominal returns illustrates a relationship often called the **Fisher effect**. Since investors are ultimately concerned with what they can buy with their money, they require compensation for inflation. Let R stand for the nominal return and r stand for the real return. The Fisher effect tells us that the relationship between nominal returns, real returns and inflation can be written as:

Fisher effect
relationship between nominal returns, real returns and inflation

$$(1 + R) = (1 + r) \times (1 + h) \qquad (10.3)$$

where h is the inflation rate.

From the example above, the nominal return was 15.50 per cent and the inflation rate was 5 per cent. What was the real return? We can determine it by plugging in these numbers:

$$(1 + 0.155) = (1 + r) \times (1 + 0.05)$$
$$(1 + r) = (1.155)/(1.05) = 1.10$$
$$r = 10\%$$

This real return is the same as we had before. If we take another look at the Fisher effect, we can rearrange things a little as follows:

$$(1 + R) = (1 + r) \times (1 + h) \qquad (10.4)$$
$$R = r + h + r \times h$$

What this tells us is that the nominal return has three components. First, there is the real return on the investment, r. Next, there is the compensation for the decrease in the value of the money originally invested because of inflation, h. The third component represents compensation for the fact that the dollars earned on the investment are also worth less because of the inflation.

This third component is usually small, so it is often dropped. The nominal rate is then approximately equal to the real rate plus the inflation rate:

$$R \approx r + h \qquad (10.5)$$

The Fisher effect

EXAMPLE 10.2

If investors require a 10 per cent real return, and the inflation rate is 8 per cent, what must be the approximate nominal rate? The exact nominal rate?

First of all, the nominal rate is approximately equal to the sum of the real rate and the inflation rate: 10% + 8% = 18%. From the Fisher effect, we have:

$$(1 + R) = (1 + r) \times (1 + h)$$
$$= (1.10) \times (1.08)$$
$$= 1.1880$$

Therefore, the nominal rate will actually be closer to 19 per cent.

It is important to note that financial rates, such as interest rates, discount rates and rates of return, are almost always quoted in nominal terms. To remind you of this, we will henceforth use the symbol R instead of r in most of our subsequent discussions about such rates.

Concept questions

10.2a *What is the difference between a nominal and a real return? Which is more important to a typical investor?*

10.2b *What is the Fisher effect?*

 ## 10.3 The historical record

Roger Ibbotson and Rex Sinquefield conducted a famous set of studies dealing with rates of return in US financial markets.[1] We have duplicated their studies using Australian financial market data. We present quarter-to-quarter historical rates of return on four important types of financial investment. The returns can be interpreted as what you would have earned if you held portfolios of the following:

1. *Ordinary shares*. The ordinary share portfolio is based on 500 of the largest companies (in terms of total market value of outstanding equity) in Australia.
2. *Small shares*. This is a portfolio composed of the smallest of the companies listed on the Australian Stock Exchange (ASX), again as measured by market value of outstanding equity.
3. *Ten-year government bonds*. This is a portfolio of government bonds with a 10-year maturity.
4. *Bank bills*. This a portfolio of bank bills with a 90-day maturity.

Roger Ibbotson

⟨⟨⟨ In their own words

Roger Ibbotson* on capital market history

The financial markets are the most carefully documented human phenomena in history. Every day, approximately 2,000 NYSE stocks are traded, and at least 6,000 more stocks are traded on other exchanges and in over-the-counter markets. Bonds, commodities, futures and options also provide a wealth of data. These data daily fill more than a dozen pages of The Wall Street Journal *(and numerous other newspapers), and these pages are only summaries of the day's transactions. A record actually exists of every transaction, providing not only a real-time database, but a historical record extending back, in many cases, more than a century.*

The global market adds another dimension to this wealth of data. The Japanese stock market trades a billion shares on active days, and the London exchange reports trades on over 10,000 domestic and foreign issues a day.

The data generated by these transactions are quantifiable, quickly analysed and disseminated, and made easily accessible by computer. Because of this, finance has increasingly come to resemble one of the exact sciences. The use of financial market data ranges from the simple, such as using the S&P 500 to measure the performance of a portfolio, to the incredibly complex. For example, only a quarter of a century ago, the bond market was the most staid province on Wall Street. Today, it attracts swarms of traders seeking to exploit arbitrage opportunities—small temporary mispricings—using real-time data and computers to analyse them.

Financial market data are the foundation for the extensive empirical understanding we now have of the financial markets. The following is a list of some of the principal findings of such research:

- *Risky securities, such as stocks, have higher average returns than riskless securities such as Treasury bills.*
- *Stocks of small companies have higher average returns than those of larger companies.*
- *Long-term bonds have higher average yields and returns than short-term bonds.*
- *The cost of capital for a company, project, or division can be predicted using data from the markets.*

Because phenomena in the financial markets are so well measured, finance is the most readily quantifiable branch of economics. Researchers are able to do more extensive empirical research than in any other economic field, and the research can be quickly translated into action in the marketplace.

* Roger Ibbotson is Professor in the Practice of Management at the Yale School of Management. He is the founder and President of Ibbotson Associates, a major supplier of financial databases to the financial services industry. An outstanding scholar, he is best known for his original estimates of the historical rates of return realised by investors in different markets and for his research on new issues.

These returns are not adjusted for inflation or taxes; thus, they are nominal, pre-tax returns.

In addition to the quarter-to-quarter returns on these financial instruments, the quarter-to-quarter percentage change in the Consumer Price Index (CPI) is also computed. This is a commonly used measure of inflation, so we can calculate real returns using this as the inflation rate.

The period studied is from the middle of 1978 to the middle of 2002. In 1987 the government introduced dividend imputation.[2] The introduction of this system means that equity returns during the 1980s may be different to the returns during the 1990s. We will see if this is the case. If it happens that returns are different, we cannot say that the effect is due to dividend imputation as there were many other events besides dividend imputation. We have not tested to see if the effect (if any) is due to dividend imputation.

A first look

Before looking closely at the different portfolio returns, we take a look at the 'big picture'. Figure 10.4 shows what happened to returns in these different portfolios from 1978. The growth in value for each of the different portfolios over the period is given separately. The vertical axis starts at $1. We have tracked what would have happened to the one dollar over time.

FIGURE 10.4

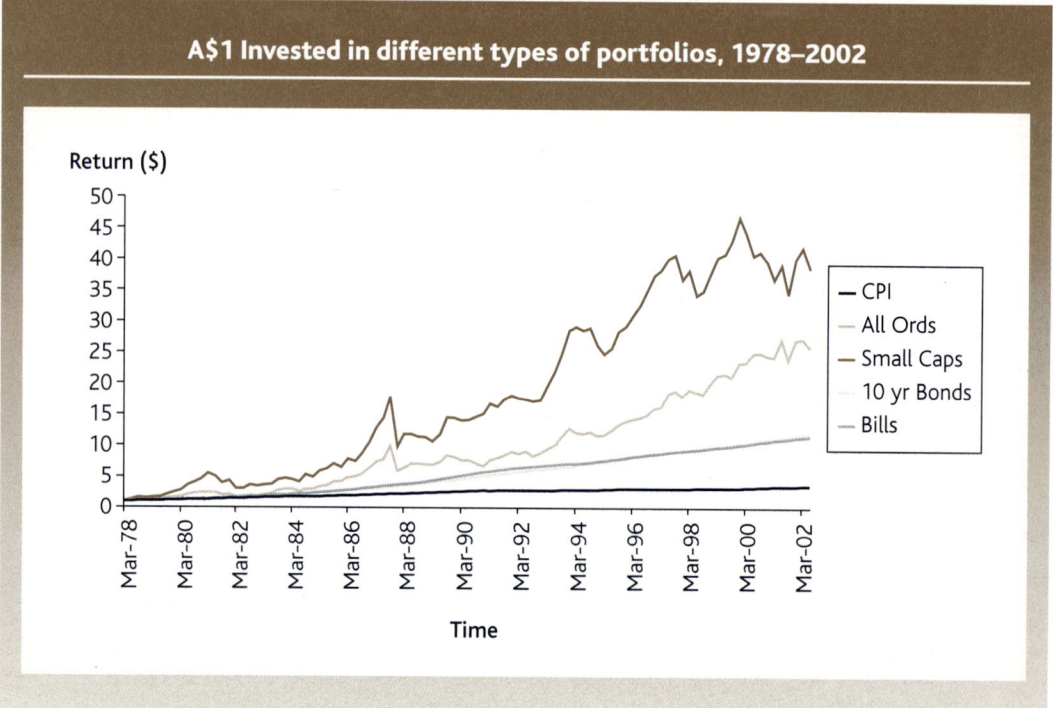

A$1 Invested in different types of portfolios, 1978–2002

Looking at Figure 10.4, we see that the 'small cap' (short for small capitalisation) investment did the best overall. Every dollar invested grew to $38.43 (approximately 3,800% growth) over the 22 years. The larger ordinary share portfolio did less well; a dollar invested in it grew to $25.76 (approximately 2,500%).

At the other end, the 90-day bank bill portfolio grew to only $11.52. This is even less impressive when we consider the inflation over this period. The increase in the price level was such that $3.60 was needed just to replace the original $1.

Given the historical record, why would anybody buy anything other than small cap shares? If you look closely at Figure 10.4, you will probably see the answer. The bank bill portfolio and the long-term government bond portfolio grew more slowly than did the share portfolios, but they also grew much more steadily. The small shares ended up on top, but as you can see, they grew quite erratically at times. For example, in the 1987 share market crash and after September 11, the small share portfolio lost the most value.

A closer look

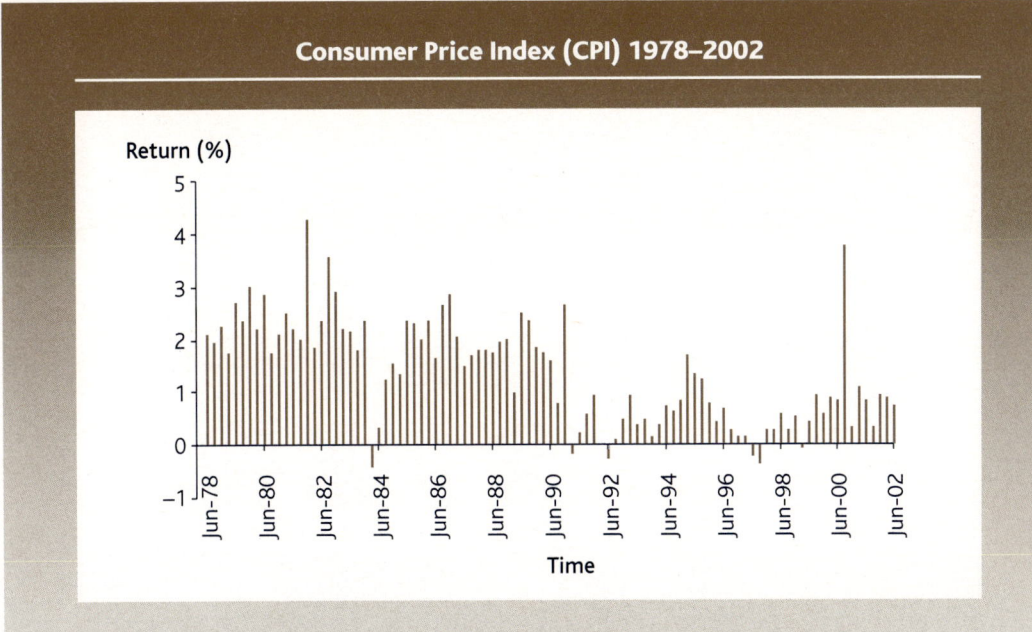

Consumer Price Index (CPI) 1978–2002

FIGURE
10.5

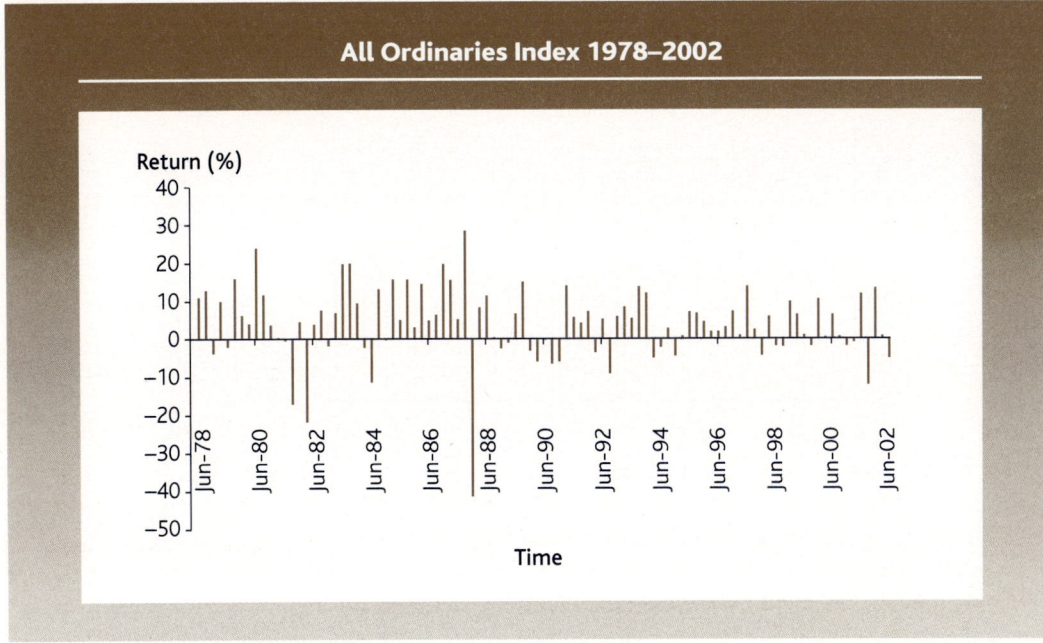

All Ordinaries Index 1978–2002

FIGURE
10.6

FIGURE
10.7

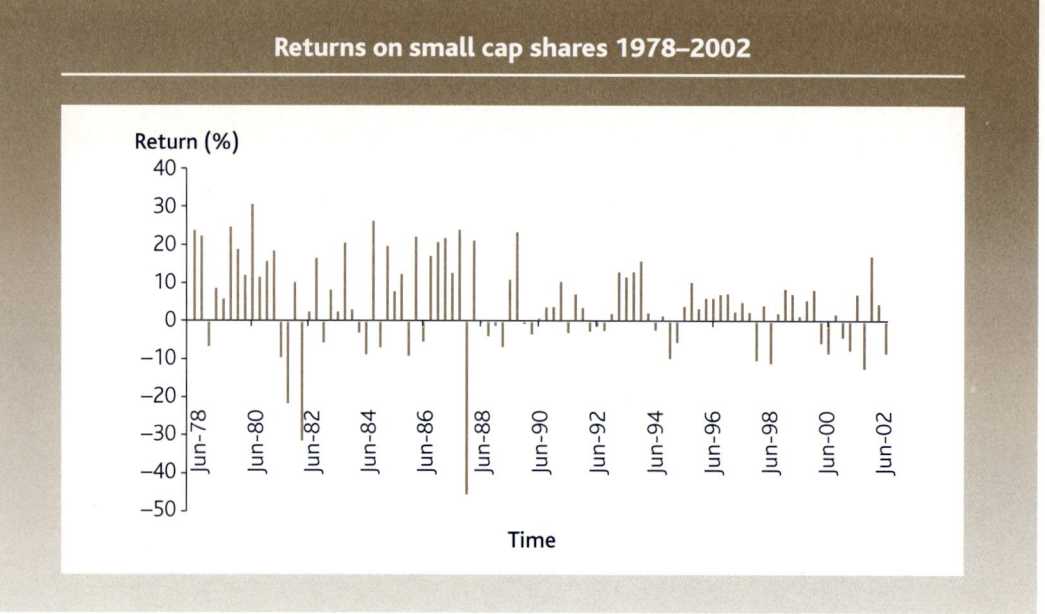

Returns on small cap shares 1978–2002

FIGURE
10.8

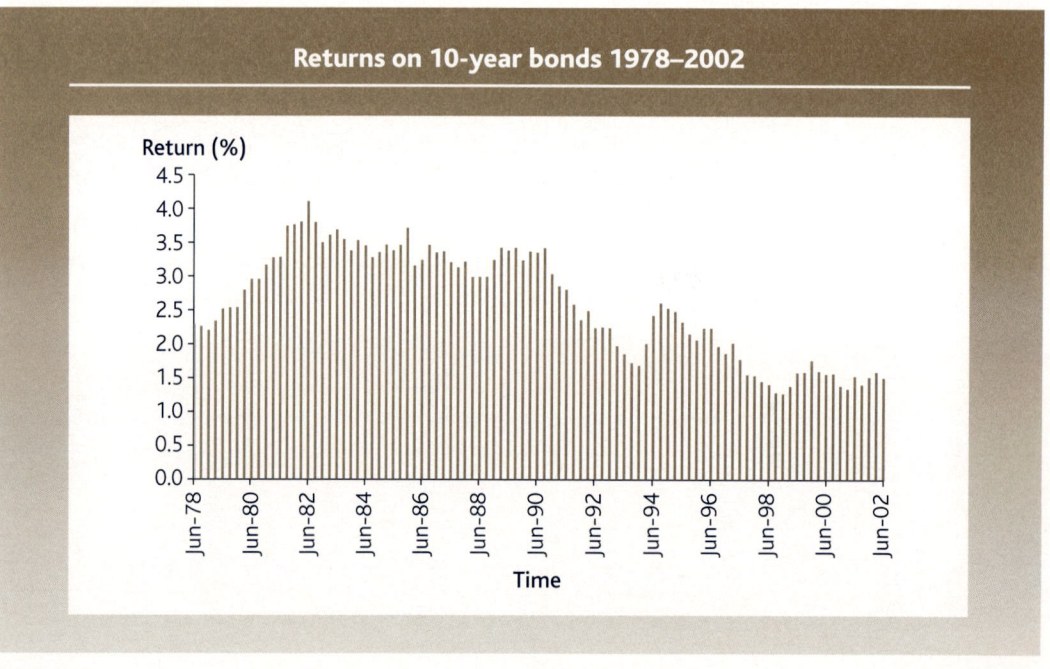

Returns on 10-year bonds 1978–2002

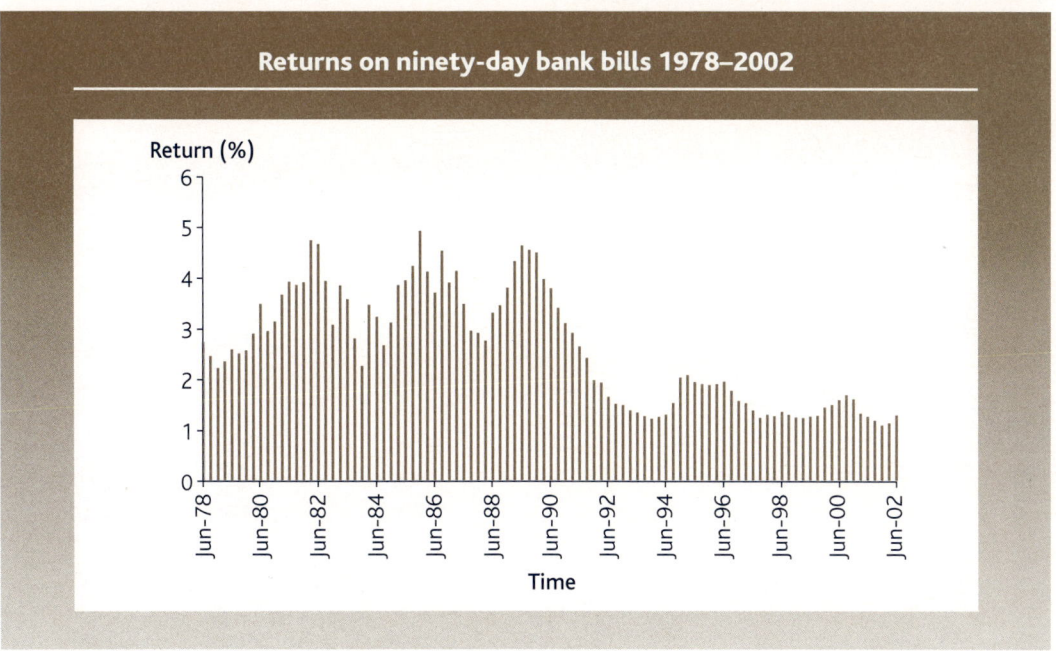

Returns on ninety-day bank bills 1978–2002

FIGURE
10.9

To illustrate the variability of the different investments, Figures 10.5 to 10.9 plot the quarter-to-quarter percentage returns in the form of vertical bars drawn from the horizontal axis. The height of the bar tells us the return for the particular quarter. For example, looking at the long-term government bonds (Figure 10.8), we see the largest historical quarterly return (4.1%) occurred in 1982. This was a good period for bonds. Today quarterly returns are much closer to 1.5%. In comparing these charts, notice the differences in the vertical axis scales. With this in mind, you can see how predictably the bank bills (Figure 10.9) behaved compared to the small shares (Figure 10.7).

The actual quarter-to-quarter returns used to draw these bar graphs are displayed in Table 10.1. Looking at this table, we see, for example, that the largest single-quarter return is a remarkable 45.22 per cent (negative) for the small share portfolio in the 1987 quarter that includes October.

Quarter-to-quarter total returns, 1978–2002

Date	CPI	All Ords	Small caps	10yr bonds	Bills
30/6/78	2.09%	10.95%	23.87%	2.28%	2.66%
30/9/78	1.95%	12.59%	22.39%	2.25%	2.43%
31/12/78	2.21%	−3.68%	−5.88%	2.20%	2.19%
31/3/79	1.70%	9.76%	8.74%	2.34%	2.29%
30/6/79	2.69%	−2.16%	5.90%	2.50%	2.56%
30/9/79	2.33%	15.72%	24.61%	2.52%	2.47%
31/12/79	2.97%	6.16%	18.98%	2.52%	2.53%
31/3/80	2.19%	4.09%	12.20%	2.80%	2.87%
30/6/80	2.84%	23.59%	30.65%	2.94%	3.46%
30/9/80	1.70%	11.51%	11.39%	2.95%	2.92%

TABLE
10.1

Quarter-to-quarter total returns, 1978–2002 (*continued*)

Date	CPI	All Ords	Small caps	10yr bonds	Bills
31/12/80	2.09%	3.76%	15.87%	3.15%	3.11%
31/3/81	2.46%	0.44%	18.32%	3.28%	3.66%
30/6/81	2.20%	−0.37%	−9.02%	3.28%	3.89%
30/9/81	1.96%	−16.82%	−21.08%	3.75%	3.84%
31/12/81	4.22%	4.60%	10.30%	3.75%	3.89%
31/3/82	1.84%	−21.42%	−31.06%	3.79%	4.72%
30/6/82	2.35%	3.81%	2.50%	4.10%	4.64%
30/9/82	3.53%	7.47%	16.40%	3.80%	3.87%
31/12/82	2.90%	−1.75%	−5.00%	3.50%	3.03%
31/3/83	2.16%	6.84%	8.03%	3.60%	3.81%
30/6/83	2.11%	19.40%	2.29%	3.68%	3.56%
30/9/83	1.75%	19.58%	20.77%	3.54%	2.77%
31/12/83	2.34%	9.34%	2.82%	3.37%	2.22%
31/3/84	−0.46%	−2.30%	−2.75%	3.53%	3.44%
30/6/84	0.31%	−11.18%	−8.35%	3.44%	3.20%
30/9/84	1.22%	12.96%	26.33%	3.28%	2.63%
31/12/84	1.51%	−0.30%	−6.56%	3.35%	3.09%
31/3/85	1.34%	15.47%	19.54%	3.45%	3.82%
30/6/85	2.35%	4.96%	7.60%	3.37%	3.94%
30/9/85	2.30%	15.42%	12.08%	3.45%	4.20%
31/12/85	1.96%	2.99%	−8.71%	3.71%	4.89%
31/3/86	2.34%	14.25%	21.87%	3.15%	4.11%
30/6/86	1.61%	4.93%	−4.94%	3.24%	3.67%
30/9/86	2.65%	6.32%	16.92%	3.46%	4.52%
31/12/86	2.84%	19.42%	20.53%	3.35%	3.88%
31/3/87	2.01%	15.30%	21.83%	3.36%	4.10%
30/6/87	1.47%	5.20%	12.50%	3.20%	3.42%
30/9/87	1.69%	28.02%	23.73%	3.13%	2.93%
31/12/87	1.79%	−40.66%	−45.22%	3.21%	2.86%
31/3/88	1.75%	8.10%	20.94%	2.97%	2.74%
30/6/88	1.72%	11.28%	−0.03%	2.99%	3.28%
30/9/88	1.92%	0.36%	−3.39%	2.99%	3.41%
31/12/88	2.00%	−2.36%	−0.72%	3.24%	3.78%
31/3/89	0.98%	−0.87%	−6.20%	3.41%	4.31%
30/6/89	2.48%	6.58%	10.86%	3.37%	4.59%
30/9/89	2.31%	14.75%	23.33%	3.41%	4.53%
31/12/89	1.85%	−3.16%	−0.24%	3.22%	4.47%
31/3/90	1.71%	−5.96%	−2.86%	3.36%	3.96%
30/6/90	1.59%	−0.40%	0.60%	3.35%	3.76%
30/9/90	0.78%	−6.35%	3.56%	3.41%	3.38%
31/12/90	2.61%	−5.97%	3.52%	3.02%	3.05%
31/3/91	−0.19%	13.77%	10.53%	2.85%	2.87%
30/6/91	0.19%	5.67%	−2.56%	2.79%	2.60%
30/9/91	0.57%	4.18%	7.09%	2.58%	2.39%

Date	CPI	All Ords	Small caps	10yr bonds	Bills
31/12/91	0.94%	7.18%	3.26%	2.35%	1.96%
31/3/92	0.00%	−3.53%	−2.29%	2.47%	1.88%
30/6/92	−0.28%	5.23%	−0.73%	2.23%	1.60%
30/9/92	0.09%	−9.13%	−2.13%	2.24%	1.49%
31/12/92	0.47%	5.90%	1.48%	2.24%	1.47%
31/3/93	0.93%	8.42%	12.87%	1.96%	1.34%
30/6/93	0.37%	5.35%	11.65%	1.84%	1.31%
30/9/93	0.46%	13.72%	13.00%	1.71%	1.22%
31/12/93	0.18%	11.91%	15.53%	1.67%	1.21%
31/3/94	0.36%	−4.84%	2.00%	1.99%	1.22%
30/6/94	0.72%	−2.19%	−2.12%	2.41%	1.28%
30/9/94	0.63%	2.72%	1.31%	2.58%	1.48%
31/12/94	0.80%	−4.48%	−9.63%	2.51%	1.99%
31/3/95	1.68%	0.66%	−5.31%	2.46%	2.03%
30/6/95	1.31%	7.02%	3.86%	2.30%	1.89%
30/9/95	1.20%	6.69%	10.21%	2.14%	1.87%
31/12/95	0.77%	4.57%	3.13%	2.05%	1.86%
31/3/96	0.42%	1.96%	5.79%	2.22%	1.88%
30/6/96	0.67%	1.83%	5.78%	2.22%	1.89%
30/9/96	0.25%	3.01%	6.80%	1.95%	1.73%
31/12/96	0.17%	7.15%	7.26%	1.84%	1.53%
31/3/97	0.17%	0.85%	2.32%	2.00%	1.51%
30/6/97	−0.25%	13.70%	4.94%	1.76%	1.34%
30/9/97	−0.42%	2.40%	1.29%	1.53%	1.19%
31/12/97	0.25%	−4.41%	−9.75%	1.51%	1.27%
31/3/98	0.25%	5.88%	4.03%	1.44%	1.24%
30/6/98	0.58%	−1.92%	−10.43%	1.39%	1.33%
30/9/98	0.25%	−2.04%	1.93%	1.27%	1.26%
31/12/98	0.49%	9.74%	8.47%	1.25%	1.20%
31/3/99	−0.08%	6.43%	6.69%	1.37%	1.20%
30/6/99	0.41%	0.81%	1.26%	1.57%	1.23%
30/9/99	0.90%	−1.96%	5.42%	1.57%	1.25%
31/12/99	0.57%	10.37%	8.41%	1.74%	1.41%
31/3/00	0.89%	0.34%	−5.31%	1.59%	1.47%
30/6/00	0.80%	6.39%	−8.16%	1.54%	1.56%
30/9/00	3.72%	0.55%	1.50%	1.55%	1.64%
31/12/00	0.31%	−1.97%	−4.14%	1.36%	1.55%
31/3/01	1.07%	−0.92%	−7.21%	1.32%	1.28%
30/6/01	0.83%	11.67%	6.62%	1.51%	1.24%
30/9/01	0.30%	−11.84%	−12.08%	1.38%	1.14%
31/12/01	0.89%	13.12%	16.78%	1.50%	1.06%
31/3/02	0.89%	0.69%	4.37%	1.58%	1.12%
30/6/02	0.73%	−5.09%	−8.15%	1.50%	1.27%

In the June quarter 2002, inflation was 0.73 per cent (3% per annum equivalent), government bonds returned 1.5 per cent (or 6% per annum), bank bills were 1.27 per cent (or 5.08% per annum), large shares 'only' lost 5.09 per cent (or 20.36% per annum) while small shares lost 8.15 per cent (or a per annum equivalent return of 32.6%).

Concept questions

10.3a *With 20–20 hindsight, what was the best investment for the period 1978–2002?*

10.3b *Why doesn't everyone just buy small shares as investments?*

10.3c *What was the smallest return observed over the 15 years for each of these investments? When did it occur?*

10.3d *How many times did ordinary shares return more than 10 per cent per quarter? How many times did they return less than –10 per cent per quarter?*

10.3e *What was the longest 'winning streak' (quarters without a negative return) for ordinary shares? For long-term government bonds?*

10.3f *How often did the bank bill portfolio have a negative return?*

10.4 ■ Average returns: The first lesson

As you have probably begun to notice, the history of capital market returns is too complicated to be of much use in its undigested form. We need to begin summarising all these numbers. Accordingly, we discuss how to go about condensing the detailed data. We start out by calculating average returns.

Calculating average returns

A way to calculate the average returns on the different investments in Table 10.1 is simply to add up the returns and divide by 97. The result is the historical average of the individual values per quarter.

What we will do is convert the quarterly returns to an equivalent annual return and average this return.

Average returns: The historical record

Table 10.2 shows the average returns computed from Table 10.1. As shown, in a typical year, the small shares increased in value by 18.36 per cent (using an equivalent rate of return). Notice also how much larger the share returns are than the bond returns.

TABLE 10.2

Average equivalent returns, 1978–2002			
	Average Equivalent Return		
Investment	Total period	1980s	1990s
Ordinary share	15.50%	19.96%	11.39%
Small share	18.36%	23.63%	12.62%
90-day bank bill	10.23%	14.61%	7.16%
10-year government bond	10.35%	13.45%	8.51%
Inflation	5.34%	8.06%	2.25%

PART 5 · RISK AND RETURN

These averages are, of course, nominal since we haven't worried about inflation. Notice that the average inflation rate was 5.34 per cent per year over this 24-year span. During the eighties inflation averaged 8.06% while during the nineties inflation averaged only 2.25%. The nominal return on government bonds was 10.35 per cent per year. The average real return on government bonds was thus approximately 5 per cent per year; so the real return on the bonds has been quite low historically. At the other extreme, small shares had an average real return of about 18.36% − 5.34% = 13.02% which is relatively high. Notice also that the real value of the ordinary share portfolio increased by approximately 10.16 per cent (15.50% − 5.34%) in a typical year.

Risk premiums

Now that we have computed some average returns, it seems logical to see how they compare with each other. Based on our discussion above, one such comparison involves government-issued securities. These are free of much of the variability we see in, for example, the share market.

The government borrows money by issuing bonds. Because the government can always raise taxes to pay its bills, this debt is virtually free of any default risk over its life. Thus, we will call the rate on such debt the risk-free return, and we will use it as a kind of benchmark.

A particularly interesting comparison involves the virtually risk-free return on government bonds and the very risky return on ordinary shares. The difference between these two returns can be interpreted as a measure of the excess return on the average risky asset (assuming that a share of a large Australian company has about average risk compared to all risky assets).

We call this the 'excess' return since it is the additional return we earn by moving from a relatively risk-free investment to a risky one. Because it can be interpreted as a reward for bearing risk, we will call it a **risk premium**.

From Table 10.2, we can calculate the risk premiums for the different investments. We report only the nominal risk premium in Table 10.3 because there is only a slight difference between the historical nominal and real risk premiums.

The risk premium on a government bond is shown as zero in the table because we have assumed that they are riskless.

risk premium
the excess return required from an investment in a risky asset over a risk-free investment

Average equivalent returns and risk premiums, 1978–2002		
Investment	Annual equivalent returns	Risk premium
Ordinary share	15.50%	5.15%
Small share	18.36%	8.01%
90-day bank bill	10.23%	−0.12%
10-year government bond	10.35%	0.00%

TABLE 10.3

THE BASIC IDEA

The first lesson

Looking at Table 10.3, we see that the average risk premium earned by a typical large ordinary share is 15.5% − 10.35% = 5.15%. This is a significant reward. The fact that it exists historically is an important observation, and it is the basis for our first lesson:

> Risky assets, on average, earn a risk premium.

Put another way, there is a reward for bearing risk.

Why is this so? Why, for example, is the risk premium for small shares so much larger than the risk premium for large shares? More generally, what determines the relative sizes of the risk premiums for the different assets? The answers to these questions are at the heart of modern finance, and the next chapter is devoted to them. For now, part of the answer can be found by looking at the historical variability of the returns of these different investments. So, to get started, we now turn our attention to measuring variability in returns.

Concept questions

10.4a *What do we mean by excess return and risk premium?*
10.4b *What was the real (as opposed to nominal) risk premium on the ordinary share portfolio?*
10.4c *What was the nominal risk premium on bank bills? The real risk premium?*
10.4d *What is the first lesson from capital market history?*

10.5 | The variability of returns: The second lesson

We have already seen that the equivalent quarter-to-quarter returns on ordinary shares tend to be more volatile than the returns on long-term government bonds (compare Figures 10.6 and 10.8). We now discuss measuring this variability so we can begin examining the subject of risk.

Frequency distributions and variability

To get started, we can draw a frequency distribution for the ordinary share returns like the one in Figure 10.10. What we have done here is to count up the number of times that the equivalent annual return on the ordinary share portfolio falls within each 20 per cent range. For example, in Figure 10.10, the height of 14 in the range 40–60 per cent means that 14 of the 97 equivalent annual returns were in that range. Notice also that the most common returns are in the ranges of 0–20 per cent and 20–40 per cent. The ordinary share portfolio had a return in these ranges of 22 times in 97 equivalent years.

What we need to do now is to actually measure the spread in returns. We know, for example, that the return on small shares in a typical year was 18.36 per cent. We now want to know how far the actual return deviates from this average in a typical year. In other words, we need a measure of how volatile the return is. The variance and its square root, the standard deviation, are the most commonly used measures of volatility. We describe how to calculate them next.

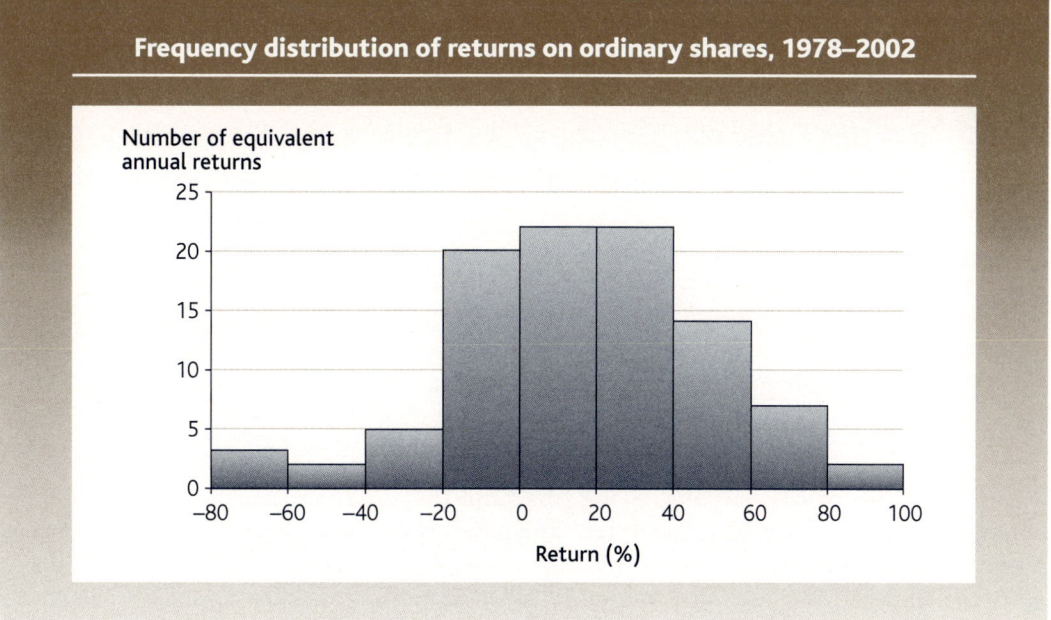

Frequency distribution of returns on ordinary shares, 1978–2002

FIGURE
10.10

The historical variance and standard deviation

The **variance** essentially measures the average squared difference between the actual returns and the average return. The bigger this number is, the more the actual returns tend to differ from the average return. Also, the larger the variance or standard deviation is, the more spread-out the returns will be.

The way that we will calculate the variance and standard deviation depends on the specific situation. In this chapter, we are looking at historical returns; so the procedure we describe here is the correct one for calculating the historical variance and standard deviation. If we were examining projected future returns, then the procedure would be different. We describe this procedure in the next chapter.

To illustrate how we calculate the historical variance, suppose a particular investment had returns of 10 per cent, 12 per cent, 3 per cent, and −9 per cent over the last four years. The average return is (0.10 + 0.12 + 0.03 − 0.09)/4 = 4%. Notice that the return is never actually equal to 4 per cent. Instead, the first return deviates from the average by 0.10 − 0.04 = 0.06, the second return deviates from the average by 0.12 − 0.04 = 0.08, and so on. To compute the variance, we square each of these deviations, add them up, and divide the result by the number of returns less one, which is three in this case. This information is summarised below:

variance
the average squared deviation between the actual return and the average return

	(1) Actual return	(2) Average return	(3) Deviation (1) − (2)	(4) Squared deviation
	0.10	0.04	0.06	0.0036
	0.12	0.04	0.08	0.0064
	0.03	0.04	−0.01	0.0001
	−0.09	0.04	−0.13	0.0169
Total	0.16		0.00	0.0270

In the first column, we write down the four actual returns. In the third column, we calculate the difference between the actual returns and the average by subtracting 4 per cent. Finally, in the fourth column, we square the numbers in column 3 to get the squared deviations from the average.

The variance can now be calculated by dividing 0.0270, the sum of the squared deviations, by the number of returns less one. Let Var(R) or σ^2 (read this as 'sigma squared') stand for the variance of the return:

$$\text{Var}(R) = \sigma^2 = 0.027/(4 - 1) = 0.009$$

The **standard deviation** is the square root of the variance. So, if SD(R) or σ stands for the standard deviation5 of return:

$$\text{SD}(R) = \sigma = \sqrt{0.009} = 0.09487$$

The square root of the variance is used because the variance is measured in 'squared' percentages and thus is hard to interpret. The standard deviation is an ordinary percentage, so the answer here could be written as 9.487.

In the table above, notice that the sum of the deviations is equal to zero. This will always be the case, and it provides a good way to check your work. In general, if we have T historical returns, where T is some number, we can write the historical variance as:

$$\textbf{Var}(R) = 1/(T - 1) \times [(R_1 - R)^2 + \ldots + (R_T - R)^2] \tag{10.6}$$

This formula tells us to do just what we did above: take each of the T individual returns (R_1, R_2, ...) and subtract the average return; square the result, and add them all up; finally, divide this total by the number of returns less one ($T - 1$). The standard deviation is always the square root of Var(R).

10.3 Calculating the variance and standard deviation

Suppose the Asset Company and the Pricing Company have experienced the following returns in the last four years:

Year	Asset returns	Pricing returns
200X–3	–0.20	0.05
200X–2	0.50	0.09
200X–1	0.30	–0.12
200X	0.10	0.20

What are the average returns? The variances? The standard deviations? Which investment was more volatile?

To calculate the average returns, we add up the returns and divide by four. The results are:

Asset average return = R = 0.70/4 = 0.175
Pricing average return = R = 0.22/4 = 0.055

PART 5 · RISK AND RETURN

To calculate the variance for Asset, we can summarise the relevant calculations as follows:

Year	(1) Actual return	(2) Average return	(3) Deviation (1) – (2)	(4) Squared deviation
200X–3	–0.20	0.175	–0.375	0.140625
200X–2	0.50	0.175	0.325	0.105625
200X–1	0.30	0.175	0.125	0.015625
200X	0.10	0.175	–0.075	0.005625
Totals	0.70		0.00	0.267500

Since there are four years of returns, we calculate the variances by dividing 0.2675 by $(4 - 1) = 3$.

To calculate the variance for Pricing, we can summarise the relevant calculations as follows:

Year	(1) Actual return	(2) Average return	(3) Deviation (1) – (2)	(4) Squared deviation
200X–3	0.05	0.055	–0.005	0.000025
200X–2	0.09	0.055	0.035	0.001225
200X–1	–0.12	0.055	–0.175	0.030625
200X	0.20	0.055	0.145	0.021025
Totals	0.22		0.00	0.0529

Since there are four years of returns, we calculate the variances by dividing .0529 by $(4 - 1) = 3$.

	Asset	Pricing
Variance (σ^2)	$0.2675/3 = 0.0892$	$0.0529/3 = 0.0176$
Standard deviation (σ)	$\sqrt{0.0892} = 0.2987$	$\sqrt{0.0176} = 0.1327$

Notice that the standard deviation for Asset, 29.87 per cent, is a little more than twice Pricing's 13.27 per cent; Asset is thus the more volatile investment.

The historical record

Table 10.4 (overleaf) summarises much of our discussion of capital market history so far. It displays average returns, standard deviations and frequency distributions of annual returns on a common scale. In Table 10.4, notice, for example, that the standard deviation for the small share portfolio (48.03% equivalent per year) is more than 15 times larger than the government bond standard deviation (3.17% equivalent per year). We will return to these figures in a moment.

TABLE
10.4

Historical returns, standard deviations and frequency distributions, 1978–2002

Series	Average annual return	Standard deviation	Distribution
Ordinary shares	15.50%	37.55%	
Small shares	18.36%	48.03%	
90-day bank bills	10.23%	4.53%	
10-year government bonds	10.35%	3.17%	
Inflation	5.34%	3.99%	

Normal distribution

For many different random events in nature, a particular frequency distribution, the **normal distribution** (or bell curve), is useful for describing the probability of ending up in a given range. For example, the idea behind 'grading on a curve' comes from the fact that exam scores often resemble a bell curve.

normal distribution
a symmetric, bell-shaped frequency distribution that can be defined by its mean and standard deviation

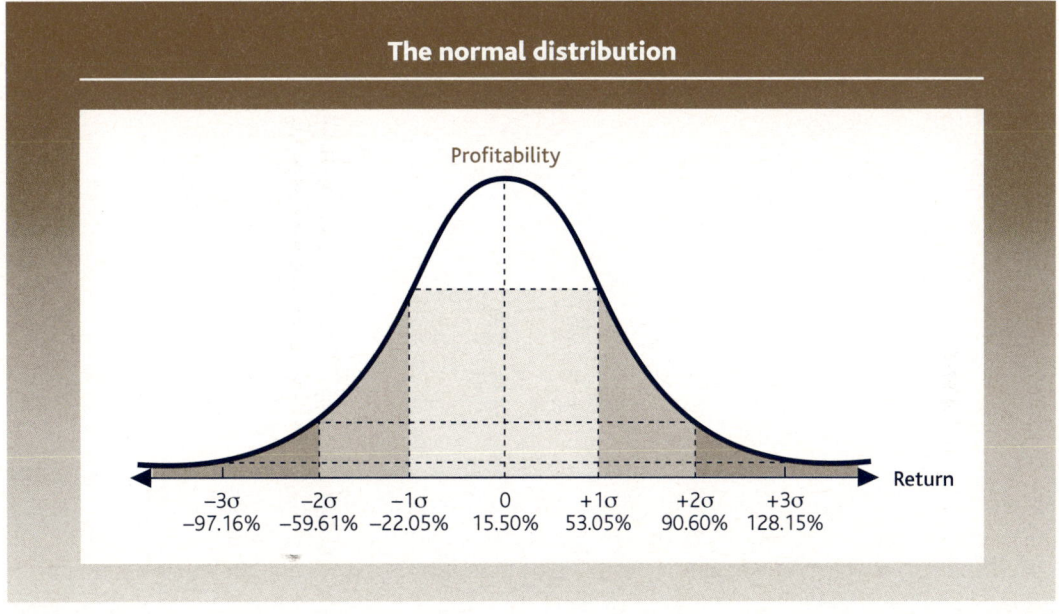

The normal distribution

Profitability

Return

	−3σ	−2σ	−1σ	0	+1σ	+2σ	+3σ
	−97.16%	−59.61%	−22.05%	15.50%	53.05%	90.60%	128.15%

FIGURE 10.11

Figure 10.11 illustrates a normal distribution and its distinctive bell shape. As you can see, this distribution has a much cleaner appearance than the actual return distributions illustrated in Table 10.4. Even so, like the normal distribution, the actual distributions do appear to be at least roughly mound-shaped and symmetrical. When this is true, the normal distribution is often a very good approximation.

Also, keep in mind that the distributions in Table 10.4 are based on only 97 equivalent yearly observations, while Figure 10.11 is, in principle, based on an infinite number. So, if we had been able to observe returns for, say, 1,000 years, we might have filled in a lot of the irregularities and ended up with a much smoother picture. For our purposes, it is enough to observe that the returns are at least roughly normally distributed.

The usefulness of the normal distribution stems from the fact that it is completely described by the average and standard deviation. If you have these two numbers, then there is nothing else to know. For example, with a normal distribution, the probability that we end up within one standard deviation of the average is about 66.6 per cent. The probability that we end up within two standard deviations is about 95 per cent. Finally, the probability of being more than three standard deviations away from the average is less than 1 per cent. These ranges and the probabilities are illustrated in Figure 10.11.

To see why this is useful, recall from Table 10.4 that the standard deviation of returns on the ordinary shares is 37.55 per cent. The average return is 15.5 per cent. So, assuming that the frequency distribution is at least approximately normal, the probability that the return in a given year is in the range −22.05 to 53.05 per cent (15.5% plus or minus one standard deviation, 37.55%) is about 66.6 per cent. This range is illustrated in Figure 10.11. In other words, there is about one chance in three that the return will be outside this range. This tells you that if you buy shares in large companies, you should expect to be outside this range in one year out of every three. This reinforces our earlier observations about stock market volatility.

The second lesson

Our observations concerning the quarter-to-quarter variability in returns are the basis for our second lesson from capital market history. On average, bearing risk is handsomely rewarded but, in a given year, there is a significant chance of a dramatic change in value. Thus, our second lesson is:

> The greater the potential reward, the greater the risk.

Using capital market history

Based on the discussion in this section, you should begin to have an idea of the risks and rewards from investing. For example, in 2000 government bonds were paying about 6.2 per cent. Suppose we had an investment that we thought had about the same risk as a portfolio of large-firm ordinary shares. At a minimum, what return would this investment have to offer for us to be interested?

From Table 10.3, the risk premium on larger ordinary shares has been 5.1 per cent historically, so a reasonable estimate of our required return would be this premium plus the government bond rate, 6.2% + 5.1% = 11.3%. This may strike you as high, but if we were thinking of starting a new business, then the risks of doing so might resemble investing in small company shares. In this case, the risk premium is 8.01 per cent, so we might require as much as 14.21 per cent from such an investment at a minimum.

We will discuss the relationship between risk and required return in more detail in the next chapter. For now, you should notice that a projected internal rate of return (IRR) on a risky investment depends on how much risk there is. This, too, is an important lesson from capital market history.

EXAMPLE 10.4 ▪ **Investing in growth shares**

The phrase 'growth share' is frequently a euphemism for a small company share. Are such investments suitable for 'widows and orphans'? Before answering, you should consider the historical volatility. For example, from the historical record, what is the approximate probability that you will actually lose 30 per cent or more of your money in a single year if you buy a portfolio of such companies?

Looking back at Table 10.4, the average return on small shares is 18.36 per cent and the standard deviation is 48.03 per cent. Assuming that the returns are approximately normal, then there is about a $1/3$ (33.3 per cent) probability that you will experience a return outside the range −29.67 to 66.39 per cent (18.36% ± 48.03%).

Because the normal distribution is symmetric, the odds of being above or below this range are equal. There is thus a 1/6 chance (half of $1/3$) that you will lose more than −29.67 per cent. So you should expect this to happen once in every six years, on average. Such investments can thus be very volatile, and they are not well-suited to those who cannot afford the risk.

10.6 ◼ Capital market efficiency

Capital market history suggests that the market values of shares, debentures and bonds can fluctuate widely from year to year. Why does this occur? At least part of the answer is that prices change because new information arrives, and investors reassess asset values based on that information.

The behaviour of market prices has been extensively studied. A question that has received particular attention is whether prices adjust quickly and correctly when new information arrives. A market is said to be 'efficient' if this is the case. To be more precise, in an **efficient capital market**, current market prices fully reflect available information. By this we simply mean that, based on available information, there is no reason to believe that the current price is too low or too high.

efficient capital market
market in which security prices reflect available information

The concept of market efficiency is a rich one, and much has been written about it. A full discussion of the subject goes beyond the scope of our study of corporate finance. However, because the concept figures so prominently in studies of market history, we briefly describe the key points here.

Price behaviour in an efficient market

To illustrate how prices behave in an efficient market, suppose the Able Performance Company (APC) has, through years of secret research and development, developed a car that will reduce fuel consumption of cars that are available now. APC's capital budgeting analysis suggests that launching the new car is a highly profitable move; in other words, the NPV appears to be positive and substantial. The key assumption thus far is that APC has not released any information about the new car; so, the fact of its existence is 'inside' information only.

Now consider a share in APC. In an efficient market, its price reflects what is known about APC's current operations and profitability, and it reflects market opinion about APC's potential for future growth and profits. The value of the new fuel-saving system is not reflected, however, because the market is unaware of its existence.

If the market agrees with APC's assessment of the value of the new project, APC's share price will rise when the decision to launch is made public. For example, assume that the announcement is made in a press release on Wednesday morning. In an efficient market, the price of shares in APC will adjust quickly to this new information. Investors should not be able to buy a share on Wednesday afternoon and make a profit on Thursday. This would imply that it took the stock market a full day to realise the implication of the APC press release. If the market is efficient, the price of shares of APC on Wednesday afternoon will already reflect the information contained in the Wednesday morning press release.

Figure 10.12 presents three possible share price adjustments for APC. In Figure 10.12, day 0 represents the announcement day. As illustrated, before the announcement, APC's shares sell for $1.40 each. The NPV per share of the new system is, say, $0.40, so the share price will be $1.80 once the value of the new project is fully reflected.

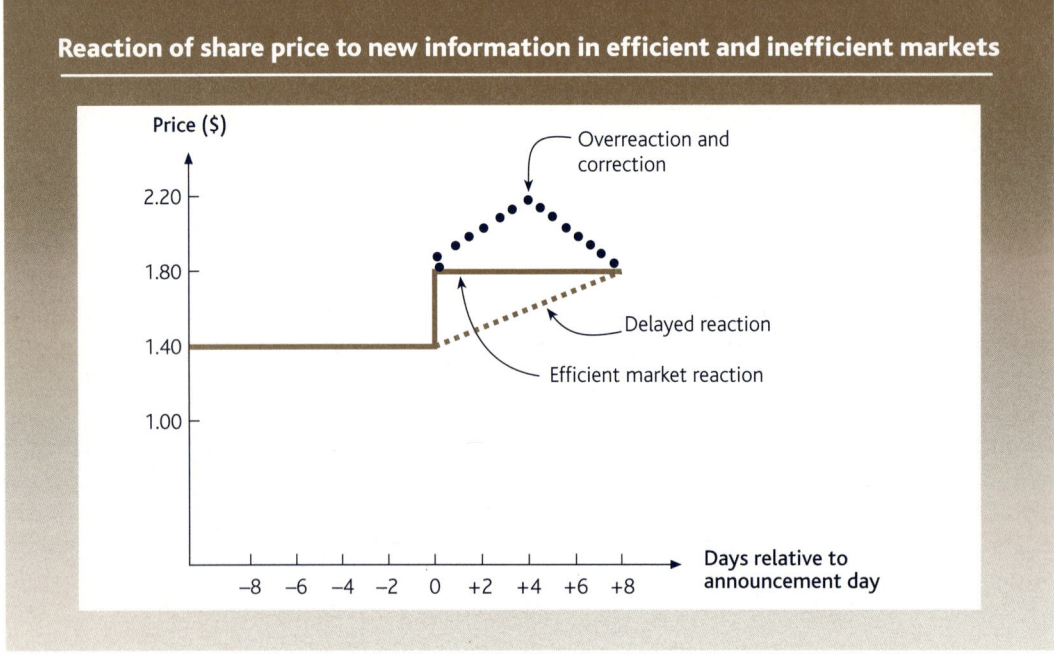

Reaction of share price to new information in efficient and inefficient markets

FIGURE 10.12

The solid line in Figure 10.12 represents the path taken by the share price in an efficient market. In this case, the price adjusts immediately to the new information and no further changes in the price of the share take place. The broken line in Figure 10.12 depicts a delayed reaction. Here it takes the market eight days or so to fully absorb the information. Finally, the dotted line illustrates an over-reaction and subsequent adjustment to the correct price.

The broken line and the dotted line in Figure 10.12 illustrate paths that the share price might take in an inefficient market. If, for example, share prices don't adjust immediately to new information (the broken line), then buying shares immediately following the release of new information and then selling them several days later would be a positive NPV activity because the price is too low for several days after the announcement.

The efficient market hypothesis

efficient market hypothesis (EMH)
the hypothesis that actual capital markets, such as the NYSE or ASX, are efficient

The **efficient market hypothesis (EMH)** asserts that well-organised capital markets such as the ASX are efficient markets, at least as a practical matter. In other words, an advocate of the EMH might argue that while inefficiencies may exist, they are relatively small and not common.

If a market is efficient, then there is a very important implication for market participants:

> All investments in an efficient market are zero NPV investments.

The reason is not complicated. If prices are neither too low nor too high, then the difference between the market value of an investment and its cost is zero; hence, the NPV is zero. As a result, in an efficient market, investors get exactly what they pay for when they buy securities, and firms receive exactly what their shares and bonds are worth when they sell them.

In their own words

Richard Roll* on market efficiency

Richard Roll

The concept of an efficient market is a special application of the 'no free lunch' principle. In an efficient financial market, costless trading policies will not generate 'excess' returns. After adjusting for the riskiness of the policy, the trader's return will be no larger than the return of a randomly selected portfolio, at least on average. This is often thought to imply something about the amount of 'information' reflected in asset prices. However, it really doesn't mean that prices reflect all information nor even that they reflect publicly available information. Instead, it means that the connection between information not reflected and prices is too subtle and tenuous to be easily or costlessly detected. Relevant information is difficult and expensive to uncover and evaluate. Thus, if costless trading policies are ineffective, there must exist some traders who make a living by 'beating the market'. They cover their costs (including the opportunity cost of their time) by trading. The existence of such traders is actually a necessary precondition for markets to become efficient. Without such professional traders, prices would fail to reflect everything that is cheap and easy to evaluate. Efficient market prices should approximate a random walk, meaning that they will appear to fluctuate more or less randomly. Prices can fluctuate non-randomly to the extent that their departure from randomness is expensive to discern. Also, observed price series can depart from apparent randomness due to changes in preferences and expectations, but this is really a technicality and does not imply a 'free-lunch' relative to current investor sentiments.

* **Richard Roll** is Allstate Professor of Finance at UCLA. He is a prominent financial researcher, and has written extensively in almost every area of modern finance. He is particularly well-known for his insightful analyses and great creativity in understanding empirical phenomena.

What makes a market efficient is competition among investors. Many individuals spend their entire lives trying to find mispriced shares. For any given share, they study what has happened in the past to the share price and its dividends. They learn, to the extent possible, what a company's earnings have been, how much it owes to creditors, what taxes it pays, what businesses it is in, what new investments are planned, how sensitive it is to changes in the economy, and so on.

Not only is there a great deal to know about any particular company, there is a powerful incentive for knowing it, namely, the profit motive. If you know more about some company than other investors in the marketplace, you can profit from that knowledge by investing in the company's shares if you have good news and selling it if you have bad news.

The logical consequence of all this information being gathered and analysed is that mispriced shares will become fewer and fewer. In other words, because of competition among investors, the market will become increasingly efficient. A kind of equilibrium comes into being where there is just enough mispricing around for those who are best at identifying it to make a living at it. For most other investors, the activity of information gathering and analysis will not pay.[3]

The following chart displays the US market around September 11. One index of the US market is the S&P 500. The market closed the night of September 10, 2001, and before it opened on September 11, the US experienced the terrorist attack. The market did not open for one week. When it did open the reaction was immediate, as the chart illustrates.

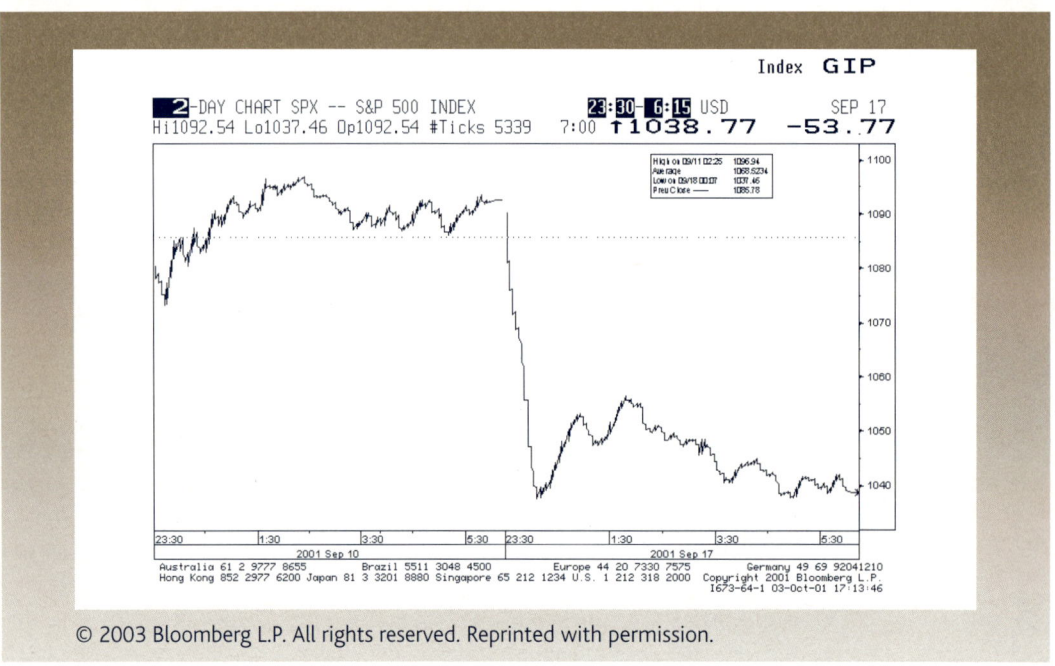

Some common misconceptions about the EMH

No idea in finance has attracted as much attention as that of efficient markets, and not all of the attention has been flattering. Rather than rehash the arguments here, we will be content to observe that some markets are more efficient than others. For example, financial markets on the whole are probably much more efficient than real asset markets.

Having said this, it is the case that much of the criticism of the EMH is misguided because it is based on a misunderstanding of what the hypothesis says and what it doesn't say. For example, when the notion of market efficiency was first publicised and debated in the popular financial press, it was often characterised by words to the effect that: 'throwing darts at the financial page will produce a portfolio that can be expected to do as well as any managed by professional security analysts'.[4]

Confusion over statements of this sort has often led to a failure to understand the implications of market efficiency. For example, sometimes it is wrongly argued that market efficiency means it doesn't matter how you invest your money because the efficiency of the market will protect you from making a mistake. However, a random dart thrower might wind up with all of the darts sticking into one or two high-risk shares that deal in genetic engineering. Would you really want all of your money in two such firms?

What efficiency does imply is that the price that a firm will obtain when it sells a share is a 'fair' price in the sense that it reflects the value of that share given the information available about it. Shareholders do not have to worry that they are paying too much for a share with a low dividend or some other sort of characteristic because the market has already incorporated that characteristic into the price. We sometimes say that the information has been 'priced out'.

The concept of efficient markets can be explained further by replying to a frequent objection. It is sometimes argued that the market cannot be efficient because share prices fluctuate from day to day. If the prices are right, the argument goes, then why do they change so much and so often? From our discussion above, these price movements are in no way inconsistent with efficiency. Investors are bombarded with information every day. The fact that prices fluctuate is, at least in part, a reflection of that information flow. In fact, the absence of price movements in a world that changes as rapidly as ours would suggest inefficiency.

The forms of market efficiency

It is common to distinguish between three forms of market efficiency. Depending on the degree of efficiency, we say that markets are either weak form efficient, semi-strong form efficient, or strong form efficient. The difference between these forms relates to what information is reflected in prices.

We start with the extreme case. If the market is strong form efficient, then all information of every kind is reflected in share prices. In such a market, there is no such thing as inside information. Thus, in our APC example above, we apparently were assuming that the market was not strong form efficient.

Casual observation, particularly in recent years, suggests that inside information does exist and it can be valuable to possess. Whether it is lawful or ethical to use that information is another issue. In any event, we conclude that private information about a particular share may exist that is not currently reflected in the price of the share. For example, prior knowledge of a take-over attempt could be very valuable.

The second form of efficiency, semi-strong efficiency, is the most controversial. If a market is semi-strong form efficient, then all public information is reflected in the share price. The reason that this form is controversial is that it implies that a security analyst who tries to identify mispriced shares using, for example, financial statement information is wasting his time because that information is already reflected in the current price.

The third form of efficiency, weak form efficiency, suggests that, at a minimum, the current price of a share reflects its own past prices. In other words, studying past prices in an attempt to identify mispriced securities is futile if the market is weak form efficient. While this form of efficiency might seem rather mild, it implies that searching in historical prices for patterns that are useful in identifying mispriced shares will not work (this practice is quite common).

What does capital market history say about market efficiency? Here again, there is great controversy. At the risk of going out on a limb, the evidence does seem to tell us three things:

1   Prices do appear to respond very rapidly to new information, and the response is at least not grossly different from what we would expect in an efficient market.
2   The future of market prices, particularly in the short run, is very difficult to predict based on publicly available information.
3   If mispriced shares do exist, then there is no obvious means of identifying them. Put another way, simple-minded schemes based on public information will probably not be successful.

Concept questions

10.6a *What is an efficient market?*
10.6b *What are the forms of market efficiency?*

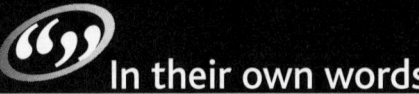

In their own words

Philip Gray* on efficient markets and football betting

Philip Gray

In its semi-strong form, the efficient market hypothesis states that all publicly-available information is reflected in market prices. This hypothesis has been examined in a variety of contexts, including stock, bond, commodities, and foreign exchange markets. However, testing this hypothesis is not always easy. For example, if stock markets are efficient, the share price is an unbiased view of the 'true' share price. The problem is that the true share price is never known—the market is continually forming and revising expectations of future cash flows.

In contrast, sports betting markets are ideal for testing the notion of efficiency. Betting on Rugby League games in Australia is conducted by SportsTAB (and no doubt many illegal bookmakers). In the week before the game, SportsTAB sets an opening 'points start'. For example, if the Sydney Roosters are expected to beat the Brisbane Broncos by around 12 points, SportsTAB might set the start at 12.5 points. I will bet on the Roosters if I believe they will win by more than this start. As the week progresses, new information comes to the market (e.g. weather, player injuries, suspensions) and the start will be altered to reflect revised expectations about the game outcome.

In the same way that we expect stock-market participants to fully incorporate new information so that share price reflects an unbiased view of the true value of the share, the points start at the time of kick-off should be an unbiased estimate of the true outcome of the game. However, unlike stock markets where true value is never known, the true outcome of a football game is revealed at the conclusion of the game. In sports betting markets, therefore, it is possible to make a clear assessment of the ability of punters to form accurate expectations and incorporate new information into prices. The implications flow over to share markets.

Given that sports betting is so amenable to testing market efficiency, it is not surprising that researchers have examined many 'markets', including basketball, baseball, American college football, Australian Rules football, one-day cricket, and horse racing. For the record, Australian research has shown that betting markets for Rugby League are not entirely efficient.† Systematic biases exist in points starts, leading to profitable betting strategies. In particular, home teams and underdogs tend to perform better than the start predicts. A strategy that bets on underdogs playing at home has a success rate significantly better than could be attributed to chance. Happy betting!

* **Philip Gray** is Associate Professor of Finance at the UQ Business School, University of Queensland.
† See Brailsford, T.J., Easton, S.A., Gray, P. and Gray, S.F. 'The efficiency of Australian football betting markets', *Australian Journal of Management*, Vol. 20, 1995, pp. 167–95.

◾10.7◾ Summary and conclusions

This chapter explores the subject of capital market history. Such history is useful because it tells us what to expect in the way of returns from risky assets. We summed up our study of market history with two key lessons:

1   Risky assets, on average, earn a risk premium. There is a reward for bearing risk.

2   The greater the potential reward from a risky investment, the greater the risk.

These lessons have significant implications for the financial manager. We will be considering these implications in the chapters ahead.

We also discussed the concept of market efficiency. In an efficient market, prices adjust quickly and correctly to new information. Consequently, asset prices in efficient markets are rarely too high or too low. How efficient capital markets (such as the ASX) are is a matter of debate, but, at a minimum, they are probably much more efficient than most real asset markets.

Key terms

Efficient capital market *339*
Efficient market hypothesis (EMH) *340*
Fisher effect *321*

Nominal returns *320*
Normal distribution *337*
Real returns *320*

Risk premium *331*
Standard deviation *334*
Variance *333*

Endnotes

1   Ibbotson, R.G. and Sinquefield, R.A. 'Stocks, Bonds, Bills and Inflation' [SBBI], Financial Analysis Research Foundation, Charlottesville, Va., 1982.

2   Under this scheme shareholders obtain a credit in their tax returns for company tax paid on the profits generating the dividends. A more detailed explanation is provided later.

3   The idea behind the EMH can be illustrated by the following short story: A student was walking down the hall with her finance professor when they both saw a $20 note on the ground. As the student bent down to pick it up, the professor shook his head slowly and, with a look of disappointment on his face, said patiently to the student, 'Don't bother. If it were really there, someone else would have picked it up already.' The moral of the story reflects the logic of the efficient market hypothesis: If you think you have found a pattern in share prices or a simple device for picking winners, you probably have not.

4   Malkiel, B.G. *A Random Walk Down Wall Street*, 2nd college edn, Norton, New York, 1981.

On the web

The information providers can help:
http://www.bloomberg.com (Bloomberg news services specialise in financial information)
http://www.afr.com.au (the *Australian Financial Review*—this newspaper constantly evaluates Australian financial information)
http://www.abc.net.au (the Australian Broadcasting Corporation offers financial review and analysis).

The Australian Stock Exchange is another relevant site: **http://www.asx.com.au**

There are some sites which offer advice and assistance, though be wary of their commercial interests:
http://www.incomeinvest.com.au (operated by Macquarie Equities).

Maximise Your Marks!
There are 30 interactive questions on lessons from capital market history waiting online for you at www.mhhe.com/au/ross3e. The questions are written with additional feedback for incorrect answers, and text excerpts with page references for follow-up study.

International Articles!
To read more on lessons from capital market history and to see current international articles, just go to www.mhhe.com/au/ross3e and click on *PowerWeb Articles* for this chapter.

Chapter review problems and self-test

10.1 · Recent return history

Use Table 10.1 to calculate the return over the year ending June 2002 for ordinary shares, small shares, and 10-year bonds. Calculate an equivalent annual return first for each quarter.

10.2 · More recent return history

Calculate the per-quarter standard deviations for ordinary shares, small shares and 10-year bonds for the year ending June 2002. Which of the investments was the most volatile in this year?

Answers to self-test problems

10.1 · We calculate the averages as follows:

Ordinary shares = −11.84 + 13.12 + 0.69 + −5.09
= −3.12%

Small shares = −12.08 + 16.78 + 4.37 + −8.15
= 0.92%

Bonds = 1.38 + 1.50 + 1.58 + 1.50
= 5.96%

10.2

Ordinary shares

Quarter	Actual Return	Average Return	Deviation	Squared Deviation
Sept	−0.1183	−0.0078	−0.1105	0.0122
Dec	0.1312	−0.0078	0.1390	0.0193
Mar	0.0069	−0.0078	0.0147	0.0002
June	−0.0509	−0.0078	−0.0431	0.0019
Total	−0.0311			0.0336
		Standard Deviation		0.1058

Small shares

Quarter	Actual Return	Average Return	Deviation	Squared Deviation
Sept	−0.1208	0.0023	−0.1231	0.0152
Dec	0.1678	0.0023	0.1655	0.0274
Mar	0.0437	0.0023	0.0414	0.0017
June	−0.0814	0.0023	−0.0837	0.0070
Total	0.0093			0.0513
		Standard Deviation		0.1307

Bonds

Quarter	Actual Return	Average Return	Deviation	Squared Deviation
Sept	0.0138	0.0149	−0.0011	0.000001
Dec	0.0150	0.0149	0.0001	0.000000
Mar	0.0158	0.0149	0.0009	0.000001
June	0.0150	0.0149	0.0001	0.000000
Total	0.0596			0.000002
		Standard Deviation		0.0008

As expected, the small shares were the most volatile.

Questions and problems

1 · Calculating returns

Delight shares have an initial price of $4.20 per share, paid a dividend of $0.24 per share during the year, and had an ending price of $3.10 per share. Compute the percentage return.

2 · Calculating yields

In problem 1, what was the dividend yield? The capital gains yield?

3 · Return calculations

Rework Problems 1 and 2 assuming that the ending price is $6.00 per share.

4 · Calculating real rate of return

If government bonds are currently paying 9 per cent and the inflation rate is 5 per cent, what is the approximate real rate? The exact real rate?

5 · Inflation and nominal returns

Suppose the real rate is 3 per cent and the inflation rate is 12 per cent. What rate would you expect to see on a Government bond?

6 · Nominal and real returns

Pipedream Voluntary Investment offers a 20 per cent return. You think that the real return will only be 12 per cent. What inflation rate is implicit in your calculation?

7 · Nominal versus real returns

Refer to Table 10.1. What was the average annual return on ordinary shares from 1996 through 2002?

a   In nominal terms?
b   In real terms?

8 · Bond returns

What is the historical real return on long-term government bonds? On 90-day bank bills? Small company shares? The real return on small company shares is higher than the real return on government bonds. Does this mean that small company shares represent a better long-term investment?

9 · Using return distributions

Suppose that the return on bank bills is normally distributed. Based on the historical record, what is the approximate probability that your return will be less than 5 per cent in a given year? What range of returns would you expect to see 95 per cent of the time? 99 per cent of the time?

10 · Negative rates

Is a negative real rate of interest possible ahead of time? After the fact? A negative inflation rate? Explain.

11 · Using return distributions

Assuming that the return from holding small company shares is normally distributed, what is the approximate probability that your money will double in value in a single year?

12 · Distributions

In Problem 11, what is the probability that the return is less than −100 per cent? (Think!) What are the implications for the distribution of returns?

13 · Calculating returns and deviations

Using the following returns, calculate the average returns and the standard deviations for Extra (X) and Flat (F).

	Returns	
Year	X	F
2001	15%	18%
2002	4	−3
2003	−9	−10
2004	8	12
2005	9	5

14 · Risk premiums

The following returns for ordinary shares and 10-year government bonds have been derived from Table 10.1 by adding the quarterly returns.

	Ordinary shares	Bonds
1997	24.71%	7.55%
1998	1.94%	5.88%
1999	14.94%	5.46%
2000	15.13%	6.45%
2001	9.34%	5.74%
2002	–3.11%	5.96%

a Calculate the observed risk premium in each year for the ordinary shares versus the 10-year Government bonds.
b Calculate the average returns and the average risk premium over this period.
c Calculate the standard deviation of the returns and the risk premium.
d Is it possible that the observed risk premium can be negative? Explain how this can happen and what it means.

15 · Effects of inflation

Look at Table 10.1 (and Figure 10.8). When were 10-year government bond rates at their highest over the period 1978–2002? Why do you think they were so high during this period? What relationship underlies your answer?

16 · Intuition and EMH

If a market is semi-strong form efficient, is it also weak form efficient? Explain.

17 · EMH

A share market analyst is able to identify mispriced shares by comparing the average price for the last 5 days to the average price for the last 20 days. If this is true, what do you know about the market?

18 · EMH

What are the implications of the efficient markets hypothesis for investors who buy and sell shares in an attempt to 'beat the market'?

19 · EMH and NPV

Explain why a characteristic of an efficient market is that investments in that market have zero NPV.

20 · EMH and speculation

Critically evaluate the following statement: 'Playing the stock market is like gambling. Such speculative investing has no social value, other than the pleasure people get from this form of gambling.'

21 · Nominal versus real risk premiums

This is a challenge question. What is the exact relationship between the nominal risk premium and the real risk premium on an investment?

22 · Inflation

T J Jones has invested $700,000 in P Q Super Investment. He has 60 per cent of his funds invested in the Diversified Portfolio and 40 per cent invested in the Fixed Interest Portfolio. He withdraws $32,800 at the end of each year for his living expenses. Even though the current rate of inflation is 3.5 per cent, T J finds that this is sufficient money for him to live comfortably and spend time at his club. The earnings of the portfolios per year have been:
Diversified: 10.43 per cent
Fixed Interest: 7.31 per cent
It is expected that these rates will continue into the foreseeable future.

a If the portfolios continued to earn the same rate, does T J's withdrawal allow him to stay in front of inflation and not be withdrawing his real capital?
b What would be the necessary split of funds across the portfolios that T J would have to maintain so that his current withdrawals match inflation?

CHAPTER 11

Return,
risk and the security market line

Objective

On completion of this chapter the relationship between expected return and risk should be understood. It will be appreciated that it is risk, which is related to the market, that is important in determining expected return. Students will know how to calculate the return for combinations of investments. They will understand the risk when investments are combined, reinforcing how it is the market-related risk that is important. The beta statistic will also be introduced and with it a clear understanding of all the components of the expected return equation will be developed.

Study tips ▷ This chapter introduces a number of concepts that are essential to contemporary finance. There is the *Capital Asset Pricing Model* (shortened to the CAPM). This model explains the *Capital Market Line* for evaluating the expected returns of combinations of investments where there is no diversifiable risk remaining, and the *Security Market Line*, which evaluates the expected returns of individual investments as well as combinations of investments. Note clearly what is meant by systematic and non-systematic risk, the relative measure of systematic risk (beta), and the covariance and correlation statistics. The work is all new but if it is read carefully and understood a strong foundation will be laid for your current course and all future studies in finance.

In Chapter 10, we learned some important lessons from capital market history. Most importantly, there is a reward, on average, for bearing risk. We called this reward a risk premium. The second lesson is that this risk premium is larger for riskier investments. The principle that higher returns can be earned only by taking greater risks appeals to our moral sense that we cannot have something for nothing. This chapter explores the economic and managerial implications of this basic idea.

This far, we have concentrated mainly on the return behaviour of a few large portfolios. We need to expand our consideration to include individual assets. Accordingly, the purpose of this chapter is to provide the background necessary for learning how the risk premium is determined for individual assets.

When we examine the risks associated with individual assets, we find that there are two types of risk: systematic and non-systematic. This distinction is crucial because, as we will see, systematic risks affect almost all assets in the economy, at least to some degree, while a non-systematic risk affects at most a small number of assets. We then develop the principle of diversification, which shows that highly diversified portfolios will tend to have almost no non-systematic risk.

The principle of diversification has an important implication: to a diversified investor, only systematic risk matters. It follows that in deciding whether or not to buy a particular individual asset, a diversified investor will be concerned only with that asset's systematic risk. This is a key observation, and it allows us to say a great deal about the risks and returns on individual assets. In particular, it is the basis for a famous relationship between risk and return called the security market line, or SML. To develop the SML, we introduce the equally famous 'beta' coefficient, one of the centrepieces of modern finance. Beta and the SML are key concepts because they supply us with at least part of the answer to the question of how to go about determining the required return on an investment.

 **Expected returns and variances**

In our previous chapter, we discussed how to calculate average returns and variances using historical data. We now begin to discuss how to analyse returns and variances when the information we have concerns future possible returns and their probabilities.

expected return

return on a risky asset expected in the future

Expected return

We start with a straightforward case. Consider a single period of time, say a year. We have two shares, Lamb and Unicorn, which have the following characteristics: Lamb shares are expected to have a return of 25 per cent in the coming year. Unicorn shares are expected to have a return of 20 per cent for the same period.

In a situation like this, if all investors agreed on the expected returns, why would anyone want to hold Unicorn shares? After all, why invest in one share when the expectation is that another will do better? Clearly, the answer must depend on the risk of the two investments. The return on a Lamb share, although it is expected to be 25 per cent, could actually turn out to be higher or lower.

For example, suppose the economy booms. In this case, we think Lamb shares will have a 70 per cent return. If the economy enters a recession, we think the return will be −20 per cent. In this case, we say that there are two states of the economy, which means that these are the only two possible situations. This setup is oversimplified, of course, but it allows us to illustrate some key ideas without a lot of computation.

Suppose we think that a boom and a recession are equally likely to happen, that there is a 50–50 chance of each. Table 11.1 illustrates the basic information we have described and some additional information about Unicorn shares. Notice that Unicorn shares earn 30 per cent if there is a recession and 10 per cent if there is a boom.

Obviously, if you buy one of these shares, say Unicorn, what you earn in any particular year depends on what the economy does during that year. However, suppose that the probabilities stay the same through time. If you hold Unicorn for a number of years, you'll earn 30 per cent about half the time and 10 per cent the other half. In this case, we say that your expected return on share Unicorn, $E(R_U)$, is 20 per cent:

$$E(R_U) = .50 \times 30\% + .50 \times 10\% = 20\%$$

In other words, you should expect to earn 20 per cent from this share, on average.

 TABLE 11.1

States of the economy and share returns			
State of the economy	Probability of the state of the economy	Security if state occurs Lamb	Unicorn
Recession	0.5	−20%	30%
Boom	0.5	70%	10%
	1.0		

For Lamb shares, the probabilities are the same, but the possible returns are different. Here we lose 20 per cent half the time, and we gain 70 per cent the other half. The expected return on Lamb, $E(R_L)$, is thus 25 per cent:

$$E(R_L) = 0.50 \times -20\% + 0.50 \times 70\% = 25\%$$

Table 11.2 illustrates these calculations.

TABLE 11.2

Calculation of expected return

(1) State of economy	(2) Probability of state of economy	Lamb		Unicorn	
		(3) Rate of return if state occurs	(4) Product (2) × (3)	(5) Rate of return if state occurs	(6) Product (2) × (5)
Recession	0.5	−0.20	−0.10	0.30	0.15
Boom	0.5	0.70	0.35	0.10	0.05
	1.0	$E(R_L)$	25%	$E(R_U)$	20%

In our previous chapter, we defined the risk premium as the difference between the return on a risky investment and a risk-free investment, and we calculated the historical risk premiums on some different investments. Using our projected returns, we can calculate the projected or expected risk premium as the difference between the expected return on a risky investment and the certain return on a risk-free investment.

For example, suppose that risk-free investments are currently offering 8 per cent. We will say that the risk-free rate, which we label as R_f, is 8 per cent. Given this, what is the projected risk premium on Unicorn? On Lamb? Since the expected return on Unicorn, $E(R_U)$, is 20 per cent, the projected risk premium is:

$$
\begin{aligned}
\textbf{Risk premium} &= \textbf{Expected return} - \textbf{Risk-free rate} \qquad \text{(11.1)} \\
&= E(R_U) - R_f \\
&= 20\% - 8\% \\
&= 12\%
\end{aligned}
$$

Similarly, the risk premium on Lamb is 25% − 8% = 17%.

In general, the expected return on a security or other asset is simply equal to the sum of the possible returns multiplied by their probabilities. So, if we have 100 possible returns, we would multiply each one by its probability and then add the results up. The result would be the expected return. The risk premium would then be the difference between this expected return and the risk-free rate.

EXAMPLE 11.1

Unequal probabilities

Look back at Tables 11.1 and 11.2. Suppose you thought that a boom would only occur 20 per cent of the time instead of 50 per cent. What are the expected returns on Unicorn and Lamb in this case? If the risk-free rate is 10 per cent, what are the risk premiums?

The first thing to notice is that a recession must occur 80 per cent of the time (1 − 0.20 = 0.80) since there are only two possibilities. With this in mind, Unicorn has a 30 per cent return in 80 per cent of the years and a 10 per cent return in 20 per cent of the years. To calculate the expected return, we again just multiply the possibilities by the probabilities and add up the results:

$$E(R_U) = 0.80 \times 30\% + 0.20 \times 10\% = 26\%$$

(continued)

EXAMPLE 11.1 · Unequal probabilities (*continued*)

Table 11.3 summarises the calculations for both shares. Notice that the expected return on Lamb is −2 per cent.

TABLE 11.3

(1) State of economy	(2) Probability of state of economy	Lamb		Unicorn	
		(3) Rate of return if state occurs	(4) Product (2) × (3)	(5) Rate of return if state occurs	(6) Product (2) × (5)
Recession	0.8	−0.20	−0.16	0.30	0.24
Boom	0.2	0.70	0.14	0.10	0.02
	1.0	$E(R_L)$	−2%	$E(R_U)$	26%

The risk premium for share Unicorn is 26% − 10% = 16% in this case. The risk premium for share Lamb is negative: −2% − 10% = −12%. This is a little odd, but it is not impossible.

Calculating the variance

To calculate the variances of the returns on our two shares, we first determine the squared deviations from the expected return. We then multiply each possible squared deviation by its probability. We add these up, and the result is the variance. The standard deviation, as always, is the square root of the variance.

To illustrate, Unicorn above has an expected return of $E(R_U)$ = 20%. In a given year, it will actually return either 30 per cent or 10 per cent. The possible deviations are thus 30% − 20% = 10% or 10% − 20% = −10%. In this case, the variance is:

$$\text{Variance} = \sigma^2 = 0.50 \times (0.1)^2 + 0.50 \times (-0.1)^2 = 0.01$$

The standard deviation is the square root of this:

$$\text{Standard deviation} = \sigma = \sqrt{0.01} = 0.10 = 10\%$$

Table 11.4 summarises these calculations for both shares. Notice that Lamb has a much larger variance.

When we put the expected return and variability information for our two shares together, we have:

	Lamb	Unicorn
Expected return, $E(R)$	25%	20%
Variance, σ^2	0.2025	0.0100
Standard deviation, σ	45%	10%

TABLE 11.4

Calculation of variance

(1) State of economy	(2) Probability of state of economy	(3) Return deviation from expected return	(4) Squared return deviation from expected return	(5) Product (2) × (4)
Share Lamb				
Recession	0.5	−0.20 − 0.25 = −0.45	$(-0.45)^2$ = 0.2025	0.10125
Boom	0.5	0.70 − 0.25 = 0.45	$(0.45)^2$ = 0.2025	0.10125
			σ^2_L = 0.2025	
			σ_L = 0.45	

TABLE
11.4

			Calculation of variance (*continued*)	

(1) State of economy	(2) Probability of state of economy	(3) Return deviation from expected return	(4) Squared return deviation from expected return	(5) Product (2) × (4)
Share Unicorn				
Recession	0.50	0.30 − 0.20 = 0.10	$(0.10)^2 = 0.01$	0.005
Boom	0.50	0.10 − 0.20 = −0.10	$(-0.10)^2 = 0.01$	0.005
			$\sigma^2_U = 0.010$	
			$\sigma_U = 0.1$	

Lamb has a higher expected return, but Unicorn has less risk. You could get a 70 per cent return on your investment in Lamb, but you could also lose 20 per cent.

Which of these two shares should you buy? We can't really say; it depends on your personal preferences. We can be reasonably sure, however, that some investors would prefer Lamb to Unicorn and some would prefer Unicorn to Lamb.

You've probably noticed that the way we calculated expected returns and variances here is somewhat different from the way we did it in the last chapter. The reason is that in Chapter 10 we were examining actual historical returns, so we estimated the average return and the variance based on some actual events. Here, we have projected future returns and their associated probabilities, so this is the information with which we must work.

More unequal probabilities

EXAMPLE
11.2

Going back to Example 11.1, what are the variances on the two shares once we have unequal probabilities? The standard deviations?

We can summarise the needed calculations as follows:

(1) State of economy	(2) Probability of state of economy	(3) Return deviation from expected return	(4) Squared return deviation from expected return	(5) Product (2) × (4)
Share Lamb				
Recession	0.8	−0.20 − (−0.02) = −0.18	0.0324	0.02592
Boom	0.2	0.70 − (−0.02) = 0.72	0.5184	0.10368
			$\sigma^2_L = 0.12960$	
Share Unicorn				
Recession	0.8	0.30 − 0.26 = 0.04	0.0016	0.00128
Boom	0.2	0.10 − 0.26 = −0.16	0.0256	0.00512
			$\sigma^2_U = 0.00640$	

Based on these calculations, the standard deviation for Lamb is $\sigma_L = \sqrt{0.1296} = 36\%$. The standard deviation for Unicorn is much smaller, $\sigma_U = \sqrt{0.0064} = 0.08$ or 8%.

Concept questions

11.1a *How do we calculate the expected return on a security?*
11.1b *In words, how do we calculate the variance of the expected return?*

11.2 Portfolios

portfolio
group of assets such as shares and debentures held by an investor

Thus far in this chapter, we have concentrated on individual assets considered separately. However, most investors actually hold a **portfolio** of assets. All we mean by this is that investors tend to own more than just a single share, debenture, or other asset. Given that this is so, portfolio return and portfolio risk are of obvious relevance. Accordingly, we now discuss portfolio expected returns and variances.

Portfolio weights

portfolio weight
percentage of a portfolio's total value in a particular asset

There are many equivalent ways of describing a portfolio. The most convenient approach is to list the percentages of the total portfolio's value that are invested in each portfolio asset. We call these percentages the **portfolio weights**.

For example, if we have $50 in one asset and $150 in another, then our total portfolio is worth $200. The percentage of our portfolio in the first asset is $50/$200 = 0.25. The percentage of our portfolio in the second asset is $150/$200, or 0.75. Our portfolio weights are thus 0.25 and 0.75. Notice that the weights have to add up to 1.00 since all of our money is invested somewhere.[1]

Portfolio expected returns

Let us go back to Lamb and Unicorn. You put half your money in each. The portfolio weights are obviously 0.50 and 0.50. What is the pattern of returns on this portfolio? The expected return?

To answer these questions, suppose the economy actually enters a recession. In this case, half your money (the half in L) loses 20 per cent. The other half (the half in Unicorn) gains 30 per cent. Your portfolio return, R_P, in a recession will thus be:

$$R_P = 0.50 \times (-20\%) + 0.50 \times 30\% = 5\%$$

Table 11.5 summarises the remaining calculations. Notice that when a boom occurs, your portfolio would return 40 per cent:

$$R_P = 0.50 \times 70\% + 0.50 \times 10\% = 40\%$$

As indicated in Table 11.5, the expected return on your portfolio, $E(R_P)$, is 22.5 per cent.

TABLE 11.5

Expected return on an equally weighted portfolio of Lamb and Unicorn			
(1) State of economy	(2) Probability of state of economy	(3) Portfolio return If state occurs	(4) Product (2) × (3)
Recession	0.50	1/2 × (−20%) + 1/2 × (30%) = 5%	2.5%
Boom	0.50	1/2 × (70%) + 1/2 × (10%) = 40%	20%
			$E(R_P) = 22.5\%$

We can save ourselves some work by calculating the expected return more directly. Given these portfolio weights, we could have reasoned that we expect half of our money to earn 25 per cent (the half in Lamb) and half of our money to earn 20 per cent (the half in Unicorn). Our portfolio expected return is thus:

$$
\begin{aligned}
E(R_P) &= 0.50 \times E(R_L) + 0.50 \times E(R_U) \\
&= 0.50 \times 25\% + 0.50 \times 20\% \\
&= 22.5\%
\end{aligned}
$$

This is the same portfolio expected return we had before.

This method of calculating the expected return on a portfolio works no matter how many assets there are in the portfolio. Suppose we had n assets in our portfolio, where n is any number. If we let x_i stand for the percentage of our money in asset i, then the expected return is:

$$E(R_P) = x_1 \times E(R_1) + x_2 \times E(R_2) + \ldots + x_n \times E(R_n) \qquad (11.2)$$

This says that the expected return on a portfolio is a straightforward combination of the expected returns on the assets in that portfolio. This seems somewhat obvious, but, as we will examine next, the obvious approach is not always the right one.

Portfolio expected return

EXAMPLE 11.3

Suppose we have the following projections on three shares:

State of economy	Probability of state	Returns		
		Share A	Share B	Share C
Boom	0.40	10%	15%	20%
Bust	0.60	8%	4%	0%

What would be the expected return on a portfolio with equal amounts invested in each of the three shares? What would the expected return be if half of the portfolio were in A, with the remainder equally divided between B and C?

From our earlier discussions, the expected returns on the individual shares are (check these for practice):

$$
\begin{aligned}
E(R_A) &= 8.8\% \\
E(R_B) &= 8.4\% \\
E(R_C) &= 8.0\%
\end{aligned}
$$

If a portfolio has equal investments in each asset, the portfolio weights are all the same. Such a portfolio is said to be equally weighted. Since there are three shares in this case, the weights are all equal to $1/3$. The portfolio expected return is thus:

$$E(R_P) = (1/3) \times 8.8\% + (1/3) \times 8.4\% + (1/3) \times 8.0\% = 8.4\%$$

Portfolio variance

From our discussion above, the expected return on a portfolio that contains equal investment in Unicorn and Lamb is 22.5 per cent. What is the standard deviation of return on this portfolio? Simple intuition might suggest that half of the money has a standard deviation of

45 per cent and the other half has a standard deviation of 10 per cent, so the portfolio's standard deviation might be calculated as:

$$\sigma_P = 0.50 \times 45\% + 0.50 \times 10\% = 27.5\%$$

Unfortunately, this approach is completely incorrect.

Let us see what the standard deviation really is. Table 11.6 summarises the relevant calculations. As we see, the portfolio's variance is about 0.031, and its standard deviation is less than we thought—it's only 17.5 per cent. What is illustrated here is that the variance on a portfolio is not generally a simple combination of the variances of the assets in the portfolio.

TABLE 11.6

	Variance on an equally weighted portfolio of Lamb and Unicorn			
(1) State of economy	(2) Probability of state of economy	(3) Portfolio return if state occurs	(4) Squared return deviation from expected return	(5) Product (2) × (4)
Recession	0.5	5%	$(0.05 - 0.225)^2 = 0.030625$	0.0153125
Boom	0.5	40%	$(0.40 - 0.225)^2 = 0.030625$	0.0153125
			$\sigma^2_p =$	0.030625
			$\sigma_p = \sqrt{0.030625} =$	17.5%

We can illustrate this point a little more dramatically by considering a slightly different set of portfolio weights. Suppose we put 2/11 (about 18%) in Lamb and the other 9/11 (about 82%) in Unicorn. If a recession occurs, this portfolio will have a return of:

$$R_P = (2/11) \times (-20\%) + (9/11) \times (30\%) = 20.91\%$$

If a boom occurs, this portfolio will have a return of:

$$R_P = (2/11) \times (70\%) + (9/11) \times (10\%) = 20.91\%$$

Notice that the return is the same no matter what happens. No further calculations are needed: this portfolio has a zero variance. Apparently, combining assets into portfolios can substantially alter the risks faced by the investor. This is a crucial observation, and we explore its implications in the next section.

EXAMPLE 11.4 Portfolio variance and standard deviation

In Example 11.3, what are the standard deviations on the two portfolios? To answer, we first have to calculate the portfolio returns in the two states. We will work with the second portfolio, which has 50 per cent in share A and 25 per cent in each of shares B and C. The relevant calculations can be summarised as follows:

State of economy	Probability of state	Returns			
		Share A	Share B	Share C	Portfolio
Boom	0.4	10%	15%	20%	13.75%
Bust	0.6	8%	4%	0%	5.00%

EXAMPLE

11.4

Portfolio variance and standard deviation (*continued*)

The portfolio return when the economy booms is calculated as:

$$0.50 \times 10\% + 0.25 \times 15\% + 0.25 \times 20\% = 13.75\%$$

The return when the economy goes bust is calculated the same way:

$$0.5 \times 8\% + 0.25 \times 4\% + 0.25 \times 0\% = 5\%$$

The expected return on the portfolio is 8.5 per cent. The variance is thus:

$$\sigma^2 = 0.40 \times (0.1375 - 0.085)^2 + 0.60 \times (0.05 - 0.085)^2$$
$$= 0.0018375$$

The standard deviation is thus about 4.3 per cent. For our equally weighted portfolio, check that the standard deviation is about 5.4 per cent.

Concept questions

11.2a *What is a portfolio weight?*

11.2b *How do we calculate the expected return on a portfolio?*

11.2c *Is there a simple relationship between the standard deviation on a portfolio and the standard deviations of the assets in the portfolio?*

11.3 ■ Announcements, surprises and expected returns

Now that we know how to construct portfolios and evaluate their returns, we begin to describe more carefully the risks and returns associated with individual securities. Thus far, we have measured volatility by looking at the differences between the actual returns on an asset or portfolio, R, and the expected return, $E(R)$. We now look at why those deviations exist.

Expected and unexpected returns

To begin, we consider the return on the share of a company called Findings. What will determine this share's return in, say, the coming year? The return on any share traded in a financial market is composed of two parts. First, the normal or expected return from the share is the part of the return that shareholders in the market predict or expect. This return depends on the information shareholders have that bears on the share, and it is based on the market's understanding today of the important factors that will influence the share in the coming year.

The second part of the return on the share is the uncertain or risky part. This is the portion that comes from unexpected information revealed within the year. A list of all possible sources of such information is endless, but here are a few examples:

- News about Findings' research.
- Government figures released on gross national product (GNP).
- The world commodity price level changes.
- The news that Findings' sales figures are higher than expected.
- A sudden, unexpected drop in interest rates.

Based on this discussion, one way to write the return on Findings' shares in the coming year would be:

$$\text{Total return} = \text{Expected return} + \text{Unexpected return} \qquad (11.3)$$
$$R = E(R) + U$$

where R stands for the actual total return in the year, $E(R)$ stands for the expected part of the return, and U stands for the unexpected part of the return. What this says is that the actual return, R, differs from the expected return, $E(R)$, because of surprises that occur during the year.

Announcements and news

We need to be careful when we talk about the effect of these and other news items on the return. For example, suppose that Findings' business is such that the company prospers when GNP (gross national product) grows at a relatively high rate and suffers when GNP is relatively stagnant. In this case, in deciding what return to expect this year from owning share in Findings, shareholders either implicitly or explicitly must think about what GNP is likely to be for the year.

When the government actually announces GNP figures for the year, what will happen to the value of Findings' shares? Obviously, the answer depends on what figure is released. More to the point, however, the impact depends on how much of that figure is new information.

At the beginning of the year, market participants will have some idea or forecast of what the yearly GNP will be. To the extent that shareholders had predicted GNP, that prediction will already be factored into the expected part of the return on the shares, $E(R)$. On the other hand, if the announced GNP is a surprise, then the effect will be part of U, the unanticipated portion of the return.

As an example, suppose shareholders in the market had forecast that the GNP increase this year would be 0.5 per cent. If the actual announcement this year is exactly 0.5 per cent, the same as the forecast, then the shareholders didn't really learn anything, and the announcement isn't news. There would be no impact on the share price as a result. This is like receiving confirmation of something that you suspected all along; it doesn't reveal anything new.

A common way of saying that an announcement isn't news is to say that the market has already 'discounted' the announcement. The use of the word 'discount' here is different from the use of the term in computing present values, but the spirit is the same. When we discount a dollar in the future, we say it is worth less to us because of the time value of money. When we discount an announcement or a news item, we mean that it has less of an impact on the market because the market already knew much of it.

For example, going back to Findings, suppose the government announced that the actual GNP increase during the year was 1.5 per cent. Now shareholders have learned something—that the increase is 1 percentage point higher than they had forecast. This difference between the actual result and the forecast, 1 percentage point in this example, is sometimes called the innovation or the surprise.

An announcement, then, can be broken into two parts, the anticipated or expected part and the surprise or innovation:

$$\text{Announcement} = \text{Expected part} + \text{Surprise} \qquad (11.4)$$

The expected part of any announcement is part of the information that the market uses to form the expectation, $E(R)$, of the return on the share. The surprise is the news that influences the unanticipated return on the share, U.

To take another example, if shareholders knew in January that the chief executive officer of the firm was going to resign, the official announcement in February would be fully expected and would be discounted by the market. Because the announcement was expected before February, its influence on the share would have taken place before February. The announcement itself will contain no surprise, and the share's price shouldn't change at all when it is actually made.

Our discussion of market efficiency in the previous chapter bears on this discussion. We are assuming that relevant information that is known today is already reflected in the expected return. This is identical to saying that the current price reflects relevant publicly available information. We are thus implicitly assuming that markets are at least reasonably efficient in the semi-strong form sense.

Henceforth, when we speak of news, we will mean the surprise part of an announcement and not the portion that the market has expected and therefore already discounted.

Concept questions

11.3a *What are the two basic parts of a return?*
11.3b *Under what conditions will an announcement have no effect on ordinary share prices?*

 # 11.4 ▪ Risk: Systematic and non-systematic

The unanticipated part of the return, that portion resulting from surprises, is the true risk of any investment. After all, if we always receive exactly what we expect, then the investment is perfectly predictable and, by definition, risk-free. In other words, the risk of owning an asset comes from surprises—unanticipated events.

There are important differences, though, among various sources of risk. Look back at our list of news stories. Some of these stories are directed specifically at Findings, and some are more general. Which of the news items are of specific importance to Findings?

Announcements about interest rates or GNP are clearly important for nearly all companies, whereas the news about Findings' chief executive officer, its research, or its sales are of specific interest to Findings. We will distinguish between these two types of event however because, as we shall see, they have very different implications.

Systematic and non-systematic risk

The first type of surprise, the ones that affect a large number of assets, we will label **systematic risk**. A systematic risk is one that influences a large number of assets, each to a greater or lesser extent. Because systematic risks are market-wide effects, they are sometimes called market risks.

The second type of surprise we will call **non-systematic risk**. A non-systematic risk is one that affects a single asset or a small group of assets. Because these risks are unique to individual companies or assets, they are sometimes called unique or asset-specific risks. We will use these terms interchangeably.

As we have seen, uncertainties about general economic conditions, such as GNP, interest rate, or inflation, are examples of systematic risks. These conditions affect nearly all companies to some degree. An unanticipated increase or surprise in inflation, for example, affects wages and the costs of the supplies that companies buy; it affects the value of the assets that companies own; and it affects the prices at which companies sell their products. Forces such as these, to which all companies are susceptible, are the essence of systematic risk.

systematic risk
a risk that influences a large number of assets. Also market risk

non-systematic risk
a risk that affects at most a small number of assets. Also unique or asset-specific risks

In contrast, the announcement of an oil strike by a company will primarily affect that company and, perhaps, a few others (such as primary competitors and suppliers). It is unlikely to have much of an effect on the world oil market, however, or on the affairs of companies that are not in the oil business.

Systematic and non-systematic components of return

The distinction between a systematic risk and a non-systematic risk is never really as exact as we make it out to be. Even the most narrow and peculiar bit of news about a company ripples through the economy. This is true because every enterprise, no matter how tiny, is a part of the economy. It is like the tale of a kingdom that was lost because one horse lost a shoe. This is mostly hair-splitting, however. Some risks are clearly much more general than others. We will see some evidence on this point in a moment.

The distinction between the types of risk allows us to break down the surprise portion, U, of the return on Findings' shares into two parts. From before, we had the actual return broken down into its expected and surprise components:

$$R = E(R) + U$$

We now recognise that the total surprise for Findings, U, has a systematic and a non-systematic component, so:

$$R = E(R) + \textbf{Systematic portion} + \textbf{Non-systematic portion} \quad (11.5)$$

Because it is traditional, we will use the Greek letter epsilon, ε, to stand for the non-systematic portion. Since systematic risks are often called market risks, we will use the letter m to stand for the systematic part of the surprise. With these symbols, we can rewrite the total return:

$$\begin{aligned} R &= E(R) + U \\ &= E(R) + m + \varepsilon \end{aligned}$$

The important thing about the way we have broken down the total surprise, U, is that the non-systematic portion, ε, is more or less unique to Findings. For this reason, it is unrelated to the non-systematic portion of return on most other assets. To see why this is important, we need to return to the subject of portfolio risk.

Concept questions

11.4a *What are the two basic types of risk?*
11.4b *What is the distinction between the two types of risk?*

 ## 11.5 Diversification and portfolio risk

We saw earlier that portfolio risks can, in principle, be quite different from the risks of the assets that make up the portfolio. We now look more closely at the riskiness of an individual asset versus the risk of a portfolio of many different assets. We will once again examine some market history to get an idea of what happens with actual investments in Australian capital markets.

The effect of diversification: another lesson from market history

To examine the relationship between portfolio size and portfolio risk, Table 11.7 illustrates typical average monthly standard deviations for equally weighted portfolios that contain different numbers of randomly selected securities.[2]

In column 2 of Table 11.7, we see that the standard deviation for a 'portfolio' of one security is about 11.5 per cent. What this means is that, if you randomly selected a single share and put all your money into it, your standard deviation of return would typically have been a substantial 11.5 per cent per month. If you were to select five shares at random and invest your money equally in each, your standard deviation would have been about 7.9 per cent on average, and so on.

TABLE 11.7

Standard deviations of monthly portfolio returns

(1) Number of shares	(2) Average standard deviation	(3) Ratio of portfolio standard deviation to the standard deviation of an individual share
1	11.49%	1.00
5	7.91%	0.69
10	6.61%	0.58
15	6.08%	0.53
20	5.71%	0.50
25	5.60%	0.49
30	5.50%	0.48
35	5.50%	0.48
40	5.26%	0.46
45	5.12%	0.45

The important thing to notice in Table 11.7 is that the standard deviation declines as the number of securities is increased. By the time we have 10 randomly chosen shares, the portfolio's standard deviation has declined from 11.49 per cent to about 6.61 per cent, which is about 60 per cent of 11.49. With 20 securities, the standard deviation is 5.71 per cent, which is about 50 per cent of 11.49—it has halved.

The principle of diversification

Figure 11.1 (overleaf) illustrates the point we have been discussing. What we have plotted is the standard deviation of return versus the number of shares in the portfolio. Notice in Figure 11.1 that the benefit in terms of risk reduction from adding securities drops off as we add more and more. By the time we have 10 securities, most of the effect is already realised, and by the time we get to 30 or so, there is very little remaining benefit.

Figure 11.1 illustrates two key points. First of all, some of the riskiness associated with individual assets can be eliminated by forming portfolios. The process of spreading an investment across assets (and thereby forming a portfolio) is called diversification. The **principle of diversification** tells us that spreading an investment across many assets will

principle of diversification

principle stating that spreading an investment across a number of assets will eliminate some, but not all, of the risk

FIGURE
11.1

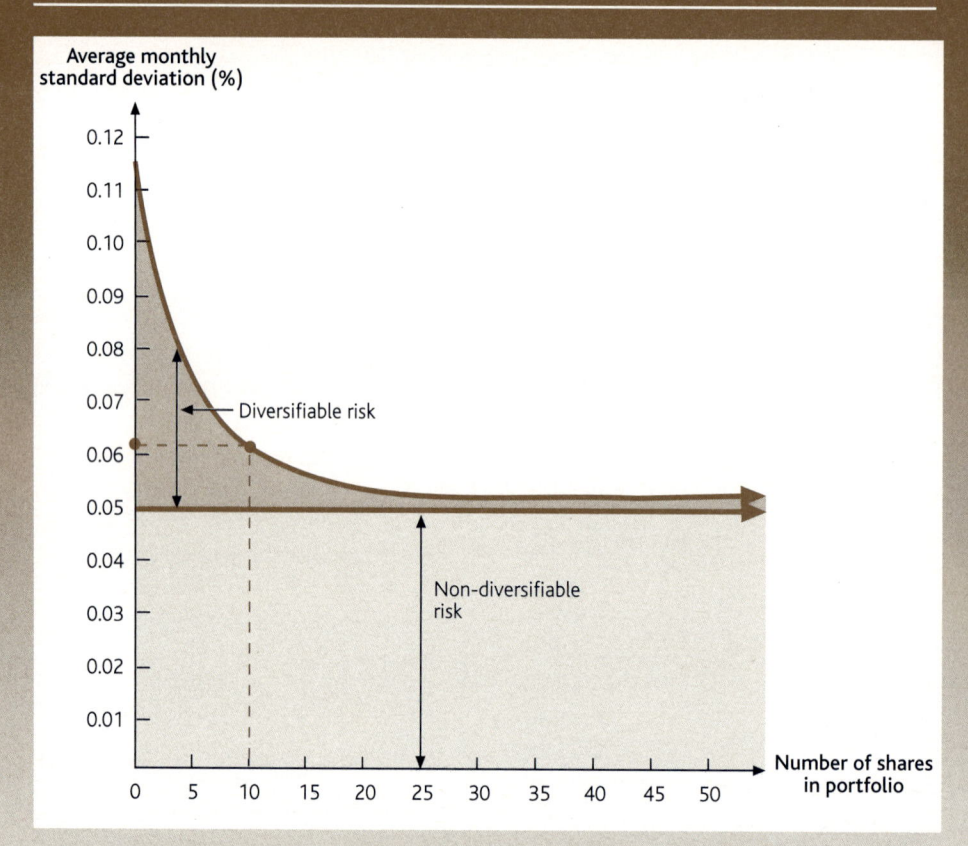

Portfolio diversification

eliminate some of the risk. The shaded area in Figure 11.1, labelled 'diversifiable risk', is the part that can be eliminated by diversification.

The second point is equally important. There is a minimum level of risk that cannot be eliminated simply by diversifying. This minimum level is labelled 'non-diversifiable risk' in Figure 11.1. Taken together, these two points are another important lesson from capital market history:

> Diversification reduces risk, but only up to a point, as market risk will always be present.

Put another way, some risk is diversifiable and some is not.

Diversification and non-systematic risk

From our discussion of portfolio risk, we know that some of the risk associated with individual assets can be diversified away and some cannot. We are left with an obvious question: Why is this so? It turns out that the answer hinges on the distinction we made earlier between systematic and non-systematic risk.

By definition, a non-systematic risk is one that is particular to a single asset or, at most, a small group of assets. For example, if the asset under consideration is a shareholding in a single company, the discovery of positive NPV projects such as successful new products and innovative cost savings will tend to increase the value of the shares. Unanticipated lawsuits, industrial accidents, strikes and similar events will tend to decrease future cash flows and thereby reduce share values.

Here is the important observation: if we only held a single share, then the value of our investment would fluctuate because of company-specific events. If we held a large portfolio, on the other hand, some of the shares in the portfolio would go up in value because of positive company-specific events and some would go down in value because of negative events. The net effect on the overall value of the portfolio will be relatively small, however, as these effects would tend to cancel each other out.

Now we see why some of the variability associated with individual assets is eliminated by diversification. By combining assets into portfolios, the unique or non-systematic events—both positive and negative—tend to 'wash out' once we have more than just a few assets.

This is an important point that bears repeating:

> Non-systematic risk is essentially eliminated by diversification, so a relatively large portfolio has almost no non-systematic risk.

In fact, the terms 'diversifiable risk' and 'non-systematic risk' are often used interchangeably.

Diversification and systematic risk

We have seen that non-systematic risk can be eliminated by diversifying. What about systematic risk? Can it also be eliminated by diversification? The answer is no because, by definition, a systematic risk affects almost all assets to some degree. As a result, no matter how many assets we put into a portfolio, the systematic risk doesn't go away. Thus, for obvious reasons, the terms systematic risk and non-diversifiable risk are used interchangeably.

Because we have introduced so many different terms, it is useful to summarise our discussion before moving on. What we have seen is that the total risk of an investment, as measured by the standard deviation of its return, can be written as:

$$
\begin{aligned}
\text{Total risk} \ &= \ \textbf{Systematic risk} \ + \ \textbf{Non-systematic risk} \qquad (11.6)\\
&= \ \textbf{Non-diversifiable risk} \ + \ \textbf{Diversifiable risk}\\
&= \ \textbf{Market risk} \ + \ \textbf{Non-market risk}
\end{aligned}
$$

Systematic risk is also called non-diversifiable risk or market risk. Non-systematic risk is also called diversifiable risk, unique risk, or asset-specific risk. For a well-diversified portfolio, the non-systematic risk is negligible. For such a portfolio, essentially all of the risk is systematic.

Concept questions

11.5a *What happens to the standard deviation of return for a portfolio if we increase the number of securities in the portfolio?*

11.5b *What is the principle of diversification?*

11.5c *Why is some risk diversifiable? Why is some risk not diversifiable?*

11.5d *Why can't systematic risk be diversified away?*

11.6 ■ Systematic risk and beta

The question that we now begin to address is: What determines the size of the risk premium on a risky asset? Put another way, why do some assets have a larger risk premium than other assets? The answer to these questions, as we discuss next, is also based on the distinction between systematic and non-systematic risk.

The systematic risk principle

Thus far, we've seen that the total risk associated with an asset can be decomposed into two components: systematic and non-systematic risk. We have also seen that non-systematic risk can be essentially eliminated by diversification. The systematic risk present in an asset, on the other hand, cannot be eliminated by diversification.

Based on our study of capital market history, we know that there is a reward, on average, for bearing risk. However, we now need to be more precise about what we mean by risk. The **systematic risk principle** states that the reward for bearing risk depends only on the systematic risk of an investment. The underlying rationale for this principle is straightforward: since non-systematic risk can be eliminated at virtually no cost (by diversifying), there is no reward for bearing it. Put another way, the market does not reward risks that are borne unnecessarily.

The systematic risk principle has a remarkable and very important implication:

> The expected return on an asset depends only on that asset's systematic risk.

There is an obvious corollary to this principle: no matter how much total risk an asset has, only the systematic portion is relevant in determining the expected return (and the risk premium) on that asset.

Measuring systematic risk

Since systematic risk is the crucial determinant of an asset's expected return, we need some way of measuring the level of systematic risk for different investments. The specific measure that we will use is called the **beta coefficient**, for which we will use the Greek symbol β. A beta coefficient, or beta for short, tells us how much systematic risk a particular asset has relative to an average asset. By definition, an average asset has a beta of 1.0 relative to itself. An asset with a beta of 0.50, therefore, has half as much systematic risk as an average asset; an asset with a beta of 2.0 has twice as much.

Table 11.8 contains the estimated beta coefficients for the shares of some well-known companies. (This particular source rounds to the nearest 0.01.) The range of betas in Table 11.8 is typical for shares of large Australian companies. Betas outside this range occur, but they are less common.

systematic risk principle

principle stating that the expected return on a risky asset depends only on that asset's systematic risk

beta coefficient

amount of systematic risk present in a particular risky asset relative to an average risky asset

TABLE 11.8

Beta coefficients for selected companies	
	Beta coefficient (β_i)
Amcor	0.78
BHP	1.33
Boral	0.85

Beta coefficients for selected companies (*continued*)	

TABLE 11.8

	Beta coefficient (β_i)
Caltex Aust	1.38
CSR	0.96
Coles Myer	0.45
Mayne Nickless	0.68
National Australia Bank	1.27

Source: Bloomberg, 2003 data.

The important thing to remember is that the expected return, and thus the risk premium, on an asset depends only on its systematic risk. Since assets with larger betas have greater systematic risks, they will have greater expected returns. Thus, according to Table 11.8, an investor who buys shares in Coles Myer, with a beta of 0.45, should expect to earn less, on average, than an investor who buys shares in National Australia Bank, with a beta of 1.27.

EXAMPLE 11.5

Total risk versus beta

Consider the following information on two securities. Which has greater total risk? Which has greater systematic risk? Greater non-systematic risk? Which asset will have a higher risk premium?

	Standard deviation	Beta
Security A	40%	0.50
Security B	20%	1.50

From our discussion in this section, security A has greater total risk, but it has substantially less systematic risk. Since total risk is the sum of systematic and non-systematic risk, security A must have greater non-systematic risk. Finally, from the systematic risk principle, security B will have a higher risk premium and a greater expected return, despite the fact that it has less total risk.

Portfolio betas

Earlier, we saw that the riskiness of a portfolio has no simple relationship to the risks of the assets in the portfolio. A portfolio beta, however, can be calculated just like a portfolio expected return. For example, looking back at Table 11.8, suppose you put half of your money in Amcor and half in Boral. What would the beta of this combination be? Since Amcor has a beta of 0.78 and Boral has a beta of 0.85, the portfolio's beta, β_P, would be:

$$\begin{aligned} \beta_P &= 0.50 \times \beta_A + 0.50 \times \beta_B \\ &= 0.50 \times 0.78 + 0.50 \times 0.85 \\ &= 0.815 \end{aligned}$$

In general, if we had a large number of assets in a portfolio, we would multiply each asset's beta by its portfolio weight and then add the results up to get the portfolio's beta.

EXAMPLE
11.6 ◼ **Portfolio betas**

Suppose we had the following investments:

Security	Amount invested	Expected return	Beta
Share A	$1,000	8%	0.80
Share B	2,000	12	0.95
Share C	3,000	15	1.10
Share D	4,000	18	1.40

What is the expected return on this portfolio? What is the beta of this portfolio? Does this portfolio have more or less systematic risk than an average asset?

To answer, we first have to calculate the portfolio weights. Notice that the total amount invested is $10,000. Of this, $1,000/$10,000 = 10% is invested in share A. Similarly, 20 per cent is invested in share B, 30 per cent in share C, and 40 per cent in share D. The expected return, $E(R_P)$, is thus:

$$E(R_P) = 0.10 \times E(R_A) + 0.20 \times E(R_B) + 0.30 \times E(R_C) + 0.40 \times E(R_D)$$
$$= 0.10 \times 8\% + 0.20 \times 12\% + 0.30 \times 15\% + 0.40 \times 18\%$$
$$= 14.9\%$$

Similarly, the portfolio beta, β_P, is:

$$\beta_P = 0.10 \times \beta_A + 0.20 \times \beta_B + 0.30 \times \beta_C + 0.40 \times \beta_D$$
$$= 0.10 \times 0.80 + 0.20 \times 0.95 + 0.30 \times 1.10 + 0.40 \times 1.40$$
$$= 1.16$$

This portfolio thus has an expected return of 14.9 per cent and a beta of 1.16. Since the beta is larger than 1.0, this portfolio has greater systematic risk than an average asset.

Concept questions

11.6a *What is the systematic risk principle?*
11.6b *What does a beta coefficient measure?*
11.6c *How do you calculate a portfolio beta?*
11.6d *The expected return on a risky asset depends on that asset's risk. True or false? Explain.*

 ◼ # The security market line

We are now in a position to see how risk is rewarded in the marketplace. To begin, suppose that asset A has an expected return of $E(R_A) = 20\%$ and a beta of $\beta_A = 1.6$. Furthermore, the risk-free rate is $R_f = 8\%$. Notice that a risk-free asset, by definition, has no systematic risk (or non-systematic risk), so a risk-free asset has a beta of 0.

Beta and the risk premium

Consider a portfolio made up of asset A and a risk-free asset. We can calculate some different possible portfolio expected returns and betas by varying the percentages invested in these

PART 5 · RISK AND RETURN

two assets. For example, if 25 per cent of the portfolio is invested in asset A, then the expected return is:

$$
\begin{aligned}
E(R_P) &= 0.25 \times E(R_A) + (1 - 0.25) \times R_f \\
&= 0.25 \times 20\% + 0.75 \times 8\% \\
&= 11.0\%
\end{aligned}
$$

Similarly, the beta on the portfolio, β_P, would be:

$$
\begin{aligned}
\beta_P &= 0.25 \times \beta_A + (1 - 0.25) \times 0 \\
&= 0.25 \times 1.6 \\
&= 0.40
\end{aligned}
$$

Notice that, since the weights have to add up to 1, the percentage invested in the risk-free asset is equal to 1 minus the percentage invested in asset A.

One thing that you might wonder about is whether it is possible for the percentage invested in asset A to exceed 100 per cent. The answer is yes. The way this can happen is for the investor to borrow at the risk-free rate. For example, suppose an investor has $100 and borrows an additional $50 at 8 per cent, the risk-free rate. The total investment in asset A would be $150, or 150 per cent of the investor's wealth. The expected return in this case would be:

$$
\begin{aligned}
E(R_P) &= 1.50 \times E(R_A) + (1 - 1.50) \times R_f \\
&= 1.50 \times 20\% - 0.50 \times 8\% \\
&= 26.0\%
\end{aligned}
$$

The beta on the portfolio would be:

$$
\begin{aligned}
\beta_P &= 1.50 \times \beta_A + (1 - 1.50) \times 0 \\
&= 1.50 \times 1.6 \\
&= 2.4
\end{aligned}
$$

We can calculate some other possibilities as follows:

Percentage of portfolio in asset A	Portfolio expected return	Portfolio beta
0%	8%	0.0
25	11	0.4
50	14	0.8
75	17	1.2
100	20	1.6
125	23	2.0
150	26	2.4

In Figure 11.2 (overleaf), these portfolio expected returns are plotted against the portfolio betas. Notice that all the combinations fall on a straight line.

FIGURE
11.2

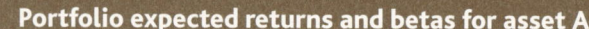

Portfolio expected returns and betas for asset A

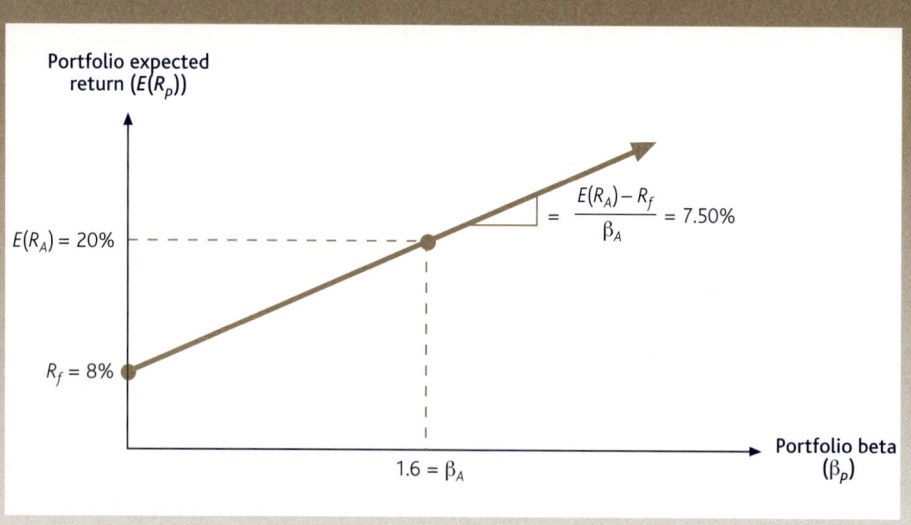

The reward-to-risk ratio

What is the slope of the straight line in Figure 11.2? As always, the slope of a straight line is equal to the 'rise over the run'. In this case, as we move out of the risk-free asset into asset A, the beta increases from zero to 1.6 (a 'run' of 1.6). At the same time, the expected return goes from 8 per cent to 20 per cent, a 'rise' of 12 per cent. The slope of the line is thus 12%/1.6 = 7.50%.

Notice that the slope of our line is just the risk premium on asset A, $E(R_A) - R_f$, divided by asset A's beta, β_A:

$$
\begin{aligned}
\text{Slope} &= \frac{E(R_A) - R_f}{\beta_A} \\
&= \frac{20\% - 8\%}{1.6} \\
&= 7.50\%
\end{aligned}
$$

What this tells us is that asset A offers a reward-to-risk ratio of 7.50 per cent.[3] In other words, asset A has a risk premium of 7.50 per cent per 'unit' of systematic risk.

The basic argument

Now suppose we consider a second asset, asset B. This asset has a beta of 1.2 and an expected return of 16 per cent. Which investment is better, asset A or asset B? You might think that, once again, we really cannot say. Some investors might prefer A; some investors might prefer B. Actually, however, we can say: A is better because, as we shall demonstrate, B offers inadequate compensation for its level of systematic risk, at least relative to A.

To begin, we calculate different combinations of expected returns and betas for portfolios of asset B and a risk-free asset, just as we did for asset A. For example, if we put 25 per cent in asset B and the remaining 75 per cent in the risk-free asset, the portfolio's expected return would be:

$$E(R_P) = 0.25 \times E(R_B) + (1 - 0.25) \times R_f$$
$$= 0.25 \times 16\% + 0.75 \times 8\%$$
$$= 10.0\%$$

Similarly, the beta on the portfolio, β_P, would be:

$$\beta_P = 0.25 \times \beta_B + (1 - 0.25) \times 0$$
$$= 0.25 \times 1.2$$
$$= 0.30$$

Some other possibilities are as follows:

Percentage of portfolio in asset B	Portfolio expected return	Portfolio beta
0%	8%	0.0
25	10	0.3
50	12	0.6
75	14	0.9
100	16	1.2
125	18	1.5
150	20	1.8

When we plot these combinations of portfolio expected returns and portfolio betas in Figure 11.3, we get a straight line just as we did for asset A.

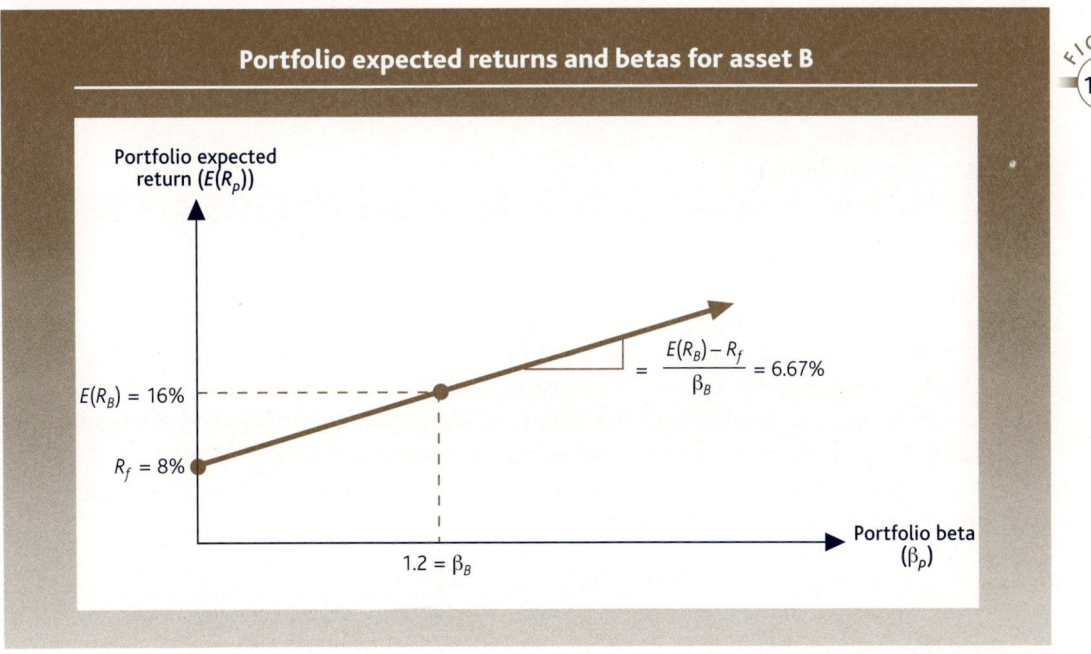

FIGURE 11.3

Portfolio expected returns and betas for asset B

The key thing to notice is that when we compare the results for assets A and B, as in Figure 11.4 (overleaf), the line describing the combinations of expected returns and betas for asset A is higher than the one for asset B. What this tells us is that for any given level of systematic risk (as measured by β), some combination of asset A and the risk-free asset always offers a larger return. This is why we were able to state that asset A is a better investment than asset B.

FIGURE
11.4

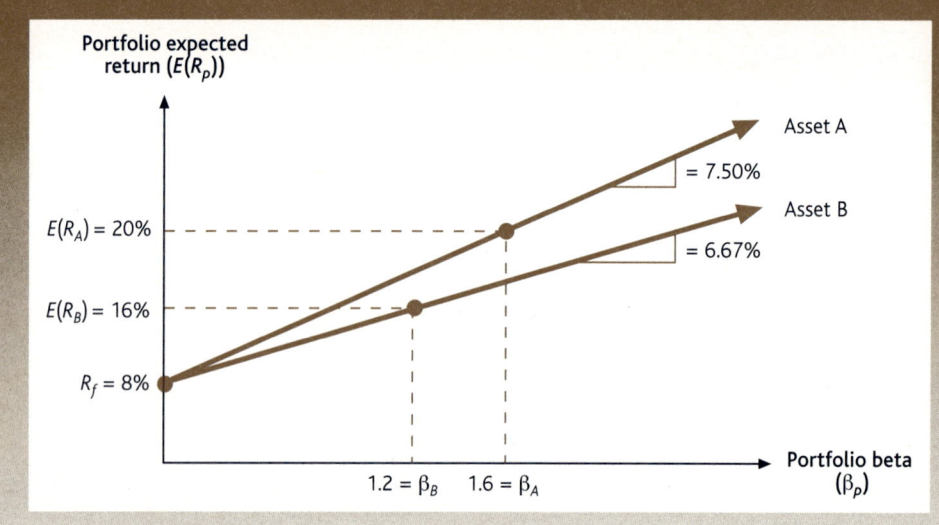

Portfolio expected returns and betas for both assets

Another way of seeing that A offers a superior return for its level of risk is to note that the slope of our line for asset B is:

$$\text{Slope} = \frac{E(R_B) - R_f}{\beta_B}$$
$$= \frac{16\% - 8\%}{1.2}$$
$$= 6.67\%$$

Thus, asset B has a reward-to-risk ratio of 6.67 per cent, which is less than the 7.5 per cent offered by asset A.

The fundamental result

The situation we have described for assets A and B cannot persist in a well-organised, active market, because investors would be attracted to asset A and away from asset B. As a result, asset A's price would rise and asset B's price would fall. Since prices and returns move in opposite directions, the result is that A's expected return would decline and B's would rise.

This buying and selling would continue until the two assets plotted on exactly the same line, which means they offer the same reward for bearing risk. In other words, in an active, competitive market, it must hold true:

$$\frac{E(R_A) - R_f}{\beta_A} = \frac{E(R_B) - R_f}{\beta_B}$$

This is the fundamental relationship between risk and return.

Our basic argument can be extended to more than just two assets. In fact, no matter how many assets we had, we would always reach the same conclusion:

> The reward-to-risk ratio must be the same for all the assets in the market.

This result is really not so surprising. What it says, for example, is that, if one asset has twice as much systematic risk as another asset, its risk premium will simply be twice as large.

Since all of the assets in the market must have the same reward-to-risk ratio, they all must plot on the same line. This argument is illustrated in Figure 11.5. As shown, assets A and B plot directly on the line and thus have the same reward-to-risk ratio. If an asset plotted above the line, such as C in Figure 11.5, its price would rise, and its expected return would fall until it plotted exactly on the line. Similarly, if an asset plotted below the line, such as D in Figure 11.3, its expected return would rise until it too plotted directly on the line.

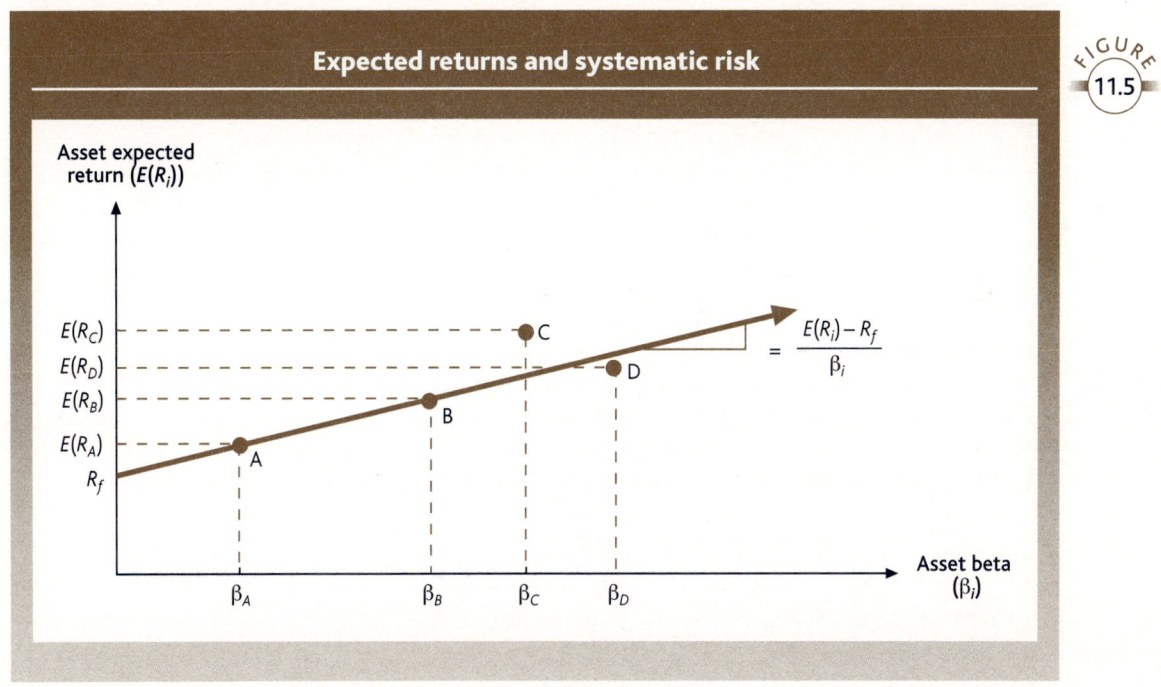

Expected returns and systematic risk

FIGURE 11.5

The arguments we have presented apply to active, competitive, well-functioning markets. The financial markets, such as the Australian financial markets, best meet these criteria. Other markets, such as real asset markets, may or may not. For this reason, these concepts are most useful in examining financial markets. We will thus focus on such markets here. However, as we discuss in a later section, the information about risk and return gleaned from financial markets is crucial in evaluating the investments that a corporation makes in real assets.

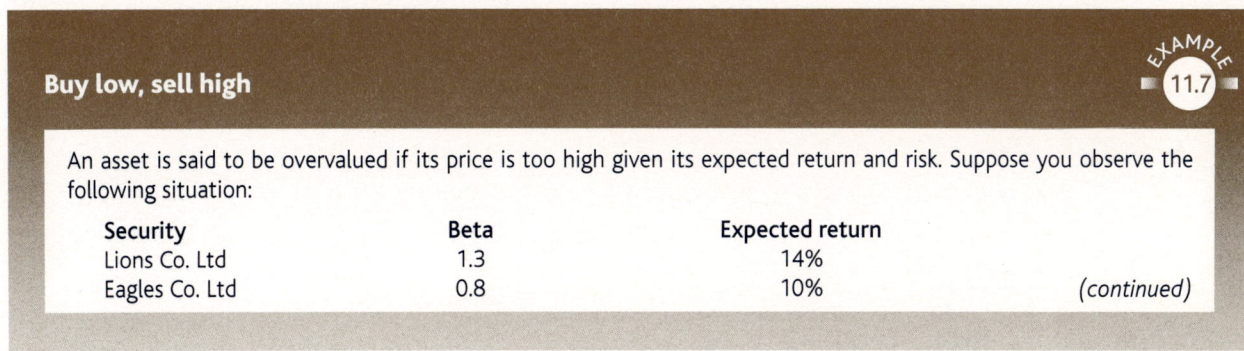

EXAMPLE 11.7

Buy low, sell high

An asset is said to be overvalued if its price is too high given its expected return and risk. Suppose you observe the following situation:

Security	Beta	Expected return
Lions Co. Ltd	1.3	14%
Eagles Co. Ltd	0.8	10%	*(continued)*

EXAMPLE 11.7 ◾ **Buy low, sell high (*continued*)**

The risk-free rate is currently 6 per cent. Is one of the two securities above overvalued relative to the other?

To answer, we compute the reward-to-risk ratio for both. For Lions, this ratio is $(14\% - 6\%)/1.3 = 6.15\%$. For Eagles, this ratio is 5 per cent. What we conclude is that Eagles offers an insufficient expected return for its level of risk, at least relative to Lions. Since its expected return is too low, its price is too high. In other words, Eagles is overvalued relative to Lions, and we would expect to see its price fall relative to Lions. Notice that we could also say that Lions is undervalued relative to Eagles.

The security market line

security market line (SML)

positively sloped straight line displaying the relationship between expected return and beta

The line that results when we plot expected returns and beta coefficients is obviously of some importance, so it's time we gave it a name. This line, which we use to describe the relationship between systematic risk and expected return in financial markets, is usually called the **security market line (SML)**. After NPV, the SML is arguably the most important concept in modern finance.

Market portfolios

It will be very useful to know the equation of the SML. There are many different ways that we could write it, but one way is particularly common. Suppose we were to consider a portfolio made up of all of the assets in the market. Such a portfolio is called a market portfolio, and we will write the expected return on this market portfolio as $E(R_M)$.

Since all the assets in the market must plot on the SML, so must a market portfolio made of those assets. To determine where it plots on the SML, we need to know the beta of the market portfolio, β_M. Since this portfolio is representative of all the assets in the market, it must have average systematic risk. In other words, it has a beta of one. We could therefore write the slope of the SML as:

$$\text{SML slope} = \frac{E(R_M) - R_f}{\beta_M} = \frac{E(R_M) - R_f}{1}$$
$$= E(R_M) - R_f$$

market risk premium

slope of the SML, the difference between the expected return on a market portfolio and the risk-free rate

The term $E(R_M) - R_f$ is often called the **market risk premium** since it is the risk premium on a market portfolio.

The capital asset pricing model

To finish up, if we let $E(R_i)$ and β_i stand for the expected return and beta, respectively, on any asset in the market, then we know that it must plot on the SML. As a result, we know that its reward-to-risk ratio is the same as the overall market's:

$$\frac{E(R_i) - R_f}{\beta_i} = E(R_M) - R_f$$

If we rearrange this, then we can write the equation for the SML as:

$$E(R_i) = R_f + [E(R_M) - R_f] \times \beta_i \tag{11.7}$$

This result is identical to the famous **capital asset pricing model (CAPM)**.[4]

What the CAPM shows is that the expected return for a particular asset depends on three things:

1 *The pure time value of money*. As measured by the risk-free rate, R_f, this is the reward for merely waiting for your money, without taking any risk.
2 *The reward for bearing systematic risk*. As measured by the market risk premium, $[E(R_M) - R_f]$, this component is the reward the market offers for bearing an average amount of systematic risk in addition to waiting.
3 *The amount of systematic risk*. As measured by β_i, this is the amount of systematic risk present in a particular asset, relative to an average asset.

capital asset pricing model (CAPM)
equation of the SML showing relationship between expected return and beta

Figure 11.6 summarises our discussion of the SML and the CAPM. As before, we plot expected return against beta. Now we recognise that, based on the CAPM, the slope of the SML is equal to the market risk premium, $[E(R_M) - R_f]$.

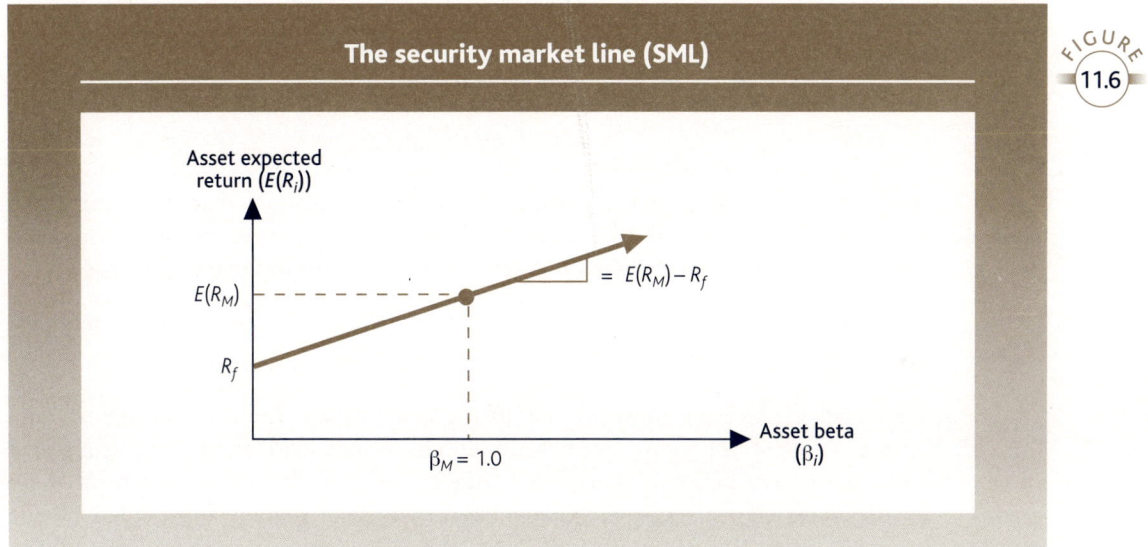

The security market line (SML)

FIGURE 11.6

Risk and return

EXAMPLE 11.8

Suppose the risk-free rate is 4 per cent, the market risk premium is 8.6 per cent, and a particular share has a beta of 1.3. Based on the CAPM, what is the expected return on this share? What would the expected return be if the beta were to double?

With a beta of 1.3, the risk premium for the share would be 1.3 × 8.6%, or 11.18 per cent. The risk-free rate is 4 per cent, so the expected return is 15.18 per cent. If the beta doubles to 2.6, the risk premium would double to 22.36 per cent, so the expected return would be 26.36 per cent.

Concept questions

11.7a *What is the fundamental relationship between risk and return in well-functioning markets?*

11.7b *What is the security market line? Why must all assets plot directly on it in a well-functioning market?*

11.7c *What is the capital asset pricing model (CAPM)? What does it tell us about the required return on a risky investment?*

11.8 The capital market line

systematic risk
cannot be avoided or reduced

Beta has been defined as the amount of **systematic risk** present in a particular risky asset relative to an average risky asset. Thus beta is a relative measure of systematic risk. But what is systematic risk? In order to simplify the discussion, we provide a definition of this market related risk as:

$$\text{Systematic risk of asset } i = \frac{\text{Change in the return on asset } i \text{ as the market changes}}{\text{Total risk of the return on the market}}$$

Let us look at the total risk of the market. It has been explained that the variance or standard deviation will measure the total risk of an asset. Similarly, the variance or standard deviation of the return on the market will measure the total risk of the market, so that:

$$\text{Total risk of the return on the market} = \text{Standard deviation of market return}$$
$$= \sigma_M$$

The statistics, which measure how two variables change together, are the covariance and the correlation coefficient. The two statistics are closely related, with the latter just a scaled version of the former (see below). Therefore a measure of how the expected return on an asset will change with changes in the expected return on the market is provided by the covariance, $\text{Cov}(\tilde{R}_i, \tilde{R}_M)$. It is convention to delete the E( ) symbol from the returns and to include a tilde (~) to denote that the terms in the covariance are random distributions.

We are now able to express systematic risk as:

systematic risk
is covariance risk

$$\textbf{Systematic risk of asset } i = \textbf{Cov } (\tilde{R}_i, \tilde{R}_M)/\sigma_M \tag{11.8}$$

where

Cov = covariance
$\tilde{R}_i$ = the random distribution of return for asset i,
$\tilde{R}_M$ = the random distribution of return for the market, and
σ_M = the standard deviation of return on the market (average asset).

beta
systematic risk divided by the standard deviation of return on the market

It has been stated that β_i is a relative measure of systematic risk so that:

$$\text{Beta of asset } i = \frac{\text{Systematic risk of asset } i}{\text{Total risk of the return on the market}}$$

$$\beta_i = [\text{Systematic risk}]/\sigma_M$$
$$\beta_i = [\text{Cov}(\tilde{R}_i,\tilde{R}_M)/\sigma_M]/\sigma_M$$
$$\beta_i = \text{Cov}(\tilde{R}_i, \tilde{R}_M)/\sigma^2_M \qquad (11.9)$$

We can now write the equation for the SML (11.7) in a revised format as:

$$E(R_i) = R_f + [E(R_M) - R_f] \times \beta_i \qquad (11.7)$$

$$E(R_i) = R_f + [E(R_M) - R_f] \times \text{Cov}(\tilde{R}_i,\tilde{R}_M)/\sigma^2_M$$

$$E(R_i) = R_f + [E(R_M) - R_f]/\sigma_M \times \text{Cov}(\tilde{R}_i,\tilde{R}_M)/\sigma_M \qquad (11.10)$$

Equation (11.10) demonstrates that:

Expected return = Risk free return + Universal premium for risk × Units of risk

where units of risk are systematic risk.

Consider again the covariance term, $\text{Cov}(\tilde{R}_i,\tilde{R}_M)$. This term measures how returns change together. The weakness of this term from a mathematical point of view is that its value depends upon the absolute values of returns.[5] To overcome this problem the measure used to evaluate how variables change together is the correlation coefficient. The correlation coefficient has a range from −1, when variables are perfectly negatively correlated, to +1, when variables are perfectly positively correlated. When variables are perfectly negatively correlated, a change in one variable will induce an identical change in the second variable but in the opposite direction. For example, if the return on an asset was perfectly negatively correlated with the return on the market and the market return increased by 5 per cent, the return on the asset would decrease by 5 per cent. When variables are perfectly positively correlated, a change in one variable will induce an identical change in the second variable in the same direction. A five per cent increase in the first variable would be matched by a 5 per cent increase in the second variable. The returns on most assets demonstrate a small positive correlation with each other—why? Their return depends upon their systematic (market-related) risk so that all assets will change as market returns change. The correlation coefficient is calculated as:

$$\text{Correlation coefficient } \rho_{iM} = \frac{\text{Cov}(\tilde{R}_i,\tilde{R}_M)}{\sigma_i \times \sigma_M} \qquad (11.11)$$

where

$\text{Cov}(\tilde{R}_i,\tilde{R}_M)$ = covariance of the return on asset i with the return on the market,
σ_i = the standard deviation of the return on asset i, and
σ_M = the standard deviation of the return on the market.

The symbol 'ρ' is called 'rho' and it is the Greek letter 'r'. From equation (11.11) it can be seen that:

$$\rho_{iM} \times \sigma_i \times \sigma_M = \text{Cov}(\tilde{R}_i,\tilde{R}_M) \qquad (11.12)$$

If the expression for covariance in equation (11.12) is substituted into equation (11.10) we have:

$$E(R_i) = R_f + [E(R_M) - R_f]/\sigma_M \times \rho_{iM} \times \sigma_i \times \sigma_M/\sigma_M$$
$$E(R_i) = R_f + [E(R_M) - R_f]/\sigma_M \times \rho_{iM} \times \sigma_i \qquad (11.13)$$

Now let us consider the case of portfolios that are fully diversified. These portfolios would have diversified away all non-systematic risk so that their total risk is equal to systematic risk. Changes in the returns to these portfolios would be totally dependent upon their systematic (market) risk. Because the returns are totally dependent on the market, these portfolios have expected returns that are perfectly positively correlated with the expected returns on the market so that $\rho_{PM} = 1$. The subscript on rho has been changed from 'i' to 'P' to denote that we are considering efficient portfolios and not individual assets.

Returning to equation (11.13) and considering efficient portfolios where $\rho_{PM} = 1$, we have:

$$E(R_P) = R_f + [E(R_M) - R_f]/\sigma_M \times 1 \times \sigma_P$$
$$E(R_P) = R_f + [E(R_M) - R_f]/\sigma_M \times \sigma_P \qquad (11.14)$$

Equation (11.13) is the expression for the capital market line (CML).

This equation shows the expected return for all **efficient portfolios** where total risk (σ_P) is rewarded. The rewarded risk is still systematic risk, but because the portfolios are efficient this is total risk.

Table 11.9 provides hypothetical data for an inefficient asset, an efficient portfolio and the market. It has been assumed that the risk-free rate is 0.08 and the expected return on the market is 0.12. The expected returns for the inefficient asset and the efficient portfolio may be derived using the equation for the SML (equation 11.7). For the inefficient asset total risk (σ_j) is greater than systematic risk ($Cov(\tilde{R}_j,\tilde{R}_M)/\sigma_M$) because the asset has an element of diversifiable risk. For the efficient portfolio and the market, total risk must equal systematic risk. Obviously the converse of this statement is that the diversifiable risk of the efficient portfolio and the market must be zero. It is the non-existence of diversifiable risk that identifies the efficiency of the portfolios.

TABLE 11.9

Hypothetical statistics for an inefficient asset, an efficient portfolio and the market

Statistic	Inefficient asset	Efficient portfolio	Market
Expected return $E(R_j)$	0.13	0.136	0.12
Total risk σ_j	0.45	0.28	0.20
Diversible risk	0.20	nil	nil
Systematic risk $Cov(\tilde{R}_j,\tilde{R}_M)/\sigma_M$	0.05/0.20 = 0.25	0.056/0.20 = 0.28	$Cov(\tilde{R}_M,\tilde{R}_M)/\sigma_M$ $= \sigma^2_M/\sigma_M$ $= 0.20*$
Covariance $Cov(\tilde{R}_j,\tilde{R}_M)$	0.05	0.056	$Cov(\tilde{R}_M,\tilde{R}_M)$ $= \sigma^2_M$ $= 0.04$

TABLE
11.9

Hypothetical statistics for an inefficient asset, an efficient portfolio and the market (*continued*)

Statistic	Inefficient asset	Efficient portfolio	Market
Beta $Cov\,(\tilde{R}_j,\tilde{R}_M)/\sigma^2_M$	0.05/0.04 = 1.25	0.056 /0.04 = 1.4	$Cov\,(\tilde{R}_M,\tilde{R}_M)/\sigma^2_M$ $= \sigma^2_M/\sigma^2_M$ $= 1.00$
Correlation ρ_{iM} $= \dfrac{Cov\,(\tilde{R}_j,\tilde{R}_M)}{\sigma_j,\sigma_M}$	0.05/(0.45 × 0.2) $= 0.555$	0.056/(0.28 × 0.2) $= 1$	$\dfrac{Cov\,(\tilde{R}_j,\tilde{R}_M)}{\sigma_M,\sigma_M}$ $= \sigma^2_M/\sigma^2_M$ $= 1.00$

*It is a mathematical fact that the covariance of an asset with itself is the variance of the asset so the covariance of the expected return on the market with the expected return on the market is the variance of the expected return on the market.

The betas are derived by dividing the covariance with the market by the variance of the market, or they could have been derived by dividing systematic risk by the standard deviation of the market. Because of the close relationship between systematic risk and the covariance, some texts call systematic risk covariance risk. Note that the efficient portfolio has a beta greater than one, however its correlation with the market is one. To be efficient the return of the portfolio must be perfectly positively correlated with the return on the market. Its return must be totally market-dependent. The equation for the **SML**, equation (11.7) or equation (11.9), will explain the expected return for all assets, efficient and inefficient. The equation for the **CML**, equation (11.13), will only explain expected return for efficient portfolios.

The returns on individual assets cannot be explained by the CML because their total risk contains non-systematic risk which is not rewarded within the context of the capital asset pricing model.

SML
the SML equation explains the expected return for all assets

CML
the CML equation explains the expected return for efficient portfolios

Concept questions

11.8a *Why is beta identified as a measure of relative risk?*

11.8b *Explain why the expected return on all efficient assets has a correlation with the market expected return equal to one.*

11.8c *Can an inefficient asset have a beta of one? Explain.*

11.8d *If efficient assets have a correlation coefficient equal to one, does this mean they must have betas equal to one? Explain.*

11.9 Portfolio characteristics

Because the portfolio characteristics introduced above are so important, we are going to have another look at them. Why do we gain from diversification when we add investments to our portfolio? We have explained earlier that this may be because, as one investment goes down in value, another may go up in value. In the real world share price movements are not always as precise as this as most investments tend to move together however some may move more than others. The statistics that identify the relationship between investments are the covariance and the closely related correlation coefficient. The correlation coefficient is a scaled version of the covariance. Remember, we derive the correlation coefficient by dividing the covariance by the product of the standard deviations. Consequently the correlation coefficient is the covariance scaled by the standard deviations (statisticians say it is the standardised covariance).

In the case of expected returns the covariance is the covariance of the expected return on the first investment with the expected return on the second investment, so we have Covariance$(E(R_1), E(R_2))$ and if we drop the expectation symbol it is Covariance$(\tilde{R}_1, \tilde{R}_2)$.

Note: Earlier we discussed the covariance of the expected return on an investment with the expected return on the market but here we are considering the covariance between investments not the investment and the market.

When investments are combined a portfolio is created and the characteristics of that portfolio are:

expected return of the portfolio = *the weighted sum of the individual returns*
beta of the portfolio = *the weighted sum of the individual betas*
covariance of the portfolio = *the weighted sum of the individual covariances*

However, the variance of the portfolio is not the weighted sum of the individual variances nor is the standard deviation a weighted sum of individual standard deviations. For example, when two investments are combined in a portfolio the variance of the portfolio's expected return is provided by:

weighted variance of the expected return on the first investment

+

weighted variance of the expected return on the second investment

+

twice the weighted covariance of the expected return on the first investment with the expected return on the second

As more investments are added to the portfolio the variance formula becomes more difficult as more and more covariance relationships have to be considered. Eventually the variance terms in the calculation become insignificant and the variance of the portfolio is driven by the average covariance value.

Let us demonstrate the relationships by revisiting Lions and Eagles. We have added to the information provided earlier and expressed the returns as decimals in the following table:

	Beta	Expected return	Standard deviation of expected return	Covariance of expected return with the market
Lions Co Ltd	1.3	0.14	0.24	0.03328
Eagles Co Ltd	0.8	0.10	0.20	0.02048
Market	1.0	0.12	0.16	0.02560

Further, we are told that 40 per cent (0.4) of our wealth will be invested in Lions and the remaining 60 per cent (0.6) in Eagles. The covariance of the expected return on Lions and the expected return on Eagles is estimated to be 0.0096. Using this information and the knowledge gained earlier we can calculate the following:

Expected Return on the Portfolio 40% Lions 60% Eagles

$$\text{Expected return} = 0.4 \times 0.14 + 0.6 \times 0.10$$
$$= 0.056 + 0.06$$
$$= 0.116 \text{ or } 11.6\%$$

Beta of the Portfolio 40% Lions 60% Eagles

$$\text{Beta} = 0.4 \times 1.3 + 0.6 \times 0.80$$
$$= 0.52 + 0.48$$
$$= 1$$

Covariance of the Portfolio 40% Lions 60% Eagles

$$\text{Covariance} = 0.4 \times 0.03328 + 0.6 \times 0.02048$$
$$= 0.013312 + 0.012288$$
$$= 0.0256$$

Checking the calculation

$$\text{Beta} = \text{Covariance with the market/variance of the market}$$
$$= 0.0256/(0.16 \times 0.16)$$
$$= 0.0256/0.0256$$
$$= 1 \text{ as above}$$

Variance of the Portfolio 40% Lions 60% Eagles

$$\text{Variance} = (0.4 \times 0.24)^2 + (0.6 \times 0.2)^2 + 2 \times 0.4 \times 0.6 \times 0.0096$$
$$= 0.009216 + 0.0144 + 0.004608$$
$$= 0.028224$$

The standard deviation is the square root of the variance $= 0.168$

Note that the variance and standard deviation of the portfolio are not the weighted sum of the individual variances or standard deviations. These are:

$$\text{Weighted variance sum} = (0.4 \times 0.24)^2 + (0.6 \times 0.2)^2$$
$$= 0.023616$$
$$\text{Weighted standard deviation sum} = 0.4 \times 0.24 + 0.6 \times 0.2$$
$$= 0.216$$

Finally we can work out the correlation between the expected return on Lions with the expected return on Eagles.

$$\text{Correlation coefficient} = \text{Covariance/product of the standard deviations}$$
$$= 0.0096/(0.24 \times 0.2)$$
$$= 0.2$$

The correlation between the investments is not to be confused with the correlation of each investment's expected return with that of the market, which is calculated as: the covariance of the investment's expected return with the market expected return divided by the product of the standard deviation of expected return on the investment and the standard deviation of the market expected return. In this example the correlations of the investments with the market are calculated as:

$$\text{Lions} = 0.03328/0.24 \times 0.16 = 0.87$$
$$\text{Eagles} = 0.02048/0.2 \times 0.16 = 0.64$$

If an investment is perfectly positively correlated with the market it is said to be an efficient asset and its correlation coefficient would be equal to one. This simply means that its total risk is systematic risk and all risk is being rewarded. The expected return on the investment would be explained by the capital market line (CML) equation.

To reinforce our understanding, let us revisit the example of Lamb and Unicorn. From Tables 11.2, 11.4, 11.5 and 11.6 we note that a portfolio comprising 50 per cent investment in each company results in:

	Lamb	Unicorn	Portfolio
Expected return	0.25	0.20	0.225
Variance	0.2025	0.01	0.030625
Standard deviation	0.45	0.1	0.175

Using this information we can work out the covariance and correlation between Lamb and Unicorn.

$$\begin{aligned}
\text{Portfolio variance} &= (0.5 \times \sigma_L)^2 + (0.5 \times \sigma_U)^2 + 2(0.5)(0.5)\,\text{Covariance(Lamb,Unicorn)} \\
0.030625 &= (0.5 \times 0.45)^2 + (0.5 \times 0.1)^2 + 0.5\,\text{Covariance(Lamb,Unicorn)} \\
0.030625 &= 0.050625 + 0.0025 + 0.5\,\text{Covariance(Lamb,Unicorn)} \\
-0.0225 &= 0.5\,\text{Covariance(Lamb,Unicorn)} \\
-0.045 &= \text{Covariance(Lamb,Unicorn)}.
\end{aligned}$$

We may now calculate the correlation as:

$$\begin{aligned}
\text{Correlation} &= \text{Covariance(Lamb,Unicorn)/product of the standard deviations} \\
&= -0.045/0.45 \times 0.1 \\
&= -0.045/0.045 \\
&= -1
\end{aligned}$$

The two investments are perfectly negatively correlated, which means that if Lamb goes up (or down) by $x\%$ then Unicorn will go down (or up) by $x\%$. It is interesting to note that despite this special correlation a portfolio comprising the two investments equally still has risk with a variance of 0.030625.

Concept questions

11.9a *Which characteristics of the portfolio are weighted sums of the component investments' characteristics?*

11.9b *When creating a portfolio, is it more important to look at the relationship between investments or specific investments?*

11.9c *Does an efficient investment have to have a beta of one?*

11.10 The SML and the cost of capital: a preview

Our goal in studying risk and return is twofold. First, risk is an extremely important consideration in almost all business decisions, so we want to discuss just what risk is and how it is rewarded in the market. Our second purpose is to learn what determines the appropriate discount rate for future cash flows. We briefly discuss this second subject now; we discuss it in more detail in Chapter 18.

The basic idea

The security market line tells us the reward for bearing risk in financial markets. At an absolute minimum, any new investment that our firm undertakes must offer an expected return that is no worse than what the financial markets offer for the same risk. The reason for this is simply that our shareholders can always invest for themselves in the financial markets.

The only way we benefit our shareholders is by finding investments with expected returns that are superior to what the financial markets offer for the same risk. Such investments will have a positive NPV. So, if we ask 'What is the appropriate discount rate?', the answer is that we should use the expected return offered in financial markets on investments with the same systematic risk.

In other words, to determine whether or not an investment has a positive NPV, we essentially compare the expected return on that new investment to what the financial market offers on an investment with the same beta. This is why the SML is so important; it tells us the 'going rate' for bearing risk in the economy.

The cost of capital

The appropriate discount rate on a new project is the minimum expected rate of return an investment must offer to be attractive. This minimum required return is very often called the **cost of capital** associated with the investment. It is called this because the required return is what the firm must earn on its capital investment in a project just to break even. It can thus be interpreted as the opportunity cost associated with the firm's capital investment.

cost of capital
the minimum required return on a new investment

Notice that when we say an investment is attractive if its expected return exceeds what is offered in financial markets for investments of the same risk, we are effectively using the internal rate of return (IRR) criterion that we developed and discussed in Chapter 7. The only difference is that now we have a much better idea of what determines the required return on an investment. This understanding will be critical when we discuss cost of capital and capital structure in Part Eight.

Concept questions

11.10a *If an investment has a positive NPV, would it plot above or below the SML? Why?*
11.10b *What is meant by the term 'cost of capital'?*

11.11 Problems with the CAPM

The CAPM states that in equilibrium an asset should be valued so that its expected return is equal to the risk-free rate of return plus a premium for risk. This risk premium is the beta of the asset times the market risk premium, which is the difference in the expected return of

---

the market and the risk-free return. *The CAPM is a model based on expectations*. The *expected* return of the asset, the *expected* return of the market, the *expected* beta and the *expected* risk-free rate. The risk-free rate is expected because the model specifies that the rate will be constant across the period of the model and this is contrary to real world experience. All interest rates change as they are influenced by Reserve Bank changes to the base rate. We do not know how expectations are formed although some of the early finance research looked at this issue only to confine it to the too-hard basket. Research is forced to use historical data in the hope of anticipating what the future (expected) data will be. Because of this weakness we need to be careful when we use the model and when we compare the research results to the predictions of the model. We will now present a brief summary of the estimation difficulties that have been identified by finance research.

Difficulties in estimating beta

The first problem we look at is when shares are infrequently traded. This is known as the 'thin trading problem'. In theory, trading in shares occurs continuously so that observed returns would always equal the 'true' returns. In practice, even the most frequently traded shares would not be traded continuously and smaller companies' shares are traded at highly irregular intervals. In fact some firms' shares do not trade monthly. The research argues that the estimates of the 'real' beta for thinly traded shares are biased downward and the estimated beta for frequently traded shares are biased upwards.

The second problem relates to the assumption that beta is constant. When we use historic data to estimate the expected beta, the assertion is that beta is constant. There is nothing in the underlying CAPM theory to even suggest beta should not change. A firm may be considered to be a combination (portfolio) of many investments. Recall that the beta of a portfolio is the weighted sum of the betas that belong to the individual investments of the portfolio. As the investments are changed the portfolio beta changes. It follows that when a firm changes its investments its beta must change. Another way of looking at the firm is as a combination of equity and debt funding so its beta is a weighted sum of the betas of its equity and its debt. Again it follows that when the firm changes its debt, or for that matter its equity, its beta must change. Numerous research projects have looked at the estimation and stability of beta. For example Sunder (1980), Thompson (1986), Bhardwaj and Brooks (1993), Howton and Peterson (1998) and Brooks, Faff and MacKenzie (1998).

Scholes and Williams (1977) and Dimson (1979) have proposed estimation processes to help alleviate the thin trading problem but these only offer a slight improvement on simple estimation. In relation to beta stability there is even less advance. Many models have been proposed to combat the stability issue but none has emerged as being superior.

Using the CAPM

The third problem we identify is in relation to using the model to measure 'true' return. In this area the research has identified what it has labelled as anomalies in pricing securities in the market. To overcome the anomalies the CAPM has been extended to include additional explanatory variables. An industry index, a measure of consumption, firm size, a measure of interest rate levels and dividend payouts are just some of the inclusions, but none has provided consistently any additional explanation over the original CAPM.

Another focus has been the measure of market return. The CAPM stipulates that the market portfolio must comprise all assets, which is impossible to measure. Any measure must be an imperfect market estimate. The research has considered whether an equally weighted index or a valued weighted index is superior, with opinion favouring the latter slightly. The other market consideration has been whether we should use a domestic index or an international index, but neither has been accepted as being consistently superior.

Where are we?

Despite its limitations the CAPM is the best model we have within the framework of our current state of knowledge. We need to be aware of the estimation shortcomings and modify or be guarded with the derived statistics when conditions imply that we may have inaccurate estimates. The identification of anomalies may be attributed to the failure to measure expectations and should not create panic. To discard the CAPM is to surely 'throw the baby out with the bath water'.

Concept questions

11.11a *What are expectations?*

11.11b *What do you understand by thin trading? Is it selling weight-loss products?*

11.11c *Within the CAPM framework, what should cause beta to change? Would a substantial increase in the amount you owe suppliers cause it to change?*

∎11.12∎ Summary and conclusions

This chapter covered the essentials of risk. Along the way, we introduced a number of definitions and concepts. The most important of these is the security market line, or SML. The SML is important because it tells us the reward offered in financial markets for bearing risk. Once we know this, we have a benchmark against which we compare the returns expected from real asset investments to determine if they are desirable.

Because we covered quite a bit of ground, it's useful to summarise the basic economic logic underlying the SML as follows:

1 Based on capital market history, there is a reward for bearing risk. This reward is the risk premium on an asset.

2 The total risk associated with an asset has two parts: systematic risk and non-systematic risk. Non-systematic risk can be freely eliminated by diversification (this is the principle of diversification), so only systematic risk is rewarded. As a result, the risk premium on an asset is determined by its systematic risk. This is the systematic risk principle.

3 An asset's systematic risk, relative to average, can be measured by its beta coefficient, β_i. The risk premium on an asset is then given by its beta coefficient multiplied by the market risk premium, $[E(R_M) - R_f] \times \beta_i$.

4 The expected return on an asset, $E(R_i)$, is equal to the risk-free rate, R_f, plus the risk premium:

$$E(R_i) = R_f + [E(R_M) - R_f] \times \beta_i$$

This is the equation of the SML, and it is often called the capital asset pricing model (CAPM).

This chapter completes our discussion of risk and return and concludes Part Five of the book. Now that we have a better understanding of what determines a firm's cost of capital for an investment, the next several chapters examine more closely how firms raise the long-term capital needed for investment.

Key terms

Beta coefficient *366*
Capital asset pricing model (CAPM) *375*
Cost of capital *383*
Expected return *352*

Market risk premium *374*
Non-systematic risk *361*
Portfolio *356*
Portfolio weight *356*

Principle of diversification *363*
Security market line (SML) *374*
Systematic risk *361, 376*
Systematic risk principle *366*

Suggested readings

For greater detail on the subject of risk and return see Chapters 9, 10 and 11 of:

Ross, S.A., Westerfield, R.W. and Jordan, B.D. *Corporate Finance*, 6th edn, Richard D. Irwin, Homewood, Ill., 2003.

Bhardwaj, R. and Brooks, L. 'Dual Betas from Bull and Bear Markets: Reversal of the Size Effect', *Journal of Financial Research*, Vol. 16, 1993, pp. 269–83.

Brooks, R., Faff, R. and McKenzie, M. 'Time-Varying Beta Risk of Australian Industry Portfolios: A Comparison of Modelling Techniques', *Australian Journal of Management*, 23, 1998, pp. 1–22.

Dimson, E. 'Risk measurement when Shares are Subject to Infrequent Trading', *Journal of Financial Economics*, 7, 1979, pp. 197–226.

Howton, S. and Peterson, D. 'An examination of Cross-Sectional Realized Stock Returns using a Varying-Risk Beta Model', *Financial Review*, 33, 1998, pp. 199–212.

Scholes, M. and Williams, J. 'Estimating Beta from Nonsynchronous Data', *Journal of Financial Economics*, December, 1977, pp. 309–27.

Sunder, S. 'Stationarity of Market Risk: Random Coefficients Tests for Individual Stocks', *Journal of Finance*, September, 1980, pp. 883–96.

Thompson, S.C. 'An Econometric Evaluation of Parameter Estimation within the Capital Asset Pricing Model Framework', Doctoral thesis, University of Queensland, 1986.

Endnotes

1 Some of it could be in cash of course but we would then just consider the cash to be one of the portfolio assets.

2 The data is from an unpublished study conducted by S. Thompson, M. Christensen and J. McIvor in 1993.

3 This ratio is sometimes called the Treynor index, after one of its originators.

4 Our discussion leading up to the CAPM is actually much more closely related to a more recently developed theory, known as the Arbitrage Pricing Theory (APT). The theory underlying the CAPM is a great deal more complex than we have indicated here, and the CAPM has a number of other implications that go beyond the scope of this discussion. As we present it here, the CAPM and the APT have essentially identical implications, so we don't distinguish between them.

5 See Berenson, M.L. and Levine, D.M. *Basic Business Statistics: Concepts and Applications*, 4th edn, Prentice Hall, 1989, or any other elementary statistics text, for a discussion of covariance and correlation coefficients.

Maximise Your Marks!
There are 30 interactive questions on return, risk and the security market line waiting online for you at www.mhhe.com/au/ross3e. The questions are written with additional feedback for incorrect answers, and text excerpts with page references for follow-up study.

International Articles!
To read more on return, risk and the security market line and to see current international articles, just go to www.mhhe.com/au/ross3e and click on *PowerWeb Articles* for this chapter.

Chapter review problems and self-test

11.1 · Expected return and standard deviation

This problem will give you some practice calculating measures of prospective portfolio performance. There are two assets and three states of nature:

(1) State of the economy	(2) Probability of state of economy	(3) Share A rate of return if state occurs	(4) Share B rate of return if state occurs
Recession	0.10	−0.20	0.30
Normal	0.60	0.10	0.20
Boom	0.30	0.70	0.50

What are the expected returns and standard deviations for these two shares?

11.2 · Portfolio risk and return

In the previous problem, suppose you have $20,000 in total. If you put $6,000 in share A and the remainder in share B, what will the expected return and standard deviation on your portfolio be?

11.3 · Risk and return

Suppose you observe the following situation:

Security	Beta	Expected return
Over Ltd	1.6	19%
Under Ltd	1.2	16%

If the risk-free rate is 8 per cent, are these securities correctly priced? What would the risk-free rate have to be if they are correctly priced?

11.4 · CAPM

Suppose the risk-free rate is 8 per cent. The expected return on the market is 14 per cent. If a particular share has a beta of 0.60, what is its expected return based on the CAPM? If another share has an expected return of 20 per cent, what must its beta be?

11.5 · Efficiency

A portfolio has been constructed with 10 investments. The intention was to create an efficient portfolio but because the expected return is relatively low and the standard deviation of expected return relatively high the manager is afraid it is not efficient. The following values have been estimated:

Expected return on the portfolio	12%
Riskless return	6%
Expected return on the market	10%
Beta of the portfolio	1.5
Standard deviation of the investment expected return	24%
Standard deviation of the market expected return	16%
Covariance of the investment expected return with the market	3.84%

Is the portfolio efficient?

Answers to self-test problems

11.1 · The expected returns are just the possible returns multiplied by the associated probabilities:

$$E(R_A) = 0.10 \times (-0.20) + 0.60 \times (0.10) + 0.30 \times (0.70) = 25\%$$
$$E(R_B) = 0.10 \times (0.30) + 0.60 \times (0.20) + 0.30 \times (0.50) = 30\%$$

The variances are given by the sums of the squared deviations from the expected returns multiplied by their probabilities:

$$
\begin{aligned}
\sigma^2_A &= 0.10 \times (-0.20 - 0.25)^2 + 0.60 \times (0.10 - 0.25)^2 + 0.30 \times (0.70 - 0.25)^2 \\
&= 0.10 \times (-0.45)^2 + 0.60 \times (-0.15)^2 + 0.30 \times (0.45)^2 \\
&= 0.10 \times 0.2025 + 0.60 \times 0.0225 + 0.30 \times 0.2025 \\
&= 0.0945
\end{aligned}
$$

$$
\begin{aligned}
\sigma^2_B &= 0.10 \times (0.30 - 0.30)^2 + 0.60 \times (0.20 - 0.30)^2 + 0.30 \times (0.50 - 0.30)^2 \\
&= 0.10 \times (0.00)^2 + 0.60 \times (-0.10)^2 + 0.30 \times (0.20)^2 \\
&= 0.10 \times 0.00 + 0.60 \times 0.01 + 0.30 \times 0.04 \\
&= 0.0180
\end{aligned}
$$

The standard deviations are thus:

$$\sigma_A = \sqrt{0.0945} = 30.74\%$$
$$\sigma_B = \sqrt{0.0180} = 13.42\%$$

11.2 · The portfolio weights are $6,000/20,000 = 0.30$, and $14,000/20,000 = 0.70$. The expected return is thus:

$$
\begin{aligned}
E(R_P) &= 0.30 \times E(R_A) + 0.70 \times E(R_B) \\
&= 0.30 \times 25\% + 0.70 \times 30\% \\
&= 28.50\%
\end{aligned}
$$

Alternatively, we could calculate the portfolio's return in each of the states:

(1) State of the economy	(2) Probability of state of economy	(3) Portfolio return if state occurs
Recession	0.10	$0.30 \times (-0.20) + 0.70 \times (0.30) = 0.15$
Normal	0.60	$0.30 \times (0.10) + 0.70 \times (0.20) = 0.17$
Boom	0.30	$0.30 \times (0.70) + 0.70 \times (0.50) = 0.56$

The portfolio's expected return is:

$$
\begin{aligned}
E(R_P) &= 0.10 \times (0.15) + 0.60 \times (0.17) + 0.30 \times (0.56) \\
&= 28.50\%
\end{aligned}
$$

This is the same as we had before.

The portfolio's variance is:

$$
\begin{aligned}
\sigma^2_P &= 0.10 \times (0.15 - 0.285)^2 + 0.60 \times (0.17 - 0.285)^2 + 0.30 \times (0.56 - 0.285)^2 \\
&= .03245
\end{aligned}
$$

So the standard deviation is $\sqrt{0.03245} = 18.01\%$.

11.3 · If we compute the reward-to-risk ratios, we get $(19\% - 8\%)/1.6 = 6.875\%$ for Over versus 6.67% for Under. Relative to Over, Under's expected return is too low, so its price is too high.

If they are correctly priced, then they must offer the same reward-to-risk ratio. The risk-free rate would have to be such that:

$(19\% - R_f)/1.6 = (16\% - R_f)/1.2$

With a little algebra, we find that the risk-free rate must be 7 per cent:

$$(19\% - R_f) = (16\% - R_f)(1.6/1.2)$$
$$19\% - 16\% \times (4/3) = R_f - R_f \times (4/3)$$
$$R_f = 7$$

11.4 · Since the expected return on the market is 14 per cent, the market risk premium is $14\% - 8\% = 6\%$ (the risk-free rate is 8%). The first share has a beta of 0.60, so its expected return is $8\% + 0.60 \times 6\% = 11.6\%$.

For the second share, notice that the risk premium is $20\% - 8\% = 12\%$. Since this is twice as large as the market risk premium, the beta must be exactly equal to 2. We can verify this using the CAPM:

$$E(R_i) = R_f + [E(R_M) - R_f] \times \beta_i$$
$$20\% = 8\% + (14\% - 8\%) \times \beta_i$$
$$\beta_i = 12\%/6\%$$
$$= 2.0$$

11.5 · If the portfolio is efficient the expected return will be explained by the CML equation so that:

$$E(R_i) = R_f + [E(R_M) - R_f] / \sigma_M \times \sigma_i$$
$$0.12 = 0.06 + (0.10 - 0.06)/0.16 \times 0.24$$
$$0.12 = 0.12$$

OR the correlation coefficient is equal to 1.

$$\text{Correlation Coefficient} = \text{Covariance/Product of standard deviations}$$
$$= 0.0384/0.16 \times 0.24$$

Note: These are not alternative tests of efficiency but equivalent tests. If the return on a portfolio is explained by the CML it must be perfectly positively correlated with the market: $\rho = 1$

And just for interest:

$$\text{Beta} = \text{Covariance/Variance of the market}$$
$$= 0.0384/0.16 \times 0.16$$
$$= 1.5 \text{ as given in the question but not used in the answer, which is something often done by lecturers in examinations.}$$

Questions and problems

1 · Calculating expected return

Based on the following information, calculate the expected return on the security.

(1) State of the economy	(2) Probability of state of economy	(3) Rate of return if state occurs
Recession	0.5	0.12
Boom	0.5	0.18

2 · Calculating expected return

Based on the following information, calculate the expected return on the security.

(1) State of the economy	(2) Probability of state of economy	(3) Rate of return if state occurs
Recession	0.20	0.12
Boom	0.80	0.18

3 · Determining portfolio weights

What are the portfolio weights for a portfolio that has 20 shares that sell for $50 per share and 30 shares that sell for $20 per share?

4 · Portfolio expected returns

If a portfolio has a positive investment in every asset, can the expected return on the portfolio be greater than that on every asset in the portfolio? Can it be less than that on every asset in the portfolio? If you answer yes to one or both of these questions, give an example to support your answer.

5 · Calculating returns and deviations

Based on the following information, calculate the expected returns and standard deviations for the two shares.

(1) State of the economy	(2) Probability of state of economy	(3) Share X rate of return if state occurs	(4) Share Y rate of return if state occurs
Recession	0.20	0.10	0.55
Normal	0.40	0.24	0.20
Boom	0.40	0.44	0.10

6 · Individual asset variance and diversification

The most important characteristic in determining the variance of a well-diversified portfolio is the variances of the individual assets in the portfolio. Is this statement true or false? Explain.

7 · Returns and deviations

Consider the following information:

State of economy	Probability of state	Returns		
		Share A	Share B	Share C
Boom	0.40	10%	15%	20%
Bust	0.60	8%	4%	0%

a What are the expected returns on the three shares? The standard deviations?
b What is the expected return on an equally weighted portfolio of the three shares?

8 · Portfolio returns and deviations

Consider the following information:

State of the economy	Probability of state of economy	Return on A	Return on B
Boom	0.10	25%	18%
Growth	0.20	10	20
Normal	0.50	15	4
Recession	0.20	−12	0

a   What is the expected return for A? For B?
b   What is the standard deviation for A? For B?
c   What is the expected return on a portfolio of A and B that is 20 per cent invested in A and the remainder in B?
d   What is the variance of a portfolio that is 60 per cent invested in A and 40 per cent in B?

9 · Portfolio risk

If a portfolio has a positive investment in every asset, can the standard deviation on the portfolio be less than that on every asset in the portfolio? What about the portfolio beta?

10 · Types of risk

In broad terms, why is some risk diversifiable? Why are some risks non-diversifiable? Does it follow that an investor can control the level of non-systematic risk in a portfolio, but not the level of systematic risk?

11 · Announcements and security prices

Suppose that the government announces that, based on a just-completed survey, the growth rate in the economy is likely to be 4 per cent in the coming year, as compared to 6 per cent for the year just completed. Would security prices increase, decrease or stay the same following this announcement?

12 · Non-systematic risk

Evaluate the following statement: 'The only truly non-systematic events are earthquakes, volcanoes and supernovas.'

13 · Systematic versus non-systematic risk

Classify the following events as mostly systematic or mostly non-systematic. Is the distinction clear in every case?

a   Short-term interest rates increase unexpectedly.
b   The interest rate a company pays on its short-term borrowing is increased by its bank.
c   Oil prices unexpectedly decline.
d   An oil tanker ruptures, creating a large oil spill.
e   A manufacturer loses a multimillion-dollar product liability suit.
f   A High Court decision substantially broadens producer liability for injuries suffered by product users.

14 · Analysing a portfolio

Suppose we had the following investments:

Security	Amount invested	Expected return	Beta
Applaud	$5,000	8%	0.80
Barrack	5,000	9	1.00
Cheer	6,000	10	1.20
Shout	4,000	12	1.40

a   What are the portfolio weights?
b   What is the expected return on the portfolio?
c   What is the portfolio beta?

15 · Using CAPM

The risk-free rate is currently 9 per cent. A share has a beta of 0.70 and an expected return of 12 per cent. Conservative has spread his investment across the risk-free rate and the share.

a   What is the expected return on a portfolio that is equally invested in the two assets?
b   If a portfolio of the two assets has a beta of 0.50, what are the portfolio weights?

c If a portfolio of the two assets has an expected return of 10 per cent, what is its beta? What is the expected return on the market?

d If a portfolio of the two assets has a beta of 1.50, what are the portfolio weights? How do we interpret the weight for the risk-free asset?

16 · Using SML

Knowledge Ltd has an expected return of 18 per cent and a beta of 1.4. If the risk-free rate is 8 per cent, complete the following table for portfolios of Knowledge and the risk-free asset. Illustrate the relationship between portfolio expected return and portfolio beta by plotting the expected returns against the betas. What is the slope of the line that results?

Percentage of portfolio in Knowledge	Portfolio expected return	Portfolio beta
0%		
25		
50		
75		
100		
125		
150		

17 · Asset correlation

If a portfolio comprising 20 per cent of Op and 80 per cent of Rah has a variance of 12.84 per cent when the variance of Op is 25 per cent and the variance of Rah is 16 per cent, what is the correlation between Op and Rah? What is the covariance between Op and Rah?

18 · Using the SML

Suppose the risk-free rate is 8 per cent and the expected return on the overall market is 14 per cent. If Fresh Produce Ltd shares have a beta of 0.60, what is their expected return based on the CAPM? If Risky Developments Ltd shares have an expected return of 20 per cent, what must Risky's beta be?

19 · Reward to risk ratios

Suppose you observe the following situation:

Security	Beta	Expected return
Sandra Ltd	0.80	10%
Tom Co. Ltd	0.60	8%

If the risk-free rate is 6 per cent, are these securities correctly priced? What would the risk-free rate have to be if they are correctly priced?

20 · Using the SML

The beta for the History Company is 0.80. Its expected return is 12 per cent, and the risk-free rate is 8 per cent. If History plots on the SML, what is the market risk premium?

21 · SML

Suppose the expected return on the market is 10 per cent. Water Development has a beta of 1.80 and an expected return of 14 per cent. If this security plots on the SML, what is the risk-free rate? What is the slope of the SML?

22 · CAPM

Using the CAPM, show that the ratio of the risk premiums on two assets is equal to the ratio of their betas.

23 · SML

This is a challenge question. Suppose you observe the following situation:

Security	Beta	Expected return
Wild Co. Ltd	1.25	19%
Run Co. Ltd	0.75	15%

Assume these securities are correctly priced. Based on the CAPM, what is the expected return on the market? What is the risk-free rate?

24 · Beta coefficients

This is a challenge question.

a Is it possible that a risky asset could have a beta of zero? Explain.
b From the CAPM, what is the expected return on such an asset?
c Is it possible that a risky asset could have a negative beta?
d What does the CAPM predict about the expected return on such an asset? Can you give an explanation for your answer?

25 · Constructing a portfolio

This is a challenge question. X, Y, and Z are portfolios of securities. M stands for the market. The following statistics have been collected:

Portfolio	Expected return	Standard deviation of expected return	Covariance of expected returns with the market
X		0.2	0.02
Y		0.4	0.05
Z	0.2		0.104
M	0.12		0.04

The covariance of the expected return on X with the expected return on Y is 0.08.

Hint: The covariance of a variable with itself is equal to its variance. Therefore the covariance of the expected return on X with the expected return on X would be the variance of the expected return on X.

Calculate:

a the beta of X.
b the beta of Y.
c the beta of a portfolio containing 40% of the wealth in X and 60% in Y.
d the riskless rate of interest.
e the expected return for the portfolio created in (c).
f Is the portfolio created in (c) efficient?
g Should the portfolio be efficient?

26 · Selecting investments

Investment selection has been very difficult over the last five years. Austin Smarttalk is seeking your advice in investment choice. He has developed forecasts for five securities. He is very confident his forecasts are correct, but he does not know which investments to advise clients to purchase. This is where you come to the rescue. You have already told Austin that it is difficult to identify 'winners' in investments and that he should advise his clients to diversify. The statistics derived by Austin are as follows:

Investment	Expected excess return	Standard deviation of expected returns
A	6.4	6
B	3	2.5
C	4.4	5.1
D	2.5	5
E	8.8	10

The excess return is the amount of return expected to be earned over the risk-free rate. Austin is not happy with your advice and he wants you to do some ranking for him. He wants you to rank the securities if:

a the objective is maximum return
b the objective is to minimise risk
c the objective is to consider both return and risk
d Austin provides additional information regarding the covariance of the expected return with the expected return on the market as:

A	0.00064
B	0.0003
C	0.00044
D	0.0002
E	0.00088

and the covariance of the market with the market as .0004. Would your answer to (c) change, and if it does, what would your revised ranking be?

27 · Expected return and standard deviation

There are two assets and three states expected in the economy:

State	Probability of state	Rate of return if state occurs	
		Share A	Share B
Recession	0.2	−0.15	0.20
Normal	0.5	0.20	0.30
Boom	0.3	0.60	0.40

What are the expected returns and standard deviations of the two shares?

28 · Portfolio return

Using the information in Problem 27, suppose you have $20,000 to invest. You put $15,000 in share A and the balance in share B. What will the expected return on your portfolio be?

29 · Return and risk

Consider the following information:

Share	Beta	Expected return
Worn	1.8	22.00%
Out	1.6	20.44%

If the risk-free rate is 7 per cent, are these shares correctly priced? What would the risk-free rate have to be if they were correctly priced?

30 · CAPM

The risk-free rate is 8 per cent and the expected return on the market is double the risk-free rate. If a share has a beta of 0.7, what is its expected return based on the CAPM? If another share has an expected return of 24 per cent, what is its beta?

Current

investment decisions

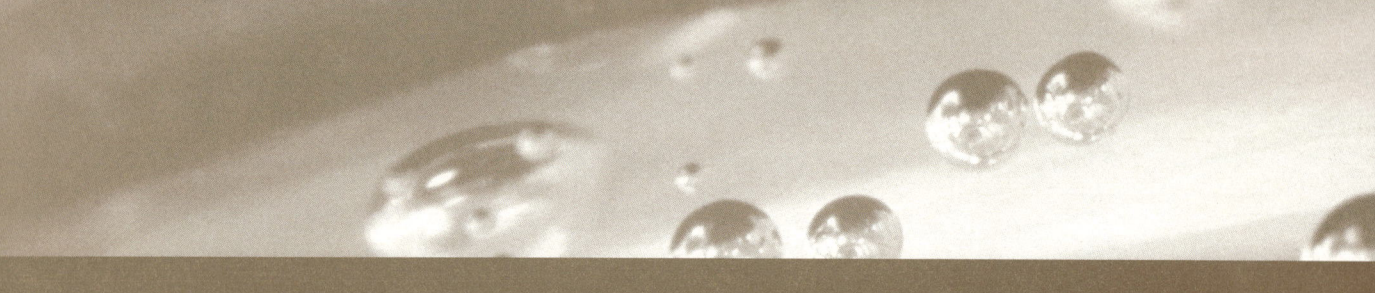

CHAPTER 12

Current
investment decisions

Objective

One of the fundamental responsibilities of the financial director is to see that the organisation does not get into difficulties due to insolvency. This area of responsibility involves the management of short-term or current assets and liabilities. The current assets and liabilities, which will be turned over within 12 months, are regarded as the working capital of the organisation. At the conclusion of this chapter students should understand how funds may be managed to ensure the organisation remains liquid at all times. In addition the chapter introduces the marginal cost form of analysis for the management of current assets as it is related to inventory control.

Introduction ▷ In Chapter 8 techniques were developed for the analysis of capital investments. Traditionally a distinction has been made between those investments in which the benefits accrue over an extended period, such as several years, and those where the benefits accrue over a relatively short period, for example within a year. The former investments are known as capital investments and the latter as current investments. The techniques that were developed for the analysis of capital investments are also appropriate for the analysis of current investments. In fact the distinction between 'capital' and 'current' is somewhat artificial for purposes of decision making.

 ## 12.1 The investments involved

Current investment decisions are almost synonymous with the management of current assets as identified in conventional Statements of Financial Position: current assets include cash and marketable securities, inventories, accounts receivable, and prepayments of expenses and accruals of income. The last group, prepayments and accruals, arise as balance day adjustments within the accounting system so that they represent book transfers and not allocation of resources. They are employed to measure periodic profit and as such are of no interest to us here. Our attention is therefore directed to the other three groups. Figure 12.1 shows how the decisions in relation to current assets are related: A casual observation of the figure is sufficient to indicate that the current asset decisions are interdependent and therefore the resolution of the current asset decisions of the firm should involve a joint consideration of all the components. Nevertheless in practice and theory, in order to reduce the problem to manageable limits, the decisions are analysed separately.

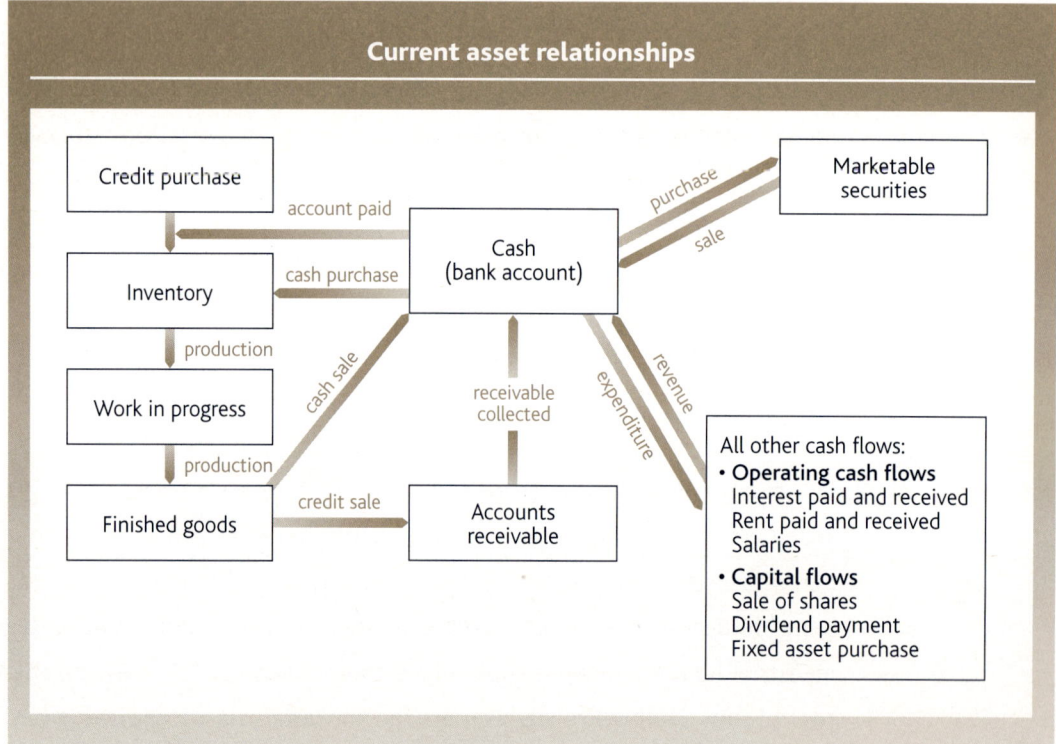

Figure 12.1 is an oversimplification of the current investment decision. Many considerations, such as cash discounts, collection costs of doubtful debts and interest on short-term loans have been ignored. Examination of Figure 12.1 highlights the similarity between a current and a capital investment decision. Both decisions involve an analysis of cash inflows and cash outflows; however, the current investment decision is clouded by a number of other considerations such as:

* How much inventory should be maintained?
* How much should be invested in short-term securities?
* How much should be held in the bank account?
* What credit terms should be allowed?

The basic problem is still one of cash inflows versus cash outflows. Figure 12.2 provides an example of a pattern that the cash flows might follow.

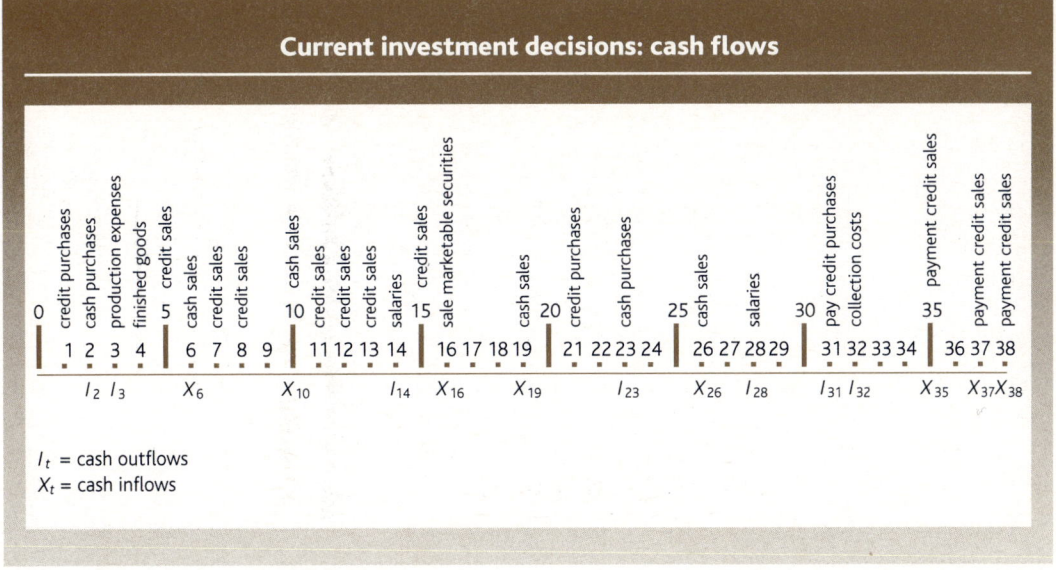

Current investment decisions: cash flows

FIGURE 12.2

I_t = cash outflows
X_t = cash inflows

It is possible to evaluate the current investment decision using the discounted cash flow techniques developed in earlier chapters, but several problems arise. It is very difficult to identify all the cash inflows and outflows associated with the current investment decision. In addition, it is extremely difficult to estimate the size of the cash flows. Selecting the time of the cash flows presents a most difficult problem because the periods involved are very short and a timing error may have a significant influence on the decision. Another problem is to determine the correct discount rate. The lack of markets for short-term investments make it almost impossible to identify the correct risk-adjusted rate. In consequence, a marginal revenue/marginal cost type of analysis is often used. This type of analysis implies that the period under consideration is too small to warrant the use of the more sophisticated discounted cash flow methods of analysis. For all practical purposes because of the time period, the discount rate may be assumed to be zero. As the length of the period of investment increases, the analysis reverts to the discounted cash flow technique.

Concept questions

12.1a *What is the timeframe within which you expect current assets to be converted to cash?*

12.1b *In what order are current assets presented in company Statements of Financial Position?*

12.1c *Why should a decision on what level of inventory to hold be related to decisions on credit policies and cash discounts?*

12.2 ▪ The operating cycle and the cash cycle

The primary concern of business in the short term is its cash flow. Many firms have been forced into liquidation because of an inability to manage their cash requirements. For a typical manufacturing firm, its short-run activities might consist of the following sequence of events and decisions:

Events	Decisions
1. Buying raw materials	1. How much inventory to order?
2. Paying cash	2. Borrow or draw down cash balance?
3. Manufacturing the product	3. What choice of production technology?
4. Selling the product	4. Should credit be extended to a particular customer?
5. Collecting cash	5. How to collect?

These activities create patterns of cash inflows and cash outflows. These cash flows are both non-synchronised and uncertain. They are non-synchronised because, for example, the payment of cash for raw materials does not happen at the same time as the receipt of cash from selling the product. They are uncertain because future sales and costs are not known with certainty.

Defining the operating and cash cycles

We can start with a simple case. One day, call it day 0, you purchase $1,000 worth of inventory on credit. You pay the bill 30 days later, and, after 30 more days, someone buys the $1,000 in inventory for $1,400. Your buyer does not actually pay for another 45 days. We can summarise these events chronologically as follows:

Day	Activity	Cash effect
0	Acquire inventory	none
30	Pay for inventory	−$1,000
60	Sell inventory on credit	none
105	Collect on sale	+$1,400

The operating cycle

There are several things to notice in our example. First, the entire cycle, from the time we acquire some inventory to the time we collect the cash, takes 105 days. This is called the **operating (or activity) cycle**.

As we illustrate, the operating cycle is the length of time it takes to acquire inventory, sell it and collect for it. This cycle has two distinct components. The first part is the time it takes to acquire and sell the inventory. This 60-day span (in our example) is called the **inventory period**. The second part is the time it takes to collect on the sale, 45 days in our example. This is called the **accounts receivable period**.

Based on our definitions, the operating cycle is obviously just the sum of the inventory and receivables periods:

$$\text{Operating cycle} = \text{Inventory period} + \text{Accounts receivable period} \quad (12.1)$$
$$105 \text{ days} = 60 \text{ days} + 45 \text{ days}$$

What the operating cycle describes is how a product moves through the current asset accounts. It begins life as inventory, it is converted to a receivable when it is sold, and it is finally converted to cash when we collect from the sale. Notice that, at each step, the asset is moving closer to cash.

The cash cycle

The second thing to notice is that the cash flows and other events that occur are not synchronised. For example, we did not actually pay for the inventory until 30 days after we acquired it. This 30-day period is called the **accounts payable period**. Next, we spend cash on day 30, but we do not collect until day 105. Somehow, we have to arrange to finance the $1,000 for 105 − 30 = 75 days. This period is called the **cash cycle**.

operating (or activity) cycle
the time period between the acquisition of inventory and when cash is collected from receivables

inventory period
the time it takes to acquire and sell inventory

accounts receivable period
the time between sale of inventory and collection of the receivable

accounts payable period
the time between receipt of inventory and payment for it

cash cycle
the time between cash disbursement and cash collection

The cash cycle, therefore, is the number of days that pass until we collect the cash from a sale, measured from when we actually pay for the inventory. Notice that, based on our definitions, the cash cycle is the difference between the operating cycle and the accounts payable period:

$$\text{Cash cycle} \ = \ \text{Operating cycle} \ - \ \text{Accounts payable period} \qquad (12.2)$$

Figure 12.3 depicts the short-term operating activities and cash flows for a typical manufacturing firm by looking at the **cash flow time line**. As shown, the cash flow time line is made up of the operating cycle and the cash cycle. In Figure 12.3, the need for short-term financial management is suggested by the gap between the cash inflows and cash outflows. This is related to the length of the operating cycle and accounts payable period.

cash flow time line
graphical representation of the operating cycle and the cash cycle

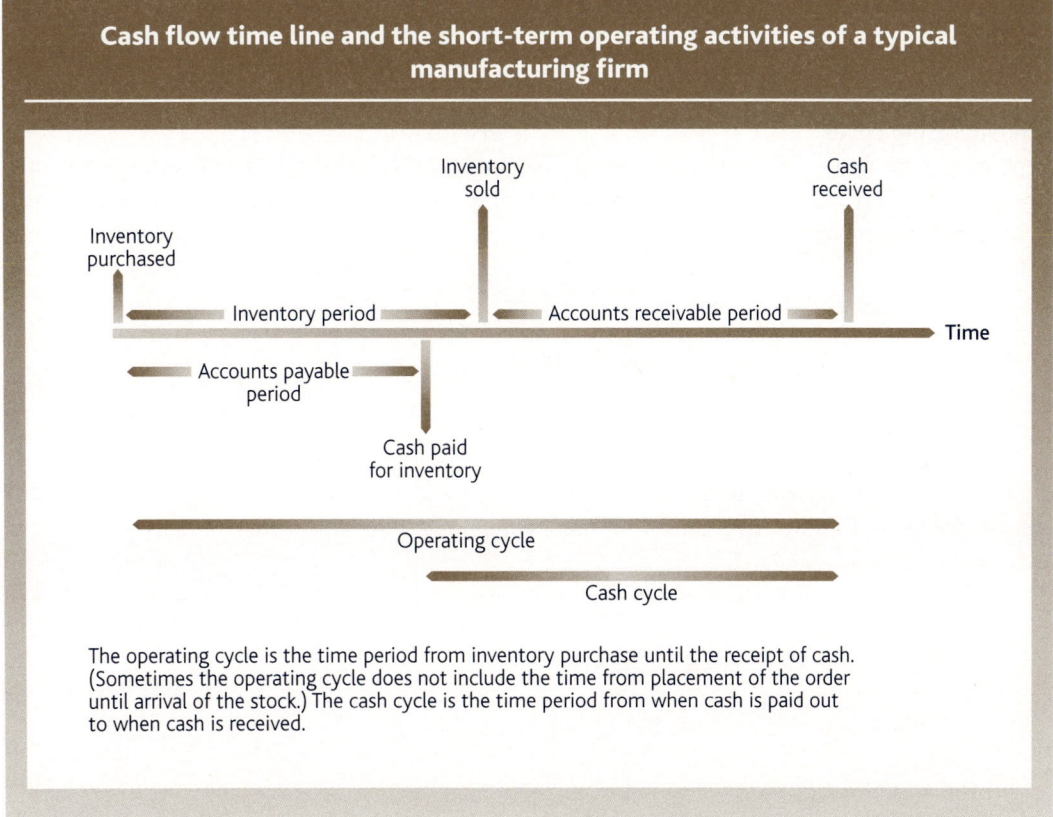

Cash flow time line and the short-term operating activities of a typical manufacturing firm

FIGURE 12.3

The operating cycle is the time period from inventory purchase until the receipt of cash. (Sometimes the operating cycle does not include the time from placement of the order until arrival of the stock.) The cash cycle is the time period from when cash is paid out to when cash is received.

The gap between short-term inflows and outflows can be filled either by borrowing or by holding a liquidity reserve in the form of cash or marketable securities. Alternatively, the gap can be shortened by changing the inventory, receivable and payable periods. These are all managerial options that we discuss below and in subsequent chapters.

Calculating the operating and cash cycles

In our example, the lengths of time that made up the different periods were obvious. If all we have is financial statement information, we will have to do a little more work. We illustrate these calculations next.

To begin, we need to determine various things like how long it takes, on average, to sell inventory and how long it takes, on average, to collect. We start by gathering some Statement of Financial Position information such as the following (in thousands):

Item	Beginning	Ending	Average
Inventory	$2,000	$3,000	$2,500
Accounts receivable	1,600	2,000	1,800
Accounts payable	750	1,000	875

Also, from the most recent Statement of Financial Performance, we might have the following figures (in thousands):

Net sales	$11,500
Cost of goods sold	8,200

We now need to calculate some financial ratios. We discussed these in some detail in Chapter 3; here we just define them and use them as needed.

The operating cycle

First of all, we need the inventory period. We spent $8.2 million on inventory (our cost of goods sold). Our average inventory was $2.5 million. We thus turned our inventory over $8.2/2.5 times during the year:[1]

$$\text{Inventory turnover} = \frac{\text{Cost of goods sold}}{\text{Average inventory}}$$

$$= \frac{\$8.2 \text{ million}}{\$2.5 \text{ million}}$$

$$= 3.28 \text{ times}$$

Loosely speaking, this tells us that we bought and sold off our inventory 3.28 times during the year. This means that, on average, we held our inventory for:

$$\text{Inventory Period} = \frac{365 \text{ days}}{\text{Average turnover}}$$

$$= \frac{365}{3.28}$$

$$= 111.3 \text{ days}$$

So the inventory period is about 111 days. On average, in other words, inventory sat for about 111 days before it was sold.[2]

Similarly, receivables averaged $1.8 million, and sales were $11.5 million. Assuming that all sales were credit sales, the receivables turnover is:[3]

$$\text{Receivables turnover} = \frac{\text{Credit sales}}{\text{Average accounts receivable}}$$

$$= \frac{\$11.5 \text{ million}}{\$1.8 \text{ million}}$$

$$= 6.4 \text{ times}$$

If we turn over our receivables 6.4 times, then the receivables period is:

$$\text{Receivables period} = \frac{365 \text{ days}}{\text{Receivables turnover}}$$

$$= \frac{365}{6.4}$$

$$= 57 \text{ days}$$

The receivables period is also called the *days' sales in receivables* or the *average collection period*. Whatever it is called, it tells us that our customers took an average of 57 days to pay.

The operating cycle is the sum of the inventory and receivables periods:

$$\text{Operating cycle} = \text{Inventory period} + \text{Accounts receivables period}$$

$$= 111 \text{ days} + 57 \text{ days}$$

$$= 168 \text{ days}$$

This tells us that, on average, 168 days elapse from the time we acquire inventory, sell it, and collect for the sale.

The cash cycle

We now need the payables period. From the information given above, average payables were $875,000, and cost of goods sold was again $8.2 million. Our payables turnover is thus:

$$\text{Payables turnover} = \frac{\text{Cost of goods sold}}{\text{Average payable}}$$

$$= \frac{\$8.2 \text{ million}}{\$0.875 \text{ million}}$$

$$= 9.4 \text{ times}$$

The payables period is:

$$\text{Payable period} = \frac{365 \text{ days}}{\text{Payable turnover}}$$

$$= \frac{365}{9.4}$$

$$= 39 \text{ days}$$

Thus, we took an average of 39 days to pay our bills.

Finally, the cash cycle is the difference between the operating cycle and the payables period:

$$\text{Cash cycle} = \text{Operating cycle} - \text{Accounts payables period}$$

$$= 168 \text{ days} - 39 \text{ days}$$

$$= 129 \text{ days}$$

So, on average, there is a 129-day delay from the time we pay for merchandise and the time we collect on the sales.

EXAMPLE
12.1
The operating and cash cycles

You have collected the following information for the Owe-it Company.

Item	Beginning	Ending
Inventory	$5,000	$7,000
Accounts receivable	1,600	2,400
Accounts payable	2,700	4,800

Sales for the year just ended were $50,000, and cost of goods sold was $30,000. How long does it take Owe-it to collect on its receivables? How long does merchandise stay around before it is sold? How long does Owe-it take to pay its bills?

We can first calculate the three turnover ratios:

Inventory turnover   = $30,000/$6,000 = 5 times
Receivables turnover = $50,000/$2,000 = 25 times
Payables turnover   = $30,000/$3,750 = 8 times

We use these to get the various periods:

Inventory period   = 365/5 = 73 days
Receivables period = 365/25 = 14.6 days
Payables period   = 365/8 = 45.6 days

All told, Owe-it collects on a sale in 14.6 days, inventory sits around for 73 days, and bills get paid after about 46 days. The operating cycle here is the sum of the inventory and receivables periods: 73 + 14.6 = 87.6 days. The cash cycle is the difference between the operating cycle and the payables period: 87.6 − 45.6 = 42 days.

Concept questions

12.2a *What does it mean to say that a firm has an inventory turnover ratio of 4?*
12.2b *Describe the operating cycle and cash cycle. What are the differences?*

12.3 Some aspects of short-term financial policy

The short-term financial policy that a firm adopts will be reflected in at least two ways:

1 *The size of the firm's investment in current assets.* This is usually measured relative to the firm's level of total operating revenues. A flexible or accommodative short-term financial policy would maintain a relatively high ratio of current assets to sales. A restrictive short-term financial policy would entail a low ratio of current assets to sales.[4]

2 *The financing of current assets.* This is measured as the proportion of short-term debt (i.e. current liabilities) and long-term debt used to finance current assets. A restrictive short-term financial policy means a high proportion of short-term debt relative to long-term financing, and a flexible policy means less short-term debt and more long-term debt.

If we take these two areas together, a firm with a flexible policy would have a relatively large investment in current assets. It would finance this investment with relatively less in short-term debt. The net effect of a flexible policy is thus a relatively high level of net working capital. Put another way, with a flexible policy, the firm maintains a larger overall level of liquidity.

The size of the firm's investment in current assets

Flexible short-term financial policies with regard to current assets include such actions as:

1 keeping large balances of cash and marketable securities;
2 making large investments in inventory;
3 granting liberal credit terms, which result in a high level of accounts receivable.

Restrictive short-term financial policies would just be the opposite of these:

1 keeping low cash balances and little investment in marketable securities;
2 making small investments in inventory;
3 allowing few or no credit sales, thereby minimising accounts receivable.

Determining the optimal investment level in short-term assets requires an identification of the different costs of alternative short-term financing policies. The objective is to trade off the cost of a restrictive policy against the cost of a flexible one to arrive at the best compromise.

Current asset holdings are highest with a flexible short-term financial policy, and lowest with a restrictive policy. So flexible short-term financial policies are costly in that they require a greater investment in cash and marketable securities, inventory and accounts receivable. However, we expect that future cash inflows will be higher with a flexible policy. For example, sales are stimulated by the use of a credit policy that provides liberal financing to customers. A large amount of finished inventory on hand ('on the shelf') provides a quick delivery service to customers and may increase sales. Similarly, a large inventory of raw materials may result in fewer production stoppages because of inventory shortages.

A more restrictive short-term financial policy probably reduces future sales levels below those that would be achieved under flexible policies. It is also possible that higher prices can be charged to customers under flexible working capital policies. Customers may be willing to pay higher prices for the quick delivery service and more liberal credit terms implicit in flexible policies.

Managing current assets can be thought of as involving a trade-off between costs that rise and costs that fall with the level of investment. Costs that rise with increases in the level of investment in current assets are called **carrying costs**. The larger the investment a firm makes in its current assets, the higher its carrying costs will be. Costs that fall with increases in the level of investment in current assets are called **shortage costs**.

In a general sense, carrying costs are the opportunity costs associated with current assets. The rate of return on current assets is very low when compared to other assets. For example, the rate of return on Australian government bonds is usually less than 10 per cent (see Table 10.2). This is very low compared to the rate of return firms would like to achieve overall. (Australian government bonds are an important component of cash and marketable securities.)

Acquisition or shortage costs are incurred when the investment in current assets is low. If a firm runs out of cash, it will be forced to sell marketable securities. Of course, if a firm runs out of cash and cannot readily sell marketable securities, it may have to borrow or default on an obligation. This situation is called a cash out. A firm will lose customers if it runs out of inventory (a stock out). The loss may be the current sale; however, it could be the current sale and all future sales to the customer. Sales may also be lost if the firm cannot extend credit to potential customers.

More generally, there are two kinds of shortage costs:

1 *Trading or order costs*. Order costs are the costs of placing an order for more cash (brokerage costs, for example) or more inventory (production set-up costs, for example).

carrying costs
costs that rise with increases in the level of investment in current assets

acquisition/shortage costs
costs that fall with increases in the level of investment in current assets

2 *Costs related to safety reserves.* These are costs of lost sales, lost customer goodwill, and disruption of production schedule.

Figure 12.4(a) illustrates the basic trade-off between carrying costs and shortage costs. On the vertical axis, we have costs measured in dollars and, on the horizontal axis, we have the amount of current assets. Carrying costs start out at zero when current assets are zero and then climb steadily as current assets grow. Shortage costs start out very high and then decline as we add current assets. The total costs of holding current assets is the sum of the two. Notice how the combined costs reach a minimum at CA*. This is the optimum level of current assets.

Current asset holdings are highest under a flexible policy. This is one in which the carrying costs are perceived to be low relative to shortage costs; Figure 12.4(b). In comparison, under restrictive current asset policies, carrying costs are perceived to be high relative to shortage costs; Figure 12.4(c).

Carrying costs and shortage costs

Dollars

Minimum point

Total cost of
holding current assets

Carrying costs

Shortage costs

**Amount of
current assets (CA)**

CA*
The optimal amount of current assets.
This point minimises costs.

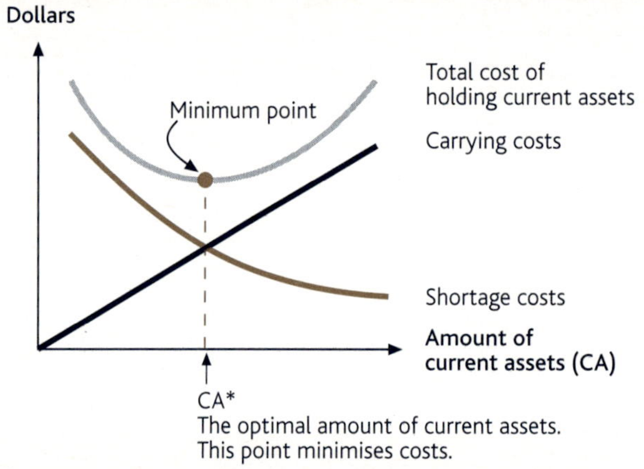

(a) Short-term financial policy: the optimal investment in current assets
Carrying costs increase with the level of investment in current assets. They include the cost of maintaining economic value and opportunity costs. Shortage costs decrease with increases in the level of investment in current assets. They include trading costs and the costs related to being short of the current asset (for example, being short of cash). The firm's policy can be characterised as flexible or restrictive.

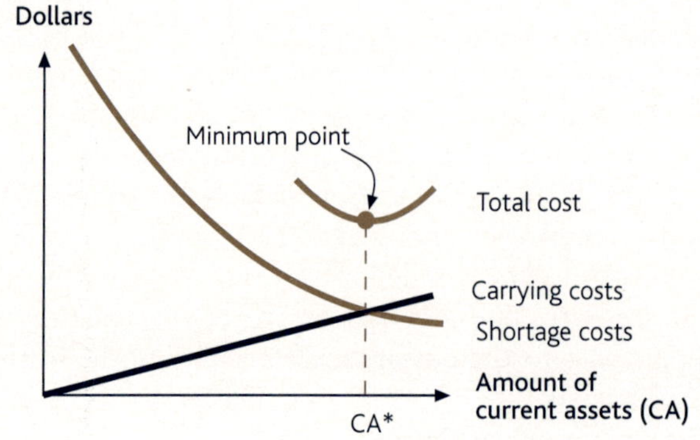

Dollars

Minimum point

Total cost

Carrying costs
Shortage costs

**Amount of
current assets (CA)**

CA*

(b) Flexible policy
A flexible policy is most appropriate when carrying costs are low relative to shortage costs.

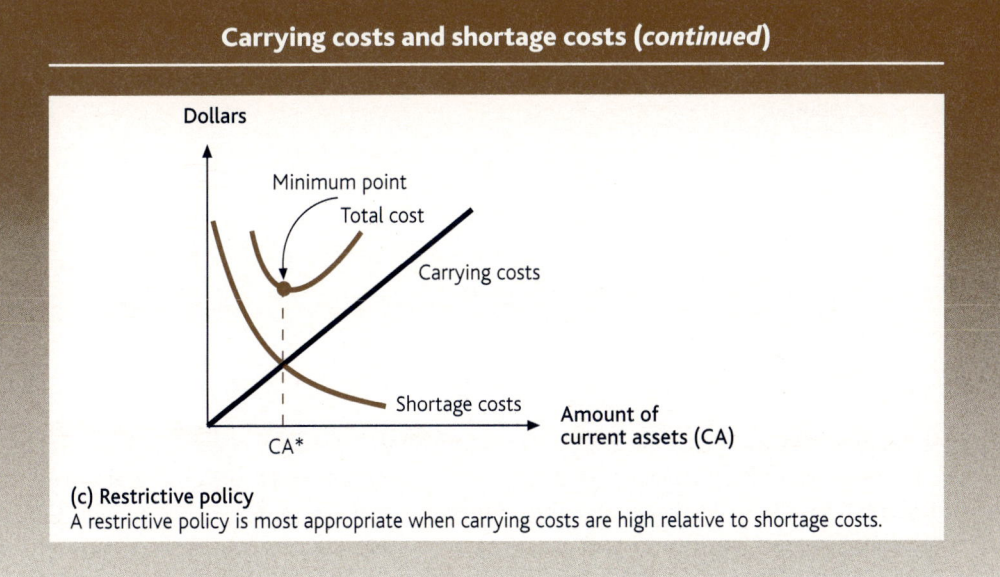

Carrying costs and shortage costs (*continued*)

FIGURE 12.4

(c) Restrictive policy
A restrictive policy is most appropriate when carrying costs are high relative to shortage costs.

The inventory model

Inventory is a most important current asset. It can comprise up to 40 per cent of the assets and 60 per cent of each sales dollar for a manufacturing firm.

The aim of the inventory model is to hold sufficient stock so that the needs of customers can be met without too many cash resources tied up in inventory. Fundamental to an inventory plan is the **economic order quantity (EOQ)** which is the quantity of inventory a company should purchase in order to minimise costs. Acquisition costs are expected to vary with the size of the inventory orders placed. These costs include:

1 ordering costs—clerical costs associated with placing and processing an order; and
2 freight and handling costs—every order placed will result in freight costs and handling costs in warehousing the inventory.

economic order quantity
the quantity of inventory a firm should order to minimise costs

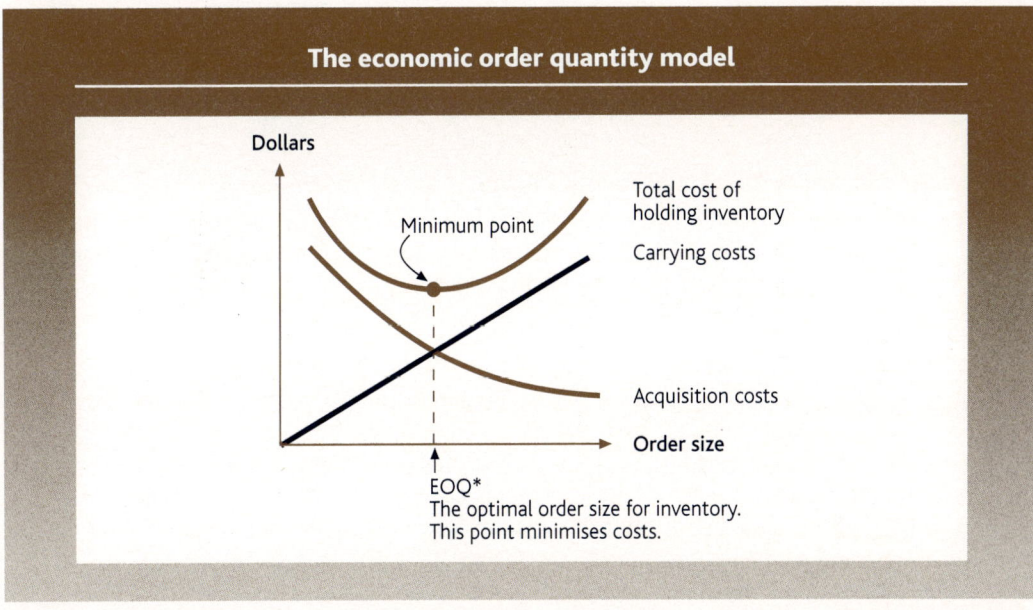

The economic order quantity model

FIGURE 12.5

EOQ*
The optimal order size for inventory.
This point minimises costs.

These costs will be lower per unit of inventory with larger orders and Figure 12.5 shows these costs related to order size. *Acquisition costs* fall as the order size increases so these are the *shortage costs* discussed in the previous section.

Carrying costs include:

1 storage costs—these costs may cover rent, insurance and other overhead costs;
2 deterioration costs—these may cover losses through wastage, spoilage or theft and they are likely to be higher for higher levels of inventory; and
3 opportunity costs—these are the costs because funds are tied up in inventory.

Again Figure 12.5 (previous page) shows how these costs are expected to behave. The total cost function for inventory may be simplified to:

$$\text{Total cost} = \text{Purchase price} + \text{Acquisition cost} + \text{Carrying cost}$$

Purchase price for inventory over a period is just total demand times the price per unit. If we specify demand as Y and price per unit as P, it is YP. Acquisition cost will equal total demand divided by the order size times the acquisition cost per order. If we specify X as the order size and A as the acquisition cost per order, it is $(Y/X)A$. Carrying cost is equal to the average level of inventory times the cost of carrying each unit. If we assume the inventory quantity ranges between X and zero, the carrying cost is $[(X + \text{zero})/2]C = (X/2)C$. We can now express the total cost of inventory as:

$$\textbf{Total cost} = \textbf{\textit{TC}} = \textbf{\textit{YP}} + (\textbf{\textit{Y/X}})\textbf{\textit{A}} + (\textbf{\textit{X/2}})\textbf{\textit{C}} \qquad (12.3)$$

The inventory plan is to establish the order quantity (X) that minimises the total cost. An application of simple calculus[5] provides the solution to this plan as:

$$\text{EOQ} = \sqrt{(2YA/C)}$$

where

$$
\begin{aligned}
EOQ &= \text{economic order quantity}\\
Y &= \text{total demand}\\
A &= \text{acquisition costs}\\
C &= \text{carrying cost}
\end{aligned}
$$

EXAMPLE 12.2 ■ Calculating EOQ

The finance officer has estimated that Slippers Ltd will require 20,000 units of product over the next 12 months. She has estimated that the cost of acquisition is $2 per unit and the carrying cost is 50 cents per unit. The cost per unit of product is $10. What would be the economic order quantity for Slippers?

$$
\begin{aligned}
\text{EOQ} &= \sqrt{(2YA/C)}\\
&= \sqrt{\frac{2 \times 20{,}000 \times \$2}{50 \text{ cents}}} \text{ units}\\
&= 400 \text{ units}
\end{aligned}
$$

It is interesting to note that the cost per unit of product ($10) for Slippers Ltd did not enter into the calculation of the EOQ. This cost can enter the calculation when quantity discounts are applicable. Quantity discounts occur where larger orders attract a discount in price. For example, suppose Slippers is offered a price of $9.99 if it

purchases more than 2,000 units and a price of $9.995 if it purchases more than 1,000 units. We now need to consider these discounts when establishing the optimal quantity. From equation (12.3) total cost is:

$$TC = YP + (Y/X)A + (X/2)C$$

so that the following total cost figures are applicable:

400 units   = 20,000 × $10 + (20,000/400)$2 + (400/2)0.5
          = $200,000 + $100 + $100
          = $200,200

1,000 units = 20,000 × $9.995 + (20,000/1,000)$2 + (1,000/2)0.5
          = $199,900 + $40 + $250
          = $200,190

2,000 units = 20,000 × $9.99 + (20,000/2,000)$2 + (2,000/2)0.5
          = $199,800 + $20 + 500
          = $200,320

Now Slippers would be better off if it purchased in lots of 1,000 rather than the 400 calculated without the price discounts, because lots of 1,000 units will reduce the total cost.

Another factor needs to be considered before we can establish an inventory plan for Slippers and this is the matter of lead time. Lead time is the time it takes from placement of an order to receipt of the goods ready for use. Let us assume that Slippers has established that its lead time is five days and its average daily usage of the product is 80 units. Slippers would have to order five days prior to its need for the new shipment or when it has 400 units (five days' supply) held in inventory. Figure 12.6 presents the inventory plan for Slippers building in the requirement for lead time. In manufacturing firms it is customary to identify reorder points in terms of quantity rather than time. An order would be placed for Slippers whenever inventory levels fell to 400 units.

Inventory plan: Slippers Ltd

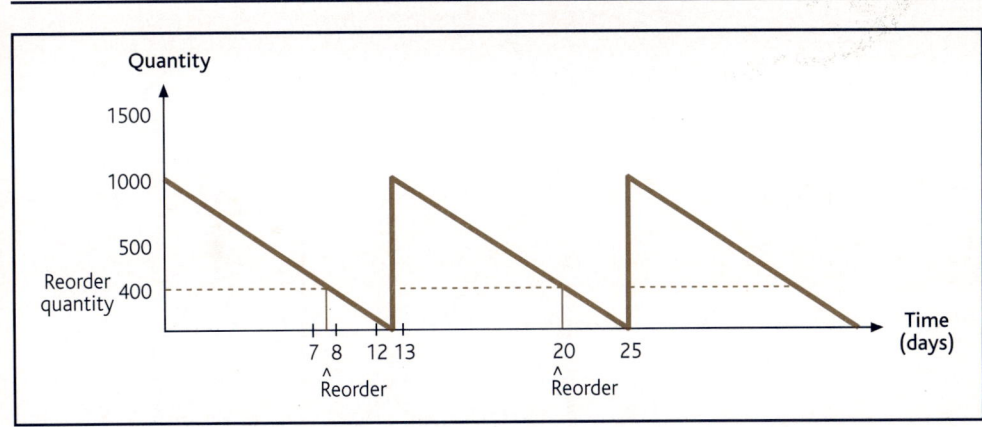

Stockout costs

To date we have considered the following costs in respect to inventory management:

* price discounts
* acquisition costs; and
* carrying costs.

cost of stockouts

the profits lost because the firm is out of a particular product

There is another cost that needs to be considered—the **cost of stockouts**. This cost is profits that are lost because the firm is out of a particular product. They may be minor when close substitutes are available, but they can be exceptionally high when the sale is lost and possibly all future sales to that customer.

Let us revisit the Slippers example with the following additional information:

1 Lead time, which is normally five days, occasionally varies by one day either way.
2 Daily usage averages 80 units.
3 Daily usage has been derived from the following distribution:

Usage	Probability
75 units	0.1
80 units	0.8
85 units	0.1

4 The costs of stockouts are considered to be very high as experience has shown that all future sales to customers are lost whenever stock is not available.

Remember that with the price discounts, the EOQ for Slippers was 1,000 units. Because stockout costs are excessive, the firm cannot afford to be out of stock so it must take the worst situation—six days' lead time and 85 units used. The level of *safety stock* would be set by considering the worst possible scenario with a normal scenario:

$$\text{Safety stock} = (85 \text{ units} \times 6 \text{ days}) - (80 \text{ units} \times 5 \text{ days})$$
$$= 110 \text{ units}$$

Now orders have to be placed whenever the level of inventory falls to 510 units (five days' normal usage plus the safety stock). Figure 12.7 shows the revised inventory plan for Slippers with a consideration of stockout cost.

FIGURE 12.7

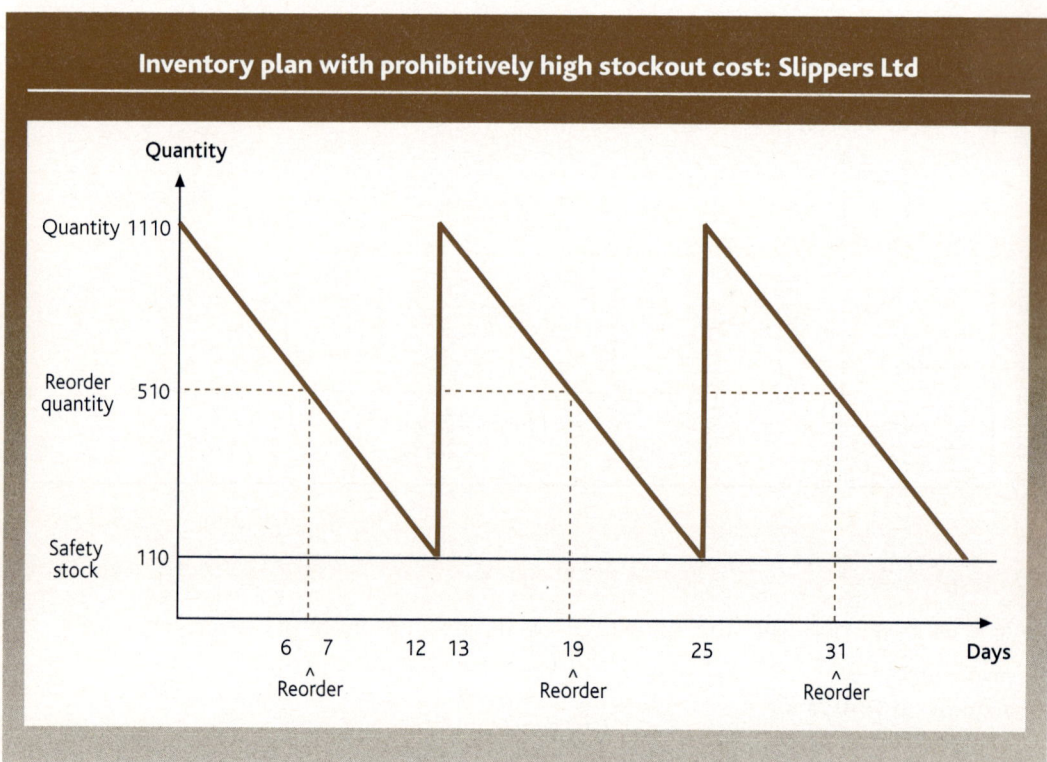

Inventory plan with prohibitively high stockout cost: Slippers Ltd

Just-in-time

Some companies use the **just-in-time** method of inventory control. Just-in-time means that the purchaser receives the goods just in time to use the goods in the production process. An example of this may be a motor vehicle manufacturer. The manufacturer produces 100 motor vehicles each day and each motor vehicle requires a battery. Using just in time, the battery supplier would deliver 100 batteries each day to be used in production.

In this case the battery manufacturer carries the inventory. The motor vehicle manufacturer would carry no inventory or a small amount of inventory. This reduces the carrying cost of inventory. The problem though is that should one of the batteries be defective, production stops. In addition if there were a transport strike then production would also stop.

Acquisition costs are also minimised as next period's production requirements are always known to the supplier. The motor vehicle manufacturer predicts that 100 motor vehicles per day will be produced, each one requiring a battery. The battery supplier would then deliver 100 per day. Effectively there is only one acquisition cost for the motor vehicle manufacturer for the scheduled production period.

The acquisition cost is passed on to the battery supplier. Instead of delivering only say once a month, the supplier now delivers batteries each day. You would expect this cost to be reflected in the price that the motor vehicle manufacturer pays to the battery supplier.

It may be doubtful whether the advantage of not carrying inventory outweighs the hidden costs of just in time.

> **just-in-time (JIT)**
> a system for managing demand-dependent inventories that minimises inventory holdings

Concept questions

12.3a *What are the marginal cost considerations in establishing an optimal inventory plan?*

12.3b *Explain why the acquisition cost per unit of product diminishes as the order size of inventory increases.*

12.3c *Why is the 'total cost of holding inventory' curve saucer-shaped like the conventional microeconomic average cost curve?*

12.4 ■ The cash budget

The **cash budget** is a primary tool in short-run financial planning. It allows the financial manager to identify short-term financial needs and opportunities. Importantly, the cash budget will help the manager explore the need for short-term borrowing. The idea of the cash budget is simple: it records estimates of cash receipts (cash in) and disbursements (cash out). The result is an estimate of the cash surplus or deficit.

> **cash budget**
> a forecast of cash receipts and disbursements for the next planning period

Sales and cash collections

We start with an example for LJT Skateboards Co. Ltd. We will prepare a quarterly cash budget. We could just as well use a monthly, weekly, or even daily basis. We choose quarters for convenience and also because a quarter is a common short-term business planning period.

All of LJT Skateboards' cash inflows come from the sale of Skateboards. Cash budgeting for LJT Skateboards must therefore start with a sales forecast for the next year, by quarter:

	Q1	Q2	Q3	Q4
Sales (in millions)	$200	$300	$250	$400

Note that these are predicted sales, so there is forecasting risk here because actual sales could be more or less. Also, LJT Skateboards started the year with accounts receivable equal to $120m.

LJT Skateboards has a 45-day receivables or average collection period. This means that half of the sales in a given quarter will be collected in the following quarter. This happens because sales made during the first 45 days of a quarter will be collected in that quarter. Sales made in the second 45 days will be collected in the next quarter. Note that we are assuming that each quarter has 90 days, so the 45-day collection period is the same as a half-quarter collection period.

Based on the sales forecasts, we now need to estimate LJT Skateboards' projected cash collections. First, any receivables that we have at the beginning of a quarter will be collected within 45 days, so all of them will be collected sometime during the quarter. Second, as we discussed, any sales made in the first half of the quarter will be collected, so total cash collections are:

$$\text{Cash collections} = \text{Beginning accounts receivable} + 1/2 \times \text{Sales} \qquad (12.4)$$

For example, in the first quarter, cash collections would be the beginning receivables of $120m plus half of sales, $1/2$ of $200m = $100m, for a total of $220m.

Since beginning receivables are all collected along with half of sales, ending receivables for a particular quarter would be the other half of sales. First quarter sales are projected at $200, so ending receivables will be $100m. This will be the beginning receivables in the second quarter. Cash collections in the second quarter will thus be $100m plus half of the projected $300m in sales, or $250m total.

Continuing this process, we can summarise LJT Skateboards' projected cash collections as shown in Table 12.1.

In Table 12.1, collections are shown as the only source of cash. Of course, this need not be the case. Other sources of cash could include asset sales, investment income and receipts from planned long-term financing.

TABLE 12.1

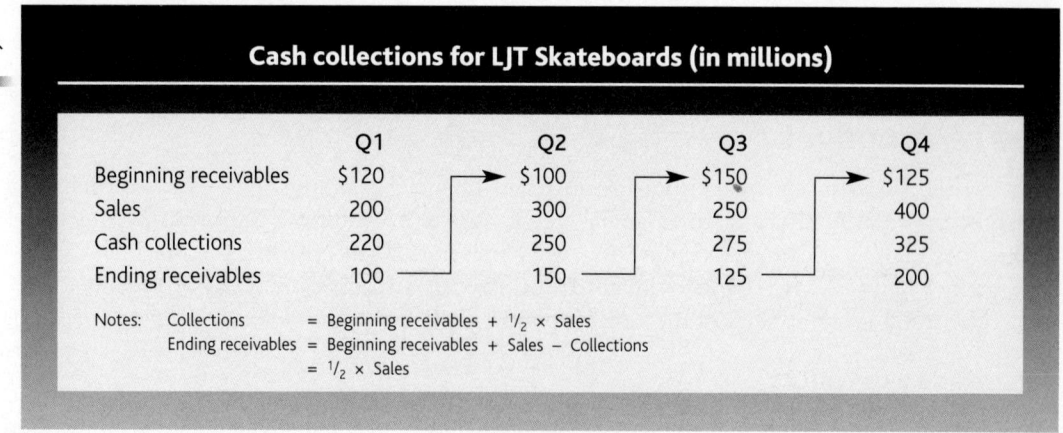

Cash collections for LJT Skateboards (in millions)

	Q1	Q2	Q3	Q4
Beginning receivables	$120	$100	$150	$125
Sales	200	300	250	400
Cash collections	220	250	275	325
Ending receivables	100	150	125	200

Notes: Collections = Beginning receivables + $1/2$ × Sales
Ending receivables = Beginning receivables + Sales − Collections
= $1/2$ × Sales

Cash outflows

Next, we consider the cash disbursements or payments. These come in four basic categories:

1 *Payments of accounts payable.* These are payments for goods or services rendered from suppliers, such as raw materials. Generally, these payments will be made sometime after purchases.

2 *Wages, taxes and other expenses*. This category includes all other regular costs of doing business that require actual expenditures. Depreciation, for example, is often thought of as a regular cost of business, but it requires no cash outflow, and is not included.

3 *Capital expenditures*. These are payments of cash for long-lived assets.

4 *Long-term financing expenses*. This category, for example, includes interest payments on long-term outstanding debt and dividend payments to shareholders.

LJT Skateboards' purchases from suppliers (in dollars) in a quarter are equal to 60 per cent of next quarter's predicted sales. LJT Skateboards' payments to suppliers are equal to the previous quarter's purchases, so the accounts payable period is 90 days. For example, in the quarter just ended, LJT Skateboards ordered $0.60 \times \$200m = \$120m$ in supplies. This will actually be paid in the first quarter (Q1) of the coming year.

Wages, taxes and other expenses are routinely 20 per cent of sales; interest and dividends are currently $20m per quarter. In addition, LJT Skateboards plans a major plant expansion (a capital expenditure) of $100m in the second quarter. If we put all this information together, the cash outflows are as shown in Table 12.2.

Cash disbursements for LJT Skateboards (in millions)				
	Q1	Q2	Q3	Q4
Payment of accounts (60% of sales)	$120	$180	$150	$240
Wages, taxes, other expenses	40	60	50	80
Capital expenditure	0	100	0	0
Long-term financing expenses (interest and dividends)	20	20	20	20
Total	$180	$360	$220	$340

TABLE 12.2

The cash balance

The predicted *net cash inflow* is the difference between cash collections and cash disbursements. The net cash inflow for LJT Skateboards is shown in Table 12.3. What we see immediately is that there is a cash surplus in the first and third quarters and a cash deficit in the second and fourth.

Net cash inflow for LJT Skateboards (in millions)				
	Q1	Q2	Q3	Q4
Total cash collections	$220	$250	$275	$325
Total cash disbursements	180	360	220	34
Net cash flow	$ 40	−$110	$ 55	−$ 15

TABLE 12.3

We will assume that LJT Skateboards starts the year with a $20m cash balance. Furthermore, LJT Skateboards maintains a $10m minimum cash balance to guard against unforeseen contingencies and forecasting errors. So we start the first quarter with $20m in cash. This rises by $40m during the quarter, and the ending balance is $60m. Of this, $10m is reserved as a minimum, so we subtract it and find that the first quarter surplus is $60m − 10m = $50m.

LJT Skateboards starts the second quarter with $60m in cash (the ending balance from the previous quarter). There is a net cash inflow of −$110m, so the ending balance is $60m − 110m = −$50m. We need another $10m as a buffer, so the total deficit is −$60m. These calculations and those for the last two quarters are summarised in Table 12.4.

TABLE 12.4

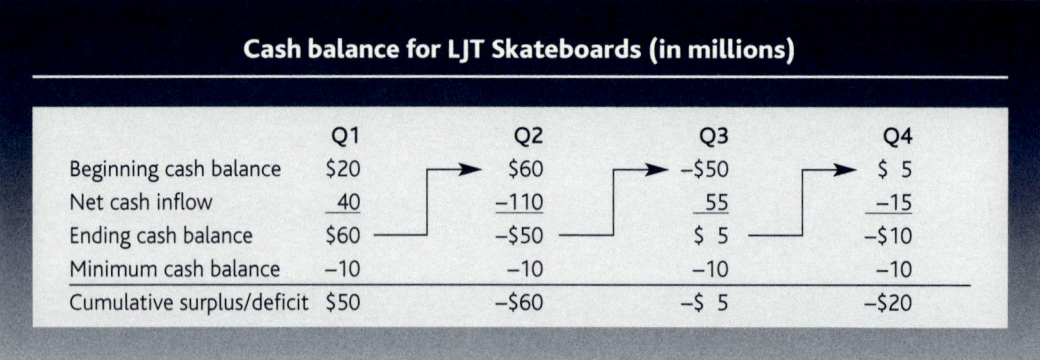

Cash balance for LJT Skateboards (in millions)				
	Q1	Q2	Q3	Q4
Beginning cash balance	$20	$60	−$50	$ 5
Net cash inflow	40	−110	55	−15
Ending cash balance	$60	−$50	$ 5	−$10
Minimum cash balance	−10	−10	−10	−10
Cumulative surplus/deficit	$50	−$60	−$ 5	−$20

Beginning in the second quarter, LJT Skateboards has a cash shortfall of $60m. This occurs because of the seasonal pattern of sales (higher towards the end of the second quarter), the delay in collections, and the planned capital expenditure.

The cash situation at LJT Skateboards is projected to improve to a $5m deficit in the third quarter but, by year's end, LJT Skateboards still has a $20m deficit. Without some sort of financing, this deficit will carry over into the next year.

For now, we can make the following general comments on LJT Skateboards' cash needs:

1 LJT Skateboards' large outflow in the second quarter is not necessarily a sign of trouble. It results from delayed collections on sales and a planned capital expenditure (presumably a worthwhile one).

2 The figures in our example are based on a forecast. Sales could be much worse (or better) than the forecast.

Concept questions

12.4a *Comment on the following: 'Firms prepare budgeted financial statements; however, a cash statement is not a required statement therefore there is no need to prepare a cash budget.'*

12.4b *What methods can be used to alleviate cash deficits highlighted in a cash budget?*

12.4c *How can a firm use cash surpluses highlighted in a cash budget?*

12.5 # A short-term financial plan

To illustrate a completed short-term financial plan, we will assume that LJT Skateboards arranges to borrow any needed funds on a short-term basis. The interest rate is 20 per cent, and it is calculated on a quarterly basis. From Chapter 5, we know that the rate is 20%/4 = 5% per quarter. We will assume that LJT Skateboards starts the year with no short-term debt.

From Table 12.4, LJT Skateboards has a second quarter deficit of $60 million. We will have to borrow this amount. Net cash inflow in the following quarter is $55 million. We now have to pay $60m × 0.05 = $3 million in interest out of that, leaving $52 million to reduce the borrowing.

We still owe $60m − $52m = $8 million at the end of the third quarter. Interest in the last quarter will thus be $8m × 0.05 = $.4 million. In addition, net inflows in the last quarter are −$15 million, so we have to borrow a total of $15.4 million, bringing our total borrowing up to $15.4m + $8m = $23.4 million. Table 12.5 extends Table 12.4 to include these calculations.

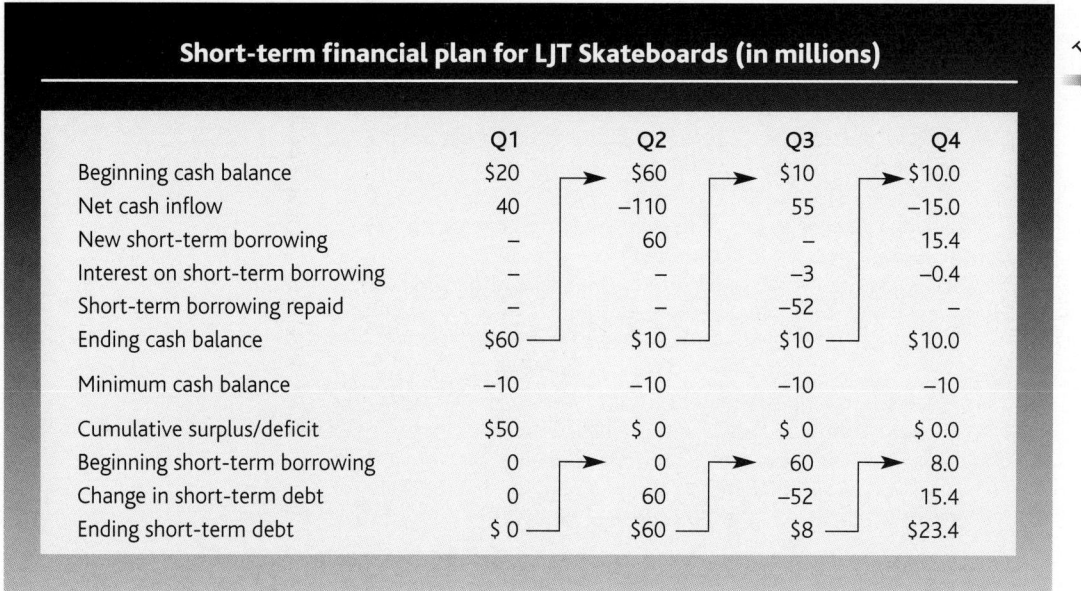

Short-term financial plan for LJT Skateboards (in millions)

TABLE 12.5

	Q1	Q2	Q3	Q4
Beginning cash balance	$20	$60	$10	$10.0
Net cash inflow	40	−110	55	−15.0
New short-term borrowing	–	60	–	15.4
Interest on short-term borrowing	–	–	−3	−0.4
Short-term borrowing repaid	–	–	−52	–
Ending cash balance	$60	$10	$10	$10.0
Minimum cash balance	−10	−10	−10	−10
Cumulative surplus/deficit	$50	$ 0	$ 0	$ 0.0
Beginning short-term borrowing	0	0	60	8.0
Change in short-term debt	0	60	−52	15.4
Ending short-term debt	$ 0	$60	$8	$23.4

Notice that the ending short-term debt is just equal to the cumulative deficit for the entire year, $20m, plus the interest paid during the year, $3m + $0.4m = $3.4m, for a total of $23.4m.

Our plan is very simple. For example, we ignored the fact that the interest paid on the short-term debt is tax deductible. We also ignored the fact that the cash surplus in the first quarter would earn some interest (which would be taxable). We could add on a number of refinements. Even so, our plan highlights the fact that in about 90 days, LJT Skateboards will need to borrow $60 million or so on a short-term basis. It is time to start lining up the source of the funds.

Our plan also illustrates that financing the firm's short-term needs will cost over $3 million in interest (before taxes) for the year. This is a starting point for LJT Skateboards to begin evaluating alternatives to reduce this expense. For example, can the $100 million planned expenditure be postponed or spread out? At 5 per cent per quarter, short-term credit is expensive.

Also, if LJT Skateboards' sales are expected to keep growing, then the $20 million plus deficit will probably also keep growing, and the need for additional financing is permanent. LJT Skateboards may wish to think about raising money on a long-term basis to cover this need.

As our example for LJT Skateboards illustrates, cash budgeting is important because it forces the firm to keep an eye on its cash flows. The following serves as an excellent reminder of why doing so is a good idea, unless the firm's owners wish to end up in the 'Poor house'.

Quoth the Banker, 'Watch Cash Flow'

Once upon a midnight dreary as I pondered weak and weary
Over many a quaint and curious volume of accounting lore,
Seeking gimmicks (without scruple) to squeeze through some new tax loophole,
Suddenly I hear a knock upon my door, Only this, and nothing more.

Then I felt a queasy tingling and I heard the cash a-jingling
As a fearsome banker entered whom I'd often seen before.
His face was money-green and in his eyes there could be seen
Dollar-signs that seemed to glitter as he reckoned up the score.
    'Cash flow,' the banker said, and nothing more.

I had always thought it fine to show a jet black bottom line.
But the banker sounded a resounding, 'No.
Your receivables are high, mounting upward toward the sky;
Write-offs loom. What matters is cash flow.'
    He repeated, 'Watch cash flow.'

Then I tried to tell the story of our lovely inventory
Which, though large, is full of most delightful stuff.
But the banker saw its growth, and with a mighty oath
He waved his arms and shouted, 'Stop! Enough!
    Pay the interest, and do not give me any guff!'

Next I looked for non-cash items which could add ad infinitum
To replace the ever-outward flow of cash,
But to keep my statement black I'd held depreciation back,
And my banker said that I'd done something rash.
    He quivered, and his teeth began to gnash.

When I asked him for a loan, he responded, with a groan,
That the interest rate would be just prime plus eight,
And to guarantee my purity he'd insist on some security—
All my assets plus the scalp upon my pate.
    Only this, a standard rate.

Though my bottom line is black, I am flat upon my back,
My cash flows out and customers pay slow.
The growth of my receivables is almost unbelievable:
The result is certain—unremitting woe!
And I hear the banker utter an ominous low mutter,
    'Watch cash flow.'
Herbert S. Bailey, Jr

To which we can only add: 'Amen.' The message of this passage cannot be overemphasised. Small business bankruptcies have been on the increase and a number are driven by the fact that the businesses over-extended themselves. They simply failed to manage the cash flows.

Source: Reprinted from *Publishers Weekly*, 13 January 1975, published by R.R. Bowker/Reed Elsevier. Copyright © 1975 Reed Elsevier.

■ 12.6 ■ Summary and conclusions

1   This chapter introduced the management of current assets. It was shown that the decisions in relation to current assets are interdependent. A firm needs to establish its level of cash and marketable securities while it considers the amount of inventory it should purchase and the level of accounts receivable. Because the time period is less significant, when current asset management is related to fixed asset management, the more sophisticated DCF methods usually give way to a marginal cost form of analysis.

2   Managing current assets involves minimising costs. The two major costs are carrying costs (including the return forgone by keeping too much invested in current assets) and acquisition or shortage costs (which includes the cost of running out of current assets). The objective of managing current assets is to find the optimal trade-off between these two costs.

3   Inventory is an important current asset. The level of inventory that should be purchased to minimise carrying and acquisition costs is called the economic order quantity (EOQ). The price of the inventory item is irrelevant in determining the EOQ except where price (quantity) discounts are provided. A final consideration in the inventory management plan is the lead time.

4   The financial manager can use the cash budget to identify short-term financial needs. The cash budget tells the manager what borrowing is required or what lending will be possible in the short run. The firm has available to it a number of possible ways of acquiring funds to meet short-term shortfalls.

Key terms

Accounts payable period *402*

Accounts receivable period *402*

Acquisition/shortage costs *407*

Cash budget deficit *413*

Cash budget surplus *413*

Cash cycle *402*

Carrying costs *407*

Cost of stockouts *412*

Current assets *400*

Economic order quantity *409*

Inventory period *402*

Just-in-time *413*

Lead time *411*

Operating (or activity) cycle *402*

Reorder points *411*

Suggested readings

Fabozzi, F. and Masonson, L.N. *Corporate Cash Management Techniques and Analysis*, Dow Jones-Irwin, Homewood, Ill., 1985.

Gallinger, G.W. and Healey, P.B. *Liquidity Analysis and Management*, Addison-Wesley Publishing Co., Reading, Mass., 1987.

Kahl, J.G. and Parkinson, K. *Current Asset Management: Cash, Credit and Inventory*, John Wiley & Sons, New York, 1984.

Vander Weide, J. and Maier, S.F. *Managing Corporate Liquidity: An Introduction to Working Capital Management*, John Wiley & Sons, New York, 1985.

Endnotes

1 Notice that we have used the cost of goods sold in calculating inventory turnover. Sales is sometimes used instead. Also, ending inventory, rather than average inventory, is often used. See Chapter 3 for some examples.

2 This measure is conceptually identical to the days' sales in inventory we discussed in Chapter 3.

3 If less than 100 per cent of our sales are credit sales, then we would just need a little more information, namely, credit sales for the year. See Chapter 3 for more discussion of this measure.

4 Some people use the term conservative in place of flexible and the term aggressive in place of restrictive.

5 The solution requires finding the value of X that provides the minimum total cost. From Figure 12.5 it can be seen that this occurs at the minimum point of the TC curve where the slope of the curve is zero. So we have:

$$TC = YP + (Y/X)A + (X/2)C$$

The slope is $= \dfrac{\delta TC}{\delta X} = -(YA/X^2) + C/2$

which is a minimum when it is equal to zero. It follows that when:

$$\frac{\delta TC}{\delta X} = \text{zero} = EOQ = -(YA/X^2) + C/2$$

it is now easy to show

$$EOQ = \sqrt{(2YA/C)}$$

On the web

The concepts discussed in this chapter are considered in detail in financial reporting and in investment issues. The site **http://www.btonline.com.au** offers some information on how BT Funds Management looks at this issue.

Other sites that consider the issue in general terms are:
http://www.afr.com.au (the *Australian Financial Review*)
http://www.asx.com.au (the Australian Stock Exchange)

Maximise Your Marks!
There are 30 interactive questions on current investment decisions waiting online for you at www.mhhe.com/au/ross3e. The questions are written with additional feedback for incorrect answers, and text excerpts with page references for follow-up study.

International Articles!
To read more on current investment decisions and to see current international articles, just go to www.mhhe.com/au/ross3e and click on *PowerWeb Articles* for this chapter.

Chapter review problems and self-test

12.1 · The operating and cash cycles

Consider the following financial statement information for the Melting Moments Company:

Item	Beginning	During	Ending
Inventory	$1,543		$1,669
Accounts receivable	4,418		3,952
Accounts payable	2,551		2,673
Net sales		$11,500	
Cost of goods sold		8,200	

Calculate the operating and cash cycles.

12.2 · Cash balance for Spancy Audio Company

Spancy Audio Company has a 60-day average collection period and wishes to maintain a $5 minimum cash balance. Based on this and the information below, complete the following cash budget. What conclusions do you draw?

Spancy Audio Company
Cash Budget (in millions)

	July to Sept Q1	Oct to Dec Q2	Jan to March Q3	April to June Q4
Beginning receivables	$120			
Sales	90	120	150	120
Cash collections				
Ending receivables				
Total cash collections				
Total cash disbursements	80	160	180	160
Net cash inflow				
Beginning cash balance	$ 5			
Net cash				
Ending cash balance				
Minimum cash balance				
Cumulative surplus (deficit)				

Answers to self-test problems

12.1 · We first need the turnover ratios. Note that we have used the average values for all Statement of Financial Position items and that we have based the inventory and payables turnover measures on cost of goods sold.

$$
\begin{aligned}
\text{Inventory turnover} &= \$8,200/[(1,543 + 1,669)/2] \\
&= 5.11 \text{ times} \\
\text{Receivables turnover} &= \$11,500/[(4,418 + 3,952)/2] \\
&= 2.75 \text{ times} \\
\text{Payables turnover} &= \$8,200/[(2,551 + 2,673)/2] \\
&= 3.14 \text{ times}
\end{aligned}
$$

We can now calculate the various periods:

$$
\begin{aligned}
\text{Inventory period} &= 365 \text{ days}/5.11 \text{ times} \\
&= 71.43 \text{ days} \\
\text{Receivables period} &= 365 \text{ days}/2.75 \text{ times} \\
&= 132.73 \text{ days} \\
\text{Payables period} &= 365 \text{ days}/3.14 \text{ times} \\
&= 116.24 \text{ days}
\end{aligned}
$$

So the time it takes to acquire inventory and sell it is about 71 days. Collection takes another 133 days, and the operating cycle is thus $71 + 133 = 204$ days. The cash cycle is this 204 days less the payables period, $204 - 116 = 88$ days.

12.2 · Since Spancy Audio has a 60-day collection period, only those sales made in the first 30 days of the quarter will be collected in the same quarter. Total cash collections in the first quarter will thus equal $30/90 =$ of sales plus beginning receivables, or $\$120 + 1/3 \times \$90 = \$150$. Ending receivables for the first quarter (and the second quarter beginning receivables) are the other $2/3$ of sales, or $2/3 \times \$90 = \$60$. The remaining calculations are straightforward, and the completed budget follows.

Spancy Audio Company
Cash Budget (in millions)

	July to Sept Q1	Oct to Dec Q2	Jan to March Q3	April to June Q4
Beginning receivables	$120	$ 60	$ 80	$100
Sales	90	120	150	120
Cash collections	150	100	130	140
Ending receivables	60	80	100	80
Total cash collections	150	100	130	140
Total cash disbursements	80	160	180	160
Net cash inflow	70	−60	−50	−20
Beginning cash balance	5	75	15	−35
Net cash	70	−60	−50	−20
Ending cash balance	75	15	−35	−55
Minimum cash balance	−5	−5	−5	−5
Cumulative surplus (deficit)	70	10	−40	−60

The primary conclusion from this schedule is that, beginning in the third quarter, Spancy Audio's cash surplus becomes a cash deficit. By the end of the year, Spancy Audio will need to arrange for $60 million in cash beyond what will be available.

Questions and problems

1 · Cash equation

The Silent Compressor Company has a book net worth of $3,000. Long-term debt is $900. Net working capital, other than cash, is $650. Fixed assets are $2,000. How much cash does the company have? If current liabilities are $800, what are current assets?

2 · Sources and uses

For the year just ended, you have gathered the following information on Novice Ltd:

a   Accounts payable declined by $6,137.
b   A $1,600 dividend was paid.
c   Inventories were decreased by $8,100.
d   Long-term debt increased by $8,000.
e   Fixed asset purchases were $6,000.

Label each as a source or use of cash and describe its effect on the firm's cash balance.

3 · Changes in the cash account

Indicate the impact of the following corporate actions on cash, using the letter I for an increase, D for a decrease, or N when no change occurs.

a   Cash is paid for raw materials purchased for inventory.
b   A dividend is paid.
c   Merchandise is sold on credit.
d   Ordinary shares are issued.
e   Raw material is purchased for inventory on credit.
f   A piece of machinery is purchased and paid for with long-term debt.
g   Payments for previous sales are collected.
h   Merchandise is sold for cash.
i   Payment is made for a previous purchase.
j   A short-term bank loan is received.
k   A dividend is paid with funds received from a sale of ordinary shares.
l   A piece of office equipment is purchased and paid for with a short-term note.
m   Marketable securities are purchased.
n   Last year's taxes are paid.
o   Interest on long-term debt is paid.

4 · Changes in the operating cycle

Indicate the effect that the following company actions will have on the operating cycle. Use the letter I to show an increase, the letter D for a decrease, and the letter N for no change.

a   Inventory turnover goes from 10 times to 5 times.
b   Receivables turnover goes from 10 times to 5 times.
c   Payables turnover goes from 10 times to 5 times.
d   Average receivables goes down.
e   Payments to suppliers are speeded up.
f   Credit sales are discontinued.

5 · Just-in-time inventory and costs

The Jay Jetskis Co. Ltd has recently installed a just-in-time (JIT) inventory system. Describe the likely effect on Jay's carrying costs, shortage costs and operating cycle.

6 · Changes in the cycles

Indicate the impact of the following company actions on the cash cycle and the operating cycle. Use the letter I to show an increase, the letter D for a decrease, and the letter N for no change.

a   The use of cash discounts offered by suppliers is decreased; so payments are made later.
b   More finished goods are being produced for order instead of for inventory.
c   A greater percentage of raw material purchases are paid for with cash.

d The terms of cash discounts offered to customers are made more favourable.

e A larger than usual amount of raw materials is purchased as a result of a price decline.

f An increased number of customers pay with cash instead of credit.

7 · Calculating cycles

Consider the following financial statement information for the Spider Mann Company:

Item		Beginning	Ending
Inventory		$2,400	$2,800
Accounts receivable		1,200	1,600
Accounts payable		5,000	5,200
Net sales	$26,600		
Cost of goods sold	13,000		

Calculate the operating and cash cycles. How do you interpret your answer?

8 · Calculating cash collections

The Crimestopper Company has projected the following quarterly sales amounts for the coming year:

	Q1	Q2	Q3	Q4
Sales (in millions)	$111	$210	$240	$120

Accounts receivable at the beginning of the year are $90m. Crimestopper has a 60-day collection period. Calculate cash collections in each of the four quarters by completing the following:

	Q1	Q2	Q3	Q4
Beginning receivables				
Sales (in millions)				
Cash collections				
Ending receivables				

What would be the effect of shortening the collection period to 30 days?

9 · Calculating payments

Fabrics Ltd has projected the following sales for the coming year:

	Q1	Q2	Q3	Q4
Projected sales	$348	$330	$430	$390

Sales in the year following this one are projected to be 20 per cent greater in each quarter.

a Calculate payments to suppliers assuming that Fabrics places orders during each quarter equal to 60 per cent of projected sales in the next quarter. Assume that Fabrics pays immediately. What is the payables period in this case?

	Q1	Q2	Q3	Q4
Payment of accounts	$	$	$	$

b Rework part (a) assuming a 90-day payables period:

	Q1	Q2	Q3	Q4
Payment of accounts	$	$	$	$

c Rework part (a) assuming a 60-day payables period:

	Q1	Q2	Q3	Q4
Payment of accounts	$	$	$	$

10 · Calculating payments

The Valerie Company's purchases from suppliers in a quarter are equal to 80 per cent of the next quarter's forecasted sales. The payables deferral period is 45 days. Wages, taxes and other expenses are 10 per cent of sales, while interest and dividends are $50 per quarter. No capital expenditures are planned. Projected quarterly sales are:

	Q1	Q2	Q3	Q4
Sales (in millions)	$500	$800	$500	$600

Sales in the first quarter of the following year are projected at $550. Calculate Valerie's cash outlays by completing the following:

	Q1	Q2	Q3	Q4
Payment of accounts	$	$	$	$
Wages, taxes other expenses				
Long-term financing expenses (interest and dividends)				
Total	$	$	$	$

11 · Cycles

Is it possible for a firm's cash cycle to be longer than its operating cycle? Explain why or why not.

12 · Calculating the cash budget

Willy's Wine has estimated sales (in millions) for the next four quarters as:

	Q1	Q2	Q3	Q4
Sales (in millions)	$340	$443	$574	$522

Sales in the first quarter of the year after this one are projected at $410. Accounts receivable at the beginning of the year were $108. Willy's has a 30-day collection period.

Willy's purchases from suppliers in a quarter are equal to 60 per cent of the next quarter's forecast sales, and suppliers are normally paid in 30 days. Wages, taxes and other expenses run to about 20 per cent of sales. Interest and dividends are $40 per quarter.

Willy's plans a major capital outlay in the third quarter of $200. Finally, Willy's started the year with a $35 cash balance and wishes to maintain a $25 minimum balance.

a Complete a cash budget for Willy's by filling in the following:

Willy's Wine Cash Budget (in millions)	Q1	Q2	Q3	Q4
Beginning cash balance	$35	$	$	$
Net cash inflow				
Ending cash balance				
Minimum cash balance	25			
Cumulative surplus (deficit)				

b Assume that Willy's can borrow any needed funds on a short-term basis at a rate of 3 per cent per quarter. Prepare a short-term financial plan by creating a schedule. What is the total interest paid for the year?

13 · Calculating cash collections

The following is the sales budget for the Fun and Games Company for the first quarter of 200X:

	January	February	March
Sales budget	$80,000	$120,000	$144,000

Credit sales are collected as follows:
> 30 per cent in the month of sale
> 40 per cent in the month after sale
> 30 per cent in the second month after sale

The amount of the accounts receivable balance at the end of the previous quarter is $36,000 ($28,000 of which is uncollected December sales).

a   Compute the sales for December.
b   Compute the cash collections from sales for each month from January through to March.

14 · Calculating the cash budget

Here are some important figures from the budget of the Duck Down Company for the second quarter of 200X:

	April	May	June
Credit sales	$160,000	$140,000	$192,000
Credit purchases	68,000	64,000	80,000
Cash disbursements			
Wages, taxes, and expenses	8,000	7,000	8,400
Interest	3,000	3,000	3,000
Equipment purchases	50,000	0	4,000

The company predicts that 10 per cent of its sales will never be collected, 50 per cent of its sales will be collected in the month of the sale, and the remaining 40 per cent will be collected in the following month. Credit purchases will be paid in the month following the purchase.

In March 200X, sales were $180,000. Using this information, complete the following cash budget:

	April	May	June
Beginning cash balances	$200,000		
Cash receipts			
Cash collections from credit sales			
Total cash available			
Cash disbursements			
Purchases	$65,000		
Wages, taxes and expenses			
Interest			
Equipment purchases			
Total cash disbursements			
Ending cash balance			

15 · Economic order quantity

Bobby Gain Ltd uses a carbon black dye in the production of its tyres. The following information has been provided in respect to the carbon black used in production:

Amount required	200,000 kg per year
Working days	365
Purchase price	$10.00 per kg
Cost of placing each order	$8.00
Carrying cost	$1.40 per kg per year, plus an imputed interest cost on the funds invested in inventory of 10 per cent per year

a   What quantity of inventory should be ordered?
b   What is the total cost per year of the inventory if you employ the order quantity derived in part (a)?

16 · Economic order quantity, imputed interest cost, safety stock

This is a challenge problem.

Part A

The Slenderer Soups Company uses the standard *economic order quantity* formula to determine how frequently it will order a particular raw material.

Estimated usage	10,000 kg per annum
Working days	200 days per year

Purchase price	$4.00 per kg
Cost of placing each order	$10.00
Carrying cost	40 cents per kg per annum, plus an imputed interest cost on the funds invested in inventory of 10 per cent per year
Lead time	3 working days

a What quantity should be ordered?
b How frequently should orders be placed?
c What is the reorder point?

Part B

The following additional information is available:

i   Stockouts are prohibitively expensive and are not to be permitted.
ii Lead time occasionally varies by one day either way.
iii Daily usage during lead time has followed this probability distribution:

	Probability
45 kg per day	0.2
50 kg per day	0.6
55 kg per day	0.2

How much safety stock should be carried?

Part C

Given the information in Part A (i.e. interest is 10%), assume now that the company's accountant calculates that interest rates prevailing throughout the economy have doubled (this will affect the carrying cost). In his excitement and haste to instruct the purchasing officer to review inventory policies, he trips over a ledger bin, strikes his head and breathes his last.

Assuming that no one in the organisation will think to review inventory policies before 12 months have elapsed, what will be the cost to the company of following a suboptimal inventory policy?

17 · Economic order quantity

Small White Pills (SWP) has derived an economic order quantity of 316 kgs for a particular drug. The cost of placing each order is 80 cents and the value of the estimated annual usage is only $200,000 with a price of $10 per kg. The pill will not be popular as it aims at improving the thought processes of finance students that are already held in high regard by university staff. What is the carrying cost SWP is using in its calculation of the EOQ?

18 · Economic order quantity

Because the mashed raw jellyfish used by Cultured Foods is delivered within a day, it is ordered in lots of 200 kgs. The cost of carrying (including refrigeration) the jellyfish is $2 per kg; the acquisition cost of each order is only $1.24. Cultured Foods uses 3,328 kgs of jellyfish per year at a cost of $10 per kg. The chef, Fries Alott, argues that too much is being ordered as it fills the cold room and he is sure that approximately $100 per year could be saved if the order size was reduced. Is Fries correct?

19 · Optimal carrying cost

A firm must order an input supply in 500 kg lots. Its annual demand is 12,500 kg and the acquisition cost is $2.50 per order. What must it keep its carrying cost per unit to if 500 kg is to be an optimal order quantity?

20 · Optimal carrying cost

Olympic Tubes must order its tube black in 500 kg lots. Its annual demand is 10,000 kg. It has reduced its administration to a minimum so that the acquisition cost of each order is only $4.00. There is concern with the efficiency of its raw materials store as Cecil, the manager, does not keep a tight control. His current carrying cost per unit of tube black is 40 cents. Cecil is sure he can reduce the cost but he does not want to overdo it. Advise Cecil what the optimal carrying cost is.

21 · Demand

Van sells copy watches that he must purchase 500 at a time. Van runs on a shoestring so his carrying cost per unit is only 20 cents and the cost of ordering and going to get the watches is $5.00 per watch. The harder he works the more he can sell, but Van enjoys his leisure so he wants to minimise his work. How many watches must Van sell if the order lot, carrying cost and acquisition cost are to be optimal?

22 · The EOQ

Danny Delito sells short-handled golf clubs. He starts each period with 10,000. This stock is used up each month and reordered at the end of the month. The carrying cost of each golf club is $1 and the fixed order cost is $5. Is Danny following an optimal inventory plan?

CHAPTER 13

Cash and liquidity management

Objective

This chapter is about how firms manage cash. The basic objective in cash management is to keep the investment in cash as low as possible while still operating the firm efficiently and effectively. We separate cash management into three steps:

1 determining the appropriate target cash balance;
2 collecting and disbursing cash efficiently; and
3 investing 'excess' cash in marketable securities.

Determining the appropriate target cash balance involves an assessment of the trade-off between the benefit and cost of liquidity. The benefit of holding cash is the convenience in liquidity it gives the firm. The cost of holding cash is the interest income that the firm could have received from investing in government bonds and other marketable securities.

If the firm has achieved its target cash balance, the value it gets from the liquidity provided by its cash will be exactly equal to the value foregone in interest on an equivalent holding of government bonds. In other words, a firm should increase its holding of cash as long as the net present value from doing so is positive.

After the optimal amount of liquidity is determined, the firm must establish procedures so that collection and disbursement of cash are done as efficiently as possible. This usually reduces to the dictum: 'Collect early and pay late.' Accordingly, we discuss some ways of accelerating collections and slowing disbursements.

While it may not be obvious, the cash management control models are simply modified inventory control models. That is why we discussed the inventory model first. The inventory item now is cash that has to be maintained at an economic level (like the economic order quantity). In the more sophisticated models probabilities of future cash flows going up or down are built into the calculation of the economic (target) level of cash. In our overview of the model, we do not need to be overly concerned with how they are built into the calculation. Our focus is upon using the models rather than understanding the theory of their development.

Introduction ▷ The following data has been derived from Statements of Financial Position presented by some leading Australian companies in 2002:

Company	Cash holdings	Cash as a percentage of total assets
BHP Billiton Limited	2,998 million	5.0%
Lend Lease Corporation Limited	904 million	10.5%
OPSM Group Limited	20 million	8.9%
Village Roadshow Limited	266 million	12.1%
Wesfarmers Limited	172 million	2.6%

Since cash earns little or no interest, why would these companies choose to hold cash? It would seem more sensible for them to put all their cash into marketable securities, such as Commonwealth Treasury bonds, and thereby earn a return on the money. Of course, one reason they hold cash is to pay for goods and services. While they may prefer to pay for these items in Commonwealth Treasury bonds, the minimum denomination of Commonwealth Treasury bonds is $1,000. In this case, cash must be used because cash is more divisible than Commonwealth Treasury bonds.[1]

Firms must invest temporarily idle cash in short-term marketable securities. As we discussed in Chapter 1, these securities can be bought and sold in the money market. As a group, they have very little default risk and most are highly marketable. There are different types of money market securities, and we discuss a few of the most important.

13.1 ▪ Reasons for holding cash

John Maynard Keynes, in his great work *The General Theory of Employment, Interest, and Money*, identified three reasons why liquidity is important: the precautionary motive, the speculative motive, and the transaction motive. We discuss these next.

Speculative and precautionary motives

speculative motive
the need to hold cash to take advantage of additional investment opportunities, such as bargain purchases

The **speculative motive** is the need to hold cash in order to be able to take advantage of, for example, bargain purchases that might arise, attractive interest rates, and (in the case of international firms) favourable exchange rate fluctuations.

For most firms, reserve borrowing ability and marketable securities can be used to satisfy speculative motives. Thus, for a modern firm, there might be a speculative motive for liquidity, but not necessarily for cash *per se*. Think of it this way: If you have a credit card with a very large credit limit, then you can probably take advantage of any unusual bargains that come along without carrying any cash.

precautionary motive
the need to hold cash as a safety margin to act as a financial reserve

This is also true, to a lesser extent, for **precautionary motives**. The precautionary motive is the need for a safety supply to act as a financial reserve. Once again, there probably is a precautionary motive for liquidity. However, given that the value of money market instruments is relatively certain and that instruments such as Commonwealth Treasury bonds are extremely liquid, there is no real need to literally hold cash for precautionary purposes.

The transaction motive

transaction motive
the need to hold cash to satisfy normal disbursement and collection activities associated with a firm's ongoing operations

Cash is needed to satisfy the **transaction motive**, the need to have cash on hand to pay bills. Transaction-related needs come from the normal disbursement and collection activities of the firm. The disbursement of cash includes the payment of wages and salaries, trade debts, taxes and dividends.

Cash is collected from sales, the selling of assets and new financing. The cash inflows (collections) and outflows (disbursements) are not perfectly synchronised, and some level of cash holdings is necessary to serve as a buffer. Perfect liquidity is the characteristic of cash that allows it to satisfy the transaction motive.

As electronic funds transfers and other high-speed, 'paperless' payment mechanisms continue to develop, even the transaction demand for cash may all but disappear. Even if it does, however, there will still be a demand for liquidity and a need to manage it efficiently.

Compensating balances

Compensating balances are another reason to hold cash. Cash balances may be kept at commercial banks to compensate for banking services the firm receives. In the United States, banks go so far as to require a minimum compensating balance for the credit services they offer to firms. The concept is not as developed in Australia; however, many banks have dropped account charges for customers who maintain a minimum balance in their accounts. As the deregulated Australian banking system becomes more sophisticated, compensating balances will probably feature more prominently.

Costs of holding cash

When a firm holds cash in excess of some necessary minimum, it incurs an opportunity cost. The opportunity cost of excess cash (held in currency or bank deposits) is the interest income that could be earned in the next best use, such as investment in marketable securities.

Given the opportunity cost of holding cash, why would a firm hold cash in excess of its requirements? The answer is that a cash balance must be maintained to provide the liquidity necessary for transaction needs—paying bills. If the firm maintains too small a cash balance, it may run out of cash. If so, the firm may have to raise cash on a short-term basis. This could involve, for example, selling marketable securities or borrowing.

Activities such as selling marketable securities and borrowing involve various costs. As we have discussed, holding cash has an opportunity cost. To determine the target cash balance, the firm must weigh the benefits of holding cash against these costs. We discuss this subject in more detail in the next section.

Concept questions

13.1a *What is the transaction motive, and how does it lead firms to hold cash?*
13.1b *What is the cost to the firm of holding excess cash?*

13.2 Determining the target cash balance

Based on our general discussion of current assets in the previous chapter, the **target cash balance** involves a trade-off between the opportunity costs of holding too much cash (the carrying costs) and the costs of holding too little (the shortage costs, also called **adjustment costs**). The nature of these costs depends on the firm's working capital policy.

If the firm has a flexible working capital policy, then it will probably maintain a marketable securities portfolio. In this case, the adjustment or shortage costs will be the trading costs associated with buying and selling securities. If the firm has a restrictive working capital policy, it will probably borrow short term to meet cash shortages. The costs in this case will be the interest and other expenses associated with arranging a loan.

In our discussion below, we will assume that the firm has a flexible policy. Its cash management then consists of moving money in and out of marketable securities. This is a very traditional approach to the subject, and it is a nice way of illustrating the costs and benefits of holding cash. Keep in mind, however, that the distinction between cash and money market investments is becoming increasingly blurred.

For example, how do we classify a money market fund with cheque-writing privileges? Such 'near-cash' arrangements are becoming more and more common. It may be that the prime reason the approaches are not universal is management of cash. We will return to this subject at various points below.

> target cash balance
> a firm's desired cash level as determined by the trade-off between carrying costs and shortage costs
>
> adjustment costs
> the costs associated with holding too little cash. Also shortage costs

The basic idea

Figure 13.1 (overleaf) presents the cash management problem for our flexible firm. If a firm tries to keep its cash holdings too low, it will find itself running out of cash more often than is desirable, and thus selling marketable securities (and perhaps later buying marketable securities to replace those sold) more frequently than would be true if the cash balance were higher. Thus, trading costs will be high when the size of the cash balance is low. These will fall as the cash balance becomes larger.

In contrast, the opportunity costs of holding cash are very low if the firm holds very little cash. These costs increase as the cash holdings rise because the firm is giving up more and more in interest that could have been earned.

At point C^* in Figure 13.1, the sum of the costs is given by the total cost curve. As shown, the minimum total cost occurs where the two individual cost curves cross. At this point, the opportunity costs and the trading costs are equal. This is the target cash balance, and it is the point the firm should try to find.

Figure 13.1 is essentially the same as one in the previous chapter. As we discuss next, however, we can now say more about the optimum investment in cash and the factors that influence it.

FIGURE 13.1

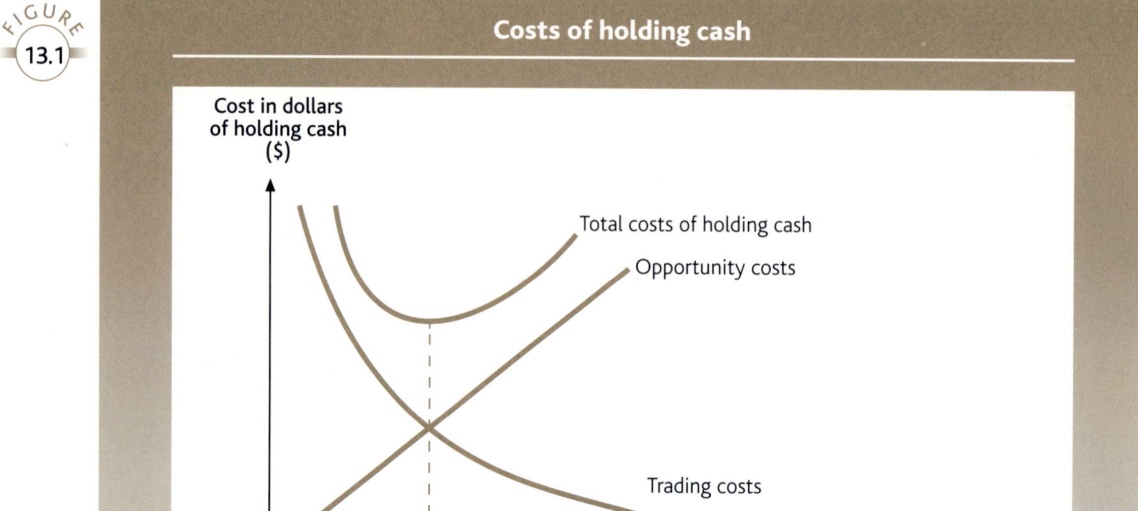

Costs of holding cash

Trading costs are increased when the firm must sell securities to establish a cash balance. Opportunity costs are increased when there is a cash balance because there is no return to cash.

The BAT model

The Baumol–Allais–Tobin (BAT) model is a classic means of analysing our cash management problem. We will illustrate how this model can be used to actually establish the target cash balance. It is a straightforward model and very useful for illustrating the factors in cash management and, more generally, current asset management.

To develop the BAT model, suppose the Easy Dough Company Limited starts off at time zero with a cash balance of C = $1.2 million. Each week, outflows exceed inflows by $600,000. As a result, the cash balance will drop to zero at the end of week two. The average cash balance will be the beginning balance ($1.2 million) plus the ending balance ($0) divided by 2, or ($1.2 million + $0)/2 = $600,000 over the two-week period. At the end of week two, Easy Dough replaces its cash by depositing another $1.2 million.

As we have described, the cash management strategy for Easy Dough is very simple and boils down to depositing $1.2 million every two weeks. This policy is shown in Figure 13.2. Notice how the cash balance declines by $600,000 per week. Since we bring the account up to $1.2 million, the balance hits zero every two weeks. This results in the 'sawtooth' pattern displayed in Figure 13.2.

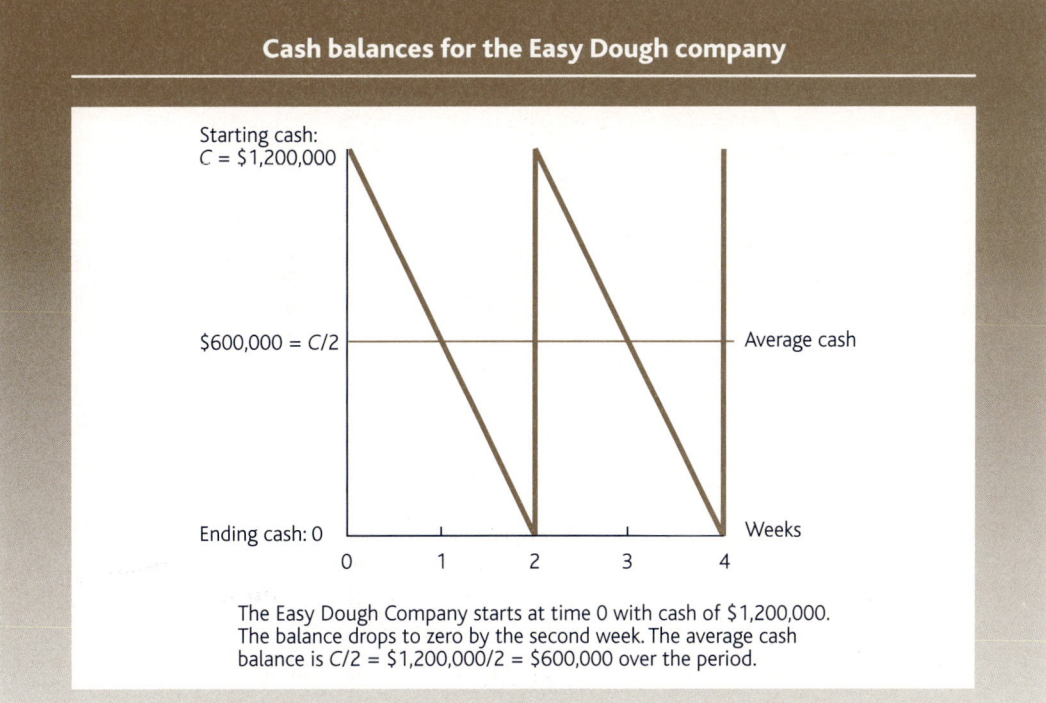

Cash balances for the Easy Dough company

FIGURE 13.2

Starting cash:
C = $1,200,000

$600,000 = C/2 — Average cash

Ending cash: 0

Weeks

0   1   2   3   4

The Easy Dough Company starts at time 0 with cash of $1,200,000. The balance drops to zero by the second week. The average cash balance is C/2 = $1,200,000/2 = $600,000 over the period.

Implicitly, we assume that the net cash outflow is the same every day and that it is known with certainty. These two assumptions make the model easy to handle. We will indicate what happens when they do not hold in the next section.

If C were set higher, say, at $2.4 million, cash would last four weeks before the firm would have to sell marketable securities, but the firm's average cash balance would increase to $1.2 million (from $600,000). If C were set at $600,000, cash would run out in one week and the firm would have to replenish cash more frequently, but its average cash balance would fall from $600,000 to $300,000.

Because transaction costs must be incurred whenever cash is replenished (e.g. the brokerage costs of selling marketable securities), establishing large initial balances will lower the trading costs connected with cash management. However, the larger the average cash balance, the greater is the opportunity cost (the return that could have been earned on marketable securities).

To determine the optimal strategy, Easy Dough needs to know the following three things:

F = the fixed cost of making a securities trade to replenish cash;
T = the total amount of new cash needed for transactions purposes over the relevant planning period, say, one year; and
R = the opportunity cost of holding cash. This is the interest rate on marketable securities.

With this information, Easy Dough can determine the total costs of any particular cash balance policy. It can then determine the optimal cash balance policy.

The opportunity costs

To determine the opportunity costs of holding cash, we have to find out how much interest is foregone. Easy Dough has, on average, $C/2$ in cash. This amount could be earning interest at rate R. So the total dollar opportunity costs of cash balances are equal to the average cash balance multiplied by the interest rate:

$$\text{Opportunity cost} = (C/2) \times R \qquad (13.1)$$

For example, the opportunity costs of various alternatives are given here assuming that the interest rate is 10 per cent:

Initial cash balance C	Average cash balance $C/2$	Opportunity cost $(R = 0.10)$ $(C/2) \times R$
$4,800,000	$2,400,000	$240,000
2,400,000	1,200,000	120,000
1,200,000	600,000	60,000
600,000	300,000	30,000
300,000	150,000	15,000

In our original case where the initial cash balance is $1.2 million, the average balance is $600,000. The interest we could have earned on this (at 10%) is $60,000, so this is what we give up with this strategy. Notice that the opportunity cost increases as the initial (and average) cash balance rises.

The trading costs

To determine the total trading costs for the year, we need to know how many times Easy Dough will have to sell marketable securities during the year. First of all, the total amount of cash disbursed during the year is $600,000 per week, or $T = \$600,000 \times 52$ weeks $= \$31.2$ million. If the initial cash balance is set at $C = \$1.2$ million, then Easy Dough will sell $1.2 million of marketable securities $T/C = \$31.2$ million/$1.2 million $= 26$ times per year. It costs F dollars each time, so trading costs are given by:

$$\$31.2 \text{ million}/\$1.2 \text{ million} \times F = 26 \times F$$

In general, the total trading costs will be given by:

$$\text{Trading costs} = (T/C) \times F \qquad (13.2)$$

In this example, if F were $1,000 (an unrealistically large amount), then the trading costs would be $26,000.

We can calculate the trading costs associated with some different strategies as follows:

Total amount of disbursements during relevant period T	Initial cash balance C	Trading costs $(F = \$1,000)$ $(T/C) \times F$
$31,200,000	$4,800,000	$ 6,500
31,200,000	2,400,000	13,000
31,200,000	1,200,000	26,000
31,200,000	600,000	52,000
31,200,000	300,000	104,000

The total cost
Now that we have the opportunity costs and the trading costs, we can calculate the total cost by adding them together:

$$\text{Total cost} = \text{Opportunity costs} + \text{Trading costs} \qquad (13.3)$$
$$= (C/2) \times R + (T/C) \times F$$

Using the numbers above, we have:

Cash balance	Opportunity costs	+	Trading costs	=	Total cost
$4,800,000	$240,000		$ 6,500		$246,500
2,400,000	120,000		13,000		133,000
1,200,000	60,000		26,000		86,000
600,000	30,000		52,000		82,000
300,000	15,000		104,000		119,000

Notice how the total cost starts out at almost $250,000 and declines to about $80,000 before starting to rise again.

The solution
We can see from the preceding schedule that a $600,000 cash balance results in the lowest total cost of the possibilities presented: $82,000. But what about $700,000 or $500,000 or other possibilities? It appears that the optimum balance is somewhere between $300,000 and $1.2 million. With this in mind, we could easily proceed by trial and error to find the optimum balance. It is not difficult to find it directly, however, so we do this next.

Take a look back at Figure 13.1. As drawn, the optimal size of the cash balance, C^*, occurs right where the two lines cross. At this point, the opportunity costs and the trading costs are exactly equal. So, at C^*, we must have:

$$\text{Opportunity costs} = \text{Trading costs}$$
$$C^*/2 \times R = (T/C^*) \times F$$

With a little algebra, we can write:

$$C^{*2} = (2T \times F)/R$$

To solve for C^*, we take the square root of both sides to get:

$$C^* = \sqrt{(2T \times F)/R} \qquad (13.4)$$

This is the optimum initial cash balance.

For Easy Dough, we have $T = \$31.2$ million, $F = \$1,000$ and $R = 10\%$. We can now find the optimum cash balance as:

$$C^* = \sqrt{(2 \times \$31,200,000 \times \$1,000/0.10)}$$
$$= \sqrt{(\$624 \text{ billion})}$$
$$= \$789,937$$

We can verify this answer by calculating the various costs at this balance as well as a little above and a little below:

Cash balance	Opportunity costs	+ Trading costs	= Total cost
$850,000	$42,500	$ 36,706	$79,206
800,000	40,000	39,000	79,000
789,937	**39,497**	**39,497**	**78,994**
750,000	37,500	41,600	79,100
700,000	35,000	44,571	79,571

The total cost at the optimum is $78,994, and it does appear to increase as we move in either direction.

The Hard Cash Company has cash outflows of $100 per day, seven days a week. The interest rate is 5 per cent, and the fixed cost of replenishing cash balances is $10 per transaction. What is the optimal initial cash balance? What is the total cost?

The total cash needed for the year is 365 days × $100 = $36,500. From the BAT model, the optimal initial balance is:

$$C^* = \sqrt{(2T \times F)/R}$$
$$C^* = \sqrt{(2 \times \$36,500 \times \$10/0.05)}$$
$$C^* = \sqrt{(14.6 \text{ million})}$$
$$= \$3,821$$

The average cash balance is $3,821/2 = $1,911, so the opportunity cost is $1,911 × 0.05 = $96. Since we need $100 per day, the $3,821 balance will last $3,821/$100 = 38.21 days. We need to refurnish the account 365/38.21 = 9.6 times, so the trading (order) cost is $96. The total cost is $192.

The BAT model is possibly the simplest because it has been stripped-down to a sensible model for determining the optimal cash position. Its chief weakness is that it assumes steady, certain cash outflows. We next discuss a more involved model designed to deal with these problems.

The Miller–Orr model: A more general approach

We now describe a cash management system designed to deal with cash inflows and outflows that fluctuate randomly from day to day. With this model, we again concentrate on the cash balance, but, in contrast to the BAT model, we assume that this balance fluctuates up and down randomly and that the average change is zero.

The basic idea

Figure 13.3 shows how the system works. It operates in terms of an upper limit to the amount of cash (U^*) and a lower limit (L), and a target cash balance (C^*). The firm allows its cash balance to wander around between the lower and upper limits. As long as the cash balance is somewhere between U^* and L, nothing happens.

FIGURE
13.3

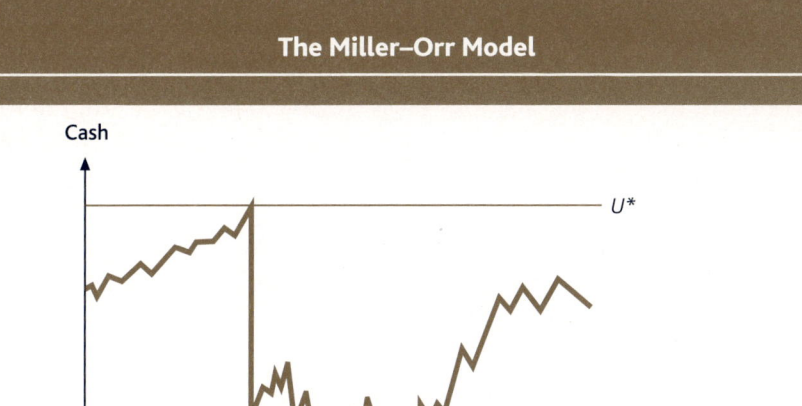

The Miller–Orr Model

Cash

U^*

C^*

L

Time

X   Y

U^* is the upper control limit. L is the lower control limit. The target cash balance is C^*. As long as cash is between L and U^*, no transaction is made.

When the cash balance reaches the upper limit (U^*), such as it does at point X, the firm moves $U^* - C^*$ dollars out of the account and into marketable securities. This action moves the cash balance down to C^*. In the same way, if the cash balance falls to the lower limit (L), as it does at point Y, the firm will sell $C^* - L$ worth of securities and deposit the cash in the account. This action takes the cash balance up to C^*.

Using the model

To get started, management sets the lower limit (L). This limit is essentially a safety stock, so where it is set depends on how much risk of a cash shortfall the firm is willing to tolerate. Alternatively, the minimum might just equal a required compensating balance.

Like the BAT model, the optimal cash balance depends on trading costs and opportunity costs. Once again, the cost per transaction of buying and selling marketable securities, F, is assumed to be fixed. Also, the opportunity cost of holding cash is R, the interest rate per period on marketable securities.

The only extra piece of information needed is σ^2, the variance of the cash flow per period. For our purposes, the period can be anything, a day or a week, for example, as long as the interest rate and the variance are based on the same length of time.

Given L, which is set by the firm, Miller and Orr[2] show that the cash balance target, C^*, and the upper limit, U^*, that minimise the total costs of holding cash are:

$$C^* = L + (\tfrac{3}{4} \times F \times \sigma^2/R)^{1/3} \qquad (13.5)$$
$$U^* = 3 \times C^* - 2 \times L \qquad (13.6)$$

Also, the average cash balance in the Miller–Orr model is:

$$\textbf{Average cash balance} = (4 \times C^* - L)/3 \qquad (13.7)$$

The derivation of these expressions is relatively complex, so we will not present it here. Fortunately, as we illustrate next, the results are not difficult to use.

For example, suppose $F = \$10$, the interest rate is 1 per cent per month, and the standard deviation of the monthly net cash flows is $200. The variance of the monthly net cash flows is:

$$\sigma^2 = (\$200)^2 = \$40,000$$

We assume a minimum cash balance of $L = \$100$. We can calculate the cash balance target, C^*, as:

$$
\begin{aligned}
C^* &= L + (^3/_4 \times F \times \sigma^2/R)^{1/3} \\
&= \$100 + (^3/_4 \times \$10 \times \$40,000/0.01)^{1/3} \\
&= \$100 + (30,000,000)^{1/3} \\
&= \$100 + 311 \\
&= \$411
\end{aligned}
$$

The upper limit, U^*, is thus:

$$
\begin{aligned}
U^* &= 3 \times C^* - 2 \times L \\
&= 3 \times \$411 - 2 \times \$100 \\
&= \$1,033
\end{aligned}
$$

Finally, the average cash balance will be:

$$
\begin{aligned}
\text{Average cash balance} &= (4 \times C^* - L)/3 \\
&= (4 \times \$411 - \$100)/3 \\
&= \$515
\end{aligned}
$$

Implications of the BAT and Miller–Orr models

Our two cash management models differ in complexity, but they have some similar implications. In both cases, all other things being equal, we see that:

1 the greater the interest rate, the lower the target cash balance;
2 the greater the order cost, the higher the target balance.

These are both fairly obvious. The advantage of the Miller–Orr model is that it improves our understanding of the problem of cash management by considering the effect of uncertainty as measured by the variation in net cash inflows.

The Miller–Orr model shows that the greater the uncertainty is (the higher σ^2 is), the greater is the difference between the target balance and the minimum balance. Similarly, the greater the uncertainty is, the higher is the upper limit and the higher is the average cash balance. These all make intuitive sense. For example, the greater the variability is, the greater is the chance that the balance will drop below the minimum. We thus keep a higher balance to guard against this happening.

Other factors influencing the target cash balance

Before moving on, we briefly discuss two additional considerations that affect the target cash balance.

First, in our discussion of cash management, we assume that cash is invested in marketable securities such as Commonwealth bonds. The firm obtains cash by selling these securities. Another alternative is to borrow cash. Borrowing introduces additional considerations to cash management:

1   Borrowing is likely to be more expensive than selling marketable securities because the interest rate is likely to be higher.
2   The need to borrow will depend on management's desire to hold low cash balances. A firm is more likely to have to borrow to cover an unexpected cash outflow the greater its cash flow variability and the lower its investment in marketable securities.

Second, for large firms, the trading costs of buying and selling securities are very small when compared to the opportunity costs of holding cash. For example, suppose a firm has $1 million in cash that will not be needed for 24 hours. Should the firm invest the money or leave it sitting?

Suppose the firm can invest the money at an average annual rate of 7.57 per cent per year. The daily rate in this case is about two basis points (.02% or .0002).[3] The daily return earned on $1 million is thus $0.0002 \times \$1$ million $= \$200$. In many cases, the order cost would be much less than this; so a large firm will buy and sell securities often before it will leave substantial amounts of cash idle.

Large firms hold significant amounts of cash for the following reasons:

1   Firms may leave cash in the bank as a compensating balance in payment for banking services.
2   Large corporations may have thousands of accounts with several dozen banks. Sometimes it makes more sense to leave cash alone than to manage each account daily and make daily transfers among them.

Bank overdraft and the Miller–Orr model

The overdraft or short-term line of credit has been one of the most popular forms of corporate loan from a bank. It is an arrangement whereby the bank agrees to lend up to a certain amount with the company borrowing all, or a portion, of the total amount as needed. The borrowing is linked to the trading account of the company so that day-to-day cash funds remaining in the account offset the debt of the company. The bank would expect the overdrawn balance of the account to fluctuate so that it would even move into credit at various points of the trading cycle. Over time the bank would aim at gradually reducing the overdraft limit; that is, the maximum amount that may be overdrawn on the account. Overdrafts are technically callable by the bank on demand so that they are regarded as short-term finance. In reality they provide an ongoing source of financing which is reviewed on a regular basis (normally annually). In more recent times banks have attempted to direct customers away from overdrafts because this form of financing is difficult to manage from the point of view of the bank—there is a lack of certainty in the amount of the commitment required by the bank.

In considering bank overdrafts and the Miller–Orr model we need to consider the relationship between the yield on long-term and short-term investments and the cost of the bank overdraft. Consider the case where:

Yield on short-term investments < Cost of bank overdraft < Yield on long-term investments

Here the cost of the bank overdraft is greater than the yield on short-term investments so that the company would not hold short-term investments as in the Miller–Orr model. This relationship would reflect normal business conditions. If the yield on short-term investments were greater than the cost of bank overdrafts, companies would always extend the overdraft to the limit and invest in short-term investments. When normal business conditions exist and a bank overdraft facility is available, the aim is to maximise long-term investments and protect liquidity requirements through the overdraft.

With a bank overdraft, the upper limit of the original Miller–Orr model becomes zero. The lower limit (overdraft limit) and the target overdrawn level of the account is established through a *target determinant* value. The target determinant is calculated as:

$$[(^3/_4 \times F \times \sigma^2)/(R - d)]^{1/3}$$

where all the terms are the same as defined earlier and d is the cost of the bank overdraft. Once the target determinant has been calculated, the lower limit (overdraft limit) and target overdrawn level are derived as:

$$\text{Lower limit} = 3 \times \text{Target determinant}$$

and

$$\text{Target overdrawn level} = 2 \times \text{Target determinant}$$

EXAMPLE 13.2 ▪ **Bank overdraft and the Miller–Orr model**

Moore Money Pty Ltd is negotiating with its bank to establish a bank overdraft. Experience has provided the following information:

- F = the fixed cost of each act of investment or disinvestment in long-term investments = $4,000
- σ^2 = the variance of the daily changes in the company's cash balance = $100,000
- R = the yield on investments = 0.00028 per day or 10.76 per cent per annum
- d = the daily overdraft rate = 0.00025 or 9.55 per cent per annum

What is the overdraft limit that Moore Money should negotiate and what is the target overdrawn level of the account that should be used if the company is to employ the Miller–Orr model?

$$
\begin{aligned}
\text{Target determinant} &= [(^3/_4 \times F \times \sigma^2)/(R - d)]^{1/3} \\
&= [(^3/_4 \times \$4{,}000 \times \$100{,}000)/(0.00028 - 0.00025)]^{1/3} \\
&= (\$300{,}000{,}000/0.00003)^{1/3} \\
&= (1 \times 10^{13})^{1/3} \\
&= \$21{,}544
\end{aligned}
$$

$$
\begin{aligned}
\text{Overdraft limit} &= 3 \times \text{Target determinant} \\
&= 3 \times \$21{,}544 \\
&= \$64{,}632
\end{aligned}
$$

$$
\begin{aligned}
\text{Target overdrawn level} &= 2 \times \text{Target determinant} \\
&= 2 \times \$21{,}544 \\
&= \$43{,}088
\end{aligned}
$$

EXAMPLE 13.3 ▪ **Plotting the Miller–Orr model with a bank overdraft**

Assume Moore Money Pty Ltd has its bank overdraft arrangement from the previous example approved. Further assume that, even though the cash inflows and outflows occur randomly, by the fifth day the accumulated surplus takes the overdraft from an overdrawn balance of $17,235 to zero. The company takes the action required by the Miller–Orr model on the fifth day. From day 5 to day 9 the accumulated deficit is $21,544. The overdraft limit is not required prior to day 9. Plot the cash flows and explain the actions that the Miller–Orr model would require during the first nine days.

a On day 5, Moore Money Pty Ltd would need to transfer $43,088 ($X - Y$ on the graph) from the bank account to long-term investments. This would increase the overdrawn bank balance from zero to an overdrawn amount of $43,088, which is the target overdrawn level.

b On day 9, Moore Money Pty Ltd would need to sell long-term investments to reduce the overdraft balance. It would need to sell investments worth $21,544 ($64,632 − $43,088) and place the amount, equal to $A − B$, into the bank account to return the overdrawn balance to −$43,088.

Moore Money Pty Ltd. The Miller–Orr Model with a bank overdraft

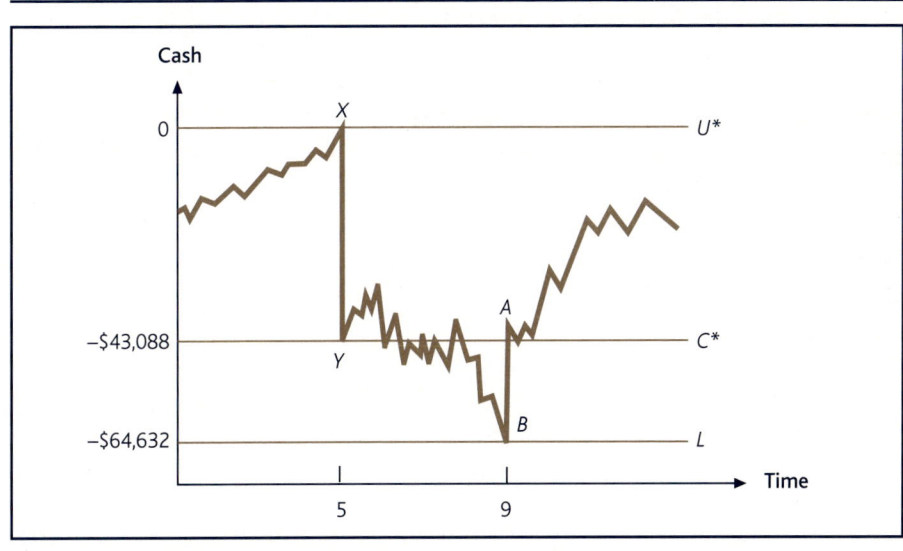

Because the target level is the amount to which the bank account is adjusted under the Miller–Orr model, it is sometimes called the *return point* of the model.

Concept questions

13.2a *What is a target cash balance?*
13.2b *What is the basic trade-off in the BAT model?*
13.2c *Describe how the Miller–Orr model works.*

13.3 ■ Managing the collection and disbursement of cash

A firm's cash balance as reported in its financial statements (its *book* or *ledger balance*) is not the same thing as the balance shown in its bank account (its *available* or *collected balance*). The difference between available balance and book balance is called **float**, and it represents the net effect of cheques in the process of clearing.

float
the difference between book cash and bank cash, representing the net effect of cheques in the process of clearing

Disbursement float

Cheques written by the firm generate *disbursement float*, causing a decrease in its book balance but no change in its available balance. For example, suppose All Beads Ltd (ABL) currently has $100,000 on deposit with its bank. On 8 June, it buys some raw materials and pays with a cheque for $100,000. The company's book balance is immediately reduced by $100,000 as a result.

ABL's bank, however, will not find out about this cheque until it is presented to ABL's bank for payment on, say, 14 June. Until the cheque is presented, the firm's available balance is greater than its book balance by $100,000. In other words, before 8 June, ABL has a zero float:

$$\text{Float} = \text{Firm's available balance} - \text{Firm's book balance}$$
$$= \$100,000 - \$100,000$$

ABL's position from 8 June to 14 June is:

$$\text{Disbursement float} = \text{Firm's available balance} - \text{Firm's book balance}$$
$$= \$100,000 - \$0$$
$$= \$100,000$$

During this period that the cheque is *clearing* (moving through the banking system), ABL has a balance with the bank of $100,000. It can obtain the benefit of this cash while the cheque is clearing. For example, the available balance could be temporarily invested in marketable securities and thus earn some interest. We will return to this subject a little later.

Collection float and net float

Cheques received by the firm create a *collection float*. A collection float increases book balances but does not immediately change available balances. For example, suppose ABL receives a cheque from a customer for $100,000 on 8 October. Assume, as before, that the company has $100,000 deposited at its bank and a zero float. It deposits the cheque and increases its book balance by $100,000 to $200,000. However, the additional cash is not available to ABL until its bank has presented the cheque to the customer's bank and received $100,000. This will occur on, say, 14 October. In the meantime, the cash position at ABL will reflect a collection float of $100,000. We can summarise these events. Before 8 October, ABL's position is:

$$\text{Float} = \text{Firm's available balance} - \text{Firm's book balance}$$
$$= \$100,000 - \$100,000$$
$$= \$0$$

ABL's position from 8 October to 14 October is:

$$\text{Collection float} = \text{Firm's available balance} - \text{Firm's book balance}$$
$$= \$100,000 - \$200,000$$
$$= -\$100,000$$

In general, a firm's payment (disbursement) activities generate a disbursement float, and its collection activities generate a collection float. The net effect—that is, the sum of the total collection and disbursement floats—is the net float. The net float at a point in time is simply the overall difference between the firm's available balance and its book balance.

If the net float is positive, then the firm's disbursement float exceeds its collection float and its available balance exceeds its book balance. In other words, the bank thinks the firm has more cash than it really does. This, of course, is desirable. If the available balance is less than the book balance, then the firm has a net collection float. This is undesirable because we actually have more cash than the bank thinks we do, but we cannot use it.

A firm should be concerned with its net float and available balance more than its book balance. If a financial manager knows that a cheque will not clear for several days, he or she will be able to keep a lower cash balance at the bank than might be true otherwise. This can generate a great deal of money.

Staying afloat

Suppose you have $5,000 on deposit. You write a cheque for $1,000 to pay for fees, and you deposit $2,000. What are your disbursement, collection and net floats?

After you write the $1,000 cheque, you show a balance of $4,000 on your records, but the bank shows $5,000 while the cheque is clearing. This is a disbursement float of $1,000.

After you deposit the $2,000 cheque, you show a balance of $6,000. Your available balance does not rise until the cheque clears. This is a collection float of −$2,000. Your net float is the sum of the collection and disbursement floats, or −$1,000.

Overall, you show $6,000 on your records, but the bank only shows $5,000 cash. The discrepancy between your available balance and your recorded balance is the net float (−$1,000), and it is bad for you. If you write another cheque for $5,500, it might bounce (be dishonoured) even though, net, it should not. This is the reason that the financial manager has to be more concerned with available balances than recorded balances. This is also why telephone banking services tell you what your balance is and the amount of funds available.

Float management

Float management involves controlling the collection and disbursement of cash. The objective in cash collection is to speed up collections and reduce the lag between the time customers pay their bills and the time the cheques are collected. The objective in cash disbursement is to control payments and minimise the firm's costs associated with making payments.

Float can be broken down into three parts: mail float, processing float and availability float:

1 *Mail float* is the part of the collection and disbursement process where cheques are trapped in the postal system.
2 *Processing float* is the time it takes the receiver of a cheque to process the payment and deposit it in a bank for collection.
3 *Availability float* refers to the time required to clear a cheque through the banking system.

Speeding up collections involves reducing one or more of these float components. Slowing up disbursements involves increasing one of them. We will describe some procedures for managing float times below. First, we need to discuss how float is measured.

Measuring float

The size of the float depends on both the dollars and time delay involved. For example, suppose that you receive a cheque for $750 from another state each month. It takes four days in the mail to reach you (the mail float) and one day for you to get over to the bank (the processing float). The bank holds out-of-state cheques overnight (availability float). The total delay is $4 + 1 + 1 = 6$ days.

In this case, what is your average daily float? There are two equivalent ways of calculating the answer. First, you have a $750 float for six days, so we say that the total float is 6 × $750 = $4,500. Assuming 30 days in the month, the average daily float is $4,500/30 = $150.

Alternatively, your float is $750 for six days out of the month and zero for the other 24 days (again assuming 30 days in a month). Your average daily float is thus:

$$
\begin{aligned}
\text{Average daily float} &= (6 \times \$750 + 24 \times 0)/30 \\
&= 6/30 \times \$750 + 24/30 \times 0 \\
&= \$4{,}500/30 \\
&= \$150
\end{aligned}
$$

This means that, on an average day, $150 is not available to spend. In other words, on average, your book balance is $150 greater than your available balance, a $150 average collection float.

Things are only a little more complicated when there are multiple receipts. Suppose that Gamble Ltd receives two items each month as follows:

	Amount	Number of days delay	Total float
Item 1	$5,000,000	× 9	= $45,000,000
Item 2	$3,000,000	× 5	= $15,000,000
Total	$8,000,000		$60,000,000

The average daily float is equal to:

$$
\begin{aligned}
\text{Average daily float} &= \frac{\text{Total float}}{\text{Total days}} \\
&= \frac{\$60{,}000{,}000}{30} \\
&= \$2{,}000{,}000
\end{aligned}
$$

So, on an average day, there is $2,000,000 that is uncollected and not available.

Another way to see this is to calculate the average daily receipts and multiply by the weighted average delay. Average daily receipts are:

$$
\begin{aligned}
\text{Average daily receipts} &= \frac{\text{Total Receipts}}{\text{Total days}} \\
&= \frac{\$8{,}000{,}000}{30} \\
&= \$266{,}666.67
\end{aligned}
$$

Of the $8,000,000 total receipts, $5,000,000, or $5/8$ of the total, is delayed for nine days. The other $3/8$ is delayed for five days. The weighted average delay is thus:

$$
\begin{aligned}
\text{Weighted average delay} &= (5/8) \times 9 \text{ days} + (3/8) \times 5 \text{ days} \\
&= 5.625 + 1.875 \\
&= 7.50 \text{ days}
\end{aligned}
$$

The average daily float is thus:

$$\begin{aligned}
\textbf{Average daily float} &= \textbf{Average daily receipts} \times \textbf{Weighted average delay} \quad (13.8)\\
&= \$266,666.67 \times 7.50 \text{ days}\\
&= \$2,000,000
\end{aligned}$$

This is just as we had before.

Cost of the float

The basic cost of collection float to the firm is simply the opportunity cost from not being able to use the cash. At a minimum, the firm could earn interest on the cash if it were available for investing.

Suppose that Cashedup Ltd has average daily receipts of $1,000 and a weighted average delay of three days. The average daily float is thus 3 × $1,000 = $3,000. This means that, on a typical day, there is $3,000 that is not earning interest. Suppose Cashedup could eliminate the float entirely. What would be the benefit? If it costs $2,000 to eliminate the float, what is the NPV of doing it?

Table 13.1 illustrates the situation for Cashedup. Suppose Cashedup starts with a zero float. On a given day, day 1, Cashedup receives and deposits a cheque for $1,000. It does not collect the cash until three days later, on day 4. At the end of the day, the book balance is $1,000 more than the available balance, so the float is $1,000. On day 2, Cashedup receives and deposits another cheque. It collects three days later, on day 5. Now there are two uncollected cheques, and the books show a $2,000 balance. The bank, however, still shows a zero balance; so the float is $2,000. The same sequence occurs on day 3, and the float rises to a total of $3,000.

Buildup of the float					
			Day		
	1	2	3	4	5...
Beginning float	$ 0	$1,000	$2,000	$3,000	$3,000...
Cheques received	+ 1,000	1,000	1,000	1,000	1,000...
Cheques cleared (cash available)	− 0	− 0	− 0	− 1,000	− 1,000...
Ending float	$1,000	$2,000	$3,000	$3,000	$3,000...

TABLE 13.1

On day 4, Cashedup again receives and deposits a cheque for $1,000. However, it also collects $1,000 from the day 1 cheque. The change in book balance and the change in available balance are identical, +$1,000; so the float stays at $3,000. The same thing happens every day after day 4; the float therefore stays at $3,000 forever.

Table 13.2 (overleaf) illustrates what happens if the float is eliminated entirely on some day t in the future. After the float is eliminated, daily receipts are still $1,000. We collect the same day since the float is eliminated, so daily collections are also still $1,000. As Table 13.2 illustrates, the only change occurs the first day. On that day, as usual, we collect $1,000 from the sale made three days ago. Because the float is gone, we also collect on the sales made two days ago, one day ago and today, for an additional $3,000. Total collections today are thus $4,000 instead of $1,000.

TABLE
13.2

		Day		
	t	*t* + 1	*t* + 2	...
Beginning float	$3,000	$ 0	$ 0	...
Cheques received	1,000	1,000	1,000	...
Cheques cleared (cash available)	4,000	− 1,000	− 1,000	...
Ending float	$1,000	$2,000	$3,000	...

Effect of eliminating the float

What we see is that Cashedup generates an extra $3,000 today by eliminating the float. On every subsequent day, Cashedup receives $1,000 in cash just as it did before the float was eliminated. If you recall our definition of relevant cash flow, the only change in the firm's cash flows from eliminating the float is this extra $3,000 that comes in immediately. No other cash flows are affected, so Cashedup is $3,000 richer.

In other words, the PV of eliminating the float is simply equal to the total float. Cashedup could pay this amount out as a dividend, invest it in interest-bearing assets, or do anything else with it. If it costs $2,000 to eliminate the float, then the NPV is $3,000 − 2,000 = $1,000; so Cashedup should do it.

EXAMPLE 13.5 ■ Reducing the float: Part 1

Instead of eliminating the float, suppose that Cashedup can reduce it to one day. What is the maximum Cashedup should be willing to pay for this?

If Cashedup can reduce the float from three days to one day, then the amount of the float will fall from $3,000 to $1,000. From our discussion just above, we see immediately that the PV of doing this is just equal to the $2,000 float reduction. Cashedup should thus be willing to pay up to $2,000.

EXAMPLE 13.6 ■ Reducing the float: Part 2

Look back at Example 13.5. Suppose that a large bank was willing to provide the float reduction service for a cost of $175 per year, payable at the end of each year. The relevant discount rate is 8 per cent. Should Cashedup hire the bank? What is the NPV of the investment? How do you interpret this discount rate? What is the most per year that Cashedup should be willing to pay?

The PV to Cashedup is still $2,000. The $175 would have to be paid out every year forever to maintain the float reduction; so the cost is perpetual, and its PV is $175/0.08 = $2,187.50. The NPV is $2,000 − 2,187.50 = −187.50; therefore, it is not a good deal.

Ignoring the possibility of bounced cheques, the discount rate here corresponds most closely to the cost of short-term borrowing. The reason is that Cashedup could borrow $1,000 from the bank every time a cheque is deposited and pay it back three days later. The cost is the interest that Cashedup would have to pay.

The most Cashedup would be willing to pay is whatever charge results in an NPV of zero. This occurs when the $2,000 benefit exactly equals the PV of the costs, that is, when $2,000 = C/0.08, where C is the annual cost. Solving for C, we find that C = 0.08 × $2,000 = $160 per year.

Managing the float

With the increase in credit card activity and electronic settlement of accounts, the bank-clearing time for payments is being reduced. Within the states the banks are locked into a single clearing system so that cheques are cleared within a day. Interstate transfers can take two days because of the need to transfer information to different clearing systems. The amount of time that cash spends in the cash collection process depends on where the customers of the firm and the banks are located and how efficient the firm is at collecting its debts. The first element is beyond the control of the firm; however, the second is well within the firm's control. One method the firm may use to collect its accounts receivable is to factor the accounts.

Factoring

Factoring occurs when the firm sells its accounts receivable. The decision to enter into a factoring arrangement may be taken as a conscious decision to sell off existing debtors or the arrangement may be created when the sale is made. In the latter situation the sale is made through credit card facilities, such as 'Visa'. When a credit card facility is used the organisation financing the facility assumes responsibility for the debt so that the firm has immediately factored its account receivable. Factoring arrangements may be distinguished on the basis of whether they are 'notification' or 'non-notification' agreements.

factoring
the process whereby a firm sells its accounts receivable

Notification agreements

In this situation customers of the firms that make the sales are aware that the factoring arrangement exists. As is the case with Visa, the statements of account bear the name of the factoring organisation and payments are made directly to that company. The accounts receivable ledger is maintained by the factoring company. Usually the factoring company assumes all the bad-debt risk so that the agreements are known as *credit-risk agreements* or *non-recourse agreements*.

Non-notification agreements

In this situation customers of the selling company are not notified of the agreement. The statements of account bear the name of the selling company, and customers either pay the selling company, which then passes the payment on to the factoring company, or the payments are sent to a post office box rented by the factoring company. The accounts receivable ledger may be maintained by the selling company; however, the factoring company may perform this service for a higher fee. The selling company would receive immediate payment for only a specified percentage of the accounts receivable. This is usually between 60 and 80 per cent. The residual is paid, less the factoring fee, once full settlement is received from the customer.

Cost of factoring

The factoring company charges a flat percentage of the value of the accounts factored. This ranges from 2.5 to 5 per cent. A smaller percentage, approximately 1 to 2 per cent, may be charged if the factoring company delays payment. For example, in the case of *maturity factoring*, payment may be delayed until 30 days after the invoice date. Credit card services provide almost immediate cash to the sellers because the amount of the credit dockets is credited to their bank accounts when the credit card dockets are deposited (electronically) at the bank.

Credit insurance

Another way of protecting against bad debt losses is to take out *credit insurance*. The insurance cover may be *specific account* or for the *whole turnover*. Specific account policies may cover a particular account or they may extend to all accounts that fall into a specified range of dollar values. Whole turnover policies cover bad debt losses on any of the company's accounts. The insurance company does not provide a complete coverage against bad-debt losses. This is to guarantee that the insured company will try to recover the bad debt before making a claim. The premium for insurance cover ranges from 2 to 6 per cent of the value of the accounts receivable to be covered.

Delaying disbursements

Accelerating collections is one method of cash management; slowing down disbursements is another. The cash disbursement process is illustrated in Figure 13.5. Slowing down disbursements, or 'playing the float game' as it is sometimes called, generally involves increasing mail time and cheque-clearing time.

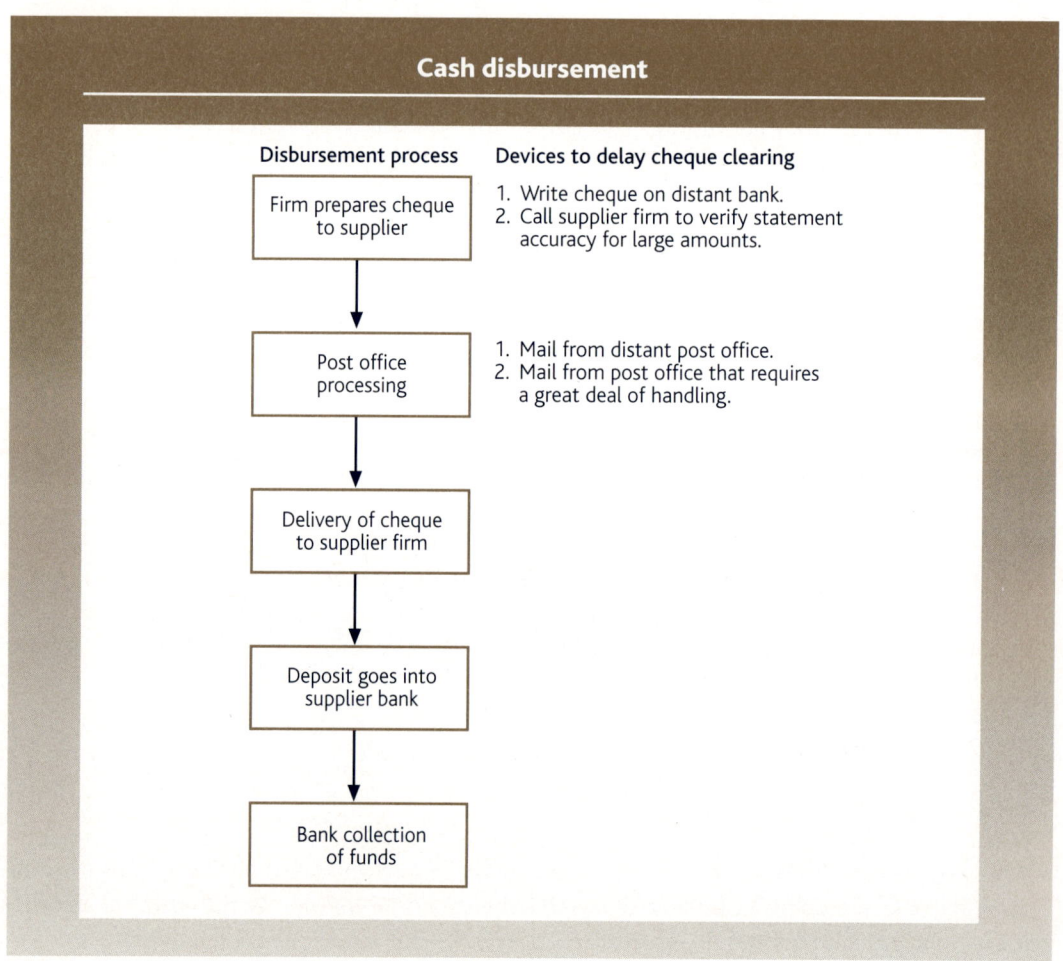

FIGURE 13.5

Cash disbursement

Disbursement process

Firm prepares cheque to supplier

Post office processing

Delivery of cheque to supplier firm

Deposit goes into supplier bank

Bank collection of funds

Devices to delay cheque clearing

1. Write cheque on distant bank.
2. Call supplier firm to verify statement accuracy for large amounts.

1. Mail from distant post office.
2. Mail from post office that requires a great deal of handling.

Increasing disbursement float

As we have seen, increasing the disbursement float in terms of slowing down payments comes from mail delivery, cheque-processing time and collection of funds. Disbursement float can be increased by writing a cheque on a geographically distant bank. Mailing cheques from remote post offices is another way firms slow down disbursement. Because there are significant ethical (and legal) issues associated with deliberately delaying disbursements in these and similar ways, such strategies appear to be disappearing.

Direct transfers

A recent business innovation, which is increasing in use, is that of direct transfer. Here the use of cheques is abandoned and funds are transferred electronically from one bank account to another. This practice eliminates the cheque clearing process and funds are available immediately for the recipient; however, the payer loses the advantage of the cheque clearing period. The payer gains from lower bank fees and avoids the costs of cheques, such as government charges and the time writing and processing the cheques.

Ethical and legal questions

The cash manager must work with collected bank cash balances and not the firm's book balance (which reflects cheques that have been deposited but not collected). If this is not done, a cash manager could be drawing on uncollected cash as a source for making short-term investments.

In May 1985, Robert Fomon, chairman of E.F. Hutton (a large US investment bank), pleaded guilty to 2,000 charges of mail and wire fraud in connection with a scheme the firm had operated from 1980 to 1982. E.F. Hutton employees wrote cheques totalling hundreds of millions of dollars against uncollected cash. The proceeds were then invested in short-term money market assets. This type of systematic overdrafting of accounts (or cheque 'kiting' as it is sometimes called) is neither legal nor ethical.

For its part, E.F. Hutton paid a $2 million fine, reimbursed the government (the US Department of Justice) $750,000, and reserved an additional $8 million for restitution to defrauded banks.

Concept questions

13.3a *What is the difference between:*
  i *a notification and a non-notification factoring agreement?*
  ii *a credit-risk factoring agreement and a non credit-risk factoring agreement?*
13.3b *Comment on the following: 'It is sometimes believed that a company which is factoring its accounts must be financially weak.'*
13.3c *Who maintains the accounts receivable ledger when a factoring agreement has been arranged?*

13.4 ▮ Investing idle cash

If a firm has a temporary cash surplus, it can invest in short-term securities. As we have mentioned at various times, the market for short-term financial assets is called the money market. The maturity of short-term financial assets that trade in the money market is one year or less.

Figure 13.6 (overleaf) identifies the securities markets that operate in Australia. Temporary cash surpluses may be invested in any of these markets; however, the firm has to be conscious of the maturity, default risk and marketability of the investments.

FIGURE 13.6

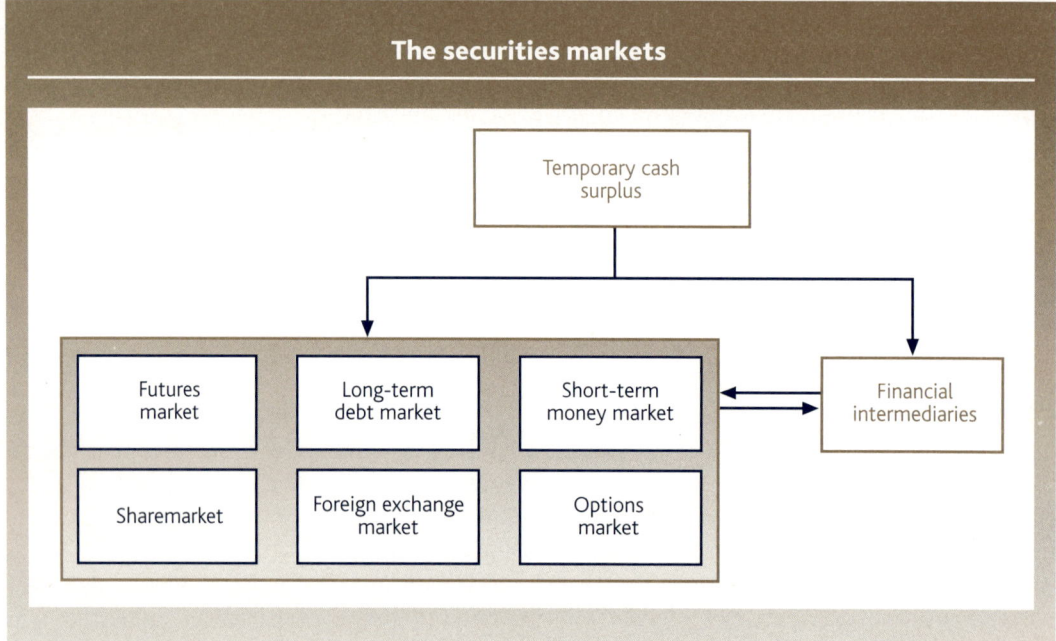

The securities markets

Temporary cash surplus

Futures market

Long-term debt market

Short-term money market

Financial intermediaries

Sharemarket

Foreign exchange market

Options market

Characteristics of short-term securities

Given that a firm has some temporarily idle cash, there are a variety of short-term securities available for investing. The most important characteristics of these short-term marketable securities are their maturity, default risk, marketability and taxability.

Maturity

Maturity refers to the time period over which interest and principal payments are made.

From Chapter 6, we know that for a given change in the level of interest rates, the prices of longer maturity securities will change more than those for shorter maturity securities. As a consequence, firms that invest in long-term securities are accepting greater risk than firms that invest in securities with short-term maturities.

We called this type of risk 'interest rate risk'. Firms often limit their investments in marketable securities to those maturing in less than 90 days to avoid the risk of losses in value from changing interest rates. Of course, the expected return on securities with short-term maturities is usually less than the expected return on securities with longer maturities.

Default risk

Default risk refers to the probability that interest and principal will not be paid in the promised amounts on the due dates (or not paid at all). In Chapter 16, we observe that various financial reporting agencies, such as Moody's Investors Service, compile and publish ratings of various corporate and public securities. These ratings are connected to default risk. Of course, some securities have negligible default risk, such as government bonds. Given the purposes of investing idle corporate cash, firms typically avoid investing in marketable securities with significant default risk.

Marketability

Marketability refers to how easy it is to convert an asset to cash; so marketability and liquidity mean much the same thing. Some money market instruments are much more marketable than others. At the top of the list are Government Treasury bonds, which can be bought and sold very cheaply and very quickly.

Most large firms manage their own short-term financial assets. Within the short-term money market sector, dealers provide a service whereby funds may be placed overnight or longer. This service is reported in the financial press as the weighted average of rates paid by the dealers on the loans outstanding and it is called the short–term money market. Banks also provide facilities for overnight, 24-hour call or longer terms through bank bills of 30-, 60- or 90-day duration.

Temporary cash surpluses

Firms have temporary cash surpluses for various reasons. Two of the most important are the financing of seasonal or cyclical activities of the firm and the financing of planned or possible expenditures.

Seasonal or cyclical activities

Some firms have a predictable cash flow pattern. They have surplus cash flows during part of the year and deficit cash flows the rest of the year. For example, major retail outlets would have seasonal cash flow patterns influenced by Christmas. These firms may buy marketable securities when surplus cash flows occur and sell marketable securities when deficits occur. Of course, bank loans are another short-term financing device. The use of bank loans and marketable securities to meet temporary financing needs is illustrated in Figure 13.7.

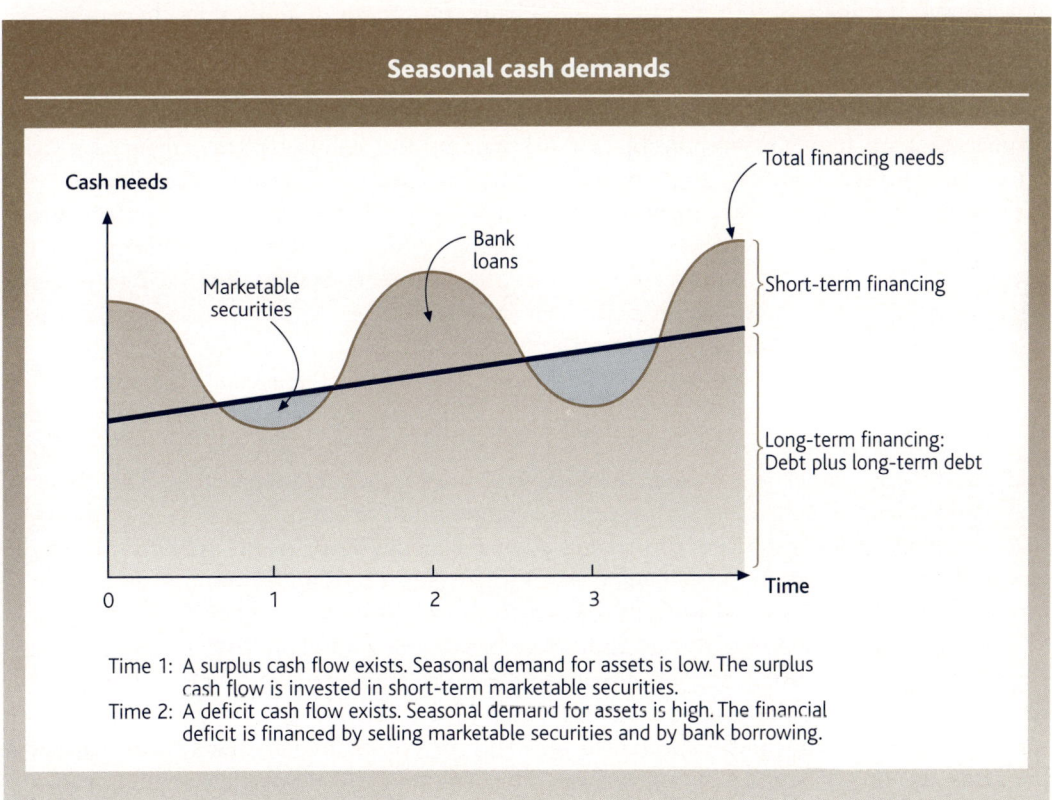

FIGURE 13.7

Seasonal cash demands

Time 1: A surplus cash flow exists. Seasonal demand for assets is low. The surplus cash flow is invested in short-term marketable securities.
Time 2: A deficit cash flow exists. Seasonal demand for assets is high. The financial deficit is financed by selling marketable securities and by bank borrowing.

Planned or possible expenditures

Firms frequently accumulate temporary investments in marketable securities to provide the cash for a plant construction program, dividend payment or other large expenditures. Thus firms may issue debt and shares before the cash is needed, investing the proceeds in short-term marketable securities and then selling the securities to finance the expenditures. Also, firms may face the possibility of having to make a large cash outlay. An obvious example would be the possibility of losing a large lawsuit. Firms may build up cash surpluses against such a contingency.

Concept questions

13.4a *What are some reasons why firms find themselves with idle cash?*
13.4b *What are some types of money market securities?*

 ## Regulation of financial intermediaries

The Australian financial markets are discussed in detail in Chapter 15. However, we shall now have a brief look at the regulation of the banking system to enhance our understanding of the management of cash and liquidity.

Intermediaries in the financial system comprise the Reserve Bank, banks and non-banks. The Reserve Bank of Australia is Australia's central bank. Over time its role has changed from that of commercial bank, central bank and supervisor (prior to 1959) to central bank and supervisor (till 1998) to now just a central bank. As a result of an inquiry chaired by Stan Wallis, supervision of banks has been transferred to the Australian Prudential Regulation Authority (APRA).

The Reserve Bank of Australia (RBA) was established in 1911 to oversee the Australian financial system. It is now responsible for maintaining the stability of the financial system. Financial stability is an essential ingredient in maintaining economic stability and the confidence of the community in undertaking their financial transactions. Within this broad goal, the Reserve Bank also has specific responsibility for the safety and efficiency of the payments system, a responsibility overseen by the Payments System Board. The Reserve Bank's objective is to help ensure that financial disturbances in any part of the financial system do not ultimately threaten the health of the economy.

In responding to financial disturbances if they occur, the Reserve Bank, unlike other regulatory agencies in Australia, is able to use its financial position to provide emergency liquidity to the financial system. It would seek to do so, wherever possible, by making funds available to the market as a whole through its domestic market operations. The Reserve Bank would lend directly to an institution in liquidity difficulties only if it were of the view that the failure of the institution to make its payments could have serious implications for the rest of the financial system. The Reserve Bank (hereafter 'the Bank') does not see its role as providing support to insolvent institutions.

The Bank's domestic market operations are carried out on a daily basis by the Domestic Markets Department. At 9.30 each morning, the Bank announces through electronic news services its estimate of the 'system cash opening position'. This is an estimate of the amount of exchange settlement funds expected to flow into or out of the banking system that day if the Bank did not undertake any operations. The Bank also states whether it intends to buy (to inject funds), sell (to withdraw funds) or do nothing on the day. Market participants can then submit bids (if the Bank is selling Commonwealth Government Securities (CGS)) or offers (if the Bank is buying CGS) up to 10.00 am. The operations are conducted in the form of an auction. The Bank accepts bids or offers in descending order of attractiveness in terms of yield and maturity, up to the volume it estimates is necessary to maintain the cash rate around the target level. It responds to counterparties as quickly as possible, and usually before 10.30 am. The Bank monitors market conditions throughout the day and, should conditions turn out to be different from those expected, it may re-enter the market for a second round of dealing. Also, as an end-of-day safety valve, other banks may borrow at their discretion from the Reserve Bank at a cost of 25 basis points above the target for the cash rate. Exchange Settlement Funds are paid an interest rate 25 basis points below the cash rate.

The 'payments system' refers to the ways in which consumers, businesses and other organisations move value between one another. It encompasses the differing forms of payment instruments—such as cash, cheques and electronic funds transfers—and the technical processes involved in transferring value from one party to another. Cash is probably the most important instrument for small retail transactions and for transfers of value between individuals. Anecdotal evidence and experience suggest that cash transactions account for the dominant share of the number of transactions, but a very small share of their value. The ready availability of cash through automated teller machines (ATMs) has sustained its use. In 2001, withdrawals from ATMs averaged around $7.6 billion a month, an average of around $390 for every man, woman and child in Australia. Non-cash payments account for most of the value of payments in the Australian economy. On average, non-cash payments worth around $130 billion are exchanged between financial institutions each day. Adding the estimated value of payments made between customers of the same financial institution suggests non-cash payments of around $160 billion each day. Around 90 per cent of the value of non-cash transactions is accounted for by a small number of high-value payments made through Australia's real-time gross settlement (RTGS) system. Most of the value of these payments is accounted for by settlement of foreign exchange and securities markets transactions.

The cheque is still the most important non-cash payment instrument in Australia but its relative importance has declined over the past two decades from around 85 per cent to around 30 per cent of the number of non-cash payments. The number of cheques written annually has steadied at around one billion in recent years and is now showing signs of declining. The Reserve Bank is interested in the payments system for both operational and policy reasons. As a participant in the system, the Bank processes a large number of payments for its customers, mainly government departments and authorities. The Bank provides Exchange Settlement Accounts (ESAs) to payment providers to allow them to settle amounts owed to other institutions as a result of payments which they have made on their own behalf and for their customers. Until recently access to ESAs was restricted to banks and Special Service Providers for building societies and credit unions. In March 1999, the Bank's Payments System Board announced the terms on which it would offer wider access.

In June 1998 the Bank introduced a real-time gross settlement (RTGS) system for high-value payments. For many years, Australia, along with most other countries, had operated a deferred net settlement system under which payment obligations between banks were settled early on the day following the transfer of payment instructions. Such a system leads to banks having large overnight exposures (i.e. settlement risk) to each other. Under RTGS, all high-value electronic payments must be settled individually at the time they are sent using credit funds from banks' ESAs. This eliminates the interbank settlement risk arising from the transfer of high-value payments. Lower-value payments will continue to be settled on a deferred net basis on the following morning.

APRA's role in supervising individual institutions and the Bank's responsibilities for overall financial system stability are largely complementary. Problems in individual institutions may give rise to broader systemic instability; in turn, systemic risks of domestic or external origin may themselves threaten the viability of even well-managed institutions. For these reasons, effective coordination between the Bank and APRA is essential.

APRA is required to prudentially supervise all *authorised deposit-taking institutions* (ADIs) including banks, credit unions, building societies and other types of entities. APRA is attempting to harmonise the regulatory requirements applicable to different institutions. The intent is to have the same prudential and operational standards for all institutions. The aim of the regulation is to ensure that ADIs keep themselves in a sound financial position, and conduct themselves with integrity, prudence and professional skill; and to promote stability in the Australian financial system.

APRA requires the management of ADIs to implement robust risk control systems. The controls are established by prudential statements and are generally based on international standards. Two key standards are capital adequacy and liquidity risk.

Capital adequacy

The purpose of the Capital Adequacy Ratio (CAR) is to ensure that ADIs have sufficient capital to absorb losses so that their solvency is not threatened. The Basle Committee on Banking Supervision developed the concept of the CAR. ADIs are required to maintain a ratio of capital to risk-weighted assets of at least 8 per cent. For example, a home loan has a risk weighting of 50 per cent. A $100,000 home loan is a risk-weighted asset of $50,000 ($100,000 × 50%) for the ADI. The loan must be funded by some capital—$4,000 (8% of $50,000). The total loan of $100,000 must be funded by at least $4,000 of shareholders' funds and up to $96,000 of ADI borrowings.

Liquidity risk

The Prime Assets Ratio (PAR) required banks to hold 3 per cent of their assets in high quality liquid assets like CGSs. This requirement has been changed for banks from 16 August 1999. APRA now agrees on a liquidity policy with each bank. This policy places greater emphasis on the internal management practices of banks and sets out how the banks plan to manage liquidity under different circumstances.

Concept questions

13.5a *Why is there a need for the financial manager to understand how the Reserve Bank influences interest rates?*
13.5b *How does the Reserve Bank ensure that the banking system does not run out of cash?*

▪ 13.6 ▪ Summary and conclusions

1 A firm holds cash to conduct transactions and to compensate banks for the various services they render.

2 The optimal amount of cash for a firm to hold depends on the opportunity cost of holding cash and the uncertainty of future cash inflows and outflows. The Baumol–Allais–Tobin (BAT) model and the Miller–Orr model are two transaction models that provide rough guidelines for determining the optimal cash position.

3 The difference between a firm's available balance and its book balance is the firm's net float. The float reflects the fact that some cheques have not cleared and are thus uncollected. The financial manager must always work with collected cash balances and not with the company's book balance. To do otherwise is to use the bank's cash without the bank knowing it, raising ethical and legal questions.

4 The firm can make use of a variety of procedures to manage the collection and disbursement of cash in such a way as to speed up the collection of cash and slow down the payments.

5 Because of seasonal and cyclical activities, to help finance planned expenditures or as a contingency reserve, firms temporarily find themselves with a cash surplus. The money market offers a variety of possible vehicles for 'parking' this idle cash.

6 Banks, merchant banks, building societies, credit unions, life offices, pension funds, cash management trusts and finance companies are all examples of financial intermediaries. All financial intermediaries perform basically the same function; that is, bringing together people wanting money and people with money. Financial intermediaries accept funds and make loans. The financial intermediaries act as 'middle men', pooling the funds of lenders (savers) and passing that money on to borrowers. Naturally, the intermediaries expect to be paid for providing the service of matching borrowing and lending requirements and taking the credit risk.

Key terms

Adjustment costs *431*
Factoring *447*
Float *441*
Maturity factoring *447*

Non-recourse factoring *447*
Precautionary motive *430*
Reserve Bank *452*
Return point *441*

Speculative motive *430*
Target cash balance *431*
Target determinant *440*
Transaction motive *430*

Suggested readings

The following are classic readings in cash management:

Batlin, C.A. and Hinko, S. 'Lockbox Management and Value Maximization', *Financial Management*, Vol. 10, Winter 1981.

Beehler, P.J. *Contemporary Cash Management: Principles, Practices, Perspectives*, 2nd edn, John Wiley & Sons, New York, 1983.

Fielitz, B.D., and White, D.L. 'A Two-Stage Procedure for the Lockbox Location Problem', *Journal of Bank Research*, Spring 1982.

Hill, N.C. and Ferguson, D.M. 'Cash Flow Timeline Management: The Next Frontier of Cash Management', Robert R. Fentress Prize Paper, Bank Administration Institute, Rolling Meadows, Ill., July 1984.

Maier, S.F. and Vander Weide, J.H. 'What Lockbox and Disbursement Models Really Do', *Journal of Finance,* Vol. 38, March 1983.

Stone, B.K. 'The Expanding Scope of Cash Management', *Journal of Cash Management*, November 1982.

Endnotes

1 Cash is liquid. One property of liquidity is divisibility; that is, how easily an asset can be divided into parts.

2 Miller, M.H. and Orr, D. 'A Model of the Demand for Money by Firms', *Quarterly Journal of Economics*, August 1966, pp. 413–35.

3 A basis point is 1 per cent of 1 per cent. Also, the annual interest rate is calculated as $(1 + R)^{365} = 1.0757$, implying a daily rate of 0.02 per cent.

On the web

Many companies publish their Statement of Financial Position results on their web sites. Also, there is usually much information relevant to a firm's cash and liquidity management policies. Try:

http://www.bhpbilliton.com (BHP Billiton Limited)
http://www.colesmyer.com.au (Coles Myer)
http://www.telstra.com (Telstra)

For information on the Reserve Bank of Australia and APRA, try:
http://www.rba.gov.au/
http://www.apra.gov.au/

For ratings services, try:
http://www.moodys.com/ (Moody's)
http://www.standardandpoors.com (Standard & Poor's)

Maximise Your Marks!
There are 30 interactive questions on cash and liquidity management waiting online for you at www.mhhe.com/au/ross3e. The questions are written with additional feedback for incorrect answers, and text excerpts with page references for follow-up study.

International Articles!
To read more on cash and liquidity management and to see current international articles, just go to www.mhhe.com/au/ross3e and click on *PowerWeb Articles* for this chapter.

Chapter review problems and self-test

13.1 · The BAT model

Given the following information, calculate the target cash balance using the BAT model:

Annual interest rate	12%
Fixed order cost	$100
Total cash needed	$240,000

What are: the opportunity cost of holding cash, the trading cost and the total cost? What would these be if $15,000 were held instead? If $25,000 were held?

13.2 · Float measurement

On a typical business day, a firm writes cheques totalling $1,000. These cheques clear in 10 days on average. Simultaneously, the firm receives $1,300. The cash is available in five days on average. Calculate the disbursement float, the collection float and the net float. How do you interpret the answer?

Answers to self-test problems

13.1 · From the BAT model, the target cash balance is:

$$C^* = \sqrt{(2F \times T/R)}$$
$$C^* = \sqrt{[22(\$100)(\$240,000)/0.12]}$$
$$C^* = \sqrt{\$400,000,000}$$
$$= \$20,000$$

The average cash balance will be $C^*/2 = \$20,000/2 = \$10,000$. The opportunity cost of holding $10,000 when the going rate is 12 per cent is $10,000 × 0.12 = $1,200. There will be $240,000/20,000 = 12 orders during the year, so the order cost, or trading cost, is also 12 × $100 = $1,200. The total cost is thus $2,400.

If $15,000 is held, then the average balance is $7,500. Check that the opportunity, trading and total costs in this case are $900, $1,600, and $2,500, respectively. At $25,000, these numbers are $1,500, $960, and $2,460, respectively.

13.2 · The disbursement float is 10 days × $1,000 = $10,000. The collection float is 5 days × −$1,300 = −$6,500. The net float is $10,000 + (−$6,500) = $3,500. In other words, at any given time, the firm typically has uncashed cheques outstanding of $10,000. At the same time, it has uncollected receipts of $6,500. Thus, the firm's book balance is, typically, $3,500 less than its available balance, a positive $3,500 net float.

Questions and problems

1 · Changes in target cash balances

Indicate the likely impact of each of the following on a company's target cash balance. Use the letter *I* to denote an increase and *D* to denote a decrease. Briefly explain your reasoning in each case.

a   Interest rates paid on money market securities rise.
b   Commissions charged by brokers increase.
c   Because of a recession, payments received from customers become irregular.
d   The cost of borrowing decreases.
e   The systematic risk of the firm's debt has increased.
f   Fluctuations in the cash receipts of the firm reduce.

2 · Using the BAT model

Smart Shirts manages its cash using the BAT model. Given the following information, calculate the target cash balance using the BAT model:

Annual interest rate	8%
Fixed order cost	$5
Total cash needed	$2,880

How do you interpret your answer?

3 · Opportunity versus trading costs

The Delightful Dora Company Pty Ltd has an average daily cash balance of $1,000. Total cash needed for the year is $100,000. The interest rate is 8 per cent, and replenishing the cash costs $4 each time. What are: the opportunity cost of holding cash, the trading cost and the total cost? What do you think of Delightful Dora's strategy?

4 · Costs and the BAT model

The Muck Free Company Pty Ltd needs a total of $5,000 in cash during the year for transactions and other purposes. Whenever cash runs low, they sell off $1,000 in securities and transfer the cash. The interest rate is 16 per cent per year, and selling off securities costs $100 per sale.

a   What is the opportunity cost under the current policy? The trading cost? Without any further calculations, does Muck keep too much or too little in cash? Explain.
b   What is the target cash balance using the BAT model?

5 · Determining optimal cash balances

The Chance Casino Company Ltd is currently holding $800,000 in cash. It projects that over the next year its cash outflows will exceed its cash inflows by $345,000 per month. How much of this cash should be retained and how much should be used to increase the company's holdings of marketable securities? Each time these securities are bought or sold through a broker, the company pays a fee of $500. The annual interest rate on money market securities is 7 per cent. After the initial investment of excess cash, how many times during the next 12 months will securities be sold?

6 · Interpreting Miller–Orr

The Superhero Corporation Ltd uses a Miller–Orr cash management approach with a lower limit of $20,000, an upper limit of $110,000, and a target balance of $30,000. Explain what each of these points represents and then explain how the system will work.

7 · Using Miller–Orr

Yearin Pty Ltd has a fixed cost associated with buying and selling marketable securities of $100. The interest rate is currently 0.02 per cent per day, and Yearin has estimated that the standard deviation of its daily net cash flows is $90. Management has set a lower limit of $1,000 on cash holdings. Calculate the target cash balance and upper limit using the Miller–Orr model. Describe how the system will work.

8 · Interpretation of Miller–Orr

Based on the Miller–Orr model, describe what will happen to each of the lower limit, the upper limit, and the spread (the distance between the two) if the variation in net cash flow grows. Give an intuitive explanation for why this happens. What happens if the variance drops to zero?

9 · Miller–Orr

The variance of the daily net cash flows for the Smart Bargain Import Company Ltd is $1.44 million. The opportunity cost to the firm of holding cash is 8 per cent per year. What should be the target cash level and the upper limit, if the tolerable lower limit has been established as $20,000? The fixed cost of buying and selling securities is $600 per transaction.

10 · Float

Which would a firm prefer: a net collection float or a net disbursement float? Why?

11 · Disbursement of float

Suppose a firm has a book balance of $1.8 million. At the ATM (automatic teller machine), the cash manager finds out that the bank balance is $2.2 million. What is the situation here? If this is an ongoing situation, what ethical dilemma arises?

12 · Calculating float

In a typical month, the Imagine Entertainment Company Ltd receives 40 cheques totalling $60,000. These are delayed 4 days on average. What is the average daily float using a 30-day month?

13 · Calculating net float

Each business day, on average, Jellybean Company writes cheques totalling $24,000 to pay its suppliers. The usual clearing time for these cheques is 5 days. Meanwhile, the company is receiving payments from its customers each day, in the form of cheques, totalling $30,000. The cash from the payments is available to the firm after 3 days.

a   Calculate the company's disbursement float, collection float, and net float.
b   How would your answer to part (a) change if the collected funds were available in 4 days instead of 3?

14 · Float and weighted average delay

A retiree in Perth drives to the post office once a month and picks up two cheques, one for $10,000 and one for $4,000. The larger cheque takes four days to clear after it is deposited; the smaller one takes eight days.

a   What is the total float for the month, using a 30-day month?
b   What is the average daily float?
c   What are the average daily receipts and weighted average delay?

15 · Using BAT

The Apple Glen Company Pty Ltd has determined that its target cash balance using the BAT model is $707. The total cash needed for the year is $10,000, and the order cost is $2. What interest rate is Apple Glen using?

16 · Costs of float

Vulgar Ltd receives an average of $5,000 per day. The delay in clearing is typically 4 days. The current interest rate is 0.02 per cent per day.

a   What is Vulgar's float?
b   What is the total opportunity cost of the float?
c   What is the daily opportunity cost of the float?

17 · Using weighted average delay

A mail order firm processes 10,000 cheques per month. Of these, 20 per cent are for $30 and 80 per cent are for $60. The $30 cheques are delayed 2 days on average; the $60 cheques are delayed 4 days on average.

a   What is the average daily collection float? How do you interpret your answer?
b   What is the weighted average delay? Use the result to calculate the average daily float.
c   How much should the firm be willing to pay to eliminate the float?
d   If the interest rate is 8 per cent per year, calculate the daily cost of the float.
e   What would the firm pay to reduce the weighted average float by 2 days?

18 · Value of delay

The Mighty Company Ltd disburses cheques every 2 weeks that average $120,000 and take 3 days to clear. How much interest can the Mighty Company earn annually if it delays transfer of funds from an interest-bearing account that pays 0.04 per cent per day for these 3 days (ignoring compounding)?

19 · NPV of reducing float

The Genius Company Ltd has an agreement with a bank whereby the bank handles $4 million in collections a day and requires a $500,000 compensating balance. Genius is contemplating cancelling the agreement and dividing its eastern region so that two other banks will handle its business. Banks 1 and 2 will each handle $2 million a day of collections, and each requires a compensating balance of $300,000. Genius's financial management expects that collections will be accelerated by one day if the eastern region is divided. The government bond rate is 7 per cent. Should the Genius Company implement the new system? What will be the annual net savings?

20 · Miller–Orr, when to use variation

This is a challenge problem that will assist with questions 21 and 22. Students have been taught two versions of the Miller–Orr model. The first version did not involve the use of a bank overdraft whereas the second one did use a bank overdraft. A second difference was that one approach involved the transfer of funds to and from short-term marketable securities and the other looked at transfers to and from long-term investments. Explain when each model should be applied.

21 · Miller–Orr with cash, investments, loan standby

You have been appointed as financial manager to a firm that has been experiencing difficulty in managing its cash balances. The firm is in an industry in which there is a fairly high degree of variability in its daily cash requirements, and the previous financial manager experienced both days with large cash surpluses and days with large cash shortages. The firm has overcome the latter problem to some extent by arranging a standby bank loan facility of $200,000; however, even with this facility, it has been forced to defer payment of some of its accounts payable beyond the due date, in most instances with a loss of a cash discount.

It has been calculated that the standard deviation of daily cash flows is $100,000 and that the fixed costs of transferring funds either to or from marketable securities are $40 per transaction. Investments in marketable securities yield 11.57 per cent per annum or 0.03 per cent per day. The firm currently has $200,000 invested in marketable securities and its loan facility is 12 per cent per annum.

The general manager who has just appointed you as financial manager has had a quick read through a financial management text looking for some possible answers to the company's problems. He likes the look of the Miller–Orr cash management model and after reading about it has formulated the following list of direct and related questions which he requires you to answer, given previous information about the company. In addition, you have perused the company's cash budget for the forthcoming 2 weeks and have discovered the following:

Day	Expected surplus	Expected deficit
1		250,000
2		50,000
3		100,000
4	200,000	
5	100,000	
6		50,000
7	150,000	
8		100,000
9		50,000
10	300,000	

The current cash on hand is $100,000 and the bank loan balance is zero.

Part A

Treat the firm as if there are three separate cash pools—cash on hand, investments and bank loan standby. The firm uses its cash first, then liquidates its investments and reverts to the bank standby loan as a final measure.

a   Briefly explain the Miller–Orr model to the general manager.
b   Calculate the optimal cash balance that the firm should hold if it institutes the Miller–Orr model.
c   Calculate the upper and lower control limits for transferring surplus cash into marketable securities, and vice versa.
d   Calculate the firm's maximum cash balance and its average cash balance for transactions purposes.
e   i   Assuming that the actual surpluses and deficits are as expected, prepare a schedule to show the changes in the marketable securities, the cash balance and the bank standby loan.
    ii Assuming that the actual surpluses and deficits are as expected, plot the behaviour of daily cash balances over time, including transfers of cash to marketable securities, and vice versa, and any use of the bank standby loan. (Assume all transfers may be made instantaneously and the cost of transacting on a bank loan is zero.)

f   At the end of day 10, calculate the following balances:
    i   cash on hand
    ii   marketable securities
    iii bank loan
g   When the firm invests its surplus cash in marketable securities, which securities will it select, and why?

Part B

Assume the firm does not have any marketable securities as in Part A but has all its funds in long-term investments. The long-term investments yield 38.87 per cent per annum or 0.09 per cent per day. The cost of each act of investment or disinvestment is $500.

Calculate the upper, lower and target levels if the firm was to arrange a bank overdraft facility. Interest on the bank overdraft is 12 per cent per annum.

22 · Miller–Orr with a bank overdraft

You have been appointed as a financial manager to a firm that has been experiencing difficulty in managing its current assets. The firm is in an industry in which there is a fairly high degree of variability in daily cash requirements. It has been calculated that the standard deviation of daily cash flows is $10,000 and the fixed cost of each act of investment (buying) or disinvestment (selling) is $200. The yield on investments is 20.016 per cent per year or 0.05 per cent per day. You have been asked to negotiate a bank overdraft facility in order to overcome short-term cash shortages. The bank is quoting a rate of 14 per cent per year, or 0.036 per cent per day.

Currently the firm has $60,000 in investments and it has overdrawn its bank account by $50,000.

a   Calculate the upper, lower and target level that should be established for the bank overdraft.
b   Assume that the following net cash flows occur:

Day 1	Deficit	$100,000
Day 2	Surplus	$ 50,000
Day 3	Surplus	$ 50,000

Draw a diagram to show what will happen to the bank overdraft over these 3 days and show the level of the bank overdraft and investments on day 3.

23 · The BAT model

Given the following information, calculate the target cash balance using the BAT model.

Annual interest rate	12%
Fixed order cost	$100
Total cash needed	$240,000

a   What are the opportunity cost of holding cash, the trading cost and the total cost?
b   What would these be if $15,000 was the target cash balance?
c   What would these be if the target cash balance was $25,000?

24 · Credit policy

Cold and Cranky is considering a new credit policy. The current policy is cash only. The new policy would extend credit for one period. The interest rate per period is 2 per cent. Its product sells at $175 and costs $130 per unit. If sales were to increase from 1,000 to 1,100 per period, should Cold and Cranky adopt the new policy?

25 · Is the customer worth it?

You are deciding whether or not to extend credit to a particular customer. Your variable cost is $15 and the selling price $22 per unit. It is a one-time sale and the customer wants to buy 1,000 units and pay in 30 days. There is a 15 per cent chance he will default. If the required return for 30 days is 3 per cent, should you accept the order?

CHAPTER 14

Credit
management

Objective

It would seem to be an excellent principle that when someone owes us money we should collect it; but the collection of money owed to an organisation is not that simple. Accounts receivable represent the funds owed to an organisation for goods and services sold in the ordinary course of business. A key factor in this definition is 'the ordinary course of business'. It is a business decision to create accounts receivable and it is a business decision to determine how they will be collected. Allowing the creation of accounts receivable is an investment decision. A dollar invested in accounts receivable is a dollar that cannot be invested in other assets and, like other investments, the decision to invest a dollar in accounts receivable must earn a competitive return for the organisation. The function of this chapter is to explain the creation and management of accounts receivable.

Study tips ▷ We have returned to NPVs. Evaluation of credit policies in relation to accounts receivable reduce to simple problems in financial mathematics where NPVs have to be calculated. The relevant cash flows are positive and negative and the time periods are short, as days—not months or years—are involved. These variations may complicate the calculations a little, but remember: the evaluation is just a simple NPV calculation.

Introduction ▷ When a firm sells goods and services, it can demand cash on or before the delivery date or it can extend credit to customers and allow some delay in payment. This chapter provides an idea of what is involved in the firm's decision to grant credit to its customers. Granting credit is investing in a customer, an investment tied to the sale of a product or service.

Why do firms grant credit? Not all do, but the practice is extremely common. The obvious reason is that offering credit is a way of stimulating sales. The costs associated with granting credit are not trivial. First, there is the chance that the customer will not pay. Second, the firm has to bear the costs of carrying the receivables. The credit policy decision thus involves a trade-off between the benefits of increased sales versus the costs of granting credit. We examine this trade-off in the sections below.

 **14.1** Credit and receivables

From an accounting perspective, when credit is granted an account receivable is created. Receivables include credit to other firms, called *trade credit*, and credit granted to consumers, called *consumer credit*. A large proportion of the assets of all Australian industrial firms are in the form of accounts receivable, so receivables obviously represent a major investment of financial resources by Australian businesses.[1] Furthermore, trade credit is a very important source of financing for corporations.

However we look at it, receivables and receivables management are very important aspects of a firm's short-term financial policy.

Components of credit policy

If a firm decides to grant credit to its customers, then it must establish procedures for extending credit and collecting. In particular, the firm will have to deal with the following components of credit policy:

terms of sale

conditions on which a firm sells its goods and services for cash or credit

1 **Terms of sale**. The terms of sale establish how the firm proposes to sell its goods and services. A basic distinction is whether the firm will require cash or will extend credit. If the firm does grant credit to a customer, the terms of sale will specify (perhaps implicitly) the credit period, the cash discount and discount period, and the type of credit instrument.

credit analysis

the process of determining the probability that customers will or will not pay

2 **Credit analysis**. In granting credit, a firm determines how much effort to expend trying to distinguish between customers who will pay and customers who will not pay. Firms use a number of devices and procedures to determine the probability that customers will not pay and, put together, these are called credit analysis.

collection policy

procedures followed by a firm in collecting accounts receivable

3 **Collection policy**. After credit has been granted, the firm has the potential problem of collecting the cash when it becomes due, for which it must establish a collection policy.

In the next several sections, we will discuss these components of credit policy that collectively make up the decision to grant credit. In a previous chapter, we described the accounts receivable period as the time it takes to collect on a sale. There are several events that occur during that period. These are the cash flows associated with granting credit, and they can be illustrated with a cash flow diagram (Figure 14.1).

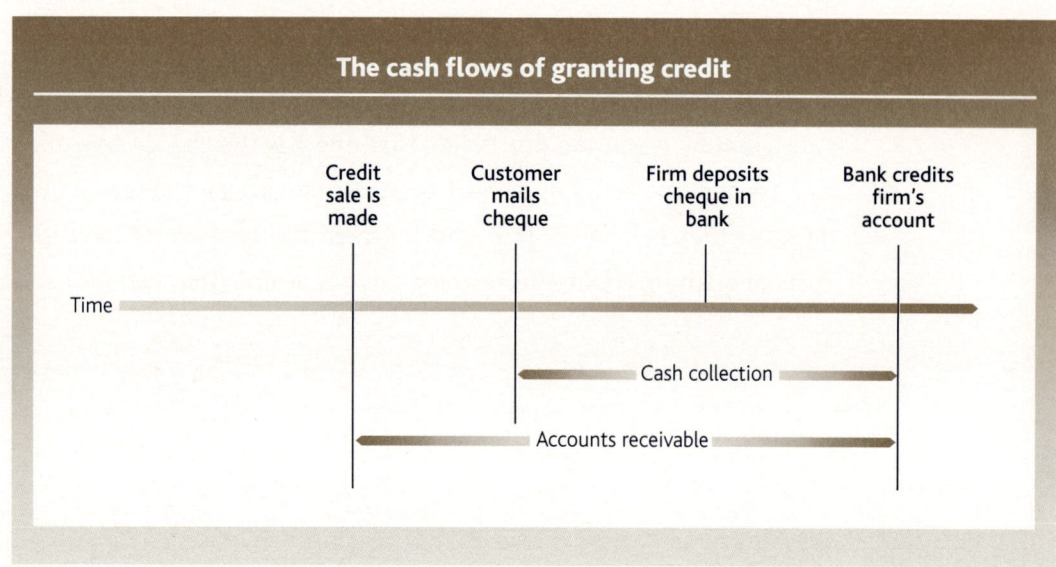

The cash flows of granting credit

The cash flows from granting credit

As our time line indicates, the typical sequence of events when a firm grants credit is (1) the credit sale is made, (2) the customer sends a cheque to the firm, (3) the firm deposits the cheque, and (4) the firm's account is credited for the amount of the cheque.

Note that many transactions also occur through the use of credit cards; however, the process of collection is similar to that of cheque payment. The firm deposits the credit card transaction slip just like a cheque, and the firm's account is credited.

Based on our discussion in the previous chapter, it is apparent that one of the factors influencing the receivables period is the float. Thus, one way to reduce the receivables period is to speed up the cheque mailing, processing and clearing. Because we covered this subject in the previous chapter, we will ignore the float in subsequent discussion and focus on what is likely to be the major determinant of the receivables period: credit policy.

The investment in receivables

The investment in accounts receivable for any firm depends on the amount of credit sales and the average collection period. For example, if a firm's average collection period (ACP) is 30 days, then at any given time there will be 30 days' worth of sales outstanding. If sales are $1,000 per day, the firm's accounts receivable will then be equal to 30 days × $1,000 per day = $30,000.

As our example illustrates, a firm's receivables will generally be equal to its average daily sales multiplied by its average collection period (ACP):

$$\text{Accounts receivable} = \text{Average daily sales} \times \text{ACP} \qquad (14.1)$$

Thus a firm's investment in accounts receivable depends on factors that influence credit sales and collections.

We have seen the average collection period in various places, including Chapter 3 and Chapter 12. Recall that we use the terms *days' sales in receivables*, *receivables period*, and *average collection period* interchangeably to refer to the length of time it takes for the firm to collect on a sale.

Concept questions

14.1a *What are the basic components of credit policy?*
14.1b *What are the basic components of the terms of sale if a firm chooses to sell on credit?*

 14.2 ■ Terms of the sale

As we described above, the terms of a sale are made up of three distinct elements:

1   the period for which credit is granted (the credit period);
2   the cash discount and the discount period;
3   the type of credit instrument.

Within a given industry, the terms of sale are usually fairly standard, but these terms vary quite a bit across industries. In many cases, the terms of sale are remarkably archaic and were established hundreds of years ago. Organised systems of trade credit that resemble current practice can be easily traced to the great fairs of medieval Europe, and they almost surely existed long before then. A twenty-first century variation is to offer 'a long credit-free period': for example, furniture and electrical retailers offer goods with no payment for twelve months.

The basic form

The easiest way to understand the terms of sale is to consider an example. For Hardware Supplies Ltd, terms of 2/10, net 60 are common. This means that customers have 60 days from the invoice date (discussed below) to pay the full amount. However, if payment is made within 10 days, a 2 per cent cash discount can be taken.

Consider a buyer who places an order for $1,000, and assume that the terms of the sale are 2/10, net 60. The buyer has the option of paying $1,000 × (1 − 0.02) = $980 in 10 days, or paying the full $1,000 in 60 days. If the terms were stated as just net 30, then the customer has 30 days from the invoice date to pay the entire $1,000, and no discount is offered for early payment.

In general, credit terms are quoted in the following form:

> Take *'this discount'* off the full invoice price if you pay in *'this many days'*, or else pay *'the full invoice amount'* in *'this many days'*.

Thus 5/10, net 45 means take a 5 per cent discount from the full price if you pay within 10 days, or else pay the full amount in 45 days.

The credit period

credit period

the length of time that credit is granted

The **credit period** is the basic length of time that credit is granted. The credit period varies widely from industry to industry, but it is almost always between 30 and 120 days. If a cash discount is offered, then the credit period has two components: the net credit period and the cash discount period.

The net credit period is the length of time the customer has to pay. The cash discount period, as the name suggests, is the time during which the discount is available. With 2/10, net 30, for example, the net credit period is 30 days and the cash discount period is 10 days.

The invoice date

invoice

bill for goods or services provided by the seller to the purchaser

The invoice date is the beginning of the credit period. An **invoice** is a written account of merchandise shipped to the buyer. For individual items, by convention, the invoice date is usually the shipping date or the billing date, not the date that the buyer receives the goods or the bill.

Many other arrangements exist. For example, the terms of sale might be ROG, for 'receipt of goods'. In this case, the credit starts when the customer receives the order. This might be used when the customer is in a remote location.

End-of-month (EOM) terms are fairly common. With EOM dating, all sales made during a particular month are assumed to be made at the end of that month. This is useful when a buyer makes purchases throughout the month, but the seller only bills once a month.

For example, terms of 2/10th EOM tell the buyer to take a 2 per cent discount if payment is made by the 10th of the month, otherwise the full amount is due after that. Confusingly, the end of the month is sometimes taken to be the 25th day of the month. MOM, for middle of month, is another variation.

Seasonal dating is sometimes used to encourage sales of seasonal products during the off-season. A product that is sold primarily in the summer (such as sunscreen) can be shipped in August with credit terms of 2/10, net 30. However, the invoice might be dated 1 December, so the credit period actually begins at that time. This practice encourages buyers to order early.

Length of the credit period

A number of factors influence the length of the credit period. One of the most important is the *buyer's* inventory period and operating cycle. All other things being equal, the shorter these are, the shorter the credit period will normally be.

Based on our discussion in Chapter 12, the operating cycle has two components: the inventory period and the receivables period. The inventory period is the time it takes the buyer to acquire inventory (from us), process it and sell it. The receivables period is the time it then takes the buyer to collect on the sale. Note that the credit period that we offer is effectively the buyer's payables period.

By extending credit, we finance a portion of our buyer's operating cycle and thereby shorten the buyer's cash cycle. If our credit period exceeds the buyer's inventory period, then we are not only financing the buyer's inventory purchases, but part of the buyer's receivables as well.

Furthermore, if our credit period exceeds our buyer's operating cycle, then we are effectively providing financing for aspects of our customer's business beyond the immediate purchase and sale of our merchandise. The reason is that the buyer effectively has a loan from us even after the merchandise is resold, and the buyer can use that credit for other purposes. For this reason, the length of the buyer's operating cycle is often cited as an appropriate upper limit to the credit period.

There are a number of other factors that influence the credit period. Many of these also influence our customers' operating cycles; so, once again, these are related subjects. Among the most important are:

1 *Perishability and collateral value*. Perishable items have relatively rapid turnover and relatively low collateral value. Credit periods are thus shorter for such goods. For example, a food wholesaler selling fresh fruit and produce might use net 7 terms. Alternatively, jewellery might be sold for 5/30, net 4 months.

2 *Consumer demand*. Products that are well established generally have more rapid turnover. Newer or slow-moving products will often have longer credit periods associated with them to entice buyers. Also, as we have seen, sellers may choose to extend much longer credit periods for off-season sales (when customer demand is low).

3 *Cost, profitability and standardisation*. Relatively inexpensive goods tend to have shorter credit periods. The same is true for relatively standardised goods and raw materials. These all tend to have lower markups and higher turnover rates, both of which lead to shorter credit periods. There are exceptions. Auto dealers, for example, generally pay for cars as they are received.

4 *Credit risk*. The greater the credit risk of the buyer, the shorter the credit period is likely to be (assuming that credit is granted at all).

5 *The size of the account*. If the account is small, the credit period will be shorter. Small accounts are more costly to manage, and the customers are less important.

6 *Competition*. When the seller is in a highly competitive market, longer credit periods may be offered as a way of attracting customers.

7 *Customer type*. A single seller might offer different credit terms to different buyers. A food wholesaler, for example, might supply groceries, bakeries, and restaurants. Each group would probably have different credit terms. More generally, sellers often have both wholesale and retail customers, and they frequently quote different terms to the two types.

Cash discounts

As we have seen, **cash discounts** are often part of the terms of sale. One reason discounts are offered is to speed up the collection of receivables. This will have the effect of reducing the amount of credit being offered, and the firm must trade this off against the cost of the discount.

Notice that when a cash discount is offered, the credit is essentially free during the discount period. The buyer only pays for the credit after the discount expires. With 2/10, net 30, a rational buyer either pays in 10 days to make the greatest possible use of the free credit or pays in 30 days to get the longest possible use of the money in exchange for giving up the discount. So, by giving up the discount, the buyer effectively gets $30 - 10 = 20$ days' credit.

Another reason for cash discounts is that they are a way of charging higher prices to customers that have had credit extended to them. In this sense, cash discounts are a convenient way of separately pricing the credit granted to customers.

Cost of the credit

In our examples, it might seem that the discounts are rather small. With 2/10, net 30, for example, early payment only gets the buyer a 2 per cent discount. Does this provide a significant incentive for early payment? The answer is yes, because the implicit interest rate is extremely high.

To see why the discount is important, we will calculate the cost to the buyer of not paying early. To do this, we will find the interest rate that the buyer is effectively paying for the trade credit. Suppose the order is for $1,000. The buyer can pay $980 in 10 days or wait another 20 days and pay $1,000. It is obvious that the buyer is effectively borrowing $980 for 20 days and that the buyer pays $20 in interest on the 'loan'. What is the interest rate?

This interest is simple interest, which we discussed in Chapter 5. With $20 in interest on $980 borrowed, the rate is $20/$980 = 2.0408\%$. This is relatively low, but remember that this is the rate per 20-day period. There are $365/20 = 18.25$ such periods in a year, so the buyer is paying an effective annual rate (EAR) of:

$$EAR = (1.020408)^{18.25} - 1 = 44.6\% \text{—using a compound interest calculation.}$$

From the buyer's point of view, this is an expensive source of financing.

Given that the interest rate is so high here, it is unlikely that the seller benefits from early payment. Ignoring the possibility of default by the buyer, the decision by a customer to forego the discount almost surely works to the seller's advantage.

EXAMPLE 14.1 ▪ What is the rate?

Ordinary tiles are often sold 3/30, net 60. What effective annual rate does a buyer pay by not taking the discount? What would the NIR (nominal interest rate) be if one were quoted?

Here we have 3 per cent discount interest on $60 - 30 = 30$ days' credit. The rate per 30 days is $0.03/0.97 = 3.093\%$. There are $365/30 = 12.17$ such periods in a year, so the effective annual rate is:

$$EAR = (1.03093)^{12.17} - 1 = 44.9\%$$

The NIR, as always, would be calculated by multiplying the rate per period by the number of periods:

$$NIR = 0.03093 \times 12.17 = 37.6\%$$

An interest rate calculated like this NIR is often quoted as the cost of the trade credit and, as this example illustrates, the true cost can be seriously understated.

Trade discounts

In some circumstances, the discount is not really an incentive for early payment and is instead a *trade discount*, a discount routinely given to some type of buyer. For example, a hardware store may offer to builders a 10 per cent discount. The builders purchase the goods more cheaply than you or I can, probably reflecting the fact that builders purchase a greater volume of goods. The trade discount is really a volume discount.

The cash discount and the ACP

To the extent that a cash discount encourages customers to pay early, it will shorten the receivables period and, all other things being equal, reduce the firm's investment in receivables.

For example, suppose a firm currently has terms of net 30 and an ACP of 30 days. If it offers terms of 2/10, net 30, then perhaps 50 per cent of its customers (in terms of volume of purchases) will pay in 10 days. The remaining customers will still take an average of 30 days to pay. What will the new average collection period (ACP) be? If the firm's annual sales are $15 million (before discounts), what will happen to the investment in receivables?

If half of the customers take 10 days to pay and half take 30, then the new average collection period will be:

$$\text{New ACP} = 0.50 \times 10 \text{ days} + 0.50 \times 30 \text{ days} = 20 \text{ days}$$

The ACP thus falls from 30 days to 20 days. Average daily sales are $15 million/365 = $41,096 per day. Receivables will thus fall by $41,096 \times 10 = $410,960.

Credit instruments

The **credit instrument** is the basic evidence of indebtedness. Most trade credit is offered on *open account*. This means that the only formal instrument of credit is the invoice, which is sent with the shipment of goods and which the customer signs as evidence that the goods have been received. Afterwards, the firm and its customers record the exchange on their books of account.

credit instrument
the evidence of indebtedness

At times, the firm may require that the customer sign a *promissory note*. This is a basic IOU and might be used when the order is large, when there is no cash discount involved, and when the firm anticipates a problem in collections. Promissory notes are not common, but they can eliminate the controversies later about the existence of debt.

One problem with promissory notes is that they are signed after delivery of the goods. One way to obtain a credit commitment from a customer before the goods are delivered is to arrange a *commercial draft*. Typically, the firm draws up a commercial draft calling for the customer to pay a specific amount by a specified date. The draft is then sent to the customer's bank with the shipping invoices.

If immediate payment on the draft is required, it is called a *sight draft*. If immediate payment is not required, then the draft is a *time draft*. When the draft is presented and the buyer 'accepts' it, meaning that the buyer promises to pay it in the future, then it is called a *trade acceptance* and is sent back to the selling firm. The seller can then keep the acceptance or sell it to someone else. If a bank accepts the draft, meaning that the bank is guaranteeing payment, then the draft becomes a *banker's acceptance*. This arrangement is common in international trade, and banker's acceptances are actively traded in the money market.

A firm can also use a conditional sales contract as a credit instrument. This is an arrangement where the firm retains legal ownership of the goods until the customer has completed payment. Conditional sales contracts usually are paid in instalments and have an interest cost built into them.

Concept questions

14.2a *What considerations enter into the determination of the terms of sale?*
14.2b *Explain what terms of '3/45, net 90' mean. What is the implicit interest rate?*

14.3 Analysing credit policy

In this section, we take a closer look at the factors that influence the decision to grant credit. Granting credit only makes sense if the NPV from doing so is positive. We thus need to look at the NPV of the decision to grant credit.

Credit policy effects

In evaluating credit policy, there will be five basic factors to consider:

1 *Revenue effects.* If the firm grants credit, then there will be a delay in revenue collections as some customers take advantage of the credit offered and pay later. However, the firm may be able to charge a higher price if it grants credit and it may be able to increase the quantity sold. Total revenues may thus increase.
2 *Cost effects.* Although the firm may experience delayed revenues if it grants credit, it will still incur the costs of sales immediately. Whether or not the firm sells for cash or credit, it will still have to acquire or produce the merchandise (and pay for it).
3 *The cost of debt.* When the firm grants credit, it must arrange to finance the resulting receivables. As a result, the firm's cost of short-term borrowing is a factor in the decision to grant credit.[2]
4 *The probability of non-payment.* If the firm grants credit, some percentage of the credit buyers will not pay. This cannot happen, of course, if the firm sells for cash.
5 *The cash discount.* When the firm offers a cash discount as part of its credit terms, some customers will choose to pay early to take advantage of the discount.

Evaluating a proposed credit policy

To illustrate how credit policy can be analysed, we will start with a relatively simple case. Simple Software has been in existence for two years, and it is one of several successful firms that develop computer programs. Currently, Simple sells for cash only.

Simple is evaluating a request from some major customers to change its current policy to net one month (30 days). To analyse this proposal, we define the following:

P = price per unit
v = variable cost per unit
Q = current quantity sold per month
Q' = quantity sold under new policy
R = monthly required return

For now, we ignore discounts and the possibility of default. Also, we ignore taxes because they do not affect our conclusions.

NPV of switching policies

To illustrate the NPV of switching credit policies, suppose we had the following for Simple:

$$P = \$49$$
$$v = \$20$$
$$Q = 100$$
$$Q' = 110$$

If the required return is 2 per cent per month, should Simple make the switch?

Currently, Simple has monthly sales of $P \times Q = \$4,900$. Variable costs each month are $v \times Q = \$2,000$, so the monthly cash flow from this activity is:

$$\text{Cash flow (old policy)} = (P - v)Q \qquad (14.2)$$
$$= (\$49 - 20) \times 100$$
$$= \$2,900$$

This is not the total cash flow for Simple, of course, but it is all that we need to look at because fixed costs and other components of cash flow are the same whether or not the switch is made.

If Simple does switch to net 30 days on sales, then the quantity sold will rise to $Q' = 110$. Monthly revenues will increase to $P \times Q'$, and costs will be $v \times Q'$. The monthly cash flow under the new policy will thus be:

$$\text{Cash flow (new policy)} = (P - v)Q' \qquad (14.3)$$
$$= (\$49 - 20) \times 110$$
$$= \$3,190$$

Going back to Chapter 8, the relevant incremental cash flow is the difference between the new and old cash flows:

$$\text{Incremental cash inflow} = (P - v)(Q' - Q)$$
$$= (\$49 - 20) \times (110 - 100)$$
$$= \$290$$

This says that the benefit each month of changing policies is equal to the contribution margin per unit sold, $(P - v) = \$29$, multiplied by the increase in sales, $(Q' - Q) = 10$. The present value of the future incremental cash flows is thus:

$$PV = [(P - v)(Q' - Q)]/R \qquad (14.4)$$

For Simple, this present value works out to be:

$$PV = (\$29 \times 10)/0.02 = \$14,500$$

Notice that we have treated the monthly cash flow as a perpetuity since the same benefit will be realised each month forever.

Now that we know the benefit of switching, what is the cost? There are two components to consider. First, since the quantity sold will rise from Q to Q', Simple will have to produce $Q' - Q$ more units today at a cost of $v(Q' - Q) = \$20 \times (110 - 100) = \$200$. Second, the sales that would have been collected this month under the current policy $(P \times Q = \$4,900)$ will not be collected. This happens because the sales made this month will not be collected until 30 days later under the new policy. The cost of the switch is the sum of these two components:

$$\text{Cost of switching} = PQ + v(Q' - Q) \qquad (14.5)$$

For Simple, this cost would be $4,900 + 200 = $5,100.

Putting it all together, the NPV of the switch is:

$$\text{NPV of switching} = -[PQ + v(Q' - Q)] + (P - v)(Q' - Q)/R \qquad (14.6)$$

For Simple, the cost of switching is $5,100. As we saw above, the benefit is $290 per month, forever. At 2 per cent per month, the NPV is:

$$
\begin{aligned}
\text{NPV} &= -\$5,100 + \$290/0.02 \\
&= -\$5,100 + 14,500 \\
&= \$9,400
\end{aligned}
$$

Therefore, the switch is very profitable.

EXAMPLE 14.2 · We'd rather fight than switch

Suppose that a company is considering a switch from all cash to net 30, but the quantity sold is not expected to change. What is the NPV of the switch? Explain.

In this case, $Q' - Q$ is zero, so the NPV is just $-P \times Q$. What this says is that the effect of the switch is simply to postpone one month's collections forever, with no benefit from doing so.

A break-even application

Based on our discussion thus far, the key variable for Simple is $Q' - Q$, the increase in unit sales. The projected increase of 10 units is only an estimate, so there is some forecasting risk. Under the circumstances, it is natural to wonder what increase in unit sales is necessary to break even.

Earlier, the NPV of the switch was defined as:

$$\text{NPV} = -[PQ + v(Q' - Q)] + (P - v)(Q' - Q)/R$$

We can calculate the break-even point explicitly by setting the NPV equal to zero and solving for $(Q' - Q)$:

$$
\begin{aligned}
\text{NPV} = 0 &= -[PQ + v(Q' - Q)] + (P - v)(Q' - Q)/R \\
Q' - Q &= (PQ)/[(P - v)/R - v] \qquad (14.7)
\end{aligned}
$$

For Simple, the break-even sales increase is thus:

$$
\begin{aligned}
Q' - Q &= \$4,900/[\$29/0.02 - \$20] \\
&= 3.43 \text{ units}
\end{aligned}
$$

This tells us that the switch is a good idea as long as we are confident that we can sell at least 3.43 more units.

Concept questions

14.3a *What are the important effects to consider in a decision to offer credit?*

14.3b *Explain how to estimate the NPV of a credit policy switch.*

PART 6 · CURRENT INVESTMENT DECISIONS

14.4 ■ More on credit policy analysis

This section takes a closer look at credit policy analysis by investigating some alternative approaches and by examining the effect of cash discounts and the possibility of non-payment.

Two alternative approaches

Now that we know how to analyse the NPV of a proposed credit policy switch, we discuss two alternative approaches: the 'one-shot' approach and the accounts receivable approach. These are very common means of analysis; our goal is to show that these two and our NPV approach are all the same. Afterwards, we will use whichever of the three is most convenient.

The one-shot approach

If the switch is not made, Simple will have a net cash flow this month of $(P - v)Q = \$29 \times 100 = \$2,900$. If the switch is made, Simple will invest $vQ' = \$20 \times 110 = \$2,200$ this month and will receive $PQ' = \$49 \times 110 = \$5,390$ next month. Suppose we ignore all other months and cash flows and view this as a one-shot investment. Is Simple better off with $2,900 in cash this month, or should Simple invest the $2,200 to get $5,390 next month?

The present value of the $5,390 to be received next month is $5,390/1.02 = $5,284.31; the cost is $2,200, so the net benefit is $5,284.31 − 2,200 = $3,084.31. If we compare this to the net cash flow of $2,900 under the current policy, then Simple should switch. The NPV is $3,084.31 − 2,900 = $184.31.

In effect, Simple can repeat this one-shot investment every month and thereby generate an NPV of $184.31 every month (including the current one). The PV of this series of NPVs is:

$$\text{Present value} = \$184.31 + \$184.31/0.02 = \$9,400$$

This PV is the same as our previous answer.

The accounts receivable approach

Our second approach is the one that is most commonly discussed and is very useful. By extending credit, the firm increases its cash flow through increased gross profits. However, the firm must increase its investment in receivables and bear the carrying cost of doing so. The accounts receivable approach focuses on the expense of the incremental investment in receivables compared to the increased gross profit.

As we have seen, the monthly benefit from extending credit is given by the contribution margin per unit $(P - v)$ multiplied by the increase in quantity sold $(Q' - Q)$. For Simple, this benefit was ($49 − 20) × (110 − 100) = $290 per month.

If Simple makes the switch, then receivables will rise from zero (since there are no credit sales) to PQ', so Simple must invest in receivables. The necessary investment has two components. The first part is what Simple would have collected under the old policy (PQ). Simple must carry this amount in receivables each month because collections are delayed by 30 days.

The second part is related to the increase in receivables that results from the increase in sales. Since unit sales increase from Q to Q', Simple must produce this quantity today even though it will not collect for 30 days. The actual cost to Simple of producing the extra quantity is equal to v per unit, so the investment necessary to provide the extra quantity sold is $v(Q' - Q)$.

In sum, if Simple switches, its investment in receivables is equal to the $P \times Q$ in revenues that are given up plus an additional $v(Q' - Q)$ in production costs:

Incremental investment in receivables $= PQ + v(Q' - Q)$

The required return on this investment (the carrying cost of the receivables) is R per month; so, for Simple, the accounts receivable carrying cost is:

$$\begin{aligned}
\text{Carrying cost} &= [PQ + v(Q' - Q)] \times R \\
&= [\$4,900 + 200] \times 0.02 \\
&= \$102 \text{ per month}
\end{aligned}$$

Since the monthly benefit is $290 and the cost per month is only $102, the net benefit per month is $290 − 102 = $188 per month. Simple earns this $188 every month, so the PV of the switch is:

$$\begin{aligned}
\text{Present value} &= \$188/0.02 \\
&= \$9,400
\end{aligned}$$

Again, this is the same figure we previously calculated.

One of the advantages of looking at the accounts receivable approach is that it helps us interpret our earlier NPV calculation. As we have seen, the investment in receivables necessary to make the switch is $PQ + v(Q' - Q)$. If you take a look back at our original NPV calculation, this is precisely what we had as the cost to Simple of making the switch. Our earlier NPV calculation thus amounts to a comparison of the incremental investment in receivables to the PV of the increased future cash flows.

There is one final thing to notice. The increase in accounts receivable is PQ', and this amount corresponds to the amount of receivables shown on the balance sheet. However, the incremental investment in receivables is $PQ + v(Q' - Q)$. It is straightforward to verify that this second quantity is smaller by $(P - v)(Q' - Q)$. This difference is the contribution of the new sales, which Simple does not actually have to put up in order to switch credit policies.

Put another way, whenever we extend credit to a new customer who would not otherwise pay cash, all we risk is our cost, not the full sales price. We will discuss this point in greater detail below.

 EXAMPLE 14.3 ■ **Extra credit**

Looking back at Simple Software, determine the NPV of the switch if the quantity sold is projected to increase by only five units instead of 10. What will be the investment in receivables? What is the carrying cost? What is the monthly net benefit from switching?

If the switch is made, Simple gives up $P \times Q$ = $4,900 today. An extra five units have to be produced at a cost of $20 each, so the cost of switching is $4,900 + 5 × $20 = $5,000. The benefit of selling the extra five units each month is 5 × ($49 − 20) = $145. The NPV of the switch is −$5,000 + $145/0.02 = $2,250, so it is still profitable.

The $5,000 cost of switching can be interpreted as the investment in receivables. At 2 per cent per month, the carrying cost is 0.02 × $5,000 = $100. Since the benefit each month is $145, the net benefit from switching is $45 per month ($145 − $100). Notice that the PV of $45 per month forever at 2 per cent is $45/0.02 = $2,250 as we calculated.

Discounts and default risk

We now take a look at cash discounts, default risk and the relationship between the two. To get started, we define the following:

π = percentage of credit sales that go uncollected
d = percentage discount allowed for cash customers
P' = credit price (the no-discount price)

Notice that the cash price (P) is equal to the credit price (P') multiplied by $(1 - d)$: $P = P'(1 - d)$ or, equivalently, $P' = P/(1 - d)$.

The situation at Simple is now a little bit more complicated. If a switch is made from the current policy of no credit, then the benefit of the switch will come from both the higher price (P') and, potentially, the increased quantity sold (Q').

Furthermore, in our previous case, it was reasonable to assume that all customers took the credit since it was free. Now, not all customers will take the credit because a discount is offered. In addition, of the customers who do take the credit offered, a certain percentage (π) will not pay.

To simplify the discussion below, we will assume that the quantity sold (Q) is not affected by the switch. This assumption is not crucial, but it does cut down on the work (see problem 25 at the end of the chapter). We will also assume that all customers take the credit terms. This assumption also is not crucial. It actually does not matter what percentage of our customers take the offered credit.[3]

NPV of the credit decision

Currently, Simple sells Q units at a price of $P = \$49$. Simple is considering a new policy that involves 30 days' credit and an increase in price to $P' = \$50$ on credit sales. The cash price will remain at \$49, so Simple is effectively allowing a discount of $(\$50 - \$49)/\$50 = 2\%$ for cash.

What is the NPV to Simple of extending credit? To answer, note that Simple is already receiving $(P - v)Q$ every month. With the new, higher price, this will rise to $(P' - v)Q$ assuming that everybody pays. However, since a percentage of sales will not be collected, Simple will only collect on $(1 - \pi) \times P'Q$; so net receipts will be $[(1 - \pi)P' - v] \times Q$.

The net effect of the switch for Simple is thus the difference between the cash flows under the new policy and the old policy:

$$\text{Net incremental cash flow} = [(1 - \pi)P' - v] \times Q - (P - v) \times Q$$

Since $P = P' \times (1 - d)$, this simplifies to:[4]

$$\textbf{Net incremental cash flow} = P'Q \times (d - \pi) \tag{14.8}$$

If Simple does make the switch, then the cost in terms of the investment in receivables is just $P \times Q$ since $Q = Q'$. The NPV of the switch is thus:

$$\textbf{NPV} = -PQ + P'Q \times (d - \pi)/R \tag{14.9}$$

For example, suppose that, based on industry experience, the percentage of 'deadbeats' (π) will be 1 per cent. What is the NPV of changing credit terms for Simple? We can plug in the relevant numbers as follows:

$$
\begin{aligned}
\text{NPV} &= -PQ + P'Q \times (d - \pi)/R \\
&= -\$49 \times 100 + \$50 \times 100 \times (0.02 - 0.01)/0.02 \\
&= -\$2{,}400
\end{aligned}
$$

Since the NPV of the change is negative, Simple should not switch.

In our expression for NPV, the key elements are the cash discount percentage (d) and the default rate (π). One thing we see immediately is that, if the percentage of sales that goes uncollected exceeds the discount percentage, then $d - \pi$ is negative. Obviously, the NPV of the switch would then be negative as well. More generally, our result tells us that the decision to grant credit here is a trade-off between getting a higher price, thereby increasing sales, versus not collecting on some fraction of those sales.

With this in mind, $P'Q \times (d - \pi)$ is the increase in sales less the portion of that increase that will not be collected. This increase is the incremental cash inflow from the switch in credit policy. If d is 5 per cent and π is 2 per cent, for example, then, loosely speaking, revenues are increasing by 5 per cent because of the higher price, but collections only rise by 3 per cent since the default rate is 2 per cent. Unless $d > \pi$, we will actually have a decrease in cash inflows from the switch.

A break-even application

Since the discount percentage (d) is controlled by the firm, the key unknown in this case is the default rate (π). What is the break-even default rate for Simple Software?

We can answer by finding the default rate that makes the NPV equal to zero.

$$NPV = 0 = -PQ + P'Q \times (d - \pi)/R$$

Rearranging things a bit:

$$PR = P'(d - \pi), \text{ substitute } P = P'(1 - d) \text{ to give}$$
$$\pi = d - R \times (1 - d)$$

For Simple, the break-even default rate works out to be:

$$\begin{aligned} \pi &= 0.02 - 0.02 \times (0.98) \\ &= 0.0004 \\ &= 0.04\% \end{aligned}$$

This is quite small because the implicit interest rate Simple will be charging its credit customers (2% discount interest per month, or about $0.02/0.98 = 2.0408\%$) is only slightly greater than the required return of 2 per cent per month. As a result, there is not much room for defaults if the switch is going to make sense.

Concept questions

14.4a *What is the incremental investment that a firm must make in receivables if credit is extended?*

14.4b *Describe the trade-off between the default rate and the cash discount.*

14.5 Optimal credit policy

So far, we have discussed how to compute net present values for a switch in credit policy. We have not discussed the optimal amount of credit or the optimal credit policy. In principle, the optimal amount of credit is determined where the incremental cash flows from increased sales are exactly equal to the incremental costs of carrying the increase in investment in accounts receivable.

The total credit cost curve

The trade-off between granting credit and not granting credit is not hard to identify, but it is difficult to quantify precisely. As a result, we can only describe an optimal credit policy.

To begin, the carrying costs associated with granting credit come in three forms:

1 the required return on receivables;
2 the losses from bad debts;
3 the costs of managing credit and credit collections.

We have already discussed the first and second of these. The third cost, the costs of managing credit, is the expenses associated with running the credit department. Firms that do not grant credit have no such department and no such expense. These three costs will all increase as credit policy is relaxed.

If a firm has a very restrictive credit policy, then all of the above costs will be low. In this case, the firm will have a 'shortage' of credit, so there will be an opportunity cost. This opportunity cost is the extra potential profit from credit sales that is lost because credit is refused. This foregone benefit comes from two sources, the increase in quantity sold, Q' versus Q, and the higher price, P' versus P. These costs go down as credit policy is relaxed.

The sum of the carrying costs and the opportunity costs of a particular credit policy is called the total **credit cost curve**. We have drawn such a curve in Figure 14.2. As Figure 14.2 illustrates, there is a point where the total credit cost is minimised. This point corresponds to the optimal amount of credit or, equivalently, the optimal investment in receivables.

If the firm extends more credit than this minimum, the additional net cash flow from new customers will not cover the carrying costs of the investment in receivables. If the level of receivables is below this amount, then the firm is foregoing valuable profit opportunities.

In general, the costs and benefits from extending credit will depend on characteristics of particular firms and industries. All other things being equal, for example, it is likely that

credit cost curve graphical representation of the sum of the carrying costs and the opportunity costs of a credit policy

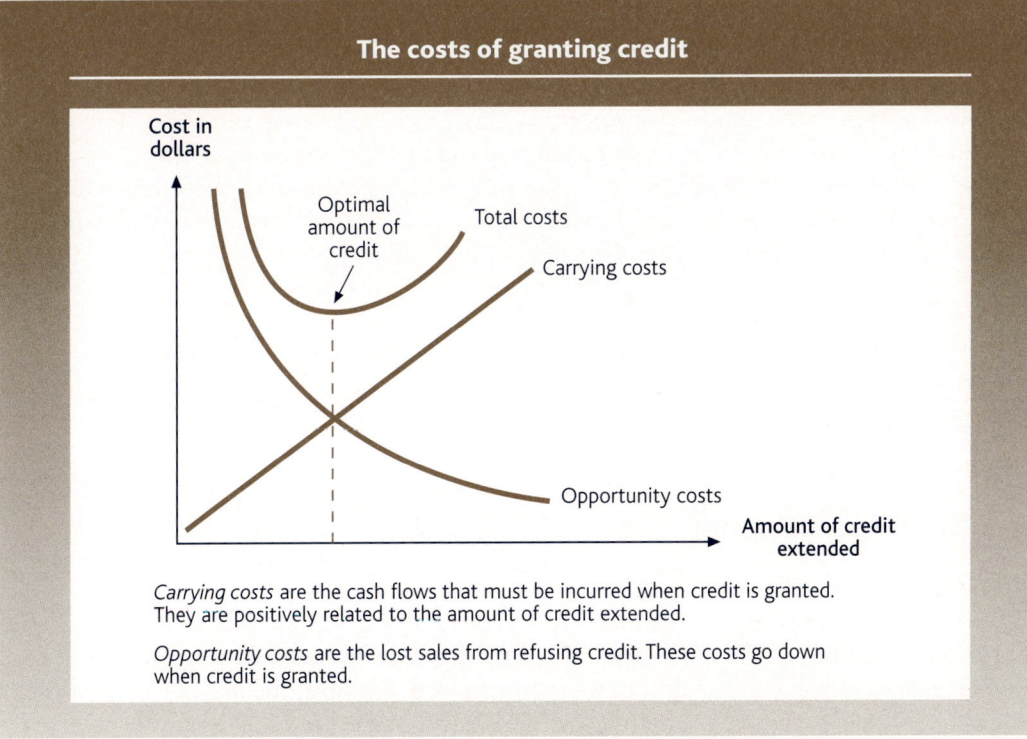

The costs of granting credit

FIGURE 14.2

Carrying costs are the cash flows that must be incurred when credit is granted. They are positively related to the amount of credit extended.

Opportunity costs are the lost sales from refusing credit. These costs go down when credit is granted.

firms with (1) excess capacity, (2) low variable operating costs, and (3) repeat customers will extend credit more liberally than otherwise. See if you can explain why each of these contributes to a more liberal credit policy.

Concept questions

14.5a *What are the carrying costs of granting credit?*

14.5b *What are the opportunity costs of not granting credit?*

 # Credit analysis

Thus far, we have focused on establishing credit terms. Once a firm decides to grant credit to its customers, it must then establish guidelines for determining who will and who will not be allowed to buy on credit. Credit analysis refers to the process of deciding whether or not to extend credit to a particular customer. It usually involves two steps: gathering relevant information and determining creditworthiness.

When should credit be granted?

Imagine that a firm is trying to decide whether or not to grant credit to a customer. This decision can get complicated. For example, the answer depends on what will happen if credit is refused. Will the customer simply pay cash or will the customer not make the purchase at all? To avoid this and other difficulties, we will use some special cases to illustrate the key points.

A one-time sale

We start by considering the simplest case. A new customer wishes to buy one unit on credit at a price of P' per unit. If credit is refused, then the customer will not make a purchase.

Furthermore, we assume that, if credit is granted, then, in one month, the customer will either pay up or default. The probability of the second of these events is π. In this case, the probability (π) can be interpreted as the percentage of new customers who will not pay. Our business does not have repeat customers, so this is strictly a one-time sale. Finally, the required return on receivables is R per month and the variable cost is v per unit.

The analysis here is straightforward. If the firm refuses credit, then the incremental cash flow is zero. If it grants credit, then it spends v (the variable cost) this month and expects to collect $(1 - \pi)P'$ next month. The NPV of granting credit is:

$$\text{NPV} = -v + (1 - \pi)P'/(1 + R) \tag{14.10}$$

For example, for Simple Software, this NPV is:

$$\text{NPV} = -\$20 + (1 - \pi) \times \$50/(1.02)$$

With, say, a 20 per cent rate of default, this works out to be:

$$\text{NPV} = -\$20 + 0.80 \times \$50/1.02 = \$19.22$$

Therefore, credit should be granted.

Our example illustrates an important point. In granting credit to a new customer, a firm risks its variable cost (v). It stands to gain the full price (P'). For a new customer, then, credit may be granted even if the default probability is high. For example, the break-even probability in this case can be determined by setting the NPV equal to zero and solving for π:

$$\text{NPV} \quad = 0 = -\$20 + (1 - \pi) \times \$50/(1.02)$$
$$(1 - \pi) = \$20/\$50 \times 1.02$$
$$\pi \quad\quad = 59.2\%$$

Simple should extend credit as long as there is at least a $1 - 0.592 = 40.8\%$ chance or better of collecting. This explains why firms with higher markups will tend to have looser credit terms.

This percentage (59.2%) is much higher than the break-even percentage we calculated earlier, because the earlier percentage was calculated assuming that $Q = Q'$, implying that there are no new customers. The percentage calculated here applies to a potential new customer only.

The important difference is that, if we extend credit to an old customer, then we risk the total sales price (P), since this is what we collect if we did not extend credit. If we extend credit to a new customer, we only risk our variable cost.

Repeat business

A second, very important factor to keep in mind is the possibility of repeat business. We can illustrate this by extending our one-time example. We make one important assumption: a new customer who does not default the first time around will remain a customer forever and never default. If the firm grants credit, it spends v this month. Next month, it either gets nothing if the customer defaults or it gets P' if the customer pays. If the customer does pay, then she will buy another unit on credit and the firm will spend v again. The net cash inflow for the month is thus $P' - v$. In every subsequent month, this same $P' - v$ will occur as the customer pays for the previous month's order and places a new one.

It follows from our discussion that, in one month, the firm will have \$0 with probability π. With probability $(1 - \pi)$, however, the firm will have a new customer. The value of a new customer is equal to present value of $(P' - v)$ every month forever:

$$\text{PV} = (P' - v)/R$$

The NPV of extending credit is therefore:

$$\textbf{NPV} = -v + (1 - \pi)(P' - v)/R \tag{14.11}$$

For Simple, this is:

$$\text{NPV} = -\$20 + (1 - \pi) \times (\$50 - \$20)/0.02$$
$$= -\$20 + (1 - \pi) \times \$1{,}500$$

Even if the probability of default is 90 per cent, the NPV is:

$$\text{NPV} = -\$20 + 0.10 \times \$1{,}500 = \$130$$

Simple should extend credit unless default is a virtual certainty. The reason is that it only costs \$20 to find out who is a good customer and who is not. A good customer is worth \$1,500, however, so Simple can afford quite a few defaults.

Our repeat business example probably exaggerates the acceptable default probability, but it does illustrate that it will often turn out that the best way to do credit analysis is simply to extend credit to almost anyone. It also points out that the possibility of repeat business is a crucial consideration. In such cases, the important thing is to control the amount of credit initially offered so that the possible loss is limited. The amount can be increased with time. Most often, the best predictor of whether or not someone will pay in the future is whether or not they have paid in the past.

Credit information

If a firm does want credit information on customers, there are a number of sources. Information commonly used to assess creditworthiness includes the following:

1 *Financial statements*. A firm can ask a customer to supply financial statement information such as the statement of financial position and the statement of financial performance. Minimum standards and rules of thumb based on financial ratios like the ones we discussed in Chapter 3 can then be used as a basis for extending or refusing credit.

2 *Credit reports on customer's payment history with other firms*. Quite a few organisations sell information on the credit strength and credit history of business firms. The best known and largest firm of this type is D&B (previously known as Dun & Bradstreet), which provides subscribers with a credit reference book and credit reports on individual firms. Ratings and information are available for a huge number of firms, including very small ones.

3 *Banks*. Banks will generally provide some assistance to their business customers in acquiring information on the creditworthiness of other firms.

4 *The customer's payment history with the firm*. The most obvious way to obtain information about the likelihood of a customer not paying is to examine whether they have paid up in the past and how much trouble collecting from them turned out to be.

Credit evaluation and scoring

five Cs of credit
the five basic credit factors to be evaluated: character, capacity, capital, collateral and conditions

There are no magical formulas for assessing the probability that a customer will not pay. In very general terms, the classic **five Cs of credit** are the basic factors to be evaluated:

1 *Character*. The customer's willingness to meet credit obligations.
2 *Capacity*. The customer's ability to meet credit obligations out of operating cash flows.
3 *Capital*. The customer's financial reserves.
4 *Collateral*. A pledged asset in the case of default.
5 *Conditions*. General economic conditions in the customer's line of business.

credit scoring
the process of quantifying the probability of default when granting consumer credit

Credit scoring refers to the process of calculating a numerical rating for a customer based on information collected and then granting or refusing credit based on the result. For example, a firm might rate a customer on a scale of 1 (very poor) to 10 (very good) on each of the five Cs of credit using all the information available about the customer. A credit score could then be calculated based on the total. From experience, a firm might choose to grant credit only to customers with a score above, say, 30.

Firms such as credit card issuers have developed elaborate statistical models for credit scoring. Usually, all of the legally relevant and observable characteristics of a large pool of customers are studied to find their historic relation to default rates. Based on the results, it is possible to determine the variables that best predict whether or not a customer will pay and then calculate a credit score based on those variables.

Because credit-scoring models and procedures determine who is and who is not creditworthy, it is not surprising that they have been the subject of government regulation. In particular, the kinds of background and demographic information that can be used in the credit decision are limited.

Concept questions

14.6a *What is credit analysis?*
14.6b *What are the five Cs of credit?*

14.7 ■ Collection policy

Collection policy is the final element in credit policy. Collection policy involves monitoring receivables to spot trouble and obtaining payment on past-due accounts.

Monitoring receivables

To keep track of payments by customers, most firms will monitor outstanding accounts. First of all, a firm will normally keep track of its average collection period through time. If a firm is in a seasonal business, the ACP will fluctuate during the year, but unexpected increases in the ACP are a cause for concern. Either customers in general are taking longer to pay, or some percentage of accounts receivable is seriously overdue.

The **ageing schedule** is a second basic tool for monitoring receivables. To prepare one, the credit department classifies accounts by age.[5] Suppose a firm has $100,000 in receivables. Some of these accounts are only a few days old, but others have been outstanding for quite some time. The following is an example of an ageing schedule.

ageing schedule
a compilation of accounts receivable by the age of each account

Ageing schedule

Age of account	Amount	Percentage of total value of accounts receivable
0–10 days	$ 50,000	50
11–60 days	25,000	25
61–80 days	20,000	20
over 80 days	5,000	5
	$100,000	100

If this firm has a credit period of 60 days, then 25 per cent of its accounts are late. Whether or not this is serious depends on the nature of the firm's collection and customers. It is often the case that accounts beyond a certain age are almost never collected. Monitoring the age of accounts is very important in such cases.

Firms with seasonal sales will find the percentages on the ageing schedule changing during the year. For example, if sales in the current month are very high, then total receivables will also increase sharply. This means that the older accounts, as a percentage of total receivables, become smaller and might appear less important. Some firms have refined the ageing schedule so that they have an idea of how it should change with peaks and valleys in their sales.

Collection effort

A firm usually goes through the following procedures for customers who are overdue:

1 It sends out a delinquency letter informing the customer of the past-due status of the account.
2 It makes a telephone call to the customer.
3 It employs a collection agency.
4 It takes legal action against the customer.

At times, a firm may refuse to grant additional credit to customers until arrears are cleared up. This may antagonise a normally good customer, and it points to a potential conflict of interest between the collections department and the sales department.

Concept questions

14.7a *What tools can a manager use to monitor receivables?*
14.7b *What is an ageing schedule?*

14.8 ▪ Summary and conclusions

This chapter covered the basics of credit policy. The major topics we discussed included:

1 *The components of credit policy.* We discussed the terms of sale, credit analysis and collection policy. Under the general subject of 'terms of sale', the credit period, the cash discount and discount period, and the credit instrument were described.

2 *Credit policy analysis.* We developed the cash flows from the decision to grant credit and showed how the credit decision can be analysed in an NPV setting. The NPV of granting credit depends on five factors: revenue effects, cost effects, the cost of debt, the probability of non-payment and the cash discount.

3 *Optimal credit policy.* The optimal amount of credit the firm offers depends on the competitive conditions under which the firm operates. These conditions will determine the carrying costs associated with granting credit and the opportunity costs of the lost sales from refusing to offer credit. The optimal credit policy minimises the sum of these two costs.

4 *Credit analysis.* We looked at the decision to grant credit to a particular customer. We saw that two considerations are very important: the cost relative to the selling price and the possibility of repeat business.

5 *Collection policy.* Collection policy is the method of monitoring the age of accounts receivable and dealing with past-due accounts. We described how an ageing schedule can be prepared and the procedures a firm might use to collect on past-due accounts.

Key terms

Ageing schedule *481*
Cash discount *468*
Collection policy *464*
Credit analysis *464*

Credit cost curve *477*
Credit instrument *469*
Credit period *466*
Credit scoring *480*

Five Cs of credit *480*
Invoice *466*
Terms of sale *464*

Suggested readings

We have benefited from reading the following material on short-term financial decisions:

Hill, N.C. and Satoris, W.L. *Short-term Financial Management: Text and Cases*, 3rd edn, Macmillan, New York, 1995.

Sartoris, W.L. and Hill, N.C. 'Evaluating Credit Policy Alternatives: A Present Value Framework', *Journal of Financial Research*, Vol. 4, Spring, 1981.

Sartoris, W.L. and Hill, N.C. 'A Generalized Cash Flow Approach to Short-Term Financial Decisions', *Journal of Finance*, Vol. 38, May, 1983.

Endnotes

1 Accounts receivable comprises 9.6 per cent of total assets for a typical Australian industrial company.

2 The cost of short-term debt is not necessarily the required return on receivables, although it is commonly assumed to be. As always, the required return on an investment depends on the risk of the investment, not the source of the financing. The buyer's cost of short-term debt is closer in spirit to the correct rate. We will maintain the implicit assumption that the seller and the buyer have the same short-term debt cost. In any case, the time periods in credit decisions are relatively short, so a relatively small error in the discount rate will not have a large effect on our estimated NPV.

3 The reason is that all customers are offered the same terms. If the NPV of offering credit is $100, assuming that all customers switch, then it will be $50 if only 50 per cent of our customers switch. The hidden assumption is that the default rate is a constant percentage of credit sales.

4 To see this, note that the net incremental cash flow is:

$$\text{Cash flow} = [(1 - \pi) \times P' - v] \times Q - (P - v) \times Q$$
$$= [(1 - \pi) \times P' - P] \times Q$$

Since $P = P' \times (1 - d)$, this can be written as:

$$\text{Net incremental cash flow} = [(1 - \pi) \times P' - (1 - d) \times P'] \times Q$$
$$= P' \times Q \times (d - \pi)$$

5 Ageing schedules are used elsewhere in business. For example, ageing schedules are often prepared for inventory items.

On the web

http://www.dnb.com
(D&B—previously known as Dun & Bradstreet—is the leading provider of business-to-business credit, marketing, purchasing, and receivables management and decision-support services worldwide.)

http://www.standardandpoors.com
(Standard & Poor's Rating Services is the world's leading provider of timely, objective credit analysis and information. They have been rating conventional-term debt and general-obligation corporate and municipal bonds since 1916.)

Maximise Your Marks!
There are 30 interactive questions on credit management waiting online for you at www.mhhe.com/au/ross3e. The questions are written with additional feedback for incorrect answers, and text excerpts with page references for follow-up study.

International Articles!
To read more on credit management and to see current international articles, just go to www.mhhe.com/au/ross3e and click on *PowerWeb Articles* for this chapter.

Chapter review problems and self-test

14.1 · Credit policy

The Advanced Microwave Co. Ltd (manufacturer of the fast-cooking domestic model) is considering a new credit policy. The current policy is cash only. The new policy would involve extending credit for one period. Based on the information below, determine if a switch is advisable. Also, check your answer by using the one-shot and accounts receivable approaches. The required return is 1.5 per cent per period, and there will be no defaults.

	Current policy	New policy
Price per unit	$150	$150
Cost per unit	$120	$120
Sales per period in units	2,000	2,200

14.2 · Discounts and default risk

The SAD Manufacturing Company Pty Ltd is considering a change in credit policy. The current policy is cash only, and sales per period are 5,000 units at a price of $95. If credit is offered, the new price will be $100 per unit and the credit will be extended for one period. Unit sales are not expected to change, and all customers will take the credit. SAD anticipates that 2 per cent of its customers will default. If the required return is 3 per cent per period, is the change a good idea? What if only half the customers take the offered credit?

14.3 · Credit where credit is due

You are trying to decide whether or not to extend credit to a particular customer. Your variable cost is $10 per unit; the selling price is $14. This customer wants to buy 100 units today and pay in 60 days. You think there is a 10 per cent chance of default. The required return is 3 per cent per 60 days. Should you extend credit? Assume that this is a one-time sale and the customer will not buy if credit is not extended.

Answers to self-test problems

14.1 · If the switch is made, an extra 200 units per period will be sold at a gross profit of $150 − 120 = $30 each. The total benefit is thus $30 × 200 = $6,000 per period. At 1.5 per cent per period forever, the PV is $6,000/0.015 = $400,000.

The cost of the switch is equal to this period's revenue of $150 × 2,000 units = $300,000 plus the cost of producing the extra 200 units, 200 × $120 = $24,000. The total cost is thus $324,000, and the NPV is $400,000 − 324,000 = $76,000. The switch should be made.

For the accounts receivable approach, we interpret the $324,000 cost as the investment in receivables. At 1.5 per cent per period, the carrying cost is $324,000 × 1.5% = $4,860 per period. The benefit per period we calculated as $6,000; so the net gain per period is $6,000 − $4,860 = $1,140. At 1.5 per cent per period, the PV of this is $1,140/0.015 = $76,000.

Finally, for the one-shot approach, if credit is not granted, the firm will generate ($150 − 120) × 2,000 = $60,000 this period. If credit is extended, the firm will invest $120 × 2,200 = $264,000 today and receive $150 × 2,200 = $330,000 in one period. The NPV of this second option is $330,000/1.015 − $264,000 = $61,123.15. The firm is $61,123.15 − 60,000 = $1,123.15 better off today and in each future period by granting credit. The PV of this stream is $1,123.15 + $1,123.15/0.015 = $76,000 (allowing for a rounding error).

14.2 · The costs per period are the same whether or not credit is offered; so we can ignore the production costs. The firm currently sells and collects $95 × 5,000 = $475,000 per period. If credit is offered, sales will rise to $100 × 5,000 = $500,000.

Defaults will be 2 per cent of sales, so the cash inflow under the new policy will be 0.98 × $500,000 = $490,000. This amounts to an extra $15,000 every period. At 3 per cent per period, the PV is $15,000/0.03 = $500,000. If the switch is made, SAD will give up this month's revenues of $475,000; so the NPV of the switch is $25,000. If only half the customers switch, then the NPV is half as large: $12,500. So SAD should be glad to make the switch.

14.3 · If the customer pays in 60 days, then you will collect $14 × 100 = $1,400. There is only a 90 per cent chance of collecting this; so you expect to get $1,400 × 0.90 = $1,260 in 60 days. The present value of this is $1,260/1.03 = $1,223.30. Your cost is $10 × 100 = $1,000; so the NPV is $223.30. Credit should be extended.

Questions and problems

1 · Credit policy components

What are the three components of credit policy?

2 · Terms of sale

The conditions under which a firm proposes to grant credit are called the terms of sale. What are the elements that make up the terms of sale?

3 · Cash discounts

You place an order for 50 video CDs at a price of $40 per CD. The supplier offers terms of 1/30, net 120.

a   How long do you have to pay before the account is overdue? If you take the full period, how much should you remit?
b   What is the discount being offered? How quickly must you pay to get the discount? If you do take the discount, how much should you remit?
c   If you do not take the discount, how much interest are you paying implicitly? How many days' credit are you receiving?

4 · Credit period length

What are some of the factors that determine the length of the credit period? Why is the length of the buyer's operating cycle often considered an upper bound on the length of the credit period?

5 · Credit period length

In each of the following, indicate which firm would probably have a longer credit period and explain your reasoning.

a   Firm A sells fresh fruit; firm B sells canned fruit.
b   Firm A sells a miracle cure for baldness; firm B sells toupees.
c   Firm A specialises in products for landlords; firm B specialises in products for tenants.
d   Firm A sells and installs carpeting; firm B sells rugs.
e   Firm A sells to customers with an inventory turnover of 10 times; firm B sells to customers with an inventory turnover of 20 times.

6 · Credit instruments

Describe each of the following:

a   time draft
b   promissory note
c   sight draft
d   trade acceptance
e   banker's acceptance

7 · Trade credit forms

In what form is trade credit most commonly offered? What is the credit instrument in this case?

8 · Credit costs

What are the costs associated with carrying receivables? What are the costs associated with not granting credit? What do we call the sum of the costs for different levels of receivables?

9 · Five Cs of credit

What are the five Cs of credit? Explain why each is important.

10 · Size of accounts receivable

Victory Autos (VAL) Ltd's annual credit sales are $12.4 million. The average collection period is 60 days. What is VAL's average investment in accounts receivable as shown on the Statement of Financial Position?

11 · ACP and size of accounts receivable

Tomorrow Ltd sells forward planning models based on the revolutionary data-dredging, factor analysis approach. Its credit terms are 5/10, net 60. Based on experience, 80 per cent of all customers will take the discount.

a   What is the average collection period for Tomorrow?
b   If Tomorrow sells 50 models at a price of $5,600 each every month, what is its average balance sheet amount in accounts receivable?

12 · Size of accounts receivable

The Feather Bed Company Ltd has monthly credit sales of $600,000, and the average collection period is 120 days. The cost of production is 70 per cent of the selling price. What is the Feather Bed Company's average accounts receivable?

13 · Terms of sale

Supaware Sales Ltd is finding trading difficult. It offers terms of 2/10, net 30. What effective annual interest rate does the firm earn when a customer does not take the discount? Without doing any calculations, explain what would happen to this effective rate if:

a   the discount were changed to 3 per cent
b   the credit period were extended to 60 days
c   the discount period were extended to 15 days
d   Explain whether the calculation of this effective rate can help in the determination of an optimal credit policy.

14 · ACP and receivables turnover

The Early Explorer Co. Pty Ltd has an average collection period of 73 days. Its average daily investment in receivables is $375,000. What are annual credit sales? What is the receivables turnover?

15 · Evaluating credit policy

The Mad Michael Corporation Ltd is in the process of considering a change in its terms of sale. The current policy is cash only; the new policy will involve one period's credit. Sales are 10,000 units per period at a price of $1,500. If credit is offered, the new price will be $1,750 per unit. Unit sales are not expected to change, and all customers will take the credit. Mad estimates that 5 per cent of credit sales will not be collected. If the required return is 10 per cent per period, is the change a good idea?

16 · Size of accounts receivable

Foxy Repair Ltd supplies off-the-shelf TV components to television repairers. A new customer has placed an order for 100 electronic diodes. The variable cost is $20 per unit, and the credit price is $30 each. Credit is extended for one period and, based on historical experience, about 1 out of every 10 such orders is never collected. The required return is 2.5 per cent per period.

a   Assuming that this is a one-time order, should it be filled? The customer will not buy if credit is not extended.
b   What is the break-even probability of default in part (a)?
c   Suppose that customers who do not default become repeat customers and place the same order every period forever. Further assume that repeat customers never default. Should the order be filled? What is the break-even probability of default?
d   Describe in general terms why credit terms will be more liberal when repeat orders are a possibility.

17 · Size of accounts receivable

The Barking Dogs Co. Ltd sells 10,000 pairs of jogging shoes per month at a cash price of $78 per pair. Barking Dogs is considering a new policy that involves 30 days' credit and an increase in price to $80 per pair on credit sales. The cash price will remain at $78, and the new policy is not expected to affect the quantity sold. The discount period will be 10 days. The required return is 1 per cent per month.

a   How would the new credit terms be quoted?
b   What is the investment in receivables required under the new policy?
c   Explain why the variable cost of manufacturing the shoes is not relevant here.
d   If the default rate is anticipated to be 3 per cent, should the switch be made? What is the break-even credit price? The break-even cash discount?

18 · Credit policy evaluation

Easy Listening Ltd sells 97,000 personal stereos each year at a price per unit of $35. All sales are on credit, with the terms being 3/15, net 40. The discount is taken by 40 per cent of the customers. What is Easy's accounts receivable?

In reaction to a competitor, Easy Listening is considering changing its credit terms to 5/15, net 40 to preserve its sales level. How will this affect accounts receivable?

19 · Credit policy evaluation

The Findaword Co. Ltd sells dictionaries on credit terms of net 45. Its accounts are on the average 28 days past due. If annual credit sales are $5 million, what is the company's balance sheet amount in accounts receivable?

20 · Credit analysis

The Fine Music Co. Ltd is considering changing its cash-only policy. The new terms would be net 2 months. Based on the information below, determine if Fine should proceed or not. Describe the build-up of receivables in this case. The required return is 1 per cent per period, and defaults are not a problem.

	Current policy	New policy
Price per unit	$840	$840
Cost per unit	690	690
Sales per month in units	345	390

21 · Credit analysis

Bonding Bodies Co. Ltd (BBC) is debating whether or not to extend credit to a particular customer. BBC's product, a knee replacement fitting, sells for $1,200 per unit. The variable cost is $600 per unit. The order under consideration is for 6 units today. Payment is promised in 90 days.

a If there is a 20 per cent chance for a default, should BBC fill the order? The required return is 4 per cent per quarter. This is a one-time sale, and the customer will not buy if credit is not extended.

b What is the break-even probability in part (a)?

c This part is a little harder. In general terms, how do you think your answer to part (a) will be affected if the customer would purchase the merchandise for cash if the credit is refused? The cash price is $1,100 per unit.

22 · Credit policy evaluation

This is a challenge problem. Consider the following information concerning two credit strategies:

	Refuse credit	Grant credit
Price per unit	$25	$27
Cost per unit	$15	$16
Quantity sold (per quarter)	3,000	3,300
Probability of payment	1.0	0.90

The higher cost per unit reflects the expense associated with credit orders, and the higher price per unit reflects the existence of a cash discount. The credit period will be 90 days, and the cost of debt is 1 per cent per month.

a Based on this information, should credit be granted?

b In part (a), what does the sale price have to be to break even?

c In part (a), suppose we can obtain a credit report for 25 cents per customer. Assuming that each customer buys one unit and that the credit report identifies all customers who would not pay, should credit be extended?

23 · Credit policy evaluation

This is a challenge problem. Fitsall Clothing Co. Ltd currently has a credit policy of 'in God we trust, everybody else pays cash'. It is considering altering this policy by going to terms of net 30 days. Based on the following information, what do you recommend? The required return is 1 per cent per month, and there will be no defaults.

	Current policy	New policy
Price per unit	$10	$12
Cost per unit	$ 6	$ 7
Sales per period in units	40,000	40,000

24 · NPV of credit policy switch

This is a challenge problem. The More Competitive Co. Ltd is considering changing its cash-only policy. The new terms would be net 1 month. Based on the information below, determine if More Competitive should proceed or not. Evaluate the switch by calculating the NPV and then check your answer with the one-shot and accounts receivable approaches. The required return is 2 per cent per period, and there will be no defaults.

	Current policy	New policy
Price per unit	$20	$22
Cost per unit	$12	$12
Sales per period in units	2,000	2,150

25 · NPV of credit policy switch

This is a challenge question. Suppose a company currently sells Q units per month for a cash-only price of P. Under a new credit policy that allows one month's credit, the quantity sold will be Q' and the price per unit will be P'. Defaults will be π per cent of credit sales. The variable cost is v per unit and is not expected to change. The percentage of customers who will take the credit is α, and the required return is R per month. What is the NPV of the decision to switch? Interpret the various parts of your expression.

CHAPTER 15

Australian

financial markets: short-term financing

Objective

On completion of this chapter, the structure of the financial system should be understood. The main forms of short-term borrowing for the organisation will be identified. Understanding will be provided of how borrowing, particularly from a bank, may be structured to meet the needs of the organisation. The process of how bills of exchange and promissory notes may be used to meet business needs will be understood. The ability to calculate prices and yields of these instruments will also be derived.

Study tips ▷ This chapter contains a lot of detailed description. It is necessary to read the material and check that it is understood. Other than the approach for calculating the price and yield on bills, it is not necessary to commit the detail to memory, mainly because the short-term market is one of change. New products in the form of structured financial packages are being introduced continuously in a highly competitive market.

Introduction ▷ Up to this point, we have developed the tools required for financial decision making and concentrated on the investment decision. We now turn our attention to the methods of financing the investments; to be specific, we now address the financing decision. Before we can identify the specific sources of funds that may be accessed by businesses, it is necessary to understand the Australian financial markets. After we have identified the components that make up the financial markets, we turn our attention towards the financing of the firm. This chapter looks at short-term borrowing, the next chapter introduces long-term financing and Chapter 17 looks specifically at raising funds by issuing securities in the market. Firms are not able to generate internally all the funds necessary to finance their investments, nor should they be expected to do so. Firms wishing to obtain funds must use the *financial system*.

∎ 15.1 ∎ The financial system

the financial system

consists of individuals, companies, markets and governments that are involved in the process of exchanging financial assets

The **financial system** consists of individuals, companies, markets and governments that are involved in the process of exchanging financial assets (Figure 15.1). The system aids in the mobilisation of the economy's savings to sectors that can make productive use of them. The Federal Government is a key player in the financial system. The system has relied heavily on Government participation to influence the level of economic activity, the rate of inflation, the level of employment and the value of the Australian dollar. Traditionally government and business have been the main borrowers, while the main lenders have been households and overseas investors. In 1998 the Commonwealth Government had $96 billion in bonds on issue. This had reduced to $70 billion in 2001 with a daily turnover of $4.5 billion. The Commonwealth Government wants to reduce the debt to zero by 2005. It is argued that this could be achieved by selling the remaining 50 per cent of Telstra to the public. However, Telstra performed poorly throughout 2000–2003. In 2003 it lost $2 billion on a failed Asian growth strategy. In consequence the share price fell from around $9.50 in 2000 to around $4.00 in 2003. The government had maintained it would only sell Telstra to the public for a price around $7.00 so it is unlikely that the sale will be completed by 2005. Even if it was, State Government debt would still exist.

FIGURE 15.1

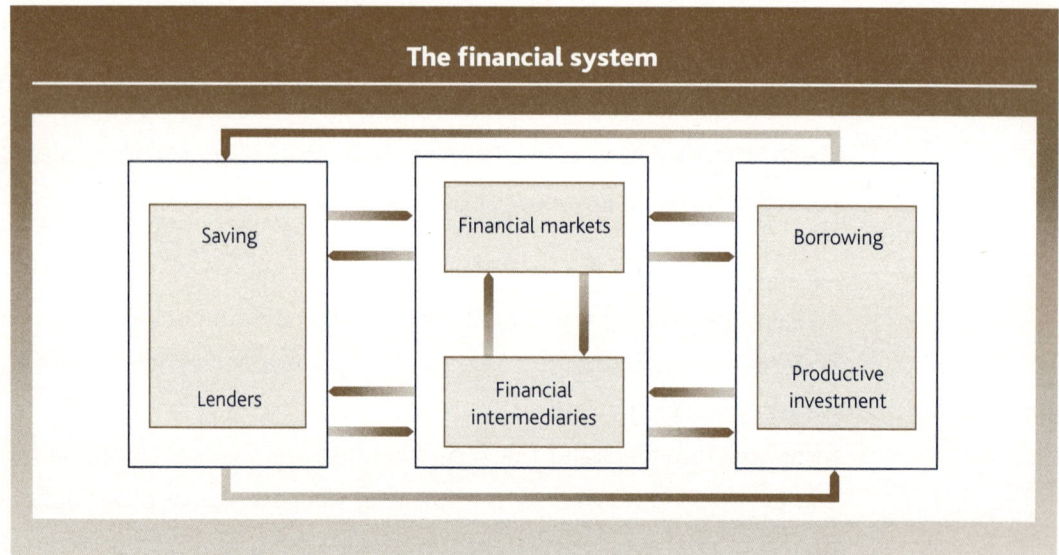

financial intermediary

an institution that acts as a principal in accepting funds from depositors and lending them to borrowers

Important players in the financial system are the **financial intermediaries**. Financial intermediaries introduce the funds from savers (lenders) to productive investors (borrowers). Examples of intermediaries include banks, life insurance companies, merchant banks, finance companies, unit trusts, building societies, credit unions, cash management trusts, and the stock exchange. Financial intermediaries act as 'middlemen' both in relation to marrying funds from savers to borrowers and in matching deals. For example, a small investor would probably rather invest short term with a building society than invest long term in the primary security, a house mortgage, which is the ultimate investment of the building society. By depositing with the building society, the small investor has security, a moderate return on the investment and ready access to cash when required. The building society bears the risk of default on the housing loan, but obtains a higher return than the small investor (depositor) with the building society. As well as matching funds, the intermediaries are keen participants in the financial markets, which will be described in the next section.

Concept questions

15.1a *Under what conditions would the government be a net lender/borrower in the financial system?*

15.1b *Would a company wishing to borrow $20 million be more likely to borrow from thousands of individual small lenders or go to financial intermediaries? Why?*

15.1c *Who would be the main investors in Commonwealth Government Securities (CGSs)?*

15.2 ▪ Financial markets

A **market** is an arrangement whereby participants buy and sell. Some markets have a physical location, such as product markets or livestock markets. Others, such as the share market, futures market, money market and foreign exchange, are not centred on a physical marketplace where participants gather to trade; instead business is conducted by video screens or telephones and confirmed by telex, fax or linked computers. For example, shares are traded using a connected system of Stock Exchange Automated Trading System (SEATS) terminals. As a result, a retiree in Noosa can trade as easily as a CEO in Melbourne.

Financial markets include:

- foreign exchange markets;
- futures and options markets;
- long-term debt markets;
- short-term debt markets; and
- share markets.

The term **primary market** is used to describe new lending and borrowing where the securities are traded in the first instance. For example, Treasury bonds or Treasury notes sold by the Reserve Bank in tenders are primary market securities. The term **secondary market** is used to represent the subsequent buying and selling of securities that have already been issued. Sale of Treasury notes from one dealer to another in the money market is an example of a secondary market transaction.

> **market**
> an arrangement whereby participants buy and sell

> **primary market**
> a market where securities are traded for the first time

> **secondary market**
> a market where subsequent trading of securities occurs

The listed market

In 1988 there were 1,429 companies listed on the main board of the Australian Stock Exchange (ASX); by 1999 the number had declined to 1,159 and by December 2001 the number was back up to 1,410 for a total value of $1,109,601 million ($1,109 billion). The ASX is the 12th largest equity market, with approximately 54,000 trades each day. Australia has the highest participation rate of any country in the share market and the ASX reports that more than 40 per cent of adult Australians now own shares. Several large privatisations or partial privatisations of public organisations (Telstra and the Commonwealth Bank of Australia) and the demutualisation of insurance companies (AMP, NRMA, National Mutual) have placed shares in the hands of small investors. This has boosted participation in the share market, although the failures of One.Tel Telecommunications and HIH Insurance early in 2002 have shaken investor confidence.

In addition, as the computer communication industry expands more small companies are being listed where substantial returns are being earned by early investors (some substantial losses are also being incurred). As well as listed equity investments there are listed debt securities and other listed investments. Figure 15.2 (overleaf) identifies the financial assets traded on the listed market. In order that a company may have its securities added to the official list of the market, it must meet certain criteria. Industrial companies must have aggregated operating profits of at least $1,000,000 before tax over the previous three years and operating profit of $400,000 over the last 12 months or an expert's report stating that the company can be expected to trade at a profit within three years. An alternative requirement is that net tangible assets must be at least $2,000,000. There is also a requirement on the number of shareholders, which must be at least 500 shareholders at the time of listing. As well as satisfying rules for admission to listing, other rules relating to the supply of information to the market must be met for the continuation of listing.

Some of the listed securities are discussed in detail in later chapters; however, a brief description is now provided.

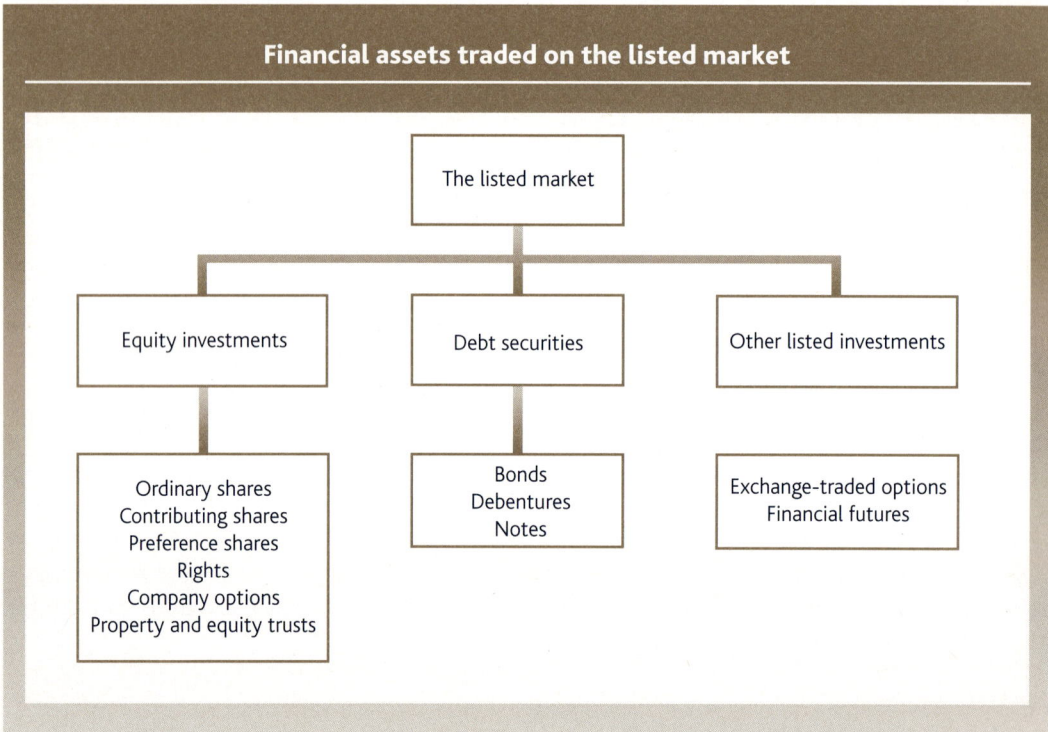

Ordinary shares

ordinary shares
the risk capital of a company, as such shares have residual and ownership rights

Ordinary shares are identified as the risk capital of a company and they represent the ownership rights or equity capital. The purchaser of ordinary shares becomes a shareholder in the assets of the company and is entitled to receive a share of the profits in the form of dividends. A share is a unit of the capital of the company, and shares no longer have a par or face value. Shares are now issued at a price determined by the directors of the company.

Voting rights attach to ordinary shares. They rank behind debentures and preference shares for interest or dividend payments. In the case of winding-up, where the company ceases to exist by an arrangement with shareholders and creditors, they rank as unsecured creditors.

Contributing shares

Contributing shares are shares that are issued and have only been part paid. When a company issues new shares it may not require the full payment for the shares immediately so it will issue the shares on a contributing or partly paid basis. The company will make a call in the future for part or all of the remaining amount. Shares paid in full are known as fully paid shares.

Preference shares

While technically a form of equity, preference shares have many of the attributes of debt. Preference shares usually have a fixed dividend rate, expressed as a percentage of the paid-up value. Preference shares have prior claim over ordinary shareholders to dividend payments and to the assets of a company if it is wound up.

Rights

Rights entitle the owner to take up an offer of additional shares in a company in proportion to their holdings. Companies make rights issues to raise money. The price of the rights, which is referred to as the application or subscription money, must be less than the market price of the existing shares—otherwise there would be no incentive for shareholders to accept the offer. Rights are often underwritten. The shareholder is not obliged to take up a rights issue but rights issues are often renounceable, which means the shareholder can sell or transfer his or her right to the shares. Rights may also be non-renounceable.

Company options

A company option is an option for existing shareholders to subscribe for capital, at some future date, to a new share, by paying the company a fixed price. There is no obligation on shareholders to exercise the option, and if it is not exercised by the expiry date, it lapses and is worthless. Company options may be sold to another investor before they are exercised.

Property and equity trusts

In the legal and commercial sense, a trust is money or property vested with an independent third party (the trustee) to administer on behalf of others (the beneficiaries of the trust). A property trust pools money from savers and invests it in property; for example, office blocks or regional shopping centres. An equity trust invests in company securities.

Bonds

Loans to a government body are called **bonds** as the borrower guarantees the principal will be repaid on a specific date and a fixed rate of interest will be paid for the period of the loan. Bonds are traded on the secondary market so that the market price may be quite different to the issuing (par) value. For example a 10 per cent bond issued at $100 paid-up value seven years ago with three years to run would sell for $113.61 if the market rate of interest fell to 5 per cent, and it would sell for $88.59 if the market rate increased to 15 per cent. The calculations are (assuming annual coupon payments):

bonds
loans made to a government body

$$\$113.61 = \$10 \times (1.05)^{-1} + \$10 \times (1.05)^{-2} + \$110 \times (1.05)^{-3}$$

or

$$\$88.59 = \$10 \times (1.15)^{-1} + \$10 \times (1.15)^{-2} + \$110 \times (1.15)^{-3}$$

Treasury bonds

Treasury bonds are securities issued by the Commonwealth Government that contain both a capital component (the principal) and a coupon (interest rate) stream. Maturities range generally from three years to 10 years. Bonds are issued by tender. On 15 October 2002 tender number 177 was for $400 million. Proceeds of the tenders mainly go towards financing the government's budget deficit, when there is one, and meeting redemptions of maturing bonds.

Company debentures and unsecured notes

debentures or unsecured notes

loans made to companies for a fixed period at a fixed rate of interest

Some loans to companies in the form of **debentures or unsecured notes** may be traded on the share market. These loans are usually for a fixed period and at a fixed rate of interest. Debentures are usually issued with a floating charge over the assets of the issuer to make them more secure than notes. Convention is that loans to government bodies are called 'bonds' whereas secured loans to companies are called 'debentures' and unsecured loans simply 'unsecured notes' or 'notes'. However, there have been efforts to adopt American terminology in calling secured company debt 'bonds'.

In 1991 the Australian Guarantee Corporation Ltd asked the Australian Securities Commission if it could call its debentures 'bonds'. AGC had conducted research that showed investors were more familiar with the word 'bonds'. Their research showed that about 43 per cent of those questioned did not know what a debenture was. As time passes the Australian market is coming closer to full use of the American terminology.

Exchange traded options

Exchange traded options are contracts which give the holder the right (but not the obligation) to buy or sell a commodity or security during a given period. The price at which the option contract can be exercised is called the strike or exercise price, and is determined at the time of issue.

Warrants

A warrant is an option which is long dated. They are normally issued by financial institutions. Warrants are issued over a variety of securities, including shares in a company, a commodity, a currency or even an index. Like options they have a limited life, but unlike options they must be owned before they can be sold. They are discussed in more detail in Chapter 21.

Unlisted markets

unlisted market trading

this trading is confined to bargaining by individual buyers and sellers and around $3 billion is invested in the unlisted equity market

Some securities are not listed on the share market, for example, shares in non-listed public companies, some semi-government bonds, some property and equity trust units, some preference shares and some mortgage securities. Transactions in these securities are broadly confined to bargaining by individual buyers and sellers. Managers of unlisted trusts usually quote 'buy and sell prices' to trade trust units. The **unlisted markets** can be quite large; for example, it is estimated that around $3 billion is invested in the unlisted equity trust market.

Concept questions

15.2a Is the Australian Stock Exchange a primary or a secondary market?
15.2b Is it true that only particular types of securities may be traded on the listed market?
15.2c Why is equity called the 'risk' capital of the company?

15.3 Financial intermediaries

In Australia financial intermediaries are the dominant source of company finance. Table 15.1 shows the market shares (in terms of total assets) attributed to each class of financial intermediary in 2001. The table shows the type of institution, who the main supervisor or regulator is, and the funds under management. The domestic banks have the largest share of the market, while the other chief players are superannuation funds and life insurance companies. In most situations the intermediaries receive their income through a system of paying the savers at one rate of interest and lending at a higher rate.

Type of institution	Main supervisor	Number of institutions	Total assets ($b)
Banks	APRA	52	835
Building societies	APRA	17	12
Credit unions	APRA	201	25
Merchant banks	ASIC	40	86
Finance companies	ASIC	73	88
Securitisers	ASIC	113	97
Life insurance companies	APRA	33	188
Friendly societies	APRA	38	6
Superannuation funds	APRA	11,072	331
Public unit trusts	ASIC	97	152
General insurance	APRA	97	64

Source: Council of Financial Supervisors Annual Report 2001, Reserve Bank of Australia.

Much pressure was placed on the Australian financial sector during the period from 1987 to 1991. Large corporations such as Bond, Hooker and the Adelaide Steamship Company failed, as did large financial institutions such as Rothwells Merchant Bank, Tricontinental Merchant Bank and Pyramid Building Society. As a result the regulation system was reconstructed to create or re-establish the authority of three bodies, the Australian Prudential Regulation Authority (APRA), the Australian Securities and Investments Commission (ASIC), and the Reserve Bank of Australia (RBA). While there is some overlap in relation to the responsibility areas, the duties of each body are clearly specified. For example, in relation to banks, ASIC assumes responsibility for monitoring the code of banking practice, the electronic funds transfer code of practice and other consumer-related practices of banking. It does not have jurisdiction over prudential regulation, the level of bank fees, bank mergers, bank branch rationalisation, credit products, consumer credit and state fair trading laws.

The changes to the regulation system have not eliminated failure, nor should they be expected to (for example, look at One.Tel and HIH), but they have facilitated the ability of the regulators to bring punitive actions against directors and executives.

Banks

The trading bank sector accounts for about 44 per cent (as at December 2001) of the total assets of the finance sector in Australia. The sector has a large established deposit base and an extensive branch network. Most banks conduct a wide range of activities through subsidiaries and affiliated companies such as savings banks, merchant banks, finance companies, general insurance companies, unit trusts, superannuation funds, sharebrokers and trustee companies. This is the concept of one-stop shopping, with the banks aiming to be complete finance houses.

The trading banks are regulated by the Australian Prudential Regulation Authority (APRA) and the Treasurer under a number of Commonwealth Acts, with some influence provided by ASIC (see above). Deregulation has seen the lifting of most of the controls previously imposed on bank operations. The only interest rate control is on savings bank housing loans made prior to April 1986. For many years the domestic banking sector was separated into saving banks and **trading banks**. The first served as a depository for savings

trading banks
these account for about 40 per cent of the total assets of the finance sector in Australia

and its major lending was for housing. The trading banks engaged in a wide range of commercial activities. In August 1987, the Treasurer removed any distinctions between trading banks and savings banks.

There have been significant changes in the source of bank funds. In 1950, for example, non-interest-bearing deposits accounted for some 76 per cent of total trading bank deposits. Today the figure is a lot less. Westpac's 2002 Annual Report indicates that 10 per cent of deposits are non-interest-bearing. Where businesses in the 1950s provided over 65 per cent of trading bank deposits, today the figure is again somewhat less. **Retail** investors (the general public) have taken up the difference, primarily in the form of fixed interest deposits. This is mainly because of the removal of the ceiling on interest rates that trading banks could pay on deposits, and also because trading banks are now able to pay interest on cheque accounts.

Lending patterns have also changed. Trading banks have moved away from relatively inexpensive overdrafts (these are described later in the chapter) to more costly forms of lending. The retail borrower now receives more expensive types of finance, such as personal loans or credit card advances. Some **wholesale** borrowers (corporations or businesses) have found their access to traditional overdrafts somewhat restricted and there are various fees to be met. The overdraft facility is often replaced by the fully drawn advance, the advantage to the bank being that the amount in question is fully advanced and the interest charged on the full amount. In addition to overdrafts and fully drawn advances, banks offer commercial bill lines, leasing and syndicate lending, frequently involving foreign lenders. Syndicate lending occurs when a group of financial institutions pool funds on a specific financing project to spread the risk. Individual return from the investment is proportionate to the degree of risk or amount of funds that each has underwritten or put up. An example of syndicate lending was the refinancing of the North-West Shelf project which occurred in October 1989. National Australia Bank Limited, together with three major offshore banks, underwrote the refinancing of the project—US$1.75 billion. A total of 28 banks were involved in the syndicate.

Merchant banks

Merchant banks or money market corporations have been a significant force in Australia's financial markets since the development of the official money market in the late 1950s and the subsequent escalation of the unofficial money market. Unlike the other financial institutions, the merchant banks have little direct involvement with the retail sector; they are primarily concerned with wholesale finance.

The growth of merchant banks until the early 1970s was strong; however, during the late 1970s and the 1980s the expansion was quite dramatic. The sector constituted the second largest group of financial corporations in 1989, with 16 per cent of total assets. Today, in terms of size, merchant banks form a relatively small part of the overall financial system— about 5 per cent of assets. In December 2001 total assets of these corporations was $86 billion. This figure does not give a true indication of their role. In the past 40 years, merchant banks have been prominent because of their ability to introduce important financial innovations. Merchant banks have been responsible for the development of cash management trusts, rebatable preference shares, the commercial bills market, the currency hedge market, the promissory note market, and the unofficial deposit market. They have traditionally been heavily involved in Treasury areas such as money market and corporate lending activities. While these activities continue to account for the bulk of merchant banking operations in asset terms, increased competition in these markets has led merchant banks to expand into other areas which in some cases are less transaction-based.

retail banking
this involves transactions with the general public

wholesale banking
involves transactions with companies or businesses

merchant banks
have little direct involvement in the retail banking sector as they are primarily concerned with wholesale banking. Have been responsible for the development of cash management trusts, rebatable preference shares, the commercial bills market, the currency hedge market, the promissory note market and the unofficial deposit market

Merchant banks are participants in the markets for the newer Treasury instruments such as foreign exchange, swaps, futures and options (these instruments are described later). Their activities now include the area usually described as investment banking. In general, investment banking covers fee-for-service activities such as corporate advisory work, investment management, placement and underwriting of issues, and other similar non-funding roles. Merchant banks have been able to survive and prosper following deregulation. The majority are owned by large international financial organisations that appear to see a continuing strong role for them in the Australian financial market. Because merchant banks are operating at the competitive edge of the financial market, they tend to fund ventures that are considered to be too risky for the more traditional domestic banks. The domestic banks have also established merchant banking arms.

In the late 1980s, merchant banks began to report large losses. In the case of bank-owned merchant banks, the parents stepped in with support and tightened control. Since late 1988, six non-bank-owned merchant banks have been placed into voluntary liquidation, including Rothwells and Equiticorp. These failures have inhibited growth. However, merchant banks remain an integral part of the Australian financial markets.

Superannuation and life insurance companies

The Australian taxation system plays a critical part in allocating funds between the various competing financial intermediaries. This issue in part explains the resurgence of insurance-type savings products. The traditional life policy, which combined both a life insurance policy and an investment policy, was replaced with new products. These separate the insurance cover and the savings function. The life protective element is covered by term insurance and the savings element is achieved separately through insurance bonds. For example, during the 1980s there was a more active promotion by the life offices of single premium products, known as 'life assurance' bonds. The life offices have responded to increasing competition by diversifying from their ordinary and industrial insurance business and superannuation fund management into such areas as general insurance, short-term money market dealing and merchant banking. Life insurance companies are now amongst the largest financial institutions in Australia. In December 2001 APRA reported 33 life insurance offices in Australia. These offices had $188 billion of assets to invest. The major portion of their investment was in equities.

The **superannuation industry** in Australia has grown rapidly throughout the last 10 years. This growth was driven by the Commonwealth Government policy to promote universal superannuation coverage. Employers have been forced to make contributions under the Commonwealth Government's Superannuation Guarantee Scheme and, when employees leave a particular employment, the funds are invested until the employee reaches retirement. Superannuation is money saved during your working life. Around 81 per cent of Australian workers are covered by superannuation. Not all superannuation funds are regulated by APRA; for example, funds with less than five members are regulated by the Australian Taxation Office. The assets of all superannuation funds total $526 billion. At December 2001, $331 billion of assets were held in superannuation funds regulated by APRA. This, coupled with life insurance, comprises almost 30 per cent of assets in the financial sector.

superannuation industry
the growth area where 98 per cent of the funds are self-managed with fewer than five members

Finance companies

Finance companies emerged in the 1950s as a major group of financial intermediaries specialising in the provision of hire purchase and instalment credit, particularly to consumers. They provide personal loans, instalment credit for retail sales, financing of motor vehicles

finance companies
these control about 6 per cent of the total assets of the finance sector in Australia

(both for individuals and vehicle dealers), home loans, construction finance, bill facilities, leasing finance and factoring.

Most finance companies are funded through the issue of debentures and, to a lesser extent, unsecured notes and deposits. Interest rates offered vary considerably depending on the term of the loan and the financial security of the finance company. The independent finance companies must pay higher rates than those owned by the major trading banks. For example, Australian Guarantee Corporation Ltd (Westpac), Custom Credit Corporation Ltd (National), and Esanda Finance Corporation Ltd (ANZ) have banks as major shareholders, which is considered more secure. The finance companies have grown more slowly since deregulation as they have struggled to cope with increasing competition, particularly from the banks.

legislation
uniform legislation has been adopted in Australia to control the non-bank financial institutions

During the 1980s, the **legislation** and regulations that led to the creation of bank-owned finance companies have disappeared, removing the need for finance subsidiaries. In consequence, parent banks, such as Westpac (AGC Ltd), National Australia Bank (Custom Credit), Suncorp Metway (Perpetual Finance) and State Bank of South Australia (Beneficial Finance), have absorbed a number of the finance subsidiaries' activities.

Building societies

Building societies basically mobilise funds for housing. Today their role is to provide a secure medium for regular, mainly small, savers, and to provide funds for home buyers. The 17 remaining building societies are controlled and regulated by APRA. Building societies are now permitted to diversify lending activities. By offering low deposit, long-term loans, building societies widened the market for home purchases even though their mortgage interest rates were higher than the controlled mortgage rates of the banks. Their ability to charge higher mortgage interest rates than the banks allowed them to win funds from the banks by offering higher deposit rates. Since deregulation, the banks have become more competitive so that the deposit growth rate has slowed for the societies.

Credit unions

Credit unions (also known as credit co-operatives) are a comparatively small part of the Australian financial scene. The 201 unions had only 1.3 per cent of the assets as at December 2001. Credit unions based in the public service or in public sector enterprises tend to be relatively large. Most, however, are based in private enterprise, or groups where there is a strong sense of local identity or a dominant local industry. According to the Reserve Bank, credit unions have traditionally concentrated on providing consumer-type finance and lending for housing. Very limited commercial lending is undertaken. Credit unions and building societies have also expanded strongly into fee-based operations, often through subsidiary companies. These operations include investment and retirement advisory services, insurance, travel and various payments services. Along with other financial institutions, credit unions and building societies have been adapting to deregulation by making greater use of technology and upgrading organisational and managerial arrangements to improve their services and increase efficiency.

Unit trusts

The concept of a unit trust is that small investors are able to pool funds. This enables them to earn a greater return than if each investor acted individually. The most popular forms of unit trusts in Australia are:

- cash management trusts;
- equity trusts; and
- property trusts.

Cash management trusts

Cash management trusts took off in the 1970s in the United States where they are known as money market mutual funds. Cash management trusts were launched in Australia in 1981 when interest rates were relatively high. Cash management trusts attract the savings dollar from the household sector by offering the same, or similar, interest rates as money market companies offer corporate sector savers. Cash management trusts operate by pooling investors' funds into higher yielding short-dated securities normally restricted to large professional investors or corporations. The share of cash management trusts in the finance market was $22 billion in 2000.

Equity trusts, property trusts and mortgage trusts

Equity trusts are unit trusts where unitholders' funds are invested in a range of shares in the stock market, either locally or overseas.

Property trusts pool their unitholders' funds into real estate investments, mainly locally, although some trusts are now investing in overseas property.

Mortgage trusts pool their unitholders' funds into residential, commercial and industrial property mortgages, usually for a term of three to five years and offering a variable rate of interest.

Authorised foreign exchange dealers

On 12 December 1983, the Reserve Bank's trade-weighted index system of valuing the Australian dollar was abandoned, leaving the market to determine the value of the dollar. In June 1984, some 18 financial institutions were granted authority to deal in foreign exchange. In December 1985, the Reserve Bank issued a list of all financial institutions authorised under the Banking Foreign Exchange Regulations to undertake a full range of foreign exchange transactions. By February 2003 the list comprised some 52 organisations, including the major trading banks and the bigger merchant banks. They are known as institutions authorised to deal in foreign exchange. The list includes over 40 non-bank dealers, including Credit Suisse First Boston and NM Rothschild & Sons (Australia) Limited. The list also includes some of the newer banks, like the Bendigo Bank.

Australian companies have increased their overseas borrowing substantially in recent years. The borrowers would have used the services of the foreign exchange dealers to set up the loans, hedge foreign currency risk and the like. Importers, Australians borrowing overseas and Australian investors in overseas securities would have used the services of the foreign exchange dealers extensively in recent years to hedge against likely currency changes.

Stock exchange and sharebrokers

The **Australian Stock Exchange (ASX)** is the central marketplace in which Australian corporations raise funds. It offers investors an efficient facility for buying and selling shares and other listed securities. In 2001 the market capitalisation of listed companies totalled $1,109 billion, which had grown from $261 billion in 1991. Table 15.2 (overleaf) shows how the market has increased over the 10 years from 1991 to 2001.

Australian Stock Exchange (ASX)
Australia's central marketplace for companies raising funds

TABLE
15.2

Stock Exchange data 1991–2001

Year ended 31 December
Market statistics

		1991	2001
Number of companies with equities traded on ASX Main Board 31 December	Domestic	968	1,334
	Total	1,005	1,410
Added to/removed from	Main board last 12 months	80	76
Net change over last 12 months		−131	4
Market capitalisation 31 December	Domestic equities (A$ million)	190,659	732,818
	Overseas-based equities (A$ million)	70,612	376,783
	All equities (A$ million)	261,271	1,109,601
	Bonds/fixed interest (A$ million)	65,192	100,512
Equity trading	Transactions ('000)	1,733	13,269
	Volume (million shares)	27,919	135,244
	Value (A$ million)	60,126	476,433
Daily averages	Transactions	6,850	52,447
	Value of turnover (A$ million)	237.7	1,883.1
	Number of trading days	253	253
Fixed interest	Value of turnover (A$ million)	22,162	1,192
Market liquidity, equities: Turnover value as % of average domestic market Capitalisation		35.8%	68.2%
Equity capital raisings from new shares quoted during year (A$ million)		9,125	12,972
Equity capital raisings as % of average domestic market capitalisation		5.4%	1.9%
ASX indices			
All Ordinaries share price index (base 31/12/79 = 500)	31 December	1,651.4	3,359.9
	High	1,696.3	3,425.4
	Low	1,204.5	2,867.4
All Ordinaries accumulation (gross) index (base 31/12/79 = 1000) 31 December		5,634.9	16,701.8
Number of companies on All Ordinaries index 31 December		235	484
Market capitalisation of stocks on All Ordinaries index (A$ million) 31 December		179,095	722,955
All Industrials share price index (base 31/12/79 = 500) 31 December		2,609.7	5,752.5
All Industrials Accumulation (gross) index (base 31/12/79 = 1000) 31 December		10,048.7	33,479.7
Average P/E ratios and yields 31 December			
Index linked P/E ratio (all companies on all ordinaries index)		19.1	25.2
Index-linked P/E ratio (excluding companies reporting losses)		15.8	17.4
Index-linked dividend yield (all companies on All Ordinaries index)		3.81%	3.3%
10-year government bond yield		9.38%	6.01%
90-day bank bill yield		7.7%	4.26%

Stock Exchange data 1991–2001 (*continued*)

TABLE 15.2

Year ended 31 December
Market statistics

		1991	2001
ASX derivatives market			
Put and call options traded over 12 months ('000) (1000 shares per contract)		9,172	13,698
Value of premiums paid on option contracts (A$ million)		2,643	13,237
Warrants traded on SEATS over 12 months ('000)			445
Value of premiums paid on warrants (A$ million)			1,071
Exchange rates and other statistics			
A$ expressed in US$	31 December	0.7598	0.5106
	12-month average	0.7785	0.5160
Trade-weighted index December 31		55.9	50.2
Inflation (Consumer price index increase)		1.5%	3.1%
Number of security firms active on ASX 31 December		87	90
ASX and the Australian economy			
Market capitalisation domestic equities 12-month average (A$ billion)		168.0	698.7
Gross domestic product: subject to adjustment by ABS (A$ billion)		399.4	690.8
Average market capitalisation of domestic equities expressed as a % of GDP		42.1%	101.1%

Source: 2001 ASX Fact Book.

After the sharemarket crash of October 1987, stock exchange turnovers decreased, cutting the brokerage and profitability of sharebrokers in what is a very competitive industry. This fall in broking profitability was a factor in the merging of brokers and the takeover of some brokers by banks.

The stock exchanges have introduced 'screen trading', trading done on computer screens for shares. The computer-based system is known as *SEATS (Stock Exchange Automated Trading System)*. It provides a single market in which sharebrokers can trade via a computer terminal. Essentially sharebrokers are able to execute orders automatically. SEATS transforms the market by taking the action away from the traditional trading floor. SEATS allows Australia to tap into international trading, on a 24-hour basis. The aim is to attract back to Australia some of the trading in our major listed companies which has increasingly moved to London and New York. (Many Australian sharebrokers have set up overseas offices in London and New York to deal directly with United Kingdom, American and European institutions in Australian equities.)

Australia has a fully electronic settlement and transfer system based on a clearing house subregister system (CHESS). This system records securities and does not require share certificates.

Another major innovation in the Australian broking system is the introduction of T + 3. This change requires contracts between brokers and clients, and transactions between brokers and the Stock Exchange, to be settled by the third business day after the date of the transaction.

Equity capital in excess of $160 billion was raised through different types of capital from 1995 to 2001. Table 15.3 looks at the percentages of the various types of equity raising used by companies over this period.

TABLE 15.3

	Types of equity capital						
Year	Rights issues ($ million)	Place	Reinvested dividends	Options, calls staff plans	Total excluding floats	New floats	Total raisings
1995	2,867.0	2,103.8	3,264.0	1,632.8	9,867.6	4,111.8	13,979.4
1996	1,662.0	5,423.0	3,188.9	1,300.9	11,574.8	3,711.2	15,286.0
1997	4,010.9	2,861.4	3,347.4	2,241.5	12,461.2	12,861.9	25,323.1
1998	3,436.2	10,887.7	3,631.7	2,026.6	19,982.2	8,856.0	28,838.2
1999	3,081.2	17,701.5	3,349.9	3,975.8	28,108.0	4,930.2	33,038.2
2000	2,146.8	12,357.9	3,718.9	3,068.5	21,292.1	10,249.6	31,541.7
2001	619.1	3,578.0	3,833.6	2,768.5	10,799.2	2,172.6	12,971.8

Source: Australian Stock Exchange Fact Book, 2001.

Friendly societies

Friendly societies are non-profit intermediaries founded by groups of people who make small periodic contributions to a common fund. The funds so saved can be withdrawn by contributors when needed for funerals, sickness and so on, or they may be left in the society as savings. They are state-controlled organisations based on the concept of small investors pooling funds together to enable them to earn a higher return. Friendly societies represent a small part of the finance market.

Concept questions

15.3a *Why are there so many different types of financial intermediaries operating in the Australian financial market?*

15.3b *How do financial intermediaries earn their profits?*

15.4 Short-term financing

short-term financial decisions
these decisions typically involve cash inflows and outflows that occur within a year or less

There is no universally accepted definition of short-term finance. The most important feature of **short-term financial decisions** is that they typically involve cash inflows and outflows that occur within a year or less. For example, short-term financial decisions are involved when a firm orders raw materials, pays in cash, and anticipates selling finished goods in one year for cash. In contrast, long-term financial decisions are involved when a firm purchases a special machine that will reduce operating costs over, say, the next five years.

In Chapters 12, 13 and 14, we looked at the basic determinants of the level of investment in current assets, and we thus focused on the asset side of the Statement of Financial Position. Now we turn to the liabilities side, and the financing question for current assets. Here we are concerned with the relative amounts of short-term and long-term debt, assuming the investment in current assets is constant.

We start off with the simplest possible case: an 'ideal' economy. In such an economy, short-term assets can always be financed with short-term debt, and long-term assets can be financed with long-term debt and equity. In this economy, net working capital is always zero.

Consider a simplified case for a flour mill. Flour mills buy crops after harvest, store them, and sell them during the year. They have high inventories of grain after the harvest and end up with low inventories just before the next harvest.

Bank loans with maturities of less than one year could be used to finance the purchase of grain and the storage costs. These loans would be paid off from the proceeds of the sale of grain.

The situation is shown in Figure 15.3. Long-term assets are assumed to grow over time, whereas current assets increase at the end of the harvest and then decline during the year. Short-term assets end up at zero just before the next harvest. Current (short-term) assets are financed by short-term debts, and long-term assets are financed with long-term debt and equity. Net working capital—current assets minus current liabilities—is always zero. Figure 15.3 displays the 'sawtooth' pattern that we saw when we discussed cash management in Chapter 13. For now, we shall discuss some alternative policies for financing current assets under less idealised conditions.

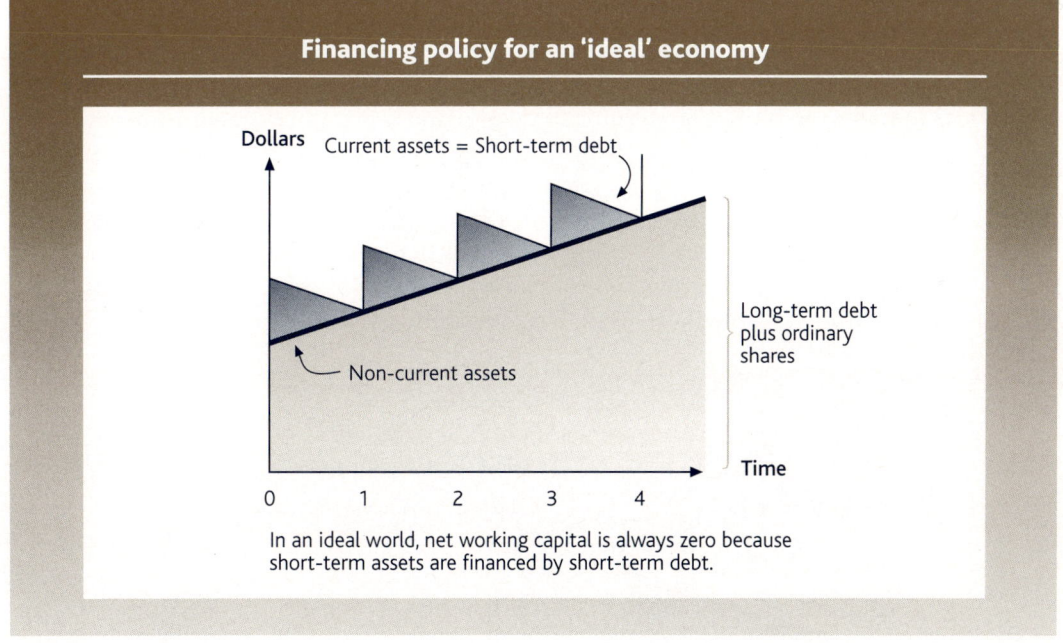

Financing policy for an 'ideal' economy

FIGURE 15.3

In an ideal world, net working capital is always zero because short-term assets are financed by short-term debt.

Different policies in financing current assets

In the real world, it is not likely that current assets will ever drop to zero. For example, a long-term rising level of sales will result in some permanent investment in current assets. Moreover, the firm's investments in long-term assets may show a great deal of variation.

A growing firm can be thought of as having a total asset requirement consisting of the current assets and long-term assets needed to run the business efficiently. The total asset requirement may exhibit change over time for many reasons, including (1) a general growth trend, (2) seasonal variation around the trend, and (3) unpredictable day-to-day and month-to-month fluctuations. This situation is depicted in Figure 15.4. (We have not tried to show the unpredictable day-to-day and month-to-month variations in the total asset requirement.)

FIGURE
15.4

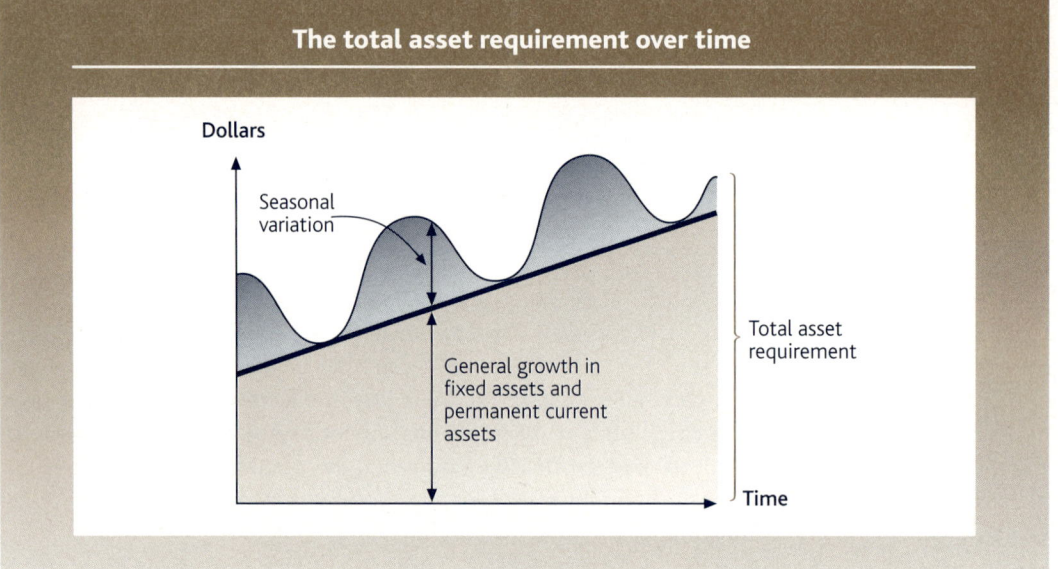

The total asset requirement over time

Dollars

Seasonal variation

General growth in fixed assets and permanent current assets

Total asset requirement

Time

When long-term financing covers more than the total asset requirements, the firm has excess cash available for investment in marketable securities. Policy F, the flexible policy in Figure 15.5, always implies a short-term cash surplus and a large investment in net working capital.

When long-term financing does not cover the total asset requirement, the firm must use short-term borrowing to make up the deficit. In Figure 15.5, Policy R, the restrictive policy, implies a persistent need for short-term borrowing. Whenever current assets rise because of seasonal variations, the firm borrows short-term to finance the growth. As these assets are worked off, the firm repays the short-term debt out of the proceeds.

FIGURE
15.5

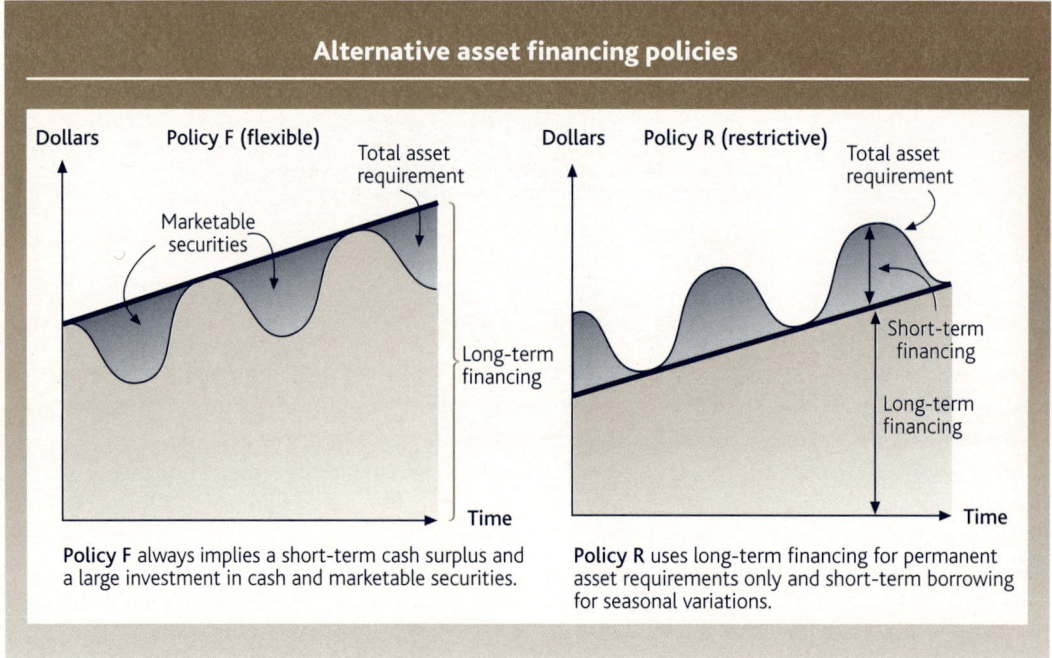

Alternative asset financing policies

Dollars   Policy F (flexible)   Total asset requirement

Marketable securities

Long-term financing

Time

Dollars   Policy R (restrictive)   Total asset requirement

Short-term financing

Long-term financing

Time

Policy F always implies a short-term cash surplus and a large investment in cash and marketable securities.

Policy R uses long-term financing for permanent asset requirements only and short-term borrowing for seasonal variations.

Which is best?

What is the most appropriate amount of short-term borrowing? There is no definite answer. Several considerations must be included in a proper analysis:

1 *Cash reserves*. The flexible financing policy implies surplus cash and little short-term borrowing. This policy reduces the probability that a firm will experience financial distress. Firms may not have to worry as much about meeting recurring, short-run obligations. However, investments in cash and marketable securities are zero net present value investments at best.

2 *Maturity hedging*. Most firms attempt to match the maturities of assets and liabilities. They finance inventories with short-term bank loans and fixed assets with long-term financing. Firms tend to avoid financing long-lived assets with short-term borrowing. This type of maturity mismatching would necessitate frequent financing and is inherently risky because short-term interest rates are more volatile than longer rates.

3 *Relative interest rates*. Short-term interest rates are usually lower than long-term rates. This implies that it is, on the average, more costly to rely on long-term borrowing than short-term borrowing.

The two policies we discussed above, F and R, are of course extreme cases. With F, the firm never does any short-term borrowing, and with R the firm never has a cash reserve (an investment in marketable securities). Figure 15.5 illustrates these two policies along with a compromise, Policy C, in Figure 15.6.

With this compromise approach, the firm borrows short-term to cover peak financing needs, but it maintains a cash reserve in the form of marketable securities during slow periods. As current assets build up, the firm draws down this reserve before doing any short-term borrowing. This allows for some run-up in current assets before the firm has to resort to short-term borrowing.

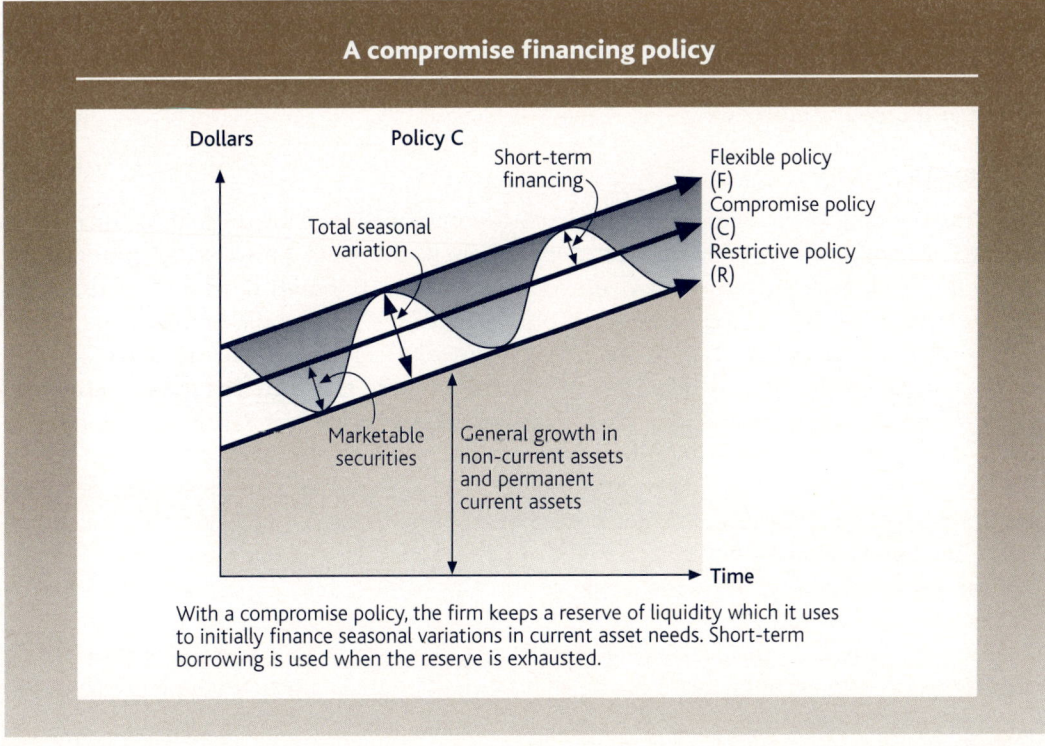

A compromise financing policy

With a compromise policy, the firm keeps a reserve of liquidity which it uses to initially finance seasonal variations in current asset needs. Short-term borrowing is used when the reserve is exhausted.

FIGURE 15.6

Concept questions

15.4a *What keeps the real world from being an ideal one where net working capital could always be zero?*

15.4b *What considerations determine the optimal size of the firm's investment in current assets?*

15.4c *What considerations determine the optimal compromise between flexible and restrictive net working capital policies?*

15.5 Short-term financing sources

It follows from the earlier discussion that short-term borrowing should be used for working capital requirements in the day-to-day operations of the business, and for transactions that are self-financing over short periods. Industries with seasonal peaks and troughs, and those engaged in international trade, will be heavy users of short-term finance. There are many methods through which a firm can secure short-term finance and these include:

- overdrafts;
- short-term loans;
- bills of exchange;
- promissory notes/commercial paper;
- inventory loans;
- letters of credit;
- short-term eurocurrency advances;
- factoring; and
- mortgage securitisation.

This list is not exhaustive as new forms of lending are developed continuously in response to market needs. Current market rates of interest applicable to some of the short-term financing are provided in the daily press. The main providers of short-term finance are trading banks, merchant banks and finance companies. Superannuation funds and brokers operate in the area as purchasers of marketable securities.

Overdrafts

overdraft
where the bank permits the customer to draw more money from the bank account than that which has been put in it

Overdraft lending by trading banks has been a common source of short-term finance in Australia. An overdraft is a credit arrangement where the bank permits the customer to extend the bank account into deficit, up to an agreed limit. Funds deposited to the bank account reduce the deficit balance so that working funds will reduce the outstanding balance and its related interest until they are used. Interest is calculated on the daily balance outstanding and it is charged quarterly in arrears. Interest rates are negotiated; however, banks publish a single indicator rate, the 'prime' rate, for overdrafts of $10,000 or more. The 'prime' rate is generally a minimum of 1 per cent above short-term bank bill rates and most overdraft arrangements are linked to rates higher than the 'prime' rate. The interest rate is variable so that it is subject to market movements. Other charges are overdraft facility fees and an unused overdraft limit fee.

Overdrafts are subject to annual reviews and the bank would expect the customer to reduce the limit. It is repayable on demand, though banks rarely exercise this discretion.

The use of overdraft finance is declining. Banks are encouraging customers to move to other forms of short-term finance because the overdraft arrangements create a high degree of uncertainty as to how much of the bank's funds will need to be committed to this line of credit. In addition, firms can operate in the short-term money market to obtain lower-cost funds.

Short-term loans

Banks are also the large providers of short-term loans. A short-term loan is an advance of funds usually made for a specific purpose rather than for working capital. Unlike the overdraft, which may be recalled on demand, a **term loan** is for a fixed period. It involves a formalised system of repayments. The repayments may be structured to include principal and interest; however, interest-only loans are available. In the case of the latter arrangement, all principal is repaid as a lump sum at the end of the term period. Interest rates may be fixed or variable; however, the rapidly increasing rates that occurred during the 1980s have encouraged lenders to write variable interest contracts. As rates declined in the early 1990s lenders moved towards fixed interest contracts until the end of 1998. The threat of increasing interest rates began to develop early in 1999 and the loan tendency shifted towards encouraging variable interest contracts.

term loan
an advance of funds made by a bank for a fixed period and a specific purpose

A form of short-term loan (though these may also be established on a long-term basis) is the *facility agreement* or *letter*. A facility arrangement will provide a source of funds that may be drawn upon at any time. For example, a real estate speculator may have a facility arrangement for $1m dollars. The speculator knows that bids may be made on property up to $1m dollars and the funds will be available. If a property is purchased for $450,000, then $550,000 will remain in the facility to be drawn at a later date. The agreement letter will specify the term, interest rate, period of notice (if any) for drawing on the facility, details of fees and the repayment pattern.

Bills of exchange

A **bill of exchange** is a negotiable instrument. The legal definition is an unconditional order in writing addressed by one person to another, signed by the person giving it, requiring the person to whom it is addressed to pay on demand, or at a fixed or determinable future time, a sum certain in money to the order of a specified person, or bearer. When a bill is used to lend money, the funds for lending may come from a third party. Some bills are accepted or endorsed by a bank so that the bank agrees to pay the third party at maturity if the borrower defaults. The main use of bills of exchange in Australia is as a means of obtaining credit, but they are not necessarily related to specific trading transactions. Bills not related to trade transactions are called *accommodation bills*. Trade bills are still used extensively for the financing of exports and imports, and there continues to be a demand for local financing of goods between Australian companies by way of trade bills. However, the bill of exchange has proved to be most adaptable to the financing of all sectors of Australian industry and commerce. The use of the bill of exchange has expanded rapidly. A significant advantage of bill financing is that it enables users of funds to defer, in the appropriate circumstances, the raising of permanent equity or debt capital. Its flexibility to meet variations in cash flow cycles is another principal advantage.

bill of exchange
a negotiable instrument that involves a drawer, acceptor and payee

There are three parties involved in a bill of exchange:

- *The drawer.* The party who issues the order is the drawer. This is usually the borrower of the funds. In the example in Figure 15.7, the drawer, M.C. Spencer Pty Ltd, has issued the order of $100,000 and agreed that the bill will be paid as stated. M.C. Spencer Pty Ltd has the obligation to repay the $100,000 on presentation of the bill at maturity.

FIGURE 15.7

Bank accepted bill of exchange

ACCEPTED PAYABLE
ON *30 November 2003*
AT *LIN Bank Australia Ltd*
90 Love Street, Sydney

1239832
DATE *3 June 2003*

AMOUNT *$A100,000*
DUE DATE *30 November 2003*

ON THE 30 *November 2003* FIXED PAY
TO THE ORDER OF *A.B. BROKER*
THE SUM OF *One hundred thousand dollars*

FOR AND ON BEHALF OF
LIN Bank Australia Ltd
– or 'the financier'

TO
LIN Bank Australia Ltd
90 Love Street, Sydney

FOR AND ON BEHALF OF
M.C. SPENCER Pty Ltd

The acceptor

The payee

The drawer

- *The acceptor.* The party who endorses the bill is the acceptor. In Figure 15.7, LIN Bank Australia Ltd has signed as acceptor to agree to pay the bill if M.C. Spencer Pty Ltd defaults.
- *The payee.* The payee is the owner of the bill. In Figure 15.7, the owner is A.B. Broker, who is entitled to be paid $100,000 on 30 November 2003. If there are successive owners, there will be endorsements to record the transfers on the back of the bill. Figure 15.8 shows that the bill has moved from A.B. Broker (on 17.8.2003) to Mary T. Fashions Pty Ltd and then from Mary T. to Hungry Investments Ltd (on 15.10.2003). If Hungry Investments holds the bill until maturity, it will collect the $100,000 from M.C. Spencer Pty Ltd.

FIGURE 15.8

Reverse side of a bank accepted bill of exchange

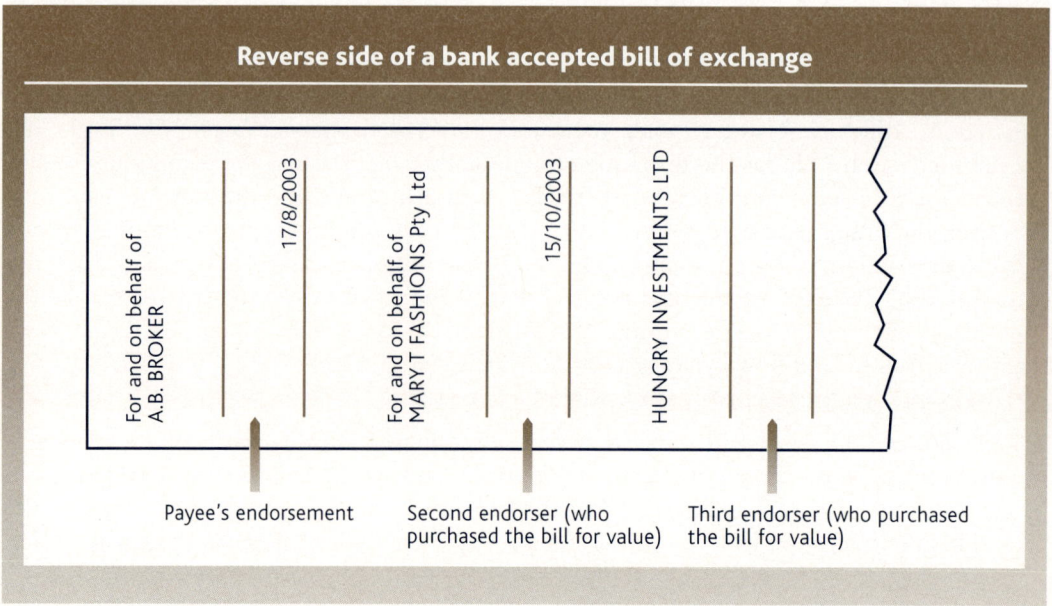

For and on behalf of A.B. BROKER — 17/8/2003

For and on behalf of MARY T FASHIONS Pty Ltd — 15/10/2003

HUNGRY INVESTMENTS LTD

Payee's endorsement

Second endorser (who purchased the bill for value)

Third endorser (who purchased the bill for value)

A bill of exchange is normally paid out by the acceptor of the bill on its due date (the acceptor is reimbursed by the drawer). The *Bills of Exchange Act* 1909 (Cth) provides for the protection of holders of bills. The liability for repayment runs from the acceptor, to the drawer, then to the endorsers (last endorser to first endorser); see question 13 for an example of this. While bank bills are bearer securities, most professional market transactions are settled in the Australian system. Securities traded through the system are lodged with Austraclear and transfer of title and cash settlements are effected electronically.

While the maximum period of a bill is 180 days, banks will arrange a bill facility so that the period may be extended from 180 days to three or five years. For a charge of about 0.5 per cent on top of the bank bill rate, the bank will guarantee the rolling over of bills so that the drawer is assured of being able to replace the maturing bill with a new bill. When funds are borrowed through a bill facility, the actual amount received is less than the face value of the bill. The face value of the bill is discounted according to the discount yield formula, which provides:

$$\text{Discounted value} = \frac{(365 \times \text{Face value})}{(365 + (\text{Yield} \times \text{Days to maturity}/100))} \qquad (15.1)$$

Discounted receipts from bills of exchange

EXAMPLE 15.1

What is the discounted receipts on the following bills of exchange?

Bill	Face value	Term	Yield per annum
A	$100,000	90 days	10%
B	$100,000	180 days	10%
C	$100,000	90 days	15%

Discounted value Bill A = (365 × $100,000)/[365 + (10 × 90/100)] = $97,593.58
Discounted value Bill B = (365 × $100,000)/[365 + (10 × 180/100)] = $95,300.26
Discounted value Bill C = (365 × $100,000)/[365 + (15 × 90/100)] = $96,433.29

It should be obvious from the formula and the calculations that the discounted receipts of a bill are dependent upon the interest rate (yield) and the term to maturity. Note that the amount received varies inversely with the interest rate.

In relation to Bill A, the interest paid would be $100,000 − $97,593.58 = $2,406.42.

The rate of interest is:

$$\frac{\$2,406.42}{\$97,593.58} \times 100\% = 2.466\% \text{ for 90 days}$$

At an annual rate, this is:

$$\frac{2.466\% \times 365}{90} = 10\%$$

which is the yield per annum specified in the problem.

Promissory notes

A promissory note is an unconditional promise in writing made by one person to another, signed by the maker, engaging to pay, on demand or at a fixed or determinable future time, a sum certain in money, to the order of a specified person, or to the bearer. A promissory note involves two parties only, the issuer and the bearer (see Figure 15.9). There is no acceptor and promissory notes are marketable without endorsement. Once a promissory note is sold, the seller has no further liability. In the case of a bill of exchange, the endorsers have a contingent liability until the bill matures. Promissory notes are unsecured borrowing and therefore their use tends to be restricted to large organisations seeking funds, such as Telstra Australia, Qantas, BHP Billiton Ltd, Boral Limited and Pacific Dunlop Ltd. There is a very active secondary market for promissory notes.

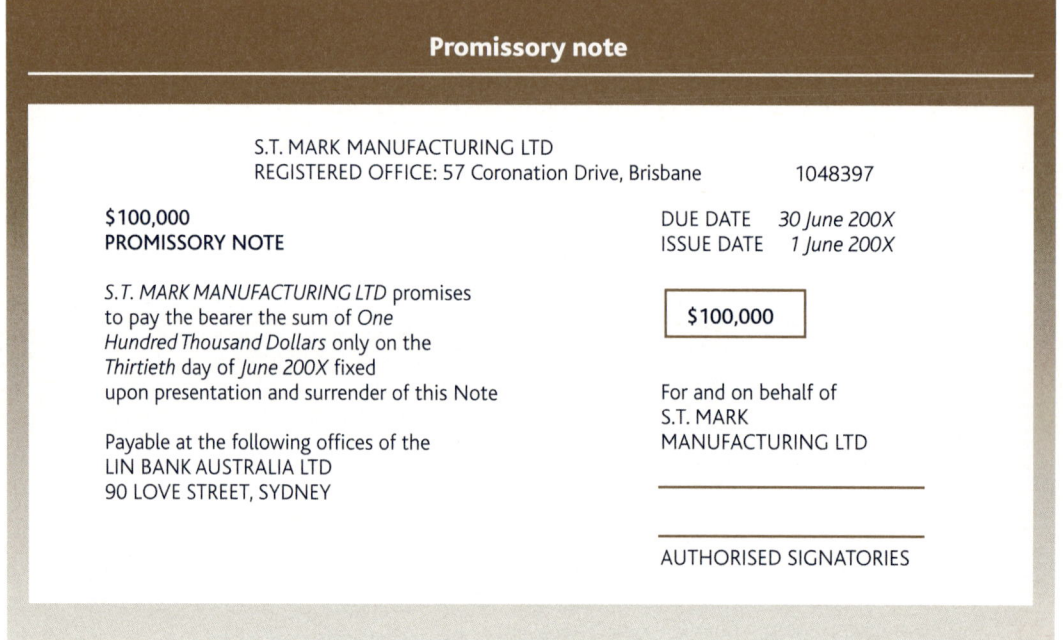

FIGURE 15.9

Promissory note

Inventory loans

Inventory loans, short-term loans to purchase inventory, come in three basic forms: blanket liens, trust receipts and field warehouse financing.

1 *Blanket inventory lien*. A blanket lien gives the lender a lien against all the borrower's inventories (the blanket 'covers' everything).
2 *Trust receipt*. A trust receipt is a device where the borrower holds specific inventory in 'trust' for the lender. Automobile dealer financing, for example, is done by trust receipts. However, it is somewhat cumbersome to use trust receipts for, say, wheat grain. Cars are much easier to identify.
3 *Field warehouse financing*. In field warehouse financing, a public warehouse company (an independent company that specialises in inventory management) acts as a control agent to supervise the inventory for the lender.

Letters of credit

A letter of credit is an irrevocable and unconditional undertaking by a bank to repay the principal and interest of a loan in the event of default by the borrower. For example, lower status borrowers can use promissory note borrowings with the backing of a letter of credit, issued under a trust deed and confirmed (guaranteed) by an Australian bank. The issue yields then reflect the borrowings status of the bank. The lender is relying on the bank should the borrower default.

Short-term eurocurrency funding

The eurocurrency market developed following World War II. American companies, followed by American banks, expanded internationally. American aid and funds financed post-war reconstruction. A lot of companies, and countries, decided to keep their US dollars in Europe; hence the development of the euromarket and eurocurrencies, which are deposits of a currency held outside the country of issue. The term 'euro' is derived from the Greek word meaning 'external' and has nothing to do with Europe. Eurocurrency loans can be provided by banks and merchant banks in a variety of currencies, such as euro–yen, euro–dollars, euro–$A. The advances are usually for six to 12 months for amounts of $5 million upwards and are drawn and repaid in one single amount. Other euromarket short-term debt instruments include euronotes and eurocommercial paper. These consist of short-term notes issued by large low-risk firms.

Factoring

Factoring or selling of accounts receivable was discussed in Chapter 13. Recall that factoring is a continuous arrangement between the company and the factor, which ensures that as soon as a sale is made, the proceeds are immediately available to the company. Funds are injected by use of this facility into the working capital of the business, thereby improving cash flow, and the company does not have to commit administrative time to the collection of debts if it does not maintain the debtors ledger.

International comparison

Table 15.4 gives some indication of the different arrangements that exist in the Australian, Hong Kong and Singapore markets. Australia has a wider range of products on offer and would tend to have a more active secondary market.

TABLE 15.4

International comparison: Short-term arrangements						
	Australian market		Hong Kong market		Singapore market	
Arrangement	Primary	Secondary	Primary	Secondary	Primary	Secondary
Bank bills	X	X				
Promissory notes	X	X	X	X		
Commercial notes	X	X	X		X	X
Exchange funded bills			X	X		
Inventory loans	X	X	X	X	X	X
Facility letters	X	X				
Factoring	X	X	X	X	X	X

Concept questions

15.5a *What are the basic differences in the short-term financing loans provided by banks?*
15.5b *Why can bills of exchange be issued by all firms whereas promissory notes can only be issued by large low-risk firms?*
15.5c *Explain factoring.*

▪15.6▪ Summary and conclusions

1 This chapter looked at Australian capital markets and then at the sources of short-term finance. The capital markets are concerned with marrying funds available from saving units with the needs of the borrowing units. The players in the markets are individuals, companies, government and the financial intermediaries.

2 Markets are often not physical locations and one has to understand primary and secondary markets, listed and unlisted markets as well as the specific markets that comprise the Australian financial markets: specific markets are the short-term debt market, the long-term debt market, the share market, the futures market and the foreign exchange market.

3 The securities traded on the listed market are shares, debt and trust units. Hybrid forms of each security are offered. Variations of shares are ordinary shares, preference shares, contributing shares, rights and options. Debt is represented by company debentures and unsecured notes and bonds. Trust units cover equity and property. The Australian markets represent dynamic environments, and products are created quickly to meet the needs of participants.

4 Much of the smooth operation of the markets must be attributed to the financial intermediaries. These are the banks, the building societies, the brokers, the cash management trusts, the credit unions, the finance companies, the friendly societies, the life insurance companies, the unit trusts, the authorised money market dealers, and other financial institutions.

5 Classification of short-term financing is just as arbitrary as the classification of assets into current and non-current; however, the typical identification is liabilities that will mature in a year or less. Sound financing policy requires that short-term assets should be funded by short-term debt.

6 The sources of short-term financing have been identified. This area does tend to be the domain of the trading banks so that bank products do provide a major part of short-term finance. In some cases the finance is linked directly to the assets; such is the case in some inventory financing. Developing areas of short-term financing are in the field of securitisation, which covers factoring and mortgage packaging, and eurocurrency funding.

7 Figure 15.10 summarises the forms of finance and identifies the source from which the funds may be obtained. Some of the funds are more readily identified as long-term funding and so are discussed in Chapter 16; however, they are presented in Figure 15.10 for completeness.

Key terms

Banks—trading, saving, merchant *495–7*
Bills of exchange *507*
Brokers *499*
Building societies *498*
Credit unions *498*
Eurocurrency funding *511*
Factoring *511*

Finance companies *497*
Financial intermediaries *490,494*
Inventory loans *510*
Letters of credit *510*
Life insurance companies *497*
Listed/unlisted markets *491,494*
Loans *507, 510*

Overdrafts *506*
Primary/secondary markets *491*
Promissory notes *509*
Securities—shares, debentures, bonds *492–4*
Superannuation industry *497*
Unit trusts *498*

Finance: form and source

FIGURE 15.10

Form of finance	Trading banks	Specialist banks	Merchant/investment banks	Finance companies	Insurance companies	Super funds	Life and pension funds	Unit trust equity/cash/property	Investment companies	Other public companies	Stock exchange/market	General public	Building societies	Specialist venture capital	Overseas banks	Overseas institutions	Overseas stock markets	Euro/bond markets
Overdraft facility unsecured or secured by fixed or floating charge	•	•	•	•											•			
Unsecured note facility	•	•	•	•	•			•	•		•				•			
Cash advance	•	•	•	•					•		•				•			
Direct term loan	•	•	•	•	•	•	•	•	•	•		•	•	•	•	•		•
Mortgage loan	•	•	•	•	•	•	•	•	•	•		•	•	•	•	•		•
Bank bill of exchange facility	•	•																
Non-bank bill facility Commercial note facility			•	•	•	•	•	•	•							•		
Promissory note facility			•	•	•	•	•	•	•	•								
Revolving credit Standby facility	•	•	•												•	•		
Trade (export) facility	•	•													•	•		
Factoring	•	•													•	•		
Bond facility	•	•	•	•	•	•	•		•	•	•			•	•	•	•	
Letter of credit or bank guarantees	•	•													•			
Euro bond facility															•	•		•
Euro note facility															•	•		•
Euro commercial note facility															•	•		•
Multi-currency euro note facility															•	•		•
Accounts receivable facility	•	•	•	•	•													
Financial lease	•	•	•	•	•	•	•		•									
Leverage lease facility	•	•	•			•	•		•						•	•		
Sale leaseback arrangement	•	•	•	•	•	•	•	•	•	•				•	•	•		
Project finances limited resource	•	•				•	•		•	•					•	•		
Project finance non-resource	•	•				•	•		•	•					•	•		
Securities issued						•	•		•	•	•	•					•	

Suggested readings

Fabozzi, F. and Masonson, L.N. *Corporate Cash Management Techniques and Analysis*, Dow Jones-Irwin, Homewood, Ill., 1985.

Gallinger, G.W. and Healey, P.B. *Liquidity Analysis and Management*, Addison-Wesley Publishing Co., Reading, Mass., 1987.

Hunt, B. and Terry, C. *Financial Instruments and Markets*, Thomas Nelson, Melbourne, 1993.

Kahl, J.G. and Parkinson, K. *Current Asset Management: Cash, Credit and Inventory*, John Wiley & Sons, New York, 1984.

McGrath, M. and Viney, C. *Financial Institutions, Instruments and Markets in Australia*, 3rd edn, McGraw-Hill, Sydney, 2000.

Vander Weide, J. and Maier, S.F. *Managing Corporate Liquidity: An Introduction to Working Capital Management*, John Wiley & Sons, New York, 1985.

On the web

The following have been mentioned in this chapter:

http://www.apra.gov.au (APRA)

http://www.rba.gov.au (Reserve Bank of Australia)

http://www.asic.gov.au (Australian Securities and Investments Commission)

http://www.westpac.com.au (Westpac)

http://www.ampbanking.com.au (AMP)

Maximise Your Marks!

There are 30 interactive questions on short-term financing waiting online for you at www.mhhe.com/au/ross3e. The questions are written with additional feedback for incorrect answers, and text excerpts with page references for follow-up study.

International Articles!

To read more on short-term financing and to see current international articles, just go to www.mhhe.com/au/ross3e and click on *PowerWeb Articles* for this chapter.

15.1 · Financing sources

Complete the table by indicating the preferred source of funds for the transaction.

Transaction / Source	Trading banks	Specialist banks	Merchant/investment banks	Finance companies	Insurance companies	Super funds	Life and pension funds	Unit trust equity/cash/property	Investment companies	Other public companies	Stock exchange/market	General public	Building societies	Specialist venture capital	Overseas banks	Overseas institutions	Overseas stock markets	Euro/bond markets
Temporary funds to meet a monthly payroll																		
Funds to finance purchase of specialist inventory from overseas																		
Funds to meet a six-monthly shortage in the cash budget																		
Funds to offset the rising level of debtors because of expanding business																		
Venture start up capital to commence a new activity																		
A subordinated short-term loan without the parent company guarantee																		
Finance for a floor plan to hold furniture for resale																		
A standby facility to cover temporary cash shortages																		

15.2 · Finance evaluation

The summarised Statement of Financial Position of Form and Fashion Pty Ltd with extracts from its Statement of Financial Performance for the year ended 30 June 200X are provided below. This small company manufactures clothing and is managed by two young, capable, working directors with a good knowledge of the rag trade.

The directors have made loans to the company to the full extent of their personal resources and they currently require funds to finance a large contract worth $600,000 from reputable first-class buyers for a quantity of suits. They are considering applying for an unsecured overdraft limit of $150,000 to help finance the contract. They are prepared to offer the bank their personal guarantees and postponement of their loans from the company. They may even convert their loans into equity.

They do not wish to offer secured debentures as a means of raising the finance as they feel this would precipitate action from the other creditors of the company.

You have been asked to write an independent report for the bank analysing the information, in the context of the request made.

Form and Fashion Pty Ltd
Statement of Financial Position as at 30 June 200X

Share capital, ordinary shares of $2 fully paid		$ 30,000
Statement of Financial Performance appropriation		5,000
Shareholders' funds		35,000
Loans by directors		55,000
Current liabilities		
Trade creditors	$550,000	
Accrued expenses	50,000	
		600,000
Shareholders' funds and liabilities		$690,000
Non-current assets		
Plant and machinery (cost less depreciation)	$105,000	
Motor vehicle (cost less depreciation)	25,000	
Goodwill	14,000	
Preliminary expenses	3,000	
		$147,000
Current assets		
Cash at bank	$118,000	
Trade debtors	170,000	
Inventory and work in progress	235,000	
Prepayments	20,000	
		543,000
Total assets		$690,000

Extracts from the Statement of Financial Performance
for the year ended 30 June 200X

Sales	$2,300,000	Cost of goods sold	1,400,000
		Profit for the year	45,500
		(after all expenses including	
		those below)	
		Depreciation	$18,000
		Taxation	nil
		Directors' remuneration	$64,000

Answers to self-test problems

15.1 · Refer to the table below

Transaction \ Source	Trading banks	Specialist banks	Merchant/investment banks	Finance companies	Insurance companies	Super funds	Life and pension funds	Unit trust equity/cash/property	Investment companies	Other public companies	Stock exchange/market	General public	Building societies	Specialist venture capital	Overseas banks	Overseas institutions	Overseas stock markets	Euro/bond markets
Temporary funds to meet a monthly payroll	●	●	●															
Funds to finance purchase of specialist inventory from overseas	●														●	●		●
Funds to meet a six-monthly shortage in the cash budget	●	●	●	●						●								●
Funds to offset the rising level of debtors because of expanding business	●									●								
Venture start up capital to commence a new activity	●	●	●						●					●				
A subordinated short-term loan without the parent company guarantee	●	●	●			●			●	●	●				●	●	●	●
Finance for a floor plan to hold furniture for resale	●	●	●	●					●	●								
A standby facility to cover temporary cash shortages	●	●	●												●	●		

15.2 · Points that should be made are:

a   Current liabilities are high relative to current assets.

b   The firm is relying upon trade credit to finance current assets and a portion of the non-current assets.

c   The firm needs to look at additional long-term finance:

    i   bank loan, or

    ii   more equity, or

    iii   development funding.

d   Equity and loans from directors finance only a small portion of the assets so maybe additional equity funding is in order.

e   Cash balance at bank is largely due to the extended trade credit and maybe valuable discounts are being lost.

f   The firm is vulnerable and would be in difficulties if creditors pressed their claims.

g   The profit for the year is good relative to the funds invested in the business. That no tax was payable indicates that there were losses carried forward even though there are accumulated profits in the Statement of Financial Performance appropriation.

h   The bank is not advised to grant an overdraft. Overdrafts are at call and it does not seem that the firm would benefit from more short-term funding.

i   The firm should look towards industry funding for the special order or even consider a commercial bill facility linked with the proposed contract.

Questions and problems

1 · Financial framework

What is the relationship between each of the following?

a   the primary market and the listed market
b   the secondary market and the listed market
c   the secondary market and the unlisted market

2 · Characteristics of securities

Consider return, risk, maturity, liquidity and marketability of each of the following investments and classify each as to whether it would be rated in relative terms as low, medium or high on the characteristics:

a   shares traded on the Stock Exchange
b   Treasury notes
c   preference shares
d   listed corporate debentures
e   non-listed corporate debentures
f   real estate in an exclusive suburb

3 · Methods of financing

The Board of Playtime Ltd, a listed company, needs to raise more funds to purchase a competitor. Members of the Board come from artistic backgrounds and are relatively naive in relation to financial matters. One member of the Board, who is a retired ballet dancer, has suggested extending the bank overdraft to cover the purchase. A second suggestion was to raise the funds by mortgaging the new season films which the firm has purchased the rights to showing. A third alternative is to issue more securities to the market, but the Board does not like this alternative as it would reduce the control of existing shareholders.

Which alternative should Playtime use, and how could it attempt to raise the funds?

4 · Role of authorised financial intermediaries

Why has the Australian Government established authorised foreign exchange dealers?

5 · Financing servies

What type of financial intermediary are you likely to approach to arrange the following?

a   a hire-purchase contract
b   an instalment credit arrangement
c   an overdraft facility
d   some wholesale finance for warehouse inventory
e   a promissory note arrangement
f   an investment of $50,000 in government securities
g   protection for an investment held in an Italian bank against fluctuations in the lira
h   a loan for a house
i   a saving arrangement with protection against income loss
j   an investment of $5,000 for 20 days
k   an investment of $10,000 into a large industrial property mortgage
l   a funeral saving plan
m   a purchase of shares in a listed public company
n   a purchase of shares in a non-listed company

6 · Cost of borrowing

Mike and Kim Makemoney have worked out a line of credit arrangement that allows them to borrow up to $10 million at any time. The interest rate is 2 per cent per quarter. In addition, 3 per cent of the amount that they borrow must be deposited in a non-interest-bearing account.

a   What is the effective annual interest rate on this lending arrangement?
b   Suppose they need $5 million today and they repay it in six months. How much interest will they pay?

7 · Cost of borrowing

Your firm has an average collection period of 60 days. Current practice is to factor all receivables immediately at a 4 per cent discount. What is the effective cost of borrowing in this case? Assume that default is extremely unlikely.

8 · Bank bill values

Slobuilding Company Ltd requires funds to meet a short-term deficit which it has identified in its cash budget. It has determined that it will require $480,000 for three or four months. It has approached three banks and obtained the following quotations for bills arranged with a minimum face value of $100,000.

	Term	Yield	Term	Yield
Wes Bank	90 days	14.36%	180 days	14.30%
Naz Bank	90 days	14.40%	180 days	14.00%
Gin Bank	90 days	14.35%	180 days	14.10%

How much would Slobuilding receive if it borrowed using the bill facilities provided by the banks? What do the banks think is going to happen to interest rates? Which borrowing arrangement would you advise Slobuilding to use?

9 · Short-term policy

Gaunt Components Ltd and Clive Bits Ltd are competing manufacturing firms. Use the information contained in their statements to answer the following questions:

a   How are the current assets of each firm financed?

b   Which firm has the larger investment in current assets on an absolute basis? On a relative basis? Which of these is more meaningful in determining working capital policy? Why?

c   Which firm is more likely to incur carrying costs, and which is more likely to incur shortage costs? Why?

GAUNT COMPONENTS LTD
Statement of Financial Position as at 30 June

	200X+1 ($000)	200X ($000)
Assets		
Cash	13,862	16,339
Accounts receivable (net)	23,887	26,778
Inventory	54,867	42,287
Total current assets	92,616	85,404
Plant, property, and equipment	101,543	99,615
less Accumulated depreciation	34,331	31,957
Other assets	14,966	14,929
Total assets	174,794	167,991
Liabilities and shareholders' equity		
Accounts payable	6,494	4,893
Notes payable	10,483	11,617
Accrued expenses	7,422	7,227
Other payables	9,924	8,460
Total current liabilities	34,323	32,197
Long-term debt	22,036	22,036
Total liabilities	56,359	54,233
Paid-up capital	38,000	38,000
Capital reserve	12,000	12,000
Retained earnings	68,435	63,758
Total shareholders' funds	118,435	113,758
Total liabilities and shareholders' equity	174,794	167,991

GAUNT COMPONENTS LTD
Statement of Financial Performance for the year ended 30 June 200X+1

Assets	($000)
Sales	$162,749
Other income	1,002
Total income	163,751
Costs of goods sold	103,570
Selling and administrative costs	28,495
Depreciation	2,274
Total expenses	134,339
Pre-tax earnings	$ 29,412
Taxes	14,890
Net earnings	14,522

Dividends	9,845
Retained earnings	4,677

CLIVE BITS LTD
Statement of Financial Position as at 30 June

	200X+1 ($000)	200X ($000)
Assets		
Cash	5,794	3,307
Accounts receivable (net)	26,177	22,133
Inventory	46,463	44,661
Total current assets	78,434	70,010
Plant, property, and equipment	31,842	31,116
less Accumulated depreciation	19,297	18,143
Goodwill	763	688
Other assets	1,601	1,385
Total assets	93,343	85,147
Liabilities and shareholders' equity		
Accounts payable	6,008	5,019
Notes payable	3,722	645
Accrued expenses	4,254	3,295
Other taxes payable	5,688	4,951
Total current liabilities	19,672	13,910
Paid-up capital	20,576	20,576
Capital reserves	5,624	5,624
Retained earnings	48,598	46,164
Outside equity interest—Loss	1,127	1,127
Total shareholders' funds	73,671	71,237
Total liabilities and shareholders' equity	93,343	85,147

CLIVE BITS LTD

Statement of Financial Performance for the year ended 30 June 200X+1

	($000)
Sales	$91,374
Other income	1,067
Total income	92,441
Costs of goods sold	59,042
Selling and administrative costs	18,068
Depreciation	1,154
Total expenses	78,264
Earnings before taxes	14,177
Taxes	6,838
Net earnings	7,339

Dividends	4,905
Retained earnings	2,434

10 · Short-term financial policy

Ozplay Ltd has produced the following abridged Statement of Financial Position. Key statistics collected from industry information suggest that the current ratio should be 0.9:1 and that the debt/equity ratio should be about 1.7:1. The Board is concerned because the working capital has fallen to an unacceptable level.

Discuss the financial position of Ozplay, considering the industry statistics and the Board's concern.

OZPLAY LTD

Statement of Financial Position as at 30 June 200X

	($000)	($000)
Current assets		
Cash	1	
Accounts receivable	26,000	
Inventory	48,000	
Total current assets	74,001	
Current liabilities		
Bank overdraft	25,000	
Accounts payable	50	
Provision for taxation	27,000	
Provision for dividend	6,500	
Accrued expenses	4,000	
Bank loan due 200X+1	10,000	
Total current liabilities	$72,550	
Working capital		$ 1,451
Fixed assets (net) and intangibles		325,000
		$326,451
Long-term liabilities—other bank loans due in 10 yrs		201,451
Shareholders' funds		125,000

11 · Bills of exchange

Define the role (if any) of each of the following in relation to a bill of exchange:

a an acceptor
b a payee
c a drawer
d an endorser
e a bearer

12 · Promissory notes

Define the role (if any) of each of the following in relation to a promissory note:

a   an acceptor
b   a payee
c   a drawer
d   an endorser
e   a bearer

13 · Contingent liabilities on bills

Patsy Hooker has drawn a bill of exchange in order to buy property from Roy Black. The bill has been accepted by Estate Bank. Roy Black has transferred the bill to Beyce White who then transferred it to LJ Alice who passed it to Profess Ltd. The bill is now due. Who is responsible for paying Profess Ltd? If the person charged with the first responsibility of paying is bankrupt, who should Profess Ltd approach as the second settler? Who would be the last person Profess Ltd is legally entitled to claim payment against?

14 · Financing with bills

In January, Fastbuck Ltd, a small private company, had current liabilities through a bank loan for $28,000. Fastbuck wished to buy real estate valued at $110,000. Super Bank was prepared to offer a deal which would provide finance for the loan and the land purchase through 180-day bank bills. Super Bank would charge 2.5 per cent on the bank bill rate for this facility. In January the bank bill rate was 8.25 per cent. Fastbuck accepted the deal.

In July, when Fastbuck had to roll over the bank bill, the bank bill rate had fallen to 6.95 per cent. In addition, Fastbuck was able to reduce the principal of the original debt because it had accumulated $12,315.89 towards repayment. How much would Fastbuck have to execute a bank bill for in January when the rollover occurred in July? How much could Fastbuck reduce the principal of the debt in July? How much is the interest payment for the July rollover?

15 · Costs of borrowing

This is a challenge problem. In exchange for a $500 million fixed commitment line of credit, your firm has agreed to do the following:

i   Pay 4 per cent per quarter of any funds actually borrowed.
ii   Maintain a 3 per cent compensating balance on any funds actually borrowed—under this arrangement the firm holds the funds in a non-interest-bearing cheque account.
iii   Pay an up-front commitment fee of 0.2 per cent of the amount of the line.

Based on this information, answer the following:

a   Ignoring the fixed commitment fee, what is the effective annual interest rate on this line of credit?
b   Suppose your firm immediately uses $40 million of the line and pays it off in a year. What is the effective annual interest rate on this $40 million loan?

PART SEVEN

Long-term
financing

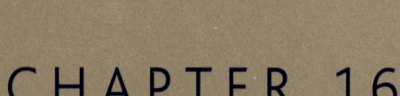

CHAPTER 16

Long-term
financing: an
introduction

Objective

This chapter explains the characteristics of corporate debt, preference shares and ordinary shares. On completion, the terms security, seniority, repayment and protective covenants of debt should be understood. The strength and weakness of preference shares will be understood, along with the basic characteristics of ordinary shares.

Study tips ▷ While the material of the chapter is not difficult, it must be understood because it provides much of the framework for later work. Students should understand the differences and roles of ordinary shares, preference shares, debentures and unsecured notes in funding the assets of the organisation. Remember that it is the risk of the security that creates the differences.

Introduction ▷ Corporate securities such as shares and debentures can be perplexing to study. Frequently, the concepts are simple and logical, but the language is unfamiliar and rich in jargon. Many of the terms and ideas we describe in this chapter and the next have appeared elsewhere in the book. Our task here and in the next several chapters is to assemble these pieces into a reasonably complete picture of long-term corporate financing.

In this chapter, we describe the main features of long-term financing and corporate securities. We begin with a look at long-term debt, preference shares and ordinary shares. We go on to briefly consider patterns of the different kinds of long-term financing. We defer to a later chapter our discussion of the institutional, legal and regulatory complexities involved in selling securities to the public.

One consequence of debt financing is the possibility of bankruptcy. Events preceding bankruptcy are referred to as *financial distress*. Because the prospect of bankruptcy is an important consideration in long-term financing, we conclude this chapter with a brief discussion of financial distress, bankruptcy and reorganisation.

16.1 ■ Corporate long-term debt

In this section, we begin our discussion of corporate debt by describing in some detail the basic terms and features that make up a typical long-term corporate debt. We discuss additional issues associated with long-term debt in subsequent sections.

Securities issued by corporations may be classified roughly as *equity securities* and *debt securities*. At its crudest level, a debt represents something that must be repaid; it is the result of borrowing money. When corporations borrow, they promise to make regularly scheduled interest payments and to repay the original amount borrowed (that is, the principal). The person or firm making the loan is called the *creditor* or *lender*. The corporation borrowing the money is called the *debtor* or *borrower*.

From a financial point of view, the main differences between debt and equity are the following:

1 Debt is not an ownership interest in the firm. Creditors generally do not have voting power.
2 The corporation's payment of interest on debt is considered a cost of doing business and is fully tax-deductible.
3 Unpaid debt is a liability of the firm. If it is not paid, the creditors can legally claim the assets of the firm. This action can result in liquidation or reorganisation, two of the possible consequences of bankruptcy. Thus, one of the costs of issuing debt is the possibility of financial failure. This problem does not arise when equity is issued.

What is debt?

In simple terms, debt is an obligation to pay a specific amount of money to another party. It involves the lender advancing a sum of money (the principal) to the borrower for a specified period. In return, the borrower pays the lender an agreed rate of interest at specified intervals and at the end of the agreed period repays the outstanding balance. Some debt arrangements may be structured with equal regular payments which incorporate part principal repayment and the period interest payment. These are *credit foncier* loans and most home mortgages operate in this way.

The description of debt can be expanded by reference to the following characteristics:

• short-term versus long-term debt;
• fixed versus floating interest rate loans;
• secured versus unsecured debt; and
• domestic versus foreign debt.

Short-term debt usually means repayment periods from between one day and up to one year, whereas *long-term* debt[1] is where the repayment period is greater than one year. Interest payable by the borrower may be set at a predetermined rate which is *fixed* for the term of the loan; or at a *floating* (or *variable*) rate, at a margin above a benchmark rate, which is reset periodically in line with movements in market interest rates. Fixed rate loans tend to have higher interest rates than variable rate loans.

Interest rates may be capped. This means that for an upfront fee a loan, set at a floating rate, is guaranteed by the lender not to exceed some predetermined rate. For example, for a fee of $1,500 a borrower may be able to undertake a loan for say 7 per cent which is capped to 8.5 per cent. The interest rate may go up or down but the highest rate (ceiling) paid will be 8.5 per cent over the term of the loan.

Secured debt provides the lender with legal access to assets of the borrower if it should be necessary to recover the original amount of the debt. When the debt is *unsecured* the lender is entirely dependent on the capacity and willingness of the borrower to repay the debt. Because of its lower risk of repayment of principal, secured debt has a *lower interest rate* than unsecured debt. A common security offered by Australian companies is a *floating charge* over the assets of the company. With a floating charge, the claim of the lender is not lodged over a specific asset or assets of the borrower but fixes on a specific asset or assets if the borrower fails to make a payment that has fallen due. The process of fixing on an asset or a group of assets is known as *crystallisation of the charge*. A floating charge allows the borrowing company to sell, buy or vary assets according to the requirements of business until there is a default in the loan repayments.

An unsecured lender can access corporate assets indirectly if the company goes into liquidation, but this class of lender ranks behind the secured lender. A *negative pledge* by a borrower is often required by the lender in conjunction with an unsecured debt. A negative pledge is an undertaking by the borrower not to use the assets to provide security (or any further security) for additional loans.

Borrowed funds may be sourced from within Australia in Australian dollars or borrowed offshore and denominated in either Australian dollars or a foreign currency. Chapter 23 looks at international corporate finance.

Long-term debt: The basics

The types of long-term debt products offered in the Australian corporate markets are:

- debentures;
- secured and unsecured notes;
- convertible notes;
- fixed deposit loans;
- mortgages;
- eurobonds;
- eurocurrency term loans (floating rate notes);
- leasing;
- project finance;
- transferable loan certificates; and
- derivative debt products.

Debentures are loans to the company offering fixed rates of interest for certain periods. They are usually secured by a fixed charge or floating charge over the assets of the company, and a trustee is appointed to protect the interests of holders. This is the most secure loan to a company.

Secured notes are for all practical purposes the same as debentures but their protection is usually a second mortgage over the assets so that they rank immediately behind the debenture holders in the situation of default.

Unsecured notes are also loans to the company but they are usually for shorter periods and no assets are set as security. The holders of the notes rank as ordinary creditors in the event of default.

Convertible notes are a cross between a loan and a share. They are similar to unsecured notes because they have fixed interest rates. However, the unique characteristic of a convertible note is that it can be converted on maturity, fully or partly, to ordinary shares or redeemed in full. The notes are usually issued at approximately the market price of the share (at the time of issue) and the interest rates offered are usually lower than the unsecured debt issue.

Fixed deposits are loans at fixed rates for definite terms. The rates are slightly higher than for unsecured notes. They rank as ordinary creditors in the event of default as no trust deed is filed. Unlike debentures or notes, they are not traded or exchanged.

Mortgages are the conveyance of property for the security of the debt. The title of the property rests with the lender until the debt is repaid and then the property is conveyed back to the borrower.

Eurobonds are fixed interest borrowings with maturities of five to 10 years. The issue is guaranteed (underwritten) by an international syndicate of financiers and sold in countries other than the country of the currency in which the issue is denominated. They are unsecured and they are only accepted in the market if the borrower is considered to be substantial. Issues are usually greater than $50 million, with an average of about $100 million. Australian companies that have raised borrowings through eurobonds are Alcoa of Australia Ltd, the BHP Billiton Ltd, Comalco Aluminium Ltd, TNT Limited, Coles Myer and Pacific Dunlop.

Eurocurrency floating rate notes (FRNs) are debt instruments with rates that are periodically adjusted to reflect market interest rates. Usually an Australian bank borrows the amount required in a foreign currency and then on-lends it to the Australian corporate borrower. The State Bank of Victoria, which subsequently managed to get into financial difficulties, in 1989 raised $375 million in United States' dollars using two eurocurrency issues, a $250 million variable rate note issue and a $125 million 10-year floating rate issue.

The simplest form of *leasing* is *direct leasing*, which involves only two parties: the supplier of the funds (as lessor) which purchases equipment and leases it to the customer (as lessee). The lease term may be about five years and repayments are at mutually suitable intervals ranging from monthly to annually. Repayments are sufficient to cover the capital cost of the leased goods plus some profit for the lessor. At the expiry of the term, the goods may be returned to the lessor, purchased by the lessee, or a further lease negotiated if the lessee wishes to continue using the goods.

The term *leveraged leasing* refers to a lease in which the lessor borrows to fund the purchase of the equipment to be leased. For example, a lessor wishing to purchase equipment costing $1 million would use say $0.2 million of its own funds, called the equity funds, and $0.8 million of borrowed funds, called the debt funds. Generally the lessee's lease repayments would cover the repayment of the debt and related interest costs while the lessor would rely on depreciation and other taxation benefits to provide a return to cover the $0.2 million equity funds. The use of leveraged leasing has almost disappeared in Australia in recent years.

Cross border leasing is basically another form of leveraged lease involving parties in two or more countries, designed to take advantage of differing tax regulations between countries. Queensland Rail and Stanwell Power Station are each involved in the cross border leasing of some of their assets. In Stanwell's case, this involves some of their generators.

Project finance is used for large projects where the level of funding exceeds $100 million, such as large mining projects like the Argyle Diamond project ($400 million), and the Sydney Harbour Tunnel. The arrangement usually involves a sponsoring company (or companies), the project and the lender. Most project finance raised in Australia is limited recourse financing. This means that before completion of the project the lenders have restricted access to the sponsoring companies for repayment of the debt if there are problems with the loan. Once a project is completed, lenders only have recourse to the project's cash flows and assets. Completion is therefore vital for the lender and the borrowing companies.

Transferable loan certificates (TLC) are certificates evidencing the existence of a debt that can be traded by the holder. The transferable certificates are generally of three- to five-year maturities.

Derivative debt products

With the deregulation of the Australian financial system, corporations, government entities and financial institutions have become concerned with managing interest rate risk. As a result derivative products have been constructed to assist in the management. These derivatives include:

- interest rate swaps;
- forward rate agreements (FRAs);
- interest rate futures; and
- options on futures contracts.

No new underlying securities are issued; however, the derivatives act as a form of insurance. For example, a forward rate agreement (FRA) is an agreement between two parties on an interest rate for a specified period from a specified future settlement date, based on an agreed notional principal amount. No commitment is made between the parties to the FRAs to lend or borrow the principal amount. The exposure to both parties in this arrangement is only the difference between the agreed interest rate and the settlement rate applicable at the date of settlement. So a borrower can combine an FRA with a variable interest loan to fix the interest rate that will be paid in the overall package. Interest rate futures and options on futures contracts are arrangements that allow borrowers and lenders to lock into interest rates. Although the arrangements are different, the outcomes are similar to the FRAs.

Interest rate swaps allow companies to use their credit standing to reduce their overall cost. Consider as an example a company and a semi-government authority. The company, due to its credit rating, may be unable to raise funds from the long-term debt market; or if so, only at a very high cost. It would therefore be willing to pay a premium to obtain fixed rate finance. On the other hand, the semi-government authority, which has a higher credit rating, can access the long-term debt market and the short-term money market at a relatively low cost.

Assume the semi-government authority can raise three-year fixed interest funds at 6.60 per cent per annum or variable rate funds at the bank bill rate which is 6.40 per cent per annum. The company can borrow long-term fixed interest funds at 10.50 per cent per annum or variable rate funds at the bank bill rate plus 2.5 per cent per annum. The interest rate charges can be summarised as:

Type of interest rate	Semi-government authority	Company	Interest rate differential
1. Floating rate	Bank bill rate	Bank bill rate + 2.5%	2.5%
2. Fixed rate	6.60% p.a.	10.50% (if available)	3.9%

Both parties can borrow in the market in which they get the best relative terms and then enter an interest rate swap to exchange the terms of their funding and achieve a lower cost than would otherwise have been available. The semi-government authority issues fixed securities and the company issues bank bills. Both parties then enter into an interest rate swap as indicated in Figure 16.1 (overleaf).

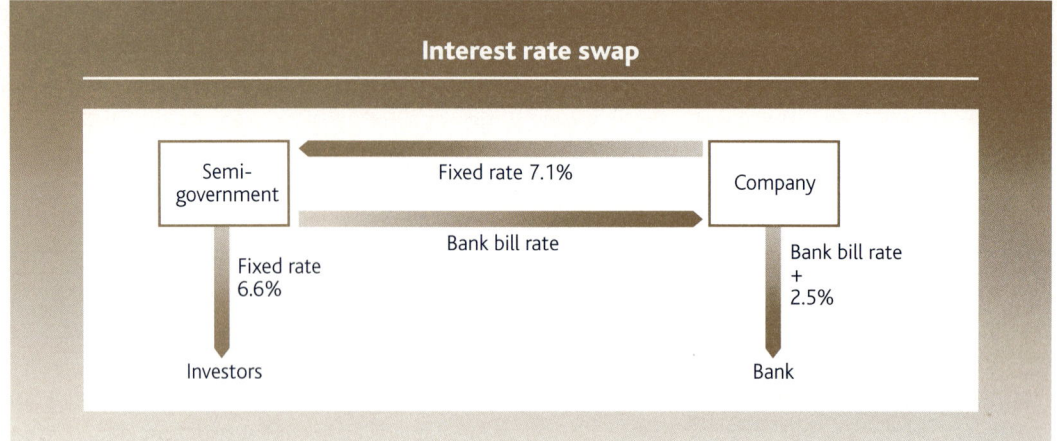

Interest rate swap

The semi-government authority is prepared to swap its fixed rate obligation for floating rate funds at the bank bill rate for a fee of say 0.50 per cent.

The cost of funds is then reduced to both borrowers as indicated below.

Type of interest rate	Semi-government authority (rate %)	Company (rate %)
Pays to investors/bank	6.60	Bank bill + 2.50
Receives from counterparty	(7.10)	(Bank bill)
Pays to counterparty	Bank bill	7.10
Net cost:	Bank bill −0.50	9.60
Alternative cost:	Bank bill	10.50 Fixed rate
Cost savings:	0.50	0.90

Because of its reimbursement of the bank bill rate from the semi-government authority, the company has converted its variable rate borrowing to a fixed rate borrowing. The rate of 9.60 per cent per annum, which it is paying, is made up of:

Semi-government authority's cost + the fee for the swap + its variable margin over bank bills

$$= 6.6\% + 0.50\% + 2.50\%$$
$$= 9.60\%$$

So an interest rate swap basically consists of the exchange between two counterparties of a fixed interest rate for a floating interest rate. The amount of interest to be paid is calculated by reference to a notionally agreed principal. Principal amounts are not physically exchanged in an interest rate swap.

Is it debt or equity?

Sometimes it is not clear if a particular security is debt or equity. For example, suppose a corporation issues a perpetual debenture with interest payable solely from corporate income if and only if earned. Whether this is really a debt or not is hard to say and is primarily a legal and semantic issue. Courts and taxing authorities would have the final say.

Corporations are very adept at creating exotic, hybrid securities that have many features of equity but are treated as debt. Obviously, the distinction between debt and equity is very important for tax purposes. So one reason that corporations try to create a debt security that is really equity is to obtain the tax benefits of debt and the bankruptcy benefits of equity.

As a general rule, equity represents an ownership interest, and it is a residual claim. This means that equityholders are paid after debtholders. As a result of this, the risks and benefits associated with owning debt and equity are different. To give just one example, the maximum reward for owning a straight debt security is ultimately fixed by the amount of the loan, whereas there is no necessary upper limit to the potential reward from owning an equity interest.

Securities with characteristics of debt and equity are called *hybrid securities* or *mezzanine debt*. Types of hybrid securities are:

- convertible notes;
- subordinated debt; and
- preference shares.

Convertible notes were explained above. Subordinate loans may be provided by a major shareholder to a company with the condition that they will not be repaid until all creditors have been paid in full. Preference shares are explained later.

For example, Woolworths Ltd completed an issue of equity hybrids to raise $583 million. Woolworths issued non-maturing perpetual notes at an interest rate of 2% above the bank bill swap rate to raise the funds. In the Statement of Financial Position, the company showed the notes as part of the group capital.

The debenture trust deed

The **debenture trust deed** is the written agreement between the corporation (the borrower) and its creditors. Usually, a trustee (a bank or public auditor) is appointed by the corporation to represent the debtholders as trustee. The trustee must (1) make sure the terms of the trust deed are obeyed, (2) manage the sinking fund (described below), and (3) represent the debtholders in default—that is, if the company defaults on its payments to them.

debenture trust deed
written agreement between the corporation and the lender detailing the terms of the debt issue

The trust deed is a legal document. It is several hundred pages in length and generally makes for very tedious reading. It is an important document, however, because it generally includes the following provisions:

1. the basic terms of the issue;
2. the amount of the debentures issued;
3. a description of property used as security;
4. the repayment arrangements;
5. the call provisions; and
6. details of the protective covenants.

We discuss these features next.

Terms of the issue

Corporate debt usually has a face value (i.e. a denomination) of $100 (note: overseas markets, in particular Japan and the United States, use a face value of $1,000). This is called the *principal value* and it is stated on the debt certificate. So, if a corporation wanted to borrow $1 million, 10,000 debentures would have to be sold.

Corporate debt is usually in **registered form**. For example, the trust deed might read as follows:

registered form
registrar of company records ownership of each note; payment is made directly to the owner of record

> **Interest is payable semi-annually on 1 July and 1 January of each year to the person in whose name the debenture is registered at the close of business on 15 June or 15 December, respectively.**

This means that the company will record the ownership of each debenture and record any changes in ownership. The company will pay the interest and principal by cheque mailed directly to the address of the owner of record.

Alternatively, the debenture could be in **bearer** form. This means that the certificate is the basic evidence of ownership, and the corporation will 'pay the bearer'.

There are two drawbacks to bearer debentures. First, they are difficult to recover if they are lost or stolen. Second, because the company does not know who owns its debt, it cannot notify debtholders of important events. Bearer debentures are not common in Australia.

bearer security

a security whose ownership is not registered by the issuer and possession of the physical document is primary evidence of ownership

Security

Debt securities are classified according to the collateral and mortgages used to protect the debtholder.

Collateral is a general term that, strictly speaking, means securities (e.g. debentures and shares) that are pledged as security for payment of debt. However, the term 'collateral' is often used much more loosely to refer to any form of security.

Mortgage securities are secured by a mortgage on the real property of the borrower. The property involved is usually real estate; for example, land or buildings. The legal document that describes the mortgage is called a mortgage trust deed. The floating charge mortgage was discussed earlier.

In Australia the term 'debentures' is used for secured company debt and 'notes' for unsecured debt. The term 'bond' is used to identify government or semi-government debt. In the United States, the term 'bond' is used to denote secured corporate debt, 'debenture' is used for unsecured debt, and 'note' for unsecured debt with a maturity date less than 10 years.

Repayment

Debt can be repaid at maturity, at which time the debtholder will receive the stated or face value of the debt, or they may be repaid in part or in entirety before maturity. Early repayment in some form is more typical and is often handled through a sinking fund.

A **sinking fund** is an account managed by the debenture trustee for the purpose of repaying the debt. The company makes annual payments to the trustee, who then uses the funds to retire a portion of the debt. The trustee does this by either buying up some of the debt in the market or calling in a fraction of the outstanding debt. This second option is discussed in the next section.

sinking fund

account managed by the debenture trustee for early debenture redemption

There are many different kinds of sinking fund arrangements, and the details would be spelled out in the trust deed.

The call provision

A call provision allows the company to repurchase or 'call' part or all of the debt issue at stated prices over a specific period. Corporate debt is usually callable.

Generally, the call price is above the debenture's face value. The difference between the call price and the face value is the **call premium**. The amount of the call premium usually becomes smaller over time. One arrangement is to initially set the call premium equal to the annual coupon payment and then make it decline to zero the closer the call date is to maturity.

call premium

amount by which the call price exceeds the paid-up value of the debenture

deferred call

call provision prohibiting the company from redeeming the debt prior to a certain date

Call provisions are not usually operative during the first part of the debt's life. This makes the call provision less of a worry for debtholders in the debt's early years. For example, a company might be prohibited from calling its debts for the first 10 years. This is a **deferred call**. During this period, the debt is said to be *call protected*.

Protective covenants

A **protective covenant** is that part of the trust deed that limits certain actions a company might otherwise wish to take during the term of the loan. Protective covenants can be classified into two types: negative covenants and positive (or affirmative) covenants.

A *negative covenant* is a 'thou shalt not'. It limits or prohibits actions that the company may take. Here are some typical examples:

1   The firm must limit the amount of dividends it pays according to some formula.
2   The firm cannot pledge any assets to other lenders.
3   The firm cannot merge with another firm.
4   The firm cannot sell or lease any major assets without approval by the lender.
5   The firm cannot issue additional long-term debt.

A *positive covenant* is a 'thou shalt'. It specifies an action that the company agrees to take or a condition the company must abide by. Here are some examples:

1   The company must maintain its working capital at or above some specified minimum level.
2   The company must periodically furnish audited financial statements to the lender.
3   The firm must maintain any collateral or security in good condition.

This is only a partial list of covenants; a particular trust deed may feature many different ones.

protective covenant
part of the trust deed limiting certain transactions that can be taken during the term of the loan, usually to protect the lender's interest

---

Concept questions

16.1a *What are the distinguishing features of debt as compared to equity?*
16.1b *What is the trust deed? What are protective covenants? Give some examples.*
16.1c *What is a sinking fund?*

 ## 16.2 ∎ Debt ratings

The two leading debt rating firms are Moody's and Standard & Poor's (S&P). John Moody (1868–1958) laid the foundations for Moody's Investors Service in 1900, when he published *Moody's Manual of Industrial and Corporation Securities*. In 1909, Moody introduced the first bond ratings as part of *Moody's Analyses of Railroad Investments*. He used the 'Aaa' through to 'C' symbols that have since become a world standard to rate some 1,500 individual securities of over 200 US railroads. From the very beginning, Moody assigned independent rating opinions to help his investor readers manage credit risk. Then—as now—Moody's ratings were based on public information and assigned without the request of issuers. See Table 16.1 for a description of the rating codes.

Current as of February 2003:

	Bonds and notes		Bank deposits	
	Long-term	**Short-term**	**Long-term**	**Short-term**
Australia	Aa2	P-1	Aa2	P-1

TABLE
16.1

Rating codes

Aaa: Bonds which are rated **Aaa** are judged to be of the best quality. They carry the smallest degree of investment risk and are generally referred to as 'gilt edged'. Interest payments are protected by a large or by an exceptionally stable margin and principal is secure. While the various protective elements are likely to change, such changes as can be visualised are most unlikely to impair the fundamentally strong position of such issues.

Aa: Bonds which are rated **Aa** are judged to be of high quality by all standards. Together with the **Aaa** group they comprise what are generally known as high-grade bonds. They are rated lower than the best bonds because margins of protection may not be as large as in **Aaa** securities or fluctuation of protective elements may be of greater amplitude or there may be other elements present which make the long-term risk appear somewhat larger than for the **Aaa** securities.

A: Bonds which are rated **A** possess many favourable investment attributes and are to be considered as upper-medium-grade obligations. Factors giving security to principal and interest are considered adequate, but elements may be present which suggest a susceptibility to impairment some time in the future.

Baa: Bonds which are rated **Baa** are considered as medium-grade obligations (i.e. they are neither highly protected nor poorly secured). Interest payments and principal security appear adequate for the present but certain protective elements may be lacking or may be characteristically unreliable over any great length of time. Such bonds lack outstanding investment characteristics and in fact have speculative characteristics as well.

Ba: Bonds which are rated **Ba** are judged to have speculative elements; their future cannot be considered as well-assured. Often the protection of interest and principal payments may be moderate, and thereby not well safeguarded during both good and bad times over the future. Uncertainty of position characterises bonds in this class.

B: Bonds which are rated **B** generally lack characteristics of the desirable investment. Assurance of interest and principal payments or of maintenance of other terms of the contract over any long period of time may be small.

Caa: Bonds which are rated **Caa** are of poor standing. Such issues may be in default or there may be present elements of danger with respect to principal or interest.

Ca: Bonds which are rated **Ca** represent obligations which are speculative in a high degree. Such issues are often in default or have other marked shortcomings.

C: Bonds which are rated **C** are the lowest rated class of bonds, and issues so rated can be regarded as having extremely poor prospects of ever attaining any real investment standing.

Short-term ratings

Moody's short-term debt ratings are opinions of the ability of issuers to punctually repay senior debt obligations. These obligations have an original maturity not exceeding one year, unless explicitly noted.

Moody's employs the following three designations, all judged to be investment grade, to indicate the relative repayment ability of rated issuers:

Prime-1: Issuers rated **Prime-1** (or supporting institutions) have a superior ability for repayment of senior short-term debt obligations. **Prime-1** repayment ability will often be evidenced by many of the following characteristics:
- Leading market positions in well-established industries.
- High rates of return on funds employed.

- Conservative capitalisation structure with moderate reliance on debt and ample asset protection.
- Broad margins in earnings coverage of fixed financial charges and high internal cash generation.
- Well-established access to a range of financial markets and assured sources of alternate liquidity.

Prime-2: Issuers rated **Prime-2** (or supporting institutions) have a strong ability for repayment of senior short-term debt obligations. This will normally be evidenced by many of the characteristics cited above but to a lesser degree. Earnings trends and coverage ratios, while sound, may be more subject to variation. Capitalisation characteristics, while still appropriate, may be more affected by external conditions. Ample alternate liquidity is maintained.

Prime-3: Issuers rated **Prime-3** (or supporting institutions) have an acceptable ability for repayment of senior short-term obligations. The effect of industry characteristics and market compositions may be more pronounced. Variability in earnings and profitability may result in changes in the level of debt protection measurements and may require relatively high financial leverage. Adequate alternate liquidity is maintained.

Source: Moody's Investors Service

Edward I. Altman

In their own words

Edward I. Altman* on junk bonds

One of the most important developments in corporate finance over the last 20 years has been the re-emergence of publicly owned and traded low-rated corporate debt. Originally offered to the public in the early 1900s to help finance some of our emerging growth industries, these high-yield, high-risk bonds virtually disappeared after the rash of bond defaults during the Depression. Recently, however, the junk bond market has been catapulted from being an insignificant element in the corporate fixed-income market to being one of the fastest-growing and most controversial types of financing mechanisms.

The term junk *emanates from the dominant type of low-rated bond issues outstanding prior to 1977 when the 'market' consisted almost exclusively of original-issue investment-grade bonds that fell from their lofty status to a higher-default risk, speculative-grade level. These so-called fallen angels amounted to about $8.5 billion in 1977. At the end of 1998, fallen angels comprised about 10 per cent of the $450 billion publicly owned junk bond market.*

Beginning in 1977, issuers began to go directly to the public to raise capital for growth purposes. Early users of junk bonds were energy-related firms, cable TV companies, airlines, and assorted other industrial companies. The emerging growth company rationale coupled with relatively high returns to early investors helped legitimise this sector.

By far the most important and controversial aspect of junk bond financing was its role in the corporate restructuring movement from 1985 to 1989. High-leverage transactions and

acquisitions, such as leveraged buyouts (LBOs), which occur when a firm is taken private, and leveraged recapitalisations (debt-for-equity swaps), transformed the face of corporate America, leading to a heated debate as to the economic and social consequences of firms being transformed with debt–equity ratios of at least 6:1.

These transactions involved increasingly large companies, and the multibillion-dollar takeover became fairly common, finally capped by the huge $251 billion RJR Nabisco LBO in 1989. LBOs were typically financed with about 60 per cent senior bank and insurance company debt, about 25–30 per cent subordinated public debt (junk bonds), and 10–15 per cent equity. The junk bond segment is sometimes referred to as 'mezzanine' financing because it lies between the 'balcony' senior debt and the 'basement' equity.

These restructurings resulted in huge fees to advisors and underwriters and huge premiums to the old shareholders who were bought out, and they continued as long as the market was willing to buy these new debt offerings at what appeared to be a favorable risk–return trade-off. The bottom fell out of the market in the last six months of 1989 due to a number of factors including a marked increase in defaults, government regulation against S&Ls† holding junk bonds, and a recession.

The default rate rose dramatically to 4 per cent in 1989 and then skyrocketed in 1990 and 1991 to 10.1 per cent and 10.3 per cent, respectively, with about $19 billion of defaults in 1991. By the end of 1990, the pendulum of growth in new junk bond issues and returns to investors swung dramatically downward as prices plummeted and the new-issue market all but dried up. The year 1991 was a pivotal year in that, despite record defaults, bond prices and new issues rebounded strongly as the prospects for the future brightened.

In the early 1990s, the financial market was questioning the very survival of the junk bond market. The answer was a resounding 'yes', as the amount of new issues soared to record annual levels of $40 billion in 1992 and almost $60 billion in 1993, and in 1997 reached an impressive $119 billion. Coupled with plummeting default rates (under 2.0 per cent each year in the 1993–97 period) and attractive returns in these years, the risk–return characteristics have been extremely favorable.

The junk bond market in the late 1990s was a quieter one compared to that of the 1980s, but, in terms of growth and returns, it was healthier than ever before. While the low default rates in 1992–98 helped to fuel new investment funds and new issues, the market experienced its ups and downs in subsequent years. Indeed, default rates started to rise in 1999 and accelerated in 2000 and 2001. The latter year saw defaults reach record levels as the economy slipped into a recession and investors suffered from the excesses of lending in the late 1990s. Despite these highly volatile events and problems with liquidity, we are convinced that high yield bonds will be a major source of corporate debt financing and a legitimate asset class for investors.

* **Edward I. Altman** is Max L. Heine Professor of Finance and Vice Director of the Salomon Center at the Stern School of Business of New York University. He is widely recognised as one of the world's experts on bankruptcy and credit analysis as well as the high-yield, or junk bond, market.

† **Saving and loans**—a US form of financial institution with similar activities to Australian non-bank institutions.

Concept questions

16.2a *What is a junk debenture?*
16.2b *What does a debenture rating say about the risk of fluctuations in a debenture's value from interest rate changes?*

16.3 ▪ Some different types of debenture

Thus far, we have considered 'plain vanilla' debentures. In this section, we look at some more unusual types: zero coupon debentures, floating-rate debentures, and others.

Zero coupon debentures

A debenture that pays no coupons at all must be offered at a price that is much lower than its stated value. Such debentures are called **zero coupon debentures**, or just zeroes.[2]

Suppose the DDB Company issues a $100 face value five-year zero coupon debenture. The initial price is set at $49.72. It is straightforward to check that, at this price, the debenture yields 15 per cent to maturity. The total interest paid over the life of the debenture is $100 − 49.72 = $50.28.

For tax purposes, the issuer of a zero coupon debenture deducts interest every year even though no interest is actually paid. Similarly, the owner must pay taxes on interest accrued every year as well, even though no interest is actually received.

> **zero coupon debenture**
> a debenture that makes no coupon payments, thus initially priced at a deep discount

Floating-rate debentures

The conventional debentures we have talked about so far have fixed-dollar obligations because the coupon rate is set as a fixed percentage of the face value. Similarly, the principal is set equal to the face value. Under these circumstances, the coupon payment and principal are completely fixed.

With *floating-rate debentures (floaters)*, the coupon payments are adjustable. The adjustments are tied to an interest rate index such as the commercial bank bill rate. For example, Citibank issued $850 million of floating-rate notes. The coupon rate was set at 1 per cent above the 90-day Treasury bill rate and adjusted semi-annually.

The value of a floating-rate debenture depends on exactly how the coupon payment adjustments are defined. In most cases, the coupon adjusts with a lag to some base rate. For example, suppose a coupon-rate adjustment is made on 1 June. The adjustment might be based on the simple average of bank bill yields during the previous three months. In addition, the majority of floaters have the following features:

1 The holder has the right to redeem the note at face value on the coupon payment date after some specified amount of time. This is called a *put* provision, and it is discussed below.
2 The coupon rate has a floor and a ceiling, meaning that the coupon is subject to a minimum and a maximum. In this case the coupon rate is said to be 'capped', and the upper and lower rates are sometimes called the 'collar'.

Other types of debenture

Since debentures are financial contracts, the possible features are only limited by the imagination of the parties involved. As a result, debentures can be fairly exotic, particularly some more recent issues. We discuss a few of the more common features and types next.

Income debentures are similar to conventional debentures, except that coupon payments are dependent on company income. Specifically, coupons are paid to debtholders only if the firm's income is sufficient. This would appear to be an attractive feature, but income debentures are not very common.

A *put debenture* allows the *holder* to force the issuer to buy the debt back at a stated price. The put feature is therefore just the reverse of the call provision and is a relatively new development. We discuss convertible debentures, call provisions and put provisions in more detail in Chapter 20.

A given debenture may have many unusual features. To give just one example, Merrill Lynch created a very popular debenture called a *liquid yield option note*, or LYON (pronounced 'lion'). A LYON is the 'kitchen sink' of debentures: a callable, puttable, convertible, zero coupon, subordinated note. Valuing a debenture of this sort can be quite complex.

A relatively recent development in Australia has been the establishment of a secondary market in mortgages. *Securitisation* is the process of taking assets that are not very marketable and turning them into financial assets that can be bought and sold in the marketplace. Briefly, mortgages are pooled and securities are issued secured by the mortgages. These securities find a ready market due to the high quality of the mortgage backing. The concept of mortgage securitisation dates back to the late 1930s in the United States, when the government deliberately encouraged securitisation of mortgages so that housing finance could become more readily available to purchasers. Mortgages, backed by the government and insured through recognised agencies, are pooled and shares in the pool sold.

The process benefits both the investor and the mortgage agency. The investor has the advantage of a security that gives both a regular income from the interest payments on the mortgages, and an additional payout once the mortgages have been paid back. The security is readily negotiable in the marketplace. The mortgage agency has the advantage of turning what would otherwise be a series of individual illiquid assets into an immediate source of funds. This gives the agency liquidity and allows it to use the funds for other purposes. This market has two segments, being *mortgage* and *non-mortgage securitisation*. In the mortgage securitisation market, home buyers borrow from a financial institution. The financial institution sells the mortgage to an originator who then pools the mortgages and issues securities to investors. Investors receive, say, fixed interest payments quarterly. Well-known mortgage originators are Aussie Home Loans and RAMS. The non-mortgage securitisation market is a lot smaller. In this relatively underdeveloped market an income stream is packaged into investment securities and sold to investors. David Bowie recently securitised the royalties to his songs. In 1998 the size of the securitisation market was $19 billion.

Concept questions

16.3a *Why might an income debenture be attractive to a corporation with volatile cash flows? Can you think of a reason why income debentures are not more popular?*

16.3b *What do you think the effect of a put feature on a debenture's coupon would be? How about a convertibility feature? Why?*

16.3c *Why would a financial institution want to sell its loans?*

Callable debentures and debenture refunding

The process of replacing all or part of an issue of outstanding debentures is called **debenture refunding**. As we have discussed, most corporate debt is callable. Typically, the first step in a debenture refunding is to take advantage of this feature to call the entire issue of debentures at the call price.

> **debenture refunding**
> the process of replacing all or part of an issue of outstanding debentures

Why would a firm want to refund a debenture issue? One reason is obvious. Suppose a firm issues long-term debt with, say, a 12 per cent coupon. Sometime after the issue, interest rates decline, and the firm finds that it could pay an 8 per cent coupon and raise the same amount of money. Under such circumstances, the firm may wish to refund the debt. Notice that, in this case, refunding a debenture issue is just a way of refinancing a higher-interest loan with a lower-interest one.

In the following discussion, we take a brief look at several issues concerning debenture refunding and the call feature. First, what is the cost to the firm of a call provision? Second, what is the value of a call provision? Third, given that the firm has issued callable debentures, when should they be refunded?

The call provision

Commonsense tells us that call provisions have value. First, almost all publicly issued debentures have such a feature. Second, a call clearly works to the advantage of the issuer. If interest rates fall and debenture prices go up, the issuer has an option to buy back the debenture at a bargain price.

On the other hand, all other things being equal, debtholders dislike call provisions. The reason is again obvious. If interest rates do fall, then the debtholder's gain is limited because of the possibility that the debenture will be called away. As a result, debtholders will take the call provision into account when they buy, and they will require compensation in the form of a higher coupon rate.

This is an important observation. A call provision is not free. Instead, the firm pays a higher coupon than otherwise. Whether or not paying this higher coupon rate is a good idea is the subject we turn to next.

Cost of the call provision

To illustrate the effect of a call feature on a debenture's coupon, suppose Coffee Supreme Company Ltd intends to issue some perpetual debentures. We will stick with perpetuities because doing so greatly simplifies some of the analysis without changing the general results.

The current interest rate on such debentures is 10 per cent, and Coffee therefore sets the annual coupon at $10. Suppose that there is an equal chance that by the end of the year interest rates will either:

1 fall to 6.7 per cent (if so, the debenture price will increase to $10/0.067 = $150); or
2 increase to 20 per cent (if so, the debenture price will fall to $10/0.20 = $50).

Notice that the debenture will sell for either $50 or $150 with equal probability, so the expected price is $100. Note also that the lower interest rate is actually 0.0666..., not 0.067. We use the exact rate in all the calculations in this section.

We now consider the market price of the debenture assuming that it is not callable, P_{NC}. This will simply be equal to the expected price of the debenture next year plus the coupon, all discounted at the current 10 per cent interest rate:

$$P_{NC} = \frac{\text{First-year coupon} + \text{Expected price at end of year}}{1.10}$$

$$= \frac{\$10 + \$100}{1.10}$$

$$= \$100$$

Thus the debenture sells at par.

Now suppose the Coffee Supreme Company decides to make the issue callable. To keep things as simple as possible, we will assume that the debentures must be called in one year or never. To call the debentures, Coffee will have to pay the $100 face value plus a call premium of $15 for a total of $115. If Coffee wants the callable debenture to sell for par, what coupon, C, must be offered?

To determine the coupon, we need to calculate what the possible prices are in one year. If interest rates decline, then the debenture will be called, and the debtholder will get $115. If interest rates rise, then the debenture will not be called, and it will thus be worth $C/0.20$. So the expected price in one year is $0.50 \times (C/0.20) + 0.50 \times (\$115)$. If the debenture sells for par, then the price, P_C, is $100 and:

$$P_C = \$100$$

$$\$100 = \frac{\text{First-year coupon} + \text{Expected price at end of year}}{1.10}$$

$$\$100 = \frac{\$C + [0.50 \times (\$C/0.20) + 0.50 \times (\$115)]}{1.10}$$

$$\$100 = [\$C + 2.5\$C + 57.5]/1.10$$

$$110 - 57.5 = 3.5\$C$$

$$\$15 = C$$

If we solve this for C, we find that the coupon will have to be

$$C = \$15$$

This is substantially higher than the $10 we had before and illustrates that the call provision is not free.

What is the cost of the call provision here? To answer, we can calculate what the debenture would sell for it if were not callable and had a coupon of $15:

$$P_C = \$100$$

$$= \frac{\text{First-year coupon} + \text{Expected price at end of year}}{1.10}$$

$$= \frac{\$15 + [0.50 \times (\$15/0.20) + 0.50 \times (\$15/0.067)]}{1.10}$$

$$= \$150$$

What we see is that the call provision effectively costs $50 per debenture in this simple case because Coffee could have raised $150 per debenture instead of $100 if the debentures were not callable.

Value of the call provision

We have seen what Coffee will have to pay to make this debenture issue callable. We now need to see what the value is to Coffee from doing so. If the value is more than $50, then the call provision has a positive NPV and should be included. Otherwise, Coffee should issue non-callable debentures.

If Coffee issues a callable debenture and interest rates drop to 6.7 per cent in a year, then Coffee can replace the 15 per cent debenture with a non-callable perpetual issue that carries a coupon of 6.7 per cent. The interest saving in this case is $15 − 6.67 = $8.33 per year every year forever (since these are perpetuities). At an interest rate of 6.7 per cent, the present value of the interest savings is $8.33/0.067 = $125.

To do the refunding, Coffee will have to pay a $15 premium, so the net present value of the refunding operation in one year is $125 − 15 = $110 per debenture. However, there is only a 50 per cent chance that the interest rate will drop, so we expect to get 0.50 × $110 = $55 from refunding in one year. The current value of this amount is $55/1.1 = $50. So we conclude that the value of the call feature to Coffee is $50.

It is not a coincidence that the cost and the value of the call provision are identical. All this says is that the NPV of the call feature is zero; the debtholders demand a coupon that exactly compensates them for the possibility of a call.

The refunding issue

In our example above, we saw that Coffee gained $110 per debenture from the refunding operation if the interest rate fell. We now need to decide when, in general, a firm should refund an outstanding debenture issue. The answer to this question can get fairly complicated, so we will stick with our simplified case. In particular, we will continue to assume that:

1   the debentures in question are perpetuities;
2   there are no taxes;
3   there are no refunding costs other than the call premium; and
4   the debentures must be called now or never.

Because of these assumptions, our example is unrealistic. Taxes and refunding costs, for example, are important, and the actual refunding decision is more complicated than we indicate here. Fortunately, the first three of these four assumptions can be eliminated without a great deal of trouble, just more arithmetic.

The last of these assumptions cannot easily be eliminated. The problem is that when we call a debenture in, we forever destroy the option to call it in later. Conceivably, it might be better to wait and call later in hopes of even lower interest rates.

When should firms refund callable debentures?

The following notation will be useful in analysing the refunding issue:

C_O = coupon rate on the outstanding debentures
C_N = coupon rate on the new issue, equal to the current market rate
C_P = call premium per debenture

We assume that the face value is $100 per debenture. If we replace the old issue, then we save $(C_O − C_N)$ × $100 in interest per debenture every year forever.

The current interest rate is C_N, so the present value of the interest saving is $(C_O − C_N)$ × $100/C_N$. It costs C_P to call the debenture, so the NPV per debenture of the refunding operation can be written simply as:

$$\text{NPV} = (C_O − C_N)/C_N \times \$100 − C_P \qquad (16.1)$$

With our Coffee example, the debentures were originally issued with a 15 per cent coupon. The going interest rate fell to 6.7 per cent, and the call premium was $15. The NPV of the refunding is:

$$
\begin{aligned}
\text{NPV} &= (C_O - C_N)/C_N \times \$100 - C_P \\
&= (0.15 - 0.067)/0.067 \times \$100 - \$15 \\
&= 1.25 \times \$100 - \$15 \\
&= \$110 \text{ per debenture}
\end{aligned}
$$

This is as we had before (ignoring a slight rounding error caused by using 0.067 not 0.06666).

EXAMPLE 16.1

Who ya gonna call?

Ghostbrekers Ltd has an outstanding perpetuity with a 10 per cent coupon rate. This issue must be called now or never. If it is called, it will be replaced with an issue that has a coupon rate of 8 per cent, equal to the current interest rate. The call premium is $20 per debenture. Should refunding commence? What is the NPV of a refunding?

Assuming a $100 face value, the interest saving will be $10 − 8 = $2 per debenture, per year, forever. The present value of this saving is $2/0.08 = $25 per debenture. Since the call premium is $20 per debenture, refunding should commence: the NPV is $5 per debenture.

Should firms issue callable debentures?

We have seen that the NPV of the call provision at the time a debenture is issued is likely to be zero. This means that whether or not the issue is callable is a matter of indifference; we get exactly what we pay for, at least on average.

A company will prefer to issue callable debentures only if it places a higher value on the call option than do the debtholders. We consider three reasons why a company might use a call provision:

1 superior interest rate predictions;
2 taxes; and
3 financial flexibility for future investment opportunities.

Superior interest rate forecasting

The company may prefer the call provision because it assigns a higher probability to a fall in the coupon rate it must pay than the debtholders do. For example, managers may be better informed about a potential improvement in the firm's credit rating. In this way, company insiders may know more about interest rate decreases than the debtholders.

Whether or not the companies truly know more than the creditors about future interest rates is debatable, but the point is they may *think* they do and thus prefer to issue callable debentures.

Taxes

We ignored taxes in our analysis above. Call provisions may have tax advantages to both debtholders and the company. This will be true if the debtholder is taxed at a lower rate than the company.

We have seen that callable debentures have higher rates than non-callable debentures. Because the coupons are a deductible interest expense to the corporation, if the corporate tax rate is higher than that of the individual holder, the corporation will gain more in interest savings than the debtholders will lose in extra taxes. Effectively, the government pays for a part of the call provision in reduced tax revenues.

Future investment opportunities

As we have seen, debenture trust deeds contain protective covenants that restrict a company's investment opportunities. For example, protective covenants may limit the company's ability to acquire another company or to sell certain assets (e.g. a division of the company). If the covenants are sufficiently restrictive, the cost to the shareholders in lost net present value can be large.

If debentures are callable, though, by paying the call premium, the company can buy back the debentures and take advantage of a superior investment opportunity.

Concept questions

16.4a *Why might a corporation call in a debenture issue? What is this action called?*
16.4b *What is the effect on a debenture's coupon rate from including a call provision? Why?*

 ## 16.5 ∎ Preference shares

Preference shares differ from ordinary shares because they have preference over ordinary shares in the payment of dividends and in the distribution of corporation assets in the event of liquidation. 'Preference' means only that the holders of the preference shares must receive a dividend (in the case of an ongoing firm) before holders of ordinary shares are entitled to anything.

Preference shares are a form of equity from a legal and tax standpoint. Importantly, however, holders of preference shares sometimes have no voting privileges.

preference shares
shares with dividend priority over ordinary shares, normally with a fixed dividend rate, sometimes without voting rights

Stated value

Preference shares have a stated liquidating value. The cash dividend is described in terms of dollars per share and is usually a fixed amount. The return on preference shares is normally higher than the return on ordinary shares. For example, Village Roadshow during 2002 issued some preference shares for $1.58 to executives. Dividends were payable at the greater of 10.175 cents per share or 3 cents above the dividends payable on ordinary shares.

Cumulative and non-cumulative dividends

A preference dividend is not like interest on a debenture. The board of directors may decide not to pay the dividends on preference shares, and their decision may have nothing to do with the current net income of the corporation.

Dividends payable on preference shares are either *cumulative* or *non-cumulative*; most are cumulative. If preference dividends are cumulative and are not paid in a particular year, they will be carried forward as an arrearage. Usually both the cumulated (past) preference dividends plus the current preference dividends must be paid before the ordinary shareholders can receive anything.

Unpaid preference dividends are not debts of the firm. Directors elected by the ordinary shareholders can defer preference dividends indefinitely. However, in such cases:

1 ordinary shareholders must also forego dividends; and
2 holders of preference shares are often granted voting and other rights if preference dividends have not been paid for some time.

Because preference shareholders receive no interest on the cumulated dividends, some have argued that firms have an incentive to delay paying preference dividends. However, if this was the expectation of investors, companies would have much difficulty in selling these types of securities.

Irredeemable or redeemable

An irredeemable preference share is similar to an ordinary share as the amount subscribed does not have to be repaid unless the company is liquidated. Preference shares may be issued so that they are automatically redeemable on the happening of some event, or redeemable at the option of the company.

Non-participating or participating

Preference shares are usually issued under terms that provide for a fixed rate of dividend. The shares are not entitled to a dividend in excess of the stated rate. In contrast, participating preference shares grant the holders the right to participate in the distribution of profit available to ordinary shareholders. The lower bound of the dividend is fixed by the stated rate; however, the participating preference share can have the rate increased because of additional profits.

> Most preference shares issued are cumulative, irredeemable and non-participating.

Because the interest paid on debt is tax deductible for the borrowing company and the preference share dividend is not tax-deductible, the cost of servicing debt is less than the cost of servicing preference shares. In consequence the interest payment on debt tends to be higher than the preference dividend, even though repayment of the preference capital ranks behind repayment of the debt. So why would any investor be interested in contributing preference capital?

Usually preference issues are made for purposes other than the direct motive of raising funds. For example, persons floating a company may take preference shares in order to demonstrate confidence in the project. In the period from 1987 to August 1989 there was a significant volume of redeemable preference shares issued in Australia (approximately $2.3 billion) to take advantage of tax laws and pass on franking benefits to the holders of the shares. In August 1989 the tax laws were changed to kill the market for franked preference shares. Redeemable preference shares are sometimes used to enhance the Statement of Financial Position by increasing the equity base. For example, James Hardie in 1988 made an issue of redeemable preference shares with detachable options over ordinary shares. James Hardie classified the redeemable preference shares as equity in its annual accounts.

Banks have an incentive to issue preference shares because as subordinate debt[3] they are treated within the capital base of the bank. The Reserve Bank regulations require banks to meet capital adequacy requirements so that their operations are limited by the amount of capital invested. The Reserve Bank regulations relating to capital adequacy show how various types of preference share issues fit into the capital base. The three classes of bank capital according to the regulations are:

1 Equity:
  - ordinary shares
  - non-cumulative irredeemable preference shares
  - retained earnings

2 Subordinate non-term debt:
  - cumulative irredeemable preference shares
  - mandatory convertible notes
  - perpetual subordinate debt

3 Subordinate term debt:
  - redeemable preference shares
  - subordinate term loans

Firms issuing preference shares can avoid the threat of bankruptcy that might otherwise exist if debt were relied on. Unpaid preference dividends are not debts of a company, and preference shareholders cannot force the company into bankruptcy because of unpaid dividends. Further, the tax advantage of interest deductibility of debt only exists for companies with significant tax liabilities; therefore companies with accumulated tax losses may favour the use of preference shares. This is particularly true when the firm finds it difficult to borrow on a long-term basis.

Another reason for issuing preference shares concerns the control of the firm. Since preference shareholders often cannot vote, preference shares may be a means of raising equity without surrendering control. In 1984 an issue of participating preference shares was proposed for John Fairfax Ltd. The objective of the issue was to simulate a non-voting ordinary share with equal dividend rights to ordinary shares (after an initial period when the preference shares would pay a higher dividend). At the time, John Fairfax was a listed public company; it needed more equity, but the family shareholders did not want to dilute their control. Hence the appeal of non-voting ordinary shares. There was no tax motive. The ASX, as a matter of principle, refused to list the shares, because it refuses to list non-voting ordinary shares and analysed the proposed issues as *de facto* ordinary shares. The issue did not proceed but this proposal provides an example of the desire to maintain control.

Concept questions

16.5a *What is a preference share?*
16.5b *Why is it arguably more like debt than equity?*
16.5c *What are two reasons why preference shares are issued?*

 # 16.6 Ordinary shares

The term **ordinary shares** means different things to different people, but it is usually applied to shares that have no special preference either in dividends or in bankruptcy. A sample shareholders' equity extract and accompanying notes are provided below for the Witch Bank Limited and Subsidiaries.

ordinary share
equity without priority for dividends or in bankruptcy

Extract from Annual Report
Witch Bank Limited and Subsidiaries

Witch Bank Limited and Subsidiaries
Statement of Financial Position
As at 30 June 200X

	Note	200X Group ($'000)
Net assets		140,000
Shareholders' equity		
Share capital	1	40,000
Reserves	2	63,000
Retained profits		12,160
Total shareholders' equity		115,160
Other capital resources		
Subordinated notes	3	24,840
Total shareholders' equity and other capital resources		140,000

The accompanying notes form part of these financial statements.

Witch Bank Limited and Subsidiaries
Notes to and forming part of the accounts
for the year ended 30 June 200X
(all figures in thousands)

1. Share capital
Issued and paid-up

79,798,000 ordinary shares of 50c each fully paid	$39,899
2,000,000 ordinary shares of 50c each 5c paid	100
2,000 non-participating shares of 50c	1
	$40,000

Movements during the year

Description	Share type	No. of shares	Paid-up capital
Dividend reinvestment plan	Fully paid	2,100,000	$0.50
Issues to staff of service companies within the group	Partly paid	160,000	$0.05
Partly paid shares converted to fully paid		280,000	$0.45

The purposes of the above issues were to support the expansion of the group's banking operations and to provide working capital. In addition, 1,500 options to purchase shares in the Bank were issued to staff of companies within the group during the year. These options, each for 100 shares, are exercisable between 30 July 200X+2 and 30 July 200X+5 at a price of $1.93 per share (including $1.43 premium). At the date of exercise, such shares are to be paid up to the same amount as has been called up on other partly paid shares. All options automatically lapse on termination of employment.

2. Reserves
Asset revaluation reserve

Balance at beginning of year	$59,879
Revaluation increments on revaluation of:	
Land	2,903
Building	218
Balance at end of year	$63,000

Other capital resources

3. Subordinated notes
    The notes are unsecured obligations of the Bank subordinated in that:
    (a) payments of principal and interest on the notes have priority over company dividend payments;
    (b) in the event of winding-up of the Bank, the rights of the note holders will rank in preference only to the rights of the ordinary shareholders.

    In accordance with banking regulations this forms part of the capital of the Bank.

Share capital

The owners of the ordinary share capital of a company are referred to as the **shareholders** or the equityholders of the company. The share capital is divided into a number of units that can be readily transferred. Traditionally, owners would receive share certificates for the shares they own; however, with the introduction of computer share registers and transfers the use of certificates has disappeared. Each share has a stated value called the nominal or paid-up value. For example, the paid-up value of Witch Bank Limited shares is 50 cents.

> **shareholders**
> owners of equity in a corporation

The *Corporations Law* prior to 1998 required a company in its Memorandum of Association to record the total number of shares and the maximum total monetary amount of share capital it will issue. The total is identified as the authorised share capital or nominal share capital or registered share capital. As a consequence of the *Company Law Review Act* 1998 (Cth), companies no longer require an authorised capital, nor a par value. Other changes include the replacement of the Memorandum of Association and Articles of Association with a Constitution.

Paid-up capital

Shares may be allotted on terms that the shareholders do not have to pay the full value of their shares all at once. For example Witch Bank Limited has issued 2,000,000 ordinary shares of 50 cents each paid up to 5 cents to provide the company with paid-up capital of $100,000. These contributing shares have 45 cents per share remaining, which is the uncalled capital at 30 June 200X. The uncalled capital could be called up by the directors, while the company is a going concern, or the liquidator in the winding-up of the company. In the 'movements during the year' Witch Bank shows it has converted partly paid shares to fully paid by making a call of 45 cents per share on 280,000 shares during the year ending 30 June 200X.

Types of companies

There are five types of company, which are identified under the *Corporations Act* 2001 according to the extent of the liability of members. These are:

- companies limited by shares;
- companies limited by guarantee;
- companies limited by both shares and guarantee;
- unlimited companies; and
- no liability companies.

A *company limited by shares* is a company formed on the principle of having the liability of its members limited by the memorandum to the amount (if any) unpaid on the shares held by them. This is by far the most common type of company.

A *company limited by guarantee* is a company formed on the principle of having the liability of members limited by the memorandum to an amount that the members undertake to contribute to the capital of the company in the event of its being wound up.

An *unlimited company* is a company formed on the principle of having no limit placed on the liability of its members.

A *no liability company* is one that does not have under its memorandum or constitution a contractual right to recover calls made on its shares from a shareholder who defaults in payment of those calls. Where a shareholder chooses not to pay a call, the shares are forfeited. Companies engaged in mining or other speculative ventures are set up as no liability companies.

Asset revaluations

When corporations believe that there has been a permanent change in the value of assets, they can revalue the assets. The revaluation may be up or down. If the revaluation is up, the company has a choice to revalue or not. If the revaluation is down the company must revalue down so as not to mislead users of the financial statements. Generally the effect of revaluations up is in the asset revaluation reserve.

Retained earnings

retained earnings
corporate earnings not paid out as dividends

Retained earnings, or retained profits, is that portion of corporate profits not paid out as dividends. The cumulative amount of retained profits of Witch Bank since its original incorporation is $12,160,000 at 30 June 200X.

The sum of issued and paid-up capital, reserves and retained profits represents the total shareholders' equity, which is usually referred to as the value (or net worth) of the firm. The **book value** represents the equity investors' entitlement to the firm.

book value
accounting per share value of firm's equity. Also net worth

Shareholders' rights

The conceptual structure of the corporation assumes that shareholders elect directors who, in turn, hire management to carry out their directives. Shareholders, therefore, control the company through the right to elect the directors. In some companies, such as special joint venture arrangements, certain shareholders have the power under the articles to appoint a number of their nominees as directors. In the case of publicly traded companies, the appointment of directors is by shareholders at the annual general meeting. Each director must be individually appointed by separate resolutions. This prevents the voting in of a director on a joint ticket with another who has strong support.

Directors are elected each year at the annual general meeting. The voting right of shareholders is one share, one vote, not one shareholder, one vote. With corporate democracy, the 'golden rule' prevails absolutely. Directors are elected by a vote of the holders of a majority of shares *present* and entitled to vote. In some companies the election of directors is staggered so that only a fraction of the directorships are up for election at a particular time. Staggering is beneficial to the company: it provides some continuity on the board of directors, and thus 'institutional memory' is retained.

Proxy voting

A proxy is a grant of authority by a shareholder allowing someone else to vote on his or her behalf. For convenience, much of the voting in large public corporations is actually done by proxy.

Each share has one vote so that the owner of 10,000 shares has 10,000 votes. Many companies have hundreds of thousands of shareholders. Shareholders can come to the annual meeting and vote in person, or they can transfer their right to vote to another party.

Obviously, the board of directors always tries to get as many proxies transferred to it as possible. However, if shareholders are not satisfied with management, an 'outside' group of shareholders can try to obtain votes via proxy. They can vote by proxy to replace management by adding enough directors. This is called a proxy fight and one recently occurred within NRMA.

Other rights

The value of a share in a corporation is directly related to the general rights of shareholders. For example, Witch Bank Limited had 2,000 non-participating shares. These shares would not be entitled to dividends or any distribution on liquidation and they are unlikely to have any voting rights. They are probably shares held by the founders who originally set up the company. They would only be worth their paid-up value, which is 50 cents per share. In addition to the right to vote for directors, shareholders usually have the following rights:

1 The right to share proportionally in dividends paid.
2 The right to share proportionally in assets remaining after liabilities have been paid in a liquidation.
3 The right to vote on shareholder matters of importance, such as a merger, usually done at the annual general meeting or a general meeting.

In addition, shareholders have the right to share proportionally in any new shares sold. This is called the *pre-emptive right*, and we will discuss it in some detail in the next chapter.

Essentially, a pre-emptive right means that a company that wishes to sell shares must offer it to the existing shareholders before offering it to the general public. The purpose is to give a shareholder the opportunity to protect his or her proportionate ownership in the corporation.

Dividends

A distinctive feature of corporations is that they have shares on which they are authorised by law to pay dividends to their shareholders. **Dividends** paid to shareholders represent a return on the capital directly or indirectly contributed to the corporation by the shareholders. The payment of dividends is at the discretion of the board of directors.

dividend
payment by a corporation to shareholders, made in either cash or shares

Some important characteristics of dividends include the following:

1 Unless a dividend is declared by the board of directors of a corporation, it is not a liability of the corporation. A corporation cannot default on an undeclared dividend. As a consequence, corporations cannot become bankrupt because of non-payment of dividends. The amount of the dividend and even whether it is paid are decisions based on the business judgment of the board of directors.
2 The payment of dividends by the corporation is not a business expense. Dividends are not deductible for corporate tax purposes. In short, dividends are paid out of after-tax profits of the corporation.

3   Dividends received by individual shareholders are for the most part considered ordinary income and are fully taxable. However, under the dividend imputation system (discussed in Chapter 19) a credit is allowed in the shareholders' tax returns for company tax paid. Dividends paid on shares with an imputation credit are called *franked dividends*.

Classes of shares

Some firms have more than one class of ordinary shares. Often, the classes are created with unequal voting rights. The Ford Motor Company, for example, has class B ordinary shares which are not publicly traded (they are held by Ford family interests and trusts). This class has about 40 per cent of the voting power. However, these shares constitute only about 15 per cent of the total outstanding shares. In principle, the stock exchanges do not allow companies to create classes of publicly traded ordinary shares with unequal voting rights. Rare exceptions (e.g. Ford) appear to have been made.

It is common for many non-listed companies to have dual classes of ordinary shares. There are several reasons why a company may wish to issue shares of different classes.

- It may wish to raise funds with the characteristics of debt but with the discretions that may be applied to equity income distributions. This can be done by issuing shares that carry a stated rate of dividend but with limited voting rights and no rights to participation in distribution of surplus assets on winding-up.
- Companies that are small or those going public for the first time may wish to concentrate some control of the company in the hands of the holders of a particular class of shares. Another example of concentrating control is where a private placement is made and rights are given to the holders to elect a certain number of directors to the board. The method used here is to give shares weighted voting rights.
- Taxation may require the issue of different classes of shares with the aim of minimising income tax for the holders.
- Frequently home unit companies issue different classes of shares, each of which entitles the shareholder to certain rights in respect of a particular unit in the building to the exclusion of the holders of other classes of shares.

The most common ways in which classes of shares differ are in relation to:

- voting rights;
- entitlement to dividend;
- the right to priority in payment of dividend;
- the right to priority of repayment of capital in winding-up; and
- the right to participate in a distribution of surplus assets on winding-up.

Concept questions

16.6a *What is a company's book value?*
16.6b *What rights do shareholders have?*
16.6c *What is a proxy?*

 ## 16.7 ▮ Size of the capital market

Both the Australian Stock Exchange and the Reserve Bank of Australia regularly report on the Australian financial market (see for example Table 16.2). The long-term *debt market* in Australia has a daily turnover of about $5.1 billion. When short-term debt is also considered this figure increases to about $15 billion. There is an active primary and secondary market in both government and corporate securities.

The *equity market* receives much more publicity than the debt market but it is much smaller. The average daily turnover is about $1.7 billion.

TABLE 16.2

Australian financial market	Daily turnover April 2001 ($A billion)
Foreign exchange (FX)	
FX turnover in Australia	170
AUD/USD transactions	54
Currency swaps	60
FX derivatives	4.2
Debt	
Government	4.1
Non-government	1
Negotiable and transferable instruments	9.8
Derivatives	76
Equity	
Physical	1.7
Derivatives	2

Source: Reserve Bank of Australia Bulletin, June 2002.

Financial distress and bankruptcy

One of the consequences of using debt is the possibility of financial distress, which can be defined in several ways:

1 *Business failure*. This is a term usually used to refer to a situation where a business has terminated, equityholders have lost all their funds, and the claims of creditors cannot be met.
2 *Legal bankruptcy*. Firms bring petitions to a federal court for bankruptcy. **Bankruptcy** is a legal proceeding for liquidating or reorganising a business.
3 *Technical insolvency*. Technical insolvency occurs when a firm defaults on a legal obligation; for example, it does not pay a bill.
4 *Accounting insolvency*. Firms with negative net worth are insolvent on the books. This happens when the total book liabilities exceed the book value of the total assets.

bankruptcy
bankruptcy is defined as a condition where all or part of the organisation's assets are transferred to creditors

For future reference, we will define bankruptcy as the transfer of some or all of the firm's assets to creditors.

Concept questions

16.7a *What type of security is more actively traded (in terms of dollar value) in Australia?*
16.7b *Why would you think that the equity market receives more publicity than the debt market?*

◗ 16.8 ◗ Summary and conclusions

The basic sources of long-term financing are long-term debt, preference shares, and ordinary shares. This chapter describes the essential features of each.

1 We emphasise that ordinary shareholders have:
   a residual risk and return in a corporation;
   b voting rights; and
   c limited liability if the corporation elects to default on its debt and must transfer some or all of the assets to the creditors.

2 Preference shares have some of the features of debt and some features of ordinary shares. Holders of preference shares have preference in liquidation and in dividend payments compared to holders of ordinary shares.

3 Long-term debt involves contractual obligations set out in trust deeds. There are many kinds of debt, but the essential feature is that debt involves a stated amount that must be repaid. If the debt is not repaid, the firm is in default and must reorganise or liquidate. Interest payments on debt are considered a business expense and are tax-deductible.

Key terms

Authorised capital *547*
Bankruptcy *551*
Book value *548*
Call premium *532*
Call protected *532*
Call provision *539*
Debenture trust deed *531*

Deferred call *532*
Dividends *549*
Note *527*
Ordinary shares *545*
Paid-up capital *547*
Preference shares *543*
Protective covenant *533*

Proxy *549*
Retained earnings *548*
Shareholders *547*
Sinking fund *532*
Zero coupon debenture *537*

Suggested readings

The following provide some evidence on the financial structure of industrial corporations:

CCH Corporations Law Editors *Australian Corporations and Securities Law Reporter*, CCH, Sydney, 1993.

Kester, W.C. 'Capital and Ownership Structure: A Comparison of the United States and Japanese Manufacturing Corporations', *Financial Management*, Vol. 15, Spring 1986.

McKern, M., Pollard, I., Skully, M. and Bruce, R. *Handbook of Australian Corporate Finance*, 5th edn, Butterworths, Sydney, 1997.

Taggart, R. 'Secular Patterns in the Financing of U.S. Corporations'. In B. Friedman (ed.) *Corporate Capital Structure in the United States*, University of Chicago Press, 1985.

Endnotes

1 There is no universally agreed-upon distinction between short-term and long-term debt. In addition, people often refer to intermediate-term debt, which has a maturity of more than one year and less than three to five, or even 10 years.

2 A debenture issued with a very low coupon rate (as opposed to a zero coupon rate) is an original issue/deep discount debenture.

3 *Subordinate debt* is a loan where the obligation of the borrower to repay the debt on maturity ranks below ordinary unsecured creditors.

On the web

Ratings agencies have elaborate sites, often as an introduction to their wide range of services. Try:

http://www.moodys.com
http://www.standardandpoors.com

More information can be obtained at the site of the Australian Stock Exchange:

http://www.asx.com.au

Maximise Your Marks!
There are 30 interactive questions on long-term financing waiting online for you at www.mhhe.com/au/ross3e. The questions are written with additional feedback for incorrect answers, and text excerpts with page references for follow-up study.

International Articles!
To read more on long-term financing and to see current international articles, just go to www.mhhe.com/au/ross3e and click on *PowerWeb Articles* for this chapter.

Chapter review problems and self-test

16.1 · Book value versus market value

The Ricefield Co. Ltd has paid up capital of 500,000 ordinary shares of $2 and 5,000 10 per cent preference shares of the same nominal value. All of the preference shares have been issued and fully paid, and only 40 per cent of the ordinary shares have been issued and fully paid. The company has the following amounts in its Statement of Financial Position:

Retained earnings	$180,000
Asset revaluation reserve	90,000
Provision for taxation	40,000
Provision for final dividend—Ordinary shares	30,000
Trademarks and patents	200,000
Goodwill	180,000
Current assets	200,000
Current liabilities	100,000
Fixed assets	570,000
Long-term liabilities	300,000

Currently ordinary shares in the company are selling for $2.50 and preference shares for $2.40. What is the book value per share of Ricefield's ordinary capital? Explain why the book value is different to the market value for the ordinary shares and the preference shares.

16.2 · Call provisions and debenture values

Skateboard Industries Pty Ltd has decided to float a perpetual debenture issue. The coupon will be 8 per cent (the current interest rate). In one year, there is an even chance that interest rates will be 5 per cent or 20 per cent. What will the market value of the debentures be if they are non-callable? If they are callable at par plus $8?

16.3 · Call provisions and coupon rates

If the Skateboard debenture in problem 16.2 is callable and sells for par, what is the coupon, C? What is the cost of the call provision in this case?

Answers to self-test problems

16.1 · The shareholders' equity would consist of:

Paid-up capital (200,000 shares of $2)	$400,000
Retained earnings	180,000
Asset revaluation reserve	90,000
Total shareholders' equity	$670,000

Two other amounts need further consideration: the provision for final dividend ($30,000) and the provision for taxation ($40,000). These amounts represent allocations from retained earnings. The first will be distributed to shareholders and the second will be used to settle a tax liability. Therefore:

Total ordinary shareholders' entitlement = $670,000 + $30,000 = $700,000
Book value per ordinary share = $700,000/200,000 = $3.50

The book value of ordinary shares is greater than the market value ($2.50). The market value is determined by the expectation of market participants of the ability of the company to produce future profits. It is not related to the historical record of the accounting transactions, which is the basis for the book value. The market value of the preference shares depends upon the fixed dividend rate and the ability of the company to pay that rate and the level of interest rates in the economy. If we assume the market feels that the company can meet its 10 per cent preference dividend rate, then the current market price ($2.40) suggests that the level of interest rates in the economy has fallen since the preference shares were issued. A return of 8.3 per cent (20 cents/$2.40) is now required, whereas 10 per cent (20 cents/$2.00) was required on issue.

16.2 · If the debenture is not callable, then, in one year, it will be worth either $8/0.05 = $160 or $8/0.2 = $40. The expected price is $100. The PV of the $100 and the first $8 coupon is $108/1.08 = $100, so the debenture will sell for par.

If the debenture is callable, then either it will be called at $108 (if rates fall to 5%) or it will sell for $40. The expected value is ($108 + 40)/2 = $74. The PV is ($74 + 8)/1.08 = $75.92.

16.3 · In one year, the debenture either will be worth C/0.20 or it will be called for $108. If the debenture sells for par, then:

$100 = [C + 0.5(C/0.20) + 0.5($108)]/1.08
$54 = [C + 0.5(C/0.20)]
    = 3.5C

The coupon, C, must be $54/3.5 = $15.429.

If the debenture had a coupon of $15.429 and was not callable, then, in one year, it would be worth either $15.429/0.05 = $308.58 or $15.429/0.20 = $77.15. There is an even chance of either of these, so we expect a value of $192.87. The debenture would sell today for ($192.87 + 15.429)/1.08 = $192.87. The cost of the call provision is thus $92.87. This is quite a bit, but, as we shall see in a later chapter, this stems from the fact that interest rates are quite volatile in this example.

Questions and problems

1 · Equity accounts

The Junkfood Co. equity accounts in 200X are as follows:

Ordinary shares	
(80,000 shares outstanding, $2 paid-up value)	(a)
Capital surplus	$ 50,000
Retained earnings	100,000
Total	(b)

Supply the missing information.

2 · Changes in equity accounts

In the previous question, suppose the company decides to issue 10,000 new shares. The current price is $5 per share. Show the effect on the different accounts. What is the market/book ratio?

3 · Interest on debt

Rank the following long-term debt arrangements in terms of the level of interest rates you would expect a company would have to pay:

a   mortgage loan by a hire purchase company secured by a charge on land
b   debentures secured by a floating charge
c   unsecured notes
d   convertible notes
e   directors' loans to the company
f   bank overdraft
g   unsecured bank fixed loan

Provide reasons for your ranking.

4 · Company control

Faymart Retailing Ltd wants to elect directors to the board of Stationery Supplies Ltd. What percentage of shares would Faymart need to acquire to be reasonably sure of electing four directors to the board of six? Does it make any difference to your answer if Stationery is a private company?

5 · Preference share

Which have a higher yield, preference shares or corporate debentures? Why is there a difference? Who are the main investors in preference shares? Why?

6 · Debt versus equity

What are the main differences between corporate debt and equity? Why do some clever firms try to issue equity in the guise of debt? Why might preference shares be called an 'equity debenture'?

7 · Patterns of financing

The Moore Gambling Company Pty Ltd has $5 million of positive NPV projects that it would like to take advantage of. What long-term financing strategy would you suggest Moore Gambling should use?

8 · Preference share

Explain what is meant by a 10 per cent $1 par non-cumulative, convertible, redeemable, non-participating preference share.

9 · Liquidate or reorganise

A petition for the receivership of the Tape View Company Pty Ltd has been filed. The liquidator estimates that the firm's liquidation value, after considering costs, is $28 million. Alternatively, the directors, using the analysis of the MT Consulting firm, predict that the reorganised business will generate $6 million annual cash flows in perpetuity. The discount rate is 20 per cent. Should Tape View be liquidated or reorganised? Why?

10 · Interest on zeroes

Exceptional Co. Ltd has issued a five-year, pure discount, 8 per cent debenture.

a   Calculate the value of the debenture at issue and the total interest.
b   If the company is allowed a tax deduction of the total interest divided by five (average interest per year) or the actual interest, which method should it use?

11 · Coupon rates and terms of trust deed

What is the effect of each of the following provisions on the coupon rate for a newly issued debenture? Give a brief explanation in each case.

a   A call provision
b   A convertibility provision
c   A put provision
d   A floating coupon

12 · Coupon rates for bonds and debentures

The market rate of interest for a certain class of debenture is 8 per cent. It is possible to identify the following four debentures in the market that meet the requirements of the class.

	Coupon rate on issue
Premium	7.5%
Average	6.0%
Medium	9.0%
Brilliant	10.0%

a   If the only characteristic of the debentures that is different is the coupon rate, rank the debentures from high to low in terms of market price.
b   How would the ranking change (if at all) if the terms to maturity are as follows?

Premium	3 years
Average	6 months
Medium	2 years
Brilliant	1 year

c   Would your answers to (a) and (b) change if the debt instruments were called 'bonds' instead of 'debentures'?

13 · Interest rate swaps

This is a challenge question. Pills Ltd is a public company that wishes to borrow at a fixed rate. Health is a public corporation that is quite happy to borrow at a floating rate. The interest rates that would be charged to both organisations are provided in the following schedule:

	Interest rates	
Organisation	Floating	Fixed
Pills Ltd	17.5%	15%
Health	17%	13%

Health faces a lower interest rate under both forms of borrowing; however, the management of both organisations believe they can enter an interest rate swap agreement that both will benefit from. They agree to share any interest savings equally.

a   What is the interest saving that is available?
b   Describe the interest rate swap arrangement the firms should enter into.
c   Complete the following schedule:

	Borrowing rate type*	Swap interest payments	Swap interest receipts	Interest Cost	Interest savings
Health					
Pills Ltd					

* Type of loan, i.e. fixed or floating.

14 · Callable debenture prices

Iceflow Air Ltd has decided to float a perpetual debenture issue. The current interest rate is 12 per cent. In one year, there is an even chance that interest rates will be 10 per cent or 15 per cent. Will this issue sell for par if the coupon is $12? What would it sell for if the coupon were $15?

15 · Pricing

In the previous question, suppose the debentures are callable at $106; what must the coupon be for the debentures to sell at par? What is the cost of the call provision?

16 · NPV and refunding

Pulse-rate Co. Ltd has an outstanding debenture issue with a total face value of $20 million and a coupon rate of 8 per cent. The debentures are callable at par plus a premium of $8 per debenture. These debentures could be reissued at 6 per cent. The total issue costs of the refunding (including the call premium) would be $3 million. The debentures must be called now or never. What would be the NPV of this refunding? Should Pulse-rate proceed?

17 · Rates

In the previous problem, what would the current interest rate have to be for Pulse-rate Co. to be indifferent to a refunding operation?

18 · NPV and maturity

In Problem 17, how would your answer be affected if the debentures had 20 years to maturity rather than an infinite number of years? What would the NPV of a refunding operation be?

19 · NPV and refunding

Leaveit Ltd has an outstanding perpetuity with a 15 per cent coupon rate. This issue must be called now or never. If it is called, it will be replaced with an issue that has a coupon rate of 9 per cent, equal to the current interest rate. The call premium is $60 per debenture. Should refunding commence? What is the NPV of a refunding?

20 · Interest rates and refunding

In the previous question, what would the current rate have to be for Leaveit to be indifferent to refunding or not refunding?

21 · NPV, refunding and taxes

This is a challenge problem. Look back at problem 19. Suppose the firm is in a 30 per cent tax bracket. The call premium is a tax-deductible expense. Interest paid on the old and new debentures is as well, of course. What is the NPV of the refunding? Note that the appropriate discount rate will be the after-tax borrowing rate. What is the net effect of worrying about taxes on the NPV of the refunding? Explain.

CHAPTER 17

Issuing
securities to the public

Objective

On completion of this chapter you will understand the basic procedure for a new issue of securities, the advantages and disadvantages of public listing, the alternative methods of making a new issue of securities, how to value a right to a new share and the effect of new issues on existing shareholders.

Study tips ▷ Some of the questions raised in this chapter remain as a challenge to contemporary finance: questions as to why initial public offerings tend to be underpriced and why there is a preference for rights issues as opposed to cash offerings in Australia when the American experience favours the cash issue. We need to be aware of these issues but we are not in a position to explain them. They are issues you might pursue in honours, masters or doctoral studies. While it is fairly straightforward, the valuation of a right does give students problems. Make sure you understand the difference between the value of a right and the value of a right per share. The value of a right is the value at which the right will trade on the market. It may require several shares in order to obtain one right to an additional share. If we subtract the value of a right per share from the share price with the rights, we will be able to calculate the theoretical ex-rights price of the share.

Introduction ▷ In Chapter 16, we looked at the different types of corporate securities. This chapter looks at how corporations sell those securities to the investing public. The general procedures we describe apply to both debt and equity, but we place more emphasis on equity.

Before securities can trade on a securities market, they must be issued to the public. A firm making a public issue must satisfy a number of requirements set out by the *Corporations Act* 2001, which is enforced by the Australian Securities and Investments Commission (ASIC), and the listing requirements of the Australian Stock Exchange (ASX). In general, investors must be given all material information in the form of a **prospectus**. In the first part of this chapter, we discuss what this entails.

prospectus
the document required by law to be issued with share offers to the public

A public issue of debt or equity can be sold directly to the public with the help of underwriters. This is called a *general cash offer*. Alternatively, a public equity issue can be sold to the firm's existing shareholders by what is called a *rights offer*. We examine the differences between an underwritten general cash offer and a rights offer. As we discuss, the direct costs of a rights offer appear to be significantly lower than those of a general cash offer. In Australia, equity issues have tended to be rights issues, which is the experience in Europe; however, in the United States issues have been predominantly general cash offers.

▪ 17.1 ▪ The public issue

Australian company law has been characterised by a lack of uniformity from state to state because the Commonwealth Parliament was not given a clear power by the Constitution to make laws with respect to all companies. In May 1988, the Commonwealth proposed legislation including the *Corporations Act* 1989 which was to bring about a single law for companies in Australia. Over the next two years there was intense political debate over the Commonwealth legislation and scheme, with most of the states hostile to the proposal. Eventually in 1990, a Heads of Agreement, Future Regulation in Australia, was signed by all states. The main features of this agreement were:

- the *Corporations Act* and the *Australian Securities Commission Act* were amended to apply as law for the Australian Capital Territory and then applied by each state and the Northern Territory as the law of that state or territory;
- the applied law was to have the characteristics and be treated for all practical purposes as Commonwealth rather than state law;
- the Australian Securities Commission (ASC) was to be the sole administering authority, replacing the National Companies and Securities Commission (NCSC) and State Corporate Affairs Commissions;
- the ASC was to be accountable to the Commonwealth Attorney-General and Parliament;
- regional offices were to be established in each capital city and the ASC was obliged to delegate the exercise of powers to Regional Commissioners to the fullest extent practicable; and
- the ASC and Commonwealth crime authorities were to replace the NCSC and state crime authorities for prosecution of offences under the legislation.

In May 1996 the Federal Government established the Financial Systems Inquiry, chaired by Stan Wallis. The Wallis inquiry completed a report and made recommendations for regulatory reform.

As a result, in 1998 the powers of the ASC were expanded and it became the Australian Securities and Investments Commission (ASIC).

The features of the Heads of Agreement sought to create a legislative scheme that 'federalised' state law so as to create a single national law. This was achieved by means of a complex arrangement set out in the *Corporations Legislation Amendment Act* 1990. This Act overcame the constitutional problems by applying the *Corporations Act* 1989 to the Australian Capital Territory and making it capable of being applied as state law.

The regulation for the raising of funds in Australia is through the *Corporations Act* 2001, which is administered by ASIC. The main areas of regulation are:

- the prospectus provisions;
- the restrictions on allotment of shares;
- the securities-hawking provisions;
- the accounts and audit provisions;
- the provisions relating to the sale of prescribed interests;
- the debenture provisions which are scattered throughout the Act;
- the takeover provisions which regulate the sale of shares during takeovers; and
- the provisions licensing persons engaged in the securities industry.

In addition to the ASIC controls, the Australian Stock Exchange (ASX) regulates the disclosure that must be provided by listed companies.

The basic procedure for a new issue

There is a series of steps involved in issuing securities to the public. In general terms, the basic procedure is as follows:

1　An analysis is made of the funding needs of the corporation and identification of the alternative methods of meeting those needs.
2　Approval from the board of directors is required before securities may be issued by management to the public.
3　Expert opinion is obtained from external parties for support of the issue.
4　a　The issue is structured and priced.
　　b　A timetable for the issue is prepared.
　　c　A prospectus for the issue is prepared.
　　d　A marketing strategy for the issue is prepared.
5　The prospectus is filed with ASIC and the ASX.
6　The underwriting agreement is executed.
7　The prospectus is registered.
8　a　A public announcement is made of the offering and any sub-underwriting arrangement by the underwriter.
　　b　The prospectus is dispatched to potential investors.
9　Funds are received.
10　Shares are allotted and holdings registered.
11　Shares are listed for trading on the ASX.

Flotation is the term used to describe the function of offering securities to the public. It is used in the sense of 'launching' a company or an investment onto the markets. When the company is going to the market for the first time it is called a ***primary issue***. Clearly a primary issue has to be a general cash offer. Primary issues are generally used to:

1　convert from a private company to a public company;
2　spin off a portion of the business of a listed company. Usually this involves the prospectus issue of new shares with shareholders of the listed company given a priority right of subscription;
3　form a new public company, commence a business or acquire a business, process or invention;
4　in recent times primary issues have been to privatise public organisations (e.g. Telstra, Commonwealth Bank (CBA), Totalisator Agency Board (TAB)) or to demutualise an insurance fund (Australian Mutual Provident Society (AMP), NRMA, National Mutual). Under mutualisation the insurance policyholders have ownership rights. When the insurance fund becomes a public company these rights move to shareholders who in some cases may be policyholders.

The decision to go public is one that requires careful analysis. The process of going public is complicated and, once listed, the management and board of the company are subject to pressures and scrutiny that are unique to the public area.

Advantages of public company listing

1　**Access to additional capital**
　　This is the principal advantage of a public flotation and listing. Private companies commonly reach a stage where the financing of further growth is beyond the capacity of

the existing shareholders. Equity funds raised from the initial public issue are available to expand operations, increase working capital or reduce borrowings. The establishment of a market for the company's securities and the broader shareholder base enhance further capital raisings and generally enable the company to satisfy its financial requirements on more favourable terms.

2 **Increased negotiability of capital**

This is an important consequence of listing, both from the vendors'/promoters' viewpoint and that of the company. Listing facilitates the realisation of investments and enables the vendors/promoters to reduce their financial commitment to the company.

3 **Growth not limited by cash resources**

From the company's standpoint, it is able to use its securities as consideration in mergers and acquisitions. Thus its capacity to grow and diversify is not constrained by limited cash resources.

4 **Corporate image enhanced**

The corporate image of the company will often be enhanced as a result of the prestige and public exposure of listing on the Stock Exchange. This can be important for consumer sales oriented companies. It is also significant for foreign companies as an offer of local participation is usually regarded most favourably by the host country. In addition, funding parties will generally look more favourably upon lending to listed companies due to the extent of reporting requirements and the controls placed upon listed companies by regulatory bodies.

5 **Can attract and retain key personnel**

The company may be in a better position to attract and retain key personnel by offering shares or options as part of their remuneration package.

6 **Independence in spin-off**

In the case of a spin-off, it enables the newly floated company to stand on its own, independent of its former owner.

Disadvantages of public company listing

1 **Dilution of control of existing owners**

Existing owners face a weakening of control as an obvious consequence following public flotation. Depending on the extent of the dilution there is the possibility of a risk of takeover.

2 **Additional responsibilities of directors**

Directors of a public company assume additional responsibilities and are legally and morally obliged to act in the best interests of all shareholders. The company is no longer the private vehicle of the original owners and all transactions between the two must be on an arm's length basis.

3 **Greater disclosure of information**

An important consequence of listing is the greater demand for disclosure of information and its wider distribution. Disclosure requirements for public companies have increased in recent years and this trend will no doubt continue. Although fears are often expressed that disclosure of such financial information as sales, material contracts, sources of revenue and expense classifications will place the company at a competitive disadvantage, subsequent performance usually suggests that such fears are ill-founded.

4 Costs

There are explicit costs associated with a public flotation. These include the initial costs of conversion to a public listed company, underwriting fees and brokerage, accounting and legal fees, listing fees, share registry costs and other continuing expenses such as the increased cost of producing annual reports. In addition executives will need to allocate time to shareholder relations and meetings with security analysts.

5 Insider trading implications

The insider trading provisions of the *Corporations Act* 2001 have significant implications for shareholders connected with the company who may wish to deal in their shares.

A company must be of sufficient size, post-issue, to comply with the ASX listing requirements on capital structure. An industrial company (as opposed to a mining and oil company) must satisfy either a Profits test or an Assets test. The Asset test requires net tangible assets of $2 million. Additionally, there is a spread of shareholders requirement: at least 500 shareholders must each hold shares to the value of at least $2,000.

Secondary issues is the term used for all issues by a company subsequent to its listing. The principal forms of secondary issues are **private placements** and *rights issues*.

Private placements are issues of ordinary shares, preference shares or debt to clients of a sharebroker and/or institutional investors, such as life insurance companies, superannuation funds and investment companies. Prior to July 1987 private placements of ordinary shares could be made only to institutional investors; however, from that date issues of voting shares to brokers' clients were permitted under certain conditions. The main conditions are that the broker should recommend the shares to the clients, the discount on market price of the issue should not be excessive, and information on the activities of the company should be sent to all clients. Because of taxation arrangements, private placements of preference shares were very popular in the early 1980s; however, these advantages have disappeared with dividend imputation and the popularity has diminished.

> **private placement**
> sale of securities to large institutional investors or selected clients of a sharebroker

Rights issues are also called *entitlement* or *pro rata issues*. When a rights issue is made, the shares are offered first to existing shareholders in proportion to their current shareholding. For example, if a 1 for 10 rights issue is made, the holder of 100 shares would be offered the right to 10 additional shares and the holder of 1,900 shares would be offered the right to 190 shares.

The factors that will determine the terms of a rights issue are:

- the amount of funds required by the company;
- the market price of the issuing company's securities;
- the state of the share market and general economic conditions;
- the desire to provide a benefit to shareholders; and
- the nature of the shareholders of the company—for example, a company with its shareholdings concentrated in the hands of a few investors would have to evaluate the support of those shareholders for the issues.

Most companies seek to maintain the current rate of dividends per share on the increased number of shares after a rights issue, although there is no economic reason for doing so. Therefore the 'cost' to the company is the increased dividend payout. The maximum issue price is determined by an assessment of what discount is necessary to ensure a high level of subscription. For an issue to be successful, the issue price (subscription price) must not be above the market price. A company that experiences substantial swings in the market price of its shares would have to fix a lower subscription price than a company whose share price is relatively constant.

Consider Awake Company and Asleep Company in Table 17.1. If share prices are assumed to be distributed normally, there is a 32 per cent[1] chance that the market price of the shares of Awake Company will fall below the proposed subscription price, $4.50, and only a 21 per cent chance that the market price of the shares of Asleep Company will fall below the subscription price. To ensure the success of the issue for Awake Company, the subscription price should be set below $4.50. If the firm wishes to have only a 20 per cent chance, the market price of Awake Company shares would fall below the subscription price; it would have to fix the price at $3.91.

TABLE 17.1

	Current market price	Previous 12 months				Proposed subscription price
		Lowest price	Highest price	Average price	Share price variance	
Awake Co.	5.00	2.00	10.00	5.30	3.00	4.50
Asleep Co.	5.00	4.00	6.00	5.30	1.00	4.50

Fixing the subscription price

The discount on market price, which acts as the incentive to ensure the success of a rights issue, translates into a positive market value for the rights. If a shareholder does not wish to take up the rights, the rights could be sold for cash. Assume we have a 1 for 4 rights issue at a subscription price of $1.20 where the market price is $1.50. The theoretical rights price is provided by the formula:

$$n\left(\frac{M - S}{n + r}\right)$$

where

n = the number of shares held to obtain a right
M = the market price
S = the subscription or issue price of the rights issue
r = the number of additional shares offered

so that:

$$4\left(\frac{\$1.50 - \$1.20}{4 + 1}\right)$$
$$= 24 \text{ cents}$$
$$= \text{the value of a right in the assumed issue}$$

Rights issues can be either renounceable or non-renounceable. Most rights issues are renounceable as non-renounceable rights issues cannot be traded.

tombstone
an advertisement announcing completion of a public offering

Tombstone advertisements are used by underwriters after the issue is fully subscribed. They provide some information about the issue, and they list the underwriters who are involved with selling the issue. Tombstones appear after the event and are edged in black, hence the name 'tombstone'.

Concept questions

17.1a *Why is an initial public offering necessarily a cash offer?*

17.1b *What are the basic procedures in selling a new issue?*

17.1c *What is the relationship between the subscription price, the new issue price and the market price of the shares of a company?*

17.1d *Is a renounceable rights issue or a non-renounceable rights issue likely to be fully subscribed?*

17.2 ▪ The cash offer

If a public issue of securities is made, whether it is a cash offer or a rights issue, underwriters are usually involved. The role of the underwriter is:

- pricing the issue—that is, setting the cash offer price or the subscription price;
- marketing the issue by timing the announcement and actively trading;
- engaging the sub-underwriters; and
- placing the shortfall.

Underwriting and sub-underwriting

Underwriting is defined as a guarantee that funds will be made available to a company at a specific time and on agreed terms and conditions. The **underwriter** is the guarantor of the availability of the funds through share sales. The underwriter may choose to reduce some of the exposure to the issue through a sub-underwriting panel. It is common to seek new large institutional shareholders for the company by including these institutions on the sub-underwriting panel. As a **sub-underwriter** the institution will receive a fee for an obligation to take up some of the shortfall. Usually the underwriter offers general sub-underwriting participation, which means that in the event of a shortfall, say 10 per cent, the sub-underwriter is responsible for subscribing a percentage (10%) of the amount of shares sub-underwritten. A less prevalent alternative in share flotations and rights issues (but not in debt issues) is an offer of specific sub-underwriting in a set parcel of shares.

Where the funds are guaranteed the situation is called a *firm* underwriting. A *standby* underwriting will generally arise in takeover situations, where the bidding company has insufficient cash if the bid is totally successful or where the bidding company wants to provide cash (from the underwriter) as an alternative to a share bid. A *best efforts* underwriting arrangement is where the underwriter is bound to use 'best efforts' to sell the securities at the agreed offering price. Beyond this, the underwriter does not guarantee any particular amount of money to the issuer company.

underwriters
investment firms that act as intermediaries between a company selling securities and the investing public

sub-underwriters
a group of underwriters formed to reduce the risk and help to sell an issue

Underwriting fees

Typically the underwriter's fee is expressed as a percentage of the capital to be raised and takes into account the degree of risk involved. Factors affecting risk will include: the relative size of the issue and the issue price; market conditions generally and the likely attitude of the market towards the shares; and the time period from when the underwriter goes firm to the opening of the issue. In addition to the risk component in the underwriting fee, allowance is made for brokerage (a selling fee) and management of the issue. On occasions a separate management fee or a prospectus preparation fee is charged by the underwriter, particularly where additional tasks are undertaken. Out of the underwriting fee, the underwriter will pass on a commission to their sub-underwriters. This commission will reflect the risk involved in the issue, though it should be noted that the underwriter's risk (and hence reward) is usually greater than that of the sub-underwriters, since the underwriter often guarantees the issue prior to seeking sub-underwriting support.

In recent times, fees for initial equity issues of industrial companies including brokerage have ranged from 3 per cent to 5 per cent. This cost can be avoided if the issue is not underwritten. A company may decide that an underwriter is not necessary as the offer is sufficiently attractive that there is little chance of a shortfall. The Telstra share offers were not underwritten.

The offering price and underpricing

Determining the correct offering price is the most difficult thing an underwriter must do for an initial public offering. The issuing firm faces a potential cost if the offering price is set too high or too low. If the issue is priced too high, it may be unsuccessful and have to be withdrawn. If the issue is priced below the market price at the time of issue, the issuer's existing shareholders will experience an opportunity loss when they sell their shares for less than they are worth.

Underpricing is a fairly common occurrence. It obviously helps new shareholders earn a higher return on the shares they buy. However, the existing shareholders of the issuing firm are not helped by underpricing. To them it is an indirect cost of issuing new securities.

Pricing

Equity issues are priced primarily by reference to the prevailing market price:

- Private placements of ordinary shares are typically made at 90–100 per cent of market price.
- Dividend reinvestment offers are typically priced at 90–95 per cent of market price.
- Rights issues are typically priced at 60–90 per cent of market price.
- Convertible notes issues typically offer an option to convert into ordinary shares at a 10–20 per cent premium over market, although recent undated convertibles have been issued with no premium (and accordingly a lower interest coupon).

Underpricing: The case of Conrail

The sale on 26 March 1987 of more than 58 million shares of Conrail, the previously US government-owned railroad company, was the largest new issue of shares in US history.

At the end of the first day after the Conrail offering, the shares were more than 10 per cent above their initial offering price level. This is a good example of underpricing. Two opposing views of the sale were prominent in the press after the offering:

1 The issue was hailed as a great success by underwriters and the US Congress. By selling 100 per cent of the railroad company, the government achieved its largest divestiture yet of state assets.
2 Others saw the sale as the largest commercial giveaway in US government history. They asked how the government could get the price so wrong.

In passing, we note that the Conrail issue raised a total of $2.20 billion. This is more than the $2 billion that AT&T obtained in 1983 in what had previously been the largest US share offering, but substantially less than, for example, the $6.34 billion raised when British Telecom (the British government-owned telephone company) went public in 1984. However, both of these issues pale in comparison to what NTT (Nippon Telephone and

Telegraph, the Japanese telephone company) raised in 1987. In November 1987, NTT sold 1.95 million shares at a price of 2.55 *million* yen *each*. At the then prevailing exchange rate, this was roughly $25,000 per share. The total issue amount was thus in the order of $48 billion. What is even more remarkable is that NTT had already sold 1.95 million shares in February of the same year.

The Conrail issue was apparently underpriced, but, as we discuss next, the underpricing was not atypical (in percentage terms). Even so, underpricing a $2.2 *billion* issue by 10 per cent or so means that the seller misses out on almost $220 million.

Evidence on underpricing

Figure 17.1 provides a more general illustration of the underpricing phenomenon. The information provided is American; the Australian experience is similar. For example:

Company	Date	Amount raised	Day 1 return
CBA	August 1991	$1,292,000,000	19.06%
Qantas	June 1995	$1,400,000,000	13.32%
St George	June 1992	$1,274,000,000	6.4%

In December 1992 there was a public float made by the Rockhampton Building Society for one dollar per share which was initially traded at more than $1.50. This discount of around 50 per cent is high—most Australian brokers admit to operating on a discount factor of 20–25 per cent, depending upon the number of new issues being floated at the time, the ability of the float to attract investors, the supply of money at the time of the float, and the buoyancy of the market at the time of the float. What is shown in Figure 17.1 is the month-by-month history of underpricing for Securities Exchange Commission (SEC) registered Initial Public Offerings (IPOs).[2] The period covered is 1960 to 1987. Figure 17.2 (overleaf) presents the number of offerings in each month for the same period.

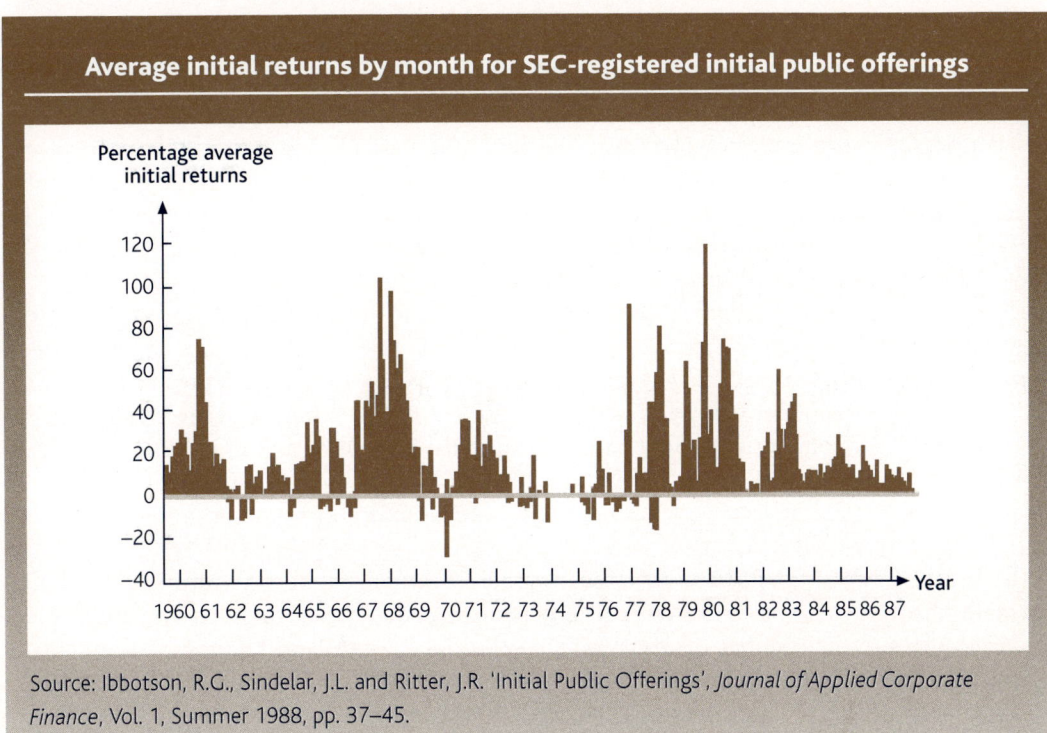

Average initial returns by month for SEC-registered initial public offerings

FIGURE 17.1

Source: Ibbotson, R.G., Sindelar, J.L. and Ritter, J.R. 'Initial Public Offerings', *Journal of Applied Corporate Finance*, Vol. 1, Summer 1988, pp. 37–45.

FIGURE
17.2

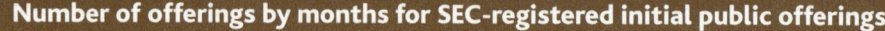

Number of offerings by months for SEC-registered initial public offerings

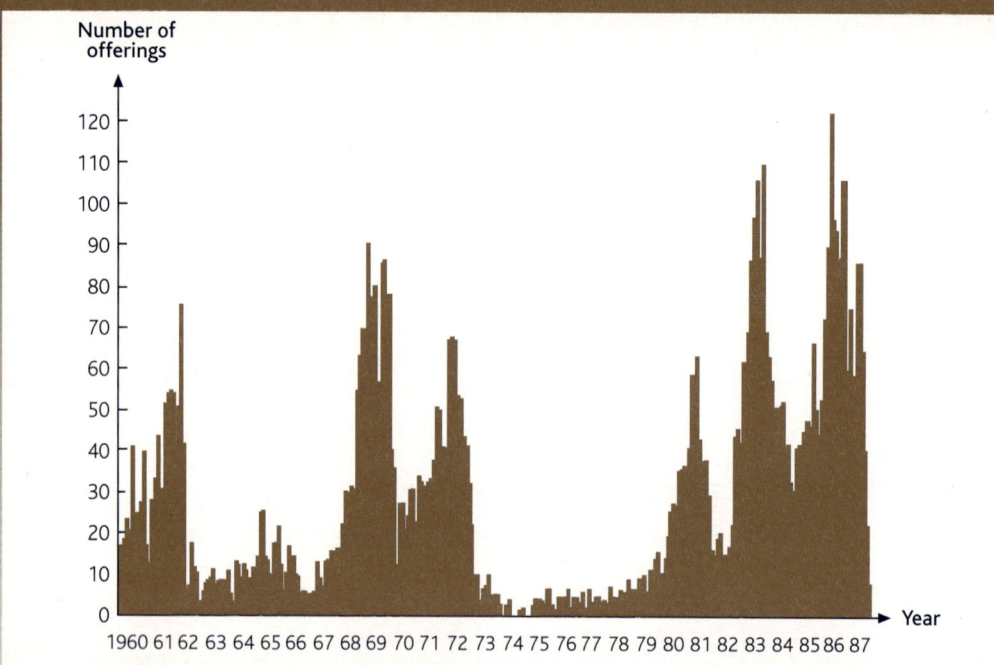

Source: Ibbotson, R.G., Sindelar, J.L. and Ritter, J.R. 'Initial Public Offerings', *Journal of Applied Corporate Finance*, Vol. 1, Summer 1988, pp. 37–45.

Figure 17.1 shows that underpricing can be quite dramatic, exceeding 100 per cent in some months. In such months, the average initial public offering more than doubled in value, sometimes in a matter of hours. Also, the degree of underpricing varies through time, and periods of severe underpricing (so-called hot issue markets) are followed by periods of little underpricing (cold issue markets). For example, in the 1960s, the average initial public offering was underpriced by 21.25 per cent. In the 1970s, the average was much smaller (8.95%), and it was actually very small or even negative for much of that time. Finally, for 1980–1987, initial public offerings were underpriced by 16.09 per cent on average.

Australian (Finn & Higham 1988) and New Zealand research (Cheung & Vos 1990) shows that an investor who subscribes to an initial public offering at the offer price and sells immediately the shares are publicly traded can earn on average an excess return of more than 28 per cent. A subsequent study by Taylor and Walter (1991) found that an average excess return of 13.4 per cent could be earned on the first day of trading for 139 IPOs. How, Izan and Monroe (1995) found this excess return to be 8.7 per cent for 340 IPOs. Easton and Pinder (1996) looked at seven government sector IPOs and also found an average first day excess return of around 8 per cent.

In Figure 17.2, it is apparent that the number of initial public offerings is also highly variable through time. Further, there are pronounced cycles in both the degree of underpricing and the number of initial public offerings. Comparing Figures 17.1 and 17.2, increases in the number of new offerings tend to follow periods of significant underpricing by roughly 6–12 months. This probably occurs because companies decide to go public when they perceive that the market is highly receptive to new issues.

Table 17.2 contains a year-by-year summary of the information presented in Figures 17.1 and 17.2. As indicated, a grand total of 8,668 companies were included in this analysis. The degree of underpricing averaged 16.37 per cent overall for the 28 years examined. Securities were overpriced on average in only five of the 28 years; the worst was 1973 when the average decrease in value was 17.82 per cent. At the other extreme, in 1968, the 368 issues were underpriced, on average, by a remarkable 55.86 per cent.

Number of offerings, average initial return and gross proceeds of intial public offerings in 1960–1987

Year	Number of offerings*	Average initial return (per cent)**	Gross proceeds ($ million)†
1960	269	17.83	553
1961	435	34.11	1,243
1962	298	−1.61	431
1963	83	3.93	246
1964	97	5.32	380
1965	146	12.75	409
1966	85	7.06	275
1967	100	37.67	641
1968	368	55.86	1,205
1969	780	12.53	2,605
1970	358	−0.67	780
1971	391	21.16	1,655
1972	562	7.51	2,724
1973	105	−17.82	330
1974	9	−6.98	51
1975	14	−1.86	264
1976	34	2.90	237
1977	40	21.02	151
1978	42	25.66	247
1979	103	24.61	429
1980	259	49.36	1,404
1981	438	16.76	3,200
1982	198	20.31	1,334
1983	848	20.79	13,168
1984	516	11.52	3,932
1985	507	12.36	10,450
1986	953	9.99	19,260
1987	630	10.39	16,380
Total	8,668	16.37	83,984

* The number of offerings excludes Regulation A offerings (small issues, raising less than $1.5 million currently). The authors have excluded real estate investment trusts (REITs) and closed-end mutual funds.

** Initial returns are computed as the percentage return from the offering price to the end-of-the-calendar-month bid price, less the market return, for offerings in 1960–76. For 1977–87, initial returns are calculated as the percentage return from the offering price to the end-of-the-first-day bid price, without adjusting for market movements.

† Gross proceeds data comes from various issues of the SEC *Monthly Statistical Bulletin* and *Going Public: The IPO Reporter.* The gross proceeds numbers reported here have been adjusted to remove REIT and closed-end mutual fund offerings.

Source: Ibbotson, R.G., Sindelar, J.L. and Ritter, J.R. 'Initial Public Offerings', *Journal of Applied Corporate Finance*, Vol. 1, Summer 1988, pp. 37–45.

Why does underpricing exist?

Based on the evidence we have examined, an obvious question is: Why does underpricing continue to exist? As we discuss, there are various explanations, but to date there is a lack of complete agreement among researchers as to which is correct.

We present some pieces of the underpricing puzzle by stressing two important caveats to our discussion above. First, the average figures we have examined tend to obscure the fact that much of the apparent underpricing is attributable to the smaller, more highly speculative issues. This point is illustrated in Table 17.3, which shows the extent of underpricing for 2,439 firms over the period 1975–84. Here, the firms are grouped based on their total sales in the 12 months prior to the initial public offering.

TABLE
17.3

Average initial returns categorised by annual sales of issuing firm		
Annual sales of issuing firm ($)*	Number of firms**	Average initial return (%)
0	386	42.9
1–999,999	678	31.4
1,000,000–4,999,999	353	14.3
5,000,000–14,999,999	347	10.7
15,000,000–24,999,999	182	6.5
25,000,000 or larger	493	5.3
All	2,439	20.7

* All sales are measured as the 12-month revenue for the year prior to going public. No adjustments for the effects of inflation have been made.

** Firms included are those using S-1 or S-18 registration forms, or with Federal Home Loan Bank Board approval, and listed in *Going Public: The IPO Reporter* for 1975–1984. Issues not using an investment banker are excluded.

† Initial returns are calculated as the percentage return from the offering price to the first recorded closing bid price. No adjustments for market movements have been made.

Source: Ibbotson, R.G., Sindelar, J.L. and Ritter, J.R. 'Initial Public Offerings', *Journal of Applied Corporate Finance*, Vol. 1, Summer 1988, pp. 37–45.

As illustrated in Table 17.3, the overall average underpricing is 20.7 per cent for this sample; however, this underpricing is clearly concentrated in the firms with little to no sales in the previous year. These firms tend to have offering prices of less than $3 per share, and such *penny shares* (as they are sometimes termed in the United States) can be very risky investments. Arguably, they must be significantly underpriced, on average, just to attract investors, and this is one explanation for the underpricing phenomenon. In fact, when the companies considered in Table 17.3 were grouped based on price per share instead of sales, the average degree of underpricing for those companies with initial offering prices of less than $3 per share was 42.8 per cent. It averaged 8.6 per cent for all the others.

The second caveat is that relatively few initial public offering buyers will actually get the initial high average returns observed in initial public offerings, and many will actually lose money. Although it is true that, on average, initial public offerings have positive initial returns, a significant fraction of them have price drops. Furthermore, when the price is too low, the issue is often 'oversubscribed'. This means investors will not be able to buy all of the shares they want, and the underwriters will allocate the shares among investors.

The average investor will find it difficult to get shares in a 'successful' offering (one where the price increases) because there will not be enough shares to go around. On the other hand, an investor blindly submitting orders for initial public offerings will find that he or she tends to get more shares in issues that go down in price.

To illustrate, consider this tale of two investors. Lara knows very accurately what the Party Corporation is worth when its shares are offered. She is confident that they are underpriced. Tim is cruising and knows only that the prices usually rise one month after an initial public offering. Armed with this information, Tim decides to buy 1,000 shares of every initial public offering. Does he actually earn an abnormally high return on the initial offering?

The answer is no, and at least one reason is Lara. Knowing about the Party Corporation, Lara invests all her money in its initial public offering. When the issue is oversubscribed, the underwriters have somehow to allocate the shares between Lara and Tim. The net result is that when an issue is underpriced, Tim does not get to buy as much of it as he wanted.

Lara also knows that the Gay Times Corporation's initial public offering is overpriced. In this case, she avoids its initial public offering altogether, and Tim ends up with a full 1,000 shares. To summarise this tale, Tim gets fewer shares when more knowledgeable investors swarm to buy an underpriced issue and gets all he wants when the smart money avoids the issue.

This is another example of the winner's curse, and it is thought to be another reason why initial public offerings have such a large average return. When the average investor 'wins' and gets her entire allocation, it may be because those who knew better avoided the issue. The only way underwriters can counteract the winner's curse and attract the average investor is to underprice new issues (on average) so that the average investor still makes a profit.

The Australian experience in relation to initial public offers is similar to that in the United States. Substantial price increases generally occur on the first day of the exchange listing. Trading arrangements for new issues in Australia differ from those in the United States. In the United States there is a well-developed over-the-counter market where the shares are sold direct by the company to the public. No such market exists in Australia and it is common practice for shares issued to the public for the first time to receive official Stock Exchange listing at the time of the issue. Official listing requirements of the Australian Stock Exchange (ASX) require that companies wishing to list must be sponsored by a member of the exchange. The sponsoring sharebroker tends to be the underwriter in most initial public floats. Underwritings of new issues in Australia take the form of a 'stand-by' agreement. In a 'stand-by' agreement, the underwriter undertakes to acquire the shortfall at the offer price if the issue is not fully subscribed. There are at least two incentives for the sponsoring underwriter to underprice a new issue of Australian shares. First, to reduce the risk of the issue being undersubscribed, and second because the underwriter/sponsor has the exclusive right to allocate all shares in the issue. There is some evidence that the brokers have retained shares in the new issue for their own account. The 1974 Final Report of the Senate Select Committee on Securities and Exchange stated that brokers were retaining shares and releasing some to selected clients.

Underwriters can only underprice new issues if they are in a position of market power and firms making new issues are forced to use their services. There are no substantial barriers to becoming an underwriter in Australia. Underwriters are required to be licensed dealers but the licensing requirements of dealers are not too onerous. Therefore the expectation is that competition to become an underwriter and competition among underwriters should ensure that new share issues will be valued fairly. The explanation for the underpricing has to be found elsewhere. It seems that there have been barriers to becoming a *sharebroker*. Membership of the exchanges has been regulated by the member brokers themselves and there is no right of appeal against their decision. The *Securities Industry Act* also placed restrictions on entry to sharebroking. If this argument is correct, the barriers would work to restrict the number of sponsoring brokers and allow the establishment of non-competitive share values. At the end of 1982, the Australian Trade Practices Commission condemned the membership provisions of the exchanges and gave them 18 months to change the provisions. The provisions were changed, but they still remained restrictive.

In 1999 the Australian Stock Exchange was listed as a public company on the exchange, with member brokers being given substantial shareholdings in the listed company, thus inhibiting further the ability of new entrants to become sharebrokers.

Concept questions

17.2a *What is the difference between firm commitment and best efforts underwriting?*

17.2b *Suppose a sharebroker calls you up out of the blue and offers to sell you 'all the shares you want' of a new issue. Do you think the issue will be more or less underpriced than average?*

In their own words

Jay Ritter

Jay Ritter* on IPO underpricing around the world

The United States is not the only country in which initial public offerings (IPOs) of common stock are underpriced. The phenomenon exists in every country with a stock market, although the extent of underpricing varies from country to country.

In general, countries with developed capital markets have more moderate underpricing than in emerging markets. During the Internet bubble of 1999–2000, however, underpricing in the developed capital markets increased dramatically. In the United States, for example, the average first-day return during 1999–2000 was 65 per cent. At the same time that underpricing in the developed capital markets increased, the underpricing of IPOs sold to residents of China moderated. The Chinese average has come down to a mere 257 per cent, which is lower than it had been in the early and mid 1990s. After the bursting of the Internet bubble in mid-2000, the level of underpricing in the United States, Germany, and other developed capital markets has returned to more traditional levels.

The table below gives a summary of the average first-day returns on IPOs in a number of countries around the world, with the figures collected from a number of studies by various authors.

Country	Sample size	Time period	Average first-day return (%)
Australia	381	1976–1995	12.1
Austria	76	1984–1999	6.5
Belgium	86	1984–1999	14.6
Brazil	62	1979–1990	78.5
Canada	500	1971–1999	6.3
Chile	55	1982–1997	8.8
China	432	1990–2000	256.9
Denmark	117	1984–1998	5.4
Finland	99	1984–1997	10.1
France	448	1983–1998	9.5
Germany	407	1978–1999	27.7
Greece	129	1987–1994	51.7
Hong Kong	334	1980–1996	15.9
India	98	1992–1993	35.3
Indonesia	106	1989–1994	15.1
Israel	285	1990–1994	12.1
Italy	164	1985–2000	23.9
Japan	1,542	1970–2000	26.4
Korea	477	1980–1996	74.3
Malaysia	401	1980–1998	104.1
Mexico	37	1987–1990	33.0
Netherlands	143	1982–1999	10.2
New Zealand	201	1979–1999	23.0
Nigeria	63	1989–1993	19.1
Norway	68	1984–1996	12.5
Philippines	104	1987–1997	22.7
Poland	149	1991–1998	35.6
Portugal	21	1992–1998	10.6
Singapore	128	1973–1992	31.4
South Africa	118	1980–1991	32.7
Spain	99	1986–1998	10.7
Sweden	251	1980–1994	34.1
Switzerland	42	1983–1989	35.8
Taiwan	293	1986–1998	31.1
Thailand	292	1987–1997	46.7
Turkey	138	1990–1996	13.6
United Kingdom	3,042	1959–2000	17.5
United States	14,760	1960–2000	18.4

* **Jay R. Ritter** is Cordell Professor of Finance at the University of Florida. An outstanding scholar, he is well respected for his insightful analyses of new issues and going public.

 ## New equity sales and the value of the firm

It seems reasonable to believe that new long-term financing is arranged by firms after positive net present value projects are put together. As a consequence, when the announcement of external financing is made, the firm's market value should go up. Interestingly, this is not what happens. Share prices tend to decline following the announcement of a new equity issue, and they tend to rise following a debt announcement. A number of researchers have studied this issue. Plausible reasons for this strange result include:

1 *Managerial information.* If management has superior information about the market value of the firm, it may know when the firm is overvalued. If it does, it will attempt to issue new shares when the market value exceeds the correct value. This will benefit existing shareholders. However, the potential new shareholders are not stupid, and they will anticipate this superior information and discount it in lower market prices at the new issue date.

2 *Debt usage.* Issuing new equity may reveal that the company has too much debt or too little liquidity. One version of this argument is that the equity issue is a bad signal to the market. After all, if the new projects are favourable ones, why should the firm let new shareholders in on them? It could just issue debt and let the existing shareholders have all the gain.

3 *Issue costs.* As we discuss next, there are substantial costs associated with selling securities.

The drop in value of the existing shares following the announcement of a new issue is an example of an indirect cost of selling securities. This drop might typically be in the order of 3 per cent for an industrial corporation, so for a large company it can be a substantial amount of money. We label this drop the *abnormal return* in our discussion of the costs of new issues below.

Concept questions

17.3a *What are some possible reasons why the price of shares drops on the announcement of a new equity issue?*

17.3b *Explain why we might expect a firm with a positive NPV investment to finance it with debt instead of equity.*

 ## The costs of issuing securities

Issuing securities to the public is not free, and the costs of different methods are important determinants of which is used. The costs associated with floating a new issue are generically called flotation costs. In this section, we take a closer look at the flotation costs associated with equity sales to the public.

The costs of selling shares are classified in Table 17.4 and fall into five categories: (1) the underwriter's commission, (2) other direct expenses, (3) indirect expenses, (4) abnormal returns (discussed above), and (5) underpricing.

The costs of issuing securities

TABLE 17.4

Underwriter's commission	This consists of direct fees paid by the issuer to the underwriting syndicate.
Other direct expenses	These are direct costs, incurred by the issuer, that are not part of the compensation to underwriters. These costs include filing fees, legal fees, and taxes—all reported on the prospectus.
Indirect expenses	These costs are not reported on the prospectus and include the costs of management time spent working on the new issue.
Abnormal returns	In a seasoned issue of shares, the price drops on average by 3 per cent upon the announcement of the issue.
Underpricing	For initial public offerings, losses arise from selling the shares below the correct value.

Table 17.5(a) reports US data on the direct costs of new equity issues in 1983 for publicly traded firms. These are all seasoned offerings; 'seasoned' indicates that other ordinary shares of the company are being traded, so we are not looking at initial public offerings. The percentages in Table 17.5(a) are as reported in the prospectuses of the issuing companies. These costs only include the underwriter's commission and other direct costs, including legal fees, accounting fees, printing costs, registration costs and taxes. Not included are indirect expenses and abnormal returns.

Flotation costs as a percentage of gross proceeds in 1983 for underwritten new issues of equity by publicly traded firms

TABLE 17.5a

United States data	
Gross proceeds ($ millions)	Direct costs reported on prospectus (per cent)
$ 0–10	10.10%
10–20	7.02
20–50	4.89
50–100	3.99
100–200	3.71
200+	3.30

Source: Hansen, R. 'Evaluating the Costs of a New Equity Issue', *Midland Corporate Finance Journal*, Vol. 4, No. 1, Spring 1986, p. 45.

TABLE
17.5b

Flotation costs as a percentage of gross proceeds for 472 issues 1983–1988		
Gross proceeds ($ millions)	Australian data Costs as a proportion of proceeds	
	Second board	Main board
$ 5	6.7%	7.1%
10		6.1%

Source: Woo, L.E. and Lange, H.P. 'Equity Raising by Australian Small Business: A Study of Access and Survival', *Small Enterprise Research, The Journal of SEAANZ*, Vol. 1, No. 1, Winter 1992, pp. 53–62.

As indicated in Table 17.5(a), the direct costs alone can be very large, particularly for smaller (less than $10 million) issues. For this group, the direct costs, as reported by the companies, average a little over 10 per cent. This means that the company, net of costs, receives 90 per cent of the proceeds of the sale on average. On a $10 million issue, this is $1 million in direct expenses—a substantial cost.

Table 17.5(b) reports similar Australian data on the costs of new equity issues for the period 1983 to 1988 for publicly traded firms. The costs of new issues are quite substantial, particularly for smaller firms.

Table 17.5 only tells part of the story. For initial public offerings, the effective costs can be much greater because of the indirect costs. Table 17.6 reports both the direct costs of going public and the degree of underpricing based on initial public offerings that took place during 1977–1982. Issues are classified by the type of underwriting (firm commitment or best efforts) and size of the issue. Again we are forced to rely on data from the United States but there is no reason to suggest that Australian information would give a different picture if it were available.

Columns (4) and (9) of Table 17.6 give some additional insight into the severity of underpricing. For example, with best efforts underwriting, the average price increase in the first full day of trading is 47.8 per cent. This means that, on average, a share offered at $10 per share sold for $14.78 at the end of the day. The underpricing was most severe for issues in the $2–3.99 million range, averaging 63.41 per cent. The underpricing was much less severe with firm commitment underwriting; the worst average is 26.92 per cent for the smallest offerings.

The total expenses of going public over these years averaged 21.22 per cent for firm commitment and 31.87 per cent for best efforts. Once again, we see that the costs of selling securities can be quite large.

The available Australian evidence supports the conclusions based upon the US research. For example, the Commonwealth Bank float of $1.36 billion recorded issuing costs of 2 per cent whereas the Industry Commission[3] reports that small floats of $250,000 would incur costs of up to 16 per cent. The data in Table 17.7 was collected for 472 Australian initial public offerings made from 1983 to 1988.

TABLE
17.6

Costs of going public—total transaction as a percentage of gross proceeds, 1977–1982

			Firm commitment offerings					Best efforts offerings		
	(1)	(2)	(3) Total	(4)	(5)	(6)	(7)	(8) Total	(9)	(10)
	Under-writing discount (per cent)	Other expenses (per cent)	direct discount (per cent) (1) + (2)	Under-pricing (per cent)	Total expenses (per cent)	Under-writing discount (per cent)	Other expenses (per cent)	direct discount (per cent) (6) + (7)	Under-pricing (per cent)	Total expenses (per cent)
Gross proceeds ($)										
1,000,000–1,999,999	9.84%	0.64%	19.48%	26.92%	31.73%	10.63%	9.52%	20.15%	39.62%	31.89%
2,000,000–3,999,999	9.83	7.60	17.43	20.70	24.93	10.00	6.21	16.21	63.41	36.28
4,000,000–5,999,999	9.10	5.67	14.77	12.57	20.90	9.86*	3.71*	13.57*	26.82*	14.49*
6,000,000–9,999,999	8.03	4.31	12.34	8.99	17.85	9.80*	3.42*	13.22*	40.79*	25.97*
10,000,000–120,174,195	7.24	2.1	9.34	10.32	16.27	8.03*	2.40*	10.43*	–5.42*	–0.17*
All offerings	8.67	5.36	14.03	14.8	21.22	10.26	7.48	17.74	47.78	31.87

The initial returns are computed as $(p - OP)/OP$, multiplied by 100 per cent, where p is the closing bid price on the first day of trading and OP is the offering price. These are not annualised returns. Total costs are computed as 100 per cent minus the net proceeds as a percentage of the market value of securities in the aftermarket. Consequently, total costs are not the sum of underwriting expenses and the average initial return. The underwriting discount is the commission paid by the issuing firm; this is listed on the front page of the firm's prospectus.

The other expense figure comprises accountable and non-accountable fees of the underwriters and cash expenses of the issuing firm for legal, printing and auditing fees and other out-of-pocket costs. These other expenses are described in footnotes on the front page of the issuing firm's prospectus. None of the expense categories includes the value of warrants granted to the underwriter, a practice that is common with best efforts offerings.

Gross proceeds categories are nominal; no price level adjustments have been made.

Also note that the –0.17% figure for the total expenses for best efforts offerings raising $10 million or more means that, on the average, these firms received net proceeds larger than the market value of the securities after the offering. It should be mentioned that there was less than one offering per year in the category.

* Based on fewer than 25 firms.

Source: Modified from Ritter, J.R. 'The Costs of Going Public', *Journal of Financial Economics*, Vol. 19, 1987 © Elsevier Science Publishers B.V. (North-Holland).

TABLE
17.7

Australian initial public offerings 1983–1988

Gross proceeds ($000s)	Average equity raised ($000s)	Formation expenses per $ (cents)	Number of firms
< 500	307	17.40	11
500–999	773	13.11	26
1,000–1,499	1,147	10.07	52
1,500–1,999	1,639	9.35	43
2,000–2,999	2,336	9.21	66
3,000–4,999	3,672	8.42	94
5,000–9,999	6,417	6.47	81
20,000–39,999	28,718	5.42	31
40,000–99,999	64,687	4.58	15
> 100,000	174,915	3.75	5
Total/Average	9,640	8.23	472

Source: Woo, L.E. and Lange, H.P. 'Equity Raising by Australian Small Business: A Study of Access and Survival', *Small Enterprise Research, The Journal of SEAANZ*, Vol. 1, No. 1, Winter 1992, pp. 53–62.

Overall, five conclusions emerge from an analysis of Tables 17.5, 17.6 and 17.7:

1 Substantial economies of size are evident. In percentage terms, the costs of selling securities decrease dramatically as the issue size grows.
2 The costs of selling securities are higher for best efforts offers.
3 The cost associated with underpricing can be substantial and can exceed the direct costs, particularly with smaller issues and best efforts underwriting.
4 Underpricing for best efforts offers is much greater than for firm commitment offers.
5 The issue costs are higher for an initial public offering than for a seasoned offering.

Concept questions

17.4a *What are the different costs associated with security offerings?*
17.4b *What lessons do we learn from studying issue costs?*

 **17.5 Rights**

When new ordinary shares are sold to the general public, the proportional ownership of existing shareholders will likely be reduced. However, if a pre-emptive right is contained in the firm's articles of incorporation, then the firm must first offer any new issue of shares to existing shareholders. If the articles of incorporation do not include a pre-emptive right, the firm has a choice of offering the issue of shares directly to existing shareholders or to the public.

An issue of ordinary shares offered to existing shareholders is called a *rights offering* or a *privileged subscription*. In a rights offering, each shareholder is issued rights to buy a specified number of new shares from the firm at a specified price within a specified time, after which time the rights are said to expire.

The mechanics of a rights offering

To illustrate the various considerations a financial manager has in a rights offering, we will examine the situation faced by the Songbird Company Ltd, whose abbreviated initial financial statements are given in Table 17.8.

As indicated in Table 17.8, Songbird earns $2 million after taxes and has 1 million shares outstanding. Earnings per share are thus $2, and the shares sell for $20, or 10 times earnings (i.e. the price–earnings ratio is 10). To fund a planned expansion, the company intends to raise $5 million of new equity funds by a rights offering.

To execute a rights offering, the financial management of Songbird will have to answer the following questions:

1 What should the subscription price per share be for the new shares?
2 How many shares will have to be sold?
3 How many shares will each shareholder be allowed to buy?
   Also management will probably want to ask:
4 What is the likely effect of the rights offering on the per-share value of the existing shares?

It turns out that the answers to these questions are highly interrelated. We will get to them in a moment.

TABLE
17.8

Songbird Company Ltd's financial statement before rights offering

Statement of Financial Position

Assets		Shareholders' equity	
		Ordinary shares	$ 5,000,000
		Retained earnings	10,000,000
Total	$15,000,000	Total	$15,000,000

Earnings summary

Earnings before taxes	$ 2,857,143
Taxes (30%)	$857,143
Net profit	$2,000,000
Earnings per share	$2
Issued shares	1,000,000
Market price per share	$20
Total market value	$20,000,000

The early stages of a rights offering are the same as for the general cash offer. The difference between a rights offering and a general cash offer lies in how the shares are sold. With a rights offer, Songbird's existing shareholders are informed that they are entitled to rights based on the number of shares they own. Songbird will then specify how many shares a shareholder needs to buy one additional share at a specified price.

To take advantage of the rights offering, shareholders have to exercise the rights by filling out a subscription form and sending it, along with payment, to the company or its agent. Shareholders of Songbird will actually have several choices: (1) exercise and subscribe for the full number of entitled shares, (2) sell their rights in the market, or (3) do nothing and let the rights expire. As we discuss below, this third course of action is inadvisable.

Number of rights attaching to each share

Songbird wants to raise $5 million in new equity. Suppose that the subscription price is set at $10 per share. How Songbird arrived at that price is something we will discuss below, but notice that the subscription price is substantially less than the current $20 per share market price.

At $10 per share, Songbird will have to issue 500,000 new shares. This can be determined by dividing the total amount of funds to be raised by the subscription price:

$$\text{Number of new shares} = \frac{\text{Funds to be raised}}{\text{Subscription price}} \qquad (17.1)$$
$$= \$5,000,000/\$10$$
$$= 500,000 \text{ shares}$$

As there are 1,000,000 old shares outstanding, Songbird will need to issue one share for every two shares currently issued if it is to reach the target of 500,000 new shares. Therefore the rights issue is a 1-for-2 issue; that is, shareholders are entitled to one right for every two shares held currently.

It should be clear that the subscription price, the number of new shares, and the number of rights attaching to each share are interrelated. For example, Songbird can lower the subscription price. If it does, more new shares will have to be issued to raise $5 million in new equity. Several alternatives are worked out here:

Subscription price	Number of new shares	Terms of rights issue
$20	250,000	1 for 4
10	500,000	1 for 2
5	1,000,000	1 for 1

The value of a right

Rights clearly have value. In the case of Songbird, the right to be able to buy a share worth $20 for $10 is definitely worth something.

Suppose a shareholder of Songbird owns two shares just before the rights offering. This situation is depicted in Table 17.9. Initially, the price of Songbird is $20 per share, so the shareholder's total holding is worth $2 \times \$20 = \$40$. The Songbird rights offer gives shareholders with two shares the opportunity to purchase one additional share for $10.

TABLE 17.9

The value of rights: the individual shareholder	
Initial position	
Number of shares	2
Share price	$20
Value of holding	$40
Terms of offer	
Subscription price	$10
Number of shares to obtain 1 new share	2
After offer	
Number of shares	3
Value of holdings	$50
Share price	16.67
Value of a right per share	
Old price − new price	$20 − 16.67 = $3.33
Value of a right	$3.33 × 2 shares = 6.67

The holding of the shareholder who exercises the right and buys a new share would increase to three shares. The total investment would be $40 + 10 = $50 (the $40 initial value plus the $10 paid to the company).

Songbird Company rights offering	
Initial position	
Number of shares	1 million
Share price	$20
Value of firm	$20 million
Terms of offer	
Subscription price	$10
Number of new shares issued	0.5 million
After offer	
Number of shares	1.5 million
Value of firm	$25 million
Share price	$16.67
Value of a right per share	
Old price − new price	$20 − 16.67 = $3.33
Value of a right	$3.33 × 2 shares = $6.67

TABLE 17.10

The shareholder now holds three shares, all of which are identical. Since the total cost of buying these three shares is $40 + 10 = $50, the price per share must end up at $50/3 = $16.67 (rounded to two decimal places).

Table 17.10 (above) summarises what happens to Songbird's share price. If all shareholders exercise their rights, the number of shares will increase to 1 million + 0.5 million = 1.5 million. The value of the firm will increase to $20 million + 5 million = $25 million. The value of each share will thus drop to $25 million/1.5 million = $16.67 after the rights offering.

The difference between the old share price of $20 and the new share price of $16.67 reflects the fact that the old shares carried rights to subscribe to the new issue. The difference must be equal to the value of the rights that attach to the share; that is, $20 − 16.67 = $3.33. Because a shareholder must hold two shares in order to obtain the right, the value of the right is $3.33 × 2 shares = $6.67 (to account for previous rounding). Using the formula presented earlier in the chapter we have:

$$\text{Value of right} = n\left(\frac{M - S}{n + r}\right)$$
$$= 2\left(\frac{20 - 10}{2 + 1}\right)$$
$$= \$6.67$$

An investor holding no shares of outstanding Songbird capital who wants to subscribe to the new issue can do so by buying rights. Suppose an outside investor buys a right. This will cost $6.67. If the investor exercises the right at a subscription price of $10, the total cost would be $10 + 6.67 = $16.67. In return for this expenditure, the investor will receive a new share which, as we have seen, is worth $16.67.

EXAMPLE 17.1 Exercising your rights

In the Songbird example, suppose the subscription price was set at $8. How many shares will have to be sold? How many shares would you need to buy a new share? What is the value of a right? What will the price per share be after the rights offer?

To raise $5 million, $5 million/$8 = 625,000 shares will need to be sold. There are 1 million shares outstanding and 625,000 more shares have to be issued: for every eight shares currently held five new shares have to be issued. You would need to own 1.6 shares currently to have the right to buy one new share. After the rights offer, there will be 1.625 million shares, worth $25 million all together, so the per-share value will be $25/1.625 = $15.38 each. The value of a right in this case is the $20 original price less the $15.38 ending price, multiplied by the number of shares to obtain a right, or:

$$n\left(\frac{M - S}{n + r}\right)$$
$$= 8\left(\frac{20 - 8}{13}\right)$$
$$= \$7.38$$

Ex rights

ex rights

period when shares are selling without a recently declared right, normally beginning four business days before the holder-of-record date

holder-of-record date

the date on which existing shareholders on company records are designated as the recipients of share rights. Also the date of record

Songbird's rights have a substantial value. In addition, the rights offering will have a large impact on the market price of Songbird's share price. It will drop by $3.33 on the day when the shares trade **ex rights**.

The standard procedure for issuing rights involves the firm setting a **holder-of-record date**—a book's closing date. Following Stock Exchange rules, the share typically goes ex rights four trading days before the book's closing date. If the share is sold before the ex-rights date—'rights-on', 'with rights', or 'cum rights'—the new owner will receive the rights. After the ex-rights date, an investor who purchases the shares will not receive the rights. This is depicted for Songbird in Figure 17.3.

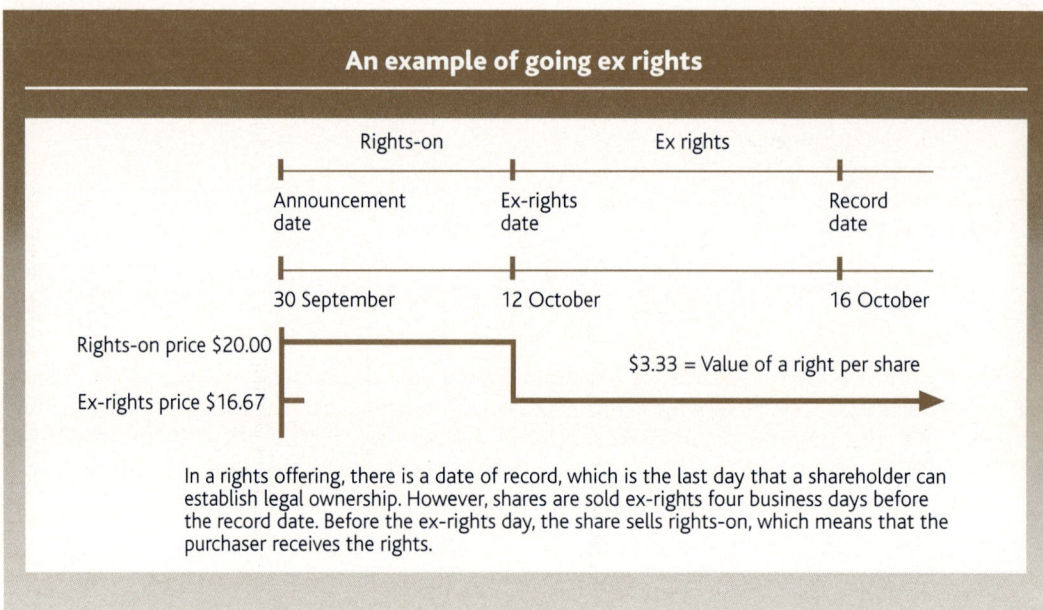

An example of going ex rights

In a rights offering, there is a date of record, which is the last day that a shareholder can establish legal ownership. However, shares are sold ex-rights four business days before the record date. Before the ex-rights day, the share sells rights-on, which means that the purchaser receives the rights.

As illustrated, on 30 September, Songbird announced the terms of the rights offering, stating that the rights would be mailed on, say, 1 November to shareholders of record as of 16 October. Since 12 October is the ex-rights date, only those shareholders who own the share on or before 11 October will receive the rights. Table 17.11 provides a timetable for rights issues (renounceable and non-renounceable) as required under the *Corporations Act 2001* and the Stock Exchange Listing Requirements.

Timetable for rights issues legal and ASX requirements

TABLE 17.11

Renounceable timetable Number of business days elapsed		Non-renounceable timetable Number of business days elapsed
0	Issue announced	0
1	Prospectus lodged with ASX and ASIC	1
12	Securities quoted 'ex-rights'	12
12	Rights trading begins	–
16	Book closing date	16
21	Prospectus dispatched to shareholders	21
36	Last day of rights trading	–
36	Applications closing date	31 (earliest)
37	Trading in 'deferred delivery' market begins	32
46	Renunciations closing date	–
56	Last allotment date	51
66	Last day for dispatch of certificates	61

EXAMPLE 17.2

Exercising your rights: Part II

The Raw Entertainment Co. has proposed a rights offering. The shares currently sell for $4. Under the terms of the offer, shareholders will be allowed to buy one new share for every five that they own at a price of $2.50 per share. What is the value of a right? What is the ex-rights price?

The value of a right is:

$$5\left(\frac{4 - 2.50}{5 + 1}\right)$$
$$= \$1.25$$

As the right value attaches to five shares, the value of a right per share is $1.25/5 = $0.25. The ex-rights price per share is $4 − $0.25 = $3.75.

In Example 17.2, suppose the rights only sold for $1 instead of the $1.25 we calculated. What could you do?

You can get rich quick, because you have found a money machine. Here is the recipe: Buy a right for $1. Exercise it and pay $2.50 to get a new share. Your total investment to get one ex-rights share is $1 + $2.50 = $3.50. Sell the share for $3.75 and pocket the $0.25 difference. Repeat as desired. This looks very easy, but remember there is no such thing as a free lunch so the situation cannot exist.

Effects on shareholders

Shareholders can exercise their rights or sell them. In either case, the shareholder will not win or lose by the rights offering. The hypothetical holder of two shares of Songbird has a portfolio worth $40. If the shareholder exercises the rights, he or she ends up with three shares worth a total of $50. In other words, by spending $10, the investor's holding increases in value by $10, which means that the shareholder is neither better nor worse off.

On the other hand, if the shareholder sells the right for $6.67, he or she would have two shares worth $16.67 and the cash from selling the right:

$$
\begin{aligned}
\text{Shares held} &= 2 \times \$16.67 = \$33.33 \\
\text{Right sold} &= \$\ 6.67 \\
\text{Total} &= \$40.00
\end{aligned}
$$

The new $33.33 market value plus $6.67 in cash is exactly the same as the original holding of $40. Thus shareholders cannot lose or gain from exercising or selling rights.

It is obvious that after the rights offering, the new market price of the firm's shares will be lower than it was before the rights offering. As we have seen, however, shareholders have suffered no loss because of the rights offering. Thus, the share price decline is very much like a share split, a device that is described in Chapter 19. The lower the subscription price, the greater the price decline of a rights offering. It is important to emphasise that because shareholders receive rights equal in value to the price drop, the rights offering does not hurt shareholders.

The new issues puzzle

In the United States, firms use general cash offers much more often than rights offerings. In Table 17.12, of the 578 (484 + 56 + 38) total issues, 94 (56 + 38), or 16 per cent, were rights offers. This reliance on general cash offers is something of a mystery because rights offerings are usually much cheaper in terms of flotation costs.

To give you an idea of the relative flotation costs, Table 17.12 shows these costs from one study expressed as a percentage of the amount raised for different issue sizes and selling procedures. Overall, general cash offers had average flotation costs equal to 6.17 per cent of the amount raised. For rights offerings with standby underwriting, total costs were 6.05 per cent. For pure rights offerings (those involving no underwriter), these costs were only 2.45 per cent of the amount raised, a significant saving.

TABLE
17.12

Costs of flotation as a percentage of proceeds*

Size of issue ($ million)	Number	Cash offers		
		Compensation as a percentage of proceeds	Other expenses as a percentage of proceeds	Total cost as a percentage of proceeds
Under 0.50	0	–	–	–
0.50 to 0.99	6	6.96%	6.78%	13.74%
1.00 to 1.99	18	10.40	4.89	15.29
2.00 to 4.99	61	6.59	2.87	9.47
5.00 to 9.99	66	5.50	1.53	7.03
10.00 to 19.99	91	4.84	0.71	5.55
20.00 to 49.99	156	4.30	0.37	4.67
50.00 to 99.99	70	3.97	0.21	4.18
100.00 to 500.00	16	3.81	0.14	3.95
Total/average	484	5.02%	1.15%	6.17%

	Rights with standby underwriting				Pure rights	
Number	Compensation as a percentage of proceeds	Other expenses as a percentage of proceeds	Total cost as a percentage of proceeds		Number	Total cost as a percentage of proceeds
0	–	–	–		3	8.99%
2	3.43%	4.80%	8.24%		2	4.59
5	6.36	4.15	10.51		5	4.90
9	5.2	2.85	8.06		7	2.85
4	3.92	2.18	6.10		6	1.39
10	4.14	1.21	5.35		3	0.72
12	3.84	0.90	4.74		1	0.52
9	3.96	0.74	4.70		2	0.21
5	3.50	0.50	4.00		9	0.13
56	4.32%	1.73%	6.05%		38	2.45%

* Based on 578 common stock issues registered under the Securities Act of 1933 during 1971–1975. The issues are subdivided by size of issue and method of financing: cash offers, rights with standby underwriting, and pure rights offering.

Issues are included only if the company's stock was listed on the NYSE, AMEX or regional exchanges before the offering; any associated secondary distribution represents less than 10 per cent of the total proceeds of the issue, and the offering contains no other types of securities. The costs reported are: (1) compensation received by investment bankers for underwriting services rendered, (2) legal fees, (3) accounting fees, (4) engineering fees, (5) trustee's fees, (6) printing and engraving expenses, (7) SEC registration fees, (8) federal reserve stamps, and (9) state taxes.

Source: Modified from Smith, C.W. Jr 'Costs of Underwritten versus Rights Issues', *Journal of Financial Economics*, Vol. 5, December 1977, p. 277 (Table I).

Overall, Table 17.12 suggests that pure rights offerings have a pronounced cost advantage. Furthermore, rights offerings protect the proportionate interest of existing shareholders. No one knows why rights offerings are not used more often, and it is an intriguing anomaly.

Various arguments in favour of general cash offerings with underwriting have been put forth:

1 Underwriters increase the share price. This is supposedly accomplished because of the selling effort of the underwriting group.

2 Underwriters provide insurance against a failed offering. This is true. If the market price goes below the offer price, the firm does not lose, because the underwriter bought the shares at an agreed-upon price. However, this insurance cannot be worth much, because the offer price is not set (in most cases) until within 24 hours of the offering when the final arrangements are made and underwriters have made careful assessment of the market for the shares.

3 Other arguments include: (a) the proceeds of underwritten issues are available sooner than with a rights offer; (b) underwriters will provide a wider distribution of ownership than would be true with a rights offering; and (c) consulting advice from investment bankers may be beneficial.

All of the preceding arguments are pieces of the puzzle, but none seems very convincing. One recent study has found that firms making underwritten rights offers suffered substantially larger price drops than did firms making underwritten cash offers.[4] This is a hidden cost, and it may be part of the reason that underwritten rights offers are uncommon in the United States.

Even though in recent years rights offerings have almost disappeared in the United States, this is not true in Australia. Table 17.13 provides data for Australian equity issues made from 1995 to 2001. If we exclude the new issues that relate to new companies being floated we can derive the cash offer figure, which was only 12 per cent of the funds raised in 1998. No doubt Australian taxation law has provided the incentive for the **dividend reinvestment schemes** (refer to Chapter 19 where dividend imputation is discussed) but again this seems to emphasise the contact with existing shareholders. This relationship could be explained by the smaller Australian market but one still wonders at the use of what seems to be a more expensive method (cash offers) as opposed to the less expensive method (rights issues) in the United States.

dividend reinvestment schemes

these offer shareholders the opportunity to apply all or part of their cash dividends to the purchase of newly issued shares, allowing the shareholder to re-invest the dividend without incurring any transaction costs

TABLE 17.13

	Rights Issues		Reinvested	Options calls, staff	Total excluding	New	Total
Year	($ million)	Placements	dividends	plans	floats	floats	raisings
1995	2,867.00	2,103.80	3,264.00	1,632.80	9,867.60	4,111.80	13,979.40
	21%	15%	23%	12%	71%	29%	100%
1996	1,662.00	5,423.00	3,188.90	1,300.90	11,574.80	3,711.20	15,286.00
	11%	35%	21%	9%	76%	24%	100%
1997	4,010.90	2,861.40	3,347.40	2,241.50	12,461.20	12,861.90	25,323.10
	16%	11%	13%	9%	49%	51%	100%
1998	3,436.20	10,887.70	3,631.70	2,026.60	19,982.20	8,856.00	28,838.20
	12%	38%	13%	7%	69%	31%	100%
1999	3,081.20	17,701.50	3,349.90	3,975.80	28,108.00	4,930.20	33,038.20
	9%	54%	10%	12%	85%	15%	100%
2000	2,146.80	12,357.90	3,718.90	3,068.50	21,292.10	10,249.60	31,541.70
	7%	39%	12%	10%	68%	32%	100%
2001	619.1	3,578.00	3,833.60	2,768.50	10,799.20	2,172.60	12,971.80
	5%	28%	30%	21%	83%	17%	100%

Types of equity capital raised by percentage

Source: Australian Stock Exchange Fact Book, 2001.

Concept questions

17.5a *How does a rights offering work?*

17.5b *What are the questions that financial management must answer before a rights offering?*

17.5c *How is the value of a right determined?*

17.5d *When does a rights offering affect the value of a company's shares?*

17.5e *Does a rights offer cause a share price decrease? How are existing shareholders affected by a rights offer?*

17.6 ∎ Dilution

A subject that comes up quite a bit in discussions involving the selling of securities is **dilution**. Dilution refers to a loss in existing shareholders' value. There are several kinds:

1 dilution of percentage ownership
2 dilution of market value
3 dilution of book value and earnings per share.

The differences between these three types can be a little confusing and there are some common misconceptions about dilution, so we discuss it in this section.

dilution

loss in existing shareholders' value, in terms of either ownership, market value, book value, or EPS

Dilution of proportionate ownership

The first type of dilution can arise whenever a firm sells shares to the general public. For example, Andrea Nibs owns 5,000 shares of Andrea's Music Company Ltd. Andrea's Music currently has 50,000 shares outstanding; each share gets one vote. Andrea thus controls 10 per cent (5,000/50,000) of the votes and gets 10 per cent of the dividends.

If Andrea's Music issues 50,000 new shares to the public via a general cash offer, Andrea's ownership in Andrea's Music may be diluted. If Andrea does not participate in the new issue, her ownership will drop to 5 per cent (5,000/100,000). Notice that the value of Andrea's shares is unaffected; she just owns a smaller percentage of the firm.

Because a rights offering would ensure Andrea Nibs an opportunity to maintain her proportionate 10 per cent share, dilution of the ownership of existing shareholders can be avoided by using a rights offering.

Dilution of value: Book versus market values

We now examine dilution of value by looking at some accounting numbers. We do this to illustrate a fallacy concerning dilution; we do not mean to suggest that accounting dilution is more important than market value dilution. As we illustrate, quite the reverse is true.

Suppose Vicki Fashions Limited (VFL) wants to build a new plant to meet future anticipated demands. VFL currently has 1 million shares outstanding and no debt. Each share is selling for $5, and the company has a $5 million market value. VFL's book value is $10 million total, or $10 per share.

VFL has experienced a variety of difficulties in the past, including cost overruns, regulatory delays in importing and below normal profits. These difficulties are reflected in the fact that VFL's market-to-book ratio is $5/$10 = 0.50 (successful firms rarely have market prices below book values).

Net profit for VFL is currently $1 million. With 1 million shares, earnings per share (EPS) are $1, and the return on equity (ROE) is $1/$10 = 10%.[5] VFL thus sells for 5 times earnings (the price/earnings ratio is 5). VFL has 200 shareholders, each of whom holds 5,000 shares. The new plant will cost $2 million, so VFL will have to issue 400,000 new shares ($5 × 400,000 = $2,000,000). There will thus be 1.4 million shares outstanding after the issue.

The ROE on the new plant is expected to be the same as for the company as a whole. In other words, net profit is expected to go up by 0.10 × $2 million = $200,000. Total net profit will thus be $1.2 million. The following things would occur:

1 With 1.4 million shares outstanding, EPS would be $1.2/1.4 = $0.857 per share, down from $1.

2 The proportionate ownership of each old shareholder drops to 5,000/1.4 million = 0.36 per cent from 0.50 per cent.

3 If the shares continue to sell for 5 times earnings, then the value would drop to 5 × 0.857 = $4.29, a loss of $0.71 per share.

4 The total book value will be the old $10 million plus the new $2 million for a total of $12 million. Book value per share will fall to $12 million/1.4 million = $8.57 per share.

If we take this example at face value, then dilution of proportionate ownership, accounting dilution, and market value dilution all occur. VFL's shareholders appear to suffer significant losses.

A misconception

Our example appears to show that selling shares when the market-to-book ratio is less than 1 is detrimental to the shareholders. Some managers claim that this dilution occurs because EPS will go down whenever shares are issued where the market value is less than the book value.

When the market-to-book ratio is less than 1, increasing the number of shares does cause EPS to go down. Such a decline in EPS is accounting dilution, and accounting dilution will always occur under these circumstances.

Is it furthermore true that market value dilution will also necessarily occur? The answer is no. There is nothing incorrect about our example, but why the market value has decreased is not obvious. We discuss this next.

The correct arguments

In this example, the market price falls from $5 per share to $4.29. This is true dilution, but why does it occur? The answer has to do with the new project. VFL is going to spend $2 million on the new plant. However, as shown in Table 17.14, the total market value of the company is going to rise from $5 million to $6 million, an increase of only $1 million. This simply means that the NPV of the new project is −$1 million. With 1.4 million shares, the loss per share is $1/1.4 = 0.71, as we calculated before.

So, true dilution takes place for the shareholders of VFL because the NPV of the project is negative, not because the market-to-book ratio is less than 1. This negative NPV causes the market price to drop, and the accounting dilution has nothing to do with it.

Suppose that the new project had a positive NPV of $1 million. The total market value would rise by $2 + 1 = $3 million. As shown in Table 17.14 (column (3)), the price per share rises to $5.71. Notice that accounting dilution still takes place because the book value per share still falls, but there is no economic consequence of that fact. The market value of the shares rise.

The $0.71 increase in share value comes about because of the $1 million NPV, which amounts to an increase in value of about $0.71 per share. Also, as shown, if the ratio of price to EPS remains at 5, then EPS must rise to $5.71/5 = $1.14. Total earnings (net income) rises to $1.14 per share × 1.4 million shares = $1.6 million. Finally, ROE would rise to $1.6 million/$12 million = 17.33%.

TABLE 17.14

New issues and dilution: the case of Vicki Fashions Ltd

	(1) Initial	After (2) Dilution	(3) No dilution
Number of shares	1,000,000	1,400,000	1,400,000
Book value (B)	$10,000,000	$12,000,000	$12,000,000
Book value per share	$10	$8.57	$8.57
Market value	$5,000,000	$6,000,000	$8,000,000
Market price (P)	$5	$4.29	$5.71
Net profit	$1,000,000	$1,200,000	$1,600,000
Return on equity (ROE)	0.10	0.10	0.1733
Earnings per share (EPS)	$1	$0.86	$1.14
EPS/P	0.20	0.20	0.20
P/EPS	5	5	5
P/B	0.5	0.5	0.67
PROJECT			
Cost $2,000,000		NPV = −$1,000,000	NPV = $1,000,000

Concept questions

17.6a *What are the different kinds of dilution?*
17.6b *Is dilution important?*

 17.7

Issuing long-term debt

The general procedures followed in a public issue of debt are the same as those for shares. The issue must be registered with ASIC, there must be a prospectus, and so on. In addition, the *Corporations Act* 2001 requires that a company that invites the public to subscribe for debentures must appoint a trustee. The second half of 1988 witnessed the re-emergence of a market in medium-term corporate debt in Australia. Eight major issuers raised around $880 million in medium-term unsecured notes. This sudden growth in the corporate debt market in the second half of 1988 was due to a number of factors, including:

- *The substantial cutback in the level of government borrowing.* Instead of government borrowing crowding out other borrowing within Australia, the substantial reduction in public sector borrowing provided much-improved opportunities for corporations to borrow within Australia.
- *The fall in interest rates from their levels over the mid-1980s.* Many corporations were loath to issue medium-term paper when interest rates were at the higher levels of several years earlier. In 1988 more companies were willing to borrow at the then lower interest rates.

- *The flight to quality*. After the share market crash in October 1987, investors looked to step up their purchases of quality, high-yielding fixed interest securities.
- *The shortage of government bonds*. The combination of banks having to meet liquidity requirements and the diminishing stock of Commonwealth government securities outstanding led to a wider gap between yields on Commonwealth government securities and those on other fixed interest securities. Life offices and pension funds began switching from government bonds to semi-government securities and to corporate securities to enhance their return.
- *The attractiveness of raising funds in the domestic market relative to that of the euromarket*. Issuers could see long-term benefits, in the form of more reliability and cheaper financing, by raising funds in the domestic market. There had to be substantial savings before an issuer would access the euromarket.

There are two basic forms of direct private long-term financing: term loans and private placement.

Term loans are direct business loans. These loans have maturities of between one year and five years. Most term loans are repayable during the life of the loan. The lenders include commercial banks, insurance companies, and other lenders that specialise in corporate finance. **Private placements** are very similar to term loans except that the maturity is longer.

The important differences between direct private long-term financing and public issues of debt are:

1 A direct long-term loan avoids the cost of Australian Securities and Investments Commission registration.
2 Direct placement is likely to have more restrictive covenants.
3 It is easier to renegotiate a term loan or a private placement in the event of a default. It is harder to renegotiate a public issue because hundreds of holders are usually involved.
4 Life insurance companies and pension funds dominate the private-placement segment of the debt market.
5 Commercial banks are significant participants in the term-loan market.

The costs of distributing debentures are lower in the private market.

The interest rates on term loans and private placements are usually higher than those on an equivalent public issue. One study found that the yield to maturity on private placement was 0.46 per cent higher than on similar public issues.[6] This finding reflects the trade-off between a higher interest rate and more flexible arrangements in the event of financial distress, as well as the lower costs associated with private placements.

An additional, and very important, consideration is that the flotation costs associated with selling debt are much less than the costs associated with selling equity.

Concept questions

17.7a *What is the difference between private and public bond issues?*
17.7b *A private placement is likely to have a higher interest rate than a public issue. Why?*

---

term loans
direct business loans of, typically, one to five years

private placements
loans, usually long-term in nature, provided directly by a limited number of investors

◐ 17.8 ▪ Summary and conclusions

This chapter looked at how corporate securities are issued. The main points are:

1   The costs of issuing securities can be quite large. They are much lower (as a percentage) for larger issues.

2   Firm commitment underwriting is far more prevalent for large issues than best efforts underwriting. This is probably connected to the uncertainty of smaller issues. For a given size offering, the direct expenses of best efforts underwriting and firm commitment underwriting are of the same magnitude.

3   The direct and indirect costs of going public can be substantial. However, once a firm is public it can raise additional capital with much greater ease.

4   Rights offerings are cheaper than general cash offers. Even so, most new equity issues in the United States are underwritten general cash offers.

Key terms

Best efforts underwriting 567
Cum rights 584
Dilution 589
Dividend reinvestment schemes 588
Ex rights 584
Firm underwriting 567
General cash offer 561

Holder-of-record date 584
Primary issue 563
Private placement 565, 592
Prospectus 561
Rights issue 565
Rights offer 561
Secondary issue 565

Standby underwriting 567
Sub-underwriters 567
Term loan 592
Tombstone 566
Underwriters 567
Underwriters' commission 568

Suggested readings

The costs of issuing new equity are documented in:
Ritter, J.R. 'The Cost of Going Public', *Journal of Financial Economics*, Vol. 19, 1987, pp. 269–82.
Smith, C.W. Jr 'Alternative Methods of Raising Capital: Rights versus Underwritten Offerings', *Journal of Financial Economics*, Vol. 5, December 1977, pp. 6–22.

Articles that examine underpricing and investment banking include:
Booth, J. and Smith, R. 'The Certification Role of the Investment Banker in New Issues Pricing', *Midland Corporate Finance Journal*, Vol. 1, Spring 1986, pp. 100–12.
Ibbotson, R.G. 'Price Performance of Common Share New Issues', *Journal of Financial Economics*, Vol. 2, 1975, pp. 235–72.
Muscarella, C.J. and Vetsuypens, M.R. 'A Simple Test of Baron's Model of Initial Public Offering Underpricing', *Journal of Financial Economics*, Vol. 24, 1989, pp. 117–35.

Ritter, J.R. ' The "Hot Issue" Market of 1980', *Journal of Business*, Vol. 57, 1984, pp. 215–41.
Rock, K. 'Why New Issues Are Underpriced', *Journal of Financial Economics*, Vol. 15, 1986, pp. 187–212.
Taylor, S.L. and Walter, T.S. 'Australian IPO Underpricing: Institutional Aspects of the Winner's Curse', working paper, Department of Accounting, University of Sydney, 1991.

The effect of seasoned new equity on share prices is discussed in:
Asquith, P. and Mullins, D. 'Equity Issues and Offering Dilution', *Journal of Financial Economics*, Vol. 15, 1986, pp. 61–90.
Masulis, R. and Korwar, A.N. 'Seasoned Equity Offerings: An Empirical Investigation', *Journal of Financial Economics*, Vol. 15, 1986, pp. 56–89.
Mikkelson, W.H. and Partch, M.M. 'The Valuation Effects of Security Offerings and the Issuance Process', *Journal of Financial Economics*, Vol. 15, 1986, pp. 165–94.

Summaries of research can be found in:

Hansen, R. 'Evaluating the Costs of a New Equity Issue', *Midland Corporate Finance Journal*, Spring 1986, pp. 45–54.

Ibbotson, R.G., Sindelar, J.L. and Ritter, J.R. 'Initial Public Offerings', *Journal of Applied Corporate Finance*, Vol. 1, Summer 1988, pp. 37–45.

Additional references:

Cheung, J. and Vos, E. 'IPO Underpricing in New Zealand', Working Paper No. 3, Accounting & Finance, University of Waikato, 1990.

Easton, S.A. and Pinder, S.M. 'Australian Government Sector Initial Public Offerings', *Applied Economic Letters*, September 1996, pp. 605–8.

Finn, F. and Higham, R. 'The Performance of Unseasoned New Equity Issues-cum-Stock Exchange Listings in Australia', *Journal of Banking and Finance*, Vol. 12, 1988, pp. 333–51.

How, J., Izan, H. and Monroe, G. 'Differential information, and the underpricing of initial public offerings: Australian evidence', *Accounting and Finance*, May 1995, pp. 87–105.

Endnotes

1 Based on the characteristics of a normal distribution, the following probabilities hold:

	Awake Company	**Asleep Company**
Standard deviation	1.732	1.00
Using Table A.5 (in the appendix)	$d_1 = \dfrac{\$4.50 - \$5.30}{1.732} = -0.4619$	$d_1 = -0.8$
Probability	$N(d_1) = 0.3228$	$N(d_1) = 0.2119$
Probability ($5.30 > share price > $4.50)	$= 0.5 - 0.3228$ $= 0.1772$	$= 0.5 - 0.2119$ $= 0.2881$

2 The discussion in this section draws on Ibbotson, R.G., Sindelar, J.L. and Ritter, J.R. 'Initial Public Offerings', *Journal of Applied Corporate Finance*, Vol. 1, Summer 1988, pp. 37–45. The degree of underpricing is calculated based on the offering price versus the price at the end of the month, less the market return for the month, over the period 1960–1976. The degree of underpricing is based on the offering price and the price at the close of the first day of trading, without adjustment for the market return, for 1977–1987.

3 Industry Commission, 'Availability of Capital', Report No. 18, 9 December 1991, AGPS, Canberra, p. 155.

4 Hansen, R.S. 'The Demise of the Rights Issue', *The Review of Financial Studies*, Vol. 1, Fall 1988, pp. 289–309.

5 Return on equity (ROE) is equal to earnings per share divided by book value per share or, equivalently, net profit divided by shareholders' funds. We discussed this and other financial ratios in some detail in Chapter 3.

6 Hays, P.A., Joehnk, M.D. and Melicher, R.W. 'Determinants of Risk Premiums in the Public and Private Bond Market', *Journal of Financial Research*, Vol. 2, Fall 1979.

On the web

Many of the concepts discussed in this chapter are given practical demonstration on the following sites:

http://www.asx.com.au (the Australian Stock Exchange)

http://www.asic.gov.au (the Australian Securities and Investments Commission)

Other information on issues and underwriting can be found at:

http://www.comsec.com.au (Commonwealth Securities, the broking arm of the Commonwealth Bank)

http://www.tdwaterhouse.com.au (T.D. Waterhouse is an online broker)

http://www.rivkin.com.au (the Rivkin Group, which offers commentary on the sharemarket)

Maximise Your Marks!
There are 30 interactive questions on issuing securities waiting online for you at www.mhhe.com/au/ross3e. The questions are written with additional feedback for incorrect answers, and text excerpts with page references for follow-up study.

International Articles!
To read more on issuing securities and to see current international articles, just go to www.mhhe.com/au/ross3e and click on *PowerWeb Articles* for this chapter.

Chapter review problems and self-test

17.1 · Flotation costs

The Blast Company Ltd is considering an equity issue to finance a new space station. A total of $10 million in new equity is needed. If the direct costs are estimated at 6 per cent of the amount raised, how large does the issue need to be? What is the dollar amount of the flotation cost?

17.2 · Rights offerings

The Delay Company Ltd currently has 40 million shares outstanding. The shares sell for $5 per share. To raise $30 million for a new particle accelerator, the firm is considering a rights offering at $2 per share. What is the value of a right in this case? The ex-rights price?

Answers to self-test problems

17.1 · The firm needs to net $10 million after paying the 6 per cent flotation costs. So the amount raised is given by:

Amount raised $\times$ (1 − 0.06) = $10 million
Amount raised = $10/0.94 = $10.638 million

The total flotation cost is thus $638,000.

17.2 · To raise $30 million at $2 per share, $30 million/$2 = 15 million shares will have to be sold. Before the offering, the firm is worth 40 million $\times$ $5 = $200 million. The issue is to raise $30 million so that there will be 55 million shares outstanding. The value of an ex-rights share will therefore be $230/55 = $4.18. The value of a right is thus:

$$(40 \div 15) \times (5 - 4.18) = \$2.18$$

or

$$(40 \div 15)\left(\frac{5 - 2}{(40 \div 15) + 1}\right) = \$2.18$$

Questions and problems

1 · Underwriting versus rights

Spendup Industries Ltd is planning to raise fresh equity capital by selling a large new issue of ordinary shares. Spendup is currently a publicly traded corporation, and it is trying to choose between an underwritten cash offer and a rights offering (not underwritten) to current shareholders. Spendup management is interested in minimising the selling costs and has asked you for advice on the choice of issue methods. What is your recommendation and why?

2 · Rights offerings

Net Buy Co. Ltd is proposing a rights offering. Presently there are 4,000,000 outstanding shares at $10.20 each. There will be 400,000 new shares issued at $8.

a   What is the value of a right?
b   What is the ex-rights price of a share?
c   What is the new market value of the company?
d   Why might a company have a rights offering rather than a cash ordinary share offering?

3 · Price dilution

Suppose the New Era Company Ltd has 100,000 shares. Each share is worth $4, and the company's market value of equity is $400,000. Suppose the firm issues 50,000 shares at the following prices: $4, $2, $1. What will be the effect of each of the alternative offering prices on the existing price per share?

4 · Initial public offering, investment and underpricing

In 200X, a certain associate professor of finance bought 12 initial public offerings of ordinary shares. He held each of these for approximately one month and then sold. The investment rule he followed was to submit a purchase order for every initial public offering of oil and gas exploration companies with a firm commitment underwriting agreement. There were 22 of these offerings, and he submitted a purchase order for approximately $1,000 for each of the companies. With 10 of these, no shares were allocated to this associate professor. With five of the 12 offerings that were purchased, fewer than the requested number of shares were allocated.

The year 200X was very good for oil and gas exploration company owners. On average, of the 22 companies that went public, the shares were selling for 80 per cent above the offering price a month after the initial offering date. The associate professor looked at his performance record and found the $8,400 invested in the 12 companies had grown to only $10,000, a return of only about 20 per cent (commissions were negligible). Did he have bad luck, or should he have expected to do worse than the average initial public offering investor? Explain.

5 · Analysis of an initial public offering

The following material contains a summary of the prospectus for the initial public offering of Wandering Wood Walk Limited (WWW), which is going public tomorrow. There is a firm commitment underwriting managed by Scat and Company with sub-underwriters MacQuary Bank Limited and Draper Broking Limited in Southern Angoria. Answer the following questions:

a   Assume that you know nothing about WWW other than the information contained in the prospectus. Based on your knowledge of finance, what is your prediction for the price of WWW tomorrow? Provide a short explanation to support your answer.
b   Assume that you are a wealthy student with several thousand dollars to invest. You receive a message from your sharebroker, whom you have not talked to for weeks, that WWW is going public tomorrow and that she can get you several thousand shares at the offering price if you call first thing in the morning. Discuss the merits of this opportunity.

(continued)

Prospectus
Wandering Wood Walk Limited

Capital Structure

Types of shares	Number of shares	Capital ($)
Authorised capital		
Ordinary shares of 50 cents each	2,000,000,000	$1,000,000,000
Issued capital		
Ordinary shares of 50 cents fully paid	3,460,010	$1,730,005
Shares to be issued to purchase Scant Hikes		
Ordinary shares of 50 cents fully paid	40,000,000	$20,000,000
*Further shares to be issued**	1,500,000	$750,000
Shares now offered for subscription		
Ordinary shares of 50 cents payable in		
full on application	100,000,000	$50,000,000

* The Treasurer of Vicapic, on behalf of the State of Vicapic, will be issued 1,500,000 fully paid ordinary shares of 50 cents at par pursuant to the advances made by it to Wandering Wood Walk. The shares will be issued after the minimum subscription of $50 million for shares to which this prospectus applies is raised.

Prospectus Summary

The company	Wandering Wood Walk has just completed two years of planning to launch a new tourist program into the Angoria market. Reports indicated that WWW will service 1.4 million customers to represent 12 per cent of the market.
The offering	100,000,000 ordinary shares of 50 cents.
Listing	Application to the Angoria Exchange for admission to the Official List of companies on the Main Board maintained by the Exchange will be made within three business days of the date of issue of this prospectus.
Purpose of the issue	Wandering Wood Walk plans to commence operations on July 1.
Profit forecast	Year ending June 30th.

	200X+1	200X+2	200X+3
Net Profit (Loss) ($000)	(7,570)	11,329	16,567
Earnings per share	N/A	8.4 cents	12.3 cents
Price earning ratio at issue price	N/A	6.0	4.1

Net asset backing	Assuming that a total of 144,960,010 shares are on issue following completion of this issue, the net asset backing per issued share of WWW will be $0.50. If deferred development expenditure and goodwill is excluded, the net asset backing will be $0.38 per share.
Dividend policy	WWW plans to maximise dividend payments subject to the financial condition and prospects of its business. The current intent is to consider declaring a five cent dividend following the second year of operations.

Because tourism in Angoria has always been a protected sector, it is difficult to estimate the expected return for the industry. With deregulation, it is expected that the risks for new entrants to the industry will be quite high, so that returns from 50 to 60 per cent should be expected.

6 · Initial public offering underpricing

Analyse the following statement: Because initial public offerings of ordinary shares are always underpriced, an investor can make money by purchasing shares in these offerings.

7 · Rights

Covariance Co. Ltd is a manufacturer of beta-blockers (consumers are just sick and tired of those pesky betas). Management has concluded that additional equity financing is required to increase production capacity and that these funds are best attained through a rights offering. It has correctly concluded that as a result of the rights offering, share price will fall from $9 to $8 ($9 is the cum-rights price; $8 is the ex-rights price). The company was seeking $6 million in additional funds with a per-share subscription price equal to $6.

How many shares were there before the offering? (Assume that the increment to the market value of the equity equals the gross proceeds from the offering.)

8 · Dilution

Sensay Holdings Ltd wishes to expand its manufacturing activities. Sensay currently has 100 million shares outstanding and no debt. The shares sells for $4 per share, but the book value per share is $6. Net income for Sensay is currently $20 million. The new facility will cost $60 million, and it will increase net income by $2 million.

Assuming a constant price/earnings ratio, what will be the effect of taking the new investment? To answer, calculate the number of shares outstanding, original EPS, new EPS, the new share price, and the new market-to-book ratio. What is going on here?

What would the new net income for Sensay have to be for the share price to remain unchanged?

9 · Funding through rights issues

Overland Motor Organisation is preparing to raise $30 million through a rights issue. The firm needs the funds to finance purchases of new mineral deposits. After public announcement the share price steadied at about $3.50 per share. There are 100 million shares on issue. OMO's financial staff have proposed two plans—plan A's subscription price is $3 while plan B's price is $1.50. Assuming both plans are successful:

a   Determine the number of shares issued under each plan.
b   How many shares currently held will be required to purchase a new share?
c   What should be the ex-rights price of the shares in each plan?
d   What should be the value of a right in each plan?
e   Which plan is preferable? Why?
f   Which plan would you recommend to OMO? Why?

10 · Dilution

The Homebake Holdings Ltd wants to diversify its operations. Some recent financial information is shown below.

Share price	$5
Number of shares	100,000
Total assets	$1,000,000
Total liabilities	$600,000
Earnings	$20,000

Homebake is considering an investment that has the same P/E ratio as the firm. The cost of the investment is $100,000, and it will be financed with a new equity issue. The return on the investment will equal Homebake's current ROE. If the P/E ratio is 21 after the investment, what is the new book value per share, the market value per share and the NPV of the investment?

11 · Dilution

In the previous problem, what would the ROE on the investment have to be if we actually want to sell new shares for $5? What is the NPV of this investment? In this case, does accounting dilution take place?

12 · Calculating flotation costs

Agecare Co. Ltd has just gone public. Under the fixed commitment agreement, Agecare received $1.50 for each of the 50 million shares sold. The initial offering price was $1.80 per share, and the share rose to $2.20 per share in the first few minutes of trading. Agecare paid $120,000 in direct legal and other costs. Indirect costs were $80,000. What was the flotation cost as a percentage of funds raised?

13 · Initial public offering underpricing

The Fit Co. Ltd and the Healthy Co. Ltd have announced initial public offerings at $5 per share. One of these is undervalued by $1, the other is overvalued by $0.50, but the fitness industry is not your speciality, so you have no way of knowing which is which. You plan on buying 100 shares of each. If an issue is underpriced, it will be rationed, and you will only get half your order. If you get 100 shares in Fit and 100 in Healthy, what will your profit be? What profit do you actually expect? What principle have you illustrated?

14 · Rights offerings

Bugrid Holdings Ltd has announced a rights offer to raise $50 million for a new operation in Plantland. Bugrid will inspect properties for white ants after the owner pays a non-refundable inspection fee of $3,000. The share currently sells for $2.50 and there are 220 million shares outstanding. Answer the following questions.

a   What is the maximum possible subscription price? What is the minimum?

b   If the subscription price is set at $1.50 per share, how many shares must be sold? How many shares will provide the right to one new share?

c   What is the ex-rights price? What is the value of a right?

d   Show how a shareholder with 100 shares and no desire (or money) to buy additional shares is not harmed by the rights offer.

15 · Rights

This is a challenge problem. The Lookaway Video Club Ltd is considering a rights offer. The company has determined that the ex-rights price will be $2.00. The current price is $2.10 per share, and there are 100 million shares outstanding. The rights offer would raise a total of $40 million. What is the subscription price?

16 · Value of a right

This is a challenge problem. Show that the value of a right can be written as:

$$\text{Value of a right per share} = P_{RO} - P_X = (P_{RO} - P_S)/(N + 1)$$

where P_{RO}, P_S and P_X stand for the rights-on price, the subscription price, and the ex-rights price, respectively, and N is the number of rights needed to buy one new share at the subscription price.

17 · Flotation costs

Overthere Corporation is considering an equity issue to finance a new refining plant. A total of $150 million is needed. If the direct cost of issuing the equity is 7 per cent, how large does the issue have to be and what are the flotation costs?

18 · Rights offering

Please Explain Corporation has 3 million shares outstanding. The shares sell for $4.00 and it wishes to raise $2 million for refugee housing. The firm is considering a rights issue with a subscription price of $2.50 per right. What will the value of a right be and what will be the ex-rights price?

PART EIGHT

Cost of capital

and long-term financial policy

CHAPTER 18

Cost
of capital

Objective

On completion of this chapter the cost of capital concept should be understood. You will be able to calculate the opportunity cost of individual sources of funds from the point of view of the organisation. These funds may be broadly classified into equity and debt funds. It will be seen that, because we are dealing with the uncertainty of the future in our calculation of the various costs, elements of subjectivity enter into the estimations. Approaches for reducing the guesswork will be explained. Once the calculation of the individual costs is mastered, the objective is to show how these costs are combined to obtain the Weighted Average Cost of Capital (WACC) for the organisation. Complications such as applying the WACC to divisional or specific project appraisal are addressed, as well as the influence of flotation costs on the evaluation.

Study tips ▷ The material covered in this chapter is very important in practice. The professional bodies incorporate its coverage into their postgraduate qualifying programs. The calculations are not difficult but the practical application of the model does require some understanding. If you experience difficulties, refer back to Chapter 6 (Valuing shares and bonds) and Chapter 11 (Return, risk and the security market line) to reinforce the basic theory for doing the calculations.

Introduction ▷ Suppose you have just become the managing director of a large company and the first decision you face is whether to go ahead with a plan to renovate the company's warehouse distribution system. The plan will cost the company $50 million, and it is expected to save $12 million per year after taxes over the next six years.

This is a familiar problem in capital budgeting. To address it, you would determine the relevant cash flows, discount them, and, if the net present value is positive, take on the project; if the NPV is negative, you would scrap it. So far so good, but what should you use as the discount rate?

From our discussion of risk and return, you know that the correct discount rate depends on the riskiness of the warehouse distribution system. In particular, the new project will have a positive NPV only if its return exceeds what the financial markets offer on investments of similar risks. We called this minimum required return the cost of capital associated with the project.

Thus, to make the right decision as managing director, you must examine what the capital markets have to offer and use this information to arrive at an estimate of the project's cost of capital. Our primary purpose in this chapter is to describe how to go about doing this. There are a variety of approaches to this task, and a number of conceptual and practical issues arise.

One of the most important concepts we develop is the weighted average cost of capital (WACC). This is the cost of capital for the firm as a whole, and it can be interpreted as the required return on the overall firm. In discussing the WACC, we will recognise the fact that a firm will normally raise capital in a variety of forms and that these different forms of capital may have different costs associated with them.

We also recognise in this chapter that taxes are an important consideration in determining the required return on an investment, because we are always interested in valuing the after-tax cash flows from a project. We will therefore discuss how to incorporate taxes explicitly into our estimates of the cost of capital.

18.1 ■ The cost of capital: Some preliminaries

In Chapter 11, we developed the security market line (SML) and used it to explore the relationship between the expected return on a security and its systematic risk. We concentrated on how the risky returns from buying securities looked from the viewpoint of, for example, a shareholder in the firm. This helped us understand more about the alternatives available to an investor in the capital markets.

In this chapter, we turn things around a bit and look more closely at the other side of the problem, which is how these returns and securities look from the viewpoint of the companies that issue them. The important fact to note is that the return an investor in a security receives is the cost of that security to the company that issued it.

Required return versus cost of capital

When we say that the required return on an investment is, say, 10 per cent, we usually mean that the investment will have a positive NPV only if its return exceeds 10 per cent. Another way of interpreting the required return is to observe that the firm must earn 10 per cent on the investment just to compensate its investors for the use of the capital needed to finance the project. This is why we could also say that 10 per cent is the cost of capital associated with the investment.

To illustrate the point further, imagine that we were evaluating a risk-free project. In this case, how to determine the required return is obvious: we look at the capital markets and observe the current rate offered by risk-free investments, and we use this rate to discount the project's cash flows. Thus the cost of capital for a risk-free investment is the risk-free rate.

If this project were risky, then, assuming that all the other information is unchanged, the required return is obviously higher. In other words, the cost of capital for this project, if it is risky, is greater than the risk-free rate, and the appropriate discount rate would exceed the risk-free rate.

We will henceforth use the terms *required return*, *appropriate discount rate* and *cost of capital* more or less interchangeably because, as the discussion in this section suggests, they all mean essentially the same thing. The key fact to grasp is that the cost of capital associated with an investment depends on the risk of that investment. This is one of the most important lessons in corporate finance, so it bears repeating:

> The cost of capital depends primarily on the use of the funds, not the source.

It is a common error to forget this crucial point and fall into the trap of thinking that the cost of capital for an investment depends primarily on how and where the capital is raised.

Financial policy and cost of capital

We know that the particular mixture of debt and equity that a firm chooses to employ—its capital structure—is a managerial variable. In this chapter, we will take the firm's financial policy as given. In particular, we will assume that the firm has a fixed debt/equity (D/E) ratio that it maintains. This D/E ratio reflects the firm's *target* capital structure. How a firm might choose that ratio is the subject of Chapter 20.

From our discussion above, we know that a firm's overall cost of capital will reflect the required return on the firm's assets as a whole. Given that a firm uses both debt and equity capital, this overall cost of capital will be a mixture of the returns needed to compensate its debtholders and its shareholders. In other words, a firm's cost of capital will reflect both its cost of debt capital and its cost of equity capital. We discuss these costs separately in the sections below.

Concept questions

18.1a *What is the primary determinant of the cost of capital for an investment?*
18.1b *What is the relationship between the required return on an investment and the cost of capital associated with that investment?*

18.2 The cost of equity

We begin with the most difficult question on the subject of cost of capital: What is the firm's overall **cost of equity**? The reason this is a difficult question is that there is no direct way of observing the return that the firm's equity investors require on their investment. Instead, we must somehow estimate it. This section discusses two approaches to determining the cost of equity: the dividend growth model approach and the security market line (SML) approach.

> **cost of equity**
> the return that equity investors require on their investment in the firm

The dividend growth model approach

The easiest way to estimate the cost of equity capital is to use the dividend growth model that we developed in Chapter 6. Recall that, under the assumption that the firm's dividend will grow at a constant rate g, the price per share, P_0, can be written as:

$$P_0 = D_0 \times (1 + g)/(R_E - g) = D_1/(R_E - g)$$

where D_0 is the dividend just paid, and D_1 is the next period's projected dividend. Notice that we have used the symbol R_E (the E stands for equity) for the required return on the share.

As we discussed in Chapter 6, we can rearrange this to solve for R_E as follows:

$$R_E = D_1/P_0 + g \qquad (18.1)$$

Since R_E is the return that the shareholders require, it can be interpreted as the firm's cost of equity capital.

Implementing the approach

To estimate R_E using the dividend growth model approach, we obviously need three pieces of information: P_0, D_0 and g.[1] Of these, for a publicly traded, dividend-paying company, the first two can be observed directly, so they are easily obtained. Only the third component, the expected growth rate in dividends, must be estimated.

For example, suppose Marsh Mellow Ltd, a large public company, paid a dividend of 20 cents per share last year. The shares currently sell for $2.60. You estimate that the dividend will grow steadily at 4 per cent per year into the indefinite future. What is the cost of equity capital for Marsh Mellow? Using the dividend growth model, the expected dividend, D_1, is:

$$\begin{aligned} D_1 &= D_0 \times (1 + g) \\ &= 0.2 \times (1.04) \\ &= \$0.208 \end{aligned}$$

Given this, the cost of equity, R_E, is:

$$
\begin{aligned}
R_E &= D_1/P_0 + g \\
&= \$0.208/\$2.60 + 0.04 \\
&= 12\%
\end{aligned}
$$

The cost of equity is thus 12 per cent.

Estimating g

To use the dividend growth model, we must come up with an estimate for g, the growth rate. There are essentially two ways of doing this: (1) use historical growth rates, or (2) use analysts' forecasts of future growth rates. Analysts' forecasts are available from a variety of sources. Naturally, different sources will have different estimates, so one approach might be to obtain multiple estimates and then average them.

Alternatively, we might observe dividends for the previous, say, five years, calculate the year-to-year growth rates, and average them. For example, suppose we observe the following for some company:

Year	Dividend
200X	$1.10
200X+1	1.20
200X+2	1.35
200X+3	1.40
200X+4	1.55

We can calculate the percentage changes in the dividend for each year as follows:

Year	Dividend	Dollar change	Percentage change
200X	$1.10	–	–
200X+1	1.20	$0.10	9.09%
200X+2	1.35	0.15	12.50
200X+3	1.40	0.05	3.70
200X+4	1.55	0.15	10.71

Notice that we calculated the change in the dividend on a year-to-year basis and then expressed the change as a percentage. Thus, in 200X+1 for example, the dividend rose from $1.10 to $1.20, an increase of $0.10. This represents a $0.10/1.10 = 9.09% increase.

If we average the four growth rates, the result is (9.09 + 12.50 + 3.70 + 10.71)/4 = 9%, so we could use this as an estimate for the expected growth rate, g. There are other, more sophisticated statistical techniques that could be used, but they all amount to using past dividend growth to predict future dividend growth.[2]

Advantages and disadvantages of the approach

The primary advantage of the dividend growth model approach is its simplicity. It is both easy to understand and easy to use. There are a number of associated practical problems and disadvantages.

First and foremost, the dividend growth model is obviously only applicable to companies that pay dividends. This means that the approach is useless in many cases. Furthermore, even for companies that do pay dividends, the key underlying assumption is that the dividend grows at a constant rate. As our example above illustrates, this will never be exactly the case. More generally, the model is really only applicable to cases where reasonably steady growth is likely to occur.

A second problem is that the estimated cost of equity is very sensitive to the estimated growth rate. An upward revision of g by just one percentage point, for example, increases the estimated cost of equity by at least a full percentage point. Since D_1 will probably be revised upwards as well, the increase will actually be somewhat larger than that.

Finally, this approach really does not explicitly consider risk. Unlike the SML approach (which we consider next), there is no direct adjustment for the riskiness of the investment. For example, there is no allowance for the degree of certainty or uncertainty surrounding the estimated growth rate in dividends. As a result, it is difficult to say whether or not the estimated return is commensurate with the level of risk.[3]

The SML approach

In Chapter 11, we discussed the security market line (SML). Our primary conclusion was that the required or expected return on a risky investment depends on three things:

1 The risk-free rate, R_f.
2 The market risk premium, $E(R_M) - R_f$.
3 The systematic risk of the asset relative to average, which we called its beta coefficient, β.

Using the SML, the expected return on the company's equity, $E(R_E)$, can be written as:

$$E(R_E) = R_f + \beta_E \times [E(R_M) - R_f]$$

where β_E is the estimated beta for the equity. For the SML approach to be consistent with the dividend growth model, we will drop the $E(\ )$s and henceforth write the required return from the SML, R_E, as:

$$R_E = R_f + \beta_E \times [R_M - R_f] \tag{18.2}$$

Implementing the approach

To use the SML approach, we need a risk-free rate, R_f, an estimate of the market risk premium, $R_M - R_f$, and an estimate of the relevant beta, β_E.

Officer[4] looked at the behaviour of returns for shares and government bonds on the Australian market from 1882 to 1987. His estimate of the risk premium over the period was 7.94 per cent. Over the same period his estimate of the risk-free rate was 5.21 per cent. Studies in the United States, Canada and the United Kingdom have found the long-term premium to be around 7 per cent.

We will use 5 per cent as an estimate of the risk-free rate and 8 per cent as an estimate of the risk premium. These can only be considered rough approximations because they are based on historic information and the SML approach is concerned with future returns. Beta coefficients for publicly traded companies are provided by several Australian services.[5]

To illustrate, let us assume that Marsh Mellow Ltd has an estimated beta of 0.875. We could thus estimate the cost of equity for Marsh Mellow Ltd as:

$$\begin{aligned} R_{GS} &= R_f + \beta_{MM} \times (R_M - R_f) \\ &= 5\% + 0.875 \times (8\%) \\ &= 12\% \end{aligned}$$

Thus using the SML approach, Marsh Mellow's cost of equity is approximately 12 per cent.

Advantages and disadvantages of the approach

The SML approach has two primary advantages. First, it explicitly adjusts for risk. Second, it is applicable to companies other than just those with steady dividend growth. Thus it may be useful in a wider variety of circumstances.

There are drawbacks, of course. The SML approach requires that two things be estimated, the market risk premium and the beta coefficient. To the extent that our estimates are poor, the resulting cost of equity will be inaccurate. For example, our estimate of the market risk premium, 8 per cent, is based on about 106 years of returns on a particular portfolio of assets. Using different time periods could result in very different estimates. For example, using the data in Chapter 10, the market risk premium for the period 1978 to 1989 was 8.3% but for the period 1990 to 2002 it was only 2.15%.

Finally, as with the dividend growth model, we essentially rely on the past to predict the future when we use the SML approach. Economic conditions can change very quickly, so, as always, the past may not be a good guide to the future. In a perfect world, the two approaches (dividend growth model and SML) are both applicable and both result in similar answers. If this happens, we might have some confidence in our estimates. We might also wish to compare the results to those for other, similar companies as a reality check.

EXAMPLE 18.1

The cost of equity

Suppose that shares in Devine Chocolate Confectionary Ltd have a beta of 1.2. The market risk premium is 8 per cent, and the risk-free rate is 5 per cent. Devine's last dividend was $2 per share, and the dividend is expected to grow at 7.5 per cent indefinitely. The shares currently sell for $30. What is Devine's cost of equity capital?

We can start off by using the SML. Doing this, we find that the expected return on the ordinary shares of Devine Chocolate Confectionary Ltd is:

$$R_E = R_f + \beta_E \times [R_M - R_f]$$
$$= 5\% + 1.2 \times 8\%$$
$$= 14.6\%$$

This suggests that 14.6 per cent is Devine's cost of equity. We next use the dividend growth model. The projected dividend is $D_0 \times (1 + g) = \$2 \times (1.075) = 2.15$, so the expected return using this approach is:

$$R_E = D_1/P_0 + g$$
$$= \$2.15/30 + 0.075$$
$$= 14.7\%$$

Our two estimates are reasonably close, so we might just average them to find that Devine's cost of equity is approximately 14.63 per cent.

Concept questions

18.2a *What do we mean when we say that a corporation's cost of equity capital is 16 per cent?*
18.2b *What are two approaches to estimating the cost of equity capital?*

The costs of debt and preference shares

In addition to ordinary equity, firms use debt and, to a lesser extent, preference shares to finance their investments. As we discuss next, determining the costs of capital associated with these sources of financing is much easier than determining the cost of equity.

The cost of debt

The **cost of debt** is the return that the firm's debtholders demand on new borrowing. In principle, we could determine the beta for the firm's debt and then use the SML to estimate the required return on debt just as we estimate the required return on equity. This is not really necessary, however.

cost of debt
the return that lenders require on the firm's debt

Unlike a firm's cost of equity, its cost of debt can normally be observed either directly or indirectly, because the cost of debt is simply the interest rate that the firm must pay on new borrowing, and we can observe interest rates in the financial markets. For example, if the firm already has debentures outstanding, then the yield to maturity on those debentures is the market-required rate on the firm's debt.

There is one thing to be careful about, though. The coupon rate on the firm's outstanding debt is irrelevant here. That just tells us roughly what the firm's cost of debt was back when the issue was made, not what the cost of debt is today.[6] This is why we have to look at the yield on the debt in today's marketplace. For consistency with our other notation, we will use the symbol R_D for the cost of debt.

EXAMPLE 18.2

The cost of debt

Suppose the Russ Saving Company issued an eight-year, 7 per cent debenture two years ago. The debenture is currently selling for $95.38. What is Russ Saving's cost of debt?

Going back to Chapter 6, we need to calculate the yield to maturity on this debenture. Since the debt is selling at a discount, the yield is apparently greater than 7 per cent – but not much greater, because the discount is fairly small. You can check that the yield to maturity is about 8 per cent, assuming annual coupons. Russ Saving's cost of debt, R_D, is thus 8 per cent.

An approximation method frequently used to estimate the cost of debt is provided by the following formula:

$$R_D = \frac{I + (PV - NP)/n}{(PV + NP)/2}$$

where

I = annual interest payment
PV = par (or face) value of the debenture
NP = net proceeds of the issue = market price less costs
n = the number of years to maturity of the debenture

The calculation for the Russ Saving Company debenture would be:

$$R_D = \frac{7 + (100 - 95.38)/6}{(100 + 95.38)/2}$$
$$= 7.95\%$$

If we assume a corporate tax rate of 30 per cent this approximate rate is adjusted for tax as follows:

$$7.95\% \times (1 - 0.3) = 5.565\%.$$

The cost of preference shares

Determining the cost of preference shares is quite straightforward. As we discussed in Chapters 5 and 6, preference shares have a fixed dividend paid every period forever, so a preference share is essentially a perpetuity. The cost of preference shares, R_P, is thus:

$$R_P = D/P_0 \qquad\qquad (18.3)$$

where D is the fixed dividend and P_0 is the current price per share of the preference share. Notice that the cost of the preference share is simply equal to the dividend yield on the preference share.

EXAMPLE 18.3 ■ **Carlton Investment Ltd: Cost of preference shares**

On 26 August 2002, Carlton Investment Ltd had an issue of preference shares that traded on the Australian Stock Exchange. On that date the quotation for the issue presented in the *Australian Financial Review* was:

Year's high	Company name & paid-up value	Last sale	Dividend cent per share	Yield %
2.11	Carlton 7% Cum pf $2	2.11	14.00	6.64

If there was an 'F' adjacent to the 'Dividend per share' it would indicate that the current dividend contained franking credits so that taxation benefits may flow to the holders. This benefit is irrelevant in determining the cost of preference shares because we are looking at the opportunity cost from the point of view of the firm, and franking provides no direct benefit to the firm.

Using the perpetuity formula the cost of preference shares is:

$$R_P = D/P_0$$

so the cost for Carlton would be:

$$= \$0.14/2.11$$
$$= 0.0664 \text{ or } 6.64\%$$

This is the percentage indicated in the dividend 'Yield %' column. It is based upon the last sale value of the shares ($2.11) and not the face value ($2.00).

Concept questions

18.3a *How can the cost of debt be calculated?*

18.3b *How can the cost of preference shares be calculated?*

18.3c *Why is the coupon rate a bad estimate of a firm's cost of debt?*

18.4 ■ The weighted average cost of capital

Now that we have the costs associated with the main sources of capital that the firm employs, we need to worry about the specific mix. As we mentioned above, we will take this mix, which is the firm's capital structure, as given for now. Also, we will focus mostly on debt and ordinary equity in this discussion.

In Chapter 3, we mentioned that financial analysts frequently focus on a firm's total capitalisation, which is the sum of its long-term debt and equity. This is particularly true in determining cost of capital; short-term liabilities are often ignored in the process. We will not explicitly distinguish between total value and total capitalisation in our discussion below; however, the general approach is applicable in either case.

The unadjusted weighted average cost of capital

We will use the symbol E (for equity) to stand for the market value of the firm's equity. We calculate this by taking the number of shares outstanding and multiplying it by the price per share. Similarly, we will use the symbol D (for debt) to stand for the market value of the firm's debt. For long-term debt, we calculate this by multiplying the market price of a single debenture by the number outstanding.

If there are multiple debenture issues (as there normally would be), then we repeat this calculation for each and then add up the results. If there is debt that is not publicly traded (because it is held by a life insurance company, for example), we must observe the yields on similar, publicly traded debt and then estimate the market value of the privately held debt using this yield as the discount rate. For short-term debt, the book (accounting) values and market values should be somewhat similar, so we might use the book values as estimates of the market values.

Finally, we will use the symbol V (for value) to stand for the combined market value of the debt and equity:

$$V = E + D \qquad (18.4)$$

If we divide both sides by V, we can calculate the percentages of the total capital represented by the debt and equity:

$$100\% = E/V + D/V \qquad (18.5)$$

These percentages can be interpreted just like portfolio weights, and they are often called the capital structure weights.

For example, if the total market value of a company's equity were calculated as $200 million and the total market value of the company's debt were calculated as $50 million, then the combined value would be $250 million. Of this total, $E/V = $200/250 = 80\%$, so 80 per cent of the firm's financing is equity and the remaining 20 per cent is debt.

At this point, we have some weights (the debt and equity percentages) and some expected returns (the costs of debt and equity). We use this information to calculate the firm's overall cost of capital in the same way that we calculated a portfolio's expected return in Chapter 11: We multiply the expected returns by their weights and then add them up. In this context, the result is called the unadjusted **weighted average cost of capital (WACC)**:

weighted average cost of capital (WACC)
the weighted average of the costs of debt and equity

$$\text{WACC (unadjusted)} = (E/V) \times R_E + (D/V) \times R_D \qquad (18.6)$$

where R_E and R_D are the required returns on (or the costs of) equity and debt, respectively.

We emphasise here that the correct way to proceed is to use the market values of the debt and equity. Under certain circumstances, such as a privately owned company, it may not be possible to get reliable estimates of these quantities. In this case, we might go ahead and use the accounting values for debt and equity. While this is probably better than nothing, we would have to approach the answer with great caution.

Taxes and the WACC

There is one final issue associated with the WACC. We called the result above the unadjusted WACC because we have not considered taxes. Recall that we are always concerned with after-tax cash flows. If we are determining the discount rate appropriate to those cash flows, then the discount rate also needs to be expressed on an after-tax basis.

As we discussed previously in various places in this book (and as we will discuss later), the interest paid by a corporation is deductible for tax purposes. Payments to shareholders, such as dividends, are not. What this means, effectively, is that the government pays some of the interest. Thus, in determining an after-tax discount rate, we need to distinguish between the pre-tax and the after-tax cost of debt.

To illustrate, suppose a firm borrows $1 million at 9 per cent interest. The corporate tax rate is 30 per cent. What is the after-tax interest rate on this loan? The total interest bill will be $90,000 per year. This amount is tax-deductible, however, so the $90,000 interest reduces our tax bill by $0.30 \times \$90,000 = \$27,000$. The after-tax interest bill is thus $\$90,000 - 27,000 = \$63,000$. The after-tax interest rate is thus $\$63,000/\$1$ million $= 6.3\%$.

As a general approximation, the after-tax interest rate is taken as the pre-tax rate multiplied by one minus the tax rate. For example, using the numbers above, we find that the after-tax interest rate is $9\% \times (1 - 0.30) = 6.3\%$. This estimate is not strictly correct, because it implies the return of the par value is tax-deductible, which is not the case. An example will explain this point.

EXAMPLE 18.4 ■ Calculating the explicit cost of debt

The Shotput Company Ltd issued a debenture seven years ago with a coupon rate of 5 per cent that will mature in three years. The corporate tax rate is 30 per cent. The current market price of the debenture is $94.75.

What is the current yield on Shotput Company debentures? What is the after-tax cost to Shotput Company on the debentures if the yield is used to estimate an approximate cost? What is the explicit after-tax cost to Shotput Company on the debentures?

$$\text{The current yield} = R_D$$
$$\text{Debenture value} = C \times (1 - 1/(1 + R_D)^t)/R_D + F/(1 + R_D)^t$$
$$\$94.75 = 5 \times (1 - 1/(1 + R_D)^3)/R_D + 100/(1 + R_D)^3$$

Using trial and error the equation may be solved to provide the current yield as 7 per cent.

$$\text{Approximate after-tax cost} = \text{Yield} \times (1 - \text{Corporate tax rate})$$
$$= 7\% \times (1 - 0.30)$$
$$= 4.9\%$$

$$\text{The explicit after-tax cost} = R_{DT}$$
$$\text{Debenture value} = C(1 - T_C) \times (1 - 1/(1 + R_{DT})^t)/(R_{DT} + F/(1 + R_{DT})^t$$

where T_C is the corporate tax rate

$$\$94.75 = 5(1 - 0.30) \times (1 - 1/(1 + R_{DT})^3)/R_{DT} + 100/(1 + R_{DT})^3$$

Using trial and error the equation may be solved to provide the explicit after-tax cost as 5.443 per cent.

While the approximation derived from the yield is a good estimate of the after-tax cost to the firm, it is not precise. We should use this approximation unless we are asked for the explicit cost.

The after-tax cost of other finance

Where funds are provided to the firm through other sources of funds, such as a long-term bank loan, the after-tax cost is the contractual rate adjusted by the corporate tax rate. For example, if the long-term bank loan contractual rate determined by the bank was 10 per cent, the cost to the firm would be 10 per cent (1 − corporate tax rate).

In summary, if we use the symbol T_C to stand for the corporate tax rate, then the after-tax rate that we use in our WACC calculation can be written as $R_D \times (1 - T_C)$. Thus, once we consider the effect of taxes, the WACC is:

$$\text{WACC} = (E/V) \times R_E + (D/V) \times R_D \times (1 - T_C) \qquad (18.7)$$

From now on, when we speak of the WACC, this is the number that we have in mind.

This WACC has a very straightforward interpretation. It is the overall return that the firm must earn on its existing assets to maintain the value of its shares. It is also the required return on any investments by the firm that have essentially the same risks as existing operations. So, if we were evaluating the cash flows from a proposed expansion of our existing operations, this is the discount rate we would use.

EXAMPLE 18.5

Calculating the WACC

The M.T.G.G. Feed Co. Ltd has 1.4 million shares outstanding. A share currently sells for $20. The firm's debt is publicly traded and was recently quoted at 93 per cent of par value. It has a total book value of $5 million, and it is currently priced to yield 11 per cent. The risk-free rate is 8 per cent, and the market risk premium is 7 per cent. You have estimated that Feed has a beta of 0.74. If the corporate tax rate is 30 per cent, what is the WACC of Feed Co.?

We can first determine the cost of equity and the cost of debt. From the SML, the cost of equity is 8% + 0.74 × 7% = 13.18%. The total value of the equity is 1.4 million × $20 = $28 million. The pre-tax cost of debt is the current yield to maturity on the outstanding debt, 11 per cent. The debt sells for 93 per cent of its face value, so its current market value is 0.93 × $5 million = $4.65 million. The total market value of the equity and debt together is $28 + 4.65 = $32.65 million.

From here, we can calculate the WACC easily enough. The percentage of equity used by M.T.G.G. Feed to finance its operations is $28/$32.65 = 85.76%. Since the weights have to add up to 1, the percentage of debt is 1 − 0.8576 = 14.24%. The WACC is thus:

$$
\begin{aligned}
\text{WACC} &= (E/V) \times R_E + (D/V) \times R_D \times (1 - T_C) \\
&= 0.8576 \times 13.18\% + 0.1424 \times 11\% \times (1 - 0.30) \\
&= 12.4\%
\end{aligned}
$$

M.T.G.G. Feed thus has an overall weighted average cost of capital of 12.4 per cent.

Calculating the WACC with various sources of funds

While the sources of funds supplied to a firm may be broadly classified into equity (funds supplied by the owners of the firm) and debt (funds supplied by the debtholders of the firm), the firm will obtain funds from many different types of debtholders at different costs. The financing arrangements might be as follows:

Source of funds	Market value	% Cost	$ Cost
Shareholders' funds			
Ordinary shares	$3,100,000	15	465,000
Long-term liabilities			
First mortgage debentures	500,000	9	45,000
Second mortgage debentures	100,000	10	10,000
Unsecured notes	300,000	11	33,000
Preference shares	100,000	13	13,000
Bank loan	900,000	6	54,000
	1,900,000		155,000
Current liabilities			
Trade creditors	500,000	3	15,000
Bank overdraft	400,000	5	20,000
	900,000		35,000
Total liabilities/equity	5,900,000		655,000

The above information includes the percentage cost and the dollar cost for each of the sources of funds. Let us look at calculating the WACC. In practice the usual tendency is to treat non-interest-bearing current liabilities like trade creditors as negative assets and ignore them in the WACC calculation. The current liabilities are set off against current assets and an asset called working capital is created. This asset, like all the other assets of the organisation, needs to be funded. The total of the relevant funds is $5,400,000 (that is, $3.1 million of shareholders' funds and $1.9 million of long-term liabilities plus the $400,000 bank overdraft). The dollar cost for servicing these funds is $640,000 (that is, $465,000 (for equity) plus $155,000 (for the long-term liabilities) and $20,000 for the bank overdraft). The WACC is calculated as:

$$\text{Weighted average cost of capital} = \frac{\text{Cost}}{\text{Market value}}$$
$$= \frac{\$640,000}{\$5,400,000} \times 100\%$$
$$= 11.85\%$$

If the capital structure of the firm remains the same, the weighted average cost of capital is unchanged.

Budgeting problems

Now we can use the WACC to solve the warehouse problem that we posed at the beginning of the chapter. However, before we rush to discount the cash flows at the WACC to estimate NPV, we need first to make sure that we are doing the right thing.

Going back to first principles, we need to find an alternative in the financial markets that is comparable to the warehouse renovation. To be comparable, an alternative must be of the same risk as the warehouse project. Projects that have the same risk are said to be in the same risk class.

The WACC for a firm reflects the risk and the target capital structure to finance the firm's existing assets as a whole. As a result, strictly speaking, the firm's WACC is the appropriate discount rate only if the proposed investment is a replica of the firm's existing operating activities.

In broader terms, whether or not we can use the firm's WACC to value the warehouse project depends on whether the warehouse project is in the same risk class as the firm. We will assume that this project is an integral part of the overall business of the firm. In such cases, it is natural to think that the cost savings will be as risky as the general cash flows of the firm, and the project will thus be in the same risk class as the overall firm. More generally, projects like the warehouse renovation, which are intimately related to the firm's existing operations, are often viewed as being in the same risk class as the overall firm.

We can now see what the managing director should do. Suppose that the firm has a target debt/equity ratio of 1/3. In this case, E/V is 0.75 and D/V is 0.25. The cost of debt is 9.4 per cent, and the cost of equity is 19.78 per cent. Assuming a 30 per cent tax rate, the WACC will be:

$$\begin{aligned} \text{WACC} &= (E/V) \times R_E + (D/V) \times R_C \times (1 - T_C) \\ &= 0.75 \times 19.78\% + 0.25 \times 9.4\% \times (1 - 0.30) \\ &= 16.48\% \end{aligned}$$

Recall that the warehouse project had a cost of $50 million and expected after-tax cash flows (the cost savings) of $12 million per year for six years. The NPV is thus:

$$\text{NPV} = -\$50 + \$12/(1 + \text{WACC})^1 + \ldots + \$12/(1 + \text{WACC})^6$$

Since the cash flows are in the form of an ordinary annuity, we can calculate this NPV using 16.48 per cent (the WACC) as the discount rate as follows:

$$\begin{aligned} \text{NPV} &= -\$50 + \$12 \times [1 - (1/(1 + 0.1648)^6)]/0.1648 \\ &= -\$50 + \$12 \times 3.6384 \\ &= -\$6.34 \end{aligned}$$

Should the firm take on the warehouse renovation? The project has a negative NPV using the firm's WACC. This means that the financial markets offer superior projects in the same risk class (namely, the firm itself). The answer is clear: the project should be rejected.

For future reference, our discussion of the WACC is summarised in Table 18.1.

Summary of capital cost calculations

TABLE 18.1

1. The cost of equity, R_E.
   a   Dividend growth model approach (from Chapter 6):

   $$R_E = D_1/P_0 + g$$

   where D_1 is the expected dividend in one period, g is the dividend growth rate, and P_0 is the current share price.
   b   SML approach (from Chapter 11):

   $$R_E = R_f + (R_M - R_f)\beta_E$$

   where R_f is the risk-free rate, R_M is the expected return on the overall market, and β_E is the systematic risk on the equity.

2. The cost of debt, R_D.
   a   For a firm with publicly held debt, the cost of debt can be measured as the yield to maturity on the outstanding debt. The coupon rate is irrelevant. Yield to maturity is covered in Chapter 6.   *(continued)*

TABLE
18.1

Summary of capital cost calculations (*continued*)

b   If the firm has no publicly traded debt, then the cost of debt can be measured as the yield to maturity on similar debt that is traded.

$$\text{Bond value} = \text{Coupon} \times (1 - 1/(1 + R_D)^t)/R_D + \text{Face Value}/(1 + R_D)^t$$

3. The weighted average cost of capital, WACC.
    a   The firm's WACC is the overall required return on the firm as a whole. It is the appropriate discount rate to use for cash flows similar in risk to the overall firm.
    b   The WACC is calculated as:

$$\text{WACC} = E/V \times R_E + D/V \times R_D \times (1 - T_C)$$

where T_C is the corporate tax rate, E is the market value of the firm's equity, D is the market value of the firm's debt, and $V = E + D$. Note that E/V is the percentage of the firm's financing (in market value terms) that is equity, and D/V is the percentage that is debt.

EXAMPLE
18.6

Using the WACC

A firm is considering a project that will result in initial cash savings of $5 million at the end of the first year. These savings will grow at the rate of 5 per cent per year. The firm has a debt/equity (D/E) ratio of 2/3, a cost of equity of 16 per cent, and a cost of debt of 8 per cent. The cost-saving proposal is closely related to the firm's core business, so it is viewed as having the same risks as the overall firm. Should the firm take on the project?

Assuming a 30 per cent tax rate, the firm should take on this project if it costs less than $73 million. To see this, first note that the PV is:

$$D/E = 2/3, \text{so that } 2D = 3E$$
$$D = 40\%$$
$$E = 60\%$$
$$\text{PV} = \$5 \text{ million}/(\text{WACC} - 0.05)$$

This is an example of a growing perpetuity as discussed in Chapter 6. The WACC is:

$$\begin{aligned}
\text{WACC} &= (E/V) \times R_E + (D/V) \times R_D \times (1 - T_C) \\
&= 0.6 \times 16\% + 0.4 \times 8\% \times (1 - 0.30) \\
&= 11.84\%
\end{aligned}$$

The PV is thus:

$$\text{PV} = \$5 \text{ million}/(0.1184 - 0.05) = \$73.099415 \text{ million}$$

The NPV will be positive only if the cost is less than $73.099415 million.

Concept questions

18.4a *How is the WACC calculated?*
18.4b *Why do we multiply the cost of debt by $(1 - T_C)$ when we compute the WACC?*
18.4c *Under what conditions is it correct to use the WACC to determine NPV?*

18.5 ■ Divisional and project costs of capital

As we have seen, using the WACC as the discount rate for future cash flows is only appropriate when the proposed investment is similar to the firm's existing activities. This is not as restrictive as it sounds. If we were in the pizza business, for example, and we were thinking of opening a new location, then the WACC is the discount rate to use. The same is true of a retailer thinking of a new store, a manufacturer thinking of expanding production, or a consumer products company thinking of expanding its markets.

Nonetheless, despite the usefulness of the WACC as a benchmark, there will clearly be situations where the cash flows under consideration have risks that are distinctly different from those of the overall firm. We consider how to cope with this problem next.

The SML and the WACC

When we are evaluating investments with risks that are substantially different from the overall firm, the use of the WACC will potentially lead to poor decisions. Figure 18.1 illustrates why.

In Figure 18.1, we have plotted an SML corresponding to a risk-free rate of 7 per cent and a market risk premium of 8 per cent. To keep things simple, we consider an all-equity company with a beta of 1. As we have indicated, the WACC and the cost of equity are exactly equal to 15 per cent for this company since there is no debt.

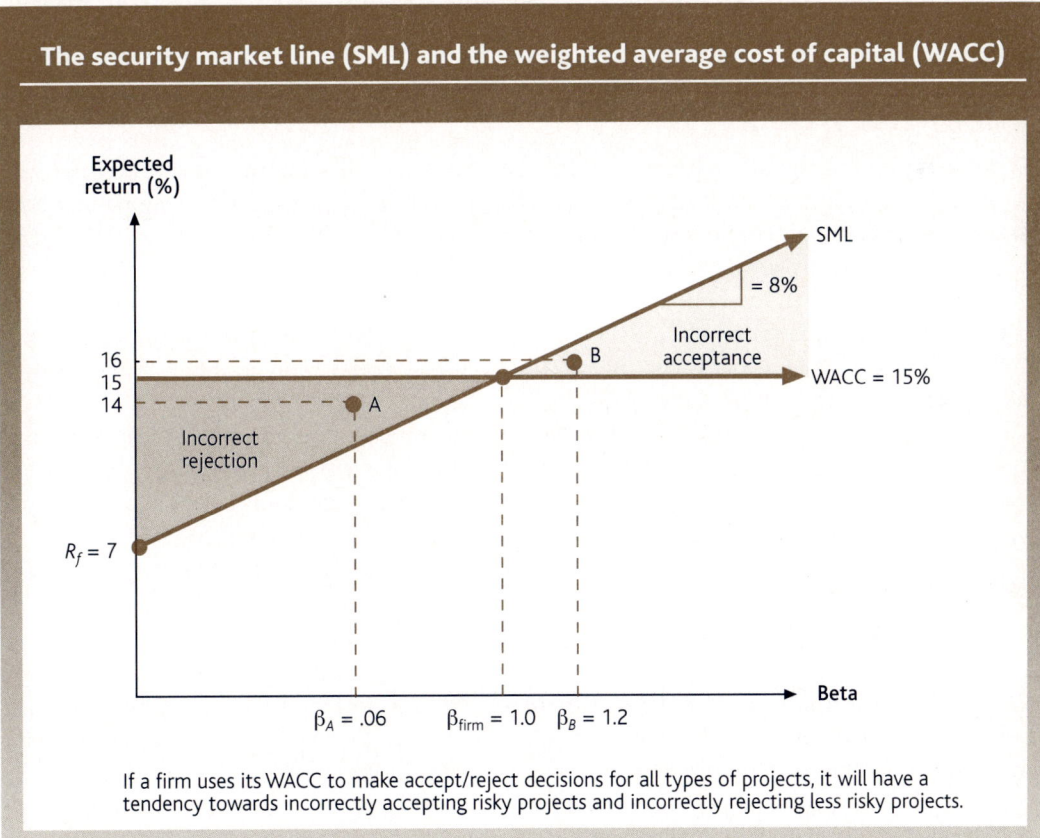

The security market line (SML) and the weighted average cost of capital (WACC)

FIGURE 18.1

If a firm uses its WACC to make accept/reject decisions for all types of projects, it will have a tendency towards incorrectly accepting risky projects and incorrectly rejecting less risky projects.

Suppose our firm uses its WACC to evaluate all investments. This means that any investment with a return of greater than 15 per cent will be accepted and any investment with a return of less than 15 per cent will be rejected. We know from our study of risk and return, however, that a desirable investment is one that plots above the SML. As Figure 18.1 illustrates, using the WACC for all types of projects can result in the firm incorrectly accepting relatively risky projects and incorrectly rejecting relatively safe ones.

For example, consider point A. This project has a β of 0.6 compared to the firm's beta of 1.0. It has an expected return of 14 per cent. Is this a desirable investment? The answer is yes, because its required return is only:

$$
\begin{aligned}
\text{Required return} &= R_f + \beta \times (R_M - R_f) \\
&= 7\% + 0.60 \times 8\% \\
&= 11.8\%
\end{aligned}
$$

However, if we use the WACC as a cut-off, then this project will be rejected because its return is less than 15 per cent. This example illustrates that a firm that uses its WACC as a cut-off will tend to reject profitable projects with risks less than those of the overall firm.

At the other extreme, consider point B. This project offers a 16 per cent return, which exceeds the firm's cost of capital. This is not a good investment, however, because, given its level of systematic risk, its return is inadequate. Nonetheless, if we use the WACC to evaluate it, it will appear to be attractive. So the second error that will arise if we use the WACC as a cut-off is that we will tend to make unprofitable investments with risks greater than the overall firm. As a consequence, through time, a firm that uses its WACC to evaluate all projects will have a tendency to both accept unprofitable investments and become increasingly risky.

Divisional cost of capital

The same type of problem with the WACC can arise in a corporation with more than one line of business. Imagine, for example, a corporation that has two divisions, a regulated bread manufacturing company and a cake manufacturing operation. The first of these (the bread operation) has relatively low risk; the second has relatively high risk.

In this case, the firm's overall cost of capital is really a mixture of two different costs of capital, one for each division. If the two divisions were competing for resources, and the firm used a single WACC as a cut-off, which division would tend to be awarded greater funds for investment?

The answer is that the riskier division would tend to have greater returns (ignoring the greater risk), so it would tend to be the 'winner'. The less glamorous operation might have great profit potential that ends up being ignored. Large corporations in Australia are aware of this problem and many work to develop separate divisional costs of capital.

The pure play approach

We have seen that using the firm's WACC inappropriately can lead to problems. How can we come up with the appropriate discount rates in such circumstances? Because we cannot observe the returns on these investments, there generally is no direct way of coming up with a beta, for example. Instead, what we must do is examine other investments outside the firm that are in the same risk class as the one we are considering and use the market-required returns on these investments as the discount rate. In other words, we will try to determine what the cost of capital is for such investments by trying to locate some similar investments in the marketplace.

For example, going back to our bread division, suppose we wanted to come up with a discount rate to use for that division. What we can do is to identify several other bread companies that have publicly traded securities. We might find that a typical bread company has a beta of .80 and a capital structure that is about 40 per cent debt and 60 per cent equity. Using this information, we could develop a WACC for a typical bread company and use this as our discount rate.

Alternatively, if we are thinking of entering a new line of business, we would try to develop the appropriate cost of capital by looking at the market-required returns on companies already in that business. In investment language, a company that focuses only on a single line of business is called a pure play. For example, if you wanted to bet on the price of crude oil by purchasing ordinary shares, you would try to identify companies that dealt exclusively with this product, since they would be the most affected by changes in the price of crude oil. Such companies would be called pure plays on the price of crude oil.

What we try to do here is to find companies that focus as exclusively as possible on the type of project in which we are interested. Our approach, therefore, is called the **pure play approach** to estimating the required return on an investment.

pure play approach
use of a WACC that is unique to a particular project

In Chapter 3, we discussed the subject of identifying similar companies for comparison purposes. The same problems that we described there come up here. The most obvious one is that we may not be able to find any suitable companies. In this case, how to determine a discount rate objectively becomes a very difficult question. Even so, the important thing is to be aware of the issue so we at least reduce the possibility of the kinds of mistakes that can arise when the WACC is used as a cut-off on all investments.

The subjective approach

Because of the difficulties that exist in establishing discount rates objectively for individual projects, firms often adopt an approach that involves making subjective adjustments to the overall WACC. To illustrate, suppose a firm has an overall WACC of 14 per cent. It places all proposed projects into four categories as follows:

Category	Examples	Adjustment factor	Discount rate
High risk	New products	+6%	20%
Moderate risk	Cost savings	+0	14%
Low risk	Expansion of existing lines	−4%	10%
Mandatory	Pollution control	n.a.*	n.a.

* n.a. = not applicable

The effect of this crude partitioning is to assume that all projects either fall into one of three risk classes or else they are mandatory. In this last case, the cost of capital is irrelevant since the project must be taken. With the subjective approach, the firm's WACC may change through time as economic conditions change. As this happens, the discount rates for the different types of projects will also change.

Within each risk class, some projects will presumably have more risk than others, and the danger of incorrect decisions still exists. Figure 18.2 (overleaf) illustrates this point. Comparing Figures 18.1 and 18.2, we see that similar problems exist, but the magnitude of the potential error is less with the subjective approach. For example, the project labelled A would be accepted if the WACC were used, but it is rejected once it is classified as a high-risk investment. What this illustrates is that some risk adjustment, even if it is subjective, is probably better than no risk adjustment.

FIGURE
18.2

The security market line (SML) and the subjective approach

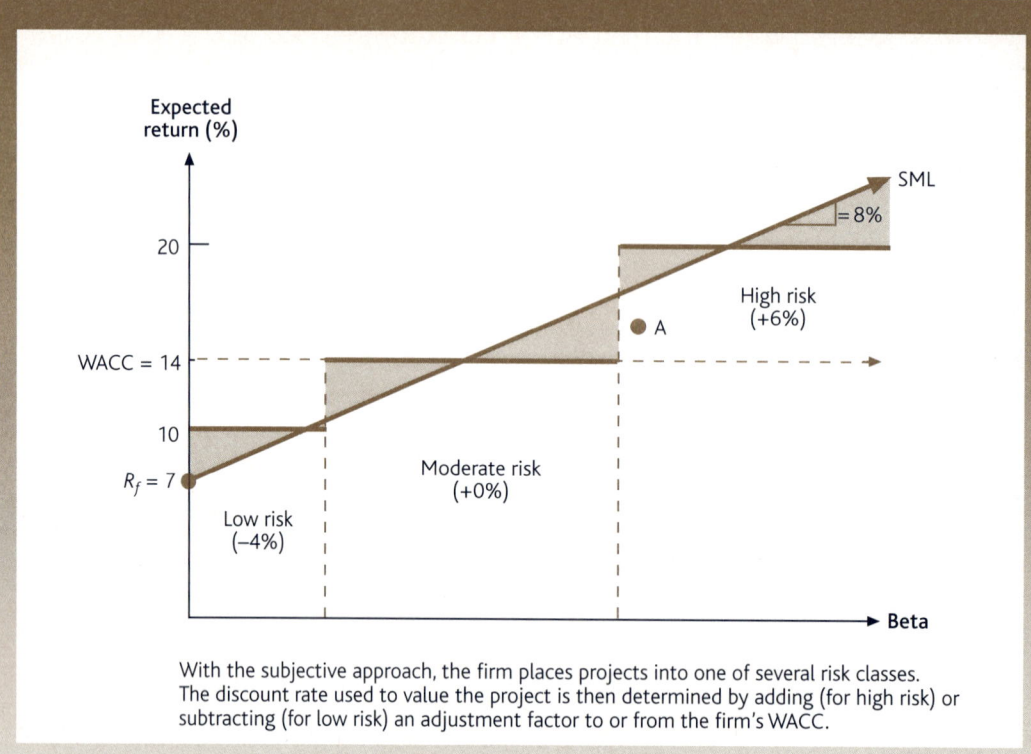

With the subjective approach, the firm places projects into one of several risk classes. The discount rate used to value the project is then determined by adding (for high risk) or subtracting (for low risk) an adjustment factor to or from the firm's WACC.

It would be better, in principle, to determine objectively the required return for each project separately. However, as a practical matter, it may not be possible to go much beyond subjective adjustments because either the necessary information is unavailable or else the cost and effort required are simply not worthwhile.

(((In their own words

Samuel Weaver* on cost of capital and hurdle rates at Hershey

Samuel Weaver

At Hershey, we re-evaluate our cost of capital annually or as market conditions warrant. The calculation of the cost of capital essentially involves three different issues, each with a few alternatives:

> *Capital structure weighting*
> *Historical book value*
> *Target capital structure*
> *Market-based weights*

Cost of debt
Historical book value
Target capital structure
Market-based interest rates

Cost of equity
Dividend growth model
Capital Asset Pricing Model (CAPM)

At Hershey, we calculate our cost of capital officially based upon the projected 'target' capital structure at the end of our three-year intermediate planning horizon. This allows management to see the immediate impact of strategic decisions related to the planned composition of Hershey's capital pool. The cost of debt is calculated as the anticipated weighted average after tax cost of debt in that final plan year based upon the coupon rates attached to that debt. The cost of equity is computed via the dividend growth model.

We recently conducted a survey of the 11 food processing companies that we consider our industry group competitors. The results of this survey indicated that the cost of capital for most of these companies was in the 10 to 12 per cent range. Furthermore, without exception, all 11 of these companies employed the CAPM when calculating their cost of equity. Our experience has been that the dividend growth model works better for Hershey. We do pay dividends, and we do experience steady, stable growth in our dividends. This growth is also projected within our strategic plan. Consequently, the dividend growth model is technically applicable and appealing to management since it reflects their best estimate of the future long-term growth rate.

In addition to the calculation described above, the other possible combinations and permutations are calculated as barometers. Unofficially, the cost of capital is calculated using market weights, current marginal interest rates and the CAPM cost of equity. For the most part, and due to rounding the cost of capital to the nearest whole percentage point, these alternative calculations yield approximately the same results.

From the cost of capital, individual project hurdle rates are developed using a subjectively determined risk premium based on the characteristics of the project. Projects are grouped into separate project categories, such as cost savings, capacity expansion, product line extension, and new products. For example, in general, a new product is more risky than a cost savings product. Consequently, each project category's hurdle rate reflects the level of risk and commensurate required return as perceived by senior management. As a result, capital project hurdle rates range from a slight premium over the cost of capital to the highest hurdle rate of approximately double the cost of capital.

* Samuel Weaver, Ph.D., was formerly Director, Financial Planning and Analysis, for Hershey Chocolate North America. He is a certified management accountant. His position combined the theoretical with the pragmatic and involved the analysis of many different facets of finance in addition to capital expenditure analysis. His current position is Professor of Finance at Lehigh University.

Bernie Wilson* on WACC in Perspective

Bernie Wilson

I'd like to give you a practical perspective on how Weighted Average Cost of Capital (WACC) principles can be used in a corporate environment; specifically, how WACC can be used in investment evaluations.

Investment decisions can be evaluated using a 'go, no go' decision framework. If the project achieves a positive Net Present Value (NPV), then it's 'go', if not, the project is 'no go'. The NPV is calculated using the WACC as the discount rate for the project. Some of the problems encountered are outlined below.

When is the WACC calculated?

The development of a project can, at times, take several months as it moves from the concept development phase to a fully fleshed out project. As this development can consume significant dollars and resources, financial evaluation will be undertaken at the various stages of development. With interest rates changing on a daily basis, a WACC rate that is regularly updated may result in a 'go' decision one day and a 'no go' decision the next day. Obviously you need to strike a balance between the theoretical approach of ensuring the WACC rate incorporates the latest information and the confusion such an approach can cause. To help with this, competition regulators have recently adopted an averaging process to overcome the potential for a WACC rate being calculated from abnormal interest rates.

How is the WACC derived?

It is important that a firm's methodology for deriving WACC is consistent. In setting the methodology, the firm will have to establish a preferred WACC formula (there are a number of competing approaches). In addition, it's a good idea to periodically agree on a number of the key inputs (e.g. beta and market risk premium). By agreeing the approach and key inputs, WACC rates can be regularly updated with minimal stress.

How precise does the WACC need to be?

Since a number of the key inputs to a WACC calculation are determined with a fair amount of subjectivity, a WACC rate calculated to more than one decimal place is usually inappropriate. A Crystal Ball simulation of the potential values for key inputs can help demonstrate the amount of subjectivity inherent in WACC calculations. There is a good argument for rounding WACC rates to the nearest quarter or half of a per cent.

Who derives the WACC?

The key to determining a WACC rate is objectivity, so it will usually be best to have the WACC methodology and actual WACC rates determined by an independent part of the organisation with the requisite skills and experience. This requires the co-operation of business managers, since they are in the best position to understand project risks.

How is the WACC applied?

It is important that the methodology for evaluating a project is internally consistent with the calculation of the WACC, so the group that determines the WACC methodology should also be asked to determine the investment evaluation methodology.

WACC rates are normally determined on a post-tax nominal basis, and cash flows need to be determined on a like basis.

Many people will argue that all approaches (i.e. nominal, real, pre-tax and post-tax) will give the same answer. This is not the case. The answers will only be the same where the project has equal cash flows in perpetuity.

Allowing multiple investment evaluation approaches in a firm increases the risk of a mismatch between the WACC and the cash flows used in the investment evaluation.

How much weight (pardon the pun) do we put on the WACC?

Rightly or wrongly, NPV has been entrenched as the key parameter for making investment decisions. Decision makers look for projects with a positive NPV. This emphasis on NPV has the following consequences:

- Project proponents need to quantify what would otherwise be qualitative criteria in order to generate a positive NPV. This can be good from the perspective that it adds a quantitative discipline to the evaluation. On the negative side, it can motivate project proponents to invent cash flows.

- A NPV approach can lead to over-evaluation. You need to ensure that an appropriate level of financial evaluation is undertaken for projects. For example, it would be inappropriate to devote the resources to financially evaluate a small 'stay-in-business' investment.

- Strategic drivers may be under-valued. Finance literature is currently promoting the use of 'real options' to overcome this problem. However, the 'real options' approach suffers from the potential for project proponents to invent 'options'.

WACC is an invaluable tool provided by finance theory. However, the key to maximising the benefit of this tool is common sense. Use it as a tool to assist in the decision-making process. Don't let the process make the decision.

* **Bernie Wilson** is Assistant Treasurer at QR (Queensland Rail).

Concept questions

18.5a *What are the likely consequences if a firm uses its WACC to evaluate all proposed investments?*

18.5b *What is the pure play approach to determining the appropriate discount rate? When might it be used?*

18.6 ■ Flotation costs and the weighted average cost of capital

So far, we have not included issue or flotation costs in our discussion of the weighted average cost of capital. If a company accepts a new project, it may be required to issue or float new debentures and shares. This means that the firm will incur some costs, which we call flotation costs. The nature and magnitude of flotation costs are discussed in some detail in earlier chapters.

Sometimes it is suggested that the firm's WACC should be adjusted upward to reflect flotation costs. This is really not the best approach, because, once again, the required return on an investment depends on the risk of the investment, not the source of the funds. This is not to say that flotation costs should be ignored. Because these costs arise as a consequence of the decision to undertake a project, they are relevant cash flows. We therefore briefly discuss how to include them in a project analysis.

The basic approach

We start with a simple case. The Magpie Company Ltd, an all-equity firm, has a cost of equity of 20 per cent. Since this firm is 100 per cent equity, its WACC and its cost of equity are the same. Magpie is contemplating a large-scale $100 million expansion of its existing operations. The expansion would be funded by selling new shares.

Based on conversations with its merchant bank adviser, Magpie believes its flotation costs will be 10 per cent of the amount issued. This means that Magpie's proceeds from the equity sale will only be 90 per cent of the amount sold. When flotation costs are considered, what is the cost of the expansion?

As we discussed in Chapter 13, Magpie needs to sell enough equity to raise $100 million after covering the flotation costs. In other words:

$$\$100 \text{ million} = (1 - 0.10) \times \text{Amount raised}$$
$$\text{Amount raised} = \$100/0.90 = \$111.11 \text{ million}$$

Magpie's flotation costs are thus $11.11 million, and the true cost of the expansion is $111.11 million once we include flotation costs.

Things are only slightly more complicated if the firm uses both debt and equity. For example, suppose that Magpie's target capital structure is 60 per cent equity, 40 per cent debt. The flotation costs associated with equity are still 10 per cent, but the flotation costs for debt are less, say 5 per cent.

Earlier, when we had different capital costs for debt and equity, we calculated a weighted average cost of capital using the target capital structure weights. Here, we will do much the same thing. We can calculate a weighted average flotation cost, f_A, by multiplying the equity flotation cost, f_E, by the percentage of equity (E/V) and the debt flotation cost, f_D, by the percentage of debt (D/V) and then adding the two together:

$$\begin{aligned} f_A &= E/V \times f_E + D/V \times f_D \\ &= 60\% \times 0.10 + 40\% \times 0.05 \\ &= 8\% \end{aligned} \tag{18.8}$$

The weighted average flotation cost is thus 8 per cent. What this tells us is that, for every dollar in outside financing needed for new projects, the firm must actually raise $1/(1 - 0.08) = \$1.087$. In our example above, the project cost is $100 million when we ignore flotation costs. If we include them, then the true cost is $100/(1 - f_A) = \$100/0.92 = \$108.7$ million.

In taking issue costs into account, the firm must be careful not to use the wrong weights. The firm should use the target weights, even if it can finance the entire cost of the project with either debt or equity. The fact that a firm can finance a specific project with debt or equity is not directly relevant. If a firm has a target debt/equity ratio of 1, for example, but chooses to finance a particular project with all debt, it will have to raise additional equity later on to maintain its target debt/equity ratio. To take this into account, the firm should always use the target weights in calculating the flotation cost.

Calculating the weighted average flotation cost

The Headpecker Corporation Ltd has a target capital structure that is 80 per cent equity, 20 per cent debt. The flotation costs for equity issues are 20 per cent of the amount raised; the flotation costs for debt issues are 6 per cent. If Headpecker needs $65 million for a new manufacturing facility, what is the true cost once flotation costs are considered?

We first calculate the weighted average flotation cost, f_A:

$$f_A = E/V \times f_E + D/V \times f_D$$
$$= 80\% \times 0.20 + 20\% \times 0.06$$
$$= 17.2\%$$

The weighted average flotation cost is thus 17.2 per cent. The project cost is $65 million when we ignore flotation costs. If we include them, then the true cost is $65/(1 - f_A)$ = $65/0.828 = $78.5 million, again illustrating that flotation costs can be a considerable expense.

Flotation costs and NPV

To illustrate how flotation costs can be included in an NPV analysis, suppose the Paper Pulping Company Ltd is currently at its target debt/equity ratio of 100 per cent. It is considering building a new $500,000 pulping plant in Tasmania. This new plant is expected to generate after-tax cash flows of $73,150 per year forever. There are two financing options:

1   A $500,000 new issue of ordinary shares. The issuance costs of the new shares would be about 10 per cent of the amount raised. The required return on the company's new equity is 20 per cent.
2   A $500,000 issue of 30-year debentures. The issuance costs of the new debt would be 2 per cent of the proceeds. The company can raise new debt at 10 per cent.

What is the NPV of the new pulping plant if the tax rate is 30 per cent?

To begin, since pulping is the company's main line of business, we will use the company's weighted average cost of capital to value the new pulping plant:

$$\text{WACC} = E/V \times R_E + D/V \times R_D \times (1 - T_C)$$
$$= 0.50 \times 20\% + 0.50 \times 10\% \times (1 - 0.30)$$
$$= 13.5\%$$

Since the cash flows are $73,150 per year forever, the PV of the cash flows at 13.5 per cent per year is:

$$\text{PV} = \$73,150/0.135 = \$541,852$$

If we ignore flotation costs, the NPV is:

$$\text{NPV} = \$541,852 - 500,000 = \$41,852$$

The project generates an NPV that is greater than zero, so it should be accepted.

What about financing arrangements and issue costs? Since new finance must be raised, the flotation costs are relevant. From the information given above, we know that the flotation costs are 2 per cent for debt and 10 per cent for equity. Since Paper uses equal amounts of debt and equity, the weighted average flotation cost, f_A, is:

$$
\begin{aligned}
f_A &= E/V \times f_E + D/V \times f_D \\
&= 0.50 \times 10\% + 0.50 \times 2\% \\
&= 6\%[7]
\end{aligned}
$$

Remember that the fact that Paper can finance the project with all debt or equity is irrelevant. Since Paper needs $500,000 to fund the new plant, the true cost, once we include flotation costs, is $\$500,000/(1 - f_A) = \$500,000/0.94 = \$531,914$.[8] Since the PV of the cash flows is $541,852, the plant has an NPV of $541,852 - 531,914 = \$9,938$, so it is still a good investment. However, its return is lower than we initially might have thought.

Concept questions

18.6a *What are flotation costs?*
18.6b *How are flotation costs included in an NPV analysis?*

◖18.7◗ Summary and conclusions

This chapter discussed cost of capital. The most important concept is the weighted average cost of capital (WACC), which we interpreted as the required rate of return on the overall firm. It is also the discount rate appropriate for cash flows that are similar in risk to the overall firm. We described how the WACC can be calculated, and we illustrated how it can be used in certain types of analyses.

We also pointed out situations in which it is inappropriate to use the WACC as the discount rate. To handle such cases, we described some alternative approaches to developing discount rates, such as the pure play approach. We also discussed how the flotation costs associated with raising new capital can be included in an NPV analysis.

Key terms

Cost of debt *609*
Cost of equity *605*

Pure play approach *619*

Weighted average cost of capital (WACC) *611*

Suggested readings

Ehrhardt, M.C. *The Search for Value: Measuring the Company's Cost of Capital*, Harvard Business School Press, Boston, Ma., 1994.

The following article contains an excellent discussion of some of the subtleties of using the WACC for project evaluation:

Miles, J. and Ezzel, R. 'The Weighted Average Cost of Capital, Perfect Capital Markets and Project Life: A Clarification', *Journal of Financial and Quantitative Analysis*, Vol. 15, September 1980.

For a good discussion on how to use the SML in project evaluation, see:

Weston, J.F. 'Investment Decisions Using the Capital Asset Pricing Model', *Financial Management*, Spring 1973.

For a discussion of estimates of the long-term risk premium, see:

Ibbotson Associates Inc. 'Stocks, Bonds, Bills and Inflation', 1996 Yearbook, Chicago, Ill. 1996.

Endnotes

1 Notice that if we have D_0 and g, we can simply calculate D_1 by multiplying D_0 by $(1 + g)$.

2 For example, we could have used the geometric mean of the historical growth rates instead of the arithmetic mean so that the estimate would be $\sqrt[4]{[(1.0909)(1.125)(1.037)(1.071)]} = 1.0805$.

3 There is an implicit adjustment for risk because the current share price is used. All other things equal, the higher the risk, the lower the share price. Further, the lower the share price, the greater the cost of equity, again assuming all the other information is the same.

4 Officer, R.R. 'Rates of Return to Shares, Bond Yields and Inflation Rates: An Historical Perspective'. In Ball, R., Brown, P., Finn, F.J. and Officer, R.R. (eds) *Share Markets and Portfolio Theory*, 2nd edn, University of Queensland Press, Brisbane, 1989, pp. 207–12.

5 Beta coefficients can be estimated directly by using historical data. For a discussion of how to do this, see Chapters 9, 10 and 11 in Ross, S.A., Westerfield, R.W. and Jordan, B.D. *Corporate Finance*, 6th edn, Irwin, Homewood, Ill., 2003.

6 The firm's cost of debt based on its historic borrowing is sometimes called the embedded debt cost.

7 This 6 per cent cost is before tax. If the flotation costs are tax-deductible, the after-tax cost is $6\% \times (1 - 0.30) = 4.2\%$.

8 If the flotation costs are tax-deductible then the cost is $\$500,000/(1 - f_{AT}) = \$521,921$.

On the web

http://www.qca.org.au
(The Queensland Competition Authority is a recognised avenue whereby both government and third parties can rely on an independent, objective appraisal of the issues subject to its review. Many reports can be found at this site on cost of capital incorporating practical issues.)

Maximise Your Marks!
There are 30 interactive questions on cost of capital waiting online for you at www.mhhe.com/au/ross3e. The questions are written with additional feedback for incorrect answers, and text excerpts with page references for follow-up study.

International Articles!
To read more on cost of capital and to see current international articles, just go to www.mhhe.com/au/ross3e and click on *PowerWeb Articles* for this chapter.

Chapter review problems and self-test

18.1 · Calculating return history

Suppose that equity of Nerd Corporation Ltd has a beta of 0.90. The market risk premium is 7 per cent, and the risk-free rate is 8 per cent. Nerd's last dividend was $0.18 per share, and the dividend is expected to grow at 7 per cent indefinitely. The shares currently sell for $2.50. What is Nerd's cost of equity capital?

18.2 · Calculating the WACC

In addition to the information in the previous problem, suppose Nerd has a target debt/equity ratio of 50 per cent. Its cost of debt is 8 per cent, before taxes. If the tax rate is 30 per cent, what is the WACC?

18.3 · Flotation costs

Suppose that in the previous question Nerd is seeking $40 million for a new project. The necessary funds will have to be raised externally.

Nerd's flotation costs for selling debt and equity are 3 per cent and 12 per cent, respectively. If flotation costs are considered, what is the true cost of the new project?

Answers to self-test problems

18.1 · We start off with the SML approach. Based on the information given, the expected return on Nerd's ordinary capital is:

$$R_E = R_f + \beta_E \times [R_M - R_f]$$
$$= 8\% + 0.9 \times 7\%$$
$$= 14.3\%$$

We now use the dividend growth model. The projected dividend is $D_0 \times (1 + g) = \$0.18 \times (1.07) = \$0.1926$, so the expected return using this approach is:

$$R_E = D_1/P_0 + g$$
$$= \$0.1926/\$2.50 + 0.07$$
$$= 14.704\%$$

Since these two estimates, 14.3 per cent and 14.7 per cent, are fairly close, we will average them. Nerd's cost of equity is approximately 14.5 per cent.

18.2 · Since the target debt/equity ratio is 0.50, Nerd uses $0.50 in debt for every $1.00 in equity. In other words, Nerd's target capital structure is $1/3$ debt and $2/3$ equity. The WACC is thus:

$$\text{WACC} = E/V \times R_E + D/V \times R_D \times (1 - T_C)$$
$$= 2/3 \times 14.5\% + 1/3 \times 8\% \times (1 - 0.30)$$
$$= 9.67 + 1.87$$
$$= 11.54\%$$

18.3 · Since Nerd uses both debt and equity to finance its operations, we first need the weighted average flotation cost. As in the previous problem, the percentage of equity financing is $2/3$, so the weighted average cost is:

$$f_A = E/V \times f_E + D/V \times f_D$$
$$= 2/3 \times 12\% + 1/3 \times 3\%$$
$$= 9\%$$

If Nerd needs $40 million after flotation costs, then the true cost of the project is $\$40/(1 - f_A) = \$40/0.91 = \$43.96$ million.

Questions and problems

1 · Calculating cost of equity

Equity in Retail Online Trading (ROT) Pty Ltd has a beta of 0.75. The market risk premium is 8 per cent, and the risk-free rate is 4 per cent. ROT's last dividend was 40 cents per share, and the dividend is expected to grow at 8 per cent indefinitely. The shares currently sell for $21.60 per share. Calculate ROT's cost of equity capital using two different methods. Comment on the answers obtained using the two methods to suggest which is the preferred answer.

2 · Calculating cost of debt

Suppose Sweet Smelling Success (SSS) Ltd issued a 30-year, 6 per cent unsecured note 5 years ago. The note is currently selling for 104 per cent of its face value, or $104.

a   What is SSS's current pre-tax cost of debt?
b   What is SSS's current after-tax cost of debt? (Assume a 30 per cent tax rate.)
c   Which is more relevant for calculating the WACC, the current pre-tax or the after-tax cost of debt? Why?

3 · Calculating WACC

The Bubble Home Co. Ltd has a target capital structure of 40 per cent debt, 60 per cent equity. Its cost of equity is 18 per cent, and its cost of debt is 8 per cent. If the relevant tax rate is 30 per cent, what is Bubble's WACC?

4 · Taxes and WACC

The Mytee Dogfood Co. Ltd has a target debt/equity ratio of 0.40. Its cost of equity is 24 per cent, and its cost of debt is 14 per cent.

a   What is Mytee's unadjusted WACC?
b   What is Mytee's WACC assuming a tax rate of 30 per cent?
c   Which is more relevant, the WACC in part (a) or the WACC in part (b)? Why?

5 · SML and WACC

Equity in the Hope Corporation Ltd has a beta of 1.4. The market risk premium is 8.5 per cent, and the risk-free rate is 6 per cent. Hope has a target debt/equity ratio of 50 per cent. Its cost of debt is 12 per cent, before taxes. If the tax rate is 30 per cent, what is the WACC?

6 · Finding target weights

You know that the Faith Corporation's overall weighted average cost of capital is 14 per cent and that Faith's tax rate is 30 per cent. Furthermore, Faith's cost of equity is 20 per cent and its cost of debt is 9 per cent. What is Faith's target debt/equity ratio?

7 · Capital costs

Tim Charity, president of Charity Enterprises Pty Ltd, is trying to determine Charity's cost of debt and cost of equity. He is not having an easy time of it.

a   The shares currently sell for $4 per share, and the dividend per share will probably be about $0.40. Tim argues, 'It will cost us $0.40 per share to use the shareholders' money this year, so the cost of equity is equal to 10 per cent ($0.40/$4).' What is wrong with this conclusion?
b   Based on the most recent financial statements, Charity's total liabilities are $8 million. Charity's total interest bill will be approximately $1 million for the coming year. Tim therefore reasons, 'We owe $8 million, and we will pay $1 million interest. Our cost of debt is obviously $1 million/$8 million = 12.5%.' What is wrong with this conclusion?
c   Based on his analysis, Tim is recommending that Charity increase its use of equity because 'debt costs 12.5 per cent, but equity only costs 10 per cent, so equity is cheaper'. Ignoring all the other problems, what do you think about the conclusion that the cost of equity is less than the cost of debt?

8 · Book value versus market value

The Cocktail Corporation Ltd has 32 million shares outstanding. The most recent price per share is $4.60. The book value per share is $1.00. Cocktail also has two debenture issues outstanding. The first issue has a face value of $25 million, a 10 per cent coupon, and sells for 96 per cent of its face value. The second issue has a face value of $14 million, an 8 per cent coupon, and sells for 90 per cent of its face value. The first issue matures in 10 years, the second in 16 years.

a   What are Cocktail's capital structure weights on a book value basis?
b   What are Cocktail's capital structure weights on a market value basis?
c   Which is more relevant, the book or market value weights? Why?

9 · SML and NPV

Both Charcoal Chemical Company Ltd, a large natural gas user, and Fastburn Oil No Liability, a major natural gas producer, are thinking of investing in natural gas in Queensland. Both are all-equity companies. The well Charcoal is thinking of investing in is located in north Queensland, while Fastburn Oil's would be in south-west Queensland; otherwise the projects are identical. Both companies have analysed their respective investments, which would involve a negative cash flow now and positive expected cash flows in the future. These cash flows would be the same for both firms. No debt would be used to finance the projects. Both companies estimate that their project would have a net present value of $1 million at an 18 per cent discount rate and a −$1.1 million NPV at a 22 per cent discount rate. Charcoal has a beta of 1.25, and Fastburn Oil has a beta of 0.75. The expected market return is 20 per cent, and risk-free investments are yielding 12 per cent. Should either company proceed? Should both? Why?

10 · SML return versus WACC

Debtless Limited, an all-equity firm, is considering the following projects:

Project	Beta	Estimated return
A	0.5	12%
B	0.8	13%
C	1.2	18%
D	1.6	19%

The government bond rate is 8 per cent, and the expected market premium is 7 per cent.

a   Which projects have a higher expected return than the firm's 15 per cent cost of capital?
b   Which projects should be accepted?
c   Which projects would be accepted or rejected incorrectly on the basis of the firm's cost of capital as a hurdle rate?

11 · WACC

The Brillcream Corporation Ltd manufactures very small particles for research purposes. Brillcream's debt/equity ratio is 0.50. Its WACC is 16 per cent, and its tax rate is 30 per cent.

a   Assuming that Brillcream's cost of equity is 22 per cent, what is its pre-tax cost of debt?
b   Assuming that Brillcream can sell debt with an interest rate of 11 per cent, what is its cost of equity?

12 · WACC and preferred shares

Kripton Power Co. Pty Ltd has a target capital structure of 35 per cent equity, 10 per cent preference shares, and 55 per cent debt. You have estimated that based on current market conditions, the costs of these components are 20 per cent, 10 per cent, and 12 per cent respectively.

a   What is Kripton's WACC? Assume a 30 per cent tax rate.
b   The company president has approached you about Kripton's capital structure. He wants to know why Kripton does not use more preference capital since, based on your estimates, preference share capital is cheaper than debt. What would you say?

13 · Market values and WACC

Colleen Catering Supply Ltd currently has 40 million shares outstanding. The shares sell for $8. The firm's debt is publicly traded and was recently quoted at 86 per cent of face value. It has a total face value of $15 million, and it is currently priced to yield 9 per cent. The risk-free rate is 8 per cent, and the expected market return is 16 per cent. You have estimated that Colleen has a beta of 1.4. If the corporate tax rate is 30 per cent, what is Colleen's WACC?

14 · Calculating cost of preferred shares

On 11 May 1990, Chase Manhattan had an issue of preference shares that traded for $80 per share. If the face value of the issue was $100 per share and the dividend was $7.60, what is Chase Manhattan's cost of preference shares? The tax rate was 39 per cent in 1990 and it is now 30 per cent.

15 · WACC and NPV

Major Investments Ltd is considering a project that will result in initial cash savings of $6 million at the end of the first year, and these savings will grow at the rate of 3 per cent per year indefinitely. The firm has a debt/equity ratio of 5.0, a cost of equity of 12 per cent, and an after-tax cost of debt of 6 per cent. The cost-saving proposal is closely related to the firm's core business, so it is viewed as having the same risks as the overall firm. Under what circumstances should the firm take on the project?

16 · Calculating flotation costs

Bud Surfskis Pty Ltd needs $600,000 for a new storage facility. Bud's target capital structure is 60 per cent equity, 40 per cent debt. The flotation cost for new equity is 12 per cent, but the flotation cost for debt is only 3 per cent. Phil Bud, the CEO, has decided to fund the new facility by borrowing the money since the flotation cost is less and the needed amount is relatively small.

a   What do you think about the rationale behind borrowing the entire amount?
b   What is Bud's weighted average flotation cost?
c   What is the true cost of the storage facility if flotation costs are included?

17 · Calculating WACC

Calculate the weighted average cost of capital for the Frazer Sitcom Company Ltd, using the following information: The company has $10 million of debt outstanding at book value. The debt is trading in the market at 90 per cent of book value. The yield to maturity at current market prices is 12 per cent. The 10 million shares of Sitcom are selling at $2. The cost of equity is 19 per cent, and the tax rate is 30 per cent.

18 · Flotation costs and NPV

The Showerarm Corporation Pty Ltd manufactures luxury plumbing supplies. It is currently at its target debt/equity ratio of 0.40. It is considering building a new $15 million manufacturing facility. This new plant is expected to generate after-tax cash flows of $3 million per year forever.

There are two financing options:

a   A new issue of ordinary shares. The flotation costs of the new share issue would be about 12 per cent of the amount raised. The required return on the company's new equity is 20 per cent.
b   A new issue of 30-year notes. The flotation costs of the new debt would be 4 per cent of the proceeds. The company can raise new debt at 10 per cent.

What is the NPV of the new plant? Assume a 30 per cent tax rate.

19 · Tax shields

In the United States when junk bonds were a real problem, legislation was proposed that would limit the deductibility of interest paid on so-called junk bonds when the bonds were issued to pay for the takeover of a corporation by another group (such bonds generally have relatively high coupon rates). What do you think is the reasoning behind the proposal?

20 · Flotation costs and NPV

The Tim Toys Company Ltd is contemplating a $20 million expansion project in its rubber toys division. It has forecast after-tax cash flows for the project of $8 million per year in perpetuity. The cost of debt capital for Tim Toys is 10 per cent, and its cost of equity capital is 20 per cent. The tax rate is 30 per cent. Tim Terrific, the company's chief financial officer, has come up with two financing options:

1   A $20 million issue of 10-year debt at 10 per cent interest. The issue costs would be 1 per cent of the amount raised.
2   A $20 million issue of ordinary shares. The issue costs of the shares would be 15 per cent of the amount raised.

The target debt/equity ratio of Tim Toys is 2. The expansion project will have about the same risk as the existing business.

Mr Terrific has advised the company to go ahead with the new project and to use debt because debt is cheaper and the issue cost will be less with debt.

a   Is Mr Terrific correct?
b   What is the NPV of the new project?

21 · Capital structure weights and WACC

The Makeacent Company Ltd has compiled the following information on its financing costs:

Type of financing	Book value	Market value	Before tax cost
Long-term debt	$6m	$2m	10%
Secured debt	$6m	$6m	8%
Paid-up capital	$12m	$16m	15%
	$24m	$24m	

The Makeacent Company is in a 30 per cent tax bracket and has a target debt/equity ratio of 100 per cent. It wants to keep its short-term debt at about the same level as its long-term debt (in market value terms).

a   Calculate the weighted average cost of capital for the Makeacent Company using (i) book value weights, (ii) market value weights, and (iii) target weights.

b   Explain the difference in the results obtained in part (a). What are the correct weights to use in the weighted average cost of capital?

22 · WACC and short-term debt

This is a challenge problem. In the previous problem, suppose that the secured debt was secured by floor stock, that is, supplies used in the business. Since this debt arises in the ordinary course of business, management feels that the cost of capital for this secured debt is simply equal to the WACC. Using the target weights, what is Makeacent's WACC in this case?

23 · WACC

This is a challenge problem. An examination of the 200X statement of financial position of Bouncing Balls Limited reveals the following information:

Paid-up capital (10,000 shares)	$10,000
Retained earnings	2,000
10% Debentures (maturing 200X+8)	3,000
12% Preference capital (1000 shares)	1,000
Long-term bank loan	2,000
Trade creditors	4,000

Note: Assume the year is 200X as above.

Further investigations reveal that:

a   The debentures were sold in 200X–7 giving the company net proceeds of $98. The current price of the debentures is $95, though an issue of similar currency if sold now would net the company $92.

b   The preference shares were issued in 200X–5 to net the company $0.95. A similar issue would now net the company $0.90.

c   The normal market price of an ordinary share is $4.

d   The firm paid $4,000 in dividends this year, which is 50 per cent of earnings. It is expected that earnings will grow at the annual rate of 5 per cent with the maintenance of the 50 per cent payout ratio.

e   It is anticipated that to float a new issue the firm would have to offer a discount of 30 cents per share below the normal market price. The cost of such an issue is expected to be 20 cents per share.

f   The firm's financial manager (Ms Bouncer) believes in an opportunity cost concept of retained earnings.

g   The marginal corporate tax rate is 30 per cent and the average marginal tax rate of the ordinary shareholders is estimated at 35 per cent.

h   The current bank loan is 9 per cent per annum. The loan revealed in the company's current financial statements is regarded as being at its normal level.

i   At present, trade creditors are at an abnormally high level. Past experience has shown that Bouncing Balls Limited consistently makes use of approximately $2,000 of trade credit on a revolving basis. It is anticipated that the current level of trade credit is transitory and that this item will fall in the near future to its previous levels.

j   Although they attempt to pay trade creditors within the period allowable for discount, Ms Bouncer sometimes neglects to check the work of her credit manager (Mr Thug) so that inadvertently, on average, Bouncing Balls forfeits $20 cash in discounts each year.

Calculate the conventional weighted average cost of capital. The approximation formula for calculation of the cost of debt may be used.

24 · Cost of equity

The equity of Woollies Retailing has a beta of 0.8. Its last dividend was 12 cents per share and a share is currently selling for $4.50. The earnings of Woollies is expected to grow at 8 per cent indefinitely. Woollies maintains a constant payout ratio. The risk-free rate is 6 per cent and the expected return on the market is twice that percentage.

Calculate the cost of equity using the CAPM and the dividend growth model. Comment on the results.

25 · WACC

Refer to Problem 24. If the cost of Woollies' debt is 9 per cent, the target debt–equity ratio is 0.5 and the current tax rate is 30 per cent, what is the weighted average cost of capital for Woollies?

26 · Flotation costs

Refer to Problems 24 and 25. Woollies is seeking to raise $30 million to establish a new outlet on Bunya Mountain. It intends to maintain its target capital ratio. The flotation cost for an equity raising is 16 per cent. Debt is much cheaper and the cost is only 2 per cent. How much will Woollies have to raise in order to establish the new outlet?

CHAPTER 19

Dividends
and dividend policy

Objective

The aim of this chapter is to make the reader aware of the economic consequences of dividend payments by corporations. The imputation tax system is explained and its effect on shareholder returns is highlighted. It will be shown that dividend policies are driven by the influences of the taxation system and the demands of business for expansion capital. The nature of share buy-back schemes, dividend reinvestment schemes, bonus shares, share splits and employee ownership plans are explained.

Study tips ▷ Dividends are relevant but dividend policy is irrelevant. How can this statement be true? This chapter explains this issue and the arguments need to be read closely. The dividend imputation system is introduced and we have all heard about how complex the Australian tax system is. There is no attempt to convert you into a taxation expert, at least as far as dividend imputation goes, but if you follow and understand the examples, you will have an excellent foundation for becoming a capable financial planner.

Introduction ▷ Dividend policy is an important subject in corporate finance, and dividends are a major cash outlay for many corporations. In 2001 alone, for example, firms listed on the Australian Stock Exchange paid out in excess of $36 billion in dividends. This represented an average dividend yield of 3.3 per cent.

At first glance, it may seem obvious that a firm would always want to give as much as possible back to its shareholders by paying dividends. It might seem equally obvious, however, that a firm can always invest the money for its shareholders instead of paying it out. The heart of the dividend policy question is just this: Should the firm pay out

money to its shareholders, or should the firm take that money and invest it for its shareholders?

It may seem surprising, but much research and economic logic suggest that dividend policy does not matter. In fact, it turns out that the dividend policy issue is much like the capital structure question. The important elements are not difficult to identify, but the interactions between those elements are complex and no easy answer exists.

Dividend policy is controversial. Many implausible reasons are given for why dividend policy might be important, and many of the claims made about dividend policy are economically illogical. Even so, in the real world of corporate finance, determining the most appropriate dividend policy is considered an important issue. It could be that financial managers who worry about dividend policy are wasting time, but it could also be true that we are missing something important in our discussions.

In part, all discussions of dividends are plagued by the 'two-handed lawyer' problem. President Truman, while discussing the legal implications of a possible presidential decision, asked his staff to set up a meeting with a lawyer. Supposedly Mr Truman said, 'But I do not want one of those two-handed lawyers.' When asked what a two-handed lawyer was, he replied, 'You know, a lawyer who says, on the one hand I recommend you do so and so because of the following reasons, but on the other hand I recommend that you do not do it because of these other reasons.'

Unfortunately, any sensible treatment of dividend policy will appear to be written by a two-handed lawyer (or, in fairness, several two-handed financial economists). On the one hand, there are many good reasons for corporations to pay high dividends, but, on the other hand, there are also many good reasons to pay low dividends.

We will cover three broad topics that relate to dividends and dividend policy in this chapter. First, we describe the various kinds of dividend and how dividends are paid. Second, we consider an idealised case in which dividend policy does not matter. We then discuss the limitations of this case and present some real-world arguments for both high and low dividend payouts. Finally, we conclude the chapter by looking at some strategies that corporations might employ to implement a dividend policy, and we discuss share repurchases as an alternative to dividends.

19.1 Cash dividends and dividend payment

dividend

payment made out of a firm's earnings to its owners, usually in the form of cash

distribution

payment made by a firm to its owners from sources other than current or accumulated earnings

The term **dividend** usually refers to cash paid out of earnings. If a payment is made from sources other than current or accumulated retained earnings, the term **distribution** rather than dividend is used. However, it is acceptable to refer to a distribution from earnings as a dividend and a distribution from capital as a liquidating dividend. More generally, any direct payment by the corporation to the shareholders may be considered a dividend or a part of dividend policy.

Dividends come in several different forms. The basic types of cash dividend are:

1 Regular cash dividends
2 Extra dividends
3 Special dividends
4 Liquidating dividends.

Later in the chapter, we discuss dividends that are paid in shares instead of cash, and we also consider an alternative to cash dividends, share repurchase.

Cash dividends

regular cash dividend

cash payment made by a firm to its owners in the normal course of business, usually made twice a year (interim and final)

The most common type of dividend is a cash dividend. Commonly, public companies pay **regular cash dividends** twice a year. This takes the form of an interim dividend and a final dividend. As the name suggests, these are cash payments made directly to shareholders, and they are made in the regular course of business. In other words, management sees nothing unusual about the dividend and no reason why it will not be continued.

Sometimes firms will pay a regular cash dividend and an *extra cash dividend*. By calling part of the payment 'extra', management is indicating that it may or may not be repeated in the future. A *special dividend* is similar, but the name usually indicates that the dividend is viewed as a truly unusual or one-time event and will not be repeated. Finally, a *liquidating dividend* usually means that some or all of the business has been liquidated; that is, sold off.

However it is labelled, a cash dividend payment reduces corporate cash and retained earnings, except in the case of a liquidating dividend (where paid-in capital may be reduced).

Standard method of cash dividend payment

The decision to pay a dividend rests in the hands of the board of directors of the organisation. When a dividend has been declared, it becomes a debt of the firm and cannot be rescinded easily. Sometime after it has been declared, a dividend is distributed to all shareholders as of some specific date.

Commonly, the amount of the cash dividend is expressed in terms of the dollars per share (*dividends per share*). As we have seen in other chapters, it is also expressed as a percentage of the market price (the *dividend yield*) or as a percentage of earnings per share (the *dividend payout*).

declaration date

date on which the board of directors passes a resolution to pay a dividend

Dividend payment: A chronology

The mechanics of a dividend payment can be illustrated by the example in Figure 19.1 and the following description:

1 **Declaration date**. On 15 May, the board of directors passes a resolution to pay a dividend of $1 per share on 16 June to all holders of record as of 30 May.

ex-dividend date

date seven business days before the date of record, establishing those individuals entitled to a dividend

2 **Ex-dividend date**. To make sure that dividend cheques go to the right people, brokerage firms and stock exchanges establish an ex-dividend date. This date is seven

business days before the date of record (discussed next). If you buy the shares before this date, then you are entitled to the dividend. If you buy on this date or after, then the previous owner will get it.

The ex-dividend date convention removes any ambiguity about who is entitled to the dividend. Since the dividend is valuable, the share price will be affected when it goes 'ex'. We examine this effect below.

In Figure 19.1, Wednesday 21 May is the ex-dividend date. Before this date, the share is said to trade 'with dividend' or 'cum dividend'. Afterwards, the share trades 'ex-dividend'.

3 **Date of record.** Based on its records, the corporation prepares a list on 30 May of all individuals believed to be shareholders as of this date. These are the holders of record and 30 May is the date of record. The word 'believed' is important here. If you buy the share just before this date, the company's records may not reflect that fact because of mailing or other delays. Without some modification, some of the dividend cheques will get mailed to the wrong people. This is the reason for the ex-dividend day convention.

date of record
date on which holders of record are designated to receive a dividend

4 **Date of payment.** The dividend cheques are mailed on 16 June.

date of payment
date that the dividend cheques are mailed

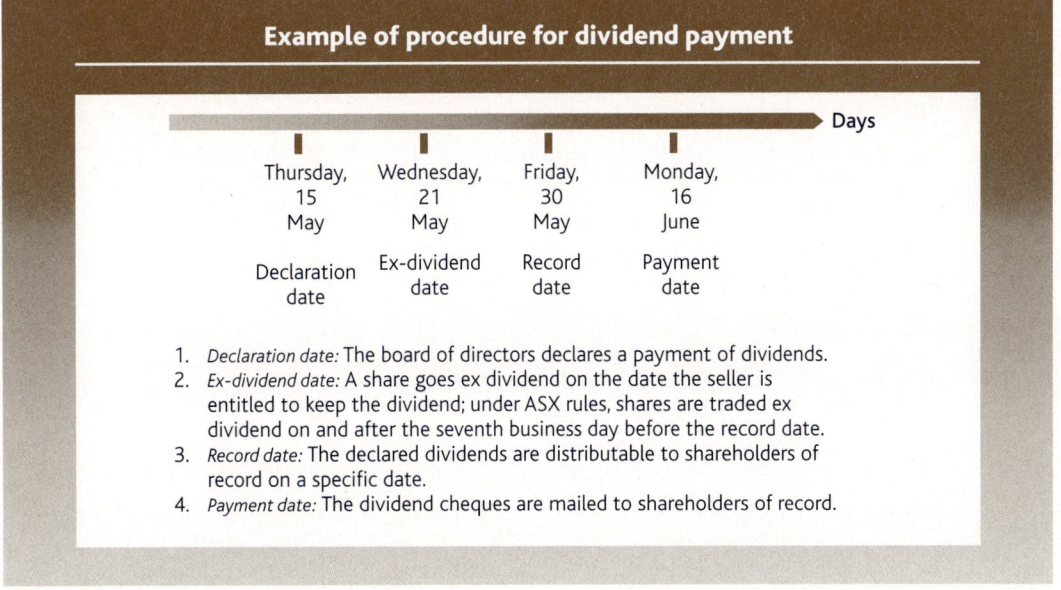

Example of procedure for dividend payment

FIGURE 19.1

Days

Thursday, 15 May	Wednesday, 21 May	Friday, 30 May	Monday, 16 June
Declaration date	Ex-dividend date	Record date	Payment date

1. *Declaration date:* The board of directors declares a payment of dividends.
2. *Ex-dividend date:* A share goes ex dividend on the date the seller is entitled to keep the dividend; under ASX rules, shares are traded ex dividend on and after the seventh business day before the record date.
3. *Record date:* The declared dividends are distributable to shareholders of record on a specific date.
4. *Payment date:* The dividend cheques are mailed to shareholders of record.

More on the ex-dividend date

The ex-dividend date is important and is a common source of confusion. We examine what happens to the share when it goes ex, meaning that the ex-dividend date arrives. To illustrate, suppose we have a share that sells for $10. The board of directors declares a dividend of $1 per share, and the record date is Thursday, 14 June. Based on our discussion above, we know that the ex date will be seven business (not calendar) days earlier on Tuesday, 5 June.

If you buy the share on Monday, 4 June, right as the market closes, you will get the $1 dividend because the share is trading cum dividend. If you wait and buy it right as the market opens on Tuesday, you will not get the $1 dividend. What will happen to the value of the share overnight?

If you think about it, the share is obviously worth about $1 less on Tuesday morning, so its price will drop by this amount between close of business on Monday and the Tuesday opening. In general, we expect that the value of a share will go down by about the dividend amount when the share goes ex-dividend. The key word here is 'about'. Depending upon the ability of the company to pass on dividend imputation credits to shareholders, the dividend may be taxed. The actual price drop might be closer to some measure of the after-tax value of the dividend. Determining this value is complicated because of the different tax rates and tax rules that apply for different buyers.

The series of events described here is illustrated in Figure 19.2.

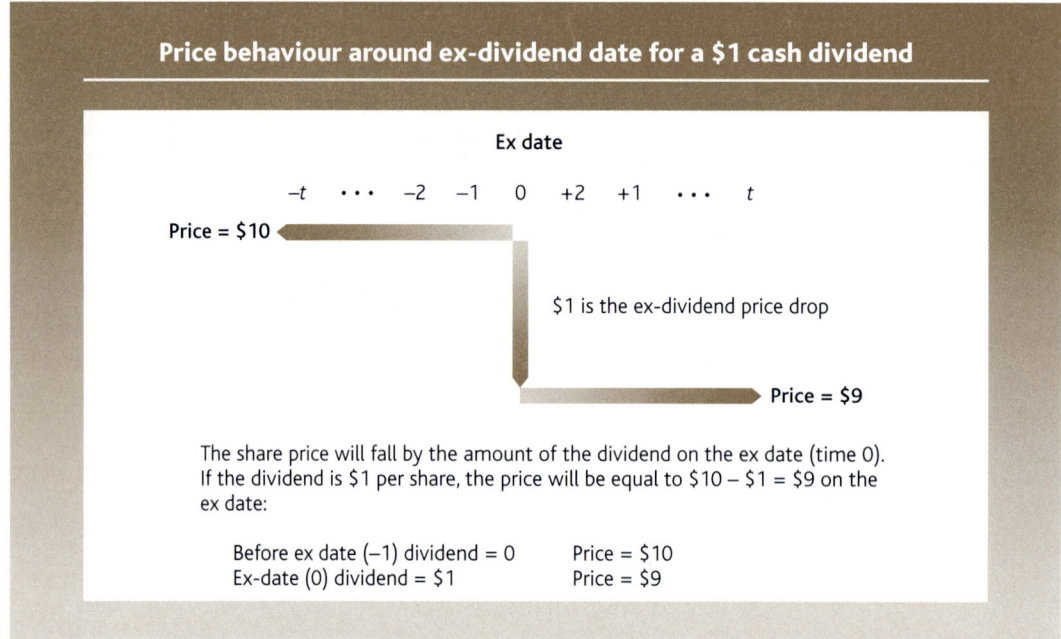

FIGURE 19.2

Price behaviour around ex-dividend date for a $1 cash dividend

Ex date

−t · · · −2 −1 0 +2 +1 · · · t

Price = $10

$1 is the ex-dividend price drop

Price = $9

The share price will fall by the amount of the dividend on the ex date (time 0). If the dividend is $1 per share, the price will be equal to $10 − $1 = $9 on the ex date:

Before ex date (−1) dividend = 0   Price = $10
Ex-date (0) dividend = $1   Price = $9

EXAMPLE 19.1   **'Ex' marks the day**

The board of directors of Club Reptile Ltd has declared a dividend of $0.25 per share on Thursday, 13 April, payable to shareholders of record as of Tuesday, 9 May. Stephen Winar buys 100 shares of Coastal on Tuesday, 2 May, for $15 per share. What is the ex date? Describe the events that will occur with regard to the cash dividend and the share price.

The ex date is *seven business days* before the date of record, Tuesday, 9 May, so the share will go ex on Friday, 28 April (note there are two weekends in the period so we have to go back 11 days from the record date to allow seven business days). Stephen buys the share on Tuesday, 2 May, so Stephen has purchased the share ex dividend. In other words, Stephen will not receive any dividends. The cheque will be mailed to the old shareholder on Tuesday, 30 May. When the share went ex on Friday, its value dropped overnight by about $0.25 per share.

Concept questions

19.1a *What are the different types of cash dividend?*
19.1b *What are the mechanics of the cash dividend payment?*
19.1c *How should the price of a share change when it goes ex dividend?*

19.2 ■ Does dividend policy matter?

To decide whether or not dividend policy matters, we first have to define what we mean by dividend *policy*. All other things being the same, of course dividends matter. Dividends are paid in cash, and cash is something that everybody likes. The question we will be discussing here is whether the firm should pay out cash now or invest the cash and pay it out later. Dividend policy, therefore, is the time pattern of dividend payout. In particular, should the firm pay out a large percentage of its earnings now or a small (or even zero) percentage? This is the dividend policy question.

An illustration of the irrelevance of dividend policy

A powerful argument can be made that dividend policy does not matter. We illustrate this by considering the simple case of Sports Stadium Company Ltd. Sports is an all-equity firm that has existed for 10 years. The current financial managers plan to dissolve the firm in two years. The total cash flows that the firm will generate, including the proceeds from liquidation, are $10,000 in each of the next two years.

Current policy: Dividends set equal to cash flow

At the present time, dividends at each date are set equal to the cash flow of $10,000. There are 100 shares outstanding, so the dividend per share will be $100. In Chapter 6, we showed that the value of the share is equal to the present value of the future dividends. Assuming a 10 per cent required return, the value of a share today, P_0, is:

$$P_0 = D_1/(1 + R)^1 + D_2/(1 + R)^2$$
$$= \$100/1.10 + \$100/1.10^2 = \$173.55$$

The firm as a whole is thus worth $100 \times \$173.55 = \$17,355$.

Several members of the board of Sports have expressed dissatisfaction with the current dividend policy and have asked you to analyse an alternative policy.

Alternative policy: Initial dividend is greater than cash flow

Another policy is for the firm to pay a dividend of $110 per share on the first date, which is, of course, a total dividend of $11,000. Because the cash flow is only $10,000, an extra $1,000 must somehow be raised. One way to do it is to issue $1,000 of debt or shares at date 1. Assume that shares are issued. The new shareholders will desire enough cash flow at date 2 so that they earn the required 10 per cent return on their date 1 investment.[1]

What is the value of the firm with this new dividend policy? The new shareholders invest $1,000. They require a 10 per cent return, so they will demand $1,000 \times 1.10 = \$1,100$ of the date 2 cash flow, leaving only $8,900 to the old shareholders. The dividends to the old shareholders will be:

	Date 1	Date 2
Aggregate dividends due to old shareholders	$11,000	$8,900
Dividends per share	110	89

The present value of the dividends per share is therefore:

$$P_0 = \$110/1.10 + \$89/1.10^2$$
$$= \$173.55$$

This is the same value we had before.

The value of the shares is not affected by this switch in dividend policy, even though we had to sell some new shares just to finance the dividend. In fact, no matter what pattern of dividend payout the firm chooses, the value of the shares will always be the same in this example. In other words, for the Sports Company, dividend policy makes no difference. The reason is simple: any increase in a dividend at some point in time is exactly offset by a decrease somewhere else, so the net effect, once we account for time value, is zero.

Home-made dividends

There is an alternative and perhaps more intuitively appealing explanation about why dividend policy does not matter in our example. Suppose that an individual investor, Margaret Muscle, prefers dividends per share of $100 at both dates 1 and 2. Would she be disappointed when informed that the firm's management is adopting the alternative dividend policy (dividends of $110 and $89 on the two dates, respectively)? Not necessarily, because she could easily reinvest the $10 of unneeded funds received on date 1 by buying some more Sports shares. At 10 per cent, this investment will grow to $11 at date 2. Thus, she would receive her desired net cash flow of $110 − 10 = $100 at date 1 and $89 + 11 = $100 at date 2.

Conversely, imagine another investor, Larry Lazabout, who prefers $110 of cash flow at date 1 and $89 of cash flow at date 2, but finds that management will pay dividends of $100 at both dates 1 and 2. This investor can simply sell $10 worth of shares to boost his total cash at date 1 to $110. Because this investment returns 10 per cent, Larry Lazabout gives up $11 at date 2 ($10 × 1.1), leaving him with $100 − 11 = $89.

Our two investors are able to transform the company's dividend policy into a different policy by buying or selling on their own. The result is that investors are able to create **home-made dividends**. This means that dissatisfied shareholders can alter the firm's dividend policy to suit themselves. As a result, there is no particular advantage to any one dividend policy that the firm might choose.

Many corporations actually assist their shareholders in creating home-made dividend policies by offering *automatic dividend reinvestment plans* (ADPs or DRIPs). As the name suggests, with such a plan shareholders have the option of automatically reinvesting some or all of their cash dividend in shares. In some cases, they actually receive a discount on the shares, thereby making such a plan very attractive.

A test

Our discussion up to this point can be summarised by considering the following true/false test questions:

1 True or false: Dividends are irrelevant.
2 True or false: Dividend policy is irrelevant.

The first statement is surely false, and the reason follows from commonsense. Clearly, investors prefer higher dividends to lower dividends at any single date if the dividend level is held constant at every other date. To be more precise regarding the first question, if the dividend per share at a given date is raised while the dividend per share at each other date is held constant, the share price will rise. The reason is that the present value of the future dividends must go up if this occurs. This action can be accomplished by management decisions that improve productivity, increase tax savings, strengthen product marketing, or otherwise improve cash flow.

The second statement is true, at least in the simple case we have been examining. Dividend policy by itself cannot raise the dividend at one date while keeping it the same at all other dates. Rather, dividend policy merely establishes the trade-off between dividends at

home-made
dividend

idea that individual
investors can undo
corporate dividend
policy by reinvesting
dividends or selling
shares

one date and dividends at another date. Once we allow for time value, the present value of the dividend stream is unchanged. Thus, in this simple world, dividend policy does not matter, because managers choosing either to raise or to lower the current dividend do not affect the current value of their firm. However, we have ignored several real-world factors that might lead us to change our minds; we pursue some of these in subsequent sections.

Concept questions

19.2a *How can an investor create a home-made dividend?*
19.2b *Are dividends irrelevant?*

19.3 ⬛ Real-world factors favouring a low payout

The example we used to illustrate the irrelevance of dividend policy ignored taxes and flotation costs. In this section, we will see that these factors might lead us to prefer a low-dividend payout.

Taxes

Australian tax laws are complex and the tax treatment of dividends paid by companies has consistently been the subject of debate and controversy. At the heart of discussions, prior to September 1985, was the issue of double taxation. Company profits were taxed and this was followed by taxation of dividends in the hands of shareholders. The only relief, until the September 1985 tax reform, had been that, under section 46 of the *Income Tax Assessment Act*, company shareholders were allowed rebates of tax paid on dividend income. From September 1985 a dividend imputation system was introduced[2] which gave some relief from the double taxation of company profits. As well as altering the taxation relating to dividends the 1985 changes affected the taxation of capital gains. Prior to 20 September 1985 capital gains tax applied to a narrow range of situations.[3] September 1985 saw the general imposition of capital gains taxation. Table 19.1 summarises the types of assets on which capital gains tax is levied at the marginal tax rate of the taxpayer. From 1 October 1999 the capital gains tax laws were changed so that one half of any gain (for an individual) is exempt from capital gains tax.

TABLE 19.1

Application of capital gains tax
Assets caught
Capital assets purchased, constructed or acquired by way of a gift or inheritance after 19 September 1985.
Specified personal-use assets purchased, constructed or acquired by way of a gift or inheritance after 19 September 1985 (e.g., works of art, stamp collections, jewellery—items expected to appreciate).
Assets exempted
Capital assets purchased, constructed (or construction begun), or acquired before 20 September 1985.
Specified personal-use assets purchased, constructed, or acquired before 20 September 1985.
Personal-use assets such as furniture.   *(continued)*

TABLE 19.1	Application of capital gains tax (*continued*)

Principal residence of a family unit and reasonable curtilage.

Motor vehicles (disposals).

Superannuation and life insurance policy proceeds.

Concessions in application

Capital gain can be rolled over where capital assets are subject to compulsory acquisition or loss or destruction and for certain business organisations.

Bodies currently exempt from income tax will also be exempt from capital gains tax. They include Commonwealth and State Governments and some of their agencies, local government bodies, religious and charitable institutions, and approved deposit funds.

Imputation

imputation system

the imputation system results in individuals receiving a tax credit for the tax actually paid by the company

The **imputation system** was designed to remove the problem of double taxation for resident individual taxpayers. The system results in the individual receiving a credit (imputation) for the tax actually paid by the company. Examples of shareholders' imputed tax situations are presented in Table 19.2.

	Examples of imputed tax credits			

Shareholders' level of taxable income	$6,001 to 20,000	$20,001 to 50,000	$50,001 to 60,000	$60,000 +
Marginal tax rate (1 July 2002)	17%	30%	42%	47%
Corporate tax	$30	$30	$30	$30
Dividend paid	$70	$70	$70	$70
Taxpayer's additional assessable income*	$100	$100	$100	$100
Tax on assessable income	$17	$30	$42	$47
Credit for company tax	$30	$30	$30	$30
Net credit (payment)	$13	nil	($12)	($17)
Tax to be paid on dividends	($13) **	nil	$12	$17

* This amount is calculated by 'grossing up' the dividend received. The dividend is divided by one minus the corporate tax rate as: $70/(1 − 0.3) = $100.

** From 1 July 2000 taxpayers can receive tax refunds for credits created by excess imputation credits; prior to this date the excess credits were lost.

The method of calculating the assessable dividend income of the taxpayer is to regard the income of the company as falling directly into the shareholder's hands. The shareholder who receives a dividend of $70 would be regarded as earning assessable dividend income of $100 (the dividend of $70 plus the $30 tax paid by the company).

Consider the situation of a shareholder who receives a dividend of $70 and has taxable income at the $6,001 to $20,000 level. The effect is that no personal tax is collected from the taxpayer on the dividend income and a net credit can be set off against tax on other income. From 1 July 2000 the credit can be collected as a tax refund—prior to that date it was lost. The imputation credit available for the resident individual taxpayer must have been matched by a payment of a corresponding amount of tax by the company. Therefore it is necessary for companies to clearly identify dividends that are paid out of profits on which tax has been levied. These dividends are called **franked dividends**.

The imputation credit can be offset against income tax on the income of shareholders, whether the income is from dividends or other sources. The imputation system affects only resident individual taxpayers. Company and non-resident shareholders do not benefit from the system.

For individual shareholders with other income sources the effective tax rates on dividend income are lower than the tax rates on capital gains. Consider the case of an individual earning in excess of $60,000 and incurring a marginal tax rate of 47 per cent. Dividend income will result in a marginal tax rate on the income equal to the marginal tax rate of the individual minus the tax rate of the company (that is $47\% - 30\% = 17\%$). As only half of the capital gains will be taxed, the effective rate is 23.5 per cent. The tax on the capital gain can be deferred until the share is sold. This will lower the effective tax rate because the present value of the tax is less. For example, assume that the individual's expected rate of return is 12 per cent; the question as to how long the capital gain has to be deferred may be presented as:

$$17\% = 23.5\%/(1.12)^n$$
$$(1.12)^n = 1.3824$$
$$n = 2.858 \text{ years}$$

The benefit of dividend imputation does not necessarily mean there should be a policy of paying all funds out as dividends. Consider a firm that has four shareholders with equal holdings. The firm has earned taxable income of $4,000 so that:

Taxable income	$4,000
Tax at 30%	1,200
Available for dividends	$2,800

Each shareholder will receive a fully franked dividend of $700. Table 19.3 provides details of the financial position of the four shareholders.

Example of dividend effects on shareholders				
	Shareholder			
	A	B	C	D
Without dividend				
Cash income	$5,000	$15,000	$40,000	$61,000
Tax payable*	nil	2,550	12,000	28,670
Net cash flow (1)	$5,000	$12,450	$28,000	$32,330
				(continued)

TABLE 19.3

franked dividends
dividends that are paid out of profits on which tax has been levied

TABLE
19.3

Example of dividend effects on shareholders (*continued*)

	Shareholder			
	A	B	C	D
With dividend				
Cash income	$5,000	$15,000	$40,000	$61,000
Assessable dividend income**	1,000	1,000	1,000	1,000
Total assessable income	$6,000	$16,000	$41,000	$62,000
Tax payable*	nil	$ 2,720	$12,300	$29,140
Dividend tax credits	$ 300	300	300	300
Net tax payable	($ 300)	$ 2,420	$12,000	$28,840
Cash income	$5,000	$15,000	$40,000	$61,000
Plus Dividend	700	700	700	700
	$5,700	$15,700	$40,700	$61,700
Less (plus) Tax	(300)	2,420	12,000	28,840
Net cash flow (2)	$6,000	$13,280	$28,700	$32,860
Additional cash flow from dividend	$1,000	$ 830	$ 700	$ 530

* The tax payable has been derived using the rates shown in Table 19.2: 0% (A), 17% (B), 30% (C), 47% (D).
** The dividend ($700) plus the proportion of tax paid by the company on the profits that provided the funds for the dividend ($1,200/4 = $300).

The last line of Table 19.3 shows that the dividend will result in a different cash flow value for each shareholder. The different cash flows are a combination of the dividend plus the difference between the taxation paid by the company on the dividend and the personal tax that is levied on the imputed dividend. The calculation is:

	Company tax paid – personal tax	**+ Dividend**	
For Shareholder A	Tax refund of $300	+ $700	= $1,000
For Shareholder B	$300 – 17% of $1,000	+ $700	= $830
For Shareholder C	$300 – 30% of $1,000	+ $700	= $700
For Shareholder D	$300 – 47% of $1,000	+ $700	= $530

Obviously the dividend has a different value for the shareholders, but does this answer the question whether the dividend should be paid? The answer depends upon what effect keeping the funds has on the value of the firm. If the firm keeps the dividend and it can use the money in profitable investments, the value of the firm must increase. In order that shareholders may use the funds generated by the increase in value, it will be necessary for them to sell shares. Capital gains tax may have to be paid on any profit arising from the sale. For example, if keeping the fund increased the value of the firm by only $2,800, all the shareholders would prefer the dividend. This is because each shareholding will increase by $700 but when it is realised capital gains tax will have to be paid on $350 (half of $700). Readers may work through a table similar to 19.3 to show that the net cash flow if we substitute the capital gain for the dividend is:

	Net cash flow	Comparison to dividend payment
Shareholder A	$ 5,700.00	less by $300.00
Shareholder B	$13,090.00	less by $189.50
Shareholder C	$28,595.00	less by $105.00
Shareholder D	$32,865.50	less by $5.50

This simple example highlights the most important consideration in the decision on dividend policy: What can the firm can do with the funds if it retains them? Will holding the funds in internal projects enhance the value of the firm? The objective of the firm is to increase the value of the owners' shares. In some situations shareholder tax rates will make higher franked dividends very attractive. In other shareholder cases, it will be preferred if the company does not pay a dividend. The optimal dividend policy for the firm will be determined by the market interaction of all these different shareholder situations.

In a competitive market situation the dividend policy of the firm does not matter. The important determination is the investment program of the firm. Once this program is determined it can be financed internally by withholding dividends or externally through a share issue or by borrowing. If the company feels it has to pay a dividend, and funds are not available from operations to finance investment and pay the dividend, it can make a share issue or it can borrow to cover the investment.

Cost of issuing new shares

In the argument that dividend policy does not matter, we saw that the firm could sell some new shares if necessary to pay a dividend. As we mentioned in Chapter 17, selling new shares can be very expensive. If we include flotation costs in our argument, then we will find that the value of the firm decreases if we sell new shares.

More generally, imagine two firms that are identical in every way except that one pays out a greater percentage of its cash flow in the form of dividends. Since the other firm ploughs back more, its equity grows faster. If these two firms are to remain identical, then the one with the higher payout will have to sell some shares periodically to catch up. Since this is expensive, a firm might be inclined to have a low payout.

Dividend restrictions

In some cases, a corporation may face restrictions on its ability to pay dividends. For example, as we discussed in Chapter 15, a common feature of a debenture trust deed is a covenant prohibiting dividend payments above some level.

Concept questions

19.3a *What are the tax benefits of high dividends?*
19.3b *Why do flotation costs favour a low payout?*

19.4 Real-world factors favouring a high payout

In this section, we consider reasons why a firm might pay its shareholders higher dividends even if it means that the firm must issue more shares to finance the dividend payments.

In a classic textbook, Graham, Dodd and Cottle (1962) argued that firms should generally have high-dividend payouts because:

1. 'The discounted value of near dividends is higher than the present worth of distant dividends.'
2. Between 'two companies with the same general earning power and same general position in an industry, the one paying the larger dividend will almost always sell at a higher price'.[4]

Two factors favouring a high-dividend payout have been mentioned frequently by proponents of this view: the desire for current income and the resolution of uncertainty.

Desire for current income

It has been argued that many individuals desire current income. The classic example is the group of retired people and others living on a fixed income, the proverbial 'widows and orphans'. It is argued that this group is willing to pay a premium to get a higher dividend yield. If this is true, then it lends support to the second claim by Graham, Dodd and Cottle.

It is easy to see, however, that this argument is not relevant in our simple case. An individual preferring high current cash flow but holding low dividend securities could easily sell off shares to provide the necessary funds. Similarly, an individual desiring a low current cash flow but holding high dividend securities can just reinvest the dividend. This is just our home-made dividend argument again. Thus, in a world of no transaction costs, a high current dividend policy would be of no value to the shareholder.

The current income argument may have relevance in the real world. Here the sale of low dividend shares would involve brokerage fees and other transaction costs. Such a sale may also trigger capital gains taxes. These direct cash expenses could be avoided by an investment in high-dividend securities. In addition, the expenditure of the shareholder's own time when selling securities and the natural (but not necessarily rational) fear of consuming out of principal might further lead many investors to buy high-dividend securities.

Even so, to put this argument in perspective, it should be remembered that financial intermediaries such as mutual funds can (and do) perform these 'repackaging' transactions for individuals at very low cost. Such intermediaries could buy low-dividend shares, and, by a controlled policy of realising gains, they could pay their investors at a higher rate.

Uncertainty resolution

We have just pointed out that investors with substantial current consumption needs will prefer high current dividends. In another classic treatment, Gordon (1961) argued that a high-dividend policy also benefits shareholders because it resolves uncertainty.[5]

According to Gordon, investors price a security by forecasting and discounting future dividends. Gordon then argues that forecasts of dividends to be received in the distant future have greater uncertainty than do forecasts of near-term dividends. Because investors dislike uncertainty, the share price should be low for those companies that pay small dividends now in order to remit higher dividends at later dates.

Gordon's argument is essentially a 'bird-in-hand' story. A $1 dividend in a shareholder's pocket is somehow worth more than that same $1 in a bank account held by the company. By now, you should see the problem with this argument. A shareholder can create a bird in hand very easily just by selling some of the shareholdings. The choice is a current dividend or a current capital gain, not a current dividend or a future dividend.

Tax and legal benefits from high dividends

Earlier, we saw that dividends were taxed favourably for individual investors. This fact is a powerful argument for a high payout. However, there are a number of other investors who do not receive favourable tax treatment from holding high-dividend rather than low-dividend yield securities; for example, retirees who live off their dividends in low or zero tax brackets would not receive any benefits.

Corporate investors have always enjoyed an exemption from paying tax on dividend income. For the corporate investor dividend income is exempt while capital gains are taxed. As a result corporate investors prefer high dividend yield shares with low capital gains. The tax advantage of dividends also leads companies to hold high-yielding shares instead of long-term debt because the interest received from the debt is taxed.

It has been pointed out that investors are attracted to the dividend policy that suits their individual tax situations; however, it is to be noted that many investors do not pay tax or their earnings are taxed at a low rate. This group includes some of the largest investors in the economy, such as superannuation funds, trust funds and endowment funds. Superannuation funds, which comply with specific conditions, are subject to tax at the concessional rate of 15 per cent on their income. These complying funds can take advantage of franking credits in respect of Australian dividends up to 15 per cent of their taxable income, so they need to select their portfolios to provide this level of franked dividend. If a company increases the level of dividend to provide a larger franking credit, it may not advantage this class of shareholders as the excess credits could not be used.

There are some legal reasons that some large institutions favour high-dividend yields. First, institutions such as superannuation funds and trust funds are often set up to manage money for the benefit of others. The managers of such institutions have a *fiduciary responsibility* to invest the money prudently. It has been considered imprudent in courts of law to buy shares in companies with no established dividend record.

Second, institutions such as university endowment funds and trust funds are frequently prohibited from spending any of the principal. Such institutions might therefore prefer high-dividend-yield shares so they have some ability to spend. Like widows and orphans, this group thus prefers current income. Unlike widows and orphans, this group is very large in terms of the number of shares owned.

Other large investors, for example superannuation funds who will have to meet large retiree payouts in 20 or 30 years, would require low current dividend cash flows and large capital gains to meet their future commitments. It can be seen that it is the overall obligations of the large institutional investors that will determine their dividend needs, not just the tax situation.

Concept questions

19.4a *Why might some individual investors favour a high dividend payout?*
19.4b *Why might some institutional investors prefer a high dividend payout?*

19.5 A resolution of real-world factors?

In the previous sections, we presented some factors that favour a low dividend policy and others that favour high dividends. In this section, we discuss two important concepts related to dividends and dividend policy: the information content of dividends and the clientele effect. The first topic illustrates both the importance of dividends in general and the importance of distinguishing between dividends and dividend policy. The second topic suggests that, despite the many real-world considerations we have discussed, the dividend payout ratio may not be as important as we originally imagined.

Information content of dividends

To begin, we quickly review some of our earlier discussion. Our previous discussion has established three different positions on dividends:

1 Based on the home-made dividend argument, dividend policy is irrelevant.
2 Because of the high taxation of some individual investors, a high-dividend policy may be best.
3 Because of new issue costs, a low-dividend policy is best.

If you wanted to decide which of these positions is the right one, an obvious way to get started would be to look at what happens to share prices when companies announce dividend changes. You would find with some consistency that share prices rise when the current dividend is unexpectedly increased, and they generally fall when the dividend is unexpectedly decreased. What does this imply about any of the three positions just stated?

At first glance, the behaviour we describe seems consistent with the second position and inconsistent with the other two. In fact, many writers have argued this. If share prices rise on dividend increases and fall on dividend decreases, then is not the market saying it approves of higher dividends?

Other authors have pointed out that this observation does not really tell us much about dividend policy. Everyone agrees that dividends are important, all other things being equal. Companies only cut dividends with great reluctance. Thus, a dividend cut is often a signal that the firm is in trouble.

More to the point, a dividend cut is usually not a voluntary, planned change in dividend policy. Instead, it usually signals that management does not think that the current dividend policy can be maintained. As a result, expectations of future dividends should generally be revised downward. The present value of expected future dividends falls and so does the share price.

In this case, the share price declines following a dividend cut because future earnings are generally lower, not because the firm changes the percentage of its earnings it will pay out in the form of dividends.

To give a particularly dramatic example, consider what happened to Consolidated Edison (Con Ed), a large United States public utility, in 1974. Faced with poor operating results and problems associated with the OPEC oil embargo, Con Ed announced after the market closed that it was omitting its regular quarterly dividend of 45 cents per share. This was somewhat surprising given Con Ed's size, prominence in the industry, and long dividend history. Also, Con Ed's earnings at that time were sufficient to pay the dividend, at least by some analysts' estimates.

The next morning was not pleasant. Sell orders were so heavy that a market could not be established for several hours. When trading finally got started, the shares opened at about $12 per share, down from $18 the day before. In other words, Con Ed, a very large company, lost about one-third of its market value overnight. As this case illustrates, shareholders can react very negatively to unanticipated cuts in dividends.

In a similar vein, an unexpected increase in the dividend signals good news. Management will raise the dividend only when future earnings, cash flow and general prospects are expected to rise enough so that the dividend will not have to be cut later. A dividend increase is management's signal to the market that the firm is expected to do well. The shares react favourably because expectations of future dividends are revised upwards, not because the firm has increased its payout.

In both these cases, the share price reacts to the dividend change. The reaction can be attributed to changes in the amount of future dividends, not necessarily a change in dividend payout policy. This signal is called the **information content effect** of the dividend. The fact that dividend changes convey information about the firm to the market makes it difficult to interpret the effect of the dividend policy on the firm.

information content effect
the market's reaction to a change in corporate dividend payout

The clientele effect

In our earlier discussion, we saw that some groups have an incentive to pursue low-payout (or zero-payout) shares.[6] Other groups have an incentive to pursue high-payout shares. Companies with high payouts will thus attract one group and low-payout companies will attract another.

These different groups are called *clienteles*, and what we have described is a **clientele effect**. The clientele effect argument states that different groups of investors desire different levels of dividends. When a firm chooses a particular dividend policy, the only effect is to attract a particular clientele. If a firm changes its dividend policy, then it just attracts a different clientele.

clientele effect
argument that stocks attract particular groups based on dividend yield and the resulting tax effects

What we are left with is a simple supply and demand argument. Suppose that 40 per cent of all investors prefer high dividends, but only 20 per cent of the firms pay high dividends. Here the high-dividend firms will be in short supply; thus, their share prices will rise. Consequently, low-dividend firms would find it advantageous to switch policies until 40 per cent of all firms have high payouts. At this point, the dividend market is in equilibrium. Further changes in dividend policy are pointless because all of the clienteles are satisfied. The dividend policy for any individual firm is now irrelevant.

The clientele effect on dividend policy is illustrated by the remarks made by John Childs of Kidder-Peabody (a US investment bank) in the following exchange:[7]

> *Joseph T. Willet*: John, you've been around public utilities for a good many years. Why do you think that utilities have such high dividend payout ratios?
>
> *John Childs*: They're raising dividends so they can raise capital . . . If you take the dividends out of utilities today, you will never sell another share. That's how important it is. In fact, if a few major utilities (with no special problems) cut their dividends, small investors would lose faith in the utility industry and that would finish the sales of utility shares.
>
> *John Childs* (again): What you are trying to do with dividend policy is to enhance and strengthen the natural interest of investors in your company. The type of shareholders you attract will depend on the type of company you are. If you're Genentech, you are going to attract the type of shareholders which have absolutely no interest in dividends. In fact, you would hurt the shares if you paid dividends. On the other hand, you go over to the other extreme such as utilities and yield banks' shares. There the shareholders are extremely interested in dividends, and these dividends have an effect on market price.

To see if you understand the clientele effect, consider the following statement: 'In spite of the theoretical argument that dividend policy is irrelevant or that firms should not pay dividends, many investors like high dividends. Because of this fact, a firm can boost its share price by having a higher dividend payout ratio.' True or false?

The answer is false if clienteles exist. As long as enough high-dividend firms satisfy the dividend-loving investors, a firm will not be able to boost its share price by paying high dividends. An unsatisfied clientele must exist for this to happen, and there is no evidence that this is the case.

Concept questions

19.5a *How does the market react to unexpected dividend changes? What does this tell us about dividends? About dividend policy?*

19.5b *What is a dividend clientele? All things considered, would you expect a risky firm with significant but highly uncertain growth prospects to have a low or high dividend payout?*

 19.6 ## Establishing a dividend policy

How do firms actually determine the level of dividends that they will pay at a particular time? As we have seen, there are good reasons for firms to pay high dividends and there are good reasons for them to pay low dividends.

We know some things about how dividends are paid in practice. Firms do not like to cut dividends. Consider the case of American Telephone and Telegraph Company (AT&T). It has been in business since 1885, and during that time it has never reduced or omitted a dividend. This is remarkable but not unusual.

In this section of our chapter, we discuss a particular dividend policy strategy. In doing so, we emphasise the real-world features of dividend policy. We also analyse an increasingly important alternative to cash dividends: a bonus issue.

 ## In their own words

Fischer Black* on why firms pay dividends

I think investors simply like dividends. They believe that dividends enhance stock value (given the firm's prospects), and they feel uncomfortable spending out of their capital.

We see evidence for this everywhere: Investment advisors and institutions treat a high-yield stock as both attractive and safe, financial analysts value a stock by predicting and discounting its dividends, financial economists study the relation between stock prices and actual dividends, and investors complain about dividend cuts.

What if investors were neutral toward dividends? Investment advisors would tell clients to spend indifferently from income and capital and, if taxable, to avoid income; financial analysts would ignore dividends in valuing stocks; financial economists would treat stock price and the discounted value of dividends as equal, even when stocks are mispriced; and a firm would apologise to its taxable investors when forced by an accumulated earnings tax to pay dividends. This is not what we observe of course.

Furthermore, changing dividends seems a poor way to tell the financial markets about a firm's prospects. Public statements can better detail the firm's prospects and have more impact on both the speaker's and the firm's reputations.

I predict that under current tax rules, dividends will gradually disappear.

* The late **Fischer Black** was a partner at Goldman Sachs & Co., an investment banking firm. Before that he was a professor of finance at MIT. He is one of the fathers of option pricing theory, and widely regarded as one of the pre-eminent financial scholars. He will remain well known for his creative ideas, many of which were dismissed at first only to become part of accepted lore when others finally came to understand them. He is sadly missed by his colleagues.

Residual dividend approach

We noted earlier that firms with higher dividend payouts will have to sell shares more often. As we have seen, such sales are not very common and they can be very expensive. Consistent with this, we will assume that the firm wishes to minimise the need to sell new equity. We will also assume that the firm wishes to maintain its current capital structure.

If a firm wishes to avoid new equity sales, then it will have to rely on internally generated equity to finance new, positive NPV projects.[8] Dividends can only be paid out of what is left over. This leftover is called the residual, and such a dividend policy is called a **residual dividend approach**.

With a residual dividend policy, the firm's objective is to meet its investment needs and maintain its desired debt/equity ratio before paying dividends. To illustrate, imagine that a firm has $1,000 in earnings and a debt/equity ratio of 0.50. Notice that, since the debt/equity ratio is 0.50, the firm has 50 cents in debt for every $1.50 in value. The firm's capital structure is thus $1/3$ debt and $2/3$ equity.

The first step in implementing a residual dividend policy is to determine the amount of funds that can be generated without selling new equity. If the firm reinvests the entire $1,000 and pays no dividend, then equity will increase by $1,000. To keep the debt/equity ratio at 0.50, the firm must borrow an additional $500. The total amount of funds that can be generated without selling new equity is thus $1,000 + 500 = $1,500.

The second step is to decide whether or not a dividend will be paid. To do this, we compare the total amount that can be generated without selling new equity ($1,500 in this case) with planned capital spending. If funds needed exceed funds available, then no dividend is paid. In addition, the firm will have to sell new equity to raise the needed finance or else (more likely) postpone some planned capital spending.

If funds needed are less than funds generated, then a dividend will be paid. The amount of the dividend is the residual; that is, that portion of the earnings that is not needed to finance new projects. For example, suppose we have $900 in planned capital spending. To maintain the firm's capital structure, this $900 must be financed $2/3$ equity and $1/3$ debt. So, the firm will actually borrow $1/3 \times $900 = $300. The firm will spend $2/3 \times $900 = $600 of the $1,000 in equity available. There is a $1,000 - 600 = $400 residual, so the dividend will be $400.

In summary, the firm has after-tax earnings of $1,000. Dividends paid are $400. Retained earnings are $600, and new borrowing totals $300. The firm's debt/equity ratio is unchanged at 0.50.

The relationship between physical investment and dividend payout is presented for six different levels of investment in Table 19.4 and illustrated in Figure 19.3 (overleaf). The first three rows of the table can be discussed together, because in each case no dividends are paid.

residual dividend approach
policy where a firm pays dividends only after meeting its investment needs while maintaining a desired debt-to-equity ratio

Example of dividend policy under the residual approach

TABLE 19.4

Row	(1) After-tax earnings	(2) New investment	(3) Additional debt	(4) Retained earnings	(5) Additional shares	(6) Dividends
1	$1,000	$3,000	$1,000	$1,000	$1,000	$ 0
2	1,000	2,000	667	1,000	333	0
3	1,000	1,500	500	1,000	0	0
4	1,000	1,000	333	667	0	333
5	1,000	500	167	333	0	667
6	1,000	0	0	0	0	1,000

FIGURE
19.3

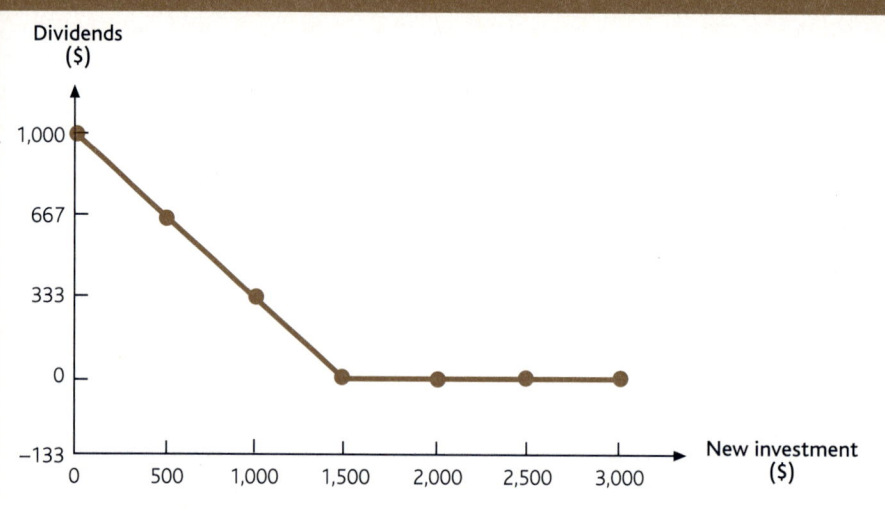

Relationship between dividends and investments in the example of residual dividend policy

This figure illustrates that a firm with many investment opportunities will pay small amounts of dividends and a firm with few investment opportunities will pay relatively large amounts of dividends.

In row 1, for example, note that new investment is $3,000. Additional debt of $1,000 and equity of $2,000 must be raised to keep the debt/equity ratio constant. Since this latter figure is greater than the $1,000 of earnings, all earnings are retained. Money to be raised from additional shares is also $1,000. In this example, since new shares are issued, dividends are not simultaneously paid out.

In rows 2 and 3, investment drops. Additional debt needed goes down as well since it is equal to $1/3$ of investment. Because the amount of new equity needed is still greater than or equal to $1,000, all earnings are retained and no dividend is paid.

We finally find a situation in row 4 where a dividend is paid. Here, total investment is $1,000. To keep our debt/equity ratio constant, $1/3$ of this investment, or $333, is financed by debt. The remaining $2/3$, or $667, comes from internal funds, implying that the residual is $1,000 − 667 = $333. The dividend is equal to this $333 residual.

In this case, note that no additional shares are issued. Since the needed investment is even lower in rows 5 and 6, new debt is reduced further, retained earnings drop, and dividends increase. Again, no additional shares are issued.

Given our discussion, we expect those firms with many investment opportunities to pay a small percentage of their earnings as dividends, and other firms with fewer opportunities to pay a high percentage of their earnings as dividends. This result appears to occur in the real world. Young, fast-growing firms commonly employ a low payout ratio, whereas older, slower-growing firms in more mature industries use a higher ratio.

Dividend stability

Companies usually increase dividend rates only when they believe that increased earnings are sustainable in the future. Dividend payout ratios have increased since the introduction of dividend imputation in 1987. This could be seen as a result of perceived pressure from shareholders for franked dividends. The practice in Australia is to pay an interim dividend in the early part of the financial year followed by a larger final dividend at the end of the financial year. Available franking credits are calculated at June irrespective of the financial year of the company. For a given year, dividends capable of being franked are limited by the level of Australian tax paid that year. The introduction of dividend imputation has brought with it a number of variations in dividend payment.

Dividend streaming

Dividend streaming occurred when a shareholder was entitled to exercise the choice of substituting a franked dividend for:

1 an unfranked dividend—a dividend selection scheme; or
2 a tax-exempt bonus share—a share dividend selection scheme; or
3 an offshore unfranked dividend—an offshore dividend scheme.

These dividend streaming schemes were stopped by tax legislation which operated from 30 June 1990. They can still occur if the equity is segregated into different classes of shares such as preference shares and ordinary shares and the dividends paid on a class of shares are franked equally. The aim of the dividend streaming schemes was to direct available tax credits to those investors who obtained the most benefit (such as Australian individuals and superannuation funds). Companies, who received no imputation benefit, and overseas shareholders, who received lower benefits, were persuaded to take higher (by 10 to 20%) but unfranked dividends.

Special dividends

Some companies with high payments of tax may wish to pass on the benefits to shareholders but do not see the increased dividend as being sustainable in future years. In such cases, the company may pay either:

1 a special dividend, which is clearly identified as a one-off extra dividend to reduce 'excess' franking credits; or
2 taxable bonus shares which are paid from retained earnings. These issues represent a frankable dividend for tax purposes but they do not involve cash payments.

On Thursday 27 February 2003, Telstra, after losing more than $2 billion on its failed Asian expansion, declared a special dividend of three cents per share. This special dividend was funded by a surge in cash flow and some asset sales. Despite the announcement of this special dividend, Telstra shares closed 2.4 per cent lower, with a turnover of shares of more than 34 million. The usual interim dividend was 12 cents per share so the special dividend was a 25 per cent increase in dividends.

Dividend reinvestment schemes

For a company with all its operations in Australia, with all of its profits taxed, the ideal dividend payout for tax-paying shareholders is an amount equal to taxable income less income tax. As well as this amount, dividends are a function of:

1 availability of future investment opportunities with positive NPVs;
2 historic dividend rates;
3 availability and ability of the company to sell new equity;
4 maintaining a target debt/equity ratio;
5 maintaining a target dividend payout ratio.

These goals are ranked more or less in order of their importance. In our strict residual approach, we assumed that the firm maintained a fixed debt/equity ratio. Under the compromise approach, that debt/equity ratio is viewed as a long-range goal. It is allowed to vary in the short run if necessary to avoid a dividend cut or the need to sell new equity.

Other issues which are important, particularly for smaller companies, are:

6 the available cash flows;
7 the debt servicing obligations and covenants placed on distributions by debt trust deeds;
8 the needs of key shareholders for cash flow;
9 the available tax credits.

Despite all of these considerations it has been established that there is a general reluctance by companies to change dividends.

In addition to a strong reluctance to cut dividends, financial managers tend to think of dividend payments in terms of a proportion of profit, and they also tend to think investors are entitled to a 'fair' share of corporate profit. This share is the long-run **target payout ratio**, and it is the fraction of the earnings that the firm expects to pay as dividends under ordinary circumstances. Again, this is viewed as a long-range goal, so it might vary in the short run if needed. As a result, in the long run, earnings growth is followed by dividend increases, but only with a lag.

The conflict between the need of the company for working capital and the pressure of shareholders for higher dividend rates has been addressed partly by the introduction of *dividend reinvestment plans (DRPs)*. DRPs offer shareholders the opportunity to apply all or part of their cash dividends to the purchase of additional newly issued shares. A DRP allows the shareholder to reinvest the dividend without incurring any transaction costs of brokerage or stamp duty. In addition, companies offer a discount on the market price of shares which ranges from 5 per cent to 10 per cent of the price. The plans differ from the special dividend bonus share offer, as a cash dividend is notionally paid with a full franking credit even if the cheque is not issued, whereas under the special dividend bonus share arrangement no notional payment is present. From the company viewpoint the DRPs are inexpensive as a prospectus does not have to be issued. Figure 19.4 indicates that in 2001, 30 per cent of equity raised came from DRPs.

target payout ratio
a firm's long-term desired dividend-to-earnings ratio

FIGURE
19.4

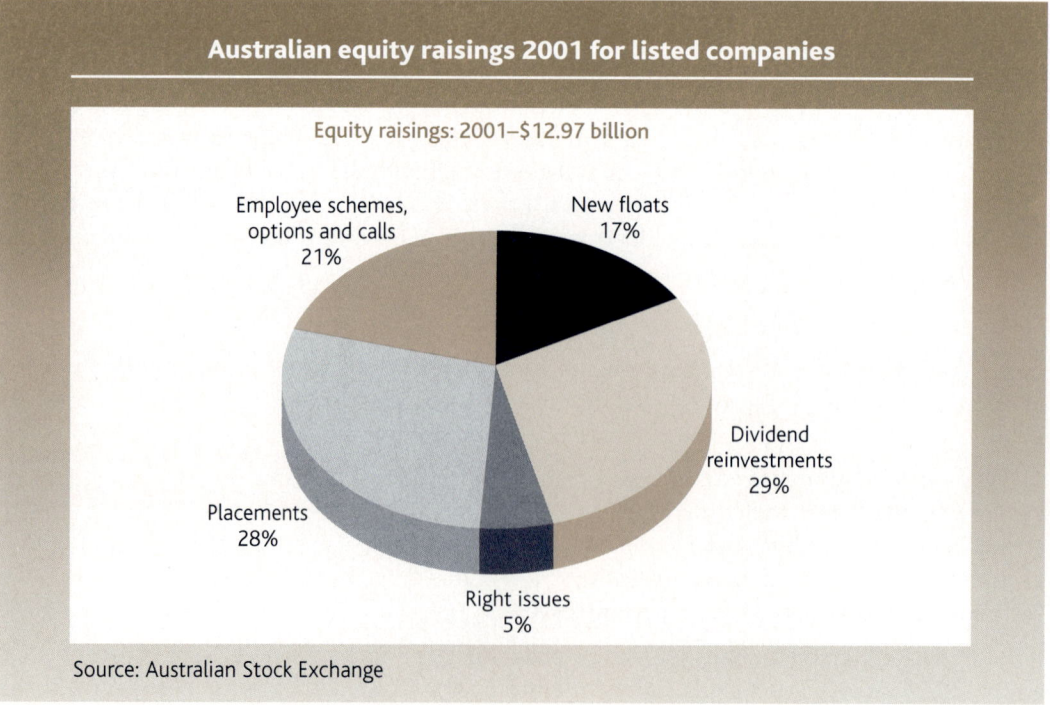

Australian equity raisings 2001 for listed companies

Equity raisings: 2001–$12.97 billion

Employee schemes, options and calls 21%

New floats 17%

Dividend reinvestments 29%

Placements 28%

Right issues 5%

Source: Australian Stock Exchange

PART 8 · COST OF CAPITAL AND LONG-TERM FINANCIAL POLICY

Concept questions

19.7 ▪ Share repurchase: An alternative to cash dividends

When a firm wants to pay cash to its shareholders, it normally pays a cash dividend. Another way is to *repurchase* its own shares. Buy-backs or repurchases are an exception to the general prohibition in Australia on a company dealing in its own shares. The law relating to buy-backs is quite strict and is covered by sections of the *Corporations Act* 2001 and Australian Stock Exchange Listing Requirements. Reform of the legislation in 1995 simplified the procedure and reduced substantially the cost. In March of 1996, Westpac repurchased 95 million shares and this was followed by the repurchase of a further 85 million shares in November of the same year. Five different types of buy-back are specified in the legislation and each type involves different legal procedures. The types are:

1 equal access buy-back where all shareholders are invited to sell to the company directly;
2 on-market buy-back where the company buys the shares through the share market;
3 employee share scheme buy-back where the company buys out shares in an employee incentive scheme;
4 selective buy-back where shares are purchased from specific shareholders; and
5 odd lot buy-backs where small parcels of shareholdings are bought.

Generally companies are able to purchase 10 per cent of their ordinary shares in a 12-month period. This is called the 10/12 limit.

Cash dividend versus repurchase

Imagine an all-equity company with excess cash of $300,000. The firm pays no dividends, and its net profit for the year just ended is $49,000. The market value Statement of Financial Position at the end of the year is represented below.

Market value Statement of Financial Position
(before paying out excess cash)

Shareholders' funds	
Paid-up capital	$1,000,000
Represented by:	
Excess cash	$ 300,000
Other assets	700,000
Total assets	$1,000,000

There are 100,000 shares outstanding. The total market value of the equity is $1 million, so the shares sell for $10 per share. Earnings per share (EPS) were $49,000/100,000 = $0.49.

One option the company is considering is a $300,000/100,000 = $3 per share extra cash dividend. Alternatively, the company is thinking of using the money to repurchase $300,000/$10 = 30,000 shares.

If commissions, taxes, and other imperfections are ignored in our example, the shareholders should not care which option is chosen. Does this seem surprising? It should not, really. What is happening here is that the firm is paying out $300,000 in cash. The new Statement of Financial Position is represented below.

If the cash is paid out as a dividend, there are still 100,000 shares outstanding, so each is worth $7.

The fact that the per-share value fell from $10 to $7 is not a cause for concern. Consider a shareholder who owned 100 shares. At $10 per share before the dividend, the total value is $1,000.

After the $3 dividend, this same shareholder has 100 shares worth $7 each, for a total of $700, plus 100 × $3 = $300 in cash, for a combined total of $1,000. This just illustrates what we saw early on: A cash dividend does not affect a shareholder's wealth if there are no imperfections. In this case, the share price simply fell by $3 when the share went ex dividend.

Also, since total earnings and the number of shares outstanding have not changed, EPS is still 49 cents. The price/earning ratio (P/E), however, falls to $7/$0.49 = 14.3. Why we are looking at accounting earnings and P/E ratios will be apparent just below.

Alternatively, if the company repurchases 30,000 shares, there will be 70,000 left outstanding. The Statement of Financial Position looks the same.

Market value Statement of Financial Position
(before paying out excess cash)

Shareholders' funds	
Paid-up capital	$700,000
Represented by:	
Other assets	700,000
Total assets	$700,000

The company is worth $700,000 again, so each remaining share is worth $700,000/70,000 = $10 each. Our shareholder with 100 shares is obviously unaffected. For example, if she were so inclined, she could sell 30 shares and end up with $300 in cash and $700 in shares, just as she has if the firm pays the cash dividend. This is another example of a home-made dividend.

In this second case, EPS goes up since total earnings are the same while the number of shares goes down. The new EPS will be $49,000/70,000 = $0.70 per share. However, the important thing to notice is that the P/E ratio is $10/$0.70 = 14.3, just as it was following the dividend.

This example illustrates the important point that, if there are no imperfections, a cash dividend and a share repurchase are essentially the same thing. This is just another illustration of dividend policy irrelevance when there are no taxes or other imperfections.

Real-world considerations in a repurchase

Buy-back and taxation

The taxation consequences of participating in a buy-back scheme, for a shareholder, depend upon when the shares were purchased and whether the purchase is on-market or off-market. Generally assets acquired before 20 September 1985 are exempt from capital gains tax. If the situation is an on-market buy-back[9] this exemption holds and the transaction does not give rise to a tax liability. If the shares are transferred in an off-market buy-back, any excess of the price over the amount against paid-up capital and the share premium account in the books of the company is taxed as a dividend in the shareholders' income and is frankable in the normal way. For a shareholder who acquired the shares after September 1985, the proceeds of sale under an on-market offer are subject to capital gains tax.

Share repurchase and EPS

You may read in the popular financial press that a share repurchase is beneficial because earnings per share increase. As we have seen, this will happen. The reason is simply that a share repurchase reduces the number of shares, but it has no effect on total earnings. As a result, EPS rises.

However, the financial press may place undue emphasis on EPS figures in a repurchase agreement. In our example above, we saw that the value of the share was not affected by the EPS change. In fact, the price/earning ratio was exactly the same when we compared a cash dividend to a repurchase.

Since the increase in earnings per share is exactly tracked by the increase in the price per share, there is no net effect. Put another way, the increase in EPS is just an accounting adjustment that reflects (correctly) the change in the number of shares.

In the real world, to the extent that repurchases benefit the firm, we would argue that they do so primarily because of the tax considerations we discussed above.

Concept questions

19.7a *Would a shareholder prefer an on-market buy-back or a fully franked extra cash dividend?*
19.7b *Why do not all firms use off-market buy-backs instead of cash dividends?*

19.8 ■ Share dividends and share splits

Another type of dividend is paid out in shares. This type of dividend is called a *share dividend* or **bonus share issue**. A bonus issue is not a true dividend because it is not paid in cash. The effect of a bonus issue is to increase the number of shares that each owner holds. Since there are more shares outstanding, each is simply worth less.

A bonus issue (share dividend) is commonly expressed as a ratio; for example, a one-for-five issue means that a shareholder receives one new share as a bonus for every five shares currently owned. Since every shareholder owns 20 per cent more equity, the total number of shares outstanding rises by 20 per cent. As we will see in a moment, the result would be that each share is worth about 20 per cent less.

A **share split** is essentially the same thing as a share dividend. When a split is declared, each share is split up to create additional shares. For example, in a three-for-one share split, each old share is split into three new shares.

> **bonus share issue**
> payment made by a firm to its owners in the form of shares, diluting the value of each share outstanding

> **share split**
> an increase in a firm's shares outstanding without any change in owners' equity

Some details on share splits and bonus issues

Share splits and bonus issues have essentially the same impacts on the corporation and the shareholder: They increase the number of shares outstanding and reduce the value per share. The accounting treatment is not the same, however, and it depends on two things:

1 whether the distribution is a share split or a bonus issue; and
2 the size of the bonus issue if it is called a dividend.

By convention, bonus issues of less than 20–25 per cent are called small bonus issues. The accounting procedure for such a dividend is discussed below. A bonus issue greater than this 20–25 per cent is called a large bonus issue. Large bonus issues are not uncommon. For example, in 1973, Walt Disney declared a 100 per cent bonus issue, thereby doubling the number of outstanding shares. Except for some relatively minor accounting differences, this has the same effect as a two-for-one share split.

Example of a small bonus issue

The Cosmetic Calculation Co. Pty Ltd, a consulting firm specialising in difficult accounting problems, has 100,000 shares, each selling at $6.60. The total market value of the equity is

$6.60 \times 100,000 = \$660,000$. With a 10 per cent bonus issue, each shareholder receives one additional share for each 10 that they own, and the total number of shares outstanding after the dividend is 110,000.

Before the bonus issue, the equity portion of Cosmetic Calculation's statement of financial position might look like this:

Paid-up capital	$100,000
(100,000 shares outstanding)	
Capital reserve	200,000
Retained earnings	200,000
Total shareholders' funds	$500,000

Since 10,000 new shares are issued, the only change to the Statement of Financial Position is the number of shares issued. Total shareholders' funds is unaffected by the bonus issue because no cash has come in or out. The net effect of these machinations is that Cosmetic Calculation's equity accounts now look like this:

Paid-up capital	$100,000
(110,000 shares outstanding)	
Capital reserve	200,000
Retained earnings	200,000
Total shareholders' funds	$500,000

Example of a share split

A share split is conceptually similar to a bonus issue, but it is commonly expressed as a ratio. For example, in a three-for-two split, each shareholder receives one additional share for each two held originally, so a three-for-two split amounts to a 50 per cent bonus issue. Again, no cash is paid out, and the percentage of the entire firm that each shareholder owns is unaffected.

Suppose that Cosmetic Calculation decides to declare a two-for-one share split. The number of shares outstanding will double to 200,000. The shareholders' equity after the split is represented as:

Paid-up capital	$100,000
(200,000 shares outstanding)	
Capital reserve	200,000
Retained earnings	200,000
Total shareholders' funds	$500,000

Note that, for all three of the categories, the figures on the right are completely unaffected by the split, as was the case with the bonus issue. The only change is in the number of shares so that the paid-up value per share is 50 cents.

Example of a large bonus issue

In our example above, if a 100 per cent bonus issue were declared, 100,000 new shares would be distributed. The result might be the following:

Paid-up capital	$100,000
(200,000 shares outstanding)	
Capital reserve	200,000
Retained earnings	200,000
Total shareholders' funds	$500,000

Value of share splits and bonus issues

The laws of logic tell us that share splits and bonus issues can (1) leave the value of the firm unaffected, (2) increase its value, or (3) decrease its value. Unfortunately, the issues are complex enough that one cannot easily determine which of the three relationships holds.

The benchmark case

A strong case can be made that bonus issues and splits do not change either the wealth of any shareholder or the wealth of the firm as a whole. In our example above, the market value of equity was worth a total of $660,000. With the small bonus issue, the number of shares increased to 110,000, so it seems that each would be worth $660,000/110,000 = $6.

For example, a shareholder who had 1,000 shares worth $6.60 each before the dividend would have 1,100 shares worth $6 each afterwards. The total value of the shares is $6,600 either way; so the bonus issue does not really have any economic effect.

With the share split, there were 200,000 shares outstanding, so each should be worth $660,000/200,000 = $3.30. In other words, the number of shares doubles and the price halves. From these calculations, it appears that bonus issues and splits are just paper transactions.

Although these results are relatively obvious, there are reasons that are often given to suggest that there may be some benefits to these actions. The typical financial manager is aware of many real-world complexities and, for that reason, the share split or bonus issue decision is not treated lightly in practice.

Popular trading range

Proponents of bonus issues and share splits frequently argue that a security has a popular **trading range**. When the security is priced above this level, many investors do not have the funds to buy the common trading unit of 100 shares, called a *round lot*. Although securities can be purchased in *odd-lot* form (fewer than 100 shares), the commissions are greater. Thus, firms will split the shares to keep the price in this trading range.

> **trading range**
> price range between highest and lowest prices at which a stock is traded

Although this argument is a popular one, its validity is questionable for a number of reasons. Mutual funds, pension funds and other institutions have steadily increased their trading activity since World War II and now handle a sizeable percentage of total trading volume. Because these institutions buy and sell in huge amounts, the individual share price is of little concern.

Furthermore, we sometimes observe share prices that are quite large without appearing to cause problems. To take an extreme case, the largest company in the world (in terms of the total market value of outstanding equity) is the Japanese telecommunications giant, NTT. In early 1989, NTT shares were selling for about $12,000 *each*, so a round lot would have cost a cool $1.2 million. This is fairly expensive, but the shares have sold for more than $20,000 each.

Finally, there is evidence that share splits may actually decrease the marketability of the company's shares. Following a two-for-one split, the number of shares traded should more than double if marketability is increased by the split. This does not appear to happen, and the reverse is sometimes observed.

Reverse splits

A less frequently encountered financial manoeuvre is the **reverse split**. In a one-for-three reverse split, each investor exchanges three old shares for one new share. As mentioned previously with reference to share splits and bonus issues, a case can be made that a reverse split changes nothing substantial about the company.

> **reverse split**
> procedure where a firm's number of shares outstanding is reduced

Given real-world imperfections, three related reasons are cited for reverse splits. First, transaction costs to shareholders may be less after the reverse split. Second, the marketability of a company's shares might be improved when its price is raised to the popular trading range. Third, shares selling below a certain level are not considered respectable, meaning that investors underestimate these firms' earnings, cash flow, growth and stability. Some financial analysts argue that a reverse split can achieve instant respectability. Stock exchanges have minimum price per share requirements so a reverse split may be used to bring the share price to such a minimum. As with share splits, none of these reasons is particularly compelling, especially the third one.

Concept questions

19.8a *What is the effect of a share split on shareholder wealth?*

19.8b *How does the accounting treatment of a share split differ from that used with a small share dividend?*

 ## 19.9 Employee share ownership plans

While employee share ownership plans do not fit within the definition of company dividends, they can be seen as part of the return to the labour production factor. Dividends are part of the return to the capital production factor. An increasing number of companies have introduced schemes to encourage the financial participation of employees in the company. This participation is seen as a benefit to employees and a method of increasing productivity for the company. The Australian Government has sought to encourage growth of employee share ownership through special tax concessions.

Share ownership plans

Fully paid shares

The issue of ordinary shares to employees at a price close to market value is the most common ownership plan. The company finances most of the initial cost with a loan, usually interest-free, secured by the shares. These plans require the employee to pay for the shares over an extended period or upon termination of employment. Often a trustee holds the shares until the loan is repaid. In some cases, there is no financial support but the shares are issued to eligible employees at a discounted market price.

Partly paid shares

Shares can be issued to employees at market price but with the payment of all but a small initial amount (0.05 per cent for example) deferred to a specific future date or until the employee resigns or retires. These shares are like a share option but they establish the cost base for calculating capital gains tax as the current market price and the scheme involves the actual immediate issue of shares. Problems arise with partly paid schemes when the market price falls below the issue price as the employee has a commitment to pay the issue price.

Special classes of shares

In some plans, employee share issues have different rights and entitlements to those of ordinary shares. Voting rights may be restricted, or the shares may be entitled to a preference dividend or a right might be established for the holder to receive a regular bonus issue of shares. For example, OPSM Industries Ltd issues 'B' class shares to its employees. The shares are paid for by instalments over a number of years. The shares are held in trust (see below) until fully paid and they carry no entitlement to cash dividends. The shares are converted to fully paid ordinary shares when payment has been made in full.

Option

Another mode of obtaining employee commitment to the future of the company has been through the issue of options. These were the earliest types of employee share ownership schemes used in Australia. Employees would be granted options to subscribe to ordinary shares at a future date at an issue price based on the current market price. The options normally have a fixed exercise date so that they cannot be exercised before the date. They are not transferable and usually lapse if an employee resigns prior to normal retirement. For capital gains purposes the shares are deemed to be acquired when the option is exercised.

Phantom or shadow shares

When a company is not listed or it is a wholly owned subsidiary of another company, it is not practical to issue ordinary shares or options. In these circumstances, profit-sharing plans may be established by creating phantom or shadow shares. The phantom shares carry rights to financial rewards based on profit sharing and established measures of performance.

Employee share trusts

While many fully paid or partly paid share plans involve a trust arrangement until the employee becomes fully entitled, some create a pooled share interest in which the underlying shares are held in trust for all employees. The shares are not specifically allocated to individual employees. Employees receive a share of the dividends received by the trust on a pro-rata basis, but they are not entitled to draw on their proportion of the shares. While the shares are held in trust the company usually has access to the instalment share capital. For example, in the case of OPSM the trustee advances the instalment income to the company for use in its operations.

Taxation

Australian taxation legislation allows a company to offer employees a discount of up to $200 per annum per employee, provided the discount is no greater than 10 per cent of the market price. To qualify for tax exemption the employee share acquisition scheme must:

- be open to participation by all permanent employees on an equal basis;
- relate to ordinary shares and options only;
- restrict the disposal by an employee of the shares for three years or when the employee ceases employment.

When the shares do not qualify for the $200 (or 10%) concession, the full amount of the discount is treated as ordinary assessable income to the employee. Employees' shares are subject to capital gains tax. Prior to 1 October 1999, the capital cost, as is the case with all asset purchases, is an indexed capital cost. The index represents the movement in price levels since the purchase of the asset. The capital cost base used for indexation in relation to employee scheme shares is the market value less the tax-free discount. From 1 October 1999, half of the capital gain would be taxed using the capital cost base without indexation. In effect, capital gains tax nullifies the tax benefit although the taxpayer is able to postpone the payment.

Employee share plans are free from fringe benefits tax to the company; however, some state laws (New South Wales and Victoria) may result in payroll tax being applicable.

Concept questions

19.9a *Why would a firm consider issuing employee shares?*
19.9b *What is the detrimental aspect of employee share trusts?*

19.10 Summary and conclusions

In this chapter, we discussed the types of dividend and how they are paid. We then defined dividend policy and examined whether or not dividend policy matters. Finally, we illustrated how a firm might establish a dividend policy and described an important alternative to cash dividends, a share repurchase.

In covering these subjects, we saw that:

1 Dividend policy is irrelevant when there are no taxes or other imperfections because shareholders can effectively undo the firm's dividend strategy. If a shareholder receives a dividend greater than desired, he or she can reinvest the excess. Conversely, if the shareholder receives a dividend that is smaller than desired, he or she can sell off extra shares.

2 The franking dividend scheme would cause some shareholders to favour a high dividend payout if the dividends are being paid from company profits that have been taxed.

3 New issue flotation costs and the demand of some shareholders for high dividend payout has led companies to develop dividend reinvestment plans.

4 There are tax exempt groups in the economy that will favour low dividend payout. Recognising that some groups prefer a low payout and others prefer a high payout, the clientele effect supports the concept that dividend policies will respond to the needs of shareholders. Thus the dividend policy of individual firms should not influence the market prices of the firms and firms should be reluctant to change dividend policy.

5 A firm wishing to pursue a strict residual dividend payout will have an unstable dividend. Dividend stability is usually viewed as highly desirable.

6 A share buy-back acts much like a cash dividend. Share buy-backs are therefore a very useful part of overall dividend policy. Employee share ownership plans are seen, in the first instance, as a means of rewarding the labour factor of production. As the employee entitlement under the scheme expands, the interests of employees are merged with the interests of the original shareholders.

To close out our discussion of dividends, we emphasise one last time the difference between dividends and dividend policy. Dividends are important, because the value of a share is ultimately determined by the dividends that will be paid. What is less clear is whether or not the time pattern of dividends (more now versus more later) matters. This is the dividend policy question, and it is not easy to give a definitive answer to it.

Key terms

Bonus share issue *657*
Buy-backs *655*
Clientele effect *649*
Date of payment *637*
Date of record *637*
Declaration date *636*

Distribution *636*
Dividend *636*
Ex-dividend date *636*
Home-made dividends *640*
Imputation system *642*
Information content effect *649*

Regular cash dividends *636*
Residual dividend approach *651*
Reverse split *659*
Share split *657*
Target payout ratio *654*
Trading range *659*

Suggested readings

Our dividend irrelevance argument is based on a classic article:

Miller, M.H. and Modigliani, F. 'Dividend Policy, Growth and the Valuation of Shares', *Journal of Business*, Vol. 34, October 1961, pp. 411–33.

Higgins describes the residual dividend approach in:

Higgins, R.C. 'The Corporate Dividend-Saving Decision', *Journal of Financial and Qualitative Analysis*, Vol. 7, March 1972, pp. 1527–41.

Discussion and evidence in relation to dividend imputation may be found in:

Bellamy, D. 'Evidence of imputation clienteles in the Australian equity market', *Asia Pacific Journal of Management*, October 1994, pp. 275–87.

Share price behaviour after dividend payments or capital repurchases is covered in:

Brown, P. and Clarke, A. 'The ex-dividend day behaviour of Australian share prices before and after dividend imputation', *Australian Journal of Management*, June 1993, pp. 1–40.

Dann, L. 'Common stock repurchases: what do they really accomplish?', in J. Stern and D. Chews (eds), *The Revolution in Corporate Finance*, 2nd edn, Blackwell, Oxford, 1992, pp. 173–80.

Endnotes

1   The same results would occur after an issue of debt, though the arguments would be less easily presented.

2   The imputation system was publicly announced in September 1985; however the legislation introducing it did not take effect until 1 July 1987.

3   For example, section 26AAA of the *Income Tax Assessment Act* 1936 (this section was maintained after September 1985) was drafted to catch short-term property sales. Section 25A (this section was deleted after September 1985) was designed to catch profit made from the sale of property acquired for the purpose of profit making, as opposed to income-producing property.

4   Graham, G., Dodd, D. and Cottle, S. *Security Analysis*, McGraw-Hill, New York, 1962.

5   Gordon, M. *The Investment, Financing and Valuation of the Corporation*, Irwin, Homewood, Ill., 1961.

6   A quick glance at Table 6.3 in Chapter 6 shows that about 50 per cent of the shares listed do not have dividends.

7   Willett, J.T. (moderator) 'A Discussion of Corporate Policy', in D.H. Chew (ed.) *Six Roundtable Discussions of Corporate Finance with Joel Stern*, Blackwell, Basel, 1986. The panellists included Robert Litzenberger, Pat Hess, Bill Kealy, John Childs and Joel Stern.

8   Our discussion of sustainable growth in Chapter 4 is relevant here. We assumed there that a firm has a fixed capital structure, profit margin and capital intensity. If the firm raises no new equity and wishes to grow at some target rate, then there is only one payout ratio consistent with these assumptions.

9   When shares are purchased through the stock exchange this is regarded as an on-market buy-back.

On the web

Dividends and dividend policy are discussed on the web sites of individual businesses. Useful sites are:

http://www.colesmyer.com.au (Coles–Myer Ltd)
http://www.telstra.com (Telstra)
http://www.bhpbilliton.com (BHP Billiton)

The Australian Stock Exchange and the Australian Prudential Regulation Authority also provide information on dividends and dividend policy:

http://www.asx.com.au
http://www.apra.gov.au

Taxation issues relating to dividends can be followed through at:

http://www.ato.gov.au (Australian Taxation Office)

Maximise Your Marks!
There are 30 interactive questions on dividends and dividend policy waiting online for you at www.mhhe.com/au/ross3e. The questions are written with additional feedback for incorrect answers, and text excerpts with page references for follow-up study.

International Articles!
To read more on dividends and dividend policy and to see current international articles, just go to www.mhhe.com/au/ross3e and click on *PowerWeb Articles* for this chapter.

Chapter review problems and self-test

19.1 · Dividends, imputation credits and cash flow

The Pampered Pooch Company Ltd has earnings of $2,500 for the year, after paying company tax at 30 per cent, which it intends to pay out as a dividend. Mr Yap owns 20 per cent of the share capital. His other taxable income is $100,000 so that his marginal tax rate is 47 per cent. Mrs Growl also owns 20 per cent of the company; however, her other taxable income is only $15,000. Her marginal tax rate is 17 per cent. Does the dividend imputation scheme result in the dividend income being more valuable in the hands of Mr Yap or Mrs Growl?

19.2 · Repurchase versus cash dividend

Bankful Corporation Ltd is deciding whether to pay out $300 in excess cash in the form of an extra dividend or to reduce its share capital. Assume the current legal requirements allow Bankful to repurchase its shares or to make a pro rata distribution of capital to shareholders. The paid-up capital book value of the shares is $1,000. Current earnings are $1.50 per share and the market price of a share is also $1.50. The Statement of Financial Position before paying out the $300 is as follows:

Market value Statement of Financial Position

Shareholders' funds	
Paid-up capital	$1,500
Represented by:	
Excess cash	$300
Other assets	1,600
	$1900
Less Debt	400
Net assets	$1,500

Book values

Shareholders' funds	
Paid-up capital	$1,000
Capital reserve	500
Total shareholders' funds	$1,500
Represented by:	
Excess cash	$300
Other assets	1,600
	1,900
Less Debt	400
Net assets	$1,500

Evaluate the two alternatives in terms of the effect on the price per share, the EPS and the P/E ratio.

Answers to self-test problems

19.1 · The dividend and the imputation credits that will accrue to Mr Yap and Mrs Growl because of their 20 per cent holdings in Pampered Pooch Company Ltd is:

Dividend: 20% of $2,500	$500
Imputation credit: 20% of 30% of $2,500/0.7	214
Grossed up income $500/0.7	$714

The tax situations are as follows:

	Mr Yap	Mrs Growl
Grossed up dividend income	$714	$714
Tax at the shareholder's marginal rate	$336	$121
Imputation credit	(214)	(214)
Tax payment (refund) on dividend	$122	($93)
Dividend received	$500	$500
Tax (payable) credited	($122)	$93
Net gain from dividend	$378	$593

The dividend is more valuable to Mrs Growl.

19.2 · The market value of the equity is $1,500. The price per share is $1.50, so there are 1,000 shares outstanding. The cash dividend would amount to $300/1,000 = 30 cents per share. When the shares go ex dividend, the price will drop by 30 cents per share to $1.20. Put another way, the total assets decrease by $300, so the equity value goes down by this amount to $1,200. With 1,000 shares, this is $1.20 per share. After the dividend, EPS will be the same, $1.50, but the P/E ratio will be $1.20/1.50 = 0.8 times.

With the repurchase, $300/1.50 = 200 shares will be bought up, leaving 800. The equity will again be worth $1,200 total. With 800 shares, this is $1,200/800 = $1.50 per share, so the price does not change. Total earnings for Bankful must be $1.50 × 1,000 = $1,500. After the repurchase, EPS will be higher at $1,500/800 = 1.875. The P/E ratio, however, will still be $1.50/1.875 = 0.8 times. With the capital reduction, the paid-up value of the shares will reduce from $1,000 to $700; that is, from $1 to 70 cents per share. As there will still be 1,000 shares on issue, the price per share will fall to $700 + $500 (capital reserve)/1,000 = $1.20. The earnings per share will remain at $1.50 and the P/E ratio becomes $1.20/$1.50 = 0.8 times.

Questions and problems

1 · Accounting for splits

The owner's equity accounts for the Tweed Co. Ltd are shown below (in millions):

Ordinary shares paid-up value	$ 50
Capital reserve	500
Retained earnings	5,000
	$5,550

Tweed shares currently sell for $5 per share.

a If Tweed makes a 1-for-10 bonus issue, how would these accounts change?
b If Tweed makes a 1-for-10 rights issue with a subscription price of $4, how would these accounts change?
c If Tweed declared a 10-for-1 split, how would the accounts change?
d If Tweed declares a dividend equal to 0.4 per cent of retained earnings and the shareholders, through a dividend reinvestment scheme, purchase shares at $4 per share, how would the accounts change?

2 · Dividends and taxes

The University of New World pays no taxes on its capital gains nor on its dividend income and interest payments. Would it be irrational to find low-dividend, high-growth shares in its portfolio? Would it be irrational to find government (tax-free) bonds which carry tax concessions? Explain.

3 · Determining ex-dividend rate

On Thursday, 16 July, Busyday's board of directors declares a dividend of 45 cents per share payable on Thursday, 20 August, to shareholders of record as of Tuesday, 4 August. When is the ex-dividend date? If a shareholder buys shares before that date, what events will take place?

4 · Dividends and share prices

The statement of financial position for Pricechange Co. Ltd is shown below in market value terms. There are 1,000 shares outstanding.

Shareholders' funds	
Paid-up capital	$20,000
Represented by:	
Cash	$ 2,000
Fixed assets	18,000
Total assets	$20,000

Pricechange has declared a final dividend of 10 cents per share. The shares go ex tomorrow. What is it selling for today? What will it sell for tomorrow? Ignore taxes in answering.

5 · Dividends and capital yields

In the previous question, suppose that the 10 cent final dividend represents a cut in the total dividend of 2 per cent. Also assume that all shareholders have a marginal tax rate of 20 per cent and there are no imputation credits associated with the dividend. The marginal tax rate would apply to both dividends and capital gains. With the reduction in dividends the management of Pricechange has announced it is changing the firm's investment in a number of key areas and it requires the funds that have been retained for that purpose. What price would you expect Pricechange shares to trade at tomorrow? If Pricechange shares fall to $1.60, what is the likely cause of this reduction? When is the fall in price likely to occur?

6 · Dividends and taxes

Antigerm Co. Ltd has declared a 20 cent per share dividend. Suppose that capital gains are not taxed, but dividends are taxed at 30 per cent. Australian Tax Office withholding regulations require that taxes be withheld at the time the dividend is paid. Antigerm sells for $2 per share and the share is about to go ex dividend. What do you think the ex-dividend price will be?

7 · Bonus issues

The market value Statement of Financial Position for Grog Ltd is shown below. Grog has declared a 1-for-4 bonus issue. The shares go ex bonus tomorrow. There are 500 shares outstanding. What will the ex-bonus price be?

Shareholders' funds	
Paid-up capital	$ 950
Represented by:	
Cash	$ 800
Fixed assets	$ 800
	1,600
Less debt	650
Net assets	$ 950

8 · Dividends versus capital gains

Church Supplies Pty Ltd has an expected dividend yield of 8 per cent, while Biblical Pty Ltd pays no dividends. The equity in both firms has the same risk. The required return on Biblical is 15 per cent. Capital gains are not taxed, but dividends are taxed at 16 per cent. What is the required pre-tax return on Church Supplies? If dividends are not taxed but capital gains are taxed at 16 per cent, what is the required pre-tax return on Church Supplies?

9 · Home-made dividends

You own 100 shares in Mountain Adventures Pty Ltd. You will receive a 35 cent per share dividend in one year. In 2 years, Mountain will pay a liquidating dividend of $15. The required return is 16 per cent. How much is your investment worth per share (ignoring taxes)? If you would rather have equal dividends in each of the next 2 years, show how you can accomplish this by home-made dividends.

10 · Home-made dividends

In the previous question, suppose you want only $20 total in dividends the first year. What will your home-made dividend be in 2 years?

11 · Residual dividend policy

Combined Exterminators Ltd predicts that earnings in the coming year will be $10 million. There are 10 million shares outstanding, and Combined Exterminators maintains a total debt ratio of 0.50.

a   Calculate the increase in total value if all the earnings are invested and the total debt ratio is maintained. What is the resultant increase in borrowing?

b   Suppose Combined Exterminators uses a residual dividend policy. Planned capital expenditures total $12 million. Based on this information, what will the dividend per share amount be?

c   In part (b), how much borrowing will take place? What are retained earnings?

d   Suppose Combined plans no capital outlays for the coming year. What will the dividend be under a residual policy? What would new borrowing be?

12 · Alternative dividends

a   Some corporations, like one British company that offers its large shareholders free crematorium use, or Coles-Myer which offers shareholders discounts on purchases from their various stores, pay dividends in kind (i.e. offer their services to shareholders at below-market cost). Should mutual funds invest in shares that pay these dividends in kind?

b   In 2002 Coles-Myer began to progressively get rid of discounts which were offered to shareholders at all its stores. Would this reduction in dividends in kind (that is, services or goods given to shareholders at below market cost) make Coles-Myer's shares more attractive to a Mutual Fund?

13 · Dividend policy

If increases in dividends tend to be followed by (immediate) increases in share prices, how can it be said that dividend policy is irrelevant?

14 · Changes in dividends

Last month, Toowoomba Telecommunications Company, which had been having trouble with cost overruns on a power line that it had been building for a local council, announced that it was 'temporarily suspending payments due to the cash flow crunch associated with its investment program'. The company's share price dropped from $28.50 to $25 when this announcement was made. How would you interpret this change in the share price (i.e., what caused it)?

15 · Accounting for bonus issues

A company, whose equity accounts follow, has declared a 1-for-20 bonus issue at a time when the market value of its shares is $6 per share. What effects on the equity accounts will the distribution of the bonus issue have?

Paid-up value	$1,000,000
Capital reserve	2,000,000
Retained earnings	5,000,000
Total shareholders' funds	$8,000,000

The book value of each share is one dollar.

16 · Accounting for share splits

In the previous question, suppose that the company instead decides on a 4-for-1 share split. The firm's 20 cent cash dividend on the new (split) shares represents an increase of 5 per cent over last year's dividend on pre-split shares. What effect does this have on the equity accounts? What was last year's dividend per share?

17 · DRIPs

The Morecash Corporation Ltd has recently developed a dividend reinvestment plan. The plan allows investors to reinvest cash dividends automatically in Morecash in exchange for new shares. Over time, investors in Morecash will be able to build their holding by reinvesting dividends to purchase additional shares of the company.

About 150 companies offer dividend reinvestment plans. Most companies with dividend reinvestment plans charge no brokerage or service fees. In fact, the shares of Morecash will be purchased at a 10 per cent 'discount' from the market price.

A consultant for Morecash estimates that about 75 per cent of Morecash's shareholders will take part in this plan. This is somewhat higher than the average.

Evaluate Morecash's dividend reinvestment plan. Will it increase shareholder wealth? Give the pros and cons.

18 · Dividend policy

In 1983 in the United States, 888 firms made initial public offerings of ordinary shares raising over US$10 billion. Except for the bank shares, hardly any of the firms were paying cash dividends in 1989. Does this mean that most of these firms represented poor investments as indicated by their lack of cash dividends?

19 · Policy

Consider the following article from the *Philadelphia Bulletin*, 16 April 1976:

The dividend question at Clark Equipment

If you're one of the 13,000 shareholders of Clark Equipment Co., you can look forward to an increase in the $1.60 annual dividend—but don't spend the money yet.

Says Leonard M. Savoie, vice president and controller, 'We will have to raise it some day. There's a lot of pressure for an increase.'

The $1.60 rate has been in effect since 1973. What with the ravages of inflation, the purchasing power of the $1.60 is considerable less than in 1973.

But an increase is not likely soon, Bert E. Phillips, president and chief executive, strongly indicated. The two officials of the Buchanan, Michigan, maker of materials-handling and construction equipment were in town yesterday for a meeting with the Financial Analysts of Philadelphia at the Racquet Club.

Two Reasons

Clark's first-quarter earnings were not 'very good', according to Phillips, who said the first half 'will likely be somewhat depressed' too. That's no time to raise the dividend.

On top of that, Phillips thinks that Clark can reinvest the money in the business at a higher return than shareholders could on their own.

That's unlikely to cut much ice with shareholders who depend on dividends. But Phillips thinks it's foolish for a company to pay a higher dividend and then have to borrow the money it needs for expansion and modernisation of its plants.

In effect, he told analysts, that's borrowing to pay dividends. Traditionally, Clark has been paying out between 45 per cent and 50 per cent of earnings in dividends. Phillips hopes to be able to persuade directors to let the payout ratio shrink as earnings pick up later this year and the next, as he expects.

Some directors might resist, worrying about the 'little old lady in tennis shoes out in Iowa' who wants an increase in the $1.60 dividend, according to Phillips.

Said Phillips, 'I think she died, but they do not know it yet.'

Next year might be different, the Clark official indicated.

'We think the downturn has bottomed,' Phillips said, 'and that the second half (of 1976) will see improvement as the whole capital-goods sector comes back to a healthier state.' Sales and earnings of capital-goods producers like Clark generally lag behind the economy by six to nine months.

Omen

Clark's shipments of forklifts and other industrial trucks declined throughout 1975. But in the past few months, according to Phillips, shipments have been 'trending upward, and we expect this to continue gradually over the remainder of the year.' Construction machinery, however, continues flat.

In 1975, Clark earned $46.6 million, or $3.43 a share, on sales of $1.4 billion. Some Wall Street analysts are forecasting 1976 earnings between $3.60 and $4 a share.

Evaluate 'The Dividend Question at Clark Equipment' in light of what you have learned about dividend policy. In particular:

a   What do you think of the two reasons for not raising the $1.60 dividend this year?
b   What do you think of 'borrowing to pay dividends'?
c   Should Clark base its dividend policy on the payout ratio? On the dividend per share?
d   Assuming that she's still alive, how much should the company worry about the little old lady in Iowa?

20 · Residual dividend policy

I.M. Lazy Ltd, had declared an annual dividend of 19 cents per share. For the year just ended, earnings were 76 cents per share.

a   What is I.M. Lazy's payout ratio?
b   Suppose I.M. Lazy has 5 million shares outstanding. Borrowing for the coming year is planned at $7 million. What are planned investment outlays assuming a residual dividend policy? What target capital structure is implicit in these calculations?

21 · Residual policy

The Handclap Pty Ltd follows a strict residual dividend policy. Its debt/equity ratio is 1.

a   If earnings for the year are $600,000, what is the maximum amount of capital spending possible with no new equity?
b   If planned investment outlays for the coming year are $1.5 million, will Handclap pay a dividend? If so, how much?
c   Does the Handclap Corporation maintain a constant dividend payout? Why or why not?

22 · Share repurchase

Natural Gas Company Pty Ltd is evaluating an extra dividend versus a share repurchase. In either case, $1,000 would be spent. Current earnings are $5 per share, and the share currently sells for $10 per share. There are 200 shares outstanding. Ignore taxes and other imperfections in answering the first two questions.

a   Evaluate the two alternatives in terms of the effect on the price per share and shareholder wealth.
b   What will be the effect on Natural Gas's EPS and P/E ratio?
c   In the real world, which of these actions would you recommend? Why?

23 · Residual policy versus a compromise

What is the chief drawback to a strict residual dividend policy? Why is this a problem? How does a compromise policy work? How does it differ from a strict residual policy?

24 · Residual dividend policy

Verbate Limited uses a strict residual dividend policy. Its target capital structure is 60 per cent debt and 40 per cent equity. Earnings for the year are $5,000.

What is the maximum amount of capital spending possible without selling any new equity?

Assume the planned investment outlay for the coming year is $12,000. How much will Verbate be able to pay as a dividend?

25 · Repurchase versus cash dividend

Elaine Sparky, the manager of M J Electric Corporation, is deciding whether to pay out $50 million in excess cash in the form of an extra dividend or make a share repurchase. Current earnings are 25 cents per share, and shares sell for $2.50 each. Market value statistics before paying out the $50 million are:

Excess cash	$ 50 million
Other assets	$250 million
Total assets	$300 million
Debt	$ 50 million
Equity	$250 million
Total	$300 million

Elaine is worried about the effect of the alternatives on the price per share, the EPS and the P/E ratio. Show her what the effect will be.

CHAPTER 20

Financial
leverage and capital structure policy

Objective

The aim of this chapter is to explain the principles of capital structure. The effects of debt in the capital structure are explained. Business and financial risk are distinguished and the roles of taxation, bankruptcy and other influences on capital structure are explained. The capital structure theories of Modigliani and Miller are introduced. Finally the empirical evidence from selected recent studies on capital structure is outlined with explanations of theories indicating the real-world influence on capital structure decisions.

Study tips ▷   What we will see in this chapter is that capital structure decisions can have important implications for the value of the firm and its cost of capital. We will also find that important elements of the capital structure decision are easy to identify, but precise measures of these elements are generally not obtainable. As a result, we are only able to give an incomplete answer to the question of what the best capital structure might be for a particular firm at a particular time.

The two propositions of Modigliani and Miller are part of the foundation of contemporary finance. The propositions are:

1   the value of the firm is independent of the capital structure; and
2   the cost of equity of the firm is a positive linear function of its capital structure.

Light may be shed on many of the highly complex corporate finance decisions by revisiting these simple fundamental theories. Make sure you understand the propositions and realise that the value of the firm is driven by its investments and not how the firm packages claims to those investments or how the firm distributes the returns from them.

Introduction ▷ Thus far, we have taken the firm's capital structure as given. Debt/equity ratios do not just drop on firms from the sky, of course, so now it is time to wonder where they do come from. Going back to Chapter 1, we call decisions about a firm's debt/equity ratio capital structure decisions.[1]

For the most part, a firm can choose any capital structure that it wants. If management so desired, a firm could issue some debentures and use the proceeds to buy back some shares, thereby increasing the debt/equity ratio. Alternatively, it can issue shares and use the money to pay off some debt, thereby reducing the debt/equity ratio. Activities such as these, that alter the firm's existing capital structure, are called capital restructurings. In general, such restructurings take place whenever the firm substitutes one capital structure for another while leaving the firm's assets unchanged.

Since the assets of a firm are not directly affected by a capital restructuring, we can examine the firm's capital structure decision separately from its other activities. This means that a firm can consider capital restructuring decisions in isolation from its investment decisions. In this chapter, then, we will ignore investment decisions and focus on the long-term financing, or capital structure, question.

20.1 ■ The capital structure question

How should a firm go about choosing its debt/equity ratio? Here, as always, we assume that the guiding principle is to choose the course of action that maximises the value of a share. As we discuss next, however, when it comes to capital structure decisions, this is essentially the same thing as maximising the value of the whole firm, and, for convenience, we will tend to frame our discussion in terms of firm value.

Firm value and share value: An example

The following example illustrates that the capital structure that maximises the value of the firm is the one that financial managers should choose for the shareholders, so there is no conflict in our goals. To begin, suppose the market value of the World Cup Company Ltd is $1,000. The company currently has no debt, and World Cup's 100 shares sell for $10 each. Further suppose that World Cup restructures itself by borrowing $500 and then paying out the proceeds to shareholders as an extra dividend of $500/100 = $5 per share.

This restructuring will change the capital structure of the firm with no direct effect on the firm's assets. The immediate effect will be to increase debt and decrease equity. However, what will be the final impact of the restructuring? Table 20.1 illustrates three possible outcomes in addition to the original no-debt case. Notice that, in scenario II, the value of the firm is unchanged at $1,000. In scenario I, firm value rises by $250; it falls by $250 in scenario III. We have not yet said what might lead to these changes. For now, we just take them as possible outcomes to illustrate a point.

Since our goal is to benefit the shareholders, we next examine, in Table 20.2, the net payoffs to the shareholders in these scenarios. We see that, if the value of the firm stays the same, then shareholders will experience a capital loss that will exactly offset the extra dividend. This is outcome II. In outcome I, the value of the firm increases to $1,250 and the shareholders come out ahead by $250. In other words, the restructuring has an NPV of $250 in this scenario. The NPV in scenario III is –$250.

The key observation to make here is that the change in the value of the firm is the same as the net effect on the shareholders. Financial managers can therefore try to find the capital structure that maximises the value of the firm. Put another way, the NPV rule applies to capital structure decisions, and the change in the value of the overall firm is the NPV of a restructuring. Thus, World Cup should borrow $500 if it expects outcome I. The crucial question in determining a firm's capital structure is, of course, which scenario is likely to occur.

 TABLE 20.1

		Debt plus dividend		
	No debt	I	II	III
Debt	Nil	$500	$500	$500
Equity	$1,000	750	500	250
Firm value	$1,000	$1,250	$1,000	$750

Possible firm values: No debt versus debt plus dividend

Possible payoffs to shareholders: Debt plus dividends			
	Debt plus dividend		
	I	II	III
Equity value reduction	−$250	−$500	−$750
Dividends	500	500	500
Net effect	+$250	$ 0	−$250

TABLE 20.2

Capital structure and the cost of capital

In Chapter 18, we discussed the concept of the firm's weighted average cost of capital (WACC). You may recall that the WACC tells us that the firm's overall cost of capital is a weighted average of the costs of the various components of the firm's capital structure. When we described the WACC, we took the firm's capital structure as given. Thus, one important issue that we will want to explore in this chapter is what happens to the cost of capital when we vary the amount of debt financing or the debt/equity ratio.

A primary reason for studying the WACC is that the value of the firm is maximised when the WACC is minimised. To see this, recall that the WACC is the discount rate that is appropriate for the firm's overall cash flows. Since values and discount rates move in opposite directions, minimising the WACC will maximise the value of the firm's cash flows.

Thus, we will want to choose the firm's capital structure so that the WACC is minimised. For this reason, we will say that one capital structure is better than another if it results in a lower weighted average cost of capital. Further, we say that a particular debt/equity ratio represents the *optimal capital structure* if it results in the lowest possible WACC. This is sometimes called the firm's *target* capital structure as well.

Concept questions

20.1a *Why should financial managers choose the capital structure that maximises the value of the firm?*

20.1b *What is the relationship between the WACC and the value of the firm?*

20.1c *What is an optimal capital structure?*

20.2 ▪ The effect of financial leverage

The previous section describes why the capital structure that produces the highest firm value (or the lowest cost of capital) is the one most beneficial to shareholders. In this section, we examine the impact of financial leverage on the payoffs to shareholders. As you may recall, financial leverage refers to the extent to which a firm relies on debt. The more debt financing a firm uses in its capital structure, the more financial leverage it employs.

As we describe, financial leverage can dramatically alter the payoffs to shareholders in the firm. Remarkably, however, financial leverage may not affect the overall cost of capital. If this is true, then a firm's capital structure is irrelevant because changes in capital structure will not affect the value of the firm. We will return to this issue a little later.

The impact of financial leverage

We start by illustrating how financial leverage works. For now, we ignore the impact of taxes. Also, for ease of presentation, we describe the impact of leverage in terms of its effects on earnings per share (EPS) and return on equity (ROE). These are, of course, accounting numbers and, as such, are not our primary concern. Using cash flows instead of these accounting numbers would lead to precisely the same conclusions, but a little more work would be required. We discuss the impact on market values in a subsequent section.

Financial leverage, EPS and ROE: An example

The Steve Entertainment Company Ltd currently has no debt in its capital structure. The financial manager, Ms Crock, is considering a restructuring that would involve issuing debt and using the proceeds to buy back some of the outstanding equity. Table 20.3 presents both the current and proposed capital structures. As shown, the firm's assets have a value of $8 million, and there are 400,000 shares outstanding. Because Steve Entertainment is an all-equity firm, the price per share is $20.

TABLE 20.3

Current and proposed capital structures for the Steve Entertainment Company Ltd		
	Current	**Proposed**
Assets	$8,000,000	$8,000,000
Debt	Nil	$4,000,000
Equity	$8,000,000	$4,000,000
Debt/equity ratio	0	1
Share price	$20	$20
Shares outstanding	400,000	200,000
Interest rate	10%	10%

The proposed debt issue would raise $4 million; the interest rate would be 10 per cent. The $4 million raised would be used to reduce equity capital from 400,000 shares to 200,000 shares. Thus the value of equity would reduce to $4 million. After the restructuring, Steve Entertainment would have a capital structure that was 50 per cent debt, so the debt/equity ratio would be 1. Notice that for now, we assume that the share price will remain at $20.

To investigate the impact of the proposed restructuring, Ms Crock has prepared Table 20.4, which compares the firm's current capital structure to the proposed capital structure under three scenarios. The scenarios reflect different assumptions about the firm's earnings before interest and taxation (EBIT). Under the expected scenario, the EBIT is $1 million. In the recession scenario, EBIT falls to $500,000. In the expansion scenario, it rises to $1.5 million.

To illustrate some of the calculations in Table 20.4, consider the expansion case. EBIT is $1.5 million. With no debt (the current capital structure) and no taxes, net profit is also $1.5 million. In this case, there are 400,000 shares worth $8 million total. EPS is therefore $1.5 million/400,000 = $3.75 per share. Also, since accounting return on equity (ROE) is net profit divided by total equity, ROE is $1.5 million/$8 million = 18.75%.[2]

Capital structure scenarios for the Steve Entertainment Company Ltd				TABLE 20.4

Current capital structure: No debt

	Recession	Expected	Expansion
EBIT	$500,000	$1,000,000	$1,500,000
Interest	0	0	0
Net profit	$500,000	$1,000,000	$1,500,000
ROE	6.25%	12.50%	18.75%
EPS	$1.25	$2.50	$3.75

Proposed capital structure: Debt = $4 million

	Recession	Expected	Expansion
EBIT	$500,000	$1,000,000	$1,500,000
Interest	400,000	400,000	400,000
Net profit	$100,000	$ 600,000	$1,100,000
ROE	2.50%	15.00%	27.50%
EPS	$0.50	$3.00	$5.50

With $4 million in debt (the proposed capital structure), things are somewhat different. Since the interest rate is 10 per cent, the interest bill is $400,000. With EBIT of $1.5 million, interest of $400,000, and no taxes, net profit is $1.1 million. Now there are only 200,000 shares worth $4 million total. EPS is therefore $1.1 million/200,000 = $5.50 per share versus the $3.75 per share that we calculated above. Furthermore, ROE is $1.1 million/$4 million = 27.5%. This is well above the 18.75 per cent we calculated for the current capital structure.

EPS versus EBIT

The impact of leverage is evident when the effect of the restructuring on EPS and ROE is examined. In particular, the variability in both EPS and ROE is much larger under the proposed capital structure. This illustrates how financial leverage acts to magnify gains and losses to shareholders.

In Figure 20.1 (overleaf), we take a closer look at the effect of the proposed restructuring. This figure plots earnings per share (EPS) against earnings before interest and taxes (EBIT) for the current and proposed capital structures. The first line, labelled 'No debt', represents the case of no leverage. This line begins at the origin, indicating that EPS would be zero if EBIT were zero. From there, every $400,000 increase in EBIT increases EPS by $1 (because there are 400,000 shares outstanding).

The second line represents the proposed capital structure. Here, EPS is negative if EBIT is zero. This follows because $400,000 of interest must be paid regardless of the firm's profits. Since there are 200,000 shares in this case, the EPS is −$2 per share as shown. Similarly, if EBIT were $400,000, EPS would be exactly zero.

The important thing to notice in Figure 20.1 is that the slope of the line in this second case is steeper. In fact, for every $400,000 increase in EBIT, EPS rises by $2, so the line is twice as steep. This tells us that EPS is twice as sensitive to changes in EBIT because of the financial leverage employed.

A CLOSER LOOK

FIGURE
20.1

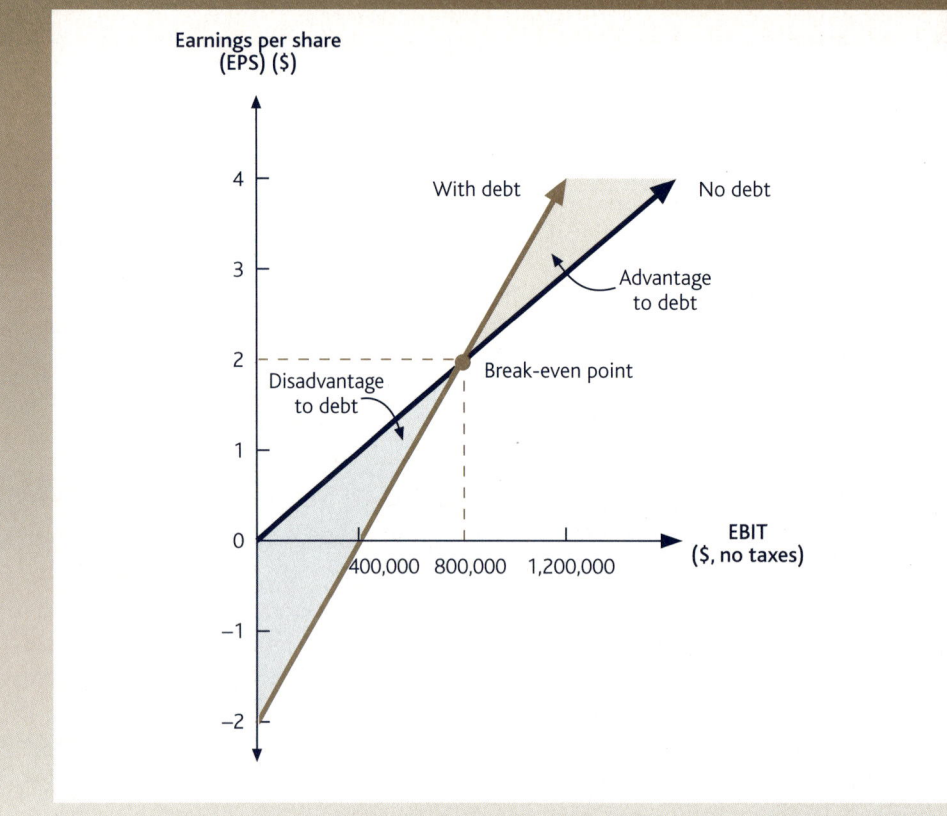

Financial leverage, EPS and EBIT for the Steve Entertainment company

Another observation to make in Figure 20.1 is that the lines intersect. At that point, EPS is exactly the same for both capital structures. To find this point, note that EPS is equal to EBIT/400,000 in the no-debt case. In the with-debt case, EPS is (EBIT − $400,000)/200,000. If we set these equal to each other, EBIT is:

$$\text{EBIT}/400{,}000 = (\text{EBIT} - \$400{,}000)/200{,}000$$
$$\text{EBIT} = 2 \times (\text{EBIT} - \$400{,}000)$$
$$\text{EBIT} = \$800{,}000$$

When EBIT is $800,000, EPS is $2 per share under either capital structure. This is labelled as the break-even point in Figure 20.1. If EBIT is above this level, leverage is beneficial; if it is below this point, it is not.

There is another, more intuitive, way of seeing why the break-even point is $800,000. Notice that, if the firm has no debt and its EBIT is $800,000, its net profit is also $800,000. In this case, the ROE is 10 per cent. This is precisely the same as the interest rate on the debt, so the firm earns a return that is just sufficient to pay the interest.

EXAMPLE

20.1

Break-even EBIT

The Soccer Italy Company Ltd (SIC) has decided to restructure its capital. Currently, SIC uses no debt financing. Following the restructuring, however, debt will be $1 million. The interest rate on the debt will be 9 per cent. SIC currently has 200,000 shares outstanding, and the price per share is $20. If the restructuring is expected to increase EPS, what is the minimum level for EBIT that SIC's management must be expecting? Ignore taxes in answering.

To answer, we calculate the break-even EBIT. At any EBIT above this, the increased financial leverage will increase EPS, so this will tell us the minimum level for EBIT. Under the old capital structure, EPS is simply EBIT/200,000. Under the new capital structure, the interest expense will be $1 million × 0.09 = $90,000. Furthermore, with the $1 million proceeds, SIC will refund $1 million/$20 = 50,000 shares, leaving 150,000 outstanding. EPS is thus (EBIT − $90,000)/150,000.

Now that we know how to calculate EPS under both scenarios, we set them equal to each other and solve for the break-even EBIT:

$$EBIT/200,000 = (EBIT − \$90,000)/150,000$$
$$EBIT = (^4/_3) \times (EBIT − \$90,000)$$
$$EBIT = \$360,000$$

Check that, in either case, EPS is $1.80 when EBIT is $360,000. Management at SIC is apparently of the opinion that EPS will exceed $1.80.

Corporate borrowing and home-made leverage

Based on Tables 20.3 and 20.4 and Figure 20.1, Ms Crock draws the following conclusions:

1   The effect of financial leverage depends on the company's EBIT. When EBIT is relatively high, leverage is beneficial.
2   Under the expected scenario, leverage increases the returns to shareholders, as measured by both ROE and EPS.
3   Shareholders are exposed to more risk under the proposed capital structure since the EPS and ROE are much more sensitive to changes in EBIT in this case.
4   Because of the impact that financial leverage has on both the expected return to shareholders and the riskiness of the shares, capital structure is an important consideration.

The first three of these conclusions are clearly correct. Does the last conclusion necessarily follow? Surprisingly, the answer is no. As we discuss next, the reason is that shareholders can adjust the amount of financial leverage by borrowing and lending on their own. This use of personal borrowing to alter the degree of financial leverage is called **home-made leverage**.

We will now illustrate that it actually makes no difference whether or not Steve Entertainment adopts the proposed capital structure, because any shareholder who prefers the proposed capital structure can simply create it using home-made leverage. To begin, the first part of Table 20.5 (overleaf) shows what would happen to an investor who buys $2,000 worth of Steve Entertainment shares if the proposed capital structure were adopted. This investor purchases 100 shares. From Table 20.4, EPS will either be $0.50, $3 or $5.50, so the total earnings for 100 shares will either be $50, $300 or $550 under the proposed capital structure.

home-made leverage

the use of personal borrowing to change the overall amount of financial leverage to which the individual is exposed

TABLE
20.5

Proposed capital structure versus original capital structure with home-made leverage

Proposed capital structure

	Recession	Expected	Expansion
EPS	$ 0.50	$ 3.00	$ 5.50
Earnings for 100 shares	50.00	300.00	550.00

Net cost = 100 shares at $20 = $2,000

Original capital structure and home-made leverage

	Recession	Expected	Expansion
EPS	$ 1.25	$ 2.50	$ 3.75
Earnings for 200 shares	250.00	500.00	750.00
Less interest on $2,000.00 at 10%	200.00	200.00	200.00
Net earnings	$ 50.00	$300.00	$550.00

Net cost = 200 shares at $20 a share − Amount borrowed = $4,000 − $2,000 = $2,000

Now, suppose that Steve Entertainment does not adopt the proposed capital structure. In this case, EPS will be $1.25, $2.50 or $3.75. The second part of Table 20.5 demonstrates how a shareholder who preferred the payoffs under the proposed structure can create them using personal borrowing. To do this, the shareholder borrows $2,000 at 10 per cent on her own. Our investor uses this amount, along with her original $2,000, to buy 200 shares. As shown, the net payoffs are exactly the same as those for the proposed capital structure.

How did we know to borrow $2,000 to create the right payoffs? We are trying to replicate Steve Entertainment's proposed capital structure at the personal level. The proposed capital structure results in a debt/equity ratio of 1. To replicate it at the personal level, the shareholder must borrow enough to create this same debt/equity ratio. Since the shareholder has $2,000 in equity invested, borrowing another $2,000 will create a personal debt/equity ratio of 1.

This example demonstrates that investors can always increase financial leverage themselves to create a different pattern of payoffs. It thus makes no difference whether or not Steve Entertainment chooses the proposed capital structure.

EXAMPLE
20.2   **Unlevering the equity**

In our Steve Entertainment example, suppose that management adopts the proposed capital structure. Further, suppose that an investor who owned 100 shares preferred the original capital structure. Show how this investor could 'unlever' the equity to recreate the original payoffs.

To create leverage, investors borrow on their own. To undo leverage, investors must lend money. For Steve Entertainment, the company borrowed an amount equal to half its value. The investor can unlever the equity by simply lending money in the same proportion. In this case, the investor sells 50 shares for $1,000 total and then lends the $1,000 at 10 per cent. The payoffs are calculated in the table opposite.

Unlevering the equity (*continued*)

	Recession	Expected	Expansion
EPS (proposed structure)	$ 0.50	$ 3.00	$ 5.50
Earnings for 50 shares	25.00	150.00	275.00
Plus: Interest on $1,000	100.00	100.00	100.00
Total payoff	$125.00	$250.00	$375.00

These are precisely the payoffs that the investor would have experienced under the original capital structure.

Concept questions

20.2a *What is the impact of financial leverage on shareholders?*
20.2b *What is home-made leverage?*
20.2c *Why is Steve Entertainment's capital structure irrelevant?*

20.3 ▪ Capital structure and the cost of equity capital

We have seen that there is nothing special about corporate borrowing because investors can borrow or lend on their own. As a result, whichever capital structure Steve Entertainment chooses, the share price will be the same. Steve Entertainment's capital structure is thus irrelevant, at least in the simple world we examined.

Our Steve Entertainment example is based on a famous argument advanced by two Nobel laureates, Franco Modigliani and Merton Miller, whom we will henceforth call M&M. What we illustrated for the Steve Entertainment Company is a special case of **M&M Proposition I**. M&M Proposition I states that it is completely irrelevant how a firm chooses to arrange its finances.

M&M Proposition I
the value of the firm is independent of its capital structure

M&M Proposition I: The pie model

One way to illustrate M&M Proposition I is to imagine two firms that are identical on the left-hand side of the balance sheet. Their assets and operations are exactly the same. The right-hand sides are different because the two firms finance their operations differently. In this case, we can view the capital structure question in terms of a 'pie' model. Why we chose this name is apparent in Figure 20.2 (overleaf). Figure 20.2 gives two possible ways of cutting up this pie between the equity slice, E, and the debt slice, D: 40%–60% and 60%–40%. However, the size of the pie in Figure 20.2 is the same for both firms because the value of the assets is the same. This is precisely what M&M Proposition I states:

> The size of the pie does not depend on how it is sliced.

FIGURE 20.2

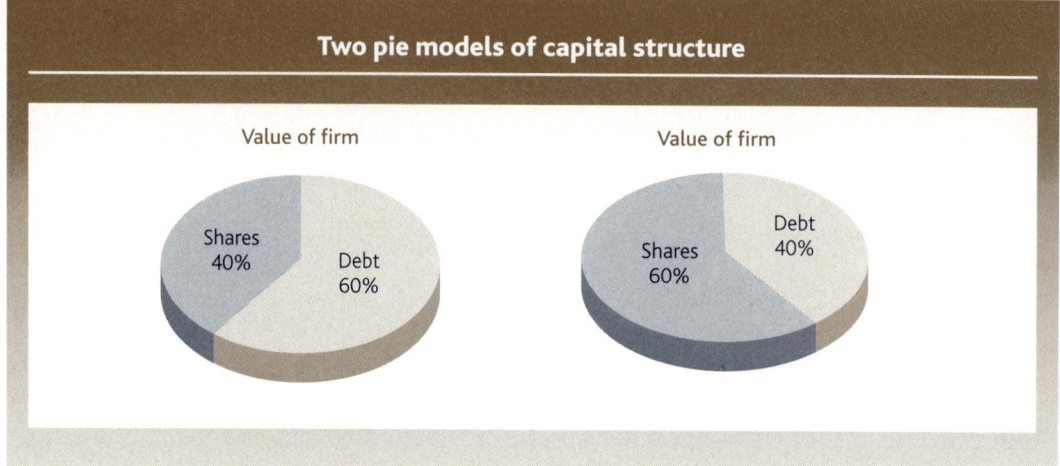

Two pie models of capital structure

Value of firm

Shares 40%
Debt 60%

Value of firm

Shares 60%
Debt 40%

The cost of equity and financial leverage: M&M Proposition II

Although changing the capital structure of the firm may not change the firm's *total* value, it does cause important changes in the firm's debt and equity. We now examine what happens to a firm financed with debt and equity when the debt/equity ratio is changed. To simplify our analysis, we will continue to ignore taxes.

M&M Proposition II

In Chapter 18, we saw that, if we ignore taxes, the weighted average cost of capital, WACC, is:

$$\text{WACC} = E/V \times R_E + D/V \times R_D$$

where $V = E + D$. We also saw that one way of interpreting the WACC is that it is the required return on the firm's overall assets. To remind us of this, we will use the symbol R_A to stand for the WACC and write:

$$R_A = E/V \times R_E + D/V \times R_D$$

If we rearrange this to solve for the cost of equity capital, we see that:

$$R_E = R_A + (R_A - R_D) \times (D/E) \tag{20.1}$$

M&M Proposition II

a firm's cost of equity capital is a positive linear function of its capital structure

This is the famous **M&M Proposition II**, which tells us that the cost of equity depends on three things: the required rate of return on the firm's assets, R_A, the firm's cost of debt, R_D, and the firm's debt/equity ratio, D/E.

Figure 20.3 summarises our discussion thus far by plotting the cost of equity capital, R_E, against the debt/equity ratio. As shown, M&M Proposition II indicates that the cost of equity, R_E, is given by a straight line with a slope of $(R_A - R_D)$. The y-intercept corresponds to a firm with a debt/equity ratio of zero, so $R_A = R_E$ in that case. Figure 20.3 shows that, as the firm raises its debt/equity ratio, the increase in leverage raises the risk of the equity and therefore the required return or cost of equity (R_E).

The cost of equity and the WACC. M&M proposition I and II with no taxes

FIGURE
20.3

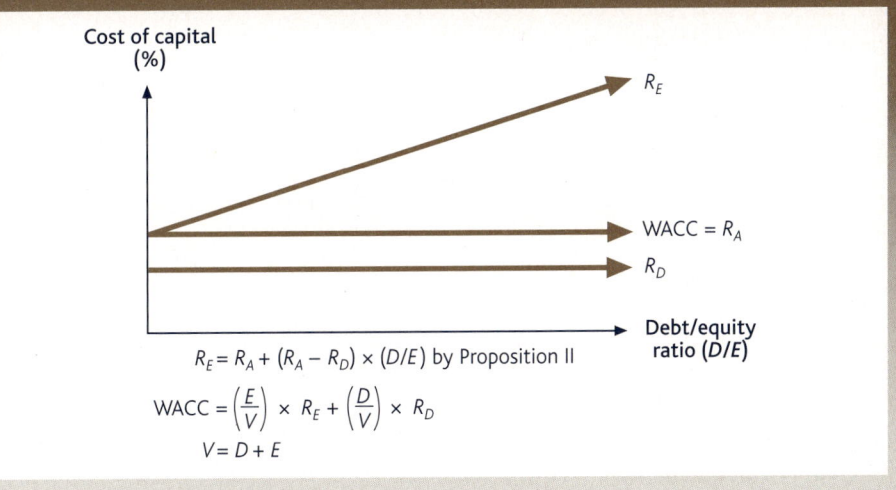

$$R_E = R_A + (R_A - R_D) \times (D/E) \text{ by Proposition II}$$

$$WACC = \left(\frac{E}{V}\right) \times R_E + \left(\frac{D}{V}\right) \times R_D$$

$$V = D + E$$

In their own words

Merton H. Miller* on capital structure—M&M 30 years later

How difficult it is to summarise briefly the contribution of these papers was brought home to me very clearly after Franco Modigliani was awarded the Nobel Prize in Economics, in part—but, of course, only in part—for the work in finance. The television camera crews from our local stations in Chicago immediately descended upon me. 'We understand,' they said, 'that you worked with Modigliani some years back in developing these M&M theorems, and we wonder if you could explain them briefly to our television viewers.' 'How briefly?' I asked. 'Oh, take 10 seconds,' was the reply.

Ten seconds to explain the work of a lifetime! Ten seconds to describe two carefully reasoned articles, each running to more than 30 printed pages and each with 60 or so long footnotes! When they saw the look of dismay on my face, they said: 'You do not have to go into details. Just give us the main points in simple, commonsense terms.'

The main point of the cost-of-capital article was, in principle at least, simple enough to make. It said that in an economist's ideal world, the total market value of all the securities issued by a firm would be governed by the earning power and risk of its underlying real assets and would be independent of how the mix of securities issued to finance it was divided between debt instruments and equity capital. Some corporate treasurers might well think that they could enhance total value by increasing the proportion of debt instruments because yields on debt instruments, given their lower risk, are, by and large, substantially below those on equity capital. But, under the ideal conditions assumed, the added risk to the shareholders from issuing more debt will raise required yields on the equity by just enough to offset the seeming gain from use of low cost debt. (continued)

Such a summary would not only have been too long, but it relied on shorthand terms and concepts that are rich in connotations to economists, but hardly so to the general public. I thought, instead, of an analogy that we ourselves had invoked in the original paper. 'Think of the firm,' I said, 'as a gigantic tub of whole milk. The farmer can sell the whole milk as is. Or he can separate out the cream and sell it at a considerably higher price than the whole milk would bring. (Selling cream is the analogue of a firm selling low yield and hence high-priced debt securities.) But, of course, what the farmer would have left would be skim milk, with low butter-fat content and that would sell for much less than whole milk. Skim milk corresponds to the levered equity. The M&M proposition says that if there were no costs of separation (and, of course, no government dairy support programs), the cream plus the skim milk would bring the same price as the whole milk.'

The television people conferred among themselves for a while. They informed me that it was still too long, too complicated, and too academic. 'Have you anything simpler?' they asked. I thought for another way that the M&M proposition is presented which stresses the role of securities as devices for 'partitioning' a firm's payoffs among the group of its capital suppliers. 'Think of the firm,' I said, 'as a gigantic pizza, divided into quarters. If now, you cut each quarter in half into eighths, the M&M proposition says that you will have more pieces, but not more pizza.'

Once again whispered conversation. This time, they shut the lights off. They folded up their equipment. They thanked me for my co-operation. They said they would get back to me. But I knew that I had somehow lost my chance to start a new career as a packager of economic wisdom for TV viewers in convenient 10-second sound bites. Some have the talent for it; and some just do not.

* The late **Merton H. Miller** was famous for his path-breaking work with Franco Modigliani on corporate capital structure, cost of capital, and dividend policy. He received the Nobel Prize in Economics for his contributions shortly after this essay was prepared.

Notice in Figure 20.3 that the WACC does not depend on the debt/equity ratio; it is the same no matter what the debt/equity ratio is. This is another way of stating M&M Proposition I: *The firm's overall cost of capital is unaffected by its capital structure.* As illustrated, the fact that the cost of debt is lower than the cost of equity is exactly offset by the increase in the cost of equity from borrowing. In other words, the change in the capital structure weights (E/V and D/V) is exactly offset by the change in the cost of equity (R_E), so the WACC stays the same.

EXAMPLE 20.3 ■ The cost of equity capital

The Jock Company Ltd has a weighted average cost of capital (unadjusted) of 12 per cent. It can borrow at 8 per cent. Assuming that Jock has a target capital structure of 80 per cent equity and 20 per cent debt, what is its cost of equity? What is the cost of equity if the target capital structure is 50 per cent equity? Calculate the unadjusted WACC using your answers to verify that it is the same.

EXAMPLE 20.3

The cost of equity capital (*continued*)

According to M&M Proposition II, the cost of equity, R_E, is:

$$R_E = R_A + (R_A - R_D) \times (D/E)$$

In the first case, the debt/equity ratio is $0.2/0.8 = 0.25$, so the cost of the equity is:

$$R_E = 12\% + (12\% - 8\%) \times (0.25)$$
$$= 13\%$$

In the second case, check that the debt/equity ratio is 1.0, so the cost of equity is 16 per cent.

We can now calculate the unadjusted WACC assuming that the percentage of equity financing is 80 per cent and the cost of equity is 13 per cent:

$$WACC = E/V \times R_E + D/V \times R_D$$
$$= 0.80 \times 13\% + 0.20 \times 8\%$$
$$= 12\%$$

In the second case, the percentage of equity financing is 50 per cent and the cost of equity is 16 per cent. The WACC is:

$$WACC = E/V \times R_E + D/V \times R_D$$
$$= 0.50 \times 16\% + 0.50 \times 8\%$$
$$= 12\%$$

As we calculated, the WACC is 12 per cent in both cases.

Business and financial risk

M&M Proposition II shows that the firm's cost of equity can be broken down into two components. The first component, R_A, is the required return on the overall firm's assets, and it depends on the nature of the firm's operating activities. The risk inherent in a firm's operations is called the **business risk** of the firm's equity. Referring back to Chapter 11, this business risk depends on the systematic risk of the firm's assets. The greater a firm's business risk, the greater R_A will be, and, all things being the same, the greater its cost of equity.

business risk
the equity risk that comes from the nature of the firm's operating activities

The second component in the cost of equity, $(R_A - R_D) \times D/E$, is determined by the firm's financial structure. For an all-equity firm, this component is zero. As the firm begins to rely on debt financing, the required return rises. This occurs because the debt financing increases the risks borne by the shareholders. This extra risk that arises from the use of debt financing is called the **financial risk** of the firm's equity.

financial risk
the equity risk that comes from the financial policy (i.e. capital structure) of the firm

The total systematic risk of the firm's equity thus has two parts: business risk and financial risk. The first part (the business risk) depends on the firm's assets and operations and is not affected by capital structure. Given the firm's business risk (and its cost of debt), the second part (the financial risk) is completely determined by financial policy. As we have illustrated, the firm's cost of equity rises when it increases its use of financial leverage because the financial risk of the equity increases while the business risk remains the same.

The SML and M&M Proposition II

In Chapter 18, we discussed the use of the security market line (SML) to estimate the cost of equity capital. We now combine the SML and M&M Proposition II. Using the SML, we can write the required return on the firm's assets as:

$$R_A = R_f + (R_M - R_f) \times \beta_A$$

The beta coefficient in this case, β_A, is called the firm's *asset* beta, and it is a measure of the systematic risk of the firm's assets. It is also called the unlevered beta because it is the beta that the equity would have if the firm had no debt.

The cost of equity from the SML is:

$$R_E = R_f + (R_M - R_f) \times \beta_E$$

Let us assume that the assets of the firm fully cover the security and the return that should accrue to the firm's debt. It follows that cost of debt, R_D, is equal to the risk-free rate, R_f. If we substitute for R_D in M&M Proposition II, we have:

$$R_E = R_A + (R_A - R_f) \times D/E$$

Now we can use the SML to replace R_A so that:

$$
\begin{aligned}
R_E &= [R_f + (R_M - R_f) \times \beta_A] + \{[R_f + (R_M - R_f) \times \beta_A] - R_f\} \times (D/E) \\
&= R_f + (R_M - R_f) \times \beta_A + [(R_M - R_f) \times \beta_A)] \times D/E \\
&= R_f + (R_M - R_f) \times \beta_A \times (1 + D/E)
\end{aligned}
$$

But from the SML:

$$R_E = R_f + (R_M - R_f) \times \beta_E$$

therefore:

$$\beta_E = \beta_A \times (1 + D/E) \tag{20.2}$$

We are now in a position to examine directly the impact of financial leverage on the firm's cost of equity. Rewriting things a bit, we see the equity beta has two components:

$$\beta_E = \beta_A + \beta_A \times (D/E)$$

We have been able to show that the systematic risk of the equity reduces to two components, the business risk (β_A) and the financial risk ($\beta_A \times (D/E)$), thus reinforcing the arguments presented above.

Concept questions

20.3a *What does M&M Proposition I state?*
20.3b *What are the two determinants of a firm's cost of equity?*

 ## 20.4 M&M propositions I and II with corporate taxes

Debt has two distinguishing features that we have not taken into proper account. First, as we have mentioned in a number of places, interest paid on debt is tax-deductible. This is good for the firm, and it may be an added benefit to debt financing. Second, failure to meet debt obligations can result in bankruptcy. This is not good for the firm, and it may be an added cost of debt financing. Since we have not explicitly considered either of these two features of debt, we may get a different answer about capital structure once we do. Accordingly, we consider taxes in this section and bankruptcy in the next one.

PART 8 · COST OF CAPITAL AND LONG-TERM FINANCIAL POLICY

We can start by considering what happens to M&M Propositions I and II when we consider the effect of corporate taxes. To do this, we will examine two firms, Firm U (unlevered) and Firm L (levered). These two firms are identical on the left-hand side of the balance sheet, so their assets and operations are the same.

We assume that EBIT is expected to be $1,000 every year forever for both firms. The difference between them is that Firm L has issued $1,000 worth of perpetual bonds on which it pays 8 per cent interest each year. The interest bill is thus $0.08 \times \$1,000 = \$80$ every year forever. Also, we assume that the corporate tax rate is 30 per cent.

For our two firms, U and L, we can now calculate the following:

	Firm U	Firm L
EBIT	$1,000	$1,000
Interest	Nil	80
Taxable income	$1,000	$ 920
Taxes (30%)	300	276
Net income	$ 700	$ 644

The interest tax shield

To simplify things, we will assume that depreciation is equal to zero. We will also assume that capital expenditure is zero and that there is no additional net working capital. In this case the cash flow from assets is equal to EBIT minus taxes. For firms U and L we thus have:

Cash flow from assets

	Firm U	Firm L
EBIT	$1,000	$1,000
Less Taxes	300	276
Total	$ 700	$ 724

We immediately see that capital structure is now having some effect because the cash flows from U and L are not the same even though the two firms have identical assets.

To see what is going on, we can compute the cash flow to shareholders and debtholders.

Cash flow

	Firm U	Firm L
To Shareholders	$700	$644
To Debtholders	Nil	80
Total	$700	$724

What we are seeing is that the total cash flow to L is $24 more. This occurs because L's tax bill (which is a cash outflow) is $24 less. The fact that interest is deductible for tax purposes has generated a tax saving equal to the interest payment ($80) multiplied by the corporate tax rate (30%): $80 \times 0.30 = \$24$. We call this tax saving the **interest tax shield**.

interest tax shield
the tax saving attained by a firm from interest expense

Taxes and M&M Proposition I

Since the debt is perpetual, the same $24 shield will be generated every year forever. The after-tax cash flow to L will thus be the same $700 that U earns plus the $24 tax shield. Since L's cash flow is always $24 greater, Firm L is worth more than Firm U by the value of this $24 perpetuity.

Because the tax shield is generated by paying interest, it has the same risk as the debt, and 8 per cent (the cost of debt) is therefore the appropriate discount rate. The value of the tax shield is thus:

$$PV = \$24/0.08 = (0.30 \times 1{,}000 \times 0.08)/0.08 = 0.30(1{,}000) = \$300$$

As our example illustrates, the value of the tax shield can be written as:

Value of the interest tax shield $= (T_C \times R_D \times D)/R_D = T_C \times D$ (20.3)

We have now come up with another famous result, M&M Proposition I with corporate taxes. We have seen that the value of Firm L, V_L, exceeds the value of Firm U, V_U, by the present value of the interest tax shield, $T_C \times D$. M&M Proposition I with taxes therefore states that:

$$V_L = V_U + T_C \times D \qquad (20.4)$$

The effect of borrowing in this case is illustrated in Figure 20.4. We have plotted the value of the levered firm, V_L, against the amount of debt, D. M&M Proposition I with corporate taxes implies that the relationship is given by a straight line with a slope of T_C and a y-intercept of V_U.

In Figure 20.4, we have also drawn a horizontal line representing V_U. As indicated, the distance between the two lines is $T_C \times D$, the present value of the tax shield.

Suppose that the cost of capital for Firm U is 10 per cent. We will call this the **unlevered cost of capital**, and we will use the symbol R_U to represent it. We can think of R_U as the cost of the capital that the firm would have if it had no debt. Firm U's cash flow is $700 every year forever, and, since U has no debt, the appropriate discount rate is $R_U = 10\%$. The value of the unlevered firm, V_U, is simply:

$$\begin{aligned} V_U &= [\text{EBIT} \times (1 - T_C)]/ R_U \\ &= 700/0.10 \\ &= \$7{,}000 \end{aligned}$$

The value of the levered firm, V_L, is:

$$\begin{aligned} V_L &= V_U + T_C \times D \\ &= \$7{,}000 + 0.30 \times \$1{,}000 \\ &= \$7{,}300 \end{aligned}$$

As Figure 20.4 indicates, the value of the firm goes up by $0.30 for every $1 in debt. In other words, the NPV *per dollar* in debt is $0.30. It is difficult to imagine why any company would not borrow to the absolute maximum under these circumstances.

The result of our analysis in this section is that, once we include taxes, capital structure definitely matters. However, we immediately reach the illogical conclusion that the optimal capital structure is 100 per cent debt.

unlevered cost of capital

the cost of capital of a firm that has no debt

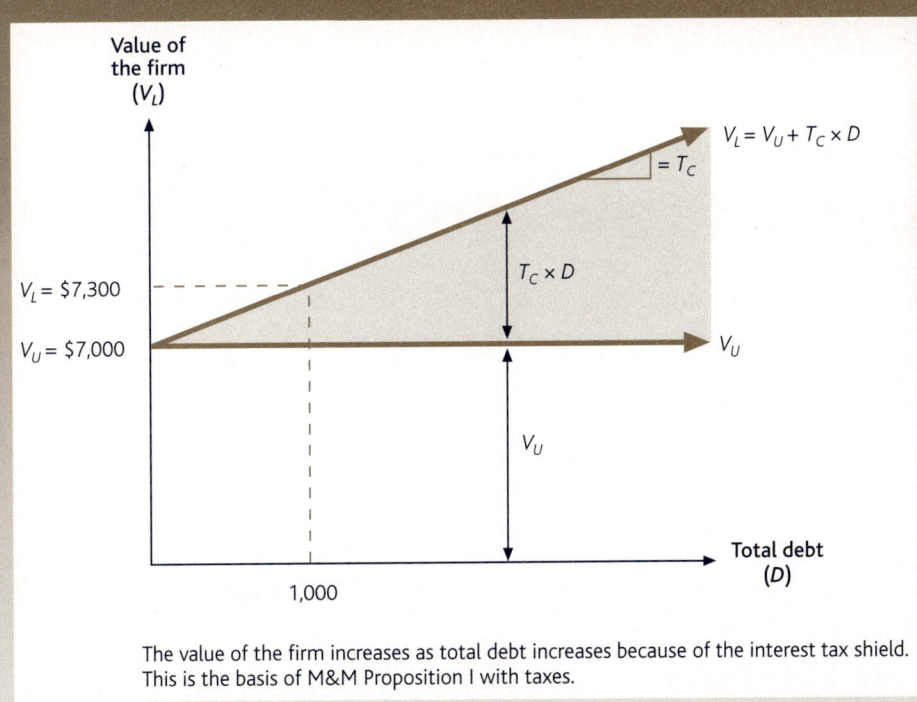

The value of the firm increases as total debt increases because of the interest tax shield. This is the basis of M&M Proposition I with taxes.

Taxes, the WACC and Proposition II

The conclusion that the best capital structure is 100 per cent debt also can be seen by examining the weighted average cost of capital. From Chapter 18, we know that, once we consider the effect of taxes, the WACC is:

$$\text{WACC} = E/V \times R_E + D/V \times R_D \times (1 - T_C)$$

To calculate this WACC, we need to know the cost of equity. M&M Proposition II with corporate taxes states that the cost of equity is:

$$R_E = R_U + (R_U - R_D) \times (D/E) \times (1 - T_C) \qquad (20.5)$$

To illustrate, we saw a moment ago that Firm L is worth $7,300 total. Since the debt is worth $1,000, the equity must be worth $7,300 - 1,000 = $6,300. For Firm L, the cost of equity is thus:

$$
\begin{aligned}
R_E &= 0.10 + (0.10 - 0.08) \times (\$1,000/\$6,300) \times (1 - 0.30) \\
&= 10.22\%
\end{aligned}
$$

The weighted average cost of capital is:

$$
\begin{aligned}
\text{WACC} &= \$6,300/\$7,300 \times 10.22\% + \$1,000/\$7,300 \times 8\% \times (1 - 0.30) \\
&= 9.6\%
\end{aligned}
$$

Without debt, the WACC is 10 per cent, and, with debt, it is 9.6 per cent. Therefore, the firm is better off with debt.

Figure 20.5 summarises our discussion concerning the relationship between the cost of equity, the after-tax cost of debt, and the weighted average cost of capital. For reference, we have included R_U, the unlevered cost of capital. In Figure 20.5, we have the debt/equity ratio on the horizontal axis. Notice how the WACC declines as the debt/equity ratio grows. This illustrates again that the more debt the firm uses, the lower is its WACC. Table 20.6 summarises the key results for future reference.

FIGURE 20.5

The cost of equity and the WACC. M&M Propositions I and II with taxes

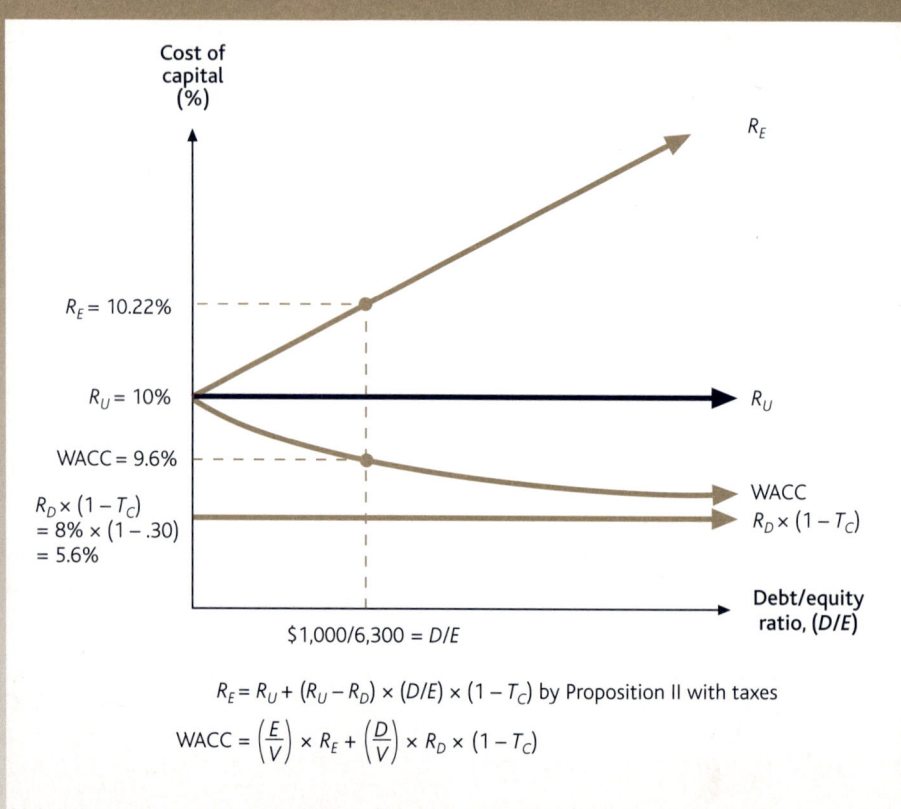

Cost of capital (%)

R_E

$R_E = 10.22\%$

$R_U = 10\%$ R_U

WACC $= 9.6\%$

$R_D \times (1 - T_C)$
$= 8\% \times (1 - .30)$
$= 5.6\%$

WACC

$R_D \times (1 - T_C)$

Debt/equity ratio, (D/E)

$\$1{,}000/6{,}300 = D/E$

$R_E = R_U + (R_U - R_D) \times (D/E) \times (1 - T_C)$ by Proposition II with taxes

$$\text{WACC} = \left(\frac{E}{V}\right) \times R_E + \left(\frac{D}{V}\right) \times R_D \times (1 - T_C)$$

TABLE 20.6

Modigliani and Miller Summary

I. *The no-tax case*

    A. Proposition I: The value of the firm leveraged (V_L) is equal to the value of the firm unleveraged (V_U):

$$V_L = V_U$$

TABLE
20.6

Modigliani and Miller Summary (*continued*)

Implications of Proposition I:
1. A firm's capital structure is irrelevant.
2. A firm's weighted average cost of capital (WACC) is the same no matter what mixture of debt and equity is used to finance the firm.

B. Proposition II: The cost of equity, R_E, is:

$$R_E = R_A + (R_A - R_D) \times D/E$$

where, R_A is the WACC, R_D is the cost of debt, and D/E is the debt/equity ratio.

Implications of Proposition II:
1. The cost of equity rises as the firm increases its use of debt financing.
2. The risk of the equity depends on two things: the riskiness of the firm's operations (business risk) and the degree of financial leverage (financial risk).

II. *With taxes:*

A. Proposition I with taxes: The value of the firm levered (V_L) is equal to the value of the firm unlevered (V_U), plus the present value of the interest tax shield:

$$V_L = V_U + T_C \times D$$

where T_C is the corporate tax rate and D is the amount of debt.

Implications of Proposition I:
1. Debt financing is highly advantageous, and, in the extreme, a firm's optimal capital structure is 100 per cent debt.
2. A firm's weighted average cost of capital (WACC) decreases as the firm relies on debt financing.

B. Proposition II with taxes: The cost of equity, R_E, is:

$$R_E = R_U + (R_U - R_D) \times D/E \times (1 - T_C)$$

where R_U is the unlevered cost of capital, i.e. the cost of capital for the firm if it had no debt.

Unlike Proposition I, the general implications of Proposition II are the same whether there are taxes or not.

EXAMPLE 20.4

The cost of equity and the value of the firm

This is a comprehensive example that illustrates most of the points we have discussed so far.

You are given the following information for the Jane Co. Pty Ltd:

$$\text{EBIT} = \$142.857$$
$$T_C = 30\% \text{ so that taxation is } \$42.857$$
$$D = \$500$$
$$R_U = 0.20$$

The cost of debt capital is 10 per cent. What is the value of Jane's equity? What is the cost of equity capital for Jane? What is the WACC? *(continued)*

EXAMPLE
20.4

The cost of equity and the value of the firm (*continued*)

This one is easier than it looks. Remember that all the cash flows are perpetuities. The value of the firm if it had no debt, V_U, is:

$$V_U = \frac{\text{EBIT} - \text{Taxes}}{R_U}$$
$$= 100/0.20$$
$$= \$500$$

From M&M Proposition I with taxes, we know that the value of the firm with debt is:

$$V_L = V_U + T_C \times D$$
$$= \$500 + 0.30 \times \$500$$
$$= \$650$$

Since the firm is worth $650 total and the debt is worth $500, the equity is worth $150.

$$E = V_L - D$$
$$= \$650 - 500$$
$$= \$150$$

Thus, from M&M Proposition II with taxes, the cost of equity is:

$$R_E = R_U + (R_U - R_D) \times (D/E) \times (1 - T_C)$$
$$= 0.20 + (0.20 - 0.10) \times (\$500/150) \times (1 - 0.30)$$
$$= 43.3\%$$

Finally, the WACC is:

$$\text{WACC} = (\$150/650) \times 43.3\% + (\$500/650) \times 10\% \times (1 - 0.30)$$
$$= 15.38\%$$

Notice that this is substantially lower than the cost of capital for the firm with no debt ($R_U = 20\%$), so debt financing is highly advantageous.

Concept questions

20.4a *What is the relationship between the value of an unlevered firm and the value of a levered firm once we consider the effect of corporate taxes?*

20.4b *If we only consider the effect of taxes, what is the optimum capital structure?*

 ## 20.5 Bankruptcy costs

One limit to the amount of debt a firm might use comes in the form of bankruptcy costs. As the debt/equity ratio rises, so too does the probability that the firm will be unable to pay its debtholders what was promised to them. When this happens, ownership of the firm's assets is ultimately transferred from the shareholders to the debtholders.

In principle, a firm is bankrupt when the value of its assets equals the value of the debt. When this occurs, the value of equity is zero and the shareholders turn over control of the firm to the debtholders. When this takes place, the debtholders hold assets whose value is exactly equal to what is owed on the debt. In a perfect world, there are no costs associated with this transfer of ownership, and the debtholders do not lose anything.

This idealised view of bankruptcy is not, of course, what happens in the real world. Ironically, it is expensive to go bankrupt. As we discuss, the costs associated with bankruptcy may eventually offset the tax-related gains from leverage.

Direct bankruptcy costs

When the value of a firm's assets equals the value of its debt, then the firm is economically bankrupt in the sense that the equity has no value. However, the formal means of turning over the assets to the debtholders is a legal process, not an economic one. There are legal and administrative costs to bankruptcy, and it has been remarked that bankruptcies are to lawyers what blood is to sharks.

Because of the expenses associated with bankruptcy, debtholders will not get all that they are owed. Some fraction of the firm's assets will 'disappear' in the legal process of going bankrupt. These are the legal and administrative expenses associated with the bankruptcy proceeding. We call these costs **direct bankruptcy costs**.

These direct bankruptcy costs are a disincentive to debt financing. If a firm goes bankrupt, then, suddenly, a piece of the firm disappears. This amounts to a bankruptcy 'tax'. So a firm faces a trade-off: Borrowing saves a firm money on its corporate taxes, but the more a firm borrows, the more likely it is that the firm will become bankrupt and have to pay the bankruptcy tax.

direct bankruptcy costs
the costs that are directly associated with bankruptcy, such as legal and administrative expenses

Indirect bankruptcy costs

Because it is expensive to go bankrupt, a firm will spend resources to avoid doing so. When a firm is having significant problems in meeting its debt obligations, we say that it is experiencing financial distress. Some financially distressed firms ultimately file for bankruptcy, but most do not because they are able to recover or otherwise survive.

The costs of avoiding a bankruptcy filing by a financially distressed firm are called **indirect bankruptcy costs**. We use the term **financial distress costs** to refer generically to the direct and indirect costs associated with going bankrupt and/or avoiding a bankruptcy filing.

When the shareholders and the debtholders are different groups, the problems that come up in financial distress are particularly severe, and the financial distress costs are thus larger. Until the firm is legally bankrupt, the shareholders control it. They, of course, will take actions in their own economic interests. Since the shareholders can be wiped out in a legal bankruptcy, they have a very strong incentive to avoid a bankruptcy filing.

The debtholders, on the other hand, are primarily concerned with protecting the value of the firm's assets and will try to take control away from shareholders. They have a strong incentive to seek bankruptcy to protect their interests and keep shareholders from further dissipating the assets of the firm. The net effect of all this fighting is that a long, drawn-out, and potentially quite expensive, legal battle gets started.

Meanwhile, as the wheels of justice turn in their ponderous way, the assets of the firm lose value because management is busy trying to avoid bankruptcy instead of running the business. Normal operations are disrupted, and sales are lost. Valuable employees leave, potentially fruitful programs are dropped to preserve cash, and otherwise profitable investments are not taken.

indirect bankruptcy costs
the difficulties of running a business that is experiencing financial distress

financial distress costs
the direct and indirect costs associated with going bankrupt or experiencing financial distress

These are all indirect bankruptcy costs, or costs of financial distress. Whether or not the firm ultimately goes bankrupt, the net effect is a loss of value because the firm chose to use debt in its capital structure. It is this possibility of loss that limits the amount of debt that a firm will choose to use.

Concept questions

20.5a *What are direct bankruptcy costs?*
20.5b *What are indirect bankruptcy costs?*

20.6 Optimal capital structure

Our previous two sections have established the basis for an optimal capital structure. A firm will borrow because the interest tax shield is valuable. At relatively low debt levels, the probability of bankruptcy and financial distress is low, and the benefit from debt outweighs the cost. At very high debt levels, the possibility of financial distress is a chronic, ongoing problem for the firm, so the benefit from debt financing may be more than offset by the financial distress costs. Based on our discussion, it would appear that an optimal capital structure exists somewhere in between these extremes.

The static theory of capital structure

static theory of capital structure

theory that a firm borrows up to the point where the tax benefit from an extra dollar in debt is exactly equal to the cost that comes from the increased probability of financial distress

The theory of capital structure that we have outlined is called the **static theory of capital structure**. It says that firms borrow up to the point where the tax benefit from an extra dollar in debt is exactly equal to the cost that comes from the increased probability of financial distress. We call this the static theory because it assumes that the firm is fixed in terms of its assets and operations and it only considers possible changes in the debt/equity ratio.

The static theory is illustrated in Figure 20.6, which plots the value of the firm, V_L, against the amount of debt, D. In Figure 20.6, we have drawn lines corresponding to three different stories. The first is M&M Proposition I with no taxes. This is the horizontal line extending from V_U, and it indicates that the value of the firm is unaffected by its capital structure. The second case, M&M Proposition I with corporate taxes, is given by the upward-sloping straight line. These two cases are exactly the same as the ones we illustrated previously in Figure 20.4.

The third case in Figure 20.6 illustrates our current discussion: The value of the firm rises to a maximum and then declines beyond that point. This is the picture that we get from our static theory. The maximum value of the firm, V_L^*, is reached at D^*, so this is the optimal amount of borrowing. Put another way, the firm's optimal capital structure is composed of D^*/V_L^* in debt and $(1 - D^*/V_L^*)$ in equity.

The final thing to notice in Figure 20.6 is that the difference between the value of the firm in our static theory and the M&M value of the firm with taxes is the loss in value from the possibility of financial distress. Also, the difference between the static theory value of the firm and the M&M value with taxes is the gain from leverage, net of distress costs.

FIGURE
20.6

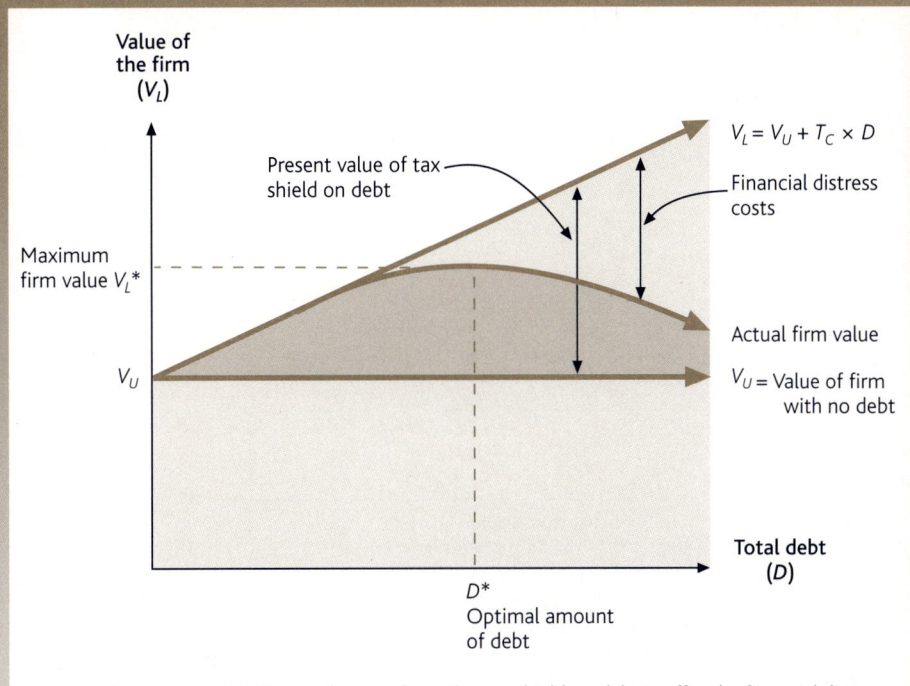

The static theory of capital structure. The optimal capital structure and the value of the firm

According to the static theory, the gain from the tax shield on debt is offset by financial distress costs. An optimal capital structure exists which just balances the additional gain from leverage against the added financial distress cost.

Optimal capital structure and the cost of capital

As we discussed earlier, the capital structure that maximises the value of the firm is also the one that minimises the cost of capital. Figure 20.7 (overleaf) illustrates the static theory of capital structure in terms of the weighted average cost of capital and the costs of debt and equity. Notice in Figure 20.7 that we have plotted the various capital costs against the debt/equity ratio, D/E.

Figure 20.7 is much the same as Figure 20.5 except that we have added a new line for the WACC. This line, which corresponds to the static theory, declines at first. This occurs because the after-tax cost of debt is cheaper than equity, at least initially, so the overall cost of capital declines.

At some point, the cost of debt begins to rise and the fact that debt is cheaper than equity is more than offset by the financial distress costs. At this point, further increases in debt actually increase the WACC. As illustrated, the minimum WACC occurs at the point D^*/E^*, just as we described above.

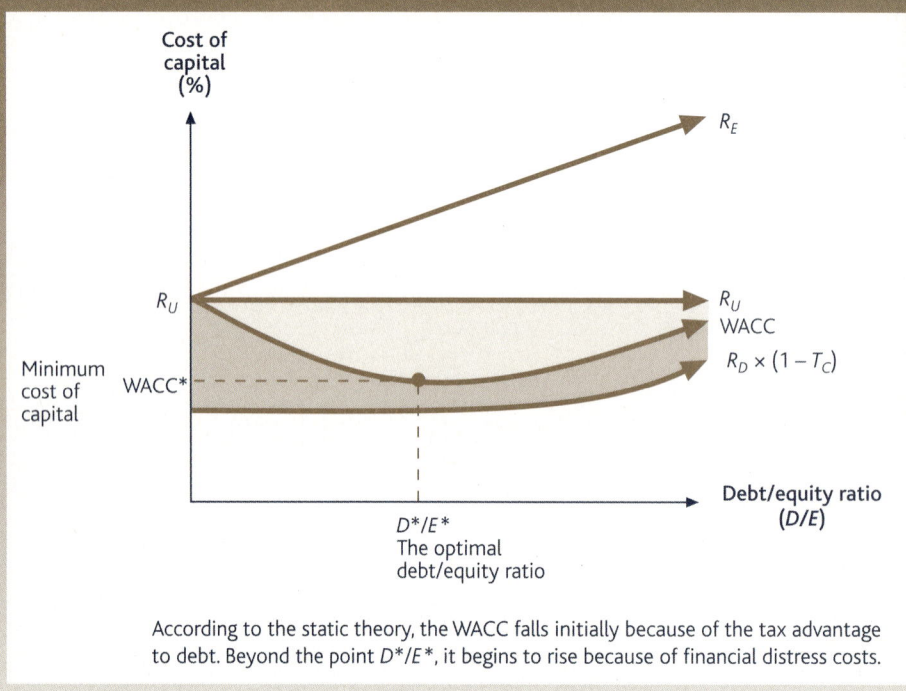

The static theory of capital structure. The optimal capital structure and the cost of capital

According to the static theory, the WACC falls initially because of the tax advantage to debt. Beyond the point D^*/E^*, it begins to rise because of financial distress costs.

Capital structure: Some managerial recommendations

The static model that we described is not capable of identifying a precise optimal capital structure, but it does point out two of the more relevant factors: taxes and financial distress. We can draw some limited conclusions concerning these.

Taxes

First of all, the tax benefit from leverage is obviously only important to firms that are in a tax-paying position. Firms with substantial accumulated losses will get little value from the tax shield. Furthermore, firms that have substantial tax shields from other sources, such as depreciation, will get less benefit from leverage.

Also, the higher the tax payable, the greater the incentive to borrow.

Financial distress

Firms with a greater risk of experiencing financial distress will borrow less than firms with a lower risk of financial distress. For example, all other things being equal, the greater the volatility in EBIT, the less a firm should borrow.

In addition, financial distress is more costly for some firms than others. The costs of financial distress depend primarily on the firm's assets. In particular, financial distress costs will be determined by how easily ownership to those assets can be transferred.

For example, a firm with mostly tangible assets that can be sold without great loss in value will have an incentive to borrow more. For firms that rely heavily on intangibles, such as employee talent or growth opportunities, debt will be less attractive since these assets effectively cannot be sold.

Concept questions

20.6a *Describe the trade-off that defines the static theory of capital structure.*
20.6b *What are the important factors in making capital structure decisions?*

20.7 ■ The pie again

Although it is comforting to know that the firm might have an optimal capital structure when we take account of such real-world matters as taxes and financial distress costs, it is disquieting to see the elegant, original M&M intuition (i.e. the no-tax version) fall apart in the face of them.

Critics of the M&M theory often say that it fails to hold as soon as we add in real-world issues and that the M&M theory is really just that, a theory that does not have much to say about the real world that we live in. In fact, they would argue that it is the M&M theory that is irrelevant, not capital structure. As we discuss next, however, taking that view blinds critics to the real value of the M&M theory.

The extended pie model

To illustrate the value of the original M&M intuition, we briefly consider an expanded version of the pie model that we introduced earlier. In the extended pie model, taxes just represent another claim on the cash flows of the firm. Since taxes are reduced as leverage is increased, the value of the government's claim, (G), on the firm's cash flows decreases with leverage.

Bankruptcy costs are also a claim on the cash flows. They come into play as the firm comes close to bankruptcy and has to alter its behaviour to attempt to stave off the event itself, and they become large when bankruptcy actually takes place. Thus, the value of the cash flows to this claim (B) rises with the debt/equity ratio.

The extended pie theory simply holds that all of these claims can be paid from only one source, the cash flows (CF) of the firm. Algebraically, we have:

$$
\begin{aligned}
CF = \ &\text{Payments to shareholders} \ + \ \text{Payments to debtholders} \\
&+ \ \text{Payments to the government} \\
&+ \ \text{Payments to bankruptcy courts and lawyers} \\
&+ \ \text{Payments to any and all other claimants to the cash flow of the firm}
\end{aligned}
$$

The extended pie model is illustrated in Figure 20.8 (overleaf). Notice that we have added a few slices for the other groups. Notice also the relative sizes of the slices as the firm's use of debt financing is increased.

With this list, we have not even begun to exhaust the potential claims to the firm's cash flows. To give an unusual example, everyone reading this book has an economic claim to the cash flows of Australian Mutual Provident Society (AMP). After all, if you are injured in an accident, you might sue AMP as the insurer and, win or lose, AMP will expend some of its cash flow in dealing with the matter. For AMP, or any other company, there should thus be a slice of the pie representing the potential lawsuits.

FIGURE
20.8

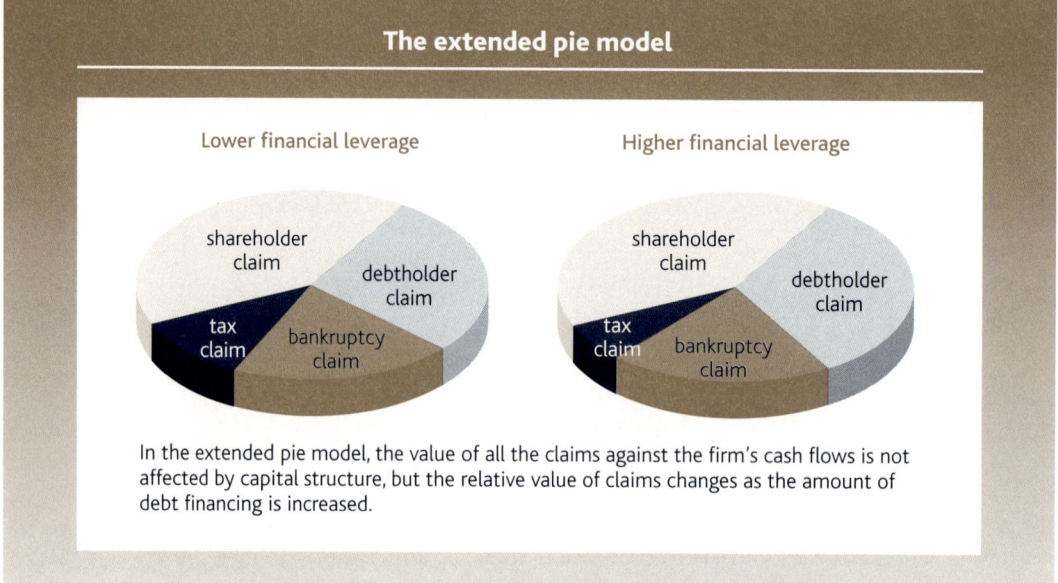

The extended pie model

In the extended pie model, the value of all the claims against the firm's cash flows is not affected by capital structure, but the relative value of claims changes as the amount of debt financing is increased.

This is the essence of the M&M intuition and theory: *the value of the firm depends on the total cash flow of the firm*. The firm's capital structure just cuts that cash flow up into slices without altering the total. What we recognise now is that the shareholders and the debtholders may not be the only ones who can claim a slice.

Marketed claims versus non-marketed claims

With our extended pie model, there is an important distinction between claims such as those of shareholders and debtholders, on the one hand, and those of the government and potential litigants in lawsuits on the other. The first set of claims are *marketed claims*, and the second set are *non-marketed claims*. A key difference is that the marketed claims can be bought and sold in financial markets and the non-marketed claims cannot be.

When we speak of the value of the firm, we are generally referring just to the value of the marketed claims, V_M, and not the value of the non-marketed claims, V_N. If we write V_T for the total value of all the claims against a company's cash flows, then:

$$V_T = E + D + G + B + \ldots$$
$$= V_M + V_N$$

The essence of our extended pie model is that this total value, V_T, of all the claims to the firm's cash flows is unaltered by capital structure. However, the value of the marketed claims, V_M, may be affected by changes in the capital structure.

By the pie theory, any increase in V_M must imply an identical decrease in V_N. The optimal capital structure is thus the one that maximises the value of the marketed claims, or, equivalently, minimises the value of non-marketed claims such as taxes and bankruptcy costs.

20.7a *What are some of the claims to a firm's cash flows?*
20.7b *What is the difference between a marketed claim and a non-marketed claim?*
20.7c *What does the extended pie model say about the value of all the claims to a firm's cash flows?*

20.8 ∎ Corporate versus personal borrowing

It was shown in our discussion of home-made leverage that personal borrowing could be used to change the overall amount of financial leverage to which the individual is exposed. The logical conclusion to this discussion is that personal borrowing must be a perfect substitute for corporate borrowing. This is the situation if there is no taxation.

Corporate borrowing and personal borrowing without taxation

EXAMPLE 20.5

Consider a manufacturer who has expanded his business and converted the business to a company. The following information is provided:

Expected business income	=	$180,000
Expected business expenses	=	$80,000
Interest on borrowed funds	=	$30,000
Corporate tax rate	=	Nil
Personal tax rate	=	Nil

All profits are to be paid out as a dividend.
Should the funds be borrowed through the company or on personal account?

	Corporate borrowing	Personal borrowing
Expected business income	$180,000	$180,000
Expected business expenses	80,000	80,000
Expected EBIT	100,000	100,000
Corporate interest	30,000	Nil
Profit = Dividend to shareholders	$70,000	$100,000
Personal interest	Nil	30,000
Funds available to shareholders	$70,000	$70,000

In both arrangements the funds available to shareholders are $70,000; therefore without taxation it does not matter whether corporate or personal borrowings are made.

Now let us introduce corporate and personal taxation but ignore dividend imputation for the time being.

EXAMPLE 20.6 ■ **Corporate borrowing and personal borrowing with taxation but no dividend imputation**

Assume the same information as in Example 20.5 but assume a corporate tax rate of 30 per cent and a personal tax rate of 47 per cent.

	Corporate borrowing	Personal borrowing
Expected business income	$180,000	$180,000
Expected business expenses	80,000	80,000
Expected EBIT	100,000	100,000
Corporate interest	30,000	Nil
Profit before corporate taxation	70,000	100,000
Corporate taxation 30%	21,000	30,000
Profit = Dividend to shareholders	$ 49,000	$ 70,000
Personal interest	Nil	30,000
	49,000	40,000
Personal taxation 47%	23,030	18,800
Funds available to shareholders	$ 25,970	$ 21,200

It can be seen that if the funds are borrowed by the company, the shareholders will be $4,770 better off. This advantage does not arise because the corporate tax rate (30%) is less than the personal tax rate (47%). It arises because there is a tax saving through the deductible corporate interest. The advantage can be calculated using the following formula:

(Corporate tax rate) × (Corporate interest) × (1 − Personal tax rate)
= 0.30 × $30,000 × (1 − 0.47)
= $4,770

EXAMPLE 20.7 ■ **Corporate borrowing and personal borrowing with imputation**

The information is the same as in Examples 20.5 and 20.6 but in addition imputation applies and we are told there are 10 shareholders who, for simplicity, all earn the same other income. We will consider the situations when the shareholders have other income of zero, $43,000, $53,000 and $63,000 each. Personal tax information used in the example is:

Taxable income	Rate	Amount of tax
0–$6,000	0%	Nil
$6,001–$20,000	17%	$2,380
$20,001–$50,000	30%	$9,000
$50,001–$60,000	42%	$4,200
$60,000+	47%	

For example, the tax on $61,000 would be $2,380 + $9,000 + $4,200 + 47% of $1,000 = $16,050.

	Corporate borrowing	Personal borrowing
Profit before corporate taxation	$70,000	$100,000
Corporate taxation 30%	21,000	30,000
Profit = Franked dividend to shareholders	$49,000	$ 70,000

Income summary with various levels of other income

Other income	Zero		$43,000	
Borrowing arrangement	Company	Personal	Company	Personal
Dividends	$ 4,900	$ 7,000	$ 4,900	$ 7,000
Franking credit*	2,100	3,000	2,100	3,000
Grossed up dividend	7,000	10,000	7,000	10,000
Personal income	Zero	Zero	43,000	43,000
Total income**	7,000	10,000	50,000	53,000
Personal interest 10%	Nil	(3,000)	Nil	(3,000)
Taxable income	7,000	7,000	50,000	50,000
Taxation	170	170	11,380	11,380
Franking credit	(2,100)	(3,000)	(2,100)	(3,000)
Tax payable (refund)	(1,930)	(2,830)	9,280	8,380
For all 10 shareholders:				
Tax (payable) refund	19,300	28,300	(92,800)	(83,800)
Dividend income	49,000	70,000	49,000	70,000
Other income	Zero	Zero	430,000	430,000
Personal interest	Nil	(30,000)	Nil	(30,000)
Combined net income	$68,300	$ 68,300	$386,200	$386,200

* The franking credit is the tax paid by the company.

** This is not the total income received but the total income for tax purposes.

Other income	$53,000		$63,000	
Borrowing arrangement	Company	Personal	Company	Personal
Dividends	$ 4,900	$ 7,000	$ 4,900	$ 7,000
Franking credit*	2,100	3,000	2,100	3,000
Grossed up dividend	7,000	10,000	7,000	10,000
Personal income	53,000	53,000	63,000	63,000
Total income**	60,000	63,000	70,000	73,000
Personal interest 10%	Nil	(3,000)	Nil	(3,000)
Taxable income	60,000	60,000	70,000	70,000
Taxation	15,580	15,580	20,280	20,280
Franking credit	(2,100)	(3,000)	(2,100)	(3,000)
Tax payable (refund)	13,480	12,580	18,180	17,280

(continued)

EXAMPLE 20.7

Corporate borrowing and personal borrowing with imputation (*continued*)

Other income	$53,000		$63,000	
Borrowing arrangement	Company	Personal	Company	Personal
For all 10 shareholders:				
Tax (payable) refund	(134,800)	(125,800)	(181,800)	(172,800)
Dividend income	49,000	70,000	49,000	70,000
Other income	530,000	530,000	630,000	630,000
Personal interest	Nil	(30,000)	Nil	(30,000)
Combined net income	$ 444,200	$ 444,200	$ 497,200	$ 497,200

* The franking credit is the tax paid by the company.
** This is not the total income received but the total income for tax purposes.

When we introduce dividend imputation, the preference for corporate borrowing changes. The advantage now depends upon the ability of the shareholders to use the franking credits the imputation system provides. Prior to 1 October 1999 this ability depended upon the taxable income that accrued to shareholders in addition to the corporate dividends. After the 1999 change, which allows taxpayers to obtain refunds for unused imputation credits, shareholders will be indifferent to corporate borrowing and personal borrowing.

Concept questions

20.8a *What is meant by the tax shield of corporate debt?*

20.8b *Would you advise the single shareholder of a private company to finance his or her business through personal borrowing or company borrowing?*

20.8c *What are franking credits? Are they different to imputation credits?*

 20.9 ## Observed capital structures

No two firms have identical capital structures. Nonetheless, there are some regular elements that we see when we start looking at actual capital structures. We discuss a few of these next.

The most striking thing that we observe about capital structures, particularly in Australia, is that most companies seem to have relatively low debt/equity ratios. In fact, most companies use less debt than equity financing. This is true even though many of these companies pay substantial taxes, and the company tax has been an important source of government revenue.

A second regularity is apparent when we compare capital structures across industries. Table 20.7 shows debt to equity ratios in Australia by industry. As shown, there is wide variation in industry debt/equity ratios. For example, firms in the beverages industry have a debt/equity ratio of 1.26 compared to 0.31 for medical firms in 2002.

Ratios of debt to equity for selected Australian industries, 2002	
Agricultural	1.14
Beverages	1.26
Building and Construction	1.62
Banks	16.59
Diversified Minerals	0.72
Food—Retail	2.57
Gold Mining	1.18
Life/Health Insurance	10.93
Medical	0.31
Property Trusts	0.83

TABLE 20.7

As extensions of the static M&M trade-off theory, dynamic capital structure theories provide theoretical arguments to explain the observed irregularities in capital structures. Research has only provided weak empirical support for the theories. One such theory is the **pecking order theory**. This theory argues firms will prefer internal financing (profits) to external financing, and then debt to equity if it is forced to raise funds externally. The cost behind this pecking order is the lack of uniformity in relation to information on the firm's prospects between investors and management. This is called the **information asymmetry cost**. The pecking order theory suggests that the debt to equity ratios should be negatively related to profits and empirical support has been found for this relationship.

A number of authors have questioned the ability of the firm to take advantage of the tax subsidy on debt which is proposed under the static M&M theory. First, Miller (1977) argued that the corporate tax advantage of debt could be offset totally by disadvantages at the investor level. Then several authors argued that firms with large non-debt tax shields (such as depreciation or losses carried forward) would be less inclined to pursue the tax advantages of issuing debt. Most of the empirical research in this area has concentrated on the relationship between non-debt tax shields and the level of debt to provide mixed results.[3]

The basic assumption of finance theory is that firms will maximise their value; however, when claims against the firm are divided between equity and debt, there is an incentive for the controlling group to maximise their value as opposed to the firm as a whole. This incentive will result in costs to the firms issuing debt. They are called the **agency costs of debt** and they must be traded off against the benefits of debt when the capital structure decision is being made. Myers (1977) argued that firms with substantial assets in place would have lower agency costs than firms whose assets are based upon the potential growth in profits. There is considerable empirical evidence to show that larger firms or firms with more assets in place will use more debt. One means the debtholders have for protecting themselves against agency costs is to raise the level of security required for the debt. They are effectively discounting the value of debt relative to the value of the firm so that they limit the debt in the capital structure. The existence of agency costs of debt would reduce the ability of the firm to issue debt. Another impediment to the firm's ability or wish to change its capital structure is the transaction costs associated with issuing or retiring securities.

pecking order theory
the process of the firm choosing profits, debt and equity in this order to finance investments

information asymmetry cost
this arises because investors do not have the same information as management in relation to the prospects of the firm

agency costs of debt
these arise because equityholders may act in their own interest rather than the interests of the firm as a whole

An aspect of debt that has not been given too much consideration in finance research is the debt maturity. Financing policy dictates that firms should match the maturity of their debt with the maturity of their assets, so the life cycle of the firm's investments may influence the amount of debt in the capital structure. Interest rate variability is another consideration that could make the consideration of debt maturity relevant. Short-term interest rates are quite volatile, so interest rate risk may direct the firm away from short-term debt financing. While short-term interest rates change a lot, there is also risk associated with long-term borrowing. In the 1980s, long-term borrowing rates were about 18 per cent; however, by 1992 these had fallen to 12 per cent and now they are half of this. Any borrower who had financed debt in the 1980s would have been looking at refinancing by 1992, and any that financed debt in 1992 would be looking at refinancing in 2003. The point that we are making is that there are considerations in relation to debt maturity that may influence the capital structure of the firm once we move to the real world.

Because different industries have different operating characteristics in terms of, for example, EBIT volatility and asset types, there does appear to be some connection between these characteristics and capital structure. Our story involving tax savings (tax benefit theory) and financial distress costs (bankruptcy theory) is undoubtedly part of the reason, but to date there is no fully satisfactory theory that explains these regularities. No doubt a complete theory on financial leverage and capital structure policy will start with the static M&M theory; however, dynamic aspects of the real world will need to be built into the model.

Table 20.8 provides a selective summary of research that has been conducted on the capital structure issue. These results indicate how inconclusive support is for the various capital structure theories. One positive outcome of the research is that there is no contrary evidence for the pecking order theory; however, much more work has to be done on modelling the research question. The evidence provided on tax benefit theory, agency theory and bankruptcy theory, at best, can be described as contradictory. The issue of explaining capital structures is far from being resolved. While it is not reported in Table 20.8, some of the researchers found different results in different countries and even different results in the same country with different samples or different time periods. As stated earlier, the starting point for making decisions on capital structure must rest with the M&M theory and this must then be modified by real-world pressures. The research indicates that the industry is a factor in identifying capital structure so a starting point for the amount of debt might be the norm for the industry.

TABLE 20.8

Summary of selected research on capital structure. Significance of variables in determining capital structure. Correlation of variables with capital structure										
Author	*I*	*tcE*	*tc*	Beta	*E*	*S*	*P*	*A*	*C*	*B*
Remmers et al. (1974)	no					no				
Toy et al. (1974)				+ve			−ve			
Ferri & Jones (1979)	yes			no		+ve				
Bowen et al. (1982)	yes	−ve								
Castanias (1983)	yes				−ve					−ve
Boquist & Moore (1984)		+ve			−ve					

Summary of selected research on capital structure. Significance of variables in determining capital structure. Correlation of variables with capital structure (*continued*)

TABLE 20.8

Author	I	tcE	tc	Beta	E	S	P	A	C	B
Bradley et al. (1984)	yes	+ve		−ve						
Long & Malitz (1985)							−ve	+ve		
Kester (1986)				no		no	−ve			
Kim & Sorensen (1986)		−ve	−ve	+ve		no				
Allen et al. (1987)	yes	−ve		no			-ve			
Davis (1987)			+ve							
Christensen (1988)		−ve				+ve	−ve	+ve		
Friend & Lang (1988)				−ve			−ve	+ve		
Baskin (1989)							−ve			
Chatterjee & Scott (1989)				+ve				+ve		
Sener (1989)	yes	+ve	−ve							
Chang & Rhee (1990)		+ve		+ve	−ve	+ve	−ve			
Prowse (1990)		−ve		−ve	−ve		−ve	+ve		
Jensen et al. (1992)				−ve			−ve	+ve		
Hamson (1993)		−ve	−ve	no		+ve		+ve		

Predictions of the various theories on capital structure for the significance of the above variables:

	I	tcE	tc	Beta	E	S	P	A	C	B
Tax benefit theory	yes	−ve	+ve	−ve						
Agency theory	yes	+ve			−ve			+ve	+ve	
Bankruptcy theory	yes	+ve		−ve		+ve		+ve		−ve
Pecking order theory	yes						−ve	+ve		

	I	tcE	tc	Beta	E	S	P	A	C	B
No. significant positive		4	1	4		4		6	1	
No. significant negative		6	3	4	4		10			1
Times not significant						3				

Variables identified as significant factors in determining capital structure:

I the industry, *tcE* the non-debt tax shields, *tc* the effective tax rate, beta the risk, *E* expenses (such as advertising and research and development), *S* the size of the firm, *P* the profit level of the firm, *A* the assets in place, *C* the capital expenditure, *B* the probability of bankruptcy costs.

Legend
+ve: significantly positively related
−ve: significantly negatively related
No: No relationship
Yes: A significant factor

Concept questions

20.9a *Do Australian companies rely heavily on debt financing?*
20.9b *What regularities do we observe in capital structures?*

Joanne Blades

 In their own words

Joanne Blades* on the debt structure puzzle: oils ain't oils and debt ain't debt

Determining how much debt an organisation can (or should) sustain on its balance sheet is one of the most important decisions in financial management. Once this has been considered, the question arises as to how this debt should be structured. That is, should it be floating rate debt, fixed rate debt or some combination? In any case, does it really matter? We propose that it does, although when put in context with the capital structure decision it can probably be considered 'second order'. While the capital structure decision deals with our organisation's capacity to sustain debt, the debt structure decision considers how we can best manage the other risks associated with its use.

We know there is no 'optimal' capital structure in practice. But there must be an 'optimal' debt structure, right? Unfortunately, there isn't. Determining an appropriate capital structure means balancing a degree of science with subjective business judgment—and this also applies to the debt structure decision. As suggested above, it is really about determining a framework for managing risk.

*A traditional view would be that the term of the funding should match the life of the assets being funded. Even if we wanted to do this, it would be difficult to do it for assets with long economic lives such as infrastructure (e.g. a power station). Also, this is not necessarily an appropriate principle to adhere to, because other factors, such as the **riskiness** of the cash flows generated by the assets and the objectives of the business as a whole, need to be considered.*

There are a couple of key risks we need to think about here: interest rate risk and refinancing risk. Interest rate risk is the risk that the value of the business will change as a result of unexpected changes in interest rates. As a starting point, we'd like to see if we could determine a structure for our debt that minimises the impact of adverse changes in interest rates on our bottom line. This is where we need to look at the risk profile of our asset base. Given that asset cash flows can also be sensitive to changing interest rates, can we construct a corresponding liability cash-flow profile that 'absorbs' this risk and protects our residual equity cash flows from unwanted shocks?

An example of this is a business with revenue cash flows indexed to inflation. As there is a positive (but less than perfect) correlation between inflation and interest rates, having a funding profile that is more sensitive to short-term interest rate changes could result in a 'natural hedge': in cash flows that are more closely matched. In this case, such a funding profile would be floating rate debt. The most practical and effective way to test this is to take a cash flow forecast for the business, plug in some alternative debt structures (e.g. from floating rate debt through to ten-year fixed rate debt) and 'stress test' the balance sheet under different interest-rate scenarios. The performance measures for these tests would be things like:

- *percentage change in equity-free cash flows;*
- *percentage change in annual interest costs; and*
- *impact on key financial ratios, such as debt service coverage ratios.*

Again, unless your business has a unique cash flow profile, these tests won't necessarily produce definitive answers. The analysis will help you identify the extremes, or unacceptable structures, potentially leaving you with a range within which you should be able to feel comfortable. This range can be quite wide and is also highly dependent on the organisation's risk appetite (e.g. can you wear some variability away from your budgeted interest costs and if so, how much?).

The other key factor that needs to be considered is refinancing risk. As debt matures, there is a risk that it cannot be refinanced at all, or that refinancing will only occur on unfavourable terms. This is particularly an issue for organisations that carry a higher credit risk. To the extent that this is an issue for an organisation, it would produce a bias away from floating rate funding. However, it also needs to be remembered that fixed rate funding comes at a cost. The other key means of managing this risk is via diversification, which should be part of any prudent debt management strategy.

In summary, risk management is all about understanding. While determining an appropriate debt structure for an organisation is more of an art than a science, the journey can lead to a greater understanding of the balance sheet's overall sensitivity to interest rates and other financial and non-financial risks. If this doesn't in itself lead to increases in shareholder value (although we're not necessarily saying that it can't), it can at least provide a framework to ensure that this value is not unnecessarily eroded by factors that are beyond our control.

* **Joanne Blades** is with the Queensland Treasury Corporation.

■20.10■ Summary and conclusions

The ideal mixture of debt and equity for a firm—its optimal capital structure—is the one that maximises the value of the firm and minimises the overall cost of capital. If we ignore taxes, financial distress costs, and any other imperfections, we find that there is no ideal mixture. Under these circumstances, the firm's capital structure is simply irrelevant.

If we consider the effect of company taxes, we find that capital structure matters a great deal. This conclusion is based on the fact that interest is tax-deductible and thus generates a valuable tax shield. Unfortunately, we also find that the optimal capital structure is 100 per cent debt, which is not something we observe for healthy firms.

We next introduced costs associated with bankruptcy or, more generally, financial distress. These costs reduce the attractiveness of debt financing. We concluded that an optimal capital structure exists when the net tax saving from an additional dollar in interest just equals the increase in expected financial distress costs. This is the essence of the static theory of capital structure.

When we examined actual capital structures, we found two regularities. First, firms in Australia typically do not use great amounts of debt, but they pay substantial taxes. This suggests that there is a limit to the use of debt financing to generate tax shields. Second, firms in similar industries tend to have similar capital structures, suggesting that the nature of their assets and operations is an important determinant of capital structure.

Key terms

Agency costs of debt *703*
Business risk *685*
Direct bankruptcy costs *693*
Financial distress costs *693*
Financial risk *685*

Home-made leverage *679*
Indirect bankruptcy costs *693*
Information asymmetry cost *703*
Interest tax shield *687*
M&M Proposition I *681*

M&M Proposition II *682*
Pecking order theory *703*
Static theory of capital structure *694*
Unlevered cost of capital *688*

Suggested readings

The classic articles on capital structure are:
Modigliani, F. and Miller, M.H. 'The Cost of Capital, Corporate Finance, and the Theory of Investment', *American Economic Review*, Vol. 48, June 1958, pp. 261–97.
—— 'Corporation Income Taxes and the Cost of Capital: A Correction', *American Economic Review*, Vol. 53, June 1963, pp. 433–43.

Some research on capital structure is summarised in:
Smith, C. 'Raising Capital: Theory and Evidence', *Midland Corporate Finance Journal*, Spring 1986.

The text of Stewart Myers' 1984 Presidential Address to the American Finance Association is in the article listed below. It summarises the academic insights on capital structure until the early 1980s and points out directions for future research:

Myers, S. 'The Capital Structure Puzzle', *Midland Corporate Finance Journal*, Fall 1985.

Additional references:
Allen, D., Johnson, J. and Mizuno, H. 'The Determinants of Australian Companies' Capital Structure: The Results of a Pilot Study', Department of Accounting and Finance, University of Western Australia, 1987.
Barclay, M. and Smith, C. 'On financial architecture: leverage, maturity and priority', *Journal of Applied Corporate Finance*, Winter 1996, pp. 4–17.
Baskin, J. 'An Empirical Investigation of the Pecking Order Hypothesis', *Financial Management*, Vol. 18, 1989, pp. 26–35.
Boquist, J. and Moore, W. 'Inter-Industry Leverage Differences and the DeAngelo-Masulis Tax Shield Hypothesis', *Financial Management*, Vol. 13, 1984, pp. 5–9.

Bowen, R., Daley, L. and Huber, C. 'Evidence on the Existence of Determinants of Inter-Industry Differences in Leverage', *Financial Management*, Vol. 11, 1982, pp. 10–20.

Bradley, M., Jarrell, G. and Kim, E. 'On the Existence of an Optimal Capital Structure: Theory and Evidence', *Journal of Finance*, Vol. 39, 1984, pp. 857–78.

Castanias, R. 'Bankruptcy Risk and Optimal Capital Structure', *Journal of Finance*, Vol. 38, 1983, pp. 1617–35.

Chang, R. and Rhee, S. 'The Impact of Personal Taxes on Corporate Dividend Policy and Capital Structure Decisions', *Financial Management*, Vol. 19, 1990, pp. 22–31.

Chatterjee, S. and Scott, J. 'Explaining Differences in Corporate Capital Structure: Theory and New Evidence', *Journal of Banking and Finance*, 1989, pp. 283–309.

Christensen, M. 'Towards Understanding an Optimal Capital Structure: Australian Evidence', Masters thesis, University of Queensland, 1988.

Davis, A. 'Effective Tax Rates as Determinants of Canadian Capital Structure', *Financial Management*, Vol. 16, 1987, pp. 22–8.

Ferri, M. and Jones, W. 'Determinants of Financial Structure: A New Methodological Approach', *Journal of Finance*, Vol. 34, 1979, pp. 631–44.

Friend, I. and Lang, L. 'An Empirical Test of the Impact of Managerial Self-Interest on Corporate Capital Structure', *Journal of Finance*, Vol. 43, 1988, pp. 271–81.

Hamson, D.F. 'An Empirical Examination of Corporate Capital Structure in Australia and the USA', unpublished thesis, Department of Commerce, University of Queensland, 1993.

Jensen, G., Solberg, D. and Zorn, T. 'Simultaneous Determination of Insider Ownership, Debt, and Dividend Policies', *Journal of Financial and Quantitative Analysis*, Vol. 27, 1992, pp. 247–63.

Kester, W. 'Capital and Ownership Structure: A Comparison of United States and Japanese Manufacturing Corporations', *Financial Management*, Vol. 16, 1986, pp. 5–16.

Kim, W.S. and Sorenson, E.H. 'Evidence of the Impact of the Agency Costs of Debt on Corporate Debt Policy', *Journal of Financial and Quantitative Analyis*, June 1986, pp. 131–44.

Long, M. and Malitz, I. 'Investment Patterns and Financial Leverage', in B. Friedman (ed.) *Corporate Capital Structures in the United States*, The University of Chicago Press, Chicago, Ill., 1985.

Myers, S.C. 'Determinants of Corporate Borrowing', *Journal of Financial Economics*, November 1977, pp. 147–75.

Prowse, S.D. 'Institutional Investment Patterns and Corporate Financial Behaviour in the United States and Japan', *Journal of Financial Economics*, Vol. 27, 1990, pp. 43–66.

Remmers, L., Stonehill, A., Wright, R. and Beekhuisen, T. 'Industry and Size as Debt Ratio Determinants in Manufacturing Internationally', *Financial Management*, Vol. 3, 1974, pp. 24–32.

Sener, T. 'An Empirical Test of the DeAngelo-Masulis Tax Shield and Tax Rate Hypothesis with Industry and Inflation Effects', *Mid-Atlantic Journal of Business*, Vol. 25, 1989.

Titman, S. and Wessels, R. 'The Determinants of Capital Structure Choice', *Journal of Finance*, March 1988, pp. 6–22.

Toy, N., Stonehill, A., Remmers, L., Wright, R. and Beekhiusen, R. 'A Comparative International Study of Growth, Profitability, and Risk as Determinants of Corporate Debt Ratios in the Manufacturing Sector', *Journal of Financial and Quantitative Analysis*, Vol. 9, 1974, pp. 875–86.

Endnotes

1   It is conventional to refer to decisions regarding debt and equity as capital structure decisions. However, the term 'financial structure' would be more accurate, and we will use the terms interchangeably.

2   ROE is discussed in some detail in Chapter 3.

3   Bradley, Jarrell and Kim (1984), Boquist and Moore (1984), Long and Malitz (1985), Sener (1989) and Chang and Rhee (1990) found that non-debt tax shields were positively related to debt. Titman and Wessels (1988) found no relationship. Bowen, Daley and Huber (1982), Kim and Sorenson (1986) and Prowse (1990) provide some evidence of a negative relationship.

On the web

The McGraw–Hill Finance SuperSite offers many links to areas of interest:

http://www.mcgraw–hill.com.au/mhhe

Sites which examine the financial world are also pertinent:

http://www.afr.com.au (*Australian Financial Review*)

http://www.bloomberg.com (the Bloomberg site offers financial news, commentary and up-to-date market reports)

Maximise Your Marks!

There are 30 interactive questions on financial leverage and capital structure policy waiting online for you at www.mhhe.com/au/ross3e. The questions are written with additional feedback for incorrect answers, and text excerpts with page references for follow-up study.

International Articles!

To read more on financial leverage and capital structure policy and to see current international articles, just go to www.mhhe.com/au/ross3e and click on *PowerWeb Articles* for this chapter.

Chapter review problems and self-test

20.1 · EBIT and EPS

Asking and his associates are considering the purchase of a business using a corporate structure. The operating company will be Asking Company Pty Ltd. Two financing proposals are being considered for Asking Company. The first will use $5 million in debt and 10 million shares which should sell for $4. The second proposal will use $25 million in debt and reduce shares accordingly. In both proposals the interest rate on debt is 12 per cent. The second proposal is expected to increase the ROE. If taxes are ignored, what is the minimum level for EBIT that is expected to be derived by Asking Company?

20.2 · M&M Proposition II (no taxes)

The Telling Company Ltd has a WACC of 20 per cent. Its cost of debt is 12 per cent, which is equal to the risk-free rate of interest. If Telling's debt/equity ratio is 2, what is its cost of equity capital? If Telling's equity beta is 1.5, what is the beta of the entire firm? Ignore taxes in your answer.

20.3 · M&M Proposition I (with corporate taxes)

The Corpse Co. Ltd (motto: 'Reach out and clutch someone') expects an EBIT of $4,000 every year forever. Corpse can borrow at 10 per cent.

Suppose that Corpse currently has no debt and its cost of equity is 14 per cent. If the corporate tax rate is 30 per cent, what is the value of the firm? What will the value be if Corpse borrows $6,000 and uses the proceeds to refund shares?

Answers to self-test problems

20.1 · To answer, we can calculate the break-even EBIT. At any EBIT above this, the increased financial leverage of the second proposal will increase EPS. Under the first proposal, the interest expense is 0.12 × $5 million = $600,000. There are 10 million shares, so, ignoring taxes, EPS is (EBIT − $600,000)/10 million.

Under the second proposal, the interest expense will be 0.12 × $25 million = $3 million. The increase in debt of $20 million allows the reduction in the number of shares issued by $20 million/$4 = 5 million shares. Thus EPS is (EBIT − $3 million)/5 million.

Now that we know how to calculate EPS under both scenarios, we set them equal and solve for the break-even EBIT as:

$$(EBIT − \$600,000)/10 \text{ million} = (EBIT − \$3 \text{ million})/5 \text{ million}$$
$$(EBIT − \$600,000) = 2 × (EBIT − \$3 \text{ million})$$
$$EBIT = \$5,400,000$$

Check that, in either proposal, EPS is 48 cents when EBIT is $5.4 million.

20.2 · According to M&M Proposition II (no taxes), the cost of equity is:

$$R_E = R_A + (R_A − R_D) × (D/E)$$
$$= 20\% + (20\% − 12\%) × 2$$
$$= 36\%$$

Also, we know that the equity beta is equal to the asset beta multiplied by the equity multiplier:

$$\beta_E = \beta_A × (1 + D/E)$$

In this case, D/E is 2 and β_E is 1.5, so the firm beta is 1.5/3 = 0.50.

20.3 · With no debt, Corpse's WACC is 14 per cent. This is also the unlevered cost of capital. The after-tax cash flow is $4,000 × (1 − 0.30) = $2,800, so the value is just V_U = $2,800/0.14 = $20,000.

After the debt issue, Corpse will be worth the original $20,000 plus the present value of the tax shield. According to M&M Proposition I with taxes, the present value of the tax shield is $T_C × D$, or 0.30 × $6,000 = $1,800, so the firm is worth $20,000 + 1,800 = $21,800.

Questions and problems

1 · Calculating effects of leverage

Start Company Ltd is being set up with no debt and it will have a total market value of $500,000. Earnings before interest and taxes (EBIT) are projected to be $50,000 if economic conditions are normal. If there is a strong expansion in the economy, then EBIT will be 20 per cent higher. If there is a recession, then EBIT will be 40 per cent lower. Start is also considering a $250,000 debt issue with an 8 per cent interest rate. If the debt issue goes ahead, fewer shares will be issued. The original plan is to issue 500,000 shares and no debt.

a Calculate earnings per share (EPS) under each of the 3 economic scenarios before any debt is issued. Also, calculate the percentage changes in EPS if the economy expands or enters a recession.

b Repeat part (a) assuming that Start goes through with its plan to issue debt. What do you observe? Ignore taxation in your answer.

2 · Leverage and break-even EBIT

The Spreading Co. Pty Ltd is comparing alternative capital structures: an all-equity plan (Plan I) and a levered plan (Plan II). Under Plan I, Spreading would have 20,000 shares outstanding. Under Plan II, Spreading would have 10,000 shares and $50,000 in debt outstanding. The interest rate is 12 per cent and there are no taxes.

a If EBIT is $10,000, which plan will result in the higher EPS?

b If EBIT is $20,000, which plan will result in the higher EPS?

c What is the break-even EBIT; that is, what EBIT generates exactly the same EPS under both plans?

3 · M&M and share value

In the previous question, what is the price per share of the equity under Plan I? Under Plan II? Ignore taxes. (*Hint*: M&M Proposition I.)

4 · Capital structure and home-made leverage

The New Company Ltd is debating whether to set up with an all-equity capital structure or one that is 40 per cent debt. An all-equity structure would have 10,000 shares outstanding and the price per share is $1.20. EBIT is expected to remain at $400 per year forever. The interest rate on the debt is 8 per cent, and there are no taxes. I.M. Leaving intends to have 1,000 shares.

a What is I.M. Leaving's cash flow under the all-equity capital structure?

b What will I.M. Leaving's cash flow be with debt in the capital structure? Assume that she holds all 1,000 shares.

c Suppose New uses debt but I.M. Leaving prefers the all-equity capital structure. Show how she could unlever her investment to re-create the original capital structure.

d Explain why the capital structure New chooses is irrelevant.

5 · Home-made leverage and WACC

M.C. Tomorrow Pty Ltd and S.T. Today Pty Ltd are identical firms in every way except for capital structure (Today uses perpetual debt). The EBIT for both is expected to be $10 million forever. The shares of Tomorrow are worth $100 million, and the shares of Today are worth $50 million. The interest rate is 8 per cent, and there are no taxes. Frankie owns $1 million of Today's shares.

a What rate of return is Frankie expecting?

b Show how Frankie could generate exactly the same cash flow and rate of return by investing in M.C. Tomorrow and using 'home-made' leverage.

c What is the cost of equity for S.T. Today? Compare your answer to your answer in part (a). What do you notice? Explain.

d What is M.C. Tomorrow's weighted average cost of capital? What is the weighted average cost of capital for Today? What principle does your answer illustrate?

6 · EPS, EBIT and leverage

Chicago and Associates need to borrow $28,000 to set up a manufacturing business. The business is to operate as a company, Chicago Co. Pty Ltd. Two different capital structures are being considered. The first capital structure, Plan I, would result in 10,000 shares, $8,000 corporate debt and $20,000 private debt. The second plan, Plan II, would result in 11,500 shares, $5,000 corporate debt and $23,000 private debt. The interest rate is 5 per cent.

a Ignoring taxes, compare both of these plans to an all-equity plan assuming that EBIT will be $4,000. Which has the highest EPS? The lowest? The largest cash flow to the owners if all earnings are paid as dividends? The all-equity plan would result in 14,000 shares outstanding.

b In part (a), what are the break-even levels of EBIT for each plan compared to an all-equity plan? Why is one higher than the other?

c Ignoring taxes, when will EPS be identical for the two plans?

d   Answer parts (a), (b) and (c) assuming that the company and personal tax rate is 40 per cent. Are the break-even levels different? Why or why not? Assume that dividend imputation does not apply.

7 · Leverage and share value
Ignoring taxes, in the previous question, what is the price per share of the equity under Plan I? Under Plan II? What principle is illustrated by your answer?

8 · Equity beta and leverage
The Wunover Co. Ltd has an asset beta of 1.20. The market return is 20 per cent, and the risk-free rate is 12 per cent. If Wunover's debt/equity ratio is 0.40, what is Wunover's cost of equity capital? What is the return on Wunover's assets if it has issued debt at the risk-free rate? Ignore taxes.

9 · Calculating WACC
Trek Corporation Ltd has a debt/equity ratio of 0.50. Its WACC is 20 per cent, and its cost of debt is 9 per cent.

a   Ignoring taxes, what is Trek's cost of equity?
b   What would Trek's cost of equity be if the debt/equity ratio were 1.0?
c   What is Trek's WACC in part (b)?

10 · WACC
Star Manufacturing Ltd has no debt, and its WACC is currently 12 per cent. Star can borrow at 9 per cent. The corporate tax rate is 30 per cent.

a   What is Star's cost of equity?
b   If Star converts to 25 per cent debt, what will its cost of equity be?
c   If Star converts to 50 per cent debt, what will its cost of equity be?
d   What is Star's WACC in part (b)? In part (c)?

11 · Value and the tax shield
The Inaheap Co. Ltd expects an EBIT of $1,000 every year forever. Inaheap can borrow at 10 per cent. Inaheap currently has no debt, and its cost of equity is 14 per cent. If the company tax rate is 30 per cent, what is the value of the firm? What will the value be if Inaheap borrows $2,000 and uses the proceeds to reduce shares?

12 · Algebra and M&M propositions
The Wayahead Co. uses no debt. The weighted average cost of capital is 10 per cent. If the current market value of the equity is $5 million and there are no taxes, what is EBIT?

13 · M&M
In the previous question, suppose the company tax rate is 20 per cent. What is EBIT in this case?

14 · M&M and taxes
Burnt Real Estate Ltd currently uses no debt. EBIT is expected to be $6,000 forever, and the cost of capital is currently 12 per cent. The corporate tax rate is a high 40 per cent.

a   What is the market value of Burnt Real Estate?
b   Suppose Burnt floats a $20,000 debt issue and uses the proceeds to reduce share capital. The interest rate is 8 per cent. What is the new value of the business? What is the new value of the equity?

15 · Leverage and WACC
In the previous question, what is the cost of equity after the debt issue? What is the weighted average cost of capital? What are the implications for capital structure?

16 · Beta, cost of equity, and leverage
Rome Rage Co. Pty Ltd is an all-equity business with a beta of 0.80. The market return is 17 per cent, and the risk-free rate is 9 per cent. Management is considering a change in capital structure that will result in a debt/equity ratio of 2. The debt will have no systematic risk, and there are no taxes.

a   What is Rome Rage's cost of equity before the debt issue?
b   What is Rome Rage's cost of equity after the debt issue?
c   What is WACC before and after the debt issue?
d   What is the beta for Rome Rage's equity after the debt issue?

17 · Asset beta versus equity beta

Korean Kapers Ltd (KKC) has an equity beta of 1.4 and a debt beta of zero. KKC's debt ratio (total debt divided by total value) is 0.5. What is the asset beta? If the market risk premium is 8 per cent and the risk-free rate is 9 per cent, what is the cost of equity? The WACC?

18 · Debt and firm value

This one is a little harder. The Donald Chump Company Ltd expects an EBIT of $5,000 every year forever. Chump currently has no debt, and its cost of equity is 18 per cent. Chump can borrow at 10 per cent. If the company tax rate is 30 per cent, what is the value of the firm? What will the value be if Chump converts to 100 per cent debt?

19 · Weighted average cost of capital

This is a challenge question. Assuming a world of company taxes only, show that the WACC can be written as $R_U \times [1 - T_C \times (D/V)]$.

20 · Cost of equity and leverage

This is another challenge question. Show that the cost of equity, R_E, with taxes is as given in the chapter by M&M Proposition II with corporate taxes. Use the result to show that the relationship between the asset beta and the equity beta for a levered firm is $\beta_E = \beta_A \times [1 + (D/E) \times (1 - T_C)]$.

21 · Dividend imputation

This is another challenge question incorporating Chapter 19 and Chapter 20 work. Jim Jives is planning to form a company. He has determined that $10,000,000 will be required as an initial capital investment. Several financial backers have indicated that they would be willing to buy the debentures of the new company or lend Jim personally the capital he needs. Jim has delineated three alternative financing plans:

1 Form the corporation with 1,000,000 shares of $10 par value, borrowing the entire $10,000,000 from his associates on a personal basis (paying 9% interest on his note).
2 Form the company with 500,000 shares of $10 par value, borrowing the $5,000,000 from his associates on a personal basis (9% note). Sell $5,000,000 worth of 9 per cent debentures to his associates.
3 Form the company with 250,000 shares of $10 par value, borrowing $2,500,000 from his associates on a personal basis (9% note). Sell $7,500,000 worth of 9 per cent debentures to his associates.

a Assuming no corporate or personal taxes, which of the three alternatives should Jim select if the firm is expected to earn $2,000,000 per year before the payment of interest and taxation (if applicable)? Assume that all of net earnings are paid out in dividends.
  i Refer to the M&M thesis. Answer (a) without making any calculations. Explain.
  ii Confirm your answer to (i) with computations.
b Assuming a 30 per cent company income tax and a personal income tax rate for Jim of 47 per cent, which of the three alternatives should Jim select if the firm were expected to earn the same amount as in (a)? Assume all earnings are paid out in dividends and dividend imputation is not applicable.
  i Once again refer to the M&M thesis. Remember particularly the conditions under which we are now operating. Answer (b) without making any calculations. Explain.
  ii Confirm your answer to (b)(i) with computations.
c Assume Jim has income from other sources and the dividend imputation system is applicable. Show the optimal financing policy given Jim earns the following different levels of income from other sources.
  i Nil
  ii $186,170
Prepare a table to show the taxable income and the net funds for Jim under each of the alternative income from other sources (nil; $186,170) and each of the alternative financing plans (plan 1; plan 2; plan 3).
d The M&M thesis is to maximise debt in the company capital structure. Does the introduction of dividend imputation change this proposal, and should the emphasis be shifted to personal borrowing?

22 · M&M Proposition II (no tax)

Livin has a WACC of 16 per cent. Its cost of debt is 13 per cent and it has a debt–equity ratio of 2. Ignoring taxes, what is Livin's cost of equity?

23 · M&M Proposition I with tax

P T Screens expects an EBIT of $10,000 every year forever. P T can borrow at 7 per cent. Assume P T Screens currently has no debt and its cost of equity is 17 per cent. If the tax rate is 30 per cent, what is the value of P T Screens?
What will the value of P T Screens be if it borrows $15,000 and uses the funds to repurchase equity?

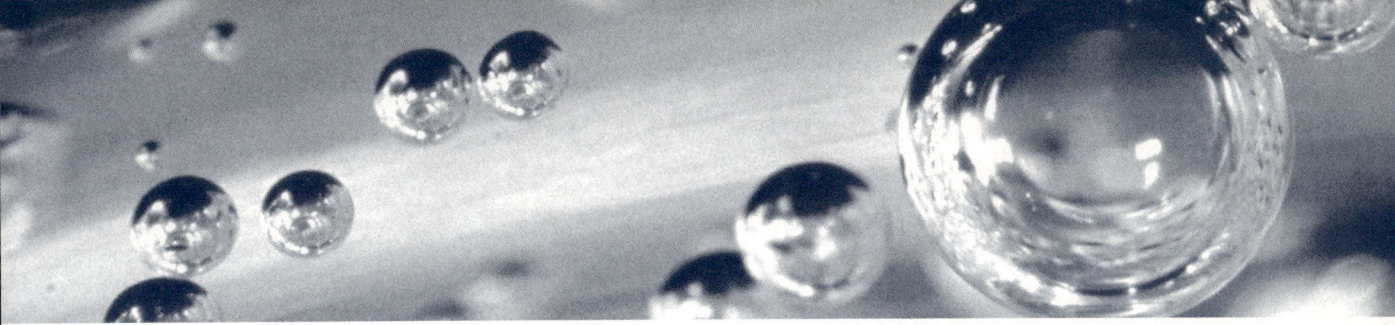

PART NINE

Special topics

in corporate finance

CHAPTER 21

Options,
corporate securities and futures

Objective

This chapter shows that almost all corporate securities have implicit or explicit option features. So that the securities that involve option features may be understood, a general knowledge of the factors that determine the value of an option is developed. The aim on completion of the chapter is to understand the main types and the characteristics of options, and to be able to determine the value of an option. Option pricing models are developed so that option prices may be calculated. This chapter starts with a description of different types of options. We identify and discuss the general factors that determine option values and show how ordinary debt and equity have option-like characteristics. For completeness we describe another derivative product, a futures contract. We show how these types of contracts can be used to hedge a position.

Study tips ▷ Valuing options is regarded as being quite difficult, but it is simply a time value of money problem. On one hand, you have the value of the underlying asset providing a value, and, on the other you have the present value of the future amount that may be paid to keep the asset reducing this value. The more complicated valuation models simply add in probabilities. For example, the Black and Scholes Option Pricing Model introduces a probability of the underlying asset having a predicted value and a probability of having to pay the future amount to keep the asset. After you have worked through the chapter, revisit this and you will see how it relates to valuing options.

Introduction ▷ Finance deals very much with the future and not with the past. As we are dealing with the future we do not know exactly what will occur. For example, if we plan to buy a machine from overseas, the price of the machine may go up or it may even go down. Additionally the exchange rate for converting one currency into another may change. To help manage changing prices, products like futures and options have been developed. This chapter examines these products.

Options are a part of everyday life. 'Keep your options open' is sound business advice, and 'we are out of options' is a sure sign of trouble. Options are obviously valuable, but actually putting a dollar value on one is not easy. How to value options is an important topic of research, and option pricing is one of the great success stories of modern finance.

In finance, an **option** is an arrangement that gives its owner the right to buy or sell an asset at a fixed price anytime on or before a given date. The most familiar options are share options. These are options to buy and sell ordinary shares, and we will discuss them in some detail below.

An option is a contract that gives its owner the right to buy or sell some asset at a fixed price on or before a given date. For example, an option on a building might give the holder of the option the right to buy the building for $1 million anytime on or before the Saturday prior to the third Wednesday in January 2010.

Options are a unique type of financial contract because they give the buyer the right, but not the obligation, to do something. The buyer uses the option only if it is profitable to do so; otherwise the option can be thrown away.

The option must relate to an asset that is clearly identifiable, for example a specific share, a particular share index, an identifiable debt instrument or a foreign currency.

There is a special vocabulary associated with options. Here are some important definitions:

1 *Exercising the option.* The act of buying or selling the underlying asset via the option contract is called **exercising the option**.

2 *Striking price or exercise price.* The fixed price specified in the option contract at which the holder can buy or sell the underlying asset is called the **striking price**, the exercise price, or just the strike price.

3 *Exercise/expiration/declaration date.* An option usually has a limited life. The option is said to expire at the end of its life. The last day on which the option can be exercised is called the **exercise date, expiration date or declaration date**.

4 *American and European options.* An **American option** may be exercised anytime up to the expiration date. A **European option** can be exercised only on the expiration date.

5 *Option writer.* The **writer of an option** or the option seller is obligated to perform according to the terms of the option if and when an exercise is enforced. Selling an option is sometimes referred to as *writing* or *granting* an option and the seller is known as the *writer* or *grantor*.

6 *Option buyer.* The **option buyer** or holder is the market participant who obtains the right conveyed by the option. Only the option buyer has a right to exercise an option. Buying an option is referred to as *taking* an option and the buyer is the *taker*.

7 *Premium.* The price paid by the buyer of an option to the writer (seller) of the option is the **premium**.

Puts and calls

Options come in two basic types: puts and calls. Call options are the more common of the two. A **call option** gives the owner the right to buy an asset at a fixed price during a particular period. It may help you to remember that a call option gives you the right to 'call in' an asset.

A **put option** is essentially the opposite of a call option. Instead of giving the holder the right to buy some asset, it gives the holder the right to *sell* that asset for a fixed exercise price. If you buy a put option, you can force the seller to buy the asset from you for a fixed price and thereby 'put it to them'.

option
a contract that gives its owner the right to buy or sell some asset at a fixed price on or before a given date

exercising the option
the act of buying or selling the underlying asset via the option contract

striking price
the fixed price in the option contract at which the holder can buy or sell the underlying asset. Also the exercise price or strike price

exercise/expiration/ declaration date
the last day on which an option can be exercised

American option
an option that can be exercised at any time until its expiration date

European option
an option that can only be exercised on the expiration date

option writer
the writer of an option is the seller of the option

option buyer
the taker of an option

premium
the price paid by the buyer to the seller for an option right

call option
the right to buy an asset at a fixed price during a particular period

put option
the right to sell an asset at a fixed price during a particular period. The opposite of a call option

What about an investor who *sells* a call option? The seller receives money upfront and has the *obligation* to sell the asset at the exercise price if the option holder wants it. Similarly, an investor who *sells* a put option receives cash upfront and is then obligated to buy the asset at the exercise price if the option holder demands it.

The asset involved in an option could be anything. The options that are most widely bought and sold, however, are share options. These are options to buy and sell shares. Because these are the best-known types of option, we will study them first. As we discuss share options, keep in mind that the general principles apply to options involving any asset, not just shares.

Share option quotations

On 26 April 1973, the Chicago Board Options Exchange (CBOE) opened and began organised trading in share options. Put and call options involving shares in some of the best-known corporations in the United States are traded there. The CBOE is still the largest organised options market, but options are traded in a number of other places today, including New York, Philadelphia, London, Amsterdam, Tokyo and the Australian Stock Exchange. Almost all such options are American (as opposed to European) type contracts. In Australia the market is known as the Australian Options Market and is operated by the ASX. Structurally all these markets are similar, offering standardised put and call options on equities. Many of the options markets have diversified to offer options on precious metals, currencies and share indices.

The Australian Options Market (AOM) was founded in 1976. It provides put and call options on a number of selected shares. The companies whose shares provide the asset base for put and call options are listed in Table 21.1. Exchange traded options turnover is shown in Table 21.2 (on page 721).

While the liquidity of the AOM has improved, not all of the companies listed have sufficient liquidity to be traded on a regular basis.

TABLE 21.1

Put and call share options. Australian Options Market—February 2003

Code	Full company name
AGL	Australian Gas Light Company
ALL	Aristocrat Leisure Limited
AMC	Amcor Limited
AMP	AMP Limited
ANN	Ansell Limited
ANZ	Australia & New Zealand Banking Group Limited
APN	APN News & Media Limited
ASX	Australian Stock Exchange Limited
AWC	Alumina Limited
AXA	AXA Asia Pacific Holdings
BBG	Billabong International Limited
BIL	Brambles Industries Limited
BHP	BHP Billiton Limited
BLD	Boral Limited
BRL	BRL Hardy Limited
BSL	BHP Steel Limited
CBA	Commonwealth Bank of Australia
CCL	Coca Cola Amatil Limited
CLI	Challenger International Limited
CML	Coles Myer Limited
COH	Cochlear Limited
CPU	Computershare Limited

(continued)

TABLE
21.1

Put and call share options. Australian Options Market—February 2003 (*continued*)

Code	Full company name
CSL	CSL Limited
CSR	CSR Limited
DJS	David Jones Limited
ERG	ERG Limited
FXJ	John Fairfax Holdings Limited
GMF	Goodman Fielder Limited
GNS	Gunns Limited
GPT	General Property Trust
HVN	Harvey Norman Holdings Limited
IAG	NRMA Insurance
JHX	James Hardie Industries NV
JUP	Jupiters Limited
LHG	Lihir Gold Limited
LLC	Lend Lease Corporation Limited
MAP	Macquarie Airports
MAY	Mayne Nickless Limited
MBL	Macquarie Bank Limited
MIG	Macquarie Infrastructure Group
MIM	MIM Holdings Limited
NAB	National Australia Bank Limited
NC1	News Corporation
NCM	Newcrest Mining Limited
NCP	News Corporation Limited
NEM	Newmont Mining Corporation
OEC	Orbital Engine Corporation Limited
ORG	Origin Energy Limited
ORI	Orica Limited
OSH	Oil Search Limited
OST	Onesteel Limited
PBL	Publishing & Broadcasting Limited
PDG	Placer Dome Inc
PPX	Paperlinx Limited
PRK	Patrick Corporation Limited
QAN	Qantas Airways Limited
QBE	QBE Insurance Group Limited
RIO	Rio Tinto Limited
SEV	Seven Network Limited
SFE	SFE Corporation Limited
SGB	St George Bank Limited
SRP	Southcorp Holdings Limited
TAB	TAB Limited
TAH	Tabcorp Holdings Limited
TEN	Ten Network Holdings Limited
TLS	Telstra Corporation Limited
TOL	Toll Holdings Limited
WBC	Westpac Banking Corporation Limited
WES	Wesfarmers Limited
WFT	Westfield Trust
WM1	WMC Limited
WMR	WMC Resources Limited
WOW	Woolworths Limited
WPL	Woodside Petroleum Limited
WSF	Westfield Holdings Limited
XJO	S&P/ASX 200 Index

| Year | Contracts millions | | | % | % | Exercise $ millions | |
	Calls	Puts	Total	Calls	Puts	Calls	Puts
1988	6.358	0.869	7.227	88	12	0.531	0.096
1989	9.962	2.26	12.221	81.5	18.5	0.68	0.183
1990	7.737	2.74	10.477	73.8	26.2	0.291	0.357
1991	7.036	2.136	9.172	76.7	23.3	0.525	0.188
1992	5.512	1.842	7.355	75	25	0.352	0.296
1993	7.276	2.234	9.51	76.5	23.5	1.046	0.139
1994	7.201	3.004	10.205	70.6	29.4	0.728	0.614
1995	6.258	2.888	9.146	68.4	31.6	0.86	0.436
1996	7.296	3.482	10.778	67.7	32.3	1.002	0.527
1997	5.66	3.211	8.871	63.8	36.2	1.016	0.541
1998	5.264	2.81	8.075	65.2	34.8	0.982	0.481
1999	6.384	3.607	9.991	63.9	36.1	1.179	0.462
2000	5.339	4.169	9.508	56.1	43.9	0.885	0.809
2001	7.548	6.149	13.697	55.1	44.9	1.093	0.942

Exchange traded options turnover 1988–2001 — TABLE 21.2

Source: *ASX 2002 Fact Book*—Derivatives Market

Contract characteristics of the AOM

Expiration month
The month in which the option expires.

Option type
All options are American options so that they can be exercised at any time prior to expiration.

Contract size
The standard contract size is 1,000 shares. When a share on which there exists a traded option undergoes a capital issue (bonus issue, share split, etc.) an adjustment is made to one or more of the exercise price, the number of options outstanding or the number of shares to which each option contract relates. Details of the adjustments that will be made are set out in the option regulations of the exchange.

Expiry
The maturity date for an option series is the last Friday of the expiration month or, if that day is not a business day, the next succeeding business day. Thus trading in an option series generally terminates on the last Thursday of the expiration month.

Exercise price
There are no strict formal criteria for the establishment of exercise prices. The general practice is that a new series is opened for trading approximately nine months prior to the expiration month, with exercise prices being set 'reasonably close' to the prevailing market price of the underlying share. Additional exercise prices are added by the Exchange on an *ad hoc* basis depending upon price movements of the underlying share. A newspaper listing for the AOM quotation of Woolworths options is presented in Table 21.3 (overleaf).

TABLE 21.3

A sample newspaper listing of call options

				Call Option Woolworths Last Sale Price $11.57				
Series	Exercise Price	Fair Value	Last Sale	Vol '000s	Open Int	Implied Volatility	Delta	Annual % Return
Apr 03	10.50	1.12	1.10	240	90		0.89	1.87
Jun 03	11.25	0.72	0.56	50	107	14.52	0.73	10.11
Sep 03	11.50	0.81	0.76	5	5	15.60	0.66	10.77
Sep 03	11.00	1.10	0.93	20		13.94	0.80	7.65
Sep 03	12.25	0.51	0.50	59	70	17.58	0.46	7.58
Jun 04	13.00	0.55	0.55	255	420	13.72	0.44	3.57
Sep 07	17.50	0.49	0.43	50	50	11.31	0.36	0.92

Source: Adapted from *Australian Financial Review*, 3 March 2003.

If we look at the last line of data in Table 21.3, we see that for an exercise price of $17.50 (second column) there is a buyer prepared to pay $0.49 (third column) and the last sale was at $0.43 (fourth column). This means the buyer sees the value of a Woolworths share as $17.99 ($0.49 plus the exercise price of $17.50). The last sale price of a Woolworths share was $11.57 (see the heading of the table). The 'volume' column indicates the number of options in the day's trading and the 'open' column indicates the total number of options. A separate listing is provided for put options for Woolworths in Table 21.4.

TABLE 21.4

A sample newspaper listing of put options

				Put Option Woolworths Last Sale Price $11.57				
Series	Exercise Price	Fair Value	Last Sale	Vol '000s	Open Int	Implied Volatility	Delta	Annual % Return
Apr 03	10.50	0.07	0.14	120	120	24.31	0.13	4.01
Jun 03	11.50	0.58	0.64	125	408	26.83	0.42	15.23
Jun 03	12.00	0.87	0.77	200	266	27.89	0.53	11.95
Sep 03	11.75	0.91	1.11	5	75	27.96	0.45	11.07
Sep 03	12.00	1.06	1.27	10	10	28.46	0.49	9.59
Jun 04	10.00	0.34	0.35	10	325	23.35	0.21	2.24
Jun 04	9.00	0.19	0.10	10	15	24.35	0.09	1.13

Source: Adapted from *Australian Financial Review*, 3 March 2003.

Clearing and margining

The Clearing House to the AOM is Options Clearing House Pty Ltd, a wholly-owned subsidiary of the Australian Stock Exchange (ASX). The premium is payable in full by the buyer (taker) and credited to the account of the seller (writer) at the time of the trade. For example, a buyer of 1,000 Woolworths call options with a striking price of $13.00 and a

June expiry would pay $550 (1,000 shares × $0.55 premium). At the same time the seller (writer) must lodge a good faith deposit with the Clearing House to ensure performance in the event of a price movement adverse to the position of the seller. For example, if Woolworths shares rose to $15.75 during the option, the seller would lose $2,750 (i.e. 1,000 shares × ($15.75 − $13.00)). Deposit levels vary depending on the value of the underlying shares and the extent to which the share price changes. The margin is comprised of two components, the *risk margin* and the *premium margin*. The premium reflects the value of the contract and the risk margin reflects the amount by which the value could change in a day. In general, the Clearing House will accept securities as collateral, or cash.

Option payoffs

Looking back at Table 21.3, suppose you were to buy 50 September 2007 $17.50 call contracts on Woolworths (last row). The seller's quote is 49 cents, so the contracts cost $490 each. You would spend a total of 50 × $490 = $24,500. You wait a while, and the expiration date rolls around.

Now what? You have a right to buy Woolworths shares for $17.50 per share. If Woolworths is selling for less than $17.50 a share, then this option is not worth anything, and you throw it away. In this case, we say that the option has finished 'out of the money' since the share price is less than the exercise price. Your $24,500 is, alas, a complete loss.

If Woolworths is selling for more than $17.50 per share, then you need to exercise your option. In this case, the option is 'in the money' since the share price exceeds the exercise price. Suppose that Woolworths rises to, say, $18.50 per share. Since you have the right to buy Woolworths at $17.50, you make a $1 profit on each share upon exercise. Each contract involves 1,000 shares, so you make $1 per share × 1,000 shares per contract = $1,000 per contract. Finally, you own 50 contracts, so the value of your options is a handsome $50,000. Notice that, since you invested $24,500, your net profit is $25,500.

As our example indicates, the gains and losses from buying call options can be quite large. To illustrate further, suppose you had simply purchased the shares with the $24,500 instead of buying call options. In this case, you would have about $24,500/$11.57 = 2,117 shares. We can now compare what you have when the option expires for different share prices:

Ending share price	Option value (50 contracts)	Option trading net profit (loss)	Share value (2,117 shares)	Share trading net profit (loss)
11.00	$0	(24,500)	23,287	(1,213)
17.00	$0	(24,500)	35,989	11,489
18.50	$50,000	25,500	39,164	14,664
19.50	$100,000	75,500	41,282	16,782
20.50	$150,000	125,500	43,399	18,899
21.50	$200,000	175,500	45,516	21,016

The option position clearly magnifies the gains and losses on the share by a substantial amount. The reason is that payoff on your 50 option contracts is based on 50 × 1,000 = 50,000 shares instead of just 2,117.

In our example, notice that, if the share price falls below the striking price, then you lose all the $24,500 with the option. With the share, you still have the shares and your losses are reduced. Also notice that the option can never be worth less than zero because you can always just throw it away. As a result, you can never lose more than your original investment (the $24,500 in our example).

It is important to recognise that share options are a zero sum game. By this we mean that whatever the buyer of a share option makes, the seller loses, and vice versa. To illustrate, suppose that, in our example just above, you had *sold* 50 option contracts. You would receive $24,500 up front, and you would be obligated to sell the share for $17.50 if the buyer of the option wished to exercise it. In this situation, if the share price ends up below $17.50, you would be $24,500 ahead. If the share price ends up above $17.50, you have to sell something for less than it is worth, so you lose the difference. For example, if the share price were $19.50, you would have to sell 50 × 1,000 = 50,000 shares at $17.50 per share, so you would lose $19.50 − 17.50 = $2 per share, or $100,000 total. Because you received $24,500 up front, your net loss is $75,500. We can summarise some other possibilities as follows:

Ending share price	Net profit (loss) to option seller
$11.00	$24,500
$17.00	$24,500
$18.50	($25,500)
$19.50	($75,500)
$20.50	($125,500)
$21.50	($175,500)

Notice that the net profits to the option buyer (calculated above) are just the opposites of these amounts.

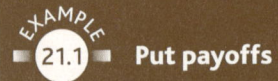

EXAMPLE 21.1 — Put payoffs

Looking at Table 21.4, suppose you buy 10 Woolworths June 2004 $9.00 put contracts. How much does this cost (ignoring commissions)? Just before the option expires, Woolworths is selling for $11.57 per share. Is this good news or bad news? What is your net profit?

The option is quoted at 19 cents, so one contract costs 1,000 × 0.19 = $190. Your 10 contracts total $1,900. You now have the right to sell 10,000 shares of Woolworths for $9.00 per share. If the share is currently selling for $11.57 per share, then this is most definitely bad news. If the share falls to $8.50 per share, you could buy 10,000 shares at $8.50 and sell them for $9.00. Your puts are thus worth $0.50 × 10,000 = $5,000. Since you paid $1,900, your net profit is $5,000 − 1,900 = $3,100.

Concept questions

21.1a *What is a call option? A put option?*

21.1b *If you thought that a share was going to drop sharply in value, how might you use share options to profit from the decline?*

21.1c *If a share on which a call option was written rose in price but the increase was less than the option premium paid, would the option be exercised? Why?*

21.2 ▪ Fundamentals of option valuation

Now that we understand the basics of puts and calls, we can discuss what determines their values. We will focus on call options in the discussion below, but the same type of analysis can be applied to put options.

Value of a call option at expiration

We have already described the payoffs from call options for different share prices. To continue this discussion, the following notation will be useful:

$$S_1 = \text{Share price at expiration (in one period)}$$
$$S_0 = \text{Share price today}$$
$$C_1 = \text{Value of the call option on the expiration date (in one period)}$$
$$C_0 = \text{Value of the call option today}$$
$$E = \text{Exercise price on the option}$$

From our previous discussion, remember that, if the share price (S_1) ends up below the exercise price (E) on the expiration date, then the call option (C_1) is worth zero. In other words:

$$C_1 = 0 \quad \text{if} \quad S_1 \leq E$$

Or, equivalently:

$$C_1 = 0 \quad \text{if} \quad (S_1 - E) \leq 0 \tag{21.1}$$

This is the case where the option is out of the money when it expires.

If the option finishes in the money, then $S_1 > E$, and the value of the option at expiration is equal to the difference:

$$C_1 = S_1 - E \quad \text{if} \quad S_1 > E$$

Or, equivalently:

$$C_1 = S_1 - E \quad \text{if} \quad (S_1 - E) > 0 \tag{21.2}$$

For example, suppose we have a call option with an exercise price of $10. The option is about to expire. If the share is selling for $8, then we have the right to pay $10 for something only worth $8. Our option is thus worth exactly zero because the share price is less than the exercise price on the option $(S_1 < E)$. If the share is selling for $12, then the option has value. Since we can buy the share for $10, it is worth $(S_1 - E) = \$12 - \$10 = \$2$.

Figure 21.1 (overleaf) plots the value of a call option at expiration against the share price. The result looks something like a hockey stick. Notice that for every share price less than E, the value of the option is zero. For every share price greater than E, the value of the call option is $(S_1 - E)$. Also, once the share price exceeds the exercise price, the option's value goes up dollar for dollar with the share price.

FIGURE
21.1

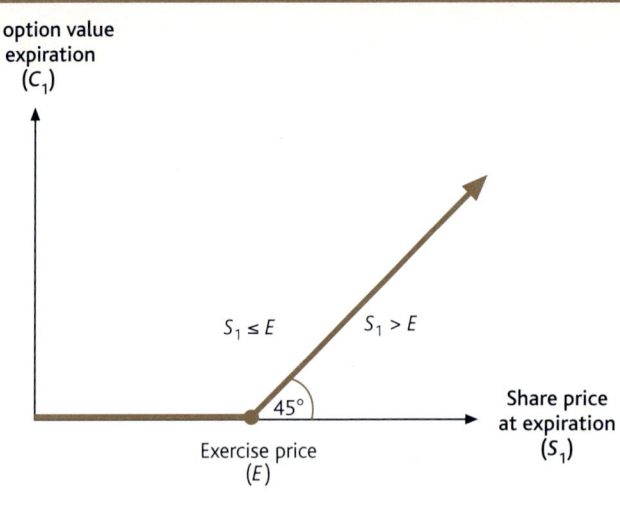

Value of a call option at expiration for different share prices

Call option value
at expiration
(C_1)

$S_1 \leq E$ $S_1 > E$

45°

Share price
at expiration
(S_1)

Exercise price
(E)

As shown, the value of a call option at expiration is equal to zero if the share price is less than or equal to the exercise price. The value of the call is equal to the share price minus the exercise price $(S_1 - E)$ if the share price exceeds the exercise price. The resulting 'hockey stick' shape is highlighted.

The upper and lower bounds on a call option's value

Now that we know how to determine C_1, the value of the call at expiration, we turn to a somewhat more challenging question: How can we determine C_0, the value sometime *before* expiration? We will be discussing this in the next several sections. For now, we will establish the upper and lower bounds for the value of a call option.

The upper bound

What is the most that a call option could sell for? If you think about it, the answer is obvious. A call option gives you the right to buy a share, so it can never be worth more than the share itself. This tells us the upper bound on a call's value: A call option will always sell for less than the underlying asset. So, in our notation, the upper bound is:

$$C_0 \leq S_0 \tag{21.3}$$

The lower bound

What is the least a call option could sell for? The answer here is a little less obvious. First of all, the call cannot sell for less than zero, so $C_0 = 0$. Furthermore, if the share price is greater than the exercise price, the call option is worth at least $S_0 - E$.

To see why, suppose we had a call option selling for $4. The share price is $10, and the exercise price is $5. Is there a profit opportunity here? The answer is yes because you could buy the call for $4 and immediately exercise it by spending an additional $5. Your total cost of acquiring the share is $4 + 5 = $9. If you turn around and immediately sell the share for $10, you pocket a certain profit of $1.

Opportunities for riskless profits such as this one are called *arbitrages* (say 'are-bi-trarzh', with the accent on the first syllable) or arbitrage opportunities. One who arbitrages is called an arbitrageur. The root for the term *arbitrage* is the same as the root for the word *arbitrate*, and an arbitrageur essentially arbitrates prices. In a well-organised market, significant arbitrages will, of course, be rare.

In the case of a call option, to prevent arbitrage, the value of the call today must be greater than the share price less the exercise price:

$$C_0 \geq S_0 - E$$

If we put our two conditions together, we have:

$$C_0 = 0 \quad \text{if} \quad S_0 - E \leq 0$$
$$\mathbf{C_0 = S_0 - E \quad if \quad S_0 - E > 0} \tag{21.4}$$

These conditions simply say that the lower bound on the call's value is either zero or $S_0 - E$, whichever is bigger.

Our lower bound is called the **intrinsic value** of the option, and it is simply what the option would be worth if it were about to expire. With this definition, our discussion thus far can be restated as follows: at expiration, an option is worth its intrinsic value; it will generally be worth more than that any time before expiration.

intrinsic value
the lower bound of an option's value, or what the option would be worth if it were about to expire

Figure 21.2 displays the upper and lower bounds on the value of a call option. Also plotted is a curve representing typical call option values for different share prices prior to maturity. The exact shape and location of this curve depends on a number of factors. We begin our discussion of these factors in the next section.

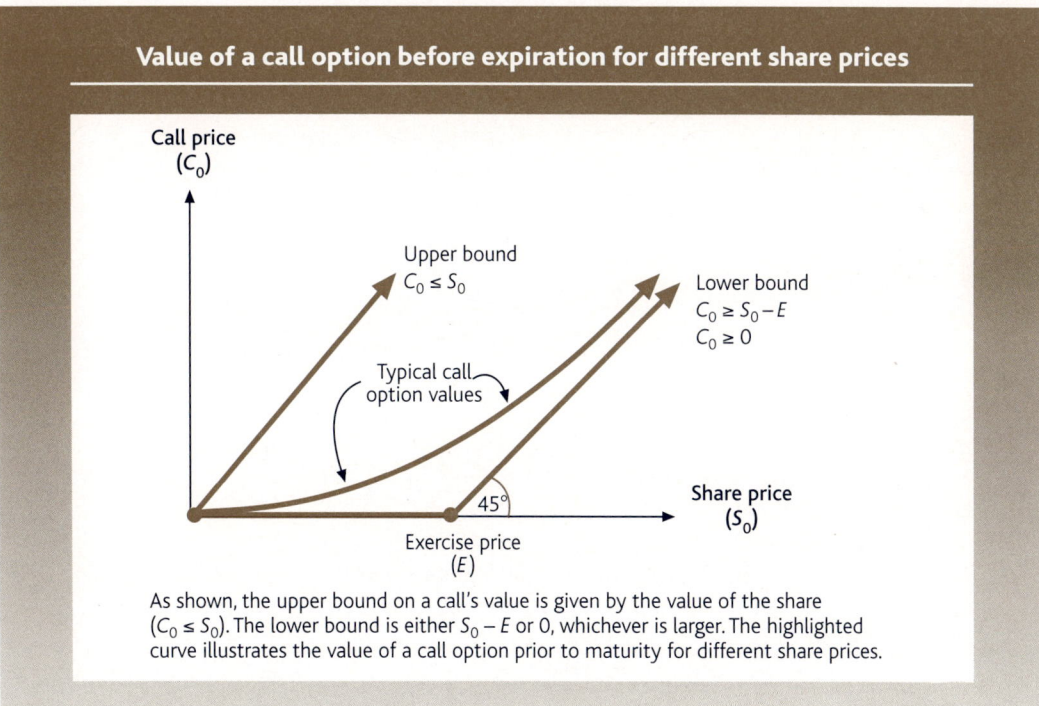

Value of a call option before expiration for different share prices

FIGURE 21.2

As shown, the upper bound on a call's value is given by the value of the share ($C_0 \leq S_0$). The lower bound is either $S_0 - E$ or 0, whichever is larger. The highlighted curve illustrates the value of a call option prior to maturity for different share prices.

A simple model

Option pricing can be a complex subject. Fortunately, as is often the case, many of the key insights can be illustrated with a simple example. Suppose that we are looking at a call option with one year to expiration and an exercise price of $10.50. The share currently sells for $10, and the risk-free rate, R_f, is 12 per cent.

The value of the share in one year is uncertain, of course. To keep things simple, suppose that we know that the share price will either be $11 or $13. Importantly, we *do not* know the odds associated with these two prices. In other words, we know the possible values for the share, but not the probabilities associated with those values.

Since the exercise price on the option is $10.50, we know that the option will be worth either $11 − 10.50 = $0.50 or $13 − 10.50 = $2.50, but, once again, we do not know which. We do know one thing, however: our call option is certain to finish in the money.

The basic approach

Here is the crucial observation: it is possible to exactly duplicate the payoffs on the share using a combination of the option and the risk-free asset. How? Buy one call option and invest $9.375 in a risk-free asset (such as Government bonds).

What will you have in a year? Your risk-free asset will earn 12 per cent, so it will be worth $9.375 × 1.12 = $10.50. Your option is worth $0.50 or $2.50, so the total value is either $11 or $13, just like the share:

Share value	Risk-free asset value	+	Call value	=	Total value
$11	$10.50	+	$0.50	=	$11
$13	$10.50	+	$2.50	=	$13

As illustrated, these two strategies—buy a share versus buy a call and invest in the risk-free asset—have exactly the same payoffs in the future.

Since these two strategies have the same future payoffs, they must have the same value today or else there would be an arbitrage opportunity. The share sells for $10 today, so the value of the call option today, C_0, is:

$$\$10 = \$9.375 + C_0$$
$$C_0 = \$0.625$$

Where did we get the $9.375? This is just the present value of the exercise price on the option, calculated at the risk-free rate:

$$E/(1 + R_f) = \$10.50/1.12 = \$9.375$$

Given this, our example shows that the value of a call option in this simple case is given by:

$$S_0 = C_0 + E/(1 + R_f)$$
$$C_0 = S_0 - E/(1 + R_f) \tag{21.5}$$

In words, the value of the call option is equal to the share price minus the present value of the exercise price.

A more complicated case

Obviously, our assumption that the share price would be either $11 or $13 is a vast oversimplification. We can now develop a more realistic model by assuming that the share price can be *anything* greater than or equal to the exercise price. Once again, we do not know how likely the different possibilities are, but we are certain that the option will finish somewhere in the money.

We again let S_1 stand for the share price in one year. Now consider our strategy of investing $9.375 in a riskless asset and buying one call option. The riskless asset will again be worth $10.50 in one year, and the option will be worth $S_1 - \$10.50$, depending on what the share price is.

When we investigate the combined value of the option and the riskless asset, we observe something very interesting:

$$
\begin{aligned}
\text{Combined value} &= \text{Riskless asset value} + \text{Option value} \\
&= \$10.50 + (S_1 - \$10.50) \\
&= S_1
\end{aligned}
$$

Just as we had before, buying a share has exactly the same payoff as buying a call option and investing the present value of the exercise price in the riskless asset.

Once again, to prevent arbitrage, these two strategies must have the same cost, so the value of the call option is equal to the share price less the present value of the exercise price:[1]

$$
C_0 = S_0 - E/(1 + R_f)
$$

Our conclusion from this discussion is that determining the value of a call option is not difficult as long as we are certain that the option will finish somewhere in the money.

Four factors determining option values

If we continue to suppose that our option is certain to finish in the money, then we can readily identify four factors that determine an option's value. There is a fifth factor that comes into play if the option can finish out of the money. We will discuss this last factor in the next section.

For now, if we assume that the option expires in t periods, then the present value of the exercise price is $E/(1 + R_f)^t$, and the value of the call is:

$$
\begin{aligned}
\text{Call option value} &= \text{Share value} - \text{Present value of the exercise price} \\
C_0 &= S_0 - E/(1 + R_f)^t \qquad \text{(21.6)}
\end{aligned}
$$

If we take a look at this expression, the value of the call obviously depends on four things:

1 *The share price.* The higher the share price (S_0) is, the more the call is worth. This comes as no surprise since the option gives us the right to buy the share at a fixed price.
2 *The exercise price.* The higher the exercise price (E) is, the less the call is worth. This is also not a surprise since the exercise price is what we have to pay to get the share.
3 *The time to expiration.* The longer the time to expiration is (the bigger t is), the more the option is worth. Once again, this is obvious. Since the option gives us the right to buy for a fixed length of time, its value goes up as that length of time increases.
4 *The risk-free rate.* The higher the risk-free rate (R_f) is, the more the call is worth. This result is a little less obvious. Normally, we think of asset values going down as rates rise. In this case, the exercise price is a cash *outflow*, a liability. The current value of that liability goes down as the discount rate goes up.

Concept questions

21.2a *What is the value of a call option at expiration?*
21.2b *What are the upper and lower bounds on the value of a call option anytime before expiration?*
21.2c *Assuming that the share price is certain to be greater than the exercise price on a call option, what is the value of the call? Why?*

 ## 21.3 ■ Valuing a call option

We now investigate the value of a call option when there is the possibility that the option will finish out of the money. We will again examine the simple case of two possible future share prices. This case will let us identify the remaining factor that determines an option's value.

A simple model: Part II

From our previous example, we have a share that currently sells for $10. It will be worth either $11 or $13 in a year, and we do not know which. The risk-free rate is 12 per cent. We are now looking at a different call option, however. This one has an exercise price of $12 instead of $10.50. What is the value of this call option?

This case is a little harder. If the share ends up at $11, the option is out of the money and worth nothing. If the share ends up at $13, the option is worth $13 − 12 = $1.

Our basic approach to determining the value of the call option will be the same. We will show once again that it is possible to combine the call option and a risk-free investment in a way that exactly duplicates the payoff from holding the share. The only complication is that it is a little harder to determine how to do it.

For example, suppose we bought one call and invested the present value of the exercise price in a riskless asset as we did before. In one year, we would have $12 from the riskless investment plus an option worth either zero or $1. The total value is either $12 or $13. This is not the same as the value of the share ($11 or $13), so the two strategies are not comparable.

Instead, consider investing the present value of $11 (the lower share price) in a riskless asset. This guarantees us an $11 payoff. If the share price is $11, then any call options we own are worthless, and we have exactly $11 as desired.

When the share is worth $13, the call option is worth $1. Our risk-free investment is worth $11, so we are $13 − 11 = $2 short. Since each call option is worth $1, we need to buy two of them to replicate the share.

Thus, in this case, investing the present value of the lower share price in a riskless asset and buying two call options exactly duplicates owning the share. When the share is worth $11, we have $11 from our risk-free investment. When the share is worth $13, we have $11 from the risk-free investment plus two call options worth $1 each.

Since these two strategies have exactly the same value in the future, they must have the same today or else arbitrage would be possible:

$$S_0 = \$10 = 2 \times C_0 + \$11/(1 + R_f)$$
$$2 \times C_0 = \$10 - \$11/1.12$$
$$= \$10 - \$9.82$$
$$C_0 = \$0.09$$

Each call option is thus worth $0.09.

EXAMPLE 21.2 ■ **Do not call us, we'll call you**

We are looking at two call options on the same share, one with an exercise price of $20 and one with an exercise price of $30. The share currently sells for $35. Its future price will either be $25 or $50. If the risk-free rate is 12 per cent, what are the values of these call options?

The first case (the \$20 exercise price) is not difficult since the option is sure to finish in the money. We know that the value is equal to the share price less the present value of the exercise price:

$$
\begin{aligned}
C_0 &= S_0 - E/(1 + R_f) \\
&= \$35 - \$20/1.12 \\
&= \$17.14
\end{aligned}
$$

In the second case, the exercise price is \$30, so the option can finish out of the money. At expiration, the option is worth \$0 if the share is worth \$25. The option is worth $\$50 - 30 = \$20$ if it finishes in the money.

As before, we start by investing the present value of the lowest share price in the risk-free asset. This costs $\$25/1.12 = \$22.32$. At expiration, we have \$25 from this investment.

If the share price is \$50, then we need an additional \$25 to duplicate the share payoff. Since each option is worth \$20 in this case, we need $\$25/\$20 = 1.25$ options. So, to prevent arbitrage, investing the present value of \$25 in a risk-free asset and buying 1.25 call options has the same value as the share:

$$
\begin{aligned}
S_0 &= 1.25 \times C_0 + \$25/(1 + R_f) \\
\$35 &= 1.25 \times C_0 + \$25/(1 + 0.12) \\
C_0 &= \$10.14
\end{aligned}
$$

Notice that this second option had to be worth less because it has the higher exercise price.

The fifth factor

We now illustrate the fifth (and last) factor that determines an option's value. Suppose that everything in our example above is the same except that the share price can be \$10.50 or \$13.50 instead of \$11 or \$13. Notice that the effect of this change is to make the share's future price more volatile than before.

We investigate the same strategy that we used above: Invest the present value of the lowest share price (\$10.50 in this case) in the risk-free asset and buy two call options. If the share price is \$10.50, then, as before, the call options have no value and we have \$10.50 in all.

If the share price is \$13.50, then each option is worth $S_1 - E = \$13.50 - 12 = \$1.50$. We have two calls, so our portfolio is worth $\$10.50 + 2 \times \$1.50 = \$13.50$. Once again, we have exactly replicated the value of the share.

What has happened to the option's value? More to the point, the variance of the return on the share has increased. Does the option's value go up or down? To find out, we need to solve for the value of the call just as we did before:

$$
\begin{aligned}
S_0 = \$10 &= 2 \times C_0 + \$10.50/(1 + R_f) \\
2 \times C_0 &= \$10 - \$10.50/1.12 \\
C_0 &= \$0.31
\end{aligned}
$$

The value of the call option has gone up from \$0.09 to \$0.31.

Based on our example, the fifth and final factor that determines an option's value is the variance of the return on the underlying asset. Furthermore, the greater that variance is, the more the option is worth. This result appears a little odd at first, and it may be somewhat surprising to learn that increasing the risk (as measured by return variance) on the underlying asset increases the value of the option.

The reason that increasing the variance on the underlying asset increases the value of the option is not hard to see in our example. Changing the lower share price to $10.50 from $11 does not hurt a bit because the option is worth zero in either case. However, moving the upper possible price to $13.50 from $13 makes the option worth more when it is in the money.

More generally, increasing the variance of the possible future prices on the underlying asset does not affect the option's value when the option finishes out of the money. The value is always zero in this case. On the other hand, increasing that variance when the option is in the money only increases the possible payoffs, so the net effect is to increase the option's value. Put another way, since the downside risk is always limited, the only effect is to increase the upside potential.

In later discussion, we will use the symbol σ^2 to stand for the variance of the return on the underlying asset.

A closer look

Before moving on, it will be useful to consider one last example. Suppose the share price is $10 and it will either move up or down by 20 per cent. The risk-free rate is 5 per cent. What is the value of a call option with a $9 exercise price?

The share price will either be $8 or $12. The option is worth zero when the share is worth $8, and it is worth $12 − 9 = $3 when the share is worth $12. We will therefore invest the present value of $8 in the risk-free asset and buy some call options.

When the share finishes at $12, our risk-free asset pays $8, leaving us $4 short. Each option is worth $3 in this case, so we need $4/$3 = $1\frac{1}{3}$ options to match the payoff on the share. The option's value must thus be given by:

$$S_0 = \text{}^4/_3 \times C_0 + \$8/1.05$$
$$C_0 = (\text{}^3/_4) \times (\$10 - \$7.62)$$
$$= \$1.79$$

To make our result a little bit more general, notice that the number of options that you need to buy to replicate the share is always equal to $\Delta S/\Delta C$, where ΔS is the difference in the possible share prices and ΔC is the difference in the possible option values. In our current case, for example, ΔS would be $12 − 8 = $4 and ΔC would be $3 − 0 = $3, so $\Delta S/\Delta C$ is $4/$3 = $\text{}^4/_3$ as we calculated.

Notice also that when the share is certain to finish in the money, $\Delta S/\Delta C$ is always exactly equal to one, so one call option is always needed. Otherwise, $\Delta S/\Delta C$ is greater than one, so more than one call option is needed.

TABLE 21.5

Five factors that determine option values		
Factor	Calls	Puts
Current value of the underlying asset	(+)	(−)
Exercise price on the option	(−)	(+)
Time to expiration on the option	(+)	(+)
Risk-free rate	(+)	(−)
Variance of return on underlying asset	(+)	(+)

This concludes our discussion of option valuation. The most important thing to remember is that the value of an option depends on five factors. Table 21.5 (opposite) summarises these factors and the direction of the influence for both puts and calls. In Table 21.5, the sign in parentheses indicates the direction of the influence.[2] In other words, the sign tells us whether the value of the option goes up or down when the value of a factor increases. For example, notice that increasing the exercise price reduces the value of a call option. Increasing any of the other four factors increases the value of the call. Notice also that the time to expiration and the variance act the same for puts and calls. The other three factors have opposite signs. We have not considered how to value a call option when the option can finish out of the money and the share price can take on more than two values. A very famous result, the Black–Scholes Option Pricing Model, is needed in this case.

Concept questions

21.3a What are the five factors that determine an option's value?

21.3b What is the effect of an increase in each of the five factors on the value of a call option? Give an intuitive explanation for your answer.

21.3c What is the effect of an increase in each of the five factors on the value of a put option? Give an intuitive explanation for your answer.

21.4 Black-Scholes option pricing model

In our discussion of call options, we did not discuss the general case where the share can take on any value *and* the option can finish out of the money. The general approach to valuing a call option falls under the heading of the **Black–Scholes Option Pricing Model (OPM)**, a very famous result in finance. This section briefly discusses the Black–Scholes model. Because the underlying development is relatively complex, we will only present the result and then focus on how to use it.

From our earlier discussion, when a *t*-period call option is certain to finish somewhere in the money, its value today, C_0, is equal to the value of the share today, S_0, less the present value of the exercise price, $E/(1 + R_f)^t$:

$$C_0 = S_0 - E/(1 + R_f)^t$$

If the option can finish out of the money, then this result needs modifying. Black and Scholes show that the value of a call option in this case is given by:

$$C_0 = S_0 \times N(d_1) - E/(1 + R_f)^t \times N(d_2) \tag{21.7}$$

where $N(d_1)$ and $N(d_2)$ are probabilities that must be calculated. This is the Black–Scholes OPM.[3]

To obtain an intuitive feel for Equation 21.7 you may like to think of it as showing:

Option value	=	Share price	×	Some probability the share price is relevant	−	Present value of exercise price	×	Some probability the exercise price is paid
C_0	=	S_0	×	$N(d_1)$	−	$E/(1 + R_f)^t$	×	$N(d_2)$

where

$$
\begin{aligned}
C_0 &= \text{option value} \\
S_0 &= \text{share price} \\
N(d_1) &= \text{a probability the share price will be relevant} \\
E/(1 + R_f)^t &= \text{the present value of the exercise price} \\
N(d_2) &= \text{a probability the exercise price will be paid}
\end{aligned}
$$

In the Black–Scholes model, $N(d_1)$ is the probability that a standardised, normally distributed random variable (widely known as a 'z' variable) is less than or equal to d_1, and $N(d_2)$ is the probability of a value that is less than or equal to d_2. Determining these probabilities requires a table such as Table 21.6.

To illustrate, suppose we were given the following information:

$$
\begin{aligned}
S_0 &= \$100 \\
E &= \$80 \\
R_f &= 1\% \text{ per month} \\
d_1 &= 1.20 \\
d_2 &= 0.90 \\
t &= 9 \text{ months}
\end{aligned}
$$

Based on this information, what is the value of the call option, C_0?

To answer, we need to determine $N(d_1)$ and $N(d_2)$. In Table 21.6, we first find the row corresponding to a d of 1.20. The corresponding probability, $N(d)$, is 0.8849, so this is $N(d_1)$. For d_2, the associated probability $N(d_2)$ is 0.8159. Using the Black–Scholes OPM, the value of the call option is thus:

$$
\begin{aligned}
C_0 &= S_0 \times N(d_1) - E/(1 + R_f)^t \times N(d_2) \\
&= \$100 \times 0.8849 - \$80/(1.01)^9 \times 0.8159 \\
&= \$88.49 - 59.68 \\
&= \$28.81
\end{aligned}
$$

TABLE 21.6

Cumulative normal distribution											
d	N(d)	d	N(d)	d	N(d)	d	N(d)	d	N(d)	d	N(d)
−3.00	.0013	−1.58	.0571	−0.76	.2236	0.06	.5239	0.86	.8051	1.66	.9515
−2.95	.0016	−1.56	.0594	−0.74	.2297	0.08	.5319	0.88	.8106	1.68	.9535
−2.90	.0019	−1.54	.0618	−0.72	.2358	0.10	.5398	0.90	.8159	1.70	.9554
−2.85	.0022	−1.52	.0643	−0.70	.2420	0.12	.5478	0.92	.8212	1.72	.9573
−2.80	.0026	−1.50	.0668	−0.68	.2483	0.14	.5557	0.94	.8264	1.74	.9591
−2.75	.0030	−1.48	.0694	−0.66	.2546	0.16	.5636	0.96	.8315	1.76	.9608
−2.70	.0035	−1.46	.0721	−0.64	.2611	0.18	.5714	0.98	.8365	1.78	.9625
−2.65	.0040	−1.44	.0749	−0.62	.2676	0.20	.5793	1.00	.8414	1.80	.9641
−2.60	.0047	−1.42	.0778	−0.60	.2743	0.22	.5871	1.02	.8461	1.82	.9656
−2.55	.0054	−1.40	.0808	−0.58	.2810	0.24	.5948	1.04	.8508	1.84	.9671
−2.50	.0062	−1.38	.0838	−0.56	.2877	0.26	.6026	1.06	.8554	1.86	.9686
−2.45	.0071	−1.36	.0869	−0.54	.2946	0.28	.6103	1.08	.8599	1.88	.9699

TABLE
21.6

Cumulative normal distribution (*continued*)

d	N(d)	d	N(d)	d	N(d)	d	N(d)	d	N(d)	d	N(d)
−2.40	.0082	−1.34	.0901	−0.52	.3015	0.30	.6179	1.10	.8643	1.90	.9713
−2.35	.0094	−1.32	.0934	−0.50	.3085	0.32	.6255	1.12	.8686	1.92	.9726
−2.30	.0107	−1.30	.0968	−0.48	.3156	0.34	.6331	1.14	.8729	1.94	.9738
−2.25	.0122	−1.28	.1003	−0.46	.3228	0.36	.6406	1.16	.8770	1.96	.9750
−2.20	.0139	−1.26	.1038	−0.44	.3300	0.38	.6480	1.18	.8810	1.98	.9761
−2.15	.0158	−1.24	.1075	−0.42	.3373	0.40	.6554	1.20	.8849	2.00	.9772
−2.10	.0179	−1.22	.1112	−0.40	.3446	0.42	.6628	1.22	.8888	2.05	.9798
−2.05	.0202	−1.20	.1151	−0.38	.3520	0.44	.6700	1.24	.8925	2.10	.9821
−2.00	.0228	−1.18	.1190	−0.36	.3594	0.46	.6773	1.26	.8962	2.15	.9842
−1.98	.0239	−1.16	.1230	−0.34	.3669	0.48	.6844	1.28	.8997	2.20	.9861
−1.96	.0250	−1.14	.1271	−0.32	.3745	0.50	.6915	1.30	.9032	2.25	.9878
−1.94	.0262	−1.12	.1314	−0.30	.3821	0.52	.6985	1.32	.9066	2.30	.9893
−1.92	.0274	−1.10	.1357	−0.28	.3897	0.54	.7054	1.34	.9099	2.35	.9906
−1.90	.0287	−1.08	.1401	−0.26	.3974	0.56	.7123	1.36	.9131	2.40	.9918
−1.88	.0301	−1.06	.1446	−0.24	.4052	0.58	.7191	1.38	.9162	2.45	.9929
−1.86	.0314	−1.04	.1492	−0.22	.4129	0.60	.7258	1.40	.9192	2.50	.9938
−1.84	.0329	−1.02	.1539	−0.20	.4207	0.62	.7324	1.42	.9222	2.55	.9946
−1.82	.0344	−1.00	.1587	−0.18	.4286	0.64	.7389	1.44	.9251	2.60	.9953
−1.80	.0359	−0.98	.1635	−0.16	.4365	0.66	.7454	1.46	.9279	2.65	.9960
−1.78	.0375	−0.96	.1685	−0.14	.4443	0.68	.7518	1.48	.9306	2.70	.9965
−1.76	.0392	−0.94	.1736	−0.12	.4523	0.70	.7580	1.50	.9332	2.75	.9970
−1.74	.0409	−0.92	.1788	−0.10	.4602	0.72	.7642	1.52	.9357	2.80	.9974
−1.72	.0427	−0.90	.1841	−0.08	.4681	0.74	.7704	1.54	.9382	2.85	.9978
−1.70	.0446	−0.88	.1894	−0.06	.4761	0.76	.7764	1.56	.9406	2.90	.9981
−1.68	.0465	−0.86	.1949	−0.04	.4841	0.78	.7823	1.58	.9429	2.95	.9984
−1.66	.0485	−0.84	.2005	−0.02	.4920	0.80	.7882	1.60	.9452	3.00	.9987
−1.64	.0505	−0.82	.2061	0.00	.5000	0.82	.7939	1.62	.9474	3.05	.9989
−1.62	.0526	−0.80	.2119	0.02	.5080	0.84	.7996	1.64	.9495		
−1.60	.0548	−0.78	.2177	0.04	.5160						

As this example illustrates, if we are given values for d_1 and d_2 (and the table), then using the Black–Scholes model is not difficult. In general, however, we will not be given the values of d_1 and d_2, and we must calculate them instead. This requires a little extra effort. The values for d_1 and d_2 for the Black–Scholes OPM are given by:

$$d_1 = [\ln(S_0/E) + (R_f + {}^1/_2 \times \sigma^2)t]/[\sigma \times \sqrt{t}] \qquad (21.8)$$
$$d_2 = d_1 - \sigma \times \sqrt{t}$$

In these expressions, σ is the standard deviation of the rate of return on the underlying asset. Also, $\ln(S_0/E)$ is the natural logarithm of the current share price divided by the exercise price (most calculators have a key labelled 'ln' to perform this calculation).

The formula for d_1 looks intimidating, but using it is mostly a matter of 'plug and chug' with a calculator. To illustrate, suppose we had the following:

$$S_0 = \$70$$
$$E = \$80$$
$$R_f = 1\% \text{ per month}$$
$$\sigma = 2\% \text{ per month}$$
$$t = 9 \text{ months}$$

With these numbers, d_1 is:

$$
\begin{aligned}
d_1 &= [\ln(S_0/E) + (R_f + {}^1/_2 \times \sigma^2) \times t]/[\sigma \times \sqrt{t}] \\
&= [\ln(0.875) + (0.01 + {}^1/_2 \times 0.02^2) \times 9]/[0.02 \times 3] \\
&= [-0.1335 + 0.0918]/0.06 \\
&= -0.70
\end{aligned}
$$

Given this result, d_2 is:

$$
\begin{aligned}
d_2 &= d_1 - \sigma \times \sqrt{t} \\
&= -0.70 - 0.02 \times 3 \\
&= -0.76
\end{aligned}
$$

Referring to Table 21.6, the values for $N(d_1)$ and $N(d_2)$ are 0.2420 and 0.2236, respectively. The value of the option is thus:

$$
\begin{aligned}
C_0 &= S_0 \times N(d_1) - E/(1 + R_f)^t \times N(d_2) \\
&= \$70 \times 0.2420 - \$80/1.01^9 \times 0.2236 \\
&= \$0.58
\end{aligned}
$$

This may seem a little small, but the share price would have to rise by $10 before the option would even be in the money.

Notice that we quoted the risk-free rate, the standard deviation and the time to maturity in months in this example. We could have used days, weeks or years as long as we are consistent in quoting all three of these using the same time units.

If we were to incorporate the continuously compounded risk-free rate into the model, we would be discounting the exercise price by the factor $e^{R_f t}$, where:

$$e = \text{the base of the natural logarithm} = 2.71828$$
$$R_f = \text{the risk-free rate}$$
$$t = \text{the time to maturity of the option}$$

Consider the following option example incorporating continuous compounding:

$$S_0 = \$9.00$$
$$E = \$10.00$$
$$t = 6 \text{ months} = 0.5 \text{ years}$$
$$\sigma = 0.5$$
$$R_f = 0.1$$

Then d_1 and d_2 can be computed as:

$$d_1 = \{\ln(9/10) + [0.10 + {}^1/_2(0.25)] \times 0.5\}/(0.5 \times \sqrt{0.5}) = 0.02$$
$$d_2 = \{\ln(9/10) + [0.10 - {}^1/_2(0.25)] \times 0.5\}/(0.5 \times \sqrt{0.5}) = -0.33$$

or

$$d_2 = d_1 - \sigma \times \sqrt{t} = 0.02 - \sqrt{0.25} \times \sqrt{0.5} = 0.02 - 0.35 = -0.33$$

so that

$$N(d_1) = N(0.02) = 0.5080$$

and

$$N(d_2) = N(-0.33) = 0.3707$$

The value of the call option is:

$$
\begin{aligned}
C_0 &= 9(0.5080) - 10/e^{(0.10)(0.5)}(0.3707) \\
&= 4.572 - 3.526 \\
&= \$1.046
\end{aligned}
$$

21.5 ∎ Equity as a call option on the firm's assets

Now that we understand the basic determinants of an option's value, we turn to examining some of the many ways that options appear in corporate finance. One of the most important insights we gain from studying options is that the ordinary shares in a leveraged firm (one that has issued debt) is effectively a call option on the assets of the firm. This is a remarkable observation, and we explore it next.

An example is the easiest way to get started. Suppose a firm has a single debt issue outstanding. The face value is $1,000, and the debt is coming due in a year. There are no interest payments between now and then, so the debt is effectively a pure discount bond. In addition, the current market value of the firm's assets is $950, and the risk-free rate is 12.5 per cent.

In a year, the shareholders will have a choice. They can pay off the debt for $1,000 and thereby acquire the assets of the firm free and clear, or they can default on the debt. If they default, the debtholders will own the assets of the firm.

In this situation, the shareholders essentially have a call option on the assets of the firm with an exercise price of $1,000. They may exercise the option by paying the $1,000, or they may not exercise the option by defaulting. Whether or not they choose to exercise obviously depends on the value of the firm's assets when the debt becomes due.

If the value of the firm's assets exceeds $1,000, then the option is in the money, and the shareholders will exercise by paying off the debt. If the value of the firm's assets is less than $1,000, then the option is out of the money, and the shareholders will optimally choose to default. What we now illustrate is that we can determine the values of the debt and equity using our option pricing results.

Case I: The debt is risk-free

Suppose that in one year the firm's assets will either be worth $1,100 or $1,200. What is the value today of the equity in the firm? The value of the debt? What is the interest rate on the debt?

To answer these questions, we first recognise that the option (the equity in the firm) is certain to finish in the money because the value of the firm's assets ($1,100 or $1,200) will always exceed the face value of the debt. In this case, from our discussion in previous sections, we know that the option value is simply the difference between the value of the underlying asset and the present value of the exercise price (calculated at the risk-free rate). The present value of $1,000 in one year at 12.5 per cent is $888.89. The current value of the firm is $950, so the option (the firm's equity) is worth $950 − 888.89 = $61.11.

What we see is that the equity, which is effectively an option to purchase the firm's assets, must be worth $61.11. The debt must therefore actually be worth $888.89. In fact, we really did not need to know about options to handle this example, because the debt is risk-free. The reason is that the debtholders are certain to receive $1,000. Since the debt is risk-free, the appropriate discount rate (and the interest rate on the debt) is the risk-free rate, and we therefore know immediately that the current value of the debt is $1,000/1.125 = $888.89. The equity is thus worth $950 − 888.89 = $61.11 as we calculated.

Case II: The debt is risky

Suppose now that the value of the firm's assets in one year will be either $800 or $1,200. This case is a little more difficult because the debt is no longer risk-free. If the value of the assets turns out to be $800, then the shareholders will not exercise their option and thereby default. The shares are worth nothing in this case. If the assets are worth $1,200, then the shareholders will exercise their option to pay off the debt and enjoy a profit of $1,200 − 1,000 = $200.

What we see is that the option (the equity in the firm) is worth either zero or $200. The assets are worth either $1,200 or $800. Based on our discussion in previous sections, a portfolio that has the present value of $800 invested in a risk-free asset and ($1,200 − $800)/($200 − $0) = 2 call options exactly replicates the assets of the firm.

The present value of $800 at the risk-free rate of 12.5 per cent is $800/1.125 = $711.11. This amount, plus the value of the two call options, is equal to $950, the current value of the firm:

$$\$950 = 2 \times C_0 + \$711.11$$
$$C_0 = \$119.44$$

Since the call option in this case is actually the firm's equity, the value of the equity is $119.44. The value of the debt is thus $950 − 119.44 = $830.56.

Finally, since the debt has a $1,000 face value and a current value of $830.56, the interest rate is $1,000/$830.56 − 1 = 20.4%. This exceeds the risk-free rate, of course, since the debt is now risky.

EXAMPLE 21.3 ▪ **Equity as a call option**

Teresa Green Ltd has a pure discount debt issue with a face value of $100. The issue is due in a year. At that time, the assets in the firm will be worth either $55 or $160, depending on the sales success of Teresa's latest product. The assets of the firm are currently worth $110. If the risk-free rate is 10 per cent, what is the value of the equity in Teresa? The value of the debt? The interest rate on the debt?

To replicate the assets of the firm, we first need to invest the present value of $55 in the risk-free asset. This costs $55/1.10 = $50. If the assets turn out to be worth $160, then the option is worth $160 − 100 = $60. Our risk-free asset will be worth $55, so we need ($160 − $55)/$60 = 1.75 call options. Since the firm is currently worth $110, we have:

$$\$110 = 1.75 \times C_0 + \$50$$
$$C_0 = \$34.29$$

The equity is thus worth $34.29; the debt is worth $110 − 34.29 = $75.71. The interest rate on the debt is about $100/$75.71 − 1 = 32.1%.

Concept questions

21.5a *Why do we say that the equity in a leveraged firm is effectively a call option on the firm's assets?*

21.5b *All other things being the same, would the shareholders of a firm prefer to increase or decrease the volatility of the firm's return on assets? Why? What about the debtholders? Give an intuitive explanation.*

In their own words

Robert C. Merton* on applications of options analysis

Organised markets for trading options on shares, fixed-income securities, currencies, financial futures, and a variety of commodities are among the most successful financial innovations of the past two decades. Commercial success is not, however, the reason that option pricing analysis has become one of the cornerstones of finance theory. Instead, its central role derives from the fact that optionlike structures permeate virtually every part of the field.

From the first observation nearly 20 years ago, that leveraged equity has the same payoff structure as a call option, option pricing theory has provided an integrated approach to the pricing of corporate liabilities, including all types of debt, preferred shares, warrants, and rights. The same methodology has been applied to the pricing of pension fund insurance, deposit insurance, and other government loan guarantees. It has also been used to evaluate various labour-contract provisions such as wage floors and guaranteed employment including tenure.

A significant and recent extension of options analysis has been to the evaluation of operating or 'real' options in capital budgeting decisions. For example, a facility that can use various inputs to produce various outputs provides the firm with operating options not available from a specialised facility that uses a fixed set of inputs to produce a single type of output. Similarly, choosing among technologies with different proportions of fixed and variable costs can be viewed as evaluating alternative options to change production levels, including abandonment of the project. Research and development projects are essentially options to either establish new markets, expand market share, or reduce production costs. As these examples suggest, options analysis is especially well-suited to the task of evaluating the 'flexibility' components of projects. These are precisely the components whose values are especially difficult to estimate by using traditional capital budgeting techniques.

* Robert C. Merton is the John and Natty McArthur University Professor at Harvard University. He was previously the J.C. Penney Professor of Management at MIT. He received the 1997 Nobel Prize in Economics for his work on pricing options and other contingent claims and for his work on risk and uncertainty.

21.6 ■ Types of equity option contracts

There are a number of option-oriented products offered in the market. The most common of these in the Australian capital markets are:

1 *Exchange traded put and call options on company shares.* These are referred to as 'share options' or 'stock options'.
2 *Exchange traded long dated option contracts issued by a financial institution to holders who can then trade them.* In Australia these are called 'warrants'.
3 *Over-the-counter options on company shares.* These are traded principal to principal and involve the company selling directly to potential shareholders. They are called 'warrants' on international markets; however, in Australia they are called 'company options'.
4 *Convertible notes issued by companies, which have both a debt and an equity component.* The option element is that of conversion.

convertible note
a note that can be exchanged for a fixed number of shares for a specified amount of time

Warrants

Warrants are a financial instrument issued by banks and other institutions and are traded on the ASX. They are tradeable securities that give the holder the right to purchase the underlying security at a fixed price for a fixed period of time. Basically warrants are long-term options. Like options, there are both call and put warrants. They are listed on the ASX and are traded in a similar way to shares. Warrants were first offered in Australia in 1991.

Types of warrants available

Equity warrants
Call and put warrants, issued over shares in ASX-listed companies, are the most popular type of warrant traded. The exercise price is usually set close to the share price at the time of issue and the expiry date is typically 12 to 18 months from the issue date. These warrants can be American or European style and, if exercised, are settled by delivery of the underlying shares.

The Top 5 by value in 2001 were:

CBAIMD	1.86	$60,337,323
NABIMD	1.71	$55,547,023
XJOWGS	.8	$25,949,113
BHPIMD	.79	$25,609,115
TLSWPF	.75	$24,449,553

Fractional warrants
Fractional warrants require a number of warrants to be exercised in order to buy or sell the underlying asset, for example four warrants for one share.

Basket warrants
A basket warrant has shares from a group of different companies as the underlying securities. These companies often carry out similar activities, for example mining or manufacturing. Basket warrants provide investors with the opportunity to profit from the performance of a select group of companies or a particular industry.

Fully covered warrants
Fully covered warrants are call warrants that are designed to reduce the level of risk attached to a particular issue by requiring the issuer to place the underlying securities in a trust or other comparable arrangement.

Index warrant

Index warrants are issued over a foreign or local index. They allow investors to benefit from moves in the market as a whole. They are usually settled via a cash payment.

Instalment warrants

Instalment warrants operate in a similar manner to ordinary warrants. The main differences are that the holder of the instalment warrant is entitled to any dividends and franking credits paid by the underlying asset during the life of the warrants. The payment to purchase the instalment warrant in the first instance may be higher than for an ordinary warrant.

Low exercise price warrants

Low exercise price warrants usually have an exercise price of one cent. They are usually European-style and the buyer pays the full premium when the warrant is purchased and receives the shares at expiry.

Endowment warrants

Endowment warrants do not have a fixed exercise price and expiry price, but an outstanding amount that changes over time. While the outstanding amount is initially determined by the warrant at the start of the issue, it will generally reduce over time as dividends paid by the underlying company and, in some cases, franking credits are applied to the balance. If the outstanding amount reduces to one cent, the warrant holder becomes the owner of the underlying shares. If the outstanding amount is not fully paid by a certain date, the issuer can request full payment or the warrant lapses.

Currency warrants

Currency warrants entitle holders to exchange an amount of foreign currency for Australian dollars on or before the expiry date. The value of the warrant rises and falls in line with movements in the Australian dollar against a foreign currency with reference to the exercise price. For example, holders of AUD/USD call warrants benefit from an increase in the AUD/USD exchange rate and holders of AUD/USD put warrants benefit from a decrease in the AUD/USD exchange rate.

Company options

A **company option** is a corporate security that gives the holder the right, but not the obligation, to buy shares directly from a company at a fixed price for a given period. Each company option specifies the number of shares that the holder can buy, the exercise price and the expiration date. Company options are often called *sweeteners* or *equity kickers* because they are usually issued in combination with privately placed loans or debenture issues. Throwing in some company options is a way of making the deal look more attractive to the lender. In most cases the company options are attached to the debentures issued. The loan agreement (debenture trust deed) will state whether the company options are detachable from the debentures. Usually the company options are detached immediately and sold by the holder as a separate security.

company option
a security that gives the holder the right to purchase shares at a fixed price over a given period

While company options have characteristics of the exchange traded option, there are differences.

The difference between company options and exchange traded options

Company options usually have much longer maturity periods. In fact some company options are actually perpetual and have no expiration date. It is usual, though, for company options to be European-type options. Remember that with European options they can only be exercised on the expiration date. Exchange traded option contracts are created by the trading in the market. That is, there are no fixed number of, say, Woolworths June $6.00 calls or puts available for trading on the AOM. On the other hand, company options are issued by the company as part of its capital-raising program; a given number of these options are in the hands of option holders; this given number may be bought and sold, following listing, in the same way as any other listed security. In the case of exchange traded options, the clearing house plays a central role, whereas there is no role for a clearing house in company options.

The economic rationale of the two forms of option are different. Company options are primarily a vehicle for capital raising by companies. It is not uncommon to see floats and new issues of shares 'sweetened' by the attachment to the issue of 'free' options. Exchange traded options increase the efficiency of securities markets by providing investors with a means of expressing their expectations regarding share price movements in a way not permitted by the share market.

In summary, company options are issued by firms whereas exchange traded options are issued by individuals. When an exchange traded option is exercised, one investor buys shares from another investor. The company is not involved. When a company option is exercised, the firm must issue a new share. Each time a company option is exercised then, the firm usually receives cash and the number of shares outstanding always increases.

To illustrate, suppose the Kert Rats Pty Ltd issues a company option giving holders the right to buy one ordinary share at $25. Further, suppose the company options are exercised. Kert must print one new share certificate. In exchange for the share certificate, it receives $25 from the holder.

In contrast, when a call option is exercised, there is no change in the number of shares outstanding. Suppose Kay Corps purchases a call option on the ordinary shares of the Kert Rats Pty Ltd from Ray Sproc. The call option gives Kay Corps the right to buy one ordinary share of the Kert Rats for $25.

If Kay Corps chooses to exercise the call option, Ray Sproc is obligated to give Kay one share of Kert in exchange for $25. If Ray Sproc does not already own a share, he must go into the share market and buy one.

The call option amounts to a side bet between Kay Corps and Ray Sproc on the value of the Kert Rats ordinary shares. When a call option is exercised, one investor gains and the other loses. The total number of shares outstanding of the Kert Rats remains constant, and no new funds are made available to the company.

Company options and the value of the firm

Since the company is not involved in buying or selling options, puts and calls have no effect on the value of the firm. However, the firm is the original seller when company options are involved, and company options do affect the value of the firm. We compare the effect of call options and company options in this section.

Imagine that Mr Peaches and Ms Cream are two investors who together purchase six ounces of platinum at a price of $500 per ounce. The total investment is $6 \times \$500 = \$3,000$, and each of the investors puts up half. They incorporate, print two share certificates, and name the firm the PC Company Pty Ltd. Each certificate represents a one-half claim to the platinum, and Mr Peaches and Ms Cream each own one certificate. The net effect of all of this is that Mr Peaches and Ms Cream have formed a company with platinum as its only asset.

The effect of a call option

Suppose Mr Peaches later decides to sell a call option to Mrs Strawberry. The call option gives Mrs Strawberry the right to buy Mr Peaches' share for $1,800 in one year.

At the end of the year, platinum is selling for $700 per ounce, so the value of the PC Company Pty Ltd is 6 × $700 = $4,200. Each share is worth $4,200/2 = $2,100. Mrs Strawberry will exercise her option, and Mr Peaches must turn over his share certificate and receive $1,800.

How would the firm be affected by the exercise? The number of shares will not be affected. There will still be two of them, now owned by Ms Cream and Mrs Strawberry. The shares are still worth $2,100 each. The only thing that happens is that, when Mrs Strawberry exercises her option, she profits by $2,100 − 1,800 = $300. Mr Peaches loses by the same amount.

The effect of a company option

This story changes if a company option is issued. Suppose that Mr Peaches does not sell a call option to Mrs Strawberry. Instead, Mr Peaches and Ms Cream get together and decide to issue a company option and sell it to Mrs Strawberry. This means that, in effect, the PC Company decides to issue a company option.

The company option will give Mrs Strawberry the right to receive a share in the company at an exercise price of $1,800. If Mrs Strawberry decides to exercise the company option, the firm will issue another share certificate and give it to Mrs Strawberry in exchange for $1,800.

Suppose again that platinum rises to $700 an ounce. The firm will be worth $4,200. Further suppose that Mrs Strawberry exercises her company option. Two things will occur:

1 Mrs Strawberry will pay $1,800 to the firm.
2 The firm will print one share certificate and give it to Mrs Strawberry. The share certificate will represent a one-third claim on the platinum of the firm.

Mrs Strawberry's one-third share seems to be worth only $4,200/3 = $1,400. This is not correct, because we have to add the $1,800 contributed to the firm by Mrs Strawberry. The value of the firm increases by this amount, so:

$$\text{New value of firm} = \text{Value of platinum} + \text{Contribution to the firm by Mrs Strawberry}$$
$$= \$4,200 + 1,800$$
$$= \$6,000$$

Because Mrs Strawberry has a one-third claim on the firm's value, her share is worth $6,000/3 = $2,000. By exercising the company option, Mrs Strawberry gains $2,000 − 1,800 = $200. This is illustrated in Table 21.7.

Effect of a call option versus a company option on PC Company Pty Ltd		
Value of firm if price of platinum per ounce	$ 700	$ 600
No company option or call option		
Mr Peaches' share	$2,100	$1,800
Ms Cream's share	$2,100	$1,800
Firm value	$4,200	$3,600
Call option		
Mr Peaches' claim	$ 0	$1,800
Ms Cream's claim	$2,100	$1,800
Mrs Strawberry's claim	$2,100	$ 0
Firm value	$4,200	$3,600 *(continued)*

TABLE 21.7

TABLE
21.7

Effect of a call option versus a company option on PC Company Pty Ltd (*continued*)

	Company option*	
Mr Peaches' share	$2,000	$1,800
Ms Cream's share	$2,000	$1,800
Mrs Strawberry's claim	$2,000	$ 0
Firm value	$6,000	$3,600

* If the price of platinum is $700, the value of the firm is equal to the value of six ounces of platinum plus the excess dollars paid into the firm by Mrs Strawberry. The amount is $4,200 + 1,800 = $6,000.

When the company options are exercised, the exercise money goes to the firm. Since Mrs Strawberry ends up owning one-third of the firm, she effectively gets back one-third of what she pays in. Since she really gives up only two-thirds of $1,800 to buy the share, the effective exercise price is $2/3 \times \$1,800 = \$1,200$.

Mrs Strawberry effectively pays out $1,200 to obtain a one-third interest in the assets of the firm (the platinum). This is worth $4,200/3 = $1,400. Mrs Strawberry's gain, from this perspective, is $1,400 − 1,200 = $200 (exactly what we calculated earlier).

Company option value and share value

What is the value of the ordinary shares of a firm that has issued company options? Let us look at the market value of the PC Company just before and just after the exercise of Mrs Strawberry's company option. Just after exercise, the statement of financial position looks like this:

Shareholders' funds	
Paid-up capital (of three shares)	$6,000
Represented by:	
Cash	$1,800
Platinum	$4,200
Total assets	$6,000

As we saw above, each share is worth $6,000/3 = $2,000.

Since whoever holds the company option will profit by $200 when the company option is exercised, the company option is worth $200 just before expiration. The statement of financial position for the PC Company just before expiration is thus:

Shareholders' funds	
Paid-up capital	$4,000
Company option issued	200
	$4,200
Represented by	
Platinum	$4,200

We calculate the value of the share as the value of the assets ($4,200) less the value of the company option ($200).

Notice that the value of each share just before expiration is $4,000/2 = $2,000 just as it is after expiration. The value of each share is thus not changed by the exercise of the company option. There is no dilution of share value from the exercise.

Earnings dilution

Company options and (as we shall see) convertible debts frequently cause the number of shares to increase. This happens (1) when the company options are exercised and (2) when the debts are converted. As we have seen, this increase does not lower the per share value of the share. However, it does cause the firm's net income to be spread over a larger number of shares and, thus, earnings per share decrease.

Firms with significant amounts of company options and convertible issues outstanding will generally calculate and report earnings per share on a fully diluted basis. This means that the calculation is based on the number of shares that would be outstanding if all the company options were exercised and all the convertibles were converted. Since this increases the number of shares, fully diluted EPS will be lower than EPS calculated only on the basis of shares actually outstanding.

Concept questions

21.6a *What is a company option?*
21.6b *Why are company options different from call options?*

21.7 ■ Futures contracts

Another common derivative is a futures contract. A futures contract is simply an agreement between two parties to exchange a specified asset at a specified price at a specified time in the future. So the agreement is today but the delivery is in the future.

To understand a futures contract it is easiest to firstly understand how a forward contract works. Consider an agreement like 'I will sell to you a new 5 Series BMW, red in colour, with leather trim and delivery is next March and the price is $85,000'. This is a forward contract. There is an agreement today between two parties to exchange a specified asset at a specified price at a specified time. It is important to realise that delivery is in the future. With this contract assume that the seller does not have a BMW. Is this a problem? The answer is no. Because delivery is not until next March the seller has a number of months to acquire a BMW to satisfy the agreement. The consequence of this is that I can sell a BMW without owning one. This is significant because in most situations buyers and sellers make a profit by first buying the article and then later selling it at a higher price. With a forward contract we can agree to buy and then sell or agree to sell and later buy. As delivery is in the future, the buying and selling can be done in either order. Unlike an option contract, the holder of the futures contract has a definite obligation – you cannot choose to let the contract lapse. However, as we shall see shortly, it is possible to 'cancel' the contract by entering into an equal and opposite futures position.

You can see that the forward contract was a tailor-made agreement between two parties. If the contract was highly standardised and traded on an exchange like the Sydney Futures Exchange then we would be dealing with a futures contract. The main reason for the existence of futures is the fact that prices of commodities fluctuate, often rapidly and within wide ranges, and producers and users of these commodities wish to avoid the uncertainty that this fluctuation brings. Buyers like to know how much they will be paying for a certain commodity in several months time, while primary producers are keen to establish, ahead of time, the price they will receive for their future output. The futures market operates by bringing together these buyers and sellers in the one place where they can agree on the price at which certain commodities will change hands at given future dates.

There is no need for the physical commodity to be present at the time, since it is described accurately within specified limits by the contract. Because it is contracts to deliver or to take delivery which are being traded, it is possible to buy and sell on the exchange without seeing or handling the commodity involved. In fact, most contracts are not settled by delivery (some cannot be settled by delivery), but by taking an opposite position in the market to the one originally held. This process is called closing out. Futures contracts to buy are cancelled by new contracts to sell.

Standardised contracts

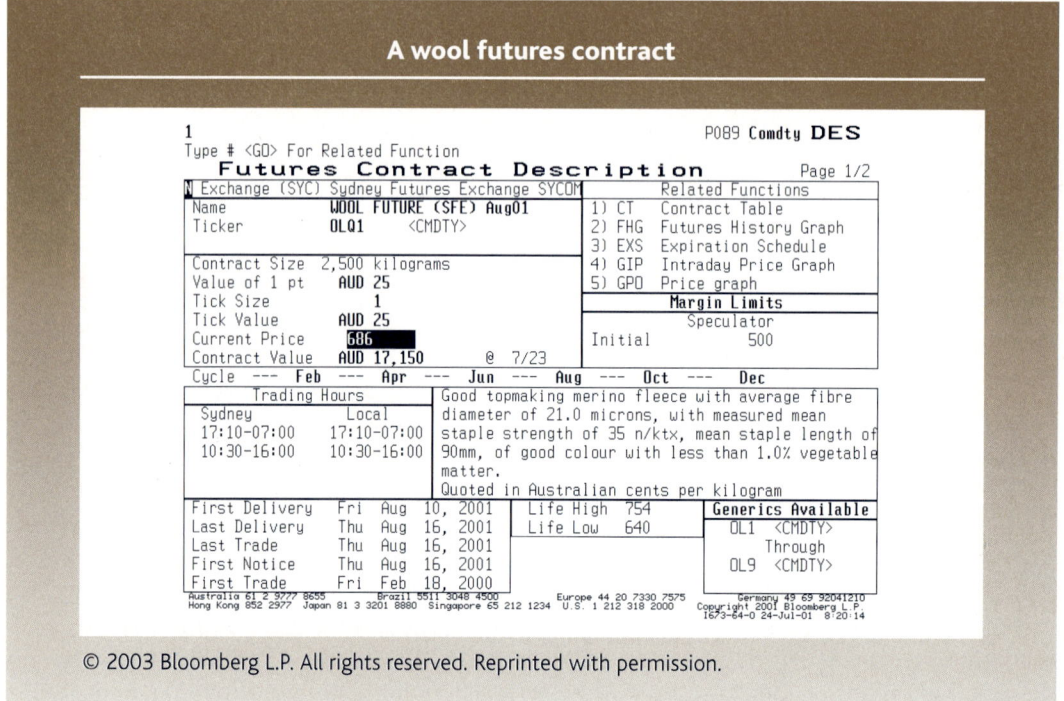

FIGURE 21.3

A wool futures contract

Figure 21.3 provides details of a wool futures contract. The contract is standardised as each contract is for 2,500 kilograms of 21.0 micron fleece. If you were to purchase two contracts you would have an exposure to the price of wool calculated on a quantity of 5,000 kilograms. The forward delivery months are February, April, June, August, October and December. You can see from Figure 21.4 the prices of the various contracts. For example the previous price on the date that this figure was taken, for a contract for delivery in October 2003, was 829 cents per kilogram. The price of one of these contacts would be 829 cents × 2,500 kilograms = $20,725.

Prices for each of the contracts fluctuate over time. Figure 21.5 displays the price of a particular contact fluctuating in price between February and July. Around 15 March a contract was trading for approximately 720 cents a kilogram. Three months later the same contract was trading for around 640 cents per kilogram. The price of these contracts fluctuate continually but the price of say a December delivery contract does approach the actual auction or spot price of wool in December. This must happen because if it did not then traders would simply sell a December contract and buy the wool at auction and make a profit on the difference in prices. It is not that easy to make a profit. If it were, many traders would be doing it and competition among the traders would compete the profit away.

The price of a wool futures contract

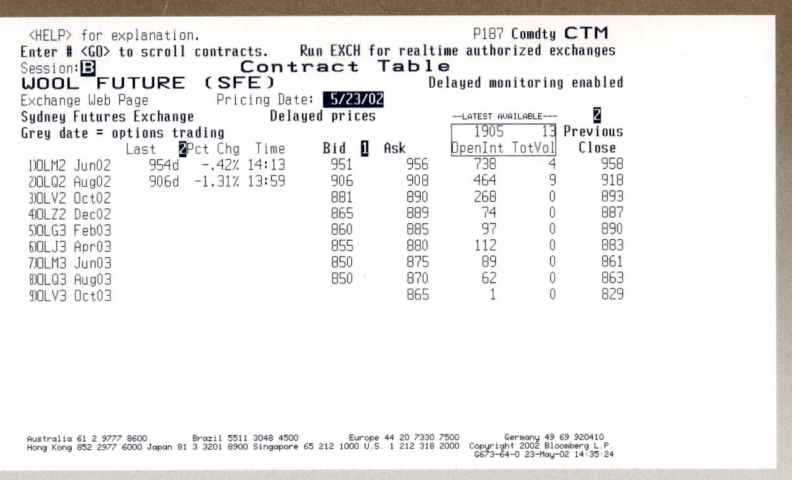

FIGURE 21.4

A wool futures contract

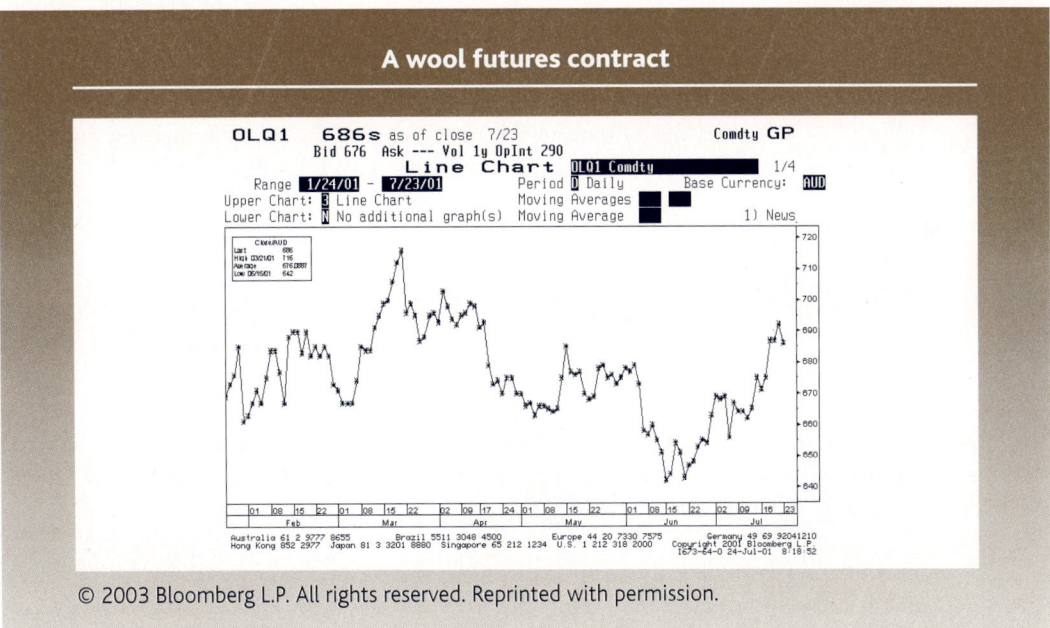

FIGURE 21.5

Basic trading

Every trader in the futures market is required to put up an initial deposit, varying according to the price volatility of the commodity, but usually representing about 5 to 10 percent of the value of the goods described by the contract. This deposit is returned at the time the contract is settled, whether by delivery or an opposite transaction on the futures market. The deposit is more of a performance bond than a down payment on the goods being traded. In addition to the deposits required to open contracts, any adverse price movements in the market must be covered daily by further deposits, known as margins. If a trader has opened a contract to buy a certain commodity and the price subsequently falls, the trader will be required to pay the broker a margin large enough to cover the current unrealised loss. The rules of the exchange require the broker to call margins from the client on a daily basis for the unrealised loss.

Rural commodities hedge example

The SFE Wool Futures contracts provide wool market participants with an easy and effective way to manage their exposure. Futures can be used by wool growers to protect their exposure to the risk that the selling price of wool will fall between the current date and the date they predict they will come to the market. In effect, hedging with wool futures enables the grower to lock-in a forward price.

A hedger will use wool futures contracts to set the price for a wool sale or purchase some time in the future. For growers, hedging using wool futures involves a series of three transactions: one transaction to open the hedge and two transactions to complete the hedge when the hedger wishes to sell their wool to the market.

Assume that in May a wool grower wishes to set a price for wool in October. By October the grower will be taking bales of wool to market. The cost of producing bales of wool with a reasonable profit is 550 cents a kilogram. Assume that in May, October delivery wool future contracts are selling for 558 cents a kilogram. The grower wishes to lock into this price. The grower will sell October contracts for 558 cents. As the grower expects 7,500 kilograms of wool, the number of contracts sold will be 3 as each are for 2,500 kilograms.

May   Sold (October delivery contracts) 7,500 × 558 cents $41,850 (Open position)

In October, the price of wool at auction falls to 525 cents per kilogram and October futures are selling for 528 cents per kilogram. The grower sells the wool at auction and buys October wool futures. This effectively cancels the earlier sale of October futures.

October   Buy (October delivery contracts) 7,500 × 528 cents $39,600 (Close out)
Profit on futures $ 2,250

October   Auction (sell the actual wool) 7,500 × 525 cents $39,375

Total $41,625
Average price $41,625/7,500 = 555 cents

What would have happened if the price of wool had risen? Assume that the price of wool at auction rises to 600 cents per kilogram and the price of an October delivery wool futures contract rises to 605 cents per kilogram.

May   Sold (October delivery contracts) 7,500 × 558 cents $41,850 (Open position)

October   Buy (October delivery contracts) 7,500 × 605 cents $45,375 (Close out)
Loss on futures $ 3,525

October Auction (sell the actual wool) 7,500 × 600 cents $45,000

Total $41,475
Average price $41,475/7,500 = 553 cents

The concept of hedging with futures is no win and no loss. The producer wants to fix the price at *around* 558 cents per kg which is the value of the first contract undertaken.

Why did the grower sell a futures contract in the first instance? The grower wants to create a hedge and the grower can either buy then sell or sell then buy. A wool grower is worried about the price falling in the future. If the price does fall, the grower wants to make a profit in the futures market. To make a profit you buy low and sell high. If the grower wants to protect against a price fall in the future, the grower will buy at the lower price in the future. If the grower is buying in the future then the grower must sell today. This sounds a bit complicated. An easier way to think about it is that the grower will be selling at auction, therefore he or she sells a futures contract first.

Short-term interest rate futures

In the bank bill market, the hedging principle is the same although the mechanics are more complicated. A bill is a lending and borrowing instrument used by large companies to arrange their funding requirements. The bill is essentially a promise to pay a specified sum (for example $1,000,000) on a designated date in the future. In the case of a 90-day bill, this future date is 90 days from the date of issue. The bill can be discounted (sold) and the amount paid for the bill is an amount less than face value, the difference representing interest earned.

Face Value	Term	Yield	Index	Price
1,000,000	90d	10%	90.00	$975,935.83
1,000,000	90d	15%	85.00	$964,332.89

Yields for bank bills are quoted according to an index system under which the interest rate per annum is deducted from 100. This is used to ensure the quoted price fluctuates in line with the contract value. If the index is 90 then the interest rate (yield) is $100 - 90 = 10$ or 10%. If the quote is 85 then the yield is 15%. The price of a contract (all contracts are for $1,000,000 and the delivery months are September, December, March and June) is calculated using a simple interest formula:

$$\text{Price of bill} = \frac{\text{Face value of bill}}{1 + (\text{Annual interest} \times t/365)} = \frac{\$1,000,000}{1 + (10\% \times 90/365)} = \$975,935.83$$

It is most important to understand that the price paid for the bill varies inversely with the interest rate: as interest rates go up, the price falls.

Hedging an interest rate

EXAMPLE 21.4

Suppose that in June, a company identifies a need to borrow $1,000,000 in the following December. The company notes that December interest rate futures are currently trading at 94.55 (which is equivalent to an interest rate of 5.45 per cent). The company is worried that the December rate may move higher than 5.45, so they decide to fix the borrowing cost at this rate. In the future a borrower would sell a bank bill therefore the company will sell a bank bill futures contract.

Assume that in December the bank bill rate is 7.05% and for futures the index is 92.90 which is a rate of 7.1%. Today in June the company would sell December futures:

$$\frac{1,000,000}{1 + 0.0545 \times 90/365} = \$986,739.84$$

(continued)

EXAMPLE
21.4 ▪ **Hedging an interest rate (*continued*)**

In December the company will close out and buy a December future contract:

$$\frac{1,000,000}{1 + 0.071 \times 90/365} = \$982,794.37$$

Profit = 3,945.47

In December the company will borrow using a $1,000,000 bank bill:

$$\frac{1,000,000}{1 + 0.0705 \times 90/365} = \$982,913.46$$

Effective borrowing = $986,858.93 (3,945.47 + 982,913.46)
Amount of interest (1,000,000 − 986,858.93) = $13,141.07

Cost of borrowing as an annual percentage cost is

$$\frac{13,141.07}{986,858.93} \times \frac{100}{1} \times \frac{365}{90} = 5.4\%$$

Bank bill futures are very heavily traded. They are used to protect against interest rate movements. Interest rates fluctuate continually. Figure 21.6 shows the yield for an Australian Government bond trading through the day. Time is on the horizontal axis. It seems that rates for this bond were at their lowest around lunchtime. During the day the rates fluctuated between 6.185% and 6.125%.

FIGURE
21.6

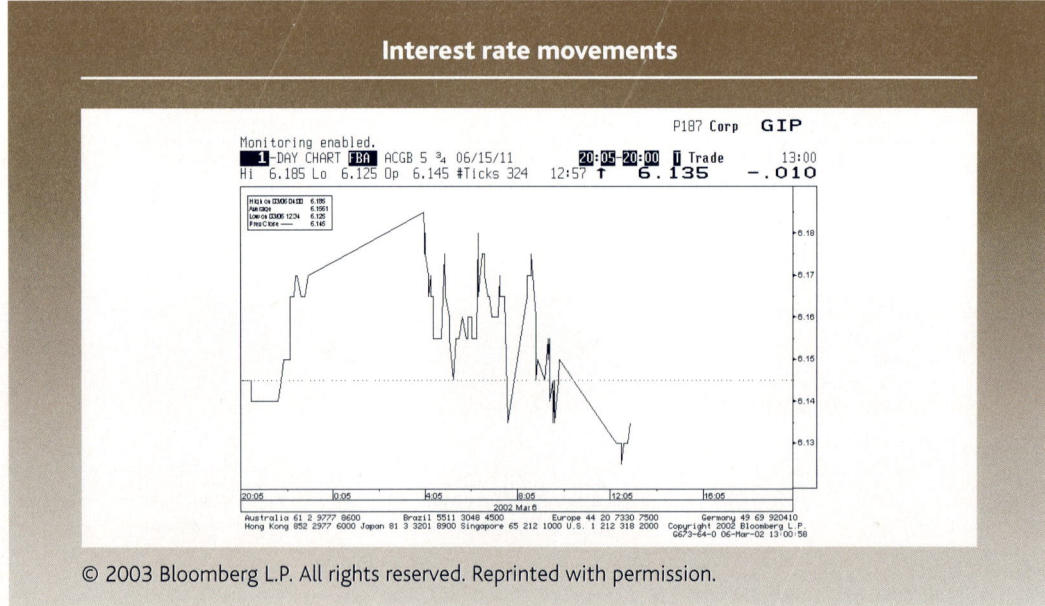

21.8 ▪ # Term structure of interest rates

In the market, at any time, we observe different interest rates depending on the period for which instruments are issued. Figure 21.7 shows yield curves for various instruments. The bottom bold line is the Australian Government bond rate. The vertical axis is the yield and the horizontal axis is time. A bond with a maturity of one year trades at a particular yield, which was about 4.5% when this yield curve was constructed. The same type of instrument with the same issuer but a different maturity has a different yield. The 10-year rate is around 6.3%. Joining theses rates for the same issuer with different maturities gives the yield curve. This curve is usually upward sloping.

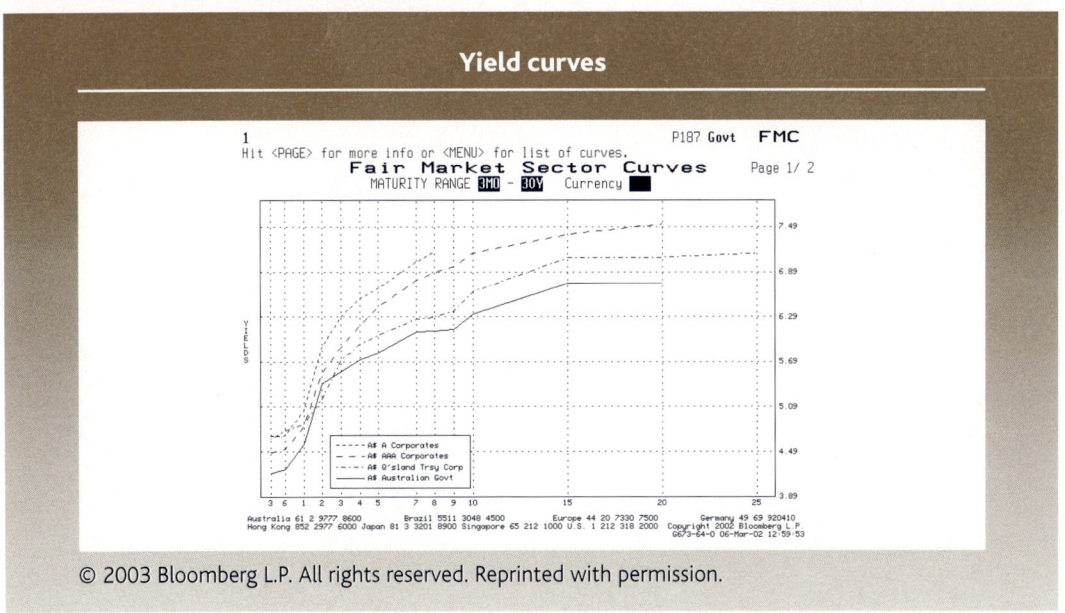

Yield curves

FIGURE 21.7

Interest rates from period to period (for example the one-year rate and the two-year rate) are related in a precise manner. This manner is called the *term structure* of interest rates.

Traditional theory argues that interest rates across time are determined by three factors: risk preferences, supply–demand conditions and future expectations.

Risk preferences

The argument is that borrowers are willing to pay more for long-term credit as they do not have to worry about future interest rates. From the lenders' point of view, the risk of default is greater on long-term loans. Lenders prefer short-term loans and will demand higher interest on longer-term loans. Both of these explain an upward sloping yield curve, but not a downward one.

Supply–demand conditions

Short-term debt capital is supplied by banks, while long-term debt is supplied mostly by pension funds and insurance companies. At the same time, certain types of borrowers are primarily interested in borrowing on a long-term basis (e.g. home buyers), while other borrowers are mainly interested in short-term credit. This suggests that the capital markets are *segmented*. Accordingly, if at a particular point in time demand is heavier in the short-term market, this will tend to produce high short-term and low long-term rates, and a downward-sloping yield curve (*of course, the opposite could apply*).

Expectations

Other things held constant, the yield curve will be upward sloping if future rates are expected to rise, downward sloping if future rates are expected to fall.

It is the last argument that most agree with. At any point in time, we see a specific relationship between long- and short-term interest rates. That relationship is called the term structure of interest rates.

A simple illustration will illustrate this relationship. The one-year rate is 10 per cent and a two-year rate is 11 per cent. Here the yield curve is upward sloping. What is the market expectation of what interest rates will be in one year's time? If the one-year rate is 10 per cent and the average of two years is 11 per cent then the expectation of what interest rates will be in one years time is about 12 per cent. The 12 per cent is called a *forward rate*.

Eleven per cent will not be the simple average because of the compounding effect. It can be calculated as follows:

$$r = \sqrt{(1 + {_0}r_1)(1 + {_1}r_2)} - 1$$

The two-year yield is the geometric average on the one-year yield and the forward rate for the second year. Given this knowledge of the term structure, and given bond prices, we can derive forward rates and yields, or vice-versa to get bond prices.

EXAMPLE 21.5 ■ Calculating the forward rate

Ten per cent $100 debentures with a one-year maturity are currently selling for $98. The two-year maturity debentures are selling for $99 and the three-year ones for $102. What are the expected interest rates per period (i.e. forward rates) and what is the yield that a two-year and three-year investor will earn?

${_0}r_1$

$98	$= \$110/(1 + {_0}r_1)$
$(1 + {_0}r_1)$	$= 110/98$
$(1 + {_0}r_1)$	$= 1.122449$
${_0}r_1$	$= 12.2449\%$, the interest rate for one year

${_1}r_2$

99	$= 10/(1 + {_0}r_1) + 110/(1 + {_0}r_1)(1 + {_1}r_2)$
99	$= 10/1.122449 + 110/1.122449 \times (1 + {_1}r_2)$
99	$= 8.91 + 98/(1 + {_1}r_2)$
90.09	$= 98/(1 + {_1}r_2)$
$(1 + {_1}r_2)$	$= 1.0878$
${_1}r_2$	$= 8.78\%$, the interest rate prevailing in the second year

${_2}r_3$

102	$= 10/(1 + {_0}r_1) + 10/(1 + {_0}r_1)(1 + {_1}r_2) + 110/(1 + {_0}r_1)(1 + {_1}r_2)(1 + {_2}r_3)$
102	$= 10/1.122449 + 10/1.122449 \times 1.0878 + 110/1.122449 \times 1.0878 \times (1 + {_2}r_3)$
102	$= 8.91 + 8.19 + 90.09/(1 + {_1}r_3)$
84.90	$= 90.09/(1 + {_2}r_3)$
$(1 + {_2}r_3)$	$= 1.06113$
${_2}r_3$	$= 6.113\%$, the interest rate in the third year

The *yield* for a two-year investor:

$$
\begin{aligned}
r &= \sqrt{(1 + {_0}r_1)(1 + {_1}r_2)} - 1 \\
&= \sqrt{1.122449 \times 1.0878} - 1 \\
&= \sqrt{1.221} - 1 \\
&= \sqrt{\text{two-year spot rate}} - 1 \\
&= 10.5\%
\end{aligned}
$$

Yield for a three-year investor:

$$
\begin{aligned}
r &= \sqrt[3]{(1 + {_0}r_1)(1 + {_1}r_2)(1 + {_1}r_3)} - 1 \\
&= \sqrt[3]{1.122449 \times 1.0878 \times 1.06113} - 1 \\
&= \sqrt[3]{1.29564} - 1 \\
&= \sqrt[3]{\text{three-year spot rate}} - 1 \\
&= 9.017\%
\end{aligned}
$$

▪21.9▪ Summary and conclusions

This chapter described the basics of option valuation and discussed option-like corporate securities. In it, we saw that:

1   Options are contracts giving the right, but not the obligation, to buy and sell underlying assets at a fixed price during a specified period.

    The most familiar options are puts and calls involving shares. These options give the holder the right, but not the obligation, to sell (the put option) or buy (the call option) ordinary shares at a given price.

    As we discussed, the value of any option depends only on five factors:

    a   the price of the underlying asset
    b   the exercise price
    c   the expiration date
    d   the interest rate on risk-free debt
    e   the volatility of the underlying asset's value

2   A company option gives the holder the right to buy ordinary shares directly from the company at a fixed exercise price for a given period. Typically, company options are issued in a package with privately placed debt. Afterward, they often can be detached and traded separately.

3   A futures contract can be used to hedge prices. For a commodity seller, a contract is sold (open position) and in the future the position is closed out by doing the opposite (buying) with the same type of contract.

4   The structure of interest rates follows a pattern, which can be seen in the yield curve. The yield curve is made up of yields for a particular instrument issued by a particular issuer for differing maturities. The curve represents a combination of forward rates. If the yield curve is upward sloping, the market expects that in the future interest rates will rise.

Key terms

American and European options *718*	Expiration date *718*	Options *718*
Call options *718*	Forward rates *752*	Put options *718*
Close out *748*	Futures contracts *745*	Striking price or exercise price *718*
Company options *741*	Intrinsic value *727*	Term structure *751*
Exercising the option *718*	Open position *748*	

Suggested reading

For a detailed discussion of options, read:

Cox, J.S. and Rubinstein, M. *Option Markets*, Prentice-Hall, Englewood Cliffs, NJ, 1985. Section 7.3 analyses corporate securities.

Endnotes

1 You are probably wondering what would happen if the share price were less than the present value of the exercise price, resulting in a negative value for the call option. This cannot happen because we are certain that the share price will be at least E in one year; we know the share price will finish in the money. If the current price of the share is less than $E/(1 + R_f)$, then the return on the share is certain to be greater than the risk-free rate, thereby creating an arbitrage opportunity. For example, if the share were currently selling for $8, then the minimum return would be ($10.50 − $8)/$8 = 31.25%. Since we can borrow at 12 per cent, we can earn a certain minimum return of 19.25 per cent per dollar borrowed. This, of course, is an arbitrage.

2 The signs in Table 21.5 are for American options. For a European put option, the effect of increasing the time to expiration is ambiguous, and the direction of the influence can be positive or negative.

3 Strictly speaking, the risk-free rate in the Black–Scholes model is the continuously compounded risk-free rate. Continuous compounding is discussed in Chapter 5.

On the web

http://www.asx.com.au (the Australian Stock Exchange)

http://www.comsec.com.au (the trading division of the Commonwealth Bank)

http://www.sfe.com.au (Sydney Futures Exchange)

Maximise Your Marks!
There are 30 interactive questions on options, corporate securities and futures waiting online for you at www.mhhe.com/au/ross3e. The questions are written with additional feedback for incorrect answers, and text excerpts with page references for follow-up study.

International Articles!
To read more on options, corporate securities and futures and to see current international articles, just go to www.mhhe.com/au/ross3e and click on *PowerWeb Articles* for this chapter.

Chapter review problems and self-test

21.1 · Value of a call option

Shares in the Lord Company Ltd are currently selling for $20 per share. In 1 year, the price will either be $20 or $30. Commonwealth Government securities with one year to maturity are paying 10 per cent. What is the value of a call option with a $20 exercise price? A $24 exercise price?

21.2 · Convertible notes

The Ring Corporation Ltd has a convertible note issue that is currently selling in the market for $90. Each note can be exchanged for 10 shares at the holder's option.

The note has a 6 per cent coupon, payable annually, and it will mature in 12 years. Debt of equivalent risk to Ring is priced in the market to yield 12 per cent. Shares in Ring are trading at $6 per share.

What is the debt part of the convertible note? What is its option value?

21.3 · Black-Scholes OPM: Part I

Calculate the Black–Scholes price for a 6-month option given the following:

$$S_0 = \$80$$
$$E = \$70$$
$$R_f = 10\% \text{ (per year)}$$
$$d_1 = 0.82$$
$$d_2 = 0.74$$

21.4 · Black-Scholes OPM: Part II

Calculate the Black–Scholes price for a 9-month option given the following:

$$S_0 = \$80$$
$$E = \$70$$
$$s = 0.30 \text{ (per year)}$$
$$R_f = 10\% \text{ (per year)}$$

Answers to self-test problems

21.1 · With a $20 exercise price, the option cannot finish out of the money (it can finish 'at the money' if the share price is $20). We can replicate the share by investing the present value of $20 in government securities and buying 1 call option. Buying the government securities will cost $20/1.1 = $18.18.

If the share ends up at $20, the call option will be worth zero and the government security will pay $20. If the share ends up at $30, the government security will again pay $20, and the option will be worth $30 − 20 = $10, so the package is worth $30. Since the government security/call option combination exactly duplicates the payoff on the share, it has to be worth $20 or arbitrage is possible. Using the notation from the chapter, we can calculate the value of the call option:

$$S_0 = C_0 + E/(1 + R_f)$$
$$\$20 = C_0 + \$18.18$$
$$C_0 = \$1.82$$

With the $24 exercise price, we start by investing the present value of the lower share price in government securities. This guarantees us $20 when the share price is $20. If the share price is $30, then the option is worth $30 − 24 = $6. We have $20 from our government security, so we need $10 from the options in order to match the share. Since each option is worth $6 in this case, we need to buy $10/$6 = 1.67 call options. Notice that the difference in the possible share prices is $10 ($\Delta S$) and the difference in the possible option prices is $6 ($\Delta C$), so $\Delta S/\Delta C$ = 1.67.

To complete the calculation, the present value of the $20 plus 1.67 call options has to be worth $20 to prevent arbitrage, so:

$$\$20 = 1.67 \times C_0 + \$20/1.1$$
$$C_0 = \$1.82/1.67$$
$$= \$1.09$$

21.2 · The straight note value is what the note would be worth if it were not convertible. The annual coupon is $6, and the note matures in 12 years. At a 12 per cent required return, the straight note value is:

$$\text{Straight note value} = \$6 \times (1 - 1/1.12^{12})/0.12 + \$100/1.12^{12}$$
$$= \$37.17 + 25.67$$
$$= \$62.84$$

The option value is the value of the convertible in excess of the debt portion of the note. Since the note is selling for $90, the option value is:

$$\text{Option value} = \$90 - 62.84$$
$$= \$27.16$$

21.3 · We need to evaluate the following:

$$C_0 = 80 \times N(0.82) - 70/(1.10)^5 \times N(0.74)$$
$$= 80 \times 0.7939 - 66.74 \times 0.7704$$
$$= \$63.51 - \$51.42$$
$$= \$12.09$$

From Table 21.6, the values for $N(0.82)$ and $N(0.74)$ are 0.7939 and 0.7704, respectively. The value of the option is about $12.09. Notice that since the interest rate (and standard deviation) is quoted on an annual basis, we used a t value of 0.50, representing a half year, in calculating the present value of the exercise price.

21.4 · $d_1 = [\ln(S/E) + (R_f + \frac{1}{2} \times \sigma^2) \times t]/(\sigma \times \sqrt{t})$

$\quad\quad = [\ln(80/70) + (0.1 + \frac{1}{2} \times 0.3^2) \times 0.75]/(0.3 \times \sqrt{0.75})$

$\quad\quad = [0.13353 + 0.145 \times 0.75]/0.25981$

$\quad\quad = 0.13353 + 0.10875/0.25981$

$\quad\quad = 0.932$

From Table 21.6, $N(d_1)$ is approximately 0.84

$\quad d_2 = d_1 - \sigma \times \sqrt{t}$

$\quad\quad = 0.932 - 0.3 \times \sqrt{0.75}$

$\quad\quad = 0.672$

From Table 21.6, $N(d_2)$ is approximately 0.75

$\quad C_0 = S \times N(d_1) - E/(1 + R_f)^t \times N(d_2)$

$\quad\quad = 80 \times 0.84 - 70/1.1^{0.75} \times 0.75$

$\quad\quad = 67.20 - 48.88$

$\quad\quad = 18.32$

Questions and problems

1 · Basic properties of options
What is a call option? A put option? Under what circumstances might you want to buy each? Which one has greater potential profit?

2 · Calls versus puts
Complete the following sentence for each of these investors:

a   A buyer of call options (pays/receives) money for the (right/obligation) to (buy/sell) a specified asset at a fixed price for a fixed length of time.

b   A buyer of put options (pays/receives) money for the (right/obligation) to (buy/sell) a specified asset at a fixed price for a fixed length of time.

c   A seller of call options (pays/receives) money for the (right/obligation) to (buy/sell) a specified asset at a fixed price for a fixed length of time.

d   A seller of put options (pays/receives) money for the (right/obligation) to (buy/sell) a specified asset at a fixed price for a fixed length of time.

3 · Arbitage and options
You notice that shares in the Lin Lun Corp. Ltd are going for $8 per share. Call options with an exercise price of $6 per share have a premium of $1.50. What is wrong here?

4 · Defining intrinsic value
What is the intrinsic value of a call option? How do we interpret this value?

5 · Defining intrinsic value
What is the value of a put option at maturity? Based on your answer, what is the intrinsic value of a put option?

6 · Understanding option quotes
Use the following option quote to answer the questions below.

15 May 200X. Pacwest Co. Last sale price $5.00

Strike price	Calls—Last			Puts—Last		
	Jun	July	Aug	Jun	July	Aug
$4.00	$0.80	$1.15	$1.20	40 cents	55 cents	80 cents

a   Are the call options in the money? What is the intrinsic value of a Pacwest Co. call option?

b   One of the options is clearly mispriced. Which one? At a minimum, what should it sell for? Explain how you could profit from the mispricing.

c   This is a little harder: What is the most the mispriced option should sell for? Explain.

7 · Calculating payoffs
Use the following option quote to answer the questions below.

15 May 200X. Pam Ltd. Last sale price $4.00

Strike price	Calls—Last			Puts—Last		
	Jun	July	Aug	Jun	July	Aug
$9.00	20 cents	29 cents	40 cents	$1.20	$1.38	$1.60

a   Suppose you buy 50 July $9.00 call contracts. How much will you pay, ignoring commissions?

b   In part (a), suppose that Pam is selling for $10 per share on the expiration date. What are your options worth?

c   Suppose you buy 10 of the Aug 200X put contracts. What is your maximum gain? On the expiration date, Pam is selling for $7.50 per share. What are your options worth?

d   In part (c), suppose you sold your 10 Aug put contracts. What is your net gain or loss if Pam is selling for $7.50? For $10? What is the break-even price; that is, the share price that results in a profit of zero?

8 · Option value and firm risk
'The unsystematic risk of a share is irrelevant in valuing the share since it can be diversified away. It is also irrelevant for valuing a call option on the share.' True or false? Explain your answer.

9 · Calls versus puts

Shares in the Citiside Co. Ltd currently sell for $8 per share. If a put option and a call option are available with $8 exercise prices, which do you think will sell for more, the put or the call? Explain.

10 · Option value and firm risk

If the risk of a share increases, what is likely to happen to the price of call options on the share? To the price of put options? Why?

11 · Calculating intrinsic risk

Government securities currently yield 8 per cent. Shares in the Tours Corporation Ltd are currently selling for $5.60 per share. There is no possibility that the share will be worth less than $4.00 in one year.

a What is the value of a call option with a $4.00 exercise price?
b What is the value of a call option with a $2.00 exercise price?
c What is the value of a put option with a $4.00 exercise price?

12 · Option value and interest rates

Suppose that the interest rate on government securities suddenly and unexpectedly rises. All other things being the same, what is the impact on call option values? On put option values?

13 · Calculating option values

The prices of Ugly Co. Ltd shares will be either $6 or $8 at the end of the year. Call options are available with 1 year to expiration. Government securities currently yield 7 per cent.

a Suppose the current price of Ugly shares is $6.50. What is the value of the call option if the exercise price is $5.50 per share?
b Suppose that the exercise price is $6.50 in part (a) above. What would the value of the call option be?

14 · Using the pricing equation

A 1-year call contract on Rich Co. Ltd shares sells for $2,000. In 1 year, the shares will be worth $4 or $8 per share. The exercise price on the call option is $5. What is the current value of the share if the risk-free rate is 10 per cent?

15 · Equity as an option

The FishRsafe Company's assets are currently worth $800 million. In a year, they will be worth $600 million or $1000 million. The risk-free rate is 8 per cent. Suppose that FishRsafe has an outstanding debt issue with a face value of $500 million.

a What is the value of the equity?
b What is the value of the debt? The interest rate on the debt if it is totally secured by the company's assets?
c Would the value of the equity go up or down if the risk-free rate were 20 per cent? Why? What does your answer illustrate?

16 · Equity as an option

The Whereru Company Ltd has a debt issue with a face value of $500 that is coming due in one year. The value of Whereru's assets is currently $600. R U Where, the CEO, believes that the assets in the firm will be worth $400 or $900 in a year. The going rate on 1-year government securities is 6 per cent.

a What is the value of the equity? The value of the debt?
b Suppose that Whereru can reconfigure its existing assets such that the value in a year will be $250 or $1,000. If the current value of the assets is unchanged, would the shareholders favour such a move? Why?

17 · Intuition and option value

Suppose a share sells for $5. The risk-free rate is 8 per cent. The price of the share in 1 year will be $5.50 or $6.00.

a What is the value of a call option with a $5.50 exercise price?
b What is wrong here? What would you do?

18 · Hedging the interest rate

A company has just completed (in May) its cash flow budget and identified a need to borrow $1,000,000 in December when it will have to pay for its large Christmas inventory. This loan will only be short-term as the company expects to have recovered the amount by March of the following year. The offer price for December 90-day bank bill futures in May is 95.19. The financial manager feels that this quote provides a level of yield that could be afforded by the company. Contrary to popular belief, the company feels interest rates will increase substantially by December.

a What is the level of yield provided by the May offer price?

b   What would be the value of a contract to cover a contract unit of $1,000,000 if the level of yield provided in (a) were to be earned?

c   Suppose that in December interest rates have risen so that the rate on 90-day bank bills is 5.45% and December bank bills futures are quoted at 94.48. What strategy should the company follow and what would be its effective borrowing cost on the bonds issued? (Express the borrowing cost as per cent per annum.)

d   Suppose that in December, interest rates have fallen on 90-day bank bills to 4.45% and December bank bills futures are quoted at 95.5. What is the borrowing cost if the company buys back on the futures market and issues bank bills to provide the funds?

19 · Hedging the cost

It is January 200X. Winter Woolies Inc is a manufacturer of the latest in winter fashion made from Australian wool. The manager, Ms McFeast, purchases wool in September each year in preparation for the following winter's fashion range. In January, wool is selling for 740c/kg on the cash market, but Ms McFeast is cautious as she has been caught by rising wool prices in the past. She has contacted your consultancy firm with the aim of managing the risk (hedging) of price rises leading up to September. After a detailed briefing, you have highlighted the following points as relevant: Winter Woolies Inc wishes to purchase 7,500 kilograms of wool in October 200X. October wool futures are quoted at 777 cents per kilogram.

a   Outline the futures strategy you would put into place on Winter Woolies' behalf. Be specific about the quantity of futures contracts taken up, whether you are buying or selling futures.

b   Assume that, come October, Ms McFeast's fears have been realised and the price of wool has risen to 790c/kg in the cash market. At the time (in October), the October maturity wool futures are quoted at 793. Explain what action you would take, given that Winter Woolies now needs to buy the wool. Again, be specific about your strategy, show what profit or loss was made and demonstrate to Ms McFeast that she has not been significantly hurt by the rise in prices.

c   Ignore part (b). Assume that in October, wool prices have dropped to 700 c/kg. The October maturity wool futures are quoted at 703. Explain what action you will take. Show Ms McFeast what price she has effectively paid for her wool.

20 · Hedging the sale price

A cotton grower anticipates a 2,000-tonne crop, due for harvest in December. A cotton futures contract is for 50 tonnes and the price of a January cotton futures contract is $230 per tonne. The grower **decides to hedge** all of the crop. In December the grower harvests 2,100 tonnes of cotton. In December the auction price for cotton is $290 per tonne and January futures contracts are trading for $285 per ton. Calculate the overall value of the harvested crop, including the profit or loss from futures trading.

21 · Calculating yields

The following 1-year 'forward' rates exist for each of the years 2004–2008

1/1/04–31/12/04	10.00%
1/1/05–31/12/05	12.00%
1/1/06–31/12/06	14.00%
1/1/07–31/12/07	11.00%
1/1/08–31/12/08	09.00%

What are the 1, 2, 3, 4 and 5-year yields?

22 · Calculating forward rates

A firm issues 7 different bonds today (31/12/03). Each has a face value of $100 and a 5% coupon rate paid annually. The bonds differ in maturity dates and issue prices, as shown below:

Bond	Maturity	Issue price
1-year	2004	$98.13
2-year	2005	$95.54
3-year	2006	$91.60
4-year	2007	$86.69
5-year	2008	$82.29
6-year	2009	$76.43
7-year	2010	$70.44

Calculate the 1-year 'forward' rates for each of the 7 years.

23 · Calculating company option values

A note with 20 detachable company options has just been offered for sale at $100. The note matures in 10 years and has an annual coupon of $8. Each company option gives the owner the right to purchase 4 shares at $1 per share. Ordinary notes (no company options) of similar quality are priced to yield 11 per cent. What is the value of a company option?

24 · Company option values and the statement of financial position

K.C. Jones Co. Ltd has 50,000 shares outstanding. The market value of K.C. Jones' assets is $700,000. The market value of outstanding debt is $200,000. K.C. Jones issued 100 company options some time ago that are about to expire. Each company option gives the owner the right to purchase 100 shares at a price of $8 per share.

a   What is the price of K.C. Jones' shares? What is the value of a company option?

b   Create a market value statement of financial position for just before and just after the company options expire.

25 · Pricing convertibles

This is a challenge question. You have been hired to value a new 30-year redeemable, convertible note. The note has a 6 per cent coupon, payable annually. The conversion price is $10, and the share currently sells for $5.012. The share price is expected to grow at 10 per cent per year. The note is redeemable at $110, but, based on prior experience, it will not be called unless the conversion value is $130. The required return on this note is 8 per cent. What value would you assign?

26 · Using the OPM

Calculate the Black–Scholes option prices in each of the cases below. The risk-free rate and the variance are quoted in annual terms. Notice that the variance is given, not the standard deviation. The last three may require some thought.

Share price	Exercise price	Risk-free rate	Maturity	Variance
$50	$60	8%	6 months	0.20
25	15	6	9 months	0.30
50	60	8	6 months	0.40
0	10	9	12 months	0.65
90	30	7	forever	0.22
50	0	8	6 months	0.44

27 · Equity as an option and the OPM

Playbox Co. Ltd has a discounted bank bill that matures in one year and requires the firm to pay $1,000. The current market value of the firm's assets is $1,200. The annual variance for the firm's return on assets is 0.30, and the annual risk-free interest rate is 6 per cent. Based on the Black–Scholes model, what is the market value of the firm's debt and equity?

28 · Changes in variance and equity value

This is a challenge problem. From the previous problem, Playbox is considering two mutually-exclusive investments. Project A has an NPV of $100, and Project B has an NPV of $150. As a result of taking Project A, the variance of the firm's return on assets will increase to 0.40. If Project B is taken, the variance will fall to 0.25.

a   What is the value of the firm's debt and equity if Project A is undertaken? If Project B is undertaken?

b   Which project do the shareholders prefer? Can you reconcile your answer with the NPV rule?

c   Suppose the shareholders and debtholders are in fact the same group of investors. Would this affect the answer to part (b)?

d   What does this problem suggest about shareholder incentives?

29 · Value of a call option

Shares in the NAZ Banking Corporation are currently selling for $25 each. In one year it is estimated that the price will increase or decrease by 20 per cent. Government bonds with one year to maturity are paying 10 per cent.

What is the value of a call option with a $20 exercise price? A $26 exercise price?

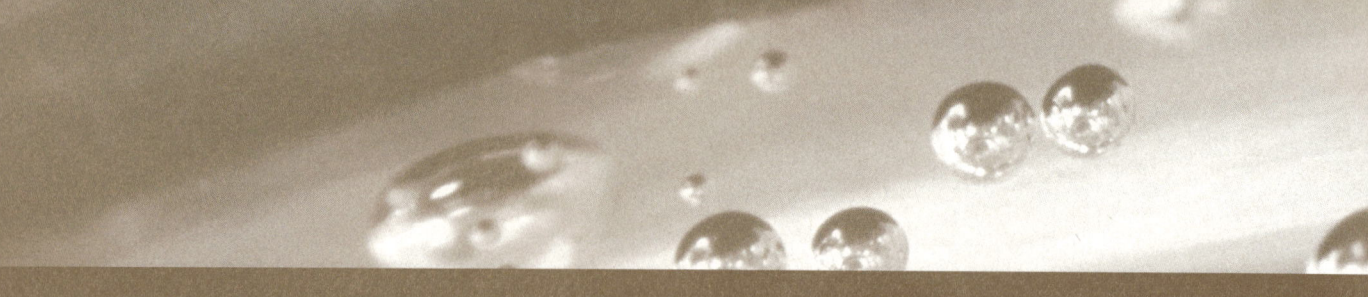

CHAPTER 22

Mergers, acquisitions and takeovers

Objective

The aim of this chapter is to evaluate reasons for mergers, acquisitions and takeovers and look at the benefits and costs. The difference between a cash offer and a share offer is examined. The empirical evidence in relation to merger activity and the effects of mergers on shareholder wealth are also highlighted.

Study tips ▷ Some of the special issues to be aware of as you read the chapter are:

1 The benefits from acquisitions can depend on such things as synergy.[1] Synergy benefits are difficult to define precisely, and it is not easy to estimate the value of synergy using discounted cash flow techniques.

2 There can be complex accounting, tax, and legal effects that must be taken into account when one firm is acquired by another.

3 Acquisitions are an important control device for shareholders. Some acquisitions are a consequence of an underlying conflict between the interests of existing managers and shareholders. Agreeing to be acquired by another firm is one way that shareholders can remove existing managers.

4 Mergers and acquisitions sometimes involve 'unfriendly' transactions. In such cases, when one firm attempts to acquire another, it does not always involve quiet, 'gentlemanly' negotiations. The sought-after firm often resists takeover and may resort to defensive tactics with exotic names, such as poison pills and white knights.

Introduction ▷ There is no more dramatic or controversial activity in corporate finance than the acquisition of one firm by another or the merger of two firms. It is the stuff of headlines in the financial press, and it is occasionally an embarrassing source of scandal.

The acquisition of one firm by another is, of course, an investment made under uncertainty, and the basic principles of valuation apply. Another firm should be acquired only if doing so generates a positive net present value to the shareholders of the acquiring firm. However, because the NPV of an acquisition candidate can be difficult to determine, mergers and acquisitions are interesting topics in their own right.

 **22.1** ## The legal forms of acquisitions

There are three basic legal procedures that one firm can use to acquire another firm:

1 merger or consolidation;
2 acquisition of shares; or
3 acquisition of assets.

Although these forms are different from a legal standpoint, the financial press frequently does not distinguish between them. If there is any distinction, the financial press consider a friendly takeover to be a *merger* and an unfriendly takeover to be an *acquisition*.

Merger or consolidation

merger

the complete absorption of one company by another, where the acquiring firm retains its identity and the acquired firm ceases to exist as a separate entity

consolidation

a merger in which an entirely new firm is created and both the acquired and acquiring firm cease to exist

A **merger** refers to the complete absorption of one firm by another. The acquiring firm retains its name and its identity, and it acquires all of the assets and liabilities of the acquired firm. After a merger, the acquired firm ceases to exist as a separate business entity.

A **consolidation** is a type of merger where an entirely new firm is created. In a consolidation, both the acquiring firm and the acquired firm terminate their previous legal existence and become part of a new firm. For this reason, the distinction between the acquiring and the acquired firm is not as important in a consolidation as it is in an ordinary merger.

The rules for mergers and consolidations are basically the same. Acquisition by merger or consolidation results in a combination of the assets and liabilities of acquired and acquiring firms; the only difference is whether or not a new firm is created. We will henceforth use the term merger to refer generically to both mergers and consolidations.

There are some advantages and some disadvantages to using a merger to acquire a firm:

1 A primary advantage is that a merger is legally simple and does not cost as much as other forms of acquisition. The reason for this is that the firms simply agree to combine their entire operations. Thus, for example, there is no need to transfer title to individual assets of the acquired firm to the acquiring firm.
2 A primary disadvantage is that a merger must be approved by a vote of the shareholders of each firm. Typically, two-thirds (or even more) of the share votes are required for approval. Obtaining the necessary votes can be time-consuming and difficult. Furthermore, as we discuss in greater detail below, the co-operation of the target firm's existing management is almost a necessity for a merger. This co-operation may not be easily or cheaply obtained.

Acquisition of assets

A company that wishes to acquire another business may effectively do so by purchasing the other company's assets. This process entails the transfer of assets and liabilities of the target company to the acquiring company. Where the target company is listed on the stock exchange, the sale of its assets must be approved at a general meeting of its shareholders.

From the target shareholders' point of view, the sale of assets may be less attractive than a sale of shares. A sale of shares for cash is more straightforward and leaves each target shareholder free to deal with the proceeds as he or she likes. If, however, the target company sold its assets and received cash, distribution of that cash to shareholders would involve liquidation of the target company. The part of the distribution that is regarded as a dividend is likely to be subject to income tax as dividend imputation credits are unlikely to apply—and the balance could be subject to capital gains tax (depending upon the date of the original purchase of the assets). In addition, the liquidation of the target company could involve a fairly lengthy process. If the members did not agree to liquidate the target company, it would have to invest the proceeds from the sale of assets and the target shareholders would have to be prepared to leave their money in essentially a new entity in the absence of a ready market for their shares.

In their own words

Michael C. Jensen* on mergers and acquisitions

Economic analysis and evidence indicate that takeovers, LBOs, and corporate restructuring are playing an important role in helping the economy adjust to major competitive changes in the last two decades. The competition among alternative management teams and organisational structures for control of corporate assets has enabled vast economic resources to move more quickly to their highest-valued use. In the process, substantial benefits for the economy as a whole as well as for shareholders have been created. Overall gains to selling-firm shareholders from mergers, acquisitions, leveraged buyouts, and other corporate restructuring in the 12-year period 1977–1988 total over $500 billion in 1988 dollars. I estimate gains to buying-firm shareholders to be at least $50 billion for the same period. These gains equal 53 per cent of the total cash dividends (valued in 1988 dollars) paid to investors by the entire corporate sector in the same period.

Mergers and acquisitions are a response to new technologies or market conditions which require a strategic change in a company's direction or use of resources. Compared to current management, a new owner is often better able to accomplish major change in the existing organisational structure. Alternatively, leveraged buyouts bring about organisational change by creating entrepreneurial incentives for management and by eliminating the centralised bureaucratic obstacles to manoeuvrability that are inherent in large public corporations.

When managers have a substantial ownership interest in the organisation, the conflicts of interest between shareholders and managers over the payout of the company's free cash flow are reduced. Management's incentives are focused on maximising the value of the enterprise, rather than building empires—often through poorly conceived diversification acquisitions—without regard to shareholder value. Finally, the required repayment of debt replaces management's discretion in paying dividends and the tendency to keep too much cash. Substantial increases in efficiency are thereby created.

* Michael C. Jensen is Edsel Bryant Ford Professor of Business Administration at Harvard University. An outstanding scholar and researcher, he is famous for his path-breaking analysis of the modern corporation and its relations with its shareholders.

Acquisition of shares

The other way in which the bidder can gain control is by acquiring shares in the target company by means of a **tender offer**. Where the takeover is by acquisition of shares, the target company continues to exist and ownership of its assets is unaffected. The acquiring company usually aims to acquire sufficient voting shares to give it management control. If the acquirer is prepared to tolerate the presence in the company of other shareholders, it can obtain control without having to buy all the shares.

tender offer

a public offer by one firm to directly buy the shares of another firm

In Australia, the term 'takeover' usually means acquisition of sufficient voting shares in the target company to gain management control.

Degrees of control

As stated above, the acquiring company will wish to purchase sufficient voting shares to give it management control. Normally this means to be able to elect directors. In a small company, the acquirer may need *majority control*, that is, more than 50 per cent of the voting shares. However, in a large company with a diversity of shareholders, a smaller percentage will give *effective control*. The *Corporations Act* 2001 sees a threshold of 20 per cent as the point at which effective control of a company can change and it imposes limits on persons acquiring a holding of more than 20 per cent. There is much debate as to what level of ownership provides effective control. It is suggested that in companies where the shareholdings are spread in many small holdings, 14 per cent of ownership will provide effective control. In companies where the shareholdings are concentrated in the hands of fewer members, much higher than 20 per cent ownership is required for effective control.

An acquiring company wishing to purchase 100 per cent of the target company must hold 90 per cent of the shares before it can compulsorily acquire the voting shares of holders who do not accept the bid. The terms on which these shares are bought out will normally be the same as those offered in a takeover scheme or takeover announcement.

An acquiring company wishing to alter the company's memorandum or articles must hold sufficient shares to enable a special resolution to be passed by not less than 75 per cent of the total votes cast at a general meeting.

Table 22.1 summarises the important percentages of voting rights in relation to control of the company as specified under common law and the legislation.

TABLE 22.1

Degrees of control	
Percentage of shares held	**Legal position**
100%	Full ownership
90%	Can compulsorily purchase remaining shares
75%	Control to pass a special resolution at a general meeting
50%	Majority control
20%	Effective control (*Corporations Act* 2001 threshold level)
5%	Must disclose shareholding (substantial shareholder)

Acquisition classifications

Financial analysts typically classify acquisitions into three types:

1   *Horizontal acquisition*. This is acquisition of a firm in the same industry as the bidder. The firms compete with each other in their product markets.
2   *Vertical acquisition*. A vertical acquisition involves firms at different steps of the production process. The acquisition by an airline company of a travel agency would be a vertical acquisition.

3   *Conglomerate acquisition*. When the bidder and the target firm are not related to each other, the merger is called a conglomerate acquisition. The acquisition of a food products firm by a computer firm would be considered a conglomerate acquisition.

A note on takeovers

Takeover is a general and imprecise term referring to the transfer of control of a firm from one group of shareholders to another. A takeover thus occurs whenever one group takes control from another.[2] This can occur in three ways: by acquisitions, proxy contests, or going-private transactions. Thus takeovers encompass a broader set of activities than just acquisitions. These activities can be depicted as follows:

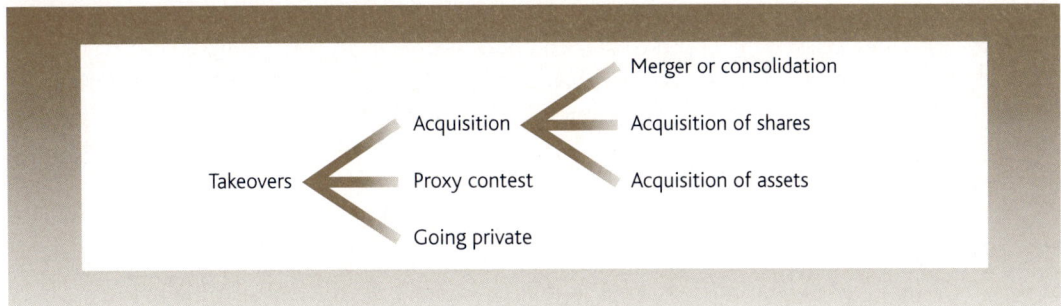

As we have mentioned above, a takeover achieved by acquisition will occur by merger, purchase of assets or purchase of shares. In mergers and share purchases, the bidder buys the voting ordinary shares of the target firm.

Takeovers can also occur with **proxy contests**. Proxy contests occur when a group attempts to gain controlling seats on the board of directors by voting in new directors. A proxy is the right to cast someone else's votes. In a proxy contest, proxies are solicited by an unhappy group of shareholders from the rest of the shareholders. A recent high-profile example of this was the NRMA proxy contest.

In **going-private transactions**, all of the equity shares of a public firm are purchased by a small group of investors. The group usually includes members of incumbent management and some outside investors. Such transactions have come to be known generically as **leveraged buyouts (LBOs)** because a large percentage of the money needed to buy up the shares is usually borrowed. Such transactions are also termed MBOs (management buyouts) when existing management is heavily involved. The shares of the firm are delisted from stock exchanges and can no longer be purchased in the open market.

LBOs have become increasingly common, and some recent ones have been quite large. One of the largest acquisitions in history (and one of the single largest private transactions ever of any kind) was the 1989 LBO of RJR Nabisco, the tobacco and food products giant. The acquisition price in that buyout was an astonishing $30.6 billion. In that LBO, as with most of the large ones, much of the financing came from junk bond sales (see Chapter 16 for a discussion of junk bonds).

proxy contest
attempt to gain control of a firm by soliciting a sufficient number of shareholder votes to replace existing management

going-private transaction
all publicly owned shares in a firm are replaced with complete equity ownership by a private group

leveraged buyout (LBO)
going-private transaction in which a large percentage of the money used to buy the shares is borrowed. Incumbent management is often involved

Concept questions

22.1a *What is a merger? How does a merger differ from other acquisition forms?*
22.1b *What is a takeover?*

▮ 22.2 ▮ Regulation of business combination

Substantial legislation has been enacted in Australia to control the acquisition of shares in target companies. Takeover activity and procedures are regulated by state and Commonwealth legislation, although there is a strong move for uniformity across the states. The most important legislation is the *Corporations Act* 2001—it replaced the *Companies (Acquisition of Shares) Amendment No. 2* 1981, the *Securities Industry Code* and the *Futures Industry Act*. This legislation provided the Australian Securities Commission (ASC) with authority to control takeovers on a national basis. The legislation is designed to prevent takeovers occurring without full public disclosure. In 1998 all the powers of the ASC were transferred to the Australian Securities and Investments Commission (ASIC). Surprisingly, bank mergers do not fall under the jurisdiction of ASIC—they remain the province of the Treasury and the Australian Competition and Consumer Commission (ACCC). The late 1990s saw a number of moves for large banking and insurance firms to merge with pure banking firms. For example, there was the Suncorp/Metway merger in Queensland in 1998, and 1999 saw the beginning of the Commonwealth Bank of Australia and the Colonial Insurance Group combination.

Statements and publications provided by ASIC indicate that the objective of the legislation is to ensure:

a that fair dealing and equity exists across all members of the companies involved in a takeover. As far as practicable, each member will have equal access to information, equal opportunity to trade in the market and equal opportunity to share in any benefits that might accrue under the takeover;

b that the market for securities is efficient, competitive and well informed;

c that any potential market manipulation is identified promptly;

d that any premium paid for control of a company is shared by all members;

e that all members of a company in receipt of a takeover offer are provided with sufficient information to assess the offer; and

f that the directors of a company receiving a takeover offer do not do anything to frustrate the offer before members have had an adequate opportunity to consider it.

Unless the procedures identified in the Acts are followed, the acquisition of additional shares in a company is prohibited if the purchase would:

a give a shareholder an entitlement to more than 20 per cent of the voting shares; or

b increase the shareholdings of members who already hold between 20 per cent and 90 per cent of the voting shares.

In our discussion, we will frequently refer to the acquiring firm as the bidder. This is the company that will make an offer to distribute cash or securities to obtain the shares or assets of another company. The firm that is sought (and perhaps acquired) is often called the target firm. The cash or securities offered to the target firm are the consideration in the acquisition.

Three procedures have been identified as leading to a takeover situation. These are a *time-delayed purchase (creeping takeover)*, an *off market bid* and a *market bid*.

A *time-delayed purchase (creeping takeover)* permits the acquisition of no more than 3 per cent of the shares of the target company every six months, provided that a threshold level of 19 per cent has been maintained for at least six months. No public statement is required in this situation.

An *off market bid* is where an acquiring company makes an offer to purchase shares of the target company. The offer may be by way of cash, a share exchange or a combination of both. This offer must remain open for one to 12 months. It may be for only a specified proportion of the target company's issued shares. A statement has to be lodged with ASIC for approval. The statement must include, among other items, the identity of the bidder, particulars of the bidder's intentions regarding the target company and any other information that is relevant to the target company's shareholders. If the statement is approved by ASIC, it is then sent to the shareholders of the target company. The target company must provide its shareholders and ASIC with the target's statement. This statement includes a recommendation as to whether the offer should be accepted and other information relevant to the offer. The statement may be accompanied by an opinion from an independent expert on the offer. The bidder can increase its offer price, but it has to pay the increased price to all shareholders who accept the offer, including the shareholders who may have already accepted the lower price.

A market bid requires an unconditional commitment by a member of the stock exchange to operate in the market and purchase for a period of one month, on behalf of the bidder, all shares offered on the exchange at a specified price. The bidder must supply ASIC and the shareholders of the target company with a statement which provides information the same to that contained in a bidder's statement above. The target company must reply through a target's statement.

In addition to this legislation some of the listing requirements of the Australian Stock Exchange have direct implications for company acquisitions. While those requirements tend to mirror the legislation, they do go further in some areas. For example, directors are required to maintain secrecy during discussions bearing on a potential takeover offer and directors of the target company are restricted from making an allotment of shares for a period of three months after receiving a takeover offer.

Other legislation which may influence the decision of a company to make an acquisition includes:

1   *Trade Practices Act* 1974. Section 50 of this Act prohibits a company from acquiring the shares or assets of another company where the acquisition is likely to place the acquiring company in a position to control or dominate a market. The Act is administered by the Australian Competition and Consumer Commission (ACCC).
2   *Foreign Takeovers Act* 1975. This Act provides the Commonwealth Treasurer with the power to prohibit acquisitions that would result in what is regarded as an excessive shareholding by foreign interests.
3   *Broadcasting and Television Act* 1942. This Act was invoked in the early 1990s to prohibit certain people from concentrating ownership of the Australian media.
4   Other Commonwealth and state legislation may inhibit acquisitions in specific industries; for example, there are controls under the *Companies (Life Insurance Holding Companies) Ordinance* 1968, *Gas Suppliers (Shareholdings) Act* 1972, *Banks (Shareholdings) Act* 1972.

While the actions of directors and officers in relation to mergers, acquisitions and takeovers are governed by specific legislation, consideration must also be given to their obligations under common law.

Figure 22.1 indicates the legal framework within which these business transactions need to be considered.

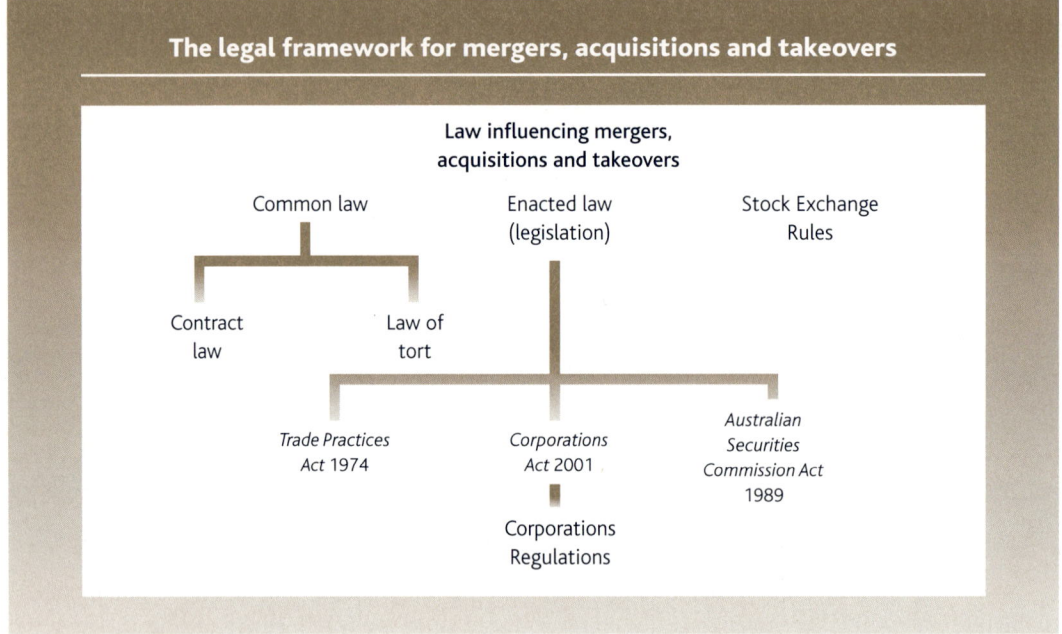

The legal framework for mergers, acquisitions and takeovers

Merger and acquisition activity has tended to fluctuate in Australia. The incidence of this form of investment has been linked with economic activity. The number of bids for listed companies was high during the 1980s, with the highest number occurring in 1988. However, the number declined during the 1990s with fairly substantial swings in the numbers from year to year. The lowest level of activity was experienced in 1992. These levels of activity have been identified as takeover 'waves'. The Australian experience of high activity in the 1920s, 1960s and the 1980s mirrors that of the United States. While there is no generally accepted theory as to why these waves occur, there is empirical evidence that merger activity is related to share prices. Bishop, Dodd and Officer (1987) have reported a close relationship between increases in the number of takeovers and share prices. Brown and da Silva Rosa (1997) found that bidding firms tended to achieve abnormally good performance in the months leading up to the takeover offer.

The largest global acquistion ever was of Time Warner Inc by AOL Time Warner in October 2000. The transaction was valued at $US186 billion. The largest successful acquistion during 2002 in Australia was the acquistion of Orogen Minerals Ltd by Oil Search Ltd for approximately $640 million.

Concept questions

22.2a *What legal restrictions stop a company from buying a controlling interest in a competitor to increase the competitor's product prices?*

22.2b *Comment on the following claims:*
  i *A creeping takeover will always see the light of day as a formal takeover offer.*
  ii *A time-delayed purchase and a formal takeover offer must eventually result in an on-market announcement.*

Taxes and acquisitions

Generally, assets purchased after 19 September 1985 and subsequently sold will be subject to capital gains tax. Special rollover provisions allow the payment of capital gains tax to be deferred on certain business reorganisations, on death and in a restricted range of other situations. Whether the rollover provisions apply depends upon complex interpretations under the Australian *Income Tax Assessment Act*. A seller will be subject to capital gains tax even where the consideration is shares in another company. In this case the seller will be deemed to have received a consideration equal to the market value of the new shares. This is still the situation where the shares of some of the members have been acquired compulsorily.

In order for assets acquired before 19 September 1985 not to be liable for capital gains tax, it is necessary that the 'Commissioner is satisfied, or considers it reasonable to assume that all times (after 19 September 1985) when the asset was held by the taxpayer, majority underlying interests in the asset were held by natural persons who, immediately before 20 September 1985, held majority underlying interests in the asset'.

In other words, once more than 50 per cent of a company's pre-20 September 1985 shareholders have changed, any assets will effectively lose their capital gains tax exempt status even though they were acquired prior to that date. Income Tax Ruling No. 2361 deals with listed companies and states that:

> . . . normal transactions in a company's shares in a stock exchange which are not associated with activity in the nature of a takeover or merger, are not required to be examined in applying the test. Major changes in the ownership of shares which accrue outside the conduct of normal stock market trading, however, will call for examination, in the course of which regard will be paid to changes to shareholdings that have occurred in the course of normal trading on stock exchanges as well as those related to events that caused the examination to be made.

This ruling suggests that when takeovers or mergers occur, the Australian Taxation Office will need to be given good grounds as to why capital gains tax should not be levied.

22.4 ■ Gains from acquisitions

To determine the gains from an acquisition, we need first to identify the relevant incremental cash flows, or, more generally, the source of value. In the broadest sense, acquiring another firm only makes sense if there is some concrete reason to believe that the target firm will somehow be worth more in our hands than it is worth now.[3] As we will see, there are a number of reasons why this might be so.

Synergy

Suppose Firm A is contemplating acquiring Firm B. The acquisition will be beneficial if the combined firm has value that is greater than the sum of the values of the separate firms. If we let V_{AB} stand for the value of the merged firm, then the merger makes sense only if:

$$V_{AB} > V_A + V_B$$

where V_A and V_B are the separate values. A successful merger thus requires that the value of the whole exceeds the sum of the parts.

The difference between the value of the combined firm and the sum of the values of the firms as separate entities is the incremental net gain from the acquisition:

$$\Delta V = V_{AB} - (V_A + V_B)$$

When ΔV is positive, the acquisition is said to generate **synergy**.

If Firm A buys Firm B, it gets a company worth V_B plus the incremental gain, ΔV. The value of Firm B to Firm A ($V_B{}^*$) is thus:

$$\text{Value of Firm B to Firm A} = V_B{}^* = \Delta V + V_B$$

We place a $*$ on $V_B{}^*$ to emphasise that we are referring to the value of Firm B to Firm A, not the value of Firm B as a separate entity.

$V_B{}^*$ can be determined in two steps: (1) estimating V_B, and (2) estimating ΔV. If B is a public company, then its market value as an independent firm under existing management (V_B) can be observed directly. If Firm B is not publicly owned, then its value will have to be estimated based on similar companies that are listed. Either way, the problem of determining a value for $V_B{}^*$ requires determining a value for ΔV.

To determine the incremental value of an acquisition, we need to know the incremental cash flows. These are the cash flows for the combined firm less what A and B could generate separately. In other words, the incremental cash flow for evaluating a merger is the difference between the cash flow of the combined company and the sum of the cash flows for the two companies considered separately. We will label this incremental cash flow as ΔCF.

EXAMPLE 22.1   **Synergy**

Firms A and B are competitors with very similar assets and business risks. Both are all-equity firms with after-tax cash flows of $10 per year forever, and both have an overall cost of capital of 10 per cent. Firm A is thinking of buying Firm B. The cash flow from the merged firm would be $21 per year. Does the merger generate synergy? What is $V_B{}^*$? What is ΔV?

The merger does generate synergy because the cash flow from the merged firm is $\Delta CF = $1 greater than the sum of the individual cash flows ($21 versus $20). Assuming that the risks stay the same, the value of the merged firm is $21/0.10 = $210. Firms A and B are each worth $10/0.10 = $100, for a total of $200. The incremental gain from the merger, ΔV, is thus $210 − 200 = $10. The total value of Firm B to Firm A, $V_B{}^*$, is $100 (the value of B as a separate company) + $10 (the incremental gain) = $110.

From our discussions in earlier chapters, we know that the incremental cash flow, ΔCF, can be broken down into four parts:

$$\Delta CF = \Delta EBIT + \Delta Depreciation - \Delta Tax - \Delta Capital\ requirements$$
$$= \Delta Revenue - \Delta Cost - \Delta Tax - \Delta Capital\ requirements$$

where $\Delta Revenue$ is the difference in revenues, $\Delta Cost$ is the difference in costs, ΔTax is the difference in taxes, and $\Delta Capital\ requirements$ is the change in new non-current assets and net working capital.

Based on this breakdown, the merger will only make sense if one or more of these cash flow components is beneficially affected by the merger. The possible cash flow benefits of mergers and acquisitions thus fall into four basic categories: revenue enhancement, cost reductions, lower taxes, and reductions in capital needs.

Revenue enhancement

One important reason for an acquisition is that the combined firm may generate greater revenues than two separate firms. Increases in revenue may come from marketing gains, strategic benefits and increases in market power.

Marketing gains

It is frequently claimed that mergers and acquisitions can produce greater operating revenues from improved marketing. For example, improvements might be made in the following areas:

1 previously ineffective media programming and advertising efforts;
2 a weak existing distribution network; and/or
3 an unbalanced product mix.

Strategic benefits

Some acquisitions promise a strategic advantage. This is an opportunity to take advantage of the competitive environment if certain things occur or, more generally, to enhance management flexibility with regard to the company's future operations. In this regard, a strategic benefit is more like an option than it is a standard investment opportunity.

For example, suppose a sewing machine firm can use its technology to enter other businesses. The small-motor technology from the original business could provide opportunities to begin manufacturing small appliances and electric typewriters. Similarly, electronics expertise gained in producing typewriters could be used to manufacture electronic printers.

The word *beachhead* has been used to describe the process of entering a new industry or market to exploit perceived opportunities. The beachhead is used to spawn new opportunities based on 'intangible' relationships. An example is Telstra's move into the Hong Kong telecommunications market. At the time of writing, Telstra and Cyberworks are attempting to purchase Cable & Wireless HKT for $64 billion. This position will complement Telstra's Australian operations.

Market power

One firm may acquire another to increase its market share and market power. In such mergers, profits can be enhanced through higher prices and reduced competition for customers. Of course, mergers that substantially reduce competition in the market may be challenged by the Australian Competition and Consumer Commission (ACCC). Section 50 of the *Trade Practices Act* 1974 prohibits the acquisition of shares or assets if a dominant market position for goods or services would result, or where the acquisition would allow the acquirer to substantially control the relevant market. In October 1988, Arnotts signed an agreement to acquire Nabisco Brands Pty Ltd. The Trade Practices Commission (an earlier equivalent of the ACCC) initiated Federal Court proceedings on the grounds that the acquisition contravened Section 50. In January 1990, the Federal Court declared void the acquisition agreement. Arnotts announced that it was prepared to appeal the decision; however, Arnotts was subsequently acquired by Campbells, a large American organisation, and the appeal did not go forward. The TPC looked long and hard at the Commonwealth Bank/Colonial merger when it was proposed before allowing negotiations to proceed.

In the middle of 2002 the ACCC dealt a body blow to two leading players in the pay television and telephony industry. The ACCC refused to ratify an alliance between Foxtel and Optus. Key platforms in the strategy behind the alliance were:

a   profitability to increase;
b   Optus to resell Foxtel programs; and
c   Telstra to also sell Foxtel services.

Telstra (50%), News Limited and Publishing and Broadcasting Ltd (PBL) were the major shareholders in Foxtel. Telstra, Australia's major telephone company, had invested in Foxtel for telephony competitive (defence) reasons. News Limited invested to develop a profit platform through the supply of profitable content to Foxtel. PBL had a role in Foxtel primarily to hedge its position in free-to-air broadcasting.

The chairman of the ACCC, Professor Alan Fels, claimed he was undecided whether Telstra's stake in Foxtel created additional competition issues. At the centre of the ACCC's rejection of the deal was the concern it would turn Foxtel into a monopoly as it was substantially lessening competition in the industry, which was dominated by Foxtel and Optus. In 2003 the ACCC revised its position after negotiating certain conditions to maintain competition among the participants. This case provides a good example of how the ACCC looks at the combinations that firms construct and the agreements they enter into that might reduce competition.

Cost reductions

One of the most basic reasons to merge is that a combined firm may operate more efficiently than two separate firms. A firm can obtain greater operating efficiency in several different ways through a merger or an acquisition.

Economies of scale

Economies of scale relate to the average cost per unit of producing goods and services. If the per-unit cost of production falls as the level of production increases, then an economy of scale exists. See Figure 22.2.

Frequently, the phrase *spreading overhead* is used in connection with economies of scale. This expression refers to the sharing of central facilities such as corporate headquarters, top management and computer services.

FIGURE 22.2

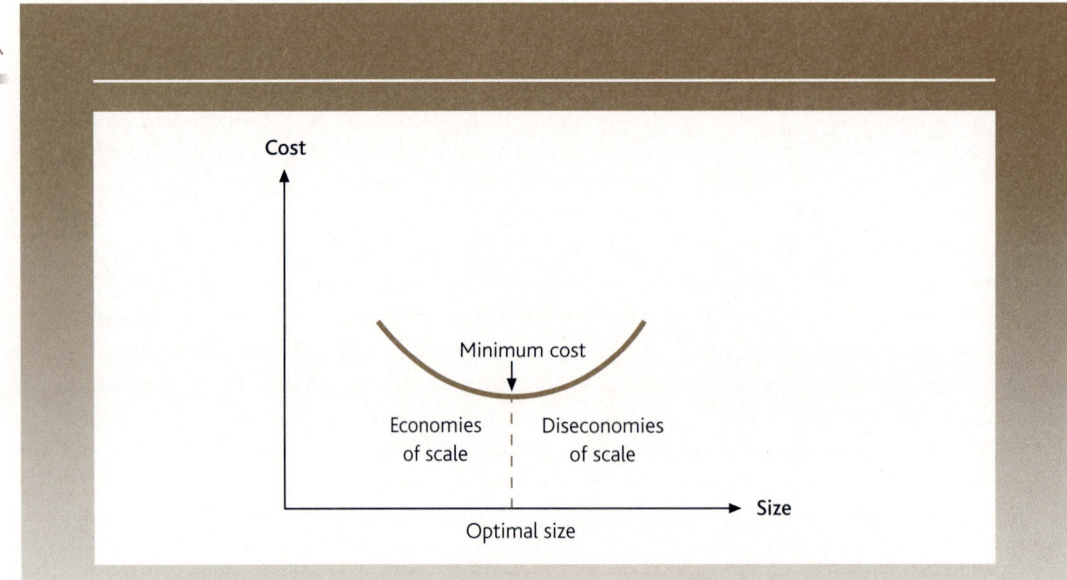

Economies of vertical integration

Operating economies can be gained from vertical combinations as well as from horizontal combinations. The main purpose of vertical acquisitions is to make co-ordinating closely related operating activities easier. Benefits from vertical integration are probably the reason that most forest product firms that cut timber also own sawmills and hauling equipment. Such economies may explain why some airline companies have purchased hotels and car rental companies.

Technology transfers are another reason for vertical integration. Consider the merger of General Motors and Hughes Aircraft in 1985. It seems natural that an automobile manufacturer might acquire an advanced electronics firm if the special technology of the electronics firm can be used to improve the quality of the automobile.

Complementary resources

Some firms acquire others to make better use of existing resources or to provide the missing ingredient for success. Think of a football equipment store that could merge with a boating equipment store to produce more even sales over both the winter and summer seasons, and thereby better use store capacity.

Tax gains

Tax gains are a powerful incentive for some acquisitions. The possible tax gains from an acquisition include the following:

1 the use of tax losses;
2 the use of franking credits;
3 the use of unused debt capacity; and
4 the ability to write up the value of depreciable assets.

Net operating losses

Firms that lose money on a pre-tax basis will not pay taxes. Such firms can end up with tax losses that they cannot use. These tax losses are referred to as NOL (an acronym for net operating losses). Under Australian tax law, NOL may be carried forward to be offset against future taxable income. A firm with net operating losses may be an attractive merger partner for a firm with significant tax liabilities. In order to take advantage of tax losses carried forward, acquisitions have to be carefully planned. Under section 50D(2) of the Australian *Income Tax Assessment Act*, the carried forward loss may be taken to account in determining taxable income if a series of continuing ownership tests are satisfied. Shares in the company incurring the loss, carrying between them:

1 the right to exercise more than half the voting power; and
2 the right to receive more than half the dividends; and
3 the right to receive more than half the distribution of capital

must be owned by natural persons at the time of the loss and at the time when the loss is to be claimed as a tax deduction. Note that the tests are cumulative and not alternatives, and they must apply at all times during the relevant loss period and the relevant income period.

Losses of one company can only be offset against profits of another company if the loss company is 100 per cent owned by the profit company.

The following examples indicate some of the difficulties in taking advantage of tax situations.

Smorgon Group successfully acquired 100 per cent of the issued ordinary shares in Humes Industries Limited; however, it only acquired 98.8 per cent of the convertible notes. A convertible note holder sought to convert 1,000 convertible notes into ordinary shares. As a result Smorgon would cease to own 100 per cent of Humes and lose the ability to group for tax purposes. For Smorgon the estimated tax saving was $28 million. Smorgon failed in an attempt to force the redemption of the convertible notes under the Trust Deed. It eventually purchased the convertible notes, which had a value of $2.80, for $10.00 per note.

Pioneer Concrete Services Limited received acceptances for 100 per cent of Ampol Limited ordinary shares but only received acceptances for 82 per cent of the preference shares. The presence of the outstanding preference shares prevented Pioneer from grouping Ampol's results for tax purposes. Pioneer called a meeting of the preference shareholders and passed a resolution for the reduction and cancellation of the outstanding preference shares. The capital reduction was initially ratified by the Supreme Court, but it was overturned on appeal so that an indirect consequence was that Pioneer could not claim the tax advantages.

Franking credits

Following the introduction in 1985 of the imputation system of taxation, the profits of companies are subject to taxation but the dividends paid to shareholders are accompanied by an imputation credit (see Chapter 19 for an explanation of the system). The amount of the credit is determined by the tax paid on the earnings of the company. Companies that have excess or unused franking credits may provide franking credits that may be used by the acquiring company to frank dividends to the acquiring company shareholders.

Unused debt capacity

Some firms do not use as much debt as they could. This makes them potential acquisition candidates. Adding debt can provide important tax savings, and many acquisitions are financed with debt. The acquiring company can deduct interest payments on the newly created debt and reduce taxes.

Australian corporate failures in the 1980s resulted in substantial losses through debt funding. The banking system incurred a serious setback through the collapses of Bond, Equiticorp, Rothwell, Tricontinental and Quintex among others. When Quintex Australia Limited went into receivership in 1989, the banks, who had lent on the security of Quintex shares, found the scrip to be worthless.

The impact of the acquisition on the amount of debt in the acquirer's capital can be an important determinant in whether the takeover should proceed. It has already been noted that the interest on the debt is a tax deduction which could be an advantage. Nevertheless, it would seem that the experiences of the 1980s have led the market to look less favourably on companies that allow debt levels to run beyond what experience considers prudent. Coca-Cola Amatil allowed its debt/equity ratio to rise to 400 per cent following a reconstruction of its activities in 1990. The share price had drifted down by 28 per cent in the first five months of 1990 despite the good performance of its soft drink and snack food operations. When the company announced that its equity base would be expanded, the market price rebounded immediately. This increase may not have been due entirely to the capital restructure, as Amatil announced a takeover of Coca-Cola Bottlers Limited at the same time.

Asset revaluations

We have previously observed that, in a taxable acquisition, the assets of the acquired firm can be revalued. If the value of the assets is increased, tax deductions for depreciation will be a gain. The Pacific Dunlop acquisition of Nucleus Limited and Repco Limited is an example where the assets were revalued to manipulate accounting profits. Pacific Dunlop had independent valuations done of the intangible assets acquired. Effectively, Pacific Dunlop revalued the identifiable intangibles, being trademarks ($70m) and patents ($130m) and wrote them off as extraordinary items. This accounting treatment had the effect of reducing 'goodwill' as defined in Accounting Standard ASRB 1013 and therefore substantially reduced 'goodwill' amortisation from future profits of Pacific Dunlop. It also ensured that no detrimental effect to profits would be suffered as a result of the possible introduction of an Intangible Assets Accounting Standard. The effect of Pacific Dunlop's actions was that profits were not reduced with a high goodwill amortisation. Some observers have suggested that this increased the value of Pacific Dunlop. Such observations are obviously incorrect as there had been no effect on the cash flows or assets of the company. It is only when the revaluation changes depreciation and reduces taxation so that cash flows are increased that asset revaluation will increase firm values.

Changing capital requirements

All firms must make investments in working capital and non-current assets to sustain an efficient level of operating activity. A merger may reduce the combined investments needed by the two firms. For example, Firm A may need to expand its manufacturing facilities while Firm B has significant excess capacity. It may be much cheaper for Firm A to buy Firm B than to build from scratch.

In addition, acquiring firms may see ways of more effectively managing existing assets. This can occur with a reduction in working capital by more efficient handling of cash, accounts receivable and inventory. Finally, the acquiring firm may also sell off certain assets that are not needed in the combined firm.

Firms will often cite a large number of reasons for merging. Consider the mergers between the then National Bank and the Commercial Banking Company of Sydney, and the Bank of New South Wales and the Commercial Bank of Australia. These organisations merged as the National Australia Bank in the first case and Westpac Banking Corporation in the second case. At the time of the mergers, boards and management of all the banks were concerned about the threat of competition from the impending entry of foreign banks into the Australian market. The banks were aiming to establish widespread branch networks so that stable, cost-effective retail deposit bases could be generated to provide a competitive advantage against any newly licensed banks. It is interesting to note that all the target company directors were given positions on the offeror (bidder) company boards and senior management positions were found for all the target executives.

It has been suggested that Thomas Nationwide Transport merged with a highly geared transport business called Alltrans (owned and managed by Peter Abeles) principally to secure the management services of the Alltrans team.

Grace Brothers was a successful organisation. However, once Bond Corporation had acquired 20 per cent of Grace Brothers and launched a bid, Grace Brothers' directors found a merger with Myer Emporium a more palatable option than the Bond bid.

Bell Resources Ltd was taken over by Bond Corporation, and the subsequent legal and commercial difficulties for that merged group revealed that the Bell Resources cash had been used by the group. One of the motivations for acquisition may be to acquire cash resources or the cash flows of the target.

Another incentive for merger may be to acquire brand names, patents, trademarks or computer software rights. A merger where brand names were not considered important is that of the Bank of New South Wales and the Commercial Bank of Australia mentioned above. These banks agreed to merge under the new name of Westpac. In the case of the Bank of New South Wales, this involved jettisoning the value of a name it had used for 150 years.

Avoiding mistakes

Evaluating the benefit of a potential acquisition is more difficult than a standard capital budgeting analysis because so much of the value can come from intangible, or otherwise difficult to quantify, benefits. Consequently, there is a great deal of room for error. Here are some general rules that should be remembered:

1 *Do not ignore market values.* There is no point and little gain in estimating the value of a publicly traded firm when that value can be directly observed. The current market value represents a consensus opinion of investors concerning the firm's value (under existing management). Use this value as a starting point. If the firm is not publicly held, then the place to start is with similar firms that are publicly held.

2 *Estimate only incremental cash flows.* It is important to estimate the cash flows that are incremental to the acquisition. Only incremental cash flows from an acquisition will add value to the acquiring firm. Acquisition analysis should thus focus only on the newly created, incremental cash flows from the proposed acquisition.

3 *Use the correct discount rate.* The discount rate should be the required rate of return for the incremental cash flows associated with the acquisition. It should reflect the risk associated with the use of funds, not the source. In particular, if Firm A is acquiring Firm B, then Firm A's cost of capital is not particularly relevant. Firm B's cost of capital is a much more appropriate discount rate because it reflects the risk of Firm B's cash flows.

4 *Be aware of transactions costs.* An acquisition may involve substantial (and sometimes astounding) transactions costs. These will include fees to investment bankers, legal fees and disclosure requirements.

A note on inefficient management

There are firms whose value could be increased with a change in management. These are firms that are poorly run or otherwise do not use their assets efficiently to create shareholder value. Mergers are a means of replacing management in such cases.

Furthermore, the fact that a firm might benefit from a change in management does not necessarily mean that existing management is dishonest, incompetent or negligent. Instead, just as some athletes are better than others, so might some management teams be better at running a business. This can be particularly true during times of technological change or other periods when innovations in business practice are occurring. In any case, to the extent that corporate raiders can identify poorly run firms or firms that otherwise would benefit from a change in management, corporate raiders provide a valuable service to target firm shareholders and society in general. By April 2000, half of the Board of AMP had been forced out of office through pressure from large institutional shareholders. The financial press of the day argued that the changes were enforced because of a bad takeover of GIO Insurance and a payout of $13 million to the retired managing director (an American) who was in control when the takeover was completed. It was revealed after the takeover that GIO had incurred serious insurance losses that were overlooked in the takeover negotiations. In February 2003 the Chairman, Stan Wallis, and a further four directors, resigned after the disclosure of huge losses in the United Kingdom. In a short period the price of AMP shares had declined from around $20 to less than $7.

Concept questions

22.4a *What are the relevant incremental cash flows for evaluating a merger candidate?*
22.4b *What are some different sources of gain from acquisition?*

22.5 ■ Some financial side-effects of acquisitions

In addition to the various possibilities we discussed above, mergers can have some purely financial side-effects; that is, things that occur regardless of whether the merger makes economic sense or not. Two such effects are particularly worth mentioning: EPS growth and diversification.

EPS growth

An acquisition can create the appearance of growth in earnings per share (EPS). This may fool investors into thinking that the firm is doing better than it really is. What happens is easiest to see with an example.

Suppose Teletalk Resources Ltd acquires Music Enterprises. The financial positions of Teletalk and Music before the acquisition are shown in Table 22.2. Since the merger creates no additional value, the combined firm (Teletalk Resources after acquiring Music) has a value that is equal to the sum of the values of the two firms before the merger.

Before the merger, both Teletalk and Music have 100 shares outstanding. However, Teletalk sells for $25 per share versus $10 per share for Music. Teletalk therefore acquires Music by exchanging 1 of its shares for every 2.5 Music shares. Since there are 100 shares in Music, it will take $100/2.5 = 40$ shares in all.

After the merger, Teletalk will have 140 shares outstanding, and several things will happen (see the 'smart' market column of Table 22.2):

1 The market value of the combined firm is $3,500. This is equal to the sum of the values of the separate firms before the merger. If the market is 'smart', it will realise that the combined firm is worth the sum of the values of the separate firms.
2 The earnings per share of the merged firm are $1.43. The acquisition enables Teletalk to increase its earnings per share from $1 to $1.43, an increase of 43 per cent.
3 Because the share price of Teletalk after the merger is the same as before the merger, the price/earnings ratio must fall. This is true as long as the market is smart and recognises that the total market value has not been altered by the merger.

If the market is 'fooled', it might mistake the 43 per cent increase in earnings per share for true growth. In this case, the price/earnings ratio of Teletalk may not fall after the merger. Suppose the price/earnings ratio of Teletalk remains equal to 25. Since the combined firm has earnings of $200, the total value of the combined firm will increase to $5,000 (25 × $200). The per-share value for Teletalk will increase to $35.71 ($5,000/140).

This is earnings growth magic. Like all good magic, it is just illusion. For it to work, the shareholders of Teletalk and Music must receive something for nothing. This, of course, is unlikely with so simple a trick.

	Teletalk Resources before merger	Music Enterprises before merger	Teletalk Resources after merger	
Financial positions of Teletalk Resources and Music Enterprises				
			The market is 'smart'	The market is 'fooled'
Earnings per share	$1.00	$1.00	$1.43	$1.43
Price per share	$25.00	$10.00	$25.00	$35.71
				(continued)

TABLE 22.2

TABLE 22.2

Financial positions of Teletalk Resources and Music Enterprises (*continued*)

	Teletalk Resources before merger	Music Enterprises before merger	Teletalk Resources after merger	
			The market is 'smart'	The market is 'fooled'
Price/earnings ratio	25	10	17.5	25
Number of shares	100	100	140	140
Total earnings	$100	$100	$200	$200
Total value	$2,500	$1,000	$3,500	$5,000

Diversification

Diversification is commonly mentioned as a benefit to a merger. The problem is that diversification *per se* does not create value.

Going back to Chapter 11, diversification reduces unsystematic risk. We also saw that the value of an asset depends on its systematic risk, and systematic risk is not directly affected by diversification. It is very easy for shareholders to reduce their exposure to unsystematic risk. All they have to do is buy shares across a range of different companies. It is much more difficult for companies to reduce their exposure to unsystematic risk. The companies would have to spread their operations into several different types of project. As it is easier and less expensive for shareholders to reduce unsystematic risk, it is not likely that they would attach any value to companies that actively pursued the reduction of unsystematic risk. Therefore unsystematic risk is not especially important from the perspective of the company and there is no particular benefit in reducing it.

An easy way to see why diversification is not an important benefit to merger is to consider the Adelaide Steamship Company Limited (Adsteam) offer for Industrial Equity Limited (IEL) in June 1990. Adsteam, through Dextran Pty Limited, bid for the outstanding shares in IEL by giving accepting shareholders the opportunity of using cash received from the bid to buy shares held by Adsteam in an associated company, Tooths and Co Limited, a brewery. Consider shareholders who held shares in Adsteam, IEL and Tooths. The merger would have in fact reduced their diversification. *The important issue is that the purchase of IEL did not do anything the shareholders could not do themselves.* Similarly in 1984, when the Broken Hill Proprietary Company (BHP) made an offer for Umal Consolidated Limited, BHP offered as consideration units in a new unit trust called Queensland Coal Trust (QCT). QCT was freely traded in the market so nothing extra was being given to shareholders.

Shareholders can get all the diversification they want by buying shares in different companies. As a result, they will not pay a premium for a merged company just for the benefit of diversification. It is more expensive for one company to buy another than it is for shareholders to purchase shares in the company.

Concept questions

22.5a *Why can a merger create the appearance of earnings growth?*
22.5b *Why is diversification by itself not a good reason for a merger?*

22.6 ▪ The cost of an acquisition

We have discussed some of the benefits of acquisition. We now need to discuss the cost of a merger.[4] We learned earlier that the net incremental gain to a merger is:

$$\Delta V = V_{AB} - (V_A - V_B)$$

Also, the total value of Firm B to Firm A, $V_B{}^*$, is:

$$V_B{}^* = V_B + \Delta V$$

The NPV of the merger is therefore:

$$\textbf{NPV} = V_B{}^* - \textbf{Cost to Firm A of the acquisition} \qquad (22.1)$$

To illustrate, suppose we have the following pre-merger information for Firm A and Firm B:

	Firm A	Firm B
Price per share	$ 20	$ 10
Number of shares	25	10
Total market value	$500	$100

Both of these firms are 100 per cent equity. You estimate that the incremental value of the acquisition, ΔV, is $100.

The board of Firm B has indicated that it will agree to a sale if the price is $150, payable in cash or shares. This price for Firm B has two parts. Firm B is worth $100 as a stand-alone, so this is the minimum value that we could assign to Firm B. The second part, $50, is called the merger premium, and it represents the amount paid above the stand-alone value.

Should Firm A acquire Firm B? Should it pay in cash or shares? To answer, we need to determine the NPV of the acquisition under both alternatives. We can start by noting that the value of Firm B to Firm A is:

$$V_B{}^* = \Delta V + V_B$$
$$= \$100 + 100 = \$200$$

The total value received by A from buying Firm B is thus $200. The question then is: How much does Firm A have to give up? The answer depends on whether cash or shares are used as the means of payment.

Case I: Cash acquisition

The cost of an acquisition when cash is used is just the cash itself. So, if Firm A pays $150 in cash to purchase all of the shares of Firm B, the cost of acquiring Firm B is $150. The NPV of a cash acquisition is:

$$\text{NPV} = V_B{}^* - \text{Cost}$$
$$= \$200 - 150 = \$50$$

The acquisition is therefore profitable.

After the merger, Firm AB will still have 25 shares outstanding. The value of Firm A after the merger is:

$$
\begin{aligned}
V_{AB} &= V_A + (V_B^* - \text{Cost}) \\
&= \$500 + 200 - 150 \\
&= \$550
\end{aligned}
$$

This is just the pre-merger value of $500 plus the $50 NPV. The price per share after the merger is $550/25 = $22, a gain of $2 per share.

Case II: Share acquisition

Things are somewhat more complicated when shares are the means of payment. In a cash merger, the shareholders in B receive cash for their shares, and they no longer participate in the company. Thus, as we have seen, the cost of the acquisition in this case is the amount of cash needed to pay off B's shareholders.

In a share merger, no cash actually changes hands. Instead, the shareholders in B come in as new shareholders in the merged firm. The value of the merged firm in this case will be equal to the pre-merger values of Firms A and B plus the incremental gain from the merger, ΔV:

$$
\begin{aligned}
V_{AB} &= V_A + V_B + \Delta V \\
&= \$500 + 100 + 100 \\
&= \$700
\end{aligned}
$$

To give $150 worth of shares for Firm B, Firm A will have to give up $150/$20 = 7.5 shares. After the merger, there will thus be 25 + 7.5 = 32.5 shares outstanding and the per-share value will be $700/32.5 = $21.54.

Notice that the per-share price after the merger is lower under the share purchase option. This has to do with the fact that B's shareholders own shares in the new firm.

It appears that Firm A paid $150 for Firm B. However, they actually paid more than that. When all is said and done, B's shareholders own 7.5 shares in the merged firm. After the merger, each of these shares is worth $21.54. The total value of the consideration received by B's shareholders is thus 7.5 × $21.54 = $161.55.

This $161.55 is the true cost of the acquisition since it is what the sellers actually end up receiving. The NPV of the merger to Firm A is:

$$
\begin{aligned}
\text{NPV} &= V_B^* - \text{Cost} \\
&= \$200 - 161.55 \\
&= \$38.45
\end{aligned}
$$

We can check this by noting that A started with 25 shares worth $20 each. The gain to A of $38.45 works out to be $38.45/25 = $1.54 per share. The value of the shares increases to $21.54 as we calculated.

When we compare the cash acquisition to the share acquisition, we see that the cash acquisition is better in this case, because Firm A gets to keep all of the NPV if it pays in cash. If it pays in shares, Firm B's shareholders share in the NPV by becoming new shareholders in A.

Of course Firm A could have protected its position by settling in terms of the value of shares after the merger. This approach would entitle Firm B shareholders to $150/$21.54 = 6.96 shares. This would leave more of the NPV of the merger to Firm A:

$$NPV = V_B^* - \text{Cost}$$
$$= \$200 - 6.96 \text{ shares} \times \$21.54$$
$$= \$50.00$$

It is questionable whether Firm B shareholders would accept an after-merger price.

Cash versus shares

The distinction between cash and share financing in a merger is an important one. If cash is used, the cost of an acquisition is not dependent on the acquisition gains. If shares are used, the cost may be higher because Firm A's shareholders may have to share the acquisition gains with the shareholders of Firm B. However, if the NPV of the acquisition is negative, then the loss will be shared between the two firms.

Whether to finance an acquisition by cash or by shares depends on several factors, including:

1 *Sharing gains*. If cash is used to finance an acquisition, the selling firm's shareholders will not participate in the potential gains of the merger. Of course, if the acquisition is not a success, the losses will not be shared, and shareholders of the acquiring firm will be worse off than if shares were used.
2 *Control*. Acquisition by cash does not affect the control of the acquiring firm. Acquisition with voting shares may have implications for control of the merged firm.

Concept questions

22.6a *Why does the true cost of a share acquisition depend on the gain from the merger?*
22.6b *What are some important factors in deciding whether to use shares or cash in an acquisition?*

22.7 ■ Defensive tactics

Target firm managers frequently resist takeover attempts. Resistance usually starts with press releases and mailings to shareholders that present management's viewpoint. It can eventually lead to legal action and solicitation of competing bids. Managerial action to defeat a takeover attempt may make target shareholders better off if it elicits a higher offer premium from the bidding firm or another firm.

Of course, management resistance may simply reflect pursuit of self-interest at the expense of shareholders. This is a controversial subject. At times, management resistance has greatly increased the amount ultimately received by shareholders. At other times, management resistance appears to have defeated all takeover attempts to the detriment of shareholders.

In this section, we describe various defensive tactics that have been used by target firms' managements to resist unfriendly attempts. The law surrounding these defences is not settled, and some of these manoeuvres may ultimately be deemed illegal or otherwise unsuitable.

Friendly shareholders

Under the Australian legal system the interests of shareholders are paramount. In practical terms it is the shareholders of the target company who are the main players in determining whether a takeover will succeed. Therefore, for a company to prevent a takeover it must have 'friendly' shareholders.

Employees

Companies seek shareholders among their employees and employee share schemes have become common. Employees are seen as a loyal group of shareholders with a long-term firm outlook. An employee share purchase plan has the added advantage of providing a base for productivity gains from employees. For example, in the case of Lend Lease, its large employee shareholdings are both a takeover defence and an embodiment of the philosophy of worker participation.

Superannuation funds

The superannuation fund of the firm can be a source of loyal shareholding. In a takeover situation the duty of the trustee is confined to serving the interests of fund members from both an investment and a job security perspective. This was a major stumbling block when the Bond Group bid for the then Waltons Limited. The only asset in Waltons' superannuation fund was a 20 per cent holding in Waltons Limited, which prevented the takeover. These types of investments by superannuation funds are now limited by a 10 per cent in-house asset rule.

Poison pills and share rights plans

poison pill
a financial device designed to make unfriendly takeover attempts unappealing, if not impossible

A **poison pill** is a tactic designed to repel would-be suitors. The term comes from the world of espionage. Agents are supposed to bite a pill of cyanide rather than permit capture. Presumably, this prevents enemy interrogators from learning important secrets.

In the equally colourful world of corporate finance, a poison pill is a financial device designed to make it impossible for a firm to be acquired without management's consent—unless the buyer is willing to commit financial suicide. Poison pill plans tend to include arrangements on special classes of shares or share rights plans or convertible notes.

It has already been pointed out that the existence of convertible notes made the Smorgon takeover of Humes Limited more difficult. In the attempted takeover of Ampol Limited by Pioneer Concrete Services Limited, it was the presence of preference shares that made the takeover less attractive. Special classes of shares or **share rights plans (SRPs)** are becoming more popular as takeover defence mechanisms.

share rights plan (SRP)
provisions allowing existing shareholders to purchase shares at some fixed price should an outside takeover bid take place, discouraging hostile takeover attempts

SRPs differ quite a bit in detail from company to company; we will describe a kind of generic approach here. In general, when a company adopts an SRP, it distributes share rights to its existing shareholders.[5] These rights allow shareholders to buy shares (or preference shares) at some fixed price.

The rights issued with an SRP have a number of unusual features. First, the exercise or subscription price on the right is usually set high enough such that the rights are well out of the money, meaning that the purchase price is much higher than the current share price. The rights will often be good for 10 years, and the purchase or exercise price is usually a reasonable estimate of what the share will be worth at that time.

In addition, unlike ordinary share rights, these rights cannot be exercised immediately, and they cannot be bought and sold separately from the share. Also, they can essentially be cancelled by management at any time; often, they can be redeemed (bought back) for a cent each, or some similarly trivial amount.

Things get interesting when, under certain circumstances, the rights are 'triggered'. This means that the rights become exercisable, they can be bought and sold separately from the share, and they are not easily cancelled or redeemed. Typically, the rights will be triggered when someone acquires 20 per cent of the ordinary shares or otherwise makes an on-market announcement.

When the rights are triggered, they can be exercised. Since they are out of the money, this fact is not especially important. Certain other features come into play, however. The most important is the *flip-over provision*.

The flip-over provision is the 'poison' in the pill. In the event of a merger, the holder of a right can pay the exercise price and receive ordinary shares in the merged firm worth twice the exercise price. In other words, holders of the right can buy shares in the merged firm at half price.

The rights issued in connection with an SRP are poison pills because anyone trying to force a merger would trigger the rights. When this happens, all the target firm's shareholders can effectively buy shares in the merged firm at half price. This greatly increases the cost of the merger to the bidder because the target firm's shareholders end up with a much larger percentage of the merged firm.

Notice that the flip-over provision does not prevent someone from acquiring control of a firm by purchasing a majority interest. It just acts to prevent a complete merger of the two firms. Even so, this inability to combine can have serious tax and other implications for the buyer.

The intention of a poison pill is to force a bidder to negotiate with management. Frequently, merger offers are made with the contingency that the rights are cancelled by the target firm.

Going private and leveraged buyouts

As we have previously discussed, going private refers to what happens when the publicly owned shares in a firm are replaced with complete equity ownership by a private group, which may include elements of existing management. As a consequence, the firm's share is taken off the market (if it is an exchange-traded share, it is delisted) and is no longer traded.

One result of going private is that takeovers via on-market announcements can no longer occur since there are no publicly held shares. In this sense, an LBO (or, more specifically, an MBO) can be a takeover defence. However, it is only a defence for management. From the shareholders' point of view, an LBO is a takeover because they are bought out.

Other devices and jargon of corporate takeovers

As corporate takeovers have become more common, a colourful new vocabulary has developed. Some of the terms are listed here, in no particular order:

1 *Golden parachutes*. Some target firms provide compensation to top-level management if a takeover occurs. Depending on your perspective and the amounts involved, this can be viewed as a payment to management to make it less concerned for its own welfare and more interested in shareholders when considering a takeover bid.
2 *Poison puts*. A poison put is a variation on the poison pill we described above. A poison put forces the firm to buy securities back at some set price.
3 *Crown jewels*. Firms often sell or threaten to sell major assets—crown jewels—when faced with a takeover threat. This is sometimes referred to as the 'scorched earth' strategy. This tactic often involves a lockup, which we discuss below.
4 *White knights*. A firm facing an unfriendly merger offer might arrange to be acquired by a different, friendly firm. The firm is rescued by a white knight. Alternatively, the firm may arrange for a friendly entity to acquire a large block of shares. So-called white squires or big brothers are individuals, firms or even mutual funds involved in friendly transactions of these types. Sometimes white knights or others are granted exceptional terms or otherwise compensated. This has recently been called whitemail. Refer to the Grace Brothers/Myer takeover discussed earlier.

5 *Lockups*. A lockup is an option granted to a friendly suitor (a white knight, perhaps) giving them the right to purchase shares or some of the assets (the crown jewels, possibly) of a target firm at a fixed price in the event of an unfriendly takeover.

6 *Shark repellent*. A shark repellent is any tactic (a poison pill, for example) designed to discourage unwanted merger offers.

Concept questions

22.7a *What can a firm do to make a takeover less likely?*

22.7b *What is a share rights plan? Explain how the rights work.*

Some evidence on acquisitions

One of the most controversial issues is whether mergers and acquisitions benefit shareholders. Several studies have attempted to estimate the effect of mergers and takeovers on the share prices of the bidding and target firms. These studies have examined the gains and losses in share value around the time of merger announcements.

Table 22.3 summarises the results of an Australian study that looks at the effects of takeovers. It shows that the shareholders of target companies in successful takeovers gain substantially. The average abnormal gains over the period of the study to the target firms' shareholders was 25.5 per cent. These gains are a reflection of the merger premium that is typically paid by the acquiring firm. These gains are excess returns; that is, the returns over and above what the shareholders would normally have earned. It is interesting to note that the bid premiums have been declining over time. It may be that impediments to takeovers make it more difficult for investors to gain and this is reflected in the premium.

Returns to participants in successful corporate takeovers		
	Abnormal returns	
	Target	Bidder
7 months around the takeover	25.5%	5%

Source: Based on research conducted and reported by Brown, P. and da Silva Rosa, R. in 'Takeovers: who wins?', *JASSA*, Issue 4, Summer 1997, pp. 2–6.

The shareholders of bidding firms do not fare nearly so well. According to the study summarised in Table 22.3, bidders experience gains of 5 per cent in takeovers. These numbers are sufficiently small to leave doubt about the precise effect on bidders, but note that they have performed very well prior to the offer. It appears that firms that are performing well enter the takeover market to build on their performance.

Why should the shareholders of bidding firms earn comparatively little from takeovers? Some studies have found that the acquiring firms actually lose value in many mergers. These findings are a puzzle, and there are a variety of explanations:

1 Anticipated merger gains may not have been completely achieved, and shareholders thus experienced losses. This can happen if managers of bidding firms tend to overestimate the gains from acquisition.

2   The bidding firms are usually much larger than the target firms. Thus, even though the dollar gains to the bidder may be similar to the dollar gains earned by shareholders of the target firm, the percentage gains will be much lower.

3   Another possible explanation for the low returns to the shareholders of bidding firms in takeovers is simply that management may not be acting in the interest of shareholders when it attempts to acquire other firms. Perhaps it is attempting to increase the size of the firm, even if this reduces its value per share.

4   The market for takeovers may be sufficiently competitive that the NPV of acquiring is zero because the prices paid in acquisitions fully reflect the value of the acquired firms. In other words, the sellers capture all of the gain.

5   Finally, the announcement of a takeover may not convey much new information to the market about the bidding firm. This can occur because firms frequently announce intentions to engage in merger 'programs' long before they announce specific acquisitions. In this case, the share price in the bidding firm may already reflect anticipated gains from mergers.

Concept questions

22.8a *What does the evidence say about the benefits of mergers and acquisitions to target company shareholders?*

22.8b *What does the evidence say about the benefits of mergers and acquisitions to acquiring company shareholders?*

22.9 ■ Summary and conclusions

This chapter introduced you to the extensive literature on mergers and acquisitions. We touched on a number of issues, including:

1 *Form of merger.* One firm can acquire another in several different ways. The three legal forms of acquisition are: merger and consolidation; acquisition of shares; and acquisition of assets.

2 *Tax issues.* Sellers under mergers and acquisitions will have to pay capital gains tax even if the consideration is shares. Where the ability to take advantage of tax losses in the target firm is a consideration, the bidder must have sufficient control to group the accounts. Accumulated profits on which taxation has been paid will provide a base for franked dividends on which tax imputation credits may be claimed.

3 *Accounting issues.* Australian standards require the purchase method of accounting for mergers and acquisition. Where companies are defined as being associated (the investor holds 20%), equity accounting has to be used. The method of accounting does not affect the after-tax cash flows of the combined firm unless depreciation deductions on assets are changed. The method of goodwill valuation may influence the level of reported accounting profit. While this may be considered important in terms of performance evaluation by managers, it will not affect the value of the firm.

4 *Merger valuation.* If Firm A is acquiring Firm B, the benefits (ΔV) from an acquisition are defined as the value of the combined firm (V_{AB}) less the value of the firms as separate entities (V_A and V_B), or:

$$\Delta V = V_{AB} - (V_A + V_B)$$

The gain to Firm A from acquiring Firm B is the increased value of the acquired firm (ΔV) plus the value of B as a separate firm. The total value of Firm B to Firm A, $V_B{}^*$, is thus:

$$V_B{}^* = \Delta V + V_B$$

An acquisition will benefit the shareholders of the acquiring firm if this value is greater than the cost of the acquisition.

The cost of an acquisition can be defined in general terms as the price paid to the shareholders of the acquired firm. The cost frequently includes a merger premium paid to the shareholders of the acquired firm.

5 The potential benefits of an acquisition come from several possible sources, including the following:

   a Revenue enhancement
   b Cost reduction
   c Lower taxes
   d Changing capital requirements

6 Some of the most colourful language of finance comes from defensive tactics in acquisition battles. Poison pills, golden parachutes and crown jewels are terms that describe various anti-takeover tactics.

7 Mergers and acquisitions have been extensively studied. The basic conclusions are that, on average, the shareholders of target firms do very well, while the shareholders of bidding firms do not appear to gain very much.

Key terms

Suggested readings

A readable book on how to quantify the value from mergers and acquisitions is:

Rappaport, A. *Creating Shareholder Value: The New Standard for Business Performance*, The Free Press, New York, 1986, Chapter 9.

Some good articles on mergers and acquisitions appear in:

Stern, J.M. and Chew, D.H. (eds) *The Revolution in Corporate Finance*, Basil Blackwell, New York, 1986.

For Australian research into takeovers, see:

Bishop, S., Dodd, P. and Officer, R.R. 'Australian Takeovers: The Evidence 1972–1985', *Policy Monograph 12*, Centre For Independent Studies, St Leonards, 1987.

Brown, P. and da Silva Rosa, R. 'Takeovers: who wins?', *JASSA*, Issue 4, Summer 1997, pp. 2–6.

Endnotes

1 A synergistic benefit might occur when a flour mill purchases wheat farms and bakeries, thus ensuring supply of ingredients and demand for its product. The value of the flour mill with wheat farms and bakeries is more valuable than the flour mill, the wheat farms and the bakeries separately.

2 Control may be defined as having a majority vote on the board of directors.

3 This has been the belief in Australia, as most acquisitions have resulted in premiums being paid on current market prices. The average premium paid in Australia for the 10 years to November 1995 has been about 20 per cent. This means that if a share is trading at $1.00, the offeror pays $1.20, on average, to purchase the shares.

4 For a more complete discussion of the costs of a merger and the NPV approach, see Myers, S.C. 'A Framework for Evaluating Mergers', in S.C. Myers (ed.) *Modern Developments in Financial Management*, Praeger Publishers, New York, 1976.

5 We discuss ordinary share rights in Chapter 16.

On the web

Taxation issues may be explored (have fun!) at: **http://www.ato.gov.au**

The Australian Stock Exchange can offer more information:

http://www.asx.com.au

So can the Australian Securities and Investments Commission:

http://www.asic.gov.au

Maximise Your Marks!

There are 30 interactive questions on mergers, acquisitions and takeovers waiting online for you at www.mhhe.com/au/ross3e. The questions are written with additional feedback for incorrect answers, and text excerpts with page references for follow-up study.

International Articles!

To read more on mergers, acquisitions and takeovers and to see current international articles, just go to www.mhhe.com/au/ross3e and click on *PowerWeb Articles* for this chapter.

22.1 · **Merger value and cost**

Consider the following information for two all-equity firms, Close and Shave:

	Close	Shave
Shares outstanding	1,000	500
Price per share	$5	$3

Close estimates that the value of the synergistic benefit from acquiring Shave is $200. Shave has indicated that it would accept a cash purchase offer of $3.50 per share. Should Close proceed?

22.2 · **Merger and EPS**

Consider the following information for two all-equity firms, Honey and Moon:

	Honey	Moon
Total earnings	$1,000	$400
Shares outstanding	1,000	800
Price per share	$8.00	$2.50

Honey is acquiring Moon by exchanging 250 of its shares for all the shares in Moon. What is the cost of the merger if the merged firm is worth $11,000? What will happen to Honey's EPS? Its P/E ratio?

Answers to self-test problems

22.1 · The total value of Shave to Close is the pre-merger value of Shave plus the $200 gain from the merger. The pre-merger value of Shave is $3 × 500 = $1,500, so the total value is $1,700. At $3.50 per share, Close is paying $3.50 × 500 = $1,750; the merger therefore has a negative NPV of −$50. At $3.50 per share, Shave is not an attractive merger partner.

22.2 · After the merger, the firm will have 1,250 shares outstanding. Since the total value is $11,000, the price per share is $11,000/1,250 = $8.80, up from $8. Since Firm Moon's shareholders end up with 250 shares in the merged firm, the cost of the merger is 250 × $8.80 = $2,200, not 250 × 8 = $2,000.

Also, the combined firm will have $1,000 + 400 = $1,400 in earnings, so EPS will be $1,400/1,250 = $1.12, up from $1,000/1,000 = $1. The old P/E ratio was $8/$1 = 8. The new one is $8.8/1.12 = 7.86.

Questions and problems

1 · Calculating synergy

Slap Manufacturing has offered $21.5 million cash for all the ordinary shares in Tickle Distribution Pty Ltd. Based on recent market information, Tickle Distribution is worth $16 million as an independent operation. If the merger makes economic sense for Slap, what is the minimum estimated value of the synergistic benefits from the merger?

2 · Cash versus shares as payment

Consider the following information about a bidding firm (Black) and a target firm (Board). Assume that both firms have no debt outstanding.

	Black	Board
Shares outstanding	100	40
Price per share	$20	$10

Black has estimated that the value of the synergistic benefits from acquiring Board is $160.

a   If Board is willing to be acquired for $12 per share, cash, what is the NPV of the merger?
b   What will the price per share be after the merger?
c   In part (a), what is the merger premium?
d   Suppose Board is agreeable to a merger by share exchange. If Black swaps one of its shares for every 2 shares in Board, what is the NPV of the merger?
e   What will the price per share be after the merger in part (d)?
f   In part (d), explain why the cost that Black is paying to acquire Board is greater than $10 per share.

3 · Mergers and taxes

What is the basic determinant of tax status in a merger? Would an LBO enable the new owners to use tax losses? Explain.

4 · Effects of a share exchange

Consider the following pre-merger information about two firms, Block and Head:

	Block	Head
Total earnings	$1,600	$600
Shares outstanding	1,000	400
Price per share	$32.00	$6.00

Assume that Block acquires Head via a share exchange at a price of $8 per share for each share of Head. Both firms are all equity.

a   What will happen to the earnings per share for Block?
b   What will the price per share be in the new firm if the market is fooled by this earnings growth (meaning that the price/earnings ratio does not change)?
c   What will the price/earnings ratio be if the market is not fooled?

5 · Economies of scale and mergers

What are economies of scale? Suppose that Maroon Power and Blue Power are located in different time zones. Both of them operate at 60 per cent of capacity except for peak periods when they operate at 100 per cent of capacity. The peak periods occur at 9.00 am and 5.00 pm, local time, and last about 45 minutes. Explain why a merger might make sense.

6 · Cash versus shares as payment

Screen Gems Pty Ltd is analysing the possible acquisition of Blank Tapes Ltd. Both firms have no debt. The forecast of Screen Gems shows that the purchase would increase its annual total after-tax cash flow by $800,000 indefinitely. The current market value of Blank Tapes is $10 million, and that of Screen Gems is $17.5 million. The appropriate discount rate for the incremental cash flows is 8 per cent.

Screen Gems is trying to decide whether it should offer 17.5 per cent of its shares or $12.5 million in cash to Blank Tapes.

a   What is the cost of each alternative?
b   What is the NPV of each alternative?
c   Which alternative should Screen Gems use?

7 · EPS, P/E and mergers

Home Insurance Ltd has voted in favour of being bought out by Big Bank Corporation Ltd. Information about each company is as shown:

	Big Bank	Home Insurance
Price/earnings ratio	16	10.8
Number of shares	100,000	50,000
Earnings	$225,000	$100,000

Shareholders in Home Insurance will receive six shares of Big Bank for every 10 shares they hold in their company.

a   How will the EPS change for these two groups of shareholders?

b   What will the effect of changes in the EPS be on the original Big Bank shareholders?

8 · Calculating NPV

This is a moderate challenge problem. Measure Hardware Ltd is considering making an offer to purchase Cement Industries Ltd. The financial manager has collected the following information:

	Measure	Cement
Price/earnings ratio	16	12
Number of shares	10,000,000	2,500,000
Earnings	$1,000,000	$750,000

She also knows that securities analysts expect the earnings and dividends (currently $0.18 per share) of Cement to grow at a constant rate of 5 per cent each year. Her research tells her, however, that the acquisition would provide Cement with some economies of scale that would improve this growth rate to 7 per cent per year.

a   What is the value of Cement to Measure?

b   What would Measure's gain be from this acquisition?

c   If Measure offers $4.00 in cash for each outstanding share of Cement, what would the NPV of the acquisition be?

d   If, instead, Measure were to offer 6,000,000 of its shares in exchange for the outstanding shares of Cement, what would the NPV be?

e   Should the acquisition be attempted, and, if so, should it be a cash or share offer?

f   Measure's management thinks that 7 per cent growth is too optimistic and that 6 per cent is more realistic. How does this change your previous answers?

9 · Merger NPV

This is a moderate challenge question. Show that the NPV of a merger can be expressed as the value of the synergistic benefits, ΔV, less the merger premium.

10 · Merger NPV

This is a challenge question. Common Ltd has a beta of 0.875. It has also been determined that the beta of equity in Common Ltd is 1.25. The ratio of its debt to equity is 3 when both are expressed as market values and 10 when they are expressed in book values. Common Ltd intends to take over People Ltd which has a beta of 0.6. People has issued no debt and the market value of its equity is twice that of the market value of Common's equity.

a   What is the beta of Common Ltd debt?

b   What is the beta of Common Ltd after it has taken over People Ltd?

c   If the beta of the debt of Common Ltd does not change after the takeover, what is the beta of equity after the takeover?

d   As a result of your answer to (c), what would you expect to happen to the return on the equity of Common as a result of the takeover?

e   As a shareholder of Common, would you desire the takeover to progress?

11 · Calculating the takeover interest rate

Interest rates have decreased in recent times so that the return on government securities is 3 per cent and the expected return on the market is 8 per cent. Prime Industries is looking at taking over Paul T Pty Ltd. Prime's capital structure is 60 per cent equity and 40 per cent debt so that the WACC is 10 per cent. Paul T has only 20 per cent debt so its WACC is 12 per cent. Prime and Paul T operate in the same industry with almost identical income earning activities however the total asset value of Prime is $20 million and Paul T is

$5 million. The beta for their industry has been estimated as 1.5. There is unlikely to be any synergy in the takeover and the combined firm's value would equal the value of Prime plus the value of Paul T.

a   What are the cost of debt and the cost of equity for Prime and Paul T?
b   If Prime takes over Paul T and changes the entire firm to its capital structure, how much debt and equity will the combined firm have?
c   What is the WACC of the combined firm if the cost of issuing the additional debt does not increase the current cost of debt?
d   What is the WACC of the combined firm if the cost of issuing the additional debt does increase the current average cost of debt by 2 per cent?
e   What rate should Prime use to evaluate whether it should proceed with the takeover of Paul T?

12 · Merge or not

Consider the following information for two all-equity firms, Dust and Bull:

	Dust	Bull
Shares outstanding	2,000	6,000
Price per share	$40	$30

Dust estimates that the value of the synergistic benefit from acquiring Bull is $6,000. Bull directors advise they would accept a cash purchase offer of $35 per share. Should Dust proceed?

13 · Share mergers and EPS

Consider the following information for two all-equity firms, Abel and Tasman:

	Abel	Tasman
Shares outstanding	600	400
Price per share	$70	$15
Total earnings	$3,000	$1,100

Abel is acquiring Tasman by exchanging 100 of its shares for all the shares in Tasman.

a   What is the cost of the merger if the combined firm is worth $63,000?
b   What will happen to Abel's EPS?
c   What will happen to Abel's P/E ratio?

CHAPTER 23

International
corporate finance

Objective

The aim of this chapter is to:

1. explain how exchange rates are quoted in the financial press;
2. explain the concept of currency arbitrage;
3. explain how interest rates and inflation rates influence exchange rate determination;
4. discuss interest rate parity and the international Fisher effect;
5. explain the relationship between spot rates and forward rates;
6. extend the principles of capital budgeting to the international scene; and
7. identify and analyse exchange rate risk.

Study tips ▷ The trick with international transactions is to watch how the exchange is quoted. For example, to state that the exchange rate for Australian dollars into United States dollars is 0.6081 is the same as claiming that one United States dollar will purchase 1.6445 Australian dollars. To convert US dollars into Australian dollars we could take:

$US100 × 1.6445 = $A164.45

or $US100/0.6081 = $A164.45.

It is not correct to multiply by 0.6081 or divide by 1.6445 because the United States dollars will give more Australian dollars and not less.

Note that you will find some rounding differences in the examples when one currency is converted into another. This is because the quoted exchange rates are truncated to four decimal places.

Introduction ▷ Corporations with significant foreign operations are often called international corporations or multinationals. Such corporations must consider many financial factors that do not directly affect purely domestic firms. These include foreign exchange rates, differing interest rates from country to country, complex accounting methods for foreign operations, foreign tax rates, and foreign government intervention.

The basic principles of corporate finance still apply to international corporations; like domestic companies, they seek to invest in projects that create more value for the shareholders than they cost and to arrange financing that raises cash at the lowest possible cost. In other words, the net present value principle holds for both foreign and domestic operations, but it is usually more complicated to apply the NPV rule to foreign investments.

One of the most significant complications of international finance is foreign exchange. The foreign exchange markets provide important information and opportunities for an international corporation when it undertakes capital budgeting and financing decisions. As we will discuss, international exchange rates, interest rates and inflation rates are closely related. We will spend much of this chapter exploring the connection between these financial variables.

We will not have much to say here about the role of cultural and social differences in international business. We also will not be discussing the implications of differing political and economic systems. These factors are of great importance to international businesses, but it would take another book to do them justice. Consequently, we will focus on some purely financial considerations in international finance and some key aspects of foreign exchange markets.

▮23.1▮ Terminology

A common buzzword in business finance is *globalisation*. The first step in learning about the globalisation of financial markets is to conquer the new vocabulary. As with any speciality, international finance is rich in jargon. Accordingly, we get started on the subject with a highly eclectic vocabulary exercise.

The terms that follow are presented alphabetically, and they are not all of equal importance. We chose these particular ones because they appear frequently in the financial press or because they illustrate some of the colourful language of international finance.

1 *Appreciation*. The rise in the value of a currency in terms of another currency or currencies.

2 *Arbitrage*. The simultaneous buying and selling of currencies to realise profits from anomalies between exchange rates prevailing at the same time in different markets.

3 *Authorised foreign exchange dealers*. Organisations granted a general authority to buy and sell foreign currency pursuant to regulation 38A of the *Banking (Foreign Exchange) Regulations*.

4 *AUD (buying) rate*. The Australian dollar exchange rate at which a bank is willing to buy a currency in exchange for another.

5 *Business day*. A day on which banks are open for business in the countries of both the currencies being exchanged. In Australia, if either Sydney or Melbourne is closed then the delivery date will be the next date when banks in both centres are open for business.

6 *Carded rates*. For small foreign exchange transactions, exchange rates quoted by banks each day and usually listed on a daily exchange rate sheet.

7 *Clean (or settlement) risk*. The exposure of one party to another on the value date of the contract. It is the risk that one party, having received settlement of one currency amount from the counterparty, is unable to effect settlement of the other currency amount.

8 *Correspondent bank*. A bank that, in its own country, handles the banking for banks from another country.

cross rates

exchange rates between two currencies derived from the exchange rates between the currencies and a third currency

9 *Cross rates*. The **cross rate** is the implicit exchange rate between two currencies when both are quoted in some third currency, usually the US dollar.

10 *Depreciation*. The fall in value of a currency in terms of another currency or currencies.

11 *Direct quotation*. In recent times, the US dollar has been the largest traded currency. An exchange rate quotation in which the US dollar is the base currency and the local currency is the quote currency is a direct quote. For example, USD1 = AUD1.4286.

12 *Discount*. The amount by which a currency is cheaper for future delivery. This will occur when the interest rates of the currency in question are greater than the interest rates of the other currency.

euro

the monetary unit for the European Monetary System (EMS)

13 *Euro*. On 1 January 1999 the **euro** was introduced. Twelve European nations, accounting for more than 20 per cent of the world GDP, now use this currency. Euro bank notes began to circulate in 2002.

eurobond

international bonds issued in multiple countries but denominated in a single currency (usually the issuer's home currency)

14 *Eurobond*. A **eurobond** is a bond issued in multiple countries, but denominated in a single currency, usually the issuer's home currency. Such bonds have become an important way to raise capital for many international companies and governments. Eurobonds are issued outside the restrictions that apply to domestic offerings and are syndicated and traded mostly from London. Trading can and does take place anywhere there is a buyer and a seller.

15 *Eurocurrency.* **Eurocurrency** is money deposited in a financial centre outside the country whose currency is involved. For instance, eurodollars—the most widely used Eurocurrency—are US dollars deposited in banks outside the US banking system.

16 *Euromarket.* An international market for the investment of currencies outside their country of origin and free from government interference.

17 *Exchange controls.* Government regulations restricting the free exchange of the domestic currency to and from foreign currencies.

18 *Exchange rate.* The price of the currency in terms of another currency.

19 *Foreign bonds.* **Foreign bonds**, unlike eurobonds, are issued in a single country and are usually denominated in that country's currency. Often, the country in which these bonds are issued will draw distinctions between them and bonds issued by domestic issuers, including different tax laws, restrictions on the amount issued, or tougher disclosure rules. Foreign bonds are often nicknamed for the country where they are issued: Yankee bonds (United States), Samurai bonds (Japan), Rembrandt bonds (the Netherlands), and Bulldog bonds (Britain). Where do you think Kangaroo bonds are issued? Partly because of tougher regulations and disclosure requirements, the foreign-bond market has not grown in past years with the vigour of the eurobond market. A substantial portion of all foreign bonds are issued in Switzerland.

20 *Forward rate.* The exchange rate used for forward transactions. The forward rate comprises two components, the spot rate (see below) plus or minus a forward margin. The forward margin can be either at a premium or a discount to the spot rate. The size of the forward margin is determined by the interest differentials between the two currencies being exchanged relative to the term of the forward transaction.

21 *Gilts.* **Gilts** are technically British and Irish government securities, although the term also includes issues of local British authorities and some overseas public-sector offerings.

22 *Hedge contract.* A contract, either spot or forward, between AUD and USD (see below), where settlement of the contract is not effected by the delivery of the two currencies but rather where settlement, in AUD, is based on the difference between the contract rate and the hedge settlement rate on the value date.

23 *Hedge settlement rate.* A spot USD/AUD exchange rate calculated by AAP-Reuters at 9.45 am each day based on the average spot USD/AUD exchange rates, quoted by certain banks and Authorised Foreign Exchange Licensees, on the Reuters screen system at that point in time.

24 *Indirect quotation.* An exchange rate quotation in which the local currency is the base currency and the foreign currency is the quote currency; for example, in Australia an indirect quotation is AUD1 = USD0.7000.

25 *London Interbank Offer Rate (LIBOR).* The **London Interbank Offer Rate (LIBOR)** is the rate that most international banks charge one another for loans of eurodollars overnight in the London market. LIBOR is a cornerstone in the pricing of money-market issues and other short-term debt issues by both government and corporate borrowers. Interest rates are frequently quoted as some spread over LIBOR, and they then float with the LIBOR rate.

26 *Margin.* The forward premium or discount component of the outright forward rate.

27 *Non-deliverable contract.* A contract, either spot or forward, where settlement of the contract is not effected by delivery of the two currencies, but rather a settlement in one of the two currencies, based on the difference between the contract rate and the spot rate on the value date.

eurocurrency
money deposited in a financial centre outside the country whose currency is involved. For instance, eurodollars—the most widely used eurocurrency—are US dollars deposited in banks outside the US banking system

foreign bond
debt issued outside the borrower's country and denominated in the currency of the country in which it is issued

gilts
these are technically British and Irish government securities; however, they also include issues by local British authorities

London Interbank Offer Rate (LIBOR)
a commonly used reference rate, derived daily from the interest rates at which major international banks in London will lend to each other

28 *Offer (selling) rate.* The exchange rate at which a bank is willing to sell a currency in exchange for another.

29 *Points.* The last decimal place of a quotation.

30 *Premium.* The amount by which one currency is dearer for future delivery than for immediate delivery. (This will occur when the interest rates of the currency in question are less than the interest rates of the other currency.)

31 *Spot rate.* The exchange rate used for delivery of settlement two business days from the quotation date.

32 *Swap.* Two transactions on which there is a simultaneous purchase and sale of a set amount of one currency against another for two different settlement dates. There are two basic kinds of **swap**: interest rate and currency. An interest rate swap occurs when two parties exchange a floating-rate payment for a fixed-rate payment or vice versa. Currency swaps are agreements to deliver one currency in exchange for another. Often both types of swap are used in the same transaction when debt denominated in different currencies is swapped.

33 *USD.* United States dollars.

34 *Value date.* The date on which a spot or forward contract is to be delivered or settled.

swaps
agreements to the exchange of two securities or currencies

Concept questions

23.1a *What are the differences between a eurobond and a foreign bond?*

23.1b *What are eurodollars?*

Foreign exchange markets and exchange rates

foreign exchange market

the market where one country's currency is traded for another's

The **foreign exchange market** is undoubtedly the world's largest financial market. It is the market where one country's currency is traded for another's. Most of the trading takes place in a few currencies: the US dollar ($), the euro (€),the British pound sterling (£), the Japanese yen (¥) and the Swiss franc (SF). Table 23.1 lists some of the more common currencies and their symbols.

The foreign exchange market is an over-the-counter market, so there is no single location where traders get together. Instead, market participants are located in the major commercial and investment banks around the world. They communicate using computer terminals, telephones, and other telecommunications devices. For example, one communications network for foreign transactions is the Society for World-wide Interbank Financial Telecommunications (SWIFT), a Belgian not-for-profit co-operative. Using data transmission lines, a bank in Sydney can send messages to a bank in London via SWIFT regional processing centres.

International currency symbols		
Country	**Currency**	**Symbol**
Australia	dollar	$A
Brazil	cruzeiro	BRC
Canada	dollar	$Can
China	yuan	CNY
Denmark	krone	DKr

Country	Currency	Symbol
European Community	euro	€
Hong Kong	dollar	$HK
India	rupee	Rs
Indonesia	rupiah	IDR
Iran	rial	RI
Japan	yen	¥
Korea	won	KRW
Kuwait	dinar	KD
Malaysia	ringgit	MYR
Mexico	peso	Ps
New Zealand	dollar	$NZ
Norway	krone	NKr
Philippines	peso	PHP
Saudi Arabia	riyal	SR
Singapore	dollar	$S
South Africa	rand	ZAR
Sweden	krona	Skr
Switzerland	franc	SF
Thailand	baht	THB
United Kingdom	pound	£
United States	dollar	$

The many different types of participants in the foreign exchange market include the following:

1 importers who pay for goods involving foreign currencies by converting foreign exchange;
2 exporters who receive foreign currency and may want to convert to the domestic currency;
3 portfolio managers who buy or sell foreign shares and bonds;
4 foreign exchange brokers who match buy and sell orders;
5 traders who 'make a market' in foreign exchange;
6 speculators who try to profit from changes in exchange rates.

Exchange rates

An **exchange rate** is simply the price of one country's currency expressed in terms of another country's currency. In practice, almost all trading of currencies takes place in terms of the US dollar. For example, the Japanese yen and the euro are often traded with their price quoted in US dollars.

exchange rate
the price of a currency in terms of another currency

Exchange rate quotations

Table 23.2 (overleaf) reproduces exchange rate quotations as they appear in the *Australian Financial Review*. If we consider the Retail Market Quotation, we see that the Westpac Banking Corporation was buying the United States dollar ($US) at 0.6083 and selling the same currency at 0.6007 on 28 February 2003. If we were converting 1,000 Australian dollars ($A1,000) into $US we would get:

$A1,000 × 0.6007 = $US600.70

Then, if we desired to convert the $US immediately back into $A, we would get:

$$\text{\$US}600.70/0.6083 = \text{\$A}987.51$$

The difference ($12.49) between the $A1,000 we started with and the $A987.51 is the charge by the bank for completing the transactions.

TABLE 23.2

Exchange rate quotation

RETAIL MARKET
Exchange Rates

	buy/sell		buy/sell
US, dollar	0.6083/0.6007	N Zealand, dollar	1.0856/1.0626
$Aust equivalent	1.6439/1.6647	Norway, krone	4.4033/4.2794
UK, pound	0.3868/0.3777	Pakistan, rupee	On Ap/30.492
$Aust equivalent	2.5853/2.6476	Papua NG, kina	On Ap/1.8871
Europe, euro	0.5697/0.5526	Philippines, peso	On Ap/31.310
$Aust equivalent	1.7553/1.8096	Saudi Arabia, riyl	2.3156/2.2224
Brunei, dollar	1.0734/1.0192	Singapore, dollar	1.0655/1.0271
Canada, dollar	0.9149/0.8898	Solomon Is, dollar	4.4590/4.0834
Denmark, kroner	4.2263/4.1034	S. Africa, rand	4.8515/4.7069
Fiji, dollar	1.2096/1.1542	Sri Lanka, rupee	On Ap/56.37
Fr Pacific, franc	67.94/65.90	Sweden, krona	5.1749/5.0316
Hong Kong, dollar	4.7779/4.6515	Switzerland, franc	0.8288/0.8061
India, rupee	On Ap/27.290	Thailand, baht	26.71/24.46
Indonesia, rupiah	On Ap/On Ap	Tonga, pa'anga	1.3360/1.2401
Japan, yen	72.01/70.08	Vanuatu, vatu	78.37/74.41
Malaysia, ringgit	On Ap/On Ap	W Samoa, tala	1.8675/1.7062
Malta, pound	0.2436/0.2298	Gold—1 oz	579.65/596.65

* For up to A$25,000 equivalent
* Other currencies, on application
Source: Westpac Banking Corporation—February 28, 2003

Representative Rates per $A

Units	Feb 24	Feb 25	Feb 26	Feb 27	Feb 28
$US	0.5987	0.6058	0.6044	0.6073	0.6054
Yen	70.84	71.33	71.00	71.13	71.25
£Stg	0.3797	0.3818	0.3840	0.3830	0.3834
$NZ	1.0697	1.0709	1.0730	1.0730	1.0768
KRW	713.71	723.02	717.42	720.44	719.46
Euro	0.5578	0.5612	0.5622	0.5628	0.5629
CHRenm	4.9557	5.0146	5.0029	5.0269	5.0111
$T'wan	20.82	21.06	21.01	21.12	21.06
$Sing	1.0435	1.0519	1.0488	1.0529	1.0518
InRuph	5336	5395	5376	5405	5389
$HK	4.6696	4.7247	4.7137	4.7365	4.7216
MlyR	2.2751	2.3020	2.2967	2.3077	2.3005
SF	0.8194	0.8215	0.8211	0.8228	0.8233
SDR	0.4360	0.4427	0.4407	0.4436	0.4408
TWI	54.2	54.7	54.6	54.7	54.7

Source: Reserve Bank of Australia

WHOLESALE MARKET

Spot Rates	Open	Close
$A/$US	0.6051	0.6049
$A/Euro	0.5623	0.5626
$A/Yen	71.13	71.17
$A/£	0.3827	0.3831
$A/Sfranc	0.8225	0.8226
$A/$NZ	1.0766	1.0769
$A/$US range	0.6048/0.6057	
Hedge Rate		0.6054

Forward Margins
'Interbank market'

$A	buy $A/sell $A
1 month	−17/−18
2 months	−35/−36
3 months	−52/−52
4 months	−69/−70
5 months	−85/−85
6 months	−101/−101
12 months	−189/−188

Cross Rates—Major Currencies

Against	NZD	USD	£Stg	Euro	Sfranc	Yen
$NZ	1	0.5617	0.3557	0.5222	0.7639	66.098
USD	1.7803	1	0.6333	0.9297	1.3601	117.68
£Stg	2.8113	1.5791	1	1.4681	2.1477	185.82
Euro	1.9149	1.0756	0.6811	1	1.4629	126.57
Sfranc	1.3090	0.7353	0.4656	0.6836	1	86.523
Yen '000	15.129	8.4980	5.3815	9.1404	11.558	1

Eurodollar Deposit Rates—%

Month	$NZD	£Stg	USD	Euro	Sfranc	Yen
1	5.47	3.62	1.24	2.60	0.52	0.02
3	5.35	3.59	1.25	2.49	0.52	0.02
6	5.35	3.51	1.25	2.42	0.52	0.01
12	5.20	3.43	1.33	2.37	0.53	0.02

Source: Commonwealth Bank—February 28, 2003

CBA Daily Commodity Price Index

US Dollar Index	103.21	−0.67
Aust Dollar Index	126.19	−0.70

Source: Commonwealth Research—February 28, 2003

Telegraphic Transfer Buying Rate

US		Japan	
1 Month	0.5986	1 Month	68.67
3 Months	0.5952	3 Months	68.11

Source: Westpac Banking Corporation—February 28, 2003

Source: *Australian Financial Review*, 3 March 2003

Under the headings for the United States, the United Kingdom and Europe there is a quote for an '$Aust equivalent'. This item represents a direct quote of the conversion into $A. For example, converting $US600.70 to $A at the selling quote would give:

$$\text{\$US}600.70 \times 1.6647 = \text{\$A}1,000[1]$$

At the buying rate the result would be:

$$\text{\$US}600.70 \times 1.6439 = \text{\$A}987.51[2]$$

Using the buying rate a conversion into United Kingdom pounds (£) would give:

$$\$A987.51 \times 0.3868 = £381.97$$

The 'Cross rates—major currencies' section of Table 23.2 shows how one foreign currency can be converted into another foreign currency. For example, $US600.70 would convert to United Kingdom pounds sterling as:

$$\$US600.70 \times 0.6333 = £380.42$$

The cross rates must be related to the buy/sell quotes or there would be opportunities for *triangle arbitrage*. For example, suppose we observed the following:

Selling Sfranc (Swiss francs) per $A1 = 0.81
(Table 23.2 shows that 0.8061 Sfrancs would be received for $A1);

Selling euro (the currency for a number of European nations) per $A1 = 0.56
(Table 23.2 shows that 0.5526 euro would be received for $A1); and

Cross rate Sfrancs for euro = 1.50
(Table 23.2 shows 1.4629 Sfrancs would be received for 1 euro).

What do you think?

The cross rate here is inconsistent with the exchange rates. To see this, suppose you have $A100. If you convert this to euro, you will receive:

$$\$A100 \times 0.56 \text{ euro per } \$A1 = 56 \text{ euro}$$

If you convert this to Swiss francs at the cross rate, you will have:

$$56 \text{ euro} \times SF1.50 \text{ per euro} = SF84$$

However, if you just convert your dollars to francs without going through euro, you will have:

$$\$A100 \times SF0.81 \text{ per } \$A = SF81$$

What we see is that the franc has two prices, SF0.81 per $A1 and SF0.84 per $A1, depending on how we get them.

To make money, we want to buy low and sell high. The important thing to note is that we get more francs if we exchange them for euro because we get 0.84 instead of 0.81 for each original dollar. If the assumed position were to be held, we should convert dollars to francs using the following method:

1 Purchase 56 euro for $A100.
2 Use the 56 euro to buy francs at the cross rate. Since it takes one euro to buy SF1.5, we will receive SF84.
3 Use the SF84 to buy Australian dollars. If the buying exchange rate[3] is SF0.81 for $A1, you will receive SF84/0.81 = $A103.70, for a round-trip profit of $3.70.
4 Repeat steps 1 to 3 as long as the difference remains.

This particular activity is called *triangle arbitrage* because the arbitrage involves moving through three different exchange rates:

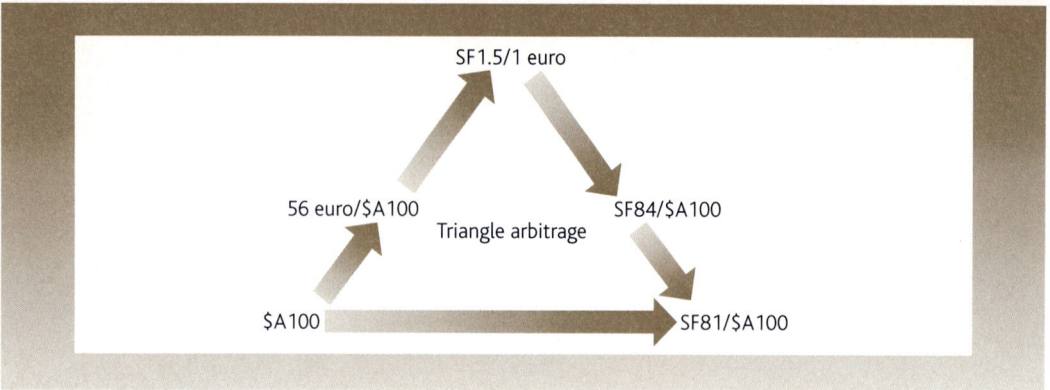

SF1.5/1 euro

56 euro/$A100

Triangle arbitrage

SF84/$A100

$A100

SF81/$A100

To prevent such opportunities, it is not difficult to see that since the dollar can be exchanged for SF0.81 or 0.56 euro, the cross rate must be:

$$(SF0.81/\$A1)/(0.56euro/\$A1) = SF1.4464/1euro$$

That is 1.4464 francs for each euro. With any other cross rate, there would be a triangle arbitrage opportunity.

Consider the information in Table 23.2 and suppose we wish to convert $1,000 into pounds sterling. We could use the bank selling exchange rate for a direct transfer of dollars into pounds as:

$$\$A1,000 \times 0.3777 = \pounds377.70$$

Alternatively we could use an indirect approach by converting into $US and using the cross rate to exchange the $US for pounds as:

$$\$1,000 \times 0.6007 = \$US600.70$$
$$\$US600.70 \times 0.6333 = \pounds380.42$$

(continued opposite)

EXAMPLE

23.1 **Shedding some pounds**

Suppose the exchange rates for the British pound and Saudi riyl are:

pounds per $A1 = 0.60
riyl per $A1 = 2.00

The official cross rate is three riyl per pound. Is this consistent? Explain how to go about making some money.

The official cross rate in the example should be 2 riyl/£0.60 = 3.33 riyl per pound. You can buy a pound for 3 riyl in one market, and you can sell a pound for 3.33 riyl in another. So we want to first get some riyl, then use the riyl to buy some pounds, and then sell the pounds. Assuming you have $A100, you could:

1 Exchange dollars for riyl: $A100 × 2 = 200 riyl
2 Exchange riyl for pounds: 200 riyl/3 = £66.67
3 Exchange pounds for dollars: £66.67/.60 = $A111.12

This would result in an $11.12 round-trip profit.

At first glance it would seem that there is scope for arbitrage here because the indirect approach yields £2.72 more (£380.42 – £377.70), but it has to be remembered that the indirect approach involves an extra conversion. Transaction charges for conversions are about 1 per cent, so that the extra conversion would use up any profit on the indirect approach.

Types of transaction

There are two basic types of deals in the foreign exchange market: spot deal and forward deals. A **spot deal** is an agreement to exchange currency 'on the spot', which actually means that the transaction will be completed or settled within two business days. The exchange rate on a spot deal is called the **spot exchange rate**. Implicitly, all of the exchange rates and transactions we have discussed so far have referred to the spot market.

Same day transactions, as the name implies, are transactions that require settlement on the day of the transaction. *Tom transactions* are transactions with settlement on the day following the day of the transaction. These are referred to as value tomorrow or 'tom' deals.

Forward exchange rates

A **forward deal** is an agreement to exchange currency at some time in the future. The exchange rate that will be used is agreed upon today and is called the **forward exchange rate**. A forward deal would normally be settled sometime in the next 12 months. However, any transaction that requires settlement in three or more business days after effecting the transaction is a forward deal.

In Table 23.2 the Swiss franc (Switzerland) was quoted at 0.8061. This is the spot exchange rate for the currency. Forward rates are not provided in the table; however, assume the 180-day forward rate was 0.7884 for Swiss francs. Notice the Swiss franc is less expensive in the forward market ($0.7884 versus $0.8061). Since the Swiss franc is less expensive in the future than it is today, it is said to be selling at a discount relative to the dollar. For the same reason, the dollar is said to be selling at a premium relative to the Swiss franc.

Why does the forward market exist? One answer is that it allows businesses and individuals to lock in a future exchange rate today, thereby eliminating any risk from unfavourable shifts in the exchange rate.

spot deal
an agreement to exchange currency within two days

spot rate
the rate for transactions for immediate delivery. In the case of foreign exchange, the spot rate is for settlement in two days

forward deal
an agreement to exchange currency in the future

forward rate
the exchange rate used for forward transactions. It comprises two components: the spot rate plus or minus a forward margin

EXAMPLE 23.3 ■ **Looking forward**

Suppose you were expecting to receive a million British pounds in six months, and you agree to a forward deal to exchange your pounds for dollars. Assuming the 180-day forward exchange rate for pounds sterling is 0.4079, how many dollars will you get in six months? Is the pound selling at a discount or a premium?

The spot exchange rate (from Table 23.2) in terms of dollars per pound is 2.5853. The forward exchange rate in terms of dollars per pound is 2.4516 (£1/0.4079). If you expect £1 million in 180 days, then you will get:

£1 million × $A2.4516 per £ = $A2.4516 million

Since it is cheaper to exchange for a pound in the forward market than in the spot market ($A2.4516 versus $A2.5853), the pound is selling at a discount relative to the dollar in the forward market.

Concept questions

23.2a *What is triangle arbitrage?*
23.2b *What do we mean by the 90-day forward exchange rate?*
23.2c *If we say that the exchange rate is € 1.90, what do we mean?*

 # 23.3 ■ Purchasing power parity

Now that we have discussed what exchange rate quotations mean, we can address an obvious question: What determines the level of the spot exchange rate? In addition, we know that exchange rates change through time. A related question is thus: What determines the rate of change in exchange rates? At least part of the answer in both cases goes by the name of **purchasing power parity (PPP)**, the idea that the exchange rate adjusts to keep purchasing power constant among currencies. As we discuss next, there are two forms of PPP, *absolute* and *relative*.

purchasing power parity (PPP)

a theory which states that the exchange rate between two currencies adjusts to reflect the relative inflation rates in the two currencies

Absolute purchasing power parity

The basic idea behind *absolute purchasing power parity* is that a commodity costs the same regardless of what currency is used to purchase it or where it is selling. This is a very straightforward concept. If a beer costs £1 in London, and the exchange rate is £0.4348 per dollar, then a beer costs £1/0.4348 = $A2.30 in Sydney. In other words, absolute PPP says that $A1 will buy you the same number of, say, cheeseburgers anywhere in the world.

More formally, let S_0 be the spot exchange rate between the British pound and the Australian dollar today (time 0), and remember that we are quoting exchange rates as the amount of foreign currency per dollar. Let P_A and P_{UK} be the current Australian and British prices, respectively, on a particular commodity, say, apples. Absolute PPP simply says that:

$$P_{UK} = S_0 \times P_A$$

This tells us that the British price for something is equal to the Australian price for that same something, multiplied by the exchange rate.

The rationale behind PPP is similar to that behind triangle arbitrage. If PPP did not hold, arbitrage would be possible (in principle) by moving apples from one country to another.

For example, suppose that apples in Sydney are selling for $4 per bushel, while in London the price is £1.525 per bushel. Absolute PPP implies that:

$$P_{UK} = S_0 \times P_A$$
$$£1.525 = S_0 \times \$A4$$
$$S_0 = £1.525/\$A4 = £0.3813$$

That is, the implied spot exchange rate is £0.3813 per $A. Equivalently, a pound is worth $1/£0.3813 = $A2.6226.

Suppose, instead, that the actual exchange rate is £0.30. Starting with $A4, a trader could buy a bushel of apples in Sydney, ship it to London, and sell it there for £1.525. Our trader then converts the £1.525 into dollars at the prevailing exchange rate, $S_0 = £0.30$, yielding a total of £1.525/0.30 = $A5.08. The round-trip gain is $A1.08.

Because of this profit potential, forces are set in motion to change the exchange rate and/or the price of apples. In our example, apples would begin moving from Sydney to London. The reduced supply of apples in Sydney would raise the price of apples there, and the increased supply in Britain would lower the price of apples in London.

In addition to moving apples around, apple traders would be busily converting pounds back into dollars to buy more apples. This activity increases the supply of pounds and simultaneously increases the demand for dollars. We would expect the value of a pound to fall. This means that the dollar is getting more valuable, so it will take more pounds to buy one dollar. Since the exchange rate is quoted as pounds per dollar, we would expect the exchange rate to rise from £0.30.

For absolute PPP to hold absolutely, several things must be true:

1 The transactions cost of trading apples—shipping, insurance, wastage, and so on—must be zero.
2 There are no barriers to trading apples, such as tariffs, taxes, or other political barriers such as VRAs (voluntary restraint agreements).
3 Finally, an apple in Sydney must be identical to an apple in London. It will not do for you to send red apples to London if the English eat only green apples or if they deteriorate during shipping.

Given the fact that the transaction costs are not zero and that the other conditions are rarely exactly met, it is not surprising that absolute PPP is really applicable only to traded goods, and then only to very uniform ones.

For this reason, absolute PPP does not imply that a Mercedes costs the same as a Ford or that a nuclear power plant in France costs the same as one in New York. In the case of the cars, they are not identical. In the case of the power plants, even if they were identical, they are expensive and very difficult to ship. On the other hand, we would be very surprised to see a significant violation of absolute PPP for gold.

Relative purchasing power parity

As a practical matter, a relative version of purchasing power parity has evolved. Relative purchasing power parity does not tell us what determines the absolute level of the exchange rate. Instead, it tells what determines the change in the exchange rate over time.

The basic idea

Suppose again that the British pound/Australian dollar exchange rate is currently $S_0 = £0.50$. Further suppose that the inflation rate in Britain is predicted to be 10 per cent over the coming year and (for the moment) the inflation rate in Australia is predicted to be zero. What do you think the exchange rate will be in a year?

If you think about it, a dollar currently costs 0.50 pounds in Britain. With 10 per cent inflation, we expect prices in Britain to generally rise by 10 per cent. So we expect that the price of a dollar will go up by 10 per cent and the exchange rate should rise to £0.50 × 1.1 = £0.55.

If the inflation rate in Australia is not zero, then we need to worry about the relative inflation rates in the two countries. For example, suppose the Australian inflation rate is predicted to be 4 per cent. Relative to prices in Australia, prices in Britain are rising at a rate of 10% − 4% = 6% per year. So we expect the price of the dollar to rise by 6 per cent, and the predicted exchange rate is £0.50 × 1.06 = £0.53.

The result

In general, relative PPP says that the change in the exchange rate is determined by the difference in the inflation rates between the two countries. To be more specific, we will use the following notation:

$$S_0 = \text{current (time 0) spot exchange rate (foreign currency per dollar)}$$
$$E[S_t] = \text{expected exchange rate in } t \text{ periods}$$
$$h_A = \text{inflation rate in Australia}$$
$$h_{FC} = \text{foreign country inflation rate}$$

Based on our discussion above, relative PPP says that the expected percentage change in the exchange rate over the next year, $(E[S_1] - S_0)/S_0$, is:

$$(E[S_1] - S_0)/S_0 = h_{FC} - h_A \tag{23.1}$$

In words, relative PPP simply says that the expected percentage change in the exchange rate is equal to the difference in inflation rates. If we rearrange this slightly, we get:

$$E[S_1] = S_0 \times [1 + (h_{FC} - h_A)] \tag{23.2}$$

This result makes a certain amount of sense, but care must be used in quoting the exchange rate.

In our example involving Britain and Australia, relative PPP tells us that the exchange rate will rise by $h_{FC} - h_A$ = 10% − 4% = 6% per year. Assuming the difference in inflation rates does not change, the expected exchange rate in two years, $E[S_2]$, will therefore be:

$$E[S_2] = E[S_1] \times (1 + 0.06)$$
$$= 0.53 \times 1.06$$
$$= 0.562$$

Notice that we could have written this as:

$$E[S_2] = 0.53 \times 1.06$$
$$= (0.50 \times 1.06) \times 1.06$$
$$= 0.50 \times 1.06^2$$

In general, relative PPP says that the expected exchange rate at sometime in the future, $E[S_t]$, is:

$$E[S_t] = S_0 \times [1 + (h_{FC} - h_A)]^t \tag{23.3}$$

As we will see, this is a very useful relationship.

Because we do not really expect absolute PPP to hold for most goods, we will focus on relative PPP in our discussion below. Henceforth, when we refer to PPP without further qualification, we mean relative PPP.

It's all relative

EXAMPLE 23.4

Suppose the Japanese exchange rate is currently 70 yen per Australian dollar. The inflation rate in Japan over the next three years will be, say, 2 per cent per year, while the Australian inflation rate will be 6 per cent. Based on relative PPP, what will the exchange rate be in three years?

Since the Australian inflation rate is higher, we expect that a dollar will become less valuable. The exchange rate change will be 2% − 6% = −4% per year. Over three years, the exchange rate will fall to:

$$
\begin{aligned}
E[S_3] &= S_0 \times [1 + (h_{FC} - h_A)]^3 \\
&= 70 \times [1 + (-0.04)]^3 \\
&= 61.93
\end{aligned}
$$

Currency appreciation and depreciation

We frequently hear things like 'the dollar strengthened (or weakened) in financial markets today' or 'the dollar is expected to appreciate (or depreciate) relative to the pound'. When we say the dollar strengthens or appreciates, we mean that the value of a dollar rises, so it takes more foreign currency to buy a dollar.

What happens to the exchange rates as currencies fluctuate in value depends on how exchange rates are quoted. Since we are quoting them as units of foreign currency per dollar, the exchange rate moves in the same direction as the value of the dollar: It rises as the dollar strengthens, and it falls as the dollar weakens.

Relative PPP tells us that the exchange rate will rise if the Australian inflation rate is lower than the foreign country's. This happens because the foreign currency depreciates in value and therefore weakens relative to the dollar.

Concept questions

23.3a *What does absolute PPP say? Why might it not hold for many goods?*
23.3b *According to relative PPP, what determines the change in exchange rates?*

23.4 Interest rate parity, unbiased forward rates and the international Fisher effect

The next issue we need to address is the relationship between the spot exchange rates, forward exchange rates and interest rates. To get started, we need some additional notation:

$$
\begin{aligned}
F_t &= \text{forward exchange rate for settlement at time } t \\
R_A &= \text{Australian nominal risk-free interest rate} \\
R_{FC} &= \text{foreign country nominal risk-free interest rate}
\end{aligned}
$$

As before, we will use S_0 to stand for the spot exchange rate. You can take the Australian nominal risk-free rate, R_A, to be the return on Commonwealth bonds.

Covered interest arbitrage

Suppose we observe the following information about the Australian dollar and the Western Samoan tala in the market:

$$S_0 = 2.00 \text{ tala} \qquad R_A = 10\%$$
$$F_1 = 1.90 \text{ tala} \qquad R_S = 5\%$$

where R_S is the nominal risk-free rate in Samoa. The period is one year, so F_1 is the 365-day forward rate.

Do you see an arbitrage opportunity here? There is one. Suppose you have $A1 to invest, and you want a riskless investment. One option you have is to invest the $A1 in a riskless Australian investment such as a 365-day Commonwealth bond. If you do this, then, in one period, your $A1 will be worth:

$$\text{\$A value in 1 period} = \text{\$A1} \times (1 + R_A)$$
$$= \$1.10$$

Alternatively, you can invest in the Samoan risk-free investment. To do this, you need to convert your $A1 to tala and simultaneously execute a forward deal to convert tala back to dollars in one year. The necessary steps would be as follows:

1 Convert your $A1 to $A1 $\times$ S_0 = 2.00 tala.
2 At the same time, enter into a forward agreement to convert tala back to dollars in one years time. Since the forward rate is 1.90 tala, you get $A1 for every 1.90 tala that you have in one year.
3 Invest your 2.00 tala in Samoa at R_S. In one year, you will have:

$$\text{Tala value in 1 year} = 2.00 \text{ tala} \times (1 + R_S)$$
$$= 2.00 \text{ tala} \times 1.05$$
$$= 2.10 \text{ tala}$$

4 Convert your 2.10 tala back to dollars at the agreed upon rate of 1.90 tala = $A1. You end up with:

$$\text{\$A value in 1 year} = 2.10 \text{ tala}/1.90$$
$$= \$A1.1053$$

Notice that the value in one year from this strategy can be written as:

$$\text{\$A value in 1 year} = \text{\$A1} \times S_0 \times (1 + R_S)/F_1$$
$$= \text{\$A1} \times 2 \times (1.05)/1.90$$
$$= \$1.1053$$

The return on this investment is apparently 10.53 per cent. This is higher than the 10 per cent we get from investing in Australia. Since both investments are risk-free, there is an arbitrage opportunity.

To exploit the difference in interest rates, you need to borrow, say, $A5 million at the Australian rate and invest it at the Samoan rate. What is the round-trip profit from doing this? To find out, we can work through the steps above:

1 Convert the $A5 million at 2 tala to get 10 million tala.
2 Agree to exchange tala for dollars in one year at 1.90 tala to the $A.
3 Invest the 10 million tala for one year at R_S = 5%. You end up with 10.5 million tala.

4   Convert the 10.5 million tala back to dollars to fulfil the forward contract. You receive 10.5 million tala/1.90 = $A5,526,316.

5   Repay the loan with interest. You owe $A5 million plus 10 per cent interest, for a total of $A5.5 million. You have $A5,526,316, so your round-trip profit is a risk-free $26,316.

The activity that we have illustrated here goes by the name of *covered interest arbitrage*. The term *covered* refers to the fact that we are covered in the event of a change in the exchange rate since we lock in the forward exchange rate today.

Interest rate parity (IRP)

If we assume that significant covered interest arbitrage opportunities do not exist, then there must be some relationship between spot exchange rates, forward exchange rates and relative interest rates. To see what this relationship is, note that, in general, strategy 1 above, investing in a riskless Australian investment, gives us $(1 + R_A)$ for every dollar we invest. Strategy 2, investing in a foreign risk-free investment, gives us $S_0 \times (1 + R_{FC})/F_1$ for every dollar we invest. Since these have to be equal to prevent arbitrage, it must be the case that:

$$(1 + R_A) = S_0 \times (1 + R_{FC})/F_1$$

Rearranging this a bit gets us the famous **interest rate parity (IRP)** condition:

$$F_1/S_0 = (1 + R_{FC})/(1 + R_A) \tag{23.4}$$

There is a very useful approximation for IRP that illustrates very clearly what is going on and is not difficult to remember. If we define the percentage forward premium or discount as $(F_1 - S_0)/S_0$, then IRP says that this per cent premium or discount is approximately equal to the difference in interest rates:

$$(F_1 - S_0)/S_0 = R_{FC} - R_A \tag{23.5}$$

Very loosely, what IRP says is that any difference in interest rates between two countries for some period is just offset by the change in the relative value of the currencies, thereby eliminating any arbitrage possibilities. Notice that we could also write:

$$F_1 = S_0 \times [1 + (R_{FC} - R_A)] \tag{23.6}$$

In general, if we have t periods instead of just one, the IRP approximation would be written as:

$$F_t = S_0 \times [1 + (R_{FC} - R_A)]^t \tag{23.7}$$

interest rate parity (IRP)

a theory which states that a forward exchange rate is given by relative interest rates in the two currencies

---

EXAMPLE 23.5

Parity check

Suppose the exchange rate for Japanese yen, S_0, is currently ¥60 = $A1. If the interest rate in Australia is R_A = 9% and the interest rate in Japan is R_J = 4%, then what must the forward rate be to prevent covered interest arbitrage?

From IRP, we have:

$$
\begin{aligned}
F_1 &= S_0 \times [1 + (R_J - R_A)] \\
&= ¥60 \times [1 + (0.04 - 0.09)] \\
&= ¥60 \times 0.95 \\
&= ¥57
\end{aligned}
$$

Notice that the yen will sell at a premium relative to the dollar (why?).

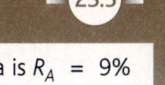

Forward rates and future spot rates

unbiased forward
rates (UFR)

a theory which
states that the
forward rate is an
unbiased predictor of
the future spot rate

In addition to PPP and IRP, there is one more basic relationship we need to discuss. What is the connection between the forward rate and the expected future spot rate? The **unbiased forward rates (UFR)** condition says that the forward rate, F_1, is equal to the expected future spot rate, $E[S_1]$:

$$F_1 = E[S_1]$$

With t periods, UFR would be written as:

$$F_t = E[S_t]$$

Loosely, the UFR condition says that, on average, the forward exchange rate is equal to the future spot exchange rate.

If we ignore risk, then the UFR condition should hold. Suppose the forward rate for the Japanese yen is consistently lower than the future spot rate by, say, 10 yen. This means that anyone who wanted to convert dollars to yen in the future would consistently get more yen by *not* agreeing to a forward exchange. The forward rate would have to rise to get anyone interested.

Similarly, if the forward rate were consistently higher than the future spot rate, then anyone who wanted to convert yen to dollars would get more dollars per yen by not agreeing to a forward deal. The forward exchange rate would have to fall to attract such traders.

For these reasons, the forward and actual future spot rates should be equal to each other on average. What the future spot rate will actually be is uncertain, of course. The UFR condition may not hold if traders are willing to pay a premium to avoid this uncertainty. If the condition does hold, then the 180-day forward rate that we see today should be an unbiased predictor of what the exchange rate will actually be in 180 days.

Putting it all together

We have developed three relationships, PPP, IRP and UFR, that describe the relationships between key financial variables such as interest rates, exchange rates and inflation rates. We now explore the implications of these relationships as a group.

Uncovered interest parity

Before we start, it is useful to collect our international financial market relationships in one place:

$$\begin{aligned}
\text{PPP:} \quad E[S_1] &= S_0 \times [1 + (h_{FC} - h_A)] \\
\text{IRP:} \quad F_1 &= S_0 \times [1 + (R_{FC} - R_A)] \\
\text{UFR:} \quad F_1 &= E[S_1]
\end{aligned}$$

uncovered interest
parity (UIP)

a theory which
states that the
difference in interest
rates between two
countries is an
unbiased predictor of
the future change in
the spot exchange
rate. Also called the
international Fisher
effect

We begin by combining UFR and IRP. Since $F_1 = E[S_1]$ from the UFR condition, we can substitute $E[S_1]$ for F_1 in IRP. The result is:

$$E[S_1] = S_0 \times [1 + (R_{FC} - R_A)] \tag{23.8}$$

This important relationship is called **uncovered interest parity (UIP)**, and it will play a key role in our international capital budgeting discussion below. With t periods, UIP becomes:

$$E[S_t] = S_0 \times [1 + (R_{FC} - R_A)]^t \tag{23.9}$$

The international Fisher effect

Next, we compare PPP and UIP. Both of them have $E[S_1]$ on the left-hand side, so their right-hand sides must be equal. We thus have:

$$S_0 \times [1 + (h_{FC} - h_A)] = S_0 \times [1 + (R_{FC} - R_A)]$$
$$h_{FC} - h_A = R_{FC} - R_A$$

This tells us that the difference in returns between Australia and a foreign country is just equal to the difference in inflation rates. Rearranging this slightly gives us the *international Fisher effect (IFE)*:

$$R_A - h_A = R_{FC} - h_{FC} \qquad (23.10)$$

The IFE says that real rates are equal across countries.[4]

The conclusion that real returns are equal across countries is really basic economics. If real returns were higher in, say, France than in Australia, money would flow out of Australian financial markets and into French markets. Asset prices in France would rise and their returns would fall. At the same time, asset prices in Australia would fall and their returns would rise. This process acts to equalise real returns.

Having said all this, we need to note several things. First of all, we have not dealt explicitly with risk in our discussion. We might reach a different conclusion about real returns once we do, particularly if people in different countries have different tastes and attitudes towards risk. Secondly, there are many barriers to the movement of money and capital around the world. Real returns might be different between two countries for long periods if money cannot move freely between them.

Despite these problems, we expect that capital markets will become increasingly internationalised. As this occurs, any differences in real rates that do exist will probably diminish. The laws of economics and the profit motive have very little respect for national boundaries.

Concept questions

23.4a *What is covered interest arbitrage?*
23.4b *What is the international Fisher effect?*

23.5 International capital budgeting

Earth Excavating Ltd, an international company based in Australia, is evaluating an overseas investment. Earth's exports of end loaders have increased to such a degree that it is considering building a plant in Hong Kong. The project will cost $HK20 million (Hong Kong dollars) to launch. The cash flows are expected to be $HK9 million a year for the next three years.

The current spot exchange rate for $HK is 5. Recall that this is $HK per Australian dollar, so $HK1 is worth $A1/5 = $A0.20. The risk-free rate in Australia is 5 per cent, and the risk-free rate in Hong Kong is 7 per cent. Notice that the exchange rate and the two interest rates are observed in financial markets, not estimated.[5] Earth's required return on investments of this sort is 10 per cent.

Should Earth take this investment? As always, the answer depends on the NPV, but how do we calculate the net present value of this project in Australian dollars? There are two basic ways to go about doing this:

1 *The home currency approach.* Convert all the $HK cash flows into $A, and then discount at 10 per cent to find the NPV in dollars. Notice that for this approach, we have to come up with the future exchange rates in order to convert the future projected $HK cash flows into dollars.

2 *The foreign currency approach.* Determine the required return on Hong Kong investments, and then discount the $HK cash flows to find the NPV in $HK. Then convert this $HK NPV to an $A NPV. This approach requires us to somehow convert the 10 per cent Australian dollar required return to the equivalent Hong Kong required return.

The difference between these two approaches is primarily a matter of when we convert from $HK to $A. In the first case, we convert before estimating the NPV. In the second case, we convert after estimating NPV.

It might appear that the second approach is superior because we only have to come up with one number, the Hong Kong discount rate. Furthermore, since the first approach requires us to forecast future exchange rates, it probably seems that there is greater room for error. As we illustrate next, however, based on our results above, the two approaches are really the same.

Method 1: The home currency approach

To convert the project future cash flows into Australian dollars, we will invoke the uncovered interest parity (UIP) relation to come up with the projected exchange rates. Based on our discussion above, the expected exchange rate at time t, $E[S_t]$, is:

$$E[S_t] = S_0 \times [1 + (R_{HK} - R_A)]^t$$

where R_{HK} stands for the nominal risk-free rate in Hong Kong. Since R_{HK} is 7 per cent, R_A is 5 per cent, and the current exchange rate (S_0) is $HK5:

$$E[S_t] = 5 \times [1 + (0.07 - 0.05)]^t$$
$$= 5 \times 1.02^t$$

The projected exchange rates for the end loader project are thus:

Year	Expected exchange rate
1	$HK5 \times 1.02^1 = $HK5.100
2	$HK5 \times 1.02^2 = $HK5.202
3	$HK5 \times 1.02^3 = $HK5.306

Using these exchange rates, along with the current exchange rate, we can convert all of the $HK cash flows to Australian dollars:

Year	(1) Cash flow in $HK	(2) Expected exchange rate	(3) Cash flow in $A (1)/(2)
0	−$HK20	$HK5.000	−$4.00
1	9	5.100	1.76
2	9	5.202	1.73
3	9	5.306	1.70

To finish off, we calculate the NPV in the ordinary way:

$$NPV = -\$4.00 + \$1.76/1.10 + \$1.73/1.10^2 + \$1.70/1.10^3$$
$$= \$0.32 \text{ million}$$

So the project appears to be profitable.

Method 2: The foreign currency approach

Earth requires a nominal return of 10 per cent on the dollar-denominated cash flows. We need to convert this to a rate suitable for \$HK-denominated cash flows. Based on the international Fisher effect, we know that the difference in the nominal rates is:

$$R_{FC} - R_A = h_{FC} - h_A$$
$$= 7\% - 5\% = 2\%$$

The appropriate discount rate for estimating the \$HK cash flows from the end loader project is approximately equal to 10 per cent plus an extra 2 per cent to compensate for the greater \$HK inflation rate.

If we calculate the NPV of the \$HK cash flows at this rate, we get:

$$NPV_{HK} = -\$HK20 + \$HK9/1.12 + \$HK9/1.12^2 + \$HK9/1.12^3$$
$$= \$HK1.6 \text{ million}$$

The NPV of this project is \$HK1.6 million. Taking this project makes us \$HK1.6 million richer today. What is this in Australian dollars? Since the exchange rate today is \$HK5, the dollar NPV of the project is:

$$NPV_{\$A} = NPV_{\$HK}/S_0 = \$HK1.6/5 = \$0.32 \text{ million}$$

This is the same Australian dollar NPV we calculated before.

The important thing to recognise from our example is that the two capital budgeting procedures are actually the same and will always give the same answer.[6] In this second approach, the fact that we are implicitly forecasting exchange rates is simply hidden. Even so, the foreign currency approach is computationally a little easier.

Unremitted cash flows

The previous example assumed that all after-tax cash flows from the foreign investment could be remitted to (paid out to) the parent firm. Actually, substantial differences can exist between the cash flows generated by a foreign project and the amount that can actually be remitted or 'repatriated' to the parent firm.

A foreign subsidiary can remit funds to a parent in many ways, including the following:

1 dividends
2 management fees for central services
3 royalties on the use of trade name and patents.

There may be current or future controls on remittances. Many governments are sensitive to the charge of being exploited by foreign national firms. In such cases, governments are tempted to limit the ability of international firms to remit cash flows. Funds that cannot currently be remitted are sometimes said to be blocked.

Concept questions

23.5a *What financial complications arise in international capital budgeting?*
23.5b *Describe two procedures for estimating NPV in international capital budgeting.*
23.5c *What are blocked funds?*

23.6 Exchange rate risk

Exchange rate risk is the natural consequence of international operations in a world where relative currency values move up and down. Managing exchange rate risk is an important part of international finance. As we discuss next, there are three different types of exchange rate risk or exposure: short-run exposure, long-run exposure and translation exposure.

Short-run exposure

The day-to-day fluctuations in exchange rates create short-run risks for international firms. Many of these firms have contractual agreements to buy and sell goods in the near future at set prices. When different currencies are involved, such transactions have an extra element of risk.

For example, imagine that you are importing cashew nuts from Pakistan and reselling them in Australia under the Paken brand name. Your largest customer has ordered 10,000 cases of Paken cashews. You place the order with your supplier today, but you will not pay until the goods arrive in 60 days. Your selling price is $9.40 per case. Your cost is 279 Pakistan rupee per case, and the exchange rate is currently 31, so it takes 31 rupee to buy $A1.

At the current exchange rate, your cost in dollars from filling the order is $279/31 = \$9.00$ per case, so your pre-tax profit on the order is $10,000 \times (\$9.40 - \$9.00) = \$4,000$. However, the exchange rate in 60 days will probably be different, so your profit will depend on what the future exchange rate turns out to be.

For example, if the rate goes to 32.26, your cost is $279/32.26 = \$8.65$ per case. Your profit goes to $7,500. If the exchange rate goes to, say, 29.69, then your cost is $279/29.69 = \$9.40$, and your profit is zero.

The short-run exposure in our example can be reduced or eliminated in several ways. The most obvious means of hedging is to enter into a forward exchange agreement to lock in an exchange rate. For example, suppose the 60-day forward rate is 32.06. What will be your profit if you hedge? What profit should you expect if you do not?

If you hedge, you lock in an exchange rate of 32.06 rupee. Your cost in dollars will thus be $279/32.06 = \$8.70$ per case, so your profit will be $10,000 \times (\$9.40 - \$8.70) = \$7,000$. If you do not hedge, then, assuming that the forward rate is an unbiased predictor (in other words, assuming the UFR condition holds), you should expect that the exchange rate will actually be 32.06 in 60 days. You should expect to make $7,000.

Alternatively, if this is not feasible, you could simply borrow the dollars today, convert them into rupee, and invest the rupee for 60 days to earn some interest. From IRP, this amounts to entering into a forward contract.

Long-run exposure

In the long run, the value of a foreign operation can fluctuate because of unanticipated changes in relative economic conditions. For example, imagine that we own a labour-intensive assembly operation located in another country to take advantage of lower wages. Through time, unexpected changes in economic conditions can raise the foreign wage levels to the point where the cost advantage is eliminated or even becomes negative.

Hedging long-run exposure is more difficult than hedging short-term risks. For one thing, organised forward markets do not exist for such long-term needs. Instead, the primary option that firms have is to try and match up foreign currency inflows and outflows. The same thing goes for matching foreign-currency-denominated assets and liabilities. For example, a firm that sells in a foreign country might try to concentrate its raw material purchases and labour expense in that country. That way, the dollar value of its revenues and costs will move up and down together.

Similarly, a firm can reduce its long-run exchange risk by borrowing in the foreign country. Fluctuations in the value of the foreign subsidiary's assets will then be at least partially offset by changes in the value of the liabilities.

Translation exposure

When an Australian company calculates its accounting net profit and EPS for some period, it must 'translate' everything into dollars. This can create some problems for the accountants when there are significant foreign operations. In particular, two issues arise:

1 What is the appropriate exchange rate to use for translating each Statement of Financial Position account?
2 How should Statement of Financial Position accounting gains and losses from foreign currency translation be handled?

To illustrate the accounting problem, suppose we started a small foreign subsidiary in Lilliputia a year ago. The local currency is the gulliver, abbreviated GL. At the beginning of the year, the exchange rate was GL2 = $A1, and the Statement of Financial Position in gullivers looked like this:

Assets	GL1,000	Liabilities	GL500
		Equity	500

At 2 gullivers to the dollar, the beginning Statement of Financial Position in dollars was:

Assets	$500	Liabilities	$250
		Equity	250

Lilliputia is a quiet place, and nothing at all actually happened during the year. As a result, net profit was zero (before consideration of exchange rate changes). However, the exchange rate did change to 4 gullivers = $1 purely because the Lilliputian inflation rate is much higher than the Australian inflation rate.

Since nothing happened, the accounting ending Statement of Financial Position in gullivers is the same as the beginning one. However, if we convert it to dollars at the new exchange rate, we get:

Assets	$250	Liabilities	$125
		Equity	125

Notice that the value of the equity has gone down by $125, even though net profit was exactly zero. Despite the fact that absolutely nothing really happened, there is a $125 accounting loss. How to handle this $125 loss has been a controversial accounting question.

One obvious and consistent way to handle this loss is simply to report the loss on the parent's Statement of Financial Performance. During periods of volatile exchange rates, this kind of treatment can dramatically impact an international company's reported EPS. This is purely an accounting phenomenon, but even so, such fluctuations are disliked by financial managers.

Managing exchange rate risk

For a large multinational firm, the management of exchange rate risk is complicated by the fact that there can be many different currencies involved in many different subsidiaries. It is very likely that a change in some exchange rate will benefit some subsidiaries and hurt others. The net effect on the overall firm depends on its net exposure.

For example, suppose a firm has two divisions. Division A buys goods in Australia for dollars and sells them in Britain for pounds. Division B buys goods in Britain for pounds and sells them in Australia for dollars. If these two divisions are of roughly equal size in terms of their inflows and outflows, then the overall firm obviously has little exchange rate risk.

In our example, the firm's net position in pounds (the amount coming in less the amount going out) is small, so the exchange rate risk is small. However, if one division, acting on its own, were to start hedging its exchange rate risk, then the overall firm's exchange risk would go up. The moral of the story is that multinational firms have to be conscious of the overall position that the firm has in a foreign currency. For this reason, exchange risk management is probably best handled on a centralised basis.

Concept questions

23.6a *What are the different types of exchange rate risk?*

23.6b *How can a firm hedge short-run exchange rate risk? Long-run exchange rate risk?*

23.7 Political risk

political risk
changes in value that arise as a consequence of political actions

One final element of risk in international investing concerns **political risk**. Political risk refers to changes in value that arise as a consequence of political actions. This is not purely a problem faced by international firms. For example, changes in Australian tax laws and regulations may benefit some Australian firms and hurt others, so political risk exists domestically as well as internationally.

Some countries do have more political risk than others, however. In such cases, the extra political risk may lead firms to require higher returns on overseas investments to compensate for the risk that funds will be blocked, critical operations interrupted, and contracts abrogated. In the most extreme case, the possibility of outright confiscation may be a concern in countries with relatively unstable political environments.

Political risk also depends on the nature of the business; some businesses are less likely to be confiscated because they are not particularly valuable in the hands of a different owner. An assembly operation supplying subcomponents that only the parent company uses would not be an attractive 'takeover' target, for example. Similarly, a manufacturing operation that requires the use of specialised components from the parent is of little value without the parent company's co-operation.

Natural resource developments, such as copper mining or oil drilling, are just the opposite. Once the operation is in place, much of the value is in the commodity. The political risk for such investments is much higher for this reason. Also, the issue of exploitation is more pronounced with such investments, again increasing the political risk.

Political risk can be hedged in several ways, particularly when confiscation or nationalisation is a concern. The use of local financing, perhaps from the government of the foreign country in question, reduces the possible loss because the company can refuse to pay on the debt in the event of unfavourable political activities. Based on our discussion above, structuring the operation such that it requires significant parent company involvement to function is another way to reduce political risk.

Concept questions

23.7a *What is political risk?*

23.7b *What are some ways of hedging political risks?*

■23.8■ Summary and conclusions

The international firm has a more complicated life than the purely domestic firm. Management must understand the connection between interest rates, foreign currency exchange rates and inflation, and it must become aware of a large number of different financial market regulations and tax systems. This chapter is intended to be a concise introduction to some of the financial issues that come up in international investing.

Our coverage was necessarily brief. The main topics we discussed include:

1   Some basic vocabulary. We briefly defined some exotic terms such as LIBOR and eurodollar.

2   The basic mechanics of exchange rate quotations. We discussed the spot and forward markets and how exchange rates are interpreted.

3   The fundamental relationships between international financial variables:

    a   absolute and relative purchasing power parity (PPP)
    b   interest rate parity (IRP)
    c   unbiased forward rates (UFR).

    Absolute purchasing power parity states that $1 should have the same purchasing power in each country. This means that an apple costs the same whether you buy it in Sydney or in Tokyo.

    Relative purchasing power parity means that the expected percentage change in exchange rates between the currencies of two countries is equal to the difference in their inflation rates.

    Interest rate parity implies that the percentage difference between the forward exchange rate and the spot exchange rate is equal to the interest rate differential. We showed how covered interest arbitrage forces this relationship to hold.

    The unbiased forward rates condition indicates that the current forward rate is a good predictor of the future spot exchange rate.

4   International capital budgeting. We showed that the basic foreign exchange relationships imply two other conditions:

    a   uncovered interest parity
    b   international Fisher effect

    By invoking these two conditions, we learned how to estimate NPVs in foreign currencies and how to convert foreign currencies into dollars to estimate NPV in the usual way.

5   Exchange rate and political risk. We described the various types of exchange rate risk and discussed some commonly used approaches to manage the effect of fluctuating exchange rates on the cash flows and value of the international firm. We also discussed political risk and some ways of managing exposure to it.

Key terms

Appreciation *796*
Authorised foreign exchange dealers *796*
Cross rate *796*
Dealers *796*
Euro *796*
Eurobond *796*
Eurocurrency *797*
Exchange rate *799*
Exchange rate risk *814*

Foreign bonds *797*
Foreign exchange market *798*
Forward deal *803*
Forward exchange rate *803*
Gilts *797*
Interest rate parity (IRP) *809*
International Fisher effect (IFE) *811*
London Interbank Offer Rate (LIBOR) *797*

Political risk *816*
Purchasing power parity (PPP) *804*
Spot deal *803*
Spot exchange rate *803*
Swaps *798*
Unbiased forward rates (UFR) *810*
Uncovered interest parity (UIP) *810*

Suggested readings

The following are good books on the modern theory of international markets:

Grabbe, J.O. *International Financial Markets*, Elsevier-North Holland Publishing, New York, 1986.

Madura, J. *International Financial Management*, 4th edn, West Publishing, St Paul, 1995.

These two articles describe budgeting for international projects:

Lessard, D.R. 'Global Competition and Corporate Finance in the 1990s', *Journal of Applied Corporate Finance*, Vol. 3, Winter 1991, pp. 59–72.

Shapiro, A.C. 'International Capital Budgeting', *Midland Corporate Finance Journal*, Vol. 3, Winter 1983, pp. 73–82.

For more information on the relationship between the forward rate and the spot rate, see:

Levich, R. M. 'Is the Foreign Exchange Market Efficient?' *Oxford Review of Economic Policy*, Vol. 5, No. 3, 1989, pp. 40–60.

Mussa, M. 'Empirical Regularities in the Behaviour of Exchange Rates and Theories of the Foreign Exchange Market', in Bruner, K. and Meltzer, A. (eds) *Policies for Employment, Prices and Exchange Rates*, Carnegie-Rochester Conference 11, North-Holland, Amsterdam, 1979.

Endnotes

1   Actually the result is $A999.98529. This is one of the rounding differences referred to in the study tips.

2   There is a rounding difference of 2 cents because the precise Australian dollar equivalent is 1.643925695, which gives the answer shown.

3   The banks' margins interfere with the true arbitrage opportunity. Table 23.2 shows the buying rate for Swiss francs is in fact 0.8288 so that you would receive SF84/0.8288 = $A101.35 not the $A103.70 shown. However, there is still an arbitrage profit of $A1.35.

4   Notice that our result here is in terms of the approximate real rate, $R - h$ (see Chapter 10), because we used approximations for PPP and IRP. For the exact result, see problem 19 at the end of this chapter.

5   For example the interest rate might be the short-term rate offered by a major bank in Hong Kong.

6   Actually there will be a slight difference because we are using the approximate relationships. If we calculate the required return as: $1.10 \times (1 + 0.02) - 1 = 12.2\%$, then we get exactly the same NPV. See Problem 19 for more detail.

On the web

Useful sites on currency exchange, with up-to-the-minute data, are:
http://www.bloomberg.com (this site, for Bloomberg financial news, also contains a currency converter)
http://www.afr.com.au (the *Australian Financial Review* site contains current information)

The Westpac site
http://www.westpac.com.au also has relevant currency information, and the same is true of the sites of other major banks.

Maximise Your Marks!
There are 30 interactive questions on international corporate finance waiting online for you at www.mhhe.com/au/ross3e. The questions are written with additional feedback for incorrect answers, and text excerpts with page references for follow-up study.

International Articles!
To read more on international corporate finance and to see current international articles, just go to www.mhhe.com/au/ross3e and click on *PowerWeb Articles* for this chapter.

Chapter review problems and self-test

23.1 · Relative review problems and self-test

The inflation rate in Australia is projected at 4 per cent per year for the next several years. The Fijian inflation rate is projected to be 2 per cent during that time. The exchange rate is currently $FJ1.20. Based on relative PPP, what is the expected exchange rate in two years?

23.2 · Covered interest arbitrage

The spot and 365-day forward rates on the Swiss franc are SF1.01 and SF0.96, respectively. The risk-free interest rate in Australia is 6 per cent, and the risk-free rate in Switzerland is 4 per cent. Is there an arbitrage opportunity here? How would you exploit it?

Answers to self-test problems

23.1 · From relative PPP, the expected exchange rate in two years, $E[S_2]$ is:

$$E[S_2] = S_0 \times [1 + (h_{FJ} - h_A)]^2$$

where h_{FJ} is the Fijian inflation rate. The current exchange rate is $FJ1.26, so the expected exchange rate is:

$$
\begin{aligned}
E[S_2] &= \$FJ1.26 \times [1 + (0.02 - 0.04)]^2 \\
&= \$FJ1.26 \times 0.962 \\
&= \$FJ1.21
\end{aligned}
$$

23.2 · From interest rate parity, the forward rate should be (approximately):

$$
\begin{aligned}
F_1 &= S_0 \times [1 + (R_{FC} - R_A)] \\
&= 1.01 \times [1 + 0.04 - 0.06] \\
&= 0.99
\end{aligned}
$$

Since the forward rate is actually SF0.96, there is an arbitrage.

To exploit the arbitrage, we first note that dollars are selling for SF0.96 each in the forward market. From IRP, this is too cheap because they should be selling for SF0.99. So we want to arrange to buy dollars with Swiss francs in the forward market. To do this, we can:

a Today: Borrow, say, $10 million for 365 days. Convert it to SF10.1 million in the spot market, and forward contract at SF0.99 to convert it back to dollars in 365 days. Invest the SF10.1 million at 4 per cent.

b In one year: Your investment has grown to SF10.1 × 1.04 = SF10.504 million. Convert this to dollars at the rate of SF0.99 = $A1. You will have SF10.504 million/0.99 = $A10,610,101. Pay off your loan with 6 per cent interest at a cost of $A10 million × 1.06 = $10,600,000 and pocket the difference of $10,101.

Questions and problems

1 · Using exchange rates

Take a look back at Table 23.2 to answer the following questions:

a   If you have $100, how many Indian rupees can you get?

b   How much is 20 Danish krones worth?

c   If you have PHP1 million (PHP stands for the Philippine peso), how many dollars do you have?

d   Which would you prefer: $HK477.79 or 2729 Indian rupees?

e   Which is worth more: a Brunei dollar or a Singapore dollar?

f   How many Swiss francs can you get for a Vanuatu vatu? What do you call this rate?

g   Per unit, based on buying quotes, what is the most valuable currency of the ones listed? The least valuable?

h   Can you think of a major world trading power that is not listed in Table 23.2? Why do you think there is no listing?

2 · Using the cross rate

Use the information in Table 23.2 to answer the following questions:

a   Which would you rather have, $A100 or £50? Why?

b   Which would you rather have, 50 euro or £50? Why?

c   What is the cross rate for yen in terms of pounds? For pounds in terms of yen?

3 · Forward exchange rates

Again referring to Table 23.2:

a   If the 180-day forward rate for the Japanese yen in yen per dollar is 73, is the yen selling at a premium or a discount? Explain.

b   If the 90-day forward rate for the Swiss franc in dollars per franc is 0.80, is the dollar selling at a premium or a discount? Explain.

c   What do you think will happen to the value of the dollar relative to the yen and the Swiss franc? Explain.

4 · Using spot and forward rates

Suppose the spot exchange rate for the Canadian dollar is $Can1.12 and the 180-day forward rate is $Can1.20.

a   Which is worth more, an Australian dollar or a Canadian dollar?

b   Assuming absolute PPP, what is the cost in Australia of a Calgary Elkhead beer if the price in Canada is $Can1.40? Why might it sell for a different price in Australia?

c   Is the Canadian dollar selling at a premium or a discount relative to the Australian dollar?

d   Which currency is expected to appreciate in value?

e   What do you expect would be true concerning interest rates in Australia and Canada?

5 · Spot versus forward rates

Suppose the exchange rate for the Swiss franc is quoted as SF4.02 on the spot market and SF4.04 in the 90-day forward market.

a   Is the dollar selling at a premium or a discount relative to the franc?

b   Does the financial market expect the franc to strengthen relative to the dollar? Explain.

c   What do you suspect is true about relative economic conditions in Australia and Switzerland?

6 · Cross rates and arbitrage

Suppose the Canadian dollar exchange rate is $Can1 = $A0.60, and the Danish krone exchange rate is $A1 = 3.75 krone.

a   What is the cross rate in terms of krone per $Can?

b   Suppose the cross rate is 2.95krone = $Can1. Is there an arbitrage? Explain how to exploit it.

7 · Inflation and exchange rates

The rate of inflation in the United Kingdom will probably run about 2 per cent higher than the Australian inflation rate for the next several years. All other things being equal, what will happen to the exchange rate? What relationship are you relying on in answering?

8 · Changes in interest rates and inflation

The exchange rate for the Japanese yen is currently ¥65. This is expected to climb over the next year by 10 per cent.

a   Is the yen expected to get stronger or weaker?

b   What do you think about the relative inflation rates in Australia and Japan?

c   What do you think about the relative nominal interest rates in Australia and Japan? Relative real rates?

9 · Foreign bonds
Which of the following most accurately describes a 'Samurai' bond?

a   A bond issued by Toyota in Australia with the interest payable in yen.
b   A bond issued by Toyota worldwide with the interest payable in yen.
c   A bond issued by IBM in Japan with the interest payable in yen.
d   A bond issued by IBM in Japan with the interest payable in dollars.
e   An ancient ritual of the Secret Brotherhood of Ninja Warriors.

10 · Interest rates and arbitrage
The secretary of a major Australian firm has $A5 million to invest for three months. The annual interest rate in Australia is 1 per cent per month. The interest rate in the United Kingdom is 0.75 per cent. The spot rate of exchange is £0.50, and the three-month forward rate is £0.49. Ignoring transaction costs, in which country would the secretary want to invest the company's funds? Why?

11 · Exchange rate risk
Suppose you are importing coffee grinders from Vanuatu. The exchange rate is given in Table 23.2. You have just placed an order for 50,000 grinders at a cost to you of 1,500 vatu each. You will pay for them after they arrive in 90 days. You can sell the grinders for $A18.75 each. Calculate your profits if the exchange rate goes up or down by 10 per cent over the next 90 days. What is the break-even exchange rate?

12 · Inflation and exchange rates
Suppose the current exchange rate for the South African rand is 3 rand. The expected exchange rate in 4 years is 2.5 rand. What is the difference in the annual inflation rates for Australia and South Africa over this period? Assume that the anticipated rate is constant for both countries. What relationship are you relying on in answering?

13 · Exchange rates and arbitrage
The spot and 180-day forward rates on the Canadian dollar are $Can1.1 and $Can1.15, respectively. The annual risk-free interest rate in Australia is 8 per cent, and the risk-free rate in Canada is 9 per cent.

a   Is there an arbitrage opportunity here? How would you exploit it?
b   What must the forward rate be to prevent arbitrage?

14 · Spot versus forward rates
The spot and 90-day forward rates for the Swedish krona are Skr4.5 and Skr4.52, respectively. In Australia, government bonds are yielding 9 per cent annually.

a   Is the krona expected to get stronger or weaker?
b   What would you estimate is the difference between the inflation rates of Australia and Sweden?

15 · Expected spot rates
The spot exchange rate for Indian rupees is INR30. Interest rates in Australia are 6 per cent per year. Rates are 12 per cent in India. What do you predict the exchange rate will be in a year? In two years? What relationship are you using?

16 · Economic conditions and exchange rates
Are the following statements true or false? Explain why.

a   If the general price index in Japan rises faster than that in Australia, we would expect the value of the yen to increase relative to the dollar.
b   Suppose you are a French wine exporter who receives all payments in foreign currency and the European Economic Community begins to undertake an expansionary monetary policy. If it is certain that the result will be higher inflation in France compared to other countries outside Europe, you would be wise to use forward markets to protect yourself against future losses resulting from the deterioration of the value of the euro.
c   If you could accurately estimate differences in relative inflation between two countries over a long period (and other participants in the markets were unable to do so), you could successfully speculate in spot currency markets.

17 · International relationships
We discussed five international capital market relationships: relative PPP, IRP, UFR, UIP and the international Fisher effect. Which of these do you expect to hold most closely? Which do you think would be likely to be violated?

18 · Capital budgeting

The Three Nephews (TTN) Limited operates a comic book publishing factory in the country of Donald. It is evaluating a proposed expansion of an existing subsidary located in Duckland. The cost would be DBs9 million. The cash flows would be DBs4 million for the next three years. The Donald dollar required return is 12 per cent per year, and the current exchange rate is DL2. The going rate on Donald dollars (DL) is 6 per cent per year. It is 4 per cent per year on Duckland bills (DBs).

a What do you project will happen to exchange rates over the next three years?
b Based on your answer to part (a), convert the projected Duckland bill cash flows into Donald dollar flows and calculate the NPV.
c What is the required return on Duckland bill cash flows?

Based on your answer, calculate the NPV in Duckland bills and then convert to Donald dollars.

19 · Using the exact international Fisher effect

This is a challenge question. From our discussion of the Fisher effect in Chapter 10, we know that the actual relationship between a nominal rate, R, a real rate, r, and an inflation rate, h, can be written as:

$$1 + r = (1 + R)/(1 + h)$$

This is the **domestic** Fisher effect.

a What is the non-approximate form of the international Fisher effect?
b Based on your answer to (a), what is the exact form for UIP? (**Hint**: Recall the exact form of IRP and use UFR.)
c What is the exact form for relative PPP? (**Hint**: Combine your previous two answers.)
d Recalculate the NPV for the Earth end loader project (discussed in Section 23.5) using the exact forms for UIP and the international Fisher effect. Verify that you get precisely the same answer either way.

20 · Relative purchasing power parity

The inflation rate in Australia is projected at 3 per cent per year for the next several years. The New Zealand inflation rate is projected to be 5 per cent during that time. The exchange rate is currently $NZ1.66. Based on relative PPP, what is the expected exchange rate in two years?

21 · Covered interest arbitrage

The spot and 360-day forward rates on the Swiss franc are SF2.1 and SF1.9 respectively. The risk-free interest rate in Australia is 6 per cent, and the risk-free rate in Switzerland is 4 per cent. Is there an arbitrage opportunity here? How could it be exploited?

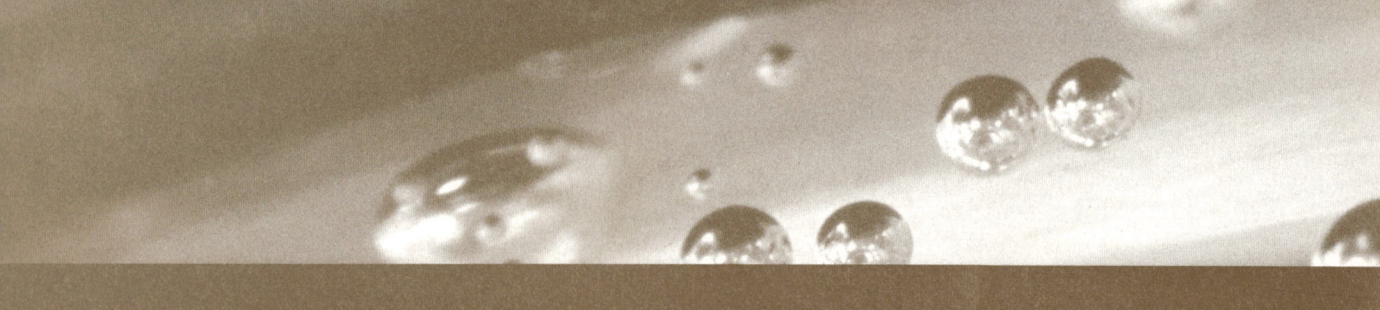

CHAPTER 24

Leasing

Objective

The aim of this chapter is to explain the main characteristics of finance leases and operating leases. The accounting and tax treatment of leases in Australia is explained. A simple approach for evaluating leases from the financing decision viewpoint is developed. An explanation of how lease premiums (payments) are determined is explained. Finally some of the claimed advantages of leasing are discussed.

The first point to note is that whether we lease or not is a financing decision. When we accept that leasing is a financing decision it is then easy for us to appreciate that the choice is do we lease or do we borrow to purchase? We are able to realise that the interest cost of leasing should be the same as the interest cost of borrowing to purchase. We are not concerned at this stage with what the asset does. That decision has been made earlier as an investment decision and now, with the leasing question, we are looking at the best method of financing to provide the highest net present value. The decision to lease or not reduces to the difference between the net tax savings through leasing and the opportunity cost of leasing. Now the challenge is to see how we calculate the net tax saving and the opportunity cost.

Introduction ▷ Leasing is a way businesses finance plant, property and equipment. Just about any asset that can be purchased can be leased, and more equipment is financed today by leasing than by any other method of equipment financing.[1] There are many good reasons for leasing. For example, when we take vacations or business trips, renting a car for a few days is a convenient thing to do. After all, buying a car and selling it a week later would be a great nuisance.

Corporations do both short-term leasing and long-term leasing, where long-term typically means more than five years. As we will discuss in greater detail shortly, leasing an asset on a long-term basis is much like borrowing the needed funds and simply buying the asset. When is leasing preferable to borrowing? This is the question we seek to answer in this chapter.

▪24.1▪ The nature of leases

A *lease* is a contractual agreement between two parties: the lessee and the lessor. The **lessee** is the user of the equipment; the **lessor** is the owner. Typically, a company first decides on the asset that it needs. It then negotiates a lease contract with a lessor for use of that asset. The lease agreement establishes that the lessee has the right to use the asset and, in return, must make periodic payments to the lessor, the owner of the asset. The lessor is usually either the asset's manufacturer or an independent leasing company. If the lessor is an independent leasing company, it must buy the asset from a manufacturer. The lessor then delivers the asset to the lessee, and the lease goes into effect.

Consideration for the contract is a periodic payment, called a **lease premium**, paid by the lessee to the lessor. The contract is known as a lease agreement and sets out:

1 the period of the lease;
2 the amount and frequency of the lease payments;
3 whether the lease is cancellable by either party, and under what conditions;
4 the minimum amount of asset maintenance, and who is to bear the costs of such (maintenance lease—lessor; net lease—lessee);
5 what is to become of the asset at the end of the lease period:

   a returned to lessor
   b purchased by lessee
   c sold
   d lease of asset may be renewed;

6 how the asset's residual value is to be accounted for.

The lessor may be an independent leasing company that purchases the asset from the manufacturer and leases it to the lessee. Leases of this type are called *direct leases*. Some companies have set up wholly owned subsidiaries called *captive finance companies* to lease out their products.[2]

Concept questions

24.1a *In a leasing agreement who is the owner of the property, the lessee or the lessor?*
24.1b *Is the leasing decision an investment, financing or dividend decision made by the firm?*

 ## ▪24.2▪ Types of leases

There are two broad categories of leases: operating leases and financial leases. Distinguishing features between the two are: the lease period, and the lease's cancellability.

For example, operating leases are usually short-lived and cancellable, while financial leases are usually long-lived and non-cancellable.

Operating leases

Years ago, a lease where the lessee received an equipment operator along with the equipment was called an **operating lease**. Today, an operating lease (or *service lease*) is difficult to define precisely, but this form of leasing has several important characteristics. An operating lease is essentially a rental agreement where the principal features are:

1 It is cancellable, prior to expiry date, with little or no cost, upon giving due notice. The expiry date is usually readily extendible on similar terms and conditions.

2 It is a maintenance lease—meaning the lessor provides service, maintenance and insurance.

3 The contracts are usually for short periods relative to the life of the asset.

4 The sum of the lease premiums does not provide for full recovery of the asset's costs.

Examples of such leases include telephones, televisions, photocopiers, motor vehicles, construction equipment, some computers, trucks, and some office rental. Note that the assets leased tend to be non-specific to individual firms; that is, the assets are in general use. While the lessor is responsible for maintenance and the other costs, these are passed on to the lessee in the form of a higher lease premium. The value of the cancellation clause depends on whether technological and/or economic conditions are likely to make the value of the asset to the lessee less than the value of the future lease payments under the lease.

Financial leases

Financial leases are essentially a means of financing the 'acquisition' of an asset without immediately paying cash for it. Main features of financial leases include:

1 They are non-cancellable prior to expiry date by either lessor or lessee.

2 Leases of this type are usually 'net leases'. Maintenance, insurance and repairs are carried out by the lessee; however, 'gross' or 'maintenance leases' can exist.

3 The lease period closely approximates the asset's economic life.

4 The sum of the lease premiums exceeds the purchase price of the asset.

In Australia, many or all of these conditions may be violated. One of the critical identification marks of a financial lease in this country is the existence of a **residual value clause**. Assets acquired by financial leases tend to be assets specific to one class of firm and therefore of little or no use to anyone else; therefore they are usually disposed of at the end of the lease period. Examples of financial leases are neon signs, specialist equipment, long-term lease of motor vehicles, heavy industrial equipment and ships.

Residual value clause

There are two cases to consider:

A. Lease continues for its full term

The lessee has three options available:

1 To purchase the asset from the lessor for its residual value.

2 To return the asset to the lessor, who sells the asset. If the selling price is less than the residual value, the lessee must compensate the lessor for the balance.

3 To renew the lease of the asset. The terms will be renegotiated and there will be a new lease agreement where the new premiums are obviously lower.

Alternative (1) is most common since the residual value is usually less than the market value of the asset. The lessee can therefore make a capital gain. Of course this need not always be the case. When a capital gain is obtained this is subject to taxation. The tax is calculated by reference to a notional depreciated value for the asset. The notional depreciated value is a value derived by assuming that the asset was purchased at the beginning of the lease contract and depreciated according to usual accepted tax practice. Where it can be demonstrated there is an identifiable market price this value will override the notional depreciated value.

B. Lease is cancelled during its initial term

This is similar to cancelling a hire-purchase contract. It is carried out with agreement of both parties, and the lessee has to pay outstanding premiums, plus the residual value of the

financial lease
this is essentially a means of financing acquisition of an asset without immediately paying for it. Typically, a longer-term, fully amortised lease under which the lessee is responsible for upkeep. Usually not cancellable without penalty

residual value clause
this clause in the lease agreement describes what happens to the leased item at the end of the lease contract

asset. However, the lessee gets an interest rebate based on the 78 rule for the interest component of the lease premiums.

Because financial leases are usually sufficient to cover fully the lessor's cost of purchasing the asset and to provide a return on the investment, they are said to be fully-amortised or full-payout leases, whereas operating leases are said to be partially amortised. Financial leases are often called *capital* leases.

There are two special types of financial leases that are of particular interest, *sale and leaseback* agreements and *leveraged leases*. We consider these next.

Sale and leaseback agreements

sale and leaseback
a financial lease in which the lessee sells an asset to the lessor and then leases it back

A **sale and leaseback** occurs when a company sells an asset it owns to another firm and immediately leases it back. In a sale and leaseback, two things happen:

1 The lessee receives cash from the sale of the asset.
2 The lessee continues to use the asset.

Sale and leasebacks are very common. For example in 1998, Motel 6 completed an innovative sale leaseback program for a significant number of its properties. The strategy freed up Motel 6's financial resources, while still retaining management of its properties. In the program, 288 Motel 6 locations, totalling 33,000 rooms, were sold at a price of $1.1 billion. Most of the Australian banks and large retailers operate their branches using this scheme.

Leveraged leases

leveraged lease
a financial lease where the lessor borrows a substantial fraction of the cost of the leased asset

A **leveraged lease** is a tax-oriented lease involving three parties: a lessee, a lessor and a lender. A typical arrangement might go as follows:

1 The lessee selects the asset, gets the value of using the asset, and makes the periodic lease payment.
2 The lessor usually puts up about 20 per cent of the financing, is entitled to the lease payments, has title to the asset, and pays interest to the lenders.
3 The lenders supply the remaining financing and receive interest payments. Their recourse for non-payment is limited to the leasing payments and the asset.

The lenders in a leveraged lease typically use a non-recourse loan. This means that the lender cannot turn to the lessor in case of a default. However, the lender is protected in two ways:

1 The lender has a first lien on the asset.
2 The lender may actually receive the lease payments from the lessee. The lender deducts the principal and interest due, and then forwards whatever is left to the lessor.

Leveraged leases make the most sense when the lessee is not in a position to use tax credits or depreciation deductions that come with owning the asset. By arranging for someone else to hold title, a leveraged lease passes on these benefits. The lessee can benefit because the lessor may return a portion of the tax benefits to the lessee in the form of lower lease costs.

Concept questions

24.2a *What are the differences between an operating lease and a financial lease?*
24.2b *What is a sale and leaseback agreement?*

24.3 ■ A brief look at accounting for leases

In March 1984 the Australian Accounting Standard 17 (AAS17), 'Accounting for Leases' was released. Among other provisions AAS17 required lessee firms to capitalise financial leases. Previously, firms were not required to provide any specific disclosure so that leasing was frequently called **off Statement of Financial Position financing** (originally it was known as off Balance Sheet financing). During a transitional period until 31 December 1987, firms were allowed footnote disclosure; however, now capitalisation is mandatory. Essentially, this requirement means that the present value of the lease payments must be calculated and reported along with debt and other liabilities on the right-hand side of the lessee's Statement of Financial Position. The same amount must be shown as an asset on the left-hand side of the Statement of Financial Position. Exactly what constitutes a financial or operating lease for accounting purposes is discussed below.

off Statement of Financial Position financing

when firms are not required to provide any specific disclosure of the financing on their Statement of Financial Position

The accounting implications of AAS17 are illustrated in Table 24.1. Imagine a firm that has $100,000 in assets and no debt, implying that the equity is also $100,000. The firm needs a truck costing $100,000 (it is a big truck) that it can lease or buy. The top of the table shows the Statement of Financial Position assuming that the firm borrows the money and buys the truck.

Accounting implications of AAS17

TABLE 24.1

Statements of Financial Position

	Initial	Borrowing	Operating	Financial
Equity	$100,000	$100,000	$100,000	$100,000
Represented by:				
Other assets	$100,000	$100,000	$100,000	$100,000
Truck		100,000		
Assets under capital lease				100,000
	$100,000	$200,000	$100,000	$200,000
Debt		100,000		
Obligations under capital lease				100,000
Net assets	$100,000	$100,000	$100,000	$100,000

Borrowing: the company borrows $100,000 for the truck.
Operating: the company has an operating lease for the truck.
Financial: the company has a capital lease for the truck.

In column 2 of Table 24.1, the firm borrows $100,000 for the truck so that the truck appears as an asset and the loan appears as a liability. In column 3, an operating lease is used so that neither the truck (the asset) nor the lease payments (the liability) appear on the Statement of Financial Position. In column 4 a financial lease is used so that the truck appears as an asset and the lease payments are capitalised to appear as a liability.

As stated earlier, it is difficult to define precisely what constitutes a financial lease and what constitutes an operating lease. AAS17 has added to the confusion. The Standard states that a financial lease occurs where substantially all risks and benefits under the agreement pass to the lessee. In contrast, the American and English standards SFAS 13 and SSAP1 rely on the legal form of the contract to classify the lease. Firms in these environments avoided the capitalisation requirement by contracting to classify leases as operating. Because the Australian standard relies on the substance of the arrangement rather than the contractual legality, it should be more difficult in theory to create an operating lease. To avoid capitalisation of financial leases Australian firms have moved outside AAS17 guidelines. The specific guidelines of AAS17 provide the following tests for an arrangement to be identified as a financial lease:

1 the lease term must be for 75 per cent or more of the remaining useful life of the asset; or
2 the present value, at the beginning of the lease term, of the minimum lease payments equals or exceeds 90 per cent of the fair value of the leased property to the lessor at that date.

Methods which would avoid the tests are, for example:

1 insertion of a renewal clause or option in the lease to avoid (1) above. The original lease term is set for less than 75 per cent of the useful life; however, the option extends the term beyond 75 per cent of the useful life.
2 establishing guaranteed residuals to avoid (2) above. For example, assume the residual value of the leased asset is $10,000. The lease would only include $1,000 but the lessor would receive the salvage value up to $9,000 ($10,000 less the $1,000). Only the $1,000 reduced residual value would be included in the present value calculation. The receipt of the $9,000 would be covered in a contract quite separate to the lease payments of premium and residual.

Whether firms have resorted to such practices is an empirical issue but efforts for keeping leases off the Statement of Financial Position are probably wasting time. Of course, if leases are not on the Statement of Financial Position, traditional measures of financial leverage, such as the ratio of total debt to total assets, will understate the true degree of financial leverage. As a consequence, the Statement of Financial Position will appear 'stronger' than it really is, but it seems unlikely that this type of manipulation could mislead many people.

Concept questions

24.3a *Explain what is meant by 'AAS17 uses a substance over form approach to distinguish between operating and financial leases'.*

24.3b *Why might financial managers prefer to have a lease classified as operating rather than financial? Is the classification likely to fool the market?*

 ## 24.4 Taxation and leases

As a general rule lease premiums paid under a lease contract are considered to be taxation deductions. Section 8–1 of the Australian *Income Assessment Act* (the Act) is a general provision that authorises deductions incurred for the purpose of producing assessable income (taxable income). Any part of the payments that represents private use or partial payment towards ultimate purchase of the leased item is not deductible. From a taxation point of view the lease premiums are seen as periodic rental payments and these would qualify as deductions. The residual payment relates to purchasing the equipment so that it would not qualify as a taxation deduction; however, there are indirect taxation consequences of the residual payment.

Any amount received by a taxpayer as a result of the sale at a profit of plant or equipment previously leased by the taxpayer and used in the conduct of its business is assessable as income or subject to capital gains tax provisions. This will be the case where the lessee purchases leased plant from the lessor under the residual value clause and then sells the plant or trades it in for more than the payout residual value. If the lessee purchases the plant for the residual value and then continues to use the plant the lessee would be able to claim depreciation deductions using the residual value as the base.

Depreciating the residual value

EXAMPLE 24.1

Good-dai Enterprises Ltd currently leases highly specialised eye testing equipment it uses to test patients. Monthly lease premiums have been $5,000 for five years. The last premium for the equipment is due on 1 June 200X. On 30 June 200X, Good-dai is required to pay the residual value of $50,000 under the lease agreement. Good-dai is in a position to make the payment. Management feels that the equipment has a useful life of another seven years as its technology level matches other equipment that is available. The Commissioner for Taxation allows a depreciation rate of 15 per cent straight-line or 22.5 per cent reducing balance on eye equipment and Good-dai uses the reducing balance method of depreciation. What depreciation deduction will Good-dai be able to claim for the machine in each year if it has zero salvage value in seven years, and what will be the total deductions from assessable income?

Date			Depreciation claims
200X	Residual Value purchase 1 July	$50,000	
	Depreciation year 1 at 22.5%	11,250	$11,250
200X+1	Depreciated Value beginning year 2	$38,750	
	Depreciation year 2 at 22.5%	8,719	8,719
200X+2	Depreciated Value beginning year 3	30,031	
	Depreciation year 3 at 22.5%	6,757	6,757
200X+3	Depreciated Value beginning year 4	23,274	
	Depreciation year 4 at 22.5%	5,237	5,237
200X+4	Depreciated Value beginning year 5	18,037	
	Depreciation year 5 at 22.5%	4,058	4,058
200X+5	Depreciated Value beginning year 6	13,979	
	Depreciation year 6 at 22.5%	3,145	3,145
200X+6	Depreciated Value beginning year 7	10,834	
	Depreciation year 7 at 22.5%	2,438	2,438
200X+7	Depreciated Value end of year 7	8,396	
200X+7	Salvage Value end of year 7	zero	
Loss on salvage		8,396	8,396
Total depreciation and loss			$50,000

There are specific sections under the Act that relate to leased motor cars or station wagons. Generally, where a leased motor car or station wagon used for income-producing purposes is subsequently purchased by the lessee, who then sells it, the profit made on the sale is assessable to the lessee. The profit is taxable on a basis comparable with the sale of depreciated property. While the principle is straightforward, the application is complicated because there are limits placed on the amounts assessable. Where the consideration receivable by the lessee on the disposal of a motor car or station wagon exceeds the cost of the vehicle to the lessee, the excess is assessable to the extent that it does not exceed the lowest of the following amounts:

1 the amount of notional depreciation deemed to have been allowed to the lessee over the period of the lease agreement;
2 the amount of deductible lease charges paid under the lease agreement.

EXAMPLE 24.2 ■ Taxed profit on the disposal of leased vehicles

Bonjour Ozi Pty Ltd leased a four wheel drive vehicle on 1 March 1999. The vehicle has been used privately by the managing director, Paul Pleasant, 30 per cent of the time and the remainder of the time it has been used for carrying tourists. The cost of the four wheel drive wagon to the lessor was $70,000; however, the vehicle was subject to a motor vehicle depreciation cost limit of $55,134. The Act places a limit on the depreciable cost of motor cars and station wagons over a certain price. The limit started at $18,000 in 1980 and has been increased in subsequent years. Revised limits have been:

30 June 1990	$42,910
30 June 1996	$52,912
30 June 1999	$55,134 (this limit was still current at June 2002)

Conditions of the lease were:

1 Lease premium per month—$1,800;
2 Term of the lease—36 months;
3 Residual value on 28 February 2002, $25,000.

On 28 February 2002, Bonjour Ozi paid the residual value and then sold the wagon for $55,000. What amount would be included in the assessable income of Bonjour as a result of the transaction?

Bonjour's profit on the sale is $30,000 ($55,000 − $25,000); however, this amount may not be included in the assessable income because the amount included cannot exceed:

1 the notional depreciation;
2 the deductible lease premiums.

Calculation of notional depreciation

Deemed cost to Bonjour (because of the cost limit)	$55,134
Deemed depreciation at 15% ($55,134 × 15% × 3 years)	24,810
Notional written down value	$30,324

(**Note**: The depreciation limit provisions of the Act reduce the deemed cost from $70,000 to $55,134.)
The residual value of $25,000 paid to the lessor is adjusted in accordance with the wagon depreciation cost limit in order to calculate the deemed depreciation as follows:

$$\$25,000 \times \$55,134/70,000 = \$19,691$$

$$\text{Excess of notional written down value} = \$30,324 - \$19,691$$
$$= \$10,633$$

$$\text{Adjusted deemed depreciation} = \$24,810 + \$10,633$$
$$= \$35,443$$

As the actual profit ($30,000) is less than the adjusted deemed depreciation ($35,443), the former figure will be included in the assessable income if it is less than the deductible lease premiums.

Deductible lease premiums

$$\text{Deductible lease premiums} = \text{business use} \times \text{number} \times \text{amount}$$
$$= 70\% \times 36 \times \$1,800$$
$$= \$45,360$$

It follows that the amount included in the assessable income of Bonjour would be $30,000.

The Bonjour example (Example 24.2) provides some insight into the complexities that the Australian taxation system has introduced into the selling of leased assets, particularly motor cars and station wagons. We have not attempted to expose students to all the difficulties in the area as that is left to a text on taxation. Nevertheless, finance students have to be aware of the general principles associated with the taxation of leasing, because taxation plays such an important role in the evaluation of leasing.

Concept questions

24.4a *Is it true that borrowing to purchase is preferred to leasing because depreciation and interest payments are allowable deductions if the asset is to be used in producing assessable income? Why or why not?*

24.4b *Comment on the following: 'Leasing is good news because one can increase the premiums (which are tax-deductible) and decrease the residual value, thus buying a valuable asset at a price much less than market value.'*

24.5 ■ An evaluation of leasing

To begin our analysis of the leasing decision, we need to identify the relevant cash flows. The first part of this section illustrates how this is done. A key point, and one to watch for, is that taxation is a very important consideration in a lease analysis.

The incremental cash flows

Consider the decision confronting Pokeahole Wells Ltd, a company that sinks bores. Business has been expanding, and Pokeahole currently has a five-year backlog of bore orders.

The International Boring Machine Corporation (IBMC) Ltd makes a boring machine that can be purchased for $10,000. Pokeahole has determined that it needs a new machine, and the IBMC model will save Pokeahole $6,000 per year in reduced electricity bills for the next five years, but it does not have immediate funds.

Pokeahole has a company tax rate of 30 per cent. For simplicity, we assume five-year straight-line depreciation is used for the boring machine and that after five years the machine will be worthless. Liberal Leasing Corporation Ltd has offered to lease the same boring machine to Pokeahole for lease payments of $2,500 per year for five years. With the lease, Pokeahole would remain responsible for maintenance, insurance and operating expenses.[3]

Shelly Beach has been asked to compare the direct incremental cash flows from leasing the IBMC machine to the cash flows associated with borrowing to buy it. The first thing she realises is that, because Pokeahole will have the machine either way, the $6,000 saving will be realised whether the machine is leased or purchased through borrowing. Thus, the cost saving, and any other operating costs or revenues, can be ignored in the analysis.

Upon reflection, Ms Beach concludes that there are only two important cash flow differences between leasing and borrowing.[4] The first concerns the funds tied up in the leasing.

1 If the machine is leased, Pokeahole must make a lease payment of $2,500 each year. This will commit future funds of the firm. Alternatively, the firm can borrow $10,000 now and give up some of its borrowing potential. The choice for Pokeahole is whether it gives up future borrowing potential, by committing $2,500 per year to the lease, or it borrows the $10,000 now, giving up the borrowing potential now. The comparison of the present value of the future funds committed with the amount to be borrowed now is the **opportunity cost of leasing**.

opportunity cost of leasing

this is the borrowing potential of the firm given up if it enters the lease agreement

2   The second cash flow difference relates to taxation.

a   If the machine is leased, Pokeahole must make a lease payment of $2,500 each year. However, lease payments are fully deductible, so the tax saving because of the lease payment is $0.30 \times \$2,500 = \$750$. This is the tax subsidy attributable to leasing.

b   If Pokeahole borrows and purchases the machine, it will be entitled to two taxation deductions, one for depreciation and the other for interest. Because we have assumed five-year straight-line depreciation, the depreciation would be $\$10,000/5 = \$2,000$. A $2,000 depreciation deduction generates a tax shield of $0.30 \times \$2,000 = \$600$ per year. Let us assume that Pokeahole can borrow the funds to purchase the machine at 10 per cent per annum. We can now work out the amount of interest that will be paid each year.

For consistency we assume that the repayments are to be made at the end of each of the five years, which is the situation with the leasing arrangement. The annual repayment is:

$$\$10,000/[1 - 1/(1 + r)^t]/r$$
$$= \$10,000/[1 - 1/1 + 0.10)^5]/0.1$$
$$= \$10,000/3.7908$$
$$= \$2,638.$$

The amount of interest in each payment may be derived from the repayment schedule in Table 24.2.

TABLE
24.2

Repayment schedule, Pokeahole Wells Ltd

Year	Principal outstanding at beginning	Interest 10%	Total amount owing	Repayment	Principal carried forward
1	$10,000	$1,000	$11,000	$2,638	$8,362
2	8,362	836	9,198	2,638	6,560
3	6,560	656	7,216	2,638	4,578
4	4,578	458	5,036	2,638	2,398
5	2,398	240	2,638	2,638	nil

Ms Beach can now complete the evaluation of the leasing alternative. Pokeahole can borrow to finance the purchase of the machine at 10 per cent per annum so the relevant interest rate for the evaluation is 10 per cent.

$$\begin{matrix} \text{Opportunity cost} \\ \text{of leasing} \end{matrix} = \begin{matrix} \text{Present value of the} \\ \text{leasing payments} \end{matrix} - \begin{matrix} \text{The borrowing cost} \\ \text{of outlay for the machine} \end{matrix} \quad (24.1)$$

For the Pokeahole example this is:

$$= \$2,500 \times 3.7908 - \$10,000$$
$$= \$9,477 - \$10,000$$
$$= (\$523)$$

Because the opportunity cost is negative, leasing provides an advantage in terms of tying up borrowing potential. The evaluation now turns to the incremental taxation position.

Table 24.3 summarises the position. The borrowing to purchase alternative results in tax subsidies that provide a present value of $3,041 (panel A); while the leasing alternative provides $2,843 (panel B) for the same figure. It is now necessary to combine the opportunity cost of leasing with the tax subsidies to see if there is any advantage in leasing.

$$\begin{array}{c}\text{Net advantage} \\ \text{of leasing}\end{array} = \begin{array}{c}\text{Difference in} \\ \text{tax subsidies} \\ \text{(net tax savings)}\end{array} - \begin{array}{c}\text{Opportunity cost} \\ \text{of leasing}\end{array} \qquad (24.2)$$

$$\begin{aligned} &= \text{Tax subsidies for leasing} - \text{Tax subsidies for borrowing} - \text{Opportunity cost} \\ &= (\$2,843 - \$3,041) - (-\$523) \\ &= (-\$198) + \$523 \\ &= \$325 \end{aligned}$$

The advantage is greater than zero, so Pokeahole should lease. Leasing provides an advantage over borrowing to purchase the asset to show a positive **net advantage of leasing (NAL)**.

net advantage of leasing (NAL)

the NPV of the decision to lease an asset instead of borrowing to purchase it

---

Comparison of tax subsidies: Lease versus borrowing, Pokeahole Wells Ltd

TABLE 24.3

Panel A: Tax subsidises borrowing

Year	Depreciation deduction	Interest deduction	Total deductions	Present value factor – 10%	Present value
1	$2,000	$1,000	$3,000	$(1.1)^{-1} = 0.9091$	$ 2,727
2	2,000	836	2,836	$(1.1)^{-2} = 0.8264$	2,344
3	2,000	656	2,656	$(1.1)^{-3} = 0.7513$	1,995
4	2,000	458	2,458	$(1.1)^{-4} = 0.6830$	1,679
5	2,000	240	2,240	$(1.1)^{-5} = 0.6209$	1,391
				Total	$10,136
			Present value of the tax subsidies (30%)		$ 3,041

Panel B: Tax subsidises leasing

Year	Lease premium	Total deduction	Present value factor – 10%	Present value
1	$2,500	$2,500	$(1.1)^{-1} = 0.9091$	$2,272
2	2,500	2,500	$(1.1)^{-2} = 0.8264$	2,066
3	2,500	2,500	$(1.1)^{-3} = 0.7513$	1,878
4	2,500	2,500	$(1.1)^{-4} = 0.6830$	1,708
5	2,500	2,500	$(1.1)^{-5} = 0.6209$	1,552
			Total	$9,476
		Present value of the tax subsidies (30%)		$2,843

Put simply:

$$\text{Lease premium} \times \text{tax rate} \times [1 - 1/(1 + r)^t]/r$$
$$= \$2,500 \times 0.30 \times [1 - 1/(1.1)^5]/0.1$$
$$= \$2,500 \times 0.30 \times 3.7908$$
$$= \$2,843$$

A note on taxes

Shelly Beach has assumed that Pokeahole can use the tax benefits of the depreciation allowances and the lease payments. This may not always be the case. If Pokeahole were losing money, it would not pay taxes and the tax shelters would be worthless (unless they could be shifted to someone else).

Concept questions

24.5a *What are the cash flow consequences of leasing instead of borrowing to buy?*

24.5b *Explain why the opportunity cost of leasing in the Pokeahole example is a plus to leasing.*

▌24.6▐ The role of the residual value

residual value

the amount for which the asset may be purchased by the lessee at the end of the lease term

The **residual value** is the amount for which the asset may be purchased by the lessee from the lessor at the end of the lease term. For example, it may be a condition of the Pokeahole Wells Ltd lease with Liberal Leasing Company Ltd that Pokeahole will be able to purchase the pipe-boring machine at the end of the lease for a residual value of $1,000. As well as the consideration of the cash flow that is linked to the residual value payout, Pokeahole must also consider the taxation consequences associated with the payout. Because it is a contractual obligation, under the lease Pokeahole must pay the lessor the residual amount. When the payment is made full ownership of the pipe-boring machine passes to Pokeahole. At that point Pokeahole can continue to use the equipment or it may sell it. We will call the price that Pokeahole may obtain from selling the equipment the salvage value of the equipment. If Pokeahole continues to use the equipment, the opportunity cost of using it is the salvage value Pokeahole would have to do without.

Let us consider three situations. One, where it is estimated that at the end of the lease contract, the salvage value is zero. The second, where the salvage value is $500, and a third where the salvage value is $1,500. There will be different tax considerations in each situation; however, as we shall see, they will not change the net tax savings from one salvage value to another. The opportunity cost of leasing will change because we have to build in the residual value; however, it will be the same for all salvage values.

Opportunity cost of leasing	=	Present value of the leasing payments	+	The present value of the residual value	−	The borrowing outlay for the machine

$$= [\$2,500 \times 3.7908 + 1,000/(1 + 0.1)^5] - \$10,000$$
$$= (\$9,477 + \$621) - \$10,000$$
$$= \$10,098 - \$10,000$$
$$= \$98$$

Table 24.4 presents the tax considerations for each situation. In the analysis we are assuming that Pokeahole pays the residual value and sells or scraps the equipment immediately for its salvage value. Even if Pokeahole does not take this action, the results of the assumption represent the opportunity costs to Pokeahole. We see from Table 24.4 and from the above calculation that for the three salvage values:

$$\text{NAL} = \text{Net tax saving} - \text{Opportunity cost of leasing}$$
$$(\$110) = (\$12) - \$98$$

TABLE
24.4

Residual value with different salvage values, Pokeahole Wells Ltd

Panel A: Pokeahole leases the equipment

	Situation 1	Situation 2	Situation 3
Salvage value	Zero	$500	$1,500
Residual value	$1,000	$1,000	$1,000
Gain (loss) on leasing	($1,000)	($500)	$500
Tax savings (payment) in year 5 @ 30%	$300	$150	($150)
Present value tax savings (payment)	$186	$93	($93)
Add tax subsidies from Table 24.3	$2,843	$2,843	$2,843
Total tax subsidies (A)	$3,029	$2,936	$2,750

Panel B: Pokeahole borrows to purchase

	Situation 1	Situation 2	Situation 3
Salvage value	Zero	$500	$1,500
Depreciated value	Zero	Zero	Zero
Gain on salvage	Nil	$500	$1,500
Tax savings (payment) in year 5 @ 30%	Nil	($150)	($450)
Present value of tax (payment)	Nil	($93)	($279)
Add tax subsidies from Table 24.3	$3,041	$3,041	$3,041
Total tax subsidies (B)	$3,041	$2,948	$2,762
Net tax savings A − B	($12)	($12)	($12)

By introducing the salvage and the residual value we have shifted the advantage away from leasing to the borrowing to purchase alternative. The NAL is now negative.

When a residual value component is introduced into the lease evaluation, the cash flow associated with the residual value commitment at the end of the lease and the tax consequences associated with the salvage value of the asset must both be taken into account.

The interest component

There is much debate in the literature as to the correct interest rate to be used in the economic evaluation of leases. The alternatives proposed are:

1 the risk-adjusted rate for the operations of the leased equipment;
2 the weighted average cost of capital of the firm;
3 the risk-free interest rate;
4 the borrowing rate of the firm; and
5 the borrowing rate of the firm after tax.

Some theorists suggest that different rates should be used for different cash flows in the analysis.

In identifying the correct rate we must focus upon the opportunity we are evaluating. In an evaluation of leasing it is the financing of the purchase of an asset. It is not the operational need or use of the asset itself. That evaluation would have been completed prior to looking at the best method of financing the purchase. It has been stated earlier that leasing is just another method of borrowing funds to finance the purchase of an asset. The next best opportunity to 'leasing an asset' is 'borrowing to purchase the asset'. It follows that, if we accept these alternatives, then the 'correct' interest rate is the borrowing rate of the firm.

Why not the borrowing rate of the firm after tax? When we complete the economic evaluation of leasing, one of the important elements is the difference in the tax savings between leasing and borrowing to purchase. When we consider cash flows and tax savings, we are reducing the cash flows by the amount of tax we save. If we were to reduce the interest rate as well as the cash flows, we would be ignoring the taxation effect. Perhaps an example will explain this point.

Consider the following:

$$
\begin{aligned}
\text{Cash expenses paid in perpetuity} &= \$5,000 \\
\text{Taxation rate} &= 30\% \\
\text{Borrowing rate} &= 10\% \\
\text{Borrowing rate after tax} &= 10(1 - 0.30) \\
&= 7\%
\end{aligned}
$$

The present value of all future cash expenses if we ignore taxation is:

$$\$5,000/0.1 = \$50,000$$

However, if we introduce taxation the cash expenses will be reduced by the taxation saved (if we assume the firm has assessable income) so that the present value of all future cash expenses becomes:

$$\$5,000(1 - 0.30)/0.1 = \$35,000$$

Now, if we were also to adjust the interest rate for taxation, we have the present value of all future cash expenses as:

$$\$5,000(1 - 0.30)/0.07 = \$50,000$$

We have ignored the tax saving we can make because we can deduct the cash expenses from assessable income. We repeat, *the correct interest rate is the borrowing rate of the firm without any adjustment for taxation.*

Concept questions

24.6a *Explain why each of the following is true or false:*
  i *The residual value requirement will always increase the opportunity cost of leasing.*
  ii *The residual value requirement will always reduce the net advantage of leasing (NAL).*
  iii *The influence of a residual value requirement is uncertain in relation to the difference in tax subsidies between leasing and borrowing to purchase.*
24.6b *How will the residual value feature in the lease evaluation if it is equal to the salvage value?*
24.6c *Why shouldn't we use the risk-free rate as the interest rate for the economic evaluation of leases?*

24.7 ▪ Setting lease premiums

We have identified leasing as a form of borrowing to purchase an asset so it is not surprising that the lease premium will include a component for the use of capital (interest) and a component for the return of capital (loan repayment). The capital recovery component of the lease premium represents the amortisation by the lessor of the debt that is due because of the lease. The procedure for setting a lease premium is as follows:

Asset value
Less   Residual payout
Lease debt amortisation

Lease base = Lease debt amortisation/Present value annuity factor

Lease premium = Lease base + Interest × Residual payout

Setting lease premiums in arrears

EXAMPLE 24.3

Howdy Finance Ltd is preparing a two-year lease for a motor vehicle which has a purchase price of $40,000. Howdy is prepared to supply funds for the lease at 12.68 per cent per annum which is 1 per cent per month. It has been agreed with the lessee that there will be a residual value of $8,000 at the end of the two years. What will be the lease premium if payments are made in arrears?

	Asset value	$40,000
Less	Residual payout	8,000
	Lease debt amortisation	$32,000

$$\text{Lease base} = \frac{\text{Lease debt amortisation}}{\text{Present value annuity factor}}$$

$$= \frac{\$32,000}{[1 - 1/(1.01)^{24}]/0.01}$$

$$= \$32,000/21.2434$$

$$= \$1,506.35$$

$$\begin{aligned}\text{Lease premium} &= \text{Lease base} + \text{Interest} \times \text{Residual payout}\\ &= \$1,506.35 + 0.01 \times \$8,000\\ &= \$1,586.35\end{aligned}$$

Australian commercial practice in relation to leasing is to have lease premiums paid in advance; that is, at the beginning of each period. In Example 24.3, if Howdy were to adopt the usual practice, the lease premium would have to be converted from an end of the month payment to a payment at the beginning of the month. The lease premium paid in advance in the Howdy example is $1,586.35/1.01 = $1,570.64.

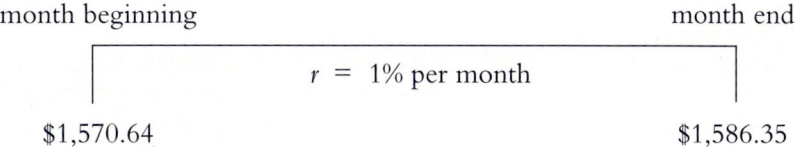

month beginning   month end

$r = 1\%$ per month

$1,570.64 $1,586.35

We could have calculated the lease premium in advance directly instead of going through the process of calculating the lease premium in arrears and converting it. The formula is:

$$\text{Lease premium in advance} = \frac{(\text{Asset value} - \text{Present value of the residual value})}{1 + \text{Present value annuity factor for } t - 1 \text{ payments}} \quad (24.3)$$

where t represents the total payments of lease premiums. For the Howdy example the calculation is:

$$\text{Lease premium in advance} = \frac{\$40,000 - \$8,000(1.01)^{-24}}{1 + [1 - 1/(1.01)^{23}]0.01}$$
$$= \$33,699.47/(1 + 20.4558)$$
$$= \$1,570.64$$

In the Howdy Finance example (Example 24.3) we were given the monthly leasing interest rate as 1 per cent per month. Suppose this rate was equal to the rate at which the lessee could borrow the funds to purchase the asset. What would be the opportunity cost of the alternative methods of financing the purchase? Obviously it will be zero because both alternatives are charging the same rate of interest. The calculation using the lease premiums in arrears data is:

$$\text{Opportunity cost of leasing} = [\$1,586.35 \times 21.2434 + \$8,000 \, (1.01)^{-24}] - \$40,000$$
$$= (\$33,699.47 + \$6,300.53) - \$40,000$$
$$= \$40,000 - \$40,000$$
$$= \text{zero}$$

This is precisely what the opportunity cost should be in a competitive market where the rate used to determine lease premiums is the opportunity cost of borrowing. When these rates are different then advantages or disadvantages will occur. In a competitive and frictionless market, the expected net advantage of leasing (NAL) is zero. However, in a market that has a tendency towards competitive equilibrium but has yet to reach equilibrium, positive net present values will exist and NAL is just one of these. The NAL may be positive or negative so that it is not possible to make generalised statements that leasing has more advantages or disadvantages than borrowing to purchase.

Concept questions

24.7a *Explain why it is better to pay lease premiums in arrears or in advance.*
24.7b *Explain whether the lease repayments represent a recovery of just principal for the lessor or a recovery of principal and interest.*

24.8 Alleged advantages and disadvantages of leasing

Proponents of leasing make many claims about why firms should lease assets rather than buy them. The advantages usually feature prominently in the promotional material supplied by finance companies marketing leasing. We have already made the point that the NAL is related to the specific analysis and no general statement can be made about leasing. The asserted advantages are questionable and they break down under rigorous analysis. The following are the most frequently encountered alleged advantages and disadvantages.

Advantages

Financial

- Leasing places no restrictions on future borrowing by the company.
- Leasing provides a source of funds that may be tailored to the firm's specific needs.
- Leasing eliminates the need to raise additional capital to finance expansion.
- Leasing relieves the company of unnecessary financial outlay.
- Some leasing arrangements do not have to be disclosed in the Statement of Financial Position so that no liability appears.
- Leasing facilitates financing capital additions on a piecemeal basis.
- Leasing is an allowable cost under government contracting.
- Leasing offers a tax advantage.

Operating

- Leasing frees capital of the company for alternative uses.
- Leasing increases the company's pool of working capital.
- Leasing gives greater control as future outlays are known with greater certainty.
- Leasing assures more competent maintenance and servicing of equipment.

Risk

- Leasing avoids the risk of obsolescence.
- Leasing avoids the equipment disposal problem.
- The bulk of the dollars outlaid are future dollars, which in times of inflation are worth less than current dollars in real terms.

Disadvantages

- Interest cost of leasing is higher.
- Leasing may provide no right to the residual value of the asset.
- Leasing enables line executives to acquire equipment without submitting to formal capital expenditure procedures.
- Leasing may cause distortions in the evaluation of interfirm and interdivision performance.
- Leasing lacks the prestige associated with the ownership of assets.

We do not intend to discuss the claims in detail; however, some general areas require some discussion. These are taxation, uncertainty, 100 per cent financing, transaction costs, and leasing and accounting income.

Taxation

One of the things we do in evaluating leasing is look at the difference in tax savings so that it should be obvious that taxation reduction is one of the driving forces of leasing. Leasing may exist simply because of the difference in the tax situations of the lessor and the lessee. They may be taxed at different marginal rates so that taxation deductions are more valuable to one than the other. If this is the case, the negotiated lease premium may reflect transfer of some of the value of the tax deduction between the parties. Another tax incentive for lease arrangements could be where one party can claim a higher rate of deduction. For example, the depreciation deduction rate for the lessor could be higher than the rate allowed for the borrowing buyer. In determining the depreciation rates for taxation deductions, the Australian Taxation Office permits the owner of rented equipment a higher depreciation rate than the owner of equipment that is not rented or hired.

A reduction of uncertainty

We have noted that the lessee does not own the property when the lease expires. The value of the property at this time is called the *residual value*. At the time the lease contract is signed, there may be substantial uncertainty as to what the residual value of the asset will be. A lease contract is a method that transfers this uncertainty from the lessee to the lessor.

Transferring the uncertainty about the residual value of an asset to the lessor makes sense when the lessor is better able to bear the risk. For example, if the lessor is the manufacturer, then the lessor may be better able to assess and manage the risk associated with the residual value. The transfer of uncertainty to the lessor amounts to a form of insurance for the lessee.

Obsolescence

The reduction of uncertainty motive for leasing is the one that is most cited by companies. For example, computers have a way of becoming technologically outdated very quickly, and computers are very commonly leased instead of purchased. In a recent survey, 82 per cent of the responding firms cited the risk of obsolescence as an important reason for leasing, whereas only 57 per cent cited the potential for cheaper financing. It must be remembered that, if there is a risk of obsolescence, there is the same element of risk to the lessor and to the lessee. In consequence the lessor is going to see that the risk reflects in a higher lease premium so the lessee is paying for the risk reduction. It is simply a case of lower risk for lower return (higher cost in this case for the lessee).

100 per cent financing

It is often claimed that an advantage to leasing is that it provides 100 per cent financing, whereas secured equipment loans require an initial downpayment. Of course, a firm can simply borrow the downpayment from another source that provides unsecured credit. Moreover, leases do usually involve a downpayment in the form of an advance lease payment. Even when they do not, leases may implicitly be secured by assets of the firm other than those being leased (leasing may give the appearance of 100 per cent financing, but not the substance).

Transaction costs

The costs of changing ownership of an asset many times over its useful life will frequently be greater than the costs of writing a lease agreement. Consider the choice that confronts a person who lives in Melbourne but must do business in Sydney for two days. It seems obvious that it will be cheaper to rent a hotel room for two nights than it would be to buy a home unit for two days and then to sell it. Thus, transaction costs may be the major reason for short-term leases (operating leases). However, this is probably not the major reason for financial leases.

Leasing and accounting income

Leasing can have a significant effect on the appearance of the firm's financial statements. If a firm is successful at keeping its leases off the books, the Statement of Financial Position and income statement can be made to look better. As a consequence, accounting-based performance measures such as return on assets (ROA) can appear to be higher.

For example, off-the-book leases (that is, operating leases) result in an expense, namely, the lease payment. However, in the early years of the lease, the expense will usually be lower than that which would occur (in accounting terms) if the asset were purchased. If an asset is purchased with debt financing, depreciation and interest expenses will be subtracted from revenues to determine accounting net income. When accelerated depreciation is used, the total of the depreciation deduction and the interest expense will almost always exceed the lease payments. Thus, accounting net income is greater with leasing.

In addition, because an operating lease does not appear on the Statement of Financial Position, total assets (and total liabilities) will be lower than they would be if the firm borrowed the money and bought the asset. From Chapter 3, ROA is computed as net income divided by total assets. With an operating lease, the net income is bigger and total assets are smaller, so ROA will be larger.

The impact that leasing has on a firm's accounting statements is not likely to fool anyone. As always, what matters are the cash flow consequences, and whether or not a lease has a positive NPV has little to do with its effect on a firm's financial statements.

Concept question

24.8a *Consider the alleged advantages and disadvantages of leasing identified in the section and see if you can analyse each to show how it breaks down.*

24.9 ■ **Summary and conclusions**

Leasing is an alternative method of financing an asset. A large proportion of Australian financing is conducted through lease contracts. This chapter describes different leases, accounting and tax implications of leasing, how to evaluate financial leases and how lease premiums are calculated.

1 Leases can be separated into two types, financial and operating. Financial leases are generally longer-term, fully amortised and not cancellable. Operating leases are usually shorter-term, partially amortised, and cancellable.

2 The distinction between financial and operating leases is important in financial accounting. Financial leases must be reported on a firm's Statement of Financial Position; operating leases are not. We discussed the specific accounting criteria for classifying leases as financial or operating.

3 Taxes are an important consideration in leasing, both in relation to the tax savings that must be considered in evaluating leases and the taxable gain or loss that relates to the residual value at the end of the lease contract.

4 A long-term financial lease is a source of financing much like long-term borrowing. We showed how to go about an NPV analysis of the leasing decision to decide whether leasing is cheaper than borrowing. A key insight was that the appropriate discount rate is the firm's borrowing rate.

5 The lease premium is set by the lessor to recover the principal that is tied up in the asset and a component for interest on that principal.

6 Many of the claimed advantages and disadvantages of leasing are not acceptable under close analysis; however, three elements may create economic advantages for the parties to a lease. These are differential taxation rates, reducing uncertainty and avoiding transaction costs.

Key terms

Financial lease *827*	Lessor *826*	Operating lease *826*
Lease premium *826*	Leveraged lease *828*	Residual value *836*
Lessee *826*	Net advantage of leasing *835*	Sale and leaseback *828*

Suggested readings

A classic article on lease valuation is:

Myers, S., Dill, D.A. and Bautista, A.J. 'Valuation of Financial Lease Contracts', *Journal of Finance*, June 1976, pp. 799–819.

See also:

Ross, S.A., Westerfield, R.W. and Jordan, B.D. *Corporate Finance*, 6th edn, Irwin/McGraw-Hill, New York, 2003, Chapter 26.

A good review and discussion of leasing is contained in:

Smith, C.W. Jr and Wakeman, L.M. 'Determinations of Corporate Leasing Policy', *Journal of Finance*, July 1985, pp. 895–908.

Evidence mentioned in the chapter is from:

Mukherjee, T.K. 'A Survey of Corporate Leasing Analysis', *Financial Management*, Autumn 1991.

Bazley, M., Brown, P. and Izan, H.Y. 'An Analysis of Lease Disclosures by Australian Companies', *Abacus*, Vol. 21, No. 1, 1985, pp. 44–62.

Endnotes

1 Equipment leasing can now be easily done on the Internet.

2 Captive finance companies may not be limited in their operations to leasing; for example, some purchase the parent company's accounts receivable as a factoring agent.

3 We have assumed that all lease payments are made in arrears; that is, at the end of the year. Actually, most leases require payments to be made at the beginning of the year.

4 There is a third consequence that we do not discuss here. If the machine has a non-trivial salvage value, then, if we lease, we give up that salvage value. We will address this issue later.

On the web

Now that you have arrived at this point, use your own web skills to find evidence of leasing being available through Internet transactions. A good place to start will be some of the sites we have listed in the preceding chapters.

Maximise Your Marks!
There are 30 interactive questions on leasing waiting online for you at www.mhhe.com/au/ross3e. The questions are written with additional feedback for incorrect answers, and text excerpts with page references for follow-up study.

International Articles!
To read more on leasing and to see current international articles, just go to www.mhhe.com/au/ross3e and click on *PowerWeb Articles* for this chapter.

Chapter review problems and self-test

24.1 · Opportunity cost of leasing

Your company wants to purchase a new network file server for its wide area computer network. The server costs $24,000. It will be completely obsolete in 3 years. Your options are to borrow the money at 10 per cent or lease the machine. If you lease it, the payments will be $9,000 per year, payable at the end of each year. If you buy the server, you can depreciate it straight-line to zero over 3 years. The tax rate is 30 per cent. Should you lease or borrow to purchase?

24.2 · Setting the lease premium

In the previous problem, assume that there will be a scrap value at the end of year 3 so that the lessor will require a residual value of $4,000. What will be the revised lease premium if we assume the lessor charges 10 per cent per annum? If the lessor charges 6.13 per cent per annum?

Answers to self-test problems

24.1 · Opportunity cost of leasing

$$
\begin{aligned}
&= \text{PV of the lease payments} - \text{Borrowing outlay}\\
&= \$9{,}000 \times [1 - 1/(1.1)^3/0.1] - \$24{,}000\\
&= \$22{,}382 - \$24{,}000\\
&= (\$1{,}618)
\end{aligned}
$$

Difference in tax savings

$$
\begin{aligned}
\text{Tax saving lease} &= 0.30 \times \$9{,}000 \times [1 - 1/(1.1)^3/0.1]\\
&= \$6{,}715
\end{aligned}
$$

$$
\begin{aligned}
\text{Periodic repayment on borrowing} &= \$24{,}000/[1 - 1/(1.1)^3/0.1]\\
&= \$9{,}651
\end{aligned}
$$

Repayment schedule borrowing

Year	Principal outstanding at beginning	Interest 10%	Total amount owing	Repayment	Principal carried forward
1	$24,000	$2,400	$26,400	$9,651	$16,749
2	16,749	1,675	18,424	9,651	8,773
3	8,773	878	9,651	9,651	nil

Depreciation straight-line = $24,000/3 = $8,000 per year

Tax saving borrowing

Year	Depreciation deduction	Interest deduction	Total deductions	Present value factor 10%	Present value
1	$8,000	$2,400	$10,400	0.9091	$9,455
2	8,000	1,675	9,675	0.8264	7,995
3	8,000	878	8,878	0.7513	6,670
				Total	$24,120

Present value of tax saving = 0.30 × $24,120 = $7,236

$$
\begin{aligned}
\text{Net advantage of leasing} &= \text{Difference in tax subsidies} - \text{Opportunity cost of leasing}\\
\text{NAL} &= \$6{,}715 - \$7{,}236 - (\$1{,}618)\\
&= (\$521) + \$1{,}618\\
&= \$1{,}097
\end{aligned}
$$

We should lease because the NAL is $1,097.

24.2 · If we assume the lessor's interest rate is 10 per cent per annum:

	Asset value	$24,000
Less	Residual value	4,000
	Lease debt amortisation	$20,000

Lease base = Lease debt amortisation/Present value annuity factor

$$
\begin{aligned}
\text{Lease base} &= \$20{,}000/[1 - 1/(1.1)^3/0.1] \\
&= \$20{,}000/2.4869 \\
&= \$8{,}042
\end{aligned}
$$

$$
\begin{aligned}
\text{Lease premium} &= \text{Lease base} + \text{Interest} \times \text{Residual payout} \\
&= \$8{,}042 + 10\% \times \$4{,}000 \\
&= \$8{,}442
\end{aligned}
$$

If we assume the lessor's interest rate is 6.13 per cent per annum:

Note: 6.13 per cent is very close to the interest rate used by the lessor to set the lease premium in question 24.1 as

$$
\$24{,}000 = \$9{,}000 \times [1 - 1/(1.0613)^3/0.0613]
$$
$$
\$24{,}000 = \$9{,}000 \times 2.666\dot{6}
$$

(the present value factor for 6.13% is 2.666595 which is very close to 2.666$\dot{6}$). Let us now see how the lease premium is reduced when a residual value of $4,000 is introduced.

$$
\begin{aligned}
\text{Lease base amortisation} &= \$24{,}000 - \$4{,}000 = \$20{,}000 \\
\text{Lease base} &= \$20{,}000/2.6666 = \$7{,}500 \\
\text{Lease premium} &= \$7500 + 6.13\% \times \$4{,}000 \\
&= \$7{,}745.20
\end{aligned}
$$

Questions and problems

1 · Leasing and alleged advantages/disadvantages

Respond to the following remarks:

a   Leasing reduces risk and can reduce a firm's cost of capital.
b   Leasing provides 100 per cent financing.
c   If there were no taxation consequences associated with leasing, this form of financing would disappear.

2 · Accounting for leases

What is meant by the phrase 'off Statement of Financial Position financing'? When do leases provide such financing, and what are the accounting and economic consequences of such activity?

3 · Sale and leaseback

Why might a firm choose to engage in a sale and leaseback transaction? Give two reasons.

4 · Setting lease premiums

Easy Rider Ltd acts as the lessor for financing motor vehicles which sell for $36,000. Easy requires a return of 12.12 per cent per annum on its leases which run for two and a half years. Customers are allowed to choose the residual values that are written into the lease contract; however, the Australian Taxation Office has ruled that for the lease to be accepted as a legitimate arrangement the values must fall between $15,000 and $20,000. Popular residual values have been:

    i $15,000
    ii $16,000
    iii $18,000
    iv $20,000

What will be the lease premiums that Easy Rider will require:

a   if premiums are paid monthly in arrears?
b   if premiums are paid monthly in advance?
c   If the cost of borrowing to purchase is 1 per cent per month, which leasing contract is preferred in terms of the opportunity cost of leasing?

5 · An economic evaluation of leasing

A. The management of the Cutaway Excavations Company Ltd is considering the purchase of a piece of equipment which costs $50,000. The expected useful life of the equipment is 3 years.

The financial manager has suggested the alternative of leasing the equipment from the Smallcost Lease Company Ltd, which has offered a non-cancellable lease with annual payments due at the end of each of the next 3 years.

For tax purposes the depreciation on the equipment is:

    Year 1 $15,000
    Year 2 $10,500
    Year 3 $7,350

The equipment is expected to have a trade-in value of $10,000 in 3 years time. The company tax rate is 30 cents in the dollar and is payable in the year of income.

The cost of debt (and leasing) is 8 per cent per annum. The required rate of return is 10 per cent per annum.

Present an analysis to show whether the company should lease if:

a   the residual value equals the book value at the end of 3 years;
b   the residual value is $12,000 at the end of 3 years;
c   the residual value is zero and the lessee has residual rights.

B. One of the directors has pointed out that it is possible to obtain the $50,000 purchase price by means of a bank overdraft at a rate of interest of 7 per cent per annum, and suggests that it is this rate that should be used to discount the cash flows. Comment.

6 · An economic evaluation of leasing

Flasher Photography Pty Ltd requires a new developing press which will cost $500,000. This press will greatly reduce turnaround time and allow Flasher to compete favourably. The expected useful life of the press is 3 years. Because of the nature of the Photography industry, customers are slow in paying their accounts so that Flasher has a cash flow problem. Nevertheless Flasher's bank has arranged for an associated finance company to lend Flasher the funds at 18 per cent. As Flasher's marginal tax rate is 30 per cent, the after-tax cost of borrowing is 12.6 per cent. The rate of 18 per cent is felt to be justified in the current market situation.

The expected useful life of a press is only 3 years because of technological advances, so that at the end of 3 years the press is expected to have a salvage value of $40,000; however, depreciation over the same period will be allowed for tax purposes at 40 per cent diminishing value. If Flasher borrows to purchase, repayment of the debt will be in 3 equal annual instalments paid at the end of each year. As an alternative to borrowing to purchase the machine the company could lease through Taxsaver Leasing Ltd. If the press is leased the annual premium is $160,000 for a 4-year period with the premium being paid at the beginning of each year. The lease is to have a zero residual value clause.

Regardless of which method of financing is used, the contract will be signed on 1 July—the beginning of the company's tax year. It may be assumed that all tax payments are made at the end of the year in which the expense is incurred.

a   Present an analysis to show which method of financing Flasher should use.
b   The bank manager insists that Flasher should borrow to purchase, since this method provides the entire $500,000 required for the press, whereas, if Flasher leases, it will be necessary for Flasher to find the first lease payment of $160,000 outside the lease. Is this a valid criticism of the leasing alternative?

7 · An economic evaluation with asset salvage

This is a challenge problem. A company is considering whether it should lease or borrow to purchase a piece of equipment. The term of the debt will be 4 years. The piece of equipment would cost $20,000 if purchased for cash. Lease and taxation payments will be made at the end of each financial year. The financial manager has calculated the following tax savings, using a 39 per cent taxation rate and a 12 per cent borrowing rate. The interest rate charged by the lessor is not known but it is greater than the borrowing rate of 12 per cent.

Present value of tax savings through lease premiums when the residual value is zero: $9,151.74.

Present value of tax savings through depreciation and interest if funds are borrowed to make the purchase: $6,693.00.

a   What is the present value of the lease premiums?
b   What is the opportunity cost of leasing if the leasing contract stipulates a residual value in 4 years time at the date of the last lease payment of:

i   zero
ii   2,500
iii 4,802
iv   6,000?

In addition, explain why the opportunity cost of leasing is changing as the residual value changes.

c   If the depreciation rate used to calculate the borrowing tax saving was 30 per cent reducing balance, calculate the net advantage of leasing for each of the residual values provided in part (b). The salvage value for the piece of equipment at the end of year 4 will be $4,000 and in all cases the lessee has residual rights.

appendix a

mathematical tables

Table A.1   Future value of $1 at the end of t periods $= (1 + r)^t$

	Interest rate								
Period	1%	2%	3%	4%	5%	6%	7%	8%	9%
1	1.0100	1.0200	1.0300	1.0400	1.0500	1.0600	1.0700	1.0800	1.0900
2	1.0201	1.0404	1.0609	1.0816	1.1025	1.1236	1.1449	1.1664	1.1881
3	1.0303	1.0612	1.0927	1.1249	1.1576	1.1910	1.2250	1.2597	1.2950
4	1.0406	1.0824	1.1255	1.1699	1.2155	1.2625	1.3108	1.3605	1.4116
5	1.0510	1.1041	1.1593	1.2167	1.2763	1.3382	1.4026	1.4693	1.5386
6	1.0615	1.1262	1.1941	1.2653	1.3401	1.4185	1.5007	1.5869	1.6771
7	1.0721	1.1487	1.2299	1.3159	1.4071	1.5036	1.6058	1.7138	1.8280
8	1.0829	1.1717	1.2668	1.3686	1.4775	1.5938	1.7182	1.8509	1.9926
9	1.0937	1.1951	1.3048	1.4233	1.5513	1.6895	1.8385	1.9990	2.1719
10	1.1046	1.2190	1.3439	1.4802	1.6289	1.7908	1.9672	2.1589	2.3674
11	1.1157	1.2434	1.3842	1.5395	1.7103	1.8983	2.1049	2.3316	2.5804
12	1.1268	1.2682	1.4258	1.6010	1.7959	2.0122	2.2522	2.5182	2.8127
13	1.1381	1.2936	1.4685	1.6651	1.8856	2.1329	2.4098	2.7196	3.0658
14	1.1495	1.3195	1.5126	1.7317	1.9799	2.2609	2.5785	2.9372	3.3417
15	1.1610	1.3459	1.5580	1.8009	2.0789	2.3966	2.7590	3.1722	3.6425
16	1.1726	1.3728	1.6047	1.8730	2.1829	2.5404	2.9522	3.4259	3.9703
17	1.1843	1.4002	1.6528	1.9479	2.2920	2.6928	3.1588	3.7000	4.3276
18	1.1961	1.4282	1.7024	2.0258	2.4066	2.8543	3.3799	3.9960	4.7171
19	1.2081	1.4568	1.7535	2.1068	2.5270	3.0256	3.6165	4.3157	5.1417
20	1.2202	1.4859	1.8061	2.1911	2.6533	3.2071	3.8697	4.6610	5.6044
21	1.2324	1.5157	1.8603	2.2788	2.7860	3.3996	4.1406	5.0338	6.1088
22	1.2447	1.5460	1.9161	2.3699	2.9253	3.6035	4.4304	5.4365	6.6586
23	1.2572	1.5769	1.9736	2.4647	3.0715	3.8197	4.7405	5.8715	7.2579
24	1.2697	1.6084	2.0328	2.5633	3.2251	4.0489	5.0724	6.3412	7.9111
25	1.2824	1.6406	2.0938	2.6658	3.3864	4.2919	5.4274	6.8485	8.6231
30	1.3478	1.8114	2.4273	3.2434	4.3219	5.7435	7.6123	10.063	13.268
40	1.4889	2.2080	3.2620	4.8010	7.0400	10.286	14.974	21.725	31.409
50	1.6446	2.6916	4.3839	7.1067	11.467	18.420	29.457	46.902	74.358
60	1.8167	3.2810	5.8916	10.520	18.679	32.988	57.946	101.26	176.03

10%	12%	14%	15%	16%	18%	20%	24%	28%	32%	36%
1.1000	1.1200	1.1400	1.1500	1.1600	1.1800	1.2000	1.2400	1.2800	1.3200	1.3600
1.2100	1.2544	1.2996	1.3225	1.3456	1.3924	1.4400	1.5376	1.6384	1.7424	1.8496
1.3310	1.4049	1.4815	1.5209	1.5609	1.6430	1.7280	1.9066	2.0972	2.3000	2.5155
1.4641	1.5735	1.6890	1.7490	1.8106	1.9388	2.0736	2.3642	2.6844	3.0360	3.4210
1.6105	1.7623	1.9254	2.0114	2.1003	2.2878	2.4883	2.9316	3.4360	4.0075	4.6526
1.7716	1.9738	2.1950	2.3131	2.4364	2.6996	2.9860	3.6352	4.3980	5.2899	6.3275
1.9487	2.2107	2.5023	2.6600	2.8262	3.1855	3.5832	4.5077	5.6295	6.9826	8.6054
2.1436	2.4760	2.8526	3.0590	3.2784	3.7589	4.2998	5.5895	7.2058	9.2170	11.703
2.3579	2.7731	3.2519	3.5179	3.8030	4.4355	5.1598	6.9310	9.2234	12.166	15.917
2.5937	3.1058	3.7072	4.0456	4.4114	5.2338	6.1917	8.5944	11.806	16.060	21.647
2.8531	3.4785	4.2262	4.6524	5.1173	6.1759	7.4301	10.657	15.112	21.199	29.439
3.1384	3.8960	4.8179	5.3503	5.9360	7.2876	8.9161	13.215	19.343	27.983	40.037
3.4523	4.3635	5.4924	6.1528	6.8858	8.5994	10.699	16.386	24.759	36.937	54.451
3.7975	4.8871	6.2613	7.0757	7.9875	10.147	12.839	20.319	31.691	48.757	74.053
4.1772	5.4736	7.1379	8.1371	9.2655	11.974	15.407	25.196	40.565	64.359	100.71
4.5950	6.1304	8.1372	9.3576	10.748	14.129	18.488	31.243	51.923	84.954	136.97
5.0545	6.8660	9.2765	10.761	12.468	16.672	22.186	38.741	66.461	112.14	186.28
5.5599	7.6900	10.575	12.375	14.463	19.673	26.623	48.039	85.071	148.02	253.34
6.1159	8.6128	12.056	14.232	16.777	23.214	31.948	59.568	108.89	195.39	344.54
6.7275	9.6463	13.743	16.367	19.461	27.393	38.338	73.864	139.38	257.92	468.57
7.4002	10.804	15.668	18.822	22.574	32.324	46.005	91.592	178.41	340.45	637.26
8.1403	12.100	17.861	21.645	26.186	38.142	55.206	113.57	228.36	449.39	866.67
8.9543	13.552	20.362	24.891	30.376	45.008	66.247	140.83	292.30	593.20	1178.7
9.8497	15.179	23.212	28.625	35.236	53.109	79.497	174.63	374.14	783.02	1603.0
10.835	17.000	26.462	32.919	40.874	62.669	95.396	216.54	478.90	1033.6	2180.1
17.449	29.960	50.950	66.212	85.850	143.37	237.38	634.82	1645.5	4142.1	10143.
45.259	93.051	188.88	267.86	378.72	750.38	1469.8	5455.9	19427.	66521.	*
117.39	289.00	700.23	1083.7	1670.7	3927.4	9100.4	46890.	*	*	*
304.48	897.60	2595.9	4384.0	7370.2	20555.	56348.	*	*	*	*

Present value of $1 to be received after t periods $= (1 + r)^{-t} = \dfrac{1}{(1 + r)^t}$

Interest rate

Period	1%	2%	3%	4%	5%	6%	7%	8%	9%
1	0.9901	0.9804	0.9709	0.9615	0.9524	0.9434	0.9346	0.9259	0.9174
2	0.9803	0.9612	0.9426	0.9246	0.9070	0.8900	0.8734	0.8573	0.8417
3	0.9706	0.9423	0.9151	0.8890	0.8638	0.8396	0.8163	0.7938	0.7722
4	0.9610	0.9238	0.8885	0.8548	0.8227	0.7921	0.7629	0.7350	0.7084
5	0.9515	0.9057	0.8626	0.8219	0.7835	0.7473	0.7130	0.6806	0.6499
6	0.9420	0.8880	0.8375	0.7903	0.7462	0.7050	0.6663	0.6302	0.5963
7	0.9327	0.8706	0.8131	0.7599	0.7107	0.6651	0.6227	0.5835	0.5470
8	0.9235	0.8535	0.7894	0.7307	0.6768	0.6274	0.5820	0.5403	0.5019
9	0.9143	0.8368	0.7664	0.7026	0.6446	0.5919	0.5439	0.5002	0.4604
10	0.9053	0.8203	0.7441	0.6756	0.6139	0.5584	0.5083	0.4632	0.4224
11	0.8963	0.8043	0.7224	0.6496	0.5847	0.5268	0.4751	0.4289	0.3875
12	0.8874	0.7885	0.7014	0.6246	0.5568	0.4970	0.4440	0.3971	0.3555
13	0.8787	0.7730	0.6810	0.6006	0.5303	0.4688	0.4150	0.3677	0.3262
14	0.8700	0.7579	0.6611	0.5775	0.5051	0.4423	0.3878	0.3405	0.2992
15	0.8613	0.7430	0.6419	0.5553	0.4810	0.4173	0.3624	0.3152	0.2745
16	0.8528	0.7284	0.6232	0.5339	0.4581	0.3936	0.3387	0.2919	0.2519
17	0.8444	0.7142	0.6050	0.5134	0.4363	0.3714	0.3166	0.2703	0.2311
18	0.8360	0.7002	0.5874	0.4936	0.4155	0.3503	0.2959	0.2502	0.2120
19	0.8277	0.6864	0.5703	0.4746	0.3957	0.3305	0.2765	0.2317	0.1945
20	0.8195	0.6730	0.5537	0.4564	0.3769	0.3118	0.2584	0.2145	0.1784
21	0.8114	0.6598	0.5375	0.4388	0.3589	0.2942	0.2415	0.1987	0.1637
22	0.8034	0.6468	0.5219	0.4220	0.3418	0.2775	0.2257	0.1839	0.1502
23	0.7954	0.6342	0.5067	0.4057	0.3256	0.2618	0.2109	0.1703	0.1378
24	0.7876	0.6217	0.4919	0.3901	0.3101	0.2470	0.1971	0.1577	0.1264
25	0.7798	0.6095	0.4776	0.3751	0.2953	0.2330	0.1842	0.1460	0.1160
30	0.7419	0.5521	0.4120	0.3083	0.2314	0.1741	0.1314	0.0994	0.0754
40	0.6717	0.4529	0.3066	0.2083	0.1420	0.0972	0.0668	0.0460	0.0318
50	0.6080	0.3715	0.2281	0.1407	0.0872	0.0543	0.0339	0.0213	0.0134

10%	12%	14%	15%	16%	18%	20%	24%	28%	32%	36%
0.9091	0.8929	0.8772	0.8696	0.8621	0.8475	0.8333	0.8065	0.7813	0.7576	0.7353
0.8264	0.7972	0.7695	0.7561	0.7432	0.7182	0.6944	0.6504	0.6104	0.5739	0.5407
0.7513	0.7118	0.6750	0.6575	0.6407	0.6086	0.5787	0.5245	0.4768	0.4348	0.3975
0.6830	0.6355	0.5921	0.5718	0.5523	0.5158	0.4823	0.4230	0.3725	0.3294	0.2923
0.6209	0.5674	0.5194	0.4972	0.4761	0.4371	0.4019	0.3411	0.2910	0.2495	0.2149
0.5645	0.5066	0.4556	0.4323	0.4104	0.3704	0.3349	0.2751	0.2274	0.1890	0.1580
0.5132	0.4523	0.3996	0.3759	0.3538	0.3139	0.2791	0.2218	0.1776	0.1432	0.1162
0.4665	0.4039	0.3506	0.3269	0.3050	0.2660	0.2326	0.1789	0.1388	0.1085	0.0854
0.4241	0.3606	0.3075	0.2843	0.2630	0.2255	0.1938	0.1443	0.1084	0.0822	0.0628
0.3855	0.3220	0.2697	0.2472	0.2267	0.1911	0.1615	0.1164	0.0847	0.0623	0.0462
0.3505	0.2875	0.2366	0.2149	0.1954	0.1619	0.1346	0.0938	0.0662	0.0472	0.0340
0.3186	0.2567	0.2076	0.1869	0.1685	0.1372	0.1122	0.0757	0.0517	0.0357	0.0250
0.2897	0.2292	0.1821	0.1625	0.1452	0.1163	0.0935	0.0610	0.0404	0.0271	0.0184
0.2633	0.2046	0.1597	0.1413	0.1252	0.0985	0.0779	0.0492	0.0316	0.0205	0.0135
0.2394	0.1827	0.1401	0.1229	0.1079	0.0835	0.0649	0.0397	0.0247	0.0155	0.0099
0.2176	0.1631	0.1229	0.1069	0.0930	0.0708	0.0541	0.0320	0.0193	0.0118	0.0073
0.1978	0.1456	0.1078	0.0929	0.0802	0.0600	0.0451	0.0258	0.0150	0.0089	0.0054
0.1799	0.1300	0.0946	0.0808	0.0691	0.0508	0.0376	0.0208	0.0118	0.0068	0.0039
0.1635	0.1161	0.0829	0.0703	0.05g6	0.0431	0.0313	0.0168	0.0092	0.0051	0.0029
0.1486	0.1037	0.0728	0.0611	0.0514	0.0365	0.0261	0.0135	0.0072	0.0039	0.0021
0.1351	0.0926	0.0638	0.0531	0.0443	0.0309	0.0217	0.0109	0.0056	O.Q029	0.0016
0.1228	0.0826	0.0560	0.0462	0.0382	0.0262	0.0181	0.0088	0.0044	0.0022	0.0012
0.1117	0.0738	0.0491	0.0402	0.0329	0.0222	0.0151	0.0071	0.0034	0.0017	0.0008
0.1015	0.0659	0.0431	0.0349	0.0284	0.0188	0.0126	0.0057	0.0027	0.0013	0.0006
0.0923	0.0588	0.0378	0.0304	0.0245	0.0160	0.0105	0.0046	0.0021	0.0010	0.0005
0.0573	0.0334	0.0196	0.0151	0.0116	0.0070	0.0042	0.0016	0.0006	0.0002	0.0001
0.0221	0.0107	0.0053	0.0037	0.0026	0.0013	0.0007	0.0002	0.0001	*	*
0.0085	0.0035	0.0014	0.0009	0.0006	0.0003	0.0001	*	*	*	*

*The factor is zero to four decimal places.

Present value of an annuity of $1 per period for the t periods $= [1 - 1/(1 + r)^t]/r$

Number of periods	Interest rate								
	1%	2%	3%	4%	5%	6%	7%	8%	9%
1	0.9901	0.9804	0.970g	0.9615	0.9524	0.9434	0.9346	0.9259	0.9174
2	1.9704	1.9416	1.9135	1.8861	1.8594	1.8334	1.8080	1.7833	1.7591
3	2.9410	2.8839	2.8286	2.7751	2.7232	2.6730	2.6243	2.5771	2.5313
4	3.9020	3.8077	3.7171	3.6299	3.5460	3.4651	3.3872	3.3121	3.2397
5	4.8534	4.7135	4.5797	4.4518	4.3295	4.2124	4.1002	3.9927	3.8897
6	5.7955	5.6014	5.4172	5.2421	5.0757	4.9173	4.7665	4.6229	4.4859
7	6.7282	6.4720	6.2303	6.0021	5.7864	5.5824	5.3893	5.2064	5.0330
8	7.6517	7.3255	7.0197	6.7327	6.4632	6.2098	5.9713	5.7466	5.5348
9	8.5660	8.1622	7.7861	7.4353	7.1078	6.8017	6.5152	6.2469	5.9952
10	9.4713	8.9826	8.5302	8.110g	7.7217	7.3601	7.0236	6.7101	6.4177
11	10.3676	9.7868	9.2526	8.7605	8.3064	7.8869	7.4987	7.1390	6.8052
12	11.2551	10.5753	9.9540	9.3851	8.8633	8.3838	7.9427	7.5361	7.1607
13	12.1337	11.3484	10.6350	9.9856	9.3936	8.8527	8.3577	7.9038	7.4869
14	13.0037	12.1062	11.2961	10.5631	9.8986	9.2950	8.7455	8.2442	7.7862
15	13.8651	12.8493	11.9379	11.1184	10.3797	9.7122	9.1079	8.5595	8.0607
16	14.7179	13.5777	12.5611	11.6523	10.8378	10.1059	9.4466	8.8514	8.3126
17	15.5623	14.2919	13.1661	12.1657	11.2741	10.4773	9.7632	9.1216	8.5436
18	16.3983	14.9920	13.7535	12.6593	11.6896	10.8276	10.0591	9.3719	8.7556
19	17.2260	15.6785	14.3238	13.1339	12.0853	11.1581	10.3356	9.6036	8.9501
20	18.0456	16.3514	14.8775	13.5903	12.4622	11.4699	10.5940	9.8181	9.1285
21	18.8570	17.0112	15.4150	14.0292	12.8212	11.7641	10.8355	10.0168	9.2922
22	19.6604	17.6580	15.9369	14.4511	13.1630	12.0416	11.0612	10.2007	9.4424
23	20.4558	18.2922	16.4436	14.8568	13.4886	12.3034	11.2722	10.3741	9.5802
24	21.2434	18.9139	16.9355	15.2470	13.7986	12.5504	11.4593	10.5288	9.7066
25	22.0232	19.5235	17.4131	15.6221	14.0939	12.7834	11.6536	10.6748	9.8226
30	25.8077	22.3965	19.6004	17.2920	15.3725	13.7648	12.4090	11.2578	10.2737
40	32.8347	27.3555	23.1148	19.7928	17.1591	15.0463	13.3317	11.9246	10.7574
50	39.1961	31.4236	25.7298	21.4822	18.2559	15.7619	13.8007	12.2335	10.9617

Interest rate									
10%	12%	14%	15%	16%	18%	20%	24%	28%	32%
0.9091	0.8929	0.8772	0.8696	0.8621	0.8475	0.8333	0.8065	0.7813	0.7576
1.7355	1.6901	1.6467	1.6257	1.6052	1.5656	1.5278	1.4568	1.3916	1.3315
2.4869	2.4018	2.3216	2.2832	2.2459	2.1743	2.1065	1.9813	1.8684	1.7663
3.1699	3.0373	2.9137	2.8550	2.7982	2.6901	2.5887	2.4043	2.2410	2.0957
3.7908	3.6048	3.4331	3.3522	3.2743	3.1272	2.9906	2.7454	2.5320	2.3452
4.3553	4.1114	3.8887	3.7845	3.6847	3.4976	3.3255	3.0205	2.7594	2.5342
4.8684	4.5638	4.2883	4.1604	4.0386	3.8115	3.6046	3.2423	2.9370	2.6775
5.3349	4.9676	4.6389	4.4873	4.3436	4.0776	3.8372	3.4212	3.0758	2.7860
5.7590	5.3282	4.9464	4.7716	4.6065	4.3030	4.0310	3.5655	3.1842	2.8681
6.1446	5.6502	5.2161	5.0188	4.8332	4.4941	4.1925	3.6819	3.2689	2.9304
6.4951	5.9377	5.4527	5.2337	5.0286	4.6560	4.3271	3.7757	3.3351	2.9776
6.8137	6.1944	5.6603	5.4206	5.1971	4.7932	4.4392	3.8514	3.3868	3.0133
7.1034	6.4235	5.8424	5.5831	5.3423	4.9095	4.5327	3.9124	3.4272	3.0404
7.3667	6.6282	6.0021	5.7245	5.4675	5.0081	4.6106	3.9616	3.4587	3.0609
7.6061	6.8109	6.1422	5.8474	5.5755	5.0916	4.6755	4.0013	3.4834	3.0764
7.8237	6.9740	6.2651	5.9542	5.6685	5.1624	4.7296	4.0333	3.5026	3.0882
8.0216	7.1196	6.3729	6.0472	5.7487	5.2223	4.7746	4.0591	3.5177	3.0971
8.2014	7.2497	6.4674	6.1280	5.8178	5.2732	4.8122	4.0799	3.5294	3.1039
8.3649	7.3658	6.5504	6.1982	5.8775	5.3162	4.8435	4.0967	3.5386	3.1090
8.5136	7.4694	6.6231	6.2593	5.9288	5.3527	4.8696	4.1103	3.5458	3.1129
8.6487	7.5620	6.6870	6.3125	5.9731	5.3837	4.8913	4.1212	3.5514	3.1158
8.7715	7.6446	6.7429	6.3587	6.0113	5.4099	4.9094	4.1300	3.5558	3.1180
8.8832	7.7184	6.7921	6.3988	6.0442	5.4321	4.9245	4.1371	3.5592	3.1197
8.9847	7.7843	6.8351	6.4338	6.0726	5.4509	4.9371	4.1428	3.5619	3.1210
9.0770	7.8431	6.8729	6.4641	6.0971	5.4669	4.9476	4.1474	3.5640	3.1220
9.4269	8.0552	7.0027	6.5660	6.1772	5.5168	4.9789	4.1601	3.5693	3.1242
9.7791	8.2438	7.1050	6.6418	6.2335	5.5482	4.9966	4.1659	3.5712	3.1250
9.9148	8.3045	7.1327	6.6605	6.2463	5.5541	4.9995	4.1666	3.5714	3.1250

Future value of an annuity of $1 per period for the t periods $= [(1 + r)^t - 1]/r$

Number of periods	Interest rate								
	1%	2%	3%	4%	5%	6%	7%	8%	9%
1	1.0000	1.0000	1.0000	1.0000	1.0000	1.0000	1.0000	1.0000	1.0000
2	2.0100	2.0200	2.0300	2.0400	2.0500	2.0600	2.0700	2.0800	2.0900
3	3.0301	3.0604	3.0909	3.1216	3.1525	3.1836	3.2149	3.2464	3.2781
4	4.0604	4.1216	4.1836	4.2465	4.3101	4.3746	4.4399	4.5061	4.5731
5	5.1010	5.2040	5.3091	5.4163	5.5256	5.6371	5.7507	5.8666	5.9847
6	6.1520	6.3081	6.4684	6.6330	6.8019	6.9753	7.1533	7.3359	7.5233
7	7.2135	7.4343	7.6625	7.8983	8.1420	8.3938	8.6540	8.9228	9.2004
8	8.2857	8.5830	8.8932	9.2142	9.5491	9.8975	10.260	10.637	11.028
9	9.3685	9.7546	10.159	10.583	11.027	11.491	11.978	12.488	13.021
10	10.462	10.950	11.464	12.006	12.578	13.181	13.816	14.487	15.193
11	11.567	12.169	12.808	13.486	14.207	14.972	15.784	16.645	17.560
12	12.683	13.412	14.192	15.026	15.917	16.870	17.888	18.977	20.141
13	13.809	14.680	15.618	16.627	17.713	18.882	20.141	21.495	22.953
14	14.947	15.971	17.086	18.292	19.599	21.015	22.550	24.215	26.019
15	16.097	17.293	18.599	20.024	21.579	23.276	25.129	27.152	29.361.
16	17.258	18.639	20.157	21.825	23.657	25.673	27.888	30.324	33.003
17	18.430	20.012	21.762	23.698	25.840	28.213	30.840	33.750	36.974
18	19.615	21.412	23.414	25.645	28.132	30.906	33.999	37.450	41.301
19	20.811	22.841	25.117	27.671	30.539	33.760	37.379	41.446	46.018
20	22.019	24.297	26.870	29.778	33.066	36.786	40.995	45.762	51.160
21	23.239	25.783	28.676	31.969	35.719	39.993	44.865	50.423	56.765
22	24.472	27.299	30.537	34.248	38.505	43.392	49.006	55.457	62.873
23	25.716	28.845	32.453	36.618	41.430	46.996	53.436	60.893	69.532
24	26.973	30.422	34.426	39.083	44.502	50.816	58.177	66.765	76.790
25	28.243	32.030	36.459	41.646	47.727	54.865	63.249	73.106	84.701
30	34.785	40.568	47.575	56.085	66.439	79.058	94.461	113.28	136.31
40	48.886	60.402	75.401	95.026	120.80	154.76	199.64	259.06	337.88
50	64.463	84.579	112.80	152.67	209.35	290.34	406.53	573.77	815.08
60	81.670	114.05	163.05	237.99	353.58	533.13	813.52	1253.2	1944.8

Interest rate										
10%	12%	14%	15%	16%	18%	20%	24%	28%	32%	36%
1.0000	1.0000	1.0000	1.0000	1.0000	1.0000	1.0000	1.0000	1.0000	1.0000	1.0000
2.1000	2.1200	2.1400	2.1500	2.1600	2.1800	2.2000	2.2400	2.2800	2.3200	2.3600
3.3100	3.3744	3.4396	3.4725	3.5056	3.5724	3.6400	3.7776	3.9184	4.0624	4.2096
4.6410	4.7793	4.9211	4.9934	5.0665	5.2154	5.3680	5.6842	6.0156	6.3624	6.7251
6.1051	6.3528	6.6101	6.7424	6.8771	7.1542	7.4416	8.0484	8.6999	9.3983	10.146
7.7156	8.1152	8.5355	8.7537	&.9775	9.4420	9.9299	10.980	12.136	13.406	14.799
9.4872	10.089	10.730	11.067	11.414	12.142	12.916	14.615	16.534	18.696	21.126
11.436	12.300	13.233	13.727	14.240	15.327	16.499	19.123	22.103	25.678	29.732
13.579	14.776	16.085	16.786	17.519	19.086	20.799	24.712	29.369	34.895	41.435
15.937	17.549	19.337	20.304	21.321	23.521	25.959	31.643	38.593	47.062	57.352
18.531	20.655	23.045	24.349	25.733	28.755	32.150	40.238	50.398	63.122	78.998
21.384	24.133	27.271	29.002	30.850	34.931	39.581	50.895	65.510	84.320	108.44
24.523	28.029	32.089	34.352	36.786	42.219	48.497	64.110	84.853	112.30	148.47
27.975	32.393	37.581	40.505	43.672	50.818	59.196	80.496	109.61	149.24	202.93
31.772	37.280	43.842	47.580	51.660	60.965	72.035	100.82	141.30	198.00	276.98
35.950	42.753	50.980	55.717	60.925	72.939	87.442	126.01	181.87	262.36	377.69
40.545	48.884	59.118	65.075	71.673	87.068	105.93	157.25	233.79	347.31	514.66
45.599	55.750	68.394	75.836	84.141	103.74	128.12	195.99	300.25	459.45	700.94
51.159	63.440	78.969	88.212	98.603	123.41	154.74	244.03	385.32	607.47	954.28
57.275	72.052	91.025	102.44	115.38	146.63	186.69	303.60	494.21	802.86	1298.8
64.002	81.699	104.77	118.81	134.84	174.02	225.03	377.46	633.59	1060.8	1767.4
71.403	92.503	120.44	137.63	157.41	206.34	271.03	469.06	812.00	1401.2	2404.7
79.543	104.60	138.30	159.28	183.60	244.49	326.24	582.63	1040.4	1850.6	3271.3
88.497	118.16	158.66	184.17	213.98	289.49	392.48	723.46	1332.7	2443.8	4450.0
98.347	133.33	181.87	212.79	249.21	342.60	471.98	898.09	1706.8	3226.8	6053.0
164.49	241.33	356.79	434.75	530.31	790.95	1181.9	2640.9	5873.2	12941.	28172.3
442.59	767.09	1342.0	1779.1	2360.8	4163.2	7343.9	22729.	69377.	*	*
1163.9	2400.0	4994.5	7217.7	10436.	21813.	45497.	*	*	*	*
3034.8	7471.6	18535.	29220.	46058.	*	*	*	*	*	*

* FVIFA > 99,9999.

Cumulative normal distribution

d	N(d)	d	N(d)	d	N(d)	d	N(d)	d	N(d)	d	N(d)
−3.00	.0013	−1.58	.0571	−0.76	.2236	0.06	.5239	0.86	.8051	1.66	.9515
−2.95	.0016	−1.56	.0594	−0.74	.2297	0.08	.5319	0.88	.8106	1.68	.9535
−2.90	.0019	−1.54	.0618	−0.72	.2358	0.10	.5398	0.90	.8159	1.70	.9554
−2.85	.0022	−1.52	.0643	−0.70	.2420	0.12	.5478	0.92	.8212	1.72	.9573
−2.80	.0026	−1.50	.0668	−0.68	.2483	0.14	.5557	0.94	.8264	1.74	.9591
−2.75	.0030	−1.48	.0694	−0.66	.2546	0.16	.5636	0.96	.8315	1.76	.9608
−2.70	.0035	−1.46	.0721	−0.64	.2611	0.18	.5714	0.98	.8365	1.78	.9625
−2.65	.0040	−1.44	.0749	−0.62	.2676	0.20	.5793	1.00	.8414	1.80	.9641
−2.60	.0047	−1.42	.0778	−0.60	.2743	0.22	.5871	1.02	.8461	1.82	.9656
−2.55	.0054	−1.40	.0808	−0.58	.2810	0.24	.5948	1.04	.8508	1.84	.9671
−2.50	.0062	−1.38	.0838	−0.56	.2877	0.26	.6026	1.06	.8554	1.86	.9686
−2.45	.0071	−1.36	.0869	−0.54	.2946	0.28	.6103	1.08	.8599	1.88	.9699
−2.40	.0082	−1.34	.0901	−0.52	.3015	0.30	.6179	1.10	.8643	1.90	.9713
−2.35	.0094	−1.32	.0934	−0.50	.3085	0.32	.6255	1.12	.8686	1.92	.9726
−2.30	.0107	−1.30	.0968	−0.48	.3156	0.34	.6331	1.14	.8729	1.94	.9738
−2.25	.0122	−1.28	.1003	−0.46	.3228	0.36	.6400	1.16	.8770	1.96	.9750
−2.20	.0139	−1.26	.1038	−0.44	.3300	0.38	.6480	1.18	.8810	1.98	.9761
−2.15	.0158	−1.24	.1075	−0.42	.3373	0.40	.6554	1.20	.8849	2.00	.9772
−2.10	.0179	−1.22	.1112	−0.40	.3446	0.42	.6628	1.22	.8888	2.05	.9798
−2.05	.0202	−1.20	.1151	−0.38	.3520	0.44	.6700	1.24	.8925	2.10	.9821
−2.00	.0228	−1.18	.1190	−0.36	.3594	0.46	.6773	1.26	.8962	2.15	.9842
−1.98	.0239	−1.16	.1230	−0.34	.3669	0.48	.6844	1.28	.8997	2.20	.9861
−1.96	.0250	−1.14	.1271	−0.32	.3745	0.50	.6915	1.30	.9032	2.25	.9878
−1.94	.0262	−1.12	.1314	−0.30	.3821	0.52	.6985	1.32	.9066	2.30	.9893
−1.92	.0274	−1.10	.1357	−0.28	.3897	0.54	.7054	1.34	.9099	2.35	.9906
−1.90	.0287	−1.08	.1401	−0.26	.3974	0.56	.7123	1.36	.9131	2.40	.9918
−1.88	.0301	−1.06	.1446	−0.24	.4052	0.58	.7191	1.38	.9162	2.45	.9929
−1.86	.0314	−1.04	.1492	−0.22	.4129	0.60	.7258	1.40	.9192	2.50	.9938
−1.84	.0329	−1.02	.1539	−0.20	.4207	0.62	.7324	1.42	.9222	2.55	.9946
−1.82	.0344	−1.00	.1587	−0.18	.4286	0.64	.7389	1.44	.9251	2.60	.9953
−1.80	.0359	−0.98	.1635	−0.16	.4365	0.66	.7454	1.46	.9279	2.65	.9960
−1.78	.0375	−0.96	.1685	−0.14	.4443	0.68	.7518	1.48	.9306	2.70	.9965
−1.76	.0392	−0.94	.1736	−0.12	.4523	0.70	.7580	1.50	.9332	2.75	.9970
−1.74	.0409	−0.92	.1788	−0.10	.4602	0.72	.7642	1.52	.9357	2.80	.9974
−1.72	.0427	−0.90	.1841	−0.08	.4681	0.74	.7704	1.54	.9382	2.85	.9978
−1.70	.0446	−0.88	.1894	−0.06	.4761	0.76	.7764	1.56	.9406	2.90	.9981
−1.68	.0465	−0.86	.1949	−0.04	.4841	0.78	.7823	1.58	.9429	2.95	.9984
−1.66	.0485	−0.84	.2005	−0.02	.4920	0.80	.7882	1.60	.9452	3.00	.9986
−1.64	.0505	−0.82	.2061	0.00	.5000	0.82	.7939	1.62	.9474	3.05	.9989
−1.62	.0526	−0.80	.2119	0.02	.5080	0.84	.7996	1.64	.9495		
−1.60	.0548	−0.78	.2177	0.04	.5160						

This table shows the probability [N(d)] of observing a value less than or equal to d. For example, as illustrated, if d is −.24 then N(d) is .4052.

appendix b

answers to selected end-of-chapter questions and problems

Chapter 1

7. (a)

Proposal	% return
1	20
2	5
3	7.5
4	9
5	12.5
6	7.5

   (b) Period 1: $6000, Period 2: $4650
   (c) Period 1: $6.00, Period 2: $4.65
   (d) Period 1: $100, Period 2: $2140
   (e) Period 1: $1590, Period 2: $500
   (f) Period 1: $1000, Period 2: $1150

9. (a) 1 and 4; or 3, 4 and 5
   NPV = $191,000

Chapter 2

1. Net profit = $105,000
3. Operating cash flow = $1,480
5. (a) Net profit (X + 1) = $398
   (b) Operating cash flow (X) = $1,583
9. Total = $182,000,000
13. Addition to NWC = −$40
17. Net profit (200X + 1) = $219
    Owners' equity (200X + 1) = $5,400

Chapter 3

1. (a) No change, assuming a cash purchase
   (c) Increase
   (e) No change
3. Equity multiplier = 1.4
5. Quick ratio = 2.84
7. Long-term debt = 6.17%
9. (a) Current ratio (200X + 1) = 0.82
   (c) Net debt/equity ratio
       (200X + 1) = 0.23
11. Days' sales in inventory = 48.47 days
13. Inventory turnover = 5 times
15. Net decrease in cash of $900
17. ROE = 20%
    Equity multiplier = 2
19. $0.1521 \times 0.391 \times 2.93 = 0.1742$
21. Interval measure = 984.9 days
23. Net profit = $0.5m
25. ROE = 28.4%

Chapter 4

1. Net profit = $120
   Equity = $300
   Dividends (the plug) = $70
3. EFN = −$200 (a surplus)
5. EFN = $263.87
9. Addition to retained earnings = $631

11. EFN = −$281
15. EFN = $445
17. $g^* = 2.04\%$
21. $g^* = 3.09\%$
23. $p = 15.87\%$
25. $936
27. $g^* = 1.52\%$
    New borrowing = $76
    With no outside financing, the maximum
    growth rate would be 1.01%.

Chapter 5

1. PV of all is $5,000
3. $r = 7.6\%$ (approximately)
5. FV = $10,254
7. $40,000 per year; the PV is $71,093.43
9. NIR = 5.91%
   NIR = 7.77%
   NIR = 11.33%
   NIR = 13.10%
11. At 10%, B has the higher PV of $253.59
    At 25%, A has the higher PV of $195.20
13. PV = $45,030.20
15. 8.0%
17. $t = 9.84$ years
    $t = 6$ years
    $t = 15$ years
    $t = 16$ years
    $t = 5$ years (factor used 1.1593)
19. PV = $671.01
    PV = $1,125.78
    PV = $1,223.35
    PV = $1,250
21. $r = 25.09\%$
    $r = 12\%$
    $r = 11\%$
    $r = 6\%$
23. There is an inverse relationship.
    At 5%, PV = $77.217
    At 10%, PV = $61.446
    At 15%, PV = $50.188
25. NIR = 9.58%
    EAR = 10.01%
27. In 8 years, FV = $22,056
    In 10 years, FV = $26,204.73
29. 4,591%
31. EAR semi-annual = 12.36%
    EAR monthly = 12.68%

33. PV = $246,978.55
35. (a) Alternative 2, $20,000
    (b) Alternative 2, $12,418.43
    (c) Alternative 1, $8,333.33
37. PV = $14,433.19
39. (a) PV = $1,201,180.55
    (b) PV = $1,131,898.53
41. EAR = 17.65%
43. $r = 10.2\%$
45. NIR = 21.29%
    EAR = 23.49%
47. (a) $592.33
    (b) $7,201.76
49. The future value of the payments is
    $297,310.25, which greatly exceeds the policy
    value.
51. PV = $335.65
    PV = $289.35

Chapter 6

1. $94.03
3. $91.35
5. (a) 6.09%
   (b) $117.06
   (c) $126.94
7. par; premium; discount
9. 7%
11. YTM = 12.5%
13. $P_0 = \$2.97$
    $P_4 = \$4.04$
14. 4%; 8%
17. $r = 14\%$
19. $P_0 = \$1.807$
21. $g = 5\%$
23. $P_0 = \$2.695$
25. $r = 17.08\%$
27. $r = 16.17\%$
29. $1 million

Chapter 7

1. 5.5 years, 6.5 years, does not exist
4. $NPV_A = \$910$, $NPV_B = \$1,530$;
   therefore B
6. 6 years, 7.461 years, does not exist
8. The NPV is positive.
10. IRR = 10%
12. $IRR_A = 80.19\%$ and −55.5%
    $IRR_B = 52.14\%$

14. $IRR_A = 0\%$ and 100%
    $IRR_B = 27\%$
16. $IRR = 10.07\%$
18. (a) A: NPV $23.34, IRR 27.71%
    B: NPV $19.60, IRR 28.23%
    (b) $42.94, the sum of the two NPVs
    (c) $IRR = 27.94\%$, a very complicated
        weighted average
22. $IRR = 20\%$
    NPV at 30% = $2,904
    NPV at 28% = $2,380
    We should take the investment when return is
    greater than 20%.
24. NPV index = PVI − 1
26. Four, being 25%, 33.33%, 42.85% and 66.67%.

Chapter 8

1. Net profit = $31,500
3. OCF = $37,949.70
5. Net proceeds = $17,200
7. NPVs = $5,234
11. $IRR = 38\%$
13. Jazzmaster AEC = $15,661
15. Method 1: AEC = $26,052
    Method 2: AEC = $22,424
16. NPV = $1,877,589

Chapter 9

1. (a) $3.75
   (b) $1,370,000
   (c) Accounting break-even = 290,323 litres
3. (a) DOL = 3.5
   (b) NPV best case = $71,549
       NPV worst case = −$13,307
5. DOL = 2.667
11. $32.50
15. (a) NPV base case = $62,118
       NPV best case = $1,028,715
       NPV worst case = −$770,236
   (c) 38 units
17. NPV = −$13,075
18. Abandon if Q is less than or equal to 496 units.
20. (a) NPV = −$4,807
    (b) Option Value = $8,269

Chapter 10

1. −20.48%
3. 48.57%, 5.71%, 42.86%

5. 15.36%
7. (a) 10.91%
   (b) 8.36%
13. Average return on X = 5.4%
    Standard deviation on X = 8.96%

Chapter 11

1. 15%
3. 62.5% and 37.5%
5. (a) $E(R_A) = 29.2\%$
       Standard deviation$_A$ = 13.12%
7. (a) $E(R_A) = 8.8\%$
       Standard deviation$_A$ = 0.98%
   (b) $E(R_B) = 8.4\%$
9. Yes, the standard deviation could be less, but
   the beta cannot be.
18. 11.6%; 2
19. If the risk free rate is 6%, they are not correctly
    priced. They are correctly priced if the risk
    free rate is 2%.
20. 5%
21. 5%
23. $E(R_M) = 17\%$, $R_f = 9\%$

Chapter 12

1. Cash = $1,250, current assets = $2,700
7. Operating cycle = 92.21 days
   Cash cycle = −50.98 days
9. (a) Q1   Q2   Q3   Q4
       $198 $258 $234 $250.56
13. (a) December sales $40,000
15. (a) 1155 kg
    (b) $2,002,771

Chapter 13

3. Holding cost $80
   Trading cost $200
   Total $280
5. $C^* = \$243,193$, so hold $556,807 in
   marketable securities. Sell 17 times.
7. $C^* = \$2,448$; $U^* = \$5,344$
9. $C^* = \$34,797$; $U^* = \$63,392$
13. (a) Disbursement float $120,000
        Collection float   −$90,000
        Net float $30,000
15. 8%
17. (a) $68,000
    (b) 3.78 days; 68,000 = 3.78 × $18,000

(c) $68,000

(d) $14.35

(e) Up to $36,000

19. NPV = $3.9 million, so the system should be implemented

Annual saving = $3.9m × 0.07

= $273,000 per year

Chapter 14

3. (a) 120 days; $2,000

(b) 1%; 30 days; $1,980

(c) $20; 90 days

13. EAR = 44.6%

(a) Increase

(b) Decrease

(c) Increase

15. NPV = $1.25 million

17. (a) 2.5/10, net 30

(b) $780,000

19. $1,000,000

21. (a) NPV = $1,938. Yes, they should fill the order.

(b) 48%

23. NPV = $3,560,000, switch

Chapter 15

5. (a) Finance company

(b) Finance company

(c) Trading bank

(d) Merchant bank

(e) Merchant bank

(f) Money market dealer

(g) Authorised foreign exchange dealer

(h) Bank, credit union or building society

(i) Life insurance company

(j) Cash management trust

(k) Property trust

(l) Friendly society

(m) Sharebroker

(n) The company shareholders

7. 28.19%

9. (c) GC inventory turnover = 1.89, CBC inventory turnover = 1.27. As CBC has the lowest inventory turnover, it is more likely to incur carrying costs; GC is more likely to incur shortage costs.

15. (a) 17.5%

(b) 17.97%

Chapter 16

1. (b) $310,000

2. BV = $4, MV = $1.25

3. c, f, g, e, b, a, d

9. PV_{ALIVE} = $30 million, PV_{DEAD} = $28 million, therefore do not liquidate.

11. (a) Increase

(b) Decrease

(c) Decrease

(d) Probably decrease, but it depends on what the coupon is tied to.

Chapter 17

3. At $4: $4.00

At $2: $3.33

At $1: $3.00

7. 2,000,000 shares

10. BVS = $4.17

Price = $4.37

EPS = $0.2083

NPV = $24,400

12. 46.93%

14. (a) Maximum = $2.50; minimum equals anything > zero

(b) 33.33 million shares; 6.6 shares needed

(c) $2.37; $0.86

(d) Before $250; After $250

Chapter 18

1. 10%. Use the disorder theory of value and the SML.

3. 13.04%

5. 14.73%

9. Both should proceed. The appropriate discount rate does **not** depend on which company is involved; it depends on the risk of the investment. Fastburn is in the business, so it is closer to a 'pure play'. The NPV thus appears to be $1million regardless of who accepts.

11. (a) 5.70%

(b) 20.15%

13. WACC = 18.70%

15. WACC = 7%, $PV_{SAVINGS}$ = $150 million; therefore, undertake if the initial investment is less than $150 million

17. 15.71%
21. (a) (i) 10.65%
    (ii) 11.98
    (iii) 10.65%
    (b) Market value

Chapter 19

3. Friday 24 July
7. $1.52 per share
9. Price per share = $11.45. To create an equal dividend each year, sell 52.45 shares in one year.
11. (a) $20 million
    (b) $0.40 a share
    (c) $6 million; $6 million
    (d) $1 a share; no new borrowing
21. (a) $1,200,000
    (b) No, as planned investment is greater than the maximum with no additional equity.
    (c) No, as a strict residual dividend policy will change with investment and earnings.
22. (a) Price per share = $5 with dividend
                        = $10 with repurchase
    Shareholder wealth unaffected
    (b) With dividend: EPS = 5; P/E = 1
        With repurchase: EPS = 10; P/E = 1

Chapter 20

1. (a) EPS = 0.12; EPS = 0.10; EPS = 0.06
   (b) EPS = 0.15; EPS = 0.11; EPS = 0.03
3. $5 (capital structure is irrelevant here)
9. (a) 25.5%
   (b) 31%
   (c) 20%
11. $4,357.14; $5,137.14
13. $625,000
15. 14.67%; 9.48%; More debt, lower WACC
17. $Beta_A$ = 0.70; R_E = 20.6%;
    WACC = 14.3%

Chapter 21

7. (a) $14,500
   (b) $50,000
   (c) $74,000; $15,000
   (d) $1,000; $16,000; $7.40
11. (a) $1.90
    (b) $3.75
    (c) $0

13. (a) $1.36
    (b) $0.67
15. (a) $356.23 million
    (b) $843.77 million, 8%
17. (a) $0
    (b) Relative to possible prices, the current share price is too low; the minimum possible return is 10%, which exceeds the risk free rate.
23. (a) $0.883
26. $3.27; $11.12; $6.00; $0; $90; $50
28. (a) A: $487.77; $812.23; B: $483.54; $866.46

Chapter 22

1. $5.5 million
4. (a) $2.00
   (b) $40
   (c) 16 times
7. (a) $2.50
   (b) An increase of 25 cents

Chapter 23

1. (a) 2729 rupees (sell quote)
   (b) $4.73 (buy quote)
   (c) About $31,939 (only sell quote available)
   (e) Singapore
   (f) SF1 = 97.22
   This is the cross rate.
   (g) Most: Malta pound = $4.105
       Worst: Vanuatu vatu = $.0128
   (h) Soviet or China, currencies are controlled
3. (a) Premium
7. (a) $2.50 is the new EPS assuming the combined earnings do not change.
   (b) Current EPS = $2.25; New EPS = $2.50; therefore the change is $0.25.
10. Invest in the UK to give $A5.2177m; the alternative will give $A5.1515m
13. (a) Yes; Forward premium too high
    (b) 1.1055
15. 1 year: 31.8; 2 years: 33.71; IRP

Chapter 24

5. (a) OC = zero
   Tax saving leasing = $10,916
   Tax saving borrowing = $10,783
   NAL = $133, therefore lease

(b) OC = zero
Tax saving leasing = $12,618
Tax saving borrowing = $12,486
NAL = $132, therefore lease

(c) OC = zero
Tax saving leasing = $12,618
Tax saving borrowing = $12,486
NAL = $132, therefore lease

7. (a) $23,466
(b) (i) $3,466
(ii) $3,640
(iii) $3,800
(iv) $3,883
(c) (i) ($2,197)
(ii) ($2,304)
(iii) ($2,401)
(iv) ($2,452)

appendix c

glossary of terms

11 a.m. rate the interest rate on 11 a.m. call money.

24-hour loans funds lent in the money market where the loan may be terminated or renegotiated after 7 days with 24 hours' notice.

A

acceptor of a bill of exchange the party agreeing to pay the holder the face value of the bill on the maturity date, usually a bank or other financial institution. Also known as the drawee.

accounting break-even the sales level that results in zero project net profit.

accounting rate of return the earnings from an investment expressed as a percentage of the investment outlay.

accounts payable a sum of money owed by a buyer as a result of goods or services bought on credit. Also known as creditors.

accounts receivable sums of money owed to a seller as a result of providing goods or services on credit. Also known as debtors.

accumulation a process by which, through the operation of interest, a present sum becomes a greater sum in the future.

acquisition/shortage costs costs that fall with increases in the level of investment in current assets.

adjustment costs the costs associated with holding too little cash. Also known as shortage costs.

ageing schedule a compilation of accounts receivable by the age of each account.

agency problem the possibility of conflicts of interest between shareholders and management of the firm.

aggregation process by which smaller investment proposals of each of a firm's operational units are added up and treated as one big project.

American option an option that can be exercised at any time until its expiration date.

annual equivalent cost (AEC) the present value of a project's costs, calculated on an annual basis.

annuity a series of cash flows of equal amount, equally spaced in time.

annuity-due an annuity in which the first cash flow is to occur at the beginning of the time period and the beginning of all subsequent periods.

anomaly a finding that appears to be inconsistent with theory.

appreciation the rise in the value of a currency in terms of another currency or currencies.

arbitrage buying and simultaneously selling an asset for a higher price, usually in another market, so as to make a risk-free profit.

arbitrage pricing model a theory of asset pricing that describes the risk premium for a risky asset as a linear combination of various risk factors.

at call money repayable immediately, whenever demanded by the lender.

AUD (buying) rate the Australian dollar exchange rate at which a bank is willing to buy the currency.

authorised foreign exchange dealers organisations granted a general authority to buy and sell foreign currency.

average tax rate total taxes paid divided by total taxable income.

B

bad debts debtors accounts that have proven to be non-collectable and are written off.

balance sheet now known as **Statement of Financial Position**.

bank bill a bill of exchange that has been accepted or endorsed by a bank.

bankruptcy costs the direct and indirect costs associated with financial difficulty that leads to control of a company being transferred to the holders of debts.

basis the difference between the spot price and the future price (for delivery at some later date) at a point in time.

bearer security a security whose ownership is not registered by the issuer, where possession of the physical document is primary evidence of ownership.

benefit/cost ratio *see* **present value index (PVI)**

beta a relative measure of an asset's market related risk. It is the systematic risk of the asset divided by the market standard deviation of expected return.

bill discount facility an agreement in which one entity (normally a bank) undertakes to discount (buy) bills of exchange drawn by another entity (the borrower).

bill facility an agreement in which one entity (normally a bank) undertakes to accept bills of exchange drawn by another entity (the borrower).

bill of exchange marketable short-term debt security in which one party (the drawer) directs another party (the acceptor) to pay a stated sum on a stated future date.

bonds long-term debt securities. In the past there was a distinction between the terms bonds and debentures but today the term bonds is preferred. Sometimes refers specifically to government securities.

bonus share issue payment made by a firm to its owners in the form of shares, diluting the value of each share outstanding.

book-to-market ratio the book value of a company's equity divided by the market value of the company's equity.

bridging finance a short-term loan, usually in the form of a mortgage, to cover a need arising from timing differences between two or more transactions.

bubble a period in which prices are high; frequently followed by a sudden decrease in prices.

business day a day in which banks are open for business. For foreign exchange, this applies to banks in both the countries of the currencies being exchanged.

business risk the risk of future net cash flows attributed to the nature of the company's operations. It is the risk shareholders face if the company is financed only by equity.

buy-and-hold policy an investment strategy in which shares are bought and then retained in the investor's portfolio.

buyout a transfer of ownership to existing employees; usually identified as a management buyout.

C

call option a right to buy an underlying asset at a fixed price.

call option on a futures contract an option that gives the buyer the right to enter into the futures contract as a buyer at a predetermined price.

capital asset pricing model (CAPM) a theory explaining the return/risk tradeoff as the relationship between expected return and beta.

capital budgeting the process of planning and managing a firm's investment in non-current assets.

capital gains yield the rate at which the value of an investment grows.

capital intensity ratio a firm's total assets divided by its sales, or the amount of assets needed to generate $1 in sales.

capital market a market in which long-term financial securities are traded.

capital market line (CML) describes the equilibrium relationship between expected return and total risk (standard deviation) when all of the risk is being rewarded because all of the risk is market related. It is derived by summing the risk free rate and the product of the expected market premium for risk and the ratio of the efficient asset's standard deviation to the standard deviation of the expected market return.

capital rationing a condition where a firm has access to limited resources for investment.

capital structure the proportion of debt to equity in relation to funding the assets of the firm.

carrying cost the cost of holding a commodity from one time period to another.

cash break-even the sales level where operating cash flow is equal to zero.

cash budget a forecast of the amount and timing of the cash receipts and payments that will result from a firm's operations over a period of time.

cash cycle the time between cash disbursement and cash collection.

cash flow a payment (cash outflow) or receipt (cash inflow) of money.

cash flow from assets the total of cash flow to debtholders and cash flow to shareholders, consisting of operating cash flow, capital spending, and additions to net working capital.

cash flow to debtholders a firm's interest payments to lenders less net new borrowings.

cash flow to shareholders dividends paid out by a firm less net new equity raised.

certainty-equivalent an approach that incorporates risk by adjusting the cash flows by subtracting a risk premium and discounting using the risk free rate.

certificate of deposit a marketable fixed rate debt instrument issued by a bank in exchange for a deposit of funds.

clientele effect the effect of investors choosing to invest in companies that have policies meeting their particular requirements. For example, investors who require high current income may choose to invest in companies that have high dividend payouts.

collection policy a policy adopted by a firm in regard to collecting slow paying accounts either internally or by the use of a debt collection agency.

commercial paper a U.S. term used to describe unsecured short-term promissory notes.

company a separate legal entity formed under the Corporations Act 2001; shareholders are the owners of a company.

compound interest interest calculated each period on the principal amount and on any interest earned on the investment up to that point.

compound option an option on an option (e.g. an option to buy an option).

conglomerate takeover a takeover of a target company in an unrelated type of business.

consol a perpetual bond. Also known as a consolidated annuity.

consolidation a merger in which an entirely new firm is created and both the acquired and acquiring firm cease to exist.

constant chain of replacement a project is assumed to be replaced at the end of its economic life by an identical project so that projects of unequal lives may be compared.

constant dividend growth model model that determines the current price of a share as its dividend next period divided by the discount rate less the dividend growth rate.

consumer credit comprises credit extended to individuals by suppliers of goods and services, or by financial institutions through credit cards.

contingency planning taking into account the management options that are implicit in a project.

contingent claim a claim that is not in existence but may come into existence by the happening of some future event.

continuous interest a method of calculating interest in which interest is charged so frequently that the time period between each charge approaches zero.

conversion ratio the relationship that determines how many ordinary shares will be received in exchange for each convertible or converting security when the conversion occurs.

corporate raiders aggressive corporate or individual investors who purchase a company's shares with the intention of achieving a controlling interest and replacing the existing management.

cost of capital the minimum rate of return needed to compensate suppliers of capital for committing resources to the firm.

cost of debt the return that lenders require on the firm's debt.

cost of equity the return that equity investors require on their investment in the firm.

coupons the fixed interest payments made on bonds, debentures and unsecured notes.

coupon payments the stated interest payments made on a bond.

coupon rate the stated interest rate for payments to be made on a debt instrument.

covenant a provision in a loan agreement to protect lenders' interests by requiring certain actions to be taken or limiting some actions such as increasing the debt.

covered interest an arbitrage movement of funds between two currencies to profit from interest rate differences while using forward contracts to eliminate exchange risk.

credit analysis the process of determining the probability that customers will or will not pay.

credit cost curve graphical representation of the sum of the carrying costs and the opportunity costs of a credit policy.

credit foncier loan a type of loan that involves regular repayments which include principal and interest.

credit period the period between the date that a purchaser is invoiced and the date when payment is due.

credit policy the seller's policy on whether credit will be offered to customers and on what terms.

credit risk the possibility of loss because a party fails to meet its obligations.

cross-border lease a finance lease, usually financed through debt, where the lessor and lessee are located in different countries.

cross rate exchange rate between two currencies derived from the exchange rates between the currencies and a third currency.

cum refers to shares and simply means 'with'.

cum dividend the period during which the purchaser of a share is qualified to receive a previously announced dividend. The cum dividend period ends on the ex-dividend date.

cum rights when shares are traded cum rights, the buyer is entitled to participate in the forthcoming rights issue.

currency swap a simultaneous borrowing and lending operation in which two parties initially exchange specific amounts of two currencies at the spot rate. Interest payments in the two currencies are also exchanged and the parties agree to reverse the initial exchange after a fixed term at a fixed exchange rate.

current assets cash, inventory, accounts receivable and other assets that will normally be converted into cash within a year.

current liabilities debt or other obligations due for payment within a year.

D

date of payment date that the dividend cheques are mailed.

date of record date on which holders of record are designated to receive a dividend.

debentures long-term debt securities. Now usually called bonds. Sometimes refers specifically to company securities.

debt a financial contract in which the receiver of the initial cash (the borrower) promises a particular cash flow, usually calculated using an interest rate, to the provider of funds (the lender).

debt capacity the ability to borrow to increase firm value.

declaration date date on which the board of directors passes a resolution to pay a dividend.

default risk the chance that a borrower will fail to meet obligations to pay interest and principal as agreed.

deferred annuity an annuity in which the first cash flow is to occur after a time period that exceeds the time period between each subsequent cash flow.

degree of operating leverage the percentage change in operating cash flow relative to the percentage change in quantity sold.

delinquent accounts accounts where payment has not been made by the due date.

depreciation the fall in value of a currency in terms of another currency or currencies. It also means the amount an owner should write off an asset as the asset is used and reduces in value.

dilution loss in existing shareholders' value, in terms of either ownership, market value, book value or EPS.

direct quote an exchange rate quotation in which the local currency is the quote currency and the foreign currency is the base currency; for example, a direct quote of the Australian dollar might be $US1 = $A1.5.

discount the amount by which a currency is cheaper for future delivery.

discount period the period during which a discount for prompt payment is available to the purchaser. discount rate expression of the price reduction a purchaser will receive if payment is made within the discount period. The interest rate that reduces a given future value to an equivalent present value.

discounted cash flow (DCF) methods of project selection that value an investment by discounting its future cash flows.

discounted payback period the length of time required for an investment's discounted cash flows to equal its initial cost.

discounter the initial purchaser of a short-term debt security such as a promissory note or a bill of exchange.

discounting the process by which, through the operation of interest, a future sum is converted to its equivalent present value.

distribution payment made by a firm to its owners from sources other than current or accumulated earnings.

diversification principle principle stating that spreading an investment across a number of assets will eliminate some, but not all, of the risk.

divestiture the sale of a subsidiary, division or collection of related assets, usually to another firm.

dividend clienteles investors who choose to invest in companies that have dividend policies which meet their particular requirements.

dividend drop-off ratio ratio of the decline in the share price on the ex-dividend day to the dividend per share.

dividend election schemes arrangements which offer shareholders the option of receiving their dividends in one or more of a number of forms.

dividend growth model a model expressing the value of a share as the sum of the present values of future dividends where the dividends are assumed to grow at a constant rate.

dividend payout ratio percentage of profit paid out to shareholders as dividends.

dividend reinvestment plan an arrangement made by a company which gives shareholders an option of reinvesting all or part of their dividends in additional shares in the company, usually at a small discount from market price.

dividend yield cash dividend per share divided by the current share price.

dividends periodic distributions, usually in cash, by a company to its shareholders.

drawer in a bill of exchange, is the party initiating the creation of the bill, usually the borrower.

Du Pont identity popular expression breaking ROE into three parts: operating efficiency, asset use efficiency, and financial leverage.

duration measure of the time period of an outstanding debt.

E

economic order quantity (EOQ) optimal quantity of inventory to be ordered that minimises the cost of purchasing and holding the inventory.

effective annual interest rate (EAR) the actual rate of interest to be earned or paid.

efficient market hypothesis (EMH) the price of a security (such as a share) accurately reflects the information available in relation to its value.

endorsement acceptance by the seller of a bill in the secondary market, of responsibility to pay the face value if there is default by the acceptor, drawer and earlier endorsers.

equipment finance a loan or lease used to finance an item of equipment where the equipment is used as security for the finance.

equivalent annual value this method involves calculating the annual cash flow of an annuity that has the same life as the project and whose present value equals the net present value of the project.

erosion the cash flows of a new project that come at the expense of a firm's existing projects.

euro the monetary unit for the European Monetary System (EMS).

eurobond a bond issued in multiple countries, but denominated in a single currency, usually the issuer's home currency. Such bonds have become an important way to raise capital for many international companies and governments. Eurobonds are issued outside the restrictions that apply to domestic offerings and are syndicated and traded mostly from London. Trading can and does take place anywhere there is a buyer and a seller.

eurocurrency money deposited in a financial centre outside the country whose currency is involved. For instance, eurodollars—the most widely used eurocurrency—are U.S. dollars deposited in banks outside the U.S. banking system.

euromarket an international market for the investment of currencies outside their country of origin and free from government interference.

euronote short-term note sold in countries other than the country of the currency in which it is denominated.

European option an option that can only be exercised on the expiration date.

event study research method that analyses the behaviour of the abnormal returns of a security around the time of a significant event such as the public announcement of the company's earnings.

event time time is defined relative to occurrences of the class of event being studied.

excess volatility a contention that share prices are more variable than they would be if they reflected only the fundamental determinants of their true value.

exchange controls government regulations restricting the free exchange of the domestic currency to and from foreign currencies.

exchange rate the price of the currency in terms of another currency.

exchange risk the changes that could occur to cash flows due to changes in exchange rates.

ex-dividend date the date on which a share begins trading ex-dividend. A share purchased ex-dividend does not include a right to the forthcoming dividend payment.

exercise price the fixed price at which the underlying asset can be traded, subject to the terms of the option contract also known as strike price.

ex-rights date the date on which a share begins trading ex-rights. After this date a share does not have attached to it the right to purchase any additional share(s) on the subscription date.

F

face value the sum promised to be paid in the future on a debt security, such as a bond, promissory note or bill of exchange. Also **par value**.

factor the provider of finance who buys the accounts receivable, manages the debtors and collects the debts on a continuing basis.

factoring the sale of a firm's accounts receivable at a discount to a financial institution.

factoring with recourse an agreement in which the factor is reimbursed by the selling firm if the debtor defaults.

factoring without recourse an agreement in which the factor is not reimbursed by the selling firm if the debtor defaults.

finance lease a long-term non-cancellable lease that effectively transfers the risks and benefits of ownership of an asset from the lessor to the lessee.

financial break-even the sales level that results in a zero NPV.

financial contract an arrangement, agreement or investment that produces cash flows.

financial distress a situation where a company's financial obligations cannot be met, or can be met only with difficulty.

financial intermediary an institution that acts as a principal in accepting funds from depositors and lending them to borrowers.

financial leverage the relationship between debt and personal contributions. Financial leverage is measured by ratios such as the debt–equity ratio in relation to companies.

financial ratios relationships determined from a firm's financial information and used for comparison purposes.

financial risk the additional risk borne by shareholders because of the use of debt as a source of finance.

Fisher effect relationship between nominal returns, real returns and inflation.

fixed costs costs that do not change when the quantity of output changes during a particular time period.

float the difference between book cash and bank cash, representing the net effect of cheques in the process of clearing.

floating charge a mortgage security for debt of a company where the security is all of the assets and not one specific asset such as land.

floating rate debt a debt security whose interest rate is adjusted periodically in line with changes in a specified reference rate.

floor members members of an exchange who are permitted to be on the trading floor and who can trade on behalf of clients. With online computer trading the tradition of being on the floor is no longer relevant. **floor-plan finance loan** a financial arrangement, usually made by a wholesaler to a retailer, that finances an inventory of durable goods such as motor vehicles. Also known as wholesale finance.

forecasting risk the possibility that errors in projected cash flows lead to incorrect decisions.

foreign bond debt issued outside the borrower's country and denominated in the currency of the country in which it is issued.

forward margin the difference between spot and forward rates.

forward rate the exchange rate used for forward transactions. The rate is established now, with payment and delivery to occur at a specified future date. A forward rate comprises two components: the spot rate plus or minus a forward margin.

franked dividend the dividend that carries a credit for income tax paid by the company.

franking premium that part of the return on shares or a share market index which is due to tax credits associated with franked dividends.

fully-drawn bill facility a bill facility in which the borrower must issue bills so that the fully-agreed amount is borrowed for the period of the facility.

future sum an amount to which a present sum, such as principal, will grow (accumulate) at a future date, through the operation of interest.

future value the amount an investment is worth after one or more periods. Also known as compound value.

G

general annuity an annuity in which the frequency of charging interest does not match the frequency of payment; thus repayments may be made either more frequently or less frequently than interest is charged.

generally accepted accounting principles (GAAP) the common set of standards and procedures by which audited financial statements are prepared.

geometric rate of return the rate of return between two dates, measured by the change in value divided by the earlier value; the average of a sequence of geometric rates of return is found by a process that resembles compounding.

gilts these are technically British and Irish government securities; however they also include issues by local British authorities.

Global Industry Classification Standard (GICS) a code used globally to classify a firm by its type of business operations.

going-private transaction all publicly owned shares in a firm are replaced with complete equity ownership by a private group.

H

hard rationing the situation that occurs when a firm cannot raise finance for a project in the external market.

hedge contract a contract, either spot or forward, between $A and $US where settlement is not affected by delivery of the two currencies.

hedge ratio the ratio of the change in an option price that results from a change in the price of the underlying asset; also known as an option's delta.

hedge settlement rate a spot $US/$A exchange rate calculated by AAP–Reuters at 9.45 a.m. each day based on average spot $US/$A exchange rates.

hedgers market participants who enter into contracts in order to reduce risk.

holder-of-record date the date on which existing shareholders on company records are designated as the recipients of share rights. Also known as the date of record.

home-made dividend idea that individual investors can undo corporate dividend policy by reinvesting dividends or selling shares.

home-made leverage the use of personal borrowing to change the overall amount of financial leverage to which the individual is exposed.

horizontal takeover a takeover of a target company operating in the same line of business as the acquiring company.

I

immunisation a strategy designed to achieve a target sum of money at a future point in time, regardless of interest rate changes.

imputation tax credit credit for Australian company tax paid which, when distributed to shareholders, can be offset against their tax liability.

imputation tax system a system under which investors in shares can use tax credits associated with franked dividends to offset their personal income tax. The system eliminates the double taxation of company profits.

incremental cash flows the difference between a firm's future cash flows with a project or without the project.

independent project one that may be accepted or rejected without affecting the acceptability of another project.

indicator rate an interest rate set and published by a lender from time to time and used as a base on which interest rates on individual loans are determined, usually by adding a margin.

indifference curve a curve showing a set of combinations such that an individual derives equal utility from (and thus is indifferent between) any combinations in the set.

indirect quotation an exchange rate quotation in which the local currency is the base currency and the foreign currency is the quoted rate; for example, in Australia an indirect quotation is $US0.595 = $A1.

information asymmetry a situation where all relevant information is not known by all interested parties. Typically this involves company 'insiders' (managers) having more information about the company's prospects than 'outsiders' (shareholders and lenders).

information content effect the market's reaction to a change in corporate dividend payout.

information efficiency a situation in which prices accurately reflect available information; different categories of information give rise to different categories of information efficiency.

interest-only loan a loan in which the borrower is required to make regular payments to cover interest accrued but is not required to make payments to reduce the principal. On the maturity date of the loan, the principal is repaid in a lump sum.

interest rate the rate of return on debt.

interest rate parity a theory which states that a forward exchange rate is given by relative interest rates in the two currencies.

interest rate swap an agreement between two parties to exchange interest payments for a specific period, related to an agreed principal amount. The most common type of interest rate swap involves an exchange of fixed interest payments for floating interest payments.

interest tax shield the tax saving attained by a firm from interest expense.

internal rate of return (IRR) the rate of return (discount rate) that would make a contract's present value equal to the initial investment; the rate that provides a zero net present value.

intrinsic value the value that traditional theorists regard as the 'true' value. In an option, it is the value if the option is exercised immediately.

inventory could comprise raw materials, work in progress, supplies used in operations or finished goods on hand ready for use.

investment opportunities opportunities to expand which are expected to be profitable but require further cash outlays to develop or maintain their value.

invoice discounting an agreement similar to a factoring agreement, in which the selling company retains the sales accounting function.

IPOs the initial public offering of securities to the market.

issue costs the costs of raising new capital by issuing securities, including underwriting fees and legal, accounting and printing expenses incurred in preparing a prospectus or other offer documents. Also known as flotation costs.

J

January effect an observation that, on average, share prices increase in January more than in other months.

just-in-time (JIT) a system for managing demand-dependent inventories that minimises inventory holdings

L

law of one price principle maintaining that an asset's price in a given currency will be the same regardless of the currency in which the price is quoted.

lead time the time it takes from placing an order to the receipt of the inventory.

lessee in a lease contract the party using the asset who is equivalent to the borrower.

lessor in a lease contract the party that owns the asset and accepts the payments (premiums) from the lessee.

leveraged buyout a takeover of a company which is largely financed using borrowed funds and the remaining equity is privately held by a small group of investors.

leveraged lease a finance lease where the lessor borrows most of the funds to acquire the asset.

limited liability a legal concept which protects shareholders whose liability to meet a company's debts is limited to the amount paid on the shares they hold.

liquid assets these comprise cash and assets that are readily convertible into cash, such as bills of exchange and treasury notes.

liquidity management this involves decisions about the composition and level of a company's liquid assets.

liquidity premium (risk premium) a theory of the term structure of interest rates that although future interest rates are determined by investors' expectations, investors require some reward (liquidity premium) to assume the increased risk of investing long term.

log price relative the natural logarithm of the ratio of successive security prices. Implicitly, it is assumed that prices have grown (or decayed) in a continuous fashion between the two dates on which the prices are observed. Also known as a logarithmic rate of return and a continuous rate of return.

London Interbank Offer Rate (LIBOR) a commonly used reference rate, derived daily from the interest rates at which major international banks in London will lend to each other.

long hedger a hedger who hedges by means of buying futures contracts now.

M

M&M Proposition I the value of the firm is independent of its capital structure.

M&M Proposition II a firm's cost of equity capital is a positive linear function of its capital structure.

maintenance lease an operating lease where the lessor is responsible for all maintenance and service of the leased asset.

management buyout a purchase of all of the issued shares of a company by a group led by the management.

managerial options opportunities that managers can exploit if certain things happen in the future.

margin call a demand for extra funds to be deposited into a trader's account because prices have moved against the position of the trader.

marginal or incremental cost the change in costs that occurs when there is a small change in output.

marginal or incremental revenue the change in revenue that occurs when there is a small change in output.

marginal tax rate amount of tax payable on the next dollar earned.

market model a time series regression of an asset's returns on the market index; it represents the empirical expression of the capital asset pricing model.

market opportunity line a line that shows the combinations of current and future consumption that an individual can achieve from a given wealth level, using capital market transactions.

market portfolio a portfolio of all risky assets, weighted according to their market value.

market risk premium slope of the SML, the difference between the expected return on a market portfolio and the risk-free rate.

marking-to-market a process of adjusting traders' account balances to reflect changes in market prices.

maturity specified date at which the principal amount of a bond is paid.

medium-term notes bearer securities with an initial term to maturity of more than 1 year and issued continually.

merchant banks have little direct involvement in the retail banking sector as they are primarily concerned with wholesale banking. Have been responsible for the development of cash management trusts, rebatable preference shares, the commercial bills market, the currency hedge market, the promissory note market and the unofficial deposit market.

merger the complete absorption of one company by another, where the acquiring firm retains its identity and the acquired firm ceases to exist as a separate entity.

money markets financial markets where short-term securities are bought and sold.

mutually exclusive projects alternative investment projects, only one of which can be accepted.

N

net present value (NPV) the difference between the present value of the net cash flows from an investment discounted at the required rate of return and the initial cash outlay of the investment.

net present value profile a graphical representation of the relationship between an investment's NPVs and various discount rates.

net working capital the current assets of a firm less the current liabilities.

nominal interest rate a quoted interest rate where interest is charged more frequently than the basis on which the interest is quoted. The interest rate actually used to calculate the interest charge is taken as a proportion of the quoted nominal rate and compounded up to the full period of the nominal rate.

nominal return return on an investment not adjusted for inflation.

non-bank bill any bill of exchange that has been neither accepted nor endorsed by a bank.

non-cash items expenses charged against revenues that do not directly affect cash flow, such as depreciation.

non-debt tax shields tax deductions for items such as depreciation, investment tax credits and tax losses carried forward.

non-recourse loan a type of loan used in leveraged leases where the lender has no recourse to the lessor in the event of default by the lessee.

non-systematic risk a risk that affects at most a small number of assets. Also unique or asset-specific risks

normal distribution a symmetric, bell-shaped frequency distribution that can be defined by its mean and standard deviation.

note issuance facility a facility provided by one or more institutions that agree to underwrite issues of short-term notes by a borrower.

notes unsecured debt securities.

O

off Statement of Financial Position financing when firms are not required to provide any specific disclosure of the financing on their Statement of Financial Positions.

open account an arrangement under which goods or services are sold to a customer on credit, but with no formal debt contract. Payment is due after an account is sent to the customer.

operating cash flow cash generated from a firm's normal business activities.

operating (or activity) cycle the time period between the acquisition of inventory and when cash is collected from receivables.

operating lease a cancellable lease which is written for a period considerably less than the useful life of the leased asset.

operating leverage the degree to which a firm or project relies on fixed costs.

opportunity cost the highest price or rate of return that would be provided by all alternative courses of action. The opportunity cost of capital is the rate of return that could be earned on another investment with the same risk.

optimal capital structure the capital structure which maximises the value of a company.

option the right but not the obligation to buy or sell underlying assets at a fixed price for a specified period.

ordinary annuity an annuity in which the time period from the date of valuation to the date of the first cash flow is equal to the time period between each subsequent cash flow. All cash flows occur at the end of the period.

ordinary perpetuity an ordinary annuity with the special feature that the cash flows are to continue forever.

ordinary shares the risk capital of a company, as such shares have residual and ownership rights; they are without priority for dividends or in bankruptcy.

overdraft where the bank permits the customer to draw more money from the bank account than that which has been put in it.

overdraft limit the level to which a firm is permitted to overdraw its account.

overnight loan funds lent in the money market on the basis that either party can terminate the loan by 11 a.m. on the following day. Also known as 11 a.m. money.

overreaction a biased response of a price to information in which the initial price movement can be expected to be reversed.

P

P/E ratio the ratio of price to earnings per share.

par value (face value) the principal amount of a debenture or note that is repaid at the maturity date.

partial takeover a takeover in which a bidder seeks to acquire no more than part of a company's issued shares.

partnership a business owned by two or more people acting as partners.

payback period the time it takes for the progressive accumulated net cash flows generated by an investment to equal the initial cash outlay.

pecking order the theory which proposes that companies follow a hierarchy of financing sources in which internal funds are preferred and, if external funds are needed, borrowing is preferred to issuing riskier securities.

percentage of sales approach financial planning method in which accounts are varied depending on a firm's predicted sales level.

perfect capital market frictionless market in which there are no taxes, no transaction costs, all relevant information is available at no cost to all participants and all participants are price takers.

perpetuity an annuity in which the cash flows continue forever.

planning horizon the long-range period that the financial planning process focuses on, usually the next two to five years.

poison pill a strategic move by a company that may become a takeover target to make its shares less attractive to an acquirer by increasing the cost of a takeover (e.g. an issue of securities which will convert to shares if a takeover bid occurs).

portfolio a combined holding of more than one asset.

post-event drift an observation that share returns display a trend after an event.

precautionary motive the need to hold cash as a safety margin to act as a financial reserve.

preference shares shares with dividend priority over ordinary shares, normally with a fixed dividend rate, sometimes without voting rights.

present value (PV) an amount that corresponds to today's value of a promised future sum.

present value index (PVI) the present value of an investment's future cash flows divided by its initial cost. Also benefit/cost ratio.

present value of a contract the value today that is equivalent to a stream of cash flows promised in a financial contract.

price–earnings ratio the share price divided by earnings per share.

primary market a market for new issues of securities where the sale proceeds go to the issuer of the securities.

principal (or principal sum) the amount borrowed at the outset of a debt contract.

principal-and-interest loans loans repaid by a sequence of equal cash flows, each of which is sufficient to cover the interest accrued since the previous payment and to reduce the current balance owing. Therefore, the debt is extinguished when the sequence of cash flows is completed. Also known as credit foncier loans.

private issue an issue of securities direct to chosen investors rather than the general public.

private placement a loan, usually long-term in nature, provided directly by a limited number of investors.

production possibilities curve (frontier) a curve that displays the investment opportunities and outcomes available to the firm; its shape therefore determines the combinations of current dividend, investment and future dividend that the firm can achieve. The shape of the curve is driven by the technical efficiency of the firm.

profit and loss account financial statement summarising a firm's performance over a period of time.

promissory note a short-term marketable debt security in which the borrower promises to pay a stated sum on a stated future date. Also known as one-name paper and commercial paper.

proportional bid a partial takeover bid to acquire a specified proportion of the shares held by each shareholder.

prospectus a document that must be provided to potential investors by a company seeking to issue shares or other securities; contains facts about a business to help investors make informed decisions.

proxy contest attempt to gain control of a firm by soliciting a sufficient number of shareholder votes to replace existing management.

purchasing power parity a theory which states that the exchange rate between two currencies adjusts to reflect the relative inflation rates in the two currencies.

pure play a firm that operates almost entirely in only one industry or line of business.

put–call parity a relationship that exists between the price of a call option and the price of the corresponding put option.

put option a right to sell an underlying asset at a fixed price.

put option on a futures contract an option that gives the buyer the right to enter into the futures contract as a seller at a predetermined price.

R

random-walk hypothesis a theory that the time sequence of returns on shares conforms to the statistical concept of a 'random walk'; this includes the implication that the time sequence is random.

real interest the interest rate after taking out the effects of inflation.

real return return adjusted for the effects of inflation.

rediscounting selling a short-term debt security in the secondary market.

residual claim the claim to profit or assets that remains after the entitlements of all other interested parties have been met.

residual dividend approach policy where a firm pays dividends only after meeting its investment needs while maintaining a desired debt-to-equity ratio.

residual value the final value in a leasing contract that must be paid by the lessee on completion of the contract.

retained earnings corporate earnings not paid out as dividends.

retention ratio current profit retained divided by the net profit. Also called the ploughback ratio.

reverse split procedure where a firm's number of shares outstanding is reduced.

revolving credit bill facility a facility in which the borrower can issue bills as required, up to the agreed limit.

risk-averse investor one who dislikes risk.

risk-neutral investor one who neither likes nor dislikes risk.

risk neutrality a situation in which investors are indifferent to risk; assets are therefore priced such that they are expected to yield the risk free interest rate.

risk premium the excess return required from an investment in a risky asset over a risk-free investment.

risk-seeking investor one who prefers risk.

S

safety stock additional inventory held when demand is uncertain, to reduce the probability of a stockout. sale and lease-back agreement an agreement in which a company sells an asset and then leases it back from the buyer.

scenario analysis the determination of what happens to NPV estimates when we ask 'what if' questions.

secondary market the market where previously issued securities are traded.

secondary market transaction the purchase or sale of an existing security.

securitisation a process whereby mortgages are pooled, insured and shares in the pool sold.

security market line graphical representation of the capital asset pricing model. Positively sloped straight line displaying the relationship between expected return and beta.

semi-strong-form efficiency where all publicly available information is reflected in the security's current market price.

sensitivity analysis analysis of the effect of changing one or more input variables to observe the effects on the results.

settlement procedures institutional arrangements for the payment and receipt of funds after a transaction.

share rights plan (SRP) provisions allowing existing shareholders to purchase shares at some fixed price should an outside takeover bid take place, discouraging hostile takeover attempts.

share split an increase in a firm's shares outstanding without any change in owners' equity.

short hedger a hedger who hedges by means of selling futures contracts today.

short selling the process of first entering into a contract to sell and later entering into a contract to buy. It is the process of selling something that is not already owned.

simple interest the method of calculating interest in which, during the entire term of the loan, interest is computed on the original sum borrowed.

simulation analysis a combination of scenario and sensitivity analyses.

size effect an observation that returns on the shares of small capitalisation companies appear to be too high compared to returns on other shares.

soft rationing the situation that occurs when management allocates limited amounts of funding to units in a firm for capital budgeting.

sole proprietorship a business owned by one person.

sources of cash a firm's activities that bring in cash.

speculative motive the need to hold cash to take advantage of additional investment opportunities, such as bargain purchases.

speculators market participants who enter into contracts in order to profit from correctly anticipating price movements.

spot price the price of the commodity when the buyer pays immediately and the seller delivers immediately.

spot rate the rate for transactions for immediate delivery. In the case of foreign exchange, the spot rate is for settlement in 2 days.

spread a long (bought) position in one maturity date, paired with a short (sold) position in another maturity date.

stakeholder someone other than a shareholder or debtholder who potentially has a claim on the firm.

stand alone principle evaluation of a project based on the project's incremental cash flows.

standard deviation the square root of the variance, a measure of dispersion around the mean.

Statement of Financial Performance financial statement summarising a firm's performance over a period of time.

Statement of Financial Position financial statement showing a firm's accounting value on a particular date.

static theory of capital structure theory that a firm borrows up to the point where the tax benefit from an extra dollar in debt is exactly equal to the cost that comes from the increased probability of financial distress.

strategic options options for future, related business products or strategies.

striking price the fixed price in an option contract at which the holder can buy or sell the underlying asset. Also known as the exercise price or strike price.

strong-form efficiency all information, whether public or private, is reflected in the security's current market price.

subordinated debt debt which ranks below other debt in the event that a company is wound up. subscription price the price that must be paid to obtain a new share.

sub-underwriters a group of underwriters formed to reduce the risk and help to sell an issue.

sunk cost the cost that has already been incurred and is irrelevant to future decision making.

sustainable growth rate the growth rate a firm can maintain given its debt capacity, ROE and retention ratio.

swap two transactions on which there is a simultaneous purchase and sale of a set amount of one currency against another for two different settlement dates. There are two basic kinds of swap: interest and currency.

syndicated loan a loan arranged by one or more leading banks which is funded by a syndicate that usually includes other banks.

synergy in takeovers the situation where the performance and therefore the value of a combined entity exceed those of the previously separate components.

systematic (market-related or non-diversifiable) risk that component of total risk which is due to economy-wide factors.

T

takeover an acquisition of control of one company by another.

target cash balance a firm's desired cash level as determined by the trade-off between carrying costs and shortage costs.

target company the object of a takeover bid.

target payout ratio a firm's long-term desired dividend-to-earnings ratio.

tax loss selling an investment strategy in which the tax rules make it attractive for an investor to sell certain shares just before the end of the tax year to take advantage of accumulated losses.

tender offer a public offer by one firm to directly buy the shares of another firm.

term loans direct business loans of, typically, one to five years.

term structure of interest rates the relationship between interest rates and term to maturity for debt securities in the same risk class.

terminal value of a contract the value as at the date of the final cash flow.

terms of sale conditions on which a firm sells its goods and services for cash or credit.

theoretical ex-rights share price the expected price of one share when shares begin to be traded ex-rights.

theoretical rights price the expected price of one right calculated on the basis of the cum rights share price.

thin-trading problem because some shares trade relatively infrequently, a current market price at a given time may be unavailable, thus causing difficulties in statistical testing.

time value the value of an option in excess of its intrinsic value.

time value of money the fundamental principle of finance that individuals prefer to receive a dollar today rather than a dollar in the future.

tombstone an advertisement announcing completion of a public offering.

trade credit an arrangement in which a seller of goods or services allows the purchaser a period of time before requiring payment; it is equivalent to a short-term loan made by the seller to the purchaser, of an amount equal to the purchase price.

trade-off theory a theory which proposes that companies have an optimal capital structure based on a trade-off between the benefits (tax) and costs (bankruptcy) of using debt.

transaction motive the need to hold cash to satisfy normal disbursement and collection activities associated with a firm's ongoing operations.

treasury stock a U.S. term for a company's own shares that have been repurchased and held rather than cancelled.

turn-of-the-month effect an observation that, on average, share prices increase around the time of a new month beginning, more than at other times.

U

unbiased forward rates a theory which states that the forward rate is an unbiased predictor of the future spot rate.

uncovered interest parity or international Fisher effect a theory which states that the difference in interest rates between two countries is an unbiased predictor of the future change in the spot exchange rate.

underreaction a biased response of a price to information in which the initial price movement can be expected to continue.

underwriters investment firms that act as intermediaries between a company selling securities and the investing public.

unlevered cost of capital the cost of capital of a firm that has no debt.

unlisted market trading this trading is confined to bargaining by individual buyers and sellers and around $3 billion is invested in the unlisted equity market.

unsubordinated debt the debt which has not been subordinated.

unsystematic (diversifiable) risk that component of total risk which is unique to the firm and may be eliminated by diversification.

uses (or applications) of cash the activities of a firm in which cash is spent.

V

variable costs costs that change when the quantity of output changes.

variable interest rate loan a loan where the lender can change the interest rate charged, usually in line with movements in the general level of interest rates in the economy.

variance a measure of dispersion around the average; the mean of the squared deviations from the mean or expected value.

vertical takeover a takeover of a target company which is either a supplier of goods to, or a consumer of goods produced by, the acquiring company.

W

weak-form efficiency the information contained in the past series of prices of a security is reflected in the security's current market price.

weighted average cost of capital (WACC) the weighted average of the costs of debt and equity.

winner's curse the problem that arises in bidding because the bidder who 'wins' is likely to be the one who most overestimates the value of the assets offered for sale.

withholding tax the tax deducted by a company from the dividend payable to a non-resident shareholder.

Y

yield curve a graph of yield to maturity against bond term at a given point in time.

yield to maturity (YTM) the market interest rate that equates a bond's present value of interest payments and principal repayments with its price.

Z

zero-coupon bonds bonds that pay only one cash flow: the payment at maturity.

index

Australian dollar, 499
  AUD (buying) rate, 796
  financial reporting, 206
Australian Financial Review, 194,
203–6, 799
Australian Options Market (AOM),
719–21
  contract characteristics, 721–2
Australian Prudential Regulation
Authority (APRA), 452–4, 495
Australian Securities and Investments
Commission (ASIC), 12, 22, 495,
768
  regulation of fund raising, 562
Australian Stock Exchange (ASX),
22, 23, 203–6, 340, 491, 499–502,
562, 573–4
  executive rewards, disclosure, 17
  industry classification, 93
  Options Clearing House Pty Ltd,
  722–3
Australian Taxation Office
  superannuation industry regulation,
  497
authorised deposit-taking institutions
(ADIs), 454
authorised foreign exchange dealers,
796
average collection period (ACP), 84
average returns, 330–1
average tax rate, 53

B

bank bill futures, 749–50
bank bills
  historical rates of return, 322–30
bank mergers, 768, 777
bank overdrafts, 81, 439–41, 496, 506
  prime rate, 506
bank-clearing time, 447
banker's acceptance, 469
Banking (Foreign Exchange)
Regulations, 796
bankruptcy, 551
  costs, direct and indirect, 692–4
banks, 495–7
  capital, classes of, 544–5
  deregulation, 495, 497, 498
  financial system, regulation, 452–4
  lending patterns, 496
  preference shares, 544
  source of funds, 496
Banks (Shareholdings) Act 1972, 769
basket warrants, 740

Basle Committee on Banking
Supervision, 454
beachhead, 773
bearer debentures, 532
bearer securities, 532
bell curve, 337–8
Bell Resources Ltd, 777
benchmark information, 93
Bendigo Bank, 499
benefit/cost ratio, 238–9
best case plan, 108
best efforts underwriting, 567
beta coefficient, 366–8
  capital market line, 376–9
  risk premium, 368–74
  security market line, 374–5, 379
  stability issue, 384
BHP, 780
BHP Billiton, 17, 204, 429, 528
bid price setting, 266–9
bidder, 768
big brothers, 785 see white squires,
white knights
bills of exchange, 507–9
  discounted value, 509
  parties involved, 507–8
Bills of Exchange Act 1909, 509
Black, Fischer, 650
Black-Scholes Option Pricing Model,
733–7
Blades, Joanne, 706–7
blanket liens, 510
blocked funds, 813
Bloomberg, 21, 22, 194–5
bonds, 188, 493, 532
  bond price reporting, 194–5
  discount bonds, 190
  face value, 188
  features and prices, 188
  interest rate risk, 192
  maturity, 188
  par value, 188
  premium bonds, 190
  priced to yield, 190
  prices and interest rates, inverse
  relationship, 192
  quoted rate, 191
  semi-annual coupons, 191
  valuation, 188–92
  value equation, 191
  values and yields, 188–92
  yield to maturity, 188, 189, 193–4
bonus share issues, 657–60
book value, 48, 49, 548
book value per share, 87

boom and recession
  share and portfolio returns, 352–9
bottom line, 50
Bowie, David, 538
break-even analysis, 289
  accounting break-even, 293–5, 298
  accounting break-even and cash
  flow, 296
  cash break-even, 298–9
  cash flow, accounting and financial
  break-even points, 297
  credit policy, 472, 476
  financial break-even, 299
  fixed and variable costs, 289–91
  operating leverage, 300–2
  sales volume and operating cash
  flow, 297
  total costs, 291–2
Broadcasting and Television Act 1942,
769
brokers, 22
building societies, 498
Bulldog bonds, 797
business day, 796
business failure, 551
business organisation forms, 11
business plan scenarios, 108
business risk, 685
buy-backs see share repurchase

C

calculations see Excel calculations
call options, 718–19
  and company options, 742–4
call premium, 541, 632
call provision, 632
callable debentures, 539–43
calls on shares, 547, 548
capital
  bank capital, classes of, 544–5
capital adequacy standard, 454, 544
"capital" and "current", 399
capital asset pricing model, 374–5
  problems with, 383–5
capital budgeting, 7, 302
  see also cost of capital
  capital investment decisions, 251
  capital rationing, 305–6
  international capital budgeting,
  811–13
  managerial options, 302–5
  practice and procedures, 239
  'Watch Cash Flow', 418
capital budgeting decision, 216–17
  options analysis, 739